what we call "civilization" is relatively recent, indeed, with the first permanent settlements occurring in the Middle East a scant 12 000 years ago. But the written record of our species' existence extends back only half this long, to the time humans invented writing and first farmed with animal-driven plows some 5000 years B.P.

Sociology came into being in the wake of the many changes to society wrought by the Industrial Revolution over the last few centuries—just the blink of an eye in evolutionary perspective. The lower time line provides a close-up look at the events and trends that have defined The Modern Era, most of which are discussed in this text. Innovations in technology are charted in the green panel below the line and provide a useful backdrop for viewing the milestones of social progress highlighted in the blue panel above the line. Major contributions to the development of sociological thought are traced along the very bottom of this time line.

This book is offered to teachers of sociology in the hope that it will help our students understand their place in today's society and in tomorrow's world.

John J. Macionis

S. Mikael Jansson

Cecilia M. Benoit

SOCIETY *the basics*

FOURTH CANADIAN EDITION

John J. Macionis
KENYON COLLEGE

S. Mikael Jansson
UNIVERSITY OF VICTORIA

Cecilia M. Benoit
UNIVERSITY OF VICTORIA

PEARSON
Prentice
Hall

Toronto

Library and Archives Canada Cataloguing in Publication

Macionis, John J.
    Society : the basics / John J. Macionis, S. Mikael Jansson, Cecilia M. Benoit.—4th Canadian ed.
Includes index.
ISBN-13: 978-0-13-173580-4
ISBN-10: 0-13-173580-2

    1. Sociology—Textbooks. I. Jansson, Mikael, 1959–
II. Benoit, Cecilia, 1954– III. Title.
HM586.M32 2008   301   C2006-905455-X

ISBN-13: 978-0-13-173580-4
ISBN-10: 0-13-173580-2

Editor-in-Chief, Vice-President of Sales: Kelly Shaw
Senior Acquisitions Editor: Laura Forbes
Executive Marketing Manager: Judith Allen
Senior Developmental Editor: Joel Gladstone
Production Editor: Kevin Leung
Copy Editor: Laurel Sparrow
Proofreader: Susan Broadhurst
Production Coordinator: Janis Raisen
Composition: Christine Velakis
Art Director: Julia Hall
Cover Design: Geoff Agnew
Interior Design: Jennifer Stimson, Anthony Leung
Cover Images: Getty Images/Wayne R Bilenduke (top), iStockphoto/Duncan Walker (middle), Getty Images (bottom)

1 2 3 4 5   12 11 10 09 08

Printed and bound in the United States of America.

BRIEF CONTENTS

CONTENTS

1

Sociology: Perspective, Theory, and Method   2

2

Culture   34

3

Socialization: From Infancy to Old Age   62

4

Social Interaction in Everyday Life   86

8

Social Stratification   196

Global Stratification   228

Gender Stratification   254

Race and Ethnicity   280

12

Economics and Politics   304

13

Family and Religion 338

14

Education, Health, and Medicine 376

15

Population, Urbanization, and Environment   412

16

Social Change: Modern and Postmodern Societies   446

MAPS

GLOBAL MAPS:
WINDOW ON THE WORLD

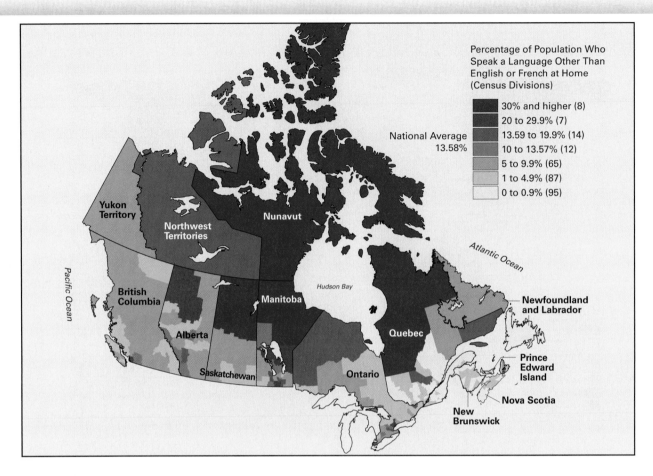

Percentage of Population Who Speak a Language Other Than English or French at Home (Census Divisions)

National Average 13.58%

- 30% and higher (8)
- 20 to 29.9% (7)
- 13.59 to 19.9% (14)
- 10 to 13.57% (12)
- 5 to 9.9% (65)
- 1 to 4.9% (87)
- 0 to 0.9% (95)

Pacific Ocean

Atlantic Ocean

Yukon Territory

Northwest Territories

Nunavut

British Columbia

Alberta

Saskatchewan

Manitoba

Hudson Bay

Ontario

Quebec

Newfoundland and Labrador

Prince Edward Island

Nova Scotia

New Brunswick

NATIONAL MAPS:
SEEING OURSELVES

BOXES

CRITICAL THINKING

CONTROVERSY & DEBATE

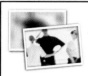

APPLYING SOCIOLOGY

PREFACE

In the same way that an earthquake makes us keenly aware of the earth beneath our feet, so changes in the world make us more aware of the society that surrounds us. The first years of the new millennium have been a challenge to us all. It has been just a few years since the tragic events of September 11, 2001, a day that changed everyone's lives. Since then, an increasing number of terrorist acts and other types of violence across the globe and the aftermath of war now prompt us to realize we cannot take the world for granted.

More to the point, these events force us to confront the question of what kind of world we live in and what kind of world we want for ourselves and for our children. It is here that readers of this book will discover the importance of the discipline of sociology.

The new fourth Canadian edition of *Society: The Basics* is authoritative, comprehensive, stimulating, and—as students' email messages testify—plain fun to read. This major revision elevates sociology's most popular text to a still higher standard of excellence and offers an unparalleled resource to today's students as they learn about both our diverse society and the changing world.

But the book is just one part of a complete learning package. Found with every new copy of *Society: The Basics,* Fourth Canadian Edition, is a Student Starter Kit for MySocLab, included with the purchase of a new text. MySocLab, Macionis edition, is a state-of-the-art, interactive and instructive online solution for introductory sociology. MySocLab combines multimedia, tutorials video, audio, tests, and quizzes to make teaching and learning fun.

In addition, students using *Society: The Basics* can log on to a full-featured website at www.pearsoned.ca/macionis, also at no cost to them. From the main page, simply click on the cover of *Society: The Basics,* Fourth Canadian Edition, to find chapter overviews and learning objectives, suggested essay questions and paper topics, multiple-choice and true-false questions that are graded instantly and online, and chapter-relevant Web destinations with learning questions.

Textbook, MySocLab, and website: A three-part multimedia package that is the foundation for sound learning in this new information age. We invite you to examine all three!

Organization of This Text

Society: The Basics carries students through sociology's basic ideas, research, and insights in sixteen logically organized chapters. Chapter 1 ("Sociology: Perspective, Theory, and Method") explains how the discipline's distinctive point of view illuminates the world in a new and exciting way. In addition, the first chapter introduces major theoretical approaches and explains the key methods sociologists use to test and refine their knowledge.

The next six chapters examine core sociological concepts. Chapter 2 ("Culture") explores the fascinating diversity of human living in our world. Chapter 3 ("Socialization: From Infancy to Old Age") investigates how people everywhere develop their humanity as they learn to participate in society. While highlighting the importance of the early years to the socialization process, this chapter describes significant transformations that occur over the entire life course, including old age. Chapter 4 ("Social Interaction in Everyday Life") takes a micro-level look at how people construct the daily realities that we often take for granted. Chapter 5 ("Groups and Organizations") focuses on social groups, within which we have many of our most meaningful experiences. It also highlights the expansion of formal organization and points up some of the problems of living in a bureaucratic age. Chapter 6 ("Sexuality and Society") explains the social foundations of human sexuality. Based on recent research, this chapter surveys sexual patterns in Canada and also explores variations in sexual practices through history and around the world today. Chapter 7 ("Deviance") analyzes how the routine operation of society promotes deviance as well as conformity.

The next four chapters provide more coverage of social inequality within Canada and cross-nationally than is found in any other brief text. Chapter 8 ("Social Stratification") introduces basic concepts that describe dimensions of social stratification throughout human history and around the world today. The chapter then highlights dimensions of social difference in present-day Canada. Chapter 9 ("Global Stratification") extends this text's commitment to global education by analyzing the social ranking of nations themselves. Why, in other words, do people in some societies have abundant wealth while, in others, people struggle every day just to survive? *Society: The Basics* also provides full-chapter coverage of two additional dimensions of social difference. Chapter 10 ("Gender Stratification") describes how gender is a central element of social stratification in Canada, as it is worldwide. Chapter 11 ("Race and Ethnicity") explores racial and ethnic diversity in our country, explaining how societies use physical and cultural traits to construct and rank categories of people in a hierarchy.

Next are three chapters that survey all the major social institutions. Chapter 12 ("Economics and Politics") looks at the economy and politics of Canadian society, beginning with a historical look at how the Industrial Revolution transformed the Western world. This chapter contrasts capitalist and socialist economic models and investigates how economic systems are linked to a society's distribution of power. It also contains coverage of the military, issues of war and peace, and a much-expanded discussion of terrorism.

Chapter 13 ("Family and Religion") spotlights two institutions central to the symbolic organization of social life. The chapter begins by focusing on the variety of family forms in Canada, making frequent comparison to kinship systems in other parts of the world. Basic elements of religious life come next, with an overview of recent religious trends.

Chapter 14 ("Education, Health and Medicine") examines two institutions with special importance in the new century. The chapter looks first at the historical expansion of schooling, noting many ways in which the scope and kind of education are linked to other social institutions. Next, we look at health, which also has become a central institution during the last century and a half. The chapter concludes by explaining the distinctive strategies various countries—including our own—employ to promote access to quality health care and also highlights the tensions in the Canadian health care system as it grapples with demographic and other societal shifts.

The final two chapters of the text focus on dimensions of social change. Chapter 15 ("Population, Urbanization, and Environment") is a synthesis that begins by spotlighting the growth of population in the world. Our attention then turns to the rise of cities in Canada and to the urban explosion now taking place in low-income countries around the world. Finally, the chapter explains how the state of the natural environment reflects social organization. Chapter 16 ("Social Change: Modern and Postmodern Societies") concludes the text with summaries of major theories of social change, a look at how people forge social movements to encourage or resist change, analysis of various benefits and liabilities of modern social patterns, and the emergence of a "postmodern" way of life.

Continuity: Established Features of Society: The Basics Fourth Canadian Edition

The extraordinary success of *Society: The Basics* results from a combination of the following distinctive features.

The best writing style. Most important, this text offers a writing style widely praised by students and faculty alike as elegant and inviting. *Society* is an enjoyable text that encourages students to read—even beyond their assignments. No one says it better than the students themselves, whose recent email includes testimonials such as these:

Thanks for writing such a brilliant book. It has sparked my sociological imagination. This was the first textbook that I have ever read completely and enjoyed. From the moment that I picked the book up I started reading nonstop. I have read four chapters ahead; it's like a good novel I can't put down! I just wanted to say thank you.

Your book is extremely well written and very interesting. I find myself reading it for pleasure, something I have never done with college texts. It is going to be the only collegiate textbook that I ever keep simply to read on my own. I am also thinking of picking up sociology as my minor due to the fact that I have enjoyed the class as well as the text so much. Your writing has my highest praise and utmost appreciation.

I am taking a Sociology 101 class using your text, a book that I have told my professor is the best textbook that I have ever seen, bar none. I've told her as well that I will be more than happy to take more sociology classes as long as there is a Macionis text to go with them.

A global perspective. *Society* was the first brief text to mainstream global content, introduce global maps, and offer comprehensive coverage of global topics like stratification and the environment. No wonder this text has been adapted and translated in half a dozen languages for use around the world. Each chapter explores the social diversity of the entire world as well as explaining why social trends and issues in Canada—from changing family patterns, increasing ethnic and racial diversity, urban sprawl, to the growing disparity of income—are influenced by what happens elsewhere. Just as important, students will learn ways that social patterns and policies at home impact low-income nations around the world.

A celebration of social diversity. *Society: The Basics* invites students from all social backgrounds to discover a fresh and exciting way to see themselves within the larger social world. Readers will discover in this text the diversity of Canadian society—people of a multitude of backgrounds ranging from Aboriginal, Asian, European, African, and other ancestries, as well as women and men of various class positions and at all points in the life course. Just as important, without flinching from the problems that marginalized people confront, this text does not treat minorities as social problems but highlights their agency and recognizes their significant achievements.

Emphasis on critical thinking. Critical-thinking skills include the ability to challenge common assumptions by formulating questions, to identify and weigh appropriate evidence, and to reach reasoned conclusions. This text not only teaches but also encourages students to discover on their own.

Engaging and instructive chapter openings. One of the most popular features of the second Canadian edition of *Society* was the engaging vignettes that begin each chapter. These openings—for instance, using the tragic sinking of the *Titanic* to illustrate the life and death consequences of social inequality, the story of Anna, a little girl who grew up tied to a chair in the attic, to show the importance of socialization, or the case of Bernard Ebbers and WorldCom to open the chapter on deviance—spark the interest of readers as they introduce important themes. This revision retains ten of the best chapter-opening vignettes found in earlier editions and offers six new ones as well.

Inclusive focus on women and men. Beyond devoting two full chapters to the important concepts of sex and gender, *Society* mainstreams gender into every chapter, showing how the topic at hand affects women and men differently, and explaining how gender operates as a basic dimension of social organization.

Theoretically clear and balanced. This text makes theory easy. The discipline's major theoretical approaches are introduced in Chapter 1 and are carried through later chapters. The text highlights the social-conflict, structural-functional, and symbolic-interaction paradigms, and also incorporates other theoretical approaches including feminism, social-exchange analysis, ethnomethodology, and sociobiology.

Recent research and the latest data. *Society: The Basics*, Fourth Canadian Edition, blends classic sociological statements with the latest research, as reported in the leading publications in the field. More than 1450 research citations support this revision, more than one-half of them published since 1990. We have used the latest government and other reputable sources to ensure that—chapter to chapter—the text's content and statistical data are the most recent available. A key feature of this edition is the continued comprehensive incorporation of the most recent data from the 2001 Census of Canada. There are almost 100 new citations referring to Statistics Canada publications from 2002 and 2003 alone, including 33 electronic databases analyzed to update statistics in this revised text.

Learning aids. This text has many features to help students learn. In each chapter, **Key Concepts** are identified by boldface type, and following each appears a *precise, italicized definition.* A listing of key concepts with their definitions appears at the end of each chapter, and a complete **Glossary** is found at the end of the book. Each chapter also contains a numbered **Summary** and four **Critical-Thinking Questions** that help students review material and

assess their understanding. Following these are **Applications and Exercises,** which provide students with activities to do on or near the campus. Each chapter ends with an annotated listing of worthwhile **Sites to See** on the Internet and a suggestion for how to use **ContentSelect™** to pursue further research. Access to ContentSelect is provided through the Research Navigator link on MySocLab. A MySocLab Student Access Kit is packaged with each text.

Outstanding images: photography and fine art. *Society: The Basics* offers the finest and most extensive program of photography and artwork available in any comparable book. We search extensively to obtain the finest images of the human condition and present them with thoughtful captions, often in the form of questions.

Thought-provoking theme boxes. Although boxed material is common to introductory texts, *Society: The Basics* provides a wealth of uncommonly good boxes. Each chapter typically contains three boxes, which fall into four types that amplify central themes of the text. **Global Sociology** boxes provoke readers to think about their own way of life by examining the fascinating social diversity that characterizes our world. **Diversity: Race, Class, and Gender** boxes, which have been expanded for this revision, focus on multicultural issues and present the voices of women and visible minorities. **Critical Thinking** boxes teach students to ask sociological questions about their surroundings, and help them evaluate important, controversial issues. Each Critical-Thinking box is followed by three "What do you think?" questions. **Controversy & Debate** boxes present several points of view on hotly debated issues and conclude with "Continue the debate" questions to stimulate thought and generate spirited class discussion.

WINDOW ON THE WORLD

GLOBAL MAP 3-1 Child Labour in Global Perspective

Industrialization extends childhood and discourages children from work and other activities considered suitable only for adults. Thus, child labour is uncommon in Canada and other high-income countries. In less economically developed nations of the world, however, children are a vital economic asset, and they typically begin working as soon as they are able.

Source: World Bank (2004) and author estimates; map projection from *Peters Atlas of the World* (1990).

Finally, **Applying Sociology** boxes, new to this revision, show readers how to apply the perspective, theory, and methods of sociology to greatest advantage; they, too, are followed by three "What do you think?" questions. A complete listing of this text's boxes appears after the table of contents.

SEEING OURSELVES

NATIONAL MAP 3-1 Aging Across Canada, 2001

The aging of the population is largely a southern phenomenon. Even though we associate Victoria, British Columbia, with the phrase "Newlyweds and Nearly Deads," the map shows that the concentration of those over age 65 is also high on the Prairies and north of Toronto. Which do you think primarily determines this pattern—social forces or individual choices?

Source: Calculated based on Statistics Canada (2003ax).

An unparalleled program of 36 global and national maps. Another popular feature of *Society: The Basics* is the program of global and national maps. Window on the World global maps—22 in all—are truly sociological maps offering a comparative look at income disparity, favoured languages and religions, the extent of prostitution, permitted marriage forms, the degree of political freedom, the incidence of HIV infection, and a host of other issues. The global maps use the non-Eurocentric projection devised by cartographer Arno Peters that accurately portrays the relative size of all the continents.

Seeing Ourselves National Maps—14 in all—help to illuminate the social diversity of Canada. Each of these maps is broken down into the 288 national census divisions, with the result that they illustrate the important differences that exist within provinces much more accurately than is possible with just provincial averages. They present at a glance the national picture on such topics as language diversity, the percentage of single-parent families across Canada, and much more. Fourteen of these maps are based on census data collected by Statistics Canada, and they are all based on the 2001 Census of Canada. A complete listing of the Seeing Ourselves national maps as well as the Window on the World global maps follows the table of contents.

CHAPTER SEVEN
Deviance

Why is deviance found in all societies?
How does *who* and *what* are defined as deviant reflect social inequality?
What effect has punishment had on reducing crime in Canada?

Innovation: Changes in the Fourth Canadian Edition
Each new edition of *Society: The Basics* has broken new ground, and this is one reason that more than 50 000 students have learned from these sociological best-sellers. A revision raises high expectations, but after three years of planning and hard work, we are pleased to offer a major revision that sets a new standard for brief texts. Here is a brief overview of the innovations that define *Society: The Basics*, Fourth Canadian Edition.

Student friendly: A new look. As instructors understand, today's students are visually oriented—in a world of rapid-fire images, they respond to what they see. Just as important, the photographs that we see in newspapers, on television, and online are more sociological than ever. As a result, this new edition of *Society: The Basics* offers more and better images, and the text has an exciting new look that is clean, attractive, and sure to boost student interest.

Society: The Basics encourages students to use images to learn. Bold, vibrant, and colourful photos pull students into the chapter material and become teaching opportunities, not just elements that add visual appeal. Combined with the chapter-opening stories that follow, students will be inspired by the visuals and educated by the context.

Student friendly: New chapter-opening questions. Each chapter of this new edition begins with three questions—a "what," a "how," and a "why" question—that alert students to key themes discussed in the chapter.

Student friendly: A new feel. A new look also calls for a new feel to the text. Our goal in this new edition can be stated in the form of a promise: Every student in every class will be able to immediately understand the material on every page of the text. This promise does not mean that we have left out any of the content you expect. What it does mean is that the authors have prepared this revision with the greatest care and with an eye toward making language and arguments as clear as they can be. Student tested—student friendly!

Student friendly: A greater focus on careers. Most students who enroll in a sociology course hope to find something useful for their future careers. They will. *Society: The Basics, Fourth Canadian Edition,* reflects the discipline's *career relevance* more than ever before. Many chapters now apply sociological insights to careers—for example, read how today's marketing is learning to be more multicultural (Chapter 2, "Culture") and why physicians should understand the social dynamics of an office visit or a medical examination (Chapter 4, "Social Interaction in Everyday Life"). In addition, there is coverage of the changes in labour unions (Chapter 12, "Economics and Politics"), as well as a new discussion of nursing as part of the medical establishment (Chapter 14, "Education, Health and Medicine").

For additional connections between sociology and careers, look for the Sociology@Work icon. Found in most chapters, these icons draw student attention to discussion that has particular importance to the world of work.

Student friendly: More applied sociology. The value of sociology depends on students' ability to apply what they learn to their own lives. This revision illustrates concepts in ways that encourage students to see these connections.

In addition, there is a new box theme: Applying Sociology. Ten of these boxed features show sociology at work in people's everyday lives.

Student friendly: Encouraging active reading. This book encourages students to be active readers. Of course, the lively and easy-to-understand writing style and current examples are important. In addition, all of the boxes in this revision now include three follow-up questions that invite students to think critically and to apply what they have learned to new situations.

Student friendly: A better way to teach theory. Sociological theory is important, but it is sometimes challenging to

students. To ensure that students learn the important lessons, all theoretical discussions are followed by a "Critical review" section. In this revision, we have also added new "Applying Theory" tables, which summarize, at a glance, how the various theoretical approaches view the topic at hand.

APPLYING THEORY
CULTURE

	Structural-Functional Approach	Social-Conflict Approach	Sociobiological Approach
What is the level of analysis?	Macro-level	Macro-level	Macro-level
What is culture?	Culture is a system of behaviour by which members of societies cooperate to meet their needs.	Culture is a system that benefits some people and disadvantages others.	Culture is a system of behaviour that is partly shaped by human biology.
What is the foundation of culture?	Cultural patterns are rooted in a society's core values and beliefs.	Cultural patterns are rooted in a society's system of economic production.	Cultural patterns are rooted in humanity's biological evolution.
What core questions does the approach ask?	How does a cultural pattern help society to operate? What cultural patterns are found in all societies?	How does a cultural pattern benefit some people and harm others? How does a cultural pattern support social inequality?	How does a cultural pattern help a species adapt to its environment?

Improved high-tech. For this edition, a student access kit for MySocLab is packaged free with each new text. For students, MySocLab combines a complete e-book version of the fourth Canadian edition of Society, The Basics, along with video, audio, animations, research support, practice tests, exams and more. For instructors, MySocLab provides quick and easy access to a vast array of resources to teach and administer a Sociology course.

New chapter-opening vignettes. This revision keeps the best of the popular chapter-opening vignettes and adds six new ones.

Many new boxes. Over 50 boxes support five themes of the text: Global Sociology, Diversity: Race, Class, & Gender, Critical Thinking, Controversy & Debate, and—new to this edition—Applying Sociology. Many boxes are revised and updated or new for this edition.

A small change in chapter ordering. In this revision, "Sexuality and Society" is moved up one spot to fall before, rather than after, the chapter on "Deviance." This small change results in a more logical flow of topics.

The latest statistical data. Instructors count on this text to include the very latest statistical data. The fourth edition comes through again, making use of the latest data from various government agencies and private organizations. The authors have worked together to ensure that the newest statistics are used throughout the text—in many cases as recent as the statistics from 2006 publications In addition, instructors will find dozens of new research citations as well as many familiar current events that raise the interest of students.

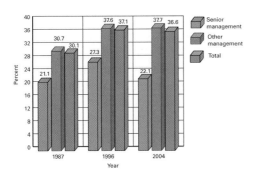

DIVERSITY SNAPSHOT

FIGURE 5–4 Women as a Percent of Total Canadians Employed in Management Positions

Source: Data from Statistics Canada, 2006d.

Keeping up with the field. As surprising as it may seem, some textbooks do not reflect new work in the field, making few references to sociology's journals and taking little notice of new books. In preparing this revision, the author has reviewed new publications—including *American Journal of Sociology, American Sociological Review, Canadian Review of Sociology and Anthropology, Rural Sociology, Social Forces, Sociological Focus, Sociological Forum, Society, The Public Interest, Social Problems, Population Bulletin, Teaching Sociology, Contemporary Sociology,* and *Social Science Quarterly*—as well as popular press publications that keep us abreast of current trends and events. Of course, material selected for inclusion in an introductory textbook must be both interesting and relevant to the lives of students.

New topics. The fourth edition of *Society: The Basics* is completely updated with new and expanded discussions in every chapter. Here is a partial listing, by chapter.

- **Chapter 1 Sociology: Perspective, Theory, and Method**: New data on suicide by gender show the power of society; the global map on economic development is updated, there are updates on race and sports; a new Applying Theory table helps students understand the three main sociological theories; the methods discussion has been greatly expanded and now includes discussion of the authors' and others' studies to illustrate each of the major methods; and there is new discussion of Human Research Ethics Committees.

- **Chapter 2 Culture**: A new chapter opening points out the gains businesses can make by better understanding cultural diversity; a new Applying Sociology box looks at the new cyber-symbols found in our computer culture; there is an expanded, more critical discussion of the Sapir-Whorf thesis; an updated discussion of Canadian value conflicts; and a new Applying Theory table helps students use theory to understand culture.

- **Chapter 3 Socialization**: This chapter offers an expanded discussion of the role of the family in socialization and incorporates recent research on street-involved youth; and look for a new Critical Thinking box on the social transitions that define "adulthood" in Canada.

- **Chapter 4 Social Interaction in Everyday Life**: A reorganized and revised discussion of status improves the presentation of this important topic. A new Critical Thinking box describes how anyone can detect lying.

- **Chapter 5 Groups and Organizations**: An update applies the concept of groupthink to the invasion of Iraq; find a new global map on Internet users around the world; there is an update on bureaucratic ritualism, new material on changes in Japanese organizations in light of that nation's economic downturn, and an update on the gradual loss of privacy.

- **Chapter 6 Sexuality and Society:** A new chapter opening discusses the pressures and problems linked to becoming sexually active at a young age; there are new data on homosexuality in Canada and attitudes towards gay people in different countries, a new Diversity Snapshot identifies four sexual orientations; there is expanded discussion of teen pregnancy; also find a new Applying Theory table that helps students use theory to study sexuality, and a new Applying Sociology box on the campus culture of "hooking up."

- **Chapter 7 Deviance:** A new chapter opening highlights one of the corporate scandals that has changed the look of "criminals" in Canada; a new Critical Thinking box asks whether cheating has become more common today in Canada; a new Applying Theory table helps students use theory to understand deviance; and there is more applied material on criminal justice.

- **Chapter 8 Social Stratification**: This chapter now includes a new discussion of emerging social classes in China; a new Applying Theory table helps students apply theory to stratification issues; the global map showing income inequality is updated

- **Chapter 9 Global Stratification:** A new chapter opening describes a deadly fire that ended the lives of fifty-two people in a Bangladesh sweatshop; a new Applying Theory table helps students apply theory to the issue of global poverty; find new data showing which global regions are prospering and which are not.

- **Chapter 10 Gender Stratification:** This chapter contains updates on the achievements of males and females in the Canadian education system, share of women in the labour force as well as the gender composition of national parliaments; a new Applying Theory table helps students use theory to understand gender.

- **Chapter 11 Race and Ethnicity:** The discussion of race now includes the trend towards increasing mixture of races; there is expanded discussion of the social construction of race and ethnicity; a new expanded discussion of prejudice contains new research findings showing patterns of prejudice in different nations.

- **Chapter 12 Economics and Politics**: A new chapter opening highlights the economic power of Wal-Mart; new data show the career plans of college and university students; new data on employment and unemployment; find updates on the extent of political freedom in the world and support for different political parties in Canada; a new Applying Theory table helps students use theory to understand politics; there are updates on the war in Iraq and the global war against terror; the chapter includes a new discussion of the role of the mass media in war; a new Controversy & Debate box examines the link between Islam and political freedom.

- **Chapter 13 Family and Religion**: A new chapter-opening story points to the diversity of families; a new Applying Theory table helps students use theory to understand the family; the chapter offers statistical updates on birthrates, the "sandwich generation"; divorce; custody of children after divorce; family violence; an updated discussion of same sex families; a new discussion of childcare in Canada; another new Applying Theory table is found in the religion discussion;

- **Chapter 14 Education, Health and Medicine**: There are statistical updates for illiteracy, education, gender and earnings; a new Diversity box asks whether school discipline operates as a type of racial profiling; the health section includes a new diary entry showing the authors experience with the health care system in Cuba; an update on income and health, smoking; a new discussion on the shortage of nurses; find a new Global Sociology box dealing with culture and eating disorders; there is an update on AIDS around the world and HIV infection in Canada.

- **Chapter 15 Population, Urbanization, and Environment**: Find updates on all the demographic indicators for Canada and the world; there is a new discussion of the $I = PAT$ formula of environmental impact, as well as updates on the composition of community solid waste and the state of the global environment; there is a new Diversity Box on visible minorities in Canada.

- **Chapter 16 Social Change: Modern and Postmodern Societies**: Revised discussions of mass society and class society takes a more critical view of both analyses; find updates from the National Opinion Research Center on people's attitudes toward social change and modernity in different countries.

A WORD ABOUT LANGUAGE

This text's commitment to representing the social diversity of Canada and the world carries with it the responsibility to use language thoughtfully. For example, we prefer the term Aboriginal to the word Indian. Most tables and figures refer to "Visible Minorities" and "Aboriginals" separately because Statistics Canada employs these terms in collecting statistical data about our population, and because that is the preference of many Aboriginals themselves.

Students should realize, however, that many individuals do not describe themselves using these terms. Although the term "Aboriginal" is commonly used in Canada, across Canada people of Aboriginal descent identify with a particular Aboriginal nation, whether it be the Métis Nation of Ontario or the Haida or Nisga'a of British Columbia.

The same holds true for visible minorities. Although this term is a useful shorthand in sociological analysis, most people think of themselves in terms of a specific country of origin (say, Japan, the Philippines, India, or Vietnam).

Throughout the text we have used the term "low-income" rather than "poor" (and "high-income" rather than "rich") for two reasons. First, while there are many consequences of poverty, the labelling of individuals, families, and nations as "poor" is primarily based on income, reflecting the primary, or direct, cause of poverty. So "low-income" is a more accurate description. Second, using the term "low-income" emphasizes the importance of thinking about the causes and consequences of poverty in an all-encompassing framework that includes individuals, families, and nations with high income.

A WORD ABOUT WEBSITES

Because of the increasing importance of the Internet, each chapter of this new edition of *Society: The Basics* links discussion to websites and ends with a listing of additional **Sites to See**. The goal is to provide sites that are current, informative, and, above all, relevant to the topic at hand.

However, students should be mindful of several potential problems. First, websites change all the time. Prior to publication, we make every effort to ensure that the sites listed meet our high standards. But readers may find that sites have changed substantially and some may have gone away entirely. Obviously, this problem is beyond our control.

Second, sites have been selected in order to provide different perspectives on various issues. The listing of a site does not imply that the author or publisher agrees with everything—or even anything—on the site. Indeed, we urge students to examine all sites critically.

Third, many of the websites listed in this text are popular. Because many people visit them, the sites may be slow in responding. Please be patient or, if a site is too busy, simply move on.

Supplements

Society: The Basics, Fourth Canadian Edition, is the heart of a multimedia learning package that includes a wide range of proven instructional aids as well as several new ones. The supplements for this revision have been thoroughly updated, improved, and expanded.

FOR THE INSTRUCTOR

Instructor's Resource CD-ROM (0-13-236769-6). This CD-ROM is a one-stop shop for instructors, containing all of the teaching tools developed specifically to accompany the Canadian Edition of *Society: The Basics*. Included on this Instructor's Resource CD-ROM are:

- *Data File* Revised by Deborah Gural (Red River College), this is an "instructor's manual" that is of interest even to those who have never used one before. The Data File provides far more than detailed chapter outlines and discussion questions; it contains statistical profiles of Canada and other nations, summaries of important developments and significant research, and supplemental lecture material for every chapter of the text.

- *Test Item File* Written by John Macionis and revised by Deborah Gural (Red River College) for the fourth Canadian edition, this file contains over 2000 items—at least 100 per chapter—in multiple-choice, true-false, and essay formats. Questions are identified as simple "recall" items or more complex inferential issues, and the answers to all questions are page referenced to the text. The Test Item File is available on this CD-ROM in two formats: Microsoft Word and MyTest. MyTest for *Society: The Basics*, Fourth Canadian Edition from Pearson Education Canada is a powerful assessment generation program that helps instructors easily create and print quizzes, tests, exams, as well as homework or practice handouts. Questions and tests can all be authored online, allowing instructors ultimate flexibility and the ability to efficiently manage assessments at anytime, from anywhere.

- *PowerPoints* Created by Edward Thompson (McMaster University), each chapter of the text is supported by a PowerPoint presentation specific to *Society*, Fourth Canadian Edition. There are well over 200 slides in total.

- *Personal Response System Questions* Gauge your students' course progress with this Personal Response System that enables instructors to pose questions, record results, and display those results instantly in your classroom. Questions are provided in PowerPoint format.

- *Image Library* This file offers selected figures and tables from the text that can be incorporated into PowerPoint presentations as desired.

Most of these instructor supplements are also available for download from a password protected section of Pearson Education Canada's online catalogue (vig.pearsoned.ca). Navigate to your book's catalogue page to view a list of those supplements that are available. See your local Pearson representative for details and access.

MEDIA SUPPLEMENTS

MySocLab MySocLab combines a complete electronic version of the fourth Canadian edition of *Society: The Basics*, with video, audio, animations, research support, practice tests, exams, and more. Included with MySocLab is access to ResearchNavigator™, which includes three databases of reliable source material, EBSCO's Content Select, The New York Times Search-By-Subject Archive™, and Link Library, editorially selected "Best of the Web" sites for sociology. MySocLab engages students and gives them the opportunities and tools they need to extend their learning experience and enhance their performance. Go to **www.pearsoned.ca/ mysoclab** to find out more.

MySocLab is a state-of-the-art interactive solution for introductory sociology. A Student Starter Kit for MySocLab is provided with every new copy of this edition.

Companion Website™. In tandem with the text, students and professors can now take full advantage of the Internet to enrich their study of sociology. The Macionis Companion Website™ continues to lead the way in providing students with avenues for delving deeper into the topics covered in the text. Features of the site include chapter objectives, study questions, and links to interesting material and information from other sites on the Web that will reinforce and enhance the content of each chapter. It is free to both students and faculty. Please visit the site at **www.pearsoned.ca/macionis** and click on the cover of *Society: The Basics*, Fourth Canadian Edition.

Pearson Education Canada's Sociology Video Library. New for 2007, Volume 5, "Media and Society," of Pearson Education Canada's Sociology Video Library is now available, with eight clips selected by Marc Belanger (Vanier College) (ISBN 0-13-241363-9). (Professor Belanger has also written an accompanying Faculty Guide with a synopsis of each segment, teaching ideas, and discussion questions.)

Volume 5 accompanies the previously published 4-volume video library, selected by Paul Lamy (University of Ottawa) and Vicki Nygaard (University of Victoria) (DVD ISBN 0-13-123344-0; VHS ISBN 0-13-121865-4). The complete Pearson Education Canada Sociology Video Library offers seven hours of video clips, ranging in length from 10 minutes up to 25 minutes. The clips offer a wealth of exciting material to use in the classroom. For adopters only, contact your Pearson Education Canada sales representative for more information.

Pearson Advantage. For qualified adopters, Pearson Education is proud to introduce the Pearson Advantage.

The Pearson Advantage is the first integrated Canadian service committed to meeting the customization, training, and support needs for your course. Our commitments are made in writing and in consultation with faculty. Your local Pearson Education sales representative can provide you with more details on this service program.

Content Media Specialists. Pearson's Content Media Specialists work with faculty and campus course designers to ensure that Pearson technology products, assessment tools, and online course materials are tailored to meet your specific needs. This highly qualified team is dedicated to helping schools take full advantage of a wide range of educational technology, by assisting in the integration of a variety of instructional materials and media formats.

Distance Learning Solutions. Pearson Education Canada is committed to providing our leading content to the growing number of courses being delivered over the Internet by developing relationships with the leading vendors—Blackboard™, Web CT™, and CourseCompass™, Pearson Education's own easy- to-use course management system powered by Blackboard™. Please visit our technology solutions site at www.pearsoned.ca/highered/main_content/technologysolutions/index.html.

FOR STUDENTS

Study Guide (0-13-238926-6). Revised and updated by Sandy Isfeld (Lakehead Univeristy), this complete guide helps students to review and reflect on the material presented in *Society: The Basics*, Fourth Canadian Edition. Each of the sixteen chapters in the study guide provides an overview of the corresponding chapter in the text, summarizes its major topics and concepts, offers applied exercises, and features end-of-chapter tests with solutions.

 VangoNotes. Study on the go with VangoNotes. Just download chapter reviews from your text and listen to them on any mp3 player or computer. Now wherever you are—whatever you're doing—you can study by listening to the following for each chapter of your textbook:

- **Big Ideas:** Your "need to know" for each chapter
- Practice Test: A gut check for the Big Ideas – tells you if you need to keep studying
- **Key Terms:** audio "flashcards" to help you review key concepts and terms
- **Rapid Review:** A quick drill session – use it right before your test

VangoNotes are **flexible**; download all the material directly to your player, or only the chapters you need. And they're **efficient**.

Use them in your car, at the gym, walking to class, wherever. So get yours today. And get studying. **VangoNotes.com**

In Appreciation

First of all, we want to acknowledge the vast amount of work that went into the U.S. version of this text by John Macionis and by the people at Prentice Hall. We also would like to thank the following friends and colleagues for helping out in the myriad tasks directly involved in the writing of this and earlier editions: Megan Alley (Victoria); Beverley Maclean-Alley (Victoria); Fran Rose (University of Victoria); Alan Hedley (University of Victoria); Lori Sugden (University of Victoria); Bill McCarthy (University of California, Davis); and Zheng Wu (University of Victoria), Helga Hallgrimsdottir (University of Victoria), Josephine MacIntoch (University of Victoria), and Peyman Vahabzadeh (University of Victoria).

We would like to thank the people we worked with at Pearson Education Canada on this edition for their many hours of hard work: Ky Pruesse, acquisitions editor; Joel Gladstone, developmental editor; Kevin Leung, production editor; and Laurel Sparrow, copyeditor.

It goes without saying that every colleague knows more about some topics covered in this book than the authors do. For that reason, we are grateful to the hundreds of faculty and students who have written to offer comments and suggestions. More formally, we are grateful to the following people who have reviewed some or all of this manuscript, or the manuscript of the previous Canadian edition:

Robert H. Cartwright (Grant MacEwan College)
Elinor Malus (Champlain College)
Fred Neale (Lethbridge Community College)
Laurie Forbes (Lakehead University)
John Steckley (Humber College)
Mark Ihnat (Humber College)

Finally, we remain in debt to David Stover and Dawn du Quesnay, who started us on this project and guided our earliest efforts in ways that remain influential.

We dedicate this book to our daughter, Annika, who at thirteen years of age has shown tremendous understanding of her parents' need to work long hours finishing yet another chapter. We are unable to express in words the love we feel for you, Annika. Thanks so much for asking the most important sociological questions: WHAT? and WHY? and more recently WHY NOT? We hope that you will always listen to our attempts at answering your questions.

S. Mikael Jansson and Cecilia Benoit

ABOUT THE AUTHORS

John Macionis

John J. Macionis (pronounced ma-SHOW-nis) was born and raised in Philadelphia, Pennsylvania. He earned a bachelor's degree from Cornell University and a doctorate in sociology from the University of Pennsylvania.

His publications are wide-ranging, focusing on community life in the United States, interpersonal intimacy in families, effective teaching, humour, new information technology, and the importance of global education. He and Nijole V. Benokraitis have edited the anthology Seeing Ourselves: Classic, Contemporary, and Cross-Cultural Readings in Sociology. Macionis has also authored Sociology, the leading comprehensive text in the field, and he collaborates on international editions of the texts: Sociology: Canadian Edition; Society: The Basics, Canadian Edition; Seeing Ourselves, Canadian Edition; and Sociology: A Global Introduction. Sociology is also available for high school students and in various foreign language editions. In addition, Macionis and Vincent Parrillo have written the urban studies text Cities and Urban Life (Prentice Hall). Macionis's most recent textbook is Social Problems (Prentice Hall). The latest on all the Macionis textbooks, as well as information and dozens of Internet links of interest to students and faculty in sociology, are found at the author's personal Web site: www.macionis.com or www.TheSociologyPage.com. Additional information, instructor resources, and online student study guides for the texts are found at the Prentice Hall site: www.prenhall.com/macionis.

John Macionis is Professor and Distinguished Scholar of Sociology at Kenyon College in Gambier, Ohio. In 2003, he received the Philander Chase Medal for completing twenty-five years of teaching at Kenyon. During that time, he has chaired the Sociology Department, directed the college's multidisciplinary program in humane studies, presided over the campus senate and the college's faculty, and most importantly, taught sociology to thousands of students.

In 2002, the American Sociological Association named Macionis recipient of the Award for Distinguished Contributions to Teaching, citing his innovative use of global material as well as introduction of new teaching technology in the development of his textbooks.

Professor Macionis has been active in academic programs in other countries, having traveled to some fifty nations. During his last study tour, he directed the global education course for the University of Pittsburgh's Semester at Sea program, teaching 400 students on a floating campus that visited twelve countries as it circled the globe.

Macionis writes, "I am an ambitious traveler, eager to learn and, through the texts, to share much of what I discover with students, many of whom know little about the rest of the world. For me, traveling and writing are all dimensions of teaching. First, and foremost, I am a teacher—a passion for teaching animates everything I do." At Kenyon, Macionis offers a wide range of upper-level courses, but his favourite course is Introduction to Sociology, which he teaches every year. He enjoys extensive contact with students and each term invites members of his classes to enjoy a home-cooked meal.

The Macionis family—John, Amy, and children McLean and Whitney—live on a farm in rural Ohio. In his free time, John plays tennis and enjoys swimming and bicycling through the Ohio countryside. During the summer he is a competitive sailor, and year-round he enjoys performing oldies rock and roll and playing the Scottish bagpipes.

Professor Macionis welcomes (and responds to) comments and suggestions about this book from faculty and students. Write to the Sociology Department, Palme House, Kenyon College, Gambier, Ohio 43022, or direct e-mail to **MACIONIS@KENYON.EDU.**

Mikael Jansson

Mikael Jansson is Adjunct Assistant Professor in the Department of Sociology, research associate with the Centre for Youth and Society, and member of the Population Research Group at the University of Victoria. Mikael spent the first sixteen years of his life living in six different communities in central Sweden before moving with his family to Canada in 1975. He attended high schools in Quebec, Ontario, and Alberta before going to the University of Alberta and finally the University of Western Ontario, where he studied migration. Since graduating he has combined teaching (Introductory Sociology, Demography, Research Methods and Statistics), research, parenting, and travel.

His current research uses a combination of qualitative and quantitative approaches to understand the situation of marginalized youth and young adults. He spends most of his time working on three research projects all of which follow people over time. One project follows street youth and tries to see how their lives, and in particular their health status, changes as a result of their street involvement. A second project follows a group of randomly selected youth in part to understand how their live experiences differ from the street involved youth. A third project involves service workers in three different occupations; hair dressers, food and beverage servers and sex workers—in Canada and the United states in an effort to try to understand how these workers lives differ from each other. Most recently, he has become interested in the transition into adulthood and hopes to find out more about the determinants (and consequences) of where and when different groups of people enter the occupational hierarchy. You can read more about the research projects he is involved in by searching for his name at the University of Victoria website (www.uvic.ca). You can reach Mikael at mjansson@uvic.ca.

Cecilia Benoit

Cecilia Benoit is a Professor in the Department of Sociology at the University of Victoria and serves on the executive of one of the five national Centres of Women's Health, NNEWH (located at York University). She was born and raised in Newfoundland and comes from a family of eleven children. After completing her Ph.D. at the University of Toronto, she moved to the University of Victoria. She has taught Introductory Sociology for over a decade, and receives high evaluations from her students because of her friendly approach, up-to-date knowledge, and international and gendered perspectives.

Across her research career, Cecilia has been involved in trying to shed light on the situation of members of our society who are marginalized due to circumstances beyond their control. This began with a study of midwives. Her 1980s field study of three generations of midwives in Newfoundland and Labrador, and subsequent comparative research on midwifery in Sweden, helped to illustrate the positive benefits of midwifery care and the occupation's relatively high status in earlier historical periods in Canada and in the modern period in other countries. Cecilia has continued to conduct research on the "new midwifery" and has helped organize a major exhibit on the history of female healers (including midwives) that will open in early 2005 at the Museum of Civilization in Ottawa and later will travel the country. Cecilia is the author of Midwives in Passage (1991) and Women, Work and Social Rights (2000), and co-editor of Professional Identities in Transition (1999), Birth By Design (2001), and Reconceiving Midwifery (2004).

Her most recent research projects have focused on the social determinants of health and access to health services of specific marginalized populations, including Aboriginal women in Vancouver's Downtown Eastside, street-involved youth, youth involved in the sex trade and workers in low-paying and low-status personal service occupations. These have developed through partnerships with the various community groups serving these populations. You can find out about Cecilia's research by checking out her website at: **http://web.uvic.ca/~cbenoit/** or contact her at **cbenoit@uvic.ca**.

The Benoit-Jansson family (or should that be the Jansson-Benoit family?) live in a small house close to the University of Victoria. Together with their daughter, Annika, they enjoy the lakes and forests on Vancouver Island, spending their leisure time fly-fishing in the spring, swimming in the summer, and gathering wild mushrooms in the fall (these being the only three seasons in Victoria).

CHAPTER ONE

Sociology: Perspective, Theory, and Method

What sets human beings apart
from all other forms of life?

Why is sociology an important tool for your future?

How should you respond to people whose
way of life differs from your own?

The sociological perspective shows us patterns of behaviour common within a society. Here, a member of Brazil's Pataxo tribe offers a traditional greeting to a visitor.

If you were to ask 100 people why couples marry, it is a safe bet that at least 90 would reply, "People marry because they fall in love." Indeed, it is hard for us to imagine a happy marriage without love; likewise, when people fall in love, we expect them to think about marriage.

But is the decision about whom to marry really so simple and so personal? There is plenty of evidence that if love is the key to marriage, Cupid's arrow is carefully aimed by the society around us.

In short, society has a number of "rules" about whom we should marry. Until very recently, Canadian society ruled out half the population as possible marriage partners because our laws did not allow people to marry someone of the same sex even if the couple was deeply in love. But many rules remain. Sociologists have found that people—especially when they are young—are very likely to marry someone close to them in age, and men and women of all ages typically marry someone of the same race, of a similar social class background, of much the same level of education, and of about equal physical attractiveness (Chapter 13 gives details). Although it may be true that we make choices about whom to marry, society certainly narrows the field (Gardyn, 2002; Zipp, 2002).

When it comes to love and most other dimensions of our lives, the decisions we make do not result from what philosophers call "free will." The essential wisdom we gain from sociology is that our social world guides our actions and life choices in much the same way that the seasons influence our clothing and activities.

The Sociological Perspective

Sociology is *the systematic study of human society*. At the heart of this discipline is a distinctive point of view called "the sociological perspective."

SEEING THE GENERAL IN THE PARTICULAR

Peter Berger (1963) described the sociological perspective as *seeing the general in the particular*. That is, sociology helps us see *general* patterns in the behaviour of *particular* people. Although every individual is unique, society shapes the lives of people in various *categories* (such as children and adults, women and men, high-income earners and low-income

earners) very differently. We begin to think sociologically by realizing how the general categories into which we fall shape our particular life experiences.

This text explores the power of society to guide our actions, thoughts, and feelings. We may think of marriage as the simple product of personal feelings. Yet the sociological perspective shows us that patterns involving our gender, age, race, and social class guide our selection of a partner. Indeed, it might be more accurate to think of "love" as a feeling we have for others who match up with what society teaches us to want in a mate.

SEEING THE STRANGE IN THE FAMILIAR

At first, using the sociological perspective amounts to *seeing the strange in the familiar*. Consider how you would react if someone were to say to you, "You fit all the right categories; you would make a wonderful spouse. Let's get married!" Looking at life sociologically requires giving up the *familiar* idea that we live our lives only in terms of what we decide, in favour of the initially *strange* notion that society shapes these decisions, as it does all our experiences.

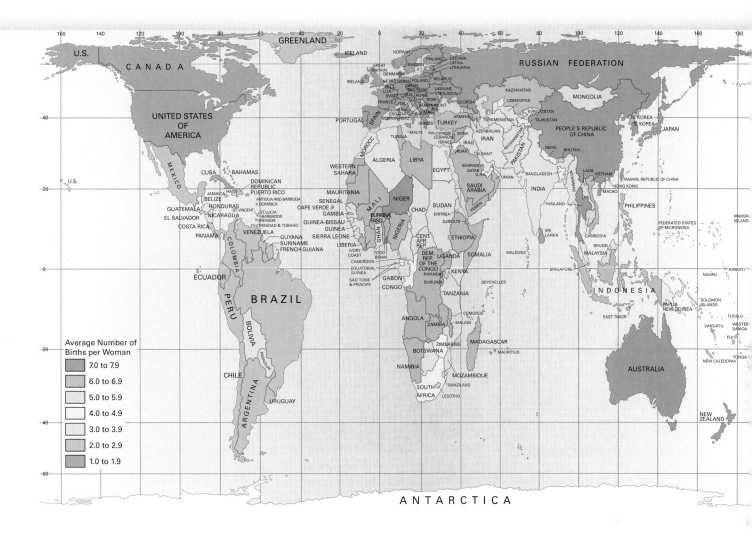

WINDOW ON THE WORLD

GLOBAL MAP 1-1 Women's Childbearing in Global Perspective

Is childbearing simply a matter of personal choice? A look around the world shows that it is not. In general, women living in low-income countries have many more children than women in high-income nations. Can you identify some of the reasons for this global disparity? In simple terms, such differences mean that if you had been born into another society (whether you are female or male), your life might be quite different from what it is now.

Source: Data from Mackay (2000). Map projection from *Peters Atlas of the World* (1990).

For individualistic North Americans, learning to see how society affects us may take a bit of practice. Consider the decision by women to bear children. Like the selection of a mate, the choice of how many children to have would seem to be a personal one. Yet there are social patterns here as well. As shown in Global Map 1–1, the average woman in Canada and the United States has slightly fewer than two children during her lifetime. In India, however, the "choice" is about

three; in South Africa, about four; in Cambodia, about five; in Saudi Arabia, about six; and in Niger, about seven.

What accounts for these striking differences? As later chapters explain, women in low-income countries have less schooling and fewer economic opportunities, are more likely not to work outside the home, and are less likely to use contraception. Clearly, society has much to do with the decisions women and men make about childbearing.

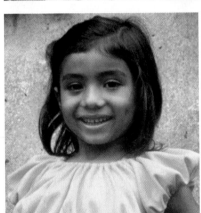

We can easily see the power of society over the individual by imagining how different our lives would be had we been born in place of any of these children from Bolivia, Ethiopia, Thailand, Botswana, South Korea, and El Salvador.

SEEING INDIVIDUALITY IN SOCIAL CONTEXT

What could be a more lonely, personal act than taking your own life? Emile Durkheim (1858–1917), one of sociology's pioneers, showed that social forces are at work even in such an intensely personal action as suicide, providing strong evidence of how social forces affect individual behaviour.

In examining official records in and around his native France, Durkheim (1966, orig. 1897) found that people in some categories were more likely than others to take their own lives. He found that men, Protestants, wealthy people, and the unmarried all had much higher suicide rates than women, Catholics and Jews, the poor, and married people. Thinking over these differences, Durkheim observed that the key to the pattern was *social integration:* People in some categories with strong social ties had low suicide rates, and more individualistic people had high suicide rates.

In the male-dominated societies Durkheim studied, men certainly had more freedom than women. But despite its advantages, freedom also contributes to social isolation and a higher suicide rate. Likewise, self-reliant Protestants were more prone to suicide than traditional Catholics and Jews, whose rituals foster stronger social ties. The wealthy, too, have more freedom than the poor but, once again, at the cost of a higher suicide rate. Finally, can you see why single people are at greater risk than married people?

A century later, Durkheim's analysis still holds some truth. Figure 1–1 shows suicide rates for women and men in Canada. In 2002, there were 11.6 recorded suicides for every 100 000 people. Suicide was more common among men than among women across the life cycle. Men (18.3 per 100 000) are more than three times as likely as women (5.0 per 100 000) to take their own lives. Following Durkheim's logic, the higher suicide rate among men reflects their greater wealth and freedom. Conversely, the lower rate among women follows from their limited social choices. Yet we also know today that while males commit suicide more often than females, females are more likely to *attempt* suicide. The reason behind this complex gender patterning requires that we build on Durkheim's ideas but go beyond them if we are to understand the personal actions of men and women in our society.

Some situations can stimulate sociological insights for everyone. Observing the diversity of people in our own society, we might wonder why others think and act differently than we do. As we continue to interact with people from social backgrounds that initially seem strange to us, we grasp the power of society to shape our lives and find ourselves easing into the use of the sociological perspective. The ability to think sociologically comes more quickly to people our society labels as "different." Those who routinely experience *social marginality*—that is, being set apart as "outsiders"—rapidly sense the power of society. For example, most Aboriginals in Canada are keenly aware of how much race affects our lives. Many whites—being the dominant majority—think about race only from time to time and may imagine that race affects only other people, not realizing its effect on themselves as well.

Finally, the U.S. sociologist C. Wright Mills (1959) pointed out that periods of social crisis also spark sociological thinking. For example, when the Great Depression of the 1930s threw one-third of the labour force out of work, unemployed workers could not help but see general social forces shaping their particular lives. Rather than thinking, "There must be something wrong with me; I can't find a job," they were likely to say, "We're all out of work because the economy has collapsed!" Of course, just as change stimulates sociological thinking, thinking sociologically suggests possibilities for change. The 1930s were a period of activism and saw the birth of both the Social Credit party (a party still in existence today in Western Canada) and the Co-operative Commonwealth Federation (which later merged into the NDP).

 For a description of the birth of the Social Credit movement and the Co-operative Commonwealth Federation, search for these two terms on Wikipedia at **http://en.wikipedia.org**.

BENEFITS OF THE SOCIOLOGICAL PERSPECTIVE

Applying the sociological perspective to our daily lives benefits us in four ways:

1. **The sociological perspective helps us critically assess "common sense" ideas.** Ideas we take for granted are not always true. One good example, noted earlier, is the notion that we are free individuals personally responsible for our lives. If we think that people decide their own fate, we may be quick to praise successful people as superior and consider people with fewer achievements as personally lacking. A sociological approach encourages us to ask how factors outside the control of individuals shape their successes and failures.

2. **The sociological perspective helps us see the opportunities and constraints in our lives.** Sociological think-

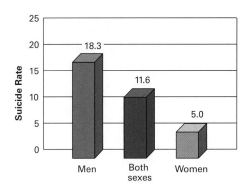

FIGURE 1-1 Rate of Death by Suicide, by Gender, for Canada

Rates indicate the number of deaths by suicide for every 100 000 people in each category for 2002.

Source: Calculated based on data in Statistics Canada (2003b, 2006a, 2006b, 2006c).

ing leads us to see that, in the game of life, we may have a say in how to play our cards, but it is society that deals us the hand. The more we understand the game, the better players we will be. Sociology helps us size up the world around us so that we can more effectively pursue our goals.

 To see how family income affects university and college attendance, go to **http://www.statcan.ca/Daily/English/050216/d050216b.htm**.

3. **The sociological perspective empowers us to be active participants in our society.** The better we understand how society operates, the more effective citizens we become. For some, this may mean supporting society as it is; others may attempt to change the world in some way. Whatever your goal, evaluating any aspect of social life includes identifying social forces and understanding their consequences.

4. **The sociological perspective helps us live in a diverse world.** North Americans make up just 5 percent of the world's population, and as this book's remaining chapters explain, many of the other 95 percent lead lives very different from our own. Still, like people everywhere, we tend to view our own way of life as "right," "natural," and "better." The sociological perspective prompts us to think critically about the strengths and weaknesses of all ways of life, including our own.

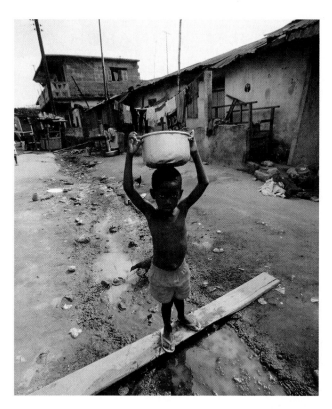

One important reason to gain a global understanding is that, living in a high-income country, we hardly can appreciate the suffering that goes on in much of the world. This boy is growing up in the African nation of Ghana, where he carries water for cooking and drinking from a public faucet and sewage flows freely over unpaved streets. In low-income countries like this, children have only a 50–50 chance of growing to adulthood.

APPLIED SOCIOLOGY

The benefits of sociology go well beyond our personal growth. As you read this text, you will learn that sociologists have helped shape public policy and law in countless ways involving issues such as healthcare, education, juvenile justice, divorce law, and social welfare. Canadian researcher Robin Bagley's work on sex offences against minors had a major impact on public policy (1984), among other things leading to the 1988 enactment of section 212 of the *Criminal Code*, which prohibits attempts to purchase sex from persons under 18 years of age (Lowman, 1987). According to the Canadian Association of University Teachers, sociologists are hired for hundreds of jobs in fields such as advertising, banking, criminal justice, education, government, healthcare, public relations, and research.

Most men and women who pursue advanced degrees in sociology go on to careers in teaching and research. But professional sociologists also work in many applied fields. For example, clinical sociologists work with troubled clients much as clinical psychologists do, focusing on a person's web of social relationships rather than on the individual alone. Another type of applied sociology is evaluation research. In today's cost-conscious political climate, administrators must evaluate the effectiveness of virtually every program and policy. Sociologists, especially those with advanced research skills, are in high demand for this kind of work.

In a short video, John Macionis offers a personal response to the question, "Why would someone want to be a sociologist?" See the Video Gallery at **http://www.TheSociologyPage.com**.

THE IMPORTANCE OF A GLOBAL PERSPECTIVE

As new communication technology draws even the farthest reaches of the Earth closer together, many academic disciplines take a **global perspective**, *the study of the larger world and our society's place in it.* What is the importance of a global perspective for sociology?

First, global awareness is a logical extension of the sociological perspective. Sociology shows us that our place in society profoundly affects our life experiences. It stands to reason, then, that the position of our society in the larger world system affects everyone in Canada.

Global Map 1–2 shows the relative economic development of the world's countries. **High-income countries** are *the richest nations with the highest overall standards of living.* High-income countries include Canada and the United States, the nations of Western Europe, Israel, Saudi Arabia, Japan, and Australia. Taken together, these 60 nations generate most of the world's goods and services and control most of its wealth. On average, individuals in these countries live well, not because they are smarter than anyone else, but because they had the good luck to be born in a wealthy region of the world.

The world's **middle-income countries** are *nations with a standard of living about average for the world as a whole.* Individuals living in any of these roughly 90 nations—many of the countries of Eastern Europe, some of Africa, and almost all of Latin America and Asia—are as likely to live in villages as in cities and to walk or ride animals, bicycles, scooters, or tractors as they are to drive cars, and they generally receive only a few years of schooling. Like high-income countries, middle-income countries are marked by pronounced social inequality, meaning that some people are extremely rich, but many more lack safe housing and adequate nutrition.

Finally, almost half the world's people live in the 60 **low-income countries**, *nations with a low standard of living in which most people are poor.* As Global Map 1–2 shows,

GLOBAL MAP 1-2 Economic Development in Global Perspective

In high-income countries—including Canada, the United States, the nations of Western Europe, Israel, Saudi Arabia, Australia, and Japan—a highly productive economy provides people, on average, with material plenty. Middle-income countries—including most of Latin America and Asia—are less economically productive, with a standard of living about average for the world as a whole but far below that of Canada. These nations also have a significant share of poor people who are barely able to feed and house themselves. In the low-income countries of the world, poverty is severe and widespread. Although small numbers of elites live very well in the poorest nations, most people struggle to survive on a small fraction of the income common in Canada.

Note: Data for this map are provided by the World Bank. Each country's economic productivity is measured in terms of its gross national income (GNI), which is the total value of all goods and services produced each year plus income from abroad. Dividing each country's GNI by the country's population gives us the per capita (per person) GNI and allows us to compare the income levels of countries of different population sizes. High-income countries have a per capita GNI of more than US$13 000. Many are far richer than this, however; the figure for Canada exceeds US$30 000. Middle-income countries have a per capita GNI ranging from US$3000 to US$13 000. Low-income countries have a per capita GNI of less than US$3000. Figures used here reflect the United Nations' "purchasing power parities" system, which is an estimate of what people can buy using their income in the local economy.

Source: Prepared by the authors using data from the World Bank (2005). Map projection from *Peters Atlas of the World* (1990).

most of the poorest societies in the world are in Africa. In these nations, a small number of people are well-off, but the majority struggle to get by with unclean water, too little food, little or no sanitation, and perhaps worst of all, little chance to improve their lives.

Chapter 9 ("Global Stratification") discusses the causes and consequences of global wealth and poverty. But every chapter highlights life in the world beyond our own borders for four reasons:

1. **Where we live makes a great deal of difference in shaping our lives.** As we saw in Global Map 1–1, women who live in high- and low-income countries lead strikingly different lives. To understand ourselves and appreciate the situation of others, we must grasp the social landscape of the world—one good reason to pay attention to the dozens of global maps found in this text.

2. **Societies throughout the world are increasingly interconnected.** Historically, Canada has paid little attention to the countries beyond its own borders. In recent decades, however, Canada and the rest of the world have become linked as never before. Electronic technology now transmits pictures, sounds, and written documents around the globe in a matter of seconds.

   One consequence of new technology, as later chapters explore, is that people all over the world now share many tastes in music, clothing, and food. With their economic power, high-income countries such as Canada influence other nations, whose people eagerly gobble up our hamburgers, dance to our music, and—more and more—speak the English language.

   But the larger world also has an impact on us. About 250 000 immigrants enter Canada each year, and we are quick to adopt many of their favourite sounds, tastes, and customs as our own, which greatly increases the cultural diversity of this country.

   Business across national borders has also created a global economy. Corporations make and market goods worldwide, just as global financial centres linked by satellite now operate around the clock. Stock traders in Toronto follow the financial markets in Tokyo and Hong Kong, just as wheat farmers in Saskatchewan watch the price of grain in the former Soviet republic of Georgia. With increasing numbers of Canadian jobs involving international trade, gaining greater global understanding has never been more important.

3. **Many social problems that we face in Canada are far more serious elsewhere.** Poverty is a serious problem in this country, but as Chapter 9 ("Global Stratification") explains, poverty in Latin America, Africa, and Asia is both more widespread and more severe. Similarly,

although women have lower social standing than men in Canada, gender inequality is much greater in the world's low-income countries.

4. **Thinking globally is a good way to learn more about ourselves.** We cannot walk the streets of a foreign city without becoming keenly aware of what it means to live in Canada. Making these comparisons often leads to unexpected lessons. For instance, in Chapter 9, we visit a squatter settlement in Madras, India. There, despite a desperate lack of basic material goods, people thrive in the love and support of family members. Why, then, does poverty in Canada lead to isolation and anger? Are material goods, so central to our definition of a "rich" life, the best means of measuring human well-being?

In sum, in an increasingly interconnected world, we can understand ourselves only to the extent that we understand others.

The Origins of Sociology

Like the "choices" made by individuals, major historical events rarely just "happen." Sociology was born as a result of powerful and complex social forces.

SOCIAL CHANGE AND SOCIOLOGY

Striking changes in eighteenth- and nineteenth-century Europe caused the social ground to tremble under people's feet. Understandably, people focused their attention on society, leading to the rise of the new science of sociology.

Industrial technology. In the Middle Ages, most people in Europe farmed near their homes or engaged in small-scale *manufacturing* (derived from Latin, meaning "to make by hand"). By the end of the eighteenth century, inventors had harnessed new sources of energy—the power of moving water and then steam—to operate large machines in mills and factories. As a result, instead of labouring at home or in tightly knit groups, workers became part of a large and anonymous labour force, toiling for strangers who owned the large factories. This change in the system of production separated families and weakened traditions that had guided members of small communities for centuries.

The growth of cities. Across Europe, factories drew people in need of work. Along with this "pull" came the "push" of the enclosure movement. Land owners fenced off more and more land, turning farms into pasture for sheep, the source of wool for the thriving textile mills. Deprived of their land, countless tenant farmers left the countryside in search of work in the new factories.

Cities grew to enormous sizes, and streets churned with strangers. Widespread social problems—including pollution,

Here we see Galileo, one of the great pioneers of the scientific revolution, defending himself before Roman Catholic Church officials, who were greatly threatened by his claims that science could explain the operation of the universe. Just as Galileo challenged the common sense of his day, pioneering sociologists such as Auguste Comte later argued that society is neither rigidly fixed by God's will nor set by human nature. On the contrary, Comte claimed, society is a system we can study scientifically, and based on what we learn, we can act intentionally to improve our lives.

North Wind Picture Archives

crime, and homelessness—further stimulated development of the sociological perspective.

Political change.   Economic development and the growth of cities also brought new ways of thinking. In the writings of Thomas Hobbes (1588–1679), John Locke (1632–1704), and Adam Smith (1723–1790), we find less concern with people's moral duties to God and to political rulers and more focus on the pursuit of self-interest. Indeed, the key phrases in the new political climate were *individual liberty* and *individual rights*. Echoing the thoughts of Locke, our own *Charter of Rights and Freedoms* spells out that everyone in Canada has "fundamental freedoms," including "conscience and religion," "thought, belief, opinion and expression," "peaceful assembly," and "assembly."

The political revolution in France that began in 1789 symbolized the Western world's break with the old political and social traditions. As the French social analyst Alexis de Tocqueville (1805–1859) declared after the French Revolution, the change in society amounted to "nothing short of the regeneration of the whole human race" (1955:13, orig. 1856). As the new industrial economy, enormous cities, and fresh political ideas combined to draw attention to society, sociology flowered in France, Germany, and England, the countries experiencing the greatest changes.

SCIENCE AND SOCIOLOGY

The nature of society has fascinated people since ancient times, including the brilliant philosophers K'ung Fu-tzu (or Confucius, 551–479 BCE) in China, and Plato (427–347 BCE) and Aristotle (384–322 BCE) in Greece.[1] Later, the

Roman emperor Marcus Aurelius (121–180), the medieval thinkers Saint Thomas Aquinas (c. 1225–1274) and Christine de Pizan (c. 1363–1431), and the great English playwright William Shakespeare (1564–1616) took up the question.

Yet these men and women were more interested in envisioning the ideal society than they were in analyzing society as it really was. In creating their new discipline, sociology's pioneers certainly cared how society could be improved, but their major goal was to understand how it operates. It was the French social thinker Auguste Comte (1798–1857) who coined the term *sociology* in 1838 to describe this new way of thinking. Thus, sociology is among the youngest of the academic disciplines—far newer than history, physics, or economics, for example.

 For a biographical sketch of Comte, go to the Gallery of Sociologists at **http://www. TheSociologyPage.com**.

Comte (1975, orig. 1851–54) saw sociology as the product of three stages of historical development. During the earliest *theological stage,* up to the end of the European Middle Ages, people took a religious view that society expressed God's will. With the Renaissance, this theological approach gradually gave way to a *metaphysical stage* in which people saw society as a natural rather than a supernatural phenomenon. The English philosopher

[1]This text uses the abbreviation BCE ("before the Common Era.") rather than BC ("before Christ") to respect the religious diversity of Canadian society. Similarly, we use the abbreviation CE ("Common Era") in place of AD (*Anno Domini*, "in the year of our Lord").

Daniel Grafton Hill (1923–2003) is a well-known authority on black history and a Canadian sociologist, civil servant, and human rights specialist. Helen Caroline Abell (1917–) is a well-known and respected Canadian sociologist involved with international studies in the field of rural sociolog.

Thomas Hobbes, for example, suggested that society reflected not the perfection of God so much as the failings of a selfish human nature.

What Comte called the *scientific stage* began with the work of early scientists such as the Polish astronomer Nicolaus Copernicus (1473–1543), the Italian astronomer and physicist Galileo Galilei (1564–1642), and the English physicist and mathematician Isaac Newton (1642–1727). Comte's contribution came in applying the scientific approach—first used to analyze the physical world—to the study of society.

Comte thus favoured **positivism**, *a way of understanding based on science.* As a positivist, Comte believed that society operates according to certain laws, just as the physical world operates according to gravity and other laws of nature.

At the beginning of the twentieth century, sociology took hold as an academic discipline in the United States (two decades earlier than in Canada), strongly influenced by Comte's ideas. Today, most sociologists still consider science a crucial element of sociology. But we now realize that human behaviour is far more complex than the movement of planets or even the actions of other living things. We are creatures of imagination and spontaneity, so human behaviour can never be explained by any rigid "laws of society." In addition, early sociologists such as Karl Marx (1818–1883) were deeply troubled by the striking inequality of the new industrial society. They wanted the new discipline of sociology not just to understand society but also to bring about change toward social justice.

MARGINALIZED VOICES

Auguste Comte and Karl Marx stand among the giants of sociology. But in recent years, we have come to see the important contributions made by others who were pushed to the margins of society because of their gender or race.

Harriet Martineau (1802–1876), who is regarded as the first female sociologist, was born to a wealthy English family. She first made her mark in 1853 by translating the writings of Auguste Comte from French into English. Later, she became a noted scholar in her own right, documenting the evils of slavery and arguing for laws to protect factory workers and to advance the standing of women.

In Canada, Nellie McClung (1873–1951) was a pioneer of women's rights who started school at 10 years of age and received a teaching certificate six years later. McClung was a supporter of suffrage for women and a well-known advocate for Prohibition, factory laws for women, formal compulsory education, reform for Canadian prisons, and equal representation for women in the political realm. While an elected Liberal MLA in Alberta, she became a member of the "Famous Five," who in 1927 petitioned the government of Canada to include women in the definition of "person" in the *British North America Act.* Their success in 1929 meant that women could vote and be appointed to the Senate.

An important contribution to understanding race in the United States was made by another sociological pioneer, William Edward Burghardt Du Bois (1868–1963). Born to a poor Massachusetts family, Du Bois enrolled at Fisk University in Nashville, Tennessee, and then at Harvard University, where he earned the first doctorate awarded by that university to a black person. Like Martineau and McClung, Du Bois believed that sociologists should try to solve contemporary problems. He therefore studied the black community (1967, orig. 1899), spoke out against racial inequality, and served as a founding member of the National Association for the Advancement of Colored People (NAACP).

The fact that women and black people were second-class citizens reduced the attention paid to the work of Martineau, McClung, and Du Bois. By the mid-twentieth century, however, Canadian sociologists were detailing their accomplishments to new generations of students.

Sociological Theory

Weaving observations into understanding brings us to another aspect of sociology: theory. A **theory** is *a statement of how and why specific facts are related*. To illustrate, recall Emile Durkheim's theory that categories of people with low social integration (men, Protestants, the wealthy, and the unmarried) are at higher risk of suicide.

Like all scientists, sociologists conduct research to test and refine their theories. Figure 1–2, which shows the suicide rates for women and men in different countries, gives you a chance to do some theorizing of your own.

In building theory, sociologists face two basic questions: "What issues should we study?" and "How should we connect the facts?" In answering these questions, sociologists look to one or more theoretical approaches or "road maps." Think of a **theoretical approach** as *a basic image of society that guides thinking and research*. Sociologists make use of the *structural-functional approach,* the *social-conflict approach*, and the *symbolic-interaction approach*.

THE STRUCTURAL-FUNCTIONAL APPROACH

The **structural-functional approach** is *a framework for building theory that sees society as a complex system whose parts work together to promote solidarity and stability*. As its name suggests, this approach points to the importance of **social structure**, *any relatively stable pattern of social behaviour*. Social structure gives our lives shape in families, the workplace, or the university classroom. Second, this approach looks for any structure's **social functions**, *the consequences of any social pattern for the operation of society as a whole*. All social patterns—from a simple handshake to complex religious rituals—function to keep society going, at least in its present form.

The structural-functional approach owes much to Auguste Comte, who pointed out the need for social integration during a time of rapid change. Emile Durkheim,

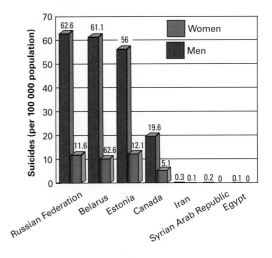

FIGURE 1-2 Suicide Rates of Men and Women in Selected Countries, 2003

Canada's suicide rate is high compared with those of some other nations and low when compared with still other nations. How do these data support or contradict Durkheim's theory of suicide?

Source: WHO, 2003.

who helped establish sociology in French universities, also based his work on this view. A third structural-functional pioneer was the English sociologist Herbert Spencer (1820–1903). Spencer compared society to the human body: just as the structural parts of the human body—the skeleton, muscles, and various internal organs—function together to help the entire organism survive, social structures work together to preserve society. The structural-functional approach, then, leads sociologists to identify various structures of society and investigate their functions.

Find biographical sketches of Durkheim and Spencer in the Gallery of Sociologists at http://www.TheSociologyPage.com.

The U.S. sociologist Robert K. Merton (1910–2003) expanded our understanding of social function by pointing out that any social structure probably has many functions, some more obvious than others. He distinguished between **manifest functions**, *the recognized and intended consequences of any social pattern*, and **latent functions**, *the unrecognized and unintended consequences of any social pattern*. To illustrate, the obvious function of this country's system of higher education is to give young people the information and skills they will need to perform jobs after

The painting *Furnishings*, by Paul Marcus, presents the essential wisdom of social-conflict theory: Society operates in a way that conveys wealth, power, and privilege to some at the expense of others. What categories of people are advantaged and disadvantaged, as suggested by the artist?

Paul Marcus, *Furnishings*, oil painting on canvas, 64 in. × 48 in., Studio SPM, Inc.

graduation. Perhaps just as important, although less often acknowledged, is post-secondary education's function as a "marriage broker," bringing together young people of similar social backgrounds. Another latent function of higher education is to limit unemployment by keeping millions of people out of the labour market, where many of them may not easily find jobs.

But Merton also recognized that the effects of social structure are not all good and certainly not good for everybody. Thus, a **social dysfunction** is *any social pattern that may disrupt the operation of society*. People usually disagree on what is helpful and what is harmful. Moreover, what is functional for one category of people (say, high profits for factory owners or landlords) may well be dysfunctional for another category of people (say, low wages for factory workers or high rents for tenants).

Critical review. The main idea of the structural-functional approach is its vision of society as stable and orderly. The main goal of sociologists who use this approach, then, is to figure out "what makes society tick."

In the mid-1900s, most sociologists favoured the structural-functional approach. In recent decades, however, its influence has declined. By focusing attention on social stability and unity, critics point out, structural-functionalism ignores inequalities of social class, race, ethnicity, and gender, which can generate tension and conflict. In general, its focus on stability at the expense of conflict makes this approach somewhat conservative. As a critical response, sociologists developed the social-conflict approach.

THE SOCIAL-CONFLICT APPROACH

The **social-conflict approach** is *a framework for building theory that sees society as an arena of inequality that generates conflict and change.* Unlike the structural-functional emphasis on solidarity, this approach highlights conflict. Guided by this approach, sociologists investigate how factors such as class, race, ethnicity, gender, and age are linked to the unequal distribution of money, power, education, and social prestige. A conflict analysis rejects the idea that social structure promotes the operation of society as a whole, focusing instead on how any social pattern benefits some people while hurting others.

Sociologists use the social-conflict approach to look at ongoing conflict between dominant and disadvantaged categories of people: high-income earners in relation to low-income earners, white people in relation to visible minorities, or men in relation to women. They find that, typically, people in advantaged positions try to protect their privileges while the disadvantaged try to gain more for themselves.

A conflict analysis of our educational system shows how schooling reproduces class inequality in every new generation. For example, secondary schools assign students to either post-secondary preparatory or vocational training programs. From a structural-functional point of view, such "tracking" benefits everyone by providing schooling that fits students' abilities. But conflict analysis counters that tracking often has less to do with talent than with social background, so that well-to-do students are placed in higher tracks and poor children end up in lower tracks. In this way, young people from privileged families get the best schooling and later pursue high-income careers. The children of low-income families, on the other hand, are not prepared for college or university and, like their parents before them, typically enter low-paying jobs. In both cases, the social standing of one generation is passed on to the next, with schools justifying the practice in terms of individual merit (Davis & Guppy, 1997; Bowles & Gintis, 1976; Oakes, 1982, 1985).

Many sociologists who use social-conflict analysis try not just to understand society but also to reduce inequality. This was the goal of W.E.B. Du Bois, who was guided by the social-conflict approach to raise the standing of black people. Likewise, Karl Marx championed the workers against those who owned the factories. In a well-known statement (inscribed on his monument in London's Highgate Cemetery), Marx declared, "The philosophers have only interpreted the world, in various ways; the point, however, is to change it."

Critical review. The social-conflict approach has gained a large following in recent decades, but like other approaches, it has met with its share of criticism. Because this analysis focuses on inequality, it largely ignores how shared values and interdependence can unify members of a society. In addition, to the extent that it pursues political goals, the social-conflict approach cannot claim scientific objectivity. Supporters of social-conflict analysis respond that *all* theoretical approaches have political consequences.

A final criticism of both the structural-functional and social-conflict approaches is that they paint society in broad strokes—in terms of "family," "social class," "race," and so on. A third theoretical approach views society less in general terms and more as the specific, everyday experiences of individual people.

THE SYMBOLIC-INTERACTION APPROACH

The structural-functional and social-conflict approaches share a **macro-level orientation**, meaning *a broad focus on social structures that shape society as a whole.* Macro-level sociology takes in the big picture, rather like observing a city from a helicopter and seeing how highways help people move from place to place or how housing differs from high-income to low-income neighbourhoods. Sociology also uses a **micro-level orientation**, *a close-up focus on social interaction in specific situations.* Exploring city life in this way occurs at street level, where you might watch how children invent games on a school playground or observe how pedestrians respond to homeless people. The **symbolic-interaction approach**, then, is *a framework for building theory that sees society as the product of the everyday interactions of individuals.*

How does "society" result from the ongoing experiences of tens of millions of people? One answer, detailed in Chapter 4 ("Social Interaction in Everyday Life"), is that society is nothing more than the reality people construct for themselves as they interact with one another. That is, human beings are creatures who live in a world of symbols, attaching *meaning* to virtually everything. "Reality," therefore, is simply how we define our surroundings, our duties toward others, and even our own identities.

The symbolic-interaction approach has roots in the thinking of Max Weber (1864–1920), a German sociologist who emphasized understanding a particular setting from

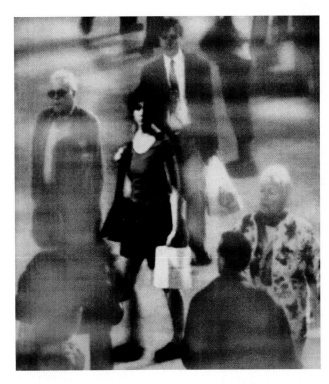

To understand how the symbolic-interaction approach views society, consider Sherry Karver's painting, *Faces in the Crowd III.* Just as the images seem to flow together in new and never quite predictable ways, society is never at rest; it is an ongoing process by which interacting people define and redefine reality.

Sherry Karver, *Faces in the Crowd III,* 2001, oil and photography on panel, 24 in. × 19 in. Courtesy of Lisa Harris Gallery, Seattle, Washington.

the point of view of the people in it. Since Weber's time, sociologists have taken micro-level sociology in a number of directions. Chapter 3 ("Socialization: From Infancy to Old Age") discusses the ideas of George Herbert Mead (1863–1931), who explored how the self is continuously shaped through social interaction. Chapter 4 ("Social Interaction in Everyday Life") presents the work of Erving Goffman (1922–1982), whose *dramaturgical analysis* describes how we resemble actors on a stage as we play out our various roles. Other sociologists, including George Homans and Peter Blau, have developed *social-exchange analysis,* the idea that interaction is guided by what each person stands to gain and lose from others. In the ritual of courtship, for example, people seek mates who can offer them at least as much—in terms of physical attractiveness, intelligence, and social background—as they offer in return.

Critical review. Without denying the existence of macro-level social structures such as "the family" and "social class," the symbolic-interaction approach reminds us that society basically amounts to *people interacting.* That is, micro-level

APPLYING THEORY
MAJOR THEORETICAL APPROACHES

	Structural-Functional Approach	Social-Conflict Approach	Symbolic-Interaction Approach
What is the level of analysis?	Macro-level	Macro-level	Micro-level
What image of society does the approach have?	Society is a system of inter-related parts that is relatively stable. Each part works to keep society operating in an orderly way. Members have general agreement about what is morally right.	Society is a system of social inequality. Society operates to benefit some categories of people and harm others. Social inequality causes conflict that leads to social change.	Society is an ongoing process. People interact in countless settings using symbolic communications. The reality people experience is variable and changing.
What core questions does the approach ask?	How is society held together? What are the major parts of society? How are these parts linked? What does each part do to help society work?	How does society divide a population? How do advantaged people protect their privileges? How do disadvantaged people challenge the system seeking change?	How do people experience society? How do people shape the reality they experience? How do behaviour and meaning change from person to person and from one situation to another?

sociology tries to show how individuals actually experience society. But on the other side of the coin, by emphasizing what is unique in each social scene, this approach risks overlooking the widespread influence of culture, as well as factors such as class, gender, and race.

The Applying Theory table summarizes the features of the structural-functional approach, the social-conflict approach, and the symbolic-interaction approach. As you read the chapters in this book, keep in mind that each approach is helpful in answering particular types of questions. As the Applying Sociology box about sports on pages 18–19 shows, the fullest understanding of society comes from using all three approaches.

Three Ways to Do Sociology

All sociologists want to learn about the social world. But, in the same way that they may prefer one theoretical approach to another, so they may prefer one methodological orientation. The following sections describe three ways to do sociological research.

SCIENTIFIC SOCIOLOGY

The first, and probably most popular, way to do sociological research is based on **science**, *a logical system that bases knowledge on direct, systematic observation.* Scientific knowledge is based on empirical evidence, information we can verify with our senses.

A scientific orientation often challenges what we accept as "common sense." Here are three examples of widely held beliefs that are contradicted by scientific evidence:

1. **"Differences in the behaviour of females and males reflect 'human nature.'"** Wrong. Much of what we call human nature is constructed by the society in which we live. We know this because researchers have documented how definitions of "feminine" and "masculine" change over time and vary from one society to another (see Chapter 10, "Gender Stratification").

2. **"Canada is a middle-class society in which most people are more-or-less equal."** Not true. As Chapter 8 ("Social Stratification") explains, the richest 5 percent of Canadian families control more than 40 percent of the country's wealth, while the poorest 5 percent of Canadian families have a negative wealth—they live in debt.

3. **"People marry because they are in love."** Not exactly. In our own society, as we have already explained, various social rules guide the selection of mates. Around the world, research indicates that marriages in most societies have little to do with love. Chapter 13 ("Family and Religion") explains why.

These examples confirm the old saying that "It's not what we don't know that gets us into trouble as much as the things we *do* know that just aren't so." Scientific sociology is a useful way to assess many kinds of information.

Concepts, variables, and measurement. A basic element of science is the **concept**, *a mental construct that represents some part of the world in a simplified form.* Sociologists use concepts to label aspects of social life, including "the family" and "the economy," and to categorize people in terms of their "gender" or "social class."

A **variable** is *a concept whose value changes from case to case.* The familiar variable "price," for example, changes from item to item in a supermarket. Similarly, people use the concept "social class" to size up others as "upper class," "middle class," "working class," or "lower class."

The use of variables depends on **measurement**, *a procedure for determining the value of a variable in a specific case.* Some variables are easy to measure, as when a checkout clerk adds up the cost of our groceries. But measuring sociological variables can be far more difficult. For example, how would you measure a person's social class? You might be tempted to look at clothing, listen to patterns of speech, or note a home address. Or, trying to be more precise, you might ask about income, occupation, and education. Because there are many ways to measure almost anything, researchers must operationalize their variables; that is, they must specify exactly what they are measuring in each case.

Sociologists also face the problem of dealing with large numbers of people. For example, how do you report income for thousands or even millions of individuals? Listing streams of numbers would carry little meaning and tell us nothing about the people as a whole. Therefore, sociologists use descriptive statistics to state what is "average" for a large population. Most commonly used are the mean (the arithmetic average of all measures, obtained by adding them up and dividing by the number of cases), the median (the middle score that divides a set of numbers in half), and the mode (the single score that appears most often).

Reliability and validity. Beyond carefully operationalizing variables, useful measurement must be reliable and valid. **Reliability** is *consistency in measurement.* For measurement to be reliable, in other words, the process must yield the same results when repeated. However, even consistent results may not be valid. **Validity** is *actually measuring exactly what you intend to measure.* Valid measurement means more than

hitting the same spot somewhere on a target again and again; it means hitting the precise target, the bull's-eye.

Say you want to know just how religious people are. You might ask how often your subjects attend religious services. But is going to a church or temple or mosque really the same thing as being religious? Maybe not, because people take part in religious rituals for many reasons, not all of them religious, and some strong believers avoid organized religion altogether. Thus, even when a measure yields consistent results (making it reliable), it can still miss the real, intended target (and lack validity). In sum, sociological research depends on careful measurement, which is always a challenge to researchers.

Correlation and cause. The real payoff in scientific research is determining how variables are related. **Correlation** means *a relationship in which two (or more) variables change together.* But sociologists want to know not just how variables change but why. The scientific ideal, then, is mapping out **cause and effect**, which means *a relationship in which change in one variable causes change in another.* As we noted earlier, Emile Durkheim found that the degree of social integration (the cause) affected the suicide rate (the effect) among categories of people. Scientists refer to the causal factor as the *independent variable* and call the effect the *dependent variable.* Understanding cause and effect is valuable because it allows researchers to *predict* how one pattern of behaviour will produce another.

Just because two variables change together does not necessarily mean that they have a cause-and-effect relationship. For instance, the marriage rate in Canada falls to its lowest point in January, exactly the same month in which the national death rate is highest. This hardly means that people drop dead if they decide not to marry (or that they don't marry because they die). More likely, it is the dreary weather across much of the country during January (perhaps combined with the post-holiday "blahs") that causes both the low marriage rate and the high death rate.

When two variables change together but neither one causes the other, sociologists describe the relationship as a *spurious,* or false, correlation. A spurious correlation between two variables usually results from some third factor. For example, delinquency rates are high where young people live in crowded housing, but both of these factors result from being poor. To be sure of a real cause-and-effect relationship, we must show that (1) the two variables are correlated, (2) the independent (or causal) variable occurs before the dependent variable, and (3) there is no evidence that the correlation is spurious because of some third variable.

The ideal of objectivity. A guiding principle of scientific study is *objectivity,* or personal neutrality, in conducting research. The ideal of objective research is to allow the facts

APPLYING SOCIOLOGY

Sports: Playing the Theory Game

Who among us doesn't enjoy sports? Many children as young as six or seven play two or three sports. For adults, weekend television is filled with sporting events, and whole sections of our newspapers report the scores. What can we learn by applying sociology's three theoretical paradigms to this familiar element of life in Canada?

A structural-functional approach asks what sports do for our society as a whole. The manifest functions of sports include recreation, physical conditioning, and a relatively harmless way to let off steam. Sports have important latent functions as well, from fostering social relationships to creating countless jobs. Perhaps most importantly, though, sports encourage competition, which is central to this nation's way of life (Coakley, 1990).

Sports also have dysfunctional consequences, of course. For example, universities intent on fielding winning teams sometimes recruit students for their athletic ability rather than their academic aptitude. This practice not only pulls down a school's academic standards, but also shortchanges athletes who devote little time to academic work.

A social-conflict analysis might begin by pointing out how sports are linked to social inequality. Some sports (such as tennis, swimming, golf, and skiing) are expensive, so participation is largely limited to the well-to-do. However, football, baseball, and basketball are accessible to people of all income levels. Thus, the

games people play are not simply a matter of choice but also a reflection of people's social standing.

Moreover, men dominate sports. The first modern Olympic Games, which were held in 1896, excluded women from competition. In Canada, through most of the twentieth century, hockey teams barred girls from the ice on the unfounded notions that girls lack the strength and stamina to play hockey and that they compromise their femininity if they do. Women competed in hockey for the first time at the 1998 Olympic Games. In the world of sports, women still take a back seat to men, particularly in sports that yield the greatest earnings and social prestige.

Although our society long excluded black people from professional sports, opportunities have expanded in recent decades. In 1947, Jackie Robinson broke through the "colour line" to become the first black player in Major League Baseball; he played for the Brooklyn Dodgers. In 1958, Canadian-born William O'Ree made headlines as the first black hockey player to be recruited to the National Hockey League. More than 50 years later, professional baseball retired the legendary Robinson's number 42 on *all* teams and in 2002, black Americans (12 percent of the U.S. population) accounted for 10 percent of Major

Take a look at a brief CBC documentary on Jackie Robinson at **http://archives. cbc.ca/1DC-1-41-621-3322-11/ that_was_then/sports/jackie-robinson.**

League Baseball players, 65 percent of National Football League (NFL) players, and 78 percent of National Basketball Association (NBA) players (Lapchick, 2003).

One reason for the increasing share of black people in professional sports is the fact that athletic performance—in terms of batting average or number of points scored per game—is measured objectively and is not influenced by racial prejudice. It is also true that some black people make a special effort to excel in athletics, where they see more opportunity than in other careers (Steele, 1990; Edwards, 2000). In recent years, in fact, black athletes have earned higher salaries, on average, than white players.

But racial discrimination still taints professional sports in Canada and the United States. For one thing, race is linked to the positions athletes play on the field, a pattern called "stacking." The figure opposite shows the results of a study of race in American football. Notice that white players dominate the offence and also play the central positions on both sides of the line. More broadly, black players figure prominently in only five major sports: basketball, football, baseball, boxing, and track. And across all professional sports, the vast majority of managers, head coaches, and team owners are still white (Lapchick, 2003).

Overall, who benefits most from professional sports? Although individual players may get sky-high salaries and

to speak for themselves and not become coloured by the personal values and biases of the researcher. In reality, of course, achieving total neutrality is impossible for anyone. But carefully observing the rules of scientific research will maximize objectivity.

The German sociologist Max Weber noted that people usually choose *value-relevant* research topics—topics they care about. But, he cautioned, once their work is underway,

researchers should try to be *value-free*. That is, we must be dedicated to finding truth as it *is* rather than as we think it *should be*. For Weber, this difference sets science apart from politics. Researchers (unlike politicians) must try to stay open-minded and be willing to accept whatever results come from their work, whether they like them or not.

Weber's argument still carries much weight in sociology, although most researchers admit that we can millions of fans love following their teams, the vast profits sports generate are controlled by a small number of people (predominantly white men). In sum, sports in North America are bound up with inequalities based on gender, race, and wealth.

At a micro level, a sporting event is a complex face-to-face interaction. In part, play is guided by assigned positions and, of course, by the rules of the game. But players are also spontaneous and unpredictable. The symbolic-interaction paradigm sees sports less as a system than as an ongoing process. Also, we expect each player to understand the game a little differently. Some enjoy stiff competition, whereas for others love of the game may be greater than the need to win.

Team members also shape their particular realities according to the prejudices, jealousies, and ambitions they bring to the field. Moreover, the behaviour of any single player changes over time. A rookie in professional baseball, for example, typically feels self-conscious during the first few games in the big leagues but goes on to develop a comfortable sense of fitting in with the team. Jackie Robinson played minor baseball in 1946 in Montreal and was revered in that cosmopolitan city. Coming to feel at home on the field in New York the next year was a different story. At first, he was painfully aware that many white players and millions of white fans resented his presence. In time, however, his outstanding ability and his confident, cooperative manner won him respect throughout North America.

The three theoretical paradigms differ in their approaches to sports, but none is entirely correct. Each generates its own insights; to fully appreciate the power of the sociological perspective, you should try to apply all three to any given issue.

WHAT DO YOU THINK?

1. Describe how a macro-level approach to sports differs from a micro-level approach. Which theoretical approaches are macro-level and which one is micro-level?
2. Make up three questions about sports, one that reflects the focus of each of the three theoretical paradigms.
3. How might you apply these three paradigms to other social patterns, such as the workplace or family life?

Race and Sport: "Stacking" in Professional Football

Source: Lapchick (2003).

never be completely value-free or even aware of all our biases (Demerath, 1996). Moreover, sociologists are not "average" people: most are white people who are highly educated and more politically liberal than the population as a whole. Sociologists need to remember that they, too, are influenced by their social backgrounds.

INTERPRETIVE SOCIOLOGY

Not all sociologists agree that the scientific orientation is the best way to study human society. Unlike planets or other elements of the natural world, humans do not simply move about; we engage in *meaningful* action. A second type of research is **interpretive sociology**, *the study of society that*

Myths are an important dimension of human existence. In his painting, *Creation of North Sacred Mountain,* Navajo artist Harrison Begay offers a mythic account of creation. A myth (from the Greek, meaning "story" or "word") may or may not be factual in the literal sense. Yet it conveys some basic truth about the meaning and purpose of life. It is the meanings that shape social behaviour that the interpretive sociologist seeks to understand.

35464/13 *Creation of North Sacred Mountain* by Harrison Begay, Haskey-Yah-Ne-Yah, Navajo. In the Collections of the Museum of Indian Arts and Culture/Laboratory of Anthropology, Museum of New Mexico. Photograph by Blair Clark.

focuses on the meanings people attach to their social world. Max Weber, the pioneer of this framework, argued that the proper focus of sociology is interpretation, or understanding the meaning people create in their everyday lives.

The importance of meaning. Interpretive sociology differs from scientific—or positivist—sociology in three ways. First, scientific sociology focuses on action, what people do; interpretive sociology, by contrast, focuses on the meaning people attach to behaviour. Second, whereas scientific sociology sees an objective reality "out there," interpretive sociology sees reality constructed by people themselves in the course of their everyday lives. Third, whereas scientific sociology tends to favour *quantitative* data—numerical measurements of social behaviour—interpretive sociology favours *qualitative* data, researchers' perceptions of how people understand their surroundings. In sum, the scientific orientation is well suited for research in a laboratory, where investigators stand back and take careful measurements. The interpretive orientation is better suited for research in a natural setting, where investigators interact with people to learn how they make sense of their everyday lives.

Weber's concept of *Verstehen.* Max Weber claimed that the key to interpretive sociology lies in *Verstehen,* the German word for "understanding." It is the interpretive sociologist's job not just to observe *what* people do but also to share in their world of meaning, coming to appreciate *why* they act as they do. Subjective thoughts and feelings—which science tends to dismiss as "bias"—now move to the centre of the researcher's attention.

CRITICAL SOCIOLOGY

Like the interpretive orientation, critical sociology developed in reaction to the limitations of scientific sociology. In the case of this third way to do research, however, the problem was the foremost principle of scientific research: objectivity.

Scientific sociology holds that reality is "out there," and the researcher's job is to study and document this reality. But Karl Marx, who founded the critical orientation, rejected the idea that society exists as a "natural" system with a fixed order. Assuming this, he claimed, amounts to saying that society cannot be changed. Scientific sociology, in his view, ends up supporting the status quo.

The importance of change. **Critical sociology**, then, is *the study of society that focuses on the need for social change.* Rather than asking the scientific question "How does society work?", critical sociologists ask moral and political questions, especially, "Should society exist in its present form?" Their answer, typically, is that it should not. The point, said Marx (1972:109, orig. 1845), is not just to study the world as it is but to change it. In making value judgments about how society should be improved, critical sociology rejects the scientific claim that research should be value-free.

Sociologists using the critical orientation seek to change not only society but also the character of research itself. They consider their research subjects as equals and encourage their participation in deciding what to study and how to do the work. Often researchers and subjects use their findings to provide a voice for less powerful people and advance the political goal of a more equal society (Wolf, 1996; Hess, 1999).

Sociology as politics. Scientific sociologists object to taking sides in this way, charging that critical sociology (whether feminist, Marxist, or some other critical orientation) is political and gives up any claim to objectivity. Critical sociologists respond that *all* research is political in that either it calls for change or it does not; sociologists thus have no choice about their work being political, but they can choose which positions to support. Critical sociology, therefore, is an activist approach tying knowledge to action and seeks not just to understand the world but also to improve it. Generally speaking, scientific sociology tends to appeal to researchers with more conservative political views; critical sociology appeals to those with liberal and radical-left politics.

SUMMING UP

Three Methodological Orientations in Sociology

	Scientific	Interpretive	Critical
What is reality?	Society is an orderly system. There is an objective reality "out there."	Society is ongoing interaction. People construct reality as they attach meanings to their behaviour.	Society is patterns of inequality. Reality is that some categories of people dominate others.
How do we conduct research?	Researcher gathers empirical, ideally quantitative, data. Researcher tries to be a neutral observer.	Researcher develops a qualitative account of the subjective sense people make of their world. Researcher is a participant.	Research is a strategy to bring about desired social change. Researcher is an activist.
Corresponding theoretical approach	Structural-functional approach	Symbolic-interaction approach	Social-conflict approach

METHODS AND THEORY

What about the link between methodological orientations and theory? In general, each of the three ways to do sociology is related to one of the theoretical approaches presented earlier in this chapter. The scientific orientation corresponds to the structural-functional approach, the interpretive orientation to the symbolic-interaction approach, and the critical orientation to the social-conflict approach. The Summing Up table reviews the differences among the three ways to do sociology. Keep in mind that, although sociologists may favour one orientation over another, most make use of all three.

RESEARCH ETHICS

Like all other scientific investigators, sociologists must remember that their work can harm as well as help subjects and communities. For this reason, the Canadian Sociology and Anthropology Association (CSAA)—the major professional association for sociologists in Canada—provides formal guidelines for conducting research (1994).

Sociologists must try to be both technically competent and fair-minded in their work. They must report their findings without omitting significant data, and they are ethically bound to share their work with other sociologists who may want to conduct the same study.

Sociologists must also ensure the safety of subjects taking part in a research project and must stop work immediately if they suspect that a subject is at risk of any harm. Researchers are also required to protect the privacy of individuals involved in a research project, even if they come under pressure from authorities, such as the police or the courts, to release confidential information. Researchers must also get the *informed consent* of participants, which means that the subjects understand their responsibilities and risks and agree—before the work begins—to take part in the study.

Another guideline concerns funding. Sociologists must reveal all sources of financial support in their published results. Furthermore, sociologists are required to avoid conflicts of interest (or even the appearance of such conflicts) that may call their results into question. For example, researchers must never accept funding from any organization that seeks to influence the research results for its own purposes.

The federal government plays a part in research ethics as well. Every college and university that seeks federal funding for research involving human subjects must have a Human Research Ethics Committee that reviews grant applications and ensures that the proposed research will not violate ethical standards.

There are also global dimensions to research ethics. Before beginning work in another nation, investigators must become familiar enough with that society to understand what people *there* are likely to regard as a violation of privacy or a source of personal danger. In a diverse society such as our own, the same rule applies to studying people with different backgrounds. The Diversity: Race, Class, & Gender box on the following page offers tips on the sensitivity outsiders should employ when studying minorities in Canada.

DIVERSITY: RACE, CLASS, & GENDER

Studying Canada's Aboriginal People

In a society as racially, ethnically, and religiously diverse as Canada, sociological investigators will inevitably encounter people who differ from themselves. Learning—in advance—some of the distinctive traits of any category of people being studied can both facilitate the research and ensure that no hard feelings remain when the work is completed. Research with Aboriginals in Canada provides clues for conducting research in general. The success of the research process requires that investigators pay particular attention to a number of factors that are not obvious.

1. **Consider the impact of the investigators' characteristics.** Differences in culture and status have an impact on observations. For example, Aboriginal children are more likely to identify themselves as Aboriginals when interviewed by another Aboriginal than when interviewed by a non-Aboriginal. Large differences between cultures necessitate large considerations.

2. **Be careful with language.** Terms have different meanings in different cultures and even within cultures. For example, Cree, an Aboriginal language, is highly inflected and words may be nonsensical in isolation. Also, Cree speakers (and northern Natives generally) tend to be more comfortable with silence after questions than

are southern mainstream Canadians; there is no mandatory gender "he" or "she" in Cree; and there are two forms of the first person plural "we" (inclusive and exclusive) depending upon whether or not the speaker is including the listener(s).

3. **Recognize that minority groups are heterogeneous.** "Aboriginal" is a term used by Statistics Canada to describe a category of individuals that includes many different nations that have different languages and dialects (Satzewich, 1998). Among as few as eight Aboriginal women in a study conducted in Alberta, there were two different nations and three different religions (not counting "no religion") represented. Many Aboriginals, in fact, identify themselves primarily as a member of a particular nation and not as a member of the census category "Aboriginal."

4. **Recognize differences in family life.** Generally speaking, Aboriginal cultures favour having many children. Aboriginal women are honoured as givers and creators of life. It is understandable, then, that Aboriginal women are reluctant to use birth control during sex with a steady partner, even if unprotected sex exposes them to HIV.

5. **Take your time to build a relationship.** Many respondents are more con-

cerned with the quality of the relationship with the researcher than with simply answering a series of questions. Thus, the researcher who tries to rush through an interview in order to cover all questions may in the end not get a true (that is, valid or reliable) response because personal trust has not first been established. This especially concerns personal and sensitive topics, such as loss of custody of one's children.

In short, researchers must always remain respectful of subjects and mindful of their well-being. In part, this means investigators must become familiar—well ahead of time—with the cultural patterns of those they wish to study.

WHAT DO YOU THINK?

1. What are some likely consequences of researchers' not being sensitive to the culture of their subjects?
2. What do researchers need to do to avoid these problems?
3. Discuss the research process with classmates from various cultural backgrounds. What similar or different concerns would be raised by these people when taking part in research?

Sources: Annis (1986), Mill (1997), and Rudmin (1994).

GENDER AND RESEARCH

In trying to be ethical in their research, sociologists must pay special attention to **gender**, *the personal traits and social positions that members of a society attach to being female or male.* Margrit Eichler (1988) identifies four ways in which gender can influence research, to which can be added a fifth:

1. **Androcentricity.** *Androcentricity* (*andro* is the Greek word for "male"; *centricity* refers to "being centred on")

means acting as if only the actions of men are important, ignoring what women do. The parallel concept of *gynocentricity*—seeing the world from a female perspective—is a problem, too, but one that is far less common in our male-dominated society.

2. **Overgeneralizing.** This problem occurs when sociologists use data obtained from men to make conclusions about all people. For example, a researcher might

gather information from a handful of male public officials and draw conclusions about an entire community.

3. **Gender blindness.** Failing to consider gender at all is called "gender blindness." A study of growing old in Canada that overlooks the fact that most elderly men live with spouses while elderly women generally live alone would be limited by gender blindness.

4. **Double standards.** Researchers must be careful not to judge men and women differently. For example, a family researcher who labels a couple "man and wife" (rather than "husband and wife") implies that the marital status of one sex is more significant than that of the other.

5. **Interference.** We can add to Eichler's list the problem of subjects reacting to the gender of the investigator in ways that interfere with the research project. For instance, while conducting research in Sicily, Maureen Giovannini (1992) found that many men reacted to her as a *woman* rather than as a *researcher*. Gender dynamics also kept her from certain activities, such as private conversations with men that were considered inappropriate for single women.

There is nothing wrong with focusing research on people of one gender or the other. But all sociologists, as well as people who read their work, should be mindful of how gender can affect an investigation.

Philip Zimbardo's research helps to explain why violence is a common element in our society's prisons. At the same time, his work demonstrates the dangers that sociological investigation poses for subjects and the need for investigators to observe ethical standards that protect the welfare of people who participate in research.

Research Methods

A **research method** is *a systematic plan for doing research.* Here we examine four widely used methods of sociological investigation: experiments, surveys, participant observation, and use of existing sources. None is better or worse than any other. Rather, just as a carpenter selects a particular tool for a particular job, researchers choose a method according to whom they want to study and what they want to learn.

TESTING A HYPOTHESIS: THE EXPERIMENT

The **experiment** is *a research method for investigating cause and effect under highly controlled conditions.* Experiments test a specific *hypothesis,* a statement of a possible relationship between two (or more) variables. A hypothesis is really an educated guess about how variables are linked. An experimenter gathers the evidence needed to accept or reject the hypothesis in three steps: (1) measuring the dependent variable (the "effect"), (2) exposing the dependent variable to the independent variable (the "cause" or "treatment"), and (3) measuring the dependent variable again to see whether the predicted change took place. If the expected change took place, the experiment supports the hypothesis; if not, the hypothesis must be modified.

Successful experiments depend on careful control of all factors that might affect what the experiment is trying to measure. Control is easiest in a research laboratory. But experiments in an everyday location—"in the field," as sociologists say—have the advantage of letting researchers observe subjects in their natural settings.

An illustration: The "Stanford County Prison" experiment. Prisons can be violent settings, but is this due simply to the "bad" people who end up there? Or, as Philip Zimbardo suspected, does prison itself somehow create violent behaviour? To answer this question, Zimbardo devised a fascinating experiment, which he called the "Stanford County Prison" (Zimbardo, 1972; Hanley, Banks, & Zimbardo, 1973).

Zimbardo thought that once inside a prison, even emotionally healthy people are prone to violence. Thus, Zimbardo treated the *prison setting* as the independent variable capable of causing *violence,* the dependent variable.

To test this hypothesis, Zimbardo's research team first constructed a realistic-looking "prison" in the basement of the psychology building on the campus of Stanford University in California. Then they placed an ad in a Palo Alto newspaper, offering to pay young men to help with a two-week research project. They administered a series of physical and psychological tests to each of the 70 who responded, and then selected the healthiest 24.

The next step was to assign randomly half the men to be "prisoners" and half to be "guards." The plan called for the guards and prisoners to spend the next two weeks in the mock prison. The prisoners began their part of the experiment soon afterward when the Palo Alto police "arrested" them at their homes. After searching and handcuffing the men, the police drove them to the local police station, where they were fingerprinted. Then police transported their captives to the Stanford prison, where the guards locked them up. Zimbardo started his video camera rolling and watched to see what would happen next.

The experiment turned into more than anyone had bargained for. Both guards and prisoners soon became embittered and hostile toward one another. Guards humiliated the prisoners by giving them jobs such as cleaning out toilets with their bare hands. The prisoners, for their part, resisted and insulted the guards. Within four days, the researchers removed five prisoners who displayed "extreme emotional depression, crying, rage and acute anxiety" (Hanley, Banks, & Zimbardo, 1973:81). Before the end of the first week, the situation had become so bad that the researchers had to cancel the experiment.

The events that unfolded at the "Stanford County Prison" supported Zimbardo's hypothesis that prison violence is rooted in the social character of jails themselves, not in the personalities of guards and prisoners. This finding raises questions about our society's prisons, suggesting the need for basic reform. Zimbardo was not surprised by the recent scandal over the abuse of prisoners in Iraq (Schwartz, 2004).

But also note that Zimbardo's experiment reveals the potential of research to threaten the physical and mental well-being of subjects. Such dangers are not always as obvious as they were in this case. Therefore, researchers must consider carefully the potential harm to subjects at all stages of their work and end any study, as Zimbardo did, if subjects may suffer harm of any kind.

ASKING QUESTIONS: THE SURVEY

A **survey** is *a research method in which subjects respond to a series of statements or questions in a questionnaire or an interview.* The most widely used of all research methods, the survey is well suited to studying what cannot be observed directly, such as political attitudes or religious beliefs or sexual practices.

A survey targets some *population,* such as unmarried mothers or adults living in rural areas of Alberta. Sometimes every adult in the country is the survey population, as in polls taken during national political campaigns. Of course, contacting a vast number of people is all but impossible, so researchers usually study a *sample,* a much smaller

number of subjects selected to represent the entire population. Surveys commonly give accurate estimates of national opinions based on samples of only 1500 people.

Beyond selecting subjects, the survey must have a specific plan for asking questions and recording answers. The most common way to do this is to give subjects a *questionnaire* with a series of written statements or questions. Often the researcher lets subjects choose possible responses to each item, as in a multiple-choice examination. Sometimes, though, a researcher may want subjects to respond freely, to permit all opinions to be included. Of course, this free-form approach means that the researcher later has to make sense out of what can be a bewildering array of answers.

In an *interview,* a researcher personally asks subjects a series of questions, thereby solving one problem common to the questionnaire method: the failure of some subjects to return the questionnaire to the researcher. A further difference is that interviews give participants freedom to respond as they wish. Researchers often ask follow-up questions to clarify an answer or to probe a bit more deeply. In doing this, however, a researcher must avoid influencing the subject even in subtle ways, such as by raising an eyebrow as the subject offers an answer.

An illustration: Longitudinal studies of hidden populations. How do you contact and stay in touch with research participants who are not members of mainstream society? Some individuals cannot be reached through a straightforward survey because they belong to what academics call *hard-to-reach* or *hidden* populations (Spreen & Zwaagstra, 1994). Such populations share three main characteristics: (1) there is no known list of the members of the population; (2) acknowledgment of belonging to the group is threatening because membership involves fear of prosecution or being the object of hate or scorn; and (3) members are distrustful of non-members and do whatever they can to avoid revealing their identities and are likely to refuse to cooperate with outsiders or to give unreliable answers to questions about themselves and their networks. Intravenous drug users and those who trade sex for money are examples of two hidden populations. Yet the need for reliable research on the individuals who are members of these populations has become urgent, given public concern over high rates of sexually transmitted infections (STIs), hepatitis, HIV infections, AIDS transmission and generally poor health status among these groups (Heckathorn, 1997).

One of the more powerful ways to understand health changes over time is to use a longitudinal research design and collect data from individuals repeatedly for as long as possible. But this again is problematic for studies of hidden populations because members are unlikely to give their real names and reliable contact information freely.

Cecilia Benoit and Mikael Jansson, two of the authors of this text, are leading a research project in British Columbia that adopts a longitudinal design in order to better understand the causal links between youth marginalization, street involvement, and health. Youth qualify for the project based on their weak attachment to parents or guardians and the school system, and strong association with the street economy. They are interviewed twice in the first month of contact and every few months for as long as they are willing to participate in the study (to a maximum of four years). Due to particular characteristics of this hidden population, combined with a distrust of academics and others in authority, several sampling techniques are being used to increase the probability of getting a reliable sample. Four non-profit community organizations are helping to establish respondent contact strategies to advertise the study and access the various subgroups of marginalized youth. The study is also widely advertised in shelters and drop-in centres and other places where marginalized youth congregate.

A final method of recruiting research participants is a technique known as *respondent-driven sampling* (Heckathorn, 1997). The technique begins with a small number of research participants who serve as "seeds." In the Benoit and Jansson project, the seeds are given three recruitment coupons to hand to peers who they believe might want to come forward for an interview (based on the rationale that reclusive youth are more likely to respond to the appeals of their peers than those from either the university or community agencies). The seeds are paid a nominal fee of $10 for each peer who comes forward to be interviewed (paid at the seed's third interview). The youths' anonymity is maintained by not collecting names or other identifying information in the data set. In order to link the questionnaires to each other over time, each youth is asked a small number of questions that will have very individual and personal answers, such as the name of their favourite teacher. So far, over 200 youths have been interviewed, and some of them have also helped to bring their peers back for follow-up interviews.

 Read more about this and other projects on hard-to-reach and hidden populations on Cecilia Benoit's homepage at **http://web.uvic.ca/~cbenoit/.**

IN THE FIELD: PARTICIPANT OBSERVATION

Participant observation is *a research method in which investigators systematically observe people while joining them in their routine activities.* This method lets researchers study social life in any natural setting, from a motorcycle club to a religious seminary. Cultural anthropologists use participant observation to study other societies, calling this method "fieldwork."

Researchers may begin with few specific hypotheses, being unsure of what the important questions will turn out to be. Compared with experiments and surveys, participant observation has few hard-and-fast rules. Flexibility can be an advantage, however, because investigators often must adapt to unexpected circumstances in an unfamiliar environment.

Participant observers try to gain entry into a setting without disturbing the routine behaviour of others. Their role is a dual one: to gain an insider's viewpoint, they must become participants in the setting, "hanging out" for months or even years, trying to act, think, and even feel the same way as the people they are observing; at the same time, they must remain observers, standing back from the action and applying the sociological perspective to social patterns that others take for granted.

Because the personal impressions of a researcher play such a central role, critics claim that participant observation lacks scientific rigour. Yet its personal approach is also a strength: Where a high-profile team of sociologists administering a formal survey might disrupt a setting, a sensitive participant observer often can gain profound insight into people's behaviour.

An illustration: Participant observation in "Cornerville." Have you ever wondered what life is like on the busy streets of an unfamiliar neighbourhood? In the late 1930s, a young graduate student at Harvard University named William Foote Whyte (1914–2000) set out to study social life in a nearby, rather rundown section of Boston. His curiosity ultimately led him to carry out four years of participant observation in this neighbourhood, which he called "Cornerville."

At the time, Cornerville was home to first- and second-generation Italian immigrants. Many were poor, and many people in other parts of Boston considered Cornerville a place to avoid—a slum inhabited by criminals. Unwilling to accept easy **stereotypes** (*exaggerated descriptions applied to every person in some category*), Whyte set out to discover for himself exactly what kind of life went on inside this community. His celebrated book, *Street Corner Society* (1981, orig. 1943), describes Cornerville as a community with its own code of values, complex social patterns, and particular social conflicts.

To start, Whyte considered a range of research methods. He could have taken questionnaires to one of Cornerville's community centres and asked local people to fill them out. Or he could have invited members of the community to come to his Harvard office for interviews. But it is easy to see that such formal strategies would have prompted little cooperation from the local people and yielded few insights. Whyte decided, therefore, to ease into Cornerville life and patiently build an understanding of this rather mysterious place.

CRITICAL THINKING

Reading Tables: An Important Skill

Marginalized Youth: Selected Background Characteristics, School Enrollment, Living Situation and Attitudes.

Sex	Age	Province of birth		Number of nights at home of parent or guardian last month		Are you lonely?		Are you happy?		Are you hopeful about the future?	
Male 63%	14 9%	BC	52%	0	71%	Always	5%	Always	9%	Always	23%
Female 37%	15 14%	Alberta	13%	1–4	3%	Almost always	5%	Almost always	17%	Almost always	19%
	16 14%	Sask.	3%	5–9	9%	Usually	9%	Usually	35%	Usually	20%
		Manitoba	2%								
	17 27%	Ontario	20%	10–14	5%	Some of the time	30%	Some of the time	30%	Some of the time	23%
		Quebec	2%	15–19	2%	Hardly ever	30%	Hardly ever	7%	Hardly ever	13%
	18+ 35%	Atlantic Provinces	2%	20–24	2%	Never	23%	Never	2%	Never	3%
		Outside of Canada	6%	25+	9%						
100%	99%		100%		101%		102%		100%		101%

Note: Calculated based on answers provided by the first 128 participants.

Source: Mikael Jansson and Cecilia Benoit. 2006. "Respect or Protect? Ethical Challenges in Conducting Community-Academic Research with Street-Involved Youth," pp. 175–189 in Bonnie Leadbeater et al. (eds.). *Ethical Issues in Community-Based Research with Children and Youth.* Toronto, Ontario: University of Toronto Press.

A table provides a lot of information in a small amount of space, so learning to read tables can increase your reading efficiency. When you spot a table, look first at the title to see what information it contains. The title of the table above tells you that the table presents a profile of the participants in a research project on marginalized youth. Across the top of the table, you will see eight variables that define these youth. Reading down each column, note the categories within each variable; even though the percentages in each column add up to a number very close to 100, they do not add up to exactly 100 percent due to rounding errors.

Starting at the top left, we see that there are more males (63 percent) than females (37 percent) within this sample. In terms of age, about a third of the respondents are 18 years of age or older (35 percent). Over half were born in British Columbia (52 percent), no doubt reflecting the fact that the study is being conducted in British Columbia.

These individuals are indeed different from other youth in that almost three-quarters of them did not sleep a single night in the household of their parent or guardian in the last month (71 percent).

Nevertheless, more than half of these youth report that they hardly ever or never feel lonely (30% + 23% = 53%), more than one-quarter of them always or almost always feel happy (9% + 17% = 26%), and almost half of them always or almost always feel hopeful about the future (23% + 19% = 42%). Despite living irregular lives, the youth who participate in this research project appear to feel pretty positive about their current situation.

WHAT DO YOU THINK?

1. Statistical data, such as those in this table, are an efficient way to convey lots of information. Can you explain why?

2. Looking at the table, can you determine the future life course of these young people? Explain.

3. Do you see any ways in which this group of youth may differ from marginalized youth in other areas of Canada? If so, what are they?

Soon enough, Whyte discovered the challenges of even getting started in field research. After all, an upper-middle-class WASP graduate student from Harvard did not exactly fit into Cornerville life. He soon found out, for example, that even a friendly overture from an outsider could seem pushy and rude. Early on, Whyte dropped in at a local bar, hoping to buy a woman a drink and encourage her to talk about Cornerville. But looking around the room, he could find no woman alone. Eventually, he thought he might have an opportunity when a fellow sat down with two women. He gamely asked, "Pardon me. Would you mind if I joined you?" Instantly, he realized his mistake:

> There was a moment of silence while the man stared at me. Then he offered to throw me down the stairs. I assured him that this would not be necessary, and demonstrated as much by walking right out of there without any assistance. (1981:289)

As this incident suggests, gaining entry to a community is the vital—and sometimes hazardous—first step in field research. "Breaking in" requires patience, ingenuity, and a little luck. Whyte's big break came in the form of a young man named "Doc," whom he met in a local social service agency. Listening to Whyte's account of his bungled efforts to make friends in Cornerville, Doc was sympathetic and decided to take Whyte under his wing and introduce him to others in the community. With Doc's help, Whyte soon became a neighbourhood regular.

Whyte's friendship with Doc illustrates the importance of a *key informant* in field research. Such people not only introduce a researcher to a community but often remain a source of information and help. But using a key informant also has its risks. Because any person has a particular circle of friends, a key informant's guidance is certain to "spin" the study in one way or another. Moreover, in the eyes of others, the reputation of the key informant—for better or worse—usually rubs off on the investigator. In sum, a key informant is helpful at the outset, but a participant observer soon must seek a broad range of contacts.

Having entered the Cornerville world, Whyte began his work in earnest. But he soon realized that a field researcher needs to know when to speak up and when simply to look, listen, and learn. One evening, he joined a group discussing neighbourhood gambling. Wanting to get the facts straight, Whyte asked innocently, "I suppose the cops were all paid off?"

> The gambler's jaw dropped. He glared at me. Then he denied vehemently that any policeman had been paid off and immediately switched the conversation to another subject. For the rest of that evening I felt very uncomfortable.

Dorothy Smith, one of Canada's pre-eminent sociologists, has developed an alternative way to study the lived experiences of people in society (Smith, 2005). Known as *institutional ethnography* (IE), and first developed as a "sociology for women," this method of inquiry allows people to explore the social relations that structure their everyday lives and is now being used by researchers across the social and human sciences as well as for policy research.

The next day, Doc offered some sound advice:

> "Go easy on that 'who,' 'what,' 'why,' 'when,' 'where' stuff, Bill. You ask those questions and people will clam up on you. If people accept you, you can just hang around, and you'll learn the answers in the long run without even having to ask the questions." (1981:303)

In the months and years that followed, Whyte became familiar with life in Cornerville and married a local woman with whom he would spend the rest of his life. In the process, he learned that this neighbourhood was hardly the stereotypical slum. On the contrary, most immigrants worked hard, many were quite successful, and some even boasted of sending children to college. In short, Whyte's book makes for fascinating reading about the deeds, dreams, and disappointments of people living in one ethnic community, and it contains a richness of detail that can only come from long-term participant observation.

Whyte's work shows that participant observation is a method based on tensions and contrasts. Its flexibility allows a researcher to respond to the unexpected but makes repeating the study difficult. Participation means getting close to people, but observation depends on keeping some distance. Because no special equipment or laboratory is needed, little expense is involved. But this method is costly

Four Research Methods

	Experiment	Survey	Participant Observation	Existing Sources
Application	For explanatory research that specifies relationships between variables; generates quantitative data	For gathering information about issues that cannot be directly observed, such as attitudes and values; useful for descriptive and explanatory research; generates quantitative or qualitative data	For exploratory and descriptive study of people in a "natural" setting; generates qualitative data	For exploratory, descriptive, or explanatory research whenever suitable data are available
Advantages	Provides the greatest opportunity to specify cause-and-effect relationships; replication of research is relatively easy	Sampling, using questionnaires, allows surveys of large populations; interviews provide in-depth responses	Allows study of "natural" behaviour; usually inexpensive	Saves time and expense of data collection; makes historical research possible
Limitations	Laboratory settings have an artificial quality; unless the research environment is carefully controlled, results may be biased	Questionnaires must be carefully prepared and may yield a low return rate; interviews are expensive and time-consuming	Time-consuming; replication of research is difficult; researcher must balance roles of participant and observer	Researcher has no control over possible biases in data; data may only partially fit current research needs

in terms of time—most studies take a year or more—which probably explains why participant observation is used less often than the other methods described in this chapter. Yet the depth of understanding gained through interpretive research of this kind greatly enriches our knowledge of many types of human communities.

USING AVAILABLE DATA: EXISTING SOURCES

Not all research involves collecting new data. In many cases, sociologists save time and money by analyzing existing sources, data collected by others.

The most widely used data are gathered by government agencies such as Statistics Canada. Data about other nations in the world are found in various publications of the United Nations and the World Bank.

Drawing on available data is appealing to sociologists with little money, and the data are often better than what researchers could hope to get on their own. However, data may not be available in the specific form a researcher may want, and

 For easy access to many data links, visit John Macionis' website at **http://www.TheSociologyPage.com**.

it may be difficult to know how accurate the data are. In his nineteenth-century study of suicide, described earlier, Emile Durkheim used official records. But Durkheim knew that some recorded suicides probably were really accidents, just as some true suicides were never recorded as such.

An illustration of the use of existing sources: Studying media narratives. Media representations of human activity constitute an important source of data collected by others. Academic analysis of media's place in the production/reproduction of dominant knowledges has been greatly influenced by the work of sociologist Stuart Hall (1978) and other contributors to the field of cultural studies (Kitzinger, 2000; Pateman, 1988; Sacks, 1996; Watkins, 2000). These approaches to media illustrate how the transmission of social knowledge, values, and meanings changes over time.

Because media representations of key social categories such as gender, class, race, and sexuality are important loci of self and personal identity construction (Seale, 2003), subjugating media stories can negatively affect a person's sense of self and emotional well-being, whether or not these stories are actually true. In addition, contemporary media create social understanding between spatially distanced and/or socially segregated groups. The standard images found in the media become taken as truth unless the audience has the empirical knowledge to reject them. Thus, in the absence of personal experience with, for example, members of ethnic and visible minorities (Ungerleider, 1991), media stories can serve as key cultural sites where negative labels are created and taken up by the majority of citizens.

Hallgrimsdottir, Phillips, and Benoit (2006) compared media stories of people who work in the sex industry with these individuals' self-reports of their personal backgrounds and experiences of what they do for a living. The authors aimed to describe the level of similarity between media depictions of sex workers and their own description of their lives.

The authors relied on two different kinds of data. First, they analyzed the print media discussion of the sex industry in one metropolitan region of Canada, the Capital Metropolitan region of Victoria, BC. In doing so, they focused on the years 1980 to 2004 in a single regional daily newspaper, the Victoria *Times Colonist*. Articles were located using both a computerized and a paper subject index; as such they represent the sum of newspaper coverage of sex industry–related work. Each article was analyzed in terms of both explicit and embedded contents in order to generate a large list of themes. A subsequent pass through the data was used to collapse these themes into a series of narrative categories, and, in a final reading of the data, each article was assigned once to each category. Second, the authors compared these media narratives with the self-reported experiences of sex industry workers—their background and personal lives, work experiences, and health and well-being—in the same city and over a comparable time period (Benoit & Millar, 2001).

Not surprisingly, the authors found that most media narratives of the sex industry were not reflected in the personal stories of sex industry workers themselves. The interview data showed instead that media narratives follow relatively rigid and standardized cultural scripts in which individuals in the sex industry are presented as having poor moral character and breaking the law, as well as causing social disruption and spreading contagious diseases. These cultural scripts organized the media narratives by directing what was included as newsworthy and what was left out from news accounts. The authors also found that the contents of these cultural scripts can be used to understand how stigma gets reproduced in our society.

Characteristics of the four major methods of sociological investigation we have introduced are found in the Summing Up table.

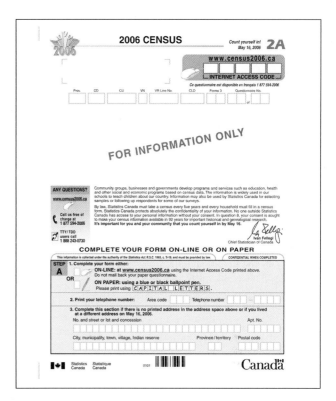

Statistics Canada holds a census every five years in Canada, and the data is used for a wide variety of purposes.

Putting It All Together: 10 Steps in Sociological Research

The following 10 questions will guide you through a research project in sociology:

1. **What is your topic?** Being curious and using the sociological perspective can generate ideas for social research at any time and in any place. Pick a topic you find important to study.

2. **What have others already learned?** You are probably not the first person with an interest in some issue. Visit the library to see what theories and methods other researchers have applied to your topic. In reviewing the existing research, note problems that have come up and knowledge gaps that warrant further investigation.

3. **What, exactly, are your questions?** Are you seeking to explore an unfamiliar setting? Are you aiming to describe some category of people? Or do you want to investigate cause and effect between variables? Clearly state the goals of your research and operationalize all variables.

CONTROVERSY & DEBATE

Is Sociology Nothing More Than Stereotypes?

"Children in public daycare suffer from maternal deprivation!"

"People in Canada? They're rich, they love to marry, and they love to divorce!"

"Everybody knows that a man cannot be a feminist!"

All people—including sociologists—make generalizations. But many beginning students of sociology may wonder how sociological generalizations differ from simple stereotypes.

All three statements at the top of this box are examples of stereotypes, *exaggerated descriptions applied to every person in some category*. First, rather than describing averages, each statement paints every individual in some category with the same brush; second, each ignores facts and distorts reality (even though many stereotypes do contain an element of truth); third, each sounds more like a "put-down" than a fair-minded assertion.

Good sociology, by contrast, involves generalizations but with three conditions. First, sociologists do not indiscriminately apply any generalization to individuals.

Second, sociologists are careful that their generalizations square with available facts. Third, sociologists offer generalizations fair-mindedly, with an interest in getting at the truth.

Recall, first, that the sociological perspective reveals "the general in the particular"; therefore, a sociological insight is a generalization about some category of people. Consider, for example, the first statement above, that children in public daycare suffer from maternal deprivation. This statement is inaccurate, since evidence shows that children in well-organized and adequately funded daycare are as socially adapted as children who spend their early years at home with their mothers. The key to successful child development, then, is quality of care—not maternal attachment.

Second, sociologists shape their generalizations to available facts. A more factual version of the second statement above is that, by world standards, the Canadian population—on average—has a very high standard of living. It is also true that our marriage rate is one of the highest in the world. And although few people take pleasure in divorcing, our divorce rate is high as well.

Third, sociologists strive to be fair-minded and have a passion for truth. The statement that a man cannot be a feminist is not good sociology for two reasons. First, the statement is simply not true because, as you know, many men identify themselves as feminists and strive to enhance women's equality. Second, it seems motivated by gender bias—in this instance, in the reverse of the usual direction.

Good sociology, then, stands apart from harmful stereotyping. But a sociology course is an excellent setting for talking over common stereotypes. The classroom encourages discussion and offers the factual information you need to decide if a particular belief is valid or just a stereotype.

CONTINUE THE DEBATE . . .

1. Do people in Canada have stereotypes of sociologists? What are they? Are they valid?
2. Do you think taking a sociology course dispels people's stereotypes? Does it generate new ones?
3. Can you identify a stereotype of your own that sociology challenges?

---

4. **What will you need to carry out research?** How much time and money are available to you? What special equipment or skills does the research require? Can you do all the work yourself?

5. **Are there ethical concerns?** Can the research harm anyone? How can you minimize the chances for injury? Will you promise your subjects anonymity? If so, how will you ensure that anonymity will be maintained?

6. **What method will you use?** Consider all major research strategies and combinations of approaches. The best method depends on the kinds of questions you are asking and the resources available to you.

7. **How will you record the data?** The research method you use guides your data collection. Be sure to record information accurately and in a way that will make sense later on (it may be months before you write up the results of your work). Watch out for any bias that may creep into your work.

8. **What do the data tell you?** Determine what the data say about your initial questions. If your study involves a specific hypothesis, you should be able to confirm, reject, or modify it based on your findings. Keep in mind that there will be several ways to interpret your results, depending on the theoretical approach you apply, and you should consider them all.

9. **What are your conclusions?** Prepare a final report indicating what you have learned. Also, evaluate your own work. What problems arose during the research process? What questions were left unanswered?

10. **How can you share what you have learned?** Consider making a presentation to a class or maybe even to a meeting of professional sociologists. The important point is to share what you have learned with others and to let them respond to your work.

To review many of the issues raised in this chapter, the final Controversy & Debate box examines how sociological generalizations differ from common stereotypes.

SUMMARY

1. The sociological perspective shows that the general operation of society affects the experiences of particular people. In this way, sociology helps us better understand barriers and opportunities in our lives.

2. Early social thinkers focused on what society *ought to be.* Sociology, named by Auguste Comte in 1838, uses scientific methods to understand society *as it is.*

3. The development of sociology was triggered by rapid change in Europe in the eighteenth and nineteenth centuries. The rise of an industrial economy, the explosive growth of cities, and the emergence of new political ideas combined to weaken tradition and make people more aware of their social world.

4. Theory is the process of linking facts to create meaning. Sociologists use theoretical approaches to guide theory building.

5. The structural-functional approach is a framework for exploring how social structures work together to promote the overall operation of society.

6. The social-conflict approach highlights dimensions of social inequality that generate conflict and promote change.

7. In contrast to these macro-level orientations, the symbolic-interaction approach is a micro-level framework for studying how people, in everyday interaction, construct reality.

8. Scientific sociology uses the logic of science, based on empirical evidence we confirm with our senses.

9. Measurement is the process of giving a value to a variable in a specific case. Sound measurement is both reliable and valid.

10. Scientific research seeks to determine how variables are related. Ideally, researchers try to identify how one (independent) variable causes change in another (dependent) variable.

11. Although researchers select topics according to their personal interests, the scientific ideal of objectivity demands that they try to suspend personal values and biases as they conduct research.

12. Interpretive sociology is a methodological orientation that focuses on the meanings that people attach to behaviour. Reality is not "out there" (as scientific sociology claims) but is constructed by people in their everyday interaction.

13. Critical sociology is a methodological orientation that uses research to bring about social change. It rejects the scientific principle of objectivity, claiming that all research has a political character.

14. Because their work can harm subjects, professional sociologists must observe ethical guidelines when doing research.

15. Scientific research is most clearly expressed in the experiment, which investigates cause-and-effect relationships between two (or more) variables under controlled laboratory conditions.

16. A survey uses either a questionnaire or an interview to gather subjects' responses to a series of questions.

17. Participant observation involves joining with people in a social setting for an extended period of time.

18. Often sociologists use existing sources rather than collecting their own data; doing so is common among researchers with limited research budgets.

19. Sociologists make generalizations about categories of people. Unlike stereotypes, these sociological statements (1) are not applied indiscriminately to all individuals, (2) are supported by research-based facts, and (3) are put forward in the fair-minded pursuit of truth.

KEY CONCEPTS

cause and effect (p. 17) a relationship in which change in one variable (the independent variable) causes change in another (the dependent variable)

concept (p. 17) a mental construct that represents some part of the world in a simplified form

correlation (p. 17) a relationship in which two (or more) variables change together

critical sociology (p. 20) the study of society that focuses on the need for social change

experiment (p. 23) a research method for investigating cause and effect under highly controlled conditions

gender (p. 22) the personal traits and social positions that members of a society attach to being female or male

global perspective (p. 8) the study of the larger world and our society's place in it

high-income countries (p. 8) the richest nations with the highest overall standards of living

interpretive sociology (p. 20) the study of society that focuses on the meanings people attach to their social world

latent functions (p. 13) the unrecognized and unintended consequences of any social pattern

low-income countries (p. 8) nations with a low standard of living in which most people are poor

macro-level orientation (p. 15) a broad focus on social structures that shape society as a whole

manifest functions (p. 13) the recognized and intended consequences of any social pattern

measurement (p. 17) a procedure for determining the value of a variable in a specific case

micro-level orientation (p. 15) a close-up focus on social interaction in specific situations

middle-income countries (p. 8) nations with a standard of living about average for the world as a whole

participant observation (p. 25) a research method in which investigators systematically observe people while joining them in their routine activities

positivism (p. 12) a way of understanding based on science

reliability (p. 17) consistency in measurement

research method (p. 23) a systematic plan for doing research

science (p. 16) a logical system that bases knowledge on direct, systematic observation

social-conflict approach (p. 14) a framework for building theory that sees society as an arena of inequality that generates conflict and change

social dysfunction (p. 14) any social pattern that may disrupt the operation of society

social functions (p. 13) the consequences of any social pattern for the operation of society as a whole

social structure (p. 13) any relatively stable pattern of social behaviour

sociology (p. 4) the systematic study of human society

stereotypes (p. 25) exaggerated descriptions applied to every person in some category

structural-functional approach (p. 13) a framework for building theory that sees society as a complex system whose parts work together to promote solidarity and stability

survey (p. 24) a research method in which subjects respond to a series of statements or questions in a questionnaire or an interview

symbolic-interaction approach (p. 15) a framework for building theory that sees society as the product of the everyday interactions of individuals

theoretical approach (p. 13) a basic image of society that guides thinking and research

theory (p. 13) a statement of how and why specific facts are related

validity (p. 17) actually measuring exactly what you intend to measure

variable (p. 17) a concept whose value changes from case to case

CRITICAL-THINKING QUESTIONS

1. In what ways does using the sociological perspective make us seem less in control of our lives? In what ways does it give us greater power over our surroundings?

2. "Sociology would not have arisen if human behaviour resulted only from biological instincts (like, say, the highly predictable behaviour of ants), nor would sociology exist if human behaviour were totally random. Sociology thrives because humans are partly guided by social structure and partly free." Do you agree or disagree with this argument? Why?

3. What factors explain why sociology developed where and when it did?

4. Guided by sociology's three major theoretical approaches, what types of questions might a sociologist ask about (a) television, (b) war, (c) humour, and (d) colleges and universities?

APPLICATIONS AND EXERCISES

1. Spend several hours exploring your local area on foot, on a bicycle, or in a car so that you can draw a sociological map of the community. This map might show the categories of people and types of buildings found in various places ("big, single-family homes," "run-down business district," "new office buildings," "student apartments," and so on). What patterns do you see?

2. Look ahead to Figure 13–4 on page 352, which shows the number of divorces in Canada over the last 40 years. What societal factors pushed the number of divorces up during this time period? How do you explain the relatively rapid rise in the 1970s, the modest decline in the early 1980s, and the rapid increase around 1985?

3. During a class, carefully observe the behaviour of the instructor and other students. What patterns do you see in how people use space? What patterns exist regarding who speaks? What categories of people are taking the class in the first place?

4. Imagine that you were going to observe your sociology teacher in order to evaluate that individual's teaching skills. How would you operationalize the concept "good teaching"? What, exactly, would you look for? Do you think students are the best judges of good and bad teaching? Why or why not?

5. Conduct a practice interview with a roommate or friend on the topic "What is the value of an education beyond high school?" Before the actual interview, prepare a list of specific questions or issues that you think are important. Afterward, give some thought to why conducting a good interview is much harder than it initially may seem.

 SITES TO SEE

www.pearsoned.ca/macionis
The authors and publisher of this book invite you to visit the interactive Companion Website™ that accompanies this text. Begin by clicking on the cover of your book. You will find a chapter-by-chapter study guide, practice tests, suggested weblinks, and links to other relevant material.

http://hdr.undp.org/Statistics/data
This site provides a range of data about most nations around the world.

www.TheSociologyPage.com
(or **www.macionis.com**)
John Macionis maintains this website (use either address), where you will find information about sociology, short videos, biographies of important sociologists, and a Links Library that will connect you to dozens of other interesting sites.

www.csaa.ca
Read the Statement of Professional Ethics at the website of the Canadian Sociology and Anthropology Association.

www40.statcan.ca/index.htm

www.cia.gov/cia/publications/factbook/index.html
The first of these sites provides statistical data and other information about Canada, the provinces, and metropolitan areas. If you navigate to the section of the site presenting the most recent census you will find, among many other things, maps showing patterns and trends of interest to sociologists. The second website offers a range of data about nations around the world.

www.cbc.ca/fifth/main_nowayhome.html
Are you interested in learning more about youth homelessness? The CBC TV program *The Fifth Estate* covered the topic in this March 2004 segment.

 INVESTIGATE WITH RESEARCH NAVIGATOR™

To access the full resources of Research Navigator™, please find the access code printed on the inside cover of the *OneSearch with Research Navigator™ Sociology* guide. You may have received this booklet if your instructor recommended this guide be packaged with new textbooks. (If your book did not come with this printed guide, you can purchase one through your school's bookstore.)

Visit our Research Navigator™ site at **www. research navigator.com.** Click on "Register" under "New Users" and enter your access code to create a personal login name and password. (When revisiting the site, use the same login name and password to enter.) Browse the features of the Research Navigator™ website and search the databases of academic journals, newspapers, magazines, and weblinks using keywords such as "sociology," "suicide," and "sports."

To reinforce your understanding of this chapter, and to identify topics for further study, visit MySocLab at **www.pearsoned.ca/mysoclab/macionis** for diagnostic tests and a multimedia ebook.

CHAPTER TWO

Culture

What is culture?

How does technology affect people's ways of life?

Why is it so important to understand
people's cultural differences?

2

Music and dress are among the many cultural elements that define a way of life. Here, accordion players at a street festival strike up tunes familiar to people in the Dordogne region of France.

Ernst & Young, one of Canada's largest corporate finance firms, pays a lot of attention these days to cultural diversity. In 2004, the company employed over 3000 full-time people at 14 offices across Canada, with just under half of its employees located at its headquarters in the hub of Toronto's financial district. With a population of over 5.6 million in 2005, Toronto is the fifth-largest and most ethnically diverse city in North America. Vancouver is similarly diverse. In 2001, 37 percent of Vancouver's total population was of a visible minority background, with immigrants of Chinese, Indian, and Filipino origin making up the three most numerous groups. Given these population statistics, it is no wonder that E&Y offices in these two cities are strong supporters of the firm's diversity initiatives. Driven by a corporate value statement calling for an "inclusive and flexible environment," over the past few years Ernst & Young has hosted a series of ethnic diversity networking events in Toronto, Vancouver, and other Canadian cities where it has branch offices. The company has a full-time director of leadership and manager of diversity with responsibilities ranging from benchmarking the company's progress in diversifying its workforce and clientele and changing corporate culture to creating a truly inclusive environment (Workplace Diversity Update, 2004).

What has been the result of this diversity initiative? A substantial increase in its share of business is with local ethnic groups. Italian, Chinese, South Asian, and Portuguese native language speakers spend more than $25.1 million annually in the Greater Toronto area alone. Any company would do well to follow Ernst & Young's lead.

Canada is among the most *multicultural* of all the world's nations, reflecting its long history of welcoming immigrants from around the world. Worldwide, cultural differences are truly astounding, involving not only musical tastes and preferred foods but also family patterns and beliefs about right and wrong. Some of the world's people have many children, while others have few; some honour the elderly, while others are obsessed with youth. Some societies are peaceful, others warlike; and segments of humanity embrace a thousand different religious beliefs as well as particular ideas about what is polite and rude, beautiful and ugly, pleasant and repulsive. This amazing human capacity for so many different ways of life is a matter of human culture.

What Is Culture?

Culture is *the values, beliefs, behaviour, and material objects that together form a people's way of life.* When studying culture, sociologists often distinguish between thoughts and things. Nonmaterial culture includes symbolic human creations ranging from art to Zen; material culture refers to physical creations of a society, everything from armaments to zippers. The terms "culture" and "society" obviously go hand in hand, but their precise meanings differ. Culture is a shared way of life or social heritage; **society** refers to *people who interact in a defined territory and share a culture.* Neither society nor culture could exist without the other.

Culture shapes not only what we do but also what we think and how we feel—elements of what we commonly but

Human beings around the globe create diverse ways of life. Such differences begin with outward appearance: Contrast the women shown here from Brazil, Kenya, New Guinea, and South Yemen, and the men from Taiwan (Republic of China), India, Canada, and New Guinea. Less obvious, but of even greater importance, are internal differences, since culture also shapes our goals in life, our sense of justice, and even our innermost personal feelings.

inaccurately describe as "human nature." The warlike Yąnomamö of the Brazilian rain forest think aggressiveness is natural, but halfway around the world, the Semai of Malaysia live in peace and cooperation with one another. The cultures of Canada and Japan both stress achievement and hard work, but members of our society value individu-

alism, whereas the Japanese value collective harmony.

Given the cultural differences in the world and people's tendency to view their own way of life as "natural," it is no wonder that travellers may suffer **culture shock**—*personal disorientation when experiencing an unfamiliar way of life.* People can experience culture shock right here in Canada,

Behaviour that people in one society consider routine can be chilling to members of another culture. In the Russian city of St. Petersburg, this young mother and her six-week-old son brave the −10°C temperatures for a dip in a nearby lake. To Russians, this is something of a national pastime. To some members of our society, however, this practice may seem cruel or even dangerous.

when, say, Jamaican-Canadians explore an Iranian neighbourhood in Montreal, university students from Toronto venture into the Amish region of Southern Ontario, or Vancouverites travel through small Native reserves in Northern British Columbia. But culture shock is most intense when we travel abroad: the Global Sociology box opposite tells the story of a researcher making his first visit to the home of the Yąnomamö people living in the Amazon region of South America.

December 1, Istanbul, Turkey. Harbours everywhere, it seems, have two things in common: ships and cats. Istanbul, the tenth port on our voyage, is awash with felines, prowling about in search of an easy meal. People certainly change from place to place—but not cats.

No way of life is "natural" to humanity, even though most people around the world view their own behaviour that way. What is natural to human beings is the capacity to create culture. Every other form of life—from ants to zebras—behaves in fixed, species-specific ways. To a world traveller, the enormous diversity of human life stands out in contrast to the behaviour of, say, cats, which is pretty much the same everywhere. This uniformity follows from the fact that most living creatures are guided by *instincts,* biological programming over which animals have no control. A few animals, notably chimpanzees and related primates, have a limited capacity for culture, and researchers have observed them using tools and teaching simple skills to their offspring. But the creative power of humans far exceeds that of any other form of life. In short, *only humans rely on culture rather than instinct to ensure their survival* (Harris, 1987). To understand how human culture came to be, we need to look back at the history of our species.

CULTURE AND HUMAN INTELLIGENCE

In a universe 15 billion years old, our planet is a much younger 4.5 billion years of age (see the timeline inside the front cover of this text). Life appeared about 1 billion years after Earth was formed. Fast-forward another 2 to 3 billion years and we find dinosaurs ruling the Earth. When these giant creatures finally disappeared, some 65 million years ago, our history took a crucial turn with the appearance of the animals we call primates.

About 12 million years ago, primates began to develop along two different lines, setting humans apart from the great apes, our closest relatives. But our common ancestry is evident in traits that humans share with chimpanzees, gorillas, and orangutans: great sociability, affectionate and long-lasting bonds that form the basis for child rearing and mutual protection, and the abilities to walk upright (normal in humans but less common among other primates), to precisely manipulate objects with our hands, and to develop shared meanings and understandings.

Fossil records show that some 3 million years ago, our distant human ancestors learned cultural basics, such as the use of fire, tools, and weapons, and were able to build simple shelters and to fashion basic clothing. These Stone Age achievements may seem modest, but they mark the point at which our ancestors embarked on a distinct evolutionary course, making culture their primary strategy for survival.

Culture, then, is a relatively recent development that was a long time in the making. As culture became a strategy for survival, our ancestors descended from the trees into the tall grasses of Central Africa. There they learned the advantages of hunting in groups. As mental capacity expanded, some 250 000 years ago our species emerged as *Homo sapiens,* Latin for "thinking person." Humans became the only species that names itself and deals with the world

GLOBAL SOCIOLOGY

Confronting the Yąnomamö: The Experience of Culture Shock

A small aluminum motorboat chugged steadily along the muddy Orinoco River, deep within South America's vast tropical rainforest. Anthropologist Napoleon Chagnon was nearing the end of a three-day journey to the home territory of the Yąnomamö, one of the most technologically simple societies on Earth.

Some 12 000 Yąnomamö live in villages scattered along the border of Venezuela and Brazil. Their way of life could hardly be more different from our own. The Yąnomamö wear little clothing and live without electricity, cars, or other conveniences most people in Canada take for granted. They use bows and arrows for hunting and warfare, as they have for centuries. Many of the Yąnomamö have had little contact with the outside world, so Chagnon would be as strange to them as they would be to him.

By two o'clock in the afternoon, Chagnon had almost reached his destination. The hot sun and humid air were becoming unbearable. Chagnon's clothes were soaked with sweat, and his face and hands were swollen from the bites of gnats swarming around him. But he scarcely noticed, so focused was he on the fact that in just a few moments he would be face to face with people unlike any he had ever known.

Chagnon's heart pounded as the boat slid onto the riverbank. He and his guide climbed from the boat and walked toward the Yąnomamö village, stooping as they pushed their way through the dense undergrowth. Chagnon describes what happened next:

> I looked up and gasped when I saw a dozen burly, naked, sweaty, hideous men staring at us down the shafts of their drawn arrows! Immense wads of green tobacco were stuck between their lower teeth and lips, making them look even more hideous, and strands of dark green slime dripped or hung from their nostrils—strands so long that they clung to their [chests] or drizzled down their chins.
>
> My next discovery was that there were a dozen or so vicious, underfed dogs snapping at my legs, circling me as if I were to be their next meal. I just stood there holding my notebook, helpless and pathetic. Then the stench of the decaying vegetation and filth hit me and I almost got sick. I was horrified. What kind of welcome was this for the person who came here to live with you and learn your way of life, to become friends with you? (1992:11–12)

Fortunately for Chagnon, the Yąnomamö villagers recognized his guide and lowered their weapons. Reassured that he would survive the afternoon, Chagnon still was shaken by his inability to make any sense of these people.

Not all anthropologists agree with Chagnon's "take" on the Yąnomamö as predominantly a violent and competitive people. Anthropologist Brian Ferguson, in his book *Yanomami Warfare: A Political History,* reveals how Chagnon might have misread the political balance between different Yąnomamö groups by favouring the more violent over the more peaceful ones. Ferguson also argues that the Yąnomamö make war not because Western influence is absent, but because it is present. Perhaps the cultural shock that Chagnon experienced, then, was his inability to "read" other meanings in his new surroundings that conveyed cooperation and negotiation and how his very presence was shaping the reactions of the Yąnomamö.

WHAT DO YOU THINK?

1. As they came to know Chagnon, might the Yąnomamö, too, have experienced culture shock? Why?
2. Can you think of an experience you had that is similar to the one described here?
3. Can studying sociology help reduce the experience of culture shock? How?

Source: Adapted from Chagnon (1992).

---

through symbols and meaning. The biological forces we call instincts gave way to a more efficient survival scheme: *human beings developed the mental power to fashion the natural environment for themselves.* Ever since, humans have made and remade their world in countless ways, which explains today's fascinating cultural diversity.

People throughout the world communicate not just with spoken words but also with bodily gestures. Because gestures vary from culture to culture, they can occasionally be the cause of misunderstandings. For instance, the commonplace thumbs-up gesture we use to express "Good job!" can get a person from Canada into trouble in Australia, where people take it to mean "Up yours!"

إِقْرَأُوا	**Read**	독서
Arabic	English	Korean
ՅԿԻՂԿ	διαβαζω	بخوانید
Armenian	Greek	Persian
ᤊᤔᤆᤖ	אֱקְרָא:	читать
Cambodian	Hebrew	Russian
閱讀	पढ़नाn	¡Ven a leer!
Chinese	Hindi	Spanish

FIGURE 2–1 Human Languages: A Variety of Symbols

Here is a single word written in 12 of the hundreds of languages humans use to communicate with each other.

The Components of Culture

Although cultures vary greatly, they all have common components, including symbols, language, values, and norms. We shall begin with the component that is the basis for all the others: symbols.

SYMBOLS

Like all other creatures, human beings sense the surrounding world, but unlike others, we also create a reality of *meaning*. Humans transform the elements of the world into **symbols**, *anything that carries a particular meaning recognized by people who share a culture*. A word, a whistle, a wall of graffiti, a flashing red light, a raised fist—all serve as symbols. We see the human capacity to create and manipulate symbols reflected in the variety of meanings associated with the simple act of winking the eye, which can convey interest, understanding, or insult.

We are so dependent on our culture's symbols that we often take them for granted. We become keenly aware of the importance of a symbol, however, when it is used in an unconventional way—say, when a young man wears an upside-down Christian cross as a symbol of Satanism. Entering an unfamiliar culture also reminds us of the power of symbols; culture shock is really the inability to "read" meaning in new surroundings. Not understanding the symbols of a culture leaves a person feeling lost and isolated, unsure of how to act, and sometimes frightened.

Culture shock is a two-way process. On one hand, the traveller *experiences* culture shock when meeting people whose way of life is different. For example, North Americans who consider dogs beloved household pets might be put off by the Masai of Eastern Africa, who pay no attention to dogs and never feed them. The same travellers might be horrified to find that in parts of Indonesia and in the northern regions of the People's Republic of China, people *roast* dogs for dinner. On the other hand, a traveller can *inflict* culture shock on others by acting in ways that offend them. A Canadian who asks for a cheeseburger in an Indian restaurant offends Hindus, who consider cows sacred and never to be eaten. Indeed, global travel provides endless opportunities for misunderstanding. When in an unfamiliar setting, we need to remember that even behaviour that seems innocent and normal to us can offend others, as the multiple meanings of the thumbs-up symbol remind us.

Symbolic meanings can also vary within a single society. In the recent debate over offshore oil rights between the government of Canada and the province of Newfoundland and Labrador, Premier Danny Williams ordered that all Canadian flags be taken down from the provincial legislature. Former prime minister Paul Martin responded that the move was "disrespectful" and insulted all Canadians.

Finally, societies create new symbols all the time. The Applying Sociology box offers a case in point, describing some of the cyber-symbols that have developed along with our increasing use of computers for communication.

APPLYING SOCIOLOGY

The New Cyber-Symbols

It all started with the "smiley" icon that means a person is happy or telling a joke. Now a new language of symbols is emerging as creative people use computer keystrokes to create *emoticons* (or *smileys*), symbols that convey thoughts and emotions. Here is a sampling of the new cyber-language. (Rotate this page 90 degrees to the right to appreciate the emoticon faces.)

:-)	I'm smiling at you.
:'-)	I'm so happy (laughing so hard) that I'm starting to cry.
:-O	Wow!
:-x	My lips are sealed!
:-II	I'm angry with you!
:-P	I'm sticking my tongue out at you!
:-(	I feel sad.
:-I	Things look grim.

%-}	I think I've had too much to drink.
-:(	Somebody cut my hair into a mohawk!
+O:-)	I've just been elected pope!
@}———>———	Here's a rose for you!

Computers are as popular in Japan as they are in Canada. The Japanese have their own emoticons or smileys, which are read vertically rather than horizontally and have more variation:

(^_^)	I'm smiling at you.
(*^o^*)	This is exciting!
(^o^)	I am happy.
\(^o^)/	Banzai! This is wonderful!

How far will this new keyboard language go? If you're creative enough, anything is possible. Here's a routine that has been making the rounds on the Internet. It's called "Mr. Asciihead learns the Macarena"! To see Mr.

Asciihead in action, go to the link at http://www.TheSociologyPage.com.

o	o	o	o	
.l.	\l.	\l/	//	
/\	>\	/<	>\	
o	<o	<o>	o>	o
X	\	l	<l	<l>
/<	>\	/<	>\	/<

WHAT DO YOU THINK?

1. What does the creation of symbols such as these suggest about culture?
2. Do you think such symbols convey meaning as well as facial expressions do? Why or why not?
3. What other recently created symbols of this kind can you point to?

Sources: Pollack (1996) and Krantz (1997). "Mr. Asciihead" is the creation of Leow Yee Ling.

LANGUAGE

The heart of a symbolic system is **language**, *a system of symbols that allows people to communicate with one another*. Humans have created many alphabets to express the hundreds of languages we speak. Several examples are shown in Figure 2–1. Even rules for writing differ: Most people in Western societies write from left to right, people in Northern Africa and Western Asia write from right to left, and people in Eastern Asia write from top to bottom. Global Map 2–1 shows where in the world we hear three of the most widely spoken languages.

Language not only allows communication but also ensures the continuity of culture. Whether spoken or written, language is a cultural heritage in coded form, the key to **cultural transmission**, *the process by which one generation passes culture to the next*. Just as our bodies contain the genes of our ancestors, our cultural heritage contains countless symbols of those who came before us. Language is the key that unlocks centuries of accumulated wisdom.

Can animals use language? To learn more, go to http://www.newscientist.com/news/news.jsp?id=ns99993218.

Language skills may link us to the past, but they also spark the human imagination to connect symbols in new ways, creating an almost limitless range of future possibilities. Language sets human beings apart as the only creatures who are self-conscious, aware of our limitations and ultimate mortality, yet able to dream and hope for a better future.

The Sapir–Whorf thesis. Does someone who speaks Cree, the language of Aboriginal people who originated from the James Bay area of Canada, experience the world differently from other Canadians who think in English or French? The answer is "yes"—each language has its own distinct symbols that serve as the building blocks of reality.

The linguist Benjamin Lee Whorf in the 1930s studied the language of the Hopi Indians in Arizona, whose

WINDOW ON THE WORLD

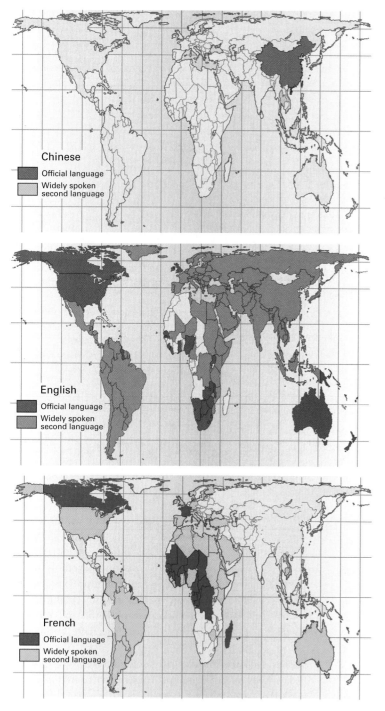

GLOBAL MAP 2–1

Language in Global Perspective

Chinese (including Mandarin, Cantonese, and dozens of other dialects) is the native tongue of one-fifth of the world's people, almost all of whom live in Asia. Although all Chinese people read and write with the same characters, they use several dozen dialects. The "official" dialect, taught in schools throughout the People's Republic of China and the Republic of Taiwan, is Mandarin (the dialect of Beijing, China's historic capital city). Cantonese, the language of Canton, is the second most common Chinese dialect; it differs in sound from Mandarin roughly the way French differs from Spanish.

English is the native tongue or official language in several world regions (spoken by one-tenth of humanity) and has become the preferred second language in most of the world.

The largest concentration of French speakers is in France and in its former African colonies. French is, of course, also one of Canada's official languages, spoken mainly as a first language in Quebec and Northern New Brunswick.

Source: *Peters Atlas of the World* (1990); updated by the authors.

language does not distinguish past, present, and future. Whorf was interested in the degree to which the languages we speak affect the ways we view the world. Along with his colleague Edward Sapir, Whorf eventually proposed that languages are not just different sets of labels for the same reality (Sapir, 1929, 1949; Whorf, 1956, orig. 1941). Rather, languages are at least partly unique, with words or expressions that have no precise counterpart in another language. As multilingual people know, a single idea may "feel" different if spoken in Hindi rather than in Persian or Dutch (Falk, 1987). The **Sapir–Whorf thesis** is built around *the idea that people perceive the world through the cultural lens of language*; it proposes that the language we use—at least to some extent—determines the way we view and think about the world around us.

In the decades since Sapir and Whorf published their work, however, scholars have taken issue with this idea. Current thinking is that while we do fashion reality out of our symbols, evidence does not support the notion that language *determines* reality the way Sapir and Whorf claimed. For example, we know that children understand the idea of "family" long before they learn that word; similarly, adults can imagine new ideas or things before devising a name for them (Kay & Kempton, 1984; Pinker, 1994).

VALUES AND BELIEFS

What accounts for the popularity of children's book and television characters like Barney, Franklin, the Berenstain Bears, and Mr. Dressup? Each teaches our children middle-class values such as hard work, competition, and respect for authority, which are all important for individual achievement in Canadian society. In applauding such characters, we are endorsing certain **values**, *culturally defined standards that people use to assess desirability, goodness, and beauty and that serve as broad guidelines for social living*. Values are statements, from the standpoint of a culture, of what ought to be.

Values are broad principles that underlie **beliefs**, *specific statements that people hold to be true*. That is, values are abstract standards of goodness, whereas beliefs are particular matters people hold to be true or false. For example, surveys show that most Canadian adults agree that their country should provide equal opportunities for all groups, including men and women (Adams, 1997). Yet in reality, fewer than one-quarter of women actually occupy ministerial positions in Canada, though this trend has been increasing ever so slowly over the last decade (Inter Parliamentary Union, 2005).

Canadian values. Because Canada is a country of native peoples and immigrants from many different countries, few values command the support of everyone. Even so, a number

Australian artist and feminist Sally Swain alters famous artists' paintings to make fun of our culture's tendency to ignore the everyday lives of women. This spoof is entitled *Mrs. Matisse Polishes the Goldfish*.

Mrs. Matisse Polishes the Goldfish from *Great Housewives of Art* by Sally Swain, copyright © 1988, 1989 by Sally Swain. Used by permission of Viking Penguin, a division of Penguin Group (USA) Inc.

of dominant values have emerged. A national report commissioned by the federal government, *Citizens' Forum on Canada's Future* (Report to the People and Government of Canada, 1991:35–45) identified seven important cultural values.

1. **Equality and fairness in a democratic society**. Canadians across the country express a belief in fairness for all citizens, including Aboriginal peoples, citizens of Quebec, and visible minorities.

2. **Consultation and dialogue**. As citizens, we should aim to settle our differences peacefully, through talking over our problems, learning about one another, and arriving at agreed-upon solutions to our problems.

3. **Importance of accommodation and tolerance**. Accommodating the traditions and customs of Canada's Aboriginal peoples and ethnic groups, including those of francophone Quebecers, is central to this cultural value.

4. **Support for diversity**. Support for the country's many diversities—regional, ethnic, linguistic, and cultural—is another central value that we share as a nation.

5. **Compassion and generosity**. People in Canada value the safety net provided by the welfare state—particularly its universal healthcare system and attractive social services, pension plans, openness toward refugees, and commitment to reducing regional disparities.

6. **Attachment to Canada's natural beauty**. Canada's wilderness is legendary, and Canadians believe that their governments should do more to protect the natural environment from pollution and other hazards of industrialization.

7. **Our world image: commitment to freedom, peace, and non-violent change**. Canadians want to be seen from abroad as a free, peaceful, and non-violent society that, as a nation, plays an active role in international peacekeeping.

Values: Sometimes in conflict. Looking over this list, we see that these dominant cultural values are often difficult to realize. For example, the federal government and national media tend to promote an image of Canada as "one" nation, bound together by shared values, traditions, and beliefs. Yet close attention to debates over "whose culture" is authentically Canadian indicates that there is little agreement on what comprises a national culture in our country. For example, it was not until 2005 that the Great Hall of the National Art Gallery of Canada finally had a solo show of First Nations art. The selected works of Anishnaabe artist Norval Morrisseau, also referred to as Copper Thunderbird and "Picasso of the North," are the first of any Aboriginal artist, producing art on Aboriginal life, to grace the walls of the Great Hall of the 126-year-old cultural institution.

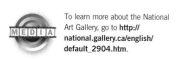 To learn more about the National Art Gallery, go to **http:// national.gallery.ca/english/ default_2904.htm**.

We may also verbally support tolerance and accommodation yet oppose such values for particular groups. This was recently the case regarding gay marriage, which was supported by a slight majority of citizens but opposed by many religious groups and some prominent politicians (Mofina, 2003). Such conflicts in values inevitably cause strain, leading to awkward balancing acts in our beliefs. Sometimes we decide that one value is more important than another; in other cases, we may simply learn to live with inconsistencies. In *A Fragile Social Fabric? Fairness, Trust, and Commitment in Canada*, sociologist Raymond Breton and colleagues (2004) attempt to assess the strength of the national social fabric, as well as the extent to which it is fragmented along the main lines of social differentiation in Canadian society.

The authors recommend ways that support for diversity according to ethnicity, social class, gender, and region can strengthen the value of "one" nation of diverse cultures.

NORMS

Middle-class Canadians are reluctant to reveal to others the size of their paycheque, while people in China tend to share such "personal" information eagerly. Both patterns illustrate the operation of **norms**, *rules and expectations by which a society guides the behaviour of its members*.

Sociologist William Graham Sumner (1959, orig. 1906) coined the term **mores** (pronounced "MORE-ayz") to refer to *norms that are widely observed and have great moral significance*. Mores, or taboos, include our society's insistence that adults not engage in sexual relations with children.

People are more casual about **folkways**, *norms for routine or casual interaction*. Examples include ideas about what are acceptable greetings and proper dress. A man who does not wear a tie to a formal dinner party may cause raised eyebrows for his violating folkways or "etiquette." Were he to arrive at the dinner party wearing *only* a tie, however, he would invite more serious punishment for violating cultural mores. Although we sometimes bristle when others pressure us to conform, norms make our encounters with others more orderly and predictable.

As we learn cultural norms, we gain the capacity to evaluate our own behaviour. Doing wrong (say, downloading a term paper from the Internet) can cause not only *shame*—the painful sense that others disapprove of our actions—but also *guilt*—a negative judgment we make of ourselves. Only cultural creatures can experience shame and guilt. This is what the writer Mark Twain had in mind when he remarked that people "are the only animals that blush—or need to."

IDEAL AND REAL CULTURE

Values and norms suggest how we *should* behave more than they describe actual behaviour. We must remember that *ideal culture* always differs from the *real culture* that actually occurs in everyday life. To illustrate, most women and men agree on the importance of sexual faithfulness in marriage. When Canadian adults take marriage vows, most promise each other sexual fidelity. However, in one national poll, almost 22 percent of males and 14 percent of females reported having had an affair while married (Angus Reid, 1997d). A number of prominent politicians from Canada and elsewhere have also publicly endorsed sexual fidelity in marriage but practised the opposite—not to mention some members of the Canadian clergy who have taken vows of celibacy during their ordination yet later broken them. But a culture's moral prodding is important all the same, calling to mind the old saying, "Do as I say, not as I do."

Technology and Culture

In addition to symbolic elements such as values and norms, every culture includes a wide range of physical human creations called *artifacts*. The Chinese eat with chopsticks rather than knives and forks, the Japanese place mats rather than rugs on the floor, and many men and women in India prefer flowing robes to the close-fitting clothing common in Canada. The material culture of a people can seem as strange to outsiders as their language, values, and norms.

A society's artifacts partly reflect underlying cultural values. The warlike Yąnomamö carefully craft their weapons and prize the poison tips on their arrows. By contrast, as Figure 2–2 shows, Canadians embrace personal autonomy through their deep attachment to the automobile. We come in near the top in regard to car ownership.

In addition to reflecting values, material culture also indicates a society's level of **technology**, *knowledge that people use to make a way of life in their surroundings*. The more complex a society's technology, the easier it is for members of a society to shape the world for themselves.

Gerhard Lenski (Nolan & Lenski, 2004) argues that a society's level of technology is crucial in determining what cultural ideas and artifacts emerge or are even possible. Thus, he sees *sociocultural evolution*—the historical change in culture caused by new technology—in terms of four major levels of development: hunting and gathering, horticulture and pastoralism, agriculture, and industry.

HUNTING AND GATHERING

The oldest and most basic way of living is **hunting and gathering**, *the use of simple tools to hunt animals and gather vegetation for food*. From the time of our earliest human ancestors 3 million years ago until about 1800, most people in the world lived as hunters and gatherers. Today, however, this technology relates to only a few societies, including the Kaska Dene Aboriginals of Northwest Canada, the Pygmies of Central Africa, the Bushmen of Southwestern Africa, the Aborigines of Australia, and the Semai of Malaysia. In most cases, hunters and gatherers spend most of their time searching for game and edible plants. Their societies stay small, generally with several dozen people living in family-like nomadic groups moving on as they deplete an area's vegetation or follow migratory animals.

Everyone participates in searching for food, with the very young and the very old helping as they can. Women usually gather vegetation—the primary food source for these people—while men do most of the hunting. Despite having different roles, the two genders have rough social parity (Leacock, 1978).

Hunters and gatherers have few formal leaders. They may look to one person as a *shaman*, or priest, but this

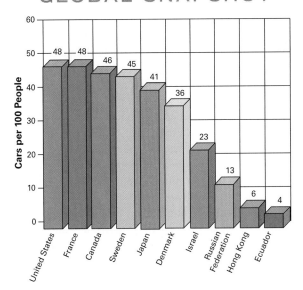

FIGURE 2–2 Car Ownership in Global Perspective

Source: World Bank (2004).

position does not excuse the person from the daily work of finding food. Overall, hunting and gathering stands as a simple and egalitarian way of life.

Limited technology leaves hunters and gatherers vulnerable to the forces of nature, however. Storms and droughts can easily destroy their food supply, and they have few effective ways to respond to accident or disease. Not surprisingly, then, many children die in childhood, and only half live to the age of 20.

As people with powerful technology steadily close in on them, hunters and gatherers are quickly vanishing from the Earth. Fortunately, studying their way of life has already produced valuable information about our sociocultural history and our fundamental ties to the natural environment.

HORTICULTURE AND PASTORALISM

Horticulture, *the use of hand tools to raise crops*, first appeared 10 000 years ago. The hoe and the digging stick (used to punch holes in the ground for seeds) first appeared in fertile regions of the Middle East and Southeast Asia, and by 6000 years ago, these tools were in use from Western Europe to China. Central and South Americans also learned to cultivate plants, but rocky soil and mountainous land forced members of many societies to continue to hunt and gather even as they adopted this new technology (Fisher, 1979; Chagnon, 1992).

In especially dry regions, societies turned not to raising crops but to **pastoralism**, *the domestication of animals.* Throughout the Americas, Africa, the Middle East, and Asia, many societies blend horticulture and pastoralism.

Growing plants and raising animals allows societies to feed hundreds of members. Whereas pastoral peoples remain nomadic, horticulturalists make permanent settlements. In a horticultural society, a material surplus means that not everyone is needed to produce food; some people are free to make crafts, become traders, or serve as full-time priests. Compared with hunters and gatherers, pastoral and horticultural societies are also more unequal, with some families operating as a ruling elite and men increasing their power at the expense of women.

Because hunters and gatherers have little control over nature, they generally believe that the world is inhabited by spirits. As they gain the power to raise plants and animals, however, people come to believe in God as the creator of the world. The pastoral roots of Judaism and Christianity are evident in the term "pastor" and the common view of God as a "shepherd" who stands watch over all.

AGRICULTURE

Five thousand years ago, further technological advances led to **agriculture**, *large-scale cultivation using plows harnessed to animals or more powerful energy sources.* Agrarian technology first appeared in the Middle East and gradually spread throughout the world. The inventions of the animal-drawn plow, the wheel, writing, numbers, and new metals were so important that historians call this era "the dawn of civilization."

By turning the soil, plows allow land to be farmed for decades, so agrarian people live in permanent settlements. With large food surpluses that can be transported by animal-powered wagons, populations easily grow into the millions. As members of agrarian societies become more and more specialized in their work, money is used as a form of common exchange, replacing the earlier system of barter. Although the development of agrarian technology expands human choices and fuels urban growth, it also makes social life more individualistic and impersonal.

Agriculture also brings about a dramatic increase in social inequality. Most people live as serfs or slaves, but a few elites are freed from labour to cultivate a "refined" way of life based on the study of philosophy, art, and literature. At all levels of such a society, men gain pronounced power over women.

People with only simple technology live in much the same way the world over, with minor differences caused by regional variations in climate. But, Lenski explains, agrarian technology gives people enough control over the world that cultural diversity increases.

INDUSTRY

Industrialization occurred as societies replaced the muscles of animals and humans with new forms of power. Formally, **industry** is *the production of goods using advanced sources of energy to drive large machinery.* The introduction of steam power, starting in England in about 1775, greatly boosted productivity and transformed culture in the process. Whereas agrarian people work in or near the home, most people in industrial societies work in large factories, under the supervision of strangers. Thus, industrialization pushes aside traditional cultural values that guided family-centred agrarian life for centuries. Industry also makes the world seem smaller. In the nineteenth century, railroads and steamships carried people across land and sea faster and farther than ever before. In the twentieth century, this process continued with the invention of the automobile, the airplane, radio, television, and the computer. Industrial technology raises living standards and extends the human life span. Acquiring education becomes the rule because industrial jobs demand more and more skills. Furthermore, industrial societies reduce economic inequality and steadily extend political rights.

It is easy to see industrial societies as more "advanced" than those relying on simpler technology. After all, industry raises living standards and stretches life expectancy to the seventies and beyond—about twice that of the Yanomamö. Even so, industry intensifies individualism, which expands personal freedom but weakens human community. Also, industry has led people to abuse the natural environment—at our peril. And although advanced technology gives us work-saving machines and miraculous forms of medical treatment, it also contributes to unhealthy levels of stress and has created weapons capable of destroying in a flash everything that our species has achieved.

POST-INDUSTRIAL INFORMATION TECHNOLOGY

Going beyond the four categories discussed by Lenski, we see that many industrial societies, including Canada, have now entered a post-industrial era in which more and more economic production makes use of *new information technology.* Production in industrial societies centres on factories that make *things,* whereas post-industrial production centres on computers and other electronic devices that create, process, store, and apply *ideas and information.*

The emergence of an information economy thus changes the skills that define a way of life. No longer are mechanical abilities the only key to success. People find that they must learn to work with symbols by speaking, writing, computing, and creating images and sounds. The overall effect of this change is that our society now has the capacity to create symbolic culture on an unprecedented scale. The Critical Thinking box opposite takes a closer look at this.

CRITICAL THINKING
Virtual Culture: Is It Good for Us?

January 16, Orlando, Florida. Walt Disney World is a delight to the kids but a little disturbing to the sociologist. It is ready-made culture: streets, stores, and events re-create a nineteenth-century small town, populated with Disney characters. Here, life is carefully controlled to ensure a good time, with the ultimate purpose of relieving us of whatever cash we have.

The Information Revolution is now generating symbols—words, sounds, and images—faster than ever before and rapidly spreading them across the continent and around the world. What does this new information technology mean for our way of life?

In centuries past, culture was a way of life transmitted from generation to generation. It was a heritage—a society's collective memory—that was authentically our own because it belonged to our ancestors (Schwartz, 1996). But in the emerging cyber-society, more and more cultural symbols are new, intentionally created by a small cultural elite of composers, writers,

filmmakers, and others who work in the expanding information economy.

To illustrate, consider the changing character of cultural heroes, people who serve as role models and represent cultural ideals. A century or so ago, our heroes were real men and women who made a difference in the life of this nation: Sir John MacDonald, Jeanne Mance, William Osler, Louis Riel, Grey Owl, Lucy Maud Montgomery, and Poundmaker. Of course, when a society makes a hero of someone (almost always

Culture used to be a way of life passed across many generations. Today, large corporations and the mass media create culture to entertain—and to make money.

well after the person has died), it "cleans up" the person's biography, highlighting the successes and overlooking the short-comings. Even so, these people were authentic parts of our history.

Today's children, by contrast, are fed a steady diet of *virtual culture,* images that spring from the minds of contemporary culture makers and that reach them through television, movie, or computer screen. Today's "heroes" include Harry Potter, the Simpsons, Aragorn, Anakin Skywalker, Rug Rats, Pokémon, Batman, Barbie, Power-puff Girls, a continuous flow of Disney characters, and the ever-smiling Ronald McDonald.

Some of these cultural icons embody values that shape our way of life. But few of them have any historical reality, and almost all have been created for a single purpose: to make money.

WHAT DO YOU THINK?

1. As the Information Revolution proceeds, do you think virtual culture will become increasingly important? Why or why not?
2. Does virtual culture erode or enhance our cultural traditions? Is that good or bad?
3. What image of Canada do North American movies and television shows give to people abroad?

Source: Thanks to Roland Johnson for the basic idea for this box.

Cultural Diversity

Take a stroll down Queen Street in Toronto or through Vancouver's Gastown, and it will soon become obvious to you that Canada is an extremely culturally diverse society. As noted at the beginning of the chapter, heavy immigration

over the past century and a half has turned Canada into one of the most *multicultural* of all high-income countries. Figure 2–3 shows that 12.8 percent of the population in 1901 were born outside of Canada. Over 75 percent of these people were born in Europe and almost 60 percent came from the United Kingdom. By 2001, the percentage of the population who were born outside of Canada had increased

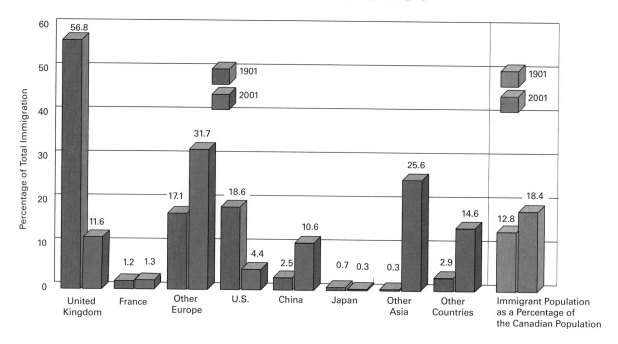

FIGURE 2–3 Birthplaces of Canadian Immigrants, 1901, 2001

Source: Statistics Canada (1999h, 2002e, 2003bj).

to 18.4 percent and more than half had been born outside of Europe. This diverging immigration is also reflected in the much greater diversity in the background of Canadians today (Table 11–1 on page 285 shows details of the ethnic diversity in Canada). To understand the reality of life in Canada, we must move beyond shared cultural patterns to consider the importance of cultural diversity.

HIGH CULTURE AND POPULAR CULTURE

Cultural diversity often involves social class. In fact, in everyday conversation, we usually reserve the term "culture" for art forms such as literature, music, dance, and painting. We describe people who attend the opera or the theatre as "cultured," thinking that they appreciate the "finer things in life."

We speak less well of ordinary people, assuming that their everyday culture is somehow less worthy. So we are tempted to judge the music of Beethoven as "more cultured" than the blues, couscous as better than cornbread, golfing as more polished than bowling, fly fishing as more refined than bait fishing, ballet as better than ultimate fighting, and the music of Ben Heppner as superior to that of Céline Dion.

In short, many cultural patterns are readily accessible to only some members of a society (Hall and Neitz, 1993). Sociologists use the shorthand term **high culture**[1] to refer to *cultural patterns that distinguish a society's elite* and **popular culture** to designate *cultural patterns that are widespread among a society's population.*

Common sense may suggest that high culture is superior to popular culture. But we should resist quick judgments about the merits of high culture over popular culture for two main reasons. First, neither elites nor ordinary people have uniform tastes and interests; people in both categories differ in numerous ways. Second, do we praise high culture because it is inherently better than popular culture or simply because its supporters have more money, power, and prestige? For example, there is no difference between a violin and a fiddle; however, we name the instrument one

---

[1]The term "high culture" is derived from the term "highbrow." A century ago, people believed that personality was affected by the shape of the human skull and praised the tastes of those they called "highbrows" while dismissing the interests of others they derided as "lowbrows."

way when it is used to produce a type of music typically enjoyed by a person of higher position, and the other way when it produces music traditionally appreciated by people with lower social standing. Therefore, sociologists are uneasy with distinctions between high and popular culture, preferring the term "culture" to refer to *all* elements of a society's way of life, including patterns of those with high incomes and low incomes alike.

SUBCULTURE

The term **subculture** refers to *cultural patterns that set apart some segment of a society's population.* People who ride "chopper" motorcycles, people who enjoy hip-hop music and fashion, Vancouver Eastside drug users, jazz musicians, Calgary cowboys, campus poets, computer "nerds," and West Coast wilderness campers—all display subcultural patterns.

It is easy but often inaccurate to put people into subcultural categories because almost everyone participates in many subcultures without having much commitment to any one of them. In some cases, ethnicity and religion set people apart from one another with tragic results. Consider the former nation of Yugoslavia in Southeastern Europe. The recent civil war there was fuelled by astounding cultural diversity. This *one* small country made use of *two* alphabets, embraced *three* major religions, spoke *four* major languages, contained *five* major nationalities, was divided into *six* separate republics, and reflected the cultural influences of *seven* surrounding countries. The cultural conflict that plunged this nation into civil war shows that subcultures are a source not only of pleasing variety but also of tension and outright violence.

Today, as in decades past, we view Canada as a "mosaic" in which many nationalities make up the Canadian cultural identity. But given our cultural diversity, how accurate is the "mosaic" image? Some authors writing on the country's two dominant groups, English- and French-speaking, maintain that Canadians make up "two solitudes" (Rocher, 1990), as is evident in the lack of formal and informal interaction among the French- and English-speaking intellectual elites within the Royal Society (Ogmundson & McLaughlin, 1994).

Others argue that subcultures involve not just difference but hierarchy. Too often, what we view as "dominant" or "mainstream" culture are patterns favoured by powerful segments of the population, while what we view as "subculture" is, in fact, the patterns of disadvantaged people, such as high school dropouts (Tanner et al., 1995). Hence, sociologist John Porter (1965) characterized Canada as a "vertical mosaic," in which a privileged male elite consists overwhelmingly of people of British origin (Bell & Tepperman, 1979; Reitz, 1980). While researchers disagree on the extent to which Canada is a closed society that has marginalized some groups at the expense of others (Curtis, Grab, & Guppy, 1999), why is it that the cultural patterns of rich skiers in Whistler, for example, tend to seem less a "subculture" than the cultural patterns of street youth in the urban core of our cities (Baron, 2004)? Or that those who alter their bodies through cosmetic surgery seem less a subculture than those who tattoo themselves (Atkinson, 2003)? Some researchers therefore prefer to level the playing field of society by emphasizing multiculturalism and shedding light on the variety of experiences of different cultural groups that find their home in Canada today (Breton, 2005).

MULTICULTURALISM

In recent years, Canada has been facing the challenge of **multiculturalism**, *an educational program recognizing the cultural diversity of Canada and promoting the equality of all cultural traditions.* This movement represents a sharp turning away from the past, when our society did not recognize the hierarchy of the cultural mosaic. Today, we spiritedly debate how to balance a celebration of cultural differences with our shared value of equality.

Multiculturalists point out that from the outset the European immigrants to the so-called New World (of course, "new" only to those who came from abroad) exploited the various Aboriginal cultures; some First Nations peoples were decimated, while others were severely reduced in numbers and marginalized on reserves (Dickason, 1992). After Confederation (1867), people of British origin gained the top political positions in the country, viewing those of other backgrounds (Aboriginal peoples, the French, Southern Europeans, the Chinese, and so on) as being of "lower stock." As Porter (1965:62) states,

> After all, Canada was a British creation, though indifferently conceived by British statesmen of the day. In the first decades of Canada's existence, who would have doubted that the British were destined to an uninterrupted epoch of imperial splendour? Although the French participated in Confederation, Canada's political and economic leaders were British and were prepared to create a British North America. Born British subjects, they intended to die as such.

As a result of this hierarchy, Canadian historians have tended to focus on the descendants of the English and other Northern Europeans, describing historical events from their point of view. And historians have tended to push to the margins the perspectives and accomplishments of Aboriginals and Canadians of African, Asian, and Latin American descent. Multiculturalists condemn this singular pattern as **Eurocentrism**, *the dominance of European (especially English) cultural patterns.* Molefi Kete Asante, a leading advocate of multiculturalism, argues that like "the 15th-century

Language Rights in Canada: Unifying or Divisive?

Widely known as Bill 101, the *Charter of the French Language* in Quebec declares that French is the official language of the courts, civil administration, work and labour relations, commerce, business, and, to a large extent, education as well. This unique piece of legislation, designed to protect the language of the majority (French speakers) from the minority (non-French speakers), has proven to be a constant source of irrita-

tion between the two groups, most recently on three fronts: (a) use of non-French store signs, including in Montreal's Chinatown; (b) use of English on Internet sites based in the province; and (c) rights of francophone parents to send their children to English schools.

Concerning the latter case, a Quebec Supreme Court judge ruled against a group of mainly francophone parents who wanted to send their children to English

schools, thereby upholding the *Charter of the French Language*. Some of the parents threaten to take the case, if necessary, all the way to the Supreme Court of Canada. The issue of a single declared language at the provincial level in the bilingual federation that is Canada is not likely to disappear overnight.

WHAT DO YOU THINK?

Source: Denis, 1990.

Europeans who could not cease believing that the earth was the centre of the universe, many today find it difficult to cease viewing European culture as the centre of the social universe" (1988:7).

Few Canadians would deny that our way of life has wide-ranging roots. But multiculturalism is controversial because it asks us to rethink norms and values that form the core of our culture. One currently contested issue surrounds language. In 1969, the *Official Languages Act* made French and English the official languages of Canada—and the country officially became bilingual. However, as noted in the excerpt from the Citizens' Forum on Canada's Future in the Diversity: Race, Class, & Gender box above, many tensions remain over the actual implementation of Canada's language policy.

Another controversy centres on how our nation's schools should teach culture. Proponents defend multiculturalism, first, as a strategy to present a more accurate picture of Canada's past. Proposed educational reforms seek, for example, to tone down the simplistic praise commonly directed at Christopher Columbus and other European explorers, by acknowledging the tragic impact of the European conquest on the Aboriginal peoples of this hemisphere. Moreover, a multicultural approach recognizes the achievements of many women and men whose cultural backgrounds have, up to now, confined them to the sidelines of history.

Second, proponents claim, multiculturalism enables students to grasp our country's even more diverse present. The 2001 census showed that Toronto has a greater proportion of immigrants (44 percent) than other major cosmo-

politan cities such as Sydney (31 percent), Los Angeles (31 percent) and New York City (24 percent) (Statistics Canada, 2003t).

Third, proponents assert, multiculturalism can strengthen the academic achievement of Canada's Aboriginal and visible minority children, who may find little personal relevance in Eurocentric education (Ghosh, 1996). National Map 2–1 takes a closer look at language diversity in different parts of Canada.

Fourth and finally, proponents see multiculturalism as needed preparation for living in a world in which nations are increasingly interdependent. Multiculturalism, in short, teaches global connectedness.

Although multiculturalism has found favour in recent years, it has provoked its share of criticism too. Most troubling to opponents of multiculturalism is its tendency to encourage divisiveness rather than unity, by encouraging people to identify only with their own category rather than with the nation as a whole. As critics see it, a multicultural approach moves Canada along the road that has led to social collapse in the former Yugoslavia and elsewhere.

Moreover, critics contend that multiculturalism erodes any claim of universal truth by evaluating ideas according to the race (and gender) of those who present them. Our common humanity, in other words, dissolves into an "Aboriginal experience," "Chinese experience," "European experience," and so on.

Finally, critics doubt that multiculturalism actually benefits minorities. On the one hand, multiculturalism

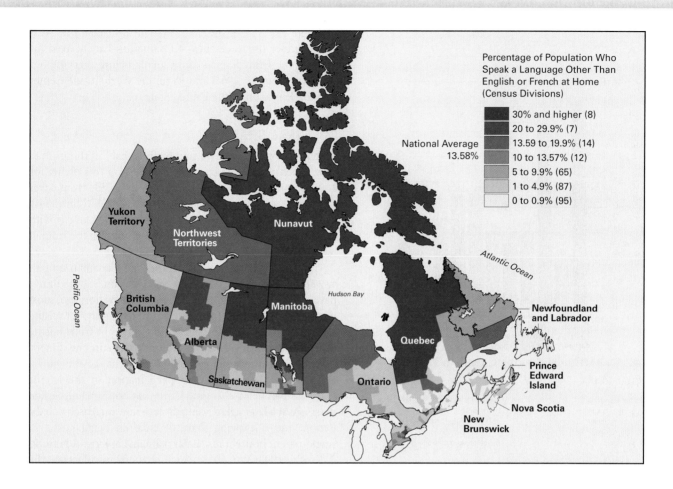

Percentage of Population Who Speak a Language Other Than English or French at Home (Census Divisions)

National Average 13.58%

- 30% and higher (8)
- 20 to 29.9% (7)
- 13.59 to 19.9% (14)
- 10 to 13.57% (12)
- 5 to 9.9% (65)
- 1 to 4.9% (87)
- 0 to 0.9% (95)

SEEING OURSELVES

NATIONAL MAP 2-1 Non-Official Home Languages Across Canada, 2001

The map shows that the percentage of households that use non-official languages at home varies greatly across Canada. The largest number of Canadians who speak a language other than French or English live in Toronto, Montreal, or Vancouver, with Toronto being the leader. What is a little surprising is the level of relative language homogeneity in large parts of Southern Quebec. What is the cause of this? What other trends do you see?

Source: Calculated based on Statistics Canada (2003z).

seems to demand precisely the kind of ethnic and racial segregation that our nation has struggled for decades to end. On the other hand, an Aboriginal-centred or Afrocentric curriculum may well deny children important knowledge and skills by forcing them to study from a single point of view. Historian Arthur Schlesinger, Jr., (1991) put the matter bluntly in regard to black people: "If a Kleagle of the Ku Klux Klan wanted to use the schools to handicap black Americans, he could hardly come up with anything more effective than the 'Afrocentric' [dominated by African cultural patterns] curriculum."

Is there any common ground in this debate? Virtually everyone agrees that we all need to gain greater appreciation of cultural diversity. But precisely where the balance is to be

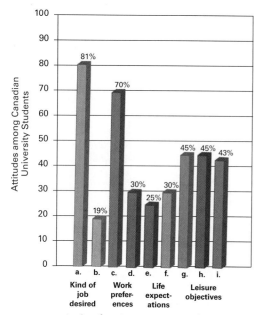

STUDENT SNAPSHOT

FIGURE 2–4 Attitudes Among Canadian University Students, 2000

a. Interesting vocations
b. High paying occupation
c. Regular hours, longer work period
d. Longer hours, shorter work period
e. Family focussed

f. Married, have two children and drive a mini-van
g. Enjoy dream home
h. Travel extensively
i. Volunteer in community

Source: Ipsos-Reid (2000b).

struck is likely to remain a divisive issue for some time to come (Davies & Guppy, 1998; Breton et al, 2004; Breton, 2005).

COUNTERCULTURE

Cultural diversity also includes outright rejection of conventional ideas or behaviour. **Counterculture** refers to *cultural patterns that strongly oppose those widely accepted within a society.*

In many societies, counterculture is linked to youth (Spates, 1976, 1983; Spates & Perkins, 1982). The youth-oriented counterculture of the 1960s, for example, rejected mainstream culture as too competitive, self-centred, and materialistic. Instead, hippies and other counterculturalists favoured a collective and cooperative lifestyle in which "being" took precedence over "doing," and personal growth—or "expanded consciousness"—was prized over material possessions such as homes and cars. Such differences led some people to "drop out" of the larger society.

Countercultures are still flourishing today. At the extreme, small bands of religious militants exist in North America, some of them engaging in violence intended to threaten our way of life. Members of al-Qaeda, one such group under the leadership of Osama bin Laden, lived for years in the United States and Canada before carrying out the September 11, 2001, attacks on the World Trade Center and the Pentagon in the United States.

CULTURAL CHANGE

Perhaps the most basic human truth is that "all things shall pass." Even the dinosaurs, which thrived on this planet for 160 million years (see the timeline on the inside front cover of the textbook), exist today only as fossils. Will humanity survive for millions of years to come? All we can say with certainty is that, given our reliance on culture, the human record will be one of continuous change.

Figure 2–4 shows recent attitudes of Canadian university students pursuing the "Canadian Dream." Some things have changed only slightly: today, as a generation ago, most women and men look forward to raising a family. Yet raising a family today is an experience quite different from raising one in earlier times. The point is that change in one dimension of a cultural system usually sparks changes in others. For example, women's rising participation in the labour force has paralleled changing family patterns, including first marriage at a later age, a rising divorce rate, increased cohabitation, and a growing share of children being raised in single-parent households (Balakrishnan, Lapierre-Adamcyk, & Krotki, 1993; Wu, 1999). Such connections illustrate the principle of **cultural integration**, *the close relationships among various elements of a cultural system.*

Some parts of a cultural system change more quickly than others. William Ogburn (1964) observed that technology moves quickly, generating new elements of material culture (such as test-tube babies) faster than nonmaterial culture (such as ideas about parenthood) can keep up with them. Ogburn called this inconsistency **cultural lag**, *the fact that some cultural elements change more quickly than others, disrupting a cultural system.* How are we to apply traditional ideas about motherhood and fatherhood in a culture where a woman can now give birth to a child by using another woman's egg, which has been fertilized in a laboratory with the sperm of a total stranger?

Cultural changes are set in motion in three ways. The first is *invention*, the process of creating new cultural elements, such as the telephone (1876), the airplane (1903), and the computer (late 1940s). The process of invention goes on constantly, as indicated by the thousands of applications submitted annually to the Canadian Intellectual Property Office. The timeline inside the front cover of this text shows other inventions that have helped change our way of life.

Discovery, a second cause of change, involves recognizing and better understanding something already in existence, from a distant star to the foods of a foreign culture to the athletic abilities of women. Many discoveries result from painstaking scientific research, and others happen by a stroke of luck, as when Marie Curie unintentionally left a rock on a piece of photographic paper in 1898 and discovered radium.

The third cause of cultural change is *diffusion*, the spread of objects or ideas from one society to another. The ability of new information technology to send information around the world in seconds means that the extent of cultural diffusion has never been greater than it is today.

Certainly, Canadian society has provided many significant cultural contributions to the world, including the renowned classical music of pianist Glenn Gould and the popular novels of Margaret Atwood, who was awarded the 2000 Booker Prize for her acclaimed novel *The Blind Assassin*. Sometimes, though, we forget that diffusion works the other way, so that much of what we assume is "Canadian" actually comes from elsewhere. Most clothing, furniture, clocks, newspapers, money, and even the English language are derived from other cultures around the world (Linton, 1937a).

ETHNOCENTRISM AND CULTURAL RELATIVISM

December 10, a small village in rural Morocco. Watching many of our shipmates browsing through this tiny ceramic factory, one can hardly doubt that North Americans are among the world's greatest shoppers. They delight in surveying hand-woven carpets in China or India, inspecting finely crafted metals in Turkey, or collecting beautifully coloured porcelain tiles here in Morocco. And of course, all these items are wonderful bargains. But the major reason for the low prices is unsettling: Many products from the world's low- and middle-income countries are produced by children—some as young as five or six—who work long days for pennies per hour.

We think of childhood as a time of innocence and freedom from adult burdens such as work. In low-income countries throughout the world, however, families depend on income earned by children. Child labour is one example of a practice that people in one society think of as right and natural and people elsewhere find puzzling and even immoral. Perhaps the Chinese philosopher Confucius had it

In the world's low-income countries, most children must work to provide their families with needed income. This young child in Dhaka, Bangladesh, is sorting discarded materials in a factory that makes recycled lead batteries. Is it ethnocentric for people living in high-income nations to condemn the practice of child labour because we think youngsters belong in school? Why or why not?

right when he noted, "All people are the same; it's only their habits that are different."

Just about every imaginable idea or behaviour is common somewhere in the world, and this cultural variation causes travellers equal measures of excitement and distress. The Australians flip light switches down to turn them on, whereas North Americans flip them up; the Japanese name city blocks rather than streets, a practice that regularly confuses North Americans, who do the opposite; Egyptians move very close to others in conversation, which irritates North Americans, who are used to maintaining several feet of personal space. Bathrooms lack toilet paper in much of rural Morocco, causing concern among Westerners unaccustomed to using the left hand for bathroom hygiene.

Given that a particular culture is the basis for everyone's reality, it is no wonder that people throughout the world exhibit **ethnocentrism**, *the practice of judging another culture by the standards of one's own culture.* Some ethnocentrism is necessary if people are to be emotionally attached to their own cultural system. But ethnocentrism also generates misunderstanding and conflict.

Even our language is culturally biased. People in North America and Europe call China the "Far East." Such a term,

The view from "Down Under"—North America should be "up" and South America "down," or so we think. But because we live on a globe, "up" and "down" have no meaning at all. The reason this map of the Western Hemisphere looks wrong to us is not that it is geographically inaccurate; it simply violates our ethnocentric assumption that Canada should be "above" the rest of the Americas.

which has little meaning to the Chinese, is an ethnocentric expression for a region that is far to the east of us. For their part, the Chinese name their country using a word translated as "Central Kingdom," suggesting that they see their society as the centre of the world. The map above challenges our ethnocentrism by presenting a "down under" view of the Western Hemisphere.

The logical alternative to ethnocentrism is **cultural relativism**, *the practice of evaluating a culture by its own standards.* Cultural relativism is a difficult attitude to adopt because it requires an understanding of unfamiliar values and norms and the suspension of lifelong cultural standards. But as people of the world increasingly come into contact with one another, the importance of understanding other cultures becomes even greater.

As noted in the opening to this chapter, businesses in Canada are realizing that success in the global economy depends on cultural sophistication. IBM, for example, now provides technical support for its products using websites in 22 languages (Fonda, 2001). In the past, companies paid little attention to cultural differences, sometime with negative consequences. General Motors learned the hard way that its Nova wasn't selling well in Spanish-speaking nations because the name in Spanish means "no go." Coors' phrase "Turn It Loose" startled Spanish-speaking customers by proclaiming that the beer would cause diarrhea. Braniff Airlines translated its slogan "Fly in Leather" into Spanish so clumsily that it read "Fly Naked"; similarly, Eastern Airlines' slogan "We Earn Our Wings Daily" became "We Fly Every Day to Heaven," discouraging timid air travellers. Even poultry giant Frank Perdue fell victim to poor marketing when his pitch "It Takes a Tough Man to Make a Tender Chicken" was transformed into the Spanish phrase "A Sexually Excited Man Makes a Chicken Affectionate" (Helin, 1992).

In two brief videos, John Macionis considers issues of cultural relativism at **http://www. TheSociologyPage.com**.

But cultural relativism introduces problems of its own. If almost any behaviour is the norm *somewhere* in the world, does that mean everything is equally right? Does the fact that some Indian and Moroccan families benefit from their children's working long hours justify child labour?

Because we are all members of a single human species, surely there must be some universal standards of proper conduct. But what are they? And in trying to identify them, how can we avoid imposing our own standards on others? There are no simple answers. But when confronting an unfamiliar cultural practice, resist making judgments before learning what the people in that culture think and why. Remember also to think about your own way of life as others might see it. After all, what we gain most from studying others is better insight into ourselves.

A GLOBAL CULTURE?

Today, more than ever before, we see many of the same cultural patterns the world over. Walking the streets of Seoul (South Korea), Kuala Lumpur (Malaysia), Madras (India), Cairo (Egypt), and Casablanca (Morocco), we find jeans, hear well-known pop music, and see advertising for many of the same products we use at home. Recall, too, from Global Map 2–1 that English is rapidly becoming the second language of most of the world. Are we witnessing the birth of a single global culture?

Societies around the world now have more contact with one another than ever before, thanks to the flow of goods, information, and people:

1. **Global economy: The flow of goods.** There has never been more international trade. The global economy has spread many consumer goods (from cars and TV shows to music and fashion) throughout the world.

2. **Global communication: The flow of information.** Satellite-based communication enables people throughout the world to experience the sights and sounds of events taking place thousands of miles away, often as they are happening.

3. **Global migration: The flow of people.** Knowing about the rest of the world motivates people to move where they imagine life will be better. Moreover, today's transportation technology, especially air travel, makes moving about faster than ever before. As a result, in most nations, significant numbers of people have been born elsewhere (including some 5.4 million people in Canada—18.4 percent of the population).

These global links have made the cultures of the world more similar. But there are three important limitations to the global culture thesis. First, the flow of information, goods, and people is uneven. Generally speaking, urban areas (centres of commerce, communication, and people) have stronger ties to one another, and rural villages remain more isolated. In addition, the greater economic and military power of North America and Western Europe means that nations in these regions influence the rest of the world more than happens the other way around.

Second, the global culture thesis assumes that people everywhere are able to afford the new goods and services. As Chapter 9 ("Global Stratification") explains, desperate poverty in much of the world deprives people of even the basic necessities of a safe and secure life (Hedley, 2000).

Third, although many cultural elements have spread throughout the world, people everywhere do not attach the same meanings to them. Do teenagers in Tokyo understand hip-hop the way young people in Vancouver or Winnipeg do? Similarly, although we may enjoy foods from around the world, we probably know little or nothing about the lives of the people who created them. In short, people everywhere look at the world through their own cultural lenses.

Theoretical Analysis of Culture

Sociologists have the special task of investigating how culture helps us make sense of ourselves and the surrounding world. Here we present several macro-level theoretical approaches to understanding culture; a micro-level approach to the personal experience of culture is the focus of Chapter 4 ("Social Interaction in Everyday Life").

STRUCTURAL-FUNCTIONAL ANALYSIS

The structural-functional approach explains culture as a complex strategy for meeting human needs. Drawing from the philosophical doctrine of *idealism,* this approach considers values to be the core of a culture (Parsons, 1966; Williams, 1970). In other words, cultural values direct our lives, give meaning to what we do, and bind people together. Countless other cultural traits have various functions that support the operation of society.

Thinking functionally helps us make sense of an unfamiliar way of life. Consider the Old Order Amish farmer in Southern Ontario plowing hundreds of acres with a team of horses. His methods may violate the Canadian cultural value of efficiency, but from the Amish point of view, hard work functions to develop the discipline necessary for a highly religious way of life. Long days of working together not only make the Amish self-sufficient but also strengthen

Following the structural-functional approach, what do you make of the Amish practice of "barn raising," by which everyone in a community joins together to raise a family's new barn in a day? Why is such a ritual almost unknown in rural areas outside of Amish communities?

family ties and unify local communities and result in lower rates of overweight and obesity compared to other Canadians.

Of course, Amish practices have dysfunctions as well. The hard work and strict religious discipline are too demanding for some, who end up leaving the community. Also, religious devotion sometimes prevents compromise, resulting in lasting divisions within the Amish world, including between the old and young and men and women (Kraybill, 1989; Kraybill & Olshan, 1994). This is not unlike the situation found in tightly controlled Mennonite communities in Manitoba, as Miriam Toews recently chronicled in her award-winning book, *A Complicated Kindness* (Toews, 2005).

If cultures are strategies for meeting human needs, we would expect to find many common patterns around the world. **Cultural universals** are *traits that are part of every known culture.* Comparing hundreds of cultures, George Murdock (1945) identified dozens of cultural universals. One common element is the family, which functions everywhere to control sexual reproduction and to oversee the care and upbringing of children. Funeral rites are also found everywhere because all human communities cope with death. Jokes are another cultural universal, serving as a safe means of releasing social tensions.

Critical review. The strength of structural-functional analysis lies in showing how culture operates to meet human needs. Yet by emphasizing a society's dominant cultural patterns, this approach overlooks cultural diversity. In addition, because this approach emphasizes cultural stability, it downplays the importance of change. In short, cultural systems are neither as stable nor a matter of as much agreement as structural-functional analysis leads us to believe.

SOCIAL-CONFLICT ANALYSIS

The social-conflict approach draws attention to the link between culture and inequality. From this point of view, any cultural trait benefits some members of society at the expense of others.

Why do certain values dominate a society in the first place? Many conflict theorists, especially Marxists, argue that culture is shaped by a society's system of economic production. Social-conflict theory, then, is rooted in the philosophical doctrine of *materialism,* which holds that a society's system of material production (such as our own capitalist economy) has a powerful effect on the rest of a culture. This materialist approach contrasts with the idealist leanings of structural-functionalism.

Social-conflict analysis ties the competitive values of North Americans to the capitalist economy, which serves the interests of the nation's wealthy elite. The culture of capitalism further teaches us that rich and powerful people have more energy and talent than others and therefore deserve their wealth and privilege. Viewing capitalism as somehow "natural" also discourages efforts to reduce economic inequality in Canada and many other Western countries.

Eventually, however, the strains of inequality erupt into movements for social change. Two recent examples in North America are the civil rights movement and the women's movement. Both seek greater equality, and both encounter opposition from defenders of the status quo.

Critical review. The social-conflict approach points out that cultural systems do not address human needs equally; rather, they allow some people to dominate others. This inequality, in turn, generates pressure toward change.

Yet by stressing the divisiveness of culture, this approach understates ways in which cultural patterns integrate members of a society. Thus, we should consider both social-conflict and structural-functional insights for a fuller understanding of culture.

SOCIOBIOLOGY

Does our biological existence influence how humans create culture? A third theoretical approach, standing with one leg in biology and the other in sociology, is **sociobiology**, *a* *theoretical approach that explores ways in which human biology affects how we create culture.*

Sociobiology rests on the theory of evolution proposed by Charles Darwin in his book *On the Origin of Species* (1859). Darwin asserted that living organisms change over long periods of time as a result of *natural selection,* a matter of four simple principles. First, all living things live to reproduce themselves. Second, the blueprint for reproduction is in the genes, the basic units of life that carry traits of one generation into the next. Third, some random variation in genes allows each species to "try out" new life patterns in a particular environment. This variation enables some organisms to survive better than others and to pass on their advantageous genes to their offspring. Fourth and finally, over thousands of generations, the genes that promote reproduction survive and become dominant. In this way, as biologists say, a species *adapts* to its environment, and dominant traits emerge as the "nature" of the organism.

Sociobiologists claim that the large number of cultural universals reflects the fact that all humans are members of a single biological species. It is our common biology that underlies, for example, the apparently universal "double standard." As sex researcher Alfred Kinsey put it, "Among all people everywhere in the world, the male is more likely than the female to desire sex with a variety of partners" (quoted in Barash, 1981:49). But why?

We all know that a child results from joining a woman's egg with a man's sperm. But the biological significance of a single sperm is very different from that of a single egg. For healthy men, sperm is a "renewable resource" produced by the testes throughout most of the life course. A man releases hundreds of millions of sperm in a single ejaculation, technically enough to fertilize every woman in North America (Barash, 1981:47). However, a newborn girl's ovaries contain her entire lifetime's supply of immature eggs. Usually a woman releases a single egg cell from the ovaries each month. So whereas men are biologically capable of fathering thousands of offspring, a woman is able to bear a much smaller number of children.

Given this biological difference, males and females have distinctive strategies for reproduction. Men reproduce their genes most efficiently by being promiscuous, engaging in sex readily and often. But this scheme opposes the reproductive interests of women. Each of a woman's pregnancies demands that she carry the child, give birth, and provide care for some time afterward. Thus, efficient reproduction on the part of the woman depends on selecting a man whose qualities (beginning with the likelihood that he will simply stay around) will contribute to her child's survival and, later, successful reproduction.

The "double standard" certainly involves more than biology; it is also a product of the historical domination of

Using an evolutionary perspective, sociobiologists explain that different reproductive strategies give rise to a double standard: Men treat women as sexual objects more than women treat men that way. While this may be so, many sociologists counter that behaviour—such as that shown in Ruth Orkin's photograph, *American Girl in Italy*—is more correctly understood as resulting from a culture of male domination.

women by men. But sociobiology suggests that this cultural pattern, like many others, has an underlying "bio-logic." Simply put, the "double standard" exists around the world because women and men everywhere tend toward distinctive reproductive strategies.

Critical review. Sociobiology provides intriguing insights into the biological roots of some cultural patterns. But this approach remains controversial for two main reasons.

First, some critics fear that sociobiology may revive the biological arguments of a century ago that claimed the superiority of one race or gender. But defenders counter that sociobiology rejects the past pseudoscience of racial superiority or male dominance. In fact, they assert, sociobiology unites all humanity because all people share a single evolutionary history. Men and women differ biologically in some ways that culture may not overcome. But far from claiming that males are somehow more important than females, they assert that both are vital to human survival.

Second, critics point out that sociobiologists have little evidence to support their theories. Research to date suggests that biological forces do not *determine* human behaviour in any rigid sense. Rather, humans *learn* behaviour within a culture. Sociobiologists have responded to this criticism by

APPLYING THEORY
CULTURE

	Structural-Functional Approach	Social-Conflict Approach	Sociobiological Approach
What is the level of analysis?	Macro-level	Macro-level	Macro-level
What is culture?	Culture is a system of behaviour by which members of societies cooperate to meet their needs.	Culture is a system that benefits some people and disadvantages others.	Culture is a system of behaviour that is partly shaped by human biology.
What is the foundation of culture?	Cultural patterns are rooted in a society's core values and beliefs.	Cultural patterns are rooted in a society's system of economic production.	Cultural patterns are rooted in humanity's biological evolution.
What core questions does the approach ask?	How does a cultural pattern help society to operate? What cultural patterns are found in all societies?	How does a cultural pattern benefit some people and harm others? How does a cultural pattern support social inequality?	How does a cultural pattern help a species adapt to its environment?

stating that some cultural patterns seem easier to learn than others (Barash, 1981).

The Applying Theory table summarizes the main lessons of each theoretical approach for an understanding of culture. Note that because any analysis of culture requires a broad focus on the workings of society, all these approaches are macro-level in scope. The symbolic-interaction approach, with its micro-level focus on people's behaviour in specific situations, will be explored in Chapter 4 ("Social Interaction in Everyday Life").

Culture and Human Freedom

Underlying the discussion throughout this chapter is an important question: To what extent are human beings, as cultural creatures, free? Does culture bind us to each other and force us to relive the past? Or does it enhance our capacity for individual thought and independent choice?

Humans cannot live without culture. But living as symbolic creatures does have some drawbacks. We may be the only animals able to name ourselves, but living in a symbolic world means that we are also the only creatures who experience alienation. Culture is largely a matter of habit, which limits our choices and drives us to repeat troubling patterns, such as racial prejudice and sex discrimination, in each new generation. In addition, in this age of new information technology, business-dominated mass media have the power to manipulate our culture in pursuit of profits.

Our insistence on competitive achievement urges us toward excellence, yet often at the cost of isolating us from one another. Material comforts do make life easy but divert us from close relationships and spiritual strength.

For better and worse, human beings are cultural creatures, just as ants and bees are prisoners of their biology. But there is a crucial difference. Biological instincts create a ready-made world; culture forces us to make choices as we create and re-create our world. No better evidence of this freedom exists than the cultural diversity of our own society and the even greater human diversity around the world.

Learning about this cultural diversity is one goal of sociology; as an example, the Global Sociology box offers some contrasts between the cultures of Canada and the United States, supporting those who argue that it is a myth that the values of the two countries are converging (Adams, 2003). Wherever we may live, the better we understand the workings of the surrounding culture, the better prepared we will be to use the freedom it offers us.

Canada and the United States: Are They Culturally Different?

Canada and the United States are two of the largest high-income nations in the world, and they share a common border of about 6400 kilometres. But do Canada and the United States share the same culture?

One important point to make right away is that both nations are *multicultural.* Not only do both countries have hundreds of Aboriginal societies, but immigration has brought people to them from all over the world. Most early immigrants to Canada and the United States came from Europe; more recent immigrants have come from nations in Asia and Latin America. The Canadian city of Vancouver, for example, has a Chinese community almost as large as the Latino community in Los Angeles.

Canada differs from the United States in one important respect. Historically, it has had *two* dominant cultures: French (about 25 percent of the population) and British (roughly 40 percent). People of French ancestry are a large majority of the province of Quebec (where French is the official language) and a large minority of New Brunswick (which is officially bilingual).

Are the dominant values of Canada much the same as those we have described for the United States? Seymour Martin Lipset (1985) found some important differences. The United States declared independence from Great Britain in 1776; Canada formally separated from Great Britain only in 1982. For this reason, Lipset concludes, the dominant culture of Canada lies between those of the United States and Great Britain.

One difference is that the culture of the United States is more individualistic, whereas Canada's is more collective. In the United States, individualism is seen in the historical importance of the cowboy, a self-sufficient type of person, and even outlaws such as Jesse James and Billy the Kid are regarded as heroes because they challenged authority. In Canada, it is the Mountie—Canada's well-known police officer on horseback—who is looked on with great respect.

Politically, people in Canada, as in Great Britain, have a strong sense that government should look after the interests of everyone. By contrast, people in the United States tend to think individuals ought to do things for themselves. This is one reason that Canada has a much broader social welfare system (which includes universal healthcare) than the United States has (it is the only high-income nation without universal healthcare). Also, Canadians are more likely to support social policy change to promote the rights of minorities, such as gay marriage, and to provide help to vulnerable populations, including safe injection sites for drug users in Vancouver's Downtown Eastside. Vancouver's first legal trial of a safer injecting facility commenced in September 2003 after a protracted debate (Fry, 2003). The facility, the first in North America, is centrally located in Vancouver's Downtown Eastside, which is the most impoverished urban neighbourhood in Canada. The federal government approved a three-year project provided it was evaluated for effectiveness in regard to its social and health effect (Wood et al., 2004). Likewise, ownership of one or more guns is common for U.S. households, and the idea that individuals are entitled to own a gun is strong—although controversial—in the U.S. In Canada, fewer households have a gun, and government greatly restricts gun ownership. This is especially in regard to handguns. According to Wendy Cukier (2000), Canada has about 1 million handguns while the U.S. has more than 77 million, and although the U.S. murder rate without guns is only 1.7 times higher than in Canada, the murder rate with handguns is 15 times the Canadian rate.

WHAT DO YOU THINK?

1. Why do some Canadians feel that their way of life is overshadowed by that of the United States?
2. Why do many people in the United States have little interest in its neighbour nations to the north (Canada) and south (Mexico)?

Sources: Lipset (1985), Adams (2000) and Macionis and Gerber (2005).

SUMMARY

1. Culture is a way of life shared by members of a society. Several species display limited capacity for culture, but only human beings rely on culture for survival.

2. As the human brain evolved, the first elements of culture appeared some 3 million years ago; culture replaced biological instincts as our species' primary strategy for survival.

3. Culture is built using symbols. Language is the symbolic system by which one generation passes on culture to the next.

4. Values are culturally defined standards of what ought to be; beliefs are statements that people who share a culture hold to be true. Norms, which guide human behaviour, are of two kinds: mores, which have great moral significance, and folkways, which are everyday matters of politeness.

5. Culture is shaped by technology. We understand technological development in terms of stages of sociocultural evolution: hunting and gathering, horticulture and pastoralism, agriculture, industry, and the post-industrial information age.

6. High culture refers to patterns that distinguish a society's elites; popular culture includes patterns widespread in a society.

7. There are many dimensions of cultural diversity in Canada. Immigration has brought cultural traits from nations around the world. Our ways of life also include distinctive subcultures as well as countercultures strongly at odds with a conventional way of life. Multiculturalism is an effort to enhance appreciation of cultural diversity.

8. Invention, discovery, and diffusion all generate cultural change. Cultural lag results when some parts of a cultural system change faster than others.

9. Ethnocentrism involves judging others using standards of one's own culture. Cultural relativism is the evaluation of another culture according to its own standards.

10. Global cultural patterns result from the worldwide flow of goods, information, and people.

11. The structural-functional approach views culture as a relatively stable system built on core values. All cultural traits play some part in the ongoing operation of society.

12. The social-conflict approach envisions culture as a dynamic arena of inequality and conflict. Cultural traits benefit some categories of people more than others.

13. Sociobiology studies how evolution shapes the human creation of culture.

14. Culture can limit social possibilities, yet as cultural creatures, we have the capacity to shape and reshape our world to meet our needs and pursue our dreams.

KEY CONCEPTS

agriculture (p. 46) large-scale cultivation using plows harnessed to animals or more powerful energy sources

beliefs (p. 43) specific statements that people hold to be true

counterculture (p. 52) cultural patterns that strongly oppose those widely accepted within a society

cultural integration (p. 52) the close relationships among various elements of a cultural system

cultural lag (p. 52) the fact that some cultural elements change more quickly than others, disrupting a cultural system

cultural relativism (p. 54) the practice of evaluating a culture by its own standards

cultural transmission (p. 41) the process by which one generation passes culture to the next

cultural universals (p. 56) traits that are part of every known culture

culture (p. 36) the values, beliefs, behaviour, and material objects that together form a people's way of life

culture shock (p. 37) personal disorientation when experiencing an unfamiliar way of life

ethnocentrism (p. 53) the practice of judging another culture by the standards of one's own culture

Eurocentrism (p. 49) the dominance of European (especially English) cultural patterns

folkways (p. 44) norms for routine or casual interaction

high culture (p. 48) cultural patterns that distinguish a society's elite

horticulture (p. 45) the use of hand tools to raise crops

hunting and gathering (p. 45) the use of simple tools to hunt animals and gather vegetation for food

industry (p. 46) the production of goods using advanced sources of energy to drive large machinery

language (p. 40) a system of symbols that allows people to communicate with one another

mores (p. 44) norms that are widely observed and have great moral significance

multiculturalism (p. 49) an educational program recognizing the cultural diversity of Canada and promoting the equality of all cultural traditions

norms (p. 44) rules and expectations by which a society guides the behaviour of its members

pastoralism (p. 46) the domestication of animals

popular culture (p. 48) cultural patterns that are widespread among a society's population

Sapir–Whorf thesis (p. 43) the idea that people perceive the world through the cultural lens of language

society (p. 36) people who interact in a defined territory and share a culture

sociobiology (p. 56) a theoretical approach that explores ways in which human biology affects how we create culture

subculture (p. 49) cultural patterns that set apart some segment of a society's population

symbols (p. 40) anything that carries a particular meaning recognized by people who share a culture

technology (p. 45) knowledge that people use to make a way of life in their surroundings

values (p. 43) culturally defined standards that people use to assess desirability, goodness, and beauty and that serve as broad guidelines for social living

CRITICAL-THINKING QUESTIONS

1. What is the cultural significance of a carefully manicured lawn in a highly mobile and largely anonymous society? What does a well-tended (or untended) front yard say about a person?

2. What cultural lessons do games such as king of the mountain, tag, or keep-away teach our children? What about a classroom spelling bee? What cultural values are expressed by children's stories such as *The Little Engine That Could* and popular board games such as Chutes and Ladders, Monopoly, and Risk?

3. To what extent, in your opinion, is a global culture emerging? Do you consider the possibility of a global culture as positive or negative? Why?

4. Do you identify with one or more subcultures? If so, describe each one, pointing out how it differs from the dominant culture.

APPLICATIONS AND EXERCISES

1. Talk to someone who grew up in another country. Discuss how the culture of that society differs from the way of life here. How does the person see Canadian culture differently than you do?

2. Make a list of words with the prefix *self-* ("self-service," "self-esteem," "self-destructive," and so on); there are hundreds of them. What does this fact suggest about our way of life?

3. Watch a Disney video such as *The Little Mermaid, Aladdin, Pocahontas,* or *Mulan.* All of these films share cultural themes, which is one reason for their popularity. In these films, what do young people strive for? What conflicts do they have with their parents? What makes these films especially "American"?

 # SITES TO SEE

www.pearsoned.ca/macionis
The authors and publisher of this book invite you to visit the interactive Companion Website™ that accompanies this text. Begin by clicking on the cover of your book. You will find a chapter-by-chapter study guide, practice tests, suggested weblinks, and links to other relevant material.

www.unb.ca/web/anthropology/internet.htm
Anthropologists study cultures all over the world. This is the website for interesting Canadian and international anthropological associations and related journals and programs, where you can find out more about this discipline, which is closely related to sociology.

www.TheSociologyPage.com
(or **www.macionis.com**)
View several short videos in which John Macionis describes the excitement and challenges of experiencing other cultures.

www.nationalgeographic.com
The National Geographic Society offers information on world cultures, including search engines and a library of maps.

www.gorilla.org
What does a 450-pound gorilla say? Anything she wants! The Gorilla Foundation offers a look at the sign language used by a 450-pound gorilla named Koko.

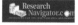 # INVESTIGATE WITH RESEARCH NAVIGATOR™

Follow the instructions on page 33 of this text to access the features of Research Navigator™. Once at the website (**www.researchnavigator.com**), enter your login name and password. Then, to use the Content Select™ database, enter keywords such as "ethnocentrism," "multiculturalism," and "immigration," and the search engine will supply relevant and recent scholarly and popular press publications.

 To reinforce your understanding of this chapter, and to identify topics for further study, visit MySocLab at **www.pearsoned.ca/mysoclab/macionis** for diagnostic tests and a multimedia ebook.

CHAPTER THREE

Socialization: From Infancy to Old Age

Why is social experience considered
the key to human personality?

What familiar social settings have special
importance to socialization?

How do people's experiences change over the life course?

Socialization is the process by which older members of a society teach their ways of life to the young. In the South Asian nation of Brunei, these Muslim fathers pass their traditional beliefs on to their sons.

On a cold winter day in 1938, a social worker knocked on the door of a rural Pennsylvania farmhouse. Investigating a case of possible child abuse, the social worker soon discovered a five-year-old girl hidden in a second-floor storage room. The child, whose name was Anna, was wedged into an old chair with her arms tied above her head so she couldn't move. Her clothes were filthy, and her arms and legs were as thin as matchsticks (Davis, 1940:554).

Anna's situation can only be described as tragic. She was born in 1932 to an unmarried, mentally impaired woman of 26 who lived with her strict father. Enraged by his daughter's "illegitimate" motherhood, the grandfather did not even want the child in his house. For her first six months, Anna was shuttled among various welfare agencies. But when her mother was no longer able to pay for care, Anna returned to the hostile home of her grandfather.

To lessen the grandfather's anger, Anna's mother kept the child in the storage room. She gave the child just enough milk to keep her alive, but she gave her no loving attention, no smiles, no hugs, no play. There in the dark and lonely world of the storage room she stayed, day after day, month after month, with almost no human contact, for five long years.

When he heard about the discovery of Anna, sociologist Kingsley Davis (1940) immediately went to see the child. He found her being cared for by local authorities at a county home. Davis was appalled by the sight of the emaciated girl, who could not laugh, speak, or even smile. Anna was completely unresponsive, as if alone in an empty world.

Social Experience: The Key to Our Humanity

Here is a horrible case of a child who was completely deprived of social contact. Although physically alive, Anna hardly seemed human. Her plight reveals that without social experience, a human being is incapable of thought, emotion, or meaningful action, seeming more an object than a person.

Sociologists use the term **socialization** to refer to *the lifelong social experience by which individuals develop their human potential and learn culture.* Unlike other living species, whose behaviour is biologically set, humans need social experience to learn their culture and survive. Social experience is also the basis of **personality**, *a person's fairly consistent patterns of acting, thinking, and feeling.* We build a personality by internalizing—taking in—our surroundings. But without social experience, as Anna's case shows, personality simply does not develop at all.

HUMAN DEVELOPMENT: NATURE AND NURTURE

Anna's case makes clear the fact that humans depend on others to provide the care needed not only for physical growth but for personality to develop. A century ago, however, people mistakenly believed that humans were born with instincts that determined their personality and behaviour.

Charles Darwin's groundbreaking study of evolution, described in Chapter 2 ("Culture"), led people to think that human behaviour was instinctive, simply our "nature." Such ideas led to claims that our economic system reflects "instinctive human competitiveness," that some people are "born criminals," or that women are "innately" emotional and men are "inherently" more rational (Witkin-Lanoil, 1984).

People trying to understand cultural diversity also misunderstood Darwin's thinking. Centuries of world exploration had taught Western Europeans that people around the world display very different behaviour. But Europeans linked these differences to biology rather than culture. It was an easy, although incorrect and very damaging, step to claim that members of technologically simple societies were biologically less evolved and therefore less human than their Western counterparts. But this ethnocentric view helped justify colonialism: if Native peoples were not human in the same sense that the colonialists were, they could be exploited, even enslaved, without a second thought. This was the experience for Canada's Aboriginal peoples, who were viewed by Canada's former colonial powers as "savages" and "barbarians" (Dickason, 1992).

Biological explanations of human behaviour came under fire in the twentieth century. Psychologist John B. Watson (1878–1958) developed a theory called *behaviourism*, which held that behaviour is not instinctive but learned. People everywhere are equally human, differing only in their cultural patterns. In short, Watson rooted human behaviour not in nature but in *nurture.*

Today, social scientists are cautious about describing *any* human behaviour as instinctive. This does not mean that biology plays no part in human behaviour. Human life, after all, depends on the functioning of the body. We also know that children often share biological traits (such as height and hair colour) with their parents and that heredity plays a part in intelligence, musical and artistic aptitude, and personality (such as how one reacts to frustration). However, whether you *realize* an inherited potential depends on your chance to develop it. In fact, unless children use their brains early in life, the brain itself does not fully develop (Goldsmith, 1983; Begley, 1995).

Without denying the importance of nature, then, nurture matters more in shaping human behaviour. More precisely, *nurture is our nature.*

SOCIAL ISOLATION

As the opening to this chapter suggests, cutting people off from the social world can be harmful indeed. Researchers can never place human beings in total isolation to study this process. But in the past, they have studied the effects of social isolation on nonhuman primates.

The personalities we develop depend largely on the environment in which we live. As William Kurelek shows in this painting, *Prairie Childhood*, based on his childhood in the Alberta prairies, a young person's life on a farm is often characterized by periods of social isolation and backbreaking work. How would such a boy's personality be likely to differ from that of his wealthy cousin raised in a large city, such as Montreal?

William Kurelek, *Prairie Childhood*. The Estate of William Kurelek and the Isaacs Gallery, Toronto.

Research with monkeys. In a classic study, psychologists Harry and Margaret Harlow (1962) placed rhesus monkeys, whose behaviour is in some ways surprisingly similar to human behaviour, in various conditions of social isolation. They found that complete isolation (with adequate nutrition) for even six months seriously disturbed the monkeys' development. When returned to their group, these monkeys were passive, anxious, and fearful.

The Harlows then placed infant rhesus monkeys in cages with an artificial "mother" made of wire mesh with a wooden head and the nipple of a feeding tube where the breast would be. These monkeys also survived but were unable to interact with others when placed in a group.

But monkeys isolated with an artificial "mother" covered with soft terry cloth did better, clinging to her more closely than those with "mothers" of just wire mesh. Because these monkeys showed less developmental damage than the earlier groups, the Harlows concluded that the monkeys benefited from the contact. The experiment confirmed how important it is that adults cradle infants lovingly.

Finally, the Harlows discovered that infant monkeys could recover from as much as three months of isolation. But by about six months, isolation caused irreversible emotional and behavioural damage.

Isolated children. The rest of Anna's story squares with the Harlows' findings. After her discovery, Anna received extensive social contact and soon showed improvement. When Kingsley Davis (1940) revisited her after ten days, he found her more alert and even smiling with obvious pleasure. Over the next year, Anna made slow but steady progress, showing more interest in other people and gradually learning to walk. After a year and a half, she could feed herself and play with toys.

As the Harlows might have predicted, however, Anna's five years of social isolation had caused permanent damage. At age eight, her mental development was still less than that of a two-year-old. Not until she was almost ten did she begin to use words. Because Anna's mother was mentally challenged, perhaps Anna was similarly so. The riddle was never solved, however, because Anna died at age ten of a blood disorder, possibly related to the years of abuse she suffered (Davis, 1940, 1947).

A more recent case of childhood isolation involves a California girl abused by her parents (Curtiss, 1977; Rymer, 1994). From the time she was two, Genie was tied to a potty chair in a dark garage. In 1970, when she was rescued at age 13, Genie weighed only 59 pounds and had the mental development of a one-year-old. With intensive treatment, she became physically healthy, but her language ability remains that of a young child. Today Genie lives in a home for developmentally disabled adults.

All evidence points to the crucial role of social experience in forming personality. Human beings can sometimes recover from abuse and isolation. Although it is unclear

 Learn more about the life of Genie at http://www.pbs.org/wgbh/nova/transcripts/2112gchild.html.

exactly when, there is a point at which isolation in infancy causes permanent developmental damage.

Understanding Socialization

Socialization is a complex, lifelong process. The following sections highlight the work of five researchers who made lasting contributions to our understanding of human development.

SIGMUND FREUD'S ELEMENTS OF PERSONALITY

Sigmund Freud (1856–1939) lived in Vienna at a time when most Europeans considered human behaviour biologically fixed. Trained as a physician, Freud soon turned to the analysis of personality and eventually developed the celebrated theory of psychoanalysis.

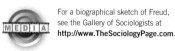 For a biographical sketch of Freud, see the Gallery of Sociologists at http://www.TheSociologyPage.com.

Basic needs. Freud claimed that biology plays a major part in human development, although not in terms of specific instincts as in other species. He theorized that humans have two basic needs or drives. First is a need for bonding, which he called the life instinct, or *eros* (from the Greek god of love). Second, we share an aggressive drive he called the death instinct, or *thanatos* (derived from the Greek word for "death"). According to Freud, these opposing forces, operating at an unconscious level, generate deep inner tension.

Freud's personality model. Freud combined basic drives and the influence of society into a model of personality with three parts: id, ego, and superego. The **id** (Latin for "it") is *the human being's basic drives*, which are unconscious and demand immediate satisfaction. Rooted in biology, the id is present at birth, making a newborn a bundle of demands for attention, touching, and food. But society opposes the self-centred id, which is why one of the first words a child usually learns is "no."

To avoid frustration, a child must learn to approach the world realistically. This is done through the **ego** (Latin for "I"), which is *a person's conscious efforts to balance innate pleasure-seeking drives with the demands of society*. The ego arises as we gain awareness of our distinct existence and face the fact that we cannot have everything we want.

In the human personality, **superego** (Latin for "above or beyond the ego") is *the cultural values and norms internalized by an individual*. The superego operates as our conscience, telling us *why* we cannot have everything we want. The superego begins to form as a child becomes aware of parental demands and matures as the child comes to understand that everyone's behaviour should take account of cultural norms.

To the id-centred child, the world is a bewildering array of physical sensations that bring either pleasure or pain. As the superego develops, however, the child learns the moral concepts of right and wrong. In other words, initially children can feel good only in a physical way, but after three or four years of age, they feel good or bad as they judge their behaviour against cultural norms.

The id and the superego remain in conflict, but in a well-adjusted person, the ego manages these opposing forces. If conflicts are not resolved during childhood, they may surface as personality disorders later on.

Culture, in the form of superego, represses selfish demands, forcing people to look beyond their own desires. Often the competing demands of self and society result in a compromise Freud called *sublimation,* which changes selfish drives into socially acceptable behaviour. For example, marriage makes the satisfaction of sexual urges socially acceptable, and competitive sports are an outlet for aggression.

Critical review. In Freud's time, few people were ready to accept sex as a basic drive. More recent critics charge that Freud's work presents humans in male terms and devalues women (Donovan & Littenberg, 1982), while other critics point to his dismissal of the reality of incest (Russell, 1986). But Freud influenced everyone who later studied human personality. Of special importance to sociology are his ideas that we internalize social norms and that childhood experiences have a lasting impact on our personalities.

JEAN PIAGET'S THEORY OF COGNITIVE DEVELOPMENT

The Swiss psychologist Jean Piaget (1896–1980) studied human *cognition:* how people think and understand. As

 To learn more about Piaget and his work, visit **http://www.piaget.org.**

Piaget watched his own three children grow, he wondered not only *what* they knew but *how* they made sense of the world; he went on to identify four stages of cognitive development.

The sensorimotor stage. Stage one is the **sensorimotor stage**, *the level of human development at which individuals experience the world only through their senses.* For about the first two years of life, infants know the world only by touching, tasting, smelling, looking, and listening. "Knowing" to young children amounts to sensory experience.

The preoperational stage. About age two, children enter the **preoperational stage**, *the level of human development at which individuals first use language and other symbols.* Now children begin to think about the world using their imagination. But "pre-op" children attach meanings only to specific experiences and objects. They can identify a special toy, for example, but they cannot describe what kinds of toys they like.

Lacking abstract concepts, a child cannot judge size, weight, or volume. In one of his best-known experiments, Piaget placed two identical glasses containing equal amounts of water on a table. He asked several five- and six-year-olds whether the amounts in both were the same. The children nodded that they were. The children then watched Piaget take one of the glasses and pour its contents into a taller, narrower glass, raising the level of the water. He asked again whether both glasses held the same amount. The typical five- or six-year-old now insisted that the taller glass held more water. By about age seven, children are able to

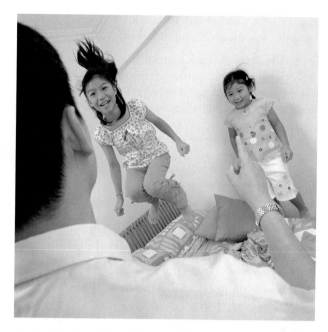

Why is it that one of the first words children come to understand is "no"? Sigmund Freud's model of personality suggests that socialization is the process of internalizing cultural values and norms, by which society controls our innate, selfish desires.

think more abstractly and realize that the amount of water stays the same.

The concrete operational stage. Next comes the **concrete operational stage**, *the level of human development at which individuals first see causal connections in their surroundings.* Between the ages of seven and eleven, children focus on how and why things happen. In addition, they attach more than one symbol to an event or object. For example, if you say to a child of five, "Today is Wednesday," she might respond, "No, it's my birthday," indicating that she can use just one symbol at a time. But an older child at the concrete operational stage would be able to respond, "Yes, and it's also my birthday."

The formal operational stage. The last step in Piaget's model is the **formal operational stage**, *the level of human development at which individuals think abstractly and critically.* At about age twelve, young people begin to reason abstractly rather than think only of concrete situations.

For example, if you ask a child of seven, "What would you like to be when you grow up?" you will get a concrete response such as "a teacher." But most teenagers can consider the question more abstractly and might respond, "I would like a job that helps others." As they gain the capacity for abstract thought, young people also learn to understand metaphors. Hearing the phrase "a penny for your thoughts" might lead a child to ask for a coin, but a teenager will recognize a gentle invitation to intimacy.

Critical review. Whereas Freud saw human beings passively torn by opposing forces of biology and culture, Piaget saw the mind as active and creative. In his view, the ability to engage the world unfolded in stages and was the result of both biological maturation and social experience.

But do people in all societies pass through all four of Piaget's stages? In fact, living in a traditional society that changes slowly probably limits the capacity for abstract, critical thought. Even in North American society perhaps 30 percent of people never reach the formal operational stage (Kohlberg & Gilligan, 1971).

LAWRENCE KOHLBERG'S THEORY OF MORAL DEVELOPMENT

Lawrence Kohlberg (1981) built on Piaget's work to study moral reasoning, that is, how people come to judge situations as right or wrong. Here, again, development of this skill occurs in stages.

Young children who experience the world in terms of pain and pleasure (Piaget's sensorimotor stage) are at the *preconventional* level of moral development. At first, "rightness" amounts to "what feels good to me."

The *conventional* level, Kohlberg's second stage, appears by the teens (corresponding to Piaget's final, formal operational stage). At this point, young people lose some of their selfishness as they learn to define right and wrong in terms of what pleases parents and conforms to cultural norms.

In the final stage of moral development, the *postconventional* level, people move beyond their society's norms to consider abstract ethical principles. As they think about ideas such as liberty, freedom, or justice, they may argue that what is lawful still may not be right.

Critical review. Like the work of Piaget, Kohlberg's model explains moral development in terms of distinct stages. But whether this model applies to people in all societies remains unclear. Furthermore, many people in Canada apparently never reach the postconventional level of moral reasoning, although exactly why is still an open question.

Another problem with Kohlberg's research is that all his subjects were boys. He committed a common research error, described in Chapter 1 ("Sociology: Perspective, Theory, and Method"), by generalizing the results of male subjects to all people. This problem led a colleague, Carol Gilligan, to investigate how gender affects moral reasoning.

CAROL GILLIGAN'S THEORY OF GENDER AND MORAL DEVELOPMENT

Carol Gilligan (1982) set out to compare the moral development of girls and boys and concluded that the two genders use different standards of rightness. Males, she claims, have a *justice perspective*, relying on formal rules to define right and wrong. Females, by contrast, have a *care and responsibility perspective*, judging a situation with an eye toward personal relationships and loyalties. For example, as boys see it, stealing is wrong because it breaks the law. However, girls are more likely to wonder why someone would steal and to be sympathetic toward someone who steals, say, to feed a hungry child.

Kohlberg treats rule-based male reasoning as morally superior to the person-based female perspective. But Gilligan notes that impersonal rules have long governed men's lives in the workplace, whereas personal relationships are more relevant to women's lives as mothers and caregivers. Why, then, Gilligan asks, should we set up male patterns as the standard by which we judge everyone?

Critical review. Gilligan's work sharpens our understanding of both human development and gender issues in research. Yet the question remains: Does nature or nurture account for the differences between females and males? In Gilligan's view, cultural conditioning is at work. Therefore, we might predict that as more women organize their lives around the workplace, the moral reasoning of women and men will become more similar. Recent cross cultural research on women's caring work also challenges Gilligan's psychological approach to gender socialization. There appears to be significant variation in the cultural shaping of women's caring work when viewed over time and across different countries (Kahne & Giele, 1992; Leira, 1992; Baker, 1995; Benoit & Heitlinger, 1998).

GEORGE HERBERT MEAD'S THEORY OF THE SOCIAL SELF

George Herbert Mead (1863–1931) developed a theory of *social behaviourism* to explain how social experience

 Mead is featured in the Gallery of Sociologists at **www.TheSociologyPage.com**.

develops an individual's personality (1962, orig. 1934).

The self. Mead's central concept is the **self**, *the part of an individual's personality composed of self-awareness and self-image.* Mead's genius lay in seeing the self as the product of social experience.

First, said Mead, *the self develops only with social experience.* The self is not part of the body and does not exist at birth. Mead rejected the idea that personality is guided by biological drives (as Freud asserted) or even biological maturation (as Piaget claimed). For Mead, self develops only as the individual interacts with others. Without interaction— as we know from isolated children—the body grows, but no self emerges.

Second, Mead explained, *social experience is the exchange of symbols.* Only people use words, a wave of the hand, or a smile to create meaning. We can train a dog using reward and punishment, but the dog attaches no meaning to its actions. By contrast, human beings find meaning in action by imagining people's underlying intentions. In short, a dog responds to *what you do,* but a human responds to *what you have in mind* as you do it. Thus you can train a dog to go to the hallway and bring back an umbrella. But without understanding intention, if the dog cannot find the umbrella, it is incapable of the *human* response: to look for a raincoat instead.

Third, Mead continues, *to understand intention, you must imagine a situation from the other's point of view.* Using symbols, we imagine ourselves in another person's shoes and see ourselves as that person does. This capacity lets us anticipate how others will respond to us even before we act. A simple toss of a ball, for example, requires stepping outside yourself to imagine how the other person will catch your throw. All symbolic interaction, then, involves seeing ourselves as others see us, a process Mead called *taking the role of the other.*

The looking-glass self. In effect, others are a mirror (which people used to call a looking glass) in which we see ourselves. What we think of ourselves, then, depends on how we think others view us. In other words, if we think others see us as clever, we will think of ourselves in the same way. But if we think others see us as clumsy, then that is how we will see ourselves. Charles Horton Cooley (1864–1929) used the phrase **looking-glass self** to mean *a self-image based on how we think others see us.*

The I and the me. Mead's fourth point is that *by taking the role of another, we become self-aware.* The self, then, has two parts. As subject, the self is active and spontaneous. Mead called the subjective side of the self the *I* (the subjective form of the personal pronoun). But the self is also an object, as we imagine ourselves as others see us. Mead called the objective side of the self the *me* (the objective form of the personal pronoun). All social experience has both components: We initiate action (the I-phase of the self), and we continue the action based on how others respond to us (the me-phase of the self).

Stages of development. The key to developing the self, then, is learning to take the role of the other. Infants, with their limited social experience, cannot do this and respond to others only through *imitation.* That is, they mimic behaviour without understanding underlying intention, and thus have no self.

As children learn to use language and other symbols, the self emerges in the form of *play.* Play involves assuming roles modelled on **significant others,** *people—such as par-*

George Herbert Mead wrote: "No hard-and-fast line can be drawn between our own selves and the selves of others." The painting *Manyness* by Rimma Gerlovina and Valeriy Gerlovin conveys this important truth. Although we tend to think of ourselves as unique individuals, each person's characteristics develop in an ongoing process of interaction with others.

Rimma Gerlovina and Valeriy Gerlovin, *Manyness,* 1990. © the artists, New City, N.Y.

ents—who have special importance for socialization. Playing "mommy" or "daddy" (often putting themselves, literally, in the shoes of a parent) begins to teach children to imagine the world from a parent's point of view.

Gradually, children learn to take the roles of several others at once. This skill lets them move from simple play (say, playing catch) involving one other person to complex games (such as baseball) involving many others. By about age seven, most children have the social experience needed to engage in team sports.

Figure 3–1 charts the progression from imitation to play to games. But a final stage in the development of self remains. Games involve dealing with a limited number of other people in one specific situation, but social life demands that we see ourselves in terms of cultural norms as anyone else might. Mead used the term **generalized other** to refer to *widespread cultural norms and values we use as a reference in evaluating ourselves.*

As life goes on, the self continues to change along with our social experiences. But no matter how much events change us, we remain creative beings. Thus, Mead concluded, we play a key role in our own socialization.

| The self is able simultaneously to take the role of: | *no one* (no ability to take the role of the other) | *one* other in *one* situation | *many* others in *one* situation | *many* others in *many* situations |

| when: | engaging in imitation | engaging in play | engaging in games | recognizing the generalized other |

FIGURE 3–1 Building on Social Experience

George Herbert Mead described the development of the self as a process of gaining social experience. That is, the self develops as we expand our capacity to take the role of the other.

Critical review. Mead's work explores the character of social experience itself. In the symbolic interaction of human beings, Mead found the root of both self and society.

Some critics say Mead's view is completely social, allowing no biological element at all. In this, he stands apart from Freud (who identified general human drives) and Piaget (whose stages of development are tied to biological maturation).

Be careful not to confuse Mead's concepts of the *I* and the *me* with Freud's terms *id* and *superego*. Freud rooted the id in the biological organism, whereas Mead rejected any biological element of self (although he never clearly spelled out the origin of the I). Moreover, whereas the superego and id are locked in continual combat, the I and the me work cooperatively together (Meltzer, 1978). We now take a closer look at these important agents of socialization.

Agents of Socialization

Every social experience we have affects us in some way, large or small. However, several familiar settings have special importance to the socialization process.

THE FAMILY

The family has the greatest impact on socialization. The responsibility for the care of infants, who are totally dependent on others, typically falls on parents and other family members. In addition, at least until children begin school, the family has the job of teaching children skills, values, and beliefs. Overall, research suggests, nothing is more likely to produce a happy, well-adjusted child than a loving family (Gibbs, 2001b).

Family learning is not all intentional. Children also learn from the kind of environment adults create. Whether children learn to see themselves as strong or weak, smart or stupid, loved or simply tolerated, or whether they see the world as trustworthy or dangerous (Erikson, 1963; orig. 1950)

depends largely on their surroundings. Children who find themselves unloved or, worse, abused by one or the other of their parents, or abandoned at an early age, may lack the basic tools needed to form and sustain social relationships. Research suggests this is the case for many street-involved youth (Ensign & Bell, 2004; Benoit, Jansson, & Murray, forthcoming).

Another crucial family function is conferring a social position on children. That is, parents not only bring children into the physical world, but also place them in society in terms of class, religious and political beliefs, race, and ethnicity. In time, these elements of social identity become part of the child's self-concept. Of course, some aspects of social position may change later on but, as discussed throughout this book, social standing at birth affects us throughout our lives. Research shows that the class position of parents influences how they raise their children (Ellison, Bartowski, & Segal, 1996) and that Canadian children from the lowest social class are twice as likely to have conduct disorders as children from the highest social class, although the reason for this is not well understood (Stevenson, 1999).

Why is class position important? Of course, affluent parents typically spend far more materially on their children than do parents of modest means. Moreover, Melvin Kohn (1977) found that middle class parents tolerate a wide range of behaviour and show greater concern for the intentions and motivation that underlie their children's actions. Working class parents, by contrast, stress behavioural conformity. But there is no conclusive evidence that poverty or affluence is directly related to the quality of parenting that children receive. Research shows that neither rich nor poor Canadians have a monopoly on child-rearing skills. Rather, children with behaviour problems and low academic achievement come from different economic backgrounds, as do children who perform well socially and academically (Bertrand, McCain, Mustard, & Willms, 1999).

Regardless of class background, Bernd Baldus and Verna Tribe (1992) argue that most children by Grade 6 (average age 11 years) use social inequality as a criterion to

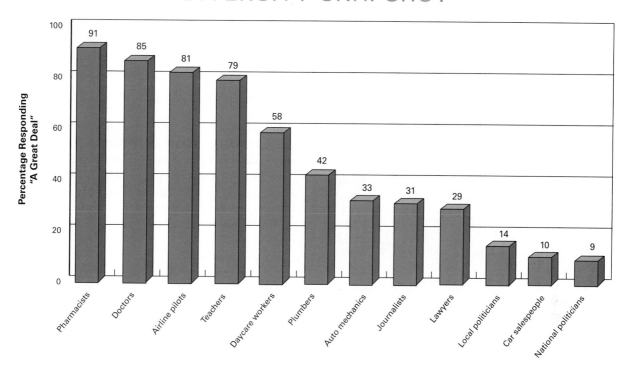

FIGURE 3–2 Whom Do You Trust? Canada, 2002

Source: Excerpted from a survey by Ipsos–Reid, Toronto. www.ipsos-reid.com

order the world around them. Further, Grade 6 students have by this age learned to acquire cognitive and affective predispositions causing them to think that less economically advantaged persons are likely to be unsuccessful in life or engage in morally questionable behaviour. Trustworthiness, on the other hand, is only partially related to class position, as Figure 3–2 illustrates.

Complicating matters still further, gender blends with class in the socialization process. Arlie Hochschild (1983:165) points out that young middle class girls are taught to "manage their feelings." Girls are taught that they will depend on men for money in adult life. Therefore, displaying more emotion or feeling is a female way of repaying their debt, argues Hochschild, especially through emotional work "that affirms, enhances, and celebrates the well-being and status of others."

THE SCHOOL

Schooling enlarges children's social world to include people with different backgrounds. In the process, they learn the importance that society attaches to ethnicity, race, and gender. Studies document that at play, children tend to cluster in groups made up of one ethnicity, race, and gender. In class, boys are more aggressive, engage in more physical activities, and spend more time outdoors, while girls are better behaved and often volunteer to help teachers with various housekeeping chores (Lever, 1978; Best, 1983; Thorne, 1993; Jordan & Cowan, 1995).

Schooling teaches children a wide range of knowledge and skills. But schools informally convey other value lessons, known as the *hidden curriculum*. Activities such as spelling bees and sports, for example, encourage the values of competition and success. Children also receive countless subtle lessons that their own society's way of life is morally good.

School is also most children's first experience with bureaucracy. The school day is based on impersonal rules and a strict time schedule. Not surprisingly, these are also the traits of the large organizations that will employ them later in life.

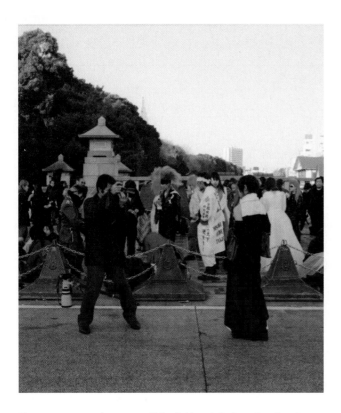

These young people come to Tokyo's Yoyogi Park on Sundays to dress up and have their picture taken.

afternoons during the week? We learn later that they put on their elaborate makeup and change into their costume in the bathroom at the Harajuku subway station around the corner. By 6:00 they have all changed back into their regular clothes and taken the subway home again. Are they rebelling or just having fun with their friends? Perhaps it is both.

By the time they enter school, children have also discovered the **peer group**, *a social group whose members have interests, social position, and age in common.* Unlike the family and the school, the peer group allows children to escape the direct supervision of adults. Among their peers, children learn how to form relationships on their own. Peer groups also offer the chance to indulge in interests that adults may not share (such as clothes and popular music) or permit (such as drugs and sex).

It is not surprising, then, that parents express concern about who their children's friends are. In a rapidly changing society, peer groups have great influence, and the attitudes of young and old may be different enough to form a "generation gap." The importance of peer groups typically peaks during adolescence, when young people begin to break away from their families and think of themselves as adults. The structure of the peer group has been shown as an important factor in trying to understand peer abuse—the abuse of children by children (Ambert, 1995). Relentless teasing by peers—girls as well as boys—can result in brutal beatings and even murder (such as in the 1997 case of 14-year-old Reena Virk of Victoria, BC), or in the suicide of the affected youth who is unable to withstand the taunting and other forms of abuse (Alphonso, 2000). The problem is that there is no single cause of bullying at our nation's schools. In addition, youth tend to condone bullying and even to join in, rather than to speak out against it (Artz, 1998).

Even during adolescence, however, parental influence on children remains strong. Peers may guide short-term choices in dress and music, but parents shape long-term goals such as pursuing post-secondary education (Davies & Kandel, 1981).

Finally, any neighbourhood or school is a social mosaic of many peer groups. As Chapter 5 ("Groups and Organizations") explains, individuals tend to view their own group in positive terms and put down other groups. Moreover, people are also influenced by peer groups they would like to join, a process sociologists call **anticipatory socialization**, *learning that helps a person achieve a desired position.* In school, for example, young people may copy the styles and slang of a group they hope will accept them. Later in life, a young lawyer may conform to the attitudes and behaviour of the firm's partners in order to win approval.

Gender differences continue through post-secondary education. While gender decisions are changing, women still tend to major in the arts, humanities, or social sciences, while men gravitate toward economics, engineering and computer science, or the natural sciences. Moreover, even for women who enter the traditionally male-dominated professions, such as medicine and law, gender stratification persists in regard to both choice of specialty and income. In brief, women tend to cluster in specialties that are lower paying and more people-oriented (for example, pediatrics or family law), while male colleagues tend to be located in specialties above the "glass ceiling," such as surgery or corporate law (Riska & Wegar, 1993; Reskin & Padavic, 1994; Hagan & Kay, 1995).

THE PEER GROUP

December 16, Yoyogi Park, Tokyo. The young people who come here on Sundays to get dressed up and have their picture taken can't be the same young people that we see in the obligatory school uniforms in the mornings and

THE MASS MEDIA

The **mass media** are *the means for delivering impersonal communications to a vast audience.* The term "media" comes from the Latin word for "middle" or "between," suggesting that media connect people. Mass media resulted as communication technology (first newspapers, then radio and television) spread information on a mass scale.

In Canada, the mass media enormously affect our attitudes and behaviour, making the media central to socialization. Television, which was introduced in 1939, has rapidly become the dominant medium in North America in particular, although its impact can be felt increasingly around the globe. Overall, the United States boasts a higher rate of television ownership than any other industrial country, but Canada is not far behind. Put another way, by 2001, a minority (40 percent) of Canadian households owned only one colour television; the majority had two or more sets and less than 1 percent did not have a set (Statistics Canada, 2003u).

Just how "glued to the television" are we? The latest statistics show that Canadian viewers watched television an average of 21.2 hours each week in the fall of 2001. Virtually everyone in Canada watches television, but not equally: Figure 3–3 identifies the amount of television viewing by gender in different regions of Canada. Women, French-speaking Quebecers, and residents of the Atlantic provinces watched more television than other Canadians. Years before children learn to read, television watching is a regular routine. Children aged two to eleven watch more than 14 hours each week. This is so despite research that suggests television makes children more passive and less likely to use their imagination (Singer & Singer, 1983; APA, 1993; Fellman, 1995). The number of hours of viewing tends to increase with age, exceeding 30 hours per week for those aged 60 and over (Statistics Canada, 2002h).

The comedian Fred Allen once quipped that we call television a "medium" because it is rarely well done. For a variety of reasons, television (like other media) provokes plenty of criticism. Some liberal critics argue that television shows mirror our society's patterns of social inequality and rarely challenge the status quo. Most programs involve men in positions of power over women. Moreover, although racial and ethnic minorities watch about 40 percent more television than white people, they are largely absent from programming (Gans, 1980; Cantor & Pingree, 1983; Ang, 1985; Parenti, 1986; Brown, 1990). The Diversity: Race, Class, & Gender box on page 74 offers an overview of the image of Canadian minorities in the media.

The number of people from minority groups who appear in the mass media has increased mainly because advertisers recognize the marketing advantages of appealing

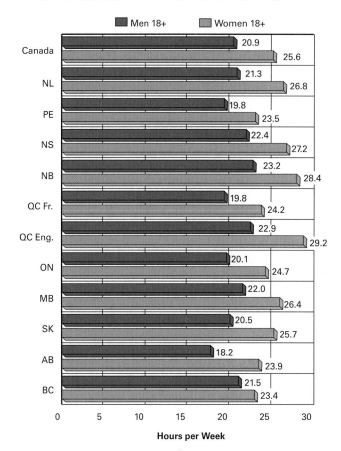

DIVERSITY SNAPSHOT

FIGURE 3–3 Television Viewing by Gender and Province

Source: Statistics Canada: Television Viewing Data Bank 2004; *Television Viewing: Television viewing: data tables*, March 2006, catalogue no 87F0006XIE.

to these large segments of North American society (Wilson & Gutiérrez, 1985). In Canada, the wide popularity of such shows as *This Hour Has 22 Minutes* is a case in point, placing at centre stage representatives from Canada's poorest province to poke fun at our national quirks. On the other side of the debate, conservative critics argue that the television and film industries constitute a liberal "cultural elite," often portraying marginalized groups as "successful" only when they adopt a middle class lifestyle and values.

A final issue concerns violence and the mass media. In 1996, the American Medical Association declared that violence in the mass media, especially television and films, has reached such a level that it poses a health hazard. More

DIVERSITY: RACE, CLASS, & GENDER

Minority Identity in Movies and Television

Visible minorities and Aboriginals are included more and more frequently in our popular media, including movies and television. But is this a reflection of a real change in societal understanding? Have the media given us genuine insight into what it is like to be a first-generation immigrant from China or India? Have minority actors really succeeded in changing the dominant group's image of race? And have minority producers succeeded in breaking through the formidable barriers of Eurocentrism to explore ethnic identities from a minority perspective?

Media observers note that we have indeed moved away from the savage and marginalized characters of yesterday's films to multifaceted representations in such popular Canadian TV shows as *The Beachcombers, North of 60,* and more recently, *Moccasin Flats.* But is this a sign of more to come, or are the recent examples merely exceptions that detract from the overall criticism articulated by Thomas Builds-the-Fire in the movie *Smoke Signals*: "The only thing more pathetic than an Indian on TV is an Indian watching an Indian on TV"?

Allan Smith (1996) argues that on the face of it, we are witnessing a revolutionary change in how most Canadians view minorities, particularly

Aboriginals, in the media. A more open and multidimensional view of an increasingly assertive minority is emerging. Nevertheless, Smith maintains that "while European-descended groups may not be as resistant to seeing what is around them as they once were, they still remain some distance from a fully engaged [quoting Charles Taylor, 1992] 'politics of recognition.'"

After analyzing the evolving imaging of Aboriginals and minorities in Canadian and U.S. film and television, Smith notes that while their portrayal is not as simplistic as it has been in the past, it is nevertheless not clear that there have been fundamental changes. For one thing, minorities still have only limited access to the resources that media production requires, and distributors are still reluctant to carry authentic minority

products to the larger market.

What, then, does the future hold? Not much change for the moment, says Smith, especially in a country such as Canada, where our need to define ourselves as one nation remains paramount (at least to the federal politicians), and where negotiation and adjustment are the main strategies for moving forward.

Yet perhaps not everyone will agree. Lorne Cardinal, who played Big Bear's less-than-admirable son in the CBC miniseries *Big Bear*, which aired in January 1999, maintains that the series was different from the typical cowboys-and-Indians dramas about "taming the West" and "civilizing the Natives." In most of these movies, according to Cardinal, the typical signal for him to appear on the scene is, "Okay, we're ready. Send out the Indians." Cardinal says that the opposite was the case with *Big Bear*: "On this set . . . they say, 'Send out the white guys'" (Dafoe, 1998:C1). At the same time, shows like *Moccasin Flats* continue to be popular among Aboriginals, which is perhaps the surest gauge as to whether the media has succeeded in capturing minority points of view.

WHAT DO YOU THINK?

1. Have the mass media improved their portrayal of minorities in Canada?

recently, a study found a link between aggressive behaviour and the amount of time elementary school children spend watching television and using video games (Robinson et al., 2001). The public seems concerned about this issue: three-fourths of U.S. adults have either walked out of a movie or turned off television because of too much violence. Moreover, almost two-thirds of television programs contain violence, and in most scenes violent characters show no remorse and are not punished (Wilson, 1998).

Like the U.S. television industry, the Canadian industry has moved to control television viewing of violent programming, especially by children. Both countries have adopted a rating system for programs. The Canadian Association of Broadcasters has a "violence code," which it uses to evaluate particular programs for violence content. The voluntary code bans the broadcast of shows containing gratuitous violence of any type, or that condone, encourage, or glamourize violence. As far as children are concerned, the code establishes a cut-off time of 9:00 P.M., prior to which violent programming aimed at adult viewers may not be broadcast.

But larger questions remain: Does viewing violent programming hurt people as much as critics say it does? More important, why do the mass media contain so much violence and sex in the first place?

In sum, television and other mass media have enriched our lives with entertaining and educational programming. The media also increase our exposure to other cultures and provoke discussion of current issues. At the same time, the power of the media—especially television—to shape how we think remains highly controversial.

Other spheres of life beyond family, school, peer group, and the media also play a part in social learning. For many people in Canada, these include religious organizations, the workplace, and social clubs. In the end, socialization is not a simple learning process but a complex balancing act as we absorb different information from different sources. In the process of sorting and weighing all the information we encounter, we form our own distinctive personalities and worldviews.

Socialization and the Life Course

Although childhood has special importance to socialization, this process continues throughout our lives. An overview of the life course reveals that our society organizes human experience according to age: childhood, adolescence, adulthood, and old age.

CHILDHOOD

A few years ago, the Nike corporation—a maker of popular athletic shoes—came under fire. The company's shoes are made in Taiwan and Indonesia, in many cases by young children who work in factories rather than going to school. In fact, some 250 million of the world's children work, half of them full-time, earning about 50 cents an hour (Human Rights Watch, 2004). Global Map 3–1 on page 76 shows that child labour is most common in the nations of Africa and Asia.

A website that reports on the state of children working as soldiers around the world is http://www.hrw.org/campaigns/crp/index.htm.

Criticism of Nike springs from the fact that most North Americans think of *childhood*—roughly the first 12 years of life—as a carefree time of learning and play. Yet childhood is a varying concept. Canadian sociologist Anthony Synnott shows how culture determines the image of children—varying from "little devils" or "little angels" to "little workers" or "a sacred trust" (Synnott, 1983). In fact, explains historian Philippe Ariès

In recent decades, some people have become concerned that Canadian society is shortening childhood, pushing children to grow up faster and faster. Do films such as *Thirteen,* which show young girls dressing and behaving as if they were much older, encourage a "hurried childhood"? Do you see this as a problem or not?

(1965), the whole idea of "childhood" is fairly new. In the Middle Ages, children of four or five were treated like adults and expected to take care of themselves. Adolescence as we know it did not exist as a stage in the life course. This meant that by age six or seven, poor children worked long and hard, just as adults did.

A look around the world today also shows that the concept of childhood is grounded not in biology but in culture (LaRossa & Reitzes, 2001). In high-income countries such as our own, we have extended childhood to allow time for young people to learn the skills they will need in a high-technology workplace, but this is by no means the norm worldwide.

ADOLESCENCE

At the same time as industrialization created childhood as a distinct stage of life, adolescence emerged as a buffer between childhood and adulthood. We generally link *adolescence,* or the teenage years, with emotional and social turmoil as young people develop their own identities. Again,

GLOBAL MAP 3-1 Child Labour in Global Perspective

Industrialization extends childhood and discourages children from work and other activities considered suitable only for adults. Thus, child labour is uncommon in Canada and other high-income countries. In less economically developed nations of the world, however, children are a vital economic asset, and they typically begin working as soon as they are able.

Source: World Bank (2004) and author estimates; map projection from *Peters Atlas of the World* (1990).

we are tempted to attribute teenage turbulence to the biological changes of puberty. But this turmoil more correctly reflects cultural inconsistency. For example, the mass media glorify sex and schools hand out condoms, even as parents urge restraint. Consider, too, that an 18-year-old may face the adult duty of going to war but lacks the adult right to drink alcohol. In short, adolescence is a time of social contradictions, when people are no longer children but not yet adults.

As is true of all stages of life, adolescence varies according to social background. Young people from working class

CRITICAL THINKING

Are We Grown Up Yet? Defining Adulthood

Are you an adult or still an adolescent? In North America, when can young people expect to be treated by others as grown up? According to U.S. sociologist Tom Smith (2003), there is no one factor that announces the onset of "adulthood." On the contrary, the results of the survey—using a representative sample of 1398 people over the age of 18—suggest that becoming an adult is a gradual process that involves a number of transitions.

According to the survey, the single most important transition in claiming adult standing is the completion of schooling. But other transitions are also important: Smith's respondents linked adult standing to taking on a full-time job, gaining the ability to support a fam-

ily financially, no longer living with parents, and finally, settling down with a partner and becoming a parent. In other words, almost everyone surveyed regarded a person who has done *all* these things as an adult.

At what age are these transitions likely to be completed? On average, according to the respondents in this study, by age 26. But this number masks an important difference based on social class. People who do not go on to higher education (more common among people growing up in lower-income families) typically finish school by about age 20, and a full-time job, independent living, marriage, and parenthood may follow in a year or two. Those from more privileged backgrounds are likely to

attend college or university and may even go on to graduate or professional school, delaying the process of becoming an adult for as long as 10 years, past the age of 30.

WHAT DO YOU THINK?

1. Do you consider yourself an adult? At what age did your adulthood begin?
2. Which of the transitions noted here do you consider the most important in becoming an adult? Why?
3. How does this research show that "adulthood" is a socially defined concept rather than a biological stage of life?

Source: Smith (2003).

families commonly work part-time while in high school and many, especially males, drop out altogether and move directly to the adult world of work and parenthood (Tanner, Krahn, & Hartnagel, 1995). Those from wealthier families, however, have privileged access to an "endless adolescence." They typically attend university, and perhaps even graduate school, until they are well into the late twenties or even thirties (Skolnick, 1996).

ADULTHOOD

If stages of the life course were based on biological changes, there would be widespread agreement about the timing of *adulthood*. However, as the Critical Thinking box explains, the definition of "growing up" turns out to be quite complex.

Regardless of exactly when it begins, adulthood is the time of life when most accomplishments occur, such as pursuing a career and raising a family. Personalities are largely formed, although marked change in a person's environment—such as unemployment, divorce, or serious illness—may result in significant change to the self.

During early adulthood—until about age 40—young adults learn to manage day-to-day affairs for themselves, often juggling conflicting priorities: parents, partner, children, schooling, and work. Women especially try to "do it all," because our culture gives them major responsibility for child rearing and household chores even if they have demanding jobs outside the home. Women in Canada find themselves occupied by an unending series of "family shifts" (Eichler, 1997) that result in little leisure and in chronic sleep deprivation. It should be noted, however, that access to public services such as quality child care (available in France and Sweden, for example) has been shown to significantly reduce women's second shift of unpaid caring work in the home (Baker, 1995).

In middle adulthood—roughly between ages 40 and 60—people sense that their life circumstances are pretty well set. They also become more aware of the fragility of health; the young typically take good health for granted. Women who have devoted many years to raising a family can find middle adulthood emotionally trying. As children grow up, they need less attention, and male partners become absorbed in their careers, leaving some women

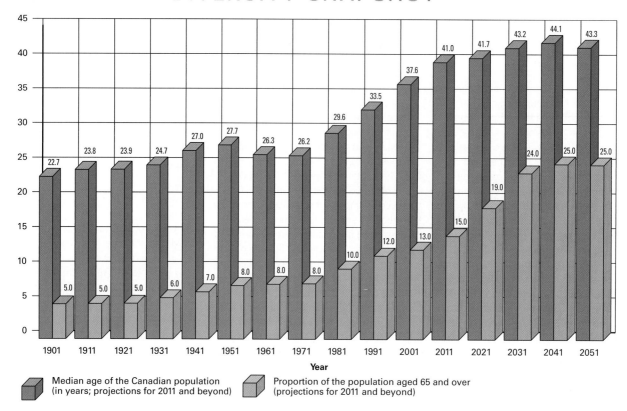

FIGURE 3–4 The Greying of the Canadian Population

Sources: George et al. (2001); Statistics Canada (1994a; 2002f).

with spaces in their lives that are difficult to fill. Many women who divorce during middle adulthood also face serious financial problems (Weitzman, 1985, 1996). For all these reasons, an increasing number of women in middle adulthood return to school and seek a new career.

For everyone, growing older means facing physical decline, a prospect our culture makes more painful for women. Because good looks are considered more important for women, the appearance of wrinkles and greying hair can be traumatic. Men have their own particular difficulties as they grow older. Some must admit that they are never going to reach their career goals. Others realize that the price of career success has been neglect of family or personal health.

OLD AGE

Old age—the later years of adulthood and the final stage of life itself—begins about the mid-60s. With people living longer, the elderly population in Canada is growing nearly as fast as

the population as a whole. As Figure 3–4 shows, about one in eight people is over age 65, and the elderly now outnumber teenagers. By 2031, the number of seniors will more than double to over 8 million, and almost 25 percent of the population will be over 65 (Statistics Canada, 2002f; George et al., 2001).

We can only begin to imagine the full consequences of the "greying of Canada." As more and more people retire from the labour force, the share of nonworking adults—already 10 times greater than in 1900—will go up, fuelling demand for health care and other social resources—although the impact may vary in different parts of Canada, as National Map 3–1 illustrates. Many middle-aged people (especially women) already think of themselves as a "sandwich generation," because they will spend as much time caring for dependent aging parents as they did for their dependent young children. But perhaps most important, elderly people will be more visible in everyday life. In the twenty-first century, the young and the old will interact a great deal.

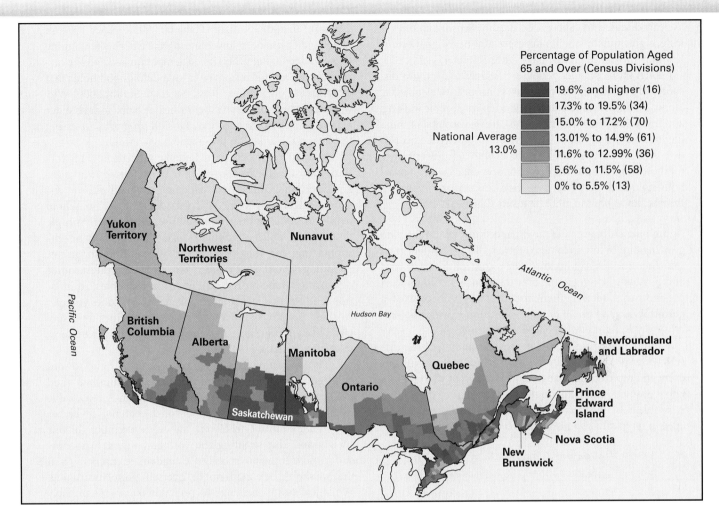

Percentage of Population Aged 65 and Over (Census Divisions)

■	19.6% and higher (16)
■	17.3% to 19.5% (34)
■	15.0% to 17.2% (70)
■	13.01% to 14.9% (61)
■	11.6% to 12.99% (36)
■	5.6% to 11.5% (58)
□	0% to 5.5% (13)

National Average 13.0%

SEEING OURSELVES

NATIONAL MAP 3-1 Aging Across Canada, 2001

The aging of the population is largely a southern phenomenon. Even though we associate Victoria, British Columbia, with the phrase "Newlyweds and Nearly Deads," the map shows that the concentration of those over age 65 is also high on the Prairies and north of Toronto. Which do you think primarily determines this pattern—social forces or individual choices?

Source: Calculated based on Statistics Canada (2003aa).

Aging In Manitoba is a 30-year research project. The website has research reports and links to aging resources:
http://www.aginginmanitoba.ca.

The aging of the Canadian population is one focus of **gerontology** (from the Greek word *geron,* meaning "old person"), *the study of aging and the elderly.* Gerontologists study both the physical and social dimensions of growing old.

For data and graphics on aging around the world, visit **www.un.org/esa/population/publications/worldageing19502050/**.

Aging and biology. For most of our population, grey hair, wrinkles, and declining energy begin in middle age. After about age 50, bones become more brittle, injuries take longer to heal, and the risks of chronic illnesses (such as arthritis and diabetes) and life-threatening conditions (such as heart disease and cancer) rise steadily. Sensory abilities—taste, sight, touch, smell, and especially hearing—become less sharp with age (Treas, 1995; Metz & Miner, 1998).

Even so, most older people are neither disabled nor discouraged by their physical condition (Chappell, MacDonald, & Stone, 2005). Only one in ten seniors reports trouble walking, and fewer than one in twenty needs care in a hospital or nursing home. No more than 1 percent of the elderly are bedridden. Overall, certainly, health declines with age. Nevertheless, for those over 65, only 5.4 percent of women living in a private household and 6.7 percent of male counterparts described their health as poor in 1997 (Statistics Canada, 2000m).

Aging and culture.   Culture shapes how we understand growing old. In low-income countries, old age confers great influence and respect because elders control the most land and possess wisdom gained over the course of a lifetime. A pre-industrial society, then, usually takes the form of a **gerontocracy**, *a form of social organization in which the elderly have the most wealth, power, and prestige.*

Industrialization lessens the social standing of the elderly. Older people typically live apart from their grown children, and rapid social change renders much of what seniors know obsolete, at least from the point of view of the young. A problem of technologically advanced societies, then, is **ageism**, *prejudice and discrimination against older people.*

> *November 1, approaching Kandy, Sri Lanka. Our little van struggles up the steep mountain incline. Breaks in the lush vegetation offer spectacular views that interrupt our conversation about growing old. "Then there are no old-age homes in your country?" I ask. "In Colombo and other cities, I am sure," our driver responds, "but not many. We are not like you Americans." "And how is that?" I ask, stiffening a bit. His eyes remain fixed on the road: "We would not leave our fathers and mothers to live alone."*

Not surprisingly, growing old in Canada is challenging. Early in life, advancing in years means taking on new roles and responsibilities. In old age, by contrast, aging means leaving behind roles that have provided social identity and prestige. Removed from familiar work routines, some people view retirement as restful recreation, but others lose their self-worth and suffer outright boredom.

Reaching old age also means living with less income. Financially, however, the Canadian elderly population as a whole is doing better than ever. The rate of poverty among the elderly, as measured by Statistics Canada's low-income cut-offs, has declined from about 21 percent in 1980, to

7 percent in 2001 (Statistics Canada, 2003v). Since 1994, in fact, poverty has been lower among the elderly than among those under 18. Put otherwise, a generation ago, old age carried the highest risk of poverty; today, childhood holds that unfortunate distinction (Ross, Scott, & Smith, 2000).Why the change? For one thing, better health helps today's older people earn more. In addition, pension programs are easing the financial burden on those who have retired.

Still, for most people in Canada, retirement leads to a significant decline in income. For many, home mortgages and children's educational expenses are paid off; yet the expenses from some medical and dental care, household help, and home utilities typically rise. Many elderly people do not have sufficient savings or pension benefits to be self-supporting; for this reason, various pension programs, including the Canada Pension Plan, are their greatest source of income. Many retirees live with fixed incomes, so inflation tends to affect them more severely than it does younger working people. Women and visible minorities are especially likely to find that growing old means growing poorer (Statistics Canada, 2000m).

The shift in poverty away from the elderly and toward children may continue, given the increasing number—and political clout—of those aged 65 and older. A reasonable question, in light of this windfall for the elderly, is whether we should continue to favour the oldest members of our society and risk slighting the youngest—those who now suffer most from poverty. But Canadian researchers warn that we should be careful not to "oversell" population aging. While a definite challenge to policy makers, it is unlikely that the greying of the Canadian population will destroy the fabric of Canadian society or lead to other apocalyptic scenarios (Gee & Gutman, 2000).

DEATH AND DYING

Throughout most of human history, low living standards and limited medical technology meant that death, caused most often by disease or accident, came at any stage of life. Today, however, 89 percent of women and 82 percent of men in Canada die after age 65 (Statistics Canada, 2002g).

After observing many dying people, the psychologist Elisabeth Kübler-Ross (1969) described death as an orderly transition involving five distinct stages. Typically, a person first reacts to the prospect of dying with *denial*. The second phase is *anger*, as the person facing death sees it as a gross injustice. Third, anger gives way to *negotiation*, as the person imagines it might be possible to avoid death by striking a bargain with God. The fourth stage, *resignation*, often is accompanied by psychological depression. Finally, a complete adjustment to death requires *acceptance*. At this point, no longer paralyzed by fear and anxiety, the person whose life is ending sets out to make the most of whatever time remains.

The reality of growing old is as much a matter of culture as it is of biology. In Canada, being elderly often means being inactive; yet, in many other countries of the world, elders often continue many familiar and productive routines.

As the share of women and men in old age steadily increases, we can expect our culture to become more comfortable with the idea of death. In recent years, for example, people in Canada and elsewhere have been discussing death more openly, and the trend is toward viewing dying as preferable to painful or prolonged suffering. More married couples are taking steps to prepare for death with legal and financial planning; this openness may ease somewhat the pain of the surviving spouse, a consideration for women who, more often than not, outlive their male partners.

THE LIFE COURSE: PATTERNS AND VARIATIONS

This brief examination of the life course points to two major conclusions. First, although each stage of life reflects the biological process of aging, the life course is largely a social construction. For this reason, people in various societies may experience a stage of life quite differently or, for that matter, not at all. Second, in any society, the stages of the life course present certain problems and transitions that involve learning something new and, in many cases, unlearning familiar routines.

Societies organize the life course according to age, but other forces such as class, race, ethnicity, and gender also shape people's lives. Thus, the general patterns described in this chapter apply somewhat differently to various categories of people. Finally, people's life experiences also vary depending on when, historically, they were born. A **cohort** is *a category of people with a common characteristic, usually*

their age. Because members of a particular age cohort generally are influenced by the same economic and cultural trends, they tend to have similar attitudes and values. Women and men born in the late 1940s and 1950s grew up during a period of economic expansion that gave them a sense of optimism. Today's post-secondary students, who have grown up in an age of economic uncertainty, are less confident about the future.

Resocialization: Total Institutions

A final type of socialization involves being confined, often against their will, in boot camps for young offenders, adult prisons, mental hospitals, and other total institutions, such as orphanages. This is the special world of the **total institution**, *a setting in which people are isolated from the rest of society and manipulated by an administrative staff.*

According to Erving Goffman (1961), total institutions have three distinctive characteristics. First, staff members supervise all aspects of daily life, including where residents (often called "inmates") eat, sleep, and work. Second, the environment of a total institution is highly standardized, with institutional food, uniforms, and one set of activities for everyone. Third, rules and schedules dictate when, where, and how inmates perform their daily routines.

The purpose of such rigid routines is **resocialization**, *radically changing an inmate's personality by carefully controlling the environment.* Prisons and mental hospitals

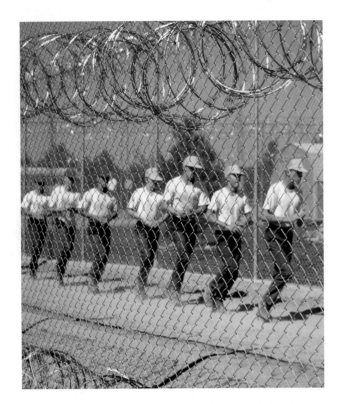

Prisons are one example of a total institution in which inmates dress alike and carry out daily routines under the direct supervision and control of the institutional staff. What do we expect prison to do to young people convicted of crimes? How well do you think prisons do what people expect them to?

physically isolate inmates behind fences, barred windows, and locked doors and control their access to the telephone, mail, and visitors. The institution is the inmate's entire world, making it easier for the staff to bring about lasting change—or at least immediate compliance—in the inmate.

Resocialization is a two-part process. First, the staff breaks down a new inmate's existing identity. For example, an inmate must surrender personal possessions, including clothing and grooming articles used to maintain a distinctive appearance. Instead, the staff provides standard-issue clothes so that everyone looks alike. The staff subjects new inmates to "mortifications of self," which can include searches, medical examinations, head shaving, fingerprinting, and assignment of a serial number. Once inside the walls, individuals also give up their privacy as guards routinely monitor their living quarters.

In the second part of the resocialization process, the staff tries to build a new self in the inmate through a system of rewards and punishments. Having a book to read, watching television, or accessing the Internet may seem like minor pleasures to the outsider, but in the rigid environment of the total institution, gaining these simple privileges can be a powerful motivation to conform. The length of incarceration typically depends on how well the inmate cooperates with the staff.

Total institutions affect people in different ways. Whereas some inmates are considered "rehabilitated" or "recovered," others may change little, and still others may become hostile and bitter. Over a long period of time, living in a rigidly controlled environment can leave some *institutionalized*, without the capacity for independent living.

But what about the rest of us? Does socialization crush our individuality or empower us? The Controversy & Debate box takes a closer look at this vital question.

CONTROVERSY & DEBATE
Are Canadians Free Within Society?

Throughout this chapter, we have stressed one key theme: society—through its agents (family, schools, peers, the mass media)—shapes how we think, feel, and act. If this is so, then in what sense are we free?

Sociologists speak with many voices when addressing this question. One response is that individuals are not free of society—in fact, as social creatures, we never could be. But if we are condemned to live in a society with power over us, it is important to do what we can to make our home as just as possible. That is, we should work to lessen class differences and other barriers to opportunity for visible minorities and women. Another approach is that we are free because society can never dictate our dreams. Our history as a country—right from early settlement to the present—is one story after another of individuals pursuing personal goals in spite of great challenges. This argument says that individual efforts rather than progressive government social policies result in the greatest freedom for citizens.

We find both attitudes in George Herbert Mead's analysis of socialization. Mead recognized that society makes demands on us, sometimes setting itself before us as a barrier. But he also reminded us that human beings are spontaneous and creative, capable of continually acting back—individually and collectively—on society. Thus Mead noted the power of society while still affirming the human capacity to evaluate, to criticize, and, ultimately, to choose and to change. A large number of children around the world are trapped in circumstances beyond their choosing, and often face lives of abuse and neglect. But some—though not all—manage to survive and sometimes flourish, emotionally, socially, and intellectually. In these more positive life histories, certain children with a deep inner drive and initiative also tend to be helped by significant others who are willing to lend economic and emotional support on a sustained basis. As Bonnie Leadbeater (forthcoming) notes about

inner-city female youth, some are able to resist dominant stereotypes of them as sexually promiscuous, impoverished, and uneducated, create new positive identities for themselves, and take control of their lives.

In the end, we are socialized into who we become as human beings and yet also able to change the world around us. As anthropologist Margaret Mead once mused, "Do not make the mistake of thinking that concerned people cannot change the world; it's the only thing that ever has."

CONTINUE THE DEBATE . . .

1. Do you think our society affords more freedom to males than to females? Why or why not?
2. What about modern, industrial countries compared to traditional, agrarian nations: are some of the world's people more free than others?
3. How does an understanding of sociology enhance personal freedom? Why?

SUMMARY

1. Socialization is the way individuals develop their humanity and particular identities. Through socialization, one generation passes on culture to the next.

2. A century ago, people thought that most human behaviour was guided by biological instinct. Today, we recognize that human behaviour results mostly from nurture rather than nature.

3. The permanently damaging effects of social isolation reveal that social experience is essential to human development.

4. Sigmund Freud's model of human personality has three parts: the id expresses innate human needs or drives (the life and death instincts); the superego represents internalized cultural values and norms; and the ego resolves competition between the demands of the id and the restraints of the superego.

5. Jean Piaget believed that human development reflects both biological maturation and increasing social experience. He identified four stages of cognitive development: sensorimotor, preoperational, concrete operational, and formal operational.

6. Lawrence Kohlberg applied Piaget's approach to moral development. Individuals first judge rightness in preconventional terms, according to their individual needs. Next, conventional moral reasoning takes account of parents' attitudes and cultural norms. Finally, postconventional moral reasoning allows people to criticize society itself.

7. Carol Gilligan discovered that males rely on abstract standards of rightness, whereas females look at the effect of decisions on interpersonal relationships.

8. To George Herbert Mead, social experience generates the self, which he characterized as partly autonomous (the I) and partly guided by society (the me). Infants engage in imitation; children engage in play and games and eventually recognize the "generalized other."

9. Charles Horton Cooley used the term "looking-glass self" to explain that we see ourselves as we imagine others see us.

10. Usually the first setting of socialization, the family is the greatest influence on a child's attitudes and behaviour.

11. Schools expose children to greater social diversity and introduce them to impersonal performance evaluations in the form of testing.

12. Peer groups free children from adult supervision and take on special significance during adolescence.

13. The mass media, especially television, also shape the socialization process. The average Canadian child spends as much time watching television as attending school or interacting with parents.

14. Each stage of the life course, from childhood to old age, is socially constructed in ways that vary from society to society.

15. People in high-income countries typically fend off death until old age. Accepting death is part of socialization for older adults.

16. Total institutions such as prisons and mental hospitals try to resocialize inmates—that is, to radically change their personalities.

17. Socialization demonstrates the power of society to shape our thoughts, feelings, and actions. Yet as humans, we have the ability to act back, shaping both ourselves and our social world.

KEY CONCEPTS

ageism (p. 80) prejudice and discrimination against older people

anticipatory socialization (p. 72) learning that helps a person achieve a desired position

cohort (p. 81) a category of people with a common characteristic, usually their age

concrete operational stage (p. 67) Piaget's term for the level of human development at which individuals first see causal connections in their surroundings

ego (p. 66) Freud's term for a person's conscious efforts to balance innate pleasure-seeking drives with the demands of society

formal operational stage (p. 67) Piaget's term for the level of human development at which individuals think abstractly and critically

generalized other (p. 69) Mead's term for widespread cultural norms and values we use as a reference in evaluating ourselves

gerontocracy (p. 80) a form of social organization in which the elderly have the most wealth, power, and prestige

gerontology (p. 79) the study of aging and the elderly

id (p. 66) Freud's term for the human being's basic drives

looking-glass self (p. 69) Charles Horton Cooley's term for a self-image based on how we think others see us

mass media (p. 73) the means for delivering impersonal communications to a vast audience

peer group (p. 72) a social group whose members have interests, social position, and age in common

personality (p. 64) a person's fairly consistent patterns of acting, thinking, and feeling

preoperational stage (p. 67) Piaget's term for the level of human development at which individuals first use language and other symbols

resocialization (p. 81) radically changing an inmate's personality by carefully controlling the environment

self (p. 68) George Herbert Mead's term for the part of an individual's personality composed of self-awareness and self-image

sensorimotor stage (p. 67) Piaget's term for the level of human development at which individuals experience the world only through their senses

significant others (p. 69) people—such as parents—who have special importance for socialization

socialization (p. 64) the lifelong social experience by which individuals develop their human potential and learn culture

superego (p. 66) Freud's term for the cultural values and norms internalized by an individual

total institution (p. 81) a setting in which people are isolated from the rest of society and manipulated by an administrative staff

CRITICAL-THINKING QUESTIONS

1. What do cases of social isolation teach us about the importance of social experience to human beings?

2. State the two sides of the "nature–nurture" debate. In what sense are human nature and nurture not opposed to each other?

3. We have all seen very young children place their hands in front of their faces and exclaim, "You can't see me!" They assume that if they cannot see you, you cannot see them. What does this behaviour suggest about a young child's ability to "take the role of the other"? Should a parent expect a young child to see things from *the parent's* point of view?

4. What are the common themes in the ideas of Freud, Piaget, Kohlberg, Gilligan, and Mead? In what ways do their theories differ?

APPLICATIONS AND EXERCISES

1. Working with several members of your sociology class, gather data by asking several classmates and friends to name traits they consider elements of "human nature." Then compare notes and discuss the extent to which these traits are the product of nature or nurture.

2. Find a copy of the book or film *Lord of the Flies,* a tale by William Golding based on a Freudian model of personality. Jack (and his hunters) represent the power of the id; Piggy consistently opposes them as the superego; Ralph stands between the two as the ego, the voice of reason. Golding was inspired to write the book after participating in the bloody D-Day landing in France during World War II. Do you agree with his belief that violence is part of human nature?

3. Make a list of the personality traits that you think characterize you. If you have the courage, ask several others who know you well to make similar lists about you, and compare them. Can you explain the origin of the traits on these lists?

4. Watch several hours of prime-time programming on network or cable television. Keep track of all the violence you see. Assign each program a "YIP rating," for the number of *years in prison* a person would serve for committing all the violent acts you witness (Fobes, 1996). On the basis of observing this small and unrepresentative sample of programs, what are your conclusions?

 # SITES TO SEE

www.pearsoned.ca/macionis
The authors and publisher of this book invite you to visit the interactive Companion Website™ that accompanies this text. Begin by clicking on the cover of your book. You will find a chapter-by-chapter study guide, practice tests, suggested weblinks, and links to other relevant material.

www.TheSociologyPage.com
(or **www.macionis.com**)
At the author's website, you can find brief biographies of George Herbert Mead, Charles Horton Cooley, and other sociologists.

www.freud-museum.at
Visit the Sigmund Freud museum of Vienna, Austria, at this site.

www.nd.edu/~rbarger/kohlberg.html
This website is dedicated to the ideas and research of Lawrence Kohlberg.

www.pearsoned.ca/macionis/massmedia.html
An online chapter on the mass media is available at the website for this text.

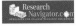 # INVESTIGATE WITH RESEARCH NAVIGATOR™

Follow the instructions on page 33 of this text to access the features of Research Navigator™. Once at the website (**www.researchnavigator.com**), enter your login name and password. Then, to use the Content Select™ database, enter keywords such as "Sigmund Freud," "childhood," and "mass media," and the search engine will supply relevant and recent scholarly and popular press publications.

 To reinforce your understanding of this chapter, and to identify topics for further study, visit MySocLab at **www.pearsoned.ca/mysoclab/macionis** for diagnostic tests and a multimedia ebook.

Social Interaction in Everyday Life

How do we create reality in our
face-to-face interactions?

Why do employers try to control their workers' feelings
as well as their on-the-job behaviour?

What are the elements that make something funny?

Sociology points to the many rules that guide behaviour in everyday situations. This waiter respectfully presents food to first-class passengers travelling on the Orient Express railroad train.

Harold and Sybil are late for their visit to another couple's home in an unfamiliar district of their city. For the last 20 minutes, they have travelled in circles, searching in vain for their destination. Harold, gripping the wheel ever more tightly, is doing a slow burn. Sybil, sitting next to him, looks straight ahead, afraid to utter a word (Tannen, 1990:62).

Harold and Sybil are lost in more ways than one: They are unable to understand why they are growing angry at their situation and at each other. Like most men, Harold cannot tolerate getting lost, and the longer he drives around, the more incompetent he feels. Sybil cannot understand why Harold does not pull over and ask someone for directions. If she were driving, she thinks to herself, they would already have arrived and would now be comfortably settled in with their friends.

Why don't men like to ask for directions? Because men value their independence, they are uncomfortable asking for help (and also reluctant to accept it). To ask someone for assistance is the same as saying, "You know something that I don't." If it takes Harold a few more minutes to find Maple Street on his own—and keep his self-respect in the process—he thinks it's a good bargain.

Women are more attuned to others and strive for connectedness. From Sybil's point of view, asking for help is right because sharing information reinforces social bonds. Asking for directions seems as natural to her as searching on his own does to Harold. Obviously, getting lost is sure to create conflict as long as neither one understands the other's point of view.

Such everyday social patterns are the focus of this chapter. The central concept is **social interaction**, *the process by which people act and react in relation to others*. We begin by presenting the rules and building blocks of common experience and then explore the almost magical way in which face-to-face interaction creates the reality in which we live.

Social Structure: A Guide to Everyday Living

September 8, Åbo, Finland. It is shortly before 8:00 a.m. when we arrive at Folkh for älsans Daghem (daycare centre) for the first time. We help our daughter discard her outside wear and change from sneakers to slippers at the space already labelled with her name. The other children are washing their hands—part of the arrival routine—and, eager to fit into her new environment, our daughter follows suit. Seated at two small square tables are a dozen or so children aged three to six, peacefully eating their breakfast with their non-parental caregivers. As Canadians, we used to attend to our daughter's dietary needs at daycare ourselves—packed lunches and a snack. The communal arrangement seems very strange (and appealing) to us. We are all the more amazed to learn that Finnish law requires that all daycare children be given a daily breakfast, hot lunch, and afternoon snack free of charge! When we pick our daughter up at the end of the day, we notice that she is the last one there at 4:30 P.M. Eager to fit in ourselves, we soon adjust our daily schedule and start to pick our daughter up around 4:00 P.M., as the other parents do.

Members of every society rely on social structure to make sense out of daily situations. As one family's introduction to the daycare system in Finland suggests, what is taken for granted in one society can seem unfamiliar and strange in another. So what, then, are the building blocks of our daily lives?

For a short video ("Sociology and Cultural Relativism") on the difficulty of travelling to unfamiliar places, go to **www.TheSociologyPage.com**.

Status

One building block of social organization is **status**, *a social position that a person holds*. In everyday use, the word "status" generally refers to "prestige," as when a university president is said to have more "status" than a university bookstore cashier. But sociologically speaking, both "president" and "cashier" are statuses, or positions, within the university organization.

Status is part of our social identity and defines our relationships to others. In the university classroom, for example, professors and students have distinct, well-defined responsibilities. As Georg Simmel (1950:307, orig. 1902), one of sociology's founders, put it, "The first condition of having to deal with somebody . . . is knowing *with whom* one has to deal."

Each of us holds many statuses at once. The term **status set** refers to *all the statuses a person holds at a given time*. A teenage girl is a daughter to her parents, a sister to her brother, a student at her school, and a goalie on her hockey team.

Status sets also change over the life course. A child turns into a parent, a student becomes a lawyer, and people marry to become intimate partners, sometimes becoming single again as a result of divorce or death. Joining an organization or finding a job enlarges our status set; retirement or withdrawing from activities makes it smaller. Over a lifetime, people gain and lose dozens of statuses.

ASCRIBED AND ACHIEVED STATUS

Sociologists analyze statuses in terms of how people attain them. An **ascribed status** is *a social position a person receives at birth or takes on involuntarily later in life*. Examples of ascribed statuses are being a daughter, a Canadian, an Aboriginal, or a widower. Ascribed statuses are matters about which people have little or no choice.

By contrast, an **achieved status** refers to *a social position a person takes on voluntarily that reflects personal ability and effort*. Examples of achieved statuses are being an honour student, an Olympic athlete, a rap artist, a computer programmer, or a drug dealer.

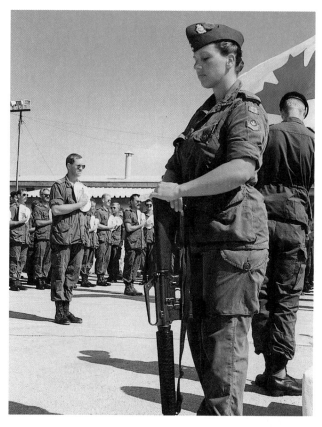
In any rigidly ranked setting, no interaction can proceed until people assess each other's social standing. Thus, military personnel wear clear insignia to designate their level of authority. Don't we size one another up in much the same way in routine interactions, noting a person's rough age, quality of clothing, and manner for clues about social position?

In practice, of course, most statuses involve a combination of ascription and achievement. That is, people's ascribed statuses influence the statuses they achieve. People who achieve the status of lawyer, for example, are likely to share the ascribed trait of having been born into well-off families. By the same token, many less desirable statuses— such as homeless person, drug addict, sex worker, or welfare recipient—are more easily achieved by people born into poverty.

MASTER STATUS

Some statuses matter more than others. A **master status** is *a status that has special importance for social identity, often shaping a person's entire life*. For most people, a job is a master status because it reveals a great deal about social background, education, and income. In a few cases, a person's

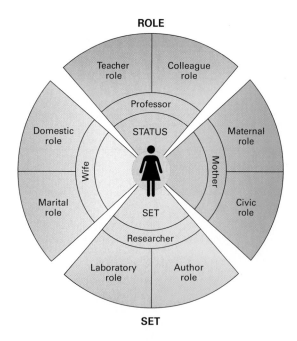

ROLE

Teacher role

Colleague role

Professor

Domestic role

STATUS

Maternal role

Wife

Mother

Marital role

Civic role

SET

Researcher

Laboratory role

Author role

SET

FIGURE 4–1 **Status Set and Role Set**

name is a master status; being an "Eaton" or a "Bronfman" is enough by itself to push an individual into the Canadian limelight.

A master status can be negative as well as positive. Consider serious illness. Sometimes people, even lifelong friends, avoid cancer patients or people with acquired immune deficiency syndrome (AIDS) because of their illness. Most societies of the world also limit opportunities for women, whatever their abilities, making gender a master status (Webster & Hysom, 1998; Reissman, 2000).

If people see an individual in terms of a physical disability, it can become a master status (Nancarrow Clarke, 1999). As one young woman who is a wife and a mother and is blind, puts it, "Most people don't expect handicapped people to grow up; they are always supposed to be children . . . You aren't supposed to date, you aren't supposed to have a job, somehow you're just supposed to disappear" (Orlansky & Heward, 1981).

Role

A second building block of social interaction is **role**, *behaviour expected of someone who holds a particular status.* A person holds a status and performs a role (Linton, 1937b). For example, holding the status of student leads you to perform the role of attending classes and completing assignments and, more broadly, devoting much of your time to personal growth through academic study.

Both statuses and roles vary by culture. In Canada, the status "uncle" refers to a brother of either mother or father; in Vietnam and Sweden, however, the word for "uncle" is different when referring to the mother's or father's side of the family, and the two men have different responsibilities. In every society, actual role performance varies according to a person's unique personality, although some societies such as Canada permit more individual expression than others.

Robert Merton (1968) introduced the term **role set** to identify *a number of roles attached to a single status*. Because we hold more than one status at a time—a status set—everyday life is a mix of many roles.

Figure 4–1 shows four statuses of one person, with each status linked to a different role set. First, as a professor, this woman interacts with students (the teacher role) and other academics (the colleague role). Second, as a researcher, she gathers data (the laboratory role) that lead to publications (the author role). Third, the woman holds the status of "wife," with a marital role (such as confidante and sexual partner) toward her husband, with whom she shares a domestic role toward the household. Fourth, she holds the status of "mother," with routine responsibilities for her children (the maternal role) as well as their school and other organizations (the civic role).

A global perspective shows us that the roles people use to define their lives differ from society to society. In low-income countries, most people work in farming or factories; high-income nations offer a far greater range of job choices. Another dimension of difference is housework. As Global Map 4–1 shows, especially in low-income nations of the world, housework falls heavily on women (Enemark, 2006). By contrast, in the high-income country of Finland, where women currently make up 49 percent of the labour force, men are much more apt to share housework with their female partners.

ROLE CONFLICT AND ROLE STRAIN

People in modern, high-income countries juggle many responsibilities demanded by their various statuses and roles. As most mothers can testify, both parenting and working outside the home are physically and emotionally draining. Sociologists thus recognize **role conflict** as *conflict among the roles corresponding to two or more statuses.*

Even roles linked to a single status can make competing demands on us. **Role strain** is *tension among the roles connected to a single status*. A plant supervisor may enjoy being friendly with other workers. At the same time, however, he has production goals and must maintain the personal distance needed to evaluate his staff. In short, performing the roles of even a single status can be a balancing act (Gigliotti & Huff, 1995).

WINDOW ON THE WORLD

GLOBAL MAP 4-1 Housework in Global Perspective

Throughout the world, housework is a major part of women's routines and identities. This is especially true in low- and middle-income societies of Latin America, Africa, and Asia, where women's work does not generally bring in a wage or salary. But our society also defines housework and childcare as "feminine" activities, even though a majority of Canadian women work in the paid economy.

Source: *Peters Atlas of the World* (1990); updated by the authors.

One strategy for minimizing role conflict is separating parts of our lives so that we perform roles for one status at one time and in one place and carry out roles for another status in a completely different setting (Nippert-Eng, 1995). A familiar example of this is deciding to "leave the job at work" before heading home to the family or, perhaps more relevant for Canadian women these days, "leaving the family at home" while at work (McDaniel, 2002).

ROLE EXIT

After she left the life of a Catholic nun to become a university sociologist, Helen Rose Fuchs Ebaugh (1988) began to

Flirting is an everyday experience in reality construction. Each person offers information to the other and hints at romantic interest. Yet the interaction proceeds with a tentative and often humorous air so that either individual can withdraw at any time without further obligation.

study *role exit,* the process by which people disengage from important social roles. In studying a range of "exes," including ex-nuns, ex-doctors, ex-husbands, and ex-alcoholics, Ebaugh saw a pattern in the process of becoming an "ex."

According to Ebaugh, the process begins as people come to doubt their ability to continue in a certain role. As they imagine alternative roles, they ultimately reach a tipping point when they decide to pursue a new life. Even at this point, however, a past role can continue to influence their lives. "Exes" carry with them a self-image shaped by an earlier role, which can interfere with building a new sense of self. For example, an ex-nun may hesitate to wear stylish clothing or makeup.

"Exes" must also rebuild relationships with people who knew them in their earlier life. Learning new social skills is another challenge. For example, Ebaugh reports, ex-nuns who enter the dating scene after decades devoted to religious life are often startled to learn that today's sexual norms are vastly different from those they knew when they were teenagers.

The Social Construction of Reality

In 1917, the Italian playwright Luigi Pirandello wrote a play titled *The Pleasure of Honesty,* about a character named Angelo Baldovino, a brilliant man with a checkered past.

Baldovino enters the fashionable home of the Renni family and introduces himself in a peculiar way:

> Inevitably we construct ourselves. Let me explain. I enter this house and immediately I become what I have to become, what I can become: I construct myself. That is, I present myself to you in a form suitable to the relationship I wish to achieve with you. And, of course, you do the same with me. (1962:157–58)

Baldovino suggests that although behaviour is guided by status and role, we have considerable ability to shape what happens from moment to moment. In other words, "reality" is not as fixed as we may think.

The phrase **social construction of reality** describes *the process by which people creatively shape reality through social interaction.* This idea is the familiar foundation of the symbolic-interaction approach, described in Chapter 1 ("Sociology: Perspective, Theory, and Method"). As Baldovino's remark suggests, quite a bit of "reality" remains unclear in everyone's mind, especially in unfamiliar situations. As we present ourselves in terms that suit the setting and our purposes, and as others do the same, reality emerges.

Social interaction, then, is a complex negotiation of reality. Most everyday situations involve at least some agreement about what's going on, but participants' perceptions of events are based on their different interests and intentions.

Our very choice of words is one way we put a "spin" on events. The Applying Sociology box provides examples of language used by the military to create (or conceal?) reality.

"STREET SMARTS"

What people commonly call "street smarts" is actually a form of constructing reality. In his autobiography, *Down These Mean Streets,* Piri Thomas remembers moving to a new apartment in Spanish Harlem. Returning home one evening, young Piri found himself cut off by Waneko, the leader of the local street gang, who was flanked by a dozen others.

> "Whatta ya say, Mr. Johnny Gringo," drawled Waneko.
> *Think man,* I told myself, *think your way out of a stomping. Make it good.* "I hear you 104th Street coolies are supposed to have heart," I said. "I don't know this for sure. You know there's a lot of streets where a whole 'click' is made out of punks who can't fight one guy unless they all jump him for the stomp." I hoped this would push Waneko into giving me a fair one. His expression didn't change.
> "Maybe we don't look at it that way."
> *Crazy, man,* I cheer inwardly, *the* cabron *is falling into my setup....* "I wasn't talking to you," I said. "Where I come from, the pres is president 'cause he got heart when it comes to dealing."

The "Spin" Game: Choosing Our Words Carefully

Military organizations choose words carefully to hide the horrors of war and make military action seem necessary and good. William Lutz, an English professor at Rutgers University, collected examples of language used by U.S. military officers. Read the military terminology and the straight-talk translations below. How do these terms put a "spin" on reality?

Military Language	Everyday Meaning
Incontinent ordnance	Bombs or shells that miss their targets and hit civilians
Area denial weapons	Cluster bombs that kill or destroy everything within a particular area
Collateral damage	Unintended death, injury, and destruction
Coercive potential	The capacity of bombs and shells to kill or injure the enemy
Suppressing assets	Reducing the enemy's ability to fight by killing people and destroying equipment
Ballistically induced aperture	Bullet hole
Scenario-dependent postcrisis	Whether we win or lose

WHAT DO YOU THINK?

1. Why, in your opinion, does the military "spin" reality in this way? Do you approve of this practice?
2. What does this example suggest about the role of power in the construction of reality? Do large organizations have the power to shape the reality experienced by individuals?
3. Can you think of another organization that shapes the reality we experience? How does it do so?

Waneko was starting to look uneasy. He had bit on my worm and felt like a sucker fish. His boys were now light on me. They were no longer so much interested in stomping me as seeing the outcome between Waneko and me. "Yeah," was his reply. . . .

I knew I'd won. Sure, I'd have to fight; but one guy, not ten or fifteen. If I lost, I might still get stomped, and if I won I might get stomped. I took care of this with my next sentence. "I don't know you or your boys," I said, "but they look cool to me. They don't feature as punks."

I had left him out purposely when I said "they." Now his boys were in a separate class. I had cut him off. He would have to fight me on his own, to prove his heart to himself, to his boys, and most important, to his turf. He got away from the stoop and asked, "Fair one, Gringo?" (1967:56–57)

This situation reveals the drama—sometimes subtle, sometimes savage—by which human beings creatively build reality. Of course, not everyone enters a situation with equal power. Should a police officer have come upon the fight that took place between Piri and Waneko, both young men might have ended up in jail.

THE THOMAS THEOREM

By using his wits and boxing with Waneko until they both tired, Piri Thomas won acceptance by the gang. What took place that evening in Spanish Harlem is an example of the **Thomas theorem**, named after W.I. Thomas (1966:301, orig. 1931): *situations that are defined as real are real in their consequences.*

Applied to social interaction, the Thomas theorem means that although reality is "soft" as it is being shaped, it can become "hard" in its effects. In the case just described, local gang members saw Piri Thomas act in a worthy way, so in their eyes, he *became* worthy.

ETHNOMETHODOLOGY

How can we become more aware of the social reality in which we play a part? Harold Garfinkel (1967) helped answer this question when he devised **ethnomethodology**, *the study of the way people make sense of their everyday surroundings.* This approach begins by pointing out that

People build reality from their surrounding culture. Yet, because cultural systems are marked by diversity and even outright conflict, reality construction always involves tensions and choices. Turkey is a nation with a mostly Muslim population, but it is also a country that has embraced Western culture. Here, women confront starkly different definitions of what is "feminine."

Staton R. Winter, *The New York Times.*

everyday behaviour rests on a number of assumptions, usually taken for granted. When someone asks the simple question, "How are you?", they might be wondering how you are physically, mentally, spiritually, or financially. Usually, you just assume that they aren't really interested in details about any of these things and you answer "Fine" no matter whether it's true or not. Both of you are "just being polite." The results of these interactions are predictable, because we all know the "rules" of everyday interaction.

But what if not everyone does know the rules? One good way to discover the assumptions we make about reality is to break the rules, whether purposely or accidentally. One of the authors learned, upon arrival in Canada from Sweden, that Canadians asked "How are you?" out of politeness, and not because they wanted to listen to an honest answer of how he was feeling. When people become confused or irritated by unexpected behaviour, it helps us to see what the rules are and how important our everyday reality is.

REALITY BUILDING: CLASS AND CULTURE

People do not build everyday experience from nothing. In part, how we act or what we see in our surroundings depends on our interests. Scanning the sky on a starry night, for example, lovers discover romance, whereas scientists see hydrogen atoms fusing into helium. Social background also directs what we see, so that residents of, say, Hull, Quebec, experience the world somewhat differently than most people living across the river in Ottawa, Ontario.

In truth, the reality construction that goes on across Canada is quite diverse. The activities people choose in one part of the country differ from those common in another. Take alternative medicine, for example. As National Map 4–1 indicates, there is considerable variation in the use of alternative medicine across Canada.

In global perspective, the construction of reality is even more variable. Consider these everyday situations: People waiting for a bus in London typically "queue up" in a straight line; people in Winnipeg, on the other hand, are rarely so orderly. The law in Saudi Arabia forbids women to drive cars, a constraint unheard of in Canada.

You can interact with all of the maps found in this text at the Companion Website™ **http://www.pearsoned.ca/macionis**.

Significant events also shape reality: Fear of crime in the big cities of the U.S. is considerably greater than it is elsewhere—including London, Paris, Rome, Calcutta, Helsinki, and Hong Kong—and this sense of public danger shapes the daily realities of a large number of U.S. citizens. Comparatively high private ownership of handguns, for example, illustrates how fear of strangers can prompt people to purchase a gun for protection.

The general conclusion is that people build reality from the surrounding culture. Chapter 2 ("Culture") explained how people the world over find different meanings in specific gestures, so travellers can find themselves building an unexpected reality. Similarly, what we see in a book or a film also depends on the assumptions we make about the world. In a study of popular culture, JoEllen Shively (1992) screened western films to two groups of males. The men in both categories claimed to enjoy the films but for different reasons. White men interpreted the films as praising rugged people striking out for the West and imposing their will on nature. Aboriginal American men saw in the same films a celebration of land and nature apart from any human ambitions.

Dramaturgical Analysis: "The Presentation of Self"

Canadian sociologist Erving Goffman (1922–1982) also analyzed social interaction, explaining how people in their everyday behaviour are very much like actors performing

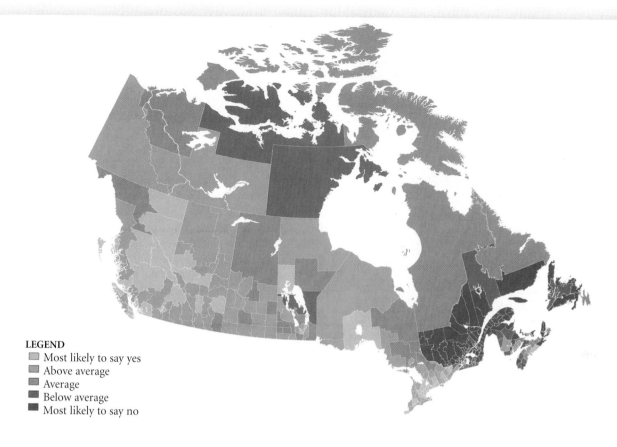

SEEING OURSELVES

NATIONAL MAP 4-1   Do You Use Alternative Medicine?

The use of alternative medicine cannot easily be explained if we only look at one important determinant. The map shows that there are probably significant differences in the usage by urban and rural residents. Do you think that there might also be east–west differences? What about other possible causes: Aboriginal status, social class and differences in how people define alternative medicine, for example?

Source: "Do you use alternative medicine?" *Saturday Night* (December 9, 2000).

on a stage. If we imagine ourselves observing what goes on in the theatre of everyday life, we are doing what Goffman called **dramaturgical analysis**, *the study of social interaction in terms of theatrical performance.*

Dramaturgical analysis offers a fresh look at the concepts of status and role. A status is like a part in a play, and a role is a script, supplying dialogue and action for the characters. Goffman described each person's performance as the **presentation of self**, *a person's efforts to create specific impressions in the minds of others.* This process, sometimes called impression management, begins with the idea of personal performance (Goffman, 1959, 1967).

PERFORMANCES

As we present ourselves in everyday situations, we reveal information—consciously and unconsciously—to others. Our performances include the way we dress (costume), the objects we carry (props), and our tone of voice and gestures (manner). In addition, we craft our performances according to the setting. We may joke loudly in a restaurant, for example,

Erving Goffman (1922–1982), born in the small town of Manville, Alberta, to Jewish immigrants from Ukraine, was one of the most important North American sociologists of the twentieth century. A Canadian Jew of short stature and researching topics at the time at the margins of the discipline, Goffman had a keen sense of the dynamics of social interaction. He relied on careful observation to capture the drama of everyday life, rather than adherence to the formal scientific method (Treviño, 2003).

but lower our voices when entering a synagogue, mosque, or church. People design settings—such as homes, offices, and corner pubs—to bring about desired reactions in others.

An application: The doctor's office. Consider how a doctor's office conveys information to an audience of patients. The fact that medical doctors enjoy high prestige and power in Canada is clear upon entering one of their offices. First, the doctor is nowhere to be seen. Instead, in what Goffman describes as the "front region" of the setting, the patient encounters a receptionist, or gatekeeper, who decides whether and when the patient can see the doctor. A simple survey of the doctor's waiting room, with patients (often impatiently) waiting to gain entry to the "back region," leaves little doubt that the doctor and his staff are in control.

The back region is composed of the examination rooms as well as the doctor's private office. In the office, the patient can see a wide range of props, such as medical books and framed degrees, which give the impression that the doctor has the specialized knowledge necessary to call the shots. The doctor usually is seated behind a desk—the larger and grander the desk, the greater the statement of power—and the patient is given only a chair.

The doctor's appearance and manner offer still more information. The usual white lab coat (costume) may have the practical function of keeping clothes from becoming dirty, but its social function is to let others know the doctor's status at a glance. A stethoscope around the neck and a black medical bag in hand (more props) have the same purpose. The doctor uses highly technical language that is often mystifying to the patient, again emphasizing that the doctor is in charge. Finally, patients use the title "doctor," but they, in turn, often are addressed only by their first names, which further shows the doctor's dominant position. The overall message of a doctor's performance is clear: "I will help you, but you must allow me to take charge."

NONVERBAL COMMUNICATION

The novelist William Sansom describes the performance of a character named Mr. Preedy, an English vacationer on a beach in Spain:

> He took care to avoid catching anyone's eye. First, he had to make it clear to those potential companions of his holiday that they were of no concern to him whatsoever. He stared through them, round them, over them—eyes lost in space. The beach might have been empty. If by chance a ball was thrown his way, he looked surprised; then let a smile of amusement light his face (Kindly Preedy), looked around dazed to see that there were people on the beach, tossed it back with a smile to himself and not a smile *at* the people. . . .
>
> [He] then gathered together his beach-wrap and bag into a neat sand-resistant pile (Methodical and Sensible Preedy), rose slowly to stretch his huge frame (Big-Cat Preedy), and tossed aside his sandals (Carefree Preedy, after all). (1956; quoted in Goffman, 1959:4–5)

Without saying a single word, Mr. Preedy offers a great deal of information about himself to anyone observing him. This illustrates the process of **nonverbal communication**, *communication using body movements, gestures, and facial expressions rather than speech.*

Many parts of the body can be used to generate *body language*, that is, to convey information to others. Facial expressions are the most significant form of body language. Smiling, for example, shows pleasure, although we can tell the difference between the deliberate smile of Kindly Preedy on the beach, a spontaneous smile of joy at seeing a friend, a pained smile of embarrassment, and the full, unrestrained smile of self-satisfaction we often associate with winning some important contest.

Eye contact is another crucial element of nonverbal communication. Generally, we use eye contact to invite social interaction. Someone across the room "catches our eye," sparking a conversation. Avoiding another's eyes, by contrast, discourages communication.

Hands also speak for us. Common hand gestures within our culture can convey, among other things, an insult, a request for a ride, an invitation for someone to join us, or a demand that others stop in their tracks. Gestures also supplement spoken words. For example, pointing in a threatening way gives greater emphasis to a word of warning, shrugging the shoulders adds an air of indifference to the phrase "I don't know," and rapidly waving the arms lends urgency to the single word "Hurry!"

Body language and deception. As any actor knows, it is very difficult to pull off a perfect performance in front of others. In everyday performances, unintended body language can contradict our planned meaning: a teenage boy explains why he is getting home so late, for example, but his mother doubts his words because he avoids looking her in the eye; the movie star on a television talk show claims that her recent flop at the box office is "no big deal," but the nervous swing of her leg suggests otherwise. Because nonverbal communication is hard to control, it provides clues to deception, in much the same way that a polygraph (lie detector) machine records the changes in breathing, pulse rate, perspiration, and blood pressure that suggest a person is lying.

Look at the two faces in the Critical Thinking box on page 98. Can you tell which one is the honest smile and which one is the deception? Uncovering phony performances is difficult, because no single bodily gesture tells us that someone is lying. But because any performance involves so many forms of body language, few people can keep up a lie without some slip-up, raising the suspicions of a careful observer. Therefore, the key to detecting lies is to view the whole performance with an eye for inconsistencies.

GENDER AND PERFORMANCES

Because women are socialized to respond to others, they tend to be more sensitive than men to nonverbal communication. In fact, as we now explain, gender is a central element in personal performances.

Demeanour. Demeanour—the way we act and carry ourselves—is a clue to social power. Simply put, powerful people enjoy more personal freedom in how they act. Off-colour remarks, swearing, or removing shoes and put-

ting one's feet up on a desk may be acceptable for the boss but rarely for employees. Similarly, powerful people can interrupt others, whereas less-powerful people are expected to show respect through silence (Smith-Lovin & Brody, 1989; Henley, Hamilton, & Thorne, 1992).

Because women generally occupy positions of lesser power, demeanour is a gender issue as well. As Chapter 10 ("Gender Stratification") explains, over 70 percent of all employed women in Canada are employed in a small number of "feminine" occupations—teaching, nursing, health-related occupations, and clerical service work—all of which are under the control of supervisors, in many cases males. Compared with men, then, women must carefully craft their personal performances on the surface and sometimes deep within themselves. Their jobs may require that they "manage their hearts" by conjuring up and displaying deep feelings of caring for those they serve (Hochschild, 1983). Women and other socially disadvantaged groups are more likely to embody their stress and unease (Lennon 1987; Krieger, 2005) and speak through their bodies about the unease they feel because of the work they do (Lock, 1993; Scheper-Hughes, 1994; Van Wolputte, 2004).

Use of space. How much space does a personal performance take? Power plays a key role here; the more power you have, the more space you use. Men typically command more space than women, whether pacing back and forth before an audience or casually sitting on a bench. Why? Our culture has traditionally measured femininity by how *little* space women occupy—the standard of "daintiness"—and masculinity by how *much* territory a man controls—the standard of "turf" (Henley, Hamilton, & Thorne, 1992).

For both sexes, **personal space** is *the surrounding area over which a person makes some claim to privacy.* In Canada and the United States, people generally stay about a metre apart when speaking; throughout the Middle East, by contrast, people stand much closer. But just about everywhere, men (with their greater social power) often intrude into women's personal space. If a woman moves into a man's personal space, however, he is likely to take it as a sexual overture, a response that helps keep women "in their place."

Staring, smiling, and touching. Eye contact encourages interaction. In conversations, women hold eye contact more than men. But men have their own brand of eye contact: staring. When men stare at women, they are claiming social dominance and defining women as sexual objects.

Although often showing pleasure, smiling is also a symbol of appeasement or submission. In a male-dominated world, it is not surprising that women smile more than men (Henley, Hamilton, & Thorne, 1992).

CRITICAL THINKING

Spotting Lies: What Are the Clues?

Deception is a common element of everyday social life. There may be no way to rid the world of dishonesty, but researchers have learned a great deal about how to tell when someone is lying. According to Paul Ekman, a specialist in analyzing social interaction, clues to deception can be found in four elements of a performance: words, voice, body language, and facial expressions.

- **Words**. People who are good liars mentally go over their lines, but they cannot always avoid inconsistencies that suggest deception. In addition, a simple slip of the tongue—something the person did not mean to say in quite that way—can occur in even the most carefully prepared performance. Any such "leak" might indicate that the person is hiding information.

- **Voice.** Tone and patterns of speech contain clues to deception because they are hard to control. A person cannot easily prevent the voice from trembling or breaking when trying to hide a powerful emotion. Speed provides another clue; an individual may speak more quickly than normal, suggesting anger, or more slowly, indicating sadness.

- **Body language.** A "leak" conveyed through body language, which is also difficult to control, may tip off an observer to deception. Subtle body movements, sudden swallowing, or rapid breathing give the impression of nervousness. Powerful emotions that flash through a performance and change body language—what Ekman calls a "hot spot"—are good clues to deception.

- **Facial expressions.** Because there are 43 distinct muscles in the face that humans use to create expressions, facial expressions are even more difficult to control than other body language. Look at the two faces in the photos. Can you tell which is the lying face? It's the one on the left. A real smile usually has a relaxed expression and lots of "laugh lines" around the eyes; a phony smile seems forced and unnatural, with fewer wrinkles around the mouth and eyes.

We all try to fake emotions—some of us more successfully than others.

 For more on detecting deception, visit **http://www. sciencenews.org/articles/ 20040731/bob8.asp.**

Obviously, the more powerful the emotion, the more difficult it is to deceive others.

WHAT DO YOU THINK?

1. Why can parents tell if their children are not being entirely truthful?
2. Might Ekman's research be useful in the war against terror? How?
3. Are there "good liars" and "bad liars"? Explain.

Sources: Ekman (1985), Golden (1999b), and Kaufman (2002).

Finally, mutual touching conveys intimacy and caring. Apart from close relationships, however, touching is generally something men do to women (and rarely, in our culture, to other men). A male doctor touches the shoulder of his female nurse as they examine a report, a young man touches the back of his female friend as he guides her across the street, or a male instructor touches the arms of young women as he teaches them to ski. In such examples, the intent of the touching may be harmless and may bring little response, but it amounts to a subtle ritual by which men claim dominance over women.

IDEALIZATION

Complex motives underlie human behaviour. Even so, Goffman suggests, we construct performances to *idealize* our intentions. That is, we try to convince others (and perhaps ourselves) that our actions reflect ideal cultural standards rather than selfish motives.

Hand gestures vary widely from one culture to another. Yet people everywhere define a chuckle, grin, or smirk in response to someone's performance as an indication that one does not take another person seriously. Therefore, the world over, people who cannot restrain their mirth tactfully cover their faces.

Idealization is easily illustrated by returning to the world of doctors and patients. In a hospital, doctors engage in a performance known as "making rounds." Upon entering a patient's room, the doctor often stops at the foot of the bed and silently examines the patient's chart. Afterward, doctor and patient talk briefly. In ideal terms, this routine represents a personal visit to check on a patient's condition.

In reality, the picture is not so perfect. A doctor may see dozens of patients a day and remember little about many of them. Reading the chart is a chance to recall the patient's name and medical problems, but revealing the impersonality of the patient's care would undermine the cultural ideal of the doctor as deeply concerned about the welfare of others.

Physicians, professors, and other professionals typically idealize their motives for entering their chosen careers. They describe their work as "making a contribution to science," perhaps "serving the community," or even "answering a call from God." Rarely do people admit the more common, less honourable motives: the income, power, prestige, and leisure that these occupations provide.

We all use idealization to some degree. When was the last time you smiled and made polite remarks to someone you did not like? Such little lies ease our way through social interactions. Even when we suspect that others are putting on an act, we are unlikely to challenge their performance, for reasons that we shall examine next.

EMBARRASSMENT AND TACT

The Marxist lecturing on the evils of capitalism nervously plays with the loose coins in his pocket; the visiting ambassador rises from the table to speak, unaware of the napkin that still hangs from her neck; the prime minister forgets himself and speaks in English to the French delegation. As carefully as people may craft their performances, slip-ups of all kinds happen. The result is *embarrassment,* or discomfort after a spoiled performance. Goffman describes embarrassment as "losing face."

Embarrassment is an ever-present danger because idealized performances typically contain some deception. In addition, most performances involve juggling so many elements that one thoughtless moment can shatter the intended impression.

A curious fact is that an audience often overlooks flaws in a performance, allowing the actor to avoid embarrassment. If we do point out a misstep ("Excuse me, but did you know your fly is open?"), we do it quietly and only to help someone avoid even greater loss of face. In Hans Christian Andersen's classic fable "The Emperor's New Clothes," the child who blurts out that the emperor is naked tells the truth but is scolded for being rude.

Often members of an audience actually help the performer recover from a flawed performance. *Tact* is helping someone "save face." After hearing a supposed expert make an embarrassingly inaccurate remark, for example, we might ignore the comment, as if it had never been spoken. Or with mild laughter we could treat what was said as a joke. Or we could simply respond, "I'm sure you didn't mean that," noting the statement but not allowing it to destroy the actor's performance.

Why is tact so common? Embarrassment creates discomfort not only for the actor but for everyone. Just as the entire audience feels uneasy when an actor forgets a line, people who observe awkward behaviour are reminded of how fragile their own performances often are. Socially constructed reality thus functions like a dam holding back a sea of chaos. Should one person's performance spring a leak, others tactfully help make repairs. After all, everyone lends a hand in building reality, and no one wants it to be suddenly swept away.

To most people in Canada, these expressions convey anger, fear, disgust, happiness, surprise, and sadness. But do people elsewhere in the world define them in the same way? Research suggests that all human beings experience the same basic emotions and display them to others in the same basic ways. But culture plays a part by specifying the situations that trigger one emotion or another.

In sum, Goffman's research shows that although behaviour is spontaneous in some respects, it is more patterned than we like to think. Almost 400 years ago, William Shakespeare captured this idea in lines that still ring true:

> All the world's a stage,
> And all the men and women merely players:
> They have their exits and their entrances;
> And one man in his time plays many parts.

> (*As You Like It*, act 2, scene 7)

Interaction in Everyday Life: Three Applications

We have now examined the major elements of social interaction. The final sections of this chapter illustrate these

lessons by focusing on three important dimensions of everyday life: emotions, language, and humour.

EMOTIONS: THE SOCIAL CONSTRUCTION OF FEELING

Emotions, more commonly called *feelings,* are an important dimension of everyday life. Indeed, what we *do* often matters less than how we *feel* about it. Emotions seem very personal because they are "inside." Even so, just as society guides our behaviour, it guides our emotional life.

The biological side of emotions. Studying people all over the world, Paul Ekman (1980a, 1980b) reported that people everywhere express six basic emotions: happiness, sadness, anger, fear, disgust, and surprise (see also Lutz & White, 1986; Lutz, 1988). Ekman also found that all people use much the same facial expressions to show these emotions. Indeed, he argues, some emotional responses seem to be "wired" into human beings, that is, biologically programmed in our facial features, muscles, and central nervous system.

Why? Complex emotions arose over the course of our species' evolution, but despite this biological root, the purpose of emotions is social: supporting group life. Emotions are powerful forces that allow us to overcome our individualism and build connections with others. Thus, the capacity for emotion arose in our ancestors along with the capacity for culture (Turner, 2000).

The cultural side of emotions. But culture does play an important role in guiding human emotions. First, Ekman explains, culture defines *what triggers* an emotion. Whether people define the departure of an old friend as joyous (causing happiness), insulting (arousing anger), a loss (creating sadness), or a mystical event (causing surprise and awe) has a lot to do with the culture. Second, culture provides rules for the *display* of emotions. For example, most people in Canada express emotions more freely with family members than with co-workers. Similarly, we expect children to express emotions to parents, although parents tend to hide their emotions from their children. Third, culture guides how we *value* emotions. Some societies encourage the expression of emotion, whereas others expect members to control their feelings and maintain a "stiff upper lip." Gender also plays a part; traditionally at least, many cultures expect women to show emotions while condemning emotional expression by men as a sign of weakness. In some cultures, of course, this pattern is less pronounced or even reversed.

 Emotions on the job. In Canada most people are freer to express their feelings at home than on the job. This is because, as Arlie Russell Hochschild (1979, 1983) explains, the typical company does indeed try to control not only the behaviour but also the emotions of its employees. Take the case of an airline flight attendant who offers passengers a pillow, a drink, and a smile. Although this smile might convey real pleasure at serving the customer, Hochschild's study of flight attendants points to a different conclusion: The smile is an emotional script demanded by the airline as the right way to do the job. Therefore, we see that the "presentation of self" described by Erving Goffman can involve not just surface acting but also the "deep acting" of emotions.

With these patterns in mind, it is easy to see that we socially construct our emotions as part of our everyday reality, a process sociologists call *emotion management*. The Diversity: Race, Class, & Gender box on page 102 tells how women who decide to have an abortion display emotions according to emotional scripts called "feeling rules."

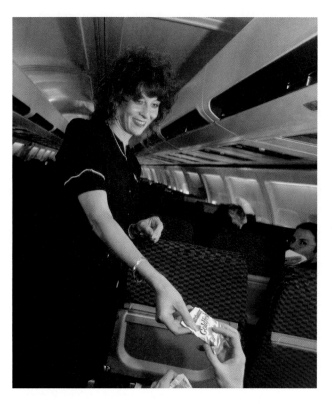

Many of us think emotions are simply part of our biological make-up. While there is a biological foundation to human emotion, sociologists have demonstrated that what triggers an emotion—as well as when, where, and to whom the emotion is displayed—is shaped by culture. For example, many jobs not only regulate a worker's behaviour, but also expect workers to display a particular emotion, as in the case of the always-smiling airline flight attendant. Can you think of other jobs that regulate emotions in this way?

LANGUAGE: THE SOCIAL CONSTRUCTION OF GENDER

As Chapter 2 ("Culture") explained, language is the thread that connects members of a society in the symbolic web we call culture. Language conveys not only a surface message but also deeper levels of meaning. One level involves gender. Language defines men and women differently in terms of both power and value.[1]

---

[1]The following sections draw primarily on Henley, Hamilton, and Thorne (1992). Additional material is drawn from Thorne, Kramarae, and Henley (1983) and other sources as noted.

Managing Feelings: The Case of Women's Abortion Experiences

Few issues today generate as much emotion as abortion. In a study of women's abortion experiences, sociologist Jennifer Keys (2002) discovered emotional scripts or "feeling rules" that guided how women felt about ending a pregnancy. Keys explains that emotional scripts arise from the political controversy surrounding abortion.

The anti-abortion movement defines abortion as a personal tragedy: the "killing of an unborn child." Given this definition, women who end a pregnancy through abortion are doing something very wrong and can expect to feel significant grief, guilt, and regret. Indeed, so intense are these feelings, according to supporters of this position, that such women often suffer from "post-abortion syndrome."

Those who take the pro-choice position have an opposing view of abortion. From this point of view, the woman's problem is the *unwanted pregnancy*; abortion is a medical solution. Therefore, the emotion common to women who end a pregnancy is not guilt but relief.

In her research, Keys conducted in-depth interviews with 40 women who had recently had abortions and found that all of them activated scripts as they "framed" their situation in an anti-abortion or pro-choice manner. In part, this construction of reality reflects the woman's own attitude about abortion. In addition, however, women's partners and friends typically encouraged specific feel-ings about the event. Ivy, one young woman in the study, had a close friend who was also pregnant. "Congratulations!" she exclaimed when she learned of Ivy's condition. "We're going to be having babies together!" Such a statement established one "feeling rule": having a baby is *good,* which sent the message to Ivy that her planned abortion should trigger guilt. Working in the other direction, Jo's partner was horrified at the news that she was pregnant. Doubting his own ability to be a father, he blurted out, "I would rather put a gun to my head than have this baby!" His panic not only defined having the child as a mistake but alarmed Jo as well. Clearly, her partner's reaction made the decision to end the pregnancy a matter of relief from a terrible problem.

Medical personnel play a part in the process of reality construction by using specific terms. Nurses and doctors who talk about "the baby" encourage the anti-abortion framing of abortion and provoke grief and guilt. On the other hand, those who use language such as "pregnancy tissue," "fetus," or "the contents of the uterus" encourage the pro-choice framing of abortion as a simple medical procedure leading to relief. Olivia began using the phrase "products of conception," which she had picked up from her doctor. Denise spoke of her procedure as "taking the extra cells out of my body. Yeah, I did feel some guilt when I thought that this was the beginning of life, but my body is full of life—you have lots of cells in you."

After the procedure, most women reported actively trying to manage their feelings. Explained Ivy, "I never used the word 'baby.' I kept saying to myself that it was not formed yet. There was nothing there yet. I kept that in my mind." On the other hand, Keys found that all of the women in her study who had undergone abortions but nevertheless leaned toward the anti-abortion position did use the term "baby." When interviewed, Gina explained, "I do think of it as a baby. The truth is that I ended my baby's life and I should not have done that. Thinking that makes me feel guilty. But—considering what I did—maybe I *should* feel guilty." Believing that what she had done was wrong, in other words, Gina actively called out the feeling of guilt—in part, Keys concluded, to punish herself.

WHAT DO YOU THINK?

1. In your own words, what are "emotional scripts" or "feeling rules"?
2. Can you apply the idea of "scripting feelings" to the experience of getting married?
3. In light of this discussion, to what extent is it correct to say that our feelings are not as personal as we might have thought?

Sources: McCaffrey and Keys (2000), and Keys (2002)..

Language and power. A young man proudly rides his new motorcycle up his friend's driveway and asks, "Isn't she a beauty?" On the surface, the question has little to do with gender. Yet why does he use the pronoun "she" rather than "he" to refer to his prized possession?

The answer is that language helps men establish control over their surroundings. That is, a man attaches a female pronoun to a motorcycle (or car, boat, or other object) because it reflects *ownership*. Perhaps this is also why, traditionally in Canada and many other parts of the world, a woman who marries takes the family name of the man she marries. While few today consider this an explicit statement of a man's ownership of a woman, many think it does reflect male dominance. For this reason, some Canadian women retain their own name after marriage and assign both family names to their children. Most likely, though, the children will want an explanation of why most of their classmates don't have hyphenated names.

Language and value. Typically, the English language treats as masculine whatever has greater value, force, or significance. For instance, the adjective "virtuous," meaning "morally worthy" or "excellent," is derived from the Latin word *vir,* meaning "man." On the other hand, the adjective "hysterical," meaning showing uncontrollable emotion, comes from the Greek word *hyster,* meaning "uterus."

In many familiar ways, language also confers a different value on women and men. Traditional masculine terms such as "king" or "lord" have a positive meaning, whereas comparable terms such as "queen," "madam," or "dame" can have a negative meaning. Similarly, the use of the suffixes "-ess" and "-ette" to indicate femininity usually devalues the words to which they are added. For example, a "major" has higher standing than a "majorette," as does a "host" in relation to a "hostess." Thus, language both mirrors social attitudes and helps perpetuate them.

Given the importance of gender in everyday life, perhaps we should not be surprised that women and men sometimes have trouble communicating clearly. In the Diversity: Race, Class, & Gender box on page 104, Harold and Sybil, whose misadventures in finding their friends' home opened this chapter, return to illustrate how the two sexes often seem to be speaking different languages.

REALITY PLAY: THE SOCIAL CONSTRUCTION OF HUMOUR

Humour plays a vital part in everyday life, and even professors include humour in their performances: Did you hear the one about the two students who slept through their exam because they had been partying too late? They told their professor that they got a flat tire on their way back from visiting their parents in the nearby town. Both were delighted to accept the offer of their considerate professor to write a make-up exam the next day, and went home to study hard that evening. However, they were both a little confused when—seated in two different rooms—they noticed that their exam paper had only one question. Their feeling of confusion was replaced by another feeling when they read the question: "Which tire?"

But although everyone laughs at a joke, few people think about what makes something funny or why humour is a part of people's lives all around the world. We can apply many of the ideas developed in this chapter to explain how, when we use humour, we "play with reality."[2]

Because humour involves challenging established social conventions, comedians have typically been "outsiders" of some sort. Rick Mercer, originally from "The Rock" (Newfoundland), is among the many comics starring on radio and television who use their cultural roots to poke fun at themselves and their audiences. Mercer's *Talking to Americans* shows that some people have a need to speak even when they don't understand the question.

The foundation of humour. Humour is produced by the social construction of reality; specifically, it arises as people create and contrast two different realities. Generally, one reality is *conventional,* that is, what people expect in some situation. The other reality is *unconventional,* an unexpected violation of cultural patterns. In short, humour arises from contradiction, ambiguity, and double meanings found in differing definitions of the same situation.

Note how this principle works in one of Woody Allen's lines: "I'm not afraid to die; I just don't want to be there when it happens." Or take the old Czech folk saying: "All mushrooms are edible—but some only once." In these examples, the first thought represents a conventional notion; the second half, however, interjects an unconventional—even absurd—meaning that collides with what we are led to expect.

This same pattern holds true for virtually all humour. Rick Mercer's New Year's resolution to "not stop drinking altogether but to explore light beer as a lunchtime beverage" ends up being not much of a resolution after all.

There are countless ways to mix realities and thereby generate humour. Contrasting realities emerge from statements that contradict themselves, such as "Nostalgia is not

---

[2]The ideas contained in this discussion are based on Macionis (1987), except as otherwise noted. The general approach draws on work presented earlier in this chapter, especially the ideas of Erving Goffman.

DIVERSITY: RACE, CLASS, & GENDER

Gender and Language: "You Just Don't Understand!"

In the story that opened this chapter, Harold and Sybil faced a situation that rings all too true to many people: when they are lost, men grumble to themselves and perhaps blame their partners but avoid asking for directions. For their part, women can't understand why.

Deborah Tannen explains that men typically define most everyday encounters as competitive. Therefore, getting lost is bad enough without asking for help and thereby letting someone else get "one up." By contrast, because women traditionally have had a subordinate position, they find it easy to ask for help. Sometimes, Tannen points out, women ask for assistance even when they don't need it.

A similar gender-linked pattern involves what women consider "trying to be helpful" and men call "nagging." Consider the following exchange (adapted from Adler, 1990:74):

SYBIL: What's wrong, honey?
HAROLD: Nothing.
SYBIL: Something is bothering you. I can tell.
HAROLD: I told you nothing is bothering me. Leave me alone.
SYBIL: But I can see that something is wrong.

HAROLD: Okay. Just why do you think something is bothering me?
SYBIL: Well, for one thing, you're bleeding all over your shirt.
HAROLD: (*now irritated*): Yeah, well, it doesn't bother me.
SYBIL: (*losing her temper*): WELL, IT SURE IS BOTHERING ME!
HAROLD: Fine. I'll go change my shirt.

The problem couples face in communicating is that what one partner *intends* by a comment is not always what the other *hears* in the words. To Sybil, her opening question is an effort at cooperative problem solving. She can see that something is wrong with Harold (who has cut himself while doing yard work), and she wants to help him. But Harold interprets her pointing out his problem as

belittling him and tries to close off the discussion. Sybil, confident that Harold would be more positive toward her if he just understood that she only wants to be helpful, repeats herself. This sets in motion a vicious circle in which Harold, thinking his wife is trying to make him feel incapable of looking after himself, responds by digging in his heels. This, in turn, makes his wife all the more sure that she needs to do something. And around it goes until somebody loses patience.

In the end, Harold agrees to change his shirt but still refuses to discuss the original problem. Mistaking his wife's concern for nagging, Harold just wants Sybil to leave him alone. For her part, Sybil fails to understand her husband's view of the situation and walks away convinced that he is a stubborn grouch.

WHAT DO YOU THINK?

1. Based on this box, how would you describe the basic difference in the ways men and women talk?
2. In your opinion, what is the reason for any gender differences in language?
3. Do you think that understanding Tannen's conclusions would help female–male couples communicate better? Why?

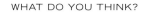

Sources: Adler (1990) and Tannen (1990).

what it used to be." Switching words also can create humour, as in Oscar Wilde's line, "Work is the curse of the drinking class;" even reordering syllables does the trick, as in the case of the country song "I'd Rather Have a Bottle in Front of Me than a Frontal Lobotomy."

Of course, a joke can be built the other way around, so that the comic leads the audience to expect an unconventional answer and then delivers a very ordinary one. When a reporter asked the famous criminal Willy Sutton why he robbed banks, for example, he replied dryly, "Because that's where the money is." However a joke is constructed, the greater the opposition or difference between the two definitions of reality, the greater the humour.

When telling jokes, the comedian can strengthen this opposition in various ways. One common technique used on the stage is to present the first, conventional remark in conversation with another actor, then turn toward the audience (or the camera) to deliver the second, unexpected line. In a Marx Brothers movie, Groucho remarks, "Outside of a dog, a book is a man's best friend." Then, dropping his voice and turning to the camera, he adds, "And *inside* of a dog, it's too dark to read!" Such "changing channels" emphasizes the difference between the conventional and unconventional realities. Following the same logic, many stand-up comedians also "reset" the audience to conventional expectations by adding "But seriously, folks . . ." between jokes.

To construct the strongest contrast in meaning, comedians pay careful attention to their performances—the precise words they use and the timing of their delivery. A joke is well told if the comic creates the sharpest possible opposition between the realities; in a careless performance, the humour falls flat. Because the key to humour lies in the collision of realities, we can see why the climax of a joke is termed the "*punch* line."

The dynamics of humour: "Getting it."   Someone who does not understand either the expected or the unexpected reality in a joke may complain, "I don't get it." To "get" humour, members of an audience must understand the two realities involved well enough to appreciate their difference.

But comics may make getting the joke harder still by leaving out some important information. In other words, the audience must pay attention to the *stated* elements of the joke and fill in the missing pieces on their own. As a simple case, consider Rick Mercer's comment on the New Democratic Party (NDP) in Canada: "I wanted to work in a political campaign and went with them because, essentially, they'd take anyone." Here, "getting" the joke depends on realizing that the NDP has a relatively marginal status in Canada and is therefore not attractive to many volunteers. Or take one of W.C. Fields' lines: "Some weasel took the cork out of my lunch!" "Some lunch!" we think to ourselves to "finish" the joke.

Here is an even more complex joke: "What do you get if you cross an insomniac, a dyslexic, and an agnostic?" Answer: "A person who stays up all night wondering if there is a dog." To get this one, you must know that insomnia is an inability to sleep, that dyslexia causes a person to reverse letters in words, and that an agnostic doubts the existence of God. Why would an audience be required to make this kind of effort to understand a joke? Simply because our enjoyment of a joke is increased by the pleasure of having completed the puzzle necessary to "get it." In addition, "getting" the joke confers a special insider status.

We can also understand the frustration of *not* getting a joke: fear of being judged as stupid, coupled with a sense of being excluded from the pleasure shared by others. Not surprisingly, outsiders in such a situation sometimes fake "getting" the joke. Sometimes someone may tactfully explain a joke so the other person doesn't feel left out.

But as the old saying goes, if a joke has to be explained, it won't be very funny. Besides taking the edge off the language and timing on which the "punch" depends, an explanation removes the mental involvement and greatly reduces the listener's pleasure.

The topics of humour.   People throughout the world smile and laugh, making humour a universal human trait. But the world's people use different languages and live in different cultures. As a result, they differ in what they find funny, and that is why humour rarely travels well.

What is humorous to the Japanese, then, may be lost on the Finns, Iraqis, or Canadians. To some degree, too, the social diversity of our own country means that people will find humour in different situations. People in Atlantic Canada and the Prairies have their own brands of humour, as do the French and English, 15- and 40-year-olds, investment bankers and construction workers. Aboriginal people and those from visible minority groups also make jokes that get back at people in more advantaged power positions.

But for everyone, topics that lend themselves to double meanings or controversy generate humour. For example, in the United States, the first jokes many of us learned as children concerned bodily functions kids are not supposed to talk about. The mere mention of "unmentionable acts" or certain parts of the body can dissolve young faces in laughter.

Are there jokes that can break through the cultural barrier? Yes, but they must touch upon universal human experiences such as, say, turning on a friend.

The controversy found in humour often walks a fine line between what is funny and what is considered "sick." During the Middle Ages, the word "humours" (derived from the Latin *humidus*, meaning "moist") referred to a balance of bodily fluids that regulated a person's health. Researchers today document the power of humour to reduce stress and improve health, confirming the old saying, "Laughter is the best medicine" (Robinson, 1983; Haig, 1988). At the extreme, however, people who always take conventional reality lightly risk being defined as deviant or even mentally ill (a common stereotype depicts insane people as laughing uncontrollably, and we have long dubbed mental hospitals "funny farms").

Then, too, every social group considers certain topics too sensitive for humorous treatment. If you joke about such things, you risk criticism for telling a "sick" joke (and being called "sick"). People's religious beliefs, tragic accidents, or appalling crimes are some of the subjects of "sick" jokes or no jokes at all. Even years later, there have been few if any jokes about the September 11, 2001, terror attacks.

The functions of humour. Humour is found everywhere because it acts as a safety valve to vent potentially disruptive sentiments. Put another way, humour provides a way to discuss an opinion on a sensitive topic without being serious. Having said something controversial, people often use humour to defuse a situation by simply stating, "I didn't mean anything by what I said—it was just a joke!"

Similarly, people use humour to relieve tension in uncomfortable situations. One study of medical examinations found that most patients begin to joke with doctors to ease their own nervousness (Baker et al., 1997).

Humour and conflict. Humour holds the potential to liberate those who laugh, but it can also be used to put others down. Men who tell jokes about women, for example, typically are voicing hostility toward them (Powell & Paton, 1988; Benokraitis & Feagin, 1995). Similarly, jokes at the expense of gay people reveal tensions about sexual orientation. Humour often is a sign of real conflict in situations in which one or both parties choose not to bring the conflict out into the open (Primeggia & Varacalli, 1990).

"Put-down" jokes make one category of people feel good at the expense of another. After analyzing jokes from many societies, Christie Davies (1990) confirmed that ethnic conflict is a driving force behind humour almost everywhere. The typical ethnic joke makes fun of some disadvantaged category of people, thereby making the jokester and the audience feel superior. In Canada, Newfoundlanders ("Newfies") have long been the "butt" of jokes, as have the Irish in Scotland, the Scots in England, the Norwegians in Sweden (and vice versa), the Sikhs in India, the Hausas in Nigeria, the Tasmanians in Australia, and the Kurds in Iraq.

In turn, disadvantaged people, of course, also make fun of the powerful. Canadian women have long joked about Canadian men, just as French Canadians portray Anglos in humorous ways, and poor people poke fun at the rich. Throughout the world, people also target their leaders with humour, and officials in some countries take such jokes seriously enough to suppress them (Speier, 1998).

In sum, the significance of humour is much greater than we may think. Humour amounts to a means of mental escape from a conventional world that is not entirely to our liking (Flaherty, 1984, 1990; Yoels & Clair, 1995). Indeed, this idea would explain why so many of our nation's comedians come from the ranks of historically marginalized peoples, including people from the Atlantic provinces. As long as we maintain a sense of humour, we assert our freedom and are never prisoners of reality. By putting a smile on our faces, we change ourselves and the world just a little.

Summary

1. Social structure provides guidelines for behaviour, making everyday life understandable and predictable.

2. A major component of social structure is status. Within a person's status set, a master status has special importance for the person's identity.

3. Ascribed statuses are involuntary, whereas achieved statuses are earned. In practice, most statuses are both ascribed and achieved.

4. Role is the active expression of a status. Tension among the roles corresponding to two or more statuses generates role conflict. Likewise, tension among the roles linked to a single status causes role strain.

5. The "social construction of reality" is the idea that we build the social world through our interactions with others.

6. The Thomas theorem states that situations defined as real are real in their consequences.

7. Ethnomethodology seeks to reveal the assumptions and understandings people have of their social world.

8. Dramaturgical analysis views everyday life as theatrical performance, noting how people try to create particular impressions in the minds of others.

9. Social power affects performances, which is one reason that men's behaviour typically differs from women's.

10. Everyday behaviour carries the ever-present danger of embarrassment. People use tact to prevent others' performances from breaking down.

11. Although the same basic emotions appear to be biologically programmed into human beings, culture guides what triggers emotions, how we display emotions, and what value we attach to emotion. In everyday life, presentations of self involve managing emotions as well as behaviour.

12. Language is vital to the process of socially constructing reality. In various ways, language defines women and men differently, generally to the advantage of men.

13. Humour stems from the difference between conventional and unconventional definitions of a situation. Because humour is an element of culture, people throughout the world find different situations funny.

KEY CONCEPTS

achieved status (p. 89) a social position a person takes on voluntarily that reflects personal ability and effort

ascribed status (p. 89) a social position a person receives at birth or takes on involuntarily later in life

dramaturgical analysis (p. 95) Erving Goffman's term for the study of social interaction in terms of theatrical performance

ethnomethodology (p. 93) Harold Garfinkel's term for the study of the way people make sense of their everyday surroundings

master status (p. 89) a status that has special importance for social identity, often shaping a person's entire life

nonverbal communication (p. 96) communication using body movements, gestures, and facial expressions rather than speech

personal space (p. 97) the surrounding area over which a person makes some claim to privacy

presentation of self (p. 95) Goffman's term for a person's efforts to create specific impressions in the minds of others

role (p. 90) behaviour expected of someone who holds a particular status

role conflict (p. 90) conflict among the roles corresponding to two or more statuses

role set (p. 90) a number of roles attached to a single status

role strain (p. 90) tension among the roles connected to a single status

social construction of reality (p. 92) the process by which people creatively shape reality through social interaction

social interaction (p. 88) the process by which people act and react in relation to others

status (p. 89) a social position that a person holds

status set (p. 89) all the statuses a person holds at a given time

Thomas theorem (p. 93) W.I. Thomas's statement that situations defined as real are real in their consequences

CRITICAL-THINKING QUESTIONS

1. Consider ways in which a physical disability can be a master status. What assumptions do people commonly make about the mental ability of someone with a physical disability such as cerebral palsy? What assumptions are made about the person's sexuality?

2. The word "conversation" has the same root as the religious term "convert," suggesting that we engage one another with the expectation of change on the part of everyone involved. In what sense, then, does a conversation require being open-minded?

3. George Jean Nathan once remarked, "I only drink to make other people interesting." What does this mean in terms of reality construction? Can you identify the elements of humour in this comment?

4. Here is a joke about sociologists: "Question: How many sociologists does it take to change a light bulb? Answer: None. There is nothing wrong with the light bulb; it's *the system* that needs to be changed!" What makes this joke funny? What sort of people are likely to get it? What kind of people probably won't? Why?

Applications and Exercises

1. Write down as many of your own statuses as you can. Do you consider any of them to be a master status? To what extent is each of your statuses ascribed or achieved?

2. During the next 24 hours, every time people ask some variation of "How are you?", stop and actually give a full and truthful answer. What happens when you respond to a polite question in an unexpected way? (Notice people's body language as well as their words.) What does this experience suggest about everyday interactions?

3. This chapter illustrated Erving Goffman's ideas with a description of a doctor's office. Investigate the offices of several professors in the same way. What furniture is there, and how is it arranged? What props do professors use? How are the offices of doctors and professors different? Which are tidier? Why?

4. Spend an hour or two walking around the businesses of your town (or shops at a local mall). Observe the number of women and men in each business. Based on your observations, would you conclude that physical space is "gendered"? Why or why not?

Sites to See

www.pearsoned.ca/macionis

The authors and publisher of this book invite you to visit the interactive Companion Website™ that accompanies this text. Begin by clicking on the cover of your book. You will find a chapter-by-chapter study guide, practice tests, suggested weblinks, and links to other relevant material.

www.familysearch.org

Many people are interested in learning more about their ancestors. This Mormon website offers free search engines to find ancestors. Can you find your ancestors? Why do you think people are interested in learning about their ancestors?

www.ai.mit.edu/projects/humanoid-robotics-group

Is it possible to build a machine capable of human interaction? That is the goal of robotics engineers at the Massachusetts Institute of Technology; this website provides details and photographs. Look over their work and think about issues raised in this chapter. In what ways are machines able, and unable, to mimic human behaviour?

www.exn.ca/Stories/2002/09/25/51.asp

Can you tell when Canadian actor Leslie Nielson is lying? Test yourself with this Discovery Channel video.

Follow the instructions on page 33 of this text to access the features of Research Navigator™. Once at the website (**www.researchnavigator.com**), enter your login name and password. Then, to use the Content Select™ database, enter keywords such as "humour," "ethnomethodology," and "emotions," and the search engine will supply relevant and recent scholarly and popular press publications. Use the *New York Times* Search-by-Subject Archive to find recent news articles related to sociology and the Link Library feature to find relevant weblinks organized by the key terms associated with this chapter.

To reinforce your understanding of this chapter, and to identify topics for further study, visit MySocLab at **www.pearsoned.ca/mysoclab/macionis** for diagnostic tests and a multimedia ebook.

CHAPTER FIVE

Groups and Organizations

How do groups affect the behaviour of members?

Why can "who you know" be as important as "what you know"?

In what ways have large business organizations changed in recent decades?

We carry out much of our daily lives as members of groups and organizations. The members of the Canadian synchronized swimming team spend long hours together training for the Olympics.

Back in 1948, people in Pasadena, California, paid little attention to the opening of a new restaurant by brothers Maurice and Richard McDonald. Yet this one small business would not only transform the restaurant industry but also introduce a new organizational model copied by countless businesses of all kinds.

The McDonald brothers' basic concept, which was soon called "fast food," was to serve meals quickly and cheaply to large numbers of people. The brothers trained employees to do highly specialized jobs: One person grilled hamburgers while others "dressed" them, made french fries, whipped up milkshakes, and handed the food to the customers in assembly-line fashion.

As the years went by, the McDonald brothers prospered, and they decided to move their restaurant to San Bernardino. It was there, in 1954, that Ray Kroc, a travelling blender and mixer salesman, paid them a visit.

Kroc was fascinated by the efficiency of the brothers' system and saw the potential for a whole chain of fast-food restaurants. The three launched the plan as partners. Soon Kroc bought out the McDonalds (who went back to running their original restaurant) and went on to become one of the greatest success stories of all time. Today, almost 50 million meals are served every day at more than 30 000 McDonald's restaurants in more than 100 nations around the world, and the company has sold more than 150 billion hamburgers (Stross, 2002).

The success of McDonald's represents more than the popularity of hamburgers and french fries. The organizational principles that guide this company are coming to dominate social life in Canada and elsewhere.

We begin this chapter with an examination of *social groups*, the clusters of people with whom we interact in our daily lives. As you will learn, the scope of group life expanded greatly during the twentieth century. From a world of families, local neighbourhoods, and small businesses, our society now turns on the operation of huge businesses and other bureaucracies that sociologists describe as *formal organizations*. Understanding this expansion of social life and appreciating what it means for us as individuals are the main objectives of this chapter.

Social Groups

Almost everyone wants a sense of belonging, which is the essence of group life. A **social group** is *two or more people who identify and interact with one another*. Human beings come together as couples, families, circles of friends, churches, clubs, businesses, neighbourhoods, and large organizations. Whatever the form, groups contain people with shared experiences, loyalties, and interests. While keeping their individuality, members of social groups also think of themselves as a special "we."

Not every collection of individuals forms a group. People with a status in common—such as "punk rocker," "civil servant," "East Asian," or "Nova Scotian"—are not a group but a category. They know that others hold the same status, but most are strangers to one another. Similarly, students sitting in a large lecture hall interact to a very limited extent. Such a loosely formed collection of people is a crowd rather than a group.

However, the right circumstances can quickly turn a crowd *into* a group. Events from power failures to terror attacks can make people bond quickly with strangers. Immediately after the September 11, 2001, terror attacks, for example, many Canadians had a renewed appreciation for neighbours and friends.

PRIMARY AND SECONDARY GROUPS

Friends often greet one another with a smile and the simple phrase, "Hi! How are you?" The response usually is, "Fine, thanks. How about you?" This answer is often more scripted than truthful. Explaining how you really are doing might make people feel so awkward that they would beat a hasty retreat.

Social groups are of one of two types, based on their members' degree of genuine personal concern for one another. According to Charles Horton Cooley (1864–1929), a **primary group** is *a small social group whose members share personal and lasting relationships.* Joined by primary relationships, people spend a great deal of time together, engage in a wide range of activities, and feel that they know one another pretty well. In short, they show real concern for one another. The family is every society's most important primary group.

To learn more about Cooley, see the Gallery of Sociologists at www.TheSociologyPage.com.

Cooley called personal and tightly integrated groups "primary" because they are among the first groups we experience in life. In addition, family and friends have primary importance in the socialization process, shaping our attitudes, behaviour, and social identity. Members of primary groups help one another in many ways, but they generally think of their group as an end in itself rather than as a means to other ends. In other words, we tend to think that family and friendship link people who "belong together." Members of a primary group also tend to view each other as unique and irreplaceable. Especially in the family, we are bound to others by emotion and loyalty. Brothers and sisters may not always get along, but they always remain siblings.

In contrast to the primary group, the **secondary group** is *a large and impersonal social group whose members pursue a specific goal or activity.* In most respects, secondary groups have characteristics precisely opposite to those of primary groups. *Secondary relationships* involve weak emotional ties and little personal knowledge of one another. Many secondary groups exist for only a short time, beginning and ending with no particular significance. Students in a first-year sociology course, who may or may not see one another after the semester ends, are one example of a secondary group.

Secondary groups include many more people than primary groups. For example, dozens or even hundreds of people may work in the same company, yet most of them pay only passing attention to one another. Sometimes the passage of time transforms a group from secondary to primary, as with co-workers who share an office for many years and develop closer relationships. But generally, members of a secondary group do not think of themselves as "we." Secondary ties need not be hostile or cold, of course.

As human beings, we live our lives as members of groups. Such groups may be large or small, temporary or long-lasting, and can be based on kinship, cultural heritage, or some shared interest.

Interactions among students, co-workers, and business associates are often quite pleasant even if they are impersonal.

Unlike members of primary groups, who display a personal orientation, people in secondary groups have a goal orientation. Whereas primary group members define each other according to who they are in terms of family ties or personal qualities, people in secondary groups look to one another for what they are, that is, what they can do for each other. In secondary groups, we tend to "keep score," aware of what we give others and what we receive in return. This goal orientation means that secondary group members usually remain formal and polite. It is in a secondary relationship, therefore, that we ask the question "How are you?" without expecting a truthful answer.

The Summing Up table reviews the characteristics of primary and secondary groups. Keep in mind that these traits define two ideal types of groups; most real groups contain elements of both. But placing these concepts at opposite ends of a continuum helps us describe and analyze group life.

Are some regions of Canada more primary in character than others? Many people think that small towns and rural areas emphasize primary relationships and that large cities are characterized by secondary ties. This generalization holds some truth, but some urban neighbourhoods, especially those populated by people of a single ethnic or religious category, can be very tightly knit. The Internet may also be helping Canadians to redefine their social interactions and even

SUMMING UP

Primary Groups and Secondary Groups

	Primary Group ←————————→	Secondary Group
Quality of relationships	Personal orientation	Goal orientation
Duration of relationships	Usually long-term	Variable; often short-term
Breadth of relationships	Broad; usually involving many activities	Narrow; usually involving few activities
Perception of relationships	As ends in themselves	As means to an end
Examples	Families, circles of friends	Co-workers, political organizations

to start new relationships via the web. Almost three in ten (28 percent) Canadian Internet users have made new friends online, and 39 percent of them have gone on to actually meet these "friends" face-to-face (Angus Reid Group Inc., 2000a).

GROUP LEADERSHIP

How do groups operate? One important element of group dynamics is leadership. Although a small circle of friends may have no leader at all, most large secondary groups place leaders in a formal chain of command.

Instrumental and expressive leaders.   Groups typically benefit from two kinds of leadership. **Instrumental leadership** refers to *group leadership that focuses on the completion of tasks.* Members look to instrumental leaders to get things done. **Expressive leadership**, by contrast, is *group leadership that focuses on the group's well-being.* Expressive leaders take less of an interest in achieving goals than in promoting the well-being of members and minimizing tension and conflict among members.

Because they concentrate on performance, instrumental leaders usually have formal, secondary relationships with other members. These leaders give orders and reward or punish people according to how much they contribute to the group's efforts. Expressive leaders build more personal, primary ties. They offer sympathy to members going through tough times, keep the group united, and lighten serious moments with humour. Whereas successful instrumental leaders enjoy more respect from members, expressive leaders generally receive more personal affection.

In the earliest types of societies, the same person combined both elements of leadership. In patriarchal societies, such as nineteenth- and early twentieth-century Canada, conventional cultural norms bestowed instrumental leadership on men. As family "breadwinners" and "heads," men

assumed primary responsibility for bringing in family income, made major decisions, and disciplined children, a responsibility that was strongly endorsed by the Canadian government of the time (Benoit, 2000a; Christie, 2000). Women were assigned an expressive leadership role, with the expectation that they would lend family members emotional support and maintain peaceful family relationships. Greater equality between men and women has blended the gender-based distinction between instrumental and expressive leadership. In most group settings, women and men now take on both leadership roles.

Leadership styles.   Sociologists also describe leadership in terms of its decision-making style. *Authoritarian leadership* focuses on instrumental concerns, takes personal charge of decision making, and demands that group members obey orders. Although this leadership style may win little affection from the group, a fast-acting authoritarian leader is appreciated in a crisis.

Democratic leadership is more expressive, making a point of including everyone in the decision-making process. Although less successful in a crisis situation, when there is little time for discussion, democratic leaders generally draw on the ideas of all members to develop creative solutions to problems.

Laissez-faire leadership (a French phrase meaning roughly "to leave alone") allows the group to function more or less on its own. This style typically is the least effective in promoting group goals (White & Lippitt, 1953; Ridgeway, 1983).

GROUP CONFORMITY

Groups influence the behaviour of their members, often promoting conformity. "Fitting in" provides a secure feeling of belonging, but at the extreme, group pressure can be unpleasant and even dangerous. Interestingly, as experiments by Solomon Asch and Stanley Milgram showed, even strangers can encourage conformity.

Asch's research.   Asch (1952) recruited students supposedly to study visual perception. Before the experiment began, he explained to all but one member of a small group that their real purpose was to put pressure on the remaining person. Placing six to eight students around a table, Asch showed them a "standard" line, as drawn on Card 1 in Figure 5–1, and asked them to match it to one of the three lines on Card 2.

Anyone with normal vision can see that the line marked "A" on Card 2 is the correct choice. Initially, as planned, everyone made the correct matches. But then Asch's accomplices began answering incorrectly, leaving the naive subject (seated at the table so as to answer next to last) bewildered and uncomfortable.

What happened? Asch found that one-third of all subjects chose to conform by answering incorrectly. Apparently, many of us are willing to compromise our own judgment to avoid the discomfort of being different, even from people we do not know.

Milgram's research.   Stanley Milgram, a former student of Solomon Asch's, conducted conformity experiments of his own. In Milgram's controversial study (Milgram, 1963, 1965; Miller, 1986), a researcher explained to male recruits that they would be taking part in a study of how punishment affects learning. One by one, he assigned them to the role of teacher and placed another person—actually an accomplice of Milgram's—in a connecting room to pose as a learner.

The teacher watched the learner sit down in a contraption resembling an electric chair. As the teacher looked on, the researcher applied electrode paste to the learner's wrist, explaining that this would "prevent blisters and burns." The researcher then attached an electrode to the learner's wrist and fastened the leather straps, explaining that they would "prevent excessive movement while the learner was being shocked." Although the shocks would be painful, the researcher reassured the teacher, they would cause "no permanent tissue damage."

The researcher then led the teacher back into the adjoining room, pointing out that the "electric chair" was connected to a "shock generator," actually a phony but realistic-looking piece of equipment with a label that read "Shock Generator, Type ZLB, Dyson Instrument Company, Waltham, Mass." On the front was a dial that supposedly regulated electric current from 15 volts (labelled "Slight Shock") to 300 volts ("Intense Shock") to 450 volts ("Danger: Severe Shock").

Seated in front of the "shock generator," the teacher was told to read aloud pairs of words. Then the teacher was to

FIGURE 5-1 Cards Used in Asch's Experiment in Group Conformity

Source: Asch (1952).

repeat the first word of each pair and wait for the learner to recall the second word. Whenever the learner failed to answer correctly, the teacher was told to apply an electric shock.

The researcher directed the teacher to begin at the lowest level (15 volts) and to increase the shock by another 15 volts every time the learner made a mistake. And so the teacher did. At 75, 90, and 105 volts, the teacher heard moans from the learner; at 120 volts, shouts of pain; by 270 volts, screams; at 315 volts, pounding on the wall; after that, deadly silence. None of the 40 subjects assigned to the role of teacher during the initial research even questioned the procedure before reaching 300 volts, and 26 of the subjects—almost two-thirds—went all the way to 450 volts. Even Milgram was surprised at how readily people obeyed authority figures.

Milgram (1964) then modified his research to see whether Solomon Asch had documented such a high degree of group conformity only because the task—matching lines—was a trivial one. What if groups could also pressure people to administer electrical shocks?

This time, Milgram formed a group of three teachers, two of whom were his accomplices. Each of the teachers was to suggest a shock level when the learner made an error; the rule was that the group would then administer the lowest of the three suggested levels. This arrangement gave the naive subject the power to deliver a lesser shock regardless of what the others proposed.

The accomplices suggested increasing the shock level with each error, putting pressure on the subject to do the same. The subjects in these groups applied voltages three to four times higher than other subjects acting alone. Thus,

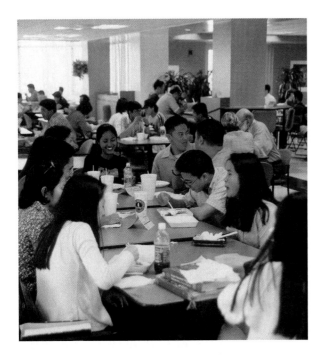

We form attitudes and plan our actions imagining how others will respond to us. Often, researchers have found, people in specific groups—called reference groups—have special importance to us. Reference groups may be groups we are already a member of or groups we would like to accept us.

Milgram's research suggests that people are surprisingly likely to follow the directions not only of legitimate authority figures but also of groups of ordinary individuals, even when it means harming another person.

Janis's research. Experts also cave in to group pressure, says Irving L. Janis (1972, 1989). Janis argues that a number of U.S. foreign policy blunders, including the failure to foresee the Japanese attack on Pearl Harbour during World War II and the country's ill-fated involvement in the Vietnam War, resulted from group conformity among highest-ranking political leaders. A Canadian example of group conformity among political leaders happened in November 1998 when RCMP officers in Vancouver pepper-sprayed unarmed student protesters during the Asia–Pacific Economic Cooperation summit.

Common sense tells us that group discussion improves decision making. Janis counters that group members often seek agreement that closes off other points of view. Janis called this process **groupthink**, *the tendency of group members to conform, resulting in a narrow view of some issue.*

Groupthink resulted in the 1961 U.S. invasion of the Bay of Pigs in Cuba, a decision that has repercussions for both countries to this day. Looking back, Arthur Schlesinger Jr., an adviser to President Kennedy, confessed feeling guilty "for having kept so quiet during those crucial discussions in the Cabinet Room," adding that the group discouraged anyone from challenging what, in hindsight, Schlesinger considered "nonsense" (quoted in Janis, 1972:30, 40). It may be that groupthink was also at work in 2003 when U.S. leaders went to war assuming that Iraq had stockpiles of weapons of mass destruction. Interestingly, many of the United States' foreign allies, including Canada, did not support either of these two decisions.

REFERENCE GROUPS

How do we assess our own attitudes and behaviour? Often we use a **reference group**, *a social group that serves as a point of reference in making evaluations and decisions.*

A young man who imagines his family's reaction to a woman he is dating is using his family as a reference group. A supervisor who tries to predict her employees' reaction to a new vacation policy is using them in the same way. As these examples suggest, reference groups can be primary or secondary. In either case, our need to conform shows how others' attitudes affect us.

We also use groups we do *not* belong to for reference. Being well prepared for a job interview means showing up dressed the way people in that company dress for work. Conforming to groups we do not belong to is a strategy to win acceptance and illustrates the process of *anticipatory socialization*, discussed in Chapter 3 ("Socialization: From Infancy to Old Age").

Stouffer's research. Samuel A. Stouffer and his colleagues conducted a classic study of reference groups during World War II. Researchers asked soldiers to rate their own, or any competent soldier's, chances of promotion in their branch of the army. One might guess that soldiers serving in outfits with high promotion rates would be optimistic about advancement. Yet Stouffer's research pointed to the opposite conclusion: soldiers in army units with low promotion rates were actually more positive about their chances to move ahead (Stouffer et al., 1949).

The key to understanding Stouffer's results lies in the groups against which soldiers measured themselves. Those assigned to units with lower promotion rates looked around them and saw people making no more headway than they were. Although they had not been promoted, neither had many others, so they did not feel deprived. However, soldiers in units with higher promotion rates could think of many people who had been promoted sooner or more often than they had. With such people in mind, even soldiers who had been promoted themselves were likely to feel shortchanged.

The point is that we do not make judgments about ourselves in isolation, nor do we compare ourselves with just anyone. Regardless of our situation in absolute terms, we form a subjective sense of our well-being by looking at ourselves relative to specific reference groups (Merton, 1968; Mirowsky, 1987).

IN-GROUPS AND OUT-GROUPS

Everyone favours some groups over others, whether because of political outlook, social prestige, or manner of dress. At a university, for example, left-leaning student activists may look down on fraternity members, whom they view as conservative; fraternity members, in turn, may snub the computer "nerds" and "grinds," who work too hard. People in virtually every social setting make similar positive and negative evaluations about members of other groups.

Such judgments illustrate another key element of group dynamics: the opposition of in-groups and out-groups. An **in-group** is *a social group toward which a member feels respect and commitment*. An **out-group**, by contrast, is *a social group toward which a person feels a sense of competition or opposition*. In-groups and out-groups are based on the idea that "we" have valued traits that "they" lack.

Tensions between groups sharpen the groups' boundaries and give people a clearer social identity. However, members of in-groups generally hold overly positive views of themselves and unfairly negative views of various out-groups (Tajfel, 1982; Bobo Hutchings, 1996).

Power also shapes intergroup relations. A powerful in-group can define others as a lower-status out-group. Historically, for example, white people viewed people of colour as an out-group and subordinated them socially, politically, and economically. Internalizing these negative attitudes, minorities often struggle to overcome negative self-images, as has been the case in Canada's Aboriginal peoples' movement for self-government. In this way, in-groups and out-groups foster loyalty but also generate conflict (Bobo Hutchings, 1996).

GROUP SIZE

The next time you go to a party, try to arrive first. If you do, you will be in a position to observe some fascinating group dynamics. Until about six people enter the room, everyone generally shares a single conversation. But as more people arrive, the group soon divides into two or more clusters. Group size plays a crucial role in how group members interact.

To understand why, note the mathematical number of relationships possible among two to seven people. As shown in Figure 5–2, two people form a single relationship; adding a third person results in three relationships; a fourth person yields six. Increasing the number of people further boosts

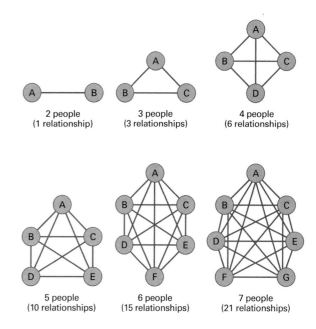

FIGURE 5–2 Group Size and Relationships

the number of relationships much more rapidly because every new individual can interact with everyone already there. Thus, by the time seven people join one conversation, 21 "channels" connect them. With so many open channels, at this point the group usually divides.

German sociologist Georg Simmel (1858–1918) explored the dynamics of the smallest social groups. Simmel (1950, orig. 1902) used the term **dyad** (from the Greek word for "pair") to describe *a social group with two members*.

Simmel explained that social interaction in a dyad typically is more intense than in larger groups because neither member shares the other's attention with anyone else. In Canada, love affairs, marriages, and the closest friendships are dyadic.

But like a stool with only two legs, dyads are unstable. Both members of a dyad must work to keep the relationship going; if either withdraws, the group collapses. Because stable marriages are important to society, the marital dyad is supported with legal, economic, and often religious ties.

A **triad**, *a social group with three members*, contains three relationships, each uniting two of the three people. A triad is more stable than a dyad because one member can act as a mediator if relations between the other two become strained. This bit of group dynamics explains why members of a dyad (say, a married couple) often seek out a third person (such as a counsellor) to discuss tensions between them.

On the other hand, two of the three can pair up to press their views on the third, or two may intensify their

Throughout the world, the most intense social bonds join two people, such as these twin sisters. Even so, the dyad is also characteristically unstable, since withdrawal of either party causes the group to collapse.

The triad, illustrated by Jonathan Green's painting *Friends,* includes three people. A triad is more stable than a dyad because conflict between any two persons can be mediated by the third member. Even so, should the relationship between any two become more intense in a positive sense, those two are likely to exclude the third.

Jonathan Green, *Friends,* 1992. Oil on masonite, 14 in. × 11 in. © Jonathan Green, Naples, Florida. Collection of Patric McCoy.

relationship, leaving the other feeling left out. For example, when two of the three members of a triad develop a romantic interest in each other, they discover the meaning of the old saying, "Two's company, three's a crowd."

As groups grow beyond three people, they become more stable and capable of withstanding the loss of one or more members. At the same time, increases in group size reduce the intense interaction possible in only the smallest groups. This is why larger groups are based less on personal attachments and more on formal rules and regulations. Such formality helps the group persist over time, although it may also undergo change. The greater the number of members, the more contact there is with the outside world, opening the door to new attitudes and behaviours (Carley, 1991).

SOCIAL DIVERSITY: RACE, CLASS, AND GENDER

Race, ethnicity, class, and gender each affect group dynamics. Peter Blau (1977; Blau, Blum, & Schwartz, 1982; South & Messner, 1986) points out three ways in which social diversity influences intergroup contact:

1. **Large groups turn inward.** Blau explains that the larger a group is, the more likely its members are to concentrate relationships among themselves. Say a university is trying to enhance social diversity by increasing the number of international students. These students may add a dimension of difference, but as their numbers rise, they become more likely to form their own social group. Thus, efforts to promote social diversity may have the unintended effect of promoting separatism.

2. **Heterogeneous groups turn outward.** The more socially diverse a group is, the more likely its members are to interact with outsiders. If you look at the various ethnic groups in your community, you are likely to find that ethnicities with a longer history in Canada are more heterogeneous and more likely to interact with others than are recent arrivals. Immigrants to Canada tend to settle in our major cities. This is one reason that residents of Montreal and Vancouver have more intergroup contact than residents of small towns and outports, which comprise people of only one or a few types. National Map 5–1 takes a closer look at the level of homogeneity in different parts of Canada.

3. **Physical boundaries create social boundaries.** To the extent that a social group is physically segregated from others (by having its own dorm or dining area, for example), its members are less likely to interact with other people. Military families in Canada and elsewhere serve as an example. As Deborah Harrison and Lucie Laliberté (1994:21) point out, "[T]he military is a portable total institution that isolates its members from

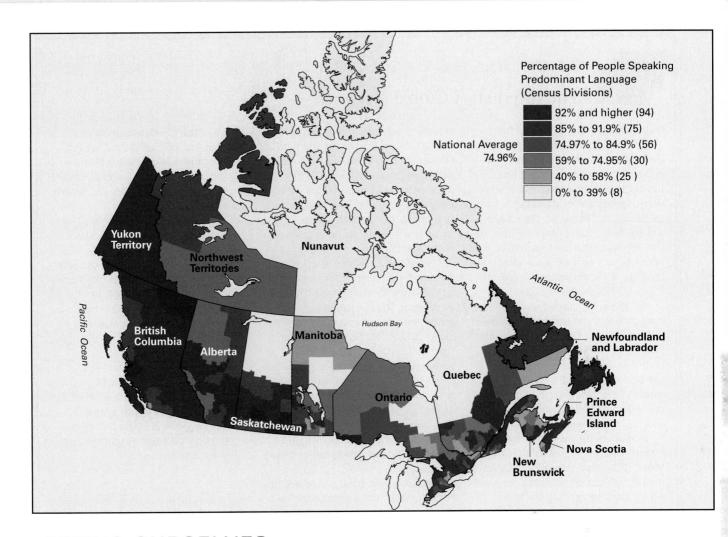

Percentage of People Speaking
Predominant Language
(Census Divisions)

■	92% and higher (94)
■	85% to 91.9% (75)
■	74.97% to 84.9% (56)
■	59% to 74.95% (30)
■	40% to 58% (25)
□	0% to 39% (8)

National Average
74.96%

SEEING OURSELVES

NATIONAL MAP 5-1 Language Homogeneity Within Census Divisions, Canada, 2001

Source: Calculated based on data in Statistics Canada (2003ab)

civilians. . . . As in the case of other total institutions, isolation from civilians facilitates control."

NETWORKS

A **network** is *a web of weak social ties.* Think of a network as a "fuzzy" group containing people who come into occasional contact but lack a sense of boundaries and belonging. If you think of a group as a "circle of friends," think of a network as a "social web" expanding outward, often reaching great distances and including large numbers of people.

Some networks come close to being groups, as in the case of school friends who stay in touch years after graduation by email and telephone. More commonly, however, a network includes people we *know of*—or who *know of us*—but with whom we interact rarely, if at all. As one woman known as a community organizer puts it, "I get calls at home, [and] someone says, 'Are you Roseann Navarro? Somebody told me to call you. I have this problem. . . .'" (Kaminer, 1984:94).

The Internet: A Global Network

Its beginnings seem right out of the 1960s Cold War film *Dr. Strangelove*. Back then, government officials and scientists were trying to figure out how to run the country after an atomic attack, which, they assumed, would knock out telephones and television. The solution was brilliant: create a communication system with no central headquarters, no one in charge, and no main power switch—in short, an electronic web that would link the country in one vast network.

By 1985, the Internet was born. Today, colleges and universities, as well as thousands of government offices, are joined by the Internet and share in the cost of its operation. Home computers can be connected to the "information superhighway" using a cable connection or a telephone line modem and a subscription to an Internet service provider.

How many people use the Internet? A rough estimate is that as of 2004, about 700 million people in 180 (out of over 200) countries around the world were connected, forming the largest network in history.

What is available on the Internet? Popular search engines such as Google (**www.google.com**) allow you to find websites for just about any topic you can imagine. The Internet also allows you to send email: You can start a cyber-romance with a pen pal, write to your textbook authors (macionis@kenyon.edu, mjansson@uvic.ca, cbenoit@uvic.ca), or even send a message to the prime minister of Canada (pm@pm.gc.ca). Through the Internet, you can join in discussion groups, visit museums through "virtual tours," access data from government agencies (a good starting point is **www.statcan.ca**), explore sites of sociological interest (try the author's website at **www.TheSociologyPage.com**), or review for exams in this course (**www.pearsoned.ca/macionis**). With no formal rules for its use, the Internet's potential is limited only by our own imaginations.

Ironically, perhaps, it is precisely this freedom that disturbs some people. Critics claim that "electronic democracy" threatens our political system, parents fear that their children will access sexually explicit "adult sites," and purists are angered as the Internet becomes flooded with advertising.

In its "anything goes" character, the Internet is very much like the real world. Not surprisingly, then, a recent trend is that more and more users now use passwords, fees, and other "gates" to create subnetworks limited to people like themselves. From one vast network, then, many social groups are emerging.

WHAT DO YOU THINK?

1. How much of your contact with other people is over the Internet?
2. How do you feel about the "anything goes" character of the Internet?
3. Can you point to both advantages and disadvantages of Internet communication?

Sources: Based on Hafner (1994) and O'Connor (1997).

Network ties may be weak, but they can be a powerful resource. For immigrants trying to become established in a new community, businesspeople seeking to expand their operations, or anyone looking for a job, *whom* you know often is just as important as *what* you know (Luo, 1997; Hagan, 1998; Petersen, Saporta, & Seidel, 2000).

Networks are based on people's academic institutions, clubs, neighbourhoods, political parties, and personal interests. Obviously, some networks are made up of people with more wealth, power, and prestige than others; that explains the importance of being "well connected." The networks of more privileged categories of people—such as the members of the prestigious Royal Society of Canada—are a valuable form of "social capital," which is more likely to lead people in these categories to higher-paying jobs (Green, Tigges, & Diaz, 1999; Lin, Cook, & Burt, 2001). And some people have denser networks than others—that is, they are connected to more people—which makes for another type of power. Typically, the most extensive social networks are maintained by people who are young, well educated, and living in urban areas (Markovsky et al., 1993; Kadushin, 1995; O'Brien, Hassinger, & Dershem, 1996; Fernandez & Weinberg, 1997; Podolny & Baron, 1997; Wellman & Hampton, 1999). Barry Wellman (1999) goes further; rather than studying geographical communities, such as neighbourhoods, he studies social networks or ties that members use to gain resources, and calls these "communities."

Gender also shapes networks. Although the networks of men and women are typically of the same size, women include more relatives (and women) in their networks,

Internet Users per 1000 People

■ High: 100 or more
■ Moderate: 10.0 to 99.9
□ Low: Fewer than 10
■ No data

Internet Users per 1000 People

High: 100 or more

Moderate: 10.0 to 99.9

Low: Fewer than 10

No data

WINDOW ON THE WORLD

GLOBAL MAP 5–1 Internet Users in Global Perspective

This map shows how the Information Revolution has affected countries around the world. In most high-income nations, at least one-third of the population uses the Internet. By contrast, only a small share of people in low-income nations do so. What effect does this have on people's access to information? What does this mean for the future in terms of global inequality?

Sources: International Telecommunication Union (2003) and United Nations Development Programme (2004).

whereas men include more co-workers (and more men). Women's ties, therefore, may not be quite as powerful as the "old boys" networks. Even so, research suggests that the networks of men and women are becoming more alike as gender inequality decreases (Mencken & Winfield, 1999; Reskin & McBrier, 2000; Torres & Huffman, 2002).

Finally, new information technology has generated a global network of unprecedented size in the form of the Internet. The Global Sociology box takes a closer look at the history and development of this twenty-first-century form of communication. Global Map 5–1 shows that Internet use around the world is linked to income levels.

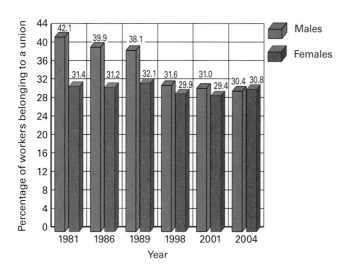

FIGURE 5-3 Union Membership, Canada, 1981–2004

Source: Morrisette, Schellenberg, & Johnson, 2005.

Formal Organizations

As noted earlier, a century ago, most people lived in small groups of family, friends, and neighbours. Today, our lives revolve more and more around **formal organizations**, *large secondary groups organized to achieve their goals efficiently.* Formal organizations such as corporations and government agencies differ from small primary groups in their impersonality and their formally planned atmosphere.

When you think about it, organizing 32.2 million members of Canadian society is a remarkable operation, involving countless jobs, from collecting taxes to delivering the mail. To carry out most of these tasks, we rely on large formal organizations, which develop lives and cultures of their own so that as members come and go, their operation can stay much the same over many years.

TYPES OF FORMAL ORGANIZATIONS

Amitai Etzioni (1975) identified three types of formal organizations, distinguished by the reasons people participate in them. Just about everyone who works for income belongs to a *utilitarian organization*. Joining a utilitarian organization usually is a matter of individual choice, although most people must join some such organization to make a living. Some people also belong to labour unions. Figure 5–3 shows that union membership declined by

almost 30 percent for Canadian males between 1981 (42.1 percent) and 2004 (30.4 percent), while union membership remained relatively constant for females.

People join *normative organizations* not for income but to pursue some goal they think is morally worthwhile. Sometimes called *voluntary associations*, these include community service groups (such as the Canadian International Development Agency [CIDA], the Lions Club, the Status of Women Canada, the Red Cross, or the whites-only organization Stormfront), political parties, and religious organizations. From a global perspective, people in the United States, Canada, and Sweden are especially likely to be members of voluntary associations (Curtis, Grabb, & Baer, 1992).

Coercive organizations have involuntary memberships. People are forced to join these organizations as a form of punishment (prisons) or treatment (psychiatric hospitals). Coercive organizations have special physical features, such as locked doors and barred windows, and are supervised by security personnel. They isolate people (whom they label "inmates" or "patients") for a period of time in order to radically change their attitudes and behaviour (Goffman, 1961).

It is possible for a single formal organization to fall into *all* of these categories. For example, a mental hospital serves as a coercive organization for a patient, a utilitarian organization for a psychiatrist, and a normative organization for a hospital volunteer.

ORIGINS OF BUREAUCRACY

Formal organizations date back thousands of years. Elites who governed early empires relied on government officials to collect taxes, undertake military campaigns, and build monumental structures, from the Great Wall of China to the pyramids of Egypt.

However, early organizations had two limitations. First, they lacked the technology to travel over large distances, to communicate quickly, and to collect and store information. Second, the pre-industrial societies they were trying to rule had a traditional culture. **Tradition**, according to German sociologist Max Weber, consists of *values and beliefs passed from generation to generation.* Tradition makes a society conservative, Weber explained, because it limits an organization's efficiency and ability to change.

By contrast, Weber described the modern worldview as **rationality**, *a way of thinking that emphasizes deliberate, matter-of-fact calculation of the most efficient means to accomplish a particular task.* A rational worldview pays little attention to the past and is open to any changes that might get the job done better or more quickly.

The rise of the "organizational society" rests on what Weber called the **rationalization of society**, *the historical change from tradition to rationality as the dominant mode of* *human thought.* Modern society, he claimed, becomes "disenchanted" as sentimental ties give way to a rational focus on science, complex technology, and the organizational structure called bureaucracy.

CHARACTERISTICS OF BUREAUCRACY

Bureaucracy is *an organizational model rationally designed to perform tasks efficiently.* Bureaucratic officials regularly create and revise policy to increase efficiency. To appreciate the power and scope of bureaucratic organization, consider that any one of the millions of phones in Canada can connect you within seconds to any other phone in a home, business, or automobile, or even one in a hiker's backpack on a remote trail in the Rocky Mountains. Such instant communication would have been beyond the imagination of people who lived in the ancient world.

Of course, the telephone system depends on technology such as electricity, fibre optics, and computers. But the system could not exist without the organizational capacity to keep track of every telephone call—recording which phone called which other phone, when, and for how long—and present all this information on the tens of millions of telephone users in the form of monthly bills.

What specific traits promote organizational efficiency? Max Weber (1978, orig. 1921) identified six key elements of the ideal bureaucratic organization:

1. **Specialization.** Our ancestors spent most of their time looking for food and finding shelter. Bureaucracy, by contrast, assigns individuals highly specialized jobs.

2. **Hierarchy of offices.** Bureaucracies arrange workers in a vertical ranking of offices. Each person is thus supervised by "higher-ups" in the organization while in turn supervising others in lower positions. Usually, with few people at the top and many at the bottom, bureaucratic organizations take the form of a pyramid.

3. **Rules and regulations.** Rationally enacted rules and regulations guide a bureaucracy's operation. Ideally, a bureaucracy seeks to operate in a completely predictable fashion.

4. **Technical competence.** Bureaucratic officials have the technical competence to carry out their duties. Bureaucracies typically hire new members according to set standards and then monitor their performance. Such impersonal evaluation contrasts with the ancient custom of favouring relatives, whatever their talents, over strangers.

5. **Impersonality.** Bureaucracy puts rules ahead of personal whim so that both clients and workers are all treated the same. From this impersonal approach comes the idea of the "faceless bureaucrat."

Although formal organization is vital to modern, high-income nations, it is far from new. Twenty-five centuries ago, the Chinese philosopher and teacher K'ung Fu-Tzu (known to Westerners as Confucius) endorsed the idea that government offices should be filled by the most talented young men. This led to what was probably the world's first system of civil service examinations. Here, would-be bureaucrats compose essays to demonstrate their knowledge of Confucian texts.

6. **Formal, written communications.** Someone once said that the heart of bureaucracy is not people but paperwork. Rather than casual, face-to-face talk, bureaucracy depends on formal written memos and reports, which accumulate in vast files.

To learn more about Max Weber, visit the Gallery of Sociologists at **www.TheSociologyPage.com**.

SUMMING UP

Small Groups and Formal Organizations

	Small Groups	Formal Organizations
Activities	Much the same for all members	Distinct and highly specialized
Hierarchy	Often informal or non-existent	Clearly defined, corresponding to offices
Norms	General norms, informally applied	Clearly defined rules and regulations
Membership criteria	Variable; often based on personal affection or kinship	Technical competence to carry out assigned tasks
Relationships	Variable and typically primary	Typically secondary, with selective primary ties
Communications	Typically casual and face-to-face	Typically formal and in writing
Focus	Person-oriented	Task-oriented

Bureaucratic organization promotes efficiency by carefully hiring workers and limiting the unpredictable effects of personal taste and opinion. The Summing Up table reviews the differences between small social groups and large formal organizations.

ORGANIZATIONAL ENVIRONMENT

No organization operates in a vacuum. How any organization performs depends not only on its own goals and policies but also on the **organizational environment**, *factors outside an organization that affect its operation.* These factors include technology, economic and political trends, and the available workforce, as well as other organizations.

Modern organizations are shaped by the *technology* of computers, telephone systems, and copiers. Computers give employees access to more information and people than ever before. At the same time, computer technology allows managers to closely monitor the activities of workers (Markoff, 1991).

Economic and political trends affect organizations. All organizations are helped or hurt by periodic economic growth or recession. Most industries also face competition from abroad as well as changes in law—such as new environmental standards—at home.

Population patterns, such as the size and composition of the surrounding population, also affect organizations. The average age, typical education, and social diversity of a local community determine the available workforce and sometimes the market for an organization's products or services.

Other organizations also contribute to the organizational environment. To be competitive, a hospital in Canada must keep open clear lines of communication with provincial medical, nursing, and allied workers' professional associations and unions, abide by federal laws governing the healthcare system, and work with regional health boards attempting to balance increasing public demands for quality health services and limited annual budgets (Armstrong & Armstrong, 1996, 2002).

THE INFORMAL SIDE OF BUREAUCRACY

Weber's ideal bureaucracy deliberately regulates every activity. In actual organizations, however, human beings are creative (and stubborn) enough to resist bureaucratic regulation. Informality may amount to simply cutting corners on the job, but it also can provide the flexibility necessary for an organization to survive and prosper (Scott, 1981).

In part, informality comes from the varying personalities of organizational leaders. Studies of large corporations show that the qualities and quirks of individuals—including personal charisma and interpersonal skills—greatly affect organizational success or failure (Halberstam, 1986; Baron, Hannan, & Burton, 1999).

Authoritarian, democratic, and laissez-faire types of leadership (described earlier in this chapter) reflect individual personality as much as any organizational plan. Then, too, in the "real world" of organizations, leaders sometimes seek to benefit personally through abuse of organizational power. Perhaps even more commonly, leaders take credit for the efforts of those who work for them. For example, many secretaries have far more authority and responsibility than their official job titles and salaries suggest.

Communication offers another example of organizational informality. Memos and other written documents are the formal way to spread information through the organization. Typically, however, people create informal networks, or "grapevines," that spread information quickly, if not always accurately. Grapevines, using word of mouth and email, are particularly important to rank-and-file workers

George Tooker's painting *Government Bureau* is a powerful statement about the human costs of bureaucracy. The artist paints members of the public in a drab sameness—reduced from human beings to mere "cases" to be disposed of as quickly as possible. Set apart from others by their positions, officials are "faceless bureaucrats" concerned more with numbers than with providing genuine assistance (notice that the artist places the fingers of the officials on calculators).

George Tooker, *Government Bureau*, 1956. Egg tempera on gesso panel, 19⅝ × 29⅝ inches. The Metropolitan Museum of Art, George A. Hearn Fund, 1956 (56.78). Photograph © 1984 The Metropolitan Museum of Art.

because higher-ups often attempt to keep important information from them.

The spread of email has "flattened" organizations somewhat, allowing even the lowest-ranking employee to bypass immediate superiors to communicate directly with the organization's leader or all fellow employees at once. Some organizations consider such "open channel" communication unwelcome and limit the use of email. Leaders also may seek to protect themselves from a flood of messages each day. Microsoft Corporation (whose leader, Bill Gates, has an "unlisted" address yet still receives hundreds of email messages a day) has developed filters that block all messages except those from approved people (Gwynne & Dickerson, 1997). In other organizations, secretaries serve as filters, reviewing all emails that go to their bosses and sending along only those that are of major importance.

Despite the highly regulated nature of bureaucracy, members of formal organizations still find ways to personalize their work and surroundings. Such efforts suggest that we now take a closer look at some of the problems of bureaucracy.

PROBLEMS OF BUREAUCRACY

We rely on bureaucracy to manage countless dimensions of everyday life, but many people are uneasy about large organizations. Bureaucracy can dehumanize and manipulate us, and some say it poses a threat to political democracy.

Bureaucratic alienation. Max Weber held up bureaucracy as a model of productivity. Yet Weber was keenly aware of bureaucracy's potential to *dehumanize* the people

it is supposed to serve. The same impersonality that fosters efficiency at the same time keeps officials and clients from responding to each other's unique personal needs. Typically, officials treat each client impersonally as a standard "case."

Formal organizations create *alienation*, according to Weber, by reducing the human being to "a small cog in a ceaselessly moving mechanism" (1978:988, orig. 1921). Although formal organizations are designed to serve humanity, Weber feared that people might well end up serving formal organizations.

Bureaucratic inefficiency and ritualism. *Inefficiency*, the failure of a formal organization to carry out the work it exists to perform, is a familiar problem. Anyone who has ever tried to complain to Canada Post about a lost or damaged package, to obtain a refund for a coupon attached to a purchased item, or to convince a librarian that an overdue book has already been returned knows that bureaucracies sometimes can be maddeningly unresponsive. According to one report, government agencies responsible for buying equipment for staff can take up to three years to process a request for a new computer. This ensures that by the time the computer arrives, it is already out of date (Gwynne & Dickerson, 1997).

The problem of inefficiency is captured in the concept of *red tape*, a term derived from the ribbon used by eighteenth-century English administrators to wrap official parcels and records (Shipley, 1985). To Robert Merton (1968), red tape amounts to a new twist on the familiar concept of group conformity. He coined the term **bureaucratic ritualism** to describe *a focus on rules and regulations to the point of undermining an organization's goals.* After the terror attacks

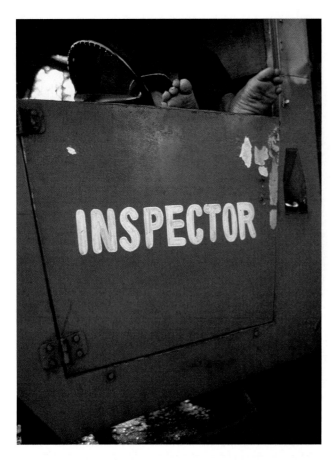

According to Max Weber, bureaucracy is an organizational strategy that promotes efficiency. Impersonality, however, also fosters alienation among employees, who may become indifferent to the formal goals of the organization. The behaviour of this municipal employee in Bombay, India, is understandable to members of formal organizations almost anywhere in the world.

in 2001, for example, the U.S. postal service continued to deliver mail addressed to Osama bin Laden to a post office in Afghanistan, despite the objections of the FBI. It took an act of Congress to change the policy (Bedard, 2002).

Bureaucratic inertia. If bureaucrats sometimes have little reason to work efficiently, they have every reason to protect their jobs. Thus, officials typically work to keep their organization going even when its goal has been realized. As Weber put it, "Once fully established, bureaucracy is among the social structures which are hardest to destroy" (1978:987, orig. 1921).

Bureaucratic inertia refers to *the tendency of bureaucratic organizations to perpetuate themselves.* Formal organizations tend to take on a life of their own beyond their formal mandate and even when their original clientele

has dwindled. This can be done, for example, by the organization taking on a broad range of work to attract a more diverse clientele. Another example is the transition that spy and military agencies have undergone since the Cold War ended: the Canadian Security Intelligence Service (CSIS) now protects us from international terrorism and economic espionage rather than from communists. Similarly, the North Atlantic Treaty Organization (NATO) now focuses on peacekeeping and humanitarian missions, and the organization includes the Czech Republic, Hungary, and Poland as member nations rather than as the foes that NATO was originally created to defend against.

Oligarchy. Early in the twentieth century, Robert Michels (1876–1936) pointed out the link between bureaucracy and political **oligarchy**, *the rule of the many by the few* (1949, orig. 1911). According to what Michels called "the iron law of oligarchy," the pyramid shape of bureaucracy places a few leaders in charge of organizational resources.

Max Weber credited a strict hierarchy of responsibility with superior organizational efficiency. Michels countered that hierarchy also undermines democracy because officials can—and often do—use their access to information, resources, and the media to promote their personal interests.

Furthermore, bureaucracy helps distance officials from the public, as in the case of the corporate president or public official who is "unavailable for comment" to the local press or the national president who claims "executive privilege" when withholding documents from scrutiny. Oligarchy, then, thrives in the hierarchical structure of bureaucracy and reduces the accountability of leaders to the people (Tolson, 1995).

Political competition, public scrutiny, and a system of checks and balances prevent Western governments from becoming an out-and-out oligarchy. Even so, some people argue that politicians should be subject to term limits because incumbents enjoy a significant advantage in politics. To illustrate, consider Canada's 2004 election. Even with spending limits and a non-partisan system for drawing districts, the system still favoured incumbents, as 83 percent were re-elected. The situation is even worse in the United States, where 99 percent of incumbents were re-elected in the same year (Pastor, 2005).

The Evolution of Formal Organizations

The problems of bureaucracy—especially the alienation it produces and its tendency toward oligarchy—stem from two organizational traits: hierarchy and rigidity. To Weber, bureaucracy is a top-down system: Rules and regulations made at the top guide every part of people's work down the chain of command. A century ago in North America, Weber's ideas took hold in an organizational model called *scientific management*. We begin with a look at this model and then examine three challenges over the course of the twentieth century that gradually led to a new model: the *flexible organization*.

SCIENTIFIC MANAGEMENT

Frederick Winslow Taylor (1911) had a simple message: Most North American businesses were sadly inefficient. The majority of managers had little idea of how to increase output, and workers relied on the same tired skills of earlier generations.

To increase efficiency, Taylor explained, business should apply the principles of science. **Scientific management** is *the application of scientific principles to the operation of a business or other large organization.*

Scientific management involves three steps. First, managers carefully observe the job performed by each worker, identifying all the operations involved and measuring the time needed for each. Second, managers then analyze their data, trying to discover ways for workers to perform each job more efficiently. For example, managers might decide to give workers different tools or reposition various work operations within the factory. Third, management provides guidance and incentives for workers to do their jobs more efficiently. If a factory worker moves 20 tonnes of pig iron in one day, for example, management would show the worker how to do the job more efficiently and then provide higher wages as the worker's productivity rises. Applying scientific principles in this way, Taylor concluded, companies become more profitable, workers earn higher wages, and in the end, consumers end up paying lower prices. Auto pioneer Henry Ford, who was enthusiastic in his support of scientific management, put it this way: "Save ten steps a day for each of 12 000 employees, and you will have saved fifty miles of wasted motion and misspent energy" (Allen & Hyman, 1999:209).

In the early 1900s, the Ford Motor Company and many other businesses followed Taylor's lead and made dramatic improvements in efficiency. As time went on, however, formal organizations faced three new challenges, involving race and gender, rising competition from abroad, and changes in the nature of work itself. Let us take a brief look at each of these challenges.

THE FIRST CHALLENGE: GENDER

In the 1960s, critics pointed out that big businesses and other organizations were inefficient—and also unfair—in their hiring practices. Rather than hiring on the basis of

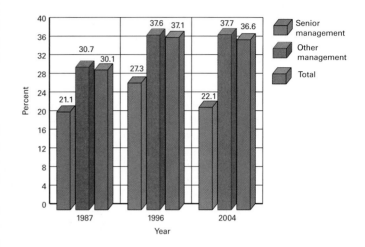

DIVERSITY SNAPSHOT

FIGURE 5-4 Women as a Percent of Total Canadians Employed in Management Positions

Source: Data from Statistics Canada, 2006d.

competence, as Weber had proposed, they routinely excluded women and other minorities. As a result, in the early 1960s, the vast majority of managers—just under 90 percent—were white men (Benoit, 2000a).

Patterns of privilege and exclusion. By 1987, 30 percent of managerial positions in Canada were held by women, and by 2004 the figure had risen to 37 percent. So even today, Canadian men still hold 63 percent of managerial jobs across the country. Moreover, all this growth in women's increased presence in management occurred in the early part of this period. The share of management positions accounted for by women actually dipped slightly between 1996 and 2004. Further, women holding managerial positions tend to be clustered in lower-level managerial positions. As Figure 5–4 shows, in 2004, women comprised only 22 percent of senior managers (Statistics Canada, 2006). The Critical Thinking box that follows discusses women's hidden burden.

Rosabeth Moss Kanter (1977; Kanter & Stein, 1979) points out that excluding women and minorities from the workplace ignores the talents of more than half the population. Furthermore, underrepresented people in an organization often feel like socially isolated out-groups:

CRITICAL THINKING

Marginalization and Women's Hidden Work Burden

Some of you might have heard of a time, not so long ago, when the food store home-delivered called-in grocery orders, when we ordered our clothes through mail-order catalogues from Eaton's or Simpsons–Sears, when attendants appeared to fill our empty gas tanks, when banks built their reputations on face-to-face services for customers, and when hospitals took pride in the bedside nursing care they provided for sick patients. But those days are no longer.

Today, we hear about the amazing efficiency and enhanced personal convenience created by the "self-service revolution." Now we can go to "clerkless" stores, where the shopper, free from the clerk's gaze, has full personal control in picking and choosing items. The only human contact left is with the checkout clerk, whose task is to scan—not to comment on or suggest additions to—one's purchases (and even the cashiers can be avoided if customers use the self-scanning checkout lanes). Warehouse stores and superstores have replaced the mail-order catalogues, corner hardware stores, and family grocery stores. These new retailers promise that with only a skeleton staff, they offer convenience, hassle-free shopping, and a greater choice of products at "rock bottom" prices. What more could we want?

As with most new developments, however, the movement from full-service to self-service is not all that it is made out to be. Who, we must ask, is this clerkless customer so much talked about by the marketing agencies? According to sociologist Nona Glaser

(1993), most clerkless customers are women from lower- and middle-class backgrounds. When the cashier replaced the salesclerk, the modern customer became the do-it-yourself buyer. As Glaser (1993:103) sees it, contrary to being free and content with her new role, the clerkless customer has actually become the unpaid "other worker" at the end of the company's chain of command. This development is even more ironic given that service has declined at a time when women with families have entered the workforce and often need extra help.

Glaser argues that the much-admired "service society" is an illusion for most women with family responsibilities, unless they have the free time and disposable income to shop at specialty stores or top-of-the-line outlets. For their less fortunate sisters, however, "[h]igh productivity in manufacturing has freed them from producing goods in the household, but not from producing services for themselves and their families. It has given them more work to do in the stores from which they buy these energy-saving goods" (pp. 103–104).

Glaser observes that a similar development is now also affecting the organization of healthcare, especially nursing services. In the U.S., the corporate takeover of medicine is already well advanced. Yet there has been much talk of late in Canada, as well, about the apparently more humane (and efficient) service that results from transferring people in hospitals, old-age homes, and mental institutions back to the commu-

nity. Such transfer depends on "home-care support." But the question that seldom gets asked is this: what does "homecare" mean in this instance (Benoit, 1998)? Who will care for the sick, the frail, and others unable to care for themselves, once they are no longer in formal institutions?

In Canada and the U.S., there are at least three likely possibilities: (1) new immigrant and visible minority women working in people's homes for low wages; (2) community volunteers, who also tend to be women; (3) dutiful sisters and daughters, whom Canadian sociologist Pat Armstrong (1994) sees as "the lowest, lowest cost care providers." In Canada, the evidence to date about the "work transfer" from nurses in public hospitals to other women in homecare is only anecdotal. But the recent cutbacks in health funding in many Canadian provinces mean that the changeover in nursing staff will increase pressure for family members to "help out"—either by doing (unpaid) shifts at the patient's hospital bedside or, better still, caring for the sick at home. For those with money to purchase private duty nurses, the situation may be disturbing but manageable. Their "carework" (including mothering, caring for elderly parents, and doing domestic work) is transferred to vulnerable women, many who are undocumented workers (Litt and Zimmerman, 2003) whose jobs are characterized by low benefits, low pay, and high turnover (Zimmerman, Litt, & Bose, 2006).

WHAT DO YOU THINK?

uncomfortably visible, taken less seriously, and given fewer chances for promotion.

Opening up an organization, Kanter claims, improves everyone's on-the-job performance by motivating employees to become "fast-trackers" who work harder and are more committed to the company. By contrast, an organization with many dead-end jobs turns workers into unproductive "zombies." An open organization also encourages leaders to seek out the ideas of everyone, which benefits the whole organization. It is officials in rigid organizations—those who have little reason themselves to be creative—who jealously guard their privileges and closely supervise their employees.

The "female advantage." Some organizational researchers argue that including more women, in particular, brings specialized management skills that strengthen an organization. According to Deborah Tannen (1994), women have a greater "information focus" and more readily ask questions in order to understand an issue. Men, by contrast, have an "image focus" that makes them wonder how asking questions in a particular situation will affect their reputation.

In another study of women executives, Sally Helgesen (1990) found three additional gender-linked patterns. First, women place greater value on communication skills and share information more than men do. Second, women are more flexible leaders who typically give their employees greater freedom. Third, women place greater emphasis on the interconnectedness of all organizational operations. She coined the term *female advantage* for these patterns, which help companies that are trying to be more flexible and democratic.

In sum, one challenge to conventional bureaucracy is increased openness and flexibility that can take advantage of everyone's experience, ideas, and creativity. The result goes right to the bottom line: greater profits.

THE SECOND CHALLENGE: THE JAPANESE WORK ORGANIZATION

In 1980, the corporate world in the United States was shaken to discover that the most popular automobile model sold in that country was not a Chevrolet, Ford, or Plymouth but the Honda Accord, made in Japan. To people old enough to remember the 1950s, the words "made in Japan" generally meant a cheap, poorly made product. But times had changed. The success of the Japanese auto industry (and shortly thereafter, companies making electronics, cameras, and other products) soon had analysts buzzing about the "Japanese organization." How else could so small a country challenge the world's economic powerhouse?

December 9, Kyoto (8:05 A.M.). After five minutes of collective warm-up, the 25 workers on the construction project next to our hotel stand in four lines. For five minutes they stand listening to something. What is it? Are they listening to the work plan for today or are they listening to an inspirational speaker? So many things are different here, even as most things are familiar.

Japanese organizations reflect that nation's strong collective spirit. That is, whereas most members of our society prize rugged individualism, the Japanese value cooperation. In effect, then, formal organizations in Japan are like very large primary groups. A generation ago, William Ouchi (1981) highlighted differences between formal organizations in Japan and in the United States. First, Japanese companies hired new workers in groups, giving everyone the same salary and responsibilities. Second, many Japanese companies hired workers for life, fostering strong loyalties. Third, many Japanese organizations trained workers in all phases of operations, again with the idea that employees will remain with the company for life. Fourth, although Japanese corporate leaders took ultimate responsibility for their organization's performance, they involved workers in "quality circles" to discuss decisions that affect them. Fifth, Japanese companies played a large role in the lives of workers, providing home mortgages, sponsoring recreational activities, and scheduling social events. These characteristics encourage loyalty among members of Japanese organizations—much more than is typically the case in countries such as Canada.

For decades, people around the world marvelled at the economic "miracle" of Japanese organizations. But the praise was premature. For one thing, the so-called Japanese Model was only ever available to workers who belonged to the core labour market, typically a privileged male core of nationals (Kiely, 1998). "The cost of employing life-time workers means an incentive to subcontract all jobs not essential to the core. The other side of the Japanese job-for-life is a majority of low-paid, fragmented peripheral workers, facing an under-funded and inadequate welfare state" (Murray, 1989:46). Further, given the recent downturn in the Japanese and some other Asian economies, the future of the core Japanese organizations remains uncertain. Does, then, the Japanese corporate model still warrant attention? Whatever the future of the model in the Japanese corporate world, there are nevertheless still important lessons to be learned, not the least of which is its people-focused strategy, which involves valuing the people who work hard to make high-performance work systems achieve (Appelbaum & Batt, 1994; Lowe, 2000).

FIGURE 5–5 Two Organizational Models

The conventional model of bureaucratic organizations has a pyramid shape, with a clear chain of command. Orders flow from the top down, and reports of performance flow from the bottom up. Such organizations have extensive rules and regulations, and their workers have highly specialized jobs. More open and flexible organizations have a flatter shape, more like a football. With fewer levels in the hierarchy, responsibility for generating ideas and making decisions is shared throughout the organization. Many workers do their jobs in teams and have a broad knowledge of the entire organization's operation.

Source: Created by the authors.

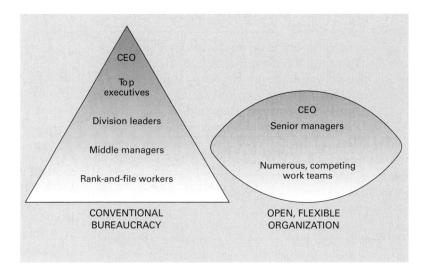

THE THIRD CHALLENGE: THE CHANGING NATURE OF WORK

Beyond rising global competition and the need to provide equal opportunity for all, pressure to modify conventional organizations is also coming from changes in the nature of work itself. In recent decades, the Canadian economy has moved from industrial to post-industrial production. In other words, rather than working in factories using heavy machinery to make *things*, more people are using computers and other electronic technology to create or process *information*. A post-industrial society, then, is characterized by information-based organizations.

Frederick Taylor developed his concept of scientific management at a time when most jobs involved tasks that, though often backbreaking, were routine. Workers shovelled coal, poured liquid iron into moulds, welded body panels to automobiles on an assembly line, or shot hot rivets into steel girders to build skyscrapers. In addition, a large part of the labour force in Taylor's day was immigrants, most of whom had little schooling and many of whom knew little English. The routine nature of industrial jobs, coupled with the limited skills of the labour force, led Taylor to treat work as a series of fixed tasks set down by management and followed by employees.

Many of today's information-age jobs are very different: The work of designers, artists, consultants, writers, editors, composers, programmers, business owners, and others now demands creativity and imagination. What does this mean for formal organizations? Here are several ways in which today's organizations differ from those of a century ago:

1. **Creative freedom.** As one Hewlett-Packard executive put it, "From their first day of work here, people are given important responsibilities and are encouraged to grow" (cited in Brooks, 2000:128). Today's organizations treat employees with information age skills as a vital resource. Executives can set production goals but cannot dictate how to accomplish tasks involving imagination and discovery. This gives highly skilled workers *creative freedom*, which means they are subject to less day-to-day supervision as long as they generate good ideas in the long run.

2. **Competitive work teams.** Many organizations give several groups of employees the freedom to work on a problem, at the same time offering the greatest rewards to the group that comes up with the best solution. Competitive work teams—a strategy first used by Japanese organizations—draw out the creative contributions of everyone and at the same time reduce the alienation often found in conventional organizations (Maddox, 1994; Yeatts, 1994).

3. **A flatter organization.** By spreading responsibility for creative problem solving throughout the workforce, organizations take on a flatter shape. That is, the pyramid shape of conventional bureaucracy is replaced by an organizational form with fewer levels in the chain of command, as shown in Figure 5–5.

4. **Greater flexibility.** The typical industrial-age organization was a rigid structure guided from the top. Such organizations may accomplish a good deal of work, but they are not especially creative or able to respond quickly to changes in their larger environment. The ideal model in the information age is a *more open, flexible* organization, one that both generates new ideas and, in a rapidly changing global marketplace, adapts quickly.

The best of today's "information-age jobs"—including working at the popular search-engine website Google—allow people a lot of personal freedom as long as they produce good ideas. At the same time, many other jobs involve the same routines and strict supervision found in factories a century ago.

As David Brooks puts it, "The machine is no longer held up as the standard that healthy organizations should emulate. Now, it's the ecosystem" (2000:128). Today's "smart" companies seek out intelligent, creative people (America Online's main building is called "Creative Center One") and encourage the growth of their talents.

Keep in mind, however, that many of today's jobs do not involve creative work at all. In reality, the post-industrial economy has created two very different types of work: highly skilled creative work and low-skilled service work. The work in the fast-food industry, for example, is routine and highly supervised and thus has much more in common with factory work of a century ago than with the creative teamwork typical of today's information organizations. Therefore, at the same time that some organizations have taken on a flatter, more flexible form, others continue to use a rigid chain of command, as the next section explains.

THE "MCDONALDIZATION" OF SOCIETY[1]

As noted in the opening to this chapter, McDonald's has enjoyed enormous success, now operating some 30 000 restaurants in Canada and around the world. Japan now has more than 2400 sets of Golden Arches, and the world's largest McDonald's is found in China's capital city of Beijing.

---

[1]The term "McDonaldization" was coined by Jim Hightower (1975); much of the material in this section is based on Ritzer (1993, 1998, 2000) and Schlosser (2002).

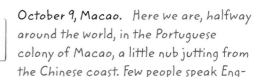 **October 9, Macao.** Here we are, halfway around the world, in the Portuguese colony of Macao, a little nub jutting from the Chinese coast. Few people speak English, and life on the streets seems a world apart from the urban rhythms of New York, Chicago, or Los Angeles. Then I turn the corner and stand face to face with (who else?) Ronald McDonald! After eating who-knows-what for many days, forgive me for giving in to the lure of the Big Mac. But the most amazing thing is that the food—the burger, fries, and drink—looks, smells, and tastes exactly the same as it does back home 15 000 kilometres away!

McDonald's can be found almost everywhere these days. In North America, in fact, it is more than a restaurant: it has become a symbol of our way of life. People around the world associate McDonald's with North America. One poll found that 98 percent of North American schoolchildren could identify Ronald McDonald, making him as well known as Santa Claus.

Even more important, the organizational principles that underlie McDonald's are coming to dominate our entire society. Our culture is becoming "McDonaldized," an awkward way of saying that many aspects of life are modelled on the famous restaurant chain. Parents buy toys at worldwide chain stores such as Toys 'R' Us; we drive in to

Jiffy Lube for a ten-minute oil change; face-to-face communication is being replaced more and more with voice mail, email, and junk mail; more vacations take the form of resort and tour packages; television presents news in the form of ten-second sound bites; university admissions officers size up students they have never met by glancing at their GPA and SAT scores; and professors assign ghostwritten textbooks[2] and evaluate students by giving tests mass-produced for them by publishing companies. The list goes on and on.

Basic principles. What do all of these developments have in common? According to George Ritzer (1993), the McDonaldization of society involves four basic organizational principles:

1. **Efficiency.** Ray Kroc, the marketing genius behind McDonald's, set out with one goal: to serve a hamburger, french fries, and a milkshake to every customer in 50 seconds or less. Today, one of the company's most popular items is the Egg McMuffin, an entire breakfast in a single sandwich. In the restaurant, customers bus their own trays or, better still, drive away from the pick-up window, taking whatever mess they make with them. Such efficiency is now central to our way of life. We tend to think that anything done quickly is, for that reason alone, good.

2. **Standardization.** The first McDonald's operating manual declared the weight of a regular raw hamburger to be 1.6 ounces, its size to be 3.875 inches across, and its fat content to be 19 percent. A slice of cheese was to weigh exactly half an ounce, and french fries were to be cut precisely 9/32 of an inch thick.

   Think about how many objects around the home, the workplace, and the campus are designed and mass-produced uniformly according to a standard plan. Not just our environment but our life experiences—from travelling the continent's highways to sitting at home viewing cookie-cutter TV shows from a handful of networks—are now more standardized than ever before.

3. **Uniformity and predictability.** A person can walk into a McDonald's restaurant almost anywhere and buy the same sandwiches, drinks, and desserts prepared in precisely the same way.[3] Uniformity results from a highly rational system that specifies every action and leaves nothing to chance.

4. **Control through automation.** The most unreliable element in the McDonald's system is human beings. After all, people have good and bad days, sometimes let their minds wander, or decide to try something a different way. To minimize the unpredictable human element, McDonald's has automated its equipment to cook food at a fixed temperature for a set length of time. Even the cash registers at McDonald's are keyed to pictures of the items so that ringing up a customer's order is as simple as possible.

   Similarly, automated teller machines are replacing banks, highly automated bakeries produce bread with scarcely any human intervention, and chickens and eggs (or is it eggs and chickens?) emerge from automated hatcheries. In supermarkets, laser scanners at self-checkouts are phasing out human checkers. Most of our shopping now occurs in malls, where everything from temperature and humidity to the kinds of stores and products are subject to continuous control and supervision (Ide & Cordell, 1994).

Can rationality be irrational? There can be no argument about the popularity or efficiency of McDonald's. But there is another side to the story.

Max Weber was alarmed at the increasing rationalization of the world, fearing that formal organizations would cage our imaginations and crush the human spirit. As he saw it, rational systems were efficient but dehumanizing. McDonaldization bears him out. Each of the four principles just discussed limits human creativity, choice, and freedom. Echoing Weber, Ritzer states that "the ultimate irrationality of McDonaldization is that people could lose control over the system and it would come to control us" (1993:145). Not surprisingly, perhaps, McDonald's itself now owns a large stake in more upscale restaurants, such as Chipotle's and Pret-à-Manger, that offer food that is more sophisticated, fresh, and healthful (Philadelphia, 2002). Read about further implications of rationality in the Controversy & Debate box that folllows.

---

[2] A number of popular sociology texts were not written by the person whose name appears on the cover. This book is not one of them.

[3] As McDonald's has "gone global," a few products have been added or changed according to local tastes. For example, in Uruguay, customers enjoy the McHuevo (hamburger with poached egg on top); Norwegians can buy McLaks (grilled salmon sandwiches); the Dutch favour the Groenteburger (vegetable burger); in Thailand, McDonald's serves Samurai pork burgers; the Japanese can purchase the Chicken Tatsuta Sandwich (chicken seasoned with soy and ginger); Filipinos eat McSpaghetti (spaghetti with tomato sauce and bits of hot dog); and in India, where Hindus eat no beef, McDonald's sells a vegetarian Maharaja Mac (Sullivan, 1995).

CONTROVERSY & DEBATE

Computer Technology, Large Organizations, and the Assault on Privacy

Late for a meeting with a new client, Sarah drives her car through a yellow light just as it turns red. A computer notes the violation, and a camera snaps a picture of the rear of the car, showing the licence plate. At the same moment, another camera photographs the side of the car, showing Sarah behind the wheel. In seven days, she receives a summons to appear in court.

Joe dials a toll-free number to check the pollen count. As he listens to a recorded message, a Caller ID computer identifies Joe and pulls up his profile from a public records database. The fact that Joe suffers from allergies is added to his profile, which is sold to a drug company, prompting the company to send Joe a free sample of a new allergy medication.

At a local department store, Nina uses her American Express card to buy an expensive new watch and some sleepwear. The store's computer adds Nina's name to its databases of "buyers of expensive jewellery" and "buyers of sexy lingerie." The store trades these databases with other companies, and within a month, Nina receives four jewellery catalogues and an adult video brochure (Bernstein, 1997; Hamilton, 2001).

Are these cases of serving the public, or are they violations of people's privacy? The answer, of course, is "both": the same systems that help organizations operate efficiently also allow them to invade our lives and manipulate us. As bureaucracy has expanded in Canada, privacy has declined.

People had little privacy in the small-town life of the past, but at least if people knew something about you, you were just as likely to know something about them. Today, unknown people "out there" can access information about any of us at any time.

In part, the loss of privacy is a result of increasingly complex computer technology. Are you aware that every time you send an email or visit a website, you leave a record in one or more computers? Most of these records can be seen by people you don't know, as well as by employers and even by police and other public officials.

Another part of today's loss of privacy reflects the increasing number and size of formal organizations. As explained in this chapter, large organizations tend to treat people impersonally, and they have a huge appetite for information. Mix large organizations with ever more complex computer technology, and it is no wonder that many people in Canada are concerned about who knows what about them—and what is being done with this information.

For decades, the level of personal privacy in our country has been declining. When the government first began issuing driver's licences, it generated a file for every licensed driver. Today, officials can dispatch this information at the touch of a button to other organizations, including police. Similarly, the Canada Revenue Agency and the federal and provincial social services all collect extensive information. Business organizations now do much the same thing, although, as these examples show, people may not be aware that their choices and activities end up in a company's database. Most people find credit cards a great convenience—the Canadian population now holds almost 50 million of them—but few people stop to think that credit card purchases automatically generate records that can end up almost anywhere.

Then there are the small cameras that are found in stores, public buildings, parking garages, and university and college campuses. The number of surveillance cameras that monitor our movements is rapidly increasing with each passing year. Such cameras may increase public safety in minor ways—say, by discouraging a mugger or even a terrorist—but only at the cost of the little privacy we have left (Walby, 2005).

Of course, some legal protections remain. The federal government and all but two provinces (Prince Edward Island and Newfoundland and Labrador) have enacted laws giving citizens rights to examine and correct records kept on them by these governments. These governments also limit the collection, use, and disclosure of personal information between government agencies, but the fact is that many private as well as public organizations now have information about us. Experts estimate that 90 percent of U.S. households are profiled in databases somewhere, and estimates for Canadian households are likely to be similar. In both countries there is public concern that current laws simply do not address the extent of the privacy problem. In the last ten years, the Internet revolution has made the problem of personal privacy more serious than ever (Crowley, 2002).

CONTINUE THE DEBATE . . .

1. Do you believe that the concern over national security is eroding privacy? Which is more important? Explain your position.
2. Internet search engines such as Yahoo! (www.yahoo.com) have "people search" programs that let you locate almost anyone. Do you think such programs pose a threat to personal privacy?
3. In your opinion, will personal privacy continue to decline in Canada in years to come? Why or why not?

Sources: Wright (1998), "Online Privacy" (2000), Rosen (2000), Hamilton (2001), and Heymann (2002).

The Future of Organizations: Opposing Trends

Early in the twentieth century, ever-larger organizations arose in Canada and other high-income countries, most taking on the bureaucratic form described by Max Weber. In many respects, these organizations were like armies led by powerful generals who passed down orders to their captains and lieutenants. Foot soldiers, working in the factories, did what they were told.

With the emergence of a post-industrial economy after 1950, as well as rising competition from abroad, many organizations evolved toward the flatter, more flexible model that encourages communication and creativity. Such "intelligent organizations" (Pinchot & Pinchot, 1993; Brooks, 2000) have become more productive than ever. Just as important, for highly skilled people who enjoy creative freedom, these organizations create less of the alienation that so worried Max Weber.

But this is only half the story. Although the post-industrial economy created many highly skilled jobs, it created even more routine service jobs, such as those offered by McDonald's. Fast-food companies now represent the largest pool of low-wage labour aside from migrant workers (Schlosser, 2002). Work of this kind—commonly called "McJobs"—offers few of the benefits that today's highly skilled workers enjoy. On the contrary, the automated routines that define work in the highly gendered fast-food industry, telemarketing, and similar fields are very much the same as those that Frederick Taylor described a century ago (Ehrenreich, 2001).

Moreover, the organizational flexibility that gives better-off workers more freedom carries, for rank-and-file employees, the ever-present threat of "downsizing" (Sennett, 1998). Organizations facing global competition are eager to attract creative employees, but they are just as eager to cut costs by eliminating as many routine jobs as possible. The net result is that some people are better off than ever while others worry about holding on to their jobs and struggle to make ends meet, a trend that Chapter 8 ("Social Stratification") explores in detail.

North American organizations remain the envy of the world for their productive efficiency. Indeed, there are few places on Earth where the mail arrives as quickly and dependably as it does in Canada. But we should remember that the future is far brighter for some than for others. In addition, as the Controversy & Debate box on page 133 explained, formal organizations pose a mounting threat to our privacy, something to keep in mind as we envision our organizational future.

To end on a positive note, we should not assume that all large formal organizations easily fit the McDonaldization thesis. This is especially the case for non-profit organizations. Take, for example, Médecins Sans Frontières—Doctors Without Borders—a large formal international organization that annually sends more than 2000 volunteers to assist in some 80 nations. The non-profit organization received the 1999 Nobel Peace Prize for its humanitarian aid. How does the principle of "lean and mean" apply to this organization that sends highly qualified volunteers to provide medical care in countries that are often violent and dangerous?

SUMMARY

1. Social groups, large and small, link members of society and perform various tasks.

2. Primary groups tend to be small and person-oriented; secondary groups typically are large and goal-oriented.

3. Instrumental leadership is concerned with realizing a group's goals; expressive leadership focuses on members' morale and well-being.

4. Because group members often seek agreement, groups can pressure members toward conformity.

5. Individuals use reference groups—both in-groups and out-groups—to evaluate situations and make decisions.

6. Georg Simmel described the dyad, a group with just two members, as intense but unstable; the three-member triad is more stable but can easily turn into a dyad with the loss of one member.

7. Peter Blau explored how group size, social diversity, and physical segregation of groups affect members' behaviour.

8. Social networks are relational webs that link people who have little common identity and limited interaction. The Internet is a vast electronic network linking millions of people worldwide.

9. Formal organizations are large secondary groups that try to perform complex tasks efficiently. They are classified as normative, coercive, or utilitarian, based on their members' reasons for joining.

10. Bureaucratic organization expands in modern societies to perform many complex tasks efficiently. Bureaucracy is based on specialization, hierarchy, rules and regulations, technical competence, impersonal interaction, and formal, written communication.

11. Technology, economic and political trends, population patterns, and other organizations are all part of the organizational environment in which a particular organization operates.

12. Ideally, bureaucracy promotes efficiency, but bureaucracy may also generate alienation and oligarchy and contribute to the erosion of personal privacy.

13. Frederick Taylor's theory of scientific management shaped North American organizations a century ago. Since then, organizations have evolved toward a more open and flexible form as they have (1) included a larger share of women and minorities; (2) responded to global competition, especially from Japan; and (3) shifted their focus from industrial production to post-industrial information processing.

14. Reflecting the collective spirit of Japanese culture, formal organizations in Japan are based more on personal ties than their North American counterparts.

15. The "McDonaldization" of society involves increasing automation and impersonality.

16. The future of organizations probably will involve opposing trends: increasing creative freedom for highly skilled information workers and increasing supervision and discipline of less-skilled service workers.

KEY CONCEPTS

bureaucracy (p. 123) an organizational model rationally designed to perform tasks efficiently

bureaucratic inertia (p. 126) the tendency of bureaucratic organizations to perpetuate themselves

bureaucratic ritualism (p. 125) a focus on rules and regulations to the point of undermining an organization's goals

dyad (p. 117) a social group with two members

expressive leadership (p. 114) group leadership that focuses on the group's well-being

formal organizations (p. 122) large secondary groups organized to achieve their goals efficiently

groupthink (p. 116) the tendency of group members to conform, resulting in a narrow view of some issue

in-group (p. 117) a social group toward which a member feels respect and commitment

instrumental leadership (p. 114) group leadership that focuses on the completion of tasks

network (p. 119) a web of weak social ties

oligarchy (p. 126) the rule of the many by the few

organizational environment (p. 124) factors outside an organization that affect its operation

out-group (p. 117) a social group toward which a person feels a sense of competition or opposition

primary group (p. 113) a small social group whose members share personal and lasting relationships

rationality (p. 122) a way of thinking that emphasizes deliberate, matter-of-fact calculation of the most efficient means to accomplish a particular task

rationalization of society (p. 122) Weber's term for the historical change from tradition to rationality as the dominant mode of human thought

reference group (p. 116) a social group that serves as a point of reference in making evaluations and decisions

scientific management (p. 127) Frederick Taylor's term for the application of scientific principles to the operation of a business or other large organization

secondary group (p. 113) a large and impersonal social group whose members pursue a specific goal or activity

social group (p. 112) two or more people who identify and interact with one another

tradition (p. 122) values and beliefs passed from generation to generation

triad (p. 117) a social group with three members

CRITICAL-THINKING QUESTIONS

1. How do primary groups differ from secondary groups? Identify examples of each in your own life.

2. According to Max Weber, what are the six characteristics of bureaucracy? In what ways do new, more flexible organizations differ from his model?

3. George Ritzer (1996:1), a critic of McDonaldization, suggests that fast-food restaurants should carry the following label:

"Sociologists warn us that habitual use of McDonald's systems are destructive to our physical and psychological well-being as well as to society as a whole." Do you agree? Why or why not?

4. The twentieth century saw the widespread use of initialisms, such as EU, IRA, IMF, IBM, RCMP, MTV, PLO, and CBC. What does this trend suggest about our future?

APPLICATIONS AND EXERCISES

1. Spend several hours observing customers at a fast-food restaurant. Think about ways in which customers as well as employees are trained to behave in certain ways. For example, customer norms include lining up to order and finding a table. Who is supposed to place garbage in waste containers? What other such norms are at work?

2. Visit a large public building with an elevator. Observe groups of people as they approach the elevator, and enter the elevator with them. Watch their behaviour: What happens to the conversations? Where do people fix their eyes? Can you account for these patterns?

3. Make a list of in-groups and out-groups on your campus. What traits account for a group's falling into each category? Ask several other people if they agree with your classifications.

4. Using available publications (and some assistance from an instructor), try to draw an "organizational pyramid" for your college or university, showing the key officials and how they supervise and report to one another.

 SITES TO SEE

www.pearsoned.ca/macionis
The authors and publisher of this book invite you to visit the interactive Companion Website™ that accompanies this text. Begin by clicking on the cover of your book. You will find a chapter-by-chapter study guide, practice tests, suggested weblinks, and links to other relevant material.

www.saturn.com
Visit the Saturn car company website to learn about Saturn's flattened organizational structure.

www.mtq.gouv.qc.ca/en/information/cameras/index.asp
Transport Quebec has many webcams in Montreal and throughout Quebec. Do you think new Internet technology of this kind threatens people's privacy? Why or why not?

http://groups.yahoo.com
At this site, people build their own social groups to chat and exchange personal information. Take a look and see what you think about "virtual groups."

Follow the instructions on page 33 of this text to access the features of Research Navigator™. Once at the website (**www.researchnavigator.com**), enter your login name and password. Then, to use the Content Select™ database, enter keywords such as "Max Weber," "bureaucracy," "social network," and "McDonald's," and the search engine will supply relevant and recent scholarly and popular press publications.

To reinforce your understanding of this chapter, and to identify topics for further study, visit MySocLab at **www.pearsoned.ca/mysoclab/macionis** for diagnostic tests and a multimedia ebook.

CHAPTER SIX

Sexuality and Society

How did the sexual revolution change Canadian society?

Why do societies control people's sexual behaviour?

What part does sexuality play in social inequality?

This kind of street dancing—common in Buenos Aires, Brazil—would probably never be seen in a city in, say, China.

Kate, Emily, and Tara stream through the door of the pizza shop a few blocks from their high school, where they have just started Grade 12. They check out the room to see who is there while pushing their bookbags beneath their favourite table, and then walk to the counter to place their order (three plain slices, three Diet Cokes). Minutes later, food in hand, the girls slide into the booth to talk about their favourite topic: sex.

Tara begins, "Now that we've had sex, Tom says I'm being a tease if we get together and I say I just want to kiss." "Me, too," Kate interrupts, scarcely waiting for her friend to finish. "It's like once you do it, you have to do it all the time! I don't know how it's supposed to be—he has a temper, and sometimes, if I don't feel like doing anything, he gets really mad." Emily, who has been listening while finishing her pizza, has not yet had sex. But listening to her friends, she is glad of that, although she would never say so (based on Mulrine, 2002).

There is nothing new about young people being interested in sex. But more of today's teens are doing more than talk—they are having sex, and at younger and younger ages. According to a recent Health Canada report (2004), *Young People in Canada: Their Health and Well-Being,* just under 20 percent of Grade 9 students in Canada in 2002 reported having had sexual intercourse. This is much lower than the rate for teens south of the border, where almost 40 percent of teens have lost their virginity by age 15.

Is more and earlier sexual activity a cause for concern? Yes, for a number of reasons. As Figure 6–1 shows, Canada has a comparatively high rate of pregnancy (births plus abortions) among teenagers when compared to some European countries, even though the rate is much lower than that of the United States. In addition, a surprisingly high number of young women are victims of sexual violence. All sexually active people (especially those with multiple partners) run the risk of infection with a sexually transmitted disease. It is also true that many young people—and a number of their parents—understand too little about sexuality to make the best choices.

But early sexual activity does not tell the whole story because there are few differences between Sweden and the United States in this regard. Rather, the big difference in access to contraceptive services and supplies between these two countries is likely causing the observed differences in pregnancy rates.

This chapter presents what researchers have learned about patterns of sexual behaviour to challenge some of the popular myths you may have heard in the local pizza shop or elsewhere. We shall examine the various ways societies define sex, the diverse ways in which people express themselves sexually, and a number of the social issues that involve sexuality, including gay rights, prostitution, and date rape.

Understanding Sexuality

How much of your day does *not* involve thoughts about sexuality? If you are like most people, the answer is "not very much," because sexuality is not just about having sex. Sexuality is a theme found throughout society—it is apparent on campus, in the workplace, and especially in the mass media. The sex industry, including pornography and prostitution, is a multibillion-dollar business in its own right. Sexuality is also an important part of how we think about ourselves as well as how others evaluate us. In truth, there are few areas of social life in which sexuality does *not* play some part.

Despite its importance, for much of our history sex has been a cultural taboo; at least in polite conversation, people usually do not even talk about it. As a result, although sex can produce much pleasure, it also causes confusion, anxi-

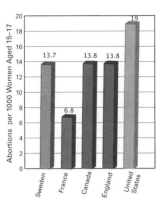

FIGURE 6-1 (a) Percentage of Women Having Had Sex by Age 18, (b) Births per 1000 Women Aged 15–17, (c) Abortions per 1000 Women Aged 15–17 (mid 1990s)

Note: Darroch et al. (2001) report that there is a significant amount of under-reporting of abortions in France.

Source: Darroch et al. (2001)

ety, and sometimes outright fear. Even scientists long considered sex off limits as a topic of research. Not until the middle of the twentieth century did researchers turn their attention to this important element of social life. Since then, as you will learn shortly, we have discovered a great deal about human sexuality.

SEX: A BIOLOGICAL ISSUE

Sex refers to *the biological distinction between females and males*. From a biological point of view, sex is the means by which humans reproduce. A woman's ovum and a man's sperm, each containing 23 chromosomes (biological codes that guide physical development), combine to form a fertilized embryo. To one of these pairs of chromosomes, which determines the child's sex, the mother contributes an X chromosome and the father contributes either an X or a Y. An X from the father produces a female (XX) embryo; a Y from the father produces a male (XY) embryo. A child's sex is determined biologically at the moment of conception.

Within weeks, the sex of an embryo starts to guide its development. If the embryo is male, testicular tissue starts to produce testosterone, a hormone that triggers the development of male genitals (sex organs). If little testosterone is present, the embryo develops female genitals. Thus, females accounted for 51 percent of the total Canadian population in 2001 (Statistics Canada, 2002f).

SEX AND THE BODY

What sets females and males apart are differences in their bodies. Right from birth, the two sexes have different **primary sex characteristics**, namely, *the genitals, organs used for reproduction*. At puberty, as people reach sexual maturity, additional sex differentiation takes place. At this point, people develop **secondary sex characteristics**, *bodily development, apart from the genitals, that distinguishes biologically mature females and males*. Mature females have wider hips for giving birth, breasts capable of producing milk for nurturing infants, and soft, fatty tissue that provides a reserve supply of nutrition during pregnancy and breastfeeding. Mature males typically develop more muscle in the upper body, more extensive body hair, and deeper voices. Of course, these are general differences; some males are smaller and have less body hair and higher voices than some females.

Keep in mind that *sex* refers to biological traits that distinguish females and males. *Gender,* by contrast, is an element of culture and refers to the personal traits and patterns of behaviour (including social opportunities and privileges) that a culture attaches to being female or male. Chapter 10 ("Gender Stratification") describes the importance of gender in social life.

Intersexed people.   Sex is not always as clear-cut as we have just described. The term **intersexed person** refers to *a*

We claim that beauty is in the eye of the beholder, which suggests the importance of culture in setting standards of attractiveness. All of the people pictured here—from Morocco, South Africa, Nigeria, Myanmar, Japan, and Ecuador—are beautiful to members of their own society. At the same time, sociobiologists point out that, in every society on Earth, people are attracted to youthfulness. The reason is that, as sociobiologists see it, attractiveness underlies our choices about reproduction, which is most readily accomplished in early adulthood.

human being with some combination of female and male genitalia. An older term for intersexed people is *hermaphrodite* (a word derived from Hermaphroditus, the child of the mythological Greek gods Hermes and Aphrodite, who embodied both sexes). A true hermaphrodite has both a female ovary and a male testis. Tens of thousands of intersexed people have been born in Canada and the U.S. with some combination of male and female genitals, and no specific pattern applies to all (Miracle, Miracle, & Baumeister, 2003).

But our culture wants sex to be clear-cut, a fact evident in the demand that parents record at birth the sex of their new child as either female or male. It is also true that some North Americans respond to intersexed people with confusion or even disgust. But in other cultures, people respond quite differently: The Pokot of Eastern Africa pay little attention to what they consider a simple biological error,

and the Navajo look on intersexed people with awe, seeing in them the full potential of both the female and the male (Geertz, 1975).

Transsexuals. **Transsexuals** are *people who feel they are one sex even though biologically they are the other.* Tens of thousands of people in North America experience the feeling of being trapped in a body of the wrong sex and a desire to be the other sex. Most become transgendered, meaning that they ignore conventional ideas about how females and males should look and behave. Many go one step further and undergo gender reassignment, surgical alteration of their genitals, usually with hormone treatment. This medical process is complex and takes months or even years, but it helps many people gain a joyful sense of becoming on the outside who they feel they are on the inside (Tewksbury &

Gagné, 1996; Gagné, Tewksbury, & McGaughey, 1997). Not all transsexuals undergo major genital surgery, however. Some "transgendered" people live with their sexual ambiguity and choose not to change their genitals. This is especially the case with female-to-male transsexuals (FTM), for whom genital surgery techniques are less satisfactorily developed than for their male-to-female (MTF) counterparts (Mackie, 1985; Devor, 1997).

SEX: A CULTURAL ISSUE

Sexuality has a biological foundation. But like all other elements of human behaviour, sexuality is also very much a cultural issue. Biology may explain some animals' mating rituals, but humans have no similar biological program. Although there is a biological "sex drive" in the sense that people find sex pleasurable and may seek to engage in sexual activity, our biology does not dictate any specific ways of being sexual any more than our desire to eat dictates any particular foods or table manners.

Cultural variation. Almost every sexual practice varies from one society to another. In his pioneering study of sexuality in the United States, Alfred Kinsey (1948) found that most couples reported having intercourse in a single position: face to face, with the woman on the bottom and the man on top. Halfway around the world, in the South Seas, most couples *never* have sex in this way. In fact, when the people of the South Seas learned of this practice from Western missionaries, they poked fun at it as the strange "missionary position."

Even the simple practice of displaying affection shows extensive cultural variation. Most people in Canada kiss in public, but the Chinese kiss only in private. The French kiss publicly, often twice (once on each cheek), and Belgians kiss three times (starting on either cheek). The Maoris of New Zealand rub noses, and most people in Nigeria don't kiss at all.

Modesty, too, is culturally variable. If a woman stepping into a bath is disturbed, what body parts does she cover? Helen Colton (1983) reports that an Islamic woman covers her face, a Laotian woman covers her breasts, a Samoan woman covers her navel, a Sumatran woman covers her knees, and a European woman covers her breasts with one hand and her genital area with the other.

Around the world, some societies restrict sexuality, and others are more permissive. In China, for example, societal norms so closely regulate sexuality that few people have sexual intercourse before they marry. The traditional cultures of many countries condemn women, but not men, who have sex before marriage. In Canada, at least in recent decades, intercourse before marriage has become the norm,

Practices for showing affection to one another vary from one culture to another. The French kiss on both cheeks; the Belgians kiss three times, alternating cheeks; the Chinese almost never kiss in public; and the Maori of New Zealand rub noses.

and some people choose to have sex even without strong commitment.

THE INCEST TABOO

When it comes to sex, do all societies agree on anything? The answer is yes. One cultural universal—an element found in every society the world over—is the **incest taboo**, *a cultural norm that forbids sex or marriage between certain relatives*. In Canada, the law, reflecting cultural mores, prohibits close relatives (including brothers and sisters, parents and children) from having sex or marrying. But in another example of cultural variation, exactly which family members are included in a society's incest taboo varies from place to place, even within our own country.

Some societies (such as the North American Navajo) apply incest taboos to the mother and others on her "side" of the family. There are also societies on record (including ancient Peru and Egypt) that have approved brother–sister marriages among the nobility (Murdock, 1965). In past decades, it was not uncommon in many parts of Newfoundland for first cousins to marry each other.

Why does some form of incest taboo exist everywhere? Part of the reason is biology: reproduction between close relatives of any species raises the odds of producing offspring with mental or physical problems. But why, of all living species, do only humans observe an incest taboo? This fact suggests that controlling sexuality between close relatives is a necessary element of *social* organization. For one thing, the incest taboo limits sexual competition

In 1925, women in Chicago were charged with indecent exposure and trucked off to the police station for wearing these "revealing" bathing suits. Today, attitudes in North America have become much more relaxed regarding matters of human sexuality.

in families by allowing sex only between intimate partners (ruling out, for example, sex between parent and child). Second, because family ties define people's rights and obligations toward one another, reproduction between close relatives would hopelessly confuse kinship; if a mother and son had a daughter, would the child consider the male a father or a brother? Third, by requiring people to "marry out," the incest taboo forges new social ties, enhances economic cooperation, and, ultimately, integrates the larger society as people look widely for partners to form new families (Lévi-Strauss, 1969).

The incest taboo has long been a sexual norm in Canada and throughout the world. But in this country, many other sexual norms have changed over time. In the twentieth century, as the next section explains, our society experienced both a sexual revolution and a sexual counter-revolution.

Sexual Attitudes in Canada

What do Canadians think about sex? Cultural orientation toward sexuality dates back to the early settlement. On one hand, most of the Europeans who came to this continent held rigid notions that, ideally, sex was only for the purpose of reproduction within marriage. Early immigrants to Upper Canada (Ontario), for example, demanded strict conformity in both attitude and behaviour, and they imposed severe penalties for any misconduct—even if the sexual "misconduct" took place in the privacy of one's home.

Efforts to regulate sexuality continued well into the twentieth century. Until 1969, for example, section 179 of

the *Criminal Code of Canada* stated the following: "Everyone is guilty of an indictable offence and liable to two years' imprisonment who knowingly, without lawful excuse or justification, offers to sell, advertises, publishes an advertisement of or has for sale or disposal any medicine, drug or article intended or represented as a means of preventing conception or causing abortion" (quoted in McLaren & McLaren, 1986:19). Today, the *Criminal Code* (159(1)) states that "every person who engages in an act of anal intercourse is guilty of an indictable offence and liable to imprisonment for a term not exceeding ten years or is guilty of an offence punishable on summary conviction." It wasn't until 1969 that an exception clause was written into the law, stating that the subsection does not apply to acts that take place in private—defined as there being only two people present in a private space—between consenting adults.

Restrictive laws are just one side of the story of sexuality in Canada. As Chapter 2 ("Culture") explains, our culture is also individualistic, and many believe in giving people freedom to do pretty much as they wish, as long as they cause no direct harm to others. Such thinking—that what people do in the privacy of their own homes is their business—makes sex a matter of individual freedom and personal choice. One of Canada's former prime ministers, the late Pierre Elliott Trudeau, while still serving as the minister of justice, stated so in what is perhaps his most famous statement while in public office: "[T]he state has no business in the bedrooms of the nation."

So which is it? Is Canada a restrictive or a permissive society when it comes to sexuality? The answer is that it is both. On one hand, many Canadians still view sexual conduct as an important indicator of personal morality. On the

FIGURE 6–2 The Sexual Revolution: Closing the Double Standard

Source: Hobart (1990).

other, sex is exploited and glorified everywhere in our culture and strongly promoted by the mass media—as if to say, "anything goes."

Within this general framework, we turn now to changes in sexual attitudes and behaviour over the course of the last hundred years. As we shall see, sexual attitudes have changed considerably over time.

THE SEXUAL REVOLUTION

Over the past century, people witnessed profound changes in sexual attitudes and practices. The first indications of this change came in the 1920s as millions of people from farms and small towns migrated to the rapidly growing cities. There, living apart from their families and meeting in the workplace, young men and women enjoyed greater sexual freedom, one reason the decade became known as the "Roaring Twenties."

In the 1930s and 1940s, the Great Depression and World War II slowed the rate of change. But in the postwar period, after 1945, Alfred Kinsey set the stage for what later came to be known as the *sexual revolution.* In 1948, Kinsey and his colleagues published their first study of sexuality in the United States, and it raised eyebrows everywhere. Although Kinsey did present some surprising results, the national uproar resulted not so much from what he said about sexual behaviour as from the fact that scientists were actually *studying sex,* a topic many people were uneasy talking about even in the privacy of their own homes.

Kinsey's two books (1948, 1953) became best-sellers because they revealed that people in North America, on average, were far less conventional in sexual matters than most had thought. These books encouraged a new openness toward sexuality, which helped set the sexual revolution in motion.

In the late 1960s, the sexual revolution truly came of age. Youth culture dominated public life, and expressions such as "if it feels good, do it" and "sex, drugs, and rock 'n' roll" summed up the new, freer attitude toward sex. Some people were turned off by the idea of "turning on," of course, but the baby boom generation, born between 1946 and 1964, became the first cohort in Canadian history to grow up with the idea that sex was part of people's lives, whether they were married or not.

Technology also played a part in the sexual revolution. The birth control pill, usually referred to simply as "the pill," introduced in 1960, not only prevented pregnancy but also made sex more convenient. Unlike a condom or a diaphragm, which has to be used at the time of intercourse, the pill could be taken anytime during the day. Now women as well as men could engage in sex without any special preparation.

The sexual revolution has special meaning for women because historically women were subject to greater sexual regulation than men. According to the *double standard,* society allows (and even encourages) men to be sexually active but expects women to be virgins until marriage and faithful to their husbands afterward. Survey data (shown in Figure 6–2) support this conclusion. Among people born in the U.S. between 1933 and 1942 (that is, people in their sixties and seventies today), 56 percent of men but just 16 percent of women report having had two or more sexual

GLOBAL MAP 6-1 Contraceptive Use in Global Perspective

The map shows the percentage of married women using modern contraception methods (such as barrier methods, contraceptive pill, implants, injectables, intrauterine contraceptive devices [IUDs], or sterilization). In general, how do high-income nations differ from low-income nations? Can you explain this difference?

Source: Data from Mackay (2000).

partners by age 20. Compare this wide gap with the pattern among those born between 1953 and 1962 (people now in their forties and fifties), who came of age after the sexual revolution. In this category, 62 percent of men and 48 percent of women say they had two or more sexual partners by age 20 (Laumann et al., 1994:198). The sexual revolution

increased sexual activity overall, but it changed behaviour among women more than among men.

Greater openness about sexuality develops as societies become richer and the opportunities for women increase. With this in mind, try to find a pattern in the global use of birth control shown in Global Map 6–1.

THE SEXUAL COUNTERREVOLUTION

The sexual revolution made sex a topic of everyday discussion and sexual activity more a matter of individual choice. However, by 1980, the climate of sexual freedom that had marked the late 1960s and 1970s was criticized by some as evidence of our country's moral decline, and the *sexual counterrevolution* began.

Politically speaking, the sexual counterrevolution was a conservative call for a return to "family values" and a change from sexual freedom back toward the sexual responsibility that had been valued by earlier generations. There was a strong push to limit sex to married couples. Critics of the sexual revolution objected not just to the idea of "free love" but to trends such as cohabitation (living together) and unmarried couples having children.

Looking back, we can see that the sexual counterrevolution did not greatly change the opinion among the majority that individuals should decide for themselves when and with whom to have a sexual relationship. But whether for moral reasons or concerns about sexually transmitted diseases, more people began limiting their number of sexual partners or choosing not to have sex at all.

 This University of Alberta website includes a program designed to help you make decisions about sexuality that are right for you: www.ualberta.ca/healthinfo/decisions/introduction.htm.

PREMARITAL SEX

In light of the sexual revolution and the sexual counterrevolution, how much has sexual behaviour in Canada and the United States really changed? One interesting trend, discussed in the opening to this chapter, involves premarital sex—sexual intercourse before marriage—among young people.

Now consider what young people do regarding premarital intercourse. For women, there has been a marked change over time. The Kinsey studies (1948, 1953; see also Laumann et al., 1994) reported that for people born in the early 1900s, about 50 percent of men but just 6 percent of women had premarital sexual intercourse before age 19. Studies of baby boomers born after World War II show a slight increase in premarital intercourse among men but a large increase—to about 33 percent—among women. The most recent studies, targeting men and women born in the 1970s, show that 76 percent of men and 66 percent of women had premarital sexual intercourse by their senior year in high school (Laumann et al., 1994:323–24). Similarly, Canadian studies show that as high a proportion as 62 percent of teenage boys and 49 percent of teenage girls are sexually active (Nelson & Robinson, 1999). A more recent Canada-wide study found that among Grade 9 students, 23 percent of boys and 19 percent of girls reported having had vaginal sexual intercourse; the rate for Grade 11 boys had increased to 40 percent and for Grade 11 girls it was even higher, as 46 percent reporting having had sexual intercourse (Council of Ministers of Education, 2003). Thus, although general public attitudes remain divided on premarital sex, this behaviour is quite widely accepted among young people.

SEX BETWEEN ADULTS

To hear the mass media tell it, Canadians are very active sexually. But do popular images exaggerate reality? According to a poll by the Angus Reid Group Inc. (1998e), the frequency of sexual activity varies widely in the Canadian population. In response to the question "How many times a month do you have sex?" the pattern breaks down like this: while on average Canadians have sex 6.2 times per month, the average is 7.5 times for Atlantic Canadians, 8.9 times for adults aged 18 to 34, 12 times for those living with a partner, and 7.3 times for high-income Canadians (defined as those with household incomes over $55 000). In short, no single pattern accurately describes sexual activity in Canada today.

We also know that sexual activity among Canadian adults is lower today (64 percent) than it was in 1984 (75 percent). But precisely why Newfoundlanders, for example, are deemed the "champions" in the nation's bedrooms (77 percent sexual activity) and British Columbians hold the unenviable position as the country's "sexual slackers"(56 percent) remains a mystery (Angus Reid Group Inc, 1998e).

Moreover, despite the widespread image of "swinging singles" promoted on television shows such as *Sex and the City*, it is actually those who are monogamous who report more sexual activity. Fixed relationships serve as a kind of "sex aid," while people who are single and more likely to go out for their entertainment are, ironically, less likely to engage in sex (Angus Reid Group Inc, 1998e).

EXTRAMARITAL SEX

What about couples having sex with someone other than their partner—that is, what people commonly call adultery (sociologists prefer more neutral-sounding terms such as "affairs" or "extramarital sex"). The research shows that Canadians' attitudes toward the acceptability of extramarital affairs also vary. A national survey shows that nearly 10 percent of married or common-law Canadians surveyed stated that they have had an extramarital affair while in their current or past relationship. Furthermore, the number jumps to close to 17 percent when asked if someone they were married to has ever had an affair. Finally, 61 percent of those surveyed answered "yes" when asked if they have a

TABLE 6-1

Reasons for Having an Extramarital Affair—Canada, 2001

Survey question: If you were to have an extramarital affair in the future, which of the following do you think would be the main reason? Would it be . . . ?

Loneliness	32%
Love	19%
Sex	18%
Don't know	13%
Other	10%
Money	7%
Power	1%

Source: Ipsos-Reid, 2001.

family member or friend who has had an affair (Ipsos-Reid, 2001). Other research shows that having an extramarital affair has become more acceptable in Canada today than it was a decade ago (Angus Reid Group Inc., 1997b).

Table 6–1 shows that Canadians don't have affairs because of sex. The top reason for which Canadians report they would have an extramarital affair is "loneliness." Those surveyed were divided about what they would do if their own spouse/partner were to be unfaithful. On the other hand, the majority said that if they knew someone else was having an affair, they would not inform the person's partner (Ipsos-Reid, 2001).

Sexual Orientation

In recent decades, public opinion about sexual orientation has shown a remarkable change. **Sexual orientation** is *a person's preference in terms of sexual partners: same sex, other sex, either sex, neither sex.* The norm in all human societies is **heterosexuality** (*hetero* is a Greek word meaning "the other of two"), *sexual attraction to someone of the other sex.* Yet in every society, a significant share of people experience **homosexuality** (*homo* is the Greek word for "the same"), *sexual attraction to someone of the same sex.* Keep in mind that people do not necessarily fall into one category or the other but may have varying degrees of sexual orientation.

The idea that sexual orientation is often not clear-cut is confirmed by the existence of a third category: **bisexuality**, *sexual attraction to people of both sexes.* Some bisexual people are attracted equally to males and females; many others

are attracted more strongly to one sex than the other. Finally, **asexuality** is *no sexual attraction to people of either sex.* Figure 6–3 places each of these sexual orientations in relation to the others.

It is important to remember that sexual attraction is not the same thing as sexual behaviour. Many people have experienced some attraction to someone of the same sex, but far fewer ever actually engage in same-sex behaviour. This is in large part because our culture discourages such actions.

Cultural systems do not value all sexual orientations equally. Throughout the world, heterosexuality is the norm because heterosexual relations permit human reproduction.

 For a summary of recent research on sexual orientation, go to http://www.davidmyers.org/Brix?pageID=16.

Even so, most societies tolerate homosexuality. Among the ancient Greeks, upper-class men considered homosexuality the highest form of relationship, partly because they looked down on women as intellectually inferior. As men saw it, heterosexuality was necessary only so they could have children; "real" men preferred homosexual relations (Kluckhohn, 1948; Ford & Beach, 1951; Greenberg, 1988).

WHAT GIVES US A SEXUAL ORIENTATION?

The question of *how* people come to have a particular sexual orientation is strongly debated. But the arguments fall into two general categories: that sexual orientation is a product of society, and that sexual orientation is a product of biology.

Sexual orientation: A product of society. This approach argues that people in any society construct a set of meanings that lets them make sense of sexuality. Therefore, an understanding of sexuality can differ from place to place and over time. As Michel Foucault (1990, orig. 1978) points out, for example, there was no distinct category of people called "homosexuals" until a century ago, when scientists and eventually the public as a whole began labelling people that way. Throughout history, many people no doubt had what we would call "homosexual experiences." But neither they nor others saw in this behaviour the basis for any special identity.

Anthropological studies show that patterns of homosexuality differ greatly from one society to another. In Siberia, for example, the Chukchee Eskimo perform a ritual during which one man dresses like a woman and does a

 The Canadian Psychological Association has a search engine where information on sexual orientation can be found, at http://www.cpa.ca/SEARCH/.

woman's work. The Sambia, who dwell in the Eastern Highlands of New Guinea, have a ritual in which young boys perform oral sex on older men in the belief that eating semen will make them more masculine. The existence of such diverse patterns in societies around the world seems to indicate that for human beings, sexual expression is socially constructed (Herdt, 1993; Blackwood & Wieringa, 1999; Murray & Roscoe, 1999).

Sexual orientation: A product of biology. A growing body of research suggests that sexual orientation is innate, or rooted in human biology in much the same way that people are born right-handed or left-handed. Arguing this position, Simon LeVay (1993) links sexual orientation to the structure of a person's brain. LeVay studied the brains of both homosexual and heterosexual men and found a small but important difference in the size of the hypothalamus, a part of the brain that regulates hormones. Such an anatomical difference, he claims, plays a part in shaping sexual orientation.

Genetics, too, may influence sexual orientation. One study of 44 pairs of brothers, all homosexual, found that 33 pairs had a distinctive genetic pattern involving the X chromosome. Moreover, the gay brothers had an unusually high number of gay male relatives, but only on their mother's side. Such evidence leads some researchers to think there may be a "gay gene" located on the X chromosome (Hamer & Copeland, 1994).

Critical review. Mounting evidence supports the conclusion that sexual orientation is rooted in biology, although the best guess at present is that both nature and nurture play a part. Remember that sexual orientation is not a matter of neat categories: most people who think of themselves as homosexual have had one or more heterosexual experiences, just as many people who think of themselves as heterosexual have had one or more homosexual experiences. Explaining sexual orientation, then, is a difficult job.

There is also a political issue here with great importance for gay men and lesbians. To the extent that sexual orientation is based in biology, homosexuals have no more choice about their sexual orientation than they do about their skin colour. If this is so, shouldn't gay men and lesbians expect the same legal protection as other groups who are discriminated against (Herek, 1991)?

HOW MANY GAY PEOPLE ARE THERE?

What share of our population is gay? This is a hard question to answer because, as we have explained, sexual orientation is not a matter of neat categories. Moreover, people are not always willing to discuss their sexuality with strangers or even family members. Pioneering sex researcher Alfred Kinsey (1948, 1953) estimated that about 4 percent of males

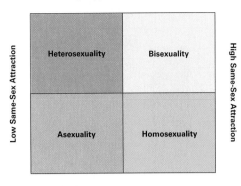

FIGURE 6–3 Four Sexual Orientations

Source: Adapted from Storms (1980).

and 2 percent of females have an exclusively same-sex orientation, although his research suggested that at least one-third of men and one-eighth of women have had at least one homosexual experience leading to orgasm.

In light of the Kinsey studies, many U.S. social scientists put the gay share of the population at 10 percent. But a more recent survey of sexuality indicates that how one operationalizes "homosexuality" makes a big difference in the results (Laumann et al., 1994). About 9 percent of U.S. men and about 4 percent of women aged 18 to 59 reported homosexual activity at some time in their lives (NORC, 2003). Though there are no comparable Canadian studies on the number of gay people, the results are likely to be about the same. The 2001 census does have data for the first time on same-sex partnerships, however. A total of 34 200 couples identified themselves in the recent census as belonging to a same-sex intimate union, which is 0.5 percent of all marital and common-law unions in the country (Statistics Canada, 2002i). Figure 6–4 shows these recent Canadian data on the percentage of people who label their sexual identity as either homosexual or bisexual.

Finally, Kinsey treated sexual orientation as an "either–or" trait: to be more homosexual was, by definition, to be less heterosexual. But same-sex and other-sex attractions can operate independently. At one extreme, then, bisexual people feel strong attractions to people of both sexes; at the other, asexual people experience little or no sexual attraction to people of either sex.

In the survey noted above, less than 1 percent of adults described themselves as bisexual. But bisexual experiences appear to be fairly common (at least for a time) among younger people, especially on university campuses (Laumann et al., 1994; Leland, 1995). Many bisexuals, then, do

DIVERSITY SNAPSHOT

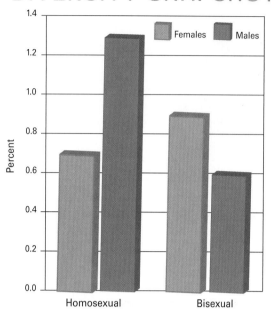

FIGURE 6–4 How Many Gay People? Canadians Aged 18–59, 2003

Source: Statistics Canada (2004a).

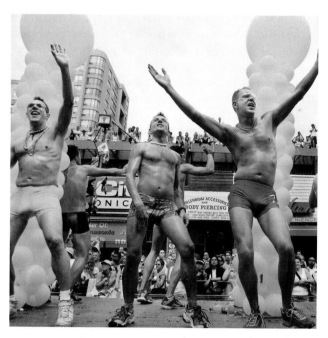

Gay parades are now a common feature in most Canadian cities despite resistance in the past by some elected officials in places like Fredericton, Hamilton, and Kelowna.

not think of themselves as either gay or straight, and their behaviour reflects elements of both gay and straight living.

THE GAY RIGHTS MOVEMENT

In the long term, the public attitude toward homosexuality is moving toward greater acceptance. In a national Canadian opinion poll (April 1998), for example, the majority in all provinces (64 percent of the population) agreed that "human rights legislation in Canada should protect gays and lesbians from discrimination based on their sexual orientation" (Angus Reid Group Inc., 1998b). This is an increase in support from a previous poll (May/June 1996), which found less public support on other gay rights issues. On the issue of same-sex spousal benefits, a majority (55 percent) of those polled said they believe that "the partners of homosexual employees should be entitled to the same spousal benefits as an employer provides to the partners of heterosexual employees," with 41 percent opposed. There was lower public support for legally recognizing same-sex marriages. When asked the question "[D]o you think homosexual couples who wish to marry should or should not qualify for legal recognition of the marriage?", 47 percent opposed and 49 percent supported the recognition.

A follow-up 2003 poll found that a slim majority—54 percent—agreed with legal recognition for same-sex marriages (Ipsos-Reid, 2003d).

In 2003, the Ontario Court of Appeal issued the first certificate of marriage to a gay couple in Canada. Since this historic moment, it is estimated that over 10 000 marriage licences have been issued to same-sex couples in Canada. Opinion polls show that Canadians have become increasingly supportive of gay "equal" marriage. A recent poll conducted by Environics Research Group (2006) asked those surveyed "whether they support equal marriage" and "whether the Conservative government should re-open the issue and have another vote or whether the issue is settled and there should not be another vote." Results show that nearly two-thirds of respondents were in favour of equal marriage and 62 percent of the respondents considered the matter settled and were thus opposed to reopening the issue and having an open vote in Parliament. Figure 6–5 shows several countries' level of acceptance of homosexuality.

In large measure, this change came about through the gay rights movement that arose in the mid-twentieth century (Chauncey, 1994). At that time, most people did not discuss homosexuality, and it was common for companies (including the federal government and the armed forces) to fire anyone who was accused of being gay. Mental health professionals, too, took a hard line, describing homosexuals as "sick" and sometimes placing them in mental hospitals where, presumably, they might be cured.

In this climate of intolerance, most lesbians and gay men remained "in the closet"—closely guarding the secret of their sexual orientation. But the gay rights movement gained strength during the 1960s. One early milestone occurred in 1973, when the American Psychological Association declared that homosexuality was not an illness but simply "a form of sexual behaviour."

The gay rights movement also began using the term **homophobia**, which describes *the fear of close personal interaction with people thought to be gay, lesbian, or bisexual* (Weinberg, 1973).

Concepts such as homophobia (literally, "fear of sameness"), and more recently "heterosexism"and "heteronormativity," turn the tables on society. Instead of asking "What's wrong with gay people?" the question becomes "What's wrong with people who can't accept a different sexual orientation?"(Martindale, 1998; Warner, 1991).

Sexual Controversies

Sexuality lies at the heart of a number of controversies in Canada today. Here we take a look at four key issues: teen pregnancy, pornography, prostitution, and sexual violence.

TEEN PREGNANCY

Being sexually active—especially having intercourse—clearly demands a high level of responsibility because pregnancy can result. Teenagers may be biologically mature, but

 Read a report from the Alan Guttmacher Institute on teenage pregnancy statistics: www.agi-usa.org/pubs/state_pregnancy_trends.pdf.

many are not socially mature and may not appreciate all the consequences of their actions. An estimated 42 161 Canadian women between the ages of 15 and 19 became pregnant in 1997 (a portion gave birth, others had an abortion, and the rest experienced fetal loss via miscarriage or stillbirth). In 1998, the teenage pregnancy rate was 41.7 pregnancies for every 1000 women aged 15 to 19, the lowest in 10 years (Statistics Canada, 2003w). In 2001, the annual rate fell further to 30.6 pregnancies for every 1000 teenage women under the age of 20 (Statistics Canada, 2004b).

These data show that the pregnancy rate among Canadian teenagers in 2001 was down by one-third from where it had been nearly three decades earlier. Yet, while Canada's rate is lower than the U.S. rate of 84 pregnancies per 1000

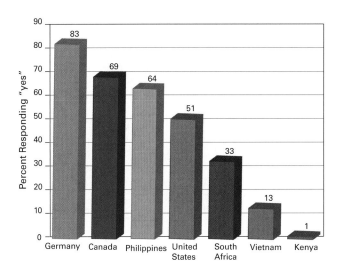

FIGURE 6–5 Acceptance of Homosexuality, 2002 Survey Question: Should homosexuality be accepted by society?

Source: Pew Research Center for the People and the Press (2003).

teenage women, many other high-income countries, including Sweden and France, have even lower teen pregnancy rates than Canada. Critics, including spokespersons from Planned Parenthood of Canada, blame the continuing comparatively high rate of unwanted teenage pregnancy in Canada on the lack of a national plan of action. Of the Canadian teens who become pregnant each year, most did not intend to do so. Pregnancy means not only that many young women (and sometimes young fathers-to-be) cannot finish school, but that they are at high risk for poverty.

Did the sexual revolution raise the rate of teenage pregnancy? Surprisingly, perhaps, the answer is no. The rate in 1950 was actually higher than the rate today, but this is because people married at a younger age back then. Also, many pregnancies led to quick marriages. As a result, there were many pregnant teenagers, but most were married women. Today, by contrast, most teenagers who become pregnant are not married. Approximately half of these women have abortions; the other half keep their babies (Voydanoff & Donnelly, 1990; Holmes, 1996b). Figure 6–6 shows the teenage pregnancy rate and live birth rate for females aged 15 to 19 in Canada from 1974 to 2003.

Concern about Canada's middle-range rate of teenage pregnancy has led to sex education programs in schools. But such programs are controversial, as the Critical Thinking box on page 153 explains.

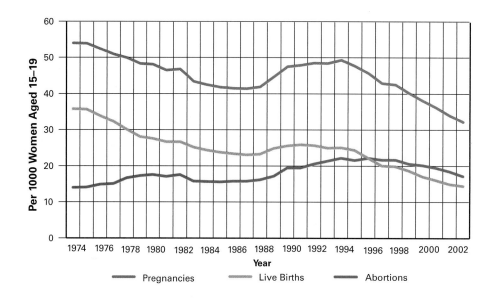

FIGURE 6-6 Teenage Pregnancies, Abortions, Live Births Canada, 1974–2003

Source: Statistics Canada (2006e, 2006f, 2006g, 2006h).

PORNOGRAPHY

In general terms, **pornography** is *sexually explicit material that causes sexual arousal*. But what—exactly—is pornographic and what separates it from erotica has long been a matter of heated debate. Recognizing that people view the portrayal of sexuality differently, the Canadian Supreme Court gives local communities the power to decide for themselves what violates "community standards" of decency and lacks any redeeming social value.

Child pornography is a very different matter, however. Section 163.1 of the *Criminal Code* states that "every person who possesses any child pornography is guilty of either a) an indictable offence and liable to imprisonment for a term not exceeding five years; or b) an offence punishable on summary conviction." Yet enforcement of even this law has proven to be difficult. In 1999 the BC Court of Appeal struck down subsection 4 of section 163.1 of the *Criminal Code*, which makes the possession of child pornography a criminal offence, because the subsection contravened the *Charter of Rights and Freedoms*. In January 2000, the Supreme Court of Canada heard arguments in an appeal of the BC court decision. During a retrial in March 2002, the

presiding judge concluded that the written document of the accused, which consisted of 17 short stories describing man–boy and boy–boy sex—including sadism, masochism, and fellatio—was "artistic" and thus not in violation of the child pornography law. The accused was, however, found guilty of the more minor offence of possessing child pornography and given a minimal sentence of house arrest for four months.

Supreme Court decisions aside, pornography and erotica are popular in Canada: X-rated videos, "900" telephone numbers for sexual conversations, and a host of sexually explicit movies and magazines together constitute a multi-billion-dollar-a-year industry. One-third of Canadians report having watched X-rated movies, and 20 percent of Canadians say that they read erotic literature or magazines (Angus Reid Group Inc., 1998e). The figure is rising as people buy more and more pornography from thousands of sites on the web.

Yet pornography has its critics. Some claim pornography is a power issue because it endorses the cultural ideal of men as the legitimate controllers of both sexuality and women (MacKinnon, 1987). While it is difficult to

CRITICAL THINKING
Sex Education: Problem or Solution?

Most schools today have sex education programs that teach the basics of sexuality. Instructors explain to young people how their bodies grow and change, how reproduction occurs, and how to avoid pregnancy by using birth control or abstaining from sex.

Because nearly half of Canadian teenage boys and girls report having had sexual intercourse by Grade 11 (Wadhera & Millar, 1996; Council of Ministers of Education, 2003; Boyce, Doherty, MacKinnon, & Fortin, 2003), "sex ed" programs seem to make sense. But critics point out that as the scope of sex education programs has expanded, the level of teenage sexual activity has actually gone up. This trend seems to suggest that sex education may not be discouraging sex among youngsters; on the contrary, learning more about sex may encourage young people to become sexually active sooner. Critics also say that it's parents who should be instructing their children about sex since, unlike teachers, parents can also teach their beliefs about what is right and wrong.

But supporters of sex education counter that there are many other influences apart from sex education that shape sexual activity among youth, not the least of which are peers and the media. Further, it is unrealistic to expect that in a culture that celebrates sexuality, children will not become sexually active. If this is the case, the sensible strategy is to ensure that they understand what they are doing and take reasonable precautions to protect themselves from unwanted pregnancy and sexually transmitted infections. The statistics show that it is comprehensive sex education—not abstinence promotion—that is linked to lower teen pregnancy rates in countries such as Sweden and France (Maticka-Tyndale, Bajos, Wellings, Danielsson, & Darroch, 2001). There the focus is on preventing HIV, STDs, and pregnancy; on contraceptives and where to obtain them; and on respect and responsibility within relationships. There are some encouraging data—only about 7 percent of Grade 9 to 11 Canadian female students reported not using any type of contraceptive measure the last time that they had sexual intercourse. However, the comparable figures for teen boys were less encouraging—18 percent for those in Grade 9 and 17 percent for those in Grade 10 (Boyce, 2004).

WHAT DO YOU THINK?

1. Schools can teach the facts about sexuality. But do you think they can address the emotional issues that often accompany sex? What about the moral issues? Why or why not?

2. What about parents? Are they doing their job as far as instructing children about sex? Ask members of your class how many received instruction in sexual matters from their parents.

3. Overall, do you think young people know too little about sexuality? Do you think they know too much? What specific changes would you suggest to address the problem of unwanted pregnancy among teens?

Sources: Gibbs (1993); Stodgill (1998); Wadhera & Millar (1996); Dryburgh (2000); Council of Ministers of Education (2003); Boyce, Doherty, MacKinnon, & Fortin (2003); Maticka-Tyndale, Bajos, Wellings, Danielsson, & Darroch (2001); Boyce (2004).

document a scientific cause-and-effect relationship between what people view and how they act, research does support the idea that pornography makes men think of women as objects rather than as people (Malamuth & Donnerstein, 1984; Attorney General's Commission on Pornography, 1986). The public share a concern about pornography and violence, with many laypeople, as well as feminist researchers, holding the opinion that pornography encourages people to commit rape (Russell, 1998).

Though people everywhere object to sexual material they find offensive, many also value free speech and want to protect artistic expression. Nevertheless, pressure to restrict pornography is building from an unlikely coalition of conservatives (who oppose pornography on moral grounds), progressives (who condemn it for political reasons), and feminists (who argue that it justifies men's oppression of women by making females into sex objects to be viewed for men's pleasure).

PROSTITUTION

Prostitution is *the selling of sexual services.* Often called "the world's oldest profession," prostitution has always been widespread, and about one in five adult men in the United States reports having paid for sex at some time (NORC, 2001:1135). Comparative data for Canada are lacking, but one Canadian survey found that 4 percent of male respondents admitted having paid for sexual favours one or more times (Peat Marwick, 1984). A more recent poll found that an even smaller number—2 percent—of Canadians have ever visited an erotic massage parlour, hired a sex worker, or used an escort service (Angus Reid Group Inc., 1998e). Even so, to the extent that people think of sex as an expression of interpersonal intimacy, they find the idea of sex for money disturbing. Even in this regard, however, there are no cross-cultural universals.

Prostitution is actually not illegal in Canada. Rather, sex workers in Canada are arrested, prosecuted, and sometimes convicted not because they sell sex for money but because they "communicate" in a public place for the purpose of engaging in prostitution (Shaver, 1993; Hackler, 1999). Meanwhile in Sweden, a recent law makes it legal for sex workers to sell sex but illegal for "johns" (customers) to purchase it (Boethus, 1999). The common belief in Canada is that "sex workers" or "sex industry workers" (less stigmatizing terms than "prostitutes") are almost always female rather than male and are more culpable and blameworthy than their customers. Regulatory strategies are much more likely to concentrate on women who sell sex rather than on their male customers, because of the assumption that most customers are "square johns who would not otherwise fall afoul with the law, while prostitutes are members of a criminal underclass whose lifestyle involves various types of law breaking" (Lowman, 1990:63–4). Consequently, as it is socially constructed and legally enforced, prostitution in Canada remains biased against women and in favour of men (Shaver, 1993; Boritch, 1997).

Around the world, prostitution also shows tremendous variation: sex workers in The Netherlands and Germany not only have legal rights to work but also pay taxes and collect social benefits that accompany most legitimate jobs. In Queensland and Victoria, Australia, brothels may operate legally if their owners and operators are investigated and licensed by state-level government and if the local council approves the brothel premises under town planning guidelines. The *Prostitution Reform Act 2003* was passed in New Zealand with the main aim of decriminalizing most aspects of sex industry work at the national level and enhancing the working conditions and health and safety of legal adult residents working in the sex industry. On the other hand, in low-income countries where patriarchy is strong and traditional cultural norms limit women's ability to earn a living, prostitution may be the only option available for women to provide for their own and their children's survival. Global Map 6-2 shows where in the world prostitution is most widespread

Types of prostitution. Most sex workers are women (estimates range from 70 to 80 percent), but they fall into different categories. Call girls (and, more rarely, call boys) are elite sex workers who are typically young, attractive, and

well educated and arrange their own "dates" with clients by telephone. The classified pages of any large city newspaper contain numerous ads for "escort services," by which women (and sometimes men) offer both companionship and sex for a fee.

A middle category of sex workers is located in "massage parlours" and brothels, which are under the control of managers. These sex workers have less choice about their clients, receive less money for their services, and get to keep no more than half of what they earn.

At the bottom of the sex-worker hierarchy are streetwalkers, women and men who "work the streets" of large cities. Some female streetwalkers are under the control of male pimps who take most of their earnings. Many streetwalkers fall victim to violence from pimps and clients (Gordon & Snyder, 1989; Davidson, 1998). Canadian research shows that sex workers located in off-street "escort agencies" tend to enjoy safer, more stable, and more lucrative work conditions than do their counterparts working on the street (Lowman & Fraser, 1995; Brock, 1998; Lewis & Maticka-Tyndale, 1999). Other research on off-street as well as on-street sex work supports this general finding but also shows that in the absence of even minimum work standards, workers in escort agencies and massage parlours and other indoor employment venues have no legal avenue to protect themselves when subject to exploitation by their employers (Benoit & Millar, 2001; Phillips & Benoit, 2005).

Most, but not all, sex workers offer heterosexual services. Gay prostitutes also trade sex for money. Researchers report that many gay sex workers have suffered rejection by family and friends because of their sexual orientation (Weisberg, 1985; Boyer, 1989; Kruks, 1991). Research on transgendered sex workers in the San Francisco Tenderloin area suggests that they face a similar situation of discrimination and rejection because of their sexual orientation (Weinberg, Shaver, & Williams, 2000).

A victimless crime? Prostitution is against the law in many countries, but many people consider it a victimless crime (see Chapter 7, "Deviance"). Consequently, instead of enforcing prostitution laws all the time, police stage only occasional crackdowns. This policy reflects a desire to control prostitution while assuming that nothing will totally eliminate it.

Is selling sex a victimless crime that hurts no one? Certainly, many people take this position, arguing that prostitution should be viewed as an occupation, as a way to make a living (Elias, Bullough, Elias, & Elders, 1998; Scambler & Scambler, 1997). Further, because of difficulties in getting jobs that provide a decent wage for marginalized people, in particular working-class female single parents, the sex trade represents a viable choice from their perspective (Chapkis,

WINDOW ON THE WORLD

GLOBAL MAP 6–2 Prostitution in Global Perspective

Generally speaking, prostitution is widespread in societies where women have low standing. Officially, at least, the People's Republic of China boasts of gender equality, including the elimination of "vice" such as prostitution, which oppresses women. By contrast, in much of Latin America, where patriarchy is strong, prostitution is common. In many Islamic societies patriarchy is also strong, but religion is a counterbalance, so prostitution is limited. Western high-income nations have a moderate amount of prostitution.

Sources: *Peters Atlas of the World* (1990) and Mackay (2000).

1997). However because it is a semi-illegal and illegitimate occupation in Canada, it is very difficult for sex workers to receive the same benefits and rights as other workers, such as sick leave, health insurance, social insurance, or workers'

Check out the Trafficking Project for research on the situation in Thailand and other Asian countries: www.unescobkk.org/culture/trafficking/publication.htm.

compensation (Shaver, 1993; Lowman & Fraser, 1995; Lewis & Maticka-Tyndale, 1999). But it is

A lot of campus rapes start here.

Whenever there's drinking or drugs, things can get out of hand.
So it's no surprise that many campus rapes involve alcohol.

But you should know that under any circumstances, sex without
the other person's consent is considered rape. A felony, punishable
by prison. And drinking is no excuse.

That's why, when you party, it's good to know what your limits are.
You see, a little sobering thought now can save you from a big
problem later.

© 1990 Rape Treatment Center, Santa Monica Hospital

Experts agree that one factor that contributes to the problem of
sexual violence on college and university campuses is the
widespread use of alcoholic beverages. What policies are in force
at your school to discourage the kind of drinking that can lead to
one person imposing sex on another?

also true that prostitution subjects many women to abuse
and outright violence, and plays a part in spreading STDs in
some nations.

SEXUAL VIOLENCE: SEXUAL ASSAULT AND DATE RAPE

Ideally, sexual activity occurs within a loving relationship,
but sex can sometimes be twisted by hatred and violence.
Here we consider two types of sexual violence: sexual
assault and date rape.

Sexual assault. Although some people think that sexual
assault is motivated only by a desire for sex, it is actually an
expression of power, a violent act that uses sex to hurt,
humiliate, or control another person. For many reasons it is
hard to collect accurate data on sexual assault. According to
the 1993 Violence Against Women Survey (Statistics Canada,

1993b), 40 percent of Canadian women have experienced at
least one incident of sexual assault since the age of 16, and
2 million Canadian women aged 18 and over have been sexually assaulted by a stranger since turning 16. Data from the
Canadian Centre for Justice Statistics indicates that 11 percent of female victims of crime in Canada in 1998 were victims of sexual assault, and 85 percent of the victims of sexual
assault were women (Statistics Canada, 2000m). More recent
data report similar findings (Statistics Canada, 2003x).
Remember that these crime statistics reflect only the
reported cases. The actual number of sexual assaults is therefore probably much higher (McCormick, 1994).

Sexual assault is a comprehensive term referring to
non-consensual sexual activity ranging from sexual touching, kissing, and sexual intercourse, to sexual violence
against a person's will. While men constitute 15 percent of
sexual assault victims, females and children make up a disproportionate share. In 2002, 61 percent of all victims of
sexual assault reported to the police in Canada were children and youth under 18 years of age and the highest rate of
sexual assault occurs for girls 13 years of age (Statistics
Canada, 2003x).

Date rape. A common myth is that rape involves strangers.
In reality, however, only about 30 percent of rapes fit this pattern. On the contrary, about 70 percent of rapes involve people who know one another—more often than not, pretty
well—and these crimes usually take place in familiar surroundings, especially the home. The term "date rape" or
"acquaintance rape" refers to forcible sexual violence against
women by men they know (Laumann et al., 1994).

A second myth, often linked specifically to date rape, is
the idea that a woman who has been raped must have done
something to encourage the man and make him think she
wanted to have sex. Perhaps the victim agreed to go out with
the offender. Maybe she even invited him into her room.
But of course, acting in this way no more justifies rape than
it would any other kind of physical assault.

Rape is a physical assault, but it also leaves emotional
and psychological scars. Beyond the brutality of being physically violated, rape by an acquaintance also undermines a
victim's sense of trust. Psychological scars are especially
serious among rape victims who are under 18, many of
whom are attacked by their own male relatives.

How common is date rape? Nowhere has date rape
been more of an issue than on the campus. The collegiate
environment brings students together in casual settings and
encourages trust. At the same time, many young people
have much to learn about relationships and about themselves. So while university and college life promotes
communication, it also invites sexual violence. A survey of
1853 university women across 44 Canadian campuses in

When Sex Is Only Sex: The Campus Culture of "Hooking Up"

Have you ever been in a sexual situation and not been sure of the right thing to do? What are the social norms on campus for sexual relationships? Most colleges and universities highlight two important rules. First, sexual activity must take place only when both participants have given clear statements of consent. The consent principle provides a clear distinction between having sex and date rape. Second, because sexual activity can spread disease, no one should knowingly expose a partner to a sexually transmitted infection, especially when that partner is unaware of the danger.

These rules are very important; yet they say little about the larger issue of what sex *means*. For example, when is it appropriate to have a sexual relationship? Does agreeing to have sex with someone mean you really like that person? Are you obligated to see the person again?

Two generations ago, there were informal rules for campus sex. In ideal terms, dating was considered part of the courtship process. That is, "going out" was a way in which women and men evaluated each other as possible marriage partners while they sharpened their own sense of what they wanted in a mate. Because, on average, marriage took place at a younger age, a number of students became engaged and married while they were still in school. Having "honourable intentions" meant that sex was a sign of a serious—potentially

marital—interest in the other person.

Of course, not all sexual activity fell under the umbrella of courtship. A fair share of men (and some women, too) have always looked for sex where they could find it. But in an era that linked sex and courtship, casual sex could easily lead to one partner feeling "used."

Today, the sexual culture of the campus is very different. Partly because people now marry much later, the culture of courtship has declined dramatically. About three-fourths of women in a recent U.S. national survey point to a new campus pattern, the culture of "hooking up." What is "hooking up"? Most describe it in words like these: "When a girl and a guy get together for a physical encounter—anything from kissing to having sex—and don't necessarily expect anything further."

Student responses to the survey suggest that "hook-ups" have three characteristics. First, most couples who hook up know little about each other. Second, a typical hook-up involves people who have been drinking alcohol, usually at a campus party. Third, most women are critical of the culture of hooking up and express little satisfaction with these encounters. Certainly, some women (and men) who hook up simply walk away, happy to have enjoyed a sexual experience free of further obligation. But given the powerful emotions that sex can unleash, hooking up often leaves at

least one of the partners wondering what to expect next. "Will you call me tomorrow?" "Will I see you again?"

The survey asked women who had experienced a recent hook-up to report how they felt, a day later, about the experience. A majority of respondents said they felt "awkward," while about half felt "disappointed" and "confused," and one in four said they felt "exploited." Clearly, for many people, sex involves something more than a physical encounter. Further, because today's campus is very sensitive to charges of sexual exploitation, there is a definite need for clearer standards of fair play.

WHAT DO YOU THINK?

1. How prevalent is hooking up on your campus? Are you aware of differences between heterosexual and homosexual encounters in this regard?

2. What are the advantages of sex without commitment? What are the disadvantages of this kind of relationship? Do you think your answers depend in part on whether you are male or female? Why or why not?

3. Do you think university and college students need more guidance about sexual issues? If so, who should provide this guidance?

Source: Based in part on Marquardt & Glenn (2001).

MEDIA

The University of Alberta has a website devoted to sexual assault resources: **www.uofaweb.ualberta.ca/sac/ index.cfm**.

1993 showed that 28.8 percent had been sexually abused in the previous year (Boritch, 1997:215). As the Applying Sociology box explains, while university life encourages commu-

nication, it also provides few social norms that help guide young people's sexual experiences. To counter the problem, many schools now actively address myths about rape. In addition, greater attention is now focused on the use of alcohol, which increases the likelihood of sexual violence.

APPLYING THEORY
SEXUALITY

	Structural-Functional Approach	Symbolic-Interaction Approach	Social-Conflict Approach
What is the level of analysis?	Macro-level	Macro-level	Micro-level
What is the importance of sexuality for society?	Society depends on sexuality for reproduction. Society uses the incest taboo and other norms to control sexuality in order to maintain social order.	Sexuality is linked to social inequality. Canadian society regulates women's sexuality more than men's, which is part of the larger pattern of men dominating women.	Sexual practices vary among the many cultures of the world. Some societies allow individuals more freedom than others in matters of sexual behaviour.
Has sexuality changed over time? How?	Yes. As advances in birth control technology separate sex from reproduction, societies relax some controls on sexuality.	Yes and no. Some sexual standards have relaxed, but society still defines women in sexual terms, just as homosexual people are harmed by society's heterosexual bias.	Yes. The meanings people attach to virginity and other sexual matters are all socially constructed and subject to change.

Theoretical Analysis of Sexuality

Applying sociology's various theoretical approaches gives us a better understanding of human sexuality. The following sections discuss the three major approaches. The Applying Theory table highlights the key insights of each approach.

STRUCTURAL-FUNCTIONAL ANALYSIS

The structural-functional approach emphasizes the contribution of any social pattern to the overall operation of society. Because sexuality is an important element of social life, society must regulate sexual behaviour.

The need to regulate sexuality. From a biological point of view, sex allows our species to reproduce. But culture and social institutions regulate *with whom* and *when* people reproduce. For example, as you have already learned, most societies condemn married people who have sex with someone other than their spouse. To do otherwise—to allow the forces of sexual passion to go unchecked—would threaten family life and, especially, the raising of children.

The fact that the incest taboo exists everywhere shows clearly that no society is willing to permit completely free choice in sexual partners. Reproduction resulting from sex between family members other than married partners would break down the system of kinship and hopelessly confuse human relationships.

Historically, the social control of sexuality was strong, mostly because sex inevitably led to childbirth. We see this in the old-fashioned distinction between "legitimate" reproduction (within marriage) and "illegitimate" reproduction (outside marriage, or "out of wedlock"). But once a society develops the technology to control births, its sexual norms become more permissive. This occurred in Canada, where, over the course of the twentieth century, sex moved beyond its basic reproductive function and became a form of intimacy and even recreation (Giddens, 1992).

Latent functions: The case of prostitution. Previously we saw why critics see prostitution as harmful. But are there latent functions that help explain why prostitution is so widespread? According to Kingsley Davis (1971), prostitution performs several useful functions. It is one way to meet the sexual needs of a large number of people who do not have ready access to sex, including soldiers, travellers, and people who are not physically attractive or who have trouble establishing relationships. Some people favour prostitution because they want sex without the "trouble" of a relationship. As one analyst said of prostitution, "Men don't pay for sex; they pay so they can leave" (Miracle, Miracle, & Baumeister, 2003:421).

Critical review. The structural-functional approach helps us appreciate the important role sexuality plays in the organization of society. The incest taboo and other cultural norms also suggest that society has always paid attention to who has sex with whom, especially who reproduces with whom.

At the same time, this approach pays little attention to the great diversity of sexual ideas and practices found within every society. In addition, the fact that sexual patterns change over time, just as they differ in remarkable ways around the world, is ignored by this perspective. To appreciate the varied and changeable character of sexuality, let us turn to the symbolic-interaction approach.

SYMBOLIC-INTERACTION ANALYSIS

The symbolic-interaction approach highlights how, as people interact, they construct everyday reality. As explained in Chapter 4 ("Social Interaction in Everyday Life"), reality construction is a highly variable process, so the views of one group or society may well differ from those of another. In the same way, our understanding of sexuality can and does change over time.

The social construction of sexuality. Almost all social patterns involving sexuality changed over the course of the twentieth century. One good illustration is the changing importance of virginity. A century ago, our society's norm—for women, at least—was virginity until marriage. This norm was strong because there was no effective means of birth control, and virginity was the only assurance a man had that his bride-to-be was not carrying another man's child. Today, because we have gone a long way toward separating sex from reproduction, the virginity norm has weakened considerably.

Another example of our society's construction of sexuality involves young people's awareness of sex. A century ago, childhood was a time of innocence in sexual matters. In recent decades, however, thinking has changed. Although few people encourage sexual activity between children, most people believe children should be educated about sex so that they can make intelligent choices about their behaviour as they grow older.

The control of women's sexuality is a common theme in human history. During the Middle Ages, Europeans devised the "chastity belt"—a metal device locked about a woman's groin that prevented sexual intercourse (and probably interfered with other bodily functions as well). While such devices are all but unknown today, the social control of sexuality continues. Can you point to examples?

Global comparisons. Around the world, different societies attach different meanings to sexuality. For example, the anthropologist Ruth Benedict (1938), who spent years learning the ways of life of the Melanesian people of Southeastern New Guinea, reported that adults paid little attention when young children engaged in sexual experimentation with one another. Parents in Melanesia shrugged off such activity because before puberty, sex cannot lead to reproduction. Is it likely that most parents in Canada would respond the same way?

Sexual practices also vary from culture to culture. Male infant circumcision (the practice of removing all or part of the foreskin of the penis) is common in Canada and the United States but rare in most other parts of the world, including European countries. A practice sometimes referred to as female circumcision but more accurately called "female genital mutilation" (involving the removal of the clitoris and sometimes much of the labia) is rare in Canada but common in parts of Africa and the Middle East (Crosette, 1995; Huffman, 2000).

The Abortion Controversy

A black van pulls up in front of the store-front in a busy section of the city. Two women get out of the front seat and cautiously scan the sidewalk. After a moment, one nods to the other, and they open the rear door to let a third young woman out of the van. Standing to the right and left of their charge, the two quickly whisk her inside the building.

Is this a description of two RCMP officers escorting a convict to a police station? It might be. But it is actually an account of two clinic workers escorting a young woman who has decided to have an abortion. Why should they be so cautious? Anyone who has read the papers in recent years knows about the heated confrontations taking place at abortion clinics across Canada and the United States. In fact, some opponents have even targeted and killed several doctors who perform abortions. Overall, abortion is probably the most hotly contested issue in North America today.

Abortion has not always been so controversial. During the colonial era, midwives and other healers performed abortions with little community opposition and with full approval of the law. But controversy arose in the course of the nineteenth century, not just in Canada but throughout the Western world (Prentice et al., 1996). Middle class reformists worried that the Anglo Saxon population was facing "race suicide," not just because of abortions but also, as noted

earlier in the chapter, due to the use of other forms of birth control (McLaren & McLaren, 1986). Ultimately the federal government passed legislation—in force until 1969—that made abortion illegal.

Such laws did not end abortion, but they greatly reduced the number of abortions. In addition, these laws drove abortion underground, so that many women—especially those who were poor—had little choice but to seek help from unlicensed "back alley" abortionists, sometimes with tragic results. In British Columbia alone, abortion-related mortalities were responsible for 20 percent of all maternal deaths between 1946 and 1968 (McLaren & McLaren, 1986:52–53).

In light of these and other developments, opposition to Canada's abortion law rose throughout the 1960s until, in 1969, the federal government amended the provisions of the *Criminal Code* dealing with contraception and abortion. Yet the criminality surrounding abortions still remained, since the amendment permitted abortion only when performed by a doctor in an accredited hospital under specified conditions. Dr. Henry Morgentaler defied the law by offering abortion services to women in private clinics in a number of Canadian cities (Morton, 1993). The *Charter of Rights and Freedoms* finally provided the opportunity for the Supreme Court in 1988 to strike down as unconstitutional the federal law

on abortion. A new abortion bill—C-43, making abortion illegal unless a doctor certified that the woman's life was in danger—was passed by the House of Commons but was narrowly defeated in the Senate. The result: abortion was left to the provinces to regulate under their own health policies. Since then, the abortion rate has risen, partly due to the increase in the number of out-of-hospital abortion clinics now operating in many provinces. In 1999, the total abortion rate (procedures in both hospitals and freestanding clinics) was 31.8 per 100 live births, which was a decrease from 32.3 in 1998 (the rate does not include Ontario due to changes in reporting requirements at the time of the survey) (Statistics Canada, 2002j).

Even so, the abortion controversy continues. On one side of the issue are people who describe themselves as "pro-choice," supporting a woman's right to choose abortion. On the other side are those who call themselves "pro-life," opposing abortion as morally wrong. These people would like to see the re-criminalization of abortions across the country.

How strong is the support for each side of the abortion controversy? A Gallup Poll (Hartley & Mazzuca, 2001) asked a sample of Canadians the question "Do you think that abortion should be legal under any circumstance, legal only under certain circumstances, or illegal in all circumstances?" In response, 32 percent

Critical review. The strength of the symbolic-interaction approach lies in revealing the constructed character of familiar social patterns. Understanding that people "construct" sexuality, we can better appreciate the variety of sexual attitudes and practices found over the course of history and around the world.

One limitation of this approach is that not everything is so variable. Throughout our own history—and around the world—men are more likely to see women in sexual terms than the other way around. If this pattern is widespread, some broader social structure must be at work, as we shall see in the following section on the social-conflict approach.

said yes to abortion being legal in all circumstances. Fifty-two percent expressed the opinion that abortion should be available only in certain circumstances, such as when a woman's health is in danger or she has a very low income. Up slightly from 2000, 14 percent of those polled would ban abortions in all circumstances, and 2 percent had no opinion on the abortion issue.

A closer look, however, shows that particular circumstances make a big difference in how people see this issue. Figure 6–7 shows that an increasingly large majority of Canadian adults favour legal abortion if a pregnancy seriously threatens a woman's health (96 percent), if she became pregnant as a result of rape or incest (89 percent), or if a fetus is very likely to have a serious defect (75 percent). The bottom line is this: between 25 and 33 percent of Canadians support access to abortion under any circumstances, but about 85 percent support access to abortion under some circumstances.

Many pro-life people feel strongly that abortion is nothing more than killing unborn children. To them, people never have the right to end innocent life in this way. But pro-choice people are no less committed to their position. As they see it, the abortion debate is really about the standing of women in society. Why? Because, they believe, women must have control over their own sexuality. If pregnancy dictates the course of women's lives, women will never be able to compete with men on equal terms, whether on campus or in the workplace. Thus, the pro-choice position concludes, women must have access to legal, safe abortion as a necessary condition to full participation in society.

CONTINUE THE DEBATE . . .

1. The more conservative pro-life people see abortion as a moral issue, while more liberal pro-choice people see abortion as a power issue. Can you see a parallel to how conservatives and liberals view the issue of pornography?
2. Surveys show that men and women have almost the same opinions about abortion. Does this surprise you? Why?
3. Why do you think the abortion controversy is often so bitter? Why has our nation been unable to find a middle ground on which all can agree?

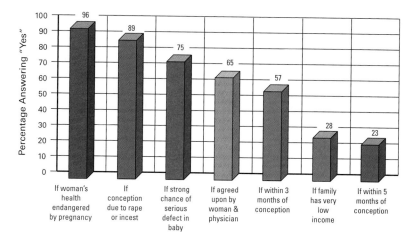

FIGURE 6–7 Acceptable Circumstances for Abortion, Canada, 2001

Source: Hartley and Mazzuca (2001).

Source: Based, in part, on Luker (1984), Tannahill (1992), and various news reports.

SOCIAL-CONFLICT ANALYSIS

As you have seen in previous chapters, the social-conflict approach highlights dimensions of inequality. Therefore, this approach shows how sexuality reflects patterns of social inequality and also how it helps perpetuate them.

Sexuality: Reflecting social inequality. Recall our discussion of prostitution, a practice outlawed in many countries and stigmatized in most. Enforcement is uneven at best, especially when it comes to who is and is not likely to be arrested. Although two people are involved, the record shows that police are far more likely to arrest (less powerful) sex workers, the majority of whom are female, than (more powerful) male clients. Of all women engaged in prostitution, it is streetwalkers—women with the least income and those most likely to be minorities—who face the highest risk of arrest (COYOTE, 2000). Furthermore, would so many women be involved in prostitution at all if they had economic opportunities equal to those of men?

Sexuality: Creating social inequality. Social-conflict theorists, especially feminists, point to sexuality as the root of inequality between women and men. Defining women in sexual terms amounts to devaluing them from full human beings to objects of men's interest and attention. Is it any wonder that the word "pornography" comes from the Greek word *porne,* meaning "a man's sexual slave"?

If men define women in sexual terms, it is easy to see pornography, almost all of which is consumed by males, as a power issue. Because pornography typically shows women focused on pleasing men, it supports the idea that men have power over women.

Some radical critics doubt that this element of power can ever be removed from heterosexual relations (Dworkin, 1987). Most social-conflict theorists do not reject heterosexuality, but they do agree that sexuality can and does degrade women. Our culture often describes sexuality in terms of sport (men "scoring" with women) and violence ("slamming," "banging," and "hitting on," for example, are verbs used for both fighting and sex).

Queer theory. Finally, social-conflict theory has taken aim not only at men dominating women but also at heterosexuals dominating homosexuals. In recent years, as many lesbians and gay men have sought public acceptance, some sociologists have tried to add a gay voice to their discipline. The term **queer theory** refers to *a growing body of research findings that challenges the heterosexual bias in North American society.*

Queer theory begins with the claim that our society is characterized by **heterosexism**, *a view stigmatizing anyone who is not heterosexual as "queer."* Our heterosexual culture victimizes a wide range of people, including gay men, lesbians, bisexuals, transsexuals, and even asexual people. Furthermore, although most people agree that bias against women (sexism) and people of colour (racism) is wrong, heterosexism is widely tolerated and sometimes well within the law. For example, U.S. military forces cannot legally discharge a female soldier for "acting like a woman" because that would be a clear case of gender discrimination. But the military forces can discharge her for homosexuality if she is a sexually active lesbian.

Heterosexism also exists at a more subtle level in our everyday understanding of the world. When we describe something as "sexy," for example, don't we really mean attractive to *heterosexuals?*

Critical review. The social-conflict approach shows how sexuality is both a cause and an effect of inequality. In particular, it helps us understand men's power over women and heterosexual people's domination of homosexual people.

At the same time, this approach overlooks the fact that sexuality is not always a power issue: Many couples enjoy a vital sexual relationship that deepens their commitment to one another. In addition, the social-conflict approach pays little attention to steps our society has made toward reducing inequality. In polite company at least, men today are less likely to describe women as sex objects than a few decades ago; moreover, our rising public concern about sexual harassment (see Chapter 10, "Gender Stratification") has reduced the abuse of sexuality in the workplace. There is also much evidence that the gay rights movement has secured greater opportunities and social acceptance for gay people.

The final topic of this chapter is perhaps the most divisive sexuality-related issue of all: **abortion,** *the deliberate termination of a pregnancy.* There seems to be no middle ground in the debate over this controversial issue, as described in the Controversy & Debate box on pages 160–161.

Summary

1. Canadian culture has long defined sex as a taboo topic. The Kinsey studies (1948, 1953) were among the first publications by social scientists on human sexuality.

2. Sex is the biological distinction between females and males, which is determined at conception as a man's sperm joins a woman's ovum.

3. Males and females are distinguished not only by their genitals (primary sex characteristics) but also by bodily development as they mature (secondary sex characteristics). Intersexed people have some combination of both male and female genitalia. Transsexuals are people who feel they are one sex although, biologically, they are the other.

4. For most species, sex is rigidly directed by biology; for human beings, sex is a matter of cultural definition and personal choice. Patterns of kissing, modesty, and beauty all vary around the world, revealing the cultural foundation of sexual practices.

5. Though in the early part of the twentieth century Canadian society held rigid attitudes toward sexuality, over time these attitudes have become more permissive.

6. The sexual revolution of the 1960s and 1970s brought a far greater openness in matters of sexuality. Research shows that changes in sexuality were greater for women than for men. By 1980, a sexual counterrevolution was taking shape, condemning permissiveness and urging a return to more conservative "family values."

7. The share of people in Canada who have premarital sexual intercourse increased over the course of the twentieth century. Research shows that about 76 percent of young men and 66 percent of young women have premarital sexual intercourse by their senior year in high school.

8. The level of sexual activity varies within the population of Canadian adults: on average Canadians have sex about six times per month, but the average is higher for three groups: Atlantic Canadians, young adults, and those living with a partner.

9. Although extramarital sex is widely condemned, about 10 percent of Canadians report being sexually unfaithful to their spouse at some time.

10. Sexual orientation refers to a person's romantic and emotional attraction to another person. Four major orientations are heterosexuality, homosexuality, bisexuality, and asexuality. Sexual orientation reflects both biological and cultural factors.

11. The share of the population that is homosexual depends on how researchers define homosexuality. More men and women report having some homosexual experience than report having a homosexual identity.

12. The gay rights movement has worked to gain greater acceptance for gay people. Largely due to this movement, the share of the Canadian population condemning homosexuality as morally wrong has steadily decreased over recent decades. The vast majority of Canadians believe that human rights legislation should protect gays and lesbians from discrimination.

13. Canadian teen girls accounted for just over 8 percent of pregnancies in 2001, down from 14 percent in 1974. The rate of teenage pregnancy has dropped since 1950, when many teens were marrying and having children. Today, however, most pregnant teens are not married, and also are at high risk of poverty, especially when the pregnancy forces them to drop out of school.

14. With no universal definition of pornography, the law allows local communities to set standards of decency. Conservatives condemn pornography as immoral; liberals and many feminists, by contrast, condemn it as demeaning to women.

15. Prostitution, the selling of sexual services, is not illegal in Canada; however, sex workers can be arrested, prosecuted, and convicted because they "communicate" in a public place for the purpose of engaging in prostitution. Although many people think of prostitution as a victimless crime, others argue that it victimizes women and spreads sexually transmitted diseases.

16. Over 60 percent of Canadian children and youth have experienced at least one incident of sexual assault or rape, and 2 million Canadian women aged 18 and over have been sexually assaulted by a stranger since turning 16. The actual number is likely even higher since many sexual assaults are never reported to the police. Although many people think of rape as a sexual act, rape is really a violent expression of power. Most sexual assaults involve people who know one another.

17. Structural-functional theory highlights society's need to regulate sexual activity. A universal norm in this regard is the incest taboo, which keeps kinship relations clear.

18. The symbolic-interaction paradigm points up how people attach various meanings to sexuality. Thus, societies differ from one another in terms of sexual attitudes and practices; similarly, sexual patterns change within any one society over time.

19. Social-conflict theory links sexuality to inequality. From this point of view, men dominate women, in part by devaluing females as sexual objects.

KEY CONCEPTS

abortion (p. 162) the deliberate termination of a pregnancy

asexuality (p. 148) no sexual attraction to people of either sex

bisexuality (p. 148) sexual attraction to people of both sexes

heterosexism (p. 162) a view stigmatizing anyone who is not heterosexual as "queer"

heterosexuality (p. 148) sexual attraction to someone of the other sex

homophobia (p. 151) the fear of close personal interaction with people thought to be gay, lesbian, or bisexual

homosexuality (p. 148) sexual attraction to someone of the same sex

incest taboo (p. 143) a cultural norm that forbids sex or marriage between certain relatives

intersexed person (p. 141) a human being with some combination of female and male genitalia

pornography (p. 152) sexually explicit material that causes sexual arousal

primary sex characteristics (p. 141) the genitals, organs used for reproduction

prostitution (p. 153) the selling of sexual services

queer theory (p. 162) a growing body of research findings that challenges the heterosexual bias in North American society

secondary sex characteristics (p. 141) bodily development, apart from the genitals, that distinguishes biologically mature females and males

sex (p. 141) the biological distinction between females and males

sexual orientation (p. 148) a person's preference in terms of sexual partners: same sex, other sex, either sex, neither sex

transsexuals (p. 142) people who feel they are one sex even though biologically they are the other

CRITICAL-THINKING QUESTIONS

1. What do sociologists mean by "the sexual revolution"? What did the sexual revolution change? Can you suggest some of the reasons these changes occurred?

2. What is sexual orientation? Why is this characteristic difficult for researchers to measure?

3. Do you think laws should regulate the portrayal of sex in books, in films, or on the Internet? Why or why not?

4. In what ways do societies regulate sexuality? In what ways does sexuality play a part in social inequality?

APPLICATIONS AND EXERCISES

1. The most complete study of sexual patterns in North America to date is the 1994 study *The Social Organization of Sexuality: Sexual Practices in the United States,* by Edward Laumann and others. You can find this book in your campus or community library. Get a copy, and browse through some of the chapters you find most interesting. As you read, think about ways in which sexuality is shaped by society.

2. Contact your school's student services office, and ask for information about the extent of sexual violence on your campus. Do people report such crimes? What policies and procedures does your school have to respond to sexual violence?

3. Sex is not always a simple matter of being female or male. Do you think that healthcare policies should cover gender reassignment surgery for adults who want it? Why or why not?

SITES TO SEE

www.pearsoned.ca/macionis
The authors and publisher of this book invite you to visit the interactive Companion Website™ that accompanies this text. Begin by clicking on the cover of your book. You will find a chapter-by-chapter study guide, practice tests, suggested weblinks, and links to other relevant material.

www.teenpregnancy.org
Visit the website of the National Campaign to Prevent Teen Pregnancy, a U.S. organization formed to guide teens toward responsible sexual behaviour. What are the key parts of this organization's program? How effective do you imagine it is? Why?

www.qrd.org/qrd
This website, the Queer Resources Directory, looks at a wide range of issues including family, religion, education, and health, from a queer theory perspective. Visit this site to see in what ways various social institutions can be considered "heterosexist." Do you agree? Why?

www.gay.com
This is a search engine for all sorts of information highlighting issues involving homosexuality.

 ## INVESTIGATE WITH RESEARCH NAVIGATOR™

Follow the instructions on page 33 of this text to access the features of Research Navigator™. Once at the website (**www.researchnavigator.com**), enter your login name and password.

Then, to use the Content Select™ database, enter keywords such as "sexuality," "incest," "transgender," and "abortion," and the search engine will supply relevant and recent scholarly and popular press publications.

To reinforce your understanding of this chapter, and to identify topics for further study, visit MySocLab at **www.pearsoned.ca/mysoclab/macionis** for diagnostic tests and a multimedia ebook.

Deviance

Why is deviance found in all societies?

How does *who* and *what* are defined as deviant reflect social inequality?

What effect has punishment had on reducing crime in Canada?

Different societies have different ways to control the behaviour of their members.

Bernard Ebbers cried on July 13, 2005. The former chief executive officer of WorldCom had just learned that he had been sentenced to 25 years in jail for his role in an accounting scandal involving US$11 billion. Ebbers was born and raised in Edmonton, and at one point or another was a milkman, a bouncer, and a student at the University of Alberta. But he is known today for his wheeling and dealing at the Mississippi-based telecommunications giant, which earned him the nickname "Telecom Cowboy." Ebbers is a devout born-again Christian who taught Sunday school at a Baptist church and credited divine intervention for his success. He was celebrated in *The Globe and Mail* in 1999 as a frugal and level-headed business leader who preferred that the executives at his company use budget hotels while on company business.

On the face of it, WorldCom appeared to be a highly successful and responsibly run corporation. But all that was to change in 2002: as it became clear that WorldCom had misreported its profits, the company suddenly collapsed, causing great harm to employees and shareholders alike. As the person in charge, Ebbers stood accused of fraud, conspiracy, and filing false documents—in short, falsifying accounting records to hide the fact that the company was losing a massive amount of money.

The rise and fall of the Ebbers fortune is staggering. From modest beginnings, Ebbers rose to become the 376th-richest person in the world, with wealth estimated at $1.4 billion in 1999. Along with the wealth came a taste for the finer things in life, with increasingly expensive yachts (culminating in a five-bedroom, 132-ft yacht), a British Columbia cattle ranch one-third the size of Prince Edward Island, and a large number of privately owned companies. In short, Ebbers lived very well—based on loans secured by his shareholdings in a company with falsified documents.

 Learn more about Bernard Ebbers and WorldCom at http://www.cbc.ca/story/business/national/2005/03/15/ebbers-050315.html.

In 2006, four years after the WorldCom accounting scandal came to light, Bernard Ebbers is out on bail during his legal appeal of his conviction and sentence. *The Globe and Mail* is no longer heralding him but rather concluded an editorial following his sentencing with the harsh words "his actions ruined thousands of lives. His sentence is severe, but richly merited" (*Globe and Mail*, 2005, p. A14). It remains to be seen whether or not Ebbers will eventually spend any actual time behind bars (McKenna, 1999; Cernetig, 2002; Pulliam et al., 2002; *The Economist*, 2005).

This chapter explores the issue of crime and criminals, showing that individuals accused of wrongdoing do not always fit the common stereotype of the "street" criminal. More broadly, it also tackles the larger question of why societies develop standards of right and wrong in the first place. As we shall see, law is simply one part of a complex system of social control: Society teaches us all to conform, at least most of the time, to countless rules. We begin our investigation by defining several basic concepts.

What Is Deviance?

Deviance is *the recognized violation of cultural norms.* Norms guide virtually all human activities, so the concept of deviance is quite broad. One category of deviance is **crime**, *the violation of a society's formally enacted criminal law.* Even criminal deviance spans a wide range, from minor traffic violations to sexual assault to murder.

Most familiar examples of nonconformity are negative instances of rule breaking, such as stealing from a convenience store, abusing a child, or driving while drunk. But we also define especially good people—students who volunteer too much in class or people who are overly enthusiastic about new computer technology—as deviant, even if we give them a measure of respect. What all deviant actions or attitudes have in common is some element of *difference* that causes us to think of another person as an "outsider" (Becker, 1966).

Not all deviance involves action or even choice. The very *existence* of some categories of people can be troublesome to others. To the young, elderly people may seem hopelessly "out of it," and to some non-Aboriginals, the mere presence of an Aboriginal person may cause discomfort. Able-bodied people often view people with disabilities as an out-group, just as rich people may avoid the poor, who appear to fall short of their standards.

All of us are subject to **social control**, *attempts by society to regulate people's thoughts and behaviour.* Often this process is informal, as when parents praise or scold their children or when friends make fun of someone's musical taste. Cases of serious deviance, however, may bring action by the **criminal justice system**, *a formal response by police, courts, and prison officials to alleged violations of the law.*

Learn more about youth justice in Canada at http://canada.justice.gc.ca/en/ps/yj.

How a society defines deviance, who is branded as deviant, and what people decide to do about deviance are all issues of social organization. Only gradually, however, have people recognized that deviance is much more than a matter of individual choice or personal failing, as the chapter now explains.

THE BIOLOGICAL CONTEXT

Chapter 3 ("Socialization: From Infancy to Old Age") explained that a century ago most people understood—or more correctly, misunderstood—human behaviour to be the result of biological instincts. Early interest in criminality thus focused on biological causes. In 1876, Cesare Lombroso (1835–1909), an Italian physician who worked in prisons, theorized that criminals stand out physically, with low foreheads, prominent jaws and cheekbones, protruding ears, hairiness, and unusually long arms. All in all, Lombroso claimed that criminals look like our apelike ancestors.

Had Lombroso looked more carefully, he would have found the physical features he linked to criminality throughout the entire population. We now know that no physical traits distinguish criminals from noncriminals (Goring, 1972, orig. 1913).

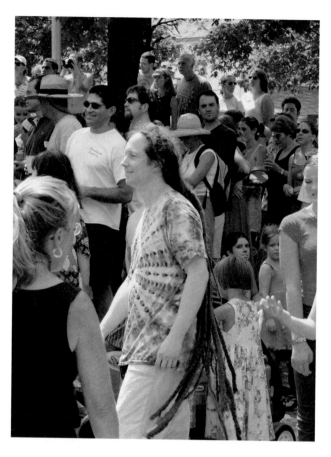
Deviance is always a matter of difference. Deviance emerges in everyday life as we encounter people whose appearance or behaviour differs from what we consider to be "right." Who is the "deviant" in this photograph? From whose point of view?

At mid-century, William Sheldon (Sheldon, Hartl, & McDermott, 1949) took a different approach, suggesting that body structure might predict criminality. He cross-checked hundreds of young men for body type and criminal history and concluded that delinquency was most common among boys with muscular, athletic builds. Sheldon Glueck and Eleanor Glueck (1950) confirmed Sheldon's conclusion but cautioned that a powerful build does not necessarily *cause* or even predict criminality. Parents, they suggested, tend to be more distant from powerfully built sons, who in turn grow up to show less sensitivity toward others. Moreover, in a self-fulfilling prophecy, people who expect muscular boys to be bullies may act in ways that bring about the aggressive behaviour they expect.

Today, genetics research seeks possible links between biology and crime. Although no conclusive evidence connects criminality to any specific genetic trait, people's overall genetic composition, in combination with social influences, probably accounts for some tendency toward criminality. In other words, biological factors may have a real but small effect on whether a person becomes a criminal (Wilson & Herrnstein, 1985; Jencks, 1987; Pallone & Hennessy, 1998).

Critical review.   At best, biological theories offer a very limited explanation of crime. Recent sociobiological research—noting, for example, that violent crimes are overwhelmingly committed by males and that parents are more likely to abuse foster children than natural children—is promising, but we know too little about the links between genes and human behaviour to draw firm conclusions (Daly & Wilson, 1988).

Furthermore, because a biological approach looks at the individual, it offers no insight into how some kinds of behaviours come to be defined as deviant in the first place. Therefore, although there is much to learn about how human biology may affect behaviour, research currently places far greater emphasis on social influences.

PERSONALITY FACTORS

Like biological theories, psychological explanations of deviance focus on individual abnormality. Some personality traits are inherited, but most psychologists think personality is shaped primarily by social experience. Deviance, then, is viewed as the result of "unsuccessful" socialization.

Research by Walter Reckless and Simon Dinitz (1967) illustrates the psychological approach. Reckless and Dinitz began by asking teachers to categorize 12-year-old male students as either likely or unlikely to get into trouble with the law. They then interviewed both the boys and their mothers to assess each boy's self-concept and how he related to others. Analyzing their results, the researchers found that the "good boys" displayed a strong conscience (or superego, in Freud's terminology), could handle frustration, and identified with cultural norms and values. The "bad boys," by contrast, had a weaker conscience, displayed little tolerance for frustration, and felt out of step with conventional culture.

As we might expect, the "good boys" went on to have fewer run-ins with the police than the "bad boys." Because all the boys lived in areas where delinquency was widespread, the investigators attributed staying out of trouble to a personality that controlled deviant impulses. Based on this conclusion, Reckless and Dinitz called their analysis *containment theory.*

Critical review.   Psychologists have shown that personality patterns have some connection to deviance. However, most serious crimes are committed by people whose psychological profiles are normal.

Overall, both biological and psychological research view deviance as an individual trait, without exploring how ideas of right and wrong initially arise, why people define some rule breakers but not others as deviant, and what role power plays in shaping a society's system of social control. To explore these issues, we now turn to a sociological analysis of deviance.

THE SOCIAL FOUNDATIONS OF DEVIANCE

Although we tend to view deviance as the free choice or personal failings of individuals, all behaviour—deviance as well as conformity—is shaped by society. Three social foundations of deviance identified here will be detailed later in this chapter:

1. **Deviance varies according to cultural norms.** No thought or action is inherently deviant; it becomes deviant only in relation to particular norms. In Saskatchewan, for example, it is illegal for businesses to offer both striptease and drinking; exotic dancing is fine, as is drinking, but the two must not occur together. Moreover, in some Canadian cities it is legal to play music on the sidewalk and to beg for money, while street musicians and panhandlers in other cities risk being fined or imprisoned.

    Around the world, deviance is even more diverse. Albania outlaws any public display of religious faith, such as "crossing" oneself; Cuba and Vietnam can prosecute citizens for meeting with foreigners; Malaysia does not allow tight-fitting jeans for women; and police in Iran can arrest a woman simply for wearing makeup.

2. **People become deviant as others define them that way.** Everyone violates cultural norms at one time or another. For example, have you ever walked around talking to yourself or "borrowed" a pen from your workplace? Whether such behaviour defines us as criminal or mentally ill depends on how others perceive, define, and respond to it.

3. **Both norms and the way people define situations involve social power.** According to Karl Marx, the law is the means by which powerful people protect their interests. A homeless person who stands on a street corner speaking out against the government risks arrest for disturbing the peace; a mayoral candidate during an election campaign does exactly the same thing and gets police protection. In short, norms and how we apply them reflect social inequality.

The Functions of Deviance: Structural-Functional Analysis

The key insight of the structural-functional approach is that deviance is a necessary element of social organization. This point was made a century ago by Emile Durkheim.

DURKHEIM'S BASIC INSIGHT

In his pioneering study of deviance, Emile Durkheim (1964a, orig. 1893; 1964b, orig. 1895) made the surprising statement that there is nothing abnormal about deviance. In fact, it performs four essential functions:

1. **Deviance affirms cultural values and norms.** As moral creatures, people must prefer some attitudes and behaviours to others. But any definition of virtue rests on an opposing idea of vice: there can be no good without evil and no justice without crime. Deviance is needed to define and sustain morality.

2. **Responding to deviance clarifies moral boundaries.** By defining some individuals as deviant, people draw a boundary between right and wrong. For example, schools draw the line between academic honesty and deviance by disciplining students who cheat on exams.

3. **Responding to deviance brings people together.** People typically react to serious deviance with shared outrage. In doing so, Durkheim explained, they reaffirm the moral ties that bind them. For example, after the September 11, 2001, terror attacks, people across the United States were joined by a common desire to protect their country and bring those responsible to justice.

4. **Deviance encourages social change.** Deviant people push a society's moral boundaries; their lives suggest alternatives to the status quo and may encourage change. Today's deviance, declared Durkheim, can become tomorrow's morality (1964b:71, orig. 1895). For example, as discussed in Chapter 6, the gay rights movement gained strength during the 1960s, eventually leading to increased public support for gay rights issues in Canada. Over time, public support for same-sex marriage climbed and eventually led to the passing of federal legislation allowing same-sex marriage in July 2005.

 Listen to and watch CBC programming about changing attitudes in Canada at http://archives.cbc.ca/ IDCC-1-69-599-3237/life_ society/gay_lesbian.

MERTON'S STRAIN THEORY

Some deviance may be necessary for a society to function, but Robert Merton

Fidel Castro erected this billboard in Havana across the street from the United States Special Interest Building. This was in response to a ticker display on the building showing news headlines from around the world.

(1938, 1968) argued that excessive deviance arises from particular social arrangements. Specifically, the extent and kind of deviance depend on whether a society provides the *means* (such as schooling and job opportunities) to achieve cultural *goals* (such as financial success).

Conformity lies in pursuing cultural goals through approved means. Thus, the Canadian "success story" is someone who gains wealth and prestige through talent, schooling, and hard work. But not everyone who wants conventional success has the opportunity to attain it. For example, people living in poverty may see little hope of becoming successful if they play by the rules. According to Merton, the strain between our culture's emphasis on wealth and the lack of opportunities to get rich gives rise, especially among the poor, to stealing, the sale of illegal drugs, and other forms of street crime. Merton called this type of deviance *innovation:* using unconventional means (street crime) to achieve a culturally approved goal (wealth). Figure 7–1 shows that innovation involves accepting the

Learn more about biker gangs in Canada at this CBC webpage: www.cbc.ca/news/background/bikergangs/.

FIGURE 7–1 Merton's Strain Theory of Deviance

Source: Merton (1968).

cultural goal (financial success) but rejecting the conventional means (hard work at a "straight" job) in favour of unconventional means (street crime).

The inability to reach a cultural goal may also prompt another type of deviance that Merton calls *ritualism* (see Figure 7–1). For example, many people may believe that they cannot achieve the cultural goal of becoming rich; therefore, they obsessively stick to the rules (the conventional means) in order at least to feel respectable.

A third response to the inability to succeed is *retreatism:* rejecting both cultural goals and means so that one, in effect, "drops out." Street people and some people dealing with addiction to drugs and alcohol are retreatists. The deviance of retreatists lies in their unconventional lifestyles and, perhaps more seriously, in what seems to be their willingness to live that way.

The fourth response to failure is *rebellion.* Like retreatists, rebels such as radical "survivalists" reject both the cultural definition of success and the conventional means of achieving it but go one step further by forming a counterculture and advocating alternatives to the existing social order.

DEVIANT SUBCULTURES

Richard Cloward and Lloyd Ohlin (1966) extended Merton's theory, proposing that crime results not simply from limited legitimate (legal) opportunity but also from readily accessible illegitimate (illegal) opportunity. In short, deviance or conformity depends on the *relative opportunity structure* that frames a person's life.

The life of Al Capone, a notorious gangster, illustrates Cloward and Ohlin's theory. As a son of poor immigrants, Capone faced barriers of poverty and ethnic prejudice, which lowered his odds of achieving success in conventional terms. Yet as a young man during the Prohibition era (when alcoholic beverages were banned in the United States, from 1920 to 1933), Capone found in his neighbourhood people who could teach him how to sell alcohol illegally—a source of illegitimate opportunity. Where the structure of opportunity favours criminal activity, Cloward and Ohlin predict the development of *criminal subcultures,* such as biker gangs.

But what happens when people are unable to find *any* opportunities, legal or illegal? Then deviance may take one of two forms: *conflict subcultures* (armed street gangs), where violence is ignited by frustration and a desire for respect, or *retreatist subcultures,* in which deviants drop out and abuse alcohol or other drugs.

Albert Cohen (1971, orig. 1955) suggests that criminality is most common among lower-class youths because they have the least opportunity to achieve conventional success. Neglected by society, they seek self-respect by creating a deviant subculture that defines as worthy the traits these youths do have. Being feared on the street may win few points with society as a whole, but it may satisfy a youth's desire to "be somebody" in a local neighbourhood.

Walter Miller (1970, orig. 1958) adds that deviant subcultures are characterized by (1) *trouble,* arising from frequent conflict with teachers and police; (2) *toughness,* the value placed on physical size, strength, and agility, especially among males; (3) *smartness,* the ability to succeed on the streets, to outsmart or "con" others; (4) *a need for excitement,* the search for thrills, risk, or danger; (5) *a belief in fate,* a sense that people lack control over their own lives; and (6) *a desire for freedom,* often expressed as anger toward all authority figures.

Finally, Elijah Anderson (1994, 2002) explains that in poor urban neighbourhoods, most people manage to conform to conventional ("decent") values. Yet faced daily with the dangers of crime and violence, hostility from police, and sometimes even neglect from their own parents, some young men decide to live by the "street code." To show that he can survive on the street, a young man displays "nerve," a willingness to stand up to any threat. Following this street code, the young man believes that even a violent death is better than being "dissed" (disrespected) by others. Some

Young people cut off from legitimate opportunity often form subcultures that many people view as deviant. Gang subcultures, including tattoos on the fingers, are one way people gain a sense of belonging and respect denied to them by the larger culture.

manage to escape the dangers, but the risk of ending up in jail—or worse—is very high for these young men, who have been pushed to the margins of our society.

Critical review. Durkheim made an important contribution by pointing out the functions of deviance. However, there is evidence that a community does not always come together in reaction to crime; sometimes fear of crime drives people to withdraw from public life (Liska & Warner, 1991; Warr & Ellison, 2000).

Merton's strain theory also has been criticized for explaining some kinds of deviance (stealing, for example) better than others (crimes of passion or mental illness). Furthermore, not everyone seeks success in conventional terms of wealth, as strain theory suggests.

The general argument of Cloward and Ohlin, Cohen, and Miller—that deviance reflects the opportunity structure of society—has been confirmed by subsequent research (Allan & Steffensmeier, 1989; Uggen, 1999). However, these theories fall short by assuming that everyone shares the same cultural standards for judging right and wrong. If we define crime as including not just street theft but the insider trading for which Martha Stewart was convicted in 2004 or the kind of corporate fraud described in the opening to this chapter, then more high-income people will be counted as criminals. There is evidence that people of all social backgrounds have become more casual about breaking the rules, as the Critical Thinking box on page 174 explains.

Finally, all structural-functional theories suggest that everyone who breaks the rules will be labelled deviant. However, becoming deviant is actually a highly complex process, as the next section explains.

Labelling Deviance: Symbolic-Interaction Analysis

The symbolic-interaction approach explains how people define deviance in everyday situations. From this point of view, definitions of deviance and conformity are surprisingly flexible.

LABELLING THEORY

The central contribution of symbolic-interaction analysis is **labelling theory**, *the assertion that deviance and conformity result not so much from what people do as from how others respond to those actions.* Labelling theory stresses the relativity of deviance, meaning that people may define the same behaviour in any number of ways. Howard Becker claims that deviance is nothing more than behaviour that people define as deviant (1966).

Consider these situations: A college student takes an article of clothing from a roommate's drawer, a married woman at a convention in a distant city has sex with an old boyfriend, and an advertising company that is a major campaign contributor to a political party receives a major federal advertising contract. We might define the first situation as carelessness, borrowing, or theft. The consequences of the second situation depend largely on whether the woman's behaviour becomes known back home. In the third situation, is the advertising company the best contractor or was it chosen merely to pay off a political debt? The social construction of reality is a highly variable process of detection, definition, and response.

CRITICAL THINKING

Deviant (Sub)Culture: Has It Become Okay to Do Wrong?

It's been a bad few years for the idea of playing by the rules. First Auditor General Sheila Fraser reports that senior civil servants broke rules when they awarded advertising contracts to Montreal advertising agencies. Then we learn that the executives of not just one but many corporations are guilty of fraud and outright stealing. Perhaps worst of all, the Roman Catholic Church, which many hold up as a model of moral behaviour, has become embroiled in a scandal of its own. In this case, hundreds of priests across Canada and the U.S. are said to have sexually abused parishioners (most of them teens and children) over many decades while church officials busied themselves covering up the crimes. By the beginning of 2004, more than 300 priests had been removed from their duties pending investigations of abuse.

Plenty of people are offering explanations for this widespread pattern of wrongdoing. Some suggest that the pressure to win in the highly competitive corporate world—by whatever means necessary—can be overwhelming. As one analyst put it, "You can get away with your

embezzlements and your lies, but you can never get away with *failing*."

Such thinking helps explain the wrongdoing among many CEOs in the corporate world, but it offers little insight into the problem of abusive priests. In some ways at least, wrongdoing seems to have become a way of life for just about everybody. For example, the Auditor General has estimated that Canadians are more and more willing to evade taxes by engaging in the underground economy, particularly in the con-

Do you consider cheating in school to be wrong? Would you turn in someone you saw cheat? Why or why not?

struction industry. The music industry claims that it has lost a vast amount of money due to illegal piracy of recordings, a practice especially common among young people. And surveys of high school students reveal that 75 percent admit to having cheated on a test at least once during the past year.

Emile Durkheim considered society to be a moral system, built on a set of rules about what people should and should not do. Years earlier, another French thinker named Blaise Pascal made the opposite claim that "cheating is the foundation of society." Today, which of the two statements is closer to the truth?

WHAT DO YOU THINK?

1. In your opinion, how widespread is wrongdoing in Canadian society today?
2. Do you think the people whose actions are described in this box consider what they are doing as wrong? Why or why not?
3. What are the reasons for this apparent increase in dishonesty?

Source: Based on "Our Cheating Hearts" (2002).

PRIMARY AND SECONDARY DEVIANCE

Edwin Lemert (1951, 1972) observed that some norm violations—say, skipping school or underage drinking—provoke slight reaction from others and have little effect on a person's self-concept. Lemert calls such passing episodes *primary deviance.*

But what happens if people take notice of someone's deviance and make something of it? For example, if people begin to describe a young man as an "alcohol abuser" and exclude him from their friendship network, he may become bitter, drink even more, and seek the company of those who approve of his behaviour. The response to primary deviance

can set in motion *secondary deviance*, by which a person repeatedly violates a norm and begins to take on a deviant identity. The development of secondary deviance is one application of the Thomas theorem (see Chapter 4, "Social Interaction in Everyday Life"), which states that situations people define as real become real in their consequences.

STIGMA

Secondary deviance marks the start of what Canadian sociologist Erving Goffman (1963) called a *deviant career.* As people develop a stronger commitment to deviant behaviour, they typically acquire a **stigma**, a *powerfully negative* *label that greatly changes a person's self-concept and social identity.* Weiss et al. (2001) define stigma as "a social process or related personal experience characterized by exclusion, rejection, blame, or devaluation that results from experience or reasonable anticipation of an adverse social judgment about a person or group." Stigma operates as a master status (see Chapter 4), overpowering other dimensions of identity so that a person is discredited in the minds of others and consequently becomes socially isolated and may suffer depression and other ill-effects (Link & Phelan, 1995). Sometimes an entire community stigmatizes a person through what Harold Garfinkel (1956) calls a degradation ceremony. A criminal prosecution is one example, operating much like a high school graduation ceremony in reverse: a person stands before the community to be labelled in a negative rather than a positive way.

Once people stigmatize a person, they may engage in *retrospective labelling*, a reinterpretation of the person's past in light of some present deviance (Scheff, 1984). For example, after discovering that a priest has sexually molested a child, others rethink his past, perhaps musing, "He always did want to be around young children." Retrospective labelling distorts a person's biography by being highly selective, a process that can deepen a deviant identity.

Similarly, people may engage in *projective labelling* of a stigmatized person. That is, people use a deviant identity to predict a person's future actions. Regarding the priest, people might say, "He's going to keep at it until he's caught." The more people in someone's social world think such things, of course, the greater the chance that they will come true.

LABELLING DIFFERENCE AS DEVIANCE

Is a homeless man who refuses to allow police to take him to a city shelter on a cold night simply trying to live independently, or is he "crazy"? People have a tendency to treat behaviour that irritates or threatens them not simply as "difference" but as deviance or even mental illness.

The psychiatrist Thomas Szasz charges that people are too quick to apply the label of mental illness to conditions that simply amount to a difference we don't like. The only way to avoid this troubling practice, Szasz concludes, is to abandon the idea of mental illness entirely (1961, 1970, 1994, 1995). As he sees it, illness is physical; therefore, mental illness is a myth. The world is full of people whose differences in thought or action may irritate others, but such differences are not grounds for defining someone as sick. Such labelling, Szasz claims, simply enforces conformity to the standards created by people powerful enough to impose their will on others.

Most mental health professionals reject the idea that there is no such thing as mental illness. But they do agree that it is important to think critically about how we define "difference." First, people who are mentally ill are no more to blame for their condition than people who suffer from cancer or some other physical problem. In other words, having a mental or physical illness is not grounds for being labelled "deviant" or "crazy." Second, ordinary people without the knowledge to diagnose mental illness should avoid applying such labels just to make people conform to our own standards of behaviour.

THE MEDICALIZATION OF DEVIANCE

Labelling theory, particularly the ideas of Szasz and Goffman, helps explain an important shift in the way our society understands deviance. Over the past 50 years, the growing influence of psychiatry and medicine has led to the **medicalization of deviance**, *the transformation of moral and legal deviance into a medical condition.*

Medicalization amounts to swapping one set of labels for another. In moral terms, we judge people or their behaviour as "bad" or "good." However, the scientific objectivity of medicine passes no moral judgment, instead using clinical diagnoses such as "sick" or "well."

To illustrate, until the mid-twentieth century, most people viewed alcoholics as morally weak people easily tempted by the pleasure of drink. Gradually, however, medical specialists redefined alcoholism so that most people now consider it a disease, making people "sick" rather than "bad." In the same way, obesity, drug addiction, child abuse, promiscuity, and other behaviours that used to be strictly moral matters are widely defined today as illnesses for which people need help rather than punishment.

Whether we define deviance as a moral or medical issue has three consequences. First, it affects *who responds* to deviance. An offence against common morality typically brings a reaction from members of the community or the police. However, applying medical labels transfers the situation to the control of clinical specialists, including counsellors, psychiatrists, and physicians.

A second issue is *how people respond.* A moral approach defines deviants as offenders subject to punishment. Medically, however, they are patients who need treatment. Whereas punishment is designed to fit the crime, treatment programs are tailored to the patient and may involve virtually any therapy that a specialist thinks might prevent future illness.

Third, and most important, the two labels differ on the issue of *the personal competence of the deviant person.* From a moral standpoint, whether we are right or wrong, at least we take responsibility for our own behaviour. Once defined as sick, however, we are seen as unable to control (or, if "mentally ill," even understand) our actions. People who are

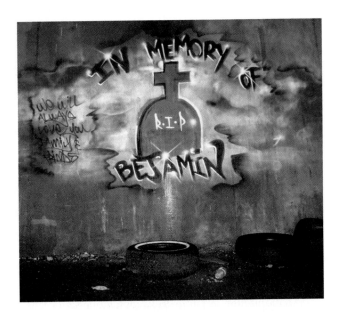

In some gangs, young people learn attitudes and skills that promote violence. Gangs offer their members a sense of belonging and social importance, but the price of membership is often high. This graffiti memorial to a fallen gang member is found in Bridgeport, Connecticut.

incompetent are in turn subject to treatment, often against their will. For this reason alone, defining deviance in medical terms should be done with extreme caution.

SUTHERLAND'S DIFFERENTIAL ASSOCIATION THEORY

Learning any social pattern, whether conventional or deviant, is a process that takes place in groups. Therefore, according to Edwin Sutherland (1940), a person's tendency toward conformity or deviance depends on the amount of contact with others who encourage—or reject—conventional behaviour. This is Sutherland's theory of *differential association*.

A number of studies confirm the idea that young people are more likely to engage in delinquency if they believe that members of their peer group encourage such activity (Akers et al., 1979; Miller & Matthews, 2001). One recent investigation focused on sexual activity among Grade 8 students in the United States. Two strong predictors of such behaviour in young girls were having a boyfriend who, presumably, encouraged sexual relations and having girlfriends they believed would approve of such activity. Similarly, boys were encouraged to become sexually active by friends who rewarded them with high status in the peer group (Little & Rankin, 2001).

HIRSCHI'S CONTROL THEORY

The sociologist Travis Hirschi (1969; Gottfredson & Hirschi, 1995) developed *control theory*, which states that social control depends on anticipating the consequences of one's behaviour. Hirschi assumes that everyone finds at least some deviance tempting. But the thought of a ruined career keeps most people from breaking the rules; for some, just imagining the reactions of family and friends is enough. On the other hand, people who think that they have little to lose from deviance are likely to become rule breakers.

Specifically, Hirschi links conformity to four different types of social control:

1. **Attachment.** Strong social attachments encourage conformity. Weak family, peer, and school relationships leave people freer to engage in deviance.

2. **Opportunity.** The greater a person's access to legitimate opportunity, the greater the advantages of conformity. By contrast, someone with little confidence in future success is freer to drift toward deviance.

3. **Involvement.** Extensive involvement in legitimate activities—such as holding a job, going to school, or playing sports—inhibits deviance (Langbein & Bess, 2002). By contrast, people who simply "hang out" waiting for something to happen have the time and energy to engage in deviant activity.

4. **Belief.** Strong beliefs in conventional morality and respect for authority figures restrain tendencies toward deviance. By contrast, people with a weak conscience (and who are left unsupervised) are more open to temptation (Stack, Wasserman, & Kern, 2004).

Hirschi's analysis combines a number of earlier ideas about the causes of deviant behaviour. Note that a person's relative social privilege and strength of moral character are crucial in generating a stake in conformity to conventional norms (Sampson & Laub, 1990; Free, 1992).

Critical review.   The various symbolic-interaction theories all see deviance as a process. Labelling theory links deviance not to *action* but to the *reaction* of others. Thus, some people are defined as deviant whereas others who think or behave in the same way are not. The concepts of secondary deviance, deviant career, and stigma show how being labelled deviant can become a lasting self-concept.

Yet labelling theory has several limitations. First, because it takes a highly relative view of deviance, labelling theory ignores the fact that some kinds of behaviour—such as murder—are condemned virtually everywhere. Therefore, labelling theory is most usefully applied to less serious issues, such as sexual promiscuity or mental illness. Second, research on the consequences of deviant labelling is inconclusive (Smith & Gartin, 1989; Sherman & Smith, 1992). Does deviant labelling produce further deviance or discourage it? Third, not everyone resists being labelled as deviant; some people actually seek it (Vold & Bernard, 1986). For example, people engage in civil disobedience and willingly subject themselves to arrest in order to call attention to social injustice.

Both Sutherland's differential association theory and Hirschi's control theory have had considerable influence in sociology. But why do society's norms and laws define certain kinds of activities as deviant in the first place? This important question is addressed by social-conflict analysis, the focus of the next section.

Deviance and Inequality: Social-Conflict Analysis

The social-conflict approach links deviance to social inequality. That is, *who* or *what* is labelled "deviant" depends on which categories of people hold power in a society.

DEVIANCE AND POWER

Alexander Liazos (1972) points out that the people we tend to define as deviants—those we dismiss as "nuts" and "sluts"—are typically those who share the trait of powerlessness. Bag ladies (not corporate polluters) and unemployed men on street corners (not international arms dealers) carry the stigma of deviance.

Social-conflict theory explains this pattern in three ways. First, all norms and especially the laws of any society generally reflect the interests of the rich and powerful. People who threaten the wealthy, either by taking their property or by pushing for a more egalitarian society, are labelled "common thieves" or "political radicals." Karl Marx, a major architect of the social-conflict approach, argued that the law (and all social institutions) supports the interests of the rich. Or as Richard Quinney puts it, "Capitalist justice is by the capitalist class, for the capitalist class, and against the working class" (1977:3).

Second, even if their behaviour is called into question, the powerful have the resources to resist deviant labels. The majority of the corporate executives involved in recent scandals have yet to be arrested; very few have gone to jail.

Third, the widespread belief that norms and laws are natural and good masks their political character. For this reason, although we may condemn the *unequal application* of the law, most of us give little thought to whether the *laws themselves* are inherently unfair (Quinney, 1977).

DEVIANCE AND CAPITALISM

In the Marxist tradition, Steven Spitzer (1980) argues that deviant labels are applied to people who interfere with the operation of capitalism. First, because capitalism is based on private control of property, people who threaten the property of others—especially the poor who steal from the rich—are prime candidates for being labelled deviant. Conversely, the rich who take advantage of the poor are less likely to be labelled deviant. For example, landlords who charge poor tenants high rents and evict those who cannot pay are not considered a threat to anyone; they are simply "doing business."

Second, because capitalism depends on productive labour, people who cannot or will not work risk being labelled deviant. Many members of our society think of unemployed people as deviant, even if they lost their jobs through no fault of their own.

Third, capitalism depends on respect for authority figures, causing people who resist authority to be labelled deviant. Examples are children who skip school or talk back to parents and teachers, and adults who do not cooperate with employers or police.

Fourth, anyone who directly challenges the capitalist status quo is likely to be defined as deviant. Such has been the case with anti-war activists, radical environmentalists, and labour organizers.

On the other side of the coin, society positively labels whatever supports the operation of capitalism. For example, winning athletes enjoy celebrity status because they make money and express the values of individual achievement and competition, both vital to capitalism. Also, Spitzer notes, we condemn using drugs of escape (marijuana, psychedelics, heroin, crack) as deviant but promote drugs (such as alcohol and caffeine) that encourage adjustment to the status quo.

The capitalist system also tries to control people who don't fit into the system. The elderly, people with mental or physical disabilities, and Robert Merton's "retreatists" (including people addicted to alcohol or other drugs) represent a "costly yet relatively harmless burden" to society. Such people, claims Spitzer, are subject to control by social welfare agencies. But people who directly challenge the capitalist system, including the inner-city "underclass" and revolutionaries—Merton's "innovators" and "rebels"—are controlled by the criminal justice system or, in times of crisis such as the 1970 FLQ crisis, military forces.

Note that both the social welfare and the criminal justice systems blame individuals, not the system, for social problems. Welfare recipients are considered unworthy freeloaders, poor people who rage at their plight are labelled rioters, anyone who actively challenges the government is

Justice John Gomery headed the commission investigating the government's sponsorship program and advertising activities. The final report was released in 2006. Jean Brault (who ran Groupaction), Paul Coffin (who ran another advertising company that benefited from the program), and Chuck Guité (who ran the program for Public Works) all received criminal convictions for their parts in the program.

The most common white-collar crimes are bank embezzlement, business fraud, bribery, and anti-trust violations. Sutherland (1940) explains that such white-collar offences typically end up in a civil hearing rather than a criminal courtroom. *Civil law* regulates business dealings between private parties; *criminal law* defines a person's moral responsibilities to society. In practice, someone who loses a civil case pays for damage or injury but is not labelled a criminal. Furthermore, corporate officials are protected by the fact that most charges of white-collar crime target the organization rather than individuals.

In the rare cases that white-collar criminals are charged and convicted, the odds are that they will not go to jail. Advertising executive Paul Coffin pleaded guilty to defrauding the government of about $1.5 million as his part of the Liberal party sponsorship scandal. In 2005 he received a sentence of two years' house arrest, although this sentence was later overturned on appeal and replaced by a jail sentence of 18 months. Nobody has been convicted in relation to the Bre-X affair.

CORPORATE CRIME

Sometimes whole companies, not just individuals, break the law. **Corporate crime** consists of *the illegal actions of a corporation or people acting on its behalf.*

Corporate crime ranges from knowingly selling faulty or dangerous products to deliberately polluting the environment (Benson & Cullen, 1998). The US$11 billion fraud at WorldCom pales in comparison to that of Enron Corporation. Following a number of alleged violations of business and accounting practices Enron collapsed in 2001. Estimates of the loss to shareholders and others exceed US$50 billion, which is four times the annual loss in the United States due to common theft (Lavella, 2002).

As with white-collar crime, most cases of corporate crime go unpunished, and many never even become a matter of public record. Furthermore, the cost of corporate crime goes beyond dollars. The collapses of WorldCom, Enron, Global Crossing, Tyco International, and other corporations in recent years cost tens of thousands of people their jobs and their pensions. Even more serious is the company wrongdoing that results in people's deaths; for example, coal mining companies have for decades knowingly put miners at risk from inhaling coal dust, so that hundreds of people die annually from "black lung" disease. The death toll from all job-related hazards that are known to companies probably exceeds 100 000 annually (Carroll, 1999; Jones, 1999).

ORGANIZED CRIME

Organized crime is *a business supplying illegal goods or services.* Sometimes criminal organizations force people to do business with them, as when a gang extorts money from

branded a radical or a Communist, and those who attempt to gain illegally what they will never acquire legally are rounded up as common criminals.

WHITE-COLLAR CRIME

In the late 1990s Bre-X Minerals Ltd. of Calgary controlled Busang, a huge Indonesian gold mine. Bre-X was the darling of the Toronto Stock Exchange, valued at more than $6 billion. The only problem was that Busang was a fraud. The valuation of the mine was based on ore samples that had been tampered with.

Bre-X's management activities exemplify **white-collar crime**, defined by Edwin Sutherland in 1940 as *crime committed by people of high social position in the course of their occupations.* White-collar crimes do not involve violence and rarely bring police with guns drawn to the scene. Rather, white-collar criminals use their powerful offices to illegally enrich themselves or others, often causing significant public harm in the process (Hagan & Parker, 1985; Vold & Bernard, 1986). For this reason, sociologists sometimes call white-collar offences crime in the suites as opposed to crime in the streets.

APPLYING THEORY

DEVIANCE

	Structural-Functional Approach	Symbolic-Interaction Approach	Social-Conflict Approach
What is the level of analysis?	Macro-level	Micro-level	Macro-level
What is deviance? What part does it play in society?	Deviance is a basic part of social organization. By defining deviance, society sets its moral boundaries.	Deviance is part of socially constructed reality that emerges in interaction. Deviance comes into being as individuals label something as such.	Deviance results from social inequality. Norms, including laws, reflect the interests of powerful members of society.
What is important about deviance?	Deviance is universal: all societies contain deviance.	Deviance is variable: any act or person may or may not be labelled as deviant.	Deviance is political: people with little power are at high risk for becoming deviant.

shopkeepers for "protection." In most cases, however, organized crime involves selling illegal goods and services—including sex, drugs, or gambling—to a willing public.

Organized crime is flourishing in Canada. The vicious scope of its operations garnered public attention in the spring of 2006 when eight members of the Bandidos motorcycle gang were murdered by other members of the gang, apparently for wanting to join the Hells Angels motorcycle gang. During the late 1990s, some 150 people died as a result of fighting between these archrival motorcycle gangs. At stake are the lucrative drug and sex trades (Canadian Press Newswire, October 21, 2000; Beltrame & Branswell, 2000).

Critical review. According to social-conflict theory, a capitalist society's inequality in wealth and power guides the creation and application of laws and other norms. The criminal justice and social welfare systems thus act as political agents, controlling categories of people who threaten the capitalist system.

Like other approaches to deviance, social-conflict theory has its critics. First, this approach suggests that laws and other cultural norms are created directly by the rich and powerful. At the very least, this is an oversimplification because the law also protects workers, consumers, and the environment, sometimes opposing the interests of corporations and the rich.

Second, social-conflict analysis argues that criminality springs up only to the extent that a society treats its members unequally. However, as Durkheim noted, deviance exists in all societies, whatever their economic system.

The sociological explanations for crime and other types of deviance are summarized in the Applying Theory table.

Deviance, Race, and Gender

What people consider deviant reflects the relative power and privilege of different categories of people. The following sections offer two examples: how racial and ethnic hostility motivates hate crimes and how gender is linked to deviance.

HATE CRIMES

The term **hate crime** refers to *a criminal act against a person or a person's property by an offender motivated by racial or other bias.* A hate crime may express hostility toward someone based on race, religion, ancestry, sexual orientation, or mental or physical disability. This is articulated in the *Criminal Code of Canada* as an aggravating circumstance that could justify increasing the sentence imposed on a person convicted of a criminal offence. The *Criminal Code* also specifies a hate propaganda crime, which is the advocation or promotion of genocide.

Most people were stunned by the brutal killing in 1998 of Nirmal Singh Gill—a Sikh temple caretaker—by five men active in white supremacist groups in British Columbia. Statistics show that almost half of hate crimes are based on race or ethnicity (Silver, Mihorean, & Taylor-Butts, 2004). People who contend with multiple stigmas—such as visible

DIVERSITY: RACE, CLASS, & GENDER

Hate Crime Laws: Do They Punish Actions or Attitudes?

Just after 2:00 A.M. on November 17, 2001, in a corner of Vancouver's Stanley Park where gays commonly meet, local resident Aaron Webster was brutally killed. His assailants were a group of five young males also from the city who told reporters that they "wanted to get into a fight."

Three years later, 22-year-old Ryan Cran, who was considered to be the ringleader, was found guilty of manslaughter in Aaron's beating death. In Cran's sentencing in February 2005, BC Supreme Court Justice Mary Humphries said the attack on Webster was "random, cowardly, and terrifying" but an individual act—not a hate crime. The gay community and members of Webster's family argued otherwise, categorizing the murder as caused by hatred against gay

Read a Statistics Canada report on hate crimes in Canada at **www. statcan.ca/english/ freepub/85-551-XIE/ 0009985-551-XIE.pdf.**

people and pointing out the need for a stiffer sentence.

As this case illustrates, hate crime laws punish a crime more severely if the offender is motivated by bias against some category of people. Supporters make three arguments in favour of hate crime legislation. First, the offender's intentions are always important in weighing criminal responsibility, so considering hatred as an intention is nothing new. Second, a crime motivated by bias against gays or discriminated groups inflames the public mood more than a crime carried out, say, for money. Third, victims of hate crimes typically suffer more serious injuries than victims of crimes with other motives.

Critics counter that while some hate crime cases involve hard-core homophobia or racism, most are impulsive acts by young people. Hate crime laws allow courts to sentence offenders not just for actions but also for their attitudes. As

Harvard University law professor Alan Dershowitz cautions, "As much as I hate bigotry, I fear much more the Court attempting to control the minds of citizens." In short, according to critics, hate crime laws open the door to punishing beliefs rather than behaviour.

In the case of Aaron Webster, the BC Supreme Court decided against the hate crime ruling and instead punished Cran for his actual behaviour rather than beliefs about gays.

WHAT DO YOU THINK?

1. Do you think crimes motivated by hate are more harmful than those motivated by, say, greed? Why or why not?
2. On balance, do you favour or oppose hate crime laws? Why?

Sources: Terry (1993) and Sullivan (2002).

---

minority and Jewish gay men—are especially likely to become victims of hate-motivated violence. The federal government does not collect data on hate crimes, and data collection varies across Canada. In addition, it is likely that many of these crimes go unreported. Nevertheless, it is estimated that there are more than 60 000 hate crimes committed every year in

Read one critic's thoughts on the attention given to groups that promote hate at **www.ccla.org/pos/columns/ heritage.shtml.**

Canada (Roberts, 1995; Statistics Canada, 2001d). Yet anyone can be a victim: A recent study found that about 25 percent of the race-based hate crimes in the United States targeted white people (Jenness & Grattet, 2001).

DEVIANCE AND GENDER

Virtually every society in the world applies stricter normative controls to women than to men. Historically, our own

society has centred women's lives around the home. In Canada even today, women's opportunities in the workplace, in politics, and in the military are limited. Elsewhere in the world, the constraints on women are greater still. In Saudi Arabia, women cannot vote or legally operate motor vehicles; in Iran, women who expose their hair or wear makeup in public can be whipped; and a Nigerian court recently convicted a divorced woman of bearing a child out of wedlock and sentenced her to death by stoning (Eboh, 2002; her life was later spared out of concern for her child).

Gender also figures in the theories about deviance noted earlier. For example, Robert Merton's strain theory defines cultural goals in terms of financial success. Traditionally at least, this goal has had more to do with the lives of men, because women have been socialized to define success in terms of relationships, particularly marriage and motherhood (Leonard, 1982). A more woman-focused theory might recognize the "strain" that results from the cultural ideal of equality clashing with the reality of gender-based inequality.

According to labelling theory, gender influences how we define deviance, because people commonly use different standards to judge the behaviour of females and males. Furthermore, because society puts men in positions of power over women, men often escape direct responsibility for actions that victimize women. In the past, at least, men who sexually harassed or assaulted women were labelled only mildly deviant and sometimes escaped punishment entirely.

By contrast, women who are victimized may have to convince others—even members of a jury—that they are not to blame for their own sexual harassment or assault. The ruling by the Ontario Court in favour of "Jane Doe," who sued the Toronto Police Services for negligence in their handling of a serial rape case, illustrates this point. Ms. Doe alleged that the police should have done more to warn women in her neighbourhood about the rapist. It took 12 years before the court finally ruled that Ms. Doe's rights under the Canadian *Charter of Rights and Freedoms* had been violated because the police failed to give her equal protection under the law. This example confirms what research tells us: whether people define a situation as deviance—and, if so, whose deviance it is—depends on the gender of both the audience and the actors (King & Clayson, 1988).

Finally, despite its focus on inequality, much social-conflict analysis does not address the issue of gender. If, as conflict theory suggests, poverty is a primary cause of crime, why do women (who are more likely to be poor than men) commit far *fewer* crimes than men?

Crime

Crime is the violation of criminal laws enacted by a locality, province or territory, or the federal government. Technically, all crimes are composed of two distinct elements: an *act* (or in a few cases, a failure to act) and *criminal intent* (in legal terminology, *mens rea,* or "guilty mind"). Intent is a matter of degree, ranging from willful conduct to negligence. Someone who is negligent does not set out deliberately to hurt anyone but acts (or fails to act) in such a way that results in harm. Prosecutors weigh the degree of intent in determining whether, for example, to charge someone with first-degree murder, second-degree murder, or negligent manslaughter. Alternatively, they may consider a killing justifiable, as in self-defence.

TYPES OF CRIME

The Canadian Centre for Justice Statistics provides summary reports on the basis of its Uniform Crime Reporting (UCR) survey. Statistics Canada originally designed the UCR survey with the agreement of, and help from, the

Violent crime is much more likely to involve victims and offenders who are males than females. While Paul Bernardo was convicted of two murders, Karla Homolka negotiated a lesser sentence before her full involvement in the murders was discovered.

Canadian Association of Chiefs of Police. Implemented in 1962, the aggregate UCR survey gathers crime statistics reported by police departments across the country. It is important to keep in mind (more on this point below) that these statistics are based only on "recorded crimes"—that is, crimes reported to the police in Canada—and not on all crimes that are actually committed.

Crimes against the person are *crimes that involve violence or the threat of violence against others.* Such "violent crimes" include murder and manslaughter (directly or indirectly causing the death of a human being), aggravated

The *Criminal Code* is available online: **http://laws.justice.gc.ca/en/C-46/index.html.**

assault (wounding, maiming, disfiguring, or endangering a person), sexual assault (forcing a victim into sexual activity without voluntary agreement), and robbery (using violence or threats to overcome resistance to stealing).

Crimes against property are *crimes that involve theft of goods belonging to others.* Property crimes include theft (unlawfully taking the property of another), break and enter (unlawfully entering a place to commit an offence), possession of stolen property (knowingly having property that was obtained unlawfully), and fraud (obtaining property, money, or a valuable security or service from the

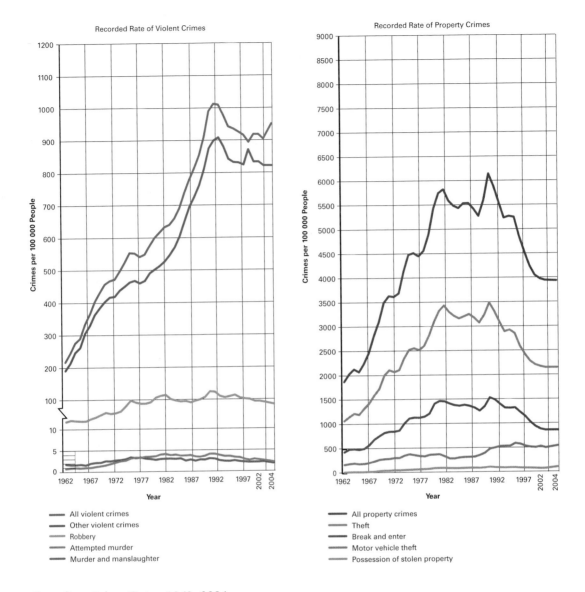

FIGURE 7-2 Canadian Crime Rates, 1962–2004

The graphs represent crime rates for various violent crimes and property crimes during recent decades. Comparable data on sexual assaults and other assaults are not available before 1983. Most "other violent crimes" before 1983 were assaults.

Source: Calculated based on data in Statistics Canada, 2006i to 2006ah.

public or any person through deceit, falsehood, or other fraudulent means).

Third and fourth categories of *Criminal Code* offences—traffic and others—include **victimless crimes**, *violations of law in which there are no obvious victims*. Such crimes include illegal drug use (technically an offence against the *Narcotics Control Act*), prostitution, and gambling. The term "victimless crime" is misleading, how-

ever. How victimless is a crime when young people purchasing drugs may be embarking on a life of crime to support a drug habit? Or when a pregnant woman, by smoking crack, permanently harms her baby? Or when a gambler falls so deeply into debt that he cannot make the mortgage payments on his house? Perhaps it is more correct to say that people who commit such crimes are themselves both offenders and victims.

Because public opinion about such activities varies considerably, the laws regulating victimless crimes differ from place to place. For example, prostitution—the exchange of money for sex—is not illegal in Canada. Nonetheless, a person can be charged who "in a public place … communicates … for the purpose of engaging in prostitution. . . ." This law is often more heavily enforced when residents of a neighbourhood complain about prostitution (Statistics Canada, 1997g).

CRIMINAL STATISTICS

Statistics gathered by police show crime rates rising from the early 1960s to 1991, but declining over the past decade. Even so, excluding traffic incidents, police tallied 2.4 million *Criminal Code* offences in 2004 (Sauve, 2005). Figure 7–2 shows the trends for various serious crimes.

You should always read crime statistics with caution, however, because they include only crimes known to the police. Almost all murders are reported, but assaults, especially between acquaintances, often are not. Police records include an even smaller proportion of property crimes, especially when the losses are small.

Researchers check official crime statistics by conducting *victimization surveys,* in which they ask a representative sample of people about their experiences with crime. According to these surveys, the overall crime rate is about three times higher than official reports indicate (Gannon & Mihorean, 2005).

THE STREET CRIMINAL: A PROFILE

The typical street criminal can be characterized in the following manner. (This profile, it should be pointed out, is shaped by different clearance rates: the rates at which police solve crimes. White-collar crimes have relatively low clearance rates compared with assault or property crimes, which police solve more successfully.)

Age.   Crime rates rise sharply during adolescence, peak at ages 15–18, and then fall sharply again. While those aged 15–24 represented just 13 percent of the Canadian population in 2002, they accounted for 46 percent of those accused of property crimes and 31 percent of those accused of violent crime (Wallace, 2003). Those charged with violent crime tend to be older (median age was 29 in 1999) than those charged with property crimes (where the median age was 23) (Tremblay, 2000).

Gender.   Although each sex makes up roughly half of the population, police collared males in about 75 percent of all property crime arrests in 2002. In other words, men are

"*You look like this sketch of someone who's thinking about committing a crime.*"

arrested more than three times as often as women for property crimes. In the case of violent crimes, the disparity is even greater for adults (18 and over): 84 percent of charges involved males compared to just 16 percent involving females (a 5:1 ratio). Among youth (ages 12–17) the disparity is less pronounced: 73 percent of charges involved males (a 3:1 ratio).

It may be that law enforcement officials are reluctant to define women as criminals. In global perspective, in fact, the greatest gender difference in crime rates occurs in societies that most severely limit the opportunities of women. In Canada, however, the difference in arrest rates for women and men has been narrowing, which probably indicates increasing gender equality in our society. Despite a decline during the late 1990s, the rate at which female youth were charged with violent crimes increased by 81 percent between 1989 and 1999, while the rate for male youth increased only 30 percent (Tremblay, 2000).

Social class.   Police do not assess the social class of arrested persons, so no statistical data of the kind given above are available. But research has long indicated that criminality is more widespread among people of lower social position (Wolfgang, Figlio, & Sellin, 1972; Clinard & Abbott, 1973; Braithwaite, 1981; Thornberry & Farnsworth, 1982; Wolfgang, Thornberry, & Figlio, 1987).

Yet the connection between class and crime is more complicated than it appears on the surface. For one thing,

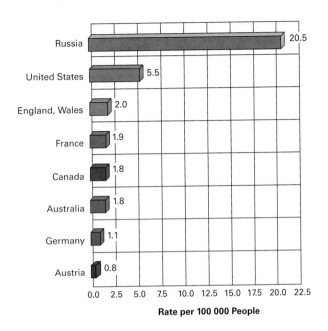

Russia — 20.5
United States — 5.5
England, Wales — 2.0
France — 1.9
Canada — 1.8
Australia — 1.8
Germany — 1.1
Austria — 0.8

0.0 2.5 5.0 7.5 10.0 12.5 15.0 17.5 20.0 22.5

Rate per 100 000 People

FIGURE 7-3 Homicide Rates for Selected Countries

Source: Savoi (2003).

many people look upon the poor as less worthy than the rich, whose wealth and power confer "respectability" (Tittle & Villemez, 1977; Tittle, Villemez, & Smith, 1978; Elias, 1986). While crime—especially violent crime—is a serious problem in the poorest inner-city neighbourhoods, most of these crimes are committed by a few hard-core offenders. The majority of poor people who live in these neighbourhoods have no criminal records at all (Wolfgang, Figlio, & Sellin, 1972; Elliott & Ageton, 1980; Harries, 1990).

Moreover, the connection between social standing and criminality depends on the kind of crime one is talking about (Braithwaite, 1981). If we expand our definition of crime beyond street offences to include white-collar crime, the "common criminal" suddenly looks much more affluent.

Race and ethnicity. In multicultural societies, such as Canada, both race and ethnicity are strongly correlated to crime rates, although the reasons are many and complex. Official U.S. statistics, for example, indicate that in 2001, 31.4 percent of arrests for property crimes and 37.6 percent of arrests for violent crimes involved black people, even

though they only made up 12.3 percent of the population (U.S. Federal Bureau of Investigation, 2002).

Firm conclusions about Canada are not as easy to come by because our police do not collect data on race and ethnicity. However, the available evidence points to the following two conclusions.

First, the situation is rather different with respect to visible ethnic minorities. In fact, they tend to be underrepresented in arrest data and prison populations.

Second, Aboriginals and black people are two exceptions. Aboriginals are dramatically overrepresented in Canada's correctional facilities: In 1998–1999, Aboriginal persons made up 17 percent of admissions to custody, even though they made up only 2 percent of the Canadian population (Thomas, 2000). Similarly, research in the Metro Toronto area on self-declared "black," "white," and "Chinese" male residents shows that black males were almost twice as likely as white males to have been stopped by the police sometime in the previous two years—the percentage of black males who reported having been stopped twice (29 percent) is greater than the proportion of white males that were stopped once (25 percent) (The Commission on Systematic Racism in the Ontario Criminal Justice System, 1995; quoted in James, 1998).

What accounts for the disproportionate number of arrests among various ethnic groups? Two factors, as mentioned above, come into play. First, prejudice related to race prompts white police to arrest Aboriginal people more readily (Schissel, 1993). Second, Aboriginal status in Canada closely relates to social standing, which, as we have already explained, affects the likelihood of engaging in street crimes. Poor people living in the midst of affluence come to see society as unjust and thus are more likely to turn to crime (Blau & Blau, 1982; Anderson, 1994).

CRIME IN GLOBAL PERSPECTIVE

By world standards, the crime rate in Canada is not high. This may seem surprising given the high crime rate characteristic of our neighbour to the south. For example, although recent crime trends are downward in Canada, the United States, and many other high-income nations, there were nonetheless 16 204 murders in the United States in 2002, which amounts to one every half-hour around the clock. In large cities such as New York, rarely does a day pass with no murder; in fact, more New Yorkers are hit with stray bullets than are deliberately gunned down in most large cities elsewhere in the world. Figure 7–3 shows that the homicide rate in Canada is only about a third as high as that in the U.S.

The rate of violent crime (but not property crime) in the United States is several times higher than in Europe. The contrast is even greater between the United States and the nations of Asia, including India and Japan, where violent crime and property crime rates are among the lowest in the world.

Elliott Currie (1985) suggests that the high crime rate in the United States arises from "a cultural emphasis on individual economic success, often at the expense of strong families and neighbourhoods." The United States also has extraordinary cultural diversity, a result of centuries of immigration. Moreover, economic inequality is higher in the U.S. than in most other high-income nations. Thus, the society's relatively weak social fabric, combined with considerable frustration among the poor, generates widespread criminal behaviour.

Proponents of gun registration in Canada point to another factor contributing to violence in the United States—the extensive private ownership of guns. About two-thirds of murder victims in the United States die from shootings. Since the early 1990s, in Texas and several other southern states, shooting deaths have exceeded automobile-related fatalities. Surveys suggest that almost half of U.S. households have at least one gun (J. Wright, 1995; NORC, 2003). Put differently, there are more guns than adults in that country, and one-third of these weapons are handguns that figure in violent crime. In large part, gun ownership reflects people's fear of crime, yet easy availability of guns in the United States makes crime more deadly. Figure 7–4 shows that the United States is the runaway leader in handgun deaths among high-income nations.

But as critics of gun control point out, waiting periods and background checks at retail gun stores do not keep guns out of the hands of criminals, who almost always obtain guns illegally (J. Wright, 1995). And gun control is not a magic bullet in the war on crime. For example, Currie (1985) notes that the number of Californians killed each year by knives alone exceeds the number of Canadians killed by weapons of all kinds. However, most experts think that stricter gun control laws would reduce the level of deadly violence.

Crime rates are soaring in some of the largest cities of the world, such as Manila (the Philippines) and São Paulo (Brazil), which have rapid population growth and millions of desperately poor people. Outside of big cities, however, the traditional character of low-income societies and their strong family structure allow local communities to control crime informally.

Some types of crime have always been multinational, such as terrorism, espionage, and arms dealing (Martin & Romano, 1992). But today, the globalization also extends to other types of crime. Consider the illegal drug trade. The problem of illegal drugs in Canada is partly a *demand* issue;

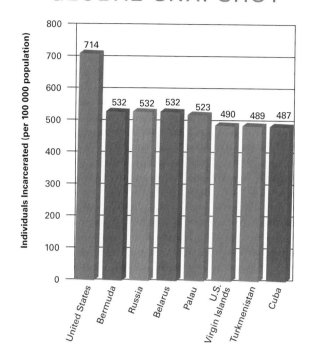

GLOBAL SNAPSHOT

FIGURE 7–4 Number of Murders by Handguns, 1996

Source: Brady Campaign to Prevent Gun Violence (2001).

the demand for cocaine and other drugs in this country is high, and many people are willing to risk arrest or even violent death for a chance to get rich in the drug trade. But the *supply* side of the issue is just as important. In the South American nation of Colombia, at least 20 percent of the people depend on cocaine production for their livelihood. Not only is cocaine Colombia's most profitable export, but it outsells all other exports—including coffee—combined. Clearly, then, drug dealing and many other crimes are closely related to social conditions both in this country and elsewhere.

Different countries have different strategies for dealing with crime. The use of capital punishment (the death penalty) is a case in point. According to Amnesty International (2003), three nations account for 81 percent of the world's executions carried out by governments. Global Map 7–1 shows which countries currently use capital punishment. The global trend is toward abolishing the death penalty: Amnesty International (2004) reports that since 1985, more than 50 nations have ended this practice.

GLOBAL MAP 7-1 Capital Punishment in Global Perspective

The map identifies 78 countries and territories in which the law allows the death penalty for ordinary crimes; in 15 more, the death penalty is reserved for exceptional crimes under military law or during times of war. The death penalty does not exist in 80 countries and territories; in 23 more, although the death penalty remains in law, no execution has taken place in more than 10 years. Compare high-income and low-income nations: what general pattern do you see? In what way do the United States and Japan stand out?

Source: Amnesty International (2004).

The Canadian Criminal Justice System

 December 10, Casablanca, Morocco. Casablanca! An exciting mix of African, European, and Middle Eastern cultures.

Returning from a stroll through the medina, the medieval section of this coastal North African city, we confront lines of police along a boulevard, standing between us and our ship in the harbour. The police are providing security for many important leaders attending an Islamic conference at a nearby hotel. Are the *streets closed? No one asks, but people stop short of an invisible line some 15 metres from the police officers. I play the brash North American and start across the street to inquire (in broken French) if we can pass by, but I stop cold as several officers draw a bead on me with their eyes. Their fingers nervously tap at the grips on their automatic weapons. This is no time to strike up a conversation.*

The criminal justice system is a society's formal response to crime. In some countries, military police keep a tight rein on people's behaviour; in others, including Canada, police have more limited powers and only respond to violations of criminal law. We shall briefly examine the key elements of the Canadian criminal justice system: police, courts, and the punishment of convicted offenders.

POLICE

The police generally serve as the point of contact between a population and the criminal justice system. In principle, the police maintain public order by enforcing the law. Of course, there is only so much that 58 414 police officers in Canada (in 2002) can do to monitor the activities of over 32 million people. As a result, the police exercise considerable discretion about which situations warrant their attention and how to handle them.

How do police carry out their duties? In a study of police behaviour in five U.S. cities, Douglas Smith and Christy Visher (1981; Smith, 1987) concluded that because they must act swiftly, police quickly size situations up in terms of six factors. First, the more serious they think the situation is, the more likely they are to make an arrest. Second, police take account of the victim's wishes in deciding whether to make an arrest. Third, the odds of arrest go up the more uncooperative a suspect is. Fourth, police are more likely to take into custody someone they have arrested before, presumably because this suggests guilt. Fifth, the presence of bystanders increases the chances of arrest. According to Smith and Visher, the presence of observers prompts police to take stronger control of a situation, if only to move the encounter from the street (the suspect's turf) to the police department (where law officers have the edge). Sixth, all else being equal, police are more likely to arrest visible minorities or Aboriginals than others, perceiving them as either more dangerous or more likely to be guilty.

COURTS

After arrest, a court determines a suspect's guilt or innocence. In principle, Canadian courts rely on an adversarial process involving attorneys—one representing the defendant and another the country—in the presence of a judge who monitors legal procedures.

In practice, however, over 90 percent of criminal cases are resolved before court appearance through **plea bargaining**, *a legal negotiation in which a prosecutor reduces a charge in exchange for a defendant's guilty plea.* For example, the Crown prosecutor may offer a defendant charged with burglary a lesser charge, perhaps possession of burglary tools, in exchange for a guilty plea. Plea bargaining is also an important tool for the Crown prosecutor who needs a witness to testify against other accused. In this instance, the accused bargains for a lesser charge in exchange for testimony against co-accused.

Plea bargaining is widespread because it spares the system the time and expense of trials. A trial is usually unnecessary if there is little disagreement as to the facts of the case. Moreover, because the number of cases entering the system has increased dramatically over the past decade, prosecutors cannot possibly bring every one to trial. By quickly resolving most of their work, then, the courts devote most of their resources to the most important cases.

But there are several problems associated with plea bargaining. First, it pressures defendants (who are presumed innocent) to plead guilty. A person can exercise the right to a trial, but only at the risk of receiving a more severe sentence if found guilty. Furthermore, low-income defendants often must rely on a public defender—typically an overworked and underpaid attorney who may devote little time to even the most serious cases (Novak, 1999). Plea bargaining may be efficient, but it undercuts the adversarial process as well as the rights of defendants.

Second, plea bargaining sometimes allows individuals to receive inadequate sentences if further facts against them are discovered after agreement with the Crown prosecutor is finalized. There is near universal condemnation of the plea bargain that the Crown prosecutor negotiated with Karla Homolka in exchange for her testimony against Paul Bernardo because of the additional facts that emerged

 Learn more about plea bargaining and the reason Homolka's agreement was not revoked at http://canada.justice.gc.ca/en/ps/inter/plea/toc.html.

against Homolka during the trial against her husband.

PUNISHMENT

When a young man is shot dead on the street after leaving a restaurant, some people may wonder why it happened, but almost everyone believes that someone should have to "pay"

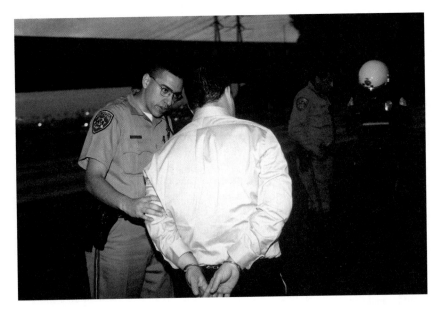

Police must be allowed discretion if they are to effectively handle the many different situations they face every day. At the same time, it is important to treat people fairly. Here, we see a police officer deciding whether or not to charge a motorist for driving while drunk. What factors do you think enter into this decision?

for the crime. Indeed, sometimes the desire to punish is so great that in the end justice may not be done.

Such cases force us to ask *why* a society should punish its wrongdoers. Scholars answer with four basic reasons: retribution, deterrence, rehabilitation, and societal protection.

Retribution. The oldest justification for punishment is to satisfy a society's need for **retribution**, *an act of moral vengeance by which society makes the offender suffer as much as the suffering caused by the crime.* Retribution rests on a view of society as being in moral balance. When criminality upsets this balance, punishment in equal measure restores the moral order, as suggested by the biblical saying, "an eye for an eye."

In the Middle Ages, most people viewed crime as sin— an offence against God as well as society—that required a harsh response. Although critics point out that retribution does little to reform the offender, many people today still consider vengeance reason enough for punishment.

Deterrence. A second justification for punishment is **deterrence**, *the attempt to discourage criminality through the use of punishment.* Deterrence is based on the eighteenth-century Enlightenment idea that as calculating and rational creatures, humans will not break the law if they think that the pains of punishment outweigh the pleasures of crime.

Deterrence emerged as a reform measure in response to harsh punishments based on retribution. Why put someone to death for stealing if theft can be discouraged by a prison sentence? As the concept of deterrence gained acceptance in

industrial societies, execution and physical mutilation of criminals were replaced by milder forms of punishment such as imprisonment.

Punishment may deter crime in two ways. *Specific deterrence* convinces an individual offender that crime does not pay. Through *general deterrence*, punishing one person serves as an example to others.

Watch CBC coverage of the last executions in Canada: **http://** archives.cbc.ca/IDC-1-69-383-2202-10/on_this_day/ life_society/last_execution.

Rehabilitation. The third justification for punishment, **rehabilitation**, is *a program for reforming the offender to prevent later offences.* Rehabilitation arose along with the social sciences in the nineteenth century. Since then, sociologists have claimed that crime and other deviance spring from a social environment marked by poverty or lack of parental supervision. Logically, then, if offenders learn to be deviant, they can also learn to obey the rules; the key is controlling the environment. Reformatories or houses of correction provided a controlled setting where people could learn proper behaviour (recall the description of total institutions in Chapter 3, "Socialization: From Infancy to Old Age").

Like deterrence, rehabilitation motivates the offender to conform. But rehabilitation emphasizes constructive improvement, whereas deterrence and retribution simply make the offender suffer. In addition, retribution demands that the punishment fit the crime, but rehabilitation tailors treatment to each offender. Thus, identical crimes would

To increase the power of punishment to deter crime, capital punishment was long carried out in public. While the last execution in Canada occurred in 1962, the last public execution took place almost 100 years earlier in 1869. Here is a photograph from the last public execution in the United States, with 22-year-old Rainey Bethea standing on the scaffold moments from death in Owensboro, Kentucky, on August 14, 1936. Children as well as adults were in the crowd.

prompt similar acts of retribution but different rehabilitation programs.

Societal protection.   A final justification for punishment is **societal protection**, *rendering an offender incapable of further offences temporarily through imprisonment or permanently by execution.* Like deterrence, societal protection is a rational approach to punishment intended to protect society from crime. The reason that there are more than 31 000 adults in Canadian prisons is partly a reflection of the widespread attitude that we should "get criminals off the streets." Remember that this number represents only about 20 percent of the total number under the supervision of the correctional system—about 66 percent of the grand total are on probation and the remainder serve a conditional sentence or are on conditional release (Beattie, 2005).

Since the early 1990s, there has been a slight decrease in the number of admissions to Canadian jails (Thomas, 2000). This is in contrast to the situation in the U.S., where currently some 2 million people are incarcerated and another 4.7 million are on parole and probation. In response to tougher public attitudes and an increasing number of drug-related arrests, the U.S. prison population has tripled since 1980. As Figure 7–5 shows, the United States incarcerates a larger share of its population than all other countries in the world (Sutton, 2000; The Sentencing Project, 2002).

Critical review.   The Summing Up table reviews the four justifications for punishment. However, an accurate assessment of the actual consequences of punishment is no simple task.

The value of retribution lies in Durkheim's claim that punishing the deviant person increases society's moral awareness. For this reason, punishment traditionally was a public event.

Certainly, punishment deters some crime. Yet our society has a high rate of **criminal recidivism**, *later offences by people previously convicted of crimes.* After being released, about half of those convicted of a *Criminal Code* offence are convicted of a new offence within three years, and some studies suggest that almost four out of five offenders are eventually convicted again (Burr et al., 2000; Hanson, Scott, & Steffy, 1995). In light of such patterns, we may well wonder about the extent to which punishment really deters crime. Then, too, only about one-third of all crimes are known to police, and of these, only about one in five results in an arrest. The old saying "crime doesn't pay" rings hollow when we consider that only a small percentage of offences are ever punished.

General deterrence is even more difficult to investigate scientifically because we have no way of knowing how people might act if they were unaware of punishments handed down to others. Opponents of capital punishment point to research suggesting that the death penalty has limited value as a general deterrent and note that the United States is the only Western, high-income nation that routinely executes serious offenders. A troubling fact is that some death sentences have been pronounced against innocent people. Between 1973 and 2003, almost 100 people were released

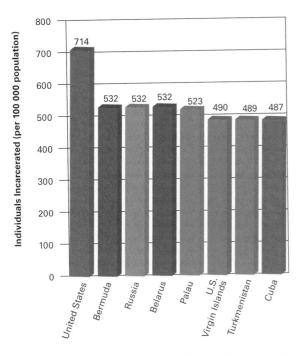

GLOBAL SNAPSHOT

Individuals Incarcerated (per 100 000 population)

- United States: 714
- Bermuda: 532
- Russia: 532
- Belarus: 532
- Palau: 523
- U.S. Virgin Islands: 490
- Turkmenistan: 489
- Cuba: 487

FIGURE 7-5 Nations With the Highest Incarceration Rates

Note: Figures are for different years. They are the most recent as of 2005.
Source: World Prism Population list, Roy Walmsley (2005)

from death row in the United States after new evidence established their innocence, which means that innocent people might have been put to death.

Prisons provide short-term societal protection by keeping offenders off the streets, but they do little to reshape attitudes or behaviour in the long term (Carlson, 1976; Wright, 1994). Perhaps rehabilitation is an unrealistic expectation because, according to Sutherland's theory of differential association, locking criminals up together for years probably strengthens criminal attitudes and skills. Imprisonment also breaks whatever social ties inmates may have in the outside world, which, following Hirschi's control theory, makes inmates likely to commit more crimes upon release.

COMMUNITY-BASED CORRECTIONS

Prisons keep convicted criminals off the streets. But the evidence suggests that locking people up does little to rehabilitate most offenders. Furthermore, prisons are expensive, costing our society over $80 000 per year to support an inmate in federal prison.

One recent alternative to the traditional prison that has been adopted in many parts of Canada is **community-based corrections**, *correctional programs operating within society at large rather than behind prison walls.* Community-based corrections have a number of advantages: They reduce the overcrowding in prisons, handle convicts at a lower cost than prisons, and allow for supervision of convicts while eliminating the hardships of prison life as well as the stigma that accompanies being imprisoned. In general, the idea of community-based corrections is not so much to punish as to reform; such programs are therefore usually offered to individuals who have committed less serious offences and who appear to be good prospects for avoiding future criminal violations (Inciardi, 2000).

Probation. One form of community-based correction is *probation*, a policy of permitting a convicted offender to remain in the community under conditions imposed by a court, including regular supervision. Courts may require that a probationer receive counselling, attend a drug treatment program, hold a job, avoid associating with "known criminals," or anything else deemed appropriate. Typically, a probationer must check in with an officer of the court (the "probation officer") on a regular schedule to make sure the guidelines are being followed. Should the probationer fail to live up to the conditions set by the court or commit a new offence, the court may revoke probation in favour of imprisonment."

Parole. *Parole* is a policy of releasing inmates from prison to serve the remainder of their sentences under the supervision of a parole officer in the local community. Although some sentences specifically deny the possibility of parole, most inmates become eligible for parole after serving a certain portion of their sentence. At this time, a parole board evaluates the risks and benefits of an inmate's early release from prison. If parole is granted, the parole board monitors the offender's conduct until the sentence is completed. Should the offender not comply with the conditions of parole or be arrested for another crime, the board can revoke parole, returning the offender to prison to complete the sentence.

Critical review. Evaluations of community-based corrections are mixed. There is little question that probation and parole programs are much less expensive than conventional imprisonment; they also free up room in prisons for people who commit more serious crimes. Yet research suggests that although probation does seem to work for some people, it does not significantly reduce criminal recidivism. Similarly, parole is useful to prison officials as a means to encourage good behaviour among inmates who hope for early release.

SUMMING UP

Four Justifications for Punishment

Retribution	The oldest justification for punishment. Punishment is society's revenge for a moral wrong. In principle, punishment should be equal in severity to the deviance itself.
Deterrence	An early modern approach. Deviance is considered social disruption, which society acts to control. People are viewed as rational and self-interested; deterrence works because the pain of punishment outweighs the pleasure of deviance.
Rehabilitation	A modern strategy linked to the development of social sciences. Deviance is viewed as the result of social problems (such as poverty) or personal problems (such as mental illness). Social conditions are improved; treatment is tailored to the offender's condition.
Societal protection	A modern approach easier to carry out than rehabilitation. If society is unable or unwilling to rehabilitate offenders or reform social conditions, people are protected by the imprisonment or execution of the offender.

Yet levels of crime among individuals who have been released on parole are high. Indeed, recidivism among parolees is so high that a number of U.S. states have ended their parole programs entirely (Inciardi, 2000).

Evaluations of all aspects of the criminal justice system point to a sobering truth: the criminal justice system cannot eliminate crime. As the Applying Sociology box on page 192 explains, while police, courts, and prisons do affect crime rates, crime and other deviant behaviours are not just the acts of "bad people" but reflect the operation of society itself.

Violent Crime Is Down—But Why?

During the 1980s, crime rates shot upward and there seemed to be no solution to the problem. In the 1990s, something good and unexpected happened: serious crime rates began to fall until by 2000, they were at levels not seen in more than a generation. Why? Researchers point to several reasons:

1. **A reduction in the youth population.** We have already noted that young people (particularly males) are responsible for much violent crime. Between 1990 and 2000, the share of the population aged 15–24 dropped significantly.

2. **Changes in policing.** Much of the drop in crime (as well as the earlier rise in crime) has taken place in large cities. Many cities have adopted a policy of community policing, which means that police are concerned not just with making arrests but with preventing crime before it happens. Officers get to know the areas they patrol and frequently stop young men for jaywalking or other minor infractions so they can check them for other things. In addition, there are more police working in Canada today. The number of police officers in Canada increased 3 percent between 1991 and 1996, and another 6 percent by 2001 (Taylor-Butts, 2004).

3. **A better economy.** The Canadian economy boomed during the 1990s. With unemployment down, more people were working, reducing the likelihood that some would turn to crime out of economic desperation. The logic here is simple: more jobs, fewer crimes. By the same token, the economic downturn of the early 2000s may well push crime rates up again.

4. **The declining drug trade.** Many analysts think that the most important factor in reducing rates of violent crime is the decline of crack cocaine. Crack came on the scene around 1985, and violence spread as young people—especially in the inner cities—became part of a booming drug trade. Facing few legitimate job opportunities but increasing opportunities to make money illegally, a generation of young people became part of a wave of violence.

By the early 1990s, however, the popularity of crack had begun to fall as people saw the damage the drug was causing to entire communities. This realization, coupled with steady economic improvement and stiffer sentences for drug offences, brought the turnaround in violent crime.

The current picture looks better relative to what it was a decade ago. The crime problem, says one researcher, "looks better, but only because the early 1990s were so bad. So let's not fool ourselves into thinking everything is resolved. It's not."

WHAT DO YOU THINK?

1. Do you support the policy of community policing? Why or why not?
2. Of all the factors mentioned here, which do you think is the most important in crime control? Which is least important? Why?

Sources: Based on Fagan, Zimring, & Kim (1998), Witkin (1998), Winship & Berrien (1999), Donahue & Levitt (2000), and Rosenfeld (2002).

SUMMARY

1. Deviance refers to norm violations, ranging from bad manners to serious violence.

2. Biological research, from Lombroso's nineteenth-century observations of convicts to recent genetic studies, has yet to offer much insight into the causes of deviance.

3. Psychological studies link deviance to a person's abnormal personality resulting from biological causes or unsuccessful socialization. Psychological theories help explain some types of deviance.

4. The roots of deviance lie in society rather than individuals because deviance varies according to cultural norms, is socially defined, and reflects patterns of social power.

5. Taking a structural-functional approach, Durkheim explained that deviance affirms norms and values, clarifies moral boundaries, brings people together, and encourages social change.

6. The symbolic-interaction approach is the basis of labelling theory, which holds that deviance lies in people's reaction to a person's behaviour, not in the behaviour itself. Acquiring the stigma of deviance can lead to secondary deviance and a deviant career.

7. Based on Karl Marx's ideas, social-conflict theory holds that laws and other norms reflect the interests of powerful members of society. Although white-collar and corporate crimes cause extensive social harm, offenders are rarely branded as criminals.

8. Official statistics indicate that arrest rates peak in late adolescence and drop steadily thereafter. About 75 percent of people arrested for property crimes and 84 percent of those arrested for violent crimes are male.

9. Poorer people commit more street crime than those with greater wealth. When white-collar crimes are included among criminal offences, however, this difference in criminal activity becomes smaller.

10. Aboriginal and black people are arrested more often than whites in proportion to their respective numbers in the population. Other visible minorities have lower than average rates of arrest.

11. Police use a great deal of personal judgment in their work. Arrest is more likely if the offence is serious, bystanders are present, or the accused is Aboriginal or black.

12. Although set up as an adversarial system, Canadian courts resolve most cases through plea bargaining. Though efficient, this method puts less powerful people at a disadvantage.

13. Justifications of punishment include retribution, deterrence, rehabilitation, and societal protection. Because its consequences are difficult to evaluate scientifically, punishment—like deviance itself—sparks controversy.

14. Community-based corrections include probation and parole. Such policies reduce the cost of supervising people convicted of crimes and reduce prison overcrowding, but have not been shown to greatly reduce recidivism.

KEY CONCEPTS

community-based corrections (p. 190) correctional programs operating within society at large rather than behind prison walls

corporate crime (p. 178) the illegal actions of a corporation or people acting on its behalf

crime (p. 168) the violation of a society's formally enacted criminal law

crimes against property (property crimes) (p. 181) crimes that involve theft of goods belonging to others

crimes against the person (violent crimes) (p. 181) crimes that direct violence or the threat of violence against others

criminal justice system (p. 169) a formal response by police, courts, and prison officials to alleged violations of the law

criminal recidivism (p. 189) later offences by people previously convicted of crimes

deterrence (p. 188) the attempt to discourage criminality through the use of punishment

deviance (p. 168) the recognized violation of cultural norms

hate crime (p. 179) a criminal act against a person or a person's property by an offender motivated by racial or other bias

labelling theory (p. 173) the assertion that deviance and conformity result not so much from what people do as from how others respond to those actions

medicalization of deviance (p. 175) the transformation of moral and legal deviance into a medical condition

organized crime (p. 178) a business supplying illegal goods or services

plea bargaining (p. 187) a legal negotiation in which a prosecutor reduces a charge in exchange for a defendant's guilty plea

rehabilitation (p. 188) a program for reforming the offender to prevent later offences

retribution (p. 188) an act of moral vengeance by which society makes the offender suffer as much as the suffering caused by the crime

social control (p. 169) attempts by society to regulate people's thoughts and behaviour

societal protection (p. 189) rendering an offender incapable of further offences temporarily through imprisonment or permanently by execution

stigma (p. 174) a powerfully negative label that greatly changes a person's self-concept and social identity

victimless crimes (crimes without complaint) (p. 182) violations of law in which there are no obvious victims

white-collar crime (p. 178) crime committed by people of high social position in the course of their occupations

CRITICAL-THINKING QUESTIONS

1. How does a sociological view of deviance differ from the common-sense idea that bad people do bad things?

2. List Durkheim's functions of deviance. From his point of view, can society ever be free from deviance? Why or why not?

3. An old saying is "sticks and stones can break my bones, but names can never hurt me." Explain how labelling theory challenges this statement.

4. The gender gap in arrest rates has narrowed in the recent past. What factors do you think will determine if this trend will continue in the future?

APPLICATIONS AND EXERCISES

1. Research computer crime. What new kinds of crime are emerging in the information age? Is computer technology also creating new ways to track down lawbreakers?

2. Rent a wheelchair (check with a local pharmacy or medical supply store), and use it as much as possible for a day or two. Not only will you gain a firsthand understanding of the physical barriers to getting around, but you will discover that people respond to you in many new ways.

3. Watch an episode of the real-action police show *COPS*. Based on this program, how would you describe the people who commit crimes?

 SITES TO SEE

www.pearsoned.ca/macionis
The authors and publisher of this book invite you to visit the interactive Companion Website™ that accompanies this text. Begin by clicking on the cover of your book. You will find a chapter-by-chapter study guide, practice tests, suggested weblinks, and links to other relevant material.

www.civilrights.org
The Leadership Conference on Civil Rights maintains this site dealing with hate crimes and other civil rights issues.

www.cbc.ca/prison
This is a CBC site about Canadian prisons.

www.johnhoward.ca
The John Howard Society has many research briefs on various aspects of the Canadian prison system.

http://justice.uaa.alaska.edu/death/intl.html
This site looks at the death penalty in global perspective.

www.unodc.org/unodc/en/analysis_and_statistics.html
The United Nations Office on Drugs and Crime conducts a survey of crime trends and the operation of the criminal justice system in individual countries around the world.

Follow the instructions on page 33 of this text to access the features of Research Navigator™. Once at the website (**www.researchnavigator.com**), enter your login name and password. Then, to use the Content Select™ database, enter keywords such as "crime," "rape," and "prison," and the search engine will supply relevant and recent scholarly and popular press publications.

To reinforce your understanding of this chapter, and to identify topics for further study, visit MySocLab at **www.pearsoned.ca/mysoclab/macionis** for diagnostic tests and a multimedia ebook.

CHAPTER EIGHT

Social Stratification

What is social stratification?

Why does social inequality exist?

How do social classes in Canada
differ from one another?

8

All societies give far more to some categories of people than to others. Though officially outlawed, the traditional caste system in India still defines some people, including this woman, as Dalits or "Untouchables"; these people remain socially scorned and very poor.

On April 10, 1912, the ocean liner *Titanic* slipped away from the docks of Southampton, England, on its first voyage across the North Atlantic to New York. A proud symbol of the new industrial age, the towering ship carried 2300 passengers, some enjoying more luxury than most travellers today could imagine. Poor people crowded the lower decks, journeying to what they hoped would be a better life in North America.

Two days out, the crew received reports of icebergs in the area but paid little notice. Then, near midnight, as the ship steamed swiftly westward, a stunned lookout reported a massive shape rising out of the dark ocean directly ahead. Moments later, the *Titanic* collided with a huge iceberg—as tall as the ship itself—that split open its side as if the grand vessel were a giant tin can.

Seawater flooded into the ship's lower levels, pulling the ship down by the bow. Within 25 minutes of impact, people were rushing for the lifeboats. By 2:00 A.M., the bow was completely submerged, and the stern rose high above the water. Clinging to the deck, quietly observed by those in lifeboats, hundreds of helpless passengers and crew solemnly passed their final minutes before the ship disappeared into the frigid Atlantic (Lord, 1976).

The tragic loss of more than 1600 lives made news around the world. Looking back on this terrible event with a sociological eye, we see that some categories of passengers had much better odds of survival than others. During this more traditional time, women and children boarded the lifeboats first, with the result that 80 percent of those who died were men. Class was also a factor. More than 60 percent of the passengers travelling on first-class tickets were saved because they were on the upper decks, where warnings were sounded first and lifeboats were accessible. Only 36 percent of the second-class passengers survived, and of the third-class passengers on the lower decks, only 24 percent escaped drowning. On board the *Titanic*, class meant more than the quality of accommodations—it was a matter of life or death.

The fate of the passengers on the *Titanic* dramatically illustrates how social inequality affects the way people live and, sometimes, whether they live at all. This chapter explores the important concept of social stratification and examines social inequality in Canada.

What Is Social Stratification?

Every society is marked by inequality, with some people having more money, schooling, health, and power than others. **Social stratification**, defined as *a system by which a society ranks categories of people in a hierarchy*, involves four basic principles:

1. **Social stratification is a trait of society, not simply a reflection of individual differences.** Many of us think of social standing in terms of personal talent and effort, exaggerating the extent to which we control our own destinies. Did a higher percentage of the first-class passengers on the *Titanic* survive because they were better swimmers than second- and third-class passengers? Hardly. They did better because of their privileged position on the ship. Similarly, children born into wealthy families are more likely than children born into poverty to enjoy good health, do well in school, succeed in a career, and live a long life. Neither the rich nor the poor are responsible for creating social stratification, yet this system shapes the lives of us all.

2. **Social stratification carries over from generation to generation.** We have only to look at how parents pass their social position on to their children to see that stratification is a trait of societies rather than individuals.

Some individuals, especially in industrial societies, do experience **social mobility**, a change in position within the social hierarchy. Social mobility may be upward or downward. We celebrate the achievements of rare individuals such as Michaëlle Jean and Wayne Gretzky, both of whom rose from modest beginnings to fame and fortune. Some people move downward in the social hierarchy because of business setbacks, unemployment, or illness. More often people move horizontally, when, say, they switch one job for another at about the same social level. The social standing of most people remains much the same over their lifetime.

3. **Social stratification is universal but variable.** Social stratification is found everywhere. Yet *what* is unequal and *how* unequal it is vary from one society to another. In some societies inequality is mostly a matter of prestige; in others, wealth or power is the key element of difference. Furthermore, some societies contain more inequality than others.

4. **Social stratification involves not just inequality but beliefs.** Any system of inequality not only gives some people more than others, but it also defines these arrangements as fair. Like the *what* of social inequality, the explanation of *why* people should be unequal differs from society to society.

Caste and Class Systems

Sociologists distinguish between *closed systems,* which allow little change in social position, and *open systems,* which permit some social mobility (Tumin, 1985). The caste system is an example of a closed system, and the class system is a more open system.

THE CASTE SYSTEM

A **caste system** amounts to *social stratification based on ascription, or birth.* A pure caste system is closed because birth alone decides a person's future, with little or no social mobility based on individual effort. People are ranked in rigid categories, in which they live out their lives.

An illustration: India.   Many of the world's societies, most of them agrarian, are caste systems. One example is India's traditional villages, where most of the country's people still live. The Indian system identifies four major castes (or *varna,* a Sanskrit word that means "colour"): Brahmin, Kshatriya, Vaishya, and Shudra. On the local level, however, each of these is composed of hundreds of subcaste (or *jati*) groups.

From birth, caste position determines the direction of a person's life. First, with the exception of farming, which is open to all, families in each caste perform one type of work, as priests, soldiers, barbers, leather workers, sweepers, and so on.

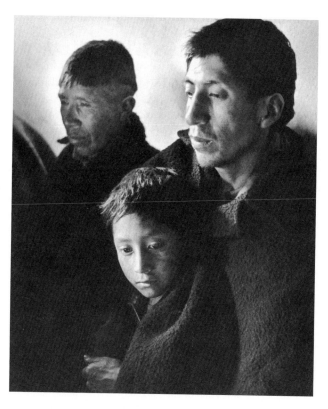

The personal experience of poverty is captured in Sebastiao Salgado's photograph, which shows how social standing is passed on from one generation to the next. The essential sociological insight is that, however strongly individuals feel its effects, our social standing is largely a consequence of the way in which a society (or a world of societies) structures opportunity and reward. To the core of our being, then, we are all the products of social stratification.

Second, a caste system demands that people marry others of the same ranking. If people were to have "mixed" marriages with members of other castes, what rank would their children hold? Sociologists call this pattern of marrying within a social category *endogamous* marriage (*endo* stems from the Greek word meaning "within"). According to tradition, Indian parents select their children's marriage partners, often before the children reach their teens.

Third, caste systems shape members' beliefs. Indian culture is built on the Hindu tradition that accepting an arranged marriage and doing the caste's life work is a moral duty.

Fourth, caste guides everyday life by keeping people in the company of "their own kind." Norms reinforce this practice by teaching, for instance, that a more "pure" person of a higher caste position is "polluted" by contact with someone of lower standing.

GLOBAL SOCIOLOGY

Race as Caste: A Report From South Africa

At the southern tip of the African continent lies South Africa, a country larger than the Northwest Territories but smaller than Quebec, with a population of about 47 million. The native Africans were joined by Dutch traders and farmers in the mid-seventeenth century. Early in the nineteenth century, a second wave of British colonization pushed the Dutch inland. By the early 1900s, the British had taken over the country, proclaiming it the Union of South Africa. In 1961, the nation declared its independence as the Republic of South Africa.

But freedom was a reality only for the white minority. To ensure their control over the black majority, whites used a policy of *apartheid,* or racial separation. Apartheid, written into law in 1948, denied blacks citizenship, ownership of land, and any voice in the government. As a lower caste, blacks received little schooling and performed menial, low-paying jobs. White people of even moderate wealth had at least one black household servant.

The white minority claimed apartheid protected their cultural traditions, and many believed blacks were inferior beings. Resistance to apartheid prompted whites to use brutal military repression to maintain their power.

Nevertheless, steady resistance—especially from younger blacks impatient for political

and economic opportunity—gradually forced change. Adding to the internal pressure was criticism from other industrial nations. By the mid-1980s, the tide began to turn as the South African government granted limited rights to people of mixed race and Asian ancestry. This was followed by the rights for all people to form labour unions, to enter various occupations once limited to whites, and to own property. Officials also repealed laws that separated the races in public places.

The pace of change increased in 1990 with the release from prison of Nelson Mandela, a revered resistance leader. In 1994, the first national election open to all races made Mandela president, ending centuries of white minority rule.

Despite this dramatic political change, social position in South Africa is still based on race. About one-third of black South Africans have no work, and

the majority remain dirt poor. The worst off are the 7 million *ukuhleleleka,* which means "marginal people" in the Xhosa language. Soweto-by-the-Sea may sound like a summer getaway, but it is home to thousands of people crammed into shacks made from packing cases, corrugated metal, cardboard, and other discarded materials. There is no electricity for lights or refrigeration. Without plumbing, people use buckets to haul sewage; women line up to take a turn at a single water tap that serves more than a thousand people. Jobs are hard to come by, and those who do find work are lucky to earn $250 a month.

South Africa's current president, Thabo Mbeki, re-elected in 2004, leads a nation still crippled by its history of racial caste. Tourism is up and holds out promise of an economic boom in years to come, but the country can shed its past only by providing real opportunity to all its people.

WHAT DO YOU THINK?

1. How has race been a form of caste in South Africa?
2. Do you think racial caste will eventually break down in South Africa? In how long?
3. Does race operate as caste in Canada? Explain your answer.

Sources: Fredrickson (1981), Wren (1991), Hawthorne (1999), and Mabry & Masland (1999).

Caste systems are typical of agrarian societies because agriculture demands a lifelong routine of hard work; by teaching a sense of moral duty, a caste system ensures that people are disciplined for a lifetime of work and are willing to perform the same jobs as their parents. Thus, caste hangs on in rural India more than half a century after being formally outlawed. People living in the industrial cities of India have many more choices about work and marriage partners than people in rural areas.

Another country dominated by caste is South Africa, although the racial system of *apartheid* is now in decline. The Global Sociology box takes a closer look.

THE CLASS SYSTEM

A modern economy, which depends on developing people's talents rather than the lifelong discipline required for farming, gives rise to a **class system**, *social stratification based on both birth and individual achievement.*

Class systems are more open than caste systems, so people who gain schooling and skills may be socially mobile in relation to their parents and siblings. Such mobility blurs class boundaries, so even blood relatives may have different social standing. Categorizing people according to their colour, sex, or social background comes to be seen as wrong in modern societies as all people gain political rights and, in principle, equal standing before the law. Furthermore, work is no longer fixed at birth but involves some personal choice. Greater individuality also translates into more freedom in selecting a marital partner.

Meritocracy. The concept of **meritocracy** refers to *social stratification based on personal merit*. Because industrial societies need to develop a broad range of abilities (beyond farming), stratification is based not just on the accident of birth but also on merit (from a Latin word meaning "worthy of praise")—in this case, the type of job held and how well it is performed. To advance meritocracy, industrial societies expand equality of opportunity, although people expect inequality of outcomes.

In a pure meritocracy, social position would depend entirely on a person's ability and effort. Such a system would have ongoing social mobility, blurring social categories as individuals continuously move up or down in the system depending on their latest performance.

Caste societies define merit in terms of loyalty to the system—that is, dutifully performing whatever job comes with a person's birth. Caste systems waste human potential, but they are very orderly. And here lies the answer to an important question: Why do modern, industrial societies keep some elements of caste—such as letting wealth pass from generation to generation—rather than becoming complete meritocracies? Simply because a pure meritocracy weakens families and other social groupings. Economic performance is not everything, after all. Would we want to evaluate our family members solely on their jobs? Probably not. Therefore, class systems in industrial societies move toward meritocracy to promote productivity and efficiency but retain some caste elements, such as family, to maintain order and social unity.

Status consistency is *the degree of consistency in a person's social standing across various dimensions of social inequality*. A caste system has little social mobility and high status consistency, so the typical person has the same relative standing with regard to wealth, power, and prestige. However, the greater mobility of class systems produces less status consistency. In Canada, a college or university professor with an advanced degree might enjoy high social prestige but earn only a modest **income** (defined as *wages or salary from work*

and earnings from investments). Low status consistency means that *classes* are less well defined than *castes*.

An illustration: The United Kingdom. The mix of meritocracy and caste in class systems is well illustrated by the United Kingdom (Great Britain—composed of England, Wales, and Scotland—and Northern Ireland), an industrial nation with a long agrarian history.

In the Middle Ages, England had a castelike system of three *estates*. The *first estate* was a hereditary nobility, making up perhaps 5 percent of the population, who controlled most of the land, which was the chief form of wealth (Laslett, 1984). Most nobles had no occupation at all, and they considered engaging in trade or doing other work for income "beneath" them. Well attended by servants, nobles used their leisure time to develop refined tastes in art, music, and literature.

To prevent vast landholdings from being divided by heirs, the law of *primogeniture* (from Latin, meaning "first born") stated that all landholdings passed to the oldest son or other male relation. Younger sons had to find other means of support. Some entered the clergy—the *second estate*—where spiritual power was supported by the church's extensive landholdings. Other men of high birth became military officers or lawyers, professions considered honourable for gentlemen. In an age when no woman could inherit her father's property and few women had the chance to earn a living on their own, a noble daughter depended for her security on marrying well.

Below the nobility and the clergy, most men and women formed the *third estate*, or commoners. Most commoners were serfs, who worked the land owned by nobles. Unlike members of the first and second estates, most commoners had little schooling and were illiterate.

As the Industrial Revolution expanded England's economy, some commoners living in cities made enough money to challenge the nobility. More emphasis on meritocracy, the growing importance of money, and the expansion of schooling and legal rights eventually blurred social rankings and gave rise to a class system.

Perhaps it is a sign of the times that these days, traditional titles are put up for sale by British nobles who need money. In 1996, for example, Earl Spencer—the brother of the late Princess Diana—sold his title, Lord of Wimbledon, to raise the $300 000 he needed to redo the plumbing in one of his large homes (McKee, 1996).

Yet the caste elements of England's past can still be seen today. A small cluster of British families still holds considerable inherited wealth and enjoys the highest prestige, the best schooling at elite universities, and political influence. A traditional monarch, Queen Elizabeth II, stands as head of

In 2002, Queen Elizabeth II celebrated her silver jubilee, marking 50 years on the throne as England's monarch. Perhaps it is a sign of more egalitarian times that the event was not a performance of the London Philharmonic but a rock and roll concert—a popular culture ritual—intended to appeal to ordinary people both in England and around the world.

state, and Parliament's House of Lords is composed of "peers," about half of whom are of noble birth. However, control of government has passed to the House of Commons, where the prime minister and other ministers typically reach their positions by achievement—winning an election—rather than by birth.

London's *Sunday Times* publishes a list of the richest people in Great Britain and other countries every year. Find the "Rich List" at http://en.wikipedia.org/wiki/Sunday_Times_Rich_List.

Further down in the hierarchy, roughly one-fourth of the British people fall into the middle class. Some earn comfortable incomes from professions and businesses and are likely to have investments in the form of stocks and bonds. Below the middle class, perhaps half of all Britons consider themselves "working class," earning modest incomes through manual labour. The remaining one-fourth of the British people make up the lower class, the poor who lack steady work. Most live in the nation's northern and western regions, which are plagued by closings of mines and factories.

Today's British class system has a mix of caste elements and meritocracy, producing a highly stratified society with some opportunity to move upward or downward. One consequence of the historical estate system is that social mobility occurs less often in the United Kingdom than in Canada (Corak, 2006). This more rigid system of inequality in the United Kingdom is reflected in the importance attached to accent. Distinctive patterns of speech develop when people are set off from one another over many generations. In Canada, accent is a clue to where a person lives or grew up (there is no mistaking a person who has worked his whole life in an outport of Newfoundland for a person who has worked his whole life on Bay Street in Toronto). In the United Kingdom, however, accent is a mark of social class (upper-class people speak the "King's English," but most people speak like "commoners"). So different are these two accents that the British seem to be, as the saying goes, "a single people divided by a common language."

CLASSLESS SOCIETIES?

Nowhere in the world do we find a society without some degree of social inequality. Yet some nations have claimed to be classless.

An illustration: The former Soviet Union.   The Union of Soviet Socialist Republics (USSR), which rivalled the United States as a military superpower in the mid- to late twentieth century, was born out of a revolution in Russia in 1917. The Russian Revolution ended the feudal estate system ruled by a hereditary nobility and transferred most farms, factories, and other productive property from private ownership to state control. Following the lead of Karl Marx, who believed that private ownership of property was the basis for social classes, Soviet leaders boasted of becoming a classless society.

Yet just 6 percent of the population belonged to the Communist Party, which ran the country. Highly placed government officials, or *apparatchiks,* ranked highest in the social order, followed by intellectuals and other professionals, manual workers, and, at the lowest level, the rural peasantry. The fact that the members of these rankings had very different standards of living shows that the former Soviet Union never really became classless.

In 1985, Mikhail Gorbachev came to power with a new economic program known as *perestroika,* meaning "restructuring." Gorbachev saw that although the Soviet system had reduced economic inequality, living standards lagged far behind those of other industrial nations. Gorbachev tried to generate economic expansion by reducing inefficient centralized government control of the economy.

Gorbachev's reforms turned into one of the most dramatic social movements in history. People throughout Eastern Europe toppled their socialist governments, and in 1991, the Soviet Union itself collapsed, remaking itself as the Russian Federation. People blamed their poverty and their lack of basic freedoms on the repressive ruling class of Communist Party officials.

The Soviet story shows that social inequality involves more than economic resources. Soviet society may not have had the extremes of wealth and poverty found in the United Kingdom and Canada, but it did have an elite class, based on power rather than wealth.

What about social mobility in so-called classless societies? In the twentieth century, there was as much upward social mobility in the Soviet Union as in the United Kingdom or Canada. Rapidly expanding industry and government drew many poor rural peasants into factories and offices. This trend illustrates what sociologists call **structural social mobility,** *a shift in the social position of large numbers of people due more to changes in society than to individual efforts.*

December 20, Tallinn, Estonia. Tallinn is located only 90 minutes across the Baltic Sea from Helsinki, Finland. Yet the visual contrast between the two capital cities—apart from the common winter snow—is so great that we wonder if we have not docked in a distant land. As we walk the cobblestone streets of the medieval part of the city with our tour guide—a retired school teacher whose pension is so low that she is forced to supplement her income by entertaining visitors such as ourselves—we marvel at the Christmas decorations in the numerous shops and restaurants. The snow starts to fall while we are enjoying a nice meal in a warmly lit restaurant off the main square. It is nearly 11:00 P.M. before we make our way back to our hotel, and on our way we notice that work crews are starting to shovel the snow away from the square. We are surprised to notice a woman who appears to be well into her seventies working beside a man a decade or two younger. They are both bundled up in large overcoats to help fend off the bitter cold while they sweep. . . . We see firsthand what happens when the pensions that people have worked 40 or more years to earn are suddenly eliminated. Independence, it seems, has not resulted in material wealth for all of Tallinn's population.

During the 1990s, structural social mobility in the Russian Federation turned downward. One indicator is that the average lifespan for men dropped by eight years and for women by two years. Many factors are involved, including Russia's poor healthcare system, but the Russian people

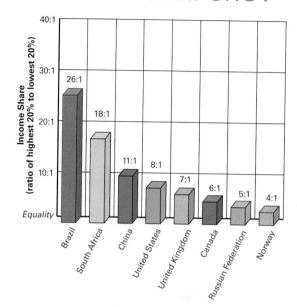

GLOBAL SNAPSHOT

FIGURE 8-1 Economic Inequality in Selected Countries

These data are the most recent available, representing income share for various years between 1998 and 2002.

Source: United Nations Development Program (2005).

clearly have suffered in the turbulent period of economic change that began in 1991 (Bohlen, 1998; Gerber & Hout, 1998).

In the long run, closing inefficient state industries may improve the Russian Federation's economic performance. But in the short run, most citizens face hard times as living standards fall. As businesses have returned to private ownership, the gulf between rich and poor has grown to about the same level as in the United States, as shown in Figure 8–1. Today, some Russians praise the recent changes while others hang on, patiently hoping for better times.

An illustration: China. Sweeping political and economic change has affected not just the Russian Federation but also the People's Republic of China. After the Communist revolution in 1949, the state took control of all farms, factories, and other productive property. Communist Party leader Mao Zedong declared all work to be equally important, so officially, social classes no longer existed.

The new program greatly reduced economic inequality. But as in the Soviet Union, social differences remained. The

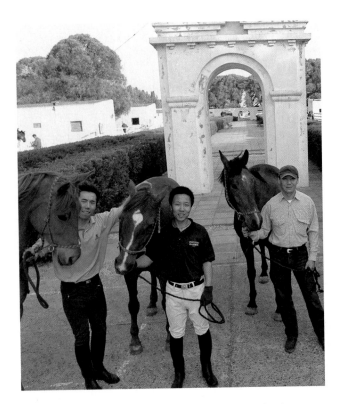

In recent decades, the government of China has permitted a market economy to operate in limited areas of the country. The result has been increased production and also the emergence of a new business class with a lifestyle similar to that of wealthy people in Canada.

country was ruled by a political elite with enormous power and considerable privilege; below them were managers of large factories and skilled professionals; next came industrial workers; at the bottom were rural peasants, who were not even allowed to leave their villages to migrate to cities.

Further economic change came in 1978, when Mao died and Deng Xiaoping became China's leader. The state gradually loosened its hold on the economy, allowing a new class of business owners to emerge. Communist Party leaders remain in control of the country, and some have prospered as they have joined the ranks of the small but wealthy elite who control new, privately run industries. Much of this new economic growth has been concentrated in coastal areas where living standards have soared far above those in China's rural interior.

Today, a new class system is emerging with a mix of the old political hierarchy and a new business hierarchy. At this early stage, scholars point to its complexity and debate its likely future. But the lesson of China is clear: with new patterns of inequality emerging over time, social stratification is highly dynamic (Bian, 2002).

IDEOLOGY: THE POWER BEHIND STRATIFICATION

How do societies persist without sharing their resources more equally? The British estate system lasted for centuries, and for 2000 years people in India accepted the idea that they should be privileged or poor based on the accident of birth.

A major reason that social hierarchies endure is **ideology**, *cultural beliefs that justify particular social arrangements, including patterns of inequality.* Any beliefs—such as the idea that the rich are smart and the poor are lazy—are ideological to the extent that they define elites as worthy and suggest that those less well off deserve their plight.

According to the ancient Greek philosopher Plato (427–347 BCE), every culture considers some type of inequality fair. Although Karl Marx understood this, he was far more critical of inequality than Plato. Marx criticized capitalist societies for defending wealth and power in the hands of a few as a "law of the marketplace." Capitalist law, he continued, defines the right to own property and ensures that money stays within the same families from one generation to the next. In short, Marx concluded, culture and institutions combine to support a society's elite, which is why established hierarchies last a long time.

Ideology changes along with a society's economy and technology. Because agrarian societies depend on the routine labour of their people, they develop caste systems that make performing the duties of a person's "station" a moral responsibility. With the rise of industrial capitalism, an ideology of meritocracy arises, defining wealth and power as prizes to be won by those who perform the best. This change means that the poor—often the targets of charity and sympathy in feudal societies—are looked down upon under industrial capitalism as personally undeserving. This harsh view is linked to the work of Herbert Spencer, as explained in the Critical Thinking box.

History shows how difficult it is to change social stratification. However, challenges to the status quo always arise. Traditional ideas about "a woman's place," for example, have given way to economic opportunity for women. The continuing struggle for racial equality in South Africa is another case of widespread rejection of the ideology of apartheid and social stratification.

The Functions of Social Stratification

Why does social stratification exist at all? According to the structural-functional approach, social stratification plays a vital part in the operation of society. This argument was

CRITICAL THINKING

Is Getting Rich "the Survival of the Fittest"?

"The survival of the fittest"—we have all heard these words used to describe society as a competitive jungle. The phrase was coined by one of sociology's pioneers, Herbert Spencer (1820–1903), whose ideas about social inequality are still widespread today.

Spencer, who lived in England, eagerly followed the work of the natural scientist Charles Darwin (1809–1882). Darwin's theory of biological evolution held that a species changes physically over many generations as it adapts to the natural environment. Spencer distorted Darwin's theory, applying it to the operation of society: society became the "jungle," with the "fittest" people rising to wealth and the "failures" sinking into miserable poverty.

It is no surprise that Spencer's views were popular among the rising industrialists of the day. John D. Rockefeller (1839–1937), who made a vast fortune building the oil industry, recited Spencer's "social gospel" to young children in Sunday school. As Rockefeller saw it, the growth of giant corporations—and the astounding wealth of their owners—was merely the result of "the survival of the fittest," a basic fact of nature. Neither Spencer nor Rockefeller had much sympathy for the poor, seeing poverty as evidence of individuals' failing to measure up in a competitive world. Spencer opposed social welfare programs because he thought they penalized society's "best" people (through taxes) and rewarded its "worst" members (through welfare benefits).

Today's sociologists are quick to point out that society is far from a meritocracy, as Spencer claimed. Moreover, it is not the case that companies or individuals who generate lots of money necessarily benefit society. Yet Spencer's view that people get what they deserve in life remains part of our individualistic culture.

WHAT DO YOU THINK?

1. What did Herbert Spencer mean when he said that society encourages "the survival of the fittest"?
2. Why do you think Spencer's ideas are still popular in Canada today?
3. In what sense do highly paid people benefit society? In what ways do they not?

presented 60 years ago by Kingsley Davis and Wilbert Moore (1945).

THE DAVIS-MOORE THESIS

The **Davis-Moore thesis** is *the assertion that social stratification exists in every society because it has beneficial consequences for the operation of society.* How else, ask Davis and Moore, can we explain the fact that some form of social stratification has been found in every society?

Davis and Moore note that modern societies have hundreds of occupational positions of varying importance. Certain jobs—say, washing windows or answering a telephone—are fairly easy and can be performed by almost anyone. Other jobs—such as designing new generations of computers or transplanting human organs—are very difficult and demand the scarce talents of people with extensive (and expensive) training.

Therefore, Davis and Moore explain, the greater the functional importance of a position, the more rewards a society attaches to it. This strategy promotes productivity and efficiency because rewarding important work with

income, prestige, power, or leisure encourages people to do these things and to work better, longer, and harder. In short, unequal rewards (which are what social stratification is) benefit society as a whole.

Davis and Moore admit that any society could be egalitarian, but only to the extent that people are willing to let *anyone* perform *any* job. Equality also demands that someone who does a job poorly be rewarded just as much as someone who performs well. Such a system clearly offers little incentive for people to try their best and thereby reduces a society's productive efficiency.

The Davis-Moore thesis suggests why some form of stratification exists everywhere; it does not state exactly what rewards a society should give to any occupational position or how unequal rewards should be. It merely points out that positions a society considers crucial must offer enough rewards to draw talented people away from less important work.

Critical review. Although the Davis-Moore thesis is an important contribution to sociological analysis, it has provoked criticism. Melvin Tumin (1953) wondered, first, how we assess the importance of a particular occupation. Perhaps the high rewards our society gives to physicians result partly from deliberate efforts by medical schools to limit the supply of physicians and thereby increase the demand for their services. Furthermore, do rewards actually reflect the contribution someone makes to society? Does multimillionaire Céline Dion contribute as much in two Las Vegas shows as the prime minister of Canada does in a whole year? Then there is the case of Larry Ellison, the chief executive officer of the U.S. software company Oracle, who earned more than $700 million even as the value of the company slid downward—an amount it would take a high school teacher 10 000 years to earn (Benjamin, 2002; Broder, 2002). Do corporate executives deserve such megasalaries for their "contributions to society"?

Second, Tumin claimed that Davis and Moore ignore how the caste elements of social stratification can *prevent* the development of individual talent. Born to privilege, rich children may develop their abilities, something many gifted poor children may never have the opportunity to do.

Third, living in a society that places so much importance on money, we tend to overestimate the importance of high-paying work; beyond making money, how do stockbrokers or people who trade international currencies really contribute to society? For the same reason, it is difficult for us to see the importance of work not oriented toward making money, such as parenting, creative writing, playing music in a symphony, or just being a good friend to someone in need (Packard, 2002).

Finally, by suggesting that social stratification benefits all of society, the Davis-Moore thesis ignores how social inequality promotes conflict and even outright revolution. This criticism leads to the social-conflict approach, which provides a very different explanation for social hierarchy.

Stratification and Conflict

Social-conflict analysis argues that rather than benefiting society as a whole, stratification provides some people with advantages over others. This analysis draws heavily on the ideas of Karl Marx, with contributions from Max Weber.

KARL MARX: CLASS CONFLICT

As Marx saw it, the Industrial Revolution promised humanity a society free from want. Yet during Marx's lifetime, the capitalist economy had done little to improve the lives of most people. Marx set out to explain a glaring contradiction: how, in a society so rich, so many could be so poor.

In Marx's view, social stratification is rooted in people's relationship to the means of production. Individuals either own productive property (such as factories and businesses)

or they labour for others. In feudal Europe, the nobility and the church owned the productive land; the peasants toiled as farmers. Under industrial capitalism, the nobility was replaced by **capitalists** (sometimes called the *bourgeoisie,* a French word meaning "town dwellers"), *people who own and operate factories and other businesses in pursuit of profits.* Peasants became the **proletarians**, *people who sell their productive labour for wages.* Capitalists and proletarians have opposing interests and are separated by a vast gulf of wealth and power, making class conflict inevitable.

Marx's analysis reflects the capitalism he observed in the nineteenth century, when industry had raised some individuals to great wealth while most made do with low wages. In this era, wealthy U.S. capitalists such as Andrew Carnegie, J.P. Morgan, and John Jacob Astor (one of the few rich passengers to drown on the *Titanic*) lived in fabulous mansions that were filled with priceless works of art and staffed by dozens of servants. Even by today's standards, their incomes were staggering. For example, Carnegie earned more than $20 million in 1900 (more than $100 million in today's dollars), when the average worker's wages totalled perhaps $500 a year (Baltzell, 1964; Pessen, 1990).

In time, Marx believed, the working majority would overthrow the capitalists once and for all. Capitalism would bring about its own downfall, Marx reasoned, by making workers poorer and poorer and giving them little control over what they made or how they made it. Under capitalism, work produces only **alienation**, *the experience of isolation and misery resulting from powerlessness.*

To replace capitalism, Marx imagined a *socialist* system that would meet the needs of all rather than just the few: "The proletarians have nothing to lose but their chains. They have a world to win" (Marx & Engels, 1972:362, orig. 1848).

Critical review.   Marx has had enormous influence on sociological thinking. But his revolutionary ideas—calling for the overthrow of capitalist society—also make his work highly controversial.

One of the strongest criticisms of the Marxist approach is that it ignores a central idea of the Davis-Moore thesis: that a system of unequal rewards is needed to motivate people to do their work well. Marx separated reward from performance; his egalitarian ideal was based on the principle "from each according to ability, to each according to need" (Marx & Engels, 1972:388, orig. 1848). However, failure to reward individual performance may be precisely what caused the low productivity of the former Soviet Union and other socialist economies around the world. Defenders respond to such criticism by asking why we assume that humanity is inherently selfish rather than social; individual rewards are not the only way to motivate people to perform their social roles (Clark, 1991; Fiske, 1991).

APPLYING THEORY
SOCIAL STRATIFICATION

	Structural-Functional Approach	Social-Conflict Approach
What is the level of analysis?	Macro-level	Macro-level
Who benefits from social inequality?	Stratification benefits society as a whole.	Stratification benefits some people and harms others.
Are unequal rewards fair?	Yes. Linking greater rewards to more important work is widely accepted by people. Unequal rewards boost economic productivity by encouraging people to work harder and try new ideas.	No. There is widespread opposition to existing social inequality. Unequal rewards only serve to divide society.
Is stratification stable?	Yes. Stratification typically lasts for generations.	No. Opposition causes ongoing social change.

A second problem is that the revolutionary change Marx predicted has failed to happen, at least in advanced capitalist societies. The next section explores this issue.

WHY NO MARXIST REVOLUTION?

Despite Marx's prediction, capitalism is still thriving. Why have industrial workers not overthrown capitalism? Ralf Dahrendorf (1959) proposed four reasons:

1. **The fragmentation of the capitalist class.** Today, tens of millions of shareholders rather than single families own most large companies. Day-to-day corporate operations are in the hands of a large class of managers, who may or may not be major shareholders. With stock so widely held—today more than 50 percent of the Canadian population are in the market—more and more people have a direct stake in the capitalist system (Angus Reid Group Inc., 1998a).

2. **A higher standard of living.** As Chapter 12 ("Economics and Politics") explains, a century ago, most Canadian workers were in factories or on farms in **blue-collar occupations**, *lower-prestige jobs that involve mostly manual labour.* Today, most workers are in **white-collar occupations**, *higher-prestige jobs that involve mostly mental activity.* These jobs are in sales, management, and other service fields. Most of today's white-collar workers do not think of themselves as an "industrial proletariat." Just as important, the average

income in Canada rose multifold over the course of the twentieth century, even allowing for inflation, and the number of hours in the work week decreased. As a result, most workers today are far better off than workers were a century ago, an example of structural social mobility helping people to accept the status quo.

3. **More worker organizations.** Workers today have the right to form labour unions that make demands of management, backed by threats of work slowdowns and strikes. Consequently, labour disputes are settled without threatening the capitalist system.

4. **Greater legal protections.** Over the past century, new laws made the workplace safer, and employment insurance, disability protection, and pension funds now provide workers with greater financial security.

A counterpoint. These developments suggest that our society has smoothed many of capitalism's rough edges. Yet many observers claim that Marx's analysis of capitalism is still largely valid (Domhoff, 1983; Stephens, 1986; Boswell & Dixon, 1993; Hout, Brooks, & Manza, 1993). First, wealth remains highly concentrated, with much of the privately controlled corporate stock in the hands of a small proportion of our population. Second, many of today's white-collar jobs offer no more income, security, or satisfaction than factory work did a century ago (Reid, 1996; Lowe, 2000). Third, many benefits enjoyed by today's workers

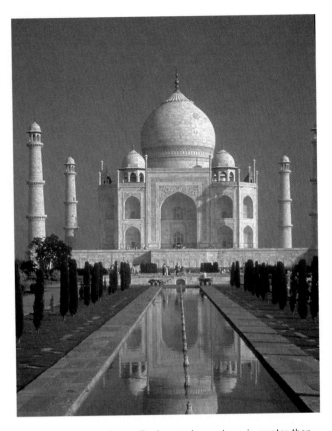

The extent of social inequality in agrarian systems is greater than that found in industrial societies. One indication of the unchallenged power of rulers is the monumental structures built over years with the unpaid labour of common people. Although the Taj Mahal in India is among the world's most beautiful buildings, it is merely a tomb for two people, Mumtaz Mahal and her husband Shah Jahan.

came about through the class conflict Marx described, and workers still struggle to hold on to what they have. Fourth, although workers have gained legal protections, the law has not helped ordinary people use the legal system as effectively as the rich. Therefore, social-conflict theorists conclude, the absence of a socialist revolution in high-income countries does not disprove Marx's analysis of capitalism.

The Applying Theory table on page 207 summarizes the two contrasting explanations of social stratification.

MAX WEBER: CLASS, STATUS, AND POWER

Max Weber agreed with Karl Marx that social stratification causes social conflict, but he viewed Marx's two-class model as simplistic. Instead, he viewed social stratification as involving three distinct types of inequality.

The first dimension is economic inequality—the issue so important to Marx—which Weber called *class* position.

Weber did not think of classes as well-defined categories but as a continuum ranging from high to low. Weber's second dimension is *status,* or social prestige, and the third is *power*.

The socioeconomic status hierarchy. Marx viewed prestige and power as simple reflections of economic position and did not treat them as distinct dimensions of inequality. But Weber noted that status consistency in modern societies often is quite low: a local official might exercise great power yet have little wealth or social prestige.

Weber, then, characterizes stratification in industrial societies as a multidimensional ranking rather than a hierarchy of clearly defined classes. In line with Weber's thinking, sociologists use the term **socioeconomic status (SES)** to refer to *a composite ranking based on various dimensions of social inequality.*

Inequality in history. Weber observed that each of his three dimensions of social inequality stands out at a different time in the evolution of human societies. Status or social prestige is the main dimension of difference in agrarian societies, taking the form of honour. Members of these societies gain prestige by carrying out the duties the culture gives to people born to a given rank.

Industrialization and the development of capitalism level traditional rankings based on birth but generate striking financial inequality. Thus, Weber argued, in an industrial society, the crucial difference between people is the economic dimension of class.

Over time, industrial societies witness the growth of a bureaucratic state. Bigger government and the spread of all types of other organizations make power more important in the stratification system. Especially in socialist societies, where government regulates many aspects of life, high-ranking officials become the new ruling elite.

This historical analysis points to a final difference between Weber and Marx. Marx thought societies could eliminate social stratification by abolishing private ownership of productive property. Weber doubted that overthrowing capitalism would significantly lessen social stratification. It might lessen economic differences, he reasoned, but socialism would increase inequality by expanding government and concentrating power in the hands of a political elite. Popular uprisings against entrenched socialist bureaucracies in Eastern Europe and the former Soviet Union support Weber's position.

Critical review. Weber's multidimensional view of social stratification has enormously influenced sociologists. But critics (particularly those who favour Marx's ideas) argue that although social class boundaries may have blurred, industrial and post-industrial nations still show striking patterns of social inequality. Moreover, as we shall see, economic inequality has increased recently in Canada. Thus, whereas some people favour Weber's multidimensional hierarchy, others think that Marx's view of the rich versus the poor is closer to the mark.

Stratification and Technology: A Global Perspective

We can weave together a number of observations made in this chapter by considering the relationship between a society's technology and its type of social stratification. This analysis draws on Gerhard Lenski's model of sociocultural evolution discussed in Chapter 2 ("Culture").

With simple technology, hunters and gatherers produce only what is necessary for day-to-day living. Some people may produce more than others, but the group's survival depends on all sharing what they have. Thus, there are only small differences in the wealth of categories of people.

As technological advances generate a surplus, social inequality increases. In horticultural and pastoral societies, a small elite controls most of the surplus. Larger-scale agriculture is more productive still, and striking inequality—as great as at any time in history—places the nobility in an almost godlike position over the masses.

Industrialization turns the tide, nudging inequality downward. Prompted by the need to develop people's talents, meritocracy takes hold and weakens the power of traditional elites. Industrial productivity also raises the living standards of the historically poor majority. Specialized work demands schooling for all, sharply reducing illiteracy. A literate population, in turn, presses for a greater voice in political decision making, reducing social inequality and lessening men's domination of women.

Over time, even wealth becomes somewhat less concentrated (countering the trend predicted by Marx). For example, when we look at the wealthiest country in the world, we notice that the richest 1 percent of U.S. families owned about 40 percent of all wealth in 1920, a figure that fell to 30 percent by the 1980s (Williamson & Lindert, 1980; Beeghley, 1989; U.S. House of Representatives, 1991). Such trends help explain why Marxist revolutions occurred in *agrarian* societies, such as Russia (1917), Cuba (1959), and Nicaragua (1979), where social inequality is most pronounced, rather than in *industrial* societies as Marx predicted. However, wealth inequality turned upward again after 1990 and is once again about the same as it was in the 1920s (Keister, 2000).

In human history, then, technological advances first increase but then moderate the intensity of social stratification. Greater inequality is functional for agrarian societies,

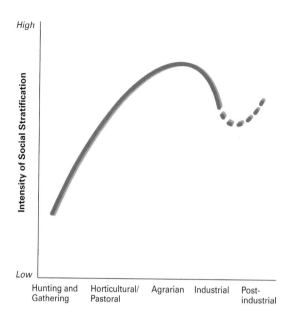

FIGURE 8-2 Social Stratification and Technological Development: The Kuznets Curve

The Kuznets curve shows that greater technological sophistication and economic productivity generally is accompanied by more pronounced social stratification. The trend reverses itself as industrial societies relax rigid, castelike distinctions in favour of greater opportunity and equality under the law. Political rights are more widely extended, and there is even some levelling of economic differences. However, the emergence of post-industrial society has brought an upturn in economic inequality, as indicated by the broken line added by the authors.

Source: Created by John Macionis, based on Kuznets (1955) and Lenski (1966).

but industrial societies benefit from a less unequal system. This historical pattern was first recognized 50 years ago by the Nobel Prize–winning economist Simon Kuznets (1955, 1966) and is illustrated by the Kuznets curve, shown in Figure 8–2.

Patterns of global inequality follow the Kuznets curve. Global Map 8–1 on page 210 shows that high-income nations that have passed through the industrial era (including Canada, the United States, and the nations of Western Europe) have somewhat less income inequality than nations in which agriculture remains a major part of the economy (as is common in Latin America and Africa). Of course, income inequality reflects not just technological development but also a society's political and economic priorities. Of all high-income nations, the United States has the greatest income inequality.

WINDOW ON THE WORLD

GLOBAL MAP 8-1 Income Inequality in Global Perspective

Societies throughout the world differ in the rigidity and extent of their social stratification and in overall standard of living. This map highlights income inequality. Generally speaking, the United States stands out among high-income nations—such as Canada, Great Britain, Sweden, Japan, and Australia—as having greater income inequality. The less economically developed countries of Latin America and Africa—including Colombia, Brazil, and the Central African Republic, as well as much of the Arab world—exhibit the most pronounced inequality of income. Is this pattern consistent with the Kuznets curve?

Source: Based on Gini coefficients obtained from World Bank (2004).

And what of the future? Notice that in Figure 8–2, the trend described by Kuznets has been extended to the post-industrial era (the broken line) to show social inequality increasing once again. As the Information Revolution moves ahead, U.S. society is experiencing greater economic inequality, suggesting that the long-term trend may differ from the one Kuznets observed half a century ago (Nielsen & Alderson, 1997).

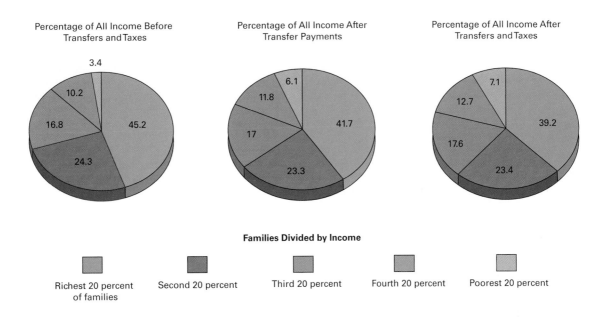

Percentage of All Income Before
Transfers and Taxes

Percentage of All Income After
Transfer Payments

Percentage of All Income After
Transfers and Taxes

Families Divided by Income

Richest 20 percent of families   Second 20 percent   Third 20 percent   Fourth 20 percent   Poorest 20 percent

FIGURE 8-3 Distribution of Income Before and After Transfer Payments and Taxes, Canada, 2001

Inequality in Canada

Canada stands apart from most European nations in never having had a titled aristocracy. Even though we have never known a caste system that rigidly ranks categories of people, our racial history shows that there is a strong relationship between race and social class.

Even so, Canadian society is highly stratified. Not only do the rich have most of the money, but they also receive the most schooling, enjoy the best health, and consume the most goods and services. Such privilege contrasts sharply with the poverty of tens of thousands of women and men who worry about paying next month's rent or putting food on the table. Many people think that Canada is a middle-class society, but is this really the case?

 Read an analysis of wealth transmission over generations in Canada and other high-income countries at **www.policyresearch.gc.ca/ v8n3_art_08**.

INCOME, WEALTH, AND POWER

Statistics Canada reports that the average market income for families (of two people or more) rose 0.8 percent in 2001 to $63 700 compared to a 4.5 percent increase in 2000 (Statistics Canada, 2003ac). The first part of Figure 8–3 shows the distribution of market income among all families in the country in 2001. The second and third parts of

Figure 8–3 illustrate the Canadian family income after transfer payments—federal and provincial payments to families and individuals—and taxes. Despite the important equalizing effect of taxes and transfer payments, large differences remain between the Canadian families earning the most and those earning the least. Before taxes and transfer payments, the 20 percent of families with the highest income received $13 in market income for every $1 received by the 20 percent with the lowest income. After taxes and transfer payments, the richest 20 percent of families in 2001 received $5.50 for every $1 received by the poorest 20 percent. Put another way, families with the lowest 20 percent of incomes earned on average $20 721 while the 20 percent of families on the other end of the continuum earned an average of $113 615 after taxes and transfer payments (Statistics Canada, 2003ad). The data also indicate that income inequality has started to increase recently. Up to 1995, the ratio had held fairly constant, with the highest-income 20 percent of families getting about $4.80 for every $1 received by the lowest-income 20 percent of families (Statistics Canada, 2003ac); as of 2001, the highest-income 20 percent were getting $5.50.

Table 8–1 on page 212 takes a closer look at the 2001 census data on income distribution after transfer payments. The highest-paid 5 percent of Canadian families earned more than $135 710 in 2000, while the lowest-paid 5 percent

TABLE 8–1
Canadian Census Family Income, 2000

Highest-paid …	Annually earns more than …
5%	$135 710
10%	112 460
20%	89 615
30%	72 400
40%	64 520
50%	55 016

Lowest-paid …	Annually earns less than …
50%	$55 016
40%	45 870
30%	37 295
20%	28 270
10%	19 480
5%	11 505

Source: Statistics Canada (2003ae). The 50th percentile quoted from this source; remaining figures estimated by the authors based on data from this source.

earned less than $11 505. In short, while a small number of people have very high incomes, the majority make do with far less.

Income is only one part of a person's or family's **wealth,** *the total value of money and other assets, minus outstanding debts.* Wealth—including shares of stock, bonds, and real estate—is distributed even more unequally than income.

The richest 5 percent of Canadian families have wealth valued at over $600 000, excluding pension plans and household articles. In contrast, the poorest 5 percent of Canadian families have a negative wealth valued at $5700—that is, they actually live in debt (Morissette, Zhang, & Drolet, 2002a). In total it is estimated that the wealthiest 5 percent of families control more than 40 percent of all wealth in Canada (Davies, 1993, quoted in Morissette, Zhang, & Drolet, 2002b).

In Canada, wealth is an important source of power. The small proportion of families that control most of the wealth also have the ability to shape the agenda of the entire society. As explained in Chapter 12 ("Economics and Politics"), some sociologists argue that such concentrated wealth weakens democracy because the political system serves the interests of the super-rich.

OCCUPATIONAL PRESTIGE

In addition to generating income, work is also an important source of prestige. We commonly evaluate one another according to the kind of work we do, giving greater respect to those who do what we consider important work and less to others with more modest jobs.

Sociologists measure the relative social prestige of various occupations (Counts, 1925; Hodge, Treiman, & Rossi, 1966; Guppy & Siltanen, 1977; NORC, 2003; Goyder, Guppy, & Thompson, 2003). Table 8–2 shows that people give high prestige to occupations that require extensive training and generate high income (such as medicine, law, and engineering). By contrast, less prestigious work—as a waitress or janitor, for example—not only pays less but requires less ability and schooling. Occupational prestige rankings are much the same in all high-income nations (Lin & Xie, 1988).

In any society, high-prestige occupations go to privileged categories of people. In Table 8–2, for example, many of the lowest-prestige jobs are commonly performed by people from visible minority groups.

SCHOOLING

Industrial societies expand opportunities for schooling, but some people still receive much more than others. In 2001, 28 percent of those aged 30–34 had no education beyond high school, while 50 percent had received a certificate, diploma, or degree from a college or university (Statistics Canada, 2003ag).

Schooling affects both occupation and income because most (but not all) of the better-paying white-collar jobs shown in Table 8–2 require a university or college degree or other advanced study. By contrast, most blue-collar jobs, which bring lower income and social prestige, require less schooling. In addition to occupation and income, schooling is also related to whether or not you have a paid job at all. Table 8–3 on page 214 shows that people with less education are more likely to be unemployed than those with more education. This relationship is particularly striking when comparing those who have some college or university education to those who have completed a college or university program.

ANCESTRY, RACE, ETHNICITY, AND GENDER

A class system rewards individual talent and effort. But nothing affects one's social standing as much as birth into a particular family. Ancestry has a strong bearing on future schooling, occupation, and income. Research suggests that at least half of the richest individuals in the U.S.—those with hundreds of millions of dollars in wealth—derived their fortunes mostly from inheritance (Thurow, 1987; Queenan, 1989). The situation is much the same in Canada (Porter, 1965; Clement, 1975; Olsen, 1980; Brym & Fox, 1989). By the same token, inherited poverty just as surely shapes the future of others.

TABLE 8-2

Occupational Prestige Scores for Selected Occupations, Canada, 2000

Occupation	Prestige Score	Occupation	Prestige Score
Physician	93	Surveyor	54
Airline pilot	83	House carpenter	52
Biologist	80	Auto mechanic	52
University professor	78	Bookkeeper	49
Registered nurse	77	Insurance agent	49
Veterinarian	76	Sales supervisor	49
CEO of large company	76	Bricklayer	49
Firefighter	75	Stay-at-home spouse	48
Physicist	75	Sheet metal worker	45
Civil engineer	75	Bus driver	44
Architect	74	Baker	43
Lawyer	74	Cook in a restaurant	42
Police constable	73	Trailer truck driver	42
Psychologist	72	Barber/hairdresser	42
Elementary teacher	70	Logger	41
Computer programmer	70	Professional babysitter	40
Chiropractor	70	Receptionist	40
Mathematician	69	Housekeeper	40
Member of Parliament	69	Mail carrier	40
Airplane mechanic	69	Farm labourer	39
High school teacher	68	Sales associate, retail	39
Financial analyst	68	Post office clerk	38
Mining engineer	68	Waitress/host	36
Accountant	67	Textile mill worker	36
Economist	66	File clerk	36
Dental hygienist	62	House painter	36
Owner of a retail store	61	Sales clerk	35
Commercial farmer	60	Taxi driver	35
Social worker	60	Bartender	35
Musician	60	Janitor	34
Funeral director	59	Stockroom attendant	33
Professional athlete	58	Worker—dry cleaner	31
Professional librarian	58	Fruit packer	27
Draftsperson	58	Flagperson, construction	27
Machinist	57	Filling station attendant	25
Administrative assistant	55	Telemarketer	24
Welder	55	Squeegee kid	9
Plumber	54		

Source: Goyder, Guppy, & Thompson, 2003.

Race and ethnicity, too, are closely linked to social position in Canada. While the average 2000 employment income for those who worked full-time for the whole year was $43 298, visible minorities earned an average $37 597 (about 12 percent less) (Statistics Canada, 2003ah). Aboriginal people are even more disadvantaged. The 2001 census showed that their income was 23 percent below non-Aboriginals' (Statistics Canada 2003bt). The larger proportion of young workers among visible minorities and Aboriginals accounts for some of this income disparity. Varying levels of education of these

TABLE 8-3

Education Level and Unemployment
Rate, Canada, 2001, 30–34-year-olds

	Percent of 30–34-year-olds	Unemployment Rate
Less than Grade 9	2.7	19.0
Grades 9–13, not a graduate	13.0	11.4
High school graduate	12.3	7.3
Trades certificate or diploma	2.9	7.8
Some college	7.4	8.3
Some university	11.7	6.4
College certificate or diploma	25.4	6.2
Bachelor's degree or higher	24.8	5.0
Total	100.0	7.1

Source: Statistics Canada (2003ag).

three populations can also be used to help us understand some of the disadvantage of Aboriginal workers. Visible minorities are more disadvantaged than these income data indicate because they tend to have a higher level of education than other Canadians, which should result in a higher income. Nevertheless, there are some signs that the incomes of visible minorities are catching up: visible minorities aged 15–24 make 2 percent less than other Canadians in that age group, which is a substantially smaller difference than that experienced by their older peers aged 25–44 (11 percent less) and 45–64 (15 percent less) (Statistics Canada, 2003ah).

Of course, both men and women are found in families at every social level. Yet, on average, women have less income, wealth, and occupational prestige than men. Even more important, households headed by women are much more likely to be poor than those headed by men. Chapter 10 ("Gender Stratification") fully examines the link between gender and social stratification.

Social Class in Canada

As we have explained, rankings in a caste system are rigid and obvious to all. Defining the social categories in a more fluid class system is not so easy. Followers of Karl Marx see two major social classes: capitalists and proletariat. Other sociologists find as many as six classes (Warner & Lunt, 1941) or even seven (Coleman & Rainwater, 1978). Still others side with Max Weber, believing that people form not clear-cut classes but a multidimensional status hierarchy.

Defining classes in Canada is difficult because of the relatively low level of status consistency. Especially toward the middle of the hierarchy, people's social position on one dimension may contradict their standing on another. For example, a government official may have the power to administer a multimillion-dollar budget yet earn a modest personal income. Similarly, many members of the clergy enjoy ample prestige but only moderate power and low pay. Or consider a lucky day trader in the stock market who wins no special respect but makes a lot of money.

Finally, the social mobility characteristic of class systems—again, most pronounced near the middle—means that social position may change during a person's lifetime, further blurring class boundaries. With these problems in mind, we can describe four general rankings: the upper class, the middle class, the working class, and the lower class.

THE UPPER CLASS

Families in the upper class—5 percent of the Canadian population—earn at least $135 000, and many earn 10 times that much. As a general rule, the more a family's income comes from inherited wealth in the form of shares of stock and bonds, real estate, and other investments, the stronger a family's claim to being upper class.

In 2003, the *Globe and Mail* estimated that there were 180 000 people in Canada with more than $1 million in the bank (Willis & MacDonald, 2003). In a different category are the estimated 7600 families who have assets exceeding $10 million, not including real estate. In 2003, *Forbes* listed 15 Canadian families or individuals worth more than US$1 billion (*Forbes*, 2003). The late Canadian media giant Ken Thomson had assets valued at US$14 billion, making him the richest person in Canada and the thirteenth-richest in the world. The upper class are Karl Marx's "capitalists"—those who own most of the means of production and, thus, most of the nation's private wealth. Many upper-class people work as top executives in large corporations and as senior government officials. Historically, though less so today, the upper class has comprised white Anglo-Saxon Protestants (WASPs) (Porter, 1965; Clement, 1975).

Upper-uppers. The *upper-upper class*, sometimes called "blue bloods" or simply "society," includes less than 1 percent of the Canadian population. Membership is almost always the result of birth, as suggested by the joke that the easiest way to become an upper-upper is to be born one. Most of these families possess enormous wealth that is mostly inherited. For this reason, members of the upper-upper class are said to have "old money."

Set apart by their wealth, members of the upper-upper class live in exclusive neighbourhoods such as Westmount in Montreal, Forest Hill in Toronto, or the Uplands in Victoria. Their children typically attend private schools with others of similar background and complete their formal education at high-prestige universities. In the historical pattern of European aristocrats, they study liberal arts rather than vocational skills. Women of the upper-upper class often do volunteer work for charitable organizations; while helping the larger community, these activities also build networks that increase this elite's power (Ostrander, 1980, 1984).

Lower-uppers. Most upper-class people actually fall into the *lower-upper class*. The Queen of England is in the upper-upper class based not on her fortune of $660 million but on her family tree. J.K. Rowling, author of the Harry Potter books, is worth even more—about $1 billion—but this woman (who was once on welfare) is a member of the lower-upper class. The major difference is that members of the lower-upper class are the "working rich": the primary source of their income is earnings, not inherited wealth. Although these "new rich" families—who make up 3 or 4 percent of the Canadian population—generally live in expensive neighbourhoods, most do not gain entry into the clubs and associations of "old money" families.

THE MIDDLE CLASS

Made up of 40 to 45 percent of the Canadian population, the large middle class has a tremendous influence on our culture. Television and movies usually show middle-class people, and most commercial advertising is directed at these average consumers. The middle class contains far more ethnic and racial diversity than the upper class.

Upper-middles. The top third in this category are referred to as the *upper-middle class*, based on their above-average income, in the range of $90 000 to $135 000 a year. Such income allows upper-middle-class families to accumulate property: a comfortable house in a fairly expensive area, several automobiles, and investments. Most upper-middle-class children go on to university or college, and postgraduate degrees are common. Many go on to high-prestige occupations as physicians, engineers, lawyers, accountants, or business executives. Lacking the power of the richest people to influence national or international events, upper-middles often play an important role in local political affairs.

Average-middles. The rest of the middle class falls close to the centre of the Canadian class structure. *Average-middles* typically work in less prestigious white-collar occupations as bank tellers, middle managers, or sales clerks, or in highly skilled blue-collar jobs such as electrical work and carpentry. Family income falls between $55 000 and $90 000 a year, which is roughly the national average.

For decades, farm families who worked hard could expect to fall within the Canadian middle class. But the trend toward large-scale agribusiness has put the future of the small family farm in doubt. Although many young people in rural areas are turning away from farming toward other careers, some carry on, incorporating high technology into their farm management in their determined efforts to succeed.

Average-middle-class people generally build up a small amount of wealth over the course of their working lives, mostly in the form of a house and a retirement account. Most middle-class men and women are likely to be high school graduates, and many send their children to seek post-secondary education at a college or university, but often close to home to save on the cost of accommodation.

THE WORKING CLASS

About one-third of the population is in the working class (sometimes called the *lower-middle class*). In Marxist terms, the working class forms the core of the industrial proletariat. The blue-collar jobs held by members of the working class generally yield a family income of between $25 000 and $55 000 a year, somewhat below the national average. Working-class families have little or no wealth and are vulnerable to financial problems caused by unemployment or illness.

Many working-class jobs provide little personal satisfaction—they require discipline but rarely imagination—and place workers under constant supervision. These jobs also offer fewer benefits, such as pension plans. About half of working-class families own their homes, usually in lower-cost neighbourhoods. College or university becomes a reality for only about one-third of working-class children.

Compared to high-income people, low-income people are half as likely to report good health and, on average, live about seven fewer years. The toll of low income—played out in inadequate nutrition, little medical care, and high stress—is easy to see on the faces of the poor, who look old before their time.

THE LOWER CLASS

The remaining 20 percent of our population make up the lower class. Low income makes their lives insecure and difficult. Many belong to the so-called "working poor." They are just slightly better off than unemployed people, holding low-prestige jobs that provide little satisfaction and minimal income. Barely half manage to complete high school, and fewer than one in three ever reach college or university.

Society segregates the lower class, especially when the poor are racial or ethnic minorities. Only some lower-class families own their own home, typically in the least desirable neighbourhoods. Although poor neighbourhoods are found in our inner cities, lower-class families also live in rural areas.

The Difference Class Makes

Social stratification affects nearly every dimension of our lives. We will briefly examine some of the ways social standing is linked to our health, values, politics, and family life.

HEALTH

Health is closely related to social standing. Children born into poor families are more likely to die from disease, neglect, accidents, or violence during their first year of life than children born into privileged families. Among adults, people with the lowest incomes are five times more likely than those from the highest income groups to describe their health as only fair or poor. Moreover, on average, richer people live longer because they eat more nutritious food, live in safer and less stressful environments, and receive better medical care (Federal, Provincial and Territorial Advisory Committee on Population Health, 1999).

VALUES AND ATTITUDES

Some cultural values vary from class to class. The "old rich" have an unusually strong sense of family history because their position is based on wealth passed down from generation to generation. Secure in their birthright privileges, upper-uppers also favour understated manners and tastes, whereas many "new rich" people practise *conspicuous consumption,* using homes, cars, and even airplanes as *status symbols* to make a statement about their social position.

Affluent people with greater education and financial security are also more tolerant of controversial behaviour such as homosexuality. Working-class people, who grow up in an atmosphere of greater supervision and discipline and are less likely to attend college or university, tend to be less tolerant (Baltzell, 1979a, orig. 1958; Lareau, 2002; NORC, 2003).

POLITICS

Political affiliations also flow along class lines. By and large, more privileged people support the Conservative or Liberal parties, while less advantaged people favour the NDP. But issue by issue, the pattern is more complex. A desire to protect wealth prompts well-off people to take a more conservative approach to economic issues, favouring, for example, lower taxes. But on social matters—such as abortion and gay rights—highly educated, more affluent people are more liberal. People of lower social standing, on the other hand, tend to be economic liberals, favouring government social programs, but support a more conservative social agenda (Angus Reid Group Inc., 1996e, 1998b; Ipsos-Reid, 2003e).

FAMILY AND GENDER

Social class also shapes family life. Generally, lower-class families are somewhat larger than middle-class families because of earlier marriage and less use of birth control. Another family pattern is that working-class parents encourage children to conform to conventional norms and respect authority figures. Parents of higher social standing pass on a different "cultural capital" to their children, teaching them to express their individuality and imagination more freely (Kohn, 1977; McLeod, 1995; Lareau, 2002).

Of course, the more money a family has, the better parents can develop their children's talents and abilities. According to some calculations, the cost of raising a child in Canada to age 18 is more than $150 000 (Scott, 1996). Given the large amount of money involved, it stands to reason that only those families with the highest incomes can afford to pay for such luxuries as private schools. Privilege leads to privilege as family life reproduces the class structure in each generation.

Class also shapes our world of relationships. Elizabeth Bott (1971, orig. 1957) found that most working-class couples divide their responsibilities according to gender roles; middle-class couples, by contrast, are more egalitarian, sharing more activities and expressing greater intimacy. More recently, Karen Walker (1995) discovered that working-class friendships typically serve as sources of material assistance; middle-class friendships are likely to involve shared interests and leisure pursuits.

Social Mobility

Ours is a dynamic society marked by significant social movement. Earning a university degree, landing a higher-paying job, or marrying someone who earns a high income contributes to *upward social mobility*; dropping out of school, losing a job, or becoming divorced (especially for women) may result in *downward social mobility*.

Over the long term, though, social mobility is not so much a matter of individual changes as changes in society itself. In the first half of the twentieth century, for example, industrialization expanded the Canadian economy, pushing up living standards. Even people who were not good swimmers rode the rising tide of prosperity. More recently, downward structural social mobility has dealt economic setbacks to many people.

Sociologists distinguish between shorter- and longer-term changes in social position. **Intragenerational social mobility** is *a change in social position occurring during a person's lifetime*. **Intergenerational social mobility**, *upward or downward social mobility of children in relation to their parents*, is important because it reveals long-term changes in society that affect almost everyone.

MYTH VERSUS REALITY

In few societies do people think about "getting ahead" as much as in Canada and the United States. Moving up has historically been seen as central to North American culture. But is there as much social mobility in our country as we like to think?

"So long, Bill. This is my club. You can't come in."

Studies of intergenerational mobility (almost all of which, unfortunately, have focused only on men) show that almost 40 percent of the sons of blue-collar workers take white-collar jobs and about 30 percent of sons born into white-collar families end up doing blue-collar work. *Horizontal social mobility*—changing jobs at the same class level—is even more common; overall, about 80 percent of sons showed some type of social mobility in relation to their fathers (Blau & Duncan, 1967; Featherman & Hauser, 1978; Hout, 1998).

Research points to four general conclusions about social mobility in Canada and the United States:

1. **Social mobility over the course of the past century has been fairly high.** Mobility is what we would expect in an industrial class system.

2. **The long-term trend in social mobility has been upward.** Industrialization, which greatly expanded the Canadian economy, and the growth of white-collar work over the course of the twentieth century have raised living standards.

3. **Within a single generation, social mobility usually is small.** Most young families increase their income over time as they gain education and skills. A typical family in which at least one partner was aged 25–34 earned

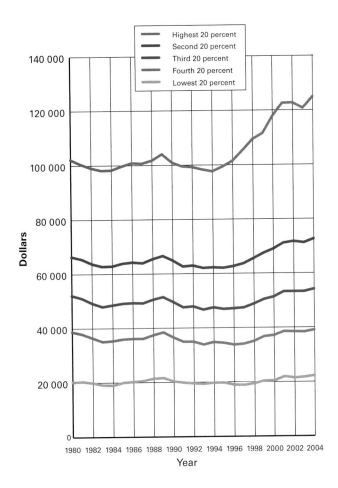

FIGURE 8–4 Mean Income, Canadian Families (two or more people), 1980–2004 (in 2002 dollars, adjusted for inflation)

Source: Statistics Canada (2006ai to 2006am).

about $65 000 in 2000; a typical family in which at least one partner was aged 35–44 earned just less than $80 000 (estimated based on Statistics Canada, 2004a). Yet only a few people move from "rags to riches" (the way J.K. Rowling did) or lose a lot of money (a number of highly paid rock stars had little money a few years after their records stopped selling). Most social mobility involves small movements *within* one class level rather than large movements *between* classes.

4. **Social mobility since the 1970s has been uneven.** Real income (adjusted for inflation) rose during the twentieth century until the 1970s. Between 1975 and 1985, gains were far smaller. During the 1980s, real income changed little for many people, rising slowly after 1990. But general trends do not show the experiences of different categories of people, as the next section explains.

MOBILITY BY INCOME LEVEL

In Figure 8–4, we see how Canadian families at different income levels made out between 1980 and 2004. Well-to-do families (the highest 20 percent, but not necessarily the same families over the entire period) saw their incomes jump 22 percent, from an average $102 200 in 1980 to $125 000 in 2001. People in the middle of the population had much more modest gains at 4 percent. The lowest-income 20 percent saw a 10 percent increase in earnings after taxes and transfers.

A comparison of the change in income level over these years reveals an interesting pattern. All income groups peaked in 1989 and had low points in the mid-eighties and nineties. However, the change in income of these five income groups was different over these two decades. In both decades, the initial decline was particularly steep for the lower income groups. During the recovery, on the other hand, the lower income groups recovered quickly in the 1980s, whereas the recovery in the latter part of the 1990s left the lower half of income earners behind. By 2000, the average income of the highest income group was over $17 000 higher than in 1990, whereas the lowest income group was only $100 higher than its 1990 income level.

In addition to these changes over time, income is quite different in different parts of Canada. National Map 8–1 on page 219 illustrates these differences.

MOBILITY BY GENDER

Historically, women have had less chance for upward mobility than men because most working women hold clerical jobs (such as secretary) and service positions (such as waitress) that offer few promotions. When marriages end in divorce (as almost half do), women commonly experience downward social mobility because they may lose not only income but a host of benefits including healthcare and insurance coverage (Weitzman, 1996; Eichler, 1997; Benoit, 2000a).

The earnings gap between women and men has been narrowing over time. Canadian women working full-time in 1967 earned 58.4 percent as much as men working full-time; by 2001, women earned just over 70 percent as much. Unfortunately, much of this change was due to a stagnation in men's earnings, while the income of women increased (Statistics Canada, 2000m, 2003ai).

THE GLOBAL ECONOMY AND THE CANADIAN CLASS STRUCTURE

Underlying the shifts in Canadian class structure is global economic change. Much of the industrial production that gave Canadian workers high-paying jobs a generation ago has moved overseas. With less industry at home, Canada now serves as a vast market for industrial goods such as

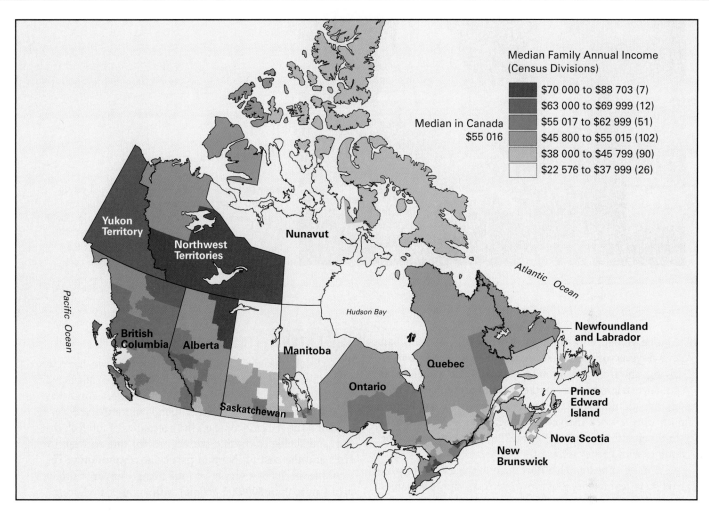

Median Family Annual Income
(Census Divisions)

- $70 000 to $88 703 (7)
- $63 000 to $69 999 (12)
- $55 017 to $62 999 (51)
- $45 800 to $55 015 (102)
- $38 000 to $45 799 (90)
- $22 576 to $37 999 (26)

Median in Canada
$55 016

SEEING OURSELVES

NATIONAL MAP 8–1 Median Income Across Canada, 2000

The map shows the median income in each of the 288 census divisions across Canada. While 50 percent of Canadian families earned less than $55 016 in 2000, there were 26 census divisions where the median income was less than $38 000. At the other end of the continuum, the high-income areas are centred on Toronto. But then there is the high-income area in the Northwest Territories. Why are incomes so high there? How much variation is there where you live? Do you notice these differences?

Source: Statistics Canada (2003am).

cars, stereos, cameras, and computers made in Japan, South Korea, and elsewhere.

High-paying jobs in manufacturing, held by 31 percent of Canadian workers in 1951, support fewthan 20 percent of workers today (Krahn & Lowe, 1998, 2002). In their place,

the economy offers service work, which pays far less. Traditionally high-paying corporations such as auto manufacturers now employ fewer people than the expanding McDonald's chain, and fast-food clerks make only a fraction of what steelworkers earn.

Many people in Canada work full-time and yet do not earn enough to escape poverty. This hotel worker washes windows to earn $7 an hour or about $14 500 per year. Do you think such workers still have the opportunity to realize their dreams for themselves and their children? Why or why not?

The global reorganization of work has not been bad news for everyone. On the contrary, the global economy is driving upward social mobility for educated people who specialize in law, finance, marketing, and computer technology. In addition, global economic expansion has helped push up the stock market (even with the recent declines) almost eightfold between 1980 and 2004, reaping profits for families with money to invest.

But the same trend has hurt many average workers, who have seen their factory jobs move overseas. Many companies have also downsized—cutting the ranks of their work-force—to stay competitive in world markets. As a result, although 62 percent of all families contain two or more workers—a notable increase from 33 percent in 1967—many families are working harder simply to hold on to what they have (Lowe, 2000; Statistics Canada, 2000o, 2003aj).

Poverty in Canada

Social stratification creates both "haves" and "have-nots." Thus, all systems of social inequality generate poverty, or at least **relative poverty**, *the deprivation of some people in relation to those who have more.* A more serious but preventable problem is **absolute poverty**, *a deprivation of resources that is life-threatening.*

As Chapter 9 ("Global Stratification") explains, almost 1 billion human beings around the world—one person in six—are at risk of absolute poverty. Even in affluent Canada, families go hungry, live in inadequate housing, and suffer poor health because of wrenching poverty.

THE EXTENT OF POVERTY

The closest measure to a poverty line that we have in Canada is the low-income cut-off level (LICO) calculated by Statistics Canada. According to this measure, a family has an income below the LICO if it spends more than 63 percent of its after-tax income on the necessities of food, clothing, and shelter, including corrections for different family sizes and the cost of living in particular communities. For example, in 2005, a family of four living in a large urban area (more than 500 000 people) with an after-tax income below $32 556 lived below the LICO. Similarly, this same family would have to have a before-tax income above $38 610 in order to be living above the LICO (Statistics Canada, 2006an). Using the after-tax LICO measure of poverty, 11 percent of Canadians (3.5 million) were poor in 2004 (Statistics Canada, 2006ao, 2006ap).[1]

WHO ARE THE POOR?

Although no single description fits all poor people, poverty is greater among certain categories of our population. Where these categories overlap, the problem is especially serious.

Age. A generation ago, the elderly were at greatest risk for poverty, but no longer. From 21 percent in 1980, the poverty rate for seniors over the age of 65 plummeted to 6 percent in 2004, or 219 000 elderly poor (Statistics Canada, 2006aq,

---

[1]These statistics refer to LICO after taxes. The proportion of the population living below LICO before taxes and transfers is considerably higher, as Figure 8–3 on page 211 shows.

2006ar). The poverty rate of the elderly has fallen due to better retirement programs from private employers and government. Still, with almost 3.5 million poor people in Canada, about 6 percent of the poor are elderly people (Statistics Canada, 2006ao).

Today, the burden of poverty falls most heavily on children. In 2004, 13 percent of people under age 18 (865 000 children and youth) were poor. Tallied another way, one in four of the Canadian poor are children and youth under age 18 (Statistics Canada, 2006as, 2006at).

The Canadian Council on Social Development has a report on children and poverty in Canada, the United States, and Mexico. Read it at **www.ccsd.ca/pubs/2006/cina**.

Race and ethnicity. The 2001 census showed that the poverty rates for visible minorities are much higher than the national average—although the census only collects data on low income before taxes. Using this measure of poverty, the poverty rate for visible minority groups at 26 percent was twice that of the national average of 12.9 percent (Statistics Canada, 2003ak). The situation is even worse for Aboriginals, with a poverty rate of 31 percent or almost one in three (Statistics Canada, 2003bu). Among Aboriginal youth aged 6–14, about one in every two is poor; this contrasts with the national average of about one in five for this age group (Statistics Canada, 1998i).

Gender and family patterns. Of all poor people, 54 percent are female and 46 percent are male. This disparity reflects the fact that women who head households bear the brunt of poverty: 36 percent of children who live in female lone-parent families live in poverty, and almost 40 percent of all children who live in poverty live with a lone mother.

The term **feminization of poverty** describes *the trend of women making up an increasing proportion of the poor.* Analyzing differences between males and females, we notice that females have higher poverty rates than males, in all age groups over 15 years of age (Statistics Canada, 2003al). Once women have fallen into poverty, they also tend to remain poor for a longer period of time than men do. Among those over age 65, 5.5 percent of the women had been poor for at least six years, whereas only 2.4 percent of the men had been poor for that long (Statistics Canada, 2003ad).

Urban and rural poverty. The greatest number of poor people are in Canada's largest cities: 41 percent of the total number of people living below the poverty line in 2001 lived in Toronto, Montreal, or Vancouver (at the time, 34 percent of Canada's population lived in these three cities). These data also show that the incidence of poverty is higher in the urban areas than rural areas, which is a phenomenon that has emerged in the last 20 years; before

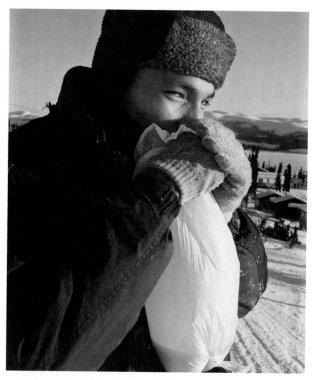
Many young disadvantaged people are faced with little opportunity to improve their lives. Does this explain high substance abuse levels in some communities?

that time, the proportion living below the LICO was higher in rural areas. National Map 8–2 on page 222 provides a picture of the shape of the housing where people live in different parts of Canada

EXPLAINING POVERTY

For one of the richest nations on Earth to contain millions of poor people raises serious questions. It is true, as some analysts remind us, that most poor people in Canada are far better off than the poor in other countries: For example, healthcare and education are publicly funded here. Nevertheless, poverty harms the overall well-being of millions of people in this country. Overwhelmingly, as Figure 8–5 on page 223 shows, Canadians feel that it is the responsibility of governments to look after the poor in our society.

But what are the causes of poverty? One view holds that *the poor are primarily responsible for their own poverty.* Throughout our history, people in Canada have placed a high value on self-reliance, convinced that social standing is mostly a matter of a person's individual talent and effort. According to this view, society offers plenty of opportunities to anyone able and willing to take advantage of them, and the poor are those who cannot or will not work—women and men with fewer skills, less schooling, and little motivation.

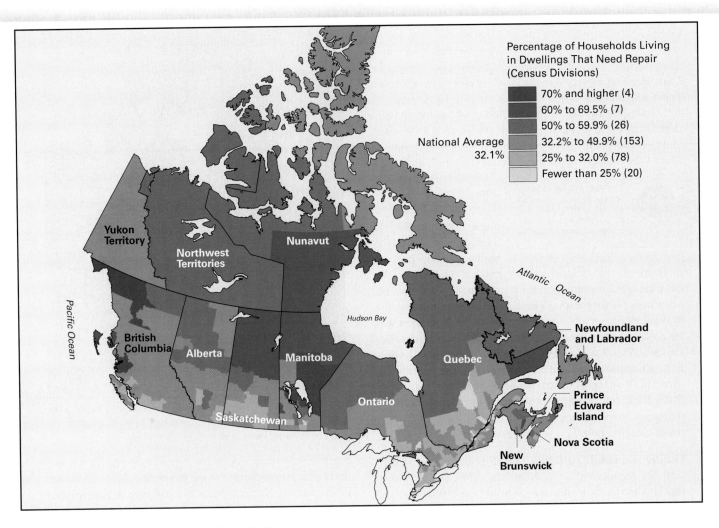

Percentage of Households Living
in Dwellings That Need Repair
(Census Divisions)

- 70% and higher (4)
- 60% to 69.5% (7)
- 50% to 59.9% (26)
- 32.2% to 49.9% (153)
- 25% to 32.0% (78)
- Fewer than 25% (20)

National Average 32.1%

SEEING OURSELVES

NATIONAL MAP 8–2 Percentage of Households Living in Dwellings
That Require Repairs, Canada, 2001

There is a relatively large amount of variation in the state of the dwellings in which people live across Canada. There are parts of Manitoba and Northwestern BC where more than 80 percent of households live in dwellings in need of repair. At the other end of the continuum are the households living in Huron and Elgin counties in Southwestern Ontario. There, the figures are less than 20 percent. What trends do you see in the map? Do you think differences are greater within provinces or between provinces?
Note: These figures are calculated only on houses built between 1981 and 1985 to minimize the impact of differences in the ages of houses in different areas.

Source: Statistics Canada (2003af).

In his study of Latin American cities, the anthropologist Oscar Lewis (1961) concluded that the poor become trapped in a *culture of poverty,* a lower-class subculture that can destroy people's ambition to improve their lives. Socialized in poor families, children become resigned to their situation, producing a self-perpetuating cycle of poverty.

A different position, argued by William Julius Wilson (1996a, 1996b), holds that *society is primarily responsible for poverty*. Wilson points to the loss of jobs in our inner cities as the primary cause of poverty, claiming that there is simply not enough work to support families. Hence, Wilson sees any apparent lack of trying on the part of the poor as a *result* of little opportunity rather than as a *cause* of poverty. From Wilson's point of view, Lewis's analysis amounts to blaming the victims for their own suffering (Ryan, 1976). To combat poverty and reduce the need for welfare, Wilson argues, the government should fund jobs and provide affordable childcare for low-income mothers and fathers.

Critical evaluation. Both sides have evidence to support their positions. Government statistics show that at least 27 percent of the non-elderly families below the LICO in 1998 did not have any member that received an income or wage during that year (Statistics Canada, 2000o). Such a fact seems to support the "blame the poor" position, since a major cause of poverty is not holding a job.

But the reasons that people do not work are more in step with the "blame society" position. Middle-class women may be able to combine working and child rearing, but this is much harder for poor women who cannot afford childcare, and few employers provide childcare programs for their employees. Moreover, as William Julius Wilson explains, many people are idle not because they are avoiding work but because there are not enough jobs. In short, most poor people in Canada find few opportunities and alternatives to improve their lives (Popkin, 1990; Schiller, 1994; Edin & Lein, 1996; Wilson, 1996a; Pease & Martin, 1997; Duncan, 1999).

But not all poor people are jobless, and the working poor command the sympathy and support of people on both sides of the poverty debate. In 1998, 20 percent of the non-elderly families with the lowest incomes had two or more wage earners, and an additional 34 percent had one wage or income recipient (Statistics Canada, 2000o). From another angle, almost 4 percent of all married and common-law couples had a total family income below the poverty line even though both partners were earners. It is clear that most poor families remained poor despite employment. A key cause for "working poverty" is that even two people working 40 hours per week, 52 weeks per year, cannot keep a family of four above the poverty line if they live in an urban area with a population of more than 500 000 and they only make minimum wage, which in 2004 ranged from $5.90 per hour in Newfoundland and Labrador to $8.50 in Nunavut.

To sum up, individual ability and personal initiative do play a part in shaping everyone's social position. However, the weight of sociological evidence points toward society—

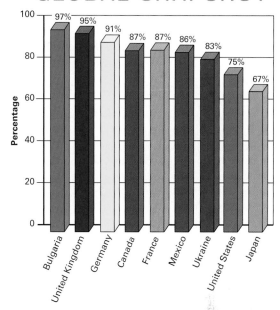

GLOBAL SNAPSHOT

FIGURE 8-5 Societal Responsibility for Poor, Selected Countries, 2002

Survey question: "It is the responsibility of the (state/government) to take care of very poor people who can't take care of themselves." Percentages reflect the percentage of respondents who replied "Completely Agree" or "Mostly Agree."

Source: Pew Research Center for the People and the Press (2003).

not individual character traits—as the primary source of poverty. Society must be at fault because the poor are categories of people—female heads of families, Aboriginal people, people isolated from the larger society in inner-city neighbourhoods—who face special barriers and limited opportunities.

HOMELESSNESS

Many low-income people in Canada cannot afford even basic housing. There is no precise count of homeless people, but experts estimate that in 1996 there were 20 000 homeless in Montreal and about the same number of street youth in Toronto (Hagan & McCarthy, 1997; Corelli, 1996).

The familiar stereotypes of homeless people—men sleeping in doorways and women carrying everything they own in shopping bags—have been replaced by the "new homeless": some thrown out of work because of plant closings, people forced out of apartments by rent increases, and others who cannot meet mortgage or rent payments because of low wages or no work at all. Today, no stereotype paints a complete picture of the homeless.

CONTROVERSY & DEBATE

The Bell Curve Debate: Are Rich People Really Smarter?

It is rare that the publication of a new book in the social sciences captures the attention of the public. But *The Bell Curve: Intelligence and Class Structure in American Life,* by Richard J. Herrnstein and Charles Murray, did that and more, igniting a firestorm of controversy over why pronounced social stratification divides society and, just as important, what should be done about it.

The Bell Curve is a lengthy book (800 pages) that addresses many important issues and resists simple summarization. But its basic thesis is captured in the following propositions:

1. Something we can describe as "general intelligence" exists; people who have more of it tend to be more successful in their careers than those who have less.

2. At least half of the variation in human intelligence (Herrnstein and Murray use figures of 60 and

70 percent) is transmitted genetically from one generation to another; the remaining variability is due to environmental factors.

3. Over the course of this century—and especially since the Information Revolution—intelligence has become more necessary to the performance of our society's top occupational positions.

4. Simultaneously, the best North American colleges and universities have shifted their admissions policies away from favouring children of inherited wealth to admitting young people who perform best on standardized tests.

5. As a result of these changes in the workplace and higher education, our society is now coming to be dominated by a "cognitive elite," who are, on average, not only better trained than most people but

actually more intelligent.

6. Because more intelligent people are socially segregated on the college or university campus and in the workplace, it is no surprise that they tend to pair up, marry, and have intelligent children, perpetuating the "cognitive elite."

7. Near the bottom of the social ladder, a similar process is at work: increasingly, poor people are individuals with lower intelligence, who live segregated from others and who tend to pass along their modest abilities to their children.

Resting on the validity of the seven assertions presented above, Herrnstein and Murray then offer, as an eighth point, a basic approach to public policy:

8. To the extent that membership in the affluent elite or the impoverished underclass is rooted in intelligence

But virtually all homeless people have one thing in common: poverty. For that reason, the approaches already used in explaining poverty also apply to homelessness. One side of the debate places responsibility on personal traits of the homeless themselves. One-third of homeless people are substance abusers, and one-fourth are mentally ill. Perhaps we should not be surprised that a fraction of 1 percent of our population, for one reason or another, is unable to cope with our complex and highly competitive society (Bassuk, 1984; Whitman, 1989).

On the other side of the debate, advocates assert that homelessness results from societal factors, including unemployment, a lack of low-income housing, and the increasing

The National Homelessness Initiative reports on homelessness initiatives across the country at **http://homelessness.gc.ca/ homelessness/index_e.asp**.

number of low-income jobs (Hagan & McCarthy, 1997; Kozol, 1988; Schutt, 1989;

Bohannan, 1991). Supporters of this position point out that one-third of all homeless people are entire families, and that children are the fastest-growing subcategory among the homeless.

No one disputes that a large proportion of homeless people are personally impaired to some degree, although it is difficult to untangle how much is cause and how much is effect. But structural changes in the Canadian economy, the closing down of mental institutions in recent decades, and limited government support for lower-income people have all certainly contributed to homelessness.

CLASS, WELFARE, POLITICS, AND VALUES

We have reviewed many facts about social inequality. In the end, however, our opinions about wealth and poverty depend not just on facts but also on our politics and values. As we might expect, the idea that social standing reflects and determined mostly by genetic inheritance, programs to assist underprivileged people (from school lunches to equity policies) will have little practical benefit.

Most social scientists joined *The Bell Curve*'s critics. In response to the book's thesis, they first questioned exactly what one means by "intelligence," doubting that anyone's innate abilities can ever be separated from the effects of socialization. Of course rich children perform better on intelligence tests, they explained: these people have had all the advantages! Some critics dismiss the concept of "intelligence" outright as a product of phony science. Others take a more moderate road, claiming that we should not think of "intelligence" as the sole cause of achievement, since recent research indicates that mental abilities and life experiences are interactive, each affecting the other.

Second, while most researchers who study intelligence agree that genetics does play some part in transmitting intelligence, the consensus is that at most 25 to 40 percent is inherited—

roughly half of what Herrnstein and Murray contend. Therefore, critics conclude, *The Bell Curve* misleads readers into thinking that social stratification is both natural and inevitable. In its assumptions and conclusions, moreover, *The Bell Curve* amounts to little more than a rehash of the social Darwinism popular a century ago, which heralded the success of industrial tycoons as merely "the survival of the fittest."

Perhaps, as one commentator suggested, the more society seems like a jungle, the more people think of stratification as a matter of blood rather than upbringing. But despite its flaws and exaggerations, *The Bell Curve*'s success raises many issues we cannot easily ignore. Can our democratic society tolerate the "dangerous knowledge" that elites (including not only rich people but our political leaders) are at least somewhat more intelligent than the rest of us? What of *The Bell Curve*'s assertion—which few challenge—that elites in such countries as Canada and the U.S. are increasingly insulating themselves from social problems, including crime, home-

lessness, and poverty? Acknowledging that such problems have become worse in recent years, how do we resist the easy explanation that poor people themselves are hobbled by limited ability? And, perhaps most basically, what should be done to ensure that all people have the opportunity to develop their abilities as fully as possible?

CONTINUE THE DEBATE . . .

1. Do you agree that "general intelligence" exists? Why or why not?
2. Overall, do you think that people of higher social position are more intelligent than those of low social status? If you think intelligence differs by social standing, which factor is cause and which is effect? How do you know?
3. Do you think sociologists should study controversial issues such as differences in human intelligence? Why or why not?

Sources: Herrnstein & Murray (1994); Jacoby, Russell, & Glauberman (1995).

---

personal merit is popular among well-off people; the opposing idea, that society should spread wealth more equally, finds favour among those who are less well off (NORC, 2003).

In comparative perspective, Figure 8–5 on page 223 shows that people in Canada are much more likely than people in the United States to believe that the government has an obligation to look after the poor. On the other hand, people in many European nations are still more likely to agree with the statement. Our cultural emphasis on individual responsibility encourages us to see successful people as personally worthy and the poor as personally lacking. Such attitudes go a long way toward explaining why our society spends much more than other high-income nations on education (to promote opportunity) but much

less on public assistance programs (which directly support the poor).

Most members of our society are willing to accept a high level of income inequality, and many hold a harsh view of the poor. To the extent that we define poor people as undeserving, we look on public assistance programs as at best a waste of money and at worst a threat to personal initiative. The Controversy & Debate box takes a closer look at the evidence of a relationship between intelligence and success.

Finally, the drama of social stratification extends far beyond Canada's borders. The most striking social inequality is found not by looking inside one country but by comparing living standards in various parts of the world. In Chapter 9, we broaden our focus by investigating global stratification.

SUMMARY

1. Social stratification refers to categories of people ranked in a hierarchy. Caste systems, common in agrarian societies, are based on ascription (birth) and permit little or no social mobility. Class systems are found in industrial societies and allow social mobility based on individual achievement.

2. The Davis-Moore thesis states that social stratification is universal because it is useful to a society. In class systems, unequal rewards attract the ablest people to the most important jobs.

3. According to Karl Marx, conflict in industrial societies places the capitalists, who own the means of production and seek profits, in opposition to the proletariat, who provide labour in exchange for wages.

4. Max Weber identified three distinct dimensions of social stratification: economic class, social status or prestige, and power. Together, these form a multidimensional hierarchy of socioeconomic status (SES).

5. Gerhard Lenski explained that historically, advancing technology tends to increase social inequality. Some reversal of this trend occurs in industrial societies, as represented by the Kuznets curve; even so, the new post-industrial society shows an increase in economic inequality.

6. The upper class (5 percent of the population) includes this country's richest, most powerful individuals. Those in the upper-upper class (the "old rich") typically inherit wealth; those in the lower-upper class ("new rich") work for their income.

7. The middle class (40 to 45 percent) enjoys reasonable financial security, but only some of these people (the upper-middle class) have significant wealth. With below-average incomes, members of the working class or lower-middle class (33 percent) typically perform blue-collar work, and only one-third of their children attend college or university.

8. About one-fifth of the Canadian population belongs to the lower class. Aboriginal people and women are disproportionately represented in the lower class.

9. Social mobility is common in Canada, as it is in other industrial societies; typically, however, there are only small changes from one generation to the next.

10. The growing global economy has increased the wealth of rich families in Canada but has had only a small impact on the standard of living of low-income families.

11. The government classifies 3.5 million people as poor. About one in four of the poor are under age 18.

12. The "culture of poverty" thesis suggests that poverty is caused by shortcomings in the poor themselves. An alternative approach claims that poverty is caused by a society's unequal distribution of income and wealth.

13. The Canadian emphasis on individual responsibility helps explain why public assistance for the poor is sometimes controversial.

KEY CONCEPTS

absolute poverty (p. 220) a deprivation of resources that is life-threatening

alienation (p. 206) the experience of isolation and misery resulting from powerlessness

blue-collar occupations (p. 207) lower-prestige jobs that involve mostly manual labour

capitalists (p. 206) people who own and operate factories and other businesses in pursuit of profits

caste system (p. 199) social stratification based on ascription, or birth

class system (p. 200) social stratification based on both birth and individual achievement

Davis-Moore thesis (p. 205) the assertion that social stratification exists in every society because it has beneficial consequences for the operation of society

feminization of poverty (p. 221) the trend of women making up an increasing proportion of the poor

ideology (p. 204) cultural beliefs that justify particular social arrangements, including patterns of inequality

income (p. 201) wages or salary from work and earnings from investments

intergenerational social mobility (p. 217) upward or downward social mobility of children in relation to their parents

intragenerational social mobility (p. 217) a change in social position occurring during a person's lifetime

meritocracy (p. 201) social stratification based on personal merit

proletarians (p. 206) people who sell their productive labour for wages

relative poverty (p. 220) the deprivation of some people in relation to those who have more

social mobility (p. 198) a change in position within the social hierarchy

social stratification (p. 198) a system by which a society ranks categories of people in a hierarchy

socioeconomic status (SES) (p. 208) a composite ranking based on various dimensions of social inequality

status consistency (p. 201) the degree of consistency in a person's social standing across various dimensions of social inequality

structural social mobility (p. 203) a shift in the social position of large numbers of people due more to changes in society than to individual efforts

wealth (p. 212) the total value of money and other assets, minus outstanding debts

white-collar occupations (p. 207) higher-prestige jobs that involve mostly mental activity

CRITICAL-THINKING QUESTIONS

1. How is social stratification a creation of society rather than simply an expression of individual differences?

2. How do caste and class systems differ? What do they have in common? In what ways does industrialization introduce a measure of meritocracy to social stratification?

3. Would you be in favour of class-based affirmative action? That is, should Canadian society give people born to lower-class families an advantage in university and college admissions and company hiring? Why or why not?

4. Our society is always ready to assist the "worthy" poor, including elderly people, whom we do not expect to take care of themselves. At the same time, we are less generous toward the "unworthy poor," healthy people who, we think, could take care of themselves but apparently do not. If this is so, why has Canadian society not done more to reduce poverty among children, who surely fall into the "worthy" category?

APPLICATIONS AND EXERCISES

1. Sit down with parents, grandparents, or other relatives, and assess the social position of your family over the last three generations. Has social mobility taken place? How much? Why?

2. Develop several simple questions that, taken together, would let you measure someone's social class position. The trick is to decide exactly what you think social class really means. Then try your questions on several adults, refining the questions as you proceed.

3. During an evening of television viewing, assess the social class of the characters you see on various shows. In each case, explain why you assign someone a specific social class position. What patterns do you find?

 ## SITES TO SEE

www.pearsoned.ca/macionis
The authors and publisher of this book invite you to visit the interactive Companion Website™ that accompanies this text. Begin by clicking on the cover of your book. You will find a chapter-by-chapter study guide, practice tests, suggested weblinks, and links to other relevant material.

www.ccsd.ca
The Canadian Council on Social Development provides many statistics and facts on poverty in Canada.

www110.hrdc-drhc.gc.ca/psait_spila/lmnec_eslc/eslc/salaire_minwage/index.cfm/doc/english
Human Resources and Social Development Canada maintains a list of the minimum wages throughout Canada.

www.cbc.ca/news/background/economy/poverty-line.html

www.swc-cfc.gc.ca/pubs/pubspr/0662281594/200003_0662281594_2_e.html

www.fraserinstitute.ca/shared/readmore.asp?sNav=pb&id=216

www.statcan.ca/english/research/13F0027XIE/13F0027XIE.htm

Here are four reports on the measurement of poverty in Canada. The first is from the CBC, the second from Status of Women Canada, the third from the Fraser Institute, and the fourth from Statistics Canada.

www.swc-cfc.gc.ca
Status of Women Canada investigates the interplay of gender and poverty.

www.iwpr.org
The Institute for Women's Policy Research investigates the links between gender and poverty.

 ## INVESTIGATE WITH RESEARCH NAVIGATOR™

Follow the instructions on page 33 of this text to access the features of Research Navigator™. Once at the website (**www.researchnavigator.com**), enter your login name and password. Then, to use the Content Select™ database, enter keywords such as "social class," "poverty," "apartheid," and "homelessness," and the search engine will supply relevant and recent scholarly and popular press publications.

 To reinforce your understanding of this chapter, and to identify topics for further study, visit MySocLab at **www.pearsoned.ca/mysoclab/macionis** for diagnostic tests and a multimedia ebook.

CHAPTER NINE

Global Stratification

What share of the world's people
live in absolute poverty?

Why do some of the world's countries have such high
incomes while others have such low incomes?

Are high-income nations making global
poverty better or worse? How?

Around the world, tens of millions of children grow up in severe poverty. This eight-year-old boy lives and works in a garbage dump in Manila, the capital city of the Philippines.

More than 1000 workers were busily sewing polo shirts on the fourth floor of the garment factory in Narsingdi, a small town about 50 kilometres northeast of Bangladesh's capital city of Dhaka. The thumping of hundreds of sewing machines produced a steady roar throughout the long working day.

But in an instant everything changed when an electric gun used to shoot spot remover onto stained fabric gave off a spark, which ignited the cloth soaked in flammable liquid. Suddenly, a whole work table burst into flames. Nearby workers rushed to smother the fire with shirts, but there was no stopping the blaze: in a room filled with combustible materials, the flames spread quickly.

The workers scrambled toward the narrow staircase that led to the street. At the bottom, however, the human wave pouring down the steep steps collided with a folding metal gate stretched across the doorway and locked to keep workers from leaving. Panicked, the people at the front turned, only to be pushed back by the hundreds behind them. In a single terrifying minute of screaming voices, thrusting legs, and pounding hearts, dozens were crushed and trampled. By the time the gates were opened and the fire put out, 52 garment workers lay dead.

Garment factories like this one are big business in Bangladesh, where clothing accounts for 75 percent of the country's total economic exports. Half of these garments end up in clothing stores in North America. The reason so much of the clothing we buy is made in low-income countries like Bangladesh is simple economics—Bangladeshi garment workers labour for close to 12 hours a day, typically every day of the week, and yet earn only $400 to $500 a year, which is just a few percent of what a garment worker makes in Canada.

Tanveer Chowdhury manages this garment factory, which is owned by his family. He complained bitterly to reporters about the tragedy. "This fire has cost me $586 373, and that does not include $70 000 for machinery and $20 000 for furniture. I made commitments to meet deadlines, and I still have the deadlines. I am now paying for air freight at $10 a dozen when I should be shipping by sea at 87 cents a dozen."

There was one other cost Mr. Chowdhury did not mention. To compensate families for the loss of their loved ones in the fire, the factory eventually agreed to pay $1952 per person. In Bangladesh, life—like labour—is cheap (based on Bearak, 2001).

These garment workers in Bangladesh are part of the roughly 1 billion of the world's people who work hard every day and yet remain poor. As this chapter explains, although poverty is a reality in Canada and other nations, the greatest social inequality is not *within* nations but *between* them (Goesling, 2001). We can understand the full dimensions of poverty only by exploring **global stratification**, *patterns of social inequality in the world as a whole.*

Global Stratification: An Overview

Chapter 8 ("Social Stratification") described inequality in Canada. In global perspective, however, social stratification is far greater. Figure 9–1 divides the world's total income by fifths of the population. Recall from Chapter 8 that the 20 percent of the Canadian population with the highest incomes earns about 45 percent of the national income (see

Figure 8–3 on page 211). However, the richest 20 percent of the global population receives over 60 percent of world income. At the other extreme, the poorest 20 percent of the Canadian population earns a little more than 3 percent of our national income, similar to the income of the poorest fifth of the world's people. Remember that Figure 8–3 also shows the impact of progressive taxation and government support to low-income earners. Because of these policies, the 20 percent of the Canadian population with the lowest incomes earn 7 percent of the national income after transfer payments and taxes.

Because global income is so concentrated, even people in Canada with income below the government's poverty line live far better than the majority of the Earth's people. The average person in a high-income nation such as Canada is extremely well-off by world standards. At the top of the pyramid, the world's richest person (Bill Gates in the United States, who was worth about $47 billion in 2004) has more wealth than the world's 46 poorest *countries* (United Nations Development Programme, 2004; Kroll & Goldman, 2004).

A WORD ABOUT TERMINOLOGY

Classifying the over 200 nations on Earth into categories ignores many striking differences. These nations have rich and varied histories, speak different languages, and take pride in their distinctive cultures. However, models have been developed that help distinguish countries on the basis of global stratification.

One such model, developed after World War II, labelled the rich, industrial countries the "First World," the less industrialized, socialist countries the "Second World," and the non-industrialized, poor countries the "Third World." But the "three worlds" model is less useful today. For one thing, it grew out of Cold War politics, when the capitalist West (the First World) faced off against the socialist East (the Second World) while other nations (the Third World) remained more or less on the sidelines. But the sweeping changes in Eastern Europe and the collapse of the former Soviet Union means that a distinctive Second World no longer exists.

A second problem is that the "three worlds" model lumped together more than 100 countries as the Third World. In reality, some better-off nations of the Third World (such as Chile in South America) have 13 times the per-person productivity seen in the poorest countries of the world (including Ethiopia in Eastern Africa).

These facts call for a modestly revised system of classification. Here, we define the 60 **high-income countries** as *the richest nations with the highest overall standards of living.* The world's 86 **middle-income countries** are somewhat

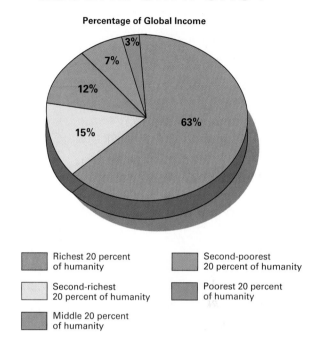

GLOBAL SNAPSHOT

Percentage of Global Income

- Richest 20 percent of humanity — 63%
- Second-richest 20 percent of humanity — 15%
- Middle 20 percent of humanity — 12%
- Second-poorest 20 percent of humanity — 7%
- Poorest 20 percent of humanity — 3%

FIGURE 9-1 Distribution of World Income

Note: Based on purchasing power parity data on 96 percent of the global population in the 163 countries with available data.

Source: Estimated based on data in World Bank (2005).

poorer; they are *nations with a standard of living about average for the world as a whole.* The remaining 63 **low-income countries** are *nations with a low standard of living in which most people are poor.*

This model has two advantages over the "three worlds" system. First, it focuses on economic development rather than whether societies are capitalist or socialist. Second, it gives a better picture of the relative economic development of various countries because it does not lump together all lower-income nations into a single "Third World" category.

Keep in mind that every country is also a stratified society. In Bangladesh, members of the Chowdhury family, who own the garment factory described in the opening vignette, earn as much as $1 million per year, which is several thousand times more than one of their workers earns. Worldwide, the full extent of global inequality is even greater than national comparisons suggest because the most well-off people in high-income countries (such as Canada) live worlds apart from the poorest people in low-income countries (such as Bangladesh, Haiti, and Sudan).

Japan represents the world's high-income countries, in which industrial technology and economic expansion have produced material prosperity. The presence of market forces is evident in this view of downtown Tokyo (above, left). The Russian Federation represents the middle-income countries of the world. Industrial development and economic performance were sluggish under socialism; as a result, Moscow residents had to wait in long lines for their daily needs (above, right). The hope is that the introduction of a market system will raise living standards, although in the short run, Russian citizens must adjust to increasing economic inequality. Bangladesh (left) represents the world's low-income countries. As the photograph suggests, these nations have limited economic development and rapidly increasing populations. The result is widespread poverty.

HIGH-INCOME COUNTRIES

In nations where the Industrial Revolution first took place more than two centuries ago, productivity increased more than one-hundredfold. Industrial technology—and the even newer technology that is part of the Information Revolution—is extremely powerful: The small European nation of the Netherlands is more productive than the vast continent of Africa south of the Sahara, and tiny South Korea outproduces all of India.

Look back at Global Map 1–2 on page 9, which identifies the 60 high-income countries of the world. They include Canada and the United States, the nations of Western Europe, Israel, Saudi Arabia, Hong Kong (now part of the People's Republic of China), Japan, South Korea, Australia, and New Zealand. These countries cover roughly 25 percent of the Earth's land area, and lie mostly in the Northern Hemisphere. In 2003, the population of these nations was about 1 billion, or about 16 percent of the Earth's people. About three-fourths of the people in high-income countries live in or near cities.

Significant cultural differences exist among high-income countries; for example, the nations of Europe

recognize more than 30 official languages. But these societies have something in common: they all produce enough economic goods to enable their people to lead a comfortable material life. Per capita annual income—that is, average income per person in a year—ranges from about US$13 000 annually in Saudi Arabia and the Slovak Republic, to US$30 040 in Canada, and more than US$35 000 annually in the United States and Norway.[1] In fact, people in high-income countries enjoy almost 60 percent of the world's total income.

Production in high-income nations is capital-intensive; that is, it is based on factories, big machinery, and advanced technology. Most of the largest corporations that design and market computers, as well as most of the world's computer users, are located in high-income countries. High-income

---

[1]High-income countries have per capita annual incomes of more than US$13 000. For middle-income countries, per capita annual income is US$3000–US$13 000 and for low-income countries, less than US$3000. All data reflect the United Nations' concept of purchasing power parities, which is an estimate of what people can buy using their income in the local economy.

When natural disasters strike high-income countries, property loss is great but loss of life is low. In low-income countries, the converse is true: Poor people have less property to lose, but many die.

countries also control the world's financial markets, so that daily events on the stock exchanges of New York, London, and Tokyo affect people throughout the world.

MIDDLE-INCOME COUNTRIES

Middle-income countries have per capita annual incomes ranging from US$3000 to US$13 000. Note that these figures are average for the world's *nations* but above that for the world's *people* because almost 70 percent of people in the world live in countries with per capita annual incomes below US$5000. Two-thirds of the people in middle-income countries live in cities, and industrial jobs are common. The remaining one-third of the people live in rural areas, where most are poor and lack access to schools, medical care, adequate housing, and even safe drinking water.

Looking back at Global Map 1–2 (page 9), we see that almost 90 of the world's nations fall in the middle-income category. At the high end are Argentina, (Latin America), South Africa (Africa), Estonia (Europe), and Malaysia (Asia), where annual per capita income tends to be at least $9000. At the low end are Ecuador (Latin America), Morocco (Africa), and Indonesia (Asia), with less than $4000 annually in per capita income.

One cluster of middle-income countries includes the countries that once made up the Soviet Union and the nations of Eastern Europe (formerly known as the Second World). These countries had mostly socialist economies until popular revolts between 1989 and 1991 swept their governments aside. Since then, these nations have begun to introduce free-market systems, but so far the results have been uneven. Some (including Poland) have improving economies, but living standards in others (including Russia) have fallen.

The remaining middle-income nations include Chile and Brazil in South America, as well as Namibia and Botswana in Africa. Recently, the People's Republic of China entered the middle-income category, which now includes large parts of Asia.

Taken together, middle-income countries span roughly 65 percent of the Earth's land area and are home to about 3 billion people, or about 45 percent of humanity. Some countries (such as Russia) are far less crowded than others (such as El Salvador), but compared with high-income countries, these societies on the whole are densely populated.

LOW-INCOME COUNTRIES

Low-income countries, where most people are very poor, are mostly agrarian societies with some industry. Most of the more than 60 low-income nations, identified in Global Map 1–2, are found in Central and East Africa as well as Asia. Low-income countries cover 25 percent of the planet's land area and are home to 37 percent of its people. Population density is generally high, although it is greater in Asian countries (such as Bangladesh and India) than in Central African nations (such as Chad and the Democratic Republic of the Congo).

In low-income countries, one-third of the people live in cities; most inhabit villages and farms as their ancestors have done for centuries. In fact, half the world's people are farmers, most of whom follow cultural traditions. With limited industrial technology, they are not very productive—one reason that many endure severe poverty. Hunger, disease, and unsafe housing frame the lives of the world's poorest people.

People living in high-income nations such as Canada find it hard to grasp the extent of human poverty in much of the world. From time to time, televised pictures of famine in countries with very low income, such as Ethiopia and Bangladesh, give us shocking glimpses into the poverty that makes every day a life-and-death struggle for many in low-income nations. Behind these images lie cultural, historical, and economic forces that we shall explore in the remainder of this chapter.

Global Wealth and Poverty

October 14, Manila, the Philippines. What caught my eye was how clean she was: a girl no more than seven or eight years old, wearing a freshly washed dress and with her hair carefully combed. She followed us with her eyes: camera-toting North Americans stand out in this, one of the poorest neighbourhoods in the entire world.

Fed by methane from the decomposing garbage, the fires never go out on Smokey Mountain, the vast garbage dump on the north side of Manila that is home to thousands of people. The smoke envelops the hills of refuse like a thick fog. It is hard to imagine a setting more hostile to human life. Amid the smoke and the squalor, men and women do what they can to survive. They pick plastic bags from the garbage and wash them in the river and collect cardboard boxes or anything else they can sell. What chance do their children have, in families that earn a few hundred dollars a year? With barely any opportunity for schooling? Year after year, breathing this air? Against this backdrop of human tragedy, one lovely little girl has put on a fresh dress and gone out to play.

Now our taxi driver threads his way through heavy traffic as we head for the other side of Manila. The change is amazing: The smoke and smell of the dump give way to neighbourhoods that could be in Toronto or Vancouver. In the distance, a cluster of yachts floats on the bay. No more rutted streets; now we glide quietly along wide, tree-lined boulevards filled with expensive Japanese cars. We pass shopping centres, upscale hotels, and high-rise office buildings. Every block or so we see the gated entrance to an exclusive residential enclave with security guards standing watch. Here, in air-conditioned homes, the rich of Manila live and many of the poor work.

Low-income nations are home to some rich and many poor people. The fact that most people live with incomes of a few hundred dollars a year means the burden of poverty is far greater than among the poor of Canada. This does not mean that poverty here is a minor problem. In so rich a country, too little food, substandard housing, and limited access to healthcare for millions of people—almost half of them children—amount to a national tragedy. While there are concentrations of extreme poverty in Canada—the Downtown Eastside in Vancouver being the largest—the Diversity: Race, Class, & Gender box profiles the striking poverty of a large population that exists not far from us along the southwestern border of the United States. Yet poverty in low-income countries is both more severe and more widespread than in Canada and the United States.

THE SEVERITY OF POVERTY

Poverty in low-income countries is more severe than it is in high-income countries. A key reason that quality of life differs so much around the world is that economic productivity is lowest in precisely the regions where population growth is highest. Figure 9–2 on page 236 shows the proportion of global population and global income for countries at each level of income. High-income countries are by far the most advantaged, with 57 percent of global income supporting just 16 percent of humanity. In middle-income nations, 47 percent of the world's people earn 33 percent of global income. This leaves 37 percent of the planet's population with just 9 percent of global income. For every $1 received by an individual in a low-income country, someone in a high-income nation takes home $14.

Table 9–1 on page 236 shows the extent of wealth and well-being in specific countries around the world. The first column of figures gives gross domestic product (GDP) for a number of high-, middle-, and low-income countries.[2]

---

[2]Gross domestic product (GDP) is the value of all the goods and services produced by a country's economy in a given year within its borders plus income received from abroad.

Las Colonias: "America's Third World"

"We wanted to have something for ourselves," explains Olga Ruiz, who has lived in the border community of College Park, Texas, for 11 years. There is no college in College Park, nor does this dusty stretch of rural land even have water or sewer lines. Yet this town is one of some 1800 settlements that have sprouted up in Southern Texas along the 2000-kilometre border with Mexico that runs from El Paso down to Brownsville; these towns are home to between 500 000 and 700 000 people, numbers expected to pass 1 million within five years.

Many people speak of *las colonias* (Spanish for "the colonies") as "America's Third World" because these desperately poor communities look much like their counterparts in Mexico or many other middle- or low-income nations. But almost all of the people living in the *colonias* are Hispanic Americans, 85 percent of them are legal residents, and more than half are U.S. citizens.

Anastacia Ledsema, now 72 years old, moved to a *colonia* called Sparks more than 40 years ago. Born in Mexico,

Ledsema married a Texas man, and together they paid $200 for a 0.1-hectare lot in a new border community. For months, they camped out on their land. Step by step, however, they invested their labour and their money to build a modest house. But only seven years ago did their small community get running water—a service promised by developers years before. After the water line came, things changed more than they expected. "When we got water," recalls Ledsema, "that's when so many people came in." The population of Sparks quickly doubled to about 3000, overwhelming the water supply.

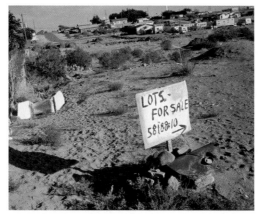

The residents of all the *colonias* know that they are poor. Indeed, the U.S. Census Bureau recently declared one *colonia* to be the poorest county in the entire United States. Concerned over the lack of basic services in so many of these communities, Texas officials have banned any new settlements. But most of the people who move here—even those who start off sleeping in their cars or trucks—see these communities as the first step on the path to the "American dream." Oscar Solis, a neighbourhood leader in Panorama Village, with a population of about 150, is proud to show visitors around the small but growing town. "All of this work we have done ourselves," he says with a smile, "to make our dream come true."

WHAT DO YOU THINK?

1. Are you surprised that such poverty exists in the United States?
2. What is the closest Canadian comparison that you can think of?
3. What special challenges do people living in these communities face in trying to improve their lives?

Source: Based on Schaffer (2002).

Canada had a GDP of almost US$1 trillion in 2003. This amount is dwarfed by the US$10 trillion GDP of the United States; Japan's GDP that same year was about $4 trillion. Some of the world's highest-income nations produce almost 1000 times more than the countries with the lowest incomes, even after we account for differences in local purchasing power.

The second column of figures in Table 9–1 divides GDP by the entire population size to give an estimate of what people can buy using their income in the local economy. The per capita GDP for the countries with the highest incomes—including Canada, the United States, and Norway—is very high, exceeding US$30 000. For middle-income countries, such as Botswana and the Russian Federation, the figures are in the US$8000 range. In the world's low-income countries, per capita GDP is as low as just a few hundred dollars. In Sierra Leone, a typical person labours all year to make what the average worker in Canada earns in less than a week.

The last column of Table 9–1 is a measure of quality of life in the various nations. This index, calculated by the United Nations, combines income, education (extent of adult literacy and average years of schooling), and longevity (how long people typically live). Index values are decimals that fall between extremes of 1 (highest) and 0 (lowest). By this calculation, Norwegians enjoy the highest quality of life

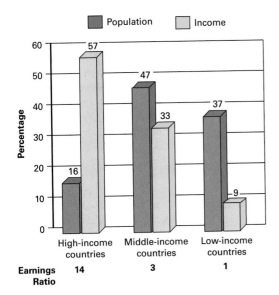

FIGURE 9–2 The Relative Share of Income and Population by Level of Income, 2003

Sources: Calculated based on data from the World Bank (2005).

(0.963), with residents of Canada close behind (0.949). At the other extreme, people in the African nation of Sierra Leone have the lowest quality of life (0.298).

Relative versus absolute poverty. The distinction between relative and absolute poverty, made in Chapter 8, has an important application to global inequality. People living in high-income countries generally focus on *relative poverty,* meaning that some people lack resources that are taken for granted by others. By definition, relative poverty exists in every society, high-income or low-income.

More important in global perspective, however, is *absolute poverty,* a lack of resources that is life-threatening. Human beings in absolute poverty lack the nutrition necessary for health and long-term survival. To be sure, some absolute poverty exists in Canada. But such immediately life-threatening poverty strikes only a small proportion of the Canadian population; in low-income countries, by contrast, one-third or more of the people are in desperate need.

Because absolute poverty is deadly, one global indicator of this problem is the median age at death. Global Map 9–1 identifies the age by which half of all people born in a nation die. In high-income countries, most people die after the age of 75, but in low-income countries, half of all deaths occur among children under the age of 10.

TABLE 9–1
Wealth and Well-Being in Global Perspective, 2002

Country	Gross National Income (US$ billions)	GNI per Capita (PPP US$)*	Quality of Life Index
High-income countries			
Norway	173	37 910	0.963
Australia	572	28 780	0.955
Sweden	239	26 710	0.949
Canada	950	30 040	0.949
United States	10 978	37 750	0.944
Japan	3 629	28 450	0.943
United Kingdom	1 643	27 690	0.939
France	1 652	27 640	0.938
South Korea	862	18 000	0.901
Middle-income countries			
Eastern Europe			
Latvia	24	10 210	0.836
Russian Federation	1 284	8 950	0.795
Romania	155	7 140	0.792
Ukraine	262	5 430	0.766
Latin America			
Mexico	919	8 980	0.814
Venezuela, RB	122	4 750	0.772
Brazil	1 326	7 510	0.792
Asia			
Malaysia	222	8 970	0.796
Thailand	462	7 450	0.778
China	6 410	4 980	0.755
Middle East			
Iran	465	7 000	0.736
Syria	60	3 430	0.721
Africa			
Algeria	189	5 930	0.722
Botswana	14	8 370	0.565
Low-income countries			
Latin America			
Bolivia	22	2 490	0.687
Haiti	15	1 730	0.475
Asia			
Pakistan	303	2 040	0.527
Bangladesh	258	1 870	0.52
Africa			
Guinea	16	2 080	0.466
Nigeria	123	900	0.453
Ethiopia	48	710	0.367
Sierra Leone	3	530	0.298

*These data are the United Nations purchasing power parity (PPP) calculations, which avoid currency rate distortion by showing the local purchasing power of each domestic currency.

Sources: The World Bank (2005); United Nations Development Program (2005).

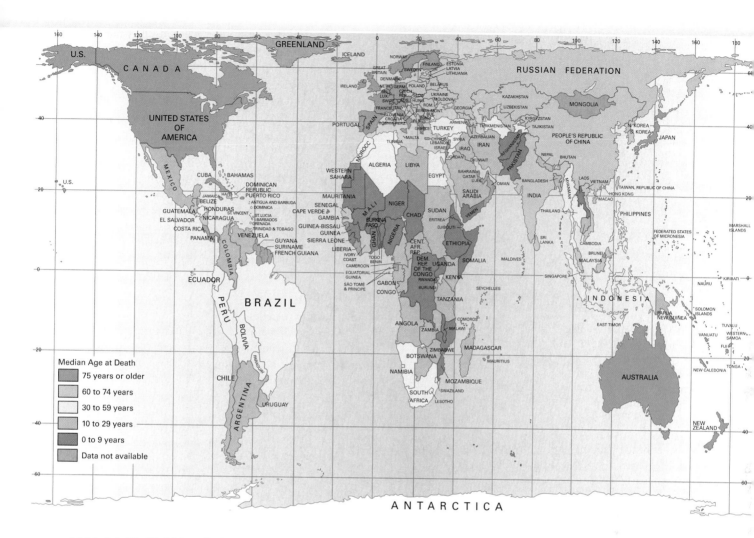

WINDOW ON THE WORLD

GLOBAL MAP 9–1 Median Age at Death in Global Perspective

This map identifies the age below which half of all deaths occur in any year. In the high-income countries of the world, including Canada, it is mostly the elderly who face death, that is, people aged 75 or older. In middle-income countries, including most of Latin America, most people die years or even decades earlier. In low-income countries, especially in Africa and parts of Asia, it is children who die, half of them never reaching their tenth birthday.

Sources: U.S. Census Bureau, International Database, accessed July 5, 2006; map projection from *Peters Atlas of the World* (1990).

THE EXTENT OF POVERTY

Poverty in low-income countries is more widespread than it is in high-income nations such as Canada. Chapter 8 ("Social Stratification") indicated that Statistics Canada officially classifies about 13 percent of the population as living below the poverty line as measured by the low-income cut-off level. In low-income countries, however, most people live no better than the poor in Canada, and many are far worse off. As Global Map 9–1 shows, the high death rates among children in Africa indicate that absolute poverty is greatest there, where half the population is malnourished. In the world as a whole, at any given time, 15 percent of the

Tens of millions of children fend for themselves on the streets of Latin America, where many fall victim to disease, drug abuse, and outright violence. What do you think must be done to put an end to scenes like this one in San Salvador, the capital city of El Salvador?

people—about 1 billion—suffer from chronic hunger, which leaves them less able to work and puts them at high risk of illness and disease (Kates, 1996; United Nations Development Programme, 2001).

The typical adult in a high-income nation such as Canada consumes about 3500 calories a day, an excess that contributes to obesity and related health problems. The typical adult in a low-income country not only does more physical labour but consumes just 2000 calories a day. The result is undernourishment: too little food or not enough of the right kinds of food.

In the 10 minutes it takes to read through this section of the chapter, about 300 people in the world who are sick and weakened from hunger will die. This amounts to about 40 000 people a day, or 15 million people each year. Clearly, easing world hunger is one of the most serious challenges facing humanity today.

POVERTY AND CHILDREN

Death comes early in low-income societies, where families lack adequate food, safe drinking water, secure housing, and access to healthcare. Organizations fighting child poverty estimate that at least 100 million city children in low-income countries beg, steal, sell sex, or work for drug gangs to provide income for their families. Such a life almost always means dropping out of school and places children at

high risk of disease and violence. Many girls become pregnant, a case of children who cannot support themselves having children of their own with little or no access to assistance from health professionals.

Analysts estimate that another 100 million of the world's children leave their families altogether, sleeping and living on the streets as best they can or perhaps trying to migrate to Canada or the United States. Roughly half of all street children are found in Latin American cities such as Mexico City and Rio de Janeiro, where perhaps half of all children grow up in poverty. Many people in Canada know these cities as exotic travel destinations, but they are also home to thousands of children living in makeshift huts, under bridges, or in alleyways (Ross, 1996; United Nations Development Programme, 2000; Collymore, 2002).

POVERTY AND WOMEN

In high-income societies, the work women do typically is undervalued, underpaid, or overlooked entirely. In low-income societies, women face even greater disadvantages. For example, most of the people who work in sweatshops like the one described in the opening to this chapter are women.

 To learn more about women labouring in sweatshops, visit www.globalexchange.org/campaigns/sweatshops.

To make matters worse, tradition keeps women out of many jobs in low-income nations; in Bangladesh, women work in garment factories because that nation's conservative Muslim religious norms bar them from most other paid work and limit their opportunities for advanced schooling (Bearak, 2001). At the same time, traditional norms give women primary responsibility for raising children and maintaining the household. The United Nations estimates that in low-income countries, men own 90 percent of the land, a far greater gender disparity in wealth than is found in high-income nations. It is no surprise, then, that about 70 percent of the world's 1 billion people living near absolute poverty are women (Hymowitz, 1995).

Finally, the fact that women in low-income countries generally do not have access to birth control raises the birth rate and keeps women at home with their children. In addition, the world's poorest women typically give birth without help from trained health workers. Figure 9–3 on page 240 shows the stark contrast between high- and low-income countries in this regard.

SLAVERY

Low-income societies have many problems in addition to hunger—including illiteracy, warfare, and even slavery. The British Empire banned slavery in 1833, followed by the

United States in 1865. But according to Anti-Slavery International (ASI), as many as 400 million men, women, and children (almost 7 percent of humanity) live today in conditions that amount to slavery.

ASI describes four types of slavery. First is *chattel slavery*, in which one person owns another. The number of chattel slaves is difficult to estimate because this practice is against the law almost everywhere. But the buying and selling of slaves still takes place in many countries in Asia, the Middle East, and especially Africa. The Global Sociology box describes the reality of one slave's life in the African nation of Mauritania.

A second, more common form of bondage is *child slavery*, in which desperately poor families let their children take to the streets to do what they can to survive. Perhaps 100 million children—many in low-income countries of Latin America—fall into this category.

Third, *debt bondage* is the practice by which employers hold workers captive by paying them too little to meet their debts. In this case, workers receive a wage, but it is too small to cover the food and housing provided by the employer; for practical purposes, they are enslaved. Many sweatshop workers in low-income nations fall into this category.

Fourth, *servile forms of marriage* may also amount to slavery. In India, Thailand, and some African nations, families marry women off against their will. Many end up as slaves to their husband's family; some are forced into prostitution.

Finally, one additional form of slavery is *human trafficking*, the movement of men, women, and children from one place to another for the purpose of performing forced labour. Women or men brought to a new country on the promise of a job and then forced to become prostitutes or farm labourers, or "parents" who adopt children from another country and then force them to work in sweatshops, are examples of trafficking in human beings. Such activity is big business: Next to trading in guns and drugs, trading in people brings the greatest profits to organized crime around the world (Orhant, 2002).

 Read the United Nations' Universal Declaration of Human Rights at www.un.org/rights/50/decla.htm.

In 1948, the United Nations issued the Universal Declaration of Human Rights, which states, "No one shall be held in slavery or servitude; slavery and the slave trade shall be prohibited in all their forms." Unfortunately, nearly six decades later, this social evil persists.

CORRELATES OF GLOBAL POVERTY

What accounts for the severe and widespread poverty throughout much of the world? The rest of this chapter

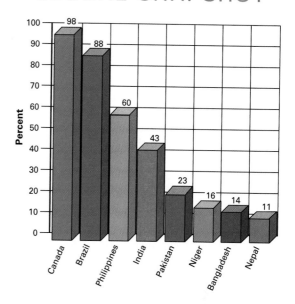

FIGURE 9-3 Percentage of Births Attended by Skilled Health Personnel

Source: United Nations Development Program (2005).

provides answers to this question using the following facts about low-income nations:

1. **Technology.** About one-quarter of people in low-income countries farm the land using human muscles or animal power. With limited energy sources, agricultural production is modest.

2. **Population growth.** As Chapter 15 ("Population, Urbanization, and Environment") explains, some of the countries with the lowest incomes have the world's highest birth rates. Despite the death toll from poverty, the populations of low-income countries in Africa double every 25 years. In these countries, half the people are teenagers or younger. With such a large share of the population just entering the childbearing years, the wave of population growth will continue to roll into the future. In recent years, for example, the population of Chad has swelled by 3.3 percent annually, so that even with economic development, living standards have fallen.

3. **Cultural patterns.** Low-income societies are usually traditional. People who hold to long-established ways of life resist change—even changes that promise a richer material life. The Global Sociology box explains why traditional people in India respond to their poverty differently than poor people in Canada.

GLOBAL SOCIOLOGY
"God Made Me to Be a Slave"

Fatma Mint Mamadou is a young woman living in North Africa's Islamic Republic of Mauritania. When asked her age, she pauses and smiles. She has no idea when she was born. Nor can she read or write. What she knows is tending camels, herding sheep, hauling bags of water, sweeping, and serving tea to her owners. This young woman is one of perhaps 90 000 slaves in Mauritania.

In the central region of this nation, having very dark skin almost always means being a slave to an Arab owner. Fatma accepts her situation, because she knows nothing else. She explains in a matter-of-fact voice that she is a slave, like her mother before her and her grandmother before that. "Just as God created a camel to be a camel," she shrugs, "he created me to be a slave."

Fatma, her mother, and her brothers and sisters live together in a squatter settlement on the edge of Nouakchott, Mauritania's capital city. Their home is a 12-square-metre hut they built from wood scraps and other building materials taken from construction sites. The roof is nothing more than a piece of cloth; there is no plumbing or furniture. The nearest water comes from a well 2 kilometres down the road.

In this region, slavery began 500 years ago, about the time Columbus sailed west toward the New World. As Arab and Berber tribes moved across the continent spreading Islam, they raided local villages and made slaves of the people, a practice that was continued for dozens of generations. In 1905, the French colonial rulers of Mauritania banned slavery. After the nation gained independence in 1961, the new government reaffirmed the ban. But such proclamations have done little to change strong traditions. Indeed, people like Fatma have no idea what freedom means.

The next question is more personal: "Are you and other girls ever raped?" Again, Fatma hesitates. With no hint of emotion, she responds, "Of course, in the night the men come to breed us. Is that what you mean by rape?"

WHAT DO YOU THINK?

1. How does tradition play a part in keeping people in slavery?
2. Why do you think the world still tolerates slavery?
3. Do you think this practice will still be found a century from now? Why or why not?

Human slavery continues to exist in the twenty-first century.

Source: Based on Burkett (1997).

4. **Social stratification.** Low-income nations distribute their wealth very unequally. Chapter 8 ("Social Stratification") explained that social inequality is greater in agrarian societies than in industrial societies. In some low-income countries, half of all farmland is owned by just 1 percent of the people (Bergamo & Camarotti, 1996).

5. **Gender inequality.** Extreme gender inequality in low-income societies keeps women from holding jobs, which typically means they have many children. An expanding population, in turn, slows economic development. Many analysts conclude that raising living standards in much of the world depends on improving the social standing of women.

6. **Global power relationships.** A final cause of global poverty lies in the relationships between the nations of the world. Historically, wealth flowed from low-income societies to high-income nations through **colonialism**, *the process by which some nations enrich themselves through political and economic control of other nations.* The countries of Western Europe colonized much of Latin America beginning roughly 500 years ago. Such global exploitation allowed some nations to develop economically at the expense of others.

Although 130 former colonies gained their independence during the twentieth century, exploitation continues through **neocolonialism** ("*neo*" is the Greek word

GLOBAL SOCIOLOGY

A Different Kind of Poverty: A Report From India

India, with a per capita gross national income (GNI) of almost US$2900, has one of the highest incomes in the group of low-income nations. Nevertheless, its per capita GNI is less than one-tenth that in Canada. For this reason, India is home to one-fourth of the world's hungry people.

But most Canadians do not easily understand the reality of poverty in India. Many of the country's 1.1 billion people live in conditions far worse than those our society labels "poor." A traveller's first experience of Indian life can be shocking. Madras, one of India's largest cities with 7 million inhabitants, seems chaotic to the outsider, with streets choked by motorbikes, trucks, carts pulled by oxen, and waves of people. Along the roadway, vendors sit on burlap cloths selling fruits, vegetables, and cooked food while people a few yards away work, talk, bathe, and sleep.

Although some people live well, Madras is dotted by more than a thousand shanty settlements, home to half a million people from rural villages who have come in search of a better life. Shantytowns are clusters of huts built with branches, leaves, and pieces of discarded cardboard and tin. These dwellings offer little privacy and lack refrigeration, running water, and bathrooms. A visitor from Canada may feel uneasy in such an area, knowing that the poorest sections of our own inner cities seethe with frustration and sometimes explode with violence.

But India's people understand poverty differently than we do. No restless young men hang out at the corner, no drug dealers work the streets, and there is little danger of violence. In Canada, poverty often means anger and isolation; in India, even shantytowns are organized around strong families—children, parents, and often grandparents—who offer a smile of welcome to a stranger.

For traditional people in India, life is

shaped by *dharma*, the Hindu concept of duty and destiny that teaches people to accept their fate, whatever it may be. Mother Teresa, who worked among the poorest of India's people, went to the heart of the cultural differences: "Americans have angry poverty," she explained. "In India, there is worse poverty, but it is a happy poverty." Perhaps we should not describe anyone who clings to the edge of survival as happy. But poverty in India is eased by the strength and support of families and communities, a sense that life has a purpose, and a worldview that encourages each person to accept whatever life offers. As a result, a visitor may come away from a first encounter with Indian poverty rather confused: "How can people be so poor and yet seem content, active, and *joyful*?"

WHAT DO YOU THINK?

1. What did Mother Teresa mean when she said that in India there is "happy poverty"?
2. How might an experience like this change the way you think about the meaning of "rich"?
3. Are there poor people in regions of Canada who behave like these people in India? Explain.

Source: Based on one of the authors' research in Madras, India, November 1988.

---

for "new"), *a new form of global power relationships that involves not direct political control but economic exploitation by multinational corporations.* A **multinational corporation** *is a large business that operates in many countries.* Corporate leaders can impose their will on countries in which they do business to create favourable economic conditions, just as colonizers did in the past.

Global Stratification: Theoretical Analysis

There are two major explanations for the unequal distribution of the world's wealth and power: *modernization theory* and *dependency theory.* Each theory suggests a different solution to the suffering of hungry people in much of the world.

MODERNIZATION THEORY

Modernization theory is *a model of economic and social development that explains global inequality in terms of technological and cultural differences between nations.* Derived from the structural-functional approach, modernization theory emerged in the 1950s, a time when Canadian society was fascinated with new technology. To counter the growing influence of the Soviet Union and socialism in much of the world, European and North American policy makers drafted a foreign policy that supported capitalism and free markets. This general policy has been with us ever since.[3]

Historical perspective. Until a few centuries ago, the entire world was low-income. Because poverty has been the norm throughout human history, modernization theory proposes that it is *affluence* that demands an explanation.

Affluence came within reach of a growing share of people in Western Europe during the late Middle Ages as world exploration and trade expanded. Soon the Industrial Revolution was underway, transforming first Western Europe and then North America. Industrial technology, together with the spirit of capitalism, created new wealth as never before. At first, this new wealth benefited only a few. But industrial technology was so productive that gradually the living standards of even the poorest people began to improve. Absolute poverty, which had plagued humanity throughout history, was finally in decline.

During the twentieth century, the standard of living in high-income countries, where the Industrial Revolution began, jumped at least fourfold. Many middle-income nations in Asia and Latin America have now industrialized, and they, too, now have a higher income on average. But with limited industrial technology, low-income countries have changed much less.

The importance of culture. Why didn't the Industrial Revolution sweep away poverty the world over? Modernization theory points out that not every society wants to adopt new technology. Doing so takes a cultural environment that emphasizes the benefits of material wealth and new ideas.

Modernization theory identifies *tradition* as the greatest barrier to economic development. A reverence for the past may discourage people from adopting new technologies that would raise their living standards. Even today, many people—from the North American Amish to traditional Islamic people in the Middle East to the Semai of Malaysia—oppose new technology as a threat to their family relationships, customs, and religious beliefs.

---

[3]The following discussion of modernization theory draws primarily on Rostow (1960, 1978), Bauer (1981), Berger (1986), Firebaugh (1996), and Firebaugh and Sandu (1998).

Max Weber (1958, orig. 1904–05) found that at the end of the Middle Ages, Western Europe's cultural environment favoured change. As Chapter 13 ("Family and Religion") explains, the Protestant Reformation reshaped traditional Catholic beliefs to generate a progress-oriented way of life. Wealth, looked on with suspicion by the Catholic church, became a sign of personal virtue, and the growing importance of individualism steadily replaced the traditional emphasis on family and community. These new cultural patterns nurtured the Industrial Revolution.

Rostow's stages of modernization. Modernization theory holds that the door to affluence is open to all. Indeed, as technological advances spread around the world, all societies should gradually industrialize. According to W.W. Rostow (1960, 1978), modernization occurs in four stages:

1. **Traditional stage.** Socialized to honour the past, people in traditional societies cannot easily imagine how life can be very different. Therefore, they build their lives around families and local communities, following well-worn paths that allow little individual freedom or change. Life is often spiritually rich but lacking in material goods.

    A century ago, much of the world was in this initial stage of economic development. Nations such as Bangladesh, Niger, and Somalia are still at the traditional stage and remain low-income countries.

2. **Take-off stage.** As a society shakes off the grip of tradition, people start to use their talents and imagination, sparking economic growth. A market emerges as people produce goods not just for their own use but to trade with others for profit. Greater individualism, a willingness to take risks, and a desire for material goods also take hold, often at the expense of family ties and time-honoured norms and values.

    Great Britain reached take-off by about 1800, the United States by 1820. Thailand, a middle-income country in Eastern Asia, is now in this stage. Such development typically is hastened by progressive influences from high-income nations, including foreign aid, the availability of advanced technology and investment capital, and opportunities for schooling abroad.

3. **Drive to technological maturity.** As this stage begins, "growth" is a widely accepted idea that fuels a society's pursuit of higher living standards. A diversified economy drives a population eager to enjoy the benefits of industrial technology. At the same time, people begin to realize (and sometimes regret) that industrialization is weakening traditional family and local community life. Great Britain entered this stage by about 1840, the

In high-income nations such as Canada, most parents expect their children to enjoy years of childhood, largely free of the responsibilities of adult life. This is not the case in low-income nations across Latin America, Africa, and Asia. Low-income families depend on whatever income their children can earn, and many children as young as six or seven work full days weaving or performing other kinds of manual labour. Child labour lies behind the low prices of many products imported for sale in this country.

United States by 1860. Today, Mexico, the U.S. territory of Puerto Rico, and South Korea are among the nations driving to technological maturity.

Absolute poverty is greatly reduced in nations in this stage. Cities swell with people who have left rural villages in search of economic opportunity; job specialization makes relationships less personal, and growing individualism generates social movements demanding greater political rights. Societies approaching technological maturity also provide basic schooling to all their people and advanced training for some. The newly educated consider tradition "backward," opening the door to further change. In addition, the social position of women steadily approaches that of men.

4. **High mass consumption.** Economic development driven by industrial technology steadily raises living standards as mass production stimulates mass consumption. Simply put, people soon learn to "need" the expanding selection of goods that their society produces.

Britain and the United States entered this stage of development by 1900, soon followed by Canada and other high-income nations. Approaching this level of economic prosperity today are two former British colonies in Eastern Asia: Hong Kong (now part of the People's Republic of China), and Singapore (independent since 1965).

The role of high-income nations. Modernization theory claims that high-income countries play four important roles in global economic development:

1. **Controlling population.** Because population growth is greatest in societies with the lowest incomes, rising population can overtake economic advances. High-income nations can help limit population growth by exporting birth control technology and promoting its use. Once economic development is underway, birth rates should decline, as they have in industrialized nations, because children are no longer an economic asset.

2. **Increasing food production.** High-income nations can export high-tech farming methods to low-income nations to help raise agricultural yields. Such techniques, collectively referred to as the "Green Revolution," include new hybrid seeds, modern irrigation methods, chemical fertilizers, and pesticides for insect control.

3. **Introducing industrial technology.** High-income nations can encourage economic growth in low-income societies by introducing machinery and information technology, which raise productivity. Industrialization also shifts the labour force from farming to skilled industrial and service jobs.

4. **Providing foreign aid.** Investment capital from high-income nations can boost the prospects of low-income societies striving to reach Rostow's take-off stage. Foreign aid can help raise agricultural productivity by enabling low-income countries to purchase more fertilizer and build irrigation systems. In addition, financial and technical assistance to build power plants and factories improves industrial output.

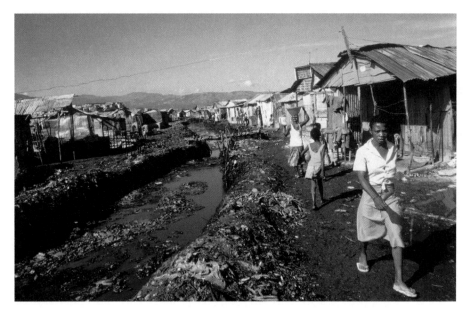

Although the world continues to grow richer, billions of people are being left behind. The shantytown of Cité Soleil ("City of the Sun") near Port-au-Prince, the capital of Haiti, is built around an open sewer. What would you estimate the life expectancy to be in such a place?

Critical review. Modernization theory has many influential supporters among social scientists (Parsons, 1966; Moore, 1977, 1979; Bauer, 1981; Berger, 1986; Firebaugh & Beck, 1994; Firebaugh, 1996; Firebaugh & Sandu, 1998). For decades it has shaped the foreign policy of Canada and other high-income nations. Supporters point to rapid economic development in Asia—including South Korea, Taiwan, Singapore, and Hong Kong—as proof that the affluence created in Western Europe and North America is within the reach of all countries.

But modernization theory faces criticism from socialist countries (and left-leaning analysts in the West) as little more than a defence of capitalism. First—its most serious flaw, according to critics—modernization simply has not occurred in many low-income countries. The United Nations reported that living standards in a number of nations—including Kenya, South Africa, the Democratic Republic of the Congo, Zambia, Swaziland, and Zimbabwe—have hardly changed since 1975 and some are actually lower today than they were then (United Nations Development Programme, 2005).

Second, modernization theory fails to recognize how high-income nations, which benefit from the status quo, often block the path to development for low-income countries. Centuries ago, high-income countries industrialized from a position of global *strength*. Can we expect low-income countries today to do so from a position of global *weakness*?

Third, modernization theory treats high-income and low-income societies as separate worlds, ignoring how international relations have affected all nations. Countries in Latin America and Asia are still struggling from the effects of their colonization, which boosted the fortunes of Europe.

Fourth, modernization theory holds up the world's most developed countries as the standard for judging the rest of humanity, revealing an ethnocentric bias. We need to remember that our Western idea of "progress" has caused us to rush headlong into a competitive, materialistic way of life, which uses up the world's scarce resources and pollutes the natural environment.

Fifth, and finally, modernization theory suggests that the causes of global poverty lie almost entirely within the low-income societies themselves. Critics see this analysis as little more than blaming the victims for their own problems. Instead, they argue, an analysis of global inequality should focus just as much on the behaviour of high-income nations as it does on the behaviour of low-income ones.

Concerns such as these reflect a second major approach to understanding global inequality: dependency theory.

DEPENDENCY THEORY

Dependency theory is *a model of economic and social development that explains global inequality in terms of the historical exploitation of low-income nations by high-income ones.* Derived from the social-conflict approach, this analysis puts primary responsibility for global poverty on high-income nations, which for centuries have systematically impoverished low-income countries and made them dependent on the high-income ones. This destructive process continues today.

Historical perspective. Everyone agrees that before the Industrial Revolution, there was little affluence in the world. However, dependency theory asserts that people living in low-income countries were actually better off economically in the past than their descendants are now. André Gunder Frank (1975), a noted supporter of this theory, argues that the colonial process that helped develop high-income nations also *underdeveloped* low-income societies.

Dependency theory is based on the idea that the economic positions of the high-income and low-income nations of the world are linked and cannot be understood apart from one another. Low-income nations are not simply lagging behind high-income ones on the "path of progress"; rather, the prosperity of the most developed countries came largely at the expense of less developed ones. In short, some nations became rich only because others became poor. Both are the result of the expansion of global commerce five centuries ago.

The importance of colonialism. Late in the fifteenth century, Europeans began surveying the Americas to the west, Africa to the south, and Asia to the east in order to establish colonies. They were so successful that a century ago, Great Britain controlled about one-fourth of the world's land, boasting, "The sun never sets on the British Empire."

Meanwhile, Europeans and Africans engaged in a brutal form of human exploitation—the slave trade—from about 1500 until 1850. Even as the world was rejecting slavery, Europeans took control of Africa itself, as Figure 9–4 shows. European powers dominated most of the continent until the early 1960s.

Formal colonialism has almost disappeared from the world. However, according to dependency theory, political liberation has not meant economic independence. Far from it: the economic relationship between low-income and high-income nations continues the colonial pattern of domination. This *neocolonialism* is the heart of the capitalist world economy.

Wallerstein's capitalist world economy. Immanuel Wallerstein (1974, 1979, 1983, 1984) explains global stratification using a model of the "capitalist world economy." Wallerstein's term "world economy" suggests that the prosperity or poverty of any country is the result of a global economic system. He traces the roots of the global economy to the beginning of colonization more than 500 years ago when Europeans began gathering wealth from the rest of the world. Because the global economy is based in high-income countries, it is capitalist in character.[4]

---

[4]Though based on Wallerstein's ideas, this section also reflects the work of Frank (1980, 1981), Delacroix and Ragin (1981), Bergesen (1983), Dixon and Boswell (1996), and Kentor (1998).

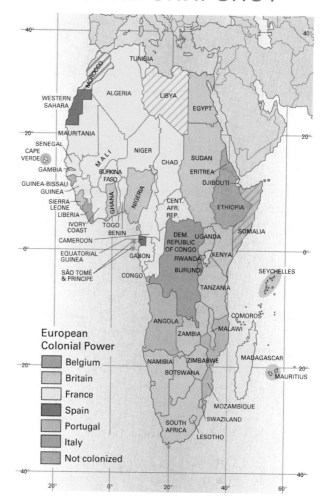

GLOBAL SNAPSHOT

European Colonial Power

- Belgium
- Britain
- France
- Spain
- Portugal
- Italy
- Not colonized

FIGURE 9–4 Africa's Colonial History

Wallerstein calls the high-income nations the *core* of the world economy. Colonialism enriched this core by funnelling raw materials from around the world to Western Europe, where they fuelled the Industrial Revolution. Today, multinational corporations operate profitably worldwide, bringing wealth to North America, Western Europe, Australia, and Japan.

Low-income countries are the *periphery* of the world economy. Drawn into the world economy by colonial exploitation, low-income nations continue to support high-income ones by providing low-cost labour and a vast market for industrial products. The remaining countries are the *semiperiphery* of the world economy. They include middle-income countries such as Mexico and Brazil that have closer ties to the global economic core.

According to Wallerstein, the world economy benefits high-income societies (by generating profits) and harms the rest of the world (by causing poverty). The world economy thus makes low-income nations dependent on high-income ones. This dependency involves three factors:

1. **Narrow, export-oriented economies.** Low-income nations produce only a few crops for export to high-income countries. Examples include coffee and fruits from Latin American nations, oil from Nigeria, hardwoods from the Philippines, and palm oil from Malaysia.

   Today's multinational corporations buy raw materials cheaply in low-income societies and transport them to core nations, where factories process them for profitable sale. Thus, low-income nations develop few industries of their own.

2. **Lack of industrial capacity.** Without an industrial base, low-income societies depend on high-income nations to buy their inexpensive raw materials and try to buy from them whatever expensive manufactured goods they can afford. In a classic example of this dependency, British colonialists encouraged the people of India to raise cotton but prevented them from weaving their own cloth. Instead, the British shipped Indian cotton to English textile mills in Birmingham and Manchester, manufactured the cloth, and shipped finished goods back to India, where the very people who harvested the cotton bought the garments.

   Dependency theorists claim the Green Revolution—widely praised by modernization theorists—works the same way. Low-income countries sell cheap raw materials to high-income nations and then try to buy expensive fertilizers, pesticides, and machinery in return. Typically, high-income countries profit from this exchange more than low-income nations.

3. **Foreign debt.** Unequal trade patterns have plunged low-income countries into debt. Collectively, the low-income nations of the world owe high-income countries $2.3 trillion; hundreds of billions of dollars are owed to Canada and the United States. Such staggering debt paralyzes a country, causing high unemployment and rampant inflation (World Bank, 2004).

The role of high-income nations. Modernization theory and dependency theory assign high-income nations very different roles. Modernization theory holds that high-income societies *produce wealth* through capital investment and new technology. Dependency theory views global inequality in terms of how countries *distribute wealth*, arguing that high-income nations have *over*developed themselves as they have *under*developed the rest of the world.

Dependency theorists do not believe that strategies by high-income countries to control population and increase agricultural and industrial output will help raise living standards in low-income countries. Instead, they claim, such programs actually benefit high-income nations and the ruling elites, not the poor majority, in low-income countries (Kentor, 2001).

Hunger activists Frances Moore Lappé and Joseph Collins (1986) maintain that the capitalist culture of Canada encourages people to think of poverty as somehow inevitable. Following this line of reasoning, poverty results from "natural" processes, including having too many children, and from natural disasters such as droughts. But according to dependency theory, global poverty is far from inevitable; it results from deliberate policies. Lappé and Collins point out that the world already produces enough food to allow every person on the planet to become quite fat. India and most of Africa actually *export* food, even though many of their own people go hungry.

According to Lappé and Collins, the existence of poverty amid plenty stems from the high-income nations' policy of producing food for profits, not people. That is, corporations in high-income nations work with elites in low-income countries to grow and export profitable crops such as coffee, which means using land that could otherwise produce basics such as beans and corn for local families. Governments of low-income countries support the practice of growing for export because they need food profits to help pay off huge foreign debt. According to Lappé and Collins, the capitalist corporate structure of the global economy is at the core of this vicious cycle.

Critical review. The main idea of dependency theory is that no nation develops (or fails to develop) in isolation, because the global economy shapes the future of all nations. Pointing to Latin America and other low-income regions of the world, dependency theorists claim that development simply cannot proceed under the constraints imposed by high-income countries. Rather, they call for radical reform of the entire world economy so that it operates in the interests of the majority of people.

Critics charge that dependency theory wrongly treats wealth as if no one gets richer without someone else getting poorer. Corporations, small business owners, and farmers can and do create new wealth through their drive and imaginative use of new technology. After all, they point out, the entire world's wealth has increased sixfold since 1950.

Second, dependency theory is wrong in blaming high-income nations for global poverty, because many of the

APPLYING THEORY
GLOBAL POVERTY

	Modernization Theory	Dependency Theory
Which theoretical approach is applied?	Structural-functional approach	Social-conflict approach
How did global poverty come about?	The whole world was low-income until some countries developed industrial technology, which allowed mass production and created affluence.	Colonialism moved wealth from some countries to others, making some nations low-income as it made other nations high-income.
What are the main causes of global poverty today?	Traditional culture and a lack of productive technology.	Neocolonialism—the operation of multinational corporations in the global, capitalist economy.
Are high-income countries part of the problem or part of the solution?	High-income countries are part of the solution, contributing new technology, advanced schooling, and foreign aid.	High-income countries are part of the problem, making low-income countries economically dependent and in debt.

world's countries with the lowest incomes (such as Ethiopia) have had little contact with high-income nations. On the contrary, a long history of trade with high-income countries has dramatically improved the economies of nations including Sri Lanka, Singapore, and Hong Kong (all former British colonies), as well as South Korea and Japan. In short, say the critics, most evidence shows that foreign investment by high-income nations encourages economic growth, as modernization theory claims, not economic decline, as dependency theory says (Vogel, 1991; Firebaugh, 1992).

Third, critics call dependency theory simplistic for pointing the finger at a single factor—world capitalism—as the cause of global inequality (Worsley, 1990). Dependency theory views low-income societies as passive victims and ignores factors inside these countries that contribute to their economic problems. Sociologists have long recognized the vital role of culture in shaping people's willingness to accept or resist change. Under the rule of the ultra-traditional Muslim Taliban, for example, Afghanistan became economically isolated, and its living standards sank to among the lowest in the world. Is it reasonable to blame capitalist societies for that country's stagnation?

Nor can high-income societies be held responsible for the reckless behaviour of foreign leaders whose corruption and militaristic campaigns impoverish their countries. Examples include the regimes of Ferdinand Marcos in the Philippines, François Duvalier in Haiti, Manuel Noriega in

Panama, Mobutu Sese Seko in Zaire (today's Democratic Republic of the Congo), and Saddam Hussein in Iraq. Some leaders even use food supplies as a weapon in internal political struggles, leaving the people starving in the African nations of Ethiopia, Sudan, and Somalia. Likewise, many countries throughout the world have done little to improve the status of women or control population growth.

Fourth, critics say dependency theory focuses on capitalist countries including Canada but downplays the economic dependency created by the former Soviet Union. The Soviet army seized control of most of Eastern Europe during World War II and then politically and economically dominated these countries. Many see the uprisings between 1989 and 1991 as a wholesale rejection of the Soviet Union's socialist colonial system.

Fifth, critics fault dependency theory for offering only vague solutions to global poverty. Most dependency theorists urge low-income nations to end all contact with high-income countries, and some call for nationalizing foreign-owned industries. In other words, dependency theory is really an argument for some sort of world socialism. Given the difficulties socialist societies (even socialist countries such as Russia with higher incomes) have had in meeting the needs of their own people, critics ask, should we really expect such a system to rescue the entire world from poverty?

The Applying Theory table summarizes the main arguments of modernization theory and dependency theory.

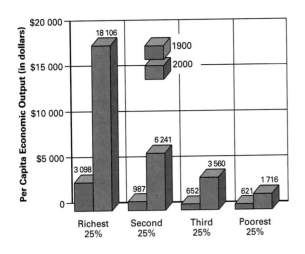

FIGURE 9-5 The World's Increasing Economic Inequality

Source: International Monetary Fund (2000).

Global Stratification: Looking Ahead

Among the most important trends of recent decades is the development of a global economy. Increased production and sales abroad have brought huge profits to many corporations and their shareholders. At the same time, the global economy has cut factory jobs in this country, hurting many average workers. The net result: economic polarization in Canada.

As this chapter has explained, social inequality is far more striking in global perspective. The concentration of wealth among high-income countries, coupled with grinding poverty in low-income nations, may well be the biggest problem facing humanity in the twenty-first century.

Finding answers to questions about global poverty is urgent. Both modernization theory and dependency theory have their strengths and their limitations. In searching for truth, we must consider empirical evidence. Over the course of the twentieth century, living standards rose in most of the world. Even the economic output of the poorest 25 percent of the world's people almost tripled over the course of the twentieth century. However, the economic output of the other 75 percent of the world's people increased about six-fold. By this measure, although all people are better off in *absolute* terms, there was almost twice as much *relative* eco-

nomic inequality in the world in 2000 as there was in 1900. Therefore, as shown in Figure 9–5, the poorest of the world's people are being left behind.

Most of this economic polarization took place between 1900 and 1970. Since 1970, the degree of economic inequality worldwide has declined. In addition, the ranks of the world's poorest people—those living on less than $1 per day—have fallen from about 600 million in 1970 to about 350 million in 2000 (Schultz, 1998; Firebaugh, 1999, 2000; Sala-i-Martin, 2002).

The greatest reduction in poverty has taken place in Asia, a region generally seen as an economic success story. Back in 1970, 75 percent of global $1-per-day poverty was found in Asia; by 2000, that figure had fallen to 15 percent (Sala-i-Martin, 2002).

Latin America represents a mixed case. During the 1970s, this world region enjoyed significant economic growth; during the 1980s and 1990s, however, there was little overall improvement. Latin America's share of global $1-per-day poverty was the same in 2000 (3 percent) as it was in 1970 (Sala-i-Martin, 2002).

Africa, specifically the countries south of the Sahara Desert, represents a region of economic decline. There, the extent of extreme poverty has become worse. In 1970, sub-Saharan Africa accounted for 11 percent of $1-per-day poverty; by 2000, this share had risen to 66 percent (Sala-i-Martin, 2002). Global Map 9–2 provides a visual picture of prosperity and stagnation around the world.

These trends in economic performance have caused both modernization and dependency theorists to revise their views. Governments have played a large role in the economic growth that has occurred in Asia and elsewhere; no nation has a market economy completely free of government involvement. This fact challenges modernization theory and its free-market approach to development. On the other hand, since the upheavals in the former Soviet Union and Eastern Europe, a global re-evaluation of socialism has been underway. Because these uprisings follow decades of poor economic performance and political repression, many low-income nations are unwilling to follow the advice of dependency theory and place economic development entirely under government control.

In the end, reducing hunger around the world is a matter not just of policy but of commitment. As the Controversy & Debate box on page 250 explains, many analysts wonder whether humanity has the determination to provide for everyone on the planet.

Although the world's future is uncertain, we have learned a great deal about global stratification. One major insight, offered by modernization theory, is that poverty is partly a *problem of technology*. A higher standard of living for a growing world population depends on raising

WINDOW ON THE WORLD

GLOBAL MAP 9-2 Prosperity and Stagnation in Global Perspective

In about 60 nations of the world, people are enjoying a higher standard of living than ever before. These prospering countries include some high-income nations (such as Canada, the United States, and the countries of Western Europe) and some low-income nations (especially in Asia). For most countries, however, living standards have remained steady or even slipped in recent decades. Especially in Eastern Europe and the Middle East, some nations have experienced economic setbacks since the 1980s. And in sub-Saharan Africa, some nations are no better off than they were in 1960. The overall pattern is economic polarization, with an increasing gap between high-income and low-income nations.

Source: United Nations Development Programme (1996); updates by the authors.

agricultural and industrial productivity. A second insight, derived from dependency theory, is that global inequality is also a *political issue.* Even with higher productivity, the human community must address crucial questions concerning the distribution of resources, both within societies and around the globe.

Although economic development raises living standards, it also places greater strains on the natural environment. As

CONTROVERSY & DEBATE

Will the World Starve?

The animals' feet leave their prints
  on the desert's face.
Hunger is so real, so very real, that
  it can make you walk around a bar-
  ren tree looking for nourishment.
Not once,
Not twice,
Not thrice . . .

These lines, by Indian poet Amit Jayaram, describe the appalling hunger found in Rajasthan, in Northwestern India. As this chapter has explained, hunger casts a menacing shadow over many regions of the world. Hundreds of millions of adults do not eat enough food to enable them to work. Most tragically, some 10 million children die each year because of hunger. As we begin the twenty-first century, what are the prospects for ending the wretched misery of daily hunger?

Pessimists point out that the population of low-income countries is currently increasing by 73 million people annually, equivalent to adding another Egypt to the world every year. Low-income countries can hardly feed the people they have now; how will they ever feed *twice* as many people a generation in the future?

In addition, hunger forces poor people to exploit the Earth's resources by using short-term strategies for food production that lead to long-term disaster. For example, farmers are cutting rain-forests in order to increase their farm-

land; without the protective canopy of trees, it is only a matter of time before much of this land turns to desert. Rising populations and shortsighted policies raise the possibility of even greater hunger and human misery.

But there are also grounds for optimism. Thanks to the Green Revolution, food production the world over has increased sharply over the last 50 years, well outpacing the growth in population. The world's economic productivity has risen steadily, so that the average person on the planet has more income now to purchase food and other necessities than ever before. This growth has increased daily caloric intake, life expectancy, access to safe water, and adult literacy; around the world, infant mortality is half what it was in 1960.

What are the prospects for ending world hunger? Overall, we see less hunger in both high-income and low-income countries, and a smaller *share* of the world's people are hungry now than in 1960. But as global population increases, with 98 percent of children born in middle- and low-income countries, the *number of lives* at risk is as great today as ever before. Many low-income countries have made solid gains, but many more are stagnating or even losing ground.

The best-case region of the world is Eastern Asia, where incomes controlled

for inflation have tripled over the last generation. Optimists point to Asia for evidence that low-income countries can raise living standards and reduce hunger. The worst-case region is sub-Saharan Africa, where living standards have fallen over the last decade, high technology is least evident, and birth rates are highest. Pessimists typically look to Africa when they argue that low-income countries are losing ground in the struggle to feed their people.

Television brings home the tragedy of hunger when news cameras focus on starving people in places such as Ethiopia and Somalia. But hunger—and early death from illness—is the plight of millions all year round. The world has the technical means to feed everyone; the question is, do we have the moral deter-mination?

CONTINUE THE DEBATE . . .

1. In your opinion, what are the primary causes of global hunger?
2. Do you place more responsibility for solving this problem on low-income countries or high-income ones? Why?
3. Do you consider yourself an optimist or a pessimist about the problem of global hunger? Why?

Sources: United Nations Development Programme (2000, 2001, 2002, 2003, 2004).

nations such as India and China—with a combined population of 2.4 billion—become more affluent, their people will consume more energy and other natural resources and produce more solid waste and other forms of pollution.

Finally, the vast gulf that separates the world's richest

and poorest people puts everyone at greater risk of war as the poorest people challenge the social arrangements that threaten their existence. In the long run, we can achieve peace on this planet only by ensuring that all people enjoy a significant measure of dignity and security.

SUMMARY

1. Around the world, social stratification is more pronounced than in Canada. About 16 percent of the world's people live in industrialized, high-income countries such as Canada and receive 57 percent of all income. Another 47 percent of humanity live in middle-income countries with significant industrialization, receiving about 33 percent of all income; 37 percent of the world's population live in low-income countries with limited industrialization and earn only 9 percent of global income.

2. Although relative poverty is found everywhere, low-income societies struggle with widespread, absolute poverty. Worldwide, the lives of some 1 billion people are at risk because of poor nutrition. About 15 million people, most of them children, die annually from diseases caused by poor nutrition.

3. Women are more likely than men to be poor nearly everywhere in the world. Gender bias against women is greatest in low-income, agrarian societies.

4. The poverty found in much of the world is a complex problem reflecting limited industrial technology, rapid population growth, traditional cultural patterns, internal social stratification, male domination, and global power relationships.

5. Modernization theory maintains that successful development requires giving up traditional cultural patterns in favour of advanced technology.

6. Modernization theorist W.W. Rostow identifies four stages of development: traditional, take-off, drive to technological maturity, and high mass consumption.

7. Arguing that high-income societies hold the keys to creating wealth, modernization theory claims that high-income

nations can help low-income nations by providing population control programs, agricultural technology such as hybrid seeds and fertilizers to increase food production, industrial technology including machinery and information technology, and foreign aid to help pay for power plants and factories.

8. Critics of modernization theory say that high-income nations do not spread economic development around the world and that low-income nations cannot follow the path to development taken by high-income nations centuries ago.

9. Dependency theory claims that global wealth and poverty are the historical products of the capitalist world economy because of colonialism and, more recently, the operation of multinational corporations.

10. Immanuel Wallerstein views the high-income countries as the advantaged "core" of the capitalist world economy; middle-income nations are the "semiperiphery," and low-income societies form the global "periphery."

11. According to dependency theory, three key factors—export-oriented economies, a lack of industrial capacity, and foreign debt—are responsible for low-income countries' dependency on high-income nations.

12. Critics of dependency theory argue that this approach overlooks the sixfold increase in the world's wealth since 1950 and note that the world's societies with the lowest incomes are not those with the strongest ties to high-income countries.

13. Both the modernization and the dependency approaches offer useful insights into the development of global inequality. The theories agree that there is an urgent need to address the various problems caused by worldwide poverty.

KEY CONCEPTS

colonialism (p. 240) the process by which some nations enrich themselves through political and economic control of other nations

dependency theory (p. 244) a model of economic and social development that explains global inequality in terms of the historical exploitation of low-income nations by high-income ones

global stratification (p. 230) patterns of social inequality in the world as a whole

high-income countries (p. 231) the richest nations with the highest overall standards of living

low-income countries (p. 231) nations with a low standard of living in which most people are poor

middle-income countries (p. 231) nations with a standard of living about average for the world as a whole

modernization theory (p. 242) a model of economic and social development that explains global inequality in terms of technological and cultural differences between nations

multinational corporation (p. 241) a large business that operates in many countries

neocolonialism (p. 240) a new form of global power relationships that involves not direct political control but economic exploitation by multinational corporations

CRITICAL-THINKING QUESTIONS

1. Based on what you have read here and elsewhere, what is your prediction about the extent of global hunger 50 years from now? Will the problem be more or less serious? Why?

2. What is the difference between relative and absolute poverty? Use these two concepts to describe social stratification in Canada and around the world.

3. Why do many analysts argue that economic development in low-income countries depends on raising the social standing of women?

4. State the basic ideas of modernization theory and dependency theory. What are several criticisms of each approach?

APPLICATIONS AND EXERCISES

1. Keep a log book of mass media advertising mentioning low-income countries (selling, say, coffee from Colombia or exotic vacations to a Caribbean island). What image of life in low-income countries does the advertising present? In light of this chapter, do you think that this image is accurate?

2. Hundreds of thousands of students from abroad study on Canadian campuses. Find a woman and a man on your campus who were raised in a low-income country. Approach

them, explain that you have been studying global stratification, and ask if they are willing to share what life is like back home. You may learn quite a bit from them.

3. Use the global maps in this text to identify social traits associated with the nations with the highest incomes and those with the lowest incomes. Try to use both modernization theory and dependency theory to build theoretical explanations of the patterns you find.

 # SITES TO SEE

www.pearsoned.ca/macionis
The authors and publisher of this book invite you to visit the interactive Companion Website™ that accompanies this text. Begin by clicking on the cover of your book. You will find a chapter-by-chapter study guide, practice tests, suggested weblinks, and links to other relevant material.

www.members.aol.com/casmasalc
This is the website for the Coalition Against Slavery in Mauritania and Sudan. This site provides information about the problem of slavery and links to similar organizations.

http://hdr.undp.org

www.worldbank.org
These sites, operated by the United Nations Development Program and the World Bank, provide data and analyses of global poverty.

www.census.gov/ipc/www/idbnew.html

www.prb.org
These two sites, operated by the U.S. Census Bureau and the Population Reference Bureau, offer a statistical profile of world nations.

www.fh.org

www.worldconcern.org

www.worldvision.org

www.care.org
Here are four additional websites that address global inequality. The first is operated by Food for the Hungry, the second takes you to the home page for World Concern, the third organization is World Vision, and the fourth is CARE. Visit them all, and watch for differences in their focus and strategies.

Follow the instructions on page 33 of this text to access the features of Research Navigator™. Once at the website (**www.researchnavigator.com**), enter your login name and password. Then, to use the Content Select™ database, enter keywords such as "colonialism," "world hunger," and "slavery," and the search engine will supply relevant and recent scholarly and popular press publications.

To reinforce your understanding of this chapter, and to identify topics for further study, visit MySocLab at **www.pearsoned.ca/mysoclab/macionis** for diagnostic tests and a multimedia ebook.

CHAPTER TEN

Gender Stratification

How is gender a creation of society?

What differences does gender make in people's lives?

Why is gender an important dimension of social stratification?

We went to the Manitoba Legislature asking for plain, common justice, an old-fashioned square deal, and in reply to that we got hat-lifting. I felt that when a man offers hat-lifting when we ask for justice we should tell him to keep his hat right on. I will go further and say that we should tell him not only to keep his hat on but to pull it right down over his face.

So wrote Nellie McClung in her book *In These Times*, which tells the story of her struggle to gain equal rights for women in the public realm. Born in Ontario in 1873, McClung migrated west as a child with her family, first settling in Manitoba and later, as an adult, moving to Alberta and British Columbia. By the time she was 40, she had given birth to five children and had become a well-known public speaker for women's rights. Back then, in much of Canada, women could not own property or keep their wages if they were married; they could not draft a will; they were barred from filing lawsuits in a court, including seeking custody of their own children; they could not attend university; and they legally could be beaten by their husbands as long as the stick used was no wider than a thumb (the origin of today's phrase "the rule of thumb").

Nor could women express their disapproval of such conditions. In this "free country," many more decades would pass before all Canadian women gained the right to vote. At that time, most people considered such a proposal absurd and outrageous. Toronto journalist Goldwin Smith argued that giving women the right to vote would lead to "national emasculation." Smith also protested the right of women to enter universities (Prentice et al., 1996:221).

Much has changed in the 130-odd years since McClung's birth. Many of the proposals she and other early feminists made are now accepted as a matter of basic fairness. But as this chapter explains, women and men still lead different lives in Canada and elsewhere in the world, and in many respects men still dominate. This chapter explores the importance of gender, and explains how gender, like class position, is a major dimension of social stratification.

Gender and Inequality

Chapter 6 ("Sexuality and Society") explained that biological differences divide the human population into categories of female and male. **Gender** refers to *the personal traits and social positions that members of a society attach to being female or male.* Gender, then, is a dimension of social organization, shaping how we interact with others and even how we think about ourselves. More important, gender also involves *hierarchy,* placing men and women in different positions in terms of power, wealth, and other resources. This is why sociologists speak of **gender stratification**, *the unequal distribution of wealth, power, and privilege between men and women.* In short, gender affects the opportunities and limitations each of us faces throughout our lives.

MALE–FEMALE DIFFERENCES

Many people think there is something "natural" about gender distinctions because biology does make one sex different from the other. But we must be careful not to think of social differences in biological terms. In 1848, for example, women were not allowed to vote because many people assumed that women did not have enough intelligence or interest in politics. Such attitudes had nothing to do with biology; they reflected the *cultural patterns* of that time and place.

Another example is athletic performance. In 1925, most people—both women and men—believed that the best women runners could never compete with men in a marathon. Today, as Figure 10–1 shows, the best women routinely post better times than the fastest men of decades past, and the performance gap between the sexes has narrowed greatly. Here, again, most of the differences between men and women turn out to be socially created.

There are some differences in physical ability between the sexes. On average, males are 10 percent taller than women, 20 percent heavier, and 30 percent stronger, especially in the upper body (Ehrenreich, 1999). On the other hand, women outperform men in the ultimate game of life itself: life expectancy for men is 77.2 years, and women can expect to live 82.1 years (Statistics Canada, 2005).

In adolescence, males show greater mathematical ability, whereas adolescent females excel in verbal skills, a difference that reflects both biology and socialization (Maccoby & Jacklin, 1974; Baker et al., 1980; Lengermann & Wallace, 1985). However, research does not point to any overall differences in intelligence between males and females. In fact, Canadian female primary and secondary school students are now outperforming their male counterparts on almost all educational achievement indicators, including high school graduation rates, reading and writing abilities, grade point average, and enrollment in college- and university-track courses (Bussière, Cartwright, & Knighton, 2003; Riordan, 2003). Moreover, over the past three decades, the well-established female disadvantage in mathematics–science performance has narrowed into small or insignificant differences, whereas male disadvantages in other educational outcomes increased.

Biologically, then, men and women differ in limited ways, with neither one naturally superior. But culture can define the two genders differently, as the global study described in the next section shows.

GENDER IN GLOBAL PERSPECTIVE

The best way to see how gender is based in culture is by comparing one society to another. Three important studies highlight just how different "masculine" and "feminine" can be.

The Israeli kibbutzim. In Israel, collective Jewish settlements are called *kibbutzim*. The kibbutz (the singular form of the word) is an important setting for gender research because gender equality is one of its stated goals; men and women share in both work and decision making. Today some 270 kibbutzim are scattered throughout the country. The number of people living in kibbutzim totals approximately 130 000, making up approximately 2.5 percent of the Israeli population.

DIVERSITY SNAPSHOT

FIGURE 10-1 Men's and Women's Athletic Performance

Do men naturally outperform women in athletic competition? The answer is not obvious. Early in the twentieth century, men outdistanced women by many kilometres in marathon races. But as opportunities for women in athletics have increased, women have been closing the performance gap. Only ten minutes separate the current world marathon records for women (set in 2003) and for men (set in 2003).

Sources: *The Christian Science Monitor*, © 1995 (**www.csmonitor.com**) and Marathonguide.com (2004). Adapted with permission of *The Christian Science Monitor*.

In kibbutzim, both men and women share most everyday jobs, including taking care of children, cooking and cleaning, repairing buildings, and making day-to-day decisions concerning life in the kibbutz. Traditionally, girls and boys were raised in the same way, and from the first weeks of life, children lived together in dormitories. However, children in the majority of kibbutzim today sleep at their parents' home until they reach high school age. Despite such changes, women and men in the kibbutzim have achieved remarkable (although not complete) social equality, evidence of the wide range that cultures have in defining what is feminine and what is masculine.

Sex is a biological distinction that develops prior to birth. Gender is the meaning that a society attaches to being female or male. Gender differences are a matter of power, as what is masculine typically has social priority over what is feminine. The importance of gender is not evident among infants, of course, but the ways in which we think of boys and girls set in motion patterns that will continue for a lifetime.

Margaret Mead's research. The anthropologist Margaret Mead carried out groundbreaking research on gender. If gender is based in the biological differences between men and women, she reasoned, people everywhere should define "feminine" and "masculine" in the same way; if gender is cultural, these concepts should vary.

Mead studied three societies in New Guinea (1963, orig. 1935). In the mountainous home of the Arapesh, Mead observed men and women with remarkably similar attitudes and behaviour. Both genders, she reported, were cooperative and sensitive to others—in short, what our culture would label "feminine."

Moving south, Mead studied the Mundugumor, whose headhunting and cannibalism stood in striking contrast to the gentle ways of the Arapesh. Both genders were typically selfish and aggressive, traits we define as more "masculine."

Finally, travelling west to the Tchambuli, Mead discovered a culture that, like our own, defined females and males differently. But, Mead reported, the Tchambuli *reversed* many of our ideas of gender: Females were dominant and rational, whereas males were submissive, emotional, and nurturing toward children. Based on her observations, Mead concluded that culture is the key to gender distinctions because what one society defines as masculine another may see as feminine.

Some critics consider Mead's findings "too neat," as if she saw in these societies just the patterns she was looking for. Deborah Gewertz (1981) challenged what she called Mead's "reversal hypothesis," pointing out that Tchambuli males are really the more aggressive gender. Gewertz explains that Mead visited the Tchambuli (who actually call themselves the Chambri) during the 1930s, after they had lost much of their property in tribal wars, and observed men rebuilding their homes, a temporary role for Chambri men.

Despite such criticisms, many researchers agree that there remains much cultural variation in gender roles throughout Melanesia, and especially in the large island of New Guinea, attesting to Mead's initial findings about the cultural underpinnings of gender arrangements in different societies.

George Murdock's research. In a broader study of more than 200 pre-industrial societies, George Murdock (1937) found some global agreement on which tasks are feminine and which are masculine. Hunting and warfare, Murdock observed, generally fall to men, and home-centred tasks such as cooking and childcare tend to be women's work. With their simple technology, pre-industrial societies apparently assign roles reflecting men's and women's physical characteristics. With their greater size and strength, men hunt game and protect the group; because women bear children, they do most work in the home.

Beyond this general pattern, Murdock found much variety. Consider agriculture: women did the farming in about the same number of societies as men; in most societies, the two genders divided this work. When it came to many other tasks, from building shelters to tattooing the body, Murdock found that pre-industrial societies were as likely to turn to either males or females.

In sum: Gender and culture. Global comparisons show that overall, societies do not consistently define tasks as feminine or masculine. With industrialization, the importance of muscle power declines, further reducing gender differences (Nolan & Lenski, 2004). In sum, gender is too variable to be a simple expression of biology; what it means to be female and male is mostly a creation of society.

PATRIARCHY AND SEXISM

Although conceptions of gender vary, everywhere in the world today we find some degree of **patriarchy** (literally, "the rule of fathers"), *a form of social organization in which males dominate females*. Despite mythical tales of societies run by female "Amazons," **matriarchy**, *a form of social organization in which females dominate males*, has never

WINDOW ON THE WORLD

GLOBAL MAP 10-1 Women's Power in Global Perspective

Women's social standing in relation to men's varies around the world. In general, women live better in high-income countries than in low-income countries. Even so, some nations stand out: In the nations of Norway, Sweden, and Australia, women come closest to social equality with men. Seager assembles data based in part on the United Nations Gender Development Index (GDI). This index compares the standing of men and women on a number of different indicators such as literacy and income. The more equality between men and women, the higher the standing of women.

Source: Data from Seager (2003).

been documented in human history (Gough, 1971; Harris, 1977; Lengermann & Wallace, 1985).

Although some degree of patriarchy may be universal, Global Map 10–1 shows the great variation in the relative power and privilege of women that exists from country to country. According to the United Nations' gender develop-

ment index, Norway, Sweden, and Australia give women the highest social standing; by contrast, women in the African nations of Niger, Burkina Faso, Mali, Guinea-Bissau, and Burundi have the lowest social standing compared with men. Of the world's nations, Canada ranked sixth in terms of gender equality (United Nations Development Programme, 2004).

In every society, people assume that certain jobs, patterns of behaviour, and ways of dressing are "naturally" feminine while others are just as obviously masculine. But in global perspective, we see remarkable variety in such social definitions. These men, Wodaabe pastoral nomads who live in the African nation of Niger, are proud to engage in a display of beauty most people in our society would consider feminine.

Sexism, *the belief that one gender is innately superior to the other*, is the ideological basis of patriarchy. Sexism is not just a matter of individual attitudes; it is built into the institutions of our society. Institutional sexism is found throughout the economy, with women highly concentrated in low-paying jobs. Similarly, the legal system has long excused violence against women, especially on the part of boyfriends, husbands, and fathers.

The costs of sexism. Sexism limits the talents and the ambitions of half the population. Although men benefit in some respects from sexism, their privilege comes at a high price. Masculinity in our culture calls for men to engage in many high-risk behaviours: using tobacco and alcohol, playing dangerous sports, and even driving recklessly. As Marilyn French (1985) argues, patriarchy drives men to relentlessly seek control, not only of women but also of themselves and their world. Thus, masculinity is linked not only to accidents but also to suicide, violence, and stress-related diseases. The *Type A personality*—marked by chronic impatience, driving ambition, competitiveness, and free-floating hostility—is a recipe for heart disease and an almost perfect match with the behaviour our culture considers masculine (Ehrenreich, 1983).

However, as Elianne Riska (2002) argues, at issue was a certain type of white middle-class masculinity that had up to then served as the norm for all male behaviour—the hard-working, achievement-oriented white middle-class male breadwinner making his way in a highly competitive, capitalist society. Riska (2000) traces the decline of the notion of the Type A man in the late 1970s and the development of a new psychological construct—the "hardy"

man. According to Suzanne Kobasa, "persons who experience high degrees of stress without falling ill have a personality structure differentiating them from persons who become sick under stress" (1979:3). In contrast to Type A man, who was driven by a seemingly irrational passion to reach extrinsic goals and rewards, the hardy man is constructed as one who is driven by intrinsic motivation. However, Riska (2002) notes that both the Type A personality and the hardy personality provide individualized explanations for differences in health of middle-class men in capitalist societies. These models need to be tested with diverse groups of men and women from different social positions and cultural backgrounds. Such research on the social patterning of health within and across the genders would help us better understand the link between social conditions and individual well-being.

Is patriarchy inevitable? In pre-industrial societies, women have little control over pregnancy and childbirth, which limits the scope of their lives. In those same societies, men's greater height and physical strength are valued resources. But industrialization, including birth control technology, gives people choices about how to live. In societies like our own, biological differences offer little justification for patriarchy.

But males remain dominant in many areas of Canadian life and a similar situation is found in many other high-income countries. Does this mean that patriarchy is inevitable? Some sociologists claim that biological factors "wire" women and men with different motivations and behaviours—especially aggressiveness in males—making patriarchy difficult, perhaps even impossible, to eliminate

(Goldberg, 1974; Rossi, 1985; Popenoe, 1993b; Udry, 2000). However, most sociologists believe that gender is socially constructed and *can* be changed. Just because no society has yet eliminated patriarchy does not mean that we must stay prisoners of the past or that no progress has been made in reducing gender inequality in private and public life.

To understand continuity and change in relations between women and men, we next examine how gender is rooted and reproduced in society, a process that begins in childhood and continues throughout our lives.

Gender and Socialization

From birth until death, gender shapes human feelings, thoughts, and actions. Children quickly learn that their society defines females and males as different kinds of people; by about age three, they begin to apply gender standards to each other and to themselves.

Table 10–1 presents traits that people in North America traditionally link to "feminine" and "masculine" behaviour. Note that the traits in each column are direct opposites, even though research shows that most people do not develop consistently feminine or masculine personalities (Bem, 1993).

Just as gender affects how we think of ourselves, so it teaches us to act in normative ways. Gender roles are attitudes and activities that a society tends to link to women and men. Insofar as our culture defines males as ambitious and competitive, we expect them to play team sports and seek out positions of leadership. To the extent that we define females as deferential and emotional, we expect them to be supportive helpers and quick to show their feelings.

GENDER AND THE FAMILY

The first question people usually ask about a newborn—"Is it a boy or a girl?"—has great importance because the answer involves not just gender but the likely direction of a child's life.

In fact, gender is at work even before a child is born because, especially in lower-income nations, parents hope their firstborn will be a boy rather than a girl. In countries such as China and India, new sex pre-determination techniques such as ultrasound are reported to be used to reinforce anti-female prejudice, resulting in unnaturally low female-to-male ratios at birth (Sen, 2003; Jhaa et al., 2006).

Soon after birth, family members welcome infants into the "pink world" of girls or the "blue world" of boys (Bernard, 1981). People even send gender messages in the way they handle infants. One researcher at an English university presented an infant dressed as either a boy or a girl

TABLE 10–1

A Traditional View of Gender Identity

Feminine Traits	Masculine Traits
Submissive	Dominant
Dependent	Independent
Unintelligent and incapable	Intelligent and competent
Emotional	Rational
Receptive	Assertive
Intuitive	Analytical
Weak	Strong
Timid	Brave
Content	Ambitious
Passive	Active
Cooperative	Competitive
Sensitive	Insensitive
Sex object	Sexually aggressive
Attractive because of physical appearance	Attractive because of achievement

to a number of women; her subjects handled the "female" child tenderly, with frequent hugs and caresses, while treating the "male" child more aggressively, often lifting him up high in the air or bouncing him on the knee (Bonner, 1984; Tavris & Wade, 2001). The lesson is clear: the female world revolves around cooperation and emotion, and the male world puts a premium on independence and action.

GENDER AND THE PEER GROUP

About the time they enter school, children move outside the family, making friends with others of the same age. Considerable research points to the fact that young children tend to form single-sex play groups (Martin & Fabes, 2001).

Peer groups teach additional lessons about gender. After spending a year watching children at play, Janet Lever (1978) concluded that boys favour team sports with complex rules and clear objectives such as scoring runs or touchdowns. Such games nearly always involve winners and losers, reinforcing masculine traits of aggression and control.

Girls, too, play team sports. But, Lever explains, girls also play hopscotch or jump rope or simply talk, sing, or dance. These activities have few rules, and rarely is "victory" the ultimate goal. Instead of teaching girls to be competitive, Lever explains, female peer groups encourage interpersonal skills of communication and cooperation, presumably the basis for girls' future roles as wives and mothers.

Lever's observations recall Carol Gilligan's gender-based theory of moral reasoning, which was introduced in Chapter 3 ("Socialization: From Infancy to Old Age"). According to Gilligan (1982), boys reason according to abstract principles. For them, "rightness" amounts to "playing by the rules." By contrast, girls consider morality a matter of responsibility to others. Thus, the games we play have serious implications for our later lives. Yet, as indicated by the 1997 murder of a teenage girl in Victoria, British Columbia, by her female classmates, violent play among female adolescents in Canada is on the rise. Although still much rarer than among males, such incidents suggest that gender polarity may be breaking down, with some girls, at least, less willing to place concern for others above their own self-interest (Campbell, 1984; Chesney-Lind & Hagedorn, 1999; Artz, 1998).

GENDER AND SCHOOLING

Gender shapes our interests and beliefs about our own abilities, guiding areas of study and, eventually, career choices (Correll, 2001). In high school, more girls than boys learn secretarial skills and take vocational classes such as cosmetology and food services. Classes in woodworking and auto mechanics attract mostly young men. In college and university, the pattern continues, with men overly represented in mathematics and the natural sciences, including physics, chemistry, and biology. Women cluster in the humanities (such as English), the fine arts (painting, music, dance, and drama), and the social sciences (including anthropology and sociology). Newer areas of study are also gender-typed: computer science enrolls mostly men, and courses in gender studies enroll mostly women.

Yet, as noted above, these traditional patterns are shifting, at least for girls. While patriarchal scripts still characterize many women's educational experiences, both national and international data from across high-income countries illustrate a historical discontinuity: female primary and secondary school students are now outperforming their male counterparts on almost all educational achievement indicators. Researchers are now struggling to find out what is happening to the boys in school performance. While some have argued that the problem stems from feminists' misguided "war against boys" (Sommers, 2000), sociologists point to gender scripts in high school that appear to lower mean school achievement among a subgroup of males by making the habits conducive to high achievement "uncool" and "unmasculine" (Cornell, 1989).

GENDER AND THE MASS MEDIA

Since television first captured the public imagination in the 1950s, white males have held centre stage; racial and ethnic minorities were all but absent from television until the early 1970s. Even when both genders appear on camera, men generally play the brilliant detectives, fearless explorers, and skilled surgeons. Women play the less capable characters who are often unnecessary except for the sexual interest they add to the story.

Historically, ads have shown women in the home, cheerfully using cleaning products, serving food, trying out appliances, and modelling clothes. Men have predominated in ads for cars, travel, banking services, industrial companies, and alcoholic beverages. The authoritative voiceover—the faceless voice that describes a product in television and radio advertising—is almost always male (Davis, 1993).

Further, a careful look at advertising in the print media reveals that men usually appear taller than women, implying male superiority. Women, by contrast, are more frequently presented lying down (on sofas and beds) or, like children, seated on the floor. Men's facial expressions and behaviour give off an air of competence and imply dominance, whereas women often appear childlike, submissive, and sexual. Sociologist Erving Goffman (1979) found that in media advertisements males tend to be positioned higher than women and women are more likely to be lying down on beds or at the floor level, physically in a form of deference to men. In recent years there has at least been a notable increase in the number of women news presenters. Research also shows that men focus on the products being advertised; women often focus on the men (Cortese, 1999). There is in fact some evidence that preteen girls may tend to find a male newsreader more believable than a woman newsreader, whereas the sex of the newsreader seems to have no noticeable effect on boys' ideas of their believability (Durkin, 1985).

Finally, advertising perpetuates what Naomi Wolf (1990) calls the "beauty myth." The Diversity: Race, Class, & Gender box takes a closer look at how this myth affects women and, increasingly, men.

Gender and Social Stratification

Gender involves more than how people think and act. It is also about social hierarchy. The reality of gender stratification can be seen, first, in the world of work.

WORKING WOMEN AND MEN

In 1891, just 11.4 percent of females in Canada were engaged in paid employment. In 2004, 57.8 percent of women aged 15 and over worked for income, and just under three-fourths of working women did so full-time (Statistics Canada, 2006au).The traditional view that earning an income is a "man's role" no longer holds true, as Figure 10–2 shows.

Factors that have changed the Canadian labour force include the decline of farming, the growth of cities, a shrinking family size, and a rising divorce rate. Thus, Canada and other industrial societies today consider women working for income to be the rule rather than the

DIVERSITY: RACE, CLASS, & GENDER

The Beauty Myth

The Duchess of Windsor once remarked, "A woman cannot be too rich or too thin." The first half of her observation might apply to men as well, but certainly not the second. After all, most ads placed by the $20 billion-a-year North American cosmetics industry and the $40 billion diet industry target women.

According to Naomi Wolf (1990), certain cultural patterns create a "beauty myth" that is damaging to women. The beauty myth arises, first, because society teaches women to measure themselves in terms of physical appearance (Backman & Adams, 1991). Yet the standards of beauty embodied by the *Playboy* centrefold or the 45-kilogram fashion model are out of reach of most women.

The way society teaches women to prize relationships with men, whom they presumably attract with their beauty, also contributes to the beauty myth. Striving for beauty not only drives women to be extremely disciplined but also

forces them to be highly attentive and responsive to men. In short, beauty-minded women try to please men and avoid challenging male power.

The beauty myth is affecting males as well these days. Historically, cosmetic surgery was viewed solely as a woman's domain. Males now make up 14 percent of all cosmetic surgery patients in North America, seeking a range of surgery options to make them feel young and beautiful. These include pectoral muscle implants, calf implants, tummy tucks, and facelifts, procedures that, as with

women's cosmetic surgery, make major demands on the wallet (Rudy, 2006).

In sum, there can be little doubt that the idea of beauty is important in everyday life. The question is whether beauty is still gendered. According to Davis (2002), the idea that there will soon be gender equality in this realm due to men's increasing option to go under the knife to beautify themselves is suspect, and cosmetic surgery will remain mainly a practice undertaken by women.

WHAT DO YOU THINK?

1. What, exactly, is the myth surrounding beauty?
2. How does the beauty myth apply differently to men and women?
3. Do you agree that the great importance attached to beauty for women and increasingly men is a problem? Why or why not?

Source: Based on Wolf (1990); Davis (2002); Rudy (2006).

---

exception. In fact, 83 percent of Canadian two-parent families have at least two income earners (Statistics Canada, 2003ad). In total, women represented 46.8 percent of the work force in Canada in 2004 (Statistics Canada, 2006au); as Global Map 10–2 shows, this is not the case in many of the low-income countries of the world.

In the past, many women in the labour force were childless but this is not the case for the majority of working women today. In 2002, 64.5 percent of women with children under age three worked for income, as did 69.5 percent whose youngest child was aged three to five, and 72.5 percent of women with children under age 16 living at home (Statistics Canada, 2006au).

Gender and occupations. While the shares of women and men in the labour force have been converging, to a large

extent the work they do remains different. Statistics Canada (2006au) reports that 67 percent of all employed women were working in teaching, nursing and related occupations, other administrative positions or sales, and services and service occupations. The percentage of men in these types of positions was just 30 percent.

Table 10–2 on page 266 shows the occupations with the highest concentrations of women. Overall, although more women now work for pay and some women have made significant inroads into traditionally male-dominated occupations, by and large they still remain segregated in the labour force in jobs at the middle and low end of the pay scale, usually supervised by men and with limited opportunity for advancement (Charles, 1992; Krahn & Lowe, 1998; Benoit, 2000a; Statistics Canada, 2000m; Statistics Canada, 2003bi; Statistics Canada, 2006au).

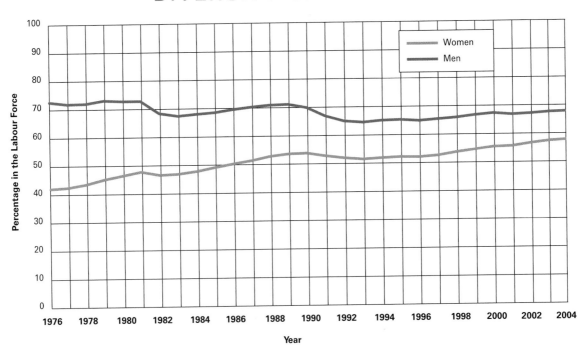

FIGURE 10-2 Women and Men in the Canadian Paid Workforce, 1976–2004

Source: Statistics Canada (2006au).

Men dominate most other job categories, such as the building trades. Virtually all brick and stone masons, structural metal workers, and heavy-equipment mechanics are men. Likewise, the majority of engineers, physicians, judges, lawyers, and corporate managers are men. At the top of the business world, men dominate senior management jobs, with just 14 percent of women holding corporate officer positions at Canada's 500 largest companies in 2002. The number of women holding "clout" jobs (CEOs, chairs, presidents, and so on) is even smaller; just 3.4 percent of these positions were held by women in the country's 500 largest companies in 2002 (Catalyst, 2003).

Read about the small number of women in top corporate jobs at www.catalystwomen.org.

Gender stratification in the workplace is easy to see: female nurses tend to assist male physicians, female secretaries serve male executives, and female flight attendants tend to be under the command of male airline pilots. Moreover, in any field, the greater a job's income and prestige, the more likely it is to be held by a man. For example,

in 2004, women made up 65 percent of full-time elementary and secondary school teachers, but only 30 percent of university teachers (Sussman & Yssaad, 2005).

HOUSEWORK: WOMEN'S "SECOND SHIFT"

Global Map 4–1 on page 91 shows that housework—maintaining the home and caring for children—is mainly the responsibility of women throughout the world. In Canada, housework has always presented a cultural contradiction: we claim that it is essential for family life, but housework carries little prestige or reward (Luxton, 1980).

With women's rapid entry into the labour force, the amount of housework performed by women has declined; however, the share women do has declined only slightly. Figure 10–3 shows that in 1998, a woman employed full-time who was living with a male partner and at least one child under age 19 put in an average of 4.9 hours of unpaid work per day. Her male partner put in an average of 3.3 hours of unpaid work per day, or about 1.5 hours less than his female counterpart. Men are also more likely than women to do zero hours of housework, as National Maps 10–1 and 10–2 on pages 268 and 269 show.

GLOBAL MAP 10-2 Women's Paid Employment in Global Perspective

This map shows the percentage of the labour force made up of women. A country's level of technological development plays an important part here. In 2004, women accounted for 46.8 percent of the labour force in Canada, a substantial increase over the preceding generation. In high-income nations, overall, nearly one-half of the labour force are women. In low-income societies, however, women work even harder than in this country, but they are less likely to be paid for their efforts. In Latin America, for example, women represent about one-third of the paid labour force; in Islamic societies of Northern Africa and the Middle East, the figure is significantly lower. One exception to this rule is Central and Southern Africa, where, traditionally, women make up a large share of farmers.

Sources: *Peters Atlas of the World* (1990); updated by the authors from World Bank (2004).

In sum, men support the idea of women entering the paid labour force, and most count on the money women earn. But many—although not all—men resist taking on an equal share of household duties (Luxton, 1980; Komarovsky, 1973; Cowan, 1992; Robinson & Spitze, 1992; Lennon & Rosenfeld, 1994; Heath & Bourne, 1995; Harpster & Monk-Turner, 1998; Lynn & Todoroff, 1998; McFarlane, Beaujot, & Haddad, 2000).

TABLE 10-2

Average Earnings of Men and Women in the 10 Highest-Paying and 10 Lowest-Paying Occupations, Full-Time, Full-Year Workers, Canada, 2000

Selected Occupational Categories	Number of Workers		Average Earnings ($)		Number of Workers per 10 000		Women's Income as a Percentage of Men's
	Men	Women	Men	Women	Men	Women	
All paid workers	4 717 575	3 441 660	49 614	35 252	10 000	10 000	71%
Total—10 highest-paying occupations	147 875	46 030	122 350	74 860	313	134	61%
Judges	1400	440	142 478	124 444	3	1	87%
Senior managers—Financial, communications carriers and other business services	30 855	8375	144 248	92 770	65	24	64%
Senior managers—Goods production, utilities, transportation and construction	37 705	4870	123 902	78 504	80	14	63%
Specialist physicians	5065	2755	126 790	73 946	11	8	58%
Senior managers—Trade, broadcasting, and other services, n.e.c.	29 645	6295	112 107	70 295	63	18	63%
Securities agents, investment dealers, and traders	10 310	6380	129 851	55 750	22	19	43%
Dentists	2860	1080	113 265	67 279	6	3	59%
General practitioners and family physicians	7665	4100	110 008	76 657	16	12	70%
Petroleum engineers	3900	435	100 574	61 491	8	1	61%
Lawyers and Quebec notaries	18 470	11 300	103 233	72 226	39	33	70%
Total—10 lowest-paying occupations	91 235	225 760	21 898	18 676	193	656	85%
Cooks	36 585	31 935	22 256	19 793	78	93	89%
Ironing, pressing, and finishing occupations	1345	2485	23 213	19 330	3	7	83%
Sewing machine operators	2535	28 200	27 158	20 035	5	82	74%
Harvesting labourers	1030	1025	21 659	18 796	2	3	87%
Cashiers	8605	50 390	23 009	19 345	18	146	84%
Bartenders	6800	9430	21 863	18 259	14	27	84%
Food counter attendants, kitchen helpers, and related occupations	15 200	39 390	20 161	19 029	32	114	94%
Service station attendants	5980	2230	19 475	15 860	13	6	81%
Food and beverage servers	12 520	42 665	22 495	16 958	27	124	75%
Babysitters, nannies, and parents' helpers	635	18 010	15 858	16 465	1	52	104%

Source: Statistics Canada (2003ak), and author calculations.

GENDER, INCOME, AND WEALTH

In 2004, the average earnings for women working full-time year-round were just under $36 500, while men working full-time earned an average of $51 700. This means that for every $1 earned by men, women earned 70.5¢ (Statistics Canada, 2006au).

While women's incomes vary by occupational status and age, it is noteworthy that their average earnings are below those of men in all but seven of more than 700 occupational groupings (Statistics Canada, 2003ak). The main reason that women earn less relates to the kind of work they do: largely clerical, sales, and service jobs. In effect, jobs and gender interact. People still perceive jobs with less clout as "women's work," just as people devalue work simply because it is performed by women (Armstrong, 1994; Krahn & Lowe, 1998; Looker & Thiessen, 1999; Benoit, 2000a; England, 1992; Bellas, 1994; Huffman, Velasco, & Bielby, 1996).

In recent decades, proponents of gender equality have proposed a policy of "comparable worth." That is, people should be paid not according to the historical double standard but according to the worth of what they actually do. Several nations—including Canada, Great Britain, and Australia—have adopted comparable worth policies, though these policies have found limited acceptance in the United States. Dedication to the pay-equity principle was tested in the summer of 1998 when the Canadian Human Rights Tribunal found that female federal workers were owed an estimated $5 billion. The federal government found itself torn between supporting the pay-equity principle and dealing with the cost of doing so (Greenspoon, 1998). Finally, on October 29, 1999, the Public Service Alliance of Canada and the federal government came to an agreement to implement the 1998 Canadian Human Rights Tribunal decision.

Another cause of gender-based income disparity has to do with the family. Both men and women have children, of course, but our culture defines parenting as more of a woman's responsibility than a man's. Being pregnant and raising small children keeps many younger women out of the labour force altogether, at a time when their male peers are making significant occupational gains. When female workers return to the labour force, they have less job seniority than their male counterparts (Fuchs, 1986; Stier, 1996; Waldfogel, 1997; Drolet, 2001; Sussman & Yssaad, 2005). Variation does exist across high-income countries, however. Countries with "women-friendly" parental leaves and benefits and publicly funded childcare programs lessen the cost of childbearing for female workers (Leira, 2000; Benoit, 2000b; Beaujot, 2006). Canada's newly extended year-long parental and maternity leave policy moves the country closer to the Nordic norm of at least one year of paid leave for parents with their newborns.

Moreover, women who choose to have children may be reluctant or unable to maintain fast-paced jobs that tie up their evenings and weekends. To avoid role strain, they may take jobs that offer a shorter commuting distance, more flexible hours, and employer childcare services. Women pursuing both a career and a family are torn between their dual responsibilities in ways that men are not. Consider this: at age 40, 90 percent of men—but only 35 percent of women—in executive positions have at least one child (Schwartz, 1989). In academia, the pattern holds: a recent study found that young women with at least one child were at least 20 percent less likely to have tenure than comparable men in the same field (Shea, 2002). This finding confirms other research that babies do alter the careers of female academics (Mason & Goulden, 2004; Sussman & Yssaad, 2005).

The two factors noted so far—type and frequency of paid work and distribution of family responsibilities—account for about two-thirds of the earnings disparity between women and men. Drolet (2001) found that gender differences in the opportunity to supervise and perform

FIGURE 10-3 Time Allocation of Married Men and Women Aged 25–44 Employed Full-Time, 1998

Source: Statistics Canada (2000m)

certain tasks accounted for about an additional 5 percent of the gender wage gap in Canada.

This finding falls under the third factor—discrimination against women—which accounts for the remainder of the earnings disparity between the genders (Pear, 1987; Fuller & Schoenberger, 1991). Because discrimination is illegal, it is practised in subtle ways. Corporate women often encounter a "glass ceiling," a barrier that is invisible because it is denied by company officials but that effectively prevents women from rising above middle management (Benokraitis & Feagin, 1995; Yamagata et al., 1997).

For all these reasons, then, women earn less than men in all major occupational categories. As shown in Table 10–2 on page 266, this disparity varies from job to job, but the difference between men and women is greater in the higher-paying occupations than in the lower-paying occupations. In only one of the highest-paying occupations—among judges—do women earn more than 75 percent of men's wages. In all but one of the lowest-paying

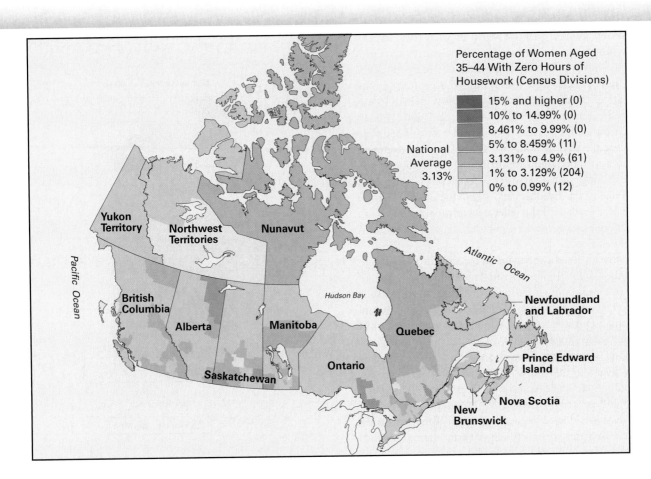

SEEING OURSELVES

NATIONAL MAP 10-1 Housework by Women, Canada, 2001

The census defined housework to include meal preparation, house maintenance, and yard work. This map shows the percentage of women aged 35–44 across Canada who did not do any housework during the week before the census in 2001. The area in Northeastern Alberta at 8 percent had the highest percentage of women who did not do any housework during this time period. Conversely, at least 99 percent of the women living in the lightest areas on the map did at least some amount of housework.

occupations do women earn more than 75 percent of men's wages. The 2001 census showed that the situation for young women is a bit brighter because women aged 25–29 earned 81¢ for every $1 earned by men (Statistics Canada, 2003bd).

Finally, perhaps because women typically outlive men, many people think that women own most of the country's wealth. None of the individuals identified in *Forbes* in 2003 as the richest people in the world was a Canadian woman, while 15 Canadian men made the billionaires' list (Forbes.com, 2003).

GENDER AND EDUCATION

In the past, our society considered schooling to be irrelevant for women because women's lives revolved around the home. But times have changed. By 1994, women earned a majority (58 percent) of all associate and bachelor's degrees and first professional degrees (Statistics Canada, 1997e); in 1997, that proportion had risen slightly to 59 percent (Statistics Canada, 2000h) and remained the same in 2000 (Statistics Canada, 2003mb).

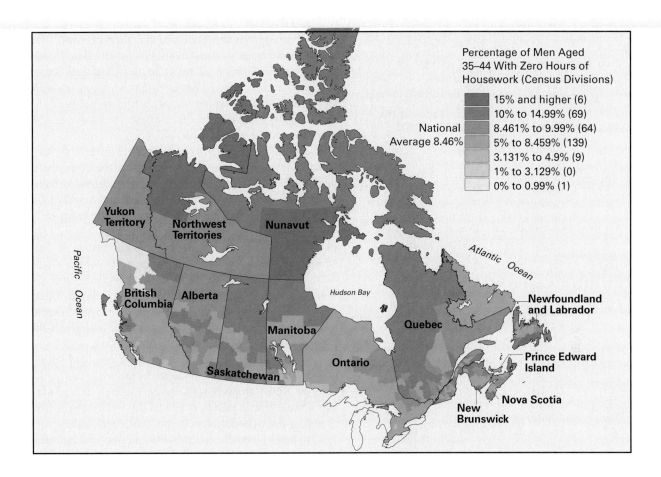

Percentage of Men Aged
35–44 With Zero Hours of
Housework (Census Divisions)

15% and higher (6)
10% to 14.99% (69)
National 8.461% to 9.99% (64)
Average 8.46% 5% to 8.459% (139)
3.131% to 4.9% (9)
1% to 3.129% (0)
0% to 0.99% (1)

SEEING OURSELVES

NATIONAL MAP 10-2 Housework by Men, Canada, 2001

The six darkest areas of this map are regions where at least 15 percent of men did not do any housework during the week before the census. Across Canada, over 8 percent of men in the 35–44 age group did no housework in the week before the census, whereas only 3 percent of women had this luxury. Beyond this obvious difference between men and women, other trends are visible. We would expect perhaps that most comparisons between the map for women and the map for men would show a trend similar to that visible for the Queen Charlotte Islands off the central coast of British Columbia and the area immediately inland, including Prince Rupert. In this area, hardly any women but relatively many men do not do any housework—meaning that women do more work as men do less. There are other areas that show a different trend. In Southwestern Saskatchewan, for example, relatively many men, as well as relatively many women, do not do any housework. How do you explain this? What other trends do you see?

Source: Calculated based on data in Statistics Canada (2003bf).

College and university doors have opened to women, and differences in men's and women's majors are becoming smaller. In 1972–73, for example, women made up just 3 percent of students in engineering and applied sciences. In 2001–02, women received 24 percent of all degrees in these fields. Women's enrollment in mathematics and physical sciences had increased from 19 to 30 percent of all graduates (Statistics Canada, 2000h; Statistics Canada, 2003be; Statistics Canada, 2006au).

In the mid-1990s, for the first time, women were earning half of postgraduate degrees, which are often a springboard to high-prestige jobs. For all areas of study in 1997, women earned 51 percent of master's degrees and 36 percent of all doctorates. In 2001–02, the proportions awarded to women at the bachelor's (58 percent), master's (51 percent), and doctoral levels (46 percent) were higher than ever before, and men outnumbered women only at the doctoral level (Statistics Canada, 2003be; Statistics Canada, 2006au).

TABLE 10–3
Women in National Parliaments, Lower or Single House, 2006, Selected Countries

Rank		Country	Women, Percent of Total	
2006	2003		2006	2003
1	1	Rwanda	48.8	48.8
2	2	Sweden	45.3	45.3
3	9	Costa Rica	38.6	35.1
4	6	Norway	37.9	36.4
5	4	Finland	37.5	37.5
6	3	Denmark	36.9	38.0
7	5	Netherlands	36.7	36.7
8	7	Cuba	36.0	36.0
8	17	Spain	36.0	28.3
10	12	Argentina	35.0	30.7
44	34	Pakistan	21.3	21.6
44	48	Portugal	21.3	19.1
47	38	Canada	20.8	20.6
47	36	Monaco	20.8	20.8
49	37	Nicaragua	20.7	20.7
50	40	Poland	20.4	20.2
51	33	China	20.3	21.8
54	54	United Kingdom	19.7	17.9
56	45	Guinea	19.3	19.3
57	47	Senegal	19.2	19.2
74	99	Zimbabwe	16.0	10.0
78	55	Philippines	15.7	17.8
80	68	United States	15.2	14.3
81	65	Angola	15.0	15.5
81	75	Chile	15.0	12.5
83	155	Bangladesh	14.8	2.0
94	120	Liberia	12.5	7.8
95	157	Niger	12.4	1.2
96	93	Azerbaijan	12.3	10.5
97	76	France	12.2	12.2
97	76	Slovenia	12.2	12.2
101	82	Jamaica	11.7	11.7
158	160	Saudi Arabia	0.0	0.0

Source: Inter-Parliamentary Union (2003, 2006) and calculations by authors. Only nations with data for both time periods are ranked.

Our society still defines high-paying professions (and the drive and competitiveness needed to succeed in them) as masculine; this fact helps explain why just as many women as men begin most pre-professional graduate programs, but women are less likely to complete their degrees (Fiorentine, 1987; Fiorentine & Cole, 1992). Even so, the proportion of women in all these professions is steadily rising.

GENDER AND POLITICS

A century ago, virtually no women held elected office in any industrial country, including Canada. In fact, women were legally barred from voting in national elections until 1918 in our country, and it was not until more than a decade later that they were permitted to sit in the Canadian Senate (Prentice et al., 1996). Women in most countries were legally barred from voting in national elections until the early decades of this century. By 2003, this picture of gender exclusion in the political life of industrial countries had changed, but not as much as one might imagine. Table 10–3 shows that there have been significant gains for women, primarily in Nordic countries, but limited progress in many other high-income countries. There are also several low-income countries that are doing very well in this respect.

In global perspective, although women are half the Earth's population, the median representation is just 16.6 percent of seats in the 180 parliaments with available data. Although this represents a small increase from 50 years ago, only in the two countries of Rwanda (48.8 percent) and Sweden (45.3 percent) does the share of parliamentary seats held by women approach their share of the population (Inter-Parliamentary Union, 2006).

Nevertheless, a small number of Canadian female politicians have achieved national prominence, as in the cases of Kim Campbell who, in 1993, served as Canada's first female prime minister, and Alexa McDonough, who served as the national New Democratic Party leader from 1997 to 2003. Nevertheless, in 2006, our provincial premiers and territorial leaders, as well as our prime minister, make up a completely male cast!

MINORITY WOMEN: INTERSECTION THEORY

If women in general are disadvantaged, what about minority women? Are they doubly handicapped? This question lies at the heart of **intersection theory**, *the investigation of the interplay of race, class, and gender, often resulting in multiple dimensions of disadvantage.* Generally speaking, the answer is yes, research shows that disadvantages linked to race, ethnicity, and gender often are additive (Ovadia, 2001).

We can demonstrate this with some income comparisons. Looking first at race and ethnicity, Aboriginal women have, on average, very low income compared to non-Aboriginal women in Canada. The average employment income in 2000 for Aboriginal women aged 15 and over was $17 979, more than $6500 less than that of non-Aboriginal women and $6800 less than that of Aboriginal men (Statistics Canada, 2003bg). Visible minority women also have relatively low average incomes. In 2000, their average employment income was $22 301, considerably higher than that of Aboriginal women but still less than that of other women in Canada ($24 693) (Statistics Canada, 2003bh).

These data confirm that although gender has a powerful effect on our lives, it never operates alone. Class position, race and ethnicity, and gender form a multilayered system of disadvantage for some and privilege for others (Arat-Koc, 1989; Ng, 1993; Ginsburg & Tsing, 1990; St. Jean & Feagin, 1998).

VIOLENCE AGAINST WOMEN

The phrase "rule of thumb" entered our language about 150 years ago when common decency of the day demanded that a man not beat his wife with a stick thicker than his thumb. Even today, a great deal of "manly" violence is directed against women. A Statistics Canada study found that 54 percent of Canadian women reported having experienced at least one instance of unwanted sexual attention (Statistics Canada, 1993b). While men also can be victims of sexual assault, 85 percent of all victims are female, indicating a strong association between gender and this type of violent activity (Statistics Canada, 2000m).

Most gender-linked violence occurs where men and women interact most: in the home. Richard Gelles (cited in Roesch, 1984) argues that, with the exception of the police and the military, the family is the most violent

Read United Nations reports on trafficking in and violence against women and children around the world at **http://www.unicef-icdc.org/ publications/**.

organization. Both sexes suffer from family violence, although, by and large, women sustain more serious injuries than men (Straus & Gelles, 1986; Schwartz, 1987; Shupe, Stacey, & Hazlewood, 1987; Gelles & Cornell, 1990; Smolowe, 1994; Johnson & Au Coin, 2003).

Violence toward women also occurs in casual relationships. As noted in Chapter 6 ("Sexuality and Society"), most rapes involve men known to and often trusted by their victims. Dianne Herman (2001) argues that the extent of sexual abuse shows that at least some tendency toward sexual violence is built into our way of life. All forms of violence against women—from the wolf whistles that intimidate women on city streets to the pinches in a crowded subway to physical assaults that occur at home—express what Herman calls a "rape culture" of men trying to dominate women. In fact, sexual violence is fundamentally about power, not sex, and therefore should be understood as a dimension of gender stratification.

Sexual harassment.   The term **sexual harassment** refers to *comments, gestures, or physical contact of a sexual nature that is deliberate, repeated, and unwelcome.* In the 1990s, sexual harassment became an issue of national importance that rewrote the rules for workplace interaction.

Most (but not all) victims of sexual harassment are women. This is because, first, our culture encourages men

The basic insight of intersection theory is that various dimensions of social stratification—including race and gender—can add up to great disadvantages for some categories of people, including women working as maids. How would you explain the fact that some categories of people are much more likely to end up in low-paying jobs like this one?

to be sexually assertive and to perceive women in sexual terms. As a result, social interaction in the workplace, on campus, and elsewhere can readily take on sexual overtones. Second, most people in positions of power—including business executives, physicians, bureau chiefs, assembly line supervisors, professors, and military officers—are men who oversee the work of women.

Sexual harassment is sometimes blatant and direct: a supervisor may solicit sexual favours from an employee with threats of reprisals if the advances are refused. Courts have declared such *quid pro quo* sexual harassment (the Latin phrase means "one thing in return for another") to be a violation of civil rights.

More often, however, the problem of unwelcome sexual attention is a matter of subtle behaviour—sexual teasing, off-colour jokes, pin-ups displayed in the workplace—that may not even be *intended* to harass anyone. But, using the *effect* standard favoured by many feminists, such actions add up to creating a *hostile environment* (Cohen, 1991; Paul, 1991). Incidents of this kind are far more complex because they involve very different perceptions of the same behaviour. For example, a man may think that complimenting a co-worker on her appearance is simply a friendly gesture; she may find that his behaviour hinders her job performance (Crocker & Kalemba, 1999).

APPLYING THEORY

GENDER

	Structural-Functional Approach	Social-Conflict Approach
What is the level of analysis?	Macro-level	Macro-level
What does gender mean?	Parsons described gender in terms of two complementary patterns of behaviour: masculine and feminine.	Engels described gender in terms of the power of one sex over the other.
Is gender helpful or harmful?	Helpful. Gender gives men and women distinctive roles and responsibilities that help society operate smoothly. Gender builds social unity as men and women come together to form families.	Harmful. Gender limits people's personal development. Gender divides society by giving power to men to control the lives of women. Capitalism makes patriarchy stronger.

Pornography. A precise definition of pornography has long eluded scholars and lawmakers. Unable to set specific standards that distinguish what is pornographic from what is not, the Supreme Court allows the provinces, territories, and smaller jurisdictions to decide for themselves what violates "community standards" of decency and lacks any redeeming social value.

Definitions aside, pornography (loosely defined) is extremely popular in Canada: X-rated videos, 1-(900) telephone numbers for sexual conversation, and a host of sexually explicit movies and magazines constitute a multimillion-dollar-a-year industry (Cheney, 2000).

Traditionally, society has cast pornography as a *moral* issue. A more recent view focuses on pornography as demeaning to women. That is, pornography is really a power issue because it implies that men should control both sexuality and women. In other words, pornography is one foundation of male dominance because it dehumanizes women as the playthings of men. Worth noting, in this context, is that the term *pornography* is derived from the Greek word *porne*, meaning a harlot who acts as a man's sexual slave.

Another way pornography involves male power, according to many analysts, is by promoting violence against women. Depicting women as merely the playthings of men amounts to defining women as weak and undeserving of respect. Men show contempt for women defined in this way by striking out against them. Surveys show that about half of adults think that pornography encourages people to commit rape (NORC, 2003:235).

Like sexual harassment, pornography raises complex and sometimes conflicting concerns. While everyone objects to offensive material, many also endorse rights of free speech and artistic expression. Nevertheless, pressure to restrict pornography has increased in recent years, both from conservative people who oppose pornography on moral grounds and liberal people who oppose it as demeaning and threatening to women.

Theoretical Analysis of Gender

Sociology's two macro-level approaches, summarized in the Applying Theory table, address the central place of gender in social organization.

STRUCTURAL-FUNCTIONAL ANALYSIS

The structural-functional approach views society as a complex system of many separate but integrated parts. From this point of view, gender serves as a means to organize social life.

As Chapter 2 ("Culture") explained, the earliest hunting and gathering societies had little power over the forces of biology. Lacking effective birth control, women were frequently pregnant, and the responsibilities of childcare kept them close to home. At the same time, men's greater strength made them better suited for warfare and hunting. Over the centuries, this gender-based division of labour became institutionalized and largely taken for granted (Lengermann & Wallace, 1985; Freedman, 2002).

Industrial technology opens up a much greater range of cultural possibilities. With human muscle power no longer the main energy source, the physical strength of men becomes less significant. In addition, the ability to control

In the 1950s, Talcott Parsons proposed that sociologists interpret gender as a matter of *differences*. As he saw it, masculine men and feminine women formed strong families and made for an orderly society. In recent decades, however, social-conflict theory has reinterpreted gender as a matter of *inequality*. From this point of view, North American society places men in a position of dominance over women.

reproduction gives women greater choice about how to live. Modern societies relax traditional gender roles as people come to recognize the enormous amount of human talent they waste; yet change comes slowly because gender is deeply rooted in culture.

Talcott Parsons: Gender and complementarity.   As Talcott Parsons (1942, 1951, 1954) observed, gender helps integrate society, at least in its traditional form. Gender forms a *complementary* set of roles that links women and men into family units for the purpose of carrying out various important tasks. Women take primary responsibility for managing the household and raising children. Men connect the family to the larger world as they participate in the labour force.

Parsons further argued that distinctive socialization teaches women and men their appropriate gender identities and skills needed for adult life. Society teaches boys—presumably destined for the labour force—to be rational, self-assured, and competitive. Parsons called this complex of traits *instrumental* qualities. To prepare girls for child rearing, socialization stresses *expressive* qualities, such as emotional responsiveness and sensitivity to others.

Society encourages gender conformity by instilling fear in men and women that straying too far from accepted standards of masculinity or femininity will cause rejection by the opposite gender. In simple terms, women learn to reject non-masculine men as sexually unattractive, and men learn to reject unfeminine women. In sum, gender integrates society both structurally (in terms of what people do) and morally (in terms of what they believe).

Critical review.   Influential a half-century ago, this approach has lost much of its standing today. First, functionalism assumes a singular vision of society that is not shared by everyone. For example, historically, many women have worked outside the home because of economic need, a fact not reflected in Parsons' conventional, middle-class view of social life. Second, Parsons' analysis ignores the personal strains and social costs of rigid gender roles. Third, in the eyes of those seeking sexual equality, Parsons' gender "complementarity" amounts to little more than women submitting to male domination.

SOCIAL-CONFLICT ANALYSIS

From a social-conflict point of view, gender involves differences not just in behaviour but in power as well. Consider the striking similarity between how traditional ideas about gender benefit men and the ways oppression of racial and ethnic minorities benefit white people (Eichler, 1997; Smith 1987). Conventional ideas about gender do not contribute to the smooth operation of society; instead, they create division and tension, with men seeking to protect their privileges as women challenge the status quo.

As earlier chapters noted, the social-conflict approach draws heavily on the ideas of Karl Marx. Yet as far as gender is concerned, Marx was a product of his times, and his writings focused almost entirely on men. However, his friend and collaborator Friedrich Engels did develop a theory of gender stratification.

Friedrich Engels: Gender and class. Looking back through history, Engels saw that in hunting and gathering societies, the activities of women and men, though different, had the same importance. A successful hunt brought men great prestige, but the vegetation gathered by women provided most of a group's food supply. As technological advances led to a productive surplus, social equality and communal sharing gave way to private property and, ultimately, a class hierarchy. At this point, men gained pronounced power over women. With surplus wealth to pass on to heirs, upper-class men needed to be sure who their sons were, which led them to control the sexuality of women. The desire to control property brought about monogamous marriage and the family. Women were taught to remain virgins until marriage, to remain faithful to their husbands thereafter, and to build their lives around bearing and raising one man's children.

According to Engels (1902, orig. 1884), capitalism intensifies this male domination. First, capitalism creates more wealth, which gives greater power to men as owners of property and as primary wage earners. Second, an expanding capitalist economy depends on turning people, especially women, into consumers who seek personal fulfillment by buying and using products. Third, society assigns women the task of maintaining the home to free men to work in factories. The double exploitation of capitalism, as Engels saw it, lies in paying low wages for male labour and paying women no wages at all.

Critical review. Social-conflict analysis is strongly critical of conventional ideas about gender, claiming that society would be better off if we minimized or even did away with this dimension of social structure. One problem with this approach is that it sees conventional families—supported by traditionalists as morally good—as a social evil. Second, social-conflict analysis minimizes the extent to which women and men live together cooperatively, and often happily, in families. A third problem with this approach lies in its claim that capitalism is the root of gender stratification. In fact, agrarian societies typically are more patriarchal than industrial-capitalist societies, and socialist nations—including the People's Republic of China and the former Soviet Union—did move women into the labour force but, by and large, provided women with very low pay in sex-segregated jobs (Moore, 1992; Rosendahl, 1997; Haney, 2002).

Feminism

Feminism is *the advocacy of social equality for men and women, in opposition to patriarchy and sexism.* The "first wave" of the feminist movement in Canada began in the mid-nineteenth century as women sought to gain equal property rights as well as voting rights. Women got to vote at the federal level in 1918; achieving the right for all Canadian women to vote in provincial elections took another 22 years—that's when the province of Quebec extended the right to women under its jurisdiction. But other disadvantages persisted, and a "second wave" of feminism arose in the 1960s.

BASIC FEMINIST IDEAS

Feminism views the personal experiences of women and men through the lens of gender. How women and men think of themselves (gender identity), how they act (gender roles), and their social standing (gender stratification) are all rooted in the operation of society.

Although people who consider themselves feminists disagree about many things, most support five general principles:

1. **Working to increase equality.** Feminist thinking is strongly political; it relates ideas to action. Feminism is critical of the status quo, pushing for change toward social equality for women and men.

2. **Expanding human choice.** Feminists argue that cultural ideas about gender divide the full range of human qualities into two opposing and limiting spheres: the female world of emotion and cooperation and the male world of rationality and competition. As an alternative, feminists propose a "reintegration of humanity" by which all individuals develop all human traits (French, 1985; Eichler, 1997).

3. **Eliminating gender stratification.** Feminism opposes laws and cultural norms that limit the education, income, and job opportunities of women.

4. **Ending sexual violence.** Today's women's movement seeks to eliminate sexual violence. Feminists argue that patriarchy distorts relationships between women and men, encouraging violence against women in the form of rape, domestic abuse, sexual harassment, and pornography (Dworkin, 1987; Freedman, 2002).

5. **Promoting sexual freedom.** Finally, feminism advocates women's control over their sexuality and reproduction. Feminists support the free availability of birth control information. As Figure 10–4 shows, contraceptives are much less available in most of the world than in Canada. Most feminists also support a woman's right to choose whether to have children or to end a pregnancy, rather than allowing men—as fathers, husbands, doctors, and legislators—to control their reproduction. Many feminists also support gay people's efforts to overcome prejudice and discrimination in a predominantly heterosexual culture (Jagger, 1983; Ferree & Hess, 1995; Armstrong, 2002).

TYPES OF FEMINISM

Although feminists agree on the importance of gender equality, they disagree on how to achieve it: through liberal feminism, socialist feminism, or radical feminism (Stacey, 1983; Vogel, 1983; Ferree & Hess, 1995; Freedman, 2002).

Liberal feminism is rooted in classic liberal thinking that individuals should be free to develop their own talents and pursue their own interests. Liberal feminism accepts the basic organization of our society but seeks to expand the rights and opportunities of women, in part laid down in Canada's *Charter of Rights and Freedoms*. Liberal feminists support reproductive freedom for all women. They respect the family as a social institution but seek changes in society, including more widely available maternity and paternity leave and childcare for parents who work.

Socialist feminism evolved from the ideas of Karl Marx and Friedrich Engels, in part as a critical response to Marx's inattention to gender. From this point of view, capitalism increases patriarchy by concentrating wealth and power in the hands of a small number of men. Socialist feminists do not think the reforms supported by liberal feminists go far enough. The family form fostered by capitalism must change in order to replace "domestic slavery" with some collective means of carrying out housework and childcare. Replacing the traditional family can come about only through a socialist revolution that creates a state-centred economy to meet the needs of all.

Like socialist feminism, *radical feminism* finds liberal feminism inadequate. Radical feminists believe that patriarchy is so firmly entrenched that even a socialist revolution would not end it. Instead, reaching the goal of gender equality means that society must eliminate gender itself. One possible way to achieve this goal is to use new reproductive technology (see Chapter 13, "Family and Religion") to separate women's bodies from the process of childbearing. With an end to motherhood, society could leave behind the entire family system, liberating women, men, and children from the oppression of family, gender, and sex itself (Dworkin, 1987). Radical feminism seeks an egalitarian and gender-free society, a revolution much more sweeping than that sought by Marx.

OPPOSITION TO FEMINISM

Feminism provokes criticism and resistance from both men and women who hold conventional ideas about gender. Some men oppose sexual equality for the same reasons that many white people have historically opposed social equality for ethnic and racial minorities: they do not want to give up their privileges. Other men and women, including those who are neither rich nor powerful, distrust a social movement (especially its radical expressions) that attacks the

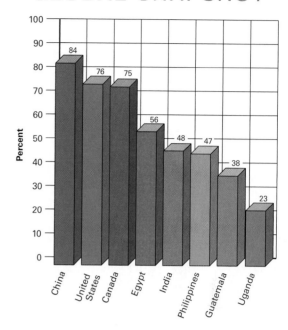

GLOBAL SNAPSHOT

FIGURE 10–4 Use of Contraception by Married Women of Childbearing Age

Source: United Nations Development Programme (2004).

traditional family and rejects patterns that have guided male–female relations for centuries. Canadians belonging to the Real Women of Canada promote their organization as Canada's "alternative women's movement," which represents the concerns of women homemakers and emphasizes the family as society's most important institution.

Men who have been socialized to value strength and dominance may feel uneasy about feminist ideals of men as gentle and warm (Doyle, 1983). Similarly, women who have built their lives around husbands and children think feminism does not value the social roles that give meaning to their lives. In general, opposition to feminism is greatest among women who have the least education and those who do not work outside the home (Marshall, 1985; Ferree & Hess, 1995).

Resistance to feminism also comes from academic circles. Some sociologists charge that feminism ignores a growing body of evidence that men and women do think and act in somewhat different ways, which may make complete gender equality impossible. Furthermore, say critics, with its drive to increase women's presence in the workplace, feminism undervalues the crucial and unique contribution women make to the development of children, especially in the first years of life (Baydar & Brooks-Gunn, 1991; Popenoe, 1993b; Gibbs, 2001b).

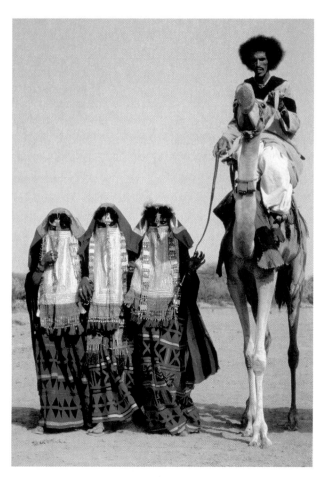

As a general rule, patriarchy is strongest in nations with traditional cultures and limited economic development. Here we see a man in Eritrea travelling to a wedding with his three wives walking alongside him as he rides his camel. Although gender stratification in Canada is not always so obvious, it remains a reality in this country as well.

Finally, there is the question of *how* women should go about improving their social standing. A large majority of Canadian adults think that women should have equal rights, but many also say women should advance individually, according to their training and abilities.

In sum, most opposition to feminism is directed toward its socialist and radical forms; support for liberal feminism is widespread. In addition, we are seeing an unmistakable trend toward gender equality, with more and more Canadian women participating in the labour force and an increasing number of male partners sharing responsibilities in the home. While gender equality in family and working life is more apparent in dual-career marriages of professional men and women (Hertz, 1986), pro-feminist men argue that their gender can be taught that both masculine and feminine identities are changing and that many of the choices open to them conflict with archaic masculine values (Morra & Smith, 1998).

Looking Ahead: Gender in the Twenty-First Century

At best, predictions about the future are no more than educated guesses. Just as economists disagree about the likely inflation rate a year from now, sociologists can offer only general observations about the likely future of gender and society.

Change so far has been remarkable. A century ago, women held a position of striking subordination. Husbands controlled property in marriage, and laws barred women from most jobs, from holding political office, and from voting. Although women remain socially disadvantaged, the movement toward equality has surged ahead. Two-thirds of people entering the work force in the 1990s were women, and in 2000, for the first time, a majority of families had both husband and wife in the paid labour force. Clearly, today's economy depends a great deal on the earnings of women.

Many factors have contributed to this transformation. Perhaps most important, industrialization and the more recent technological advances that have resulted from the Information Revolution have shifted the nature of work from physically demanding tasks that favoured male strength to jobs that require thought and imagination. This change puts women and men on a more even footing. Also, because birth control technology has given us greater control over reproduction, women's lives are less constrained by pregnancy and the demands of childrearing.

Many women and men have deliberately pursued social equality. For example, sexual harassment complaints in the workplace are taken much more seriously today than they were a generation ago. As more women assume positions of power in the corporate and political worlds, social changes in the twenty-first century may be as great as what we have already witnessed.

Gender is woven into the fabric of social life. Efforts to change deeply rooted ideas about the roles of women and men will continue to spark debate and opposition, as the Controversy & Debate box illustrates. On balance, however, although change may occur slowly, we are seeing steady movement toward a society in which women and men enjoy equal rights and opportunities.

A Closer Look: Are Men *Really* So Privileged?

Anti-male discrimination has become far greater in scope, in degree, and in damage than any which may exist against women.

—Men's rights advocate Richard F. Doyle

It is men, this chapter argues, who dominate society. Men enjoy higher earnings, control more wealth, exercise more power, do less housework, and get more respect than women do. But Doyle's assertion above states an important counterpoint advanced by the "men's rights movement"—that the male world is not nearly as privileged as some people think.

If men are so privileged in our society, why do they turn to crime more often than women? Moreover, the criminal justice system does not give men any special privileges. Probably most people would not be surprised to learn that police are reluctant to arrest a woman, especially if she has children. This fact helps explain why 80 percent of arrests for serious crime put the handcuffs on a male. Neither do men get a break from the courts, since in 2000–01 males made up 91 percent of adults admitted to provincial and territorial prisons and 95 percent of those to federal penitentiaries (Hendrick & Farmer, 2002).

Culture is not always generous to men, either. Our way of life praises as "real men" males who work, live, and play hard, and who drink, smoke, and speed on the highways. Given this view of maleness, is it any wonder that men are twice as likely as women to suffer serious assault, three times more likely to fall victim to homicide, and four times more likely to commit suicide? In light of these statistics, how do we explain our society's attention to violence against women? Perhaps, critics suggest, we are in the grip of a cultural double standard: We accept harm that comes to males while showing sympathy for the far fewer cases of violence against women. It is this same double standard, the argument continues, that moves women and children out of harm's way and expects men to "go down with the ship" or die defending their country on the battlefield.

Child custody is another sore point from the perspective of many men. Despite decades of consciousness-raising in pursuit of gender fairness, and clear evidence that men earn more than women, courts across Canada routinely award primary care of children to mothers. In 2003, mothers were awarded sole custody in 48 percent of all custody decisions settled in court; fathers, by contrast, were awarded sole custody in a paltry 8 percent of these cases (Statistics Canada, 2006au). To make matters worse, men separated from their children by the courts are often stigmatized as "runaway fathers" or "deadbeat dads."

Finally, male advocates point out that affirmative action laws now cover the majority of the population, but notably exclude white males. Therefore, in today's affirmative action climate, women have the inside track to university (where they now outnumber men) as well as the work force (where businesses know they will be called to account for hiring practices).

Even nature seems to plot against men as, on average, women live over five years longer. The controversial question is this: when society plays favourites, who is favoured?

CONTINUE THE DEBATE . . .

1. Do you think that the criminal justice system favours women over men, or do men simply get what they deserve? Why, in your opinion, are so many more men than women in prison?
2. On your campus, do men's organizations (such as fraternities and athletic teams) enjoy special privileges? What about women's organizations?
3. On balance, do you agree or disagree with the "men's rights perspective"? What specific points do you find convincing or wrong? Why?

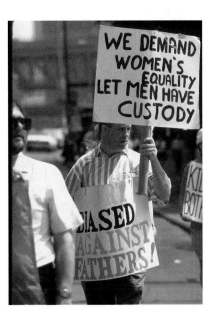

Sources: Based on Doyle (1980), Scanlon (1992), Rosenfeld (1998), Kleinfeld (1999), and Statistics Canada (2006au).

SUMMARY

1. Gender is the meaning a culture attaches to being female or male. Because society gives men more power and resources than women, gender is an important dimension of social stratification.

2. Although some degree of male dominance exists everywhere, gender varies throughout history and across cultures.

3. Through the socialization process, people build gender into their personalities (gender identity) as well as their actions (gender roles). The major agents of socialization—family, peer groups, schools, and the mass media—reinforce cultural definitions of femininity and masculinity.

4. Gender stratification shapes the workplace. Although a majority of women are now in the paid labour force, most hold clerical or service jobs. Unpaid housework remains a task performed mostly by women, whether or not they hold jobs outside the home.

5. On average, Canadian women in full-time year-round employment earn 70.5 percent as much as men. This disparity stems from differences in jobs and family responsibilities, as well as from discrimination on the part of employers.

6. Women now earn a slight majority of all bachelor's and master's degrees. Men still earn a majority of doctorates.

7. The number of women in politics has increased sharply in recent decades. Still, most elected officials, especially at the national level, are men.

8. Intersection theory investigates the intersection of race, class, and gender, which often results in multiple disadvantages.

9. Violence against women is a widespread problem in Canada. Our society is also dealing with issues of sexual harassment and pornography.

10. Structural-functional analysis suggests that in pre-industrial societies, distinct roles for females and males reflect biological differences. In industrial societies, marked gender inequality becomes dysfunctional and gradually decreases. Talcott Parsons claimed that complementary gender roles promote the social integration of families and society as a whole.

11. Social-conflict analysis views gender as a dimension of social inequality and conflict. Friedrich Engels tied gender stratification to the development of private property.

12. Feminism supports the social equality between women and men and opposes patriarchy and sexism. Feminism also seeks to end violence against women and give women control over their sexuality and reproduction.

13. There are three variations of feminist thinking. Liberal feminism seeks equal opportunity for both genders within current social arrangements, socialist feminism advocates abolishing private property as the means to social equality, and radical feminism seeks to create a gender-free society.

KEY CONCEPTS

feminism (p. 274) the advocacy of social equality for women and men, in opposition to patriarchy and sexism

gender (p. 256) the personal traits and social positions that members of a society attach to being female or male

gender stratification (p. 256) the unequal distribution of wealth, power, and privilege between men and women

intersection theory (p. 270) the investigation of the interplay of race, class, and gender, often resulting in multiple dimensions of disadvantage

matriarchy (p. 258) a form of social organization in which females dominate males

patriarchy (p. 258) a form of social organization in which males dominate females

sexism (p. 260) the belief that one sex is innately superior to the other

sexual harassment (p. 271) comments, gestures, or physical contact of a sexual nature that is deliberate, repeated, and unwelcome

CRITICAL-THINKING QUESTIONS

1. In what ways are sex and gender related? In what ways are they distinct?

2. What techniques do the mass media use to "sell" conventional ideas about gender to women and men?

3. Why is gender a dimension of social stratification? How does gender intersect other dimensions of inequality such as class, race, and ethnicity?

4. Consider the following two statements: "He fathered the child" and "She mothered the child." Describe the differences in meaning. How do you account for these differences?

5. A number of European nations, including Great Britain, Norway, Denmark, and Finland, require that at least 25 percent of candidates for national offices be women. Should Canada adopt a similar policy? Is such a policy likely?

APPLICATIONS AND EXERCISES

1. Take a walk through a business area of your local community. Which businesses are frequented almost entirely by women? by men? by both men and women? Try to explain the patterns you find.

2. Watch several hours of children's television programming on a Saturday morning. Notice the advertising, which sells mostly toys and breakfast cereal. Keep track of what share of toys are "gendered," that is, aimed at one sex or the other.

What traits do you associate with toys intended for boys and those intended for girls?

3. Do some research on the history of women's issues in your province or territory. When was the first woman elected to government? What laws have existed restricting the work women could do? Are any such laws in effect today? What percentage of political officials in your province or territory are women?

 SITES TO SEE

www.pearsoned.ca/macionis
The authors and publisher of this book invite you to visit the interactive Companion Website™ that accompanies this text. Begin by clicking on the cover of your book. You will find a chapter-by-chapter study guide, practice tests, suggested weblinks, and links to other relevant material.

www.psac.com
Visit the Public Service Alliance of Canada's website and learn about pay equity issues.

www.swc-cfc.gc.ca
Visit the site for the Status of Women Canada to discover the goals and strategies of this organization.

www.cwhn.ca
Another informative site is run by the Canadian Women's Health Network. Identify the issues this organization finds most important.

www.wwwomen.com
This site provides a search engine to locate all sorts of information concerning women.

www.educationindex.com/women
This site provides numerous and widely varied links to sites concerned with women's issues.

www.womenspace.ca
The Womenspace site discusses ways of using the Internet for women's activism.

www.catalystwomen.org
This site includes research and information on the social standing of Canadian and U.S. women in business.

www.realwomenca.com
This is the website of the Real Women of Canada.

www.feminist.com/resources/links/links_men.html
This is an informative site that lists a number of pro-feminist men's groups.

www.un.org/womenwatch
Here is the United Nations' Internet gateway on the advancement and empowerment of women.

 INVESTIGATE WITH RESEARCH NAVIGATOR™

Follow the instructions on page 33 of this text to access the features of Research Navigator™. Once at the website (**www.researchnavigator.com**), enter your login name and password. Then, to use the Content Select™ database, enter keywords such as "gender," "feminism," and "sexual harassment," and the search engine will supply relevant and recent scholarly and popular press publications.

 To reinforce your understanding of this chapter, and to identify topics for further study, visit MySocLab at **www.pearsoned.ca/mysoclab/macionis** for diagnostic tests and a multimedia ebook.

CHAPTER ELEVEN

Race and Ethnicity

What are race and ethnicity,
and how are they created by society?

Why is Canada known as a nation of immigrants?

How are race and ethnicity important dimensions
of social inequality today?

Race is an important basis of social inequality. In Johannesburg, South Africa, as in Canada, the lowest-paying jobs are commonly performed by visible minorities.

Colonial attitudes and practices, enshrined in official legislation, took a huge toll on Canada's Aboriginal peoples. The infamous *Indian Act* of 1874 legally authorized federal government jurisdiction over Aboriginal communities across the country. Among other things, the *Indian Act* institutionalized a residential school system. Federally appointed education authorities removed—by physical force, if parents objected—Aboriginal children of both sexes from their families and communities, relocating them to distant residential schools where a foreign language, religion, and culture were imposed.

Aboriginal youth who "successfully" completed the school program later faced a different set of concerns: they often found their newly acquired "foreign" knowledge wanting. They had not learned how to forge intimate relationships with others, including their elders, or how to parent effectively. The knowledge they acquired from the white teachers left them caught between two worlds; they found it difficult to accept the teachings of their elders and yet felt isolated from mainstream society. In brief, the proud and "educated" Aboriginal was left "hanging in the middle of the two cultures and he is not a white man and he is not an Indian. [The missionary teachers] washed away practically everything an Indian needed to help himself, to think the way a human person should in order to survive" (Sluman & Goodwill, quoted in Dickason, 1992:336).

Much is changing for Canada's Aboriginal people today. The federal government has started to return political control to the Aboriginal people, allowing them to decide what educational system and other social institutions are best for their children. And the United Church has formally apologized for the sexual abuse of Aboriginal children in the residential system. Yet deep scars remain. In many pockets of the country, former religious teachers are only now being brought to justice for the physical and sexual abuse they inflicted on generations of Aboriginal children, who continue to be treated in many respects as second-class citizens in a country that prides itself on its tolerance and concern for others (Benoit & Carroll, 1995).

Around the world, the pattern of inequality and conflict based on colour and culture is even more striking. Since the fall of the former Soviet Union, Ukrainians, Moldavians, Azerbaijanis, and a host of other ethnic peoples have struggled to recover their cultural identity. In the Middle East, Arabs and Jews are trying to overcome deep-rooted tensions, as are Northern Ireland's Protestants and Catholics. In dozens of the world's nations, colour and culture often flare into hateful confrontation.

This chapter examines the meaning of race and ethnicity, explains how these social constructs have shaped our history, and suggests why they will play an even greater part in social life as we move through the twenty-first century.

The Social Meaning of Race and Ethnicity

People often confuse the terms "race" and "ethnicity." For this reason, we begin with some definitions.

The range of biological variation in human beings is far greater than any system of racial classification allows. This fact is made obvious by trying to place all of the people pictured here into simple racial categories.

RACE

A **race** is *a socially constructed category composed of people who share biologically transmitted traits that members of a society consider important.* People may classify one another racially based on physical characteristics such as skin colour, facial features, hair texture, and body shape.

Racial diversity appeared among our human ancestors as the result of living in different regions of the world. In regions of intense heat, people developed darker skin (from the natural pigment melanin) that offers protection from the sun; in moderate climates, people developed lighter skin. Such traits are literally only skin deep because human beings the world over are members of a single biological species.

The striking variety of racial traits found today is also the product of migration; genetic characteristics once common to a single place are now found in many lands. Especially pronounced is the racial mix in the Middle East (that is, Western Asia), historically a crossroads of migration. Greater racial uniformity characterizes more isolated peoples such as the island-dwelling Japanese. But every population has some genetic mixture, and increasing contact ensures even more racial blending in the future.

Although we often think of race in terms of biological traits, race is a socially constructed concept. At one level, research shows that white people rate black people as darker in skin tone than black people do (Hill, 2002). Also, a number of people—especially biracial and multiracial people—define themselves and are defined by others differently, depending on the setting (Harris & Sim, 2002). More broadly, entire societies define physical traits differently. Typically, people in Canada "see" fewer racial categories (commonly Aboriginal, Asian, white, and black) than people in Brazil, who distinguish between *branca* (white), *parda* (brown), *morena* (brunette), *mulata* (mulatto), *preta* (black), and *amarela* (yellow) (Inciardi, Surratt, & Telles, 2000). In countries such as Canada, people consider racial differences more important; the people of other countries, such as Brazil, consider them less important.

In any society, definitions and meanings concerning race change over time. For example, in 1900, many people in North America viewed individuals of Irish and Italian ancestry as racially different, a practice that was far less common by 1950 (Loveman, 1999). Today, Statistics Canada allows people to describe themselves as being Aboriginal or belonging in one or more other racial categories (offering a total of nine options plus "other").

Many people today consider themselves to be multiracial. What effect will this trend have on the use of traditional racial categories?

Racial types. Scientists invented the concept of race more than a century ago as they tried to organize the world's physical diversity using three racial types. They called people with light skin and fine hair *Caucasoid,* people with dark skin and coarse hair *Negroid,* and people with yellow or brown skin and distinctive folds on the eyelids *Mongoloid.*

Sociologists consider such terms misleading at best and harmful at worst. For one thing, no society contains biologically "pure" people. The skin colour of people we might call "Caucasoid" (or "Indo-European," "Caucasian," or more commonly, "white") ranges from very light (typical in Scandinavia) to very dark (in Southern India). The same variation exists among so-called "Negroids" ("Africans" or, more commonly, "black" people) and "Mongoloids" (that is, "Asians"). In fact, many "white" people (say, in Southern India) actually have darker skin than many "black" people (such as the Negroid aborigines of Australia). Overall, the three racial categories differ in about 6 percent of their genes, less than the genetic variation *within* each category (Boza, 2002; Harris & Sim, 2002).

Why, then, do people make so much of race? Such categories allow societies to rank people in a hierarchy, allowing some people to feel that they are by nature "better" than others. Because racial ranking shapes access to wealth and prestige, societies may construct racial categories in extreme ways. Throughout much of the twentieth century, for example, many Southern U.S. states labelled as "coloured" anyone with as little as one thirty-second African ancestry (that is, one African American great-great-great-grandparent). Today, the law allows parents to declare the race of a child as

they wish. Even so, most people in the United States are still very sensitive to people's racial backgrounds.

A trend toward mixture. The population of Canada is quite mixed. Over many generations and throughout the Americas, the genetic traits of Negroid Africans, Caucasoid Europeans, and Mongoloid Native Americans (whose ancestors came from Asia) have intermingled. Many "black" people therefore have a significant Caucasoid ancestry, and many "white" people have some Negroid genes, and many "Aboriginals" have either or sometimes both. In short, whatever people may think, race is no black-and-white issue.

Today, many people define themselves as multiracial. When completing their 2001 census forms, almost 74 000 people described themselves by checking two or more racial categories (Statistics Canada, 2003bv).

ETHNICITY

Ethnicity is *a shared cultural heritage.* People define themselves—or others—as members of an ethnic category based on having common ancestors, language, and religion that confer a distinctive social identity. Canada is a multi-ethnic society in which English and French are the "official languages," yet many people speak other languages at home, including Mandarin, Cantonese, Hindi, Thai, Italian, German, Spanish, or Swedish. Similarly, while Catholicism has the largest number of followers, many Canadians identify themselves as Protestants, while many others of Greek, Ukrainian, and Russian descent are affiliated with the Eastern Orthodox Church. About 1 percent of the Canadian population claim Judaism as their faith, and others have a Muslim religious heritage. Table 11–1 presents the broad sweep of ethnic diversity in Canada, as recorded by the 2001 census.

People can fairly easily modify their ethnicity: immigrants may discard their cultural traditions over time or, like many people of Aboriginal descent recently, try to revive their heritage (Dickason, 1992; Nagel, 1994; Spencer, 1994).

Finally, ethnicity involves a great deal of variability, for most people identify with more than one ethnic background. In Canada, for example, more than one-third of the population declare themselves to belong to more than one ethnic category.

MINORITIES

March 3, Dallas, Texas. Sitting in the lobby of just about any hotel in a major U.S. city presents a lesson in contrasts: the majority of the guests checking in and out are white; the majority of the employees who carry the luggage, serve the food, and clean the rooms are visible minorities.

As Chapter 10 ("Gender Stratification") described, a **minority** is *any category of people distinguished by physical or cultural difference that a society sets apart and subordinates.* The 1996 census was the first in which "Canadian" was included in the examples accompanying the question on ethnicity. In that year, 18.7 percent of the population stated "Canadian" as their only ethnic origin and another 12.2 percent included it in among up to six permissible ethnic origins. In the 2001 census almost 40 percent of Canadians marked this down as one of their ethnicities or their only one. Table 11–1 also illustrates the ethnic diversity of Canada. If the first category, "Canadian," is disregarded, the lengthy list of sole ethnicities covers only 35 percent of the Canadian population in 2001. In addition to the 190 specific ethnic backgrounds listed in the census summary tables, there are 17 other ethnic categories that list those "not included elsewhere" (n.i.e.), down to the smallest of these—"African, n.i.e." (this category includes 155 people). Nevertheless, the numerical dominance of, first, the British, and second, the French, is evident, given that these two ethnic groups alone claim more than 20 percent of all Canadians who claim only one ethnic background.

Minorities have two important characteristics. First, they share a *distinct identity*, which may be based on physical or cultural traits. Second, minorities experience *subordination*. As the rest of this chapter shows, Canadian minorities typically have lower income, lower occupational prestige, and limited schooling. Class, race, and ethnicity, as well as gender, are overlapping and reinforcing dimensions of social stratification.

Of course, not all members of a minority category are disadvantaged. For example, some Aboriginals are quite wealthy; other Aboriginals are celebrated academic, professional, and artistic leaders. But even job success rarely allows individuals to escape their minority standing (Benjamin, 1991). As described in Chapter 4 ("Social Interaction in Everyday Life"), race or ethnicity often serves as a master status that overshadows personal accomplishments.

As noted, minorities usually—but not always—make up a small proportion of a society's population. For example, black South Africans are disadvantaged even though they are a numerical majority in their country. In Canada, women make up slightly more than half the population but are still struggling for the opportunities and privileges enjoyed by men. National Map 11–1 shows the percentage of visible minorities in different parts of Canada.

TABLE 11-1

Most Frequent Specific Ethnic Categories in Canada, 2001

Ethnic Group	Total Reponses	Percentage of Population Declaring Being Only	Percentage of Population Declaring as One of Several
Canadian	11 682 680	22.8%	16.6%
English	5 978 875	5.0%	15.2%
French	4 668 410	3.6%	12.2%
Scottish	4 157 210	2.0%	12.0%
Irish	3 822 660	1.7%	11.2%
German	2 742 765	2.4%	6.9%
Italian	1 270 370	2.5%	1.8%
Chinese	1 094 700	3.2%	0.5%
Ukrainian	1 071 060	1.1%	2.5%
North American Indian	1 000 890	1.5%	1.8%
Dutch (Netherlands)	923 310	1.1%	2.0%
Polish	817 085	0.9%	1.9%
East Indian	713 330	2.0%	0.4%
Norwegian	363 760	0.2%	1.1%
Portuguese	357 690	0.9%	0.4%
Welsh	350 365	0.1%	1.1%
Jewish	348 605	0.6%	0.5%
Russian	337 960	0.2%	0.9%
Filipino	327 550	0.9%	0.2%
Métis	307 845	0.2%	0.8%
Swedish	282 760	0.1%	0.9%
Hungarian (Magyar)	267 255	0.3%	0.6%
American (USA)	250 005	0.1%	0.8%
Greek	215 105	0.5%	0.2%
Spanish	213 105	0.2%	0.5%
Jamaican	211 720	0.5%	0.2%
Danish	170 780	0.1%	0.5%
Vietnamese	151 410	0.4%	0.1%
Austrian	147 585	0.1%	0.4%
Lebanese	143 635	0.3%	0.2%
Romanian	131 830	0.2%	0.3%
Belgian	129 780	0.1%	0.3%
Finnish	114 690	0.1%	0.3%
Swiss	110 795	0.1%	0.3%
Korean	101 715	0.3%	0.0%
Québécois	98 670	0.2%	0.1%
Croatian	97 050	0.2%	0.1%
Iranian	88 220	0.2%	0.0%
Japanese	85 230	0.2%	0.1%
Haitian	82 405	0.2%	0.0%
Czech	79 910	0.1%	0.2%
Icelandic	75 090	0.0%	0.2%
Pakistani	74 015	0.2%	0.1%
Acadian	71 590	0.1%	0.2%
Sri Lankan	61 315	0.2%	0.1%
West Indian	59 705	0.1%	0.1%
Inuit	56 330	0.1%	0.1%
Total responses	**47 998 365**	**18 307 575**	**29 690 800**
Total population	**29 639 035**	**61.8%**	**38.2%**

Source: Statistics Canada (2003s).

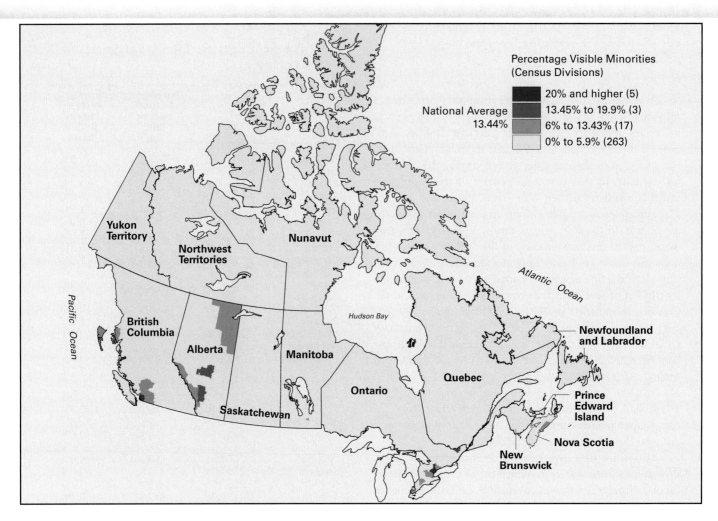

Percentage Visible Minorities
(Census Divisions)

National Average
13.44%

	20% and higher (5)
	13.45% to 19.9% (3)
	6% to 13.43% (17)
	0% to 5.9% (263)

SEEING OURSELVES

NATIONAL MAP 11-1 Visible Minorities in Canada, 2001

This map shows that there are only 25 census divisions in Canada where visible minorities make up 6 percent or more of the population. Only eight census divisions exceed the national average of 13.4 percent. Why do you think there are so few visible minorities in most of Canada?

Source: Calculated based on data in Statistics Canada (2003bk).

PREJUDICE AND STEREOTYPES

November 19, Jerusalem, Israel. We are driving along the edge of this historic city, a holy place to Jews, Christians, and Muslims, when Razi, our taxi driver, spots a small group of Falasha—Ethiopian Jews—on a street corner. "Those people over there," he begins, "they are different. They don't drive cars. They don't want to improve themselves. Even when our country offers them schooling, they don't take it." He shakes his head at the Ethiopians and drives on.

Prejudice is *a rigid and unfair generalization about an entire category of people*. Prejudice is unfair because such attitudes are supported by little or no direct evidence. Prejudice

 Take a test for different kinds of prejudices at **https://implicit. harvard.edu/implicit/demo/ measuring.html**.

Racial and ethnic stereotypes are deeply embedded in our culture and language. Many people speak of someone "gypping" another without realizing that this word insults European Gypsies, a category of people long pushed to the margins of European societies. What about terms such as "Dutch treat," "French kiss," or "Indian giver"?

may target people of a particular social class, sex, sexual orientation, age, political affiliation, race, or ethnicity.

Prejudices are prejudgments that can be either positive or negative. Our positive prejudices exaggerate the virtues of people like ourselves, and our negative prejudices condemn those who are different from us. Negative prejudice can be expressed as anything from mild dislike to outright hostility. Because such attitudes are rooted in culture, everyone has at least some measure of prejudice.

Prejudice often takes the form of **stereotypes** (*stereo* is derived from the Greek word for "hard" or "solid"), which are *exaggerated descriptions applied to every person in some category.* Many white people hold stereotypical views of minorities. Stereotyping is especially harmful to minorities in the workplace. If company officials see minority workers only in terms of a stereotype, they will make assumptions about their abilities, steer them toward certain jobs, and limit their access to better opportunities (Kaufman, 2002).

Minorities, too, stereotype whites and also other minorities (Smith, 1996; Cummings & Lambert, 1997). For example, recent surveys show that more blacks than whites express the belief that Asians engage in unfair business practices and that more Asians than whites criticize Hispanics for having too many children (Perlmutter, 2002).

MEASURING PREJUDICE: THE SOCIAL DISTANCE SCALE

One measure of prejudice is *social distance,* which refers to how closely people are willing to interact with members of some category. Eighty years ago, the sociologist Emory Bogardus developed the *social distance scale* shown in Figure 11–1. Bogardus asked students at colleges and universities in the United States how closely they were willing to interact with people in 30 racial and ethnic categories. People

express the greatest social distance (most negative prejudice) by declaring that some category of people should be barred from the country entirely (point 7 in the figure); at the other extreme, people express the least social distance (most social acceptance) by saying that they would accept a member of some category into their family through marriage.

Bogardus (1925, 1967; Owen, Elsner, & McFaul, 1977) found that people felt much more social distance toward some categories than they did toward others. In general, students in his surveys expressed the most social distance toward Hispanics, African Americans, Asians, and Turks by indicating that they would accept such people as co-workers but would not welcome them as neighbours, close friends, or family members. People expressed the least social distance toward those from Northern and Western Europe, including English and Scottish people, and also Canadians, indicating that they would be willing to include them in their families by marriage.

Bogardus' original article is available on this Brock University website: **http://spartan.ac.brocku.ca/~lward/Bogardus/Bogardus_1925c.html.**

What patterns of social distance do we find among college and university students today? A recent study using the same social distance scale reported three major findings (Parrillo, 2003b):[1]

1. Student opinions show a trend toward greater acceptance. Today's students express less social distance

---

[1]Parrillo dropped seven of the categories used by Bogardus (Armenians, Czechs, Finns, Norwegians, Scots, Swedes, and Turks), claiming they were no longer visible minorities. He added nine new categories (Africans, Arabs, Cubans, Dominicans, Haitians, Jamaicans, Muslims, Puerto Ricans, and Vietnamese), claiming that these are visible minorities today. This change probably encouraged higher social distance scores, making the trend toward decreasing social distance all the more significant.

DIVERSITY: RACE, CLASS, & GENDER

Hard Work: The Guest Worker's Life in North America

On Saturday, June 10, 2006, British Columbia's minister for transportation, Kevin Falcon, celebrated the start of the tunnel boring operation for the new rapid transit line linking Vancouver airport with other parts of the city. The boring machine—Sweet Leilani—was so sophisticated that it required specialized staffing from Costa Rica, Peru, and Colombia. The only problem was that these workers were paid as little as $3.47 per hour, a lot less than the legislated minimum wage in British Columbia. Less than a month later, a majority of the foreign workers had voted to become unionized.

Early one morning farther south, it was already hot in Houston as a line of pick-up trucks snaked slowly into a dusty yard, where 200 labourers had been gathered since dawn, hoping for a day's work. The driver of the first truck opened his window and told the foreman that he was looking for a crew to spread boiling tar on a roof. The foreman turned to the crowd, and after a few minutes, three workers stepped forward and climbed into the back of the truck. The next driver was looking for two experienced house painters. The scene was repeated over and over as men and a few women left to dig ditches, spread cement, hang drywall, open clogged septic tanks, and even crawl under houses to poison rats. As each driver entered, the foreman, Abdonel Cespedes, asked, "How much?" Most of the people in the trucks offered $5 an hour. Cespedes automatically

responded, "$6.50; the going rate is $6.50 for an hour's hard work." Sometimes he convinced people to pay that much, but usually not. The temporary workers—who had come from Mexico, El Salvador, Guatemala, and beyond—knew that dozens of them would end up with no work at all that day. Most jumped at the offer of $5 an hour because they knew that, when the day was over, they would have earned $50.

Canada today is confronting a unique problem: it no longer has enough workers, especially those in construction and the trades. Employers crying out for temporary workers argue that Canada should beef up its guest worker program and make it easier to recruit immigrants. On the other hand, critics (including trade unions) argue that guest workers depress wages for Canadian workers and worsen

working conditions. At the same time, some Canadian unions have begun to support guest workers struggling to unionize.

The hard truth is that immigrants to Canada and the United States do the jobs that no one else wants. Immigrants represent the bottom level of our national economy, working in restaurants and hotels, on construction crews, and in private homes cooking, cleaning, and caring for children. Across North America, about half of all housekeepers, household cooks, tailors, and restaurant waiters are men or women born abroad. Few immigrants make much more than the minimum wage and—unless they gain landed immigrant or citizenship status—are unlikely to receive any health or pension benefits. Like the United States and Britain, Canada has not signed a UN Convention that protects the rights of migrant workers.

WHAT DO YOU THINK?

1. In what ways do you or members of your family depend on the low-paid labour of immigrants?
2. Do you think there is anything wrong with paying someone the current minimum wage for hard work? Why or why not?
3. Do you think that guest workers to Canada should have the right to become permanent residents and eventually citizens?

Source: Based in part on Booth (1998).

toward all minorities than students did decades ago. Figure 11–1 shows that the average (mean) score on the social distance scale declined from 2.14 in 1925 to 1.93 in 1977 to 1.44 in 2001. Respondents (81 percent of whom were white) showed notably greater acceptance of African Americans, a category of people that moved

up from near the bottom in 1925 to the top one-third in 2001.

2. People see less difference among various minorities. The earliest studies found the difference between the highest- and lowest-ranked minorities equal to almost three points on the scale. As the figure shows, the most

STUDENT SNAPSHOT

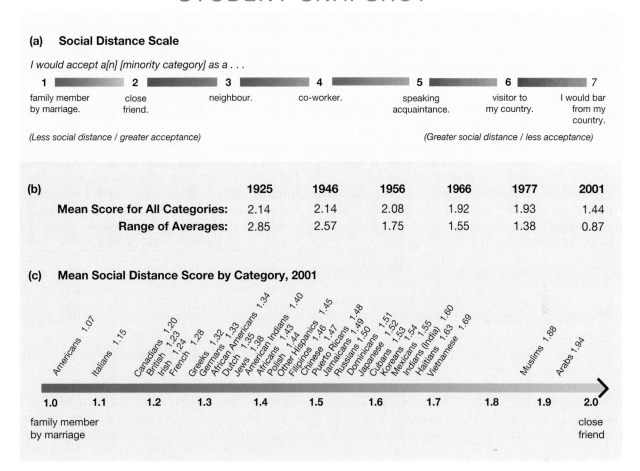

(a) Social Distance Scale

I would accept a[n] [minority category] as a . . .

1	2	3	4	5	6	7
family member by marriage.	close friend.	neighbour.	co-worker.	speaking acquaintance.	visitor to my country.	I would bar from my country.

(Less social distance / greater acceptance)   *(Greater social distance / less acceptance)*

(b)

	1925	1946	1956	1966	1977	2001
Mean Score for All Categories:	2.14	2.14	2.08	1.92	1.93	1.44
Range of Averages:	2.85	2.57	1.75	1.55	1.38	0.87

(c) Mean Social Distance Score by Category, 2001

Americans 1.07, Italians 1.15, Canadians 1.20, British 1.23, Irish 1.24, French 1.28, Greeks 1.32, Germans 1.33, African Americans 1.34, Dutch 1.35, Jews 1.38, American Indians 1.40, Polish 1.43, Other Hispanics 1.44, Filipinos 1.45, Chinese 1.46, Puerto Ricans 1.47, Jamaicans 1.48, Russians 1.49, Dominicans 1.50, Japanese 1.51, Cubans 1.52, Koreans 1.53, Mexicans 1.54, Indians (India) 1.55, Haitians 1.60, Vietnamese 1.63, ... , Muslims 1.88, Arabs 1.94

1.0 1.1 1.2 1.3 1.4 1.5 1.6 1.7 1.8 1.9 2.0

family member by marriage   close friend

FIGURE 11-1 Bogardus Social Distance Research

Source: Parrillo (2003b).

---

recent research produced a range of averages of less than one point.

3. The terror attacks of September 11, 2001, may have reduced social acceptance of Arabs and Muslims. The most recent study was conducted just a few weeks after September 11, 2001. Perhaps the fact that the 19 men who attacked the World Trade Center and the Pentagon were Arabs and Muslims is part of the reason that students ranked these categories last on the social distance scale. However, not a single student gave Arabs or Muslims a 7, indicating that they should be barred from the country. On the contrary, the 2001 scores (1.94 for Arabs and 1.88 for Muslims) show higher social acceptance than students in 1977 expressed toward 18 of the 30 categories of people.

RACISM

A powerful and destructive form of prejudice, **racism** is *the belief that one racial category is innately superior or inferior to another.* Racism has existed throughout world history. Despite their many achievements, the ancient Greeks, the peoples of India, and the Chinese were all quick to consider people unlike themselves inferior.

Racism can give rise to hate crimes. Read how the Canadian *Criminal Code* defines hate crimes, at **http://laws.justice.gc.ca/en/ c-46/41491.html**.

Canadian historical records also contain racism: we should not forget that Canada has a long history of oppression. The practice of slavery is recorded among many of the fishing communities of the Pacific Northwest coast predating European contact

(Donald, 1997). Racism was also practised in British North America prior to Canadian Confederation, and officially ended only in 1834 (Brand, 1992; Ponting, 1994; Prentice et al., 1996). More recently, evidence has been found of the interplay between racism, sexism, and immigration in our country (Ng, 1993; Ng & Das Gupta, 1993; Iacovetta, 1995).

 The Canadian Race Relations Foundation has articles and statistics about racism in Canada at **http://www.crr.ca.**

Further, racism—in thought and deed—remains a serious social problem everywhere as people still contend that some social categories of people are "better" than others (Henry et al., 1995). Indeed, some people wonder if members of one race are smarter than those of another. The Applying Sociology box explains, however, that racial differences in mental abilities result from environment rather than biology.

THEORIES OF PREJUDICE

Where does prejudice come from? Social scientists provide several answers to this vexing question, focusing on frustration, personality, culture, and social conflict.

Scapegoat theory. *Scapegoat theory* holds that prejudice springs from frustration among people who are themselves disadvantaged (Dollard, 1939). Take the case of a white woman who is frustrated by her low-paying job in a textile factory. Directing her hostility at the powerful factory owners carries the obvious risk of being fired; therefore, she may blame her low pay on the presence of minority co-workers. Her prejudice does not improve her situation, but it is a relatively safe way to express anger, and it may give her the comforting feeling that at least she is superior to someone.

A **scapegoat**, then, is *a person or category of people, typically with little power, whom people unfairly blame for their own troubles.* Because they are usually "safe targets," minorities often are used as scapegoats.

Authoritarian personality theory. Theodor Adorno and others (Adorno et al., 1950) considered extreme prejudice a personality trait of certain individuals. This conclusion is supported by research indicating that people who show strong prejudice toward one minority usually are intolerant of all minorities. These *authoritarian personalities* rigidly conform to conventional cultural values, see moral issues as clear-cut matters of right and wrong, and look upon society as naturally competitive with "better" people (like themselves) dominating those who are weaker (including all minorities).

Adorno also found that people tolerant toward one minority are likely to be accepting of all. They tend to be more flexible in their moral judgments and treat all people as equals.

Adorno thought that people with little education and those raised by cold and demanding parents tend to develop authoritarian personalities. Filled with anger and anxiety as children, they grow into hostile and aggressive adults, seeking scapegoats whom they consider inferior.

Culture theory. A third theory claims that although extreme prejudice is found in certain people, some prejudice is found in everyone. Why? Because prejudice is rooted in culture, as the Bogardus social distance studies illustrate. Bogardus found that students across the country had mostly the same attitudes toward specific racial and ethnic categories, feeling closer to some and more distant from others.

Finally, we know that prejudice is rooted in culture because minorities tend to express the same attitudes as white people toward categories other than their own. Such patterns suggest that individuals hold prejudices because we live in a "culture of prejudice" that has taught us to view certain categories of people as "better" or "worse" than others.

Conflict theory. A fourth explanation proposes that prejudice is used as a tool by powerful people to oppress others. Anglos who look down on Latino immigrants, for example, can get away with paying the immigrants low wages for hard work. Similarly, all elites benefit when prejudice divides workers along racial and ethnic lines and discourages them from working together to advance their common interests (Geschwender, 1978; Olzak, 1989).

According to another conflict-based argument, made by Shelby Steele (1990), minorities themselves encourage *race consciousness* to win greater power and privileges. Because of their historic disadvantage, minorities claim that they are victims entitled to special consideration based on their race. Although this strategy may bring short-term gains, Steele cautions that such thinking often sparks a backlash from whites or others who oppose "special treatment" on the basis of race or ethnicity.

DISCRIMINATION

Closely related to prejudice is **discrimination**, *treating various categories of people unequally.* Whereas prejudice refers to attitudes, discrimination is a matter of *action*. Like prejudice, discrimination can be either positive (providing special advantages) or negative (creating obstacles), and ranges from subtle to blatant.

Does Race Affect Intelligence?

Are Asians smarter than white people? Is the typical white person more intelligent than the average black person? Throughout the history of Canada, we have painted one category of people as intellectually more gifted than another. Moreover, people have used such thinking to justify the privileges of the allegedly superior category and even to bar supposedly inferior people from entering this country.

Scientists know that the distribution of the intelligence of individuals forms a bell-shaped curve, as shown in the figure below. By convention, average performance is defined as an *intelligence quotient* (IQ) score of 100 (technically, an IQ score is mental age as measured by a test divided by age in years, with the result multiplied by 100; thus, an eight-year-old who performs like a ten-year-old has an IQ of $10/8 = 1.25 \times 100 = 125$).

In a controversial study of intelligence and social inequality, Richard Herrnstein and Charles Murray (1994) claim that overwhelming evidence shows that race is related to measures of intelligence. More specifically, they say the average IQ of people with European ancestry is 100, the average for people of East Asian ancestry is 103, and for people of African descent, the average is 90. A University of Western Ontario psychology professor, Philippe Rushton, made a similar claim in developing his "race hierarchy" scale, which has the Chinese at the apex of the racial hierarchy, white people in the middle, and blacks at the bottom (Rushton & Bogaert, 1987).

Of course, assertions of this kind are explosive because they fly in the face of our democratic and egalitarian sentiments, which say that no racial type is inherently better than another. Such assertions have led some critics to charge that intelligence tests are not valid and even that the con-

cept of intelligence has little real meaning.

Most social scientists acknowledge that IQ tests do measure something important that we think of as intelligence, and they agree that some *individuals* vary in intellectual aptitude. But they reject the notion that any *category* of people, on average, is smarter than any other. Research does show that categories of people display small differences in measured intelligence, but the crucial question is why.

Thomas Sowell explains that most of the documented differences in intelligence result not from biology but from environment. In some skillful sociological detective work, Sowell traced IQ scores for various racial and ethnic categories throughout the twentieth century. He found that, on average, early twentieth-century immigrants to North America from European nations such as Poland, Lithuania, Italy, and Greece, as well as Asian countries including China and Japan, scored 10 to 15 points below the U.S. average, but by the end of the twentieth century, people in these same categories had IQ scores that were average or above average. Among Italian Americans, for example, average IQ jumped almost 10 points; among Polish and Chinese Americans, the increase was almost 20 points.

Because genetic changes occur over thousands of years and most people in the various categories married others

like themselves, biological factors cannot explain such a rapid rise in IQ scores. The only plausible explanation is changing cultural patterns. The descendants of early immigrants improved their intellectual performance as their standard of living rose and their opportunity for schooling increased.

Sowell found that a similar pattern applies to African Americans. Historically, the average IQ score of African Americans living in the North has been about 10 points higher than the average score of those living in the South. Furthermore, among the descendants of African Americans who migrated from the South to the North after 1940, IQ scores went up just as they did with descendants of earlier immigrants. Thus, if environmental factors are the same for various categories of people, racial IQ differences largely disappear.

What these test score differences do tell is that *cultural patterns* matter, Sowell continues. Asians who score highly on tests are no smarter than other people, but they have been raised to value learning and pursue excellence. For their part, African Americans are no less intelligent than anyone else, but they carry a legacy of disadvantage that can undermine self-confidence and discourage achievement.

WHAT DO YOU THINK?

1. If IQ scores and other measures of intelligence always reflect people's environment, to what extent are they valid measures? In what ways are they harmful?
2. Why, according to Thomas Sowell, do some racial and ethnic categories show dramatic, short-term changes in average IQ scores?
3. What could schools do to raise the IQ scores of children, especially those from disadvantaged backgrounds?

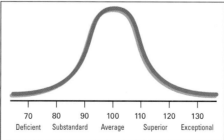

IQ: The Distribution of Intelligence

Sources: Herrnstein and Murray (1994); Sowell (1994, 1995).

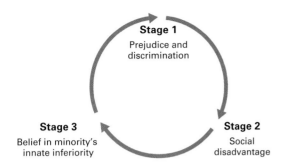

Stage 1: Prejudice and discrimination begin, often as an expression of ethnocentrism or an attempt to justify economic exploitation.

Stage 2: As a result of prejudice and discrimination, a minority is socially disadvantaged, occupying a low position in the system of social stratification.

Stage 3: This social disadvantage is then interpreted not as the result of earlier prejudice and discrimination but as evidence that the minority is innately inferior, unleashing renewed prejudice and discrimination by which the cycle repeats itself.

FIGURE 11-2 Prejudice and Discrimination: The Vicious Self-Perpetuating Circle

Prejudice and discrimination can form a vicious circle, perpetuating themselves.

INSTITUTIONAL PREJUDICE AND DISCRIMINATION

We typically think of prejudice and discrimination as the hateful ideas or actions of specific people. But Stokely Carmichael and Charles Hamilton (1967) pointed out that far greater harm results from **institutional prejudice and discrimination**, *bias built into the operation of society's institutions*, including schools, hospitals, the police, and the workplace. For example, researchers have shown that banks reject home mortgage applications from minorities at a higher rate than those from white people, even when income and quality of neighbourhood are held constant (Gotham, 1998).

Canada has its own forms of institutional discrimination, as shown by the previously mentioned *Indian Act* and its harsh rules toward Aboriginal people (Jamieson, 1986; Ponting & Kiely, 1997). The Act specifically discriminated against Aboriginal women. If a Status Indian woman married a non–Status Indian man, she lost her legal status and was denied rights and benefits under the *Indian Act*. This meant that many women and children of subsequent generations were culturally alienated from their traditional communities. According to Jeffries (1992:92-3),

The government's treatment of women under the *Indian Act* was particularly devastating and tantamount to cultural genocide, because women were responsible for maintaining culture. If a woman chose to marry a non-Indian man, she was removed from the government's list of registered Indians . . . Upon marriage, the woman could no longer live in the community in which she was born, nor could she participate in any matters respecting the community. The final insult was upon death: neither she nor any of her children could be buried in a family plot on band land.

With the passage of *Bill C-31* in 1985, this patriarchal principle was finally revoked. Yet Aboriginal women's access to land and housing remains problematic to this day (Benoit & Carroll, 1995). Since provincial divorce laws do not hold on reserves, Aboriginal women are at risk of losing all common property after separation or divorce.

PREJUDICE AND DISCRIMINATION: THE VICIOUS CIRCLE

Prejudice and discrimination reinforce each other. The Thomas theorem, discussed in Chapter 4 ("Social Interaction in Everyday Life"), offers a simple explanation of this fact: *Situations that are defined as real become real in their consequences* (Thomas, 1966:301, orig. 1931).

As Thomas recognized, stereotypes become real to people who believe them, sometimes even to those victimized by them. For example, prejudice toward Aboriginals, for example, does not produce *innate* inferiority, but it can produce *social* inferiority, pushing Aboriginals into low-paying jobs, inferior schools, and racially segregated housing. Then, as non-Aboriginals see social disadvantage as evidence that Aboriginals are inferior, they unleash a new round of prejudice and discrimination, creating a vicious circle in which each perpetuates the other, as shown in Figure 11–2.

Majority and Minority: Patterns of Interaction

Social scientists describe interaction between majority and minority members of a society in terms of four models: pluralism, assimilation, segregation, and genocide.

PLURALISM

Pluralism is *a state in which people of all races and ethnicities are distinct but have equal social standing*. In other words, people who differ in appearance or social heritage all share resources roughly equally.

Canada is pluralistic to the extent that all people have equal standing under the law. In addition, large cities contain countless "ethnic villages" where people proudly display the traditions of their immigrant ancestors. These include Chinatowns found in Victoria, Vancouver, and Toronto; the Jewish area around Avenue du Parc in Montreal; and the Portuguese neighbourhoods around Dundas Street West in Toronto.

But Canada is not really pluralistic, for three reasons. First, although many people appreciate their cultural heritage, only a small proportion want to live with others exactly like themselves (NORC, 2003). Second, our tolerance for social diversity goes only so far. One reaction to the growing proportion of minorities in Canada, for example, is the rise of white supremacist groups in many Canadian cities. Third, as we shall see later in this chapter, it is simply a fact that people of various colours and cultures have unequal social standing.

ASSIMILATION

Many people traditionally have viewed Canada as a "mosaic" in which disparate cultural groups join together to create a tolerant and peaceful multicultural society. Rather than everyone joining as equals in some new cultural pattern, however, minorities typically adopt the traits of the dominant culture established by the earliest settlers. Why? As an avenue to upward social mobility and to escape the prejudice and discrimination directed against more visible foreigners. Sociologists use the term **assimilation** to describe *the process by which minorities gradually adopt patterns of the dominant culture*. Assimilation involves changing styles of dress, values, religion, language, and friends.

The amount of assimilation varies by category. For example, Swedes have "melted" more than Italians, the Dutch more than Dominicans, Germans more than the Japanese. Multiculturalists oppose making assimilation a goal, because it suggests that minorities are "the problem" and defines them (rather than majority people) as the ones who need to do all the changing.

Note that assimilation involves changes in ethnicity but not in race. For example, many descendants of Japanese immigrants have discarded their ethnic traditions but retain their racial identity. In order for racial traits to diminish over generations, **miscegenation**, or *biological reproduction by partners of different racial categories*, must occur. Although interracial marriage is becoming more common, it still amounts to only a small percentage of all marriages.

SEGREGATION

Segregation is *the physical and social separation of categories of people*. Sometimes minorities, especially religious orders

Most Canadian cities today have distinct ethnic enclaves. Some people see this as a positive trend, arguing that it validates the uniqueness of ethnic cultures. Others argue the opposite, viewing ethnic enclaves as indicative of the ghettoization of marginalized groups in our society.

such as the Amish, voluntarily segregate themselves from the larger world by forming their own isolated communities. However, majorities usually segregate minorities by excluding them. Figure 11–3 illustrates that people in Canada are less likely than people in many other countries to feel that they would not like to have people of a different race as neighbours. Neighbourhoods, schools, occupations, hospitals, and even cemeteries can be segregated. Whereas pluralism encourages cultural distinctiveness without disadvantage, segregation enforces separation that harms members of a minority.

Racial segregation also has a long history in Canada, as mentioned above, starting with the segregation of Aboriginal peoples on reserves. Apart from the internment of Japanese Canadians during World War II (Kogawa, 1981; Omatsu, 1992), *de jure* (Latin meaning "by law") discrimination in Canada has been relatively rare, in contrast, for example, with the United States. However, *de facto* ("in fact") segregation continues to this day.

Research by Balakrishnan and Hou (1995) has documented the concentration of different groups in Canada's urban centres. The authors found that visible minorities and Jewish people tend to live in specific areas of a city rather than being dispersed throughout. This contrasts with the British, Germans, and French, who are relatively evenly distributed (the British in Montreal are an exception to this general pattern).

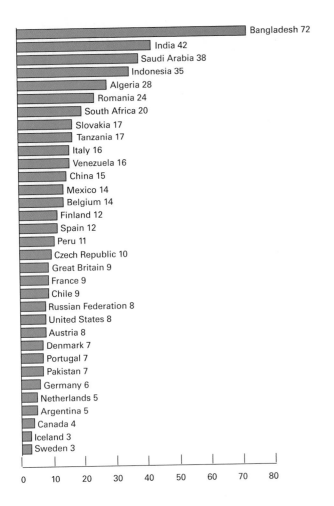

Bangladesh 72
India 42
Saudi Arabia 38
Indonesia 35
Algeria 28
Romania 24
South Africa 20
Slovakia 17
Tanzania 17
Italy 16
Venezuela 16
China 15
Mexico 14
Belgium 14
Finland 12
Spain 12
Peru 11
Czech Republic 10
Great Britain 9
France 9
Chile 9
Russian Federation 8
United States 8
Austria 8
Denmark 7
Portugal 7
Pakistan 7
Germany 6
Netherlands 5
Argentina 5
Canada 4
Iceland 3
Sweden 3

0   10   20   30   40   50   60   70   80

FIGURE 11-3 Percent of People Identifying "People of a Different Race" as a Category Not Wanted as Neighbours, Selected Countries, 1999–2003.

Survey question: "On this list are various groups of people. Could you please sort out any that you would not like to have as neighbours?"

Source: European Values Study Group and World Values Survey Association (2006).

Balakrishnan and Hou also documented the changing nature of residential segregation. First, even though the composition of the immigration stream to Canada has changed in recent decades—a larger proportion of today's immigrants are from Asia—the authors found that the distribution of Asians in urban areas is not changing. Balakrishnan and Hou attributed this to the fact that the selective nature of immigration policy has led to immigrants being highly skilled and therefore not choosing to live in the traditional low-income areas of our cities. Second, the authors pointed out, a certain amount of residential segregation comes from families and individuals choosing to live together rather than being forced into ethnic ghettos. The Jewish population is a case in point. Even though this population is above average in income and education—factors that historically imply freedom of choice—Jews are also among the most segregated ethnic groups in Canada.

GENOCIDE

Genocide is *the systematic killing of one category of people by another.* This deadly form of racism and ethnocentrism violates nearly every recognized moral standard, yet it has occurred time and again in human history.

Genocide was common in the history of contact between Europeans and the original inhabitants of the Americas. From the sixteenth century on, the Spanish, Portuguese, English, French, and Dutch forcibly colonized vast empires. Although most native people died from diseases brought by Europeans, to which they had no natural defences, many were killed deliberately (Matthiessen, 1984; Sale, 1990).

Genocide also occurred in the twentieth century. Unimaginable horror befell European Jews in the 1930s and 1940s during Adolf Hitler's reign of terror, known as the Holocaust. The Nazis murdered more than 6 million Jewish men, women, and children (along with gay people, gypsies, and people with handicaps). The Soviet dictator Josef Stalin murdered on an even greater scale, killing some 30 million real and imagined enemies during his violent rule. Between 1975 and 1980, Pol Pot's Communist regime in Cambodia butchered all "capitalists," which included anyone able to speak a Western language. In all, some 2 million people (one-fourth of the population) perished in the Cambodian "killing fields" (Shawcross, 1979).

Tragically, genocide continues even today. Recent examples include Hutus killing Tutsis in the African nation of Rwanda, and Serbs killing Bosnians in the Balkans of Eastern Europe.

These four patterns of minority–majority contact have all been played out in Canada. Although many people proudly point to patterns of pluralism and assimilation, it is also important to recognize the degree to which Canadian society has been built on segregation from one end of the country to the other (black Canadians in Eastern Canada and Japanese Canadians in British Columbia) and genocide (of Aboriginal Canadians). The remainder of this chapter examines how these four patterns have shaped the past and present social standing of major racial and ethnic categories in Canada.

Race and Ethnicity in Canada

Like all people who have nothing, I lived on dreams. I
burned my way through stone walls to get to America.

Nu, I got to America.

Ten hours I pushed a machine in a shirtwaist factory,
when I was yet lucky to get work.

And always my head was drying up with saving and
pinching and worrying to send home a little from the little
I earned.

Where are my dreams that were so real to me in the
old country?

These words by Jewish immigrant Anzia Yezierska
(quoted in Frager, 1992:10) capture the dreams and subsequent disappointments of many European immigrants who
made the difficult journey across the Atlantic to find work
in the emerging cities of the New World—including "Little
York" (Toronto) in Upper Canada and "Ville-Marie" (Montreal) in Lower Canada. As the following history of Canada's
racial and ethnic minorities reveals, our nation's golden
door has opened more widely for some than for others.

CANADA'S ABORIGINAL PEOPLES

Some 30 000 years before Columbus "discovered" the Americas, migrating peoples crossed a land bridge from Asia to
North America where the Bering Strait (off the coast of
Alaska) lies today. Gradually, they made their way throughout North and South America.

When the first Europeans arrived late in the fifteenth
century, Native Americans numbered in the millions. But by
the beginning of the twentieth century, after relentless sub-
jugation and even acts of genocide, the "vanishing Americans" numbered a mere 250 000 (Dobyns, 1966; Tyler, 1973).

It was Christopher Columbus (1446–1506) who first
referred to Native Americans as "Indians"; when he landed
in the Bahama Islands in the Caribbean, he mistakenly
thought he had reached India. Columbus found the indige-
nous people to be passive and peaceful, in stark contrast
with the more materialistic and competitive Europeans
(Matthiessen, 1984; Sale, 1990). Yet even as Europeans
seized the land of Native Americans, they demeaned their
victims as thieves and murderers to justify their actions
(Unruh, 1979; Josephy, 1982).

At the beginning of the eighteenth century there were
about 10 Aboriginal people for every European settler in
Canada; by 1881 there were about 40 Europeans for every
Aboriginal person (Jaffe, 1992). This was not primarily
because of a natural increase of European immigrants,
however. Traders and later settlers to British North America
and New France (later renamed Upper and Lower Canada)
brought with them not only trade items but also racist atti-

There has recently been a resurgence in Aboriginals' pride in their
heritage. Do you think that this resurgence is because of, or
despite, being a minority group?

tudes toward the non-Christian "savages" who resided in
the New World. The Europeans were even prepared to use
their superior military power to subdue any Aboriginal peoples unwilling to be colonized.

Europeans also brought with them deadly diseases.
Smallpox and other epidemic diseases (including measles,
influenza, and tuberculosis) had killed many Europeans in
the previous centuries. However, for the Aboriginal peoples
of the New World, these contagions were "virgin soil epi-
demics," ravaging hitherto unexposed populations without
any built-up immunity to soften the impact (Cohen, 1989).
These "diseases of civilization," along with the ill effects of
adulterated whiskey, reduced the Aboriginal population of
British Columbia, for example, by nearly two-thirds before
the end of the 1800s (Jaffe, 1992). So marginalized were
Canada's Aboriginal peoples that they were not entitled to
vote alongside non-Aboriginal Canadian citizens until
1960.

TABLE 11–2

Aboriginal Population, Canada, 2001

	Total Aboriginal Population	of Total Population	Percentage Geographic Distribution
Canada	976 305	3.3%	100.0%
Newfoundland and Labrador	18 775	3.7%	1.9%
Prince Edward Island	1345	1.0%	0.1%
Nova Scotia	17 010	1.9%	1.7%
New Brunswick	16 990	2.4%	1.7%
Quebec	79 400	1.1%	8.1%
Ontario	188 315	1.7%	19.3%
Manitoba	150 040	13.6%	15.4%
Saskatchewan	130 185	13.5%	13.3%
Alberta	156 220	5.3%	16.0%
British Columbia	170 025	4.4%	17.4%
Yukon Territory	6545	22.9%	0.7%
Northwest Territories	18 730	50.5%	1.9%
Nunavut	22 720	85.2%	2.3%

Source: Statistics Canada (2003bs).

Today, Aboriginal peoples in Canada comprise a diverse and growing population. About 1.3 million persons claimed some Aboriginal ancestry in the 2001 census, up from 1 million in 1991 (Statistics Canada, 2003o, 1998c). Within this large population, about 1 million adopted an Aboriginal identity—that is, they considered themselves Aboriginal persons; this number is expected to grow to about 1.4 million by 2017 (Statistics Canada, 2005). In 2001, the majority identified themselves as "North American Indians," a minority declared themselves to be "Métis," and a smaller number reported "Inuit" ancestry. Table 11–2 shows the geographic distribution of Canada's Aboriginal peoples.

Despite their growing number, Aboriginal peoples in Canada continue to earn far below the median average income for Canadians. Aboriginal peoples also are more likely to live in single-parent families, and they record higher rates of unemployment and have lower rates of school attendance. Their health status is also bleak when compared with that of the country's non-Aboriginal population. Aboriginal peoples have higher tuberculosis and suicide rates, and much shorter life expectancies, than their non-Aboriginal counterparts (Statistics Canada, 1995b).

Like other racial and ethnic minorities in Canada, Aboriginal peoples have recently reasserted pride in their cultural heritage. Some are finally resolving negotiations over territorial lands. Yet, as discussed in the Controversy & Debate box, not all Canadians are comfortable with special rights for Aboriginal groups, such as the Nisga'a of British Columbia.

BRITISH CANADIANS

British Canadians—sometimes referred to as White Anglo-Saxon Protestants (WASPs)—were not the first people to inhabit Canada, but they came to dominate this nation once European settlement began. Most British Canadians are of English descent, but this category also includes Scots, Welsh, and Irish. On the 2001 census, 2.6 million, or 9 percent of the national population, claimed British ancestry only and another 7.3 million Canadians claimed British as one of their ancestries (Statistics Canada, 2003s).

Historically, British immigrants were highly skilled and motivated by what we now call the "Protestant work ethic." Because of their number and power, British Canadians (with the possible exception of the Irish Catholics) were not subject to the prejudice and discrimination experienced by other categories of immigrants. The historical dominance of British Canadians has been so great that, as noted earlier, others have sought to become more like them.

And the British cultural legacy still stands: English remained, until recent decades, Canada's only official language, and it still dominates the country's media and electronic communication systems. The Canadian legal and political systems, too, reflect their British origins.

FRENCH CANADIANS

The French explorers arrived in Canada in the sixteenth century, initially involving themselves in fishing and fur trading. Eventually more French immigrated in search of a better life in "New France." By 1760, there were about 70 000 inhabitants of the colony, with approximately the same number of women as men (Prentice et al., 1996:37). When Acadia (now Nova Scotia) passed from French to British hands in 1713, men and women from that region were either deported to France or resettled in the northeastern regions of what was then "British North America." In the aftermath of the Seven Years' War (1756–1763), Canada fell under British colonial rule. Though the French retained some control over their own language, religion, and legal institutions, English Canada gained control over economic, political, and social matters.

To some extent, this remains the case even today. The historical legacy of the "two solitudes"—French and English—joined in an uneasy political union resulted in the so-called Quiet Revolution of the 1960s in Quebec. At its most intense, the Quiet Revolution involved the use of radical

CONTROVERSY & DEBATE

Should Certain Groups in Canada Enjoy Special Rights?

July 23, 1998, marked the conclusion to treaty negotiations among the federal government, the provincial government of British Columbia, and the Nisga'a people of the Nass Valley in Northwestern BC. Listed below are the highlights of the treaty, which involves sums estimated to reach $448 million. Among the gains for the Nisga'a is the right to elect their own government, with authority to make laws in several key provincial jurisdictions, including those regarding land use, culture, and employment.

Such "special rights" accompanying the groundbreaking treaty (which, it is worth noting, had been pursued by the Nisga'a people for six generations) ignited a heated debate in the province, as well as across the country. People questioned whether any group—Aboriginal or otherwise—should have legal rights that are different from those of other Canadian citizens. Some critics of the deal argued that it entrenches inequality in Canadian society and called for a province-wide referendum to let the public decide whether the treaty should become law. Others, sympathetic to the Nisga'a people's historical struggle, welcomed the agreement as a compromise that was finally acceptable to the Nisga'a. Such a compromise, argued proponents, would allow the Nisga'a to get on with tackling the high unemployment and other problems affecting their people. Supporters pointed out as well that the Nisga'a had given up other (similarly special) rights they previously held under the *Indian Act*.

Highlights of Nisga'a Treaty

Land. The Nisga'a receive 1930 square kilometres of Crown land and title to 62 square kilometres of land currently designated as Indian reserves. Nisga'a lands do not include private property held by non-Natives or agricultural leases. Provincial laws continue to apply to several parcels of land owned by non-Natives that will be surrounded by Nisga'a lands.

Self-government. Elections for a central Nisga'a government and four village governments must be held no later than six months after the treaty comes into force. Only Nisga'a can vote for the Nisga'a government, which will adopt a constitution recognizing the rights and freedoms of its citizens.

The Nisga'a government can make laws on Nisga'a citizenship, language, culture, property, public order, safety, employment, traffic, child and family services, health services, policing, and correctional and court services.

Non-Nisga'a Canadians can participate in elected bodies that directly affect them by making representations and seeking elections to public agencies such as the health board. Local laws affecting everything from traffic to garbage collection will apply to non-Nisga'a within Nisga'a lands, but most laws will apply only to Nisga'a citizens.

Nisga'a continue to be Aboriginal peoples under the Constitution and are entitled to the same rights as other Canadian citizens. The *Charter of Rights and Freedoms* and all federal and provincial laws continue to apply to Nisga'a people. However, Nisga'a people will no longer be exempt from sales and income taxes.

Resources. Ownership of all forests within Nisga'a lands, and all mineral, oil, and other subsurface resources, will be transferred to the Nisga'a, who can set conditions for their use. Current forest licences will remain in effect for five years. Nisga'a management standards must meet or exceed provincial standards.

Public access to Nisga'a lands for hunting, fishing, and recreation will be provided, although the Nisga'a government may make laws regulating public access for public safety or environmental reasons.

Nisga'a people will be guaranteed 26 percent of the Nass River allowable catch for salmon, and will be allowed to sell their salmon. Any federal commercial or recreational ban on fishing will also apply to the Nisga'a.

Key geographic features will be renamed with Nisga'a names and important cultural sites will be designated as heritage sites. The treaty states that it is the final settlement of Nisga'a Aboriginal rights.

CONTINUE THE DEBATE . . .

1. What is your interpretation of the Nisga'a treaty? Is it right that the treaty bestows special rights on a group of people?
2. Should other Aboriginal groups in Canada also be able to claim "special legal rights" to the land and resources of their forebears? Why or why not?
3. How can sociology play a part in understanding this and other debates over Aboriginal land claims?

Source: Excerpted from Matas and McInnes (1998).

terrorism as a political weapon against the English (Rocher, 1990). And though the province has undergone substantial change in subsequent decades, in many respects French Quebec and English Canada can still be said to be "two nations warring in the bosom of the same state" (Guindon, 1990:30).

In the 2001 census, about 1 million people, or 3.6 percent of the national population, identified themselves as

The Quebec language law—*Bill 101*—was upheld in April 2000, when the Quebec superior court ruled that French had to be the predominant language on commercial signs. A spray can quickly changes the familiar stop sign into a political message.

French immersion school programs, and the civil service has become increasingly staffed with bilingual francophones. Yet many issues remain unresolved regarding the future of Quebec or, indeed, of French Canadians in Canada. These issues include the "French-only" sign law, the requirement that new immigrants to the province educate their children in French, and the insistence that the lands claimed by the Aboriginal peoples of the province's North be included in the territory proposed for a sovereign Quebec.

CANADA'S OTHER IMMIGRANTS

As previously noted, Canada is a country of founding peoples, but also of immigrants. Four distinct historical eras can be distinguished when investigating international migration to the country (Gee, 1990). As mentioned above, the French were the original immigrants to the part of the New World that was later to be called "Canada." The French immigrants eventually established the colony of New France between 1608 and 1760. During the nineteenth century, a new wave of immigrants came, mainly from Britain, in two population flows: the United Empire Loyalists came from the American colonies, fleeing the American independence movement; and immigrants came directly from the British Isles. Smaller numbers of other Europeans also immigrated to Canada during this time, including Germans, Scandinavians, and Eastern Europeans.

The last decades of the nineteenth century and the first decades of the early twentieth century saw the arrival of the largest wave of immigrants to the country up to that point. Their numbers ranged from 3.7 to 4.6 million (Kalbach & McVey, 1979). Among them were 15 000 Chinese who were permitted to come to Canada as a cheap source of labour for the construction of the transcontinental railroad. Between 1886 and 1923, Canada barred all Asians from settling permanently in the country and imposed a "head tax" on all Chinese wishing to immigrate. The initial head tax was $50, later $100, and finally, in 1904, $500, a very large sum indeed at the time. The head tax on Chinese immigrants was not lifted until 1947. Everyone seemed to line up against the Chinese, as captured in a popular phrase of the time that a person "didn't have a Chinaman's chance" (Sung, 1967).

The head tax and generally racist attitude of many Canadians toward the Chinese created domestic hardship, because in Canada (and similarly in the U.S.) Chinese men outnumbered Chinese women (Hsu, 1971; Lai, 1980; Prentice et al., 1996). For the relatively few Chinese women who managed to enter the country, the situation was far from friendly. Below, a woman of Chinese background recalls her life in Nanaimo, British Columbia, in the early decades of this century:

having French-only ancestry; 22 000 of these people identified themselves as Acadian. In total, 4.7 million Canadians claimed at least partial French ancestry.

Unlike the economy of earlier times when English merchants and traders were in control, the Quebec economy today is mainly under the control of francophone entrepreneurs. Politics has also changed significantly. During the 1990s, two French political parties controlled the majority of seats in the province, with the Parti Québécois holding power in the Quebec Legislature (the National Assembly) and a new separatist party—the Bloc Québécois—leading the separatist cause at the federal level for a while as the official opposition. The razor-thin defeat of the separatists in the Quebec referendum of 1995 (by a mere 1 percent of the vote) opened the eyes of other Canadians to the very real possibility of the break-up of the country. Since then, however, the separatist parties have suffered setbacks both at the provincial and federal levels.

During Canada's 39th general election held on January 23rd, 2006, the Bloc Québécois lost support. Although it captured 51 of the province's 75 seats (only three fewer than in 2004), its share of the vote declined from 49 percent in 2004 to 42 percent, as a sizable group of Quebecers rallied late in the campaign to the surging Conservatives who won a minority government in Parliament.

Meanwhile, many English-speaking Canadian parents have, in the past few decades, enrolled their children in

On December 7, 1941, Japan attacked Pearl Harbor and Hong Kong. Just weeks later, the Canadian federal government, under the *War Measures Act*, demanded the evacuation of all Japanese Canadians residing within about 160 kilometres of the Pacific Coast. Although apparently relocated for reasons of national security, no Japanese Canadian was ever charged with disloyalty to the country. In all, 20 000 men, women, and children of Japanese descent were forced to leave their homes for camps in the interior of British Columbia and farms in Alberta and Manitoba.

Source: William Lyon Mackenzie King Collection/National Archives of Canada/C-24452.

> When I went to school in Nanaimo in the 1920s we had to go to a segregated school. In those days there was still segregation for the "Others." We had to go to a special school because we were not white … We had to walk past the better schools, which were only for the white people or westerners, to go to this "ward" school that housed all the Indians, the ethnic people, or "Others" (quoted in Yee, 1992:235–6).

With the relaxation of Canadian immigration laws after 1947, and the more open immigration polices of recent decades, Chinese immigrants to Canada have received a warmer, if not wholehearted, welcome.

The Chinese were not the only immigrants to enter the country during the early part of the twentieth century, however. Many immigrants came from the United States, some from Britain and other parts of Europe, and others from as far away as India.

The last wave of immigrants to Canada arrived in the post–World War II period—more than 5 million of them—many from middle- and low-income countries around the globe. Canada does not have a quota system in place regarding how many immigrants may enter the country annually. The current regulations emphasize "economic immigra-

TABLE 11-3
Visible Minorities in Canada, 2001

	Individuals	Percentage
Total visible minority population	3 983 845	100.0%
Chinese	1 029 395	25.8%
South Asian	917 075	23.0%
Black	662 210	16.6%
Filipino	308 575	7.7%
Latin American	216 975	5.4%
Southeast Asian	198 875	5.0%
Arab	194 680	4.9%
West Asian	109 285	2.7%
Korean	100 660	2.5%
Japanese	73 320	1.8%
Visible minority, n.i.e.[1]	98 920	2.5%
Multiple visible minorities	73 870	1.9%

[1]Includes Pacific Islanders and other visible minority groups (n.i.e. = not included elsewhere)

Source: Statistics Canada (2003bs).

tion"—that is, the preferred immigrants ideally possess the particular skills and disposable capital to establish themselves economically after migration.

The 2001 census showed that almost 5.6 million people in Canada—that is, 19 percent of the population—were born outside Canada. The top four birthplaces named in 2001 were the United Kingdom, China, India, and Italy. Together these four origins accounted for 28 percent of all immigrants (Statistics Canada, 2003bj). The composition of the immigration stream is changing substantially. Among immigrants who have arrived since 1980, there are only two European origins that make the top-10 list—Poland in fifth position and the United Kingdom in eighth. With the exception of the U.S. (ninth position) and the European part of the former USSR (tenth), the remaining top-10 positions are all of Asian origin (Statistics Canada, 2003bj).

In fact, over 70 percent of the immigrant population since 1981 are members of a visible minority group. It is to this category that we now turn.

VISIBLE MINORITIES

The Canadian *Employment Equity Act* defines visible minorities as "persons, other than Aboriginal peoples, who are non-Caucasian in race or non-white in colour." As shown in Table 11-3, based on this definition the following ethnic groups are designated as visible minorities in Canada: Chinese, South Asians, blacks, Arabs and West Asians, Filipinos,

Although sometimes portrayed as a successful "model minority," Canadians with Asian ancestry are highly diverse and, like other categories of people, include both rich and poor. These young people contend with many of the same patterns of prejudice and discrimination familiar to members of other minorities.

TABLE 11–4

Average Employment Income, Visible Minorities and All Canadians, by Gender and Age Groups, 2000

Persons Aged	Visible Minorities		All Canadians	
	Women	Men	Women	Men
15–24	$20 707	$22 394	$19 634	$23 696
25–44	$32 462	$41 638	$35 048	$47 611
45–64	$33 664	$46 626	$37 407	$55 754
65 and over	$23 663	$41 568	$28 171	$44 661
All over 14	$32 143	$42 377	$34 892	$49 224

Note: Includes only those aged 15 and over employed full-time, full-year.

Source: Statistics Canada (2003ah).

Southeast Asians, Latin Americans, Japanese, Koreans, and Pacific Islanders. These visible minorities comprise about 4 million people, representing 13.4 percent of the total population. According to the 2001 census, almost one in three visible minority persons was born in Canada. As with the Chinese immigrants who came a century earlier, Canada's visible minorities tend to live in the larger metropolitan areas, with three-quarters of visible minorities residing in just the three largest cities—Toronto, Montreal, and Vancouver—where in total 29 percent of the Canadian population lives. National Map 11–1 on page 286 shows that there are only a few areas outside of these three centres where visible minorities make up a substantial proportion of the population.

You can read the *Employment Equity Act* at the Justice Department website: http://laws.justice.gc.ca/en/ E-5.401/238505.html.

Even as the concentration of visible minorities in our three largest urban areas is predicted to remain at 75 percent, the proportions of the populations within these cities are expected to change dramatically over the next decade. By 2017, the majority of the populations of Toronto and Vancouver are expected to be members of a visible minority (Belanger & Malenfant, 2005)

It is clear that the total integration of visible minorities into Canadian society is not complete, since visible minorities are more likely to hold university degrees yet all visible minority groups (except women aged 15–24) have lower average incomes than the averages for all Canadians. As indicated in Table 11–4, and as we discussed in detail in Chapter 10 ("Gender Stratification"), gender is another kind of minority status that deepens our understanding of the Canadian mosaic. Yet, the educational aspirations of visible minority students are consistently higher than those of other students. The differences between visible minority and non-visible minority students are particularly strong in the face of adversity, when parents have low income and no post-secondary education (Taylor & Krahn, 2005).

Race and Ethnicity: Looking Ahead

Canada has been, and will remain, a land of immigrants. Immigration has brought striking cultural diversity and tales of success, hope, and struggle told in hundreds of languages.

For immigrants who came to this country during the second wave of immigration that peaked about 1910, the next generations brought gradual economic gains and at least some cultural assimilation. The government also granted basic freedoms that earlier had been denied, including citizenship and the right to vote and hold public office.

A third wave of immigration began after World War II, and swelled as immigration laws were relaxed in the 1960s. Since 1990, more than 225 000 people have come to Canada each year on average, twice the number that arrived during the "Great Immigration" a century ago (although newcomers now enter a country with a much larger population). Most contemporary immigrants come not from Europe but from middle- and low-income countries.

Many new arrivals face much the same prejudice and discrimination that were directed toward the country's Aboriginal peoples, as well as toward earlier generations of immigrants. Indeed, recent years have witnessed rising hostility toward foreigners (sometimes called xenophobia, a word with Greek roots meaning "fear of what is strange"). This is especially the case in the United States, where, in 1994, California voters passed *Proposition 187*, which mandates a cut-off in social services (including schooling) to illegal immigrants. The rise of neo-Nazi groups in Canada in the 1990s, and indeed across many high-income countries, suggests that the U.S. is not alone in its fears of foreigners.

Even so, like Canada's Aboriginal peoples, who are enjoying a cultural revival, many new immigrants now try to join Canadian society while maintaining their traditional cultures. Some have also built racial and ethnic enclaves to keep their ethnic traditions and celebrations alive for the next generation. Others have been more open to joining the Canadian mainstream, adhering to the traditional hope of their predecessors—that racial and ethnic diversity, while a dimension of difference, will not be viewed as a badge of inferiority.

SUMMARY

1. Races are socially constructed categories by which societies set apart people with various physical traits. Although a century ago scientists assigned people to one of three broad categories—Caucasoids, Negroids, and Mongoloids—there are no pure races.

2. Ethnicity is based not on biology but on shared cultural heritage.

3. Minorities, including people of certain races and ethnicities, are categories of people society sets apart, making them both distinct and disadvantaged.

4. Prejudice is a rigid and unfair generalization about a category of people. Racism, a destructive type of prejudice, asserts that one race is innately superior or inferior to another.

5. Discrimination is a pattern of action by which a person treats various categories of people unequally.

6. Pluralism means that racial and ethnic categories, although distinct, have equal social standing. Assimilation is a process by which minorities gradually adopt the patterns of the dominant culture. Segregation is the physical and social separation of categories of people. Genocide is the extermination of a category of people.

7. Native Americans—the earliest human inhabitants of the Americas—have endured genocide, segregation, and forced assimilation. Native Americans in Canada are usually referred to as "Aboriginal peoples" and include Native Indians, Métis, and Inuit. Today, Aboriginal peoples have social standing well below the national average.

8. WASPs predominated among the original European settlers of Canada, and many continue to enjoy high social standing today.

9. The French group includes both French-only ancestry and Acadians. Though the French were the first to colonize Canada, they subsequently fell under the control of British Canadians. Many French Canadians still express the desire to establish their own separate nation.

10. Canada is a country of Aboriginal peoples, the descendants of two colonial powers, and a diversity of other immigrants. Chinese and Japanese immigrants historically have suffered both racial and ethnic discrimination.

11. Chinese and Japanese immigrants in Canada are categorized as "visible minorities"—that is, persons, other than Aboriginal peoples, who are non-Caucasian in race or non-white in colour. Based on this definition, the following ethnic groups are designated as visible minorities in Canada: Chinese and South Asians, blacks, Arabs and West Asians, Filipinos,

Southeast Asians, Latin Americans, Japanese, Koreans, and Pacific Islanders.

12. The Canadian vertical mosaic also includes immigrants of other European ancestries: Germans, Scandinavians, and Eastern Europeans.

13. Immigration has increased in recent years. No longer primarily from Europe, most immigrants now arrive from Latin America and Asia.

KEY CONCEPTS

assimilation (p. 293) the process by which minorities gradually adopt patterns of the dominant culture

discrimination (p. 291) treating various categories of people unequally

ethnicity (p. 284) a shared cultural heritage

genocide (p. 294) the systematic killing of one category of people by another

institutional prejudice and discrimination (p. 292) bias built into the operation of society's institutions

minority (p. 285) any category of people distinguished by physical or cultural difference that a society sets apart and subordinates

miscegenation (p. 293) biological reproduction by partners of different racial categories

pluralism (p. 292) a state in which people of all races and ethnicities are distinct but have equal social standing

prejudice (p. 286) a rigid and unfair generalization about an entire category of people

race (p. 283) a socially constructed category composed of people who share biologically transmitted traits that members of a society consider important

racism (p. 289) the belief that one racial category is innately superior or inferior to another

scapegoat (p. 291) a person or category of people, typically with little power, whom people unfairly blame for their own troubles

segregation (p. 293) the physical and social separation of categories of people

stereotypes (p. 287) exaggerated descriptions applied to every person in some category

CRITICAL-THINKING QUESTIONS

1. What is the difference between race and ethnicity? What does it mean to say that race and ethnicity are socially constructed?

2. Do you think all Aboriginal Canadians, rich or poor, should be considered minorities? Why or why not?

3. Many historians claim the history of Canada is the history of immigrants. Do you agree with this statement? Is it as true today as it was in the past?

4. Many people assume that only white people display prejudice and engage in discrimination. To what extent do minorities exhibit prejudice and discrimination against whites? against other minorities?

APPLICATIONS AND EXERCISES

1. Does your college or university take account of race and ethnicity in its hiring practices? Ask to speak with an equity officer to see what you can learn about your school's use of race and ethnicity in hiring.

2. Give several of your friends or family members a quick quiz, asking them what share of the Canadian population is Aboriginal and in which provinces most Aboriginals live. Also ask about your province (see Table 11–2 on page 296—Aboriginal Population, Canada, 2001). Some research shows that most people will exaggerate the proportion of Aboriginals (Labovitz, 1996). What do you make of the results?

3. Ask immigrants on your campus or in your local community about their homelands and their experiences since arriving in Canada, and compare what you learn from them with what you have read in this chapter.

 ## SITES TO SEE

www.pearsoned.ca/macionis
The authors and publisher of this book invite you to visit the interactive Companion Website™ that accompanies this text. Begin by clicking on the cover of your book. You will find a chapter-by-chapter study guide, practice tests, suggested weblinks, and links to other relevant material.

www.crr.ca
The Canadian Race Relations Foundation was established as part of the 1988 Japanese Redress Agreement between the Canadian government and the National Association of Canadians. The government of Canada admitted to human rights violations during and after World War II.

www.bnaibrith.ca
B'nai Brith Canada has information on Jewish efforts to combat anti-Semitism, bigotry, and racism in Canada.

www.uottawa.ca/hrrec/links/discriminationcan_e.html
The Human Rights Research and Education Centre at the University of Ottawa has research reports and links to legislation and other organizations concerned about human rights in Canada.

 ## INVESTIGATE WITH RESEARCH NAVIGATOR™

Follow the instructions on page 33 of this text to access the features of Research Navigator™. Once at the website (**www.researchnavigator.com**), enter your login name and password.

Then, to use the Content Select™ database, enter keywords such as "race," "ethnicity," and "segregation" and the search engine will supply relevant and recent scholarly and popular press publications.

To reinforce your understanding of this chapter, and to identify topics for further study, visit MySocLab at **www.pearsoned.ca/mysoclab/macionis** for diagnostic tests and a multimedia ebook.

CHAPTER TWELVE

Economics and Politics

What is a social institution?

How does change in the economy reshape society?

Why do some critics say that Canada is not really a democracy?

Economics and politics are two social institutions that affect how wealth and power are distributed throughout a society's population. The expansion of international trade by the World Trade Organization has sparked opposition from some people, who fear it will harm working people living in low-income nations.

Here's a quick quiz about the North American economy. (Hint: All four questions have the same right answer.)

- Which business do over 100 million people in North America alone visit each week?
- Which company, on average, opens a new store every day?
- Which company is the largest employer in the world?
- Which company will create nearly 800 000 new jobs over the next five years?

You have probably guessed that the correct answer is Wal-Mart, the global discount store chain founded by Sam Walton, who opened his first store in Arkansas in 1962. By 2004, Wal-Mart was making $256 billion in sales through 5100 stores in North and South America (Saporito, 2003).

But not everyone is happy with the "Wal-Martization" of our society and others around the world. In Canada, people have formed a social movement to keep Wal-Mart out of their communities, fearing the loss of local businesses and, in some cases, local culture. Critics claim that the merchandising giant pays low wages at home, keeps out unions, and sells many products made in sweatshops abroad (Rousseau, 2002).

This chapter explores the economy and the closely related institution of politics. A number of very large corporations, including Wal-Mart, are at the centre of the Canadian economy, raising questions about just how the economy operates, whose interests it ought to serve, and to what extent big business shapes our country's political life.

Economics and politics are each a **social institution**, *a major sphere of social life, or societal subsystem, organized to meet human needs.* The two chapters that follow consider other social institutions: Chapter 13 focuses on the family and religion, and Chapter 14 highlights education and medicine. These discussions explain how social institutions have changed over the course of history, describe how they operate today, and point out controversies that are likely to shape them tomorrow.

The Economy: Historical Overview

The **economy** is *the social institution that organizes a society's production, distribution, and consumption of goods and services.* The economy operates—for better or worse—in a generally predictable manner. Goods are commodities ranging from necessities (such as food, clothing, and shelter) to luxury items (such as automobiles, swimming pools, and yachts). Services are activities that benefit others (including the work of priests, doctors, teachers, and computer software specialists).

THE AGRICULTURAL REVOLUTION

As Chapter 2 ("Culture") explained, the earliest societies were made up of hunters and gatherers living off the land. In such societies, there was no distinct economy; producing and consuming were part of family life.

Harnessing animals to plows 5000 years ago permitted the development of agriculture, which was ten times as productive as hunting and gathering. The resulting surplus meant that not everyone had to produce food, so many people took on specialized work: making tools, raising animals, and building dwellings. Soon towns sprang up, linked by networks of traders. These four factors—agricultural technology, specialized work, permanent settlements, and trade—made the economy a distinct social institution.

THE INDUSTRIAL REVOLUTION

By the mid-eighteenth century, a second technological revolution was underway, starting in England and spreading to the United States. Industrialization changed the economy in five ways:

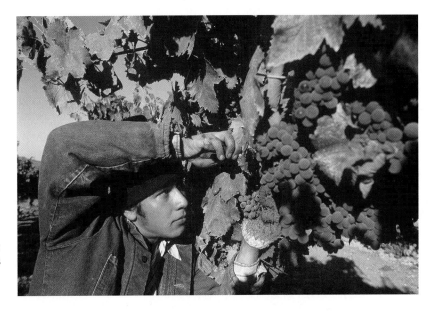

As societies industrialize, a smaller and smaller share of the labour force works in agriculture. In Canada, much of what agricultural work remains is performed by immigrants from lower-income nations.

1. **New sources of energy.** Throughout history, "energy" had meant the muscle power of people or animals. Then, in 1765, the English inventor James Watt introduced the steam engine. A hundred times more powerful than muscle power, early steam engines soon drove heavy machinery.

2. **Centralization of work in factories.** Steam-powered machinery moved work from homes to factories, centralized workplaces that housed the machines.

3. **Manufacturing and mass production.** Before the Industrial Revolution, most people grew or gathered raw materials (such as grain, wood, or wool). In an industrial economy, people working in factories turn raw materials into finished products (such as furniture and clothing).

4. **Specialization.** Historically, artisans at home made products from beginning to end. In the factory, a labourer repeats a single task over and over, making only a small contribution to the finished product.

5. **Wage labour.** Instead of working for themselves, factory workers became wage labourers who sold their labour to strangers, who often cared less for them than for the machines they operated. (Recall the story at the start of Chapter 9, in which after a tragic fire, the manager of a Bangladesh sweatshop was more concerned about the harm to his factory than the deaths of his workers.)

The Industrial Revolution raised living standards as the production of countless new products fuelled an expanding economy. However, the benefits of industrial technology were shared very unequally, especially at the beginning. Some factory owners made huge fortunes, but the majority of workers lived close to poverty. Children slaved in factories or deep in coal mines for pennies a day. With time, workers formed labour unions to collectively represent their interests to factory owners. Over the course of the twentieth century, new laws banned child labour, set minimum wage levels, improved workplace safety, and extended schooling and political rights to a larger segment of the population (Krahn & Lowe, 2002).

THE INFORMATION REVOLUTION AND POST-INDUSTRIAL SOCIETY

By about 1950, the nature of production was changing once again. Canada was creating a **post-industrial economy**, *a productive system based on service work and high technology.* Automated machinery (and more recently, robotics) reduced the role of human labour in production while expanding the ranks of clerical workers and managers. Service industries—including sales, healthcare, food service, and banking—currently employ most working people in this country. The post-industrial era, then, is marked by a shift from industrial work to service work.

Driving this economic change is a third technological breakthrough: the computer. Just as factories did two centuries ago, the Information Revolution, with new kinds of products and new forms of communication, has changed the character of work itself. In general, we see three changes:

1. **From tangible products to ideas.** The industrial era was defined by the production of goods; in the post-industrial era, work involves manipulating symbols.

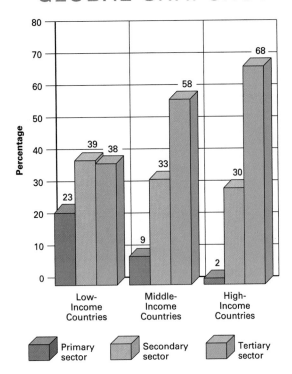

GLOBAL SNAPSHOT

FIGURE 12–1 The Size of Economic Sectors by Income Level of Country

Source: Estimates based on United Nations Development Programme (2000) and World Bank (2000).

Computer programmers, writers, financial analysts, advertising executives, architects, editors, and various types of consultants make up the labour force of the information age.

2. **From mechanical skills to literacy skills.** The Industrial Revolution required mechanical skills, but the Information Revolution requires literacy skills: speaking and writing well and, of course, using computers. People able to communicate effectively enjoy new opportunities; people without these skills face declining prospects.

3. **From factories to almost anywhere.** Industrial technology drew workers to factories that were near power sources, but computer technology allows people to work almost anywhere. Laptop computers, cell phones, palm pilots, and portable fax machines can turn a home, a car, or even an airplane into a "virtual office." In short, new information technology blurs the line between work and home life.

SECTORS OF THE ECONOMY

The three revolutions just described reflect a shifting balance among the three sectors of the economy. The **primary sector** is *the part of the economy that draws raw materials from the natural environment.* The primary sector—agriculture, ranching, fishing, forestry, and mining—is largest in low-income nations. Figure 12–1 shows that 23 percent of the economic output of low-income countries is in the primary sector, compared with 9 percent of economic activity among middle-income nations and just 2 percent in high-income countries like Canada.

The **secondary sector**, *the part of the economy that transforms raw materials into manufactured goods*, includes operations such as refining petroleum into gasoline and turning metals into automobiles. The globalization of industry means that just about all of the world's countries derive a significant share of their economic output from the secondary sector. As Figure 12–1 shows, the secondary sector accounts for a greater share of economic output in low-income nations than it does in high-income countries.

The **tertiary sector** is *the part of the economy that involves services rather than goods.* Accounting for just 38 percent of economic output in low-income countries, the tertiary sector grows with industrialization and dominates the economies of middle-income countries (58 percent) and high-income, post-industrial nations (68 percent). Approximately 75 percent of workers in the Canadian labour force perform service jobs, including clerical jobs and positions in food service, sales, law, healthcare, advertising, and teaching (Statistics Canada, 2003bm).

THE GLOBAL ECONOMY

New information technology is drawing nations of the world closer together, creating a **global economy**, *expanding economic activity that crosses national borders.* The development of a global economy has four major consequences. First, a global division of labour causes different regions of the world to specialize in different sectors of economic activity. As Global Map 12–1 shows, agriculture represents more than half of the total economic output in the world's poorest countries. Global Map 12–2 shows that most of the economic output in high-income countries, including Canada, is in the service sector.

Second, an increasing number of products pass through more than one nation. Look no further than your morning coffee: It may have been grown in Colombia and transported to Vancouver on a freighter that was registered in Liberia, made in Japan using steel from Korea, and fuelled by oil from Venezuela.

Third, national governments no longer control economic activity within their borders. In fact, governments

GLOBAL MAP 12-1 Agricultural Employment in Global Perspective

The primary sector of the economy is largest in the nations that are least developed. Thus, in low-income countries of Africa and Asia, up to half of all workers are farmers. This picture is altogether different in the world's most economically developed countries—including Canada, the United States, Great Britain, and Australia—which have 2 percent of their labour force in agriculture.

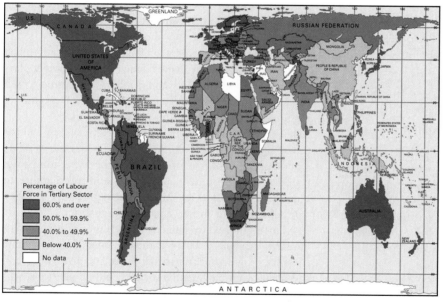

GLOBAL MAP 12-2 Service-Sector Employment in Global Perspective

The tertiary sector of the economy becomes ever larger as a nation's income level rises. In Canada, the United States and the countries of Western Europe, Australia, and Japan, about two-thirds of the labour force performs service work.

Sources: Data from United Nations Development Programme (2000) and World Bank (2000, 2001); map projection from *Peters Atlas of the World* (1990).

cannot even regulate the value of their national currencies because dollars, euros, pounds sterling, yen, and other currencies are traded around the clock in the financial centres of Tokyo, London, and New York, which are linked by satellite communications.

Fourth, a small number of businesses, operating internationally, now control a vast share of the world's economic activity. According to one estimate, the 600 largest multinational companies account for half the world's economic output (Kidron & Segal, 1991; Gergen, 2002).

The planet is divided into more than 200 politically distinct nations. But the rising level of international trade makes nationhood less important than it was even a decade ago.

Economic Systems: Paths to Justice

 October 20, Ho Chi Minh City (formerly known as Saigon), Vietnam. Sailing up the narrow Saigon River is an unsettling experience for anyone who came of age in the 1960s. We need to remember that Vietnam is a country, not a war, and that 30 years have passed since the last U.S. helicopter lifted off from the rooftop of the U.S. embassy, ending our country's presence there.

Saigon is becoming a boomtown. Neon signs bathe the city's waterfront in colour; hotels, bankrolled by Western corporations, push skyward from a dozen construction sites; taxi meters record fares in U.S. dollars, not Vietnamese dong; and Visa and American Express stickers decorate the doors of fashionable shops that cater to tourists from Canada, Japan, France, and the United States.

There is heavy irony here: after decades of fighting, millions of lives lost on both sides, and the victory of Communist forces, the Vietnamese are doing an about-face and turning toward capitalism.

Every society's economy makes a statement about justice by determining who gets what. Two general economic models are capitalism and socialism. However, no nation anywhere in the world has an economy that is purely one or the other; capitalism and socialism are two ends of a spectrum along which the actual economies of the world fall. We will look, in turn, at each of these two models.

CAPITALISM

Capitalism is *an economic system in which natural resources and the means of producing goods and services are privately owned.* An ideal capitalist economy has three distinctive features:

1. **Private ownership of property.** In a capitalist economy, individuals can own almost anything. The more capitalist an economy, the more private ownership there is of wealth-producing property such as factories, real estate, and natural resources.

2. **Pursuit of personal profit.** A capitalist society tries to create profit and wealth. The profit motive is considered the natural way of doing business.

3. **Competition and consumer choice.** A purely capitalist economy is a free-market system with no government interference (sometimes called a *laissez-faire* economy, from French words meaning "to leave alone"). According to the Scottish economist Adam Smith (1723–1790), a freely competitive economy regulates itself by the "invisible hand" of the law of demand and supply (1937, orig. 1776).

Consumers guide a market economy, Smith explained, by choosing goods and services offering the greatest value. Producers advertise their products, seeking the customer's business by providing higher-quality goods at lower prices. From narrow self-interest, as Smith put it, comes "the greatest good for the greatest number of people." Government control of an economy, on the other hand, distorts market forces, reduces producer motivation, lessens quality, and shortchanges consumers.

"Justice" in a capitalist system amounts to freedom of the marketplace, where anyone can produce, buy, and invest according to individual self-interest. The increasing popularity of Wal-Mart, described in the opening to this chapter, reflects the fact that the company offers a high level of value to customers who choose to shop there.

Canada is considered a capitalist nation because most businesses are privately owned. However, government plays a large role in Canadian economic affairs. Government itself owns—in part or completely—a number of productive organizations, including almost all of this country's schools, roads, parks, and museums, Canada Post, Via Rail, and the Canadian military. In addition, governments use taxation and other forms of regulation to influence what companies produce, to control the quality and cost of merchandise, to regulate what businesses import and export, and to motivate consumers to conserve natural resources.

Furthermore, government sets minimum wage levels, enforces workplace safety standards, regulates corporate mergers, provides farm price supports, and gives income in the form of employment insurance, public pensions, student loans, child tax credits, and subsidies for child and elder care, to a majority of people in Canada. Municipal, provincial, territorial, and federal governments together are the nation's biggest employer, with 18 percent of the labour force on their payrolls in 1999 (Statistics Canada, 2003bn).

SOCIALISM

Socialism is *an economic system in which natural resources and the means of producing goods and services are collectively owned.* In its ideal form, a socialist economy rejects each of the three characteristics of capitalism just described in favour of three opposite features:

Capitalism still thrives in Hong Kong (left); it is evident in streets choked with advertising and shoppers. Socialism is more the rule in China's capital of Beijing (right), a city dominated by government buildings rather than a downtown business district.

1. **Collective ownership of property.** A socialist economy limits rights to private property, especially property used to generate income. Government controls such property and makes housing and other goods available to all, not just to the people with the most money.

2. **Pursuit of collective goals.** The individualistic pursuit of profit goes against the collective orientation of socialism. What capitalism celebrates as the "entrepreneurial spirit," socialism condemns as greed; individuals are urged to work for the common good of all.

3. **Government control of the economy.** Socialism rejects capitalism's laissez-faire approach in favour of a *centrally controlled* or *command* economy operated by government. Commercial advertising thus plays little role in socialist economies.

"Justice" in a socialist context means not competing to gain wealth but meeting everyone's basic needs in a roughly equal manner. From a socialist point of view, a capitalist practice such as cutting back on workers' wages and benefits to boost company earnings puts profits before people and is thus an injustice.

The People's Republic of China and some two dozen other nations in Asia, Africa, and Latin America have socialist economies, with almost all wealth-generating property under state control (McColm et al., 1991; Freedom House, 2004). The extent of world socialism has declined in recent years as countries in Eastern Europe and the former Soviet Union have geared their economies toward a market system.

WELFARE CAPITALISM AND STATE CAPITALISM

Some nations in Western Europe, including Sweden and Italy, have market-based economies but also offer broad social welfare programs. Analysts call this third type of economic system **welfare capitalism**, *an economic and political system that combines a mostly market-based economy with extensive social welfare programs.*

Under welfare capitalism, the government owns some of the largest industries and services, such as transportation, the mass media, and healthcare. In Sweden and Italy, about 12 percent of economic production is "nationalized," or state-controlled. That leaves most industry in private hands but subject to extensive government regulation. High taxation (aimed especially at the rich) funds a wide range of social welfare programs, including universal healthcare and childcare (Olsen, 1996; Swank, 2002).

Yet another alternative is **state capitalism**, *an economic and political system in which companies are privately owned but cooperate closely with the government.* State capitalism is the rule in the nations along the Pacific Rim. Japan, South Korea, and Singapore are all capitalist countries, but their governments work in partnership with large companies, supplying financial assistance and controlling foreign imports to help their businesses compete in world markets (Gerlach, 1992).

Global comparisons indicate that socialist economies generate greater economic equality although living standards remain relatively low. Capitalist economies, by contrast, generate more economic inequality although living standards are relatively high. As the Russian Federation has moved from socialism toward capitalism, there is widespread evidence of increasing economic inequality, including the building of large mansions by those who have become rich. This complex is being built by a business tycoon in the suburbs of the Russian capital, an area coming to be known as "the Beverly Hills of Moscow."

RELATIVE ADVANTAGES OF CAPITALISM AND SOCIALISM

Which economic system works best? Comparing economies is difficult because all countries mix capitalism and socialism to varying degrees. Nations also differ in cultural attitudes toward work, natural resources, technological development, and patterns of trade. Despite such complicating factors, some crude comparisons are revealing.

Economic productivity. One key dimension of economic performance is productivity. A commonly used measure of economic output is *gross domestic product* (GDP), the total value of all goods and services produced annually. Per capita (per person) GDP allows us to compare the economic performance of nations of different population sizes.

The output of mostly capitalist countries at the end of the 1980s varied somewhat, but averaging the figures for Canada, the United States, and the nations of Western Europe yielded a per capita GDP of about $13 500. The comparable figure for the former Soviet Union and the nations of Eastern Europe was about $5000. This means that the capitalist countries outproduced the socialist nations by a ratio of 2.7 to 1 (United Nations Development Programme, 1990). A recent comparison of economic output found that (mostly capitalist) South Korea outproduced (mostly socialist) North Korea by about 18 to 1 (Omestad, 2003).

Economic equality. The distribution of resources within the population is another important measure of economic performance. A comparative study in the mid-1970s looked at income ratios based on the earnings of the richest 5 percent of the population and the poorest 5 percent (Wiles, 1977). Societies with mostly capitalist economies had an income ratio of about 10 to 1; the figure for socialist countries was 5 to 1. In other words, *capitalist economies support a higher overall standard of living but with greater income inequality.* Said another way, socialist economies create more economic equality but provide a lower overall living standard.

Personal freedom. One additional consideration in evaluating capitalism and socialism is the personal freedom each system gives its people. Capitalism emphasizes the *freedom to* pursue self-interest and depends on the freedom of producers and consumers to interact with little interference from the state. Socialism, by contrast, emphasizes *freedom from* basic want. The goal of equality requires the state to regulate the economy, which in turn limits personal choices and opportunities for citizens.

To date, no system has been able to offer both political freedom and economic equality. In capitalist Canada, our political system offers many personal freedoms, but they are not worth as much to a poor person as to a rich one. On the other side of the coin, North Korea has more economic equality, but people cannot speak out or travel inside and outside the country freely.

CHANGES IN SOCIALIST COUNTRIES

In 1989 and 1990, the nations of Eastern Europe, which had been seized by the former Soviet Union at the end of World War II, overthrew their socialist regimes. These nations—including the former German Democratic Republic, the Czech Republic, Slovakia, Hungary, Romania, and Bulgaria—are all moving toward capitalist market systems after decades of state-controlled socialist economies. At the end of 1991, the Soviet Union itself formally dissolved and introduced some free-market principles. Ten years later, 75 percent of businesses were partly or entirely under private ownership (Montaigne, 2001).

There were many reasons for these sweeping changes. First, the capitalist economies far outproduced their socialist counterparts. The socialist economies were successful in achieving economic equality, but living standards were low compared with those of Western Europe. Second, Soviet socialism was heavy-handed, rigidly controlling the media and restricting individual freedoms. In other words, Soviet-style socialism did away with *economic* elites, as Karl Marx predicted, but as Max Weber foresaw, socialism increased the power of *political* elites.

So far, the market reforms in Eastern Europe are proceeding unevenly. Some nations (Czech Republic, Slovakia, Poland, and the Baltic states of Latvia, Estonia, and Lithuania) are doing pretty well. But other countries (Romania, Bulgaria, and the Russian Federation) have been hit by price increases and falling living standards. Officials hope that expanding production will gradually bring a turnaround. However, introducing a market economy has also brought more economic inequality—by 2000, economic inequality in Russia was greater than in Canada and even the United States (Buraway, 1997; World Bank, 2004).

Work in the Post-Industrial Economy

Economic change is occurring not just in the socialist world but also in Canada. The latest census for which data are available showed that in 2001, there were approximately 15.8 million people in the labour force, representing approximately two-thirds of those aged 16 and over. A larger share of men (73 percent) than women (60 percent) were part of the labour force, although the gap is closing. Among men, 72 percent of those of visible minority background are in the labour force, compared to 67 percent of Aboriginal men. Among women, 60 percent of those from visible minority groups are in the labour force, compared to 56 percent of Aboriginal women (Statistics Canada, 2003bp, 2003bq).

THE CHANGING WORKPLACE

In 1911, 40 percent of Canadian workers had jobs in the primary sector. In 2006, just 4 percent were part of this economy. Figure 12–2 illustrates the shrinking role of the primary sector in the Canadian economy.

Similarly, a century ago, industrialization swelled the ranks of workers in the manufacturing sector. By the mid-1900s, however, a white-collar revolution was gaining

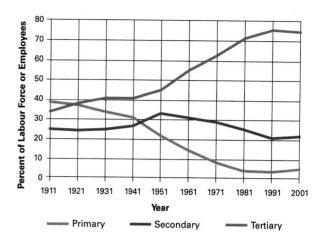

FIGURE 12-2 The Changing Pattern of Work in Canada, 1911–2001

Sources: Estimated based on data in Bowlby (2001); Leacy (1999); and CANSIM Tables D137024-D137028, D137032, D137051, D137052, D137056, D137059-D137061, D137067.

momentum. More than 90 percent of new jobs in 2002 were in the service sector, and 75 percent of the labour force performed service work (Statistics Canada, 2003bm).

As Chapter 8 ("Social Stratification") explained, much service work—including sales, clerical positions, and work in hospitals and restaurants—yields little of the income and prestige of white-collar professions, and, at the same time, offers fewer rewards than factory work. In sum, many jobs in this post-industrial era provide only a modest standard of living.

LABOUR UNIONS

The changing economy has seen a change in labour unions, organizations that seek to improve wages and working conditions. Canadian union membership increased rapidly after 1935, to more than one-third of non-farm workers by 1950. Then it fell slightly during the 1960s, but increased during the 1970s, to return to the 1950 level, where it has stabilized (Marshall, 2000).

In 2004, the unionized rate for the total employed workforce in Canada was 32 percent (Statistics Canada, 2002j, 2006au). In Japan, about 33 percent of workers belong to unions; between 30 and 40 percent are unionized in much of Europe, and 75 percent or more in the Nordic countries. Sweden has one of the highest union rates, at 77 percent (Western, 1993, 1995; Swank, 2002; International Labour Organization, 2002).

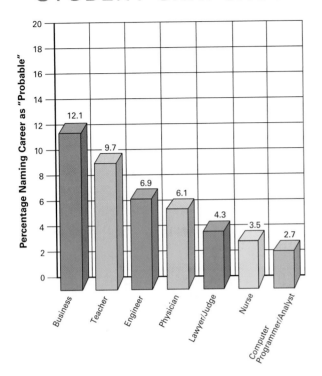

FIGURE 12-3 The Careers Most Commonly Named as Probable by First-Year College and University Students, 2003

Source: Sax et al. (2003).

even professional exterminators. As distinct from an *amateur* (from the Latin for "lover," meaning one who acts out of love for the activity itself), a professional does some task to earn a living. But what exactly is a profession?

A **profession** is *a prestigious, white-collar occupation that requires extensive formal education.* People performing this kind of work make a profession, or public declaration, of their willingness to work according to certain principles. Professions include the ministry, medicine, law, academia, and fields such as architecture, accountancy, and social work. Occupations are professional to the extent that they demonstrate the following four characteristics (Goode, 1960; Ritzer & Walczak, 1990):

1. **Theoretical knowledge.** Professionals have theoretical knowledge of their field rather than simply technical training. Anyone can learn first-aid skills, for example, but doctors have a theoretical understanding of human health. This means that tennis players, house cleaners, and exterminators do not really qualify as "professionals."

2. **Self-regulating practice.** The typical professional is self-employed, "in private practice" rather than working for a company. Professionals oversee their own work and observe a code of ethics.

3. **Authority over clients.** Because of their expertise, professionals are sought out by clients, who value their advice and follow their directions.

4. **Community orientation rather than self-interest.** The traditional professing of duty states an intention to serve the community rather than merely seek income.

In almost all cases, professional work requires a college or university degree and a graduate degree. Not surprisingly, professions are well represented among the jobs beginning university students say they hope to get after graduation, as shown in Figure 12–3.

Many new occupations in the post-industrial economy seek to *professionalize* their services. Claiming professional standing usually begins by renaming the work to suggest special, theoretical knowledge, moving the field away from its original, lesser reputation. Stockroom workers become "inventory supply managers," and exterminators are reborn as "insect control specialists."

Interested parties may also form a professional association that certifies their skills. The organization licenses its members, writes a code of ethics, and emphasizes the work's importance. To win public acceptance, a professional association may also establish schools or other training facilities and perhaps start a professional journal. Not all occupations try to claim professional status. Some *paraprofessionals,* including paralegals and medical technicians, possess

Yet, overall there has been a decline in union rates across high-income countries, though not to the extent seen in the United States, where only about 13 percent of non-farm workers are unionized.

The global decline in unions follows the shrinking industrial sector of the economy. In addition, newer service jobs are less likely to be unionized. But, as some analysts see it, decreased job security may well make unions more popular in years to come. Nevertheless, unions will have to adapt to the new global economy. Union members in Canada and the United States, used to seeing foreign workers as "the enemy," will have to build new international alliances (Church, 1994; Greenhouse, 2000).

PROFESSIONS

All kinds of jobs today are called *professional;* there are professional tennis players, professional house cleaners, and specialized skills but lack the extensive theoretical education required of full professionals.

SELF-EMPLOYMENT

Self-employment—earning a living without working for a large organization—was once common in Canada. In 1800

 Visit the website of the Canadian Federation of Independent Business at **http://www.cfib.ca**.

the vast majority of workers were self-employed, compared with just 15 percent of workers today (19 percent of men and 11 percent of women) (Statistics Canada, 2006au).

Lawyers, doctors, and other professionals are well represented among the ranks of the self-employed. But most self-employed workers are small business owners (including people who buy and sell using the Internet), farmers, plumbers, carpenters, freelance writers and editors, artists, and long-distance truck drivers. In all, more self-employed people have blue-collar than white-collar jobs.

Finally, a notable trend is that self-employment has grown faster for Canadian women than men during the past two decades (Benoit, 2000a). As a result, women accounted for 34 percent of this nation's small businesses in 2004, up from 31 percent in 1990 and 26 percent in 1976 (Statistics Canada, 2006au).

UNEMPLOYMENT

Every society has some level of unemployment. Few young people entering the labour force find a job right away. Workers temporarily leave their jobs to seek new work or to

 For a case study of unemployment among Aboriginal and visible minority populations in Toronto, go to http://www.sdc.gc.ca/asp/gateway.asp?hr=/en/lp/lo/lswe/we/special_projects/RacismFreeInitiative/George-Doyle.shtml&hs=wzp.

stay at home raising children. Union members strike. Others suffer from long-term illnesses. Still others are illiterate or without the skills to perform useful work.

But unemployment is not just an individual situation; it is also caused by the economy. Jobs disappear as occupations become obsolete, businesses close in the face of foreign competition or economic recession, and companies "downsize" to become more profitable. Since 1980, the largest Canadian businesses and different levels of government have eliminated thousands of jobs in manufacturing and the public service.

In May 2006 about 6.1 percent of Canadians were unemployed—a substantial decrease from 7.7 percent in the fall of 2003. As National Map 12–1 shows, some regions of Canada, particularly the east coast and the Prairies, had high unemployment in 2001; in some places, the unem-

This Depression-era photo is a powerful statement of the personal collapse and private despair that afflicts men and women who are out of work. How does a sociological perspective help us to understand being out of work as more than a personal problem?

ployment rate was more than three times the national rate (Statistics Canada, 2003br).

Figure 12–4 on page 318 shows that the 2001 unemployment rate among visible minority men between 25 and 44 years of age (13.2 percent) was substantially higher than that among other men in Canada (9.9 percent), and that almost three times as many Aboriginal men (27.4 percent) were unemployed than other Canadian men. In 1996, the unemployment rate for visible minority women (15.3 percent) was lower than that of Aboriginal women (21.6 percent), but higher than the unemployment rate of other females (9.4 percent) (Statistics Canada, 2003bp, 2003bq).

WORKPLACE DIVERSITY: RACE AND GENDER

Traditionally, white men have been the mainstay of the Canadian labour force. However, as explained in Chapter 11 ("Race and Ethnicity"), our country's proportion of minorities is rapidly rising. Between 1981 and 2001, the proportion of visible minorities in Canada's population has increased from 4.7 percent to 13.4 percent (Statistics Canada, 2003t). The Diversity: Race, Class, & Gender box takes a closer look at how increasing social diversity will affect the workplace.

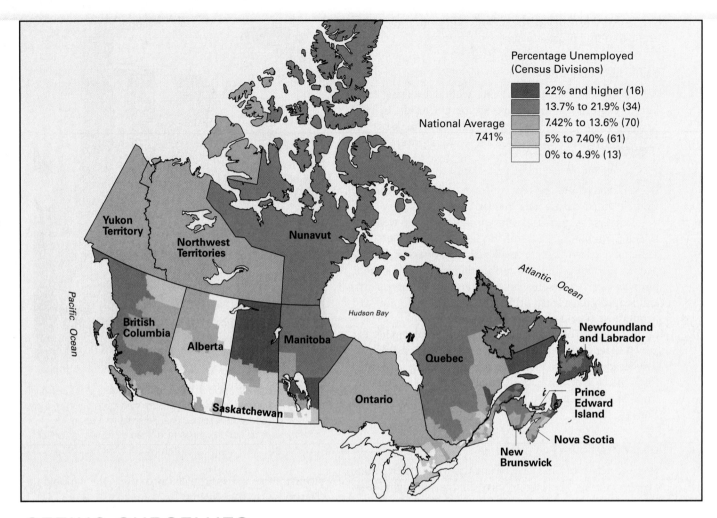

Percentage Unemployed (Census Divisions)

▨	22% and higher (16)
▨	13.7% to 21.9% (34)
▨	7.42% to 13.6% (70)
▨	5% to 7.40% (61)
☐	0% to 4.9% (13)

National Average 7.41%

SEEING OURSELVES

NATIONAL MAP 12-1 Unemployment Rates Across Canada

The 2001 census reported an unemployment rate of 7.41 percent for all of Canada. As in the 1996 census, the highest level of unemployment was in Newfoundland, where three census divisions had employment rates of 35 percent. The depiction of the unemployment rate on this map makes us think of the structural causes and consequences of unemployment. Do you usually consider structural or personal factors when you try to understand the unemployment that exists where you live?

Source: Statistics Canada (2003br).

NEW INFORMATION TECHNOLOGY AND WORK

July 2, Edmonton, Alberta. The manager of the local hardware store scans the barcodes of a bagful of items. "The computer not only totals the costs," she explains, "it also keeps track of inventory, places orders to the warehouse, and decides what products to continue to sell and which to discontinue." "Sounds like what you used to do, Maureen," I respond with a smile. "Yep," she says, with no smile at all.

Computers and new information technology play a central role in the twenty-first-century workplace. The

DIVERSITY: RACE, CLASS, & GENDER

Twenty-First Century Diversity: Changes in the Workplace

An upward trend in the Canadian visible minority population is changing the workplace. The share of visible minorities employed in Canada increased from 4.7 percent in 1981 to 13.4 percent in 2001 (Statistics Canada, 2003t). As shown in Chapter 10 ("Gender Stratification"), over this time period, the proportion of women employed markedly increased, while a significantly lower proportion of men were employed than was the case 25 years before.

The overall result? Within a decade, white men will represent a minority of all workers, and that figure will continue to drop. Therefore, companies that welcome social diversity will tap the largest talent pool and enjoy a competitive advantage.

Welcoming social diversity means, first, recruiting talented workers of both genders as well as all colours and cultural backgrounds. But developing the potential of all employees requires meeting the special needs of women and other minorities, which may not be the same as those of white men. For example, in the twenty-first century corporations will be pressed to provide childcare at the workplace.

Second, businesses need to develop effective ways to defuse tension that arises from social differences. They will have to work harder at treating workers equally and respectfully; also, no corporate culture can tolerate racial or sexual harassment.

Third, companies will have to rethink current promotion practices. At present, as noted in Chapter 10, men dominate senior management jobs in the business world, with just 14 percent of women holding corporate officer positions in Canada's 500 largest companies in 2002 and only 3.4 percent holding CEO or equivalent positions (Catalyst, 2003).

Visible minorities and Aboriginals are even less likely to have managerial jobs, especially at the top levels (Statistics Canada, 2000m).

In sum, "glass ceilings" that limit the advancement of skilled workers not only discourage effort but also deprive companies of their largest source of talent: women and other minorities.

Sources: Samuel (1992), Statistics Canada (1995a, 2000m, 2003t), and Catalyst (2003).

Information Revolution is changing what people do in some basic ways (Rule & Brantley, 1992; Vallas & Beck, 1996):

1. **Computers are deskilling labour.** Just as industrial machines replaced the master craftsworkers of an earlier era, computers now threaten the skills of managers. More business operations are based not on executive decisions but on computer modelling. A machine, not a person, decides whether to place an order, resupply a client, or approve a loan application.

2. **Computers are making work more abstract.** Most industrial workers have a hands-on relationship with their product. Post-industrial workers manipulate symbols to perform abstract tasks, such as making a company more profitable or making software more user-friendly.

3. **Computers limit workplace interaction.** As workers spend more time at computer terminals, they become isolated from one another.

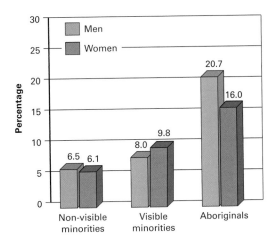

FIGURE 12–4 Unemployment Rates Among Visible Minority and Aboriginal Men and Women Aged 25–44, Canada, 2001

Source: Statistics Canada (2003bp, 2003bq).

4. **Computers increase employers' control of workers.** Computers allow supervisors to check employees' output continuously, whether they work at keyboard terminals or on assembly lines.

Such changes remind us that technology is not socially neutral. Computers not only change the way we work but also give employers more power over employees. For this reason, people welcome some aspects of the Information Revolution more than others.

Corporations

At the core of today's capitalist economy is the **corporation**, *an organization with a legal existence, including rights and liabilities, apart from that of its members.* Incorporating makes an organization a legal entity, able to enter into contracts and own property.

ECONOMIC CONCENTRATION

Most of Canada's corporations are small—more than 606 000 Canadians are self-employed and operate one or more corporations. Of these, more than one-third are without any employees (Statistics Canada, 2003bo). The largest corporations, however, dominate our nation's economy. In

2002, there were five corporations with revenues exceeding $10 billion (four car companies and one life insurer). The largest Canadian corporation in terms of sales is General Motors, which had over $37 billion in revenue in 2001 (Globeinvestor.com, 2003).

CORPORATE LINKAGES

Economic concentration creates *conglomerates,* giant corporations composed of many smaller corporations. Conglomerates form as corporations enter new markets, spin off new companies, or merge with other companies. For example, Altria is a conglomerate that includes Philip Morris (tobacco products), Nabisco and Post (food products), and Starbucks (coffee). While Canada's conglomerates make up only 1 percent of all businesses in the country, they generate more than one-third of all business income and employ about one-quarter of the workforce (Statistics Canada, 2000e).

Many conglomerates are linked because they own each other's stock, the result being worldwide corporate alliances of staggering size. General Motors, for example, owns Opel (Germany), Vauxhall (Great Britain), and half of Saab (Sweden) and has partnerships with Suzuki, Isuzu, and Toyota (Japan). Similarly, Ford owns Jaguar and Aston Martin (Great Britain) and a share of Mazda (Japan), Kia (Korea), and Volvo (Sweden).

Another type of corporate linkage is the *interlocking directorate,* a social network of people who serve as directors of many corporations (Weidenbaum, 1995; Kono et al., 1998). These boardroom connections provide access to valuable information about other companies' products and marketing strategies. While perfectly legal, such linkages encourage illegal activity, such as price fixing, as companies share information about their pricing policies.

CORPORATIONS: ARE THEY COMPETITIVE?

According to the capitalist model, businesses operate independently in a competitive market. But in light of the extensive linkages that exist between them, it is obvious that large corporations do not operate independently. Also, a few large corporations dominate many markets, so they are not truly competitive.

The law forbids a large company from establishing a **monopoly**, *the domination of a market by a single producer,* because a monopoly could simply dictate prices. But **oligopoly**, *the domination of a market by a few producers,* is both legal and common. This pattern results from the huge investment needed to enter a major market, such as the auto industry, which is beyond the reach of all but the biggest companies. In addition, true competition involves risk, which any company tries to avoid.

Federal governments seek to regulate corporations in order to protect the public interest. Yet as recent corporate scandals in Canada and the United States have shown, corporate wrongdoing harms millions of people, and regulation is often too little too late. The government is also the corporate world's single biggest customer and sometimes steps in to support struggling corporations with billion-dollar loan programs. In addition, as the Applying Sociology box on page 321 explains, provincial governments' aid to corporations has drawn fire as "corporate welfare."

CORPORATIONS AND THE GLOBAL ECONOMY

Corporations have grown so large that they now account for most of the world's economic output. The biggest corporations—based in the United States, Japan, and Western Europe—consider the entire world one huge marketplace.

Global corporations know that low-income countries contain most of the world's people and resources. In addition, as shown in Figure 12–5, labour costs there are attractively low: a manufacturing worker in Mexico labours for almost two weeks to earn about what a German worker earns in a single day.

As Chapter 9 ("Global Stratification") explained, the impact of multinational corporations on low-income countries is controversial. Modernization theorists claim that multinational corporations, by unleashing the great productivity of capitalism, raise living standards in low-income nations, offering them tax revenues, capital investment, new jobs, and advanced technology that together accelerate economic growth (Berger, 1986; Firebaugh & Beck, 1994; Firebaugh & Sandu, 1998).

Dependency theorists respond that multinationals intensify global inequality, blocking the development of local industries and pushing poor countries to make goods for export rather than food and other products for local consumption. From this standpoint, multinationals make low-income nations poorer and increasingly dependent on high-income nations (Wallerstein, 1979; Delacroix & Ragin, 1981; Bergesen, 1983; Walton & Ragin, 1990).

LOOKING AHEAD: THE ECONOMY OF THE TWENTY-FIRST CENTURY

Social institutions are a society's ways of meeting people's needs. But as we have seen, the Canadian economy only partly succeeds in this respect. Although highly productive, our economy provides for some much better than for others. In addition, the Information Revolution continues to change our economy. First, the share of the Canadian labour force engaged in manufacturing is now half of what it was in 1960; lower-paying service work, especially computer-related jobs, makes up the difference. For industrial work-

Canada is now a "post-industrial" society: industry involves just over 25 percent of the labour force, while the service sector involves nearly 75 percent of workers. How does this transformation change the nature as well as the location of work?

ers, the post-industrial economy has brought unemployment and declining wages. Our society must face up to the challenge of providing millions of men and women with the language and computer skills needed in the new economy. Yet as the economic collapse of many dot-coms in 2001 and 2002 shows, even this new type of work can experience a downturn.

A second transformation that will mark the new century is the expansion of the global economy. Two centuries ago, the ups and downs of a local economy reflected events and trends in a single town. One century ago, communities across the country became economically linked so that one town's prosperity depended on producing goods demanded by people elsewhere in the country. Today, it makes less sense to speak of a national economy because what people in a Saskatchewan farm town produce and consume may be affected as much by what happens in the wheat-growing region of Russia as by events in their own provincial capital. In short, Canadian workers are not only creating new products and services but are also working in response to factors and forces that are distant and unseen.

Finally, analysts around the world are rethinking conventional economic models. The global economy shows that socialism is less productive than capitalism, one important reason for the collapse of socialist regimes in Eastern Europe and the former Soviet Union. But capitalism, too, is

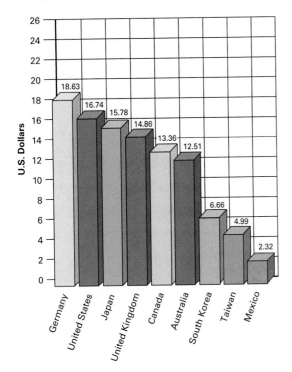

FIGURE 12–5 Average Hourly Wages for Workers in Manufacturing, 2002

Source: U.S. Department of Labor (2004).

changing and now operates with significant government regulation, partly to address the economic inequality generated by market systems.

What will be the long-term effects of these changes? Two conclusions seem certain. First, the economic future of Canada and other nations will be played out in a global arena. The new Canadian post-industrial economy is inseparable from the increasing industrial production of other nations. Second, we must address the urgent challenges of global inequality and population increase. Whether the world economy reduces or enlarges the gap between rich and poor societies may end up steering our planet toward peace or war.

Politics: Historical Overview

There is a close link between economics and **politics** (or "the polity"), *the social institution that distributes power, sets a society's goals, and makes decisions.* Early in the twentieth century, Max Weber (1978, orig. 1921) defined **power** as *the*

ability to achieve desired ends despite resistance from others. To a large degree, the exercise of power is the business of **government**, *a formal organization that directs the political life of a society.*

Brute force is the most basic form of power. But no government that gets power *only* from sheer force lasts for long, and life in such a society would be a nightmare of terror. Social organization depends on creating agreement about goals and how to attain them. This brings us to the concept of **authority**, *power that people perceive as legitimate rather than coercive.*

A society's source of authority depends, in turn, on its economy. According to Max Weber, pre-industrial societies rely on *traditional authority,* power legitimized by respect for long-established cultural patterns. Woven into a society's collective memory, traditional authority may seem almost sacred. Chinese emperors in centuries past were legitimized by tradition, as were the nobles in medieval Europe. Traditional authority declines as societies industrialize. For example, royal families still exist in ten European nations, but the democratic cultures of countries such as the United Kingdom, Sweden, and Denmark have shifted power to commoners elected to office. Weber explained that the expansion of rational bureaucracy is the modern foundation of authority. *Rational–legal authority* (sometimes called *bureaucratic authority*) is power legitimized by rationally enacted law. Traditional authority is tied to family; rational–legal authority flows from offices in governments. A traditional monarch passes power on to heirs; a modern president takes and gives up power according to law.

Weber described one additional type of authority that has surfaced throughout history. *Charismatic authority* is power legitimized by the extraordinary personal qualities—charisma—of a leader. Unlike its traditional and rational–legal counterparts, charismatic authority depends less on a person's ancestry or office and more on individual personality. Followers see in charismatic leaders some special, perhaps even divine power. Examples of charismatic leaders include Jesus of Nazareth, Nazi Germany's Adolf Hitler, the liberator of India Mahatma Gandhi, and the civil rights leader Martin Luther King Jr. All charismatic leaders aim to radically transform society, which makes them highly controversial (and explains why few charismatic leaders die of old age).

Because charismatic authority flows from a single individual, the leader's death creates a crisis. The survival of a charismatic movement, Weber explained, requires the **rout-inization of charisma**: *the transformation of charismatic authority into some combination of traditional and bureaucratic authority.* After the death of Jesus, for example, followers institutionalized his teachings in a

For more about the life of Dr. King, go to **http://www.lib.lsu.edu/hum/mlk**.

APPLYING SOCIOLOGY

Them That's Got, Gets: The Case of Corporate Welfare

Would you like the government to slash your income taxes and end sales tax on your purchases? What about to offer you money to buy a new house at a below-market interest rate? Would you like the government to hook up all your utilities for free and pay your water and electric bills?

For an ordinary person, such deals sound too good to be true. But our tax money is doing exactly that—not for families but for big corporations. All a large company has to do is declare a willingness to relocate and then wait for the offers from provincial and local governments to come pouring in.

Supporters call government aid to corporations "public–private partnerships." They point to the jobs corporations create, sometimes in areas hard hit by earlier business closings. For a city or town with a high unemployment rate, the promise of a new factory is simply too good to pass up. If incentives in the form of tax relief or free utilities are

needed to seal the deal, it is money well spent.

Critics call such arrangements "corporate welfare." They agree that companies create new jobs, but they point out that the corporations get much more than they give. On June 22, 1999, for example, the Canadian federal government gave $154 million to aerospace giant Pratt & Whitney for engine development technology. The payoff for the Canadian public was 770 jobs—but the cost was $200 000 per job! To take another example, Bombardier and its

subsidiaries have received $772 million in federal government handouts since 1982, making the company the largest beneficiary of Ottawa's corporate welfare program. Overall, government support to corporations exceeds millions of dollars each year, far more than the total welfare dollars given to people who are poor.

Although new plants do create some jobs, most jobs are simply moved from one place to another. But not all jobs pay well. Nor is there any guarantee that once settled, a corporation will stay, since businesses are free to make a better deal and move to another location.

WHAT DO YOU THINK?

1. Why do governments give tax breaks to businesses?
2. Does this policy help local communities or corporations? Why?
3. Overall, do you support the tax breaks for business described here? Why or why not?

Sources: Bartlett & Steele (1998) and various news reports.

---

church, built on tradition and bureaucracy. Routinized in this way, the Church has existed for nearly 2000 years.

Global Political Systems

The world's political systems differ in countless ways. Generally, however, they fall into four categories: monarchy, democracy, authoritarianism, and totalitarianism.

MONARCHY

Monarchy (with Latin and Greek roots meaning "one ruler") is *a type of political system in which a single family rules from generation to generation.* Monarchy is commonly found in agrarian societies; for example, the Bible tells of

great kings such as David and Solomon. In the world today, 28 nations have royal families;[1] most trace their ancestry back for centuries. In Weber's analysis, then, monarchy is legitimized by tradition.

During the Middle Ages, *absolute monarchs* in much of the world claimed a monopoly of power based on divine right. In some nations—including Kuwait, Saudi Arabia, and Bahrain—monarchs still exercise virtually absolute control over their people.

---

[1] In Europe: Sweden, Norway, Denmark, Great Britain, the Netherlands, Liechtenstein, Luxembourg, Belgium, Spain, and Monaco; in the Middle East: Jordan, Saudi Arabia, Oman, Qatar, Bahrain, and Kuwait; in Africa: Lesotho, Swaziland, and Morocco; in Asia and the Pacific: Brunei, Samoa, Tonga, Thailand, Malaysia, Cambodia, Nepal, Bhutan, and Japan.

In 2004, just 28 of the world's 192 nations were political monarchies where single families pass power from generation to generation. Here, the African nation of Swaziland celebrates the coronation of a young king.

With industrialization, however, monarchs gradually pass from the scene in favour of elected officials. All the European societies with royal families today are *constitutional monarchies,* meaning that their monarchs are little more than symbolic heads of state; actual governing is the responsibility of elected officials, led by a prime minister and guided by a constitution. In these countries, nobility formally reigns, but elected officials actually rule.

DEMOCRACY

The historical trend throughout most of the world is toward **democracy**, *a type of political system that gives power to the people as a whole.* More correctly, a system of representative democracy puts authority in the hands of leaders who, from time to time, compete for office in elections.

Most high-income countries in the world claim to be democratic (including those that still have royal families). Industrialization and democracy often go together because both require a literate populace. Also, the traditional legitimization of power in a monarchy gives way, with industrialization, to rational–legal authority. Thus, democracy and rational–legal authority are linked in the same way as monarchy and traditional authority.

But high-income countries such as Canada are not truly democratic for two reasons. First, there is the problem of bureaucracy. The number of people employed at the various levels of government in Canada (federal, provincial,

territorial, and municipal) is nearly 1 million strong. The vast majority of government officials are never elected by anyone and are not directly accountable to the people (Scaff, 1981; Edwards, 1985; Etzioni-Halevy, 1985; Light, 1999).

Second, there is the problem of economic inequality, because rich people have far more political power than poor people. Both George W. Bush and John Kerry, who ran for the presidency of the United States in 2004, are very wealthy men, and in the game of politics, "money talks." Though many of Canada's elected leaders do not come from wealthy families, some have substantial personal wealth (including our former prime minister, Paul Martin). Moreover, Canadian politicians are privileged by their education, with two-thirds of them having some background in law. The current prime minister, Stephen Harper, has a master's degree in economics. Given the even greater resources of billion-dollar corporations and labour unions, how can we think that our "democratic" system responds to—or even hears—the voices of "average people"?

Still, democratic nations do provide many rights and freedoms. Global Map 12–3 shows one assessment of political freedom around the world. According to Freedom House, an organization that tracks political trends, 88 of the world's 192 nations (with 44 percent of the global population) were "free," respecting many civil liberties, in 2004. This represents a gain for democracy: Just 76 nations were free a decade earlier (Freedom House, 2004).

AUTHORITARIANISM

Some governments actively resist involving their people in politics. **Authoritarianism** is *a political system that denies the people participation in government.* An authoritarian government is indifferent to people's needs and offers them no voice in selecting leaders. The absolute monarchies in Saudi Arabia and Bahrain are authoritarian, as is the military junta in Ethiopia.

TOTALITARIANISM

October 22, near Saigon, Vietnam. Six of our students have been arrested, allegedly for talking to Vietnamese students and taking pictures at the university. The Vietnamese minister of education has cancelled the reception tonight, claiming that our students' meeting with their students threatens Vietnam's security.

The most intensely controlled political form is **totalitarianism**, *a highly centralized political system that extensively regulates people's lives.* Totalitarian systems emerged in the twentieth century as governments gained the ability to

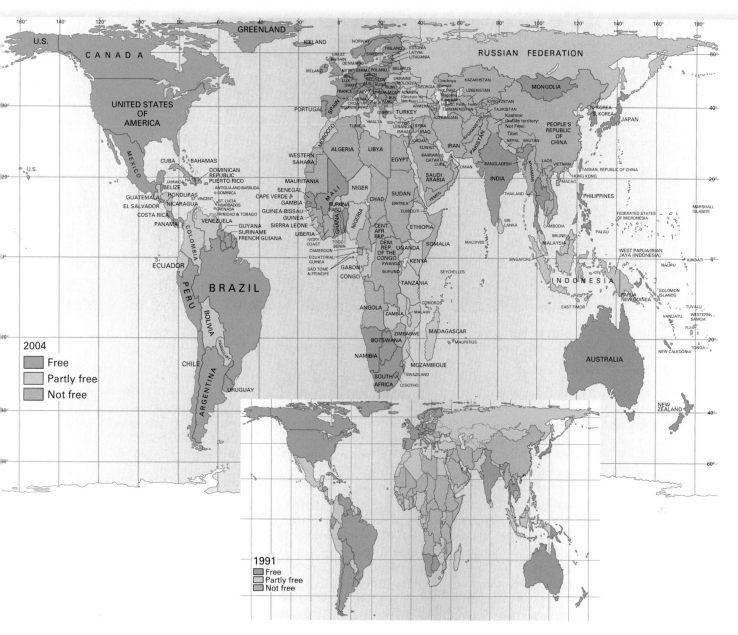

WINDOW ON THE WORLD

GLOBAL MAP 12-3 Political Freedom in Global Perspective

In 2004, a total of 88 of the world's nations, containing 44 percent of all people, were politically "free"; that is, they offered their citizens extensive political rights and civil liberties. Another 55 countries, which included 21 percent of the world's people, were "partly free," with more limited rights and liberties. The remaining 49 nations, home to 35 percent of humanity, fall into the category of "not free." In these countries, government sharply restricts individual initiative. Between 1980 and 2004, democracy made significant gains, largely in Latin America and Eastern Europe. In Asia, India (containing 1 billion people) returned to the "free" category in 1999. In 2000, Mexico joined the ranks of nations considered "free" for the first time.

Source: Freedom House (2004).

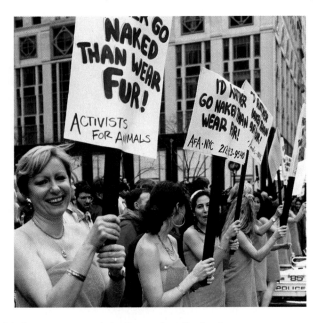

Lower-income people have more pressing financial needs and so they tend to focus on economic issues, such as the level of the minimum wage. Higher-income people, by contrast, provide support for many social issues, such as animal rights.

rigidly control a population. The Vietnamese government closely monitors the activities not just of visitors but of all its citizens. Similarly, the government of North Korea uses surveillance equipment and powerful computers to collect information about its people and to control them.

Some totalitarian governments claim to represent the will of the people, but most seek to bend people to the will of the government. Such governments are *total* concentrations of power, allowing no organized opposition. Denying people the right to assemble and controlling access to information, these governments create an atmosphere of isolation and fear. In the former Soviet Union, for example, most citizens had no access to telephone directories, copying equipment, fax machines, or even accurate city maps.

Socialization in totalitarian societies is highly political, seeking obedience and commitment to the system. In North Korea, one of the world's most totalitarian nations, pictures of leaders and political messages are everywhere, reminding citizens that they owe total allegiance to the state. Government-controlled schools and mass media present only official versions of events.

Totalitarian governments span the political spectrum from fascist (including Nazi Germany) to communist (such as North Korea). In all cases, however, one party claims total control of the society and permits no opposition.

A GLOBAL POLITICAL SYSTEM?

Is globalization changing politics in the same way that it is changing the economy? On one level, the answer is no.

Although most of today's economic activity is international, the world remains divided into nation–states just as it has been for centuries. The United Nations (founded in 1945) was a small step toward global government, but to date its political role in world affairs has been limited.

On another level, however, politics has become a global process. For some analysts, multinational corporations represent a new political order because of their enormous power to shape events throughout the world. In other words, politics is dissolving into business as corporations grow larger than governments.

Also, the Information Revolution has moved national politics onto the world stage. Email, cellular phones, satellite transmission systems, palm pilots, and fax machines mean that few countries can conduct their political affairs in complete privacy.

Finally, several thousand *non-governmental organizations* (NGOs) seek to advance global issues, such as human rights (Amnesty International) and environmental protection (Greenpeace). NGOs will continue to play a key role in expanding the global political culture.

In sum, just as individual nations are losing control of their own economies, governments cannot fully manage the political events occurring within their borders.

Politics in Canada

In contrast to the United States' revolutionary break with Great Britain, Canada's political independence came about through a peaceful transition from monarchial rule to democratic decision making. Our nation's political development reflects its distinctive history, capitalist economy, and cultural heritage.

CANADIAN CULTURE AND THE RISE OF THE WELFARE STATE

Our cultural emphasis on individualism is reflected in the Canadian *Human Rights Act* and *Charter of Rights and Freedoms*, both of which make explicit that all individuals have an equal right to make the lives for themselves that they are able to and wish to achieve. In making the best life for themselves, some people in Canada—and many more in the United States, no doubt—share the sentiment of nineteenth-century philosopher and poet Ralph Waldo Emerson: "The government that governs best is the government that governs least." Yet many other Canadians view the government in a more positive light, agreeing to pay higher taxes to support quality public services.

What is clear is that our government has grown into a vast and complex **welfare state**, *a range of government agencies and programs that provide benefits to the population.* Government benefits begin even before birth (through prenatal nutrition programs, and coverage of midwives' and physicians' fees and patients' hospital stays) and continue into old age (through public pensions). Some programs are especially important to the poor, who are not well served by our capitalist economic system; nevertheless, students, farmers, homeowners, small business operators, veterans, performing artists, and even giant corporations also get various subsidies and supports. In fact, virtually all Canadian adults look to the government to fund their healthcare services as well as public education programs for their children, and a majority of us also look to government for at least part of our income (Caplow et al., 1982; Devine, 1985; Myles, 1996; Bartlett and Steele, 1998; Benoit, 2000a).

Today's welfare state is the result of a gradual increase in the size and scope of government. At the time of Confederation in 1867, in most communities the presence of the federal government amounted to little more than a flag. Since then, the federal budget has steadily risen, reaching $212 billion in 2005–06.

As much as government has expanded in this country, the Canadian welfare state, though larger than that of our neighbour to the south, is still smaller than in many other industrial nations. Figure 12–6 shows that government is larger in most of Europe, and especially in Scandinavian countries such as Denmark and Sweden.

THE POLITICAL SPECTRUM

Who supports a bigger welfare state? Who wants to cut it back? Answers to such questions reveal attitudes that form

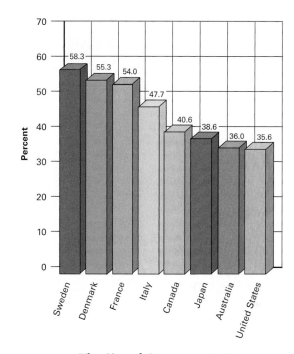

GLOBAL SNAPSHOT

FIGURE 12-6 The Size of Government: Government Expenditures as a Percentage of Gross Domestic Product, 2002

Source: U.S. Census Bureau (2003).

the *political spectrum,* which ranges from the extremely liberal on the left to the extremely conservative on the right.

One cluster of attitudes concerns economic issues. Supporters of the New Democratic Party (NDP) call for extensive government regulation of the economy in order to reduce disparities in income. Conservative Party members want to limit the hand of government in the economy and allow market forces freer rein, while Liberal Party supporters attempt to strike a balance between public and private responsibility for the individual well-being of citizens.

Social issues are moral questions ranging from abortion and the death penalty to gay rights and treatment of minorities. NDP members endorse equal rights and opportunities for all categories of people, view abortion as a matter of individual choice, and oppose the death penalty because it has been unfairly applied to minorities. The "family values" agenda of the Conservatives supports traditional gender roles and opposes gay families, affirmative action, and other "special programs" for minorities. Conservative supporters tend to condemn abortion as morally wrong and many support the death penalty. Again,

Stéphane Dion celebrates his election as the leader of the Liberal party during the Liberal Leadership convention in December 2006.

Liberal members tend to adopt a middle ground on most social issues, focusing on extending choice rather than favouring a single solution.

Until a few decades ago, there were two major political parties in Canada: the Progressive Conservatives ("Tories") and Liberals ("Grits"). A third party, the New Democratic Party, usually but not always campaigned for political office along the lines described above. But Canada's political spectrum has changed recently, with a number of newer political parties competing for the public's attention and, ultimately, their votes. These include the comparatively conservative Canadian Alliance Party (formerly the Reform Party), almost exclusively based in Western Canada, which recently merged with the Conservatives; and the provincial Parti Québécois and federal Bloc Québécois, French parties based in Quebec. Both continuity and change in the political power matrix were observable in the 2006 federal election. Stephen Harper's Conservative Party won a minority government with 124 seats. The last time this party was in office was in 1993. The second-largest number of seats (104) was won by the former reigning party, the Liberal Party. The Bloc Québécois (51 seats) picked up support from the Liberal Party as did the New Democrats with 29 seats. Canadians clearly wanted a change from the Liberal Party, cautiously choosing the Conservative Party to take the lead under the helm of Stephen Harper.

PARTY IDENTIFICATION

Because many people hold mixed political attitudes, with liberal views on some issues and conservative stands on others—party identification in Canada has historically tended to be weak. Figure 12–7 shows, however, that from the early 1990s until 2006, the Liberal Party enjoyed remarkable support from Canadians. During this time the Liberals enjoyed popular support that dropped below 40 percent only during the 1997 and 2000 elections; its support dipped to 30 percent in 2006. Meanwhile the Conservative Party (made up of the former Alliance (Reform) Party and Progressive Conservatives) recently gained in popular support from 20 percent in 2000 to 30 percent in 2006.

Although more than eight in every ten people polled preferred one party over another, most were not strongly committed to their party of choice. But most individuals do not hold views entirely consistent with either party of preference. With wealth to protect, well-to-do people generally hold conservative views on economic issues. Yet their extensive schooling and secure social standing encourage them to adopt liberal attitudes on many social issues. Individuals of low social position exhibit the opposite pattern,

To see how different polling organizations vary in their estimates of party support, go to http://www.wlu.ca/LISPOP/pollslinks.htm.

tending toward social democratic views on economic policy and embracing a socially conservative agenda (Nunn, Crocket, & Williams, 1978; Erikson, Luttbeg, & Tedin, 1980; Syzmanski, 1983; Humphries, 1984; McBroom & Reed, 1990).

SPECIAL-INTEREST GROUPS

In the wake of events such as school shootings across North America, public support for gun control has been rising. In 1995, the Canadian government passed *Bill C-68*, which radically changed firearms legislation. The keystone of the law is universal firearms registration. The Canadian Association of Police Chiefs has been a strong supporter of the legislation, arguing that it will improve police safety across the country. Yet members of the National Firearms Association and its supporters have steadily worked in opposition to the legislation.

Groups for and against the "gun lobby" are examples of *special-interest groups*, people with an interest in some economic or social issue. Special-interest groups—which include associations of senior citizens, farmers, fireworks producers, and environmentalists—flourish in nations such as Canada, where loyalty to political parties tends to be low.

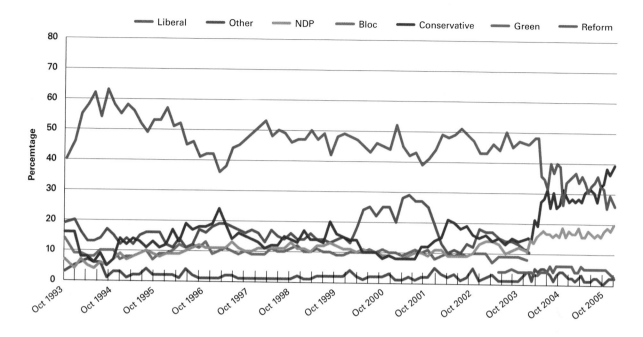

FIGURE 12-7 Political Party Popular Support, Canada, 1993–2006

Note: October 1993, June 1997, November 27, 2000, June 28, 2004, and January 23, 2006, are based on election results.

Sources: Angus Reid Group Inc. (1995, 1996b, 1997c, 1998c, 2000b); Ipsos-Reid (2001c, 2001d, 2001e, 2001f, 2001g, 2001h, 2002a, 2002b, 2002c, 2002d, 2002e, 2003g, 2003h, 2003i, 2003j, 2004a to 2004c, 2005a to 2005m, 2006a to 2006c).

Many special-interest groups employ lobbyists to work on their behalf.

VOTER APATHY

It is a disturbing fact of political life that many Canadians are indifferent about voting. In fact, Canadian citizens are less likely to vote today than they were a century ago. In the 2000 federal election, only 63 percent of eligible voters showed up at the polls. In 2004, the percentage dropped even further to 60.9 percent. More Canadian voters— 65 percent—went to the ballot box in 2006. Nevertheless, this turnout is generally lower than in almost all other industrialized nations except for the U.S.

Who is and is not likely to vote? Canadian women are less likely to cast a ballot than men. Seniors are more likely to vote than young people. White people are more likely to vote than are visible minorities, and Aboriginals are the least likely of all to vote. Generally speaking, people with a bigger stake in society—homeowners, parents with children at home, people with good jobs and extensive schooling— are most likely to vote. Income matters, too: people with incomes in the top 20 percent are much more likely to vote than are people with incomes in the bottom 20 percent

(Bennett, 1991; Hackey, 1992; Lewis, McCracken, & Hunt, 1994; DeLuca, 1998; Fetto, 1999).

Some non-voting is, of course, to be expected. At any given time, many people are sick or disabled; many more are away from home, having made no arrangement to submit an absentee ballot. Others forget to reregister after moving to a new neighbourhood. Moreover, registering and voting depend on the ability to read and write, which discourages Canadian adults who have limited literacy skills. Electoral reforms made it possible for homeless people to vote in the 2000 federal election, a privilege that was previously denied them because they had no fixed address.

Conservatives suggest that apathy amounts to *indifference* to politics because most people are, by and large, content with their lives. Liberals, and especially political radicals, counter that apathy reflects *alienation* from politics: people are so deeply dissatisfied with society that they doubt elections will make any real difference. Yet, as noted above, there is a link between income and voting: higher income is associated with greater likelihood of voting (Pammet and LeDuc, 2003). The fact that it is the disadvantaged and powerless people who are least likely to vote suggests that the liberal explanation for apathy probably is closer to the truth.

Theoretical Analysis of Politics

Sociologists have long debated how power is spread among different groups in Canada. Power is a very difficult topic to study because decision making is complex and often takes place behind closed doors. Despite this difficulty, researchers have developed three competing models of power in high-income countries such as Canada.

THE PLURALIST MODEL: THE PEOPLE RULE

The **pluralist model**, closely linked to structural-functional theory, is *an analysis of politics that sees power as spread among many competing interest groups*. Pluralists claim, first, that politics is an arena of negotiation. With limited resources, no organization can expect to achieve all of its goals. Organizations therefore operate as *veto groups,* realizing some goals but mostly keeping opponents from achieving all of their ends. The political process relies heavily on creating alliances and compromises between numerous interest groups so that policies gain wide support. In short, pluralists see power as spread widely throughout society, with all people having at least some voice in the political system (Dahl, 1961, 1982; Rothman & Black, 1998).

THE POWER-ELITE MODEL: A FEW PEOPLE RULE

The **power-elite model**, which is based on social-conflict theory, is *an analysis of politics that sees power as concentrated among the rich*. The term "power elite" was coined by C. Wright Mills (1956), a social-conflict theorist who argued that the upper class holds most of society's wealth, prestige, and power.

Mills claimed that members of the power elite are in charge of the three major sectors of societies such as Canada: the economy, government, and the military. Elites in this privileged category move easily from one sector to another, Mills continued, consolidating power as they go. Wallace Clement (1975) argues this point about the Canadian elite, concluding that the corporate elite control both the economy and the mass media, and also have a major influence over politics. Cases in point are Canadian corporate media giants Ted Rogers, André Chagnon, and Conrad Black, and, until their deaths, Ken Thomson and Izzy Asper.

Power-elite theorists say that countries such as Canada and the United States are not democracies because the concentration of wealth and power is simply too great for the average person's voice to be heard. They reject the pluralist idea that various centres of power serve as checks and balances on one another; according to the power-elite model, those at the top face no real opposition (Bartlett & Steele, 2000; Moore et al., 2002).

THE MARXIST MODEL: BIAS IN THE SYSTEM ITSELF

A third approach to understanding Canadian politics is the **Marxist political-economy model**, *an analysis that explains politics in terms of the operation of a society's economic system*. Like the power-elite model, the Marxist approach is a social-conflict model that rejects the idea of Canada as a genuine political democracy. But whereas the power-elite model focuses on the enormous wealth and power of certain individuals, the Marxist model looks to the bias rooted in this nation's institutions, especially its economy. Karl Marx believed that a society's economic system (capitalist or socialist) shapes its political system. Therefore, power elites do not simply appear on the scene: they are creations of capitalism.

From this point of view, reforming the political system—by, say, limiting the amount of money that rich people can contribute to political candidates—is unlikely to bring about true democracy. The problem does not lie in the *people* who exercise great power or the *people* who don't vote; the problem is the *system* itself—what Marxists call the "political economy of capitalism." In other words, as long as Canada has a predominantly capitalist economy, just as the majority of people are exploited in the workplace, they will also be shut out of politics.

Critical review. The Applying Theory table summarizes the three political system models discussed above. Which of the three models is correct? Over the years, research has shown support for each one. In the end, of course, how you think our political system ought to work is as much a matter of political values as it is of scientific fact.

Classic research by Nelson Polsby (1959) supports the pluralist model. Polsby studied the politics of New Haven, Connecticut, where he found that key decisions involving urban renewal, choosing political candidates, and running the city's schools were made by different groups. Polsby concluded that in New Haven, no one group—not even the upper class—ruled all the others.

Robert and Helen Lynd (1937) studied Muncie, Indiana (which they called "Middletown," to suggest it was a typical city), and documented the fortune amassed by a single family, the Balls, from their business producing glass canning jars. The Lynds' findings support the power-elite position. They showed how the Ball family dominated many aspects of the city's life, pointing to that family's name on a local bank, university, hospital, and department store. In Muncie, according to the Lynds, the power elite were more or less a single family. In Canada, such influence of wealth is observable in the province of New Brunswick, where the McCain and Irving families seem omnipotent.

APPLYING THEORY

POLITICS

	Pluralist Model	Power-Elite Model	Political-Economy Model
Which theoretical approach is applied?	Structural-functional approach	Social-conflict approach	Social-conflict approach
How is power spread throughout society?	Power is spread widely, so that all groups have some voice.	Power is concentrated in the hands of top business, political, and military leaders.	Power is directed by the operation of the capitalist economy.
Is Canada a democracy?	Yes. Power is spread widely enough to make the country a democracy.	No. Power is too concentrated for the country to be a democracy.	No. The capitalist economy sets political decision making, so the country is not a democracy.

From the Marxist perspective, the point is not which individuals make decisions. Rather, as Alexander Liazos (1982:13) explains, "The basic tenets of capitalist society shape everyone's life: the inequalities of social classes and the importance of profits over people." As long as the basic institutions of society are organized to meet the needs of the few rather than the many, Liazos concludes, a truly democratic society is impossible.

Clearly, the political system in Canada gives almost everyone the right to participate in politics through elections. But as the power-elite and Marxist models point out, the Canadian political system is, at the very least, far less democratic than most people think. Most citizens have the right to vote, but the major political parties and their candidates typically support only the positions that are acceptable to the most powerful segments of society and consistent with the operation of our capitalist economy.

Whatever the reasons, many people in Canada are losing confidence in their leaders. Canadians want more government transparency and greater accountability (Pammet & LeDuc, 2003).

Power Beyond the Rules

Politics is always a matter of disagreement over a society's goals and the means to achieve them. A political system tries to settle controversy within a system of rules. But political activity sometimes breaks the rules or even tries to do away with the entire system.

REVOLUTION

Political revolution is *the overthrow of one political system in order to establish another.* Revolution goes beyond reform, or change within a system, and even beyond a coup d'état (in French, literally "stroke of the state"), by which one leader topples another. Revolution involves change in the type of system itself.

No type of political system is immune to revolution, nor does revolution produce any one particular kind of government. The U.S. Revolutionary War (1775–76) changed colonial rule by the British monarchy into a representative democracy. French revolutionaries in 1789 also overthrew a monarch, only to set the stage for the return of a monarchy in the person of Napoleon. In 1917, the Russian Revolution replaced a monarchy with a socialist government built on the ideas of Karl Marx. In 1991, a second Russian revolution dismantled the socialist Soviet Union, and the nation was reborn as the Russian Federation, moving toward a market system and a greater political voice for its people.

Despite their striking variety, revolutions share a number of traits (Tocqueville, 1955, orig. 1856; Skocpol, 1979; Lewis, 1984; Tilly, 1986):

1. **Rising expectations.** Common sense suggests that revolution is more likely when people are severely deprived, but history shows that most revolutions occur when people's lives are improving. Rising expectations, rather than bitterness and despair, make revolution more likely.

2. **Unresponsive government.** Revolution becomes more likely when a government is unwilling to reform itself, especially when demands for change being made by powerful segments of society are not heard.

3. **Radical leadership by intellectuals.** The English philosopher Thomas Hobbes (1588–1679) claimed that intellectuals provide the justification for revolution, and universities often are at the centre of political change. For example, students played a key role in China's pro-democracy movement and in the uprisings in Eastern Europe.

4. **Establishing a new legitimacy.** Overthrowing a political system is not easy, but ensuring a revolution's long-term success is harder still. Some revolutionary movements are held together merely by hatred of the past regime and fall apart once new leaders are installed. Revolutionaries must also guard against counterrevolutionary drives led by overthrown leaders. This explains the speed and ruthlessness with which victorious revolutionaries typically dispose of former leaders.

Scientific research cannot say whether a revolution is good or bad. That judgment depends on personal values and in any case becomes clear only many years later. Fifteen years after its revolution, the future of the former Soviet Union remains uncertain.

TERRORISM

On September 11, 2001, terrorists hijacked four commercial airliners; one crashed in a wooded area, but the other three crashed into public buildings full of people. The attack killed more than 3000 innocent people (representing 68 nations, including Canada), injured many thousands more, completely destroyed the twin towers of the World Trade Center in New York City, and seriously damaged the Pentagon in Washington, D.C. Not since the attack on Pearl Harbor at the outbreak of World War II had the United States suffered such a blow. This event was the most serious terrorist act ever recorded in that country.

Terrorism refers to *acts of violence or the threat of such violence used as a political strategy by an individual or a group.* Like revolution, terrorism is a political act beyond the rules of established political systems. According to Paul Johnson (1981), terrorism has four distinguishing characteristics.

First, terrorists try to paint violence as a legitimate political tactic, despite the fact that such acts are condemned by virtually every nation. Terrorists also bypass (or are excluded from) established channels of political negotiation. Therefore, terrorism is a weak organization's strategy

against a stronger enemy. The 1970 FLQ kidnapping and subsequent murder of then Quebec labour minister Pierre Laporte was strongly condemned in all of Canada. At the same time, it served as a wake-up call for Canadians outside Quebec to the bitterness many Québécois feel about their position in Canada. Likewise, attacks against the U.S. embassies in Tanzania and Kenya in 1998 and the *U.S.S. Cole* in 2000 may have been morally wrong because they harmed innocent people, but they did raise the profile of organizations with grievances against the United States.

 Read the U.S. State Department's annual report on global terrorism at **http://www.state.gov/s/ct/**.

Today, terrorism has become commonplace in international politics. In 2003, there were 208 acts of terrorism worldwide, which claimed 625 lives and injured 3646 people. Of these, 60 (29 percent) were directed against the United States (U.S. Department of State, 2004).

Second, terrorism is used not just by groups but also by governments against their own people. *State terrorism* is the use of violence, generally without support of law, by government officials. State terrorism is lawful in some authoritarian and totalitarian states, which survive by creating widespread fear and intimidation. Saddam Hussein, for example, relied on secret police and state terror to protect his power in Iraq.

Third, democratic societies reject terrorism in principle, but they are especially vulnerable to terrorists because they give extensive civil liberties to their people and have less extensive police networks. In contrast, totalitarian regimes make widespread use of state terrorism, but their extensive police power minimizes opportunities for individual acts of terror.

Fourth, and finally, terrorism is always a matter of definition. Governments claim the right to maintain order, even by force, and may label opposition groups who use violence as "terrorists." Political differences may explain why one person's "terrorist" is another's "freedom fighter."

Hostage taking and outright killing provoke popular anger, but taking action against terrorists is difficult. Because most terrorist groups have no formal connection to any established state, identifying those responsible may be all but impossible, and a military response may risk confrontation with other governments. Yet as terrorism expert Brian Jenkins warns, the failure to respond "encourages other terrorist groups, who begin to realize that this can be a pretty cheap way to wage war" (quoted in Whitaker, 1985:29).

War and Peace

Perhaps the most critical political issue is **war**, *organized, armed conflict among the people of various nations, directed* *by their governments.* War is as old as humanity, of course, but understanding it is crucial today because humanity now has weapons that can destroy the entire planet.

At almost any moment during the twentieth century, nations somewhere in the world were engaged in violent conflict. In the "Great War" (World War I) alone, 56 500 Canadian soldiers lost their lives, and many more were injured. Other deadly conflicts since then took the lives of countless Canadians and people from all corners of the globe. To take another example, the United States has participated in eleven major wars. From the Revolutionary War to the War in Iraq, more than 1.3 million U.S. men and women have been killed in armed conflicts. Domestic and international wars continue to be waged at this time around the world, eating up a substantial portion of national budgets that could otherwise be used for more constructive purposes.

THE CAUSES OF WAR

Wars occur so often that we might think there is something "natural" about armed conflict. But there is no evidence that human beings must wage war under any particular circumstances. On the contrary, governments around the world usually have to force their people to go to war.

Like other forms of social behaviour, warfare is a product of *society* that varies in purpose and intensity from place to place. The Semai of Malaysia, among the most peace-loving of the world's peoples, rarely resort to violence. In contrast, the Ya̧nomamö (see the box on page 39) are quick to wage war.

If society holds the key to war or peace, under what circumstances do humans go to war? Quincy Wright (1987) cites five factors that promote war:

1. **Perceived threats.** Nations mobilize in response to a perceived threat to their people, territory, or culture. Some leaders justified the recent U.S.-led military campaign against Iraq, for example, by stressing the threat posed by Saddam Hussein to the United States and globally. However, Paul Martin, who was Canadian prime minister when the war started, decided not to support the U.S.-led campaign.

2. **Social problems.** When internal problems cause widespread frustration at home, a nation's leaders may divert attention by attacking an external "enemy" as a form of scapegoating. Some analysts think the lack of development toward democratic rule in the People's Republic of China, for example, led to hostility toward Vietnam, Tibet, and the former Soviet Union.

3. **Political objectives.** Poor nations, such as Vietnam, have fought wars to end foreign domination. Powerful

Not all terrorism is the work of individuals or groups. Since 1950, China has sought to maintain control of Tibet by force. This Tibetan refugee displays instruments of torture used against him by officials of the Chinese government.

countries such as the United States use a periodic "show of force" (recall the recent deployments of troops in Somalia, Haiti, Bosnia, Afghanistan, and Iraq) to increase global political standing.

4. **Moral objectives.** Nations rarely claim that they are going to war to gain wealth and power. Instead, their leaders infuse military campaigns with moral urgency. By calling the 2003 war in Iraq "Operation Iraqi Freedom," U.S. leaders portrayed the mission as a morally justified war of liberation from an evil tyrant.

5. **The absence of alternatives.** Preventing war was one reason that the United Nations was created. Although it still tries to maintain international peace, the UN has had limited success in resolving tensions among nations and thus preventing war.

IS TERRORISM A NEW KIND OF WAR?

After the terrorist attacks of September 11, 2001, U.S. government officials spoke of terrorism as a new kind of war. War has historically followed certain patterns: it is played out according to at least some basic rules; the warring parties are known to each other; and the objectives of the warring parties—which generally involve control of territory—are clearly stated.

Terrorism breaks from these patterns. The identity of terrorist individuals and organizations may not be known, those responsible may deny their responsibility, and their goals may be unclear. The recent terrorist attacks in countries such as the United States, Britain, Italy, and so forth were not attempts to defeat the nation militarily or to secure territory. They were carried out by people representing not a country but a cause, one that was not well understood in well-off Western countries. In short, they were expressions of anger and hate intended to create widespread fear.

Conventional warfare is symmetrical, with nations sending armies into battle. By contrast, terrorism is a new kind of war: an asymmetrical conflict in which a small number of attackers use terror and their own willingness to die as a means to level the playing field against a much more powerful enemy. Although the terrorists may be ruthless, the nation under attack must use caution in its response to terror because little may be known about the identity and location of those responsible. It is for this reason that U.S. officials maintain that the reaction to the September 11 attacks will unfold over a period of years.

THE COSTS AND CAUSES OF MILITARISM

The costs of war extend far beyond battlefield casualties. The world's nations spend almost $1 trillion annually (about $150 for every person on the planet) for military purposes. Such expenditures mean less money is available to aid hundreds of millions of poor people in their struggle for survival.

The United States has emerged as the world's single military superpower, with more military might than the next nine countries combined (Gergen, 2002). Defence is the U.S. government's second-biggest expenditure (after social security), accounting for 18 percent of all federal spending, or $376 billion, in 2003.

For decades, military spending went up because of the *arms race* between the United States and the former Soviet Union, which dropped out of the race after its collapse in 1991. But some analysts (who support power-elite theory) link high military spending to the domination of these societies by a **military-industrial complex**, *the close association of the federal government, the military, and defence industries.* The roots of militarism, then, lie not just in external threats but also in the institutional structures here at home (Marullo, 1987; Barnes, 2002b).

A final reason for continuing militarism is regional conflict. In the 1990s, localized wars broke out in Bosnia, Chechnya, and Zambia, and today tensions run high between Israel and the Palestinians, as well as between India and Pakistan. Even limited wars have the potential to grow and involve other countries, including the United States. India and Pakistan, both nuclear powers, moved to the brink of war in 2002. In 2003, the announcement by North Korea that it, too, had nuclear weapons raised tensions in Asia.

NUCLEAR WEAPONS

Despite the easing of superpower tensions, the world still contains 20 000 nuclear warheads, representing a destructive power equal to five tonnes of TNT for every person on the planet. If even a small fraction of this arsenal were used in war, life as we know it would end on much of the Earth. Albert Einstein, whose genius contributed to the development of nuclear weapons, reflected, "The unleashed power of the atom has changed everything *save our modes of thinking,* and we thus drift toward unparalleled catastrophe." In short, nuclear weapons make full-scale war possible in a world not yet capable of peace.

The United States, the Russian Federation, Great Britain, France, the People's Republic of China, Israel, India, Pakistan, and North Korea all have nuclear weapons. Although a few nations stopped the development of nuclear weapons—Argentina and Brazil halted work in 1990, and South Africa dismantled its arsenal in 1991—by 2010, as many as 50 countries could have the ability to fight a nuclear war. Such a trend makes any regional conflict far more dangerous.

MASS MEDIA AND WAR

The war in Iraq was the first war in which television crews travelled with troops, reporting as the campaign unfolded. The mass media provided ongoing and detailed reports of events; cable television made live coverage of the war available 24 hours a day, seven days a week.

Those media outlets critical of the war—especially the Arab news channel Al-Jazeera—tended to report the slow pace of the conflict, the casualties to the U.S. and allied forces, and the deaths and injuries suffered by Iraqi civilians, information that increased pressure to end the war. Media outlets supportive of the war tended to report the rapid pace of the war and the casualties to Iraqi forces, and to downplay harm to Iraqi civilians as minimal and unintended. In sum, the power of the mass media to provide selective information to a worldwide audience means that television and other media are almost as important to the outcome of a conflict as the soldiers who are doing the actual fighting.

PURSUING PEACE

How can the world reduce the dangers of war? Here are the most recent approaches to securing peace:

1. **Deterrence.** The logic of the arms race holds that security comes from a balance of terror between the superpowers. The principle of *mutual assured destruction* (MAD) means that a nation launching a first strike against another will face greater retaliation. This deterrence policy kept the peace for almost 50 years during the Cold War. Yet it encouraged an enormous arms race and cannot control nuclear proliferation, which poses a growing threat to peace. Deterrence also does little to stop terrorism or to prevent war started by a stronger nation against a weaker foe.

2. **High-technology defence.** If technology created the weapons, perhaps it can also protect us from them; such is the claim of the *strategic defence initiative* (SDI). Under SDI, satellites and ground installations would destroy enemy missiles soon after they were launched. Partly in response to the September 11 attacks, two-thirds of U.S. adults now support SDI (Thompson & Waller, 2001; "Female Opinion," 2002). However critics, including many Canadians, claim that the system—which they refer to as "Star Wars"—would be at best a leaky umbrella. Others worry that building such a system will spark another massive arms race.

3. **Diplomacy and disarmament.** Some analysts believe that the best road to peace is diplomacy rather than technology (Dedrick & Yinger, 1990). Teams of diplomats working together can increase security by reducing, rather than building, weapon stockpiles.

    But disarmament has limitations. No nation wants to be weakened by eliminating its defences. Successful diplomacy depends on everyone involved sharing responsibility for a common problem (Fisher & Ury, 1988). Although the United States and the Soviet Union succeeded in negotiating arms reduction agreements that remain in effect, the threat from other nations such as North Korea is increasing.

4. **Resolving underlying conflict.** In the end, reducing the dangers of war may depend on resolving the issues that have fuelled the arms race. Even as Britain and the United States claim to be fighting in Iraq to spread the values of freedom and political democracy, many Islamic people see them as fighting the entire Muslim world. Perhaps the world needs to ask whether it is wise to be spending thousands of times as much money on militarism as we spend on efforts to find peaceful solutions (Sivard, 1988; Kaplan & Schaffer, 2001).

LOOKING AHEAD: POLITICS IN THE TWENTY-FIRST CENTURY

Just as economies are changing, so are political systems. Several problems and trends are likely to be important as the twenty-first century continues to unfold.

One troublesome problem in Canada is inconsistency between our democratic ideals and our low turnout at the polls. Perhaps, as conservative pluralist theorists say, many people do not bother to vote because they are content with their lives. On the other hand, the liberal power-elite theorists may be right when they say that people withdraw from a system that concentrates wealth and power in the hands of so few people. Or perhaps, as radical Marxist critics claim, people find that our political system offers little real choice, limiting options and policies to those that support our capitalist economy. In any case, the current high level of apathy calls for significant political reform.

A second major trend is the global rethinking of political models. The Cold War cast political debate in the form of two opposing models: capitalism and socialism. Today, however, discussion includes a broader range of political systems that link government to the economy in a variety of ways. "Welfare capitalism," as found in Sweden, or "state capitalism," as found in South Korea and Japan, are just two possibilities. The Controversy & Debate box looks at the current lack of democratic governments among the world's Islamic countries.

Third, we still face the danger of war in many parts of the world. Even as the end of the Cold War has resulted in the dismantling of some warheads, vast stockpiles of nuclear weapons remain, and nuclear technology continues to spread around the world. In addition, new superpowers are likely to arise (the People's Republic of China and India are likely candidates), just as regional conflicts and terrorism are likely to continue. We can only hope (and vote!) for leaders who will find nonviolent solutions to the age-old problems that provoke war, putting us on the road to world peace.

Islam and Freedom: A "Democracy Gap"?

As the United States, Britain, and the other participating allies launched the war in Iraq, their respective heads of state spoke hopefully of liberating the Iraqi people and holding up a democratic Iraq as an example to the rest of the Islamic world. As a recent study by Freedom House shows, however, these Western leaders are up against some long odds.

Freedom House reports that 47 of the world's 192 nations have an Islamic majority population. As the figure below shows, just 11 of these 47 countries (23.4 percent) have democratic governments, and Freedom House rates only one—Mali—as "free." Of the 145 nations without a majority Islamic population, 110 (75.9 percent) have democratic governments, and 84 are rated as "free." In other words, countries without Islamic majorities are three times more likely to have democratic governments than countries with Islamic majorities. Freedom House concludes that countries with Islamic majority populations display a disturbing "democracy gap."

This relative lack of democracy holds for all world regions that have Islamic-majority nations— Africa, Central Europe, the Middle East, and Asia. The pattern is especially strong among the 16 Islamic-majority states in the Middle East and North Africa that are ethnically Arabic—none is an electoral democracy.

What explains this "democracy gap"? Freedom House points to four factors.[*]

1. Countries with Islamic-

majority populations typically are less developed economically, with limited schooling for their people and widespread poverty.

2. These countries have cultural traditions that rigidly control the lives of women, providing them with few economic, educational, or political opportunities.

3. While most countries limit the power of religious elites in government, and some even require a "separation of church and state," Islamic-majority nations support involving Islamic leaders in government. In just two recent cases—Iran under the ayatollahs and Afghanistan under the Taliban—have Islamic leaders actually taken formal control of government; in many nations, however, they exert a considerable influence on politics.

4. The enormous wealth that comes from Middle Eastern oil plays a part in preventing democratic govern-

ment. In Iraq, Saudi Arabia, Kuwait, Qatar, and other nations, this resource has provided astounding riches to a small number of families, which they use to strengthen their political control. In addition, oil wealth permits elites to build airports and other modern facilities without encouraging broader economic development that would raise the living standards of the majority.

For all these reasons, Freedom House concludes that the road to democracy for Islamic-majority nations is likely to be long. Yet there are also reasons to think that change will come. In 1950, very few Catholic-majority countries (mostly in Europe and Latin America) had democratic governments. Today, however, most of these nations are democratic. Note, too, that a majority of the world's Muslim people—who live in countries including Nigeria, Turkey, Bangladesh, India, Indonesia, the United States, and Canada—already live under democratic governments.

CONTINUE THE DEBATE . . .

1. Do you think the United States and its allies are right or wrong in seeking to bring about a democratic political system in Iraq? Why?

2. Do you expect to see greater democracy in Islamic-majority countries 50 years from now? Why or why not?

3. Can you point to several reasons that Muslim people might object to the kind of political system we call "democracy"?

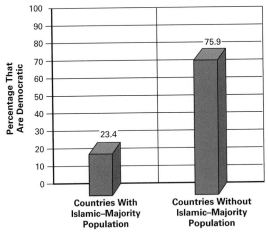

Democracy in Countries With and Without Islamic-Majority Populations

Source: Karatnycky (2002).

Source: Based on Karatnycky (2002).

SUMMARY

Economics

1. The economy is the major social institution by which a society produces, distributes, and consumes goods and services.

2. The primary sector of the economy produces raw materials; the secondary sector produces manufactured goods; the tertiary sector involves services rather than goods.

3. Capitalism is based on private ownership of productive property and the pursuit of profit in a competitive marketplace. Socialism is based on collective ownership of productive property through government control of the economy.

4. Capitalism's great productivity provides a high overall standard of living but with high income inequality; socialism is less productive, generating lower living standards but with less economic inequality.

5. The emerging global economy links many nations across national boundaries.

6. Canada is a post-industrial nation with only a small percentage of workers holding agricultural jobs; a minority have blue-collar, industrial jobs; three-quarters have white-collar, service jobs.

7. A profession is a special category of white-collar work based on theoretical knowledge, self-regulating practice, authority over clients, and emphasis on serving the community.

8. In 2006, some 6.1 percent of Canadian workers were unemployed, with young people and minorities most likely to be without jobs.

9. Women and other minorities represent an increasing share of all Canadian workers.

10. Corporations are the core of the Canadian economy. Most large conglomerates now operate in many countries.

Politics

1. Politics is the major social institution by which a society distributes power and organizes decision making. Max Weber claimed that power is legitimized by tradition, rationally enacted rules, or the personal charisma of a leader.

2. Monarchy is common to pre-industrial societies; industrialization favours the development of democracy.

3. Authoritarian political systems deny the people participation in government. Totalitarian political systems go even further, tightly controlling people's everyday lives.

4. The political spectrum—from the liberal left to the conservative right—involves attitudes on economic issues (such as how much the government regulates the economy) and social issues (including the rights and opportunities of women and other minorities).

5. Special-interest groups tend to be strong in countries like Canada and the United States that have weak political parties. Only 65 percent of eligible Canadian voters cast ballots in the 2006 national election.

6. The pluralist model of politics views power as spread widely among competing interest groups; the power-elite model believes that power is concentrated in a small, wealthy segment of society; the Marxist political-economy model says the capitalist economy makes true democracy impossible.

7. Revolution is the overthrow of one political system in order to establish another. Terrorism uses violence in pursuit of a political goal.

8. War is armed conflict between governments. The spread of nuclear weapons increases the threat of global catastrophe. Terrorism is a new form of asymmetrical conflict in which individuals or organizations use terror as a tactic against a more powerful enemy.

KEY CONCEPTS

Economics

capitalism (p. 310) an economic system in which natural resources and the means of producing goods and services are privately owned

corporation (p. 318) an organization with a legal existence, including rights and liabilities, apart from that of its members

economy (p. 306) the social institution that organizes a society's production, distribution, and consumption of goods and services

global economy (p. 308) expanding economic activity that crosses national borders

monopoly (p. 318) the domination of a market by a single producer

oligopoly (p. 318) the domination of a market by a few producers

post-industrial economy (p. 307) a productive system based on service work and high technology

primary sector (p. 308) the part of the economy that draws raw materials from the natural environment

profession (p. 314) a prestigious, white-collar occupation that requires extensive formal education

secondary sector (p. 308) the part of the economy that transforms raw materials into manufactured goods

social institution (p. 306) a major sphere of social life, or societal subsystem, organized to meet human needs

socialism (p. 310) an economic system in which natural resources and the means of producing goods and services are collectively owned

state capitalism (p. 311) an economic and political system in which companies are privately owned but cooperate closely with the government

tertiary sector (p. 308) the part of the economy that involves services rather than goods

welfare capitalism (p. 311) an economic and political system that combines a mostly market-based economy with extensive social welfare programs

Politics

authoritarianism (p. 322) a political system that denies the people participation in government

authority (p. 320) power that people perceive as legitimate rather than coercive

democracy (p. 322) a type of political system that gives power to the people as a whole

government (p. 320) a formal organization that directs the political life of a society

Marxist political-economy model (p. 328) an analysis that explains politics in terms of the operation of a society's economic system

military-industrial complex (p. 332) the close association of the federal government, the military, and defence industries

monarchy (p. 321) a type of political system in which a single family rules from generation to generation

pluralist model (p. 328) an analysis of politics that sees power as spread among many competing interest groups

political revolution (p. 329) the overthrow of one political system in order to establish another

politics (p. 320) the social institution that distributes power, sets a society's goals, and makes decisions

power (p. 320) the ability to achieve desired ends despite resistance from others

power-elite model (p. 328) an analysis of politics that sees power as concentrated among the rich

routinization of charisma (p. 320) the transformation of charismatic authority into some combination of traditional and bureaucratic authority

terrorism (p. 330) acts of violence or the threat of such violence used as a political strategy by an individual or a group

totalitarianism (p. 322) a highly centralized political system that extensively regulates people's lives

war (p. 330) organized, armed conflict among the people of various nations, directed by their governments

welfare state (p. 325) a range of government agencies and programs that provide benefits to the population

CRITICAL-THINKING QUESTIONS

1. As social institutions, what are the economy and the political system supposed to do? How well, in your opinion, does each do its job?

2. In what specific ways did the Industrial Revolution change the economy of Canada? How is today's Information Revolution changing the economy once again?

3. Compare the pluralist, power-elite, and Marxist models of political power. Which do you think is most correct? Why?

4. How are both the economy and politics becoming global in scope? What changes in each would you expect by the end of the twenty-first century?

SITES TO SEE

www.pearsoned.ca/macionis

The authors and publisher of this book invite you to visit the interactive Companion Website™ that accompanies this text. Begin by clicking on the cover of your book. You will find a chapter-by-chapter study guide, practice tests, suggested weblinks, and links to other relevant material.

www40.statcan.ca/l01/ind01/l2_2621.htm

Visit the website operated by Statistics Canada, where you will find a wide range of interesting data and reports on the Canadian labour market.

www.clc-ctc.ca

The Canadian Labour Congress unites 2.3 million Canadian workers promoting issues related to the social and economic justice of working people across the country.

www.fao.org

The Food and Agriculture Organization is a part of the United Nations concerned with how well the global economy meets the needs of the world's people. From its home page, look for the FAO's annual report, titled State of Food Insecurity in the World.

www.collectionscanada.ca/femmes/002026-801-e.html

This Internet source provides key reference sources for women in Canadian politics.

www.amnesty.org

Amnesty International operates a website that offers information about the state of human rights around the world.

www.dwatch.ca

Visit the website for Democracy Watch, an independent, non-profit, non-partisan Canadian citizen advocacy organization based in Ottawa. The organization works with Canadian citizens and organizations in helping to reform Canadian government and business institutions to bring them into line with the realities of a modern, working democracy.

 # INVESTIGATE WITH RESEARCH NAVIGATOR™

Follow the instructions on page 33 of this text to access the features of Research Navigator™. Once at the website (**www.researchnavigator.com**), enter your login name and password. Then, to use the Content Select™ database, enter keywords such as "corporations," "political economy," and "terrorism," and the search engine will supply relevant and recent scholarly and popular press publications.

To reinforce your understanding of this chapter, and to identify topics for further study, visit MySocLab at **www.pearsoned.ca/mysoclab/macionis** for diagnostic tests and a multimedia ebook.

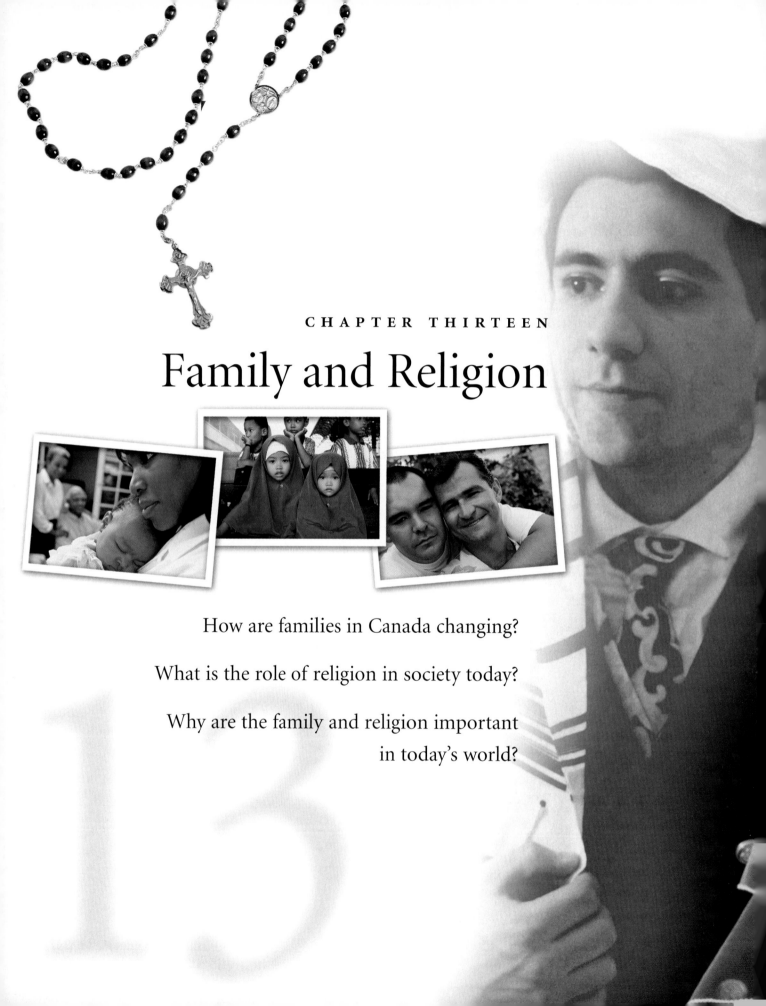

CHAPTER THIRTEEN

Family and Religion

How are families in Canada changing?

What is the role of religion in society today?

Why are the family and religion important
in today's world?

13

The family and religion are social institutions that shape people's behaviour and beliefs. The two institutions often come together in ritual events, such as this Jewish wedding ceremony.

Diane Carp had the career of her dreams: She worked as a nurse in a pediatric intensive care unit and found great satisfaction in helping children in need. Even with her long hours at the hospital, she saved time to teach nursing classes at the nearby university and also to work on several research projects. She is widely known and well respected in her home community.

With so many responsibilities at work, it may be no surprise to learn that Diane Carp never quite got around to marrying. She recalls, "I had always thought I had such a rewarding career. . . . Part of me kept saying that I did not need the other stuff, the husband and the kids. Then, suddenly I was 40 and I realized that if I were going to do something, I had better do it now."

Carp decided she wanted a child and set out to adopt an infant girl from China, one of the few countries that permit adoption by foreigners who are single and over 40. She filled out volumes of paperwork and sent off her application. Fifteen months later, she was in China for the joyful first meeting with her daughter, Kai Li. This experience has been so wonderful for them that today, five years later, Carp is going through the process once again so that Kai Li will have a little sister.

"I have friends who say, 'Hey, I have someone I'd really like you to meet.' I reply, 'Well, thanks, but I really don't have time for another relationship.' I would rather devote the extra time to helping another child" (Padawer, 2001).

Diane Carp's story illustrates an important trend: Families in high-income countries such as Canada do not conform to any one model and are more diverse than ever before. Families differ because people's desires and situations differ. But family diversity also sparks a good deal of debate. What exactly is a "family"? Are families disappearing? Such questions touch on many people's deeply held beliefs and are part of the current "family values" debate.

Consider these statistics: among women under 30, half of all pregnancies occur out of wedlock. The Canadian divorce rate has doubled over the past 25 years so that 25 percent of today's marriages last fewer than 15 years and 40 percent will eventually end in divorce. The fact that one in four children is born to an unmarried woman (though some of these women may have been living in a common-law relationship when their child was born), coupled with the high divorce rate, means that half of Canadian children will live with a single parent at some time before reaching age 18 (one reason that the share of Canadian children living in poverty has been rising steadily).

To hear some tell it, the family is fast becoming an endangered species. Others counter that families are not disappearing so much as changing. For better or worse, the family probably is changing faster than any other social institution (Bianchi & Spain, 1996; Fox, 2001). Not long ago, the cultural ideal of the family consisted of a working husband, a homemaker wife, and their young children. Today, fewer people have such a singular vision of the family, and, at any given time, only about 15 percent of Canadian households fit that description.

At the same time, religion is changing, too, as membership in long-established churches is declining and new sects are flourishing. This chapter examines the family and religion, which are closely linked as society's *symbolic institutions*. Both help establish morality, maintain traditions, and join people together. Focusing on Canada with comparisons to other countries, we will examine why many people consider the family and religion the foundations of society, while others predict—and may even encourage—the decline of both institutions.

Families vary from culture to culture and also over time. But everywhere, people celebrate the ritual of marriage that extends kinship into a new generation. This idea is expressed clearly in David Botello's painting, *Wedding Photos at Hollenbeck Park.*

David Botello, *Wedding Photos at Hollenbeck Park,* 1990.

The Family: Basic Concepts

The **family** is *a social institution that unites people in cooperative groups to oversee the bearing and raising of children.* Family ties are also called **kinship,** *a social bond based on blood, marriage, or adoption.* All societies have families, but exactly whom people call their kin has varied through history and varies today from one culture to another. In Canada, most people regard a **family unit** as *a social group of two or more people, related by blood, marriage, or adoption, who usually live together.* In this country and throughout the world, families form around **marriage**—*a legal relationship usually involving economic cooperation as well as sexual activity and childbearing*—that people expect to last.

Today, some people object to defining only married couples and children as families because it endorses a single standard of behaviour as moral. Because some business and government programs still use this conventional definition, many unmarried but committed partners of the same or opposite sex are excluded from family healthcare and other benefits. However, organizations are gradually coming to recognize *families of affinity:* people with or without legal or blood ties who feel they belong together and want to define themselves as a family.

Statistics Canada no longer employs the traditional notion of family when collecting data on the Canadian "census family," which is currently defined as "a now-married couple (with or without never-married sons or daughters of either or both spouses), a couple living common-law (again with or without never-married sons or daughters of either or both partners), or a lone parent of any marital status, with at least one never-married son or daughter living in the same dwelling. Families of now-married and common-law couples together constitute husband–wife families" (Statistics Canada, 1998i). Until the 2001 census when a question on "sexual orientation" was added, sociologists in Canada did not have access to accurate national data on gay families and the 2001 census was the first one to provide data on same-sex partnerships. In 2001, a total of 34 200 couples—0.5 percent of all couples—identified themselves as same-sex common-law couples (Statistics Canada, 2002a).

Like many European countries today, Canada has now joined the international trend toward acceptance of a wider definition of "family" (Fox & Luxton, 2001), though this has not yet occurred south of the border.

The Family: Global Variations

In pre-industrial societies, people take a broad view of family ties, recognizing the **extended family,** *a family unit that includes parents and children as well as other kin.* This group is also called the *consanguine family* because it includes everyone with "shared blood." With industrialization, however, increasing social mobility and geographic migration gave rise to the **nuclear family,** *a family unit composed of one or two parents and their children.* The nuclear family is also called the *conjugal family,* meaning "based on marriage." Although many members of our society live in extended families, the nuclear family is the most common family form.

MARRIAGE PATTERNS

Cultural norms, and often laws, identify people as suitable or unsuitable marriage partners. Some norms promote **endogamy**, *marriage between people of the same social category*. Endogamy limits marriage prospects to others of the same age, village, race, religion, or social class. By contrast, **exogamy** is *marriage between people of different social categories*. In rural India, for example, a person is expected to marry someone from the same caste (endogamy) but from a different village (exogamy). The reason for endogamy is that people of similar position pass along their standing to their children, thereby maintaining the traditional social hierarchy. Exogamy, on the other hand, links communities and encourages the spread of culture.

In higher-income nations, laws permit only **monogamy** (from Greek, meaning "one union"), *marriage that unites two partners*. Global Map 13–1 shows that monogamy is the rule throughout the Americas and Europe. But many lower-income countries—especially in Africa and Southern Asia—permit **polygamy** (Greek, "many unions"), *marriage that unites three or more people*. Polygamy has two forms. By far the more common is *polygyny* (Greek, "many women"), a form of marriage that unites one man and two or more women. For example, Islamic nations in the Middle East and Africa permit men up to four wives. Even so, most Islamic families are monogamous because few men can afford to support several wives and even more children. *Polyandry* (Greek, "many men") unites one woman and two or more men. This extremely rare pattern exists in Tibet, a mountainous land where agriculture is difficult. There, polyandry discourages the division of land into parcels too small to support a family and divides the work of farming among many men.

Most of the world's societies at some time have permitted more than one marital pattern. Even so, as noted already, most marriages have been monogamous (Murdock, 1965, orig. 1949). The historical preference for monogamy reflects two facts of life: supporting several spouses is a heavy financial burden, and the number of men and women in most societies is roughly the same. Monogamy is also the dominant marriage pattern in Canada. However, there is a polygamist colony commune called "Bountiful," a community of approximately 1000 people just outside Creston in Southeast British Columbia. This fundamentalist group broke away from the U.S.-based Mormon church or, officially, the Church of Jesus Christ of Latter-day Saints, in 1886 when the Mormon church disavowed polygamy. Polygamy is illegal in BC, but the government has up until now adopted a hands-off approach to the community because the guarantee of freedom of religion under the *Charter of Rights and Freedoms* protects church members from the law.

RESIDENTIAL PATTERNS

Just as societies regulate mate selection, they also designate where a couple lives. In pre-industrial societies, most newlyweds live with one set of parents who offer protection, support, and assistance. Most often, married couples live with or near the husband's family, an arrangement called *patrilocality* (Greek, "place of the father"). But in some societies (such as the North American Iroquois), couples live with or near the wife's family, which is called *matrilocality* ("place of the mother"). Societies that engage in frequent local warfare tend toward patrilocality, so sons are close to home to offer protection. Societies that engage in distant warfare may be patrilocal or matrilocal, depending on whether sons or daughters have greater economic value (Ember & Ember, 1971, 1991).

Industrial societies typically do not follow either of these patterns. Finances permitting, they favour *neolocality* (Greek, "new place"), in which a married couple lives apart from both sets of parents.

PATTERNS OF DESCENT

Descent refers to *the system by which members of a society trace kinship over generations*. Most pre-industrial societies trace kinship through just the father's or the mother's side of the family. Patrilineal descent, the more common pattern, traces kinship through males, so that property flows from fathers to sons. Patrilineal descent characterizes most pastoral and agrarian societies, in which men produce the most valued resources. Matrilineal descent, by which people define only the mother's side as kin and property passes from mothers to daughters, is found in horticultural societies where women are the primary food producers.

Industrial societies with greater gender equality recognize *bilateral descent* ("two-sided descent"). That is, children recognize people on both the mother's side and the father's side of the family as relatives.

PATTERNS OF AUTHORITY

Worldwide, polygyny, patrilocality, and patrilineal descent are dominant and reflect the global pattern of patriarchy. Indeed, as Chapter 10 ("Gender Stratification") explains, no truly matriarchal society has ever existed.

In high-income industrial societies such as Canada, more egalitarian families are evolving as the share of women in the labour force goes up. However, men are still typically heads of households. Moreover, though children now more commonly take both of their parents' last names, children very rarely use only their mother's last name when both parents are married and living together.

GLOBAL MAP 13-1 Marital Form in Global Perspective

Monogamy is the only legal form of marriage throughout the Western Hemisphere and in much of the rest of the world. In most African nations and in Southern Asia, however, polygamy is permitted by law. In many cases, this practice reflects the historic influence of Islam, a religion that allows a man to have up to four wives. Even so, most marriages in these countries are monogamous, primarily for financial reasons.

Source: *Peters Atlas of the World* (1990).

Theoretical Analysis of the Family

As in earlier chapters, the various theoretical approaches offer a range of insights about the family.

FUNCTIONS OF THE FAMILY: STRUCTURAL-FUNCTIONAL ANALYSIS

According to the structural-functional approach, the family performs many vital tasks. In fact, the family operates as the backbone of society.

1. **Socialization.** As noted in Chapter 3 ("Socialization: From Infancy to Old Age"), the family is the first and most important setting for child rearing. Ideally, parents help children become well-integrated and contributing members of society (Parsons & Bales, 1955). Of course, family socialization continues throughout the life cycle, from childhood to old age. Nor is this process a one-way street: as any parent knows, mothers and fathers learn as much from their children as the children learn from them.

2. **Reproduction and regulation of sexual activity.** Every sustainable culture requires reproduction. But every culture also regulates sexual activity in the interest of maintaining kinship organization and property rights. As discussed in Chapter 6 ("Sexuality and Society"), the **incest taboo** is *a norm forbidding sexual relations or marriage between certain relatives.* Although the incest taboo exists in societies around the world, exactly which relatives cannot marry varies from one culture to another (Murdock, 1965, orig. 1949).

   Reproduction between close relatives can result in mental and physical damage to offspring. Yet only humans observe an incest taboo, suggesting that the key reason for controlling incest is social. Why? First, the incest taboo limits sexual competition in families by restricting sex to spouses. Second, because kinship defines people's rights and obligations toward one another, reproduction between close relatives would hopelessly confuse kinship ties and threaten the social order. Third, forcing people to marry beyond their immediate families integrates the larger society.

3. **Social placement.** Families are not needed for people to reproduce, but they help maintain social organization. Parents pass on their own social identity—in terms of race, ethnicity, religion, and social class—to children at birth.

4. **Material and emotional security.** Many view the family as a "haven in a heartless world," offering physical protection, emotional support, and financial assistance. In support of this view, people living in families tend to be healthier than people living alone.

Critical review. Structural-functional analysis explains why society, at least as we know it, is built on families. But this approach glosses over the diversity of Canadian family life and ignores how other social institutions (such as government) could meet at least some of the same human needs. Finally, structural-functionalism overlooks the negative aspects of family life, including patriarchy and family violence.

INEQUALITY AND THE FAMILY: SOCIAL-CONFLICT ANALYSIS

Like the structural-functional approach, the social-conflict approach considers the family central to our way of life. But instead of focusing on ways in which kinship benefits society, conflict theorists point out how the family perpetuates social inequality.

1. **Property and inheritance.** Friedrich Engels (1902, orig. 1884) traced the origin of the family to men's need (especially in the higher classes) to identify heirs so that they could hand down property to their sons. Families thus concentrate wealth and reproduce the class structure in each new generation (Mare, 1991; Eichler, 1997).

2. **Patriarchy.** To know their heirs, men must control the sexuality of women. Families therefore transform women into the sexual and economic property of men. A century ago in Canada, most wives' earnings belonged to their husbands. Today, women still bear most of the responsibility for child rearing and housework (Benoit, 2000a; Statistics Canada, 2000m; Ward, 2002).

3. **Race and ethnicity.** Racial and ethnic categories persist over generations only to the degree that people marry others like themselves. Endogamous marriage supports racial and ethnic hierarchies (Lynn & Todoroff, 1998; Mandell & Duffy, 2000; Mandell & Duffy, 2004).

Critical review. Social-conflict analysis shows another side of family life: its role in social stratification. Friedrich Engels criticized the family as part and parcel of capitalism. But non-capitalist societies also have families (and family problems). The family may be linked to social inequality, as Engels argued, but it carries out societal functions not easily accomplished by other means.

CONSTRUCTING FAMILY LIFE: MICRO-LEVEL ANALYSIS

Both the structural-functional and social-conflict approaches view the family as a structural system. By contrast, micro-level analysis explores how individuals shape and experience family life.

The symbolic-interaction approach. Ideally, family living offers an opportunity for *intimacy,* a word with Latin roots that mean "sharing fear." As family members share many activities over time, they build emotional bonds. Of course, the fact that parents act as authority figures often limits their closeness with younger children. Only as young people reach adulthood do kinship ties open up to include sharing confidences as well as turning to one another for help with daily tasks and responsibilities (Macionis, 1978).

People in every society recognize the reality of physical attraction. But the power of romantic love, captured in Christian Pierre's painting, *I Do,* holds surprisingly little importance in traditional societies. In much of the world, it would be less correct to say that individuals marry individuals and more true to say that families marry families. In other words, parents arrange marriages for their children with an eye to the social position of the kin groups involved.

The social-exchange approach. Social-exchange analysis, another micro-level approach, describes courtship and marriage as forms of negotiation (Blau, 1964). Dating allows each person to assess the advantages and disadvantages of a potential spouse. In essence, exchange analysts suggest, people "shop around" to make the best "deal" they can in a partner in light of what they have to offer.

In patriarchal societies, gender roles dictate the elements of exchange: men bring wealth and power to the marriage marketplace, and women bring beauty. The importance of beauty explains women's traditional concern with their appearance and sensitivity about revealing their age. But as women have joined the labour force and have become less dependent on men to support them, the terms of exchange are becoming more similar for men and women (Harman & Remy, 2002).

Critical review. Micro-level analysis offers a useful balance to structural-functional and social-conflict visions of the family as an institutional system. Both the symbolic-interaction and social-exchange approaches focus on the individual experience of family life. However, micro-level analysis misses the bigger picture: family life is similar for people in the same social and economic categories. The Applying Theory table summarizes what we learn from the three theoretical approaches to family life.

Canadian families vary in some predictable ways according to social class and ethnicity, and as the next section explains, they typically evolve through distinct stages linked to the life course.

Stages of Family Life

Members of our society recognize several distinct stages of family life across the life course.

COURTSHIP AND ROMANTIC LOVE

November 17, 2000, Victoria, BC. It is a typical late-autumn Saturday in the city. We are at the Interfaith Chapel and attending the marriage of Jan and Nathan. Both are in their early twenties and beaming at their new status. On the surface, there is nothing at all unusual about the young couple. Their relationship is based on romantic love rather than an arrangement struck between their parents or extended families, a practice still common in parts of the world. However, the new couple is different in at least one respect. Signifying the expanding role of the Internet in both Canada and England (where Nathan comes from), the couple's courtship (which spanned several months) took place online. According to Jan, by the time she actually met Nathan in person, they were already planning their marriage.

 Check out how people use the Internet to find partners at **http://www.loveme.com.**

APPLYING THEORY

FAMILY

	Structural-Functional Approach	Social-Conflict Approach	Symbolic-Interaction Approach
What is the level of analysis?	Macro-level	Macro-level	Micro-level
What is the importance of the family for society?	The family performs vital tasks, including socializing the young and providing emotional and financial support for members. The family helps regulate sexual activity.	The family perpetuates social inequality by handing down wealth from one generation to the next. The family supports patriarchy as well as racial and ethnic inequality.	The reality of family life is constructed by members in their interaction. Courtship typically brings together people who offer the same level of advantages.

Halfway across the globe, in rural Sri Lanka, as in pre-industrial societies throughout the world, most people consider courtship too important to be left to the young (Stone, 1977). *Arranged marriages* are alliances between two extended families of similar social standing and usually involve an exchange not just of children but also of wealth and favours. Romantic love has little to do with arranged marriages, and parents may make such arrangements when their children are very young. A century ago in Sri Lanka and India, half of all girls married before age 15 (Mayo, 1927; Mace & Mace, 1960). As the Global Sociology box explains, in some parts of rural India, child marriage is still found today.

Industrialization both erodes the importance of extended families and weakens traditions. Young people who choose their own mates delay marriage until they gain the experience needed to select a suitable partner. Dating sharpens courtship skills and allows sexual experimentation.

Our culture celebrates *romantic love*—affection and sexual passion toward another person—as the basis for marriage. We find it hard to imagine marriage without love, and our popular culture, from fairy tales such as "Cinderella" to today's paperback romance novels, portrays love as the key to a successful marriage. However, as Figure 13–1 on page 348 shows, in many countries, romantic love plays a much smaller role in marriage.

Our society's emphasis on romantic love motivates young people to "leave the nest" to form families of their own; physical passion may also help a new couple through difficult adjustments in living together (Goode, 1959). On the other hand, because feelings change over time, romantic love is a less stable foundation for marriage than social

and economic considerations, one reason that the divorce rate is much higher in Canada than in nations where culture limits choices in partners.

But even in our country, sociologists point out, society aims Cupid's arrow more than we like to think. Most people fall in love with others of the same race, of comparable age, and of similar social class. Our society "arranges" marriages by encouraging **homogamy** (literally, "like marrying like"), *marriage between people with the same social characteristics.*

SETTLING IN: IDEAL AND REAL MARRIAGE

Our culture gives young people an idealized, "happily ever after" picture of marriage. Such optimism can lead to disappointment, especially for women, who are taught that marriage is the key to happiness. Also, romantic love involves a lot of fantasy: We fall in love with others not always as they are but as we want them to be.

Sexuality, too, can be a source of disappointment. In the romantic haze of falling in love, people may see marriage as an endless sexual honeymoon only to realize that sex becomes less than an all-consuming passion. Although the frequency of marital sex does decline over time, about two in three married people report that they are satisfied with the sexual dimension of their relationship. In general, couples with the best sexual relationships experience the most satisfaction in their marriages. Sex may not be the key to marital happiness, but good sex and good relationships often go together (Blumstein & Schwartz, 1983; Laumann et al., 1994).

Infidelity—sexual activity outside marriage—is another area where the reality of marriage does not match our cultural ideal. Most Canadian adults do not approve of sex outside of marriage, but many have difficulty discussing

Early to Wed: A Report From Rural India

Sumitra Jogi cries as her wedding is about to begin. Are they tears of joy? Not exactly. This "bride" is an eleven-month-old squirming in the arms of her mother. The groom? A boy of six.

In a remote village in India's western state of Rajasthan, the two families gather at midnight to celebrate a traditional wedding ritual. It is May 2, in Hindu tradition an especially good day to marry. Sumitra's father smiles as the ceremony begins; her mother cradles the infant, who has fallen asleep. The groom, wearing a special costume and a red and gold turban on his head, gently reaches up and grasps the baby's hand. Then, as the ceremony ends, the young boy leads the baby and her mother around the wedding fire three-and-one-half times while the audience beams at the couple's first steps together as husband and wife.

Child weddings are illegal in India, but traditions are strong in rural regions,

and marriage laws are hard to enforce. As a result, thousands of children marry each year. "In rural Rajasthan," explains one social worker, "all the girls are married by age 14. These are poor, illiterate families, and they don't want to keep girls past their first menstrual cycle."

For a time, Sumitra Jogi will remain with her parents. But in eight or ten years, a second ceremony will send her to live with her husband's family, and her married life will begin.

If the reality of marriage is years in the future, why do families push their

children to marry at such an early age? Parents of girls know that the younger the bride, the smaller the dowry offered to the groom's family. Also, when girls marry this young, there is no question about their virginity, which raises their value on the marriage market. No one in these situations thinks about love or the fact that the children are too young to understand what is taking place.

WHAT DO YOU THINK?

1. In traditional societies, why do parents arrange the marriages of their children?
2. What are some advantages and disadvantages of arranged marriages?
3. Arranged marriages are sometimes arranged by parents within their specific caste/Indian ethnic community in high-income countries such as the United Kingdom (as shown in the 2002 film *Bollywood/Hollywood* by Indo-Canadian director Deepa Mehta) and Canada (Gibbons, 1990). What do you think about such arrangements?

Source: Based on Anderson (1995); Gibbons (1990).

---

infidelity—in thought and in action—with their spouse. In a 2003 poll on marriage in Canada, 23 percent of married Canadians said that they had not mentioned to their spouse an attraction to another person, 16 percent of those surveyed had not discussed with their spouses doubts about their marriage, 9 percent had not mentioned using the Internet to view risqué material, and 4 percent had avoided discussing an extra-marital affair (Ipsos-Reid 2003a).

CHILD REARING

Despite the demands children make on us, a majority of adults in a recent international poll—including the major-

ity surveyed in Canada (60 percent)—identified raising children as one of life's great joys (The Gallup Organization, 1997). Today, however, few people in Canada, similar to their counterparts in a number of other countries, want more than a few children, as Figure 13–2 documents. This is a change from two centuries ago, when eight children was the Canadian average!

The trend toward smaller families is most pronounced in high-income nations. The picture differs in lower-income countries in Latin America, Asia, and especially Africa, where many women have few alternatives to bearing children. In such societies, as a glance back at

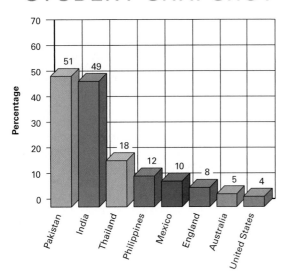

FIGURE 13-1 Percentage of Post-Secondary Students Who Express a Willingness to Marry Without Romantic Love

Source: Levine (1993).

Global Map 1–1 on page 5 shows, four to six children is still the norm.

Parenting is a very expensive, long-term commitment. As our society has given people greater choice about family life, more Canadian adults have decided to delay childbirth or to remain childless. In 2002, there were only 41 births for every 1000 females aged 15–49, just one-third the 1959 figure of 116 births for females in this age group (Statistics Canada, 2006au, p. 40).

About two-thirds of parents in Canada claim they would like to devote more of their time to child rearing (Statistics Canada, 1999f). But unless we accept a lower standard of living, economic realities demand that most parents pursue careers outside the home, even if that means giving less attention to their families (Fox, 2001).

Children of working parents spend most of the day at school. But after school, over 20 percent of our children aged 6–12 are latchkey kids, who spend time alone at home unsupervised (Child and Family Canada, 2003; Vandivere et al., 2003).

Traditionalists in the "family values" debate charge that many mothers work at the expense of their children, who receive less parenting. Progressives counter that such criticism targets women for wanting the same opportunities men have long enjoyed.

Most Northern European countries provide generous family leaves and benefits, as well as public childcare, to help ease the conflict between family and work (Baker, 1995). Changes in the Canadian *Employment Insurance Act* have brought the length of the leave (12 months as of January 2001) within the range of that found in the Nordic countries. However, the Canadian leave is accompanied by comparatively low benefits (55 percent of previous wages), compared to 80 percent in Sweden (Benoit, 2000a). Even worse off are U.S. parents. Congress took a small step toward easing the conflict between family and job responsibilities by passing the *Family and Medical Leave Act* in 1993. This law allows up to 90 days' unpaid leave from work for a new child or a serious family emergency. Still, most parents in the U.S. have to juggle parental and occupational responsibilities, and there are direct economic consequences because the U.S. leave has no monetary benefit unless parents belong to employer-sponsored parental programs.

Here is a report on the evolution of maternity and parental leave benefits in Canada: **http://www.irpp.org/choices/archive/vol12no2.pdf**.

THE FAMILY IN LATER LIFE

Increasing life expectancy in Canada means that couples who stay married do so for a long time. By age 60, most have completed the task of raising children. At this point, marriage brings a return to living with only a spouse.

Like the birth of children, their departure—the "empty nest"—requires adjustments, although a marriage often becomes closer and more satisfying. Years of living together may have lessened a couple's sexual passion, but understanding and commitment often increase.

Personal contact with children usually continues because most older adults live a short distance from at least one of their grown children. Moreover, a substantial number of Canadian adults are grandparents, many of whom help with childcare and other responsibilities. Among Latin American, South Asian, and Aboriginal Canadians, in particular, grandmothers have a central position in family life (Statistics Canada, 2000m).

The other side of the coin is that adults in midlife now provide more care for aging parents. The "empty nest" may not be filled by a parent coming to live in the home, but many adults find that caring for parents living to 80 and beyond can be more taxing than raising young children. Many of the "baby boomers"—who are now between 40 and 60 years old—are called the "sandwich generation" because they have children under 18 living at home as well as caring responsibilities for one or more of their own parents (Habtu & Popovic, 2006). While Canadian women and men are equally likely to find themselves in the role of caring for an older adult while still caring for a child, Table 13–1 shows that women are more likely to be negatively affected by the ensuing changes to their professional and personal lives.

The final, and surely the most difficult, transition in married life comes with the death of a spouse. Wives typically outlive husbands because of their greater life expectancy and the fact that women usually marry men several years older than themselves. Wives can thus expect to spend some years as widows. The challenge of living alone after the death of a spouse is especially great for men, who usually have fewer friends than widows and may lack housekeeping skills.

Canadian Families: Class, Race, and Gender

Dimensions of inequality—social class, ethnicity, race, and gender—are powerful forces that shape marriage and family life. This discussion addresses each of these factors in turn, but bear in mind that they overlap in our lives.

SOCIAL CLASS

Social class determines a family's financial security and range of opportunities. Interviewing working-class women, Lillian Rubin (1976) found that wives thought a good husband was a man who held a steady job, did not drink too much, and was not violent. Rubin's middle-class respondents, by contrast, never mentioned such things; these women simply *assumed* that a husband would provide a safe and secure home. Their ideal husband was a man with whom they could communicate easily and share feelings and experiences.

Clearly, what women (and men) hope for in marriage—and what they end up with—is linked to their social class. Much the same holds for children: boys and girls lucky enough to be born into more affluent families enjoy better mental and physical health, develop more self-confidence, and go on to greater achievement than children born to poor parents (McLeod & Shanahan, 1993; Duncan et al., 1998; Hertzman, 1999; Kohen, Brooks–Gunn, Leventhal, & Hertzman, 2002).

ETHNICITY AND RACE

Ethnicity and race, too, shape families. Analysis of Aboriginal and visible minority families must begin with the stark reality of economic disadvantage. Despite upward mobility over the generations, the incidence of low income among

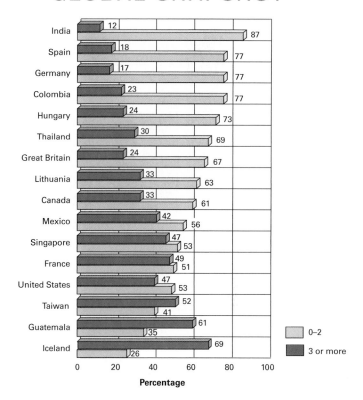

GLOBAL SNAPSHOT

FIGURE 13–2 Ideal Number of Children, Selected Countries, 1997

Survey question: "What do you think is the ideal number of children for a family to have?"

Note: No opinion omitted.

Source: The Gallup Organization (1997).

families of visible minorities is still significantly above the Canadian average (Statistics Canada, 2006au). In 2000, about 26 percent of members of visible minorities lived in families with incomes below Statistics Canada's low-income cut-off, compared with only 13 percent of all Canadians. About 34 percent of children under the age of 14 in the visible minority population were in low-income families in 2000, compared to 19 percent of all children. The incidence of low income was 16 percent among the visible minority population aged 65 and over, while the national average was 6 percent (Statistics Canada, 2003ah).

Some visible minority groups are also more likely to be single parents. Among females aged 25–44, black women (30 percent) were almost three times as likely in 2001 to be single parents as non-visible minority women (11 percent).

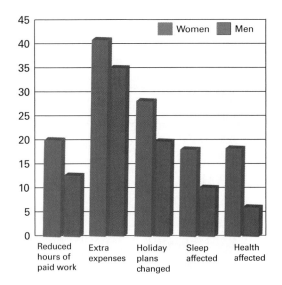

Table 13–1 Consequences of Informal Caregiving to Seniors

Source: Habtu, Roman and Andrija Popovic. "Informal Caregivers: Balancing Work and Life Responsibilities." Horizons. Vol8, No. (April 2006): 27-34.

Why, then, do many people think that marriage benefits women more than men (Bernard, 1982)? The positive stereotype of the carefree bachelor contrasts sharply with the negative image of the lonely spinster, suggesting that women are fulfilled only through being wives and mothers.

But, Bernard claims, married women have poorer mental health, less happiness, and more passive attitudes toward life than single women do. Married men, on the other hand, generally live longer, are mentally better off, and report being happier than single men. These differences suggest why, after divorce, men are more eager than women to find a new partner.

Bernard concludes that there is no better guarantor of long life, health, and happiness for a man than to have a woman well socialized to devoting her life to taking care of him and providing the security of a well-ordered home. She is quick to add that marriage could be healthful for women if husbands did not dominate wives and expect them to do almost all the housework. Indeed, research confirms that the wives and husbands with the best mental health are those who share responsibilities for earning income, raising children, and keeping the home (Ross, Mirowsky, & Huber, 1983; Mirowsky & Ross, 1984; Leira, 1992; Eichler, 1997).

Transitions and Problems in Family Life

The newspaper columnist Ann Landers once remarked that one marriage in twenty is wonderful, five in twenty are good, ten in twenty are tolerable, and the remaining four are "pure hell." Families can be a source of joy, but the reality of family life often falls short of the ideal.

DIVORCE

Canadian society strongly supports marriage, and about nine out of ten people at some point "tie the knot." But many of today's marriages unravel. Figure 13–4 on page 352 shows an increase in the Canadian divorce rate from the late 1960s (when the divorce laws were liberalized), peaking in 1987 (when restrictions were eased on marital dissolutions). Demographers estimate that if the divorce rate remained as high as it was in 1987, 50.6 percent of marriages would end in divorce by the 30th wedding anniversary. The divorce rate gradually levelled off and the estimated number of marriages ending in divorce before the 30th wedding anniversary decreased to 40 percent in 1995 and to 34.8 percent in 1997, but climbed to 37.7 percent in 2000. In 2003, the rate was 224 divorces per 100 000 population, a decrease of 3 percent (Statistics Canada, 2006au: 37; Statistics Canada, 2002c).

Apart from blacks, females from Latin America were the next most likely to be lone parents. However, among Japanese, Korean, and Chinese women, the incidence of lone parenthood is comparatively low, as illustrated in Figure 13–3 (Statistics Canada, 2003ba).

The patterns found among visible minority women are repeated for Aboriginal women. As explained in Chapter 11 ("Race and Ethnicity"), the personal incomes of Aboriginal men and women in Canada are substantially below the national incomes of non-Aboriginal men and women. People of Aboriginal ancestry are in fact more than twice as likely as non-Aboriginal people to have low incomes, so that family patterns reflect unemployment, underemployment, and, in some cases, physical environments replete with violence, alcoholism, and drug abuse.

Under these circumstances, maintaining stable family ties is difficult. Aboriginal lone mothers are especially marginalized economically (Castellano, 2002).

GENDER

Regardless of race, U.S. sociologist Jessie Bernard (1982; orig. 1973) says that every marriage is actually two different relationships: a woman's marriage and a man's marriage. Today, few marriages are composed of two equal partners. Patriarchy has diminished, but we still expect husbands to be older and taller than their wives and to have more important careers (McRae, 1986).

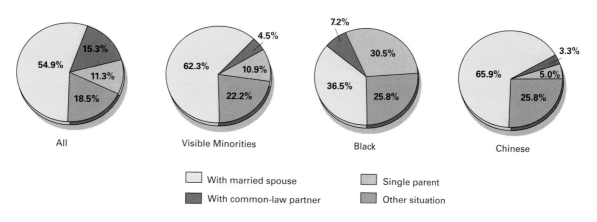

FIGURE 13-3 Living Situation of Females Aged 25–44 by Visible Minority Status, Canada, 2001

Source: Statistics Canada (2003ba).

Causes of divorce. The comparatively high Canadian divorce rate has many causes (Weitzman, 1985; Furstenberg & Cherlin, 1991; Etzioni, 1993; Popenoe, 1999; Greenspan, 2001; Luxton, 2001):

1. **Individualism is on the rise.** Today's family members spend less time together. We have become more individualistic, more concerned with our own personal happiness than with the well-being of our families and children.

2. **Romantic love often fades.** Because our culture bases marriage on romantic love, relationships may fail as sexual passion fades. Many people end a marriage in favour of a new relationship that promises renewed excitement and romance.

3. **Women are less dependent on men.** Women's increasing participation in the labour force has reduced wives' financial dependency on their husbands. Thus, women find it easier to leave unhappy marriages.

4. **Many of today's marriages are stressful.** With both partners working outside the home in most cases, jobs leave less time and energy for family life. This makes raising children harder than ever. Children do stabilize some marriages, but divorce is most common during the early years of marriage when many couples have young children.

5. **Divorce is socially acceptable.** Divorce no longer carries the powerful stigma it did a century ago. Family

and friends are now less likely to discourage couples in conflict from divorcing.

6. **Legally, a divorce is easier to get.** In the past, courts required divorcing couples to demonstrate that one or both were guilty of behaviour such as adultery or physical abuse. Today, all provinces allow divorce if a couple simply thinks their marriage has failed. Concern about easy divorce, voiced by many Canadians, has led some to advocate rewriting the marriage laws.

Who divorces? At greatest risk of divorce are young couples—especially those who marry after a brief courtship, have little money, and have yet to mature emotionally. The chance of divorce also rises if a couple marries after an unexpected pregnancy or if one or both partners have substance abuse problems. People whose parents divorced also have a higher divorce rate themselves. Researchers suggest a role-modelling effect: children who see parents go through divorce are more likely to consider divorce themselves (Amato, 2001; Williams, 2001; Statistics Canada, 2003l). Finally, people who are not religious are more likely to divorce than those who have strong religious beliefs.

Divorce is also more common if both partners have successful careers, perhaps because of the strains of a two-career marriage but also because financially secure people may not feel they have to stay in an unhappy home. Finally, men and women who divorce once are more likely to divorce again, probably because high risk factors follow them from one marriage to another (Glenn & Shelton, 1985).

FIGURE 13-4 Divorces in Canada 1970–2003

Source: Statistics Canada, 2006av.

In previous decades, the vast majority of Canadian mothers gained custody of children and, because fathers typically earn more income, the well-being of children was often dependent on fathers making court-ordered child-support payments (Statistics Canada, 1998k). In recent years, however, this trend has changed. As noted earlier, in 2003 mothers were awarded sole custody of fewer than half (48 percent) of the dependent Canadian children for whom custody was determined through divorce proceedings. This is down from 75.8 percent in 1988. A similar downward trend also occurred with husbands. Custody of a child/dependant was awarded to the husband in only 8 percent of cases in 2003, a drop from a peak of 15 percent in 1986. The other big change is that in 2003, 44 percent of dependent children for whom custody was awarded had custody given jointly to the husband and wife, a continuation of a 15-year trend of steady increases in joint custody arrangements (Statistics Canada, 2006).

Though Canadian courts tend to award child support in divorces involving children, in any given year, and despite the positive trend toward joint custody, a significant number of children legally entitled to support receive only partial payments or no payments at all (Baker, 1995). Canadian data for 1994–95 indicate that regular financial payments were received for about three-quarters of children whose parents reached an arrangement out of court; however, only just over half of children for whom financial support had been court ordered received regular custody payments (Statistics Canada, 1998k). In contrast, Sweden has a publicly financed child-support payment system that provides a minimum guaranteed level of economic support for children following separation or divorce of their parents (Baker, 1995; Boje & Leira, 2000). While all the reasons may not be clear, recent research indicates that children living in post-divorce custodial households have higher incidences of behavioural or emotional problems than children living with both of their biological parents (Williams, 2002; Strohschein, 2005).

Learn more about the Canadian Federal child support guidelines at http://www.justice.gc.ca/en/ps/sup/index.html.

REMARRIAGE

Four out of five people who divorce remarry, most within five years. Nationwide, about half of all marriages are now remarriages for at least one partner. Men, who benefit more from wedlock, are more likely than women to remarry.

Remarriage often creates *blended families,* composed of children and some combination of biological parents and stepparents. Members of blended families thus have to define precisely who is part of the nuclear family. Adjustments are necessary; for example, a former "only child" may suddenly find that she now has two older brothers. At the same time, blended families offer both young and old the chance to relax rigid family roles.

FAMILY VIOLENCE

The ideal family is a source of pleasure and support. However, the disturbing reality of many homes is *family violence,* emotional, physical, or sexual harm of one family member by another. The sociologist Richard J. Gelles calls the family "the most violent group in society with the exception of the police and the military" (quoted in Roesch, 1984:75).

Violence against women and men. Family brutality often goes unreported to police, but results from the 1999 General Social Survey estimate that nearly 700 000 women who are married or in common-law relationships or in contact with their former partners were exposed to spousal violence over the five-year period predating the survey. Data from 2001 indicate that the number of cases reported to police departments has been increasing, although there are also suggestions that victims are now more willing to report incidents to police than earlier victims were (Statistics Canada, 2000m, 2003m). In 2004, women were the victims of 51 percent of violent crimes reported to a sample of police forces; during that year, women committed 17 percent of violent crimes in Canada (Statistics Canada, 2006).

Men, too, are victims of spousal violence (Straus, 1993). In the 1999 and 2004 General Surveys on Victimization, men were victims at a rate similar to that of women (7 percent for men compared to 8 percent for women in 1999 and 6 percent each in 2004). However, women (25 percent) are much more likely than are men (10 percent) to be severely abused by their partner. Women were also more likely to be victims of repeat spousal violence (57 percent of women versus 50 percent of men in 2004). Further, women who are victims of spousal abuse are more likely than men in comparable situations to incur a physical injury: 44 percent of women versus 19 percent of men. Finally, though the overall rate is decreasing, women are at a much greater risk of spousal homicide than men. This is especially the case for women in common-law unions. In other words, women are much more likely to be killed by a family member than men are: while only 4 percent of male homicide victims were murdered by a spouse or ex-spouse in 2004, the rate for female homicide victims of spouses or ex-spouses was 37 percent (Statistics Canada, 2006). Overall, Canadian women are still more likely to be hurt by a family member than to be mugged or raped by a stranger or injured in an automobile accident (Statistics Canada, 2000m).

Historically, the law defined wives as the property of husbands, so that no man could be charged with raping his wife. In the past, too, the law regarded domestic violence as a private family matter, giving victims few options. Now, even without separation or divorce, a woman can at least obtain court protection from an abusive spouse. *Bill C-126*, known as the "Anti-Stalking Law," prohibits an ex-partner from following or otherwise threatening a woman (Statistics Canada, 1995a). Further, communities across North America have established domestic abuse shelters that provide counselling as well as temporary housing for women and children driven from their homes by domestic violence. While in 1975 there were only 15 shelters for abused women and children across the country, by 2004 this number had increased to more than 500 (Statistics Canada, 2005). On the other hand, there still are no shelters for men and their children leaving abusive relationships (Modrcin, 1998).

Violence against children. Family violence also victimizes children. Figures for 2001 show that children under 18 years old represent 21 percent of the population but were victims in more than 60 percent of all sexual abuse offences. Further, family members caused crimes against children in 37 percent of cases involving physical assaults and in 43 percent of cases involving sexual assaults (Statistics Canada, 2003m). Child abuse entails more than physical injury because abusive adults also violate trust to undermine a child's emotional well-being. Child abuse is most common among the youngest and most vulnerable children (Straus & Gelles, 1986; Van Biema, 1994).

Most child abusers are men; in 1996 fathers were the perpetrators of 73 percent of the reported physical assaults

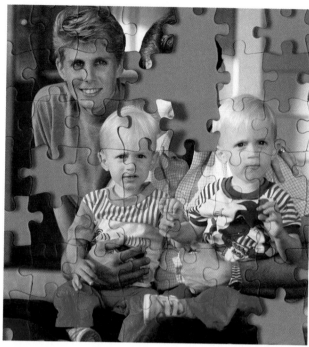

Divorce may be a solution for a couple in an unhappy marriage, but it can be a problem for children who experience the withdrawal of a parent from their social world. In what ways can divorce be harmful to children? Is there a positive side to divorce? How might separating parents better prepare their children for the transition of parental divorce?

against children, and 98 percent of the sexual assaults (Statistics Canada, 1998j). These men do not conform to a simple stereotype, but most abusers do share one trait: they were abused themselves as children. Researchers have found

 The Toronto Child Abuse Centre provides information on child abuse: **www.tcac.on.ca.**

that violent behaviour in close relationships is learned; in families, then, violence begets violence (Gwartney-Gibbs, Stockard, & Bohmer, 1987; Widom, 1996; Browning & Laumann, 1997).

Alternative Family Forms

The majority of Canadian families in the mid-twentieth century were composed of a married couple who raised children. But in recent decades, our society has displayed significant diversity in family forms.

ONE-PARENT FAMILIES

About 16 percent of Canadian families are one-parent families. Since 1981, the number of lone-parent families in Canada has grown from 712 000 to almost 1.3 million

In recent years, the proportion of young people who cohabit—that is, live together without being married—has risen sharply. This trend contributes to the debate over what is and is not a family: Do you consider a cohabiting couple a family? Why or why not?

(Statistics Canada, 2003n). One-parent families—81 percent of which in 2001 were headed by lone mothers, or four out of every five such families—may result from divorce, death, or the decision of an unmarried woman to have a child (Statistics Canada, 2002d).

In 2001, over one-third of Aboriginal children under the age of 15 lived in a one-parent family—more than twice the rate found in the population at large (Statistics Canada, 2003o). Many one-parent families are multigenerational, with single parents (most of whom are mothers) turning to their own parents (again, often mothers) for support. In countries such as Canada and the United States, then, the rise in single parenting is tied to both a declining role for fathers and a growing importance for grandparents. By contrast, in countries such as Sweden and Finland, the increasing role of the welfare state in providing social services, such as public childcare, significantly increases single parenthood (Macionis & Plummer, 1997:476–77).

Much research points to the conclusion that growing up in a one-parent family usually disadvantages children. According to some studies, a father and a mother each make a distinctive contribution to a child's social development, so it is unrealistic to expect a single parent to do as good a job. To make matters worse, most North American families with one parent—especially if that parent is a woman—contend with poverty. On average, children growing up in a single-parent family start out poorer, gain less schooling, and end

up with lower incomes as adults. Such children are also more likely to be single parents themselves (Weisner & Eiduson, 1986; Wallerstein & Blakeslee, 1989; Astone & McLanahan, 1991; Li & Wojtkiewicz, 1992; Biblarz & Raftery, 1993; Popenoe, 1993a; Shapiro & Schrof, 1995; Webster, Orbuch, & House, 1995; Wu, 1996; Duncan et al., 1998). Other research suggests, however, that single parenting itself is not the problem, and that one caring parent is much better for a child than two uncaring ones. Further, in countries where the state has reduced poverty among one-parent families, children in these families appear to do as well as their counterparts in two-parent families (Sainsbury, 1996).

Given the instability of common-law relationships, it is interesting to note that countries vary wildly in regard to their moral views on children being born outside marriage; views diverge especially in regard to the growing trend in Canada and other industrial countries of never-married women having children (almost 27 percent of Canadian female lone parents in 2000 were of this type) (Statistics Canada, 2003p).

COHABITATION

Cohabitation is *the sharing of a household by an unmarried couple.* The prevalence of cohabiting couples in Canada increased substantially over the past two decades, from a low of 6 percent in 1981 to 14 percent of all families in 2001. Nearly half of such unions involve children, sometimes born within the common-law union itself or otherwise from a former relationship (Statistics Canada, 1997b). In 2001, 13 percent of children under age 25 lived with common-law parents, more than four times the proportion of 3 percent 20 years earlier (Statistics Canada, 2002a). In fact, common-law families are the most likely to have young children, followed by female lone-parent families.

In global perspective, cohabitation as a long-term form of family life, with or without children, is common in Sweden and other Scandinavian countries, but it is rare in more traditional (especially Roman Catholic) nations such as Italy. National Map 13–1 illustrates the high proportion of cohabitation in Quebec, where 30 percent of all couples live in such a union, a rate similar to that of Sweden (Turcotte & Bélanger, 1998; Statistics Canada, 2002a). Cohabitation is gaining in popularity in Canada, and as this trend continues it may influence the future number of single-parent families because common-law unions have a higher probability of dissolution than do formal marriages (Wu, 2000). According to a recent Statistics Canada study (2000d), women whose first marriage ended in divorce tend to enter a new union, but are likely to opt for common-law rather than marriage. The same holds true for women whose first union was common-law: they are also likely to form a new

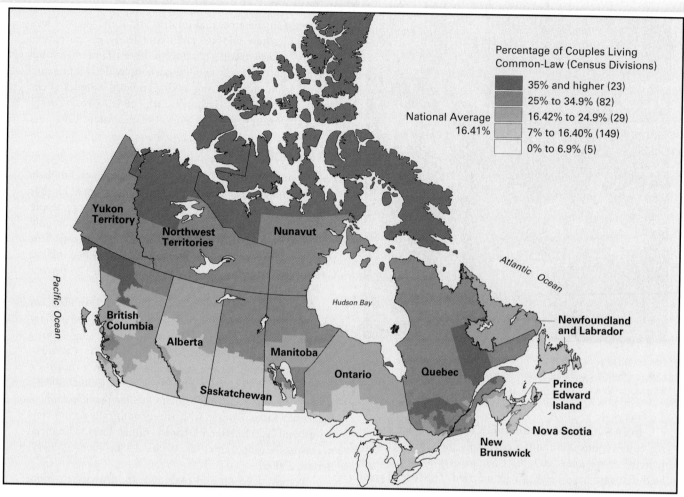

SEEING OURSELVES

NATIONAL MAP 13-1 Cohabitation Across Canada

Even though over 16 percent of all couples live in common-law relationships in Canada, this percentage varies greatly across Canada. One might think that it would be the couples in urban areas leading the way in this new trend. But as the map shows, it is Quebec and the rural areas in the other parts of Canada that are at the forefront in this trend. The lowest rate of cohabitation, on the other hand, occurs in Southern Manitoba and in York, just outside of Toronto. What do you think explains the patterns that you see in this map? Perhaps it is easier to explain why Quebec has a high rate than to explain the high rate in the rural areas.

Source: Calculated based on data in Statistics Canada (2002d).

relationship but tend to continue to live common-law. So, while marriage may be less popular, conjugal unions continue to be popular among Canadians.

GAY AND LESBIAN COUPLES

In 1989, Denmark became the first country to institute legislation granting registered same-sex partners the same rights as married couples. Norway, Sweden, and Iceland all enacted similar legislation in 1996, and Finland followed suit six years later. The Netherlands was the first country (2001) to allow civil marriage of gay couples and to permit them to adopt children. In 2003 Belgium followed suit in allowing their marriage, though it did not extend adoption rights to gay couples. Spain took this road in June 2005, allowing full legal rights for gays to marry and adopt children.

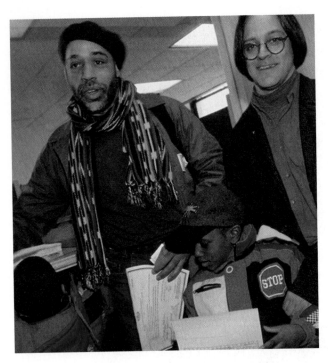

Gay couples can legally marry in Canada. Some are raising children from previous heterosexual unions, and some have adopted children.

In 1999, the Supreme Court of Canada held that same-sex couples must be granted essentially the same rights as married couples. In 2003, the Court of Appeal of Ontario held that gays have a right to get married. The federal government decided not to appeal this and similar cases, but instead to institute legislation toward the same effect. The federal government was forced to act after a series of court rulings struck down provincial marriage laws. Courts in Ontario, Quebec, and British Columbia have ruled that the exclusion of gays and lesbians unjustifiably violates equality rights. Gays and lesbians were allowed to marry immediately after the Ontario verdict, and did so, under a new right denied to them throughout most of human history. Other changes have taken place as well. A bill in 2000 extended full federal tax and social benefits to same-sex couples, and some provincial benefit plans and employers have recognized same-sex unions in their private insurance plans. In 2000, the province of British Columbia changed a variety of provincial statutes to grant same-sex couples the same rights and obligations as common-law couples. The new Conservative federal government elected in 2006 has decided to introduce a free vote in Parliament to repeal the same-sex marriage laws. The Conservatives had pledged to revisit the legislation before winning last year's election campaign. At the time of writing, then, the state of gay marriage in Canada remains uncertain.

Some gay couples with children are raising offspring from previous heterosexual unions, and some gay and lesbian couples have adopted children. Clearly, gay parenting challenges many traditional notions about families. It also indicates that many gay and lesbian couples derive the same rewards from child rearing as do "straight" couples (Bell, Weinberg, & Kiefer-Hammersmith, 1981; Gross, 1991; Pressley & Andrews, 1992; Henry, 1993; Herman, 1994).

SINGLEHOOD

Because most people in Canada marry at some point in their lives, we tend to see singlehood as a transitory stage of life that ends with marriage. In recent decades, however, more people have deliberately chosen to live alone. In the early 1950s, only one household in twelve consisted of a single person. This proportion had risen to one in four in 2001. In 1996, 3 million Canadians aged 15 and over lived alone, or about 12.5 percent of the population (Statistics Canada, 2003l).

The figure for women was almost 1.7 million, or 13.7 percent of the total female population 15 years of age and up. Most striking is the surging number of single young women. In 1960, approximately one in four Canadian women aged 20–24 were single; by 2001, the proportion had soared to 88.5 percent (Statistics Canada, 2003l). Underlying this trend is women's greater participation in the labour force. Women who are economically secure view a husband as a matter of choice rather than a financial necessity (Goldscheider & Waite, 1986; Eichler, 1997; Benoit, 2000a).

Women aged 65 and over also are now much more likely to live alone—in fact, twice as likely as their male counterparts. In large part this is because women tend to survive their husbands and to subsequently remain unmarried (Statistics Canada, 2003l).

NEW REPRODUCTIVE TECHNOLOGY

Recent medical advances, generally called new reproductive technology (NRT), are changing families, too. In the 20 years since headlines proclaimed England's Louise Brown the world's first "test-tube" baby, thousands of people have been conceived in this way. Before too long, 2–3 percent of the population of industrial societies may be the result of new birth technologies.

Technically, test-tube babies result from in vitro fertilization, whereby doctors unite a woman's egg and a man's sperm "in glass"—that is, in a laboratory dish. When successful, this complex medical procedure produces embryos, which doctors either implant in the womb of the woman who is to bear the child or freeze for use at a later time.

At present, in vitro fertilization helps some couples who cannot conceive normally to become parents. Yet numerous ethical issues remain unsolved in regard to NRT. Canada and the U.S. are almost alone among high-income nations in not adopting national regulations. Both countries leave up to medical experts such ethical issues as experimentation in the cloning of humans for body parts (for transplantation). Yet experts may not always be willing to place the public good ahead of their own self-interest. Canada has continued to resist regulating this area, even though a recent Angus Reid poll indicated that as much as 72 percent of the population finds cloning humans for body parts unacceptable (Angus Reid Group Inc., 1997a).

LOOKING AHEAD: THE FAMILY IN THE TWENTY-FIRST CENTURY

Without a doubt, family life in Canada will continue to change in years to come, and change often causes controversy. Advocates of "traditional family values" line up against those who support greater personal choice. Sociologists cannot predict the outcome of this debate, but we can suggest five likely future trends.

1. **The divorce rate is likely to remain high, even in the face of evidence that marital break-ups harm children.** Today's marriages are about as durable as they were a century ago, when many were cut short by death. The difference is that now more couples *choose* to end marriages that fail to meet their expectations. Although the divorce rate declined slightly in the 1990s, it is unlikely that we will ever return to the low rates that marked the early decades of the twentieth century.

2. **Family life in the future will be more diverse than ever.** Cohabiting couples, one-parent families, gay and lesbian families, and blended families are all on the increase. Most families are still based on marriage, and most married couples still have children. But the diversity of family forms implies a trend toward more personal choice.

3. **Men will play a limited role in child rearing.** In the 1950s, a decade many people consider the "golden age" of families, men began to withdraw from active parenting (Snell, 1990; Stacey, 1990). In recent years, a countertrend has become evident, with some older, highly educated fathers staying at home with young children, many using computer technology to continue their work. But the stay-at-home dad represents no more than 15 percent of fathers with young children (Gardner, 1996). The bigger picture is that the high Canadian divorce rate and the increase in single motherhood are weakening children's ties to fathers. For those Canadian children living with their mother, just under one-third saw their father on a weekly basis, some children saw

their father less frequently but on a regular basis, and 40 percent had irregular visits or never saw him. The absence of the non-custodial parent can lead to estrangement: research findings show that, over the long term, contact with the non-custodial parent decreases; 24 percent of children whose biological parents have been apart for at least five years do not see their fathers. Children of common-law arrangements are more likely to reside with their mother and see their father infrequently or not at all. Children from such common-law unions are also less likely to receive regular financial support from their non-custodial father

 You can visit a website for stay-at-home fathers at http://www.slowlane.com.

(Statistics Canada, 2003q). At the same time, evidence is building that the absence of fathers is detrimental to children, at the very least because such families are at high risk of being poor.

4. **Families will continue to feel the effects of economic change.** In many homes, both household partners work, reducing marriage and family to the interaction of weary men and women trying to fit a little "quality time" with their children into an already full schedule. Added to their burden is the problem of finding quality childcare. The Controversy & Debate box outlines some of the issues around childcare in Canada today. The long-term effects of the two-career couple on families as we have known them are likely to be mixed.

5. **The importance of new reproductive technology will increase.** Ethical concerns about whether what *can* be done *should* be done will surely slow these developments, but new reproductive technology will continue to alter the traditional meaning of parenthood.

Despite the changes and controversies that have shaken the family in Canada, most people still report being happy as partners and parents. Marriage and family life will likely remain a foundation of our society for some time to come.

Religion: Basic Concepts

Like the family, religion has played a central part in the drama of human history. Families have long used religious rituals to celebrate birth, recognize adulthood, and mourn the dead.

The French sociologist Emile Durkheim said religion involves "things that surpass the limits of our knowledge" (1965:62, orig. 1915). As human beings, we define most objects, events, and experiences as **profane** (from Latin,

In Search of an Imaginative Childcare Plan for Canadian Families

Non-family care for Canada's young children is high on the political radar screen today. The issue of a childcare program raises many questions of sociological interest: Who does the care? What kind of national system is needed? Whom will it be for, where will it be located, and at what cost and from what sources? Answers to any of these questions pit groups against each other and result in an array of platitudes from politicians. Seldom, however, is there an attempt to put the issues of childcare in historical and cross-national context.

In fact, childcare became an issue in Canada and other countries during the early industrial period. In the last decades of the nineteenth century, impoverished children, many of whom were the offspring of abandoned or widowed single mothers, were sometimes placed in charity founding homes and orphanages while their parent searched for employment. Single mothers who were lucky to find domestic or factory work might eventually be able to bring their child back home. Other times, a child might be permanently relinquished to authorities (Acton et al., 1974).

Some enlightened thinkers of the period argued that non-family childcare might actually be beneficial for the personal development of children from better-off families. Well-organized kindergartens (preschools/nursery schools) could enhance a child's social and intellectual advancement. This perspective was especially prominent in many

countries of continental Europe where public kindergartens had been in operation for over a century. Eventually the idea caught on in Canada as well. Non-family childcare also became more positively viewed whenever women's economic independence was deemed important for the economy and society. A shortage of labour power in virtually all industrial capitalist countries, including Canada, during World War II drew mothers of preschool- and school-aged children into paid employment in large numbers, necessitating non-family solutions for the care of children, if only temporarily until the war had ended and the

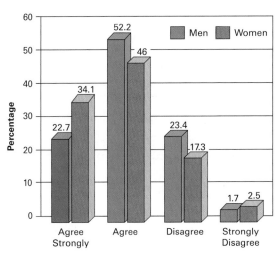

FIGURE 13-5 Working Mothers' Relationship With Children, Canada, 2000

Survey question: "A working mother can establish just as warm and secure a relationship with her children as a mother who does not work."

Source: World Values Survey (2000).

male "breadwinners" returned home (Benoit, 2000a).

With the dramatic rise in paid employment for mothers in the 1960s and 1970s, the demand for non-family childcare for preschool children at even younger ages escalated. Working parents scrambled to find a safe, dependable, and affordable place to put their preschool-age children. In the early 1980s, the advent of high-quality, affordable non-family daycare for all employed parents looked promising in Canada. All provinces had passed childcare regulations to support children's healthy development and well-being, and all offered some funding for at least targeted families unable to meet the costs out-of-pocket. The federal government at the time also indicated some willingness to accept childcare as an essential public service by sharing the cost of non-family childcare for low-income families. Yet under the Canada Assistance Plan (CAP), provinces had to initially pay up front the expenses involved in providing childcare for families in financial straits, and later apply to the federal government for matching funds. Single parents were especially affected because they had no partner to help share the responsibility and yet often could not find a space for their child, even when they were eligible for a childcare subsidy (Baker, 1995). In a move that worsened matters, the federal government in 1988 attempted to remove childcare coverage from CAP under a proposed *Child Care Act*. If enacted, the proposed legislation would have removed federal funding for childcare from social welfare assistance but it would also have made it possible for the federal contribution to the provinces to be reduced. The legislation also suggested that federal funding be extended to private/for-profit childcare facilities, and proposed no national standards for regulation of childcare centres, nor minimal formal qualifications for childcare employees. After vocal opposition from almost every interested party (apart from the federal authorities designing the proposed legislation), the federal government abandoned any change of the status quo with the result that "[b]y the mid-1990s, the childcare situation was in decline in much of Canada. Universal funding had been eliminated or decreased in a majority of jurisdictions and fee subsidies for low income parents had been reduced, frozen and capped by provincial/territorial governments" (Friendly, 1997:109).

Quebec stands out as an exception to the general case of minimum provision. Throughout 1994–95, the Quebec government consulted the public regarding how best to finance childcare services, as well as how the early childhood education system should be revamped to better serve the province's children. In 1996, the Quebec government announced its intention to implement a new family policy and to develop a comprehensive early childhood policy for children 0–12 years of age. An integral part of its family policy was the $5-a-day childcare program.

In 1997, implementation of the new family policy began to be phased in and by 2000, $5-a-day childcare was available to all children aged 0–4 for whom a space was available, whether or not the parent was in the labour force. Between 1997 and 2001, the government of Quebec increased the supply of spaces, wages of educators, and its childcare budget very substantially. Quebec became the only province in Canada to develop a universal system of childcare for its youngest citizens.

Some other countries have taken the step further to provide a national program for non-family childcare. This has been the case in countries with strong social democratic traditions—especially in Norway, Sweden, and Finland—where a *public responsibility* has led to the development of a nationwide institutionalized childcare system (Leira, 1992; Tyyskä, 1998). Canada, however, continues to view childcare essentially as a *private responsibility*, based on the viewpoint that the parental role in caring for children is paramount to their successful adaptation to adulthood and to a harmonious family life.

Meanwhile, the need has increased. In 2004, 65 percent of women with children under the age of 3 worked to support their families. For women with children between 3 and 5 years old, the number who work outside of the home had risen to 70 percent, up from 36 percent in 1976 (Statistics Canada, 2006). Opinion poll data show that the majority of both women and men agree with the statement "a working mother can establish just as warm and secure a relationship with her children as a mother who does not work" (see Figure 13–5). Yet, as of 2004, only 15.5 percent of Canada's

children had access to a regulated childcare space (Friendly, Beach, & Turiano, 2005).

Following this long history of promises and little action, the Liberal federal government in 2005 reached agreements with most provinces to provide funding to support the development of increased affordable regulated childcare opportunities. The government was subsequently defeated and the new Conservatives appear intent on undermining the progress that has been made. In the spring of 2006, Prime Minister Stephen Harper took action to replace the federal–provincial agreements with a "choice in childcare allowance." The allowance provides $100 monthly to parents for each child less than six years of age. The allowance will be taxable, and for some households, child-tax benefits and GST credits will decrease due to the allowance. Some see the decision of the new government to cancel those agreements as a huge setback for working families with young children.

CONTINUE THE DEBATE . . .

1. What do you think? Should Canada implement a national childcare policy?
2. Some argue that non-family childcare is bad for young children? Do you agree? Why or why not?
3. What are the advantages and disadvantages of subsidizing parental cost for childcare versus subsidizing spaces for children in formal care settings (the Harper government strategy)?

Sources: Acton et al. (1974); Baker (1995); Benoit (2000a); Friendly (1997); Friendly, Beach, & Turiano (2005); Leira (1992); Mahon (2005); Phipps (2006); Sainsbury (1996); Statistics Canada (2006); Tyyskä (1998).

Religion is founded on the concept of the sacred: that which is set apart as extraordinary and which demands our submission. Bowing, kneeling, or prostrating oneself are all ways of symbolically surrendering to a higher power. This monk is performing an act of "prostration circumambulation," a complicated way of saying that he falls flat on the ground every few steps as he moves around a holy shrine. In this way, he expresses his complete surrender to his faith.

meaning "outside the temple"), *an ordinary element of everyday life.* But we also consider some things **sacred**, *set apart as extraordinary, inspiring awe and reverence.* Setting the sacred apart from the profane is the essence of all religious belief. **Religion**, then, is *a social institution involving beliefs and practices based on a conception of the sacred.*

A global perspective shows great variety in matters of faith, with no one thing sacred to everyone on Earth. Although people regard most books as profane, Jews believe the Torah (the first five books of the Hebrew Bible or the Old Testament) is sacred, in the same way that Christians revere the Old and New Testaments of the Bible and Muslims exalt the Qur'an (Koran).

But no matter how a community of believers draws religious lines, Durkheim (1965:62, orig. 1915) explained, people understand profane things in terms of everyday usefulness: we log on to the Internet with our computer or turn a key to start our car. What is sacred we reverently set apart from daily life, giving it a "forbidden" aura. For example, Muslims remove their shoes before entering a mosque to avoid defiling a sacred place with soles that have touched the profane ground outside. Similarly, Sikhs eat their ceremonial meal after temple prayers seated on the floor, rather than at (profane) tables. When moderate Sikhs in British Columbia recently defied traditionalists by sitting at tables to have their ceremonial meal after temple prayers, the Sikh

religion's highest authority, the Akal Takhat, was called upon to reconfirm an edict banning tables and chairs from temples worldwide.

The sacred is embodied in *ritual*, or formal ceremonial behaviour. Holy Communion is the central ritual of Christianity; to the Christian faithful, the bread and wine consumed during Communion are never treated in a profane way as food but as the sacred symbols of the body and blood of Jesus Christ.

Because religion deals with ideas that transcend everyday experience, neither common sense nor sociology can prove or disprove religious doctrine. Religion is a matter of **faith**, *belief based on conviction rather than scientific evidence.* The New Testament of the Bible defines faith as "the conviction of things not seen" (Hebrews 11:1) and urges Christians to "walk by faith, not by sight" (2 Corinthians 5:7).

Some people with strong religious beliefs may be disturbed by the thought of sociologists turning a scientific eye on what they hold sacred. However, sociological study is no threat to anyone's faith. Sociologists study religion just as they study the family, to understand religious experiences around the world and how religion is tied to other social institutions. They make no judgments about whether a specific religion is "right" or "wrong." Sociological analysis takes a more worldly approach, seeking to understand why religion takes a particular form in one society or another and how religious activity affects society as a whole.

Theoretical Analysis of Religion

Sociologists have applied the theoretical approaches to the study of religion. Each provides distinctive insights about religious life.

FUNCTIONS OF RELIGION: STRUCTURAL-FUNCTIONAL ANALYSIS

According to Emile Durkheim (1965, orig. 1915), society has a life and power of its own beyond the life of any individual. In other words, society itself is godlike, shaping the lives of its members and living on beyond them. Thus, in practising religion, people celebrate the awesome power of their society.

No wonder people around the world transform everyday objects into sacred symbols of their collective life. Members of technologically simple societies do this with a **totem**, *an object in the natural world collectively defined as sacred.* The totem—perhaps an animal or an elaborate work of art—becomes the centrepiece of ritual and symbolizes the power of collective life over any individual. In our society, the national flag is a quasi-religious totem that is not to be used in a profane way (say, as clothing) or allowed to touch the ground.

Durkheim identified three major functions of religion that contribute to the operation of society:

1. **Social cohesion.** Religion unites people through shared symbolism, values, and norms. Religious thought and ritual establish morality and rules of fair play that make organized social life possible.

2. **Social control.** Society uses religious ideas to promote conformity. In medieval Europe, for example, monarchs claimed to rule by divine right. Even today, our leaders publicly ask for God's blessing, implying to audiences that their efforts are right and just.

3. **Providing meaning and purpose.** Religious belief offers the comforting sense that our brief lives serve some greater purpose. Strengthened by such beliefs, people are less likely to despair in the face of change or even tragedy. For this reason, we mark major life transitions—including birth, marriage, and death—with religious observances.

Critical review. In Durkheim's structural-functional analysis, religion represents the collective life of society. The major weakness of this approach is that it downplays religion's dysfunctions, especially the fact that strongly held beliefs can generate social conflict. Terrorists have claimed that God supports their actions, and nations march to war under the banner of their God. Especially in light of recent world events, few people would deny that religious beliefs have provoked more violence in the world than differences in social class have.

CONSTRUCTING THE SACRED: SYMBOLIC-INTERACTION ANALYSIS

From a symbolic-interaction point of view, religion (like all of society) is socially constructed (although perhaps with divine inspiration). Through various rituals—from daily prayer to annual events such as Easter or Passover—people sharpen the distinction between sacred and profane. Furthermore, says Peter Berger (1967:35–36), placing our small, brief lives within some "cosmic frame of reference" gives us the appearance of "ultimate security and permanence."

Marriage is a good example. If two people look on marriage as a simple contract, they can walk away whenever they want. Their bond makes much stronger claims on them when it is defined as holy matrimony, surely one reason for the lower divorce rate among people with strong religious beliefs. More generally, whenever humans face uncertainty or life-threatening situations—such as illness, natural disaster, or terrorist attack—we turn to our sacred symbols.

Reverend Lois Mike was the first Inuit female priest in the 4 million square kilometres that make up the Anglican Church of Canada's Arctic Diocese. Reverend Mike, a 40-year-old mother of four, was ordained in 1994. There are now at least five female Inuit priests in the Arctic.

Critical review. In the symbolic-interaction approach, religion gives everyday life sacred meaning. Berger adds that the sacred's ability to give meaning and stability to society depends on ignoring the fact that it is socially constructed. After all, how much strength could we gain from sacred beliefs if we saw them merely as a means of coping with tragedy? Also, this micro-level view ignores religion's link to social inequality, to which we now turn.

INEQUALITY AND RELIGION: SOCIAL-CONFLICT ANALYSIS

The social-conflict approach highlights religion's support of social inequality. Religion, proclaimed Karl Marx, serves elites by legitimizing the status quo and diverting people's attention from social inequities.

Even today, the British monarch is the formal head of the Church of England, illustrating the close alliance between religious and political elites. In practical terms, working for political change may mean opposing the church and, by implication, God. Religion also encourages people to accept the social problems of this world while

Patriarchy is found in all of the world's major religions, including Christianity, Judaism, and Islam. Male dominance can be seen in restrictions that limit religious leadership to men and also in regulations that prohibit women from worshipping along with men.

they look hopefully to a "better world to come." In a well-known statement, Marx dismissed religion as "the sigh of the oppressed creature, the sentiment of a heartless world, and the soul of soulless conditions. It is the opium of the people" (1964:27, orig. 1848).

Religion and social inequality are also linked through gender, because virtually all of the world's major religions are patriarchal. For example, the Qur'an, the sacred text of Islam, gives men social dominance over women:

> Men are in charge of women. . . . Hence good women are obedient. . . . As for those whose rebelliousness you fear, admonish them, banish them from your bed, and scourge them. (quoted in Kaufman, 1976:163)

Christianity, the major religion in the Western Hemisphere, has also supported patriarchy. Although Catholics revere Mary, the mother of Jesus, the New Testament instructs us:

> A man . . . is the image and glory of God; but woman is the glory of man. For man was not made from woman, but woman from man. Neither was man created for woman, but woman for man. (1 Corinthians 11:7–9)
>
> As in all the churches of the saints, the women should keep silence in the churches. For they are not permitted to speak, but should be subordinate, as even the law says. If there is anything they desire to know, let them ask their husbands at home. For it is shameful for a woman to speak in church. (1 Corinthians 14:33–35)
>
> Wives, be subject to your husbands, as to the Lord. For the husband is the head of the wife as Christ is the head of the church. . . . As the church is subject to Christ, so let

wives also be subject in everything to their husbands. (Ephesians 5:22–24)

Judaism also has traditionally supported patriarchy. Male Orthodox Jews recite the following prayer each day:

> Blessed art thou, O Lord our God, King of the Universe, that I was not born a gentile.
> Blessed art thou, O Lord our God, King of the Universe, that I was not born a slave.
> Blessed art thou, O Lord our God, King of the Universe, that I was not born a woman.

Despite patriarchal traditions, most religions now have women in leadership roles, and many are introducing more gender-neutral language in hymnals and prayer books. Such changes involve not just organizational patterns but conceptions of God. Theologian Mary Daly puts the matter bluntly: "If God is male, then male is God" (cited in Woodward, 1989:58).

Critical review. Social-conflict analysis emphasizes the power of religion to legitimize social inequality. Yet religion also promotes change toward equality. For example, nineteenth-century religious groups in the United States played an important role in the movement to abolish slavery. In the 1950s and 1960s, religious organizations and their leaders were at the core of the civil rights movement. In the 1960s and 1970s, many clergy actively opposed the Vietnam War, and today many support any number of progressive issues such as feminism, gay rights, and the rights of Aboriginal peoples.

The Applying Theory table summarizes the three theoretical approaches to understanding religion.

APPLYING THEORY
RELIGION

	Structural-Functional Approach	Symbolic-Interaction Approach	Social-Conflict Approach
What is the level of analysis?	Macro-level	Micro-level	Macro-level
What is the importance of religion for society?	Religion performs vital tasks, including uniting people and controlling behaviour. Religion gives life meaning and purpose.	Religion strengthens marriage by giving it (and family life) sacred meaning. People often turn to sacred symbols for comfort when facing danger and uncertainty.	Religion supports social inequality by claiming that the social order is just. Religion turns attention from problems in this world to a "better world to come."

Religion and Social Change

Religion is not just the conservative force portrayed by Karl Marx. In fact, at some points in history, as Max Weber (1958, orig. 1904–05) explained, religion has promoted dramatic social change.

MAX WEBER: PROTESTANTISM AND CAPITALISM

Weber believed that particular religious ideas set into motion a wave of change that brought about the industrialization of Western Europe. The rise of industrial capitalism was encouraged by Calvinism, a movement within the Protestant Reformation.

Central to the religious thought of John Calvin (1509–1564) is the doctrine of *predestination:* An all-knowing, all-powerful God has selected some people for salvation while condemning most to eternal damnation. Each person's fate, sealed before birth and known only to God, is either eternal glory or endless hellfire.

Driven by anxiety over their fate, Calvinists understandably looked for signs of God's favour in this world and came to see prosperity as a sign of divine blessing. Religious conviction and a rigid devotion to duty thus led Calvinists to work hard, and many amassed great wealth. But money was not for selfish spending or for sharing with the poor, whose plight they saw as a mark of God's rejection. As agents for God's work on Earth, Calvinists believed that they could best fulfill their "calling" by reinvesting profits and achieving ever-greater success in the process.

All the while, the Calvinists lived thrifty lives and embraced technological advances, thereby laying the groundwork for the rise of industrial capitalism. In time, the religious fervour that motivated early Calvinists weakened, resulting in a profane "Protestant work ethic." To Max Weber, industrial capitalism itself was a "disenchanted" religion, further showing the power of religion to change the shape of society.

LIBERATION THEOLOGY

Historically, Christianity has reached out to suffering and oppressed people, urging all to strengthen their faith in a better life to come. In recent decades, however, some church leaders and theologians have taken a decidedly political approach and endorsed **liberation theology**, *the combining of Christian principles with political activism, often Marxist in character.*

This social movement started in the late 1960s in Latin America's Roman Catholic Church. Today, Christian activists continue to help people in poor nations liberate themselves from abysmal poverty. Their message is simple: Social oppression runs counter to Christian morality, so as a matter of faith and justice, Christians must promote greater social equality.

Despite its Roman Catholic beginnings, Pope John Paul II condemned liberation theology for distorting church doctrine with left-wing politics. Nevertheless, the liberation theology movement has grown in Latin America, where many people's Christian faith drives them to improve conditions for the world's poor (Neuhouser, 1989; Williams, 2002).

In global perspective, the range of religious activity is truly astonishing. Members of this Southeast Asian cult show their devotion to God by suspending themselves in the air using ropes and sharp hooks that pierce their skin.

Church, Sect, and Cult

Sociologists categorize the hundreds of different religious organizations found in Canada along a continuum, with *churches* at one end and *sects* at the other. Drawing on the ideas of his teacher Max Weber, Ernst Troeltsch (1931) defined a **church** as *a type of religious organization that is well integrated into the larger society*. Churchlike organizations typically persist for centuries and include generations of the same families. Churches have well-established rules and regulations and expect leaders to be formally trained and ordained.

Though concerned with the sacred, a church accepts the ways of the profane world. Church members conceive of God in intellectual terms (say, as a force for good) and favour abstract moral standards ("Do unto others as you would have them do unto you"). By teaching morality in safely abstract terms, church leaders avoid social

controversy. For example, many churches that celebrate the unity of all peoples have all-white memberships. Such duality minimizes conflict between the church and political life (Troeltsch, 1931).

> **December 11, Casablanca, Morocco.**
> The waves of the Atlantic crash along the walls of Casablanca's magnificent coastline mosque, said to be the largest in the world. From the top of the towering structure, a green laser beam cuts through the sky pointing to Mecca, the holy city of Islam, toward which the faithful bow in prayer. To pay for this monumental house of worship, King Hassan II, Morocco's head of state and religious leader, levied a tax on every citizen in his realm. This example of government religion contrasts sharply with our ideas about the separation of church and state.

A church may operate as an arm of the state. A **state church** is *a church formally allied with the state*, as illustrated by Islam in Morocco. State churches have existed throughout human history; for centuries, Roman Catholicism was the official religion of the Roman Empire, as was Confucianism in China until early in the twentieth century. Today, the Anglican Church is the official church of England, and Islam is the official religion of Pakistan and Iran. State churches count everyone in a society as a member, which sharply limits tolerance of religious differences.

A **denomination**, by contrast, is *a church, independent of the state, that recognizes religious pluralism*. Denominations exist in nations that formally separate church and state, such as ours. Canada has dozens of Christian denominations, including Catholics, Baptists, Episcopalians, Methodists, and Lutherans—as well as various categories of Judaism and other traditions. Although members of any denomination hold to their own beliefs, they recognize the right of others to have alternative beliefs.

Unlike a church, which tries to fit into the larger society, a **sect** is *a type of religious organization that stands apart from the larger society*. Sect members have rigid religious convictions and deny the beliefs of others. In extreme cases, members of a sect may withdraw completely from society to practise their faith without interference. In Canada and the U.S., for example, the Amish and the Hutterites have long isolated themselves from modern life (Hostetler, 1980; Curtis & Lambert, 1990). Because North American culture generally considers religious tolerance a virtue, members of sects sometimes are accused of being narrow-minded in insisting that they alone follow the true religion (Kraybill, 1994; Williams, 2002).

In organizational terms, sects are less formal than churches. Sect members may be highly spontaneous and emotional in worship, whereas members of churches tend to listen passively to their leaders. Sects also reject the intellectualized religion of churches, stressing instead the personal experience of divine power. Rodney Stark (1985:314) contrasts a church's vision of a distant God—"Our Father, who art in Heaven"—with a sect's more immediate God—"Lord, bless this poor sinner kneeling before you now."

Churches and sects also have different patterns of leadership. The more churchlike an organization, the more likely that its leaders are formally trained and ordained. Sectlike organizations, which celebrate the personal presence of God, expect their leaders to show divine inspiration in the form of **charisma** (from Greek, meaning "divine favour"), *extraordinary personal qualities that can infuse people with emotion and turn them into followers.*

Sects generally form as breakaway groups from established religious organizations (Stark & Bainbridge, 1979). Their psychic intensity and informal structure make them less stable than churches, and many sects blossom, only to disappear soon after. Over the long term, sects typically become more like churches, losing fervour as they become more bureaucratic.

To sustain their membership, many sects actively recruit, or *proselytize,* new members. Sects highly value the experience of *conversion,* or religious rebirth. For example, Jehovah's Witnesses visit door to door to share their faith with others in the hope of attracting new members.

Finally, churches and sects differ in their social composition. Because they are more closely tied to the world, well-established churches tend to include people of high social standing. Sects attract more disadvantaged people. A sect's openness to new members and promise of salvation and personal fulfillment appeal to people who see themselves as social outsiders.

A **cult** is *a religious organization that is largely outside a society's cultural traditions.* Most sects spin off from a conventional religious organization; by contrast, a cult typically forms around a highly charismatic leader who offers a compelling message of a new and very different way of life. As many as 5000 cults exist in the United States and an unknown number exist in Canada (Marquand & Wood, 1997).

Because some cult principles or practices are unconventional, many people view cults as deviant or even evil. The suicides of 39 members of California's Heaven's Gate cult in 1997—people who claimed that dying was the doorway to a higher existence, perhaps in the company of aliens from outer space—confirmed the negative image the public holds of many cults. Also in 1997, the charred bodies of five people were found inside a house in Saint Casimir, Quebec.

The three women and two men were members of the Solar Temple, an international cult professing the belief that such ritualized suicides lead to rebirth on a planet known as "Sirius." In short, say some scholars, calling a religious community a "cult" amounts to dismissing its members as crazy (Richardson, 1990; Shupe, 1995; Gleick, 1997).

There is nothing basically wrong with this kind of religious organization. Many religions—Christianity, Islam, and Judaism included—began as cults. Of course, few cults exist for very long. One reason is that they are even more at odds with the larger society than sects. Many cults demand that members not only accept their teaching but also embrace a radically new lifestyle. This is why people sometimes accuse cults of brainwashing their members, although research suggests that most people who join cults experience no psychological harm (Kilbourne, 1983; Williams, 2002).

Religion in History

Like the family, religion is a part of every known society. Also like the family, religion shows marked variation both historically and cross-culturally.

Early hunters and gatherers embraced **animism** (from Latin, meaning "the breath of life"), *the belief that elements of the natural world are conscious life forms that affect humanity.* Animistic people view forests, oceans, mountains, and even the wind as spiritual forces. Many Aboriginal societies in Canada are animistic, which accounts for their reverence for the natural environment.

Belief in a single divine power responsible for creating the world arose with pastoral and horticultural societies. The conception of God as a "shepherd" arose because Christianity, Judaism, and Islam all had their beginnings among pastoral peoples.

Religion becomes more important in agrarian societies. The central role of religion in social life is seen in the huge cathedrals that dominated the towns of medieval Europe.

To learn more about different religions, visit http://www.adherents.com.

The Industrial Revolution introduced a growing emphasis on science. More and more, people looked to physicians and scientists for the guidance and comfort they used to get from priests. However, religion persists in industrial societies because science is powerless to address issues of ultimate meaning in human life. In other words, how this world works is a matter for scientists, but why we and the rest of the universe exist is a question of faith.

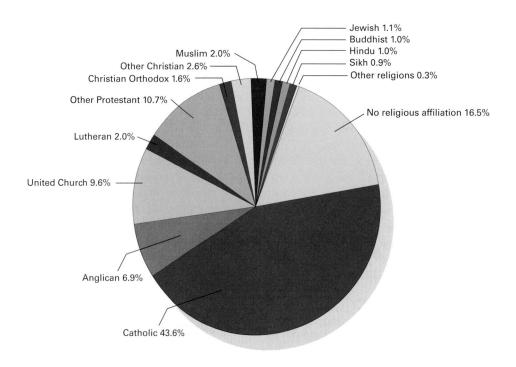

Jewish 1.1%
Buddhist 1.0%
Hindu 1.0%
Sikh 0.9%
Other religions 0.3%

Muslim 2.0%
Other Christian 2.6%
Christian Orthodox 1.6%
Other Protestant 10.7%
Lutheran 2.0%
United Church 9.6%
Anglican 6.9%
Catholic 43.6%

No religious affiliation 16.5%

FIGURE 13–6 Religious Identification in Canada, 2001

Source: Statistics Canada (2003r)

Religion in Canada

Just as people debate the health of family life in Canada, so analysts disagree about the strength of religion in our society. Research shows that changes are underway but also confirms the ongoing role of religion in social life (Collins, 1982; Greeley, 1989; Woodward, 1992; Hadaway, Marler, & Chaves, 1993; Bibby, 1993; Dawson, 1996; Bibby & Brinkeroff, 1994; Bibby, 2002).

RELIGIOUS COMMITMENT

According to the 2001 census, about 83 percent of Canadian adults identify with a particular religion. Figure 13–6 shows that 73 percent of Canadian adults identify as either Protestant or Catholic. At the same time, a variety of other religions are mentioned, identifying people as Christian Orthodox, Muslim, Jewish, Buddhist, Hindu, and Sikh (Statistics Canada, 2003r).

This makes our society one of the most religiously diverse around the globe. Canada is one of the most religious of high-income countries, though less so than the U.S. Take a look at Figure 13–7 to get a global perspective on religiosity.

Canada's religious diversity stems from a constitutional ban on any government-sponsored religion, as well as a high rate of immigration. At the national level, the largest religious group remains Catholic; 43.6 percent of Canadians identify with this religion and their membership has slightly increased over the decade. While Protestant denominations still comprised the second-largest major religious group in 2001, their numbers have declined along with their representation in the population from 35 percent in 1991 to 29 percent in 2001. Most of the decline in Protestant denominations during the decade took place within the largest six denominations such as the Anglican Church and the United Church, with Baptists being the only group bucking this downward trend. The largest increases in religious affiliations occurred among faiths such as Islam, Hinduism, Sikhism, and Buddhism, reflecting the increasing numbers of immigrants from regions outside of Europe, in particular Asia and the Middle East.

While just 16 percent of Canadians in 2001 reported "no religion," this is a major increase since 1971 when a mere 1 percent reported not having any religion. The greatest proportion of people reporting no religion was in the Yukon (37 percent), followed by British Columbia (35 percent) and Alberta (23 percent). In contrast, the people of

Newfoundland and Labrador were the least likely across the country to do so (only 2 percent), followed by Quebec (6 percent).

Religiosity is *the importance of religion in a person's life.* By global standards, people in Canada and the U.S. are relatively religious; more so, for example, than the British, French, Japanese, and Swedes. Just how religious we are, however, depends on precisely how one operationalizes this concept. While the vast majority of Canadians (78 percent) claim to definitely or partially believe in God, only 23 percent report that they attend religious services weekly (Ipsos-Reid, 2003f). Further, as shown in Figure 13–8, there is a notable pattern regarding people who attend religious services regularly. Married people are much more likely to do so, compared to single people and especially those living in common-law relationships (Clark, 2000).

Keep in mind, too, that people probably claim to be more religious than they really are. One team of researchers, which recently tallied actual church attendance in Ashtabula County in Northeast Ohio, concluded that twice as many people said they attended church on a given Sunday as really did so. Strong religious values in U.S. society encouraged a "desirability" effect in the reporting of church attendance (Campbell & Curtis, 1994). In actuality, it is estimated that no more than 20 percent of the Canadian population attend worship services regularly, while another 58 percent attend at least once a year (Bibby, 2002). Finally, religiosity varies among denominations. In Canada, weekly attendance at religious services has declined significantly for both Catholics and Protestants since World War II, although in the past decade attendance has increased slightly among fundamentalist Protestant sects, a phenomenon that is much more pronounced in the U.S.

Yet in his book, *Restless Gods: The Renaissance of Religion in Canada* (2002), well-known sociologist of religion Reginald Bibby maintains that there is a significant rejuvenation of religion currently underway in Canada, both inside and outside the churches. Bibby notes that the vast majority of Canadians are continuing to look to religion for answers to the "the big questions" about the meaning of life, birth, suffering, and life after death, and a large number of them talk to and say they have experienced God. Clearly, the question "How religious are we?" yields no easy answers.

Find online resources for the study of religion at
http://www.princeton.edu/~csrelig/links/links.html.

RELIGION: CLASS, ETHNICITY, AND RACE

Religious affiliation is related to a number of other factors. We shall consider three: social class, ethnicity, and race.

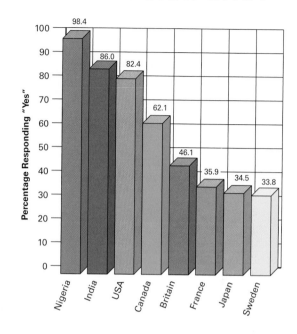

FIGURE 13-7 Religiosity in Global Perspective

Survey question: "Do you gain comfort and strength from religion?"

Note: Calculations exclude those who answered "Don't know."

Source: Inglehart et al. (2000).

Social class. Protestants of European background have traditionally occupied a privileged place in Canadian society, while Catholics—the majority from French backgrounds and residing in the poorer regions of the country, such as Quebec and the Atlantic provinces—have tended to be of more moderate social standing (Porter, 1965). Yet circumstances have changed recently: Quebec society has become more secularized, and the population has experienced increased upward mobility, while at the same time the increasing religious diversity of Canadian society has challenged the once-dominant Protestant majority.

Ethnicity. Throughout the world, religion is closely allied with ethnicity, largely because one religion may predominate in a single region or society. The Arab cultures of the Middle East, for example, are mostly Islamic; Hinduism is tightly fused with the culture of India. Christianity and Judaism diverge from this pattern; while these religions are primarily Western, followers live in nations around the world (Riis, 1998).

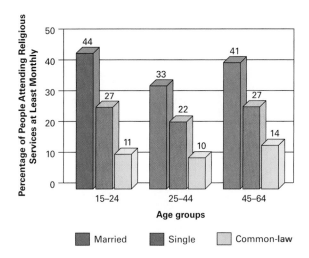

FIGURE 13-8 Religious Attendance by Marital Status and Age Group, Canada, 2001

Formal marriage makes a difference in people's religiosity, as measured by higher regular attendance at religious services for married people as compared to single people and especially couples living in common-law relationships. Can you explain why this might be the case?

Source: Clark (2000).

The link between religion and ethnicity also comes through in Canada. Our society encompasses Anglo-Saxon Protestants, Irish Catholics, Russian Jews, and Greek Orthodox. This fusion of nationality and religion derives from an influx of immigrants from countries with a single major religion. Still, nearly every Canadian ethnic group incorporates at least some religious diversity. People of English ancestry, for instance, may be Protestants, Roman Catholics, Jews, or affiliated with some other religion.

Race. Historically, the church has been central to the spiritual—and also political—lives of blacks living in Canada and the U.S. Transported to the Western Hemisphere, most people of African descent became Christians—the dominant religion in the Americas—but they blended Christian belief and practice with elements of African tribal religions. Guided by this multicultural religious heritage, many people of colour participate in religious rituals that are—by European standards—both spontaneous and emotional (Frazier, 1965; Roberts, 1980).

As black people migrated from the rural South to the industrial cities of the North, and some as far afield as Eastern Canada, the church played a key role in addressing problems of dislocation, poverty, and prejudice. Further, black churches have provided an important avenue of achievement for talented men and women. Ralph Abernathy, Martin Luther King, Jr., and Jesse Jackson all gained world recognition as religious leaders.

Religion in a Changing Society

Like family life, religion is also changing in Canada. Sociologists focus on a major aspect of change: the process of secularization.

SECULARIZATION

Secularization is *the historical decline in the importance of the supernatural and the sacred.* Secularization (from Latin, meaning "the present age") is commonly associated with modern, technologically advanced societies in which science is the dominant mode of understanding.

Today, we are more likely to experience the transitions of birth, illness, and death in the presence of physicians (with scientific knowledge) than church leaders (whose knowledge is based on faith). This shift alone suggests that religion's importance for our everyday lives has declined. Harvey Cox explains:

> The world looks less and less to religious rules and rituals for its morality or its meanings. For some [people], religion provides a hobby, for others a mark of national or ethnic identification, for still others an aesthetic delight. For fewer and fewer does it provide an inclusive and commanding system of personal and cosmic values and explanations (1971:3; orig. 1965).

Secularization does not, then, signal the death of religion. More correctly, some dimensions of religion (such as belief in life after death) may have declined, but others (such as religious affiliation) have increased. Moreover, people are of two minds about whether secularization is good or bad. Conservatives see any weakening of religion as a mark of moral decline. Progressives view secularization as liberation from the all-encompassing beliefs of the past, so people can choose what to believe. Secularization has also brought many traditional religious practices (such as ordaining only men) into line with widespread social attitudes (such as that of gender equality, exemplified by, for instance, opening ordination to women as well as men).

CIVIL RELIGION

One dimension of secularization is what Robert Bellah (1975) calls **civil religion**, *a quasi-religious loyalty binding individuals in a basically secular society.* In other words, even in a mostly secular society, citizenship has religious qualities. Many people in the United States consider their way of

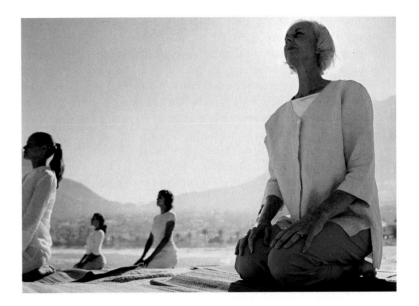

New Age "seekers" are people in pursuit of spiritual growth, often using the age-old technique of meditation. The goal of this activity is to quiet the mind so that, by moving away from everyday concerns, one can hear an inner, divine voice. Countless people attest to the spiritual value of meditation; it has also been linked to improved physical health.

life a force for moral good in the world. Some Canadians express similar sentiments. Many people also find religious qualities in political movements, whether liberal or conservative (Williams & Demerath, 1991).

Civil religion involves a range of rituals, from standing to sing the national anthem at sporting events to waving the flag at public parades. At all such events, the Canadian flag serves as a sacred symbol of our national identity, and we expect people to treat it with respect.

"NEW AGE" SEEKERS: SPIRITUALITY WITHOUT FORMAL RELIGION

In recent decades, an increasing number of people have sought spiritual development outside established religious organizations. This trend toward spirituality but away from established religious organizations has led some analysts to conclude that Canada and the United States are becoming *post-denomination societies.* In simple terms, more people seem to be spiritual seekers, believing in a vital spiritual dimension to human existence that they pursue more or less separately from any formal denomination.

What exactly is the difference between this "New Age" focus on spirituality and a traditional concern with religion? As one analysis (Cimino & Lattin, 1999:62) puts it:

> [Spirituality is] the search for … a religion of the heart, not the head. It … downplays doctrine and dogma, and revels in direct experience of the divine—whether it's called the "holy spirit" or "divine consciousness" or "true self." It's practical and personal, more about stress reduction than salvation, more therapeutic than theological. It's about feeling good rather than being good. It's as much about the body as the soul.

From a traditional point of view, this concern with spirituality may seem more like psychology than religion. Yet like civil religion, it is a new form of religious interest in the modern world.

Finally, keep in mind the effect of high immigration on religious life in Canada. As people come from Latin America, Asia, and other regions and join the Canadian cultural mix, they are likely to fuse traditional religious ideas with ideas they encounter in their new land. The result is religious innovation (Yang & Ebaugh, 2001).

RELIGIOUS REVIVAL: "GOOD OLD-TIME RELIGION"

At the same time that "New Age" spirituality is flourishing, a great deal of change has been going on in the world of organized religion. Membership in established, mainstream churches has plummeted. The largest decline occurred among Presbyterians, whose numbers fell 36 percent in the 1990s. Pentecostals recorded the second-largest drop in membership, falling 15 percent across the decade. The number of United Church adherents declined 8 percent, Anglicans by 7 percent, and Lutherans by 5 percent. During the same period, affiliation with other religious organizations (including Evangelical Missionary Church, Hutterites, Adventists, and Christian and Missionary Alliance) has risen just as dramatically. Since the 1950s, weekly attendance at conservative evangelical churches in Canada has increased from 700 000 to 1.5 million (Bibby, 2002).

Secularization itself may be self-limiting so that, as churchlike organizations become more worldly, many people leave them in favour of sectlike communities that offer a more intense religious experience (Stark & Bainbridge,

1981; Roof & McKinney, 1987; Jacquet & Jones, 1991; Warner, 1993; Iannaccone, 1994; Bibby, 2002).

One striking religious trend today is the growth of **fundamentalism**, *a conservative religious doctrine that opposes intellectualism and worldly accommodation in favour of restoring traditional, otherworldly religion.* In the United States, fundamentalism has made the greatest gains among Protestants. Southern Baptists, for example, are the largest religious community in the United States. But fundamentalist groups have also grown among Roman Catholics and Jews.

Religious "fundamentalism" such as that of the Fundamentalist Church of Jesus Christ of Latter-day Saints has mainly emerged in parts of Alberta and British Columbia, reflecting the somewhat moralistic social values (for example, anti–gay rights; traditional gender roles) and conservative political views articulated more often in Alberta and BC than in other provinces. Yet the flavour of conservative Protestantism found here tends to be less evangelical and all-encompassing than the religious fundamentalism south of the Canadian border (Dawson, 1998).

In response to what they see as the growing influence of science and the weakening of the conventional family, religious fundamentalists defend what they call "traditional values." As they see it, liberal churches are simply too open to change. Religious fundamentalism is distinctive in five ways (Hunter, 1983, 1985, 1987):

1. **Fundamentalists take the words of sacred texts literally.** Fundamentalists insist on a literal reading of sacred texts such as the Bible to counter what they consider excessive intellectualism among more liberal Christian organizations. For example, fundamentalist Christians believe God created the world in seven days precisely as described in the Book of Genesis.

2. **Fundamentalists reject religious pluralism.** Fundamentalists believe that tolerance and relativism water down personal faith. Therefore, they maintain that their religious beliefs are true and other beliefs are not.

3. **Fundamentalists pursue the personal experience of God's presence.** In contrast to the worldliness and intellectualism of other religious organizations, fundamentalists encourage a return to "good old-time religion" and spiritual revival. Being "born again" and having a personal relationship with Jesus Christ should be evident in a person's everyday life.

4. **Fundamentalists oppose "secular humanism."** Fundamentalists think accommodation to the changing world undermines religious conviction. They reject "secular humanism," our society's tendency to look to scientific experts rather than God for guidance about how to live.

5. **Many fundamentalists endorse conservative political goals.** Although fundamentalism tends to back away from worldly concerns, some fundamentalist leaders (such as Ralph Reed, Pat Robertson, and Gary Bauer) have entered politics to oppose the "liberal agenda," which includes feminism and gay rights. Fundamentalists oppose abortion, gay marriage, and liberal bias in the media; they support the traditional two-parent family, seek a return of prayer in schools, and criticize the mass media for colouring stories with a liberal bias (Ellison & Sherkat, 1993; Green, 1993; Manza & Brooks, 1997; Thomma, 1997; Rozell, Wilcox, & Green, 1998).

Opponents regard fundamentalism as rigid and self-righteous. But many people find in fundamentalism, with its greater religious certainty and emphasis on experiencing God's presence, an appealing alternative to the more intellectual, tolerant, and worldly mainstream denominations (Marquand, 1997).

Which religious organizations are fundamentalist? In recent years, the world has become familiar with an extreme form of fundamentalist Islam that supports violent attacks against Western culture. In North America, this term is most commonly applied to conservative Christian organizations in the evangelical tradition, including Pentecostals, Southern Baptists, Seventh-Day Adventists, and the Assemblies of God. Several national religious movements, including Promise Keepers (a men's organization) and Chosen Women, have a fundamentalist orientation. In national surveys, 30 percent of U.S. adults describe their upbringing as "fundamentalist," 40 percent claim a "moderate" religious upbringing, and 24 percent a "liberal" background (NORC, 2003:150). As indicated in Figure 13–6 on p. 366, Canada differs from the U.S. in this regard, with just less than 11 percent of the population claiming membership in "other" Protestant groups.

In contrast to local congregations of years past, some religious organizations, especially fundamentalist ones, have become electronic churches dominated by "prime-time preachers" (Hadden & Swain, 1981). Electronic religion, a pattern until recently found only in the U.S., has now found its way to Western Canada. It has propelled people such as Oral Roberts, Pat Robertson, and Robert Schuller to greater prominence than all but a few clergy in the past. Perhaps 5 percent of the national television audience (about 10 million people) are regular viewers of religious television, and 20 percent (about 40 million) watch some religious programming every week (NORC, 2003). Again, the data from Canada show a different trend: Canadians appear to have much smaller appetites than do their southern neighbours for viewing evangelical services on

Does Science Threaten Religion?

At the dawning of the modern age, the Italian physicist and astronomer Galileo (1564–1642) helped initiate the scientific revolution with a series of startling discoveries. Dropping objects from the Leaning Tower of Pisa, he discerned some of the laws of gravity. He also fashioned a telescope and surveyed the heavens, confirming a new proposition that the Earth orbited the sun, rather than the other way around.

But his lively scientific imagination got him into trouble: Galileo was denounced by the Roman Catholic Church, which had preached for centuries that the Earth stood motionless at the centre of the universe. Galileo only made matters worse by declaring that religious leaders and Biblical doctrine had no place in the building wave of science. Before long, he found his work banned and himself condemned to house arrest.

From its beginnings, science has maintained an uneasy relationship with religion. Indeed, as the course of Galileo's life makes clear, the claims of one sometimes infringe on the other's truth.

Through this century, too, science and religion have been at odds—this time over the issue of creation. In the wake of Charles Darwin's masterwork *On the Origin of Species* (1859), scientists concluded that humanity evolved from lower forms of life over the course of a billion years. Yet the theory of evolution seems to fly in the face of the Biblical account of creation found in Genesis,

which states that "God created the heavens and the earth," introducing the beginnings of life on the third day and then, on the fifth and sixth days, creating animal life, including human beings fashioned in God's own image.

Today—almost four centuries after the silencing of Galileo—many people still ponder the apparently conflicting claims of science and religion. But a middle ground is emerging, which acknowledges that Biblical accounts may be inspired by God and represent important philosophical truths without being literally correct in a scientific sense. That is, science and religion embody two different levels of understanding that respond to different kinds of questions. Both Galileo and Darwin devoted their lives to investigating how the natural world operates. Yet only religion can address why humans and the natural world exist in the first place.

The more scientists discover about the origins of the universe, the more overwhelming the entire process appears. Indeed, as one scientist recently noted, the mathematical odds that some cosmic "Big Bang" 12 billion years ago created the universe and led to the formation of life on Earth as we know it today are utterly infinitesimal—surely much smaller than the chance of one person winning a lottery for 20 weeks in a row. Doesn't such a scientific fact point to the operation of an intelligent and purposeful power underlying our creation? Can't one be both a scientific investigator and a religious believer?

There is another reason to acknowledge the importance of both scientific and religious thinking: rapid scientific advances continue to leave in their wake vexing ethical dilemmas. Latter-day Galileos have unleashed the power of atomic energy, yet we still struggle to find its rightful use in the world. Similarly, unravelling the secrets of human genetics has now brought us to the threshold of manipulating life itself, a power that few have the moral confidence to use. In 1992, a Vatican commission created by Pope John Paul II conceded that the church's silencing of Galileo had been in error. Today, most scientific and religious leaders agree that even though science and religion represent distinctive truths, their teachings may be complementary. And many believe—in the rush to scientific discovery—that our world has never been in more need of the moral guidance afforded by religion.

CONTINUE THE DEBATE . . .

1. In what way are science and religion similar? In what way are they different?
2. Do you think that the sociological study of religion should also include the study of science as a belief system? Why or why not?
3. Do you think that ethics in scientific research should be given priority in Canadian universities? Why or why not?

Source: Based on Gould (1981) and Huchingson (1994).

television, with 1996 estimates of less than 1 percent of viewing time being spent on religious programming (Campbell & Curtis, 1994; Statistics Canada, 1998d). One explanation is that aggressive marketing of religion by sectarian competitors is much more advanced in the U.S. than in other countries, including Canada and Britain (Bibby, 1987; Dawson, 1998).

Faith has a specific meaning for these individuals. For others, faith means something quite different. Do we need to separate religious from non-religious faiths?

LOOKING AHEAD: RELIGION IN THE TWENTY-FIRST CENTURY

The popularity of media ministries, the growth of religious fundamentalism, and the connection of millions of people to mainstream churches show that religion will remain a major part of modern society. In fact, high levels of immigration from many religious countries (in Latin America and elsewhere) should intensify as well as diversify the religious character of Canadian society as the twenty-first century progresses.

The world is becoming more complex, and social change seems to move at a faster pace than our capacity to make sense of it all. But rather than weakening religion, this process fires the religious imagination. New technology that can alter, sustain, and even create life confronts us with difficult moral dilemmas. Against this backdrop of uncertainty, it is little wonder that many people look to their faith for assurance and hope.

SUMMARY

Family

1. Although families are found everywhere in the world, the definition of a family varies across cultures and over time.

2. In higher-income nations such as Canada, marriage is monogamous. Many lower-income countries permit polygamy, of which there are two types: polygyny and polyandry.

3. In global perspective, patrilocal residence is more common than matrilocal residence. Industrial societies favour neolocality. Descent in pre-industrial societies tends to be either patrilineal or matrilineal; in industrial societies, descent is bilateral.

4. Structural-functional analysis identifies major family functions: socializing the young, regulating sexual activity, and providing social placement and emotional support. Social-conflict theory highlights how the family perpetuates inequality based on class, ethnicity, race, and gender. Symbolic-interaction analysis highlights the dynamic and changeable experience of family life.

5. In Canada and elsewhere, family life evolves over the life course, beginning with courtship, extending through child rearing, and ending with the death of a spouse, usually in old age.

6. Families in Canada are diverse, varying along with class position, ethnicity, race, gender, and personal preferences.

7. The divorce rate today is ten times higher than a century ago; 40 percent of current marriages will end in divorce. Most people who divorce, especially men, remarry.

8. Family violence is an important public issue.

9. Our society's family life is becoming more varied. Singlehood, cohabitation, one-parent families, and gay and lesbian families are on the rise.

Religion

1. Religion is a major social institution based on setting the sacred apart from the profane. Religion is grounded in faith, not scientific evidence. Sociologists study how religion affects society but make no claims as to the truth of any religious belief.

2. According to Durkheim, people celebrate the power of their society through religion. His structural-functional analysis suggests that religion promotes social cohesion and conformity and gives meaning and purpose to life.

3. Using the symbolic-interaction approach, Peter Berger explains that people socially construct religious beliefs as a response to life's uncertainties.

4. Social-conflict analyst Karl Marx claimed that religion supports inequality. By contrast, Max Weber's analysis showed how religious ideas can trigger societal change.

5. Churches (religious organizations that are well integrated into their societies) fall into two categories: state churches and denominations. Sects (the result of religious division) are marked by charismatic leadership and suspicion of the larger society. Cults represent new and unconventional religious beliefs and practices.

6. The religiosity of our society depends on how we operationalize the concept. Most people say they believe in God, but only about 20 percent of the Canadian population reports attending religious services regularly.

7. The concept of secularization refers to the diminishing importance of religion. Some measures of Canadian religiosity (including membership in mainstream churches) have declined; others (such as membership in sects and spiritual seeking) are on the rise. It is unlikely that religion will disappear.

8. Fundamentalism opposes religious accommodation to the world, advocates a literal reading of sacred texts, and pursues the personal experience of God's presence. Some fundamentalist Christians have become a conservative force in politics.

KEY CONCEPTS

Family

cohabitation (p. 354) the sharing of a household by an unmarried couple

descent (p. 342) the system by which members of a society trace kinship over generations

endogamy (p. 342) marriage between people of the same social category

exogamy (p. 342) marriage between people of different social categories

extended family (p. 341) a family unit that includes parents and children as well as other kin; also known as the *consanguine family*

family (p. 341) a social institution that unites people in cooperative groups to oversee the bearing and raising of children

family unit (p. 341) a social group of two or more people, related by blood, marriage, or adoption, who usually live together

homogamy (p. 346) marriage between people with the same social characteristics

incest taboo (p. 344) a norm forbidding sexual relations or marriage between certain relatives

kinship (p. 341) a social bond based on blood, marriage, or adoption

marriage (p. 341) a legal relationship usually involving economic cooperation as well as sexual activity and childbearing, which people expect to last

monogamy (p. 342) marriage that unites two partners

nuclear family (p. 341) a family unit composed of one or two parents and their children; also known as the *conjugal family*

polygamy (p. 342) marriage that unites three or more people

Religion

animism (p. 365) the belief that elements of the natural world are conscious life forms that affect humanity

charisma (p. 365) extraordinary personal qualities that can infuse people with emotion and turn them into followers

church (p. 364) a type of religious organization that is well integrated into the larger society

civil religion (p. 368) a quasi-religious loyalty binding individuals in a basically secular society

cult (p. 365) a religious organization that is largely outside a society's cultural traditions

denomination (p. 364) a church, independent of the state, that recognizes religious pluralism

faith (p. 360) belief based on conviction rather than scientific evidence

fundamentalism (p. 370) a conservative religious doctrine that opposes intellectualism and worldly accommodation in favour of restoring traditional, otherworldly religion

liberation theology (p. 363) the combining of Christian principles with political activism, often Marxist in character

profane (p. 357) an ordinary element of everyday life

religion (p. 360) a social institution involving beliefs and practices based on a conception of the sacred

religiosity (p. 367) the importance of religion in a person's life

sacred (p. 357) set apart as extraordinary, inspiring awe and reverence

sect (p. 364) a type of religious organization that stands apart from the larger society

secularization (p. 368) the historical decline in the importance of the supernatural and the sacred

state church (p. 364) a church formally allied with the state

totem (p. 360) an object in the natural world collectively defined as sacred

CRITICAL-THINKING QUESTIONS

1. Identify important changes in Canadian families since 1960. What factors are responsible for these changes?

2. Are Canadian families becoming weaker or simply more diverse? What evidence supports your position?

3. Explain Karl Marx's claim that religion tends to support the status quo. Develop a counterargument, based on Max Weber's analysis of Calvinism, that religion is a major force for social change.

4. What evidence suggests that the importance of religion is declining in Canada? In what ways does religion seem to be getting stronger?

APPLICATIONS AND EXERCISES

1. Parents and grandparents can be a wonderful source of information about changes in marriage and the family. Spend an hour or two with married people of two different generations, and ask them at what ages they married, what their married lives have been like, and what changes in family life today stand out to them.

2. Relationships with various family members differ. With which family member—mother, father, brother, sister—do you most easily, and least easily, share confidences? Why? To which family member would you turn first in a crisis? Why?

3. Some schools are decidedly religious; others are passionately secular. Investigate the place of religion on your campus. Is your school affiliated with a religious organization? Was it ever? Is there a chaplain or other religious official? See whether you can learn from sources on campus what share of students regularly attend any religious service.

4. Is religion getting weaker? To test the secularization idea, go to the library or local newspaper office and find an issue of your local newspaper published 50 years ago and, if possible, another from 100 years ago. Compare attention to religious issues then and now.

 # SITES TO SEE

www.pearsoned.ca/macionis
The authors and publisher of this book invite you to visit the interactive Companion Website™ that accompanies this text. Begin by clicking on the cover of your book. You will find a chapter-by-chapter study guide, practice tests, suggested weblinks, and links to other relevant material.

web.uvic.ca/hrd/cfp
This is the site of the Canadian Families Project, an interdisciplinary research project based at the University of Victoria, BC. The project team is researching Canadian families based on a special data set from the 1901 census. By the time you read this, the data set may be accessible to you.

www.fraserinstitute.ca
Browse through the various documents found at the website for the Fraser Institute, an independent public policy organization based in Vancouver, with offices in Calgary and Toronto. The Institute is well known for its conservative positions on the family and other social institutions.

www.polyamorysociety.org
Survey the increasing diversity of family life at the website for the Polyamory Society. What do you make of the society's views of family life?

www.bwanet.org

www.churchworldservice.org

www.crs.org

www.jdc.org
A number of religious organizations are involved in addressing hunger and other social problems. These websites describe the activities of the Baptist World Alliance, Church World Service, Catholic Relief Services, and American Jewish Joint Distribution Committee.

www.parishioners.org
This site offers information on a variety of religious issues, including cults and toleration of religious differences.

INVESTIGATE WITH RESEARCH NAVIGATOR™

Follow the instructions on page 33 of this text to access the features of Research Navigator™. Once at the website (**www.researchnavigator.com**), enter your login name and password. Then, to use the Content Select™ database, enter keywords such as "family," "religion," and "cults," and the search engine will supply relevant and recent scholarly and popular press publications.

To reinforce your understanding of this chapter, and to identify topics for further study, visit MySocLab at **www.pearsoned.ca/mysoclab/macionis** for diagnostic tests and a multimedia ebook.

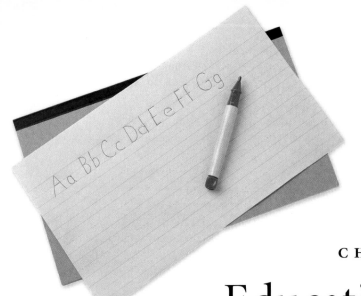

CHAPTER FOURTEEN

Education, Health, and Medicine

How are schooling and healthcare linked
to social inequality in Canada?

In what ways did the Industrial Revolution make both
schooling and healthcare widely available?

Why do people in low-income nations have little access
to schooling and healthcare services?

14

Education, health, and medicine are social institutions that have great importance in the modern world. These young people in South Africa—all HIV positive—speak out in an effort to teach others about the dangers of AIDS and to encourage those already infected to receive new treatments.

Tony doesn't know it, but he is getting the short end of the stick. He is a bright boy—teachers say he stands out among all students in Grade 4—but he barely passed the provincial proficiency tests. Many of his classmates failed the tests and, overall, children who attend Blanshard Elementary School have one of the lowest average test scores in British Columbia.

Across the city, another Grade 4 student named Sarah is doing just fine. Most teachers consider Sarah only an average student, but her test scores were satisfactory. Indeed, the children who go to Uplands Elementary School have about the highest average test scores in the entire province.

How do we explain the difference in the achievement of these two students? The answer is not so much a matter of the two children themselves as it is of their neighbourhoods. Blanshard Elementary is in one of Victoria's poorest neighbourhoods, where 37 percent of families earn less than $30 000 per year, and the school looks the part, with large classes and a building in obvious need of repair. Uplands Elementary, by contrast, is found in one of Victoria's most affluent communities, where only 12 percent of families earn less than $30 000 per year. The teachers are keen and facilities state-of-the-art.

In short, as go the schools, so go the children. Throughout Canada we find the same pattern: children attending schools in high-income neighbourhoods do better than children attending schools in low-income communities (BC Ministry of Education, 2003a, 2003b).

This chapter begins by exploring *education,* a social institution that has particular importance in high-income nations, including Canada. You will learn *why* schooling is so important in these societies and *who* receives the most benefits from schooling. The second half of the chapter examines *health and medicine,* another social institution with great importance in the modern world. Good health, like good schooling, is distributed unequally throughout our society's population. In addition, like education, access to crucial health and medical care services reveals striking variation from society to society.

Education: A Global Survey

Education is *the social institution through which society provides its members with important knowledge, including basic facts, job skills, and cultural norms and values.* Education takes place in many ways, from informal family discussions around the dinner table to lectures and labs at large universities. In high-income nations, education is largely a matter of **schooling,** *formal instruction under the direction of specially trained teachers.*

SCHOOLING AND ECONOMIC DEVELOPMENT

The extent of schooling in any society is tied to its patriarchal traditions and level of economic development. In countries with limited industrialization, which are home to most of the world's people, families and local communities teach young people important knowledge and skills. Formal schooling—especially learning that is not directly linked to work—is available mainly to wealthy people, especially well-off males. After all, the Greek root of the word *school* means "leisure." In ancient Greece, famous teachers such as Plato, Socrates, and Aristotle taught aristocratic, upper-class men; similarly, in ancient China, the famous philosopher K'ung Fu-Tzu (Confucius) shared his wisdom with just a privileged few males.

Today, schooling in low-income and middle-income countries reflects the cultural diversity and economic development of each nation. Schooling in Bangladesh (Asia), Iran (Middle East), Zimbabwe (Africa), and Nicaragua (Latin America) has been shaped by the distinctive cultural traditions of these countries. The same applies to countries such as China (Shu, 2004) and Turkey (Rankin & Aytac, 2006). All of these countries have two traits in common when it comes to schooling: there is not very much of it, and what is available tends to go to the boys. In the poorest nations (including several in Central Africa), only half of all children ever get to school and boys are much more likely than girls to attend; for the world as a whole, only half of all children ever get to the secondary grades and girls are less likely than boys to achieve this level of educational attainment. As a result, about one-third of people around the world cannot read or write. Global Map 14–1 shows the extent of illiteracy around the world, and the following national comparisons illustrate the link between schooling, gender, and economic development.

SCHOOLING IN INDIA

India is a middle-income country where people earn about 10 percent of the income of people in Canada, and most poor families depend on the earnings of children. Thus, even though India has outlawed child labour, many children continue to work in factories—weaving rugs or making handicrafts—for up to 60 hours a week, which greatly limits their chances for schooling.

Today, 77 percent of children in India complete primary school, typically in crowded schoolrooms where one teacher may face as many as 60 children. Fewer than half continue on to secondary education, and very few enter college or university. As a result, only about 60 percent of the people in this vast country are literate.

Patriarchy also shapes Indian education. Indian parents rejoice at the birth of a boy because he and his future wife both will contribute income to the family. But there are economic costs linked to raising a girl: parents must provide a dowry at the time of her marriage, and after her marriage, a daughter's work benefits her husband's family. Therefore, many Indians see little reason to invest in the schooling of girls, which is why only 30 percent of girls (compared with 45 percent of boys) reach the secondary grades. So what do the girls do while the boys are in school? Most of the children working in Indian factories are girls—their families' way of benefiting from daughters while they can (United Nations Development Programme, 1995). This gender inequality is also reflected in adult literacy rates: the literacy rate in 2000–04 in India for people aged 15–24 was 80 percent for males but only 65 percent for females (Population Reference Bureau, 2005).

SCHOOLING IN JAPAN

 September 30, Kobe, Japan. Compared to people in Canada, the Japanese are particularly orderly. Young boys and girls on their way to school stand out with their uniforms, their arms filled with books, and a look of seriousness and purpose on their faces.

Before industrialization brought mandatory education to Japan in 1872, only a privileged few received schooling. Today, Japan's educational system is widely praised for producing some of the world's highest achievers.

The early grades concentrate on transmitting Japanese traditions, including obligation to family, as well as striving to get into preschool. Starting in their early teens, students take a series of rigorous and highly competitive examinations. These tests, which resemble the Scholastic Aptitude Tests (SATs) used for university admission in the United States, determine a Japanese student's future.

More men and women graduate from high school in Japan (94 percent) than in Canada (89 percent) or the United States (88 percent) (OECD, 2002). But competitive examinations in Japan, among other factors, meant that in 2000, just 34 percent of people aged 25–64—compared with 41 percent in Canada and 37 percent in the United States—had completed a college or university degree. Understandably, then, Japanese students take these examinations very seriously, and about half attend cram schools to prepare for them.

Japanese schooling produces impressive results. In a number of fields, notably mathematics and science, Japanese students outperform most students in other high-income nations, including Canada (Benedict, 1974; Hayneman & Loxley, 1983; Rohlen, 1983; Brinton, 1988; Simons, 1989). (Note: In the last international tests, students from Hong Kong and Finland did better.)

SCHOOLING IN THE UNITED STATES

The United States was among the first countries to set a goal of mass public education for white males. By 1850, half of the U.S. population between the ages of 5 and 19 was enrolled in school. In 1918, the last of the states passed a *mandatory education* law requiring children to attend school until age 16 or completion of Grade 8. A milestone was reached in the mid-1960s, when, for the first time, a majority of U.S. adults had high school diplomas. Today, more than four out of five adults have a high school education, and more than one in four have a four-year university degree.

Schooling in the United States also tries to promote equal opportunity. National surveys show that most people think schooling is crucial to personal success, and a majority

WINDOW ON THE WORLD

GLOBAL MAP 14–1 Illiteracy in Global Perspective

Reading and writing skills are widespread in high-income countries, where illiteracy rates are generally below 5 percent. In much of Latin America, however, illiteracy is more common, one consequence of limited economic development. In 25 nations—18 of them in Africa—illiteracy is the rule rather than the exception; there, people rely on the oral tradition of face-to-face communication rather than the written word. Not represented on this illiteracy map is the fact that males are much more likely to be literate in low- and middle-income countries than females. For example, the literacy rate in 2000–04 in Mali for people aged 15–24 was 32 percent for males and 17 percent for females (Population Reference Bureau, 2005).

Sources: United Nations Development Programme (2004) and World Bank (2004); map projection from *Peters Atlas of the World* (1990).

believe that everyone has the chance to get an education consistent with personal ability and talent (NORC, 2003). This opinion expresses cultural ideals rather than actual reality. A century ago, for example, women and blacks were all but excluded from higher education; even today, most people who attend college and university come from families with above-average incomes and non-whites remain under-represented.

SCHOOLING IN CANADA

As in the U.S. and Japan, the educational system in Canada has been shaped by past patriarchal traditions and cultural norms. The result is a mixture of public schools, elite private schools, and publicly funded Roman Catholic schools. At the same time, a strong belief in social equality in regard to literacy and basic schooling has prevailed—a tradition, in fact, that predates the emergence of the modern education system as we have come to know it (Harrigan, 1990). Yet throughout the twentieth century, educational participation was influenced by gender, geographic location, and social class. And to some extent, it can be argued that this remains the case even today.

Find a Statistics Canada report on inequalities in literacy skills among Canadian and U.S. youth at **http://www.statcan.ca/bsolc/ english/bsolc?catno=89-552- M1999006**.

Nevertheless, formal education for children of all social backgrounds has changed enormously since the mid-nineteenth century in our country. Prior to this time, education for most children—apart from those of the elite—was informal and unorganized (Prentice, 1977). Even by the turn of the twentieth century, school attendance remained sporadic, and most students—boys and girls in equal proportions—dropped out after Grade 3 (Harrigan, 1990; Baldus & Kassam, 1996). This was especially true for rural children. Further, school teachers were often ill-trained and poorly paid, typically receiving lower wages than day labourers of the time. Prejudice restricted females from public teaching until the second half of the nineteenth century and, even thereafter, conditions were hardly equal between the sexes. For example, when Martha Hamm Lewis entered teachers' training school in the mid-nineteenth century in New Brunswick, her principal required that she "enter the classroom ten minutes before the male students, sit alone at the back of the room, always wear a veil, leave the classroom five minutes before the end of the lesson and leave the building without speaking to any of the young men" (MacLellan, 1972:6, cited in Wilson, 1996:99).

The early public schools in Canada did not champion class equality despite proclaiming an egalitarian ideology. Rather, they served to reproduce the existing social class system and to teach its validity to students in order to minimize conflict between the social classes (Curtis, 1988:370–371). Likewise, the early schoolbooks of Upper Canada (later to be called Ontario) were "infused with a hefty dose of class interest" (Baldus & Kassam, 1996:328), with their authors aiming mainly to curtail insubordination stemming from the "lower orders."

As the twentieth century unfolded, women came to dominate the teaching profession, the quality of instruction

TABLE 14-1

Educational Attainment in Canada, Population Aged 25–64, 1991–2001

Population Aged 25 to 64	Males		Females	
	1991	2001	1991	2001
Less than high school	31.2	23.4	31.7	22.0
High school	22.0	22.5	27.4	25.4
Trades	17.4	16.5	9.1	9.3
College	11.5	15.0	16.1	20.7
University	18.0	22.6	15.6	22.6

Source: Statistics Canada (2003c).

greatly improved, and national legislation was passed requiring that children of both sexes across Canada remain in school until at least their mid-teens. Increasingly, most groups embraced publicly funded education as a minimum requirement for future success in a modern industrial society.

Today, approximately 5.4 million students are enrolled full-time in Canada's 12 249 elementary schools and 3388 secondary schools. Many students continue their educations: annually there are about 1 million full-time students in 199 community colleges and 75 universities, which are partly supported by student tuition fees but mainly funded by public taxes (Statistics Canada, 2001c). Table 14–1 shows that Canadians have recently made great strides in regard to educational attainment, accelerating the trend that has slowly been emerging over the last century or so. The increase for females is particularly impressive; in the 2001 census, 52.6 percent of females in the working population (the population aged 25–64) had completed a post-secondary program, up from 40.8 percent in 1991. At the same time, the percentage of females in this age group who had not completed high school decreased from 31.7 percent to 22 percent in 2001 (Statistics Canada, 2003c).

The Saskatchewan Status of Women Office has a webpage on gender and education at **http://www.swo.gov.sk.ca/ education.html**.

In 2001, Canadian taxpayers spent an estimated $70.8 billion on education—the equivalent of just over $2277 for every Canadian—making it the second-largest item of public expenditure after health. Canada spent 6.1 percent of the gross domestic product (GDP) on education in 2001–02, a decrease from 6.4 percent of GDP in 1999–2000. Despite this decline, Canada ranked second in total expenditure on education in relation to GDP compared to the OECD average and G-7 countries in 2001 (Statistics Canada, 2005). The comparable figure for the U.S. was 6.5 percent yet this

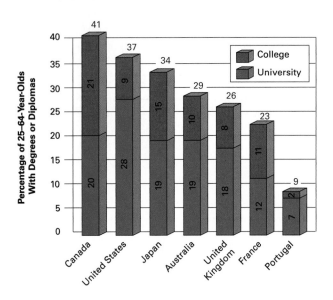

FIGURE 14-1 University Degrees in Global Perspective

Source: U.S. Census Bureau (2003, 2004).

figure hides the fact that private spending makes up 25 percent of total spending in the U.S. compared to 20 percent in Canada (OECD, 2002). What this means is that the educational system in the U.S. is more dependent on payments by students—and their parents—than our system is.

Canada also compares well internationally in regard to educational attainment. Our percentage of adults with post-secondary education is among the highest in the world. It is noteworthy that Canada has a large percentage of people with university degrees—among the five highest in the world—but what makes Canada stand out is its large proportion of people with non-university post-secondary education. If college and university educations are combined, no other OECD country tops Canada in regard to the portion of its working age population holding a post-secondary credential.

Besides trying to make schooling more widely available, educational systems in industrial societies have also stressed the value of practical learning—that is, knowledge that has a direct bearing on people's work and interests. The educational philosopher John Dewey (1859–1952) championed progressive education, emphasizing practical skills rather than a fixed body of knowledge passed from generation to generation. This is a popular sentiment even in our society today, where 60 percent of decided respondents answered that young people should acquire a trade skill rather than a general university education (Angus Reid Group Inc., 1999a). Many of today's university students are selecting areas of major study with an eye toward future jobs. As a result of the Information Revolution, the top three fields in which males in Canada attained a bachelor's degree in 2001 were engineering (19.9 percent), business and commerce (16.3 percent), and computer science and applied mathematics (9.1 percent). For women acquiring bachelor's degrees, the leading areas were education (13.2 percent), business and commerce (9.8 percent), and financial management (6.7 percent) (Statistics Canada, 2003c).

THE FUNCTIONS OF SCHOOLING

Structural-functional analysis focuses on ways in which schooling supports the operation and stability of society:

1. **Socialization.** Technologically simple societies look to families to transmit a way of life from one generation to the next. As societies gain complex technology, they turn to trained teachers to pass on specialized knowledge.

2. **Cultural innovation.** Schools invent new machines just as they create new ideas. Especially at centres of higher education, scholars conduct research that leads to discovery and changes our way of life.

3. **Social integration.** Schools mould a diverse population into one society sharing norms and values. This is one reason why provinces enacted mandatory education laws a century ago at a time when immigration was very high. In light of the ethnic diversity of many urban areas, schooling continues to serve the same purpose today.

4. **Social placement.** Schools identify talent and match instruction to ability. Schooling increases meritocracy by rewarding talent and hard work regardless of social background and provides a path to upward social mobility.

5. **Latent functions.** Schooling serves several less widely recognized functions. It provides childcare for the growing number of one-parent and two-career families. In addition, it occupies thousands of young people in their twenties who would otherwise be competing for a limited number of jobs. High schools, colleges, and universities also bring together people of marriageable age. Finally, school networks can be a valuable career resource throughout life.

Sociological research has documented the fact that young people living in low-income communities suffer in school due to large class sizes, poor-quality teaching, and insufficient budgets for technology and other instructional materials. In countries such as Canada and the United States, where people believe that schools should give everyone a chance to develop talents and abilities, should such inequalities exist?

Critical review. Structural-functional analysis stresses ways in which formal education supports the operation of a modern society. However, this approach overlooks the many problems of our educational system and how schooling helps reproduce the class structure in each generation.

SCHOOLING AND SOCIAL INEQUALITY

Social-conflict analysis challenges the structural-functional idea that schooling develops everyone's talents and abilities. Instead, this approach emphasizes how schooling causes and perpetuates social inequality:

1. **Social control.** As Samuel Bowles and Herbert Gintis (1976) see it, the demand for public education in the late nineteenth century arose just as capitalists needed an obedient and disciplined work force. Once in school, immigrants learned not only the English language but also the importance of following orders. Egerton Ryerson also saw this as a function for public schools; he argued that public schools should "in no respect intrude upon the providential arrangements of order and rank in society, [but rather] divest poverty of its meanness and its hatreds, and wealth of its arrogance and selfishness" (Ryerson, 1852, cited in Prentice, 1977:126).

2. **Testing.** Critics claim that the aptitude tests widely used by schools reflect our society's dominant culture, placing minority students at a disadvantage. By defining majority students as smarter, standardized tests transform privilege into personal merit (Crouse & Trusheim, 1988; Putka, 1990). Scott McLean (1997) argues that even the very notion of an individual assessment measure, as well as our detailed statistical system for recording students' academic performance, holds little meaning among Inuit in the Canadian Arctic.

3. **Tracking.** Despite controversy over tests and other quantitative measures, our educational system uses them for streaming, or **tracking**, *assigning students to different types of educational programs*, such as vocational or academic training. Tracking supposedly helps teachers meet a student's individual abilities and interests. Education critic Jonathan Kozol (1992), however, considers tracking one of the "savage inequalities" in our school system. Most students from privileged backgrounds get into higher tracks where they receive the best the school can offer. Students from disadvantaged backgrounds end up in lower tracks where teachers stress memorization and classroom drill (Bowles & Gintis, 1976; Persell, 1977; Davis & Haller, 1981; Oakes, 1982, 1985; Hallinan & Williams, 1989; Kilgore, 1991; Gamoran, 1992). As a result of such criticisms, some Canadian schools have destreamed their educational programs in recent years. Yet a variety of groups have opposed destreaming—including school boards, teachers, and middle-class parents; the latter worry that, without different tracks, their university-bound children will not have the required skills to compete successfully at university.

PUBLIC AND PRIVATE EDUCATION

Across Canada, virtually all elementary and secondary school students continue to attend public schools. In 1998–99, 297 798 students out of a total school population of 5 369 716 attended a private educational institution (Statistics Canada, 2001c). When examined over time, private school enrollment in Canada shows a very gradual climb, from an all-time low in 1971 of only 2.41 percent to 4 percent of elementary and secondary students in 1981–82. However, in the mid-1980s private school enrollment dropped noticeably, owing in part to a decision by the Ontario government to publicly fund Catholic secondary education for students in Grades 11, 12, and 13. Such students were subsequently excluded from private school student rolls. More recently, private school enrollment numbers have began to slowly climb again—about 5.6 percent of elementary and secondary students were enrolled in private schools in 1999—reflecting some Canadian parents' growing dissatisfaction with the quality of public school education for their children (Statistics Canada, 2003d; Maxwell & Maxwell, 1995).

Two recent Angus Reid polls attempted to capture Canadians' views on Canadian schools. These polls found, among other things, that 39 percent of respondents would seriously consider sending their child to a private school with an annual tuition fee of $5000 per student (Angus Reid, 1996e) and over 60 percent thought that students in private schools "receive much better education than public school students" (Angus Reid Groups Inc., 1999a).

The Canadian Association of Independent Schools (CAIS) is an association for elite private schools across the country. Its membership in 2003 comprised 74 "independent" (non-public) schools enrolling about 35 000 private school students (a little more than 10 percent of the total private school enrollment). According to Mary Percival Maxwell and James Maxwell (1995:335), "[d]espite their small numbers these schools have played a crucial role in the social reproduction of the upper classes ... [and] their graduates are disproportionately represented in the various institutional elites."

Over half of the CAIS private schools were established prior to 1920; 22 of them were founded in the nineteenth century. The original-member CAIS schools were not only exclusive along class lines; most were only open to a single sex, a policy that was reinforced by the sponsoring religious denomination. Before World War I, upper-class Canadian families were likely to send both their daughters and sons to board at elite private schools. Worsening economic circumstances in subsequent decades meant that many could no longer afford private educations for both daughters and sons. Instead, families tended to commit their reduced resources to their sons' private school educations, while sending their daughters to less-expensive local schools. As a result, by 1993, there remained only 16 private girls' schools (Maxwell & Maxwell, 1995). Yet even the single-sex private schools for boys have been forced to change with the times. During the 1970s, declining enrollments have forced many of them to go "co-ed." At the same time, the ethnic make-up of these schools has become more diverse, reflecting the more heterogeneous ethnic make-up of the upper and upper-middle classes in present-day Canadian society. Despite their changing student populations, Canada's elite private schools continue to prepare their students for leadership positions in the various elites of the larger society, which does not differ significantly from what sociologists have observed in earlier generations (Porter, 1965; Clement, 1975; Newman, 1975).

Public school financing does not differ very much across Canada, owing to the country's relative success in redistributing wealth through income tax (Oreopoulos, 2006). Nevertheless, Canadian data indicate that the provinces vary substantially in the number of years of education of the adult population. In 2001, in three Canadian provinces—Newfoundland and Labrador, Manitoba, and New Brunswick—and one territory—Nunavut—more than one-half of their working populations had completed only high school or less. The remainder of the provinces and territories had more than 50 percent of their working populations with some post-secondary education (Statistics Canada, 2003c).

Even if schools were exactly the same everywhere, students whose families value and encourage learning would still perform better since success in school is correlated with parents encouraging reading at home, buying books or borrowing them from public libraries, and enrolling children in extra-curricular activities (de Brouker & Lavalleé, 1998).

ACCESS TO HIGHER EDUCATION

Schooling is the main path to high-paying jobs, but only 59 percent of Canadian high school graduates enroll in post-secondary institutions within the first year following their graduation. By age 20, two in ten high-school graduates had not enrolled in a college, university, or trade school (Tomkowicz & Bushnik, 2003). National Map 14–1 shows that school attendance of those aged 15–24 in Canada also varies by geographical location, within as well as across provinces and territories.

While more young people are accessing higher education today in Canada than ever before, those from less privileged family backgrounds are not increasing their participation nearly to the extent that their more privileged friends are (Bouchard & Zhao, 2000; Lowe & Krahn, 2000;

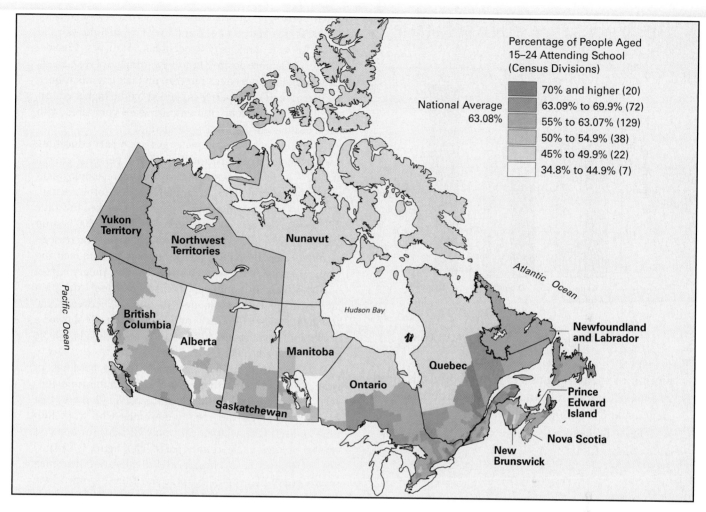

SEEING OURSELVES

NATIONAL MAP 14-1 School Attendance, People Aged 15–24, Canada, 2001

Generally speaking, school attendance is most common among youth and adults living in the urban south of the country. How would you explain this pattern? Income is one obvious consideration, but do you think that people's ideas about the importance of school attendance also vary depending on whether their environment is rural or urban? There also appears to be a higher level of attendance in Quebec. Do you think that this is related to the cost of tuition?

Note: Educational participation is defined as full- or part-time attendance in courses that could be used as credits toward certificates, diplomas, or degrees.

Source: Based on Statistics Canada (2003e).

Statistics Canada, 2005a). Post-secondary education in Canada is expensive. Government funding as a portion of overall institutional revenues has declined steadily for the past 20 years, forcing universities and colleges to look for additional funding from student tuition fees and, to a lesser extent, funding from the private sector. In 1986–87, 81 per-

cent of university operating revenue came from government funding and 16 percent from student fees. By 2000–01, government's share of university funding decreased to 61 percent, whereas revenues from student fees grew to 34 percent (Robertson, 2003). At the same time, however, post-secondary students have gained from

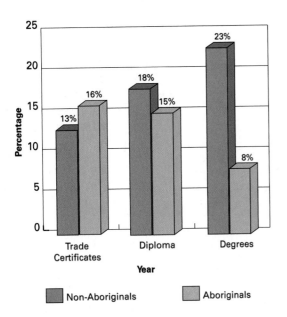

FIGURE 14-2 Aboriginals and Non-Aboriginals, Aged 25–34, With Trade Certificates, Post-Secondary Degrees, and Diplomas, Canada 2001

Source: Statistics Canada (2003c).

increased public expenditure on scholarships and bursaries, including most recently the Millennium Scholarship Fund (MSF). In fact, there has been an increase in expenditure on scholarships and bursaries recently, bringing the figure to $262.6 million in 1996–97, which excludes the $2.5 billion MSF that began in the year 2000.

Nevertheless, the amount owing by those who take out student loans is increasing. Students from the graduating class of 1995 who received student loans owed on average $11 000 at graduation—a whopping 39 percent increase over the class of 1990 and 59 percent over the class of 1986 (Statistics Canada, 2003f). It is little wonder that the financial burdens of higher education discourage many young people from less privileged backgrounds from attending. Among other factors, there is a strong relationship between a father's occupational status and the educational attainment of his children, whereas a mother's employment status has a small but positive influence (Statistics Canada, 1998u).

Over the past 25 years, educational attainment for Aboriginal people aged 20–25 has generally improved. The fact remains, however, that Aboriginal people still lag behind

other Canadians in regard to post-secondary degrees or diplomas (see Figure 14–2), and they are only one-third as likely to have university credentials (Statistics Canada, 2003c). On a more positive note, new immigrants to Canada actually attain more education than do their Canadian-born counterparts. This is partly explained by the higher educational levels of recent immigrants when compared with those of the Canadian-born population.

For those who do complete post-secondary education, rewards include not just intellectual and personal growth but also increased opportunities for secure employment and higher income. This is especially the case for women. In 2003, women with university degrees who worked full-time full-year earned $53 400, up from $48 260 in 2000 and up over 10 percent since 1968. This was the largest increase in earnings across the educational groupings for both men and women. Earnings for women with some secondary school but who had not completed their high school education increased much more slowly—4.1 percent between 1980 and 2000 to $24 914. This group in 2003 actually showed a decrease in earnings, to $22 900 (Statistics Canada, 2003g; Statistics Canada, 2006).

Despite this dramatic increase in the earnings of women with university degrees who worked full-time, full-year, they still earn less than men. Table 14–2 shows that among 25–34-year-old men and women who work full-time and full-year, women earn only 78 cents for every $1 earned by their male counterparts. This figure is inflated because women have a higher level of education than men in this group of people—61 percent of these women have earned a certificate, diploma, or degree, whereas only 45 percent of men have (Statistics Canada, 2003h). Looking at the differences in income by education level, the differences between the earnings of men and women are greater at all education levels. Table 14–2 also shows that additional years of education bring higher earnings.

PRIVILEGE AND PERSONAL MERIT

If attending college or university is a rite of passage for rich men and women, as social-conflict analysis suggests, then schooling transforms social privilege into personal merit. However, because of our cultural emphasis on individualism, we tend to see diplomas and degrees as badges of ability rather than as symbols of family wealth (Sennett & Cobb, 1973). When we congratulate the new graduate, we rarely recognize the resources—both financial and cultural—that made this achievement possible. Yet young people from families with incomes exceeding $100 000 a year average more than 200 points higher on the SAT university entrance examination than young people from families with $10 000 in annual income. The richer students are

TABLE 14–2

Average Annual Earnings, by Gender and Educational Attainment, Canada, 2003

Education	Women	Men	Women's Earnings as Percentage of Men's Earnings
All levels of education	36 500	51 700	70.5
Less than Grade 9	21 700	31 200	69.4
Some secondary school	22 900	40 000	57.3
Secondary school graduate	30 500	43 000	71.0
Some post-secondary	31 500	41 600	75.6
Post-secondary certificate or diploma	34 200	49 800	68.6
University degree	53 400	77 500	68.9

Source: Statistics Canada (2005). *Women in Canada: A Gender-Based Statistical Analysis*. Fifth edition. Ottawa: Statistics Canada. Catalogue no. 89-503-XIE.

Aboriginal students at this residential school in Port Alberni on Vancouver Island experienced rigid uniformity in the extreme. In 1998, 25 former students successfully sued the federal government and the United Church for the abuse they had suffered 30 years earlier.

thus more likely to get into university; once there, they are also more likely to get a university degree. In a *credential society*—one that evaluates people based on their schooling—companies hire those with the best education. This process ends up harming those who are already disadvantaged (Collins, 1979).

Critical review. Social-conflict analysis links formal education to social inequality to show how schooling transforms privilege into personal worthiness and disadvantage into personal deficiency. However, the social-conflict approach overlooks the extent to which schooling provides upward mobility for talented women and men from all backgrounds. In addition, despite claims that schooling supports the status quo, today's university and college curricula challenge social inequality on many fronts.

The Applying Theory table sums up what the theoretical approaches show us about education.

Problems in the Schools

An intense debate revolves around schooling in Canada. Because we expect schools to do so much—to equalize opportunity, instill discipline, and fire the individual imagination—few people think that public schools are doing an excellent job; about two-thirds of Canadians think that high school graduates do not have strong reading and writing skills, and the same proportion do not think that our high schools do a good job of preparing students for today's work force (Angus Reid Group Inc., 1999a).

DISCIPLINE AND VIOLENCE

When many of today's older teachers think back to their own student days, school "problems" consisted of talking out of turn, chewing gum, breaking the dress code, or cutting class. But today's schools are also grappling with drug and alcohol abuse, teenage pregnancy, and outright violence.

While Canadians are used to hearing about violence in the United States, our collective conscience was shocked at the 1999 fatal shooting at the W.R. Myers school in Taber, Alberta. Moreover, in a survey conducted just prior to the shooting, one-third of Canadian teenagers under 18 believed that violence had increased in their school over the last five years (Angus Reid Group Inc., 1999b). The Diversity: Race, Class, & Gender box raises the question of a racial element in the severity of school discipline.

BUREAUCRACY AND STUDENT PASSIVITY

If some schools are plagued by violence, many more are filled with passive, bored students. Some of the blame for passivity can be placed on television (which now claims more of young people's time than school), parents (who are not involved enough with their children), and the students themselves. But schools must share the blame (Coleman, Hoffer, & Kilgore, 1981).

The small, personal schools that served local communities a century ago have evolved into huge educational factories. Theodore Sizer (1984:207–09) identified five ways in which large, bureaucratic schools undermine education:

APPLYING THEORY
EDUCATION

	Structural-Functional Approach	Social-Conflict Approach
What is the level of analysis?	Macro-level	Macro-level
What is the importance of education for society?	Schooling performs many vital tasks for the operation of society, including socializing the young and encouraging discovery and invention to improve our lives. Schooling helps unite a diverse society by teaching shared norms and values.	Schooling maintains social inequality through unequal schooling for rich and poor. Within individual schools, tracking provides privileged children with better educations than poor children.

1. **Rigid uniformity.** Bureaucratic schools run by outside specialists (such as provincial education officials) generally ignore the cultural character of local communities and the personal needs of their children.

2. **Numerical ratings.** School officials focus on attendance rates, dropout rates, and achievement test scores. They overlook dimensions of schooling that are difficult to quantify, such as creativity and enthusiasm.

3. **Rigid expectations.** Officials expect 15-year-olds to be in Grade 10, and Grade 11 students to score at a certain level on a standardized verbal achievement test. Rarely are exceptionally bright and motivated students permitted to graduate early. Likewise, the system pushes poor performers on from grade to grade.

4. **Specialization.** High-school students learn French from one teacher, receive guidance from another, and are coached in sports by still others. No school official comes to know the complete student. Students experience this division of labour as a continual shuffling between periods throughout the school day.

5. **Little individual responsibility.** Highly bureaucratic schools do not empower students to learn on their own. Similarly, teachers have little say in what and how they teach their classes; they dare not accelerate learning for fear of disrupting the system.

Of course, with nearly 5.5 million elementary and secondary students in Canada, schools have to be bureaucratic to get the job done. But Sizer recommends that we "humanize" schools by eliminating rigid scheduling, reducing class size, and training teachers more broadly to make them more involved in the lives of their students. Moreover, James Coleman (1993) suggests that schools be less "administratively driven" and more "output-driven." Perhaps this transformation could begin by ensuring that graduation from high school depends on what students have learned rather than how many years they have spent in the building.

THE ACADEMY: THE SILENT CLASSROOM

Passivity is also common among college and university students (Gimenez, 1989). Sociologists rarely study the post-secondary classroom—a curious fact considering how much time they spend there. A fascinating exception is a study of a co-educational university where David Karp and William Yoels (1976) found that, even in small classes, only a few students speak up. Thus, passivity is a classroom norm, and students even become irritated if one of their number is especially talkative.

According to Karp and Yoels, most students think classroom passivity is their own fault. But as anyone who watches young people outside of class knows, they are usually active and vocal. Thus, it is schools that teach students to be passive, viewing instructors as "experts" who serve up "truth." Students see their proper role as quietly listening and taking notes. As a result, the researchers estimate, just 10 percent of class time is used for discussion.

DROPPING OUT

If many students are passive in class, others are not there at all. The problem of dropping out—quitting before earning a diploma, certificate, or degree—leaves young people (many of whom are disadvantaged to begin with) ill-equipped for the world of work and at high risk for a life of poverty.

School Discipline: A Case of Racial Profiling?

Ken Russell was known as a trouble-maker in his high school. He doesn't deny it. But he also thinks he has been punished for more than his behaviour. Why? Ken, who is black, recently got into a scuffle with another boy, who is white. It started with name calling, Ken threw a punch, and there was a fistfight. Ken took some lumps, but the white boy required five stitches to close a wound over his left eye.

The school responded with suspensions: The white boy was sent home for three days, and Ken was suspended for more than a month. The school justified the difference by pointing to the white student's more serious injuries. But after hearing school officials describe the fight as "mutual," Ken's father thought that his son's longer suspension was unfair. He filed a civil rights complaint, claiming that his son was punished more severely because he is black.

Records in the local school district and other districts across Canada and the United States indicate a clear pattern: black students are much more likely than white students to be kicked out of school for misbehaving.

Why? At least one school official claims the answer is simply that black youngsters are more likely to misbehave.

He points out that the school district also suspends far more males than females. "Does that mean," he asks, "that we discriminate against men?"

But others charge that racial bias is real. One recent study of school discipline concluded that black students were more likely than white students to be disciplined for the same behaviours, especially relatively minor issues such as making too much noise or acting disrespectfully. "You can choose not to use the word *racism*," the researcher con-

Does race play a part in which students school officials charge with behaviour problems? What about social class?

cluded, "but school districts need to look seriously at what is going on."

Perhaps both theories contain some truth. The National Association of Secondary School Principals in the United States confirms that blacks are more likely than whites to misbehave, but they claim the cause is not race but differences in social background. In other words, black children have more disciplinary problems in school because they are more likely to come from poor families where they are subject to disadvantages ranging from less parenting to exposure to lead-based paint. But if this is so, we are still left with the question, "Whose fault is that?"

WHAT DO YOU THINK?

1. Outline the arguments for and against the idea that school discipline unfairly targets black youth. What is your position?
2. Do you think the fact that black students are more likely to be disciplined than white students is a case of racial profiling? Why or why not?
3. What can schools do to ensure that all students are treated fairly?

Source: Morse (2002a), and Ruck & Wortley (2002).

A recent study of high school dropouts by Canadian sociologist Scott Davies (1994) shows that social class is only weakly related to Canadian high school dropout rates. More important are such factors as streaming (mentioned above) and students' poor academic achievement—neither of which, notes Davies, is exclusive to lower-class and minority students.

There has been a notable reduction in the Canadian high-school dropout rates in the last decade. Nevertheless, in 1999, 12 percent of 20-year-olds had not completed their secondary education and, equally disturbing, the boys' rate was 1.5 times higher than that of girls. Many of the problems that students have during their high-school years

follow them to college and university. Those who had difficulty attending, passing, and attaining high grades in high school are much more likely to drop out of their post-secondary school than their colleagues who did not have these difficulties in high school (Butlin, 2000).

ACADEMIC STANDARDS

In Canada, as in many other countries, fears have been growing about the standard of education. According to the Conference Board of Canada, Canada's position as one of the strongest economic nations in the world is "at risk

For all categories of people in Canada, dropping out of school greatly reduces the chances to get a good job and earn a secure income.

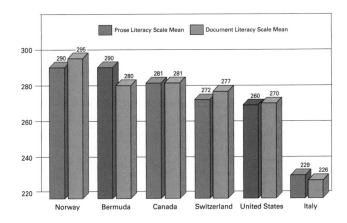

FIGURE 14-3 Adult Literacy and Life Skills Survey

Source: Statistics Canada and OECD (2005).

because of the high secondary-school dropout rate, as well as a short supply of skilled labour and high public debt (Conference Board of Canada, 2000). Similar fears surround the extent of **functional illiteracy**, *a lack of the reading and writing skills needed for everyday living* (Coulombe, Tremblay, & Marchand, 2004).

Results from the 2003 Adult Literacy and Life Skills Survey (Statistics Canada and OECD, 2005) confirmed earlier 1994 findings: many older Canadians have difficulty coping with the unfamiliar literacy and numeracy demands of employment and daily living. Depending on the country surveyed, 33–66 percent of adults did not attain the third of five skill levels, the minimum that educators consider needed to deal with our post-industrial knowledge society. As shown in Figure 14–3, Canadian adults compare well to adults in other nations on literacy performance measures.

Looking Ahead: Schooling in the Twenty-First Century

Despite the fact that Canada leads the world in sending people to post-secondary schools, the public school system struggles with serious problems, many of which have their roots in the larger society. Thus, during the twenty-first century, we cannot expect schools by themselves to provide high-quality education. Schools will only improve to the extent that students, teachers, parents, and local communities commit to educational excellence. In short, educational problems are social problems, and there is no quick fix.

For much of the twentieth century, there were just two models for education in Canada: public schools run by the government, and private schools operated by non-governmental organizations. In the last decade, however, many new ideas about schooling have come on the scene, including schooling for profit and a wide range of "choice" programs (Finn & Gau, 1998). In the decades ahead, we will likely see some significant changes in mass education guided, in part, by social science research pointing out the consequences of different strategies.

Another factor that will continue to shape schools is new information technology. Today almost all schools—and many daycare centres—use computers for instruction. Computers prompt students to be more active and allow them to progress at their own pace. Even so, computers have their limitations; they can never replace the personal insight or imagination of a motivated human teacher. Nor will technology solve the problems—including violence and rigid bureaucracy—that plague our schools. What we need is a broad plan for social change that re-ignites this country's early ambition to provide quality universal schooling to all—a goal that has so far eluded us.

Medicine and Health

According to the World Health Organization (1946:3), **health** is *a state of complete physical, mental, and social well-being.* This definition emphasizes an important idea: *health is as much a social as a*

Learn more about the World Health Organization at http://www.who.int/en.

biological issue. **Medicine**, a much narrower concept, is *a social institution that focuses on fighting disease and improving health.*

HEALTH AND SOCIETY

Society affects health in four basic ways:

1. **Cultural patterns define health.** Standards of health vary from culture to culture. A century ago, yaws, a contagious skin disease, was so common in tropical Africa that people there considered it normal (Dubos, 1980, orig. 1965). "Health," therefore, is sometimes a matter of having the same diseases as one's neighbours (Pinhey, Rubinstein, & Colfax, 1997).

    What people see as healthful also reflects what they think is morally good. People (especially men) in Canada think a competitive way of life is "healthy" because it fits our cultural mores, but stress contributes to heart disease and many other illnesses. On the other hand, people who object to homosexuality on moral grounds often call it "sick," even though it is natural from a biological point of view. Thus, ideas about health act as a form of social control, encouraging conformity to cultural norms.

2. **Cultural standards of health change over time.** Early in the twentieth century, some doctors warned women not to go to college or university because higher education strained the female brain. Others claimed that masturbation was a threat to health. We now know that both of these ideas are false. Fifty years ago, on the other hand, few doctors understood the dangers of smoking cigarettes or getting too much sun exposure, practices that we now recognize as serious health risks.

3. **A society's technology affects people's health.** In low-income nations, infectious diseases are widespread because of malnutrition and poor sanitation. As industrialization raises living standards, people become healthier. But industrial technology also creates new threats to health. As Chapter 15 ("Population, Urbanization, and Environment") explains, high-income countries endanger health by encouraging overeating, overtaxing the world's resources, and creating pollution.

4. **Social inequality affects people's health.** All societies distribute resources unequally. Overall, the rich have far better physical, mental, and emotional health than the poor.

Health: A Global Survey

Because health is closely linked to social life, human well-being improved over the long course of history as societies

Educators have long debated the proper manner in which to school children with disabilities. On the one hand, such children may benefit from distinctive facilities and specially trained teachers. On the other hand, they are less likely to be stigmatized as "different" if included in regular classroom settings. What do you consider to be the ramifications of the "special education" versus "inclusive education" debate for the classroom experience of all children, not only those who have disabilities?

developed more advanced technology. Differences in societal development are also the cause of striking differences in health around the world today.

HEALTH IN LOW-INCOME COUNTRIES

With only simple technology, our ancestors could do little to improve health. Hunters and gatherers faced frequent food shortages, which sometimes forced mothers to abandon their children. Those lucky enough to survive infancy

For information on nutrition and health, go to **http://www. hc-sc.gc.ca/fn-an/index_e.html**.

were still vulnerable to injury and illness, so half died by age 20 and few lived to 40 (Diamond, 1997; Scupin, 2000; Nolan & Lenski, 2004).

As agricultural societies developed, food became more plentiful. Yet social inequality also increased, so that elites enjoyed better health than peasants and slaves, who lived in crowded, unsanitary shelters and often went hungry. In the growing cities of medieval Europe, human waste and refuse piled up in the streets, spreading infectious diseases, and plagues periodically wiped out entire towns (Mumford, 1961).

TABLE 14-3

Cancer and Heart Disease Death Rates in Canada: 1981, 1997, and 2001

	Women		Men	
	Heart Disease	Cancer	Heart Disease	Cancer
1981	205	149	380	240
1997	130	149	231	230
2001	80	149	155	225

Deaths per 100 000 population

Figures are age-standardized to the 1991 population.

Data on heart disease for 1981 and 1997 use ICD-9 codes 390–398, 402, 404, and 410–429; for 2001 they use ICD-10 codes 100–109, 111, 113, and 120–151. Data on cancer for 1981 and 1997 use ICD-9 codes 140–208 and for 2001, they use ICD-10 codes C00–C97.

Source: Statistics Canada (2005). *Women in Canada: A Gender-Based Statistical Analysis.* Fifth edition. Ottawa: Statistics Canada. Catalogue no. 89-503-XIE.

November 1, Central India. Poverty is not just a matter of what you have; it shapes what you are. Most of the people we see in the villages here have never had the benefit of a doctor's or dentist's services. The result is easy to see: people look old before their time.

In much of the world, poverty cuts decades off the life expectancy found in high-income countries. A look back at Global Map 9–1 on page 237 shows that in the poorest low-income countries of the world, most people die before reaching their teens. To make matters worse, healthcare personnel are few and far between, so that many of the world's poorest people never see a doctor.

The World Health Organization reports that 1 billion people around the world—one person in six—suffer from serious illness due to unequal access to resources. Poor sanitation and malnutrition kill people of all ages but are especially likely to result in higher rates of morbidity and mortality for girls and women (Population Reference Bureau, 2005).

HEALTH IN HIGH-INCOME COUNTRIES

Industrialization dramatically changed patterns of health in Europe, although at first not for the better. By 1800, as the Industrial Revolution took hold, factory jobs drew people from all over the rural countryside. Cities became overcrowded, creating serious sanitation problems. Factories fouled the air with smoke, and workplace accidents were common.

However, as industrialization progressed, rising living standards translated into better nutrition and safer housing for most people, and health began to improve in Western Europe and North America. After 1850, advances in knowledge of how diseases are spread also improved health, primarily by controlling infectious diseases. For example, in 1854, a researcher named John Snow mapped the street addresses of London's cholera victims and found that they had all drunk contaminated water from the same well (Rockett, 1994). Such discoveries by Snow and others led scientists to link cholera to specific bacteria and eventually to develop a vaccine against the deadly disease. Armed with scientific knowledge, early environmentalists campaigned against common practices such as dumping raw sewage into rivers used for drinking water. By the early twentieth century, death rates from infectious diseases had fallen sharply.

The leading killers in 1900—influenza and pneumonia—account for just a few percent of deaths in Canada today. As Table 14–3 shows, chronic "lifestyle" illnesses—such as heart disease and cancer—are now the leading killers in our country. Industrialization delays death by shifting its primary causes from acute illnesses that strike at any age to the chronic illnesses of old age.

Health in Canada

Because Canada is a high-income nation, its people are generally healthy by global standards. Still, some categories of people have much better health than others.

WHO IS HEALTHY? AGE, GENDER, CLASS, AND RACE

Social epidemiology is *the study of how health and disease are distributed throughout a society's population.* Social epidemiologists examine the origin and spread of epidemic diseases and show how people's health is tied to their physical and social environments. The trend in Canada is toward a higher level of health for all people, but recent analysis shows that differences persist between high- and low-income earners, with men in the richest 20 percent of neighbourhoods living five years longer than men from the poorest 20 percent of neighbourhoods in Canada in 1996. This is an improvement from 1971, when the difference was more than six years, but the analysis shows that while the top 80 percent of neighbourhoods have almost achieved the goal of equal health for all, the bottom 20 percent remain far behind (Wilkins, Berthelot, & Ng, 2002).

Age and gender. Death is now rare among young people. Still, young people do fall victim to accidents and, more recently, to acquired immune deficiency syndrome (AIDS).

Throughout the life course, women have better health than men. First, females are less likely than males to die before or immediately after birth. Then, as socialization into gender roles proceeds, males become more aggressive and individualistic, resulting in higher rates of accidents, violence, and suicide. Yet women are more likely than men to report poor mental health (Annandale & Hunt, 2000). Studies report that the lifetime prevalence of major depression is twice the amount for adult women than men, and women are also more prone to experiencing stress caused by life events (Stephens, Dulberg, & Joubert, 2000). A number of explanations have been suggested for this pattern, including socializing practices and structural differences between the genders in work and family roles (Sachs-Ericsson & Ciarlo, 2000). Women are twice as likely as men to be given a diagnosis of unipolar depression, anxiety, panic disorder, or agoraphobia, and three times as likely to be diagnosed as having a histrionic personality and borderline personality disorder. Men, on the other hand, receive a diagnosis of alcohol abuse at the ratio of 5:1, antisocial personality disorder at 3:1, and obsessive-compulsive personality disorder at 2:1. These findings suggest that mental health problems are influenced by gender roles and, in fact, certain diagnoses are gender specific.

Social class and race. Infant mortality—the death rate among children under one year of age—is twice as high for Aboriginal children in Canada as for other children born to privilege. Although the health of the richest children in this country is the best in the world, our poorest children are as vulnerable to disease as those in low-income nations such as Lebanon and Vietnam.

Health, race, and ethnicity are also linked. As Figure 14–5 shows, reported cases of tuberculosis are substantially higher for our foreign-born and Aboriginal populations than for other Canadians.

Because Aboriginal Canadians are much more likely than other Canadians to be poor, they are more likely to die in infancy and to have a shorter life expectancy. Studies show that the life expectancy for Canada's Aboriginal population is five or more years less than that for the total Canadian population (Canadian Institute for Health Information, 2000).

However, sex is an even stronger predictor of health than race, since Aboriginal women can expect to outlive males of either race (Statistics Canada, 2006).

CIGARETTE SMOKING

Cigarette smoking tops the list of preventable health hazards in Canada. Only after World War I did smoking become popular in this country. Despite growing evidence of its dangers, smoking remained fashionable even a generation ago. Today, however, an increasing number of people consider smoking to be a mild form of social deviance.

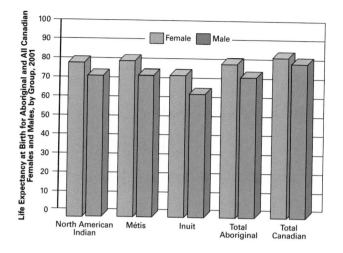

FIGURE 14-4 Life Expectancy at Birth for Aboriginal and All Canadian Females and Males, by Group, 2001

Source: Statistics Canada (2005). *Women in Canada: A Gender-Based Statistical Analysis.* Fifth edition. Ottawa: Statistics Canada. Catalogue no. 89-503-XIE.

The popularity of cigarettes peaked in 1960, when almost 45 percent of Canadian adults smoked. By 2000–01, only 21.5 percent were smoking daily (Statistics Canada, 2003j). Quitting is difficult because cigarette smoke contains nicotine, a physically addictive drug. And many people smoke to cope with stress: divorced and separated people are likely to smoke, as are lower-income people, the unemployed, and people in the armed forces. Moreover, a slightly larger share of Canadian men (23.5 percent) than women (19.4 percent) smoke. But cigarettes, the only form of tobacco use popular among women, have taken a toll on women's health. By the early 1990s, lung cancer surpassed breast cancer as a cause of death among Canadian women.

In 2003 alone, it is predicted that 21 100 new cases of lung cancer will be diagnosed and 18 880 people in Canada will die of lung cancer. Lung cancer is the leading cause of death due to cancer in Canada, representing an estimated 30 percent of the cancer deaths in males and 25 percent of the cancer deaths in females (Health Canada, 2003a).

Smokers also suffer more often from minor illnesses such as flu, and pregnant women who smoke increase the likelihood of spontaneous abortion, prenatal death, and low-birthweight babies. Even non-smokers exposed to cigarette smoke have a high risk of smoking-related diseases.

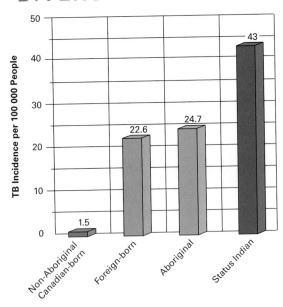

FIGURE 14-5 Reported Tuberculosis Cases, by Population Subgroup, Canada, 1996

Source: Health Canada (2001).

Tobacco is a billion-dollar industry in Canada. In 1997, the tobacco industry conceded that cigarette smoking is harmful to health and agreed to stop marketing cigarettes to young people. But despite the anti-smoking trend in Canada, the percentage of young people (aged 20–34) who smoke has been creeping upward, to 26.1 percent in 2000–01 (Statistics Canada, 2003j). In addition, the use of chewing tobacco, also a threat to health, is increasing among the young.

The tobacco industry has increased marketing abroad, where there is less regulation of sales and advertising. Figure 14–6 shows that in many countries (especially in Asia), a large majority of men smoke. Worldwide, more than 1 billion adults (about 30 percent of the total) smoke, consuming some 6 trillion cigarettes annually, and smoking is on the rise. The good news is that about ten years after quitting, an ex-smoker's health is about as good as that of someone who never smoked at all.

EATING DISORDERS

An *eating disorder* is an intense form of dieting or other unhealthy method of weight control. One eating disorder, *anorexia nervosa*, is characterized by dieting to the point of starvation; another is *bulimia,* which involves binge eating followed by induced vomiting to avoid weight gain. The (Canadian) National Eating Disorders Information Centre estimates that anorexia nervosa occurs in approximately 1–2 percent of young women, and bulimia in approximately 2–3 percent of young women.

Eating disorders have a significant cultural component: 95 percent of people who suffer from anorexia nervosa or bulimia are women, mostly from white, affluent families. For women, North American culture equates slenderness with being successful and attractive to men. Conversely, we tend to stereotype overweight women (and, to a lesser extent, men) as lazy, sloppy, and even stupid (Levine, 1987).

Research shows that most college and university-age women believe that "guys like thin girls," that being thin is crucial to physical attractiveness, and that they are not as thin as men would like. In fact, most college and university women want to be thinner than most males in this group say women should be. For their part, most men display far less dissatisfaction with their own body shape (Fallon & Rozin, 1985), though some research into young men has related body image dissatisfaction to unhealthy body-building practices, including the use of anabolic steroids (Canadian Centre for Drug-Free Sport, 1993).

Because few women are able to meet our culture's unrealistic standards of beauty, many women develop a low self-image. It is our idealized image of beauty that leads many young women to diet to the point of risking their health and even their lives. The Global Sociology box explains how the introduction of North American culture to the island of Fiji soon resulted in a sharp increase in eating disorders among its women.

SEXUALLY TRANSMITTED INFECTIONS

Sexual activity, though both pleasurable and vital to the continuation of our species, can transmit more than 50 kinds of infection, or *venereal disease* (from Venus, the Roman goddess of love). People in our society associate sex with sin, and tend also to regard sexually transmitted infections (STIs) not only as illnesses but also as marks of immorality.

STIs grabbed national attention during the "sexual revolution" of the 1960s, when infection rates rose dramatically as people began sexual activity earlier and had a greater number of partners. This means that STIs are an exception to the general decline in infectious diseases over the course of the past century. By the late 1980s, the rising danger of STIs, especially AIDS, generated a sexual counterrevolution as people moved away from casual sex (Kain, 1987; Laumann et al., 1994). The following sections briefly describe several common STIs.

Gonorrhea and syphilis. Gonococcal infection (or gonorrhea) and syphilis, among the oldest known infections, are caused by microscopic organisms that are almost always transmitted by sexual contact. Untreated, gonococcal infection causes sterility, and syphilis can damage major organs and result in blindness, mental disorders, and death.

After a steady and dramatic decline in gonorrhea rates since the early 1980s, an increase was reported in 2004 (28.9 per 100 000) up from 23.5 per 100 000 in 2002, 20.1 per 100 000 in 2000, and a low of 14.9 per 100 000 in 1997 (Public Health Agency of Canada, 2006). Syphilis rates have followed a similar pattern of significant decline over time, though the pattern has reversed in the recent period for both males and females and is especially noticeable among the country's poorer populations, such as residents of Vancouver's Downtown Eastside. Thus, even though the national rate had remained between 0.4 to 0.6 per 100 000 since the mid-1990s, the rate for 2001 rose to 0.9 per 100 000 (Health Canada, 2002a). Both STIs can easily be cured with antibiotics such as penicillin. Thus, neither is currently a major health problem in Canada.

Genital herpes. Genital herpes is not a reportable STI in Canada. It is estimated, however, that the prevalence rate is about one in five in the adult population (Steben & Sacks, 1997). Though far less serious than gonorrhea and syphilis, herpes is incurable. People with genital herpes may not have any symptoms, or they may experience periodic, painful blisters on the genitals accompanied by fever and headache. Although it is not fatal to adults, women with active genital herpes can transmit the disease during a vaginal delivery, and it can be deadly to newborns. Therefore, it is recommended that women with this infection give birth by Cesarean section even when everything else is normal with the pregnancy (Sobel, 2001).

AIDS. The most serious of all sexually transmitted infections is acquired immune deficiency syndrome (AIDS). Identified in 1981, it is incurable and almost always fatal. AIDS is caused by the human immunodeficiency virus (HIV), which attacks white blood cells, weakening the immune system. AIDS thus makes a person vulnerable to a wide range of other health problems that eventually cause death.

At the end of 1999, a total of 49 800 people were living with HIV infection in Canada. Of these, about one-third—approximately 15 000 infected individuals—were not aware of their health condition, and an estimated 15 000–17 000 individuals had died by the end of 1999 (adjusted for underreporting and delayed reporting) (Health Canada, 2003c). Globally, HIV infects some 40 million people—half of them under age 25—and the number is rising rapidly. The global death toll now exceeds 20 million.

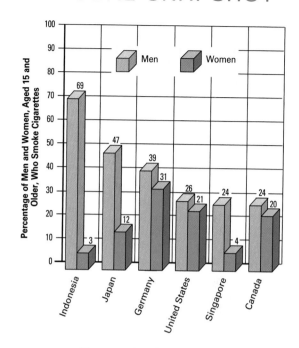

FIGURE 14-6 Cigarette Smoking in Selected Countries

Sources: Centers for Disease Control and Prevention (2004) and World Bank (2005).

Global Map 14–2 shows that Africa (more specifically, countries south of the Sahara) has the highest HIV infection rate and accounts for 66 percent of all world cases. A recent United Nations study found that across much of sub-Saharan Africa, 15-year-olds face a 50–50 chance of becoming infected with HIV. The risk is especially high for girls, not only because HIV is transmitted more easily from men to women but also because many African cultures encourage women to be submissive to men. According to some analysts, the AIDS crisis now threatens the political and economic security of Africa and, indeed, the entire world (Ashford, 2002; United Nations, 2002).

Upon infection, people with HIV display no symptoms at all, so most are unaware of their condition. Symptoms of AIDS may not appear for a year or longer, during which time an infected person may infect others. Within five years, one-third of infected people develop full-blown AIDS; half develop AIDS within 10 years, and almost all become sick within 20 years.

HIV is infectious but not contagious. That is, HIV is transmitted from person to person through blood, semen, or breast milk but not through casual contact such as shaking hands, hugging, sharing towels or dishes, swimming

GLOBAL SOCIOLOGY

Gender and Eating Disorders: A Report From Fiji

In 1995, television came to Fiji, a small group of islands in the South Pacific Ocean. A single cable channel carried programming from a small number of high-income countries—including Great Britain, the United States, and Australia. Anne Becker, a health researcher specializing in eating disorders, read the news with great interest, wondering what effect the new culture being poured in via television would have on young women there.

Traditionally, Fijian culture emphasizes good nutrition and looking strong and healthy. The idea of dieting to look very thin was almost unknown. So it is not surprising that in 1995, Becker found just 3 percent of Fijian teenage girls reported ever vomiting to control their weight. By 1998, however, a striking change had taken place, with 15 percent of teenage girls—a fivefold increase—reporting this practice. Becker also found that 62 percent of girls claimed they had dieted during the previous month and 74 percent reported feeling "too big" or "fat."

The rapid rise in eating disorders in Fiji, which Becker linked to the introduction of television, shows the power of culture to shape patterns of health. Eating disorders, including anorexia nervosa and bulimia, are even more common in North America, where about half of college and university women report engaging in such behaviour, even though most of these women, medically speaking, are not over-weight. Indeed, Fijian women are now learning what many women in countries such as our own already believe: "You are never too thin to feel fat."

WHAT DO YOU THINK?

1. How do we know that eating disorders are a social issue as well as a health issue?
2. At what age do you think girls begin to learn that "you are never too thin to feel fat"?
3. What social changes might reduce the rate of eating disorders among Canadian women?

Source: Based on Becker (1999).

together, or even coughing and sneezing. The risk of transmitting AIDS through saliva (as in kissing) is extremely low. The risk of transmitting HIV through sexual activity is greatly reduced by the use of latex condoms. However, abstinence or an exclusive relationship with an uninfected person is the only sure way to avoid infection.

Specific behaviours place people at high risk for HIV infection. The first is *anal sex,* which can cause rectal bleeding, allowing easy transmission of HIV from one person to another. The fact that many men who have sex with other men (MSM) engage in anal sex helps explain why these categories of people accounted for 58 percent of AIDS cases in Canada in 2002 (Public Health Agency of Canada, 2004).

Sharing needles used to inject drugs is a second high-risk behaviour. Sex with an intravenous drug user is also very risky. Because intravenous drug use is more common among poor people and Aboriginals in Canada, AIDS is now becoming a disease of the socially disadvantaged.

Using any drug, including alcohol, also increases the risk of being infected with HIV to the extent that it impairs judgment. In other words, even people who understand what places them at risk of infection may act less responsibly once they are under the influence of alcohol, marijuana, or some other drug.

While only 14 percent of the people with AIDS in Canada in 1999 were women, the figure had increased to 20 percent in 2004 and there is an increasing trend toward positive HIV reports among heterosexuals (Health Canada, 2003d). As Figure 14–7 shows, heterosexual activity does transmit HIV (27 percent in 2005), and the danger rises with the number of sexual partners, especially if they fall into high-risk categories. In fact, worldwide, heterosexual relations are the primary means of HIV transmission, accounting for two-thirds of all infections.

The Canadian government initially responded slowly to the AIDS crisis, largely because gays and intravenous drug users are widely viewed as deviant. But funding for AIDS research, including from the country's primary health funding agency (the Canadian Institutes for Health Research), has increased dramatically in recent years, and researchers have identified some drugs, including protease inhibitors, that suppress the symptoms of the disease. Canada has also approved on a trial basis the safe injection site in Vancouver, BC. The facility opened its doors in 2003, and is the first of its kind in North America. It operates with an exemption from Health Canada that expires in September 2006. The researchers led by Dr. Tom Kerr hope that the project will receive renewed support from Health Canada. A

WINDOW ON THE WORLD

GLOBAL MAP 14-2 HIV/AIDS Infection of Adults in Global Perspective

Almost 70 percent of all global HIV infections are in sub-Saharan Africa. In countries such as Botswana and Swaziland, more than one-third of people aged 15–49 are infected with HIV/AIDS. This very high infection rate reflects the prevalence of other sexually transmitted infections and infrequent use of condoms, two factors that promote heterosexual transmission of HIV. All of Southeast Asia accounts for about 17 percent of global HIV infections. In countries such as Cambodia and Thailand, 2–3 percent of people aged 15–49 are now infected. All of North and South America taken together account for 8 percent of global HIV infections. The incidence of infection in Muslim nations is extremely low by world standards.

Source: Population Reference Bureau (2004); map projection from *Peters Atlas of the World* (1990).

recent study published in the *New England Journal of Medicine* shows that drug users who use Vancouver's safe injection site are more likely to enter detox and other treatment facilities (Kerr, Tyndall, Li, Montaner, & Wood, 2005). Other research has shown that the safe injection site has helped to increase public order and reduces needle sharing in Vancouver's Downtown Eastside (Wood, Kerr, Small, Li, Marsh, Montaner, & Tyndall, 2004). But educational programs remain the most effective weapon against AIDS because prevention is the only way to stop a disease that has no cure.

FIGURE 14-7 Types of Transmission HIV/AIDS, Canada, 1999 and 2002

Source: Public Health Agency of Canada (2005).

ETHICAL ISSUES SURROUNDING DEATH

Now that technological advances have given human beings the power to draw the line separating life and death, people often must make the decision about how and when to do so. In other words, technology has added an ethical dimension to health and illness.

When does death occur? Common sense suggests that life ends when breathing and the heartbeat stop. But the ability to revive or replace a heart and artificially sustain respiration makes this definition of death obsolete. Thus, medical and legal experts in North America define death as an *irreversible* state involving no response to stimulation, no movement or breathing, no reflexes, and no indication of brain activity (Ladd, 1979; Wall, 1980; Jones, 1998).

Do people have a right to die? Today, medical personnel, family members, and patients themselves bear the agonizing burden of deciding when a terminally ill person should die. Among the most difficult cases are the 10 000 people in Canada in a permanent vegetative state who cannot express their own desires about life and death. Generally speaking, the first duty of doctors and hospitals is to protect a patient's life. Even so, a mentally competent person in the process of dying can refuse medical treatment or even nutrition (either at the time or, in advance, through a document called a "living will").

"Mercy killing" is the common term for **euthanasia**, *assisting in the death of a person suffering from an incurable disease.* Euthanasia (from Greek, meaning "a good death") poses an ethical dilemma, as it is considered by some to be an act of kindness and by others as a form of killing.

Whether there is a "right to die" is one of today's most difficult issues. All people with incurable diseases have a right to refuse treatment that might prolong their lives. But whether a doctor should be allowed to help bring about death is at the heart of today's debate. Though Parliament no longer views attempted suicide as a crime in Canada, it is still against the *Criminal Code* to assist a suicide. Still, many people in Canada are terminally ill, and some do express a wish for assistance to end their life. Such was the case for BC resident Sue Rodriguez, who took her case all the way to the Supreme Court in 1993. The court did not rule in her favour, though Rodriguez ultimately got her wish through the assistance of an anonymous physician. A sympathetic former BC member Parliament, Svend Robinson, was also at her side. A special prosecutor later ruled against charging either party with wrongdoing.

Supporters of *active* euthanasia—allowing a dying person to enlist the services of a doctor to bring on a quick death—argue that there are circumstances (such as when a dying person suffers from great pain) that make death preferable to life. Critics counter that permitting active euthanasia invites abuse. They fear that patients will feel pressure to end their lives to spare family members the burden of caring for them and avoid the high costs of hospitalization. Research in the Netherlands, where physician-assisted suicide is legal, indicates that about one-fifth of all such deaths have occurred without a patient explicitly requesting to die (Gillon, 1999).

In Canada, Saskatchewan farmer Robert Latimer has been in and out of court for the carbon-monoxide poisoning of his disabled daughter, Tracy, in 1993. She had a severe case of cerebral palsy. The Saskatchewan Court of Appeal ruled in November 1998 that Latimer had to return to prison to serve his life sentence, with no opportunity for parole for ten years. Latimer's lawyers appealed the case to the Supreme Court of Canada but lost. Latimer is now back in jail, completing his ten-year sentence for ending his daughter's life. The Canadian public remain torn over the case. The "right to die" debate is sure to continue.

The Medical Establishment

Throughout most of human history, healthcare was the responsibility of individuals and their families. Medicine emerges as a social institution only as societies become more productive and people take on specialized work.

Members of agrarian societies today still turn to various traditional health practitioners, including acupuncturists and herbalists. In industrial societies, medical care falls to specially trained and licensed professionals, from anesthesiologists to X-ray technicians. The medical establishment of modern, industrial societies took form over the last 150 years.

THE RISE OF SCIENTIFIC MEDICINE

In pre-Confederation times, herbalists, druggists, midwives, and ministers practised the healing arts. But not all were effective. Unsanitary instruments, lack of anesthesia, and simple ignorance made surgery a terrible ordeal, and doctors probably killed as many people as they saved. In 1795, the first *Medical Act* attempted to regulate the practices of "physic and surgery" in Upper Canada by making it illegal for untrained healers to practise medicine without licences; only those with university degrees were exempted. The impracticality of the ruling soon became apparent, and the small degree-holding segment of the medical profession was left vulnerable to public critics. The original *Medical Act* was repealed in 1806, and traditional healers, including midwives, remained immune from the licensing laws of the Ontario Medical Board for the next half-century. In 1866, however, the government changed the law so that practitioners of midwifery and other healing arts, such as naturopathy, required medical degrees. That meant the predominantly male medical profession in the province enjoyed a legal monopoly over the birthing chamber by the time of Confederation in 1867 (Benoit, 1998b). No female physicians were licensed in Ontario until the 1880s, and owing to continuing patriarchal traditions, few women entered this profession for many decades thereafter. Although some "traditionalist" physicians opposed this turn of events embraced by their "radical" colleagues and called instead for formal training and legalization of lay healers, their efforts proved unsuccessful (Biggs, 1983).

The Canadian Medical Association (CMA), founded in 1867, also symbolized the growing acceptance of a scientific model of medicine. The CMA widely publicized the successes of its members in identifying the causes of life-threatening diseases—bacteria and viruses—and developing vaccines to prevent them. Still, other approaches to healthcare, such as regulating nutrition, also had defenders. But the CMA responded boldly—some thought arrogantly—to these alternative approaches to healthcare, trumpeting the superiority of its practitioners.

The influential Flexner Report of 1910 highlighted the abysmal situation of Canadian (and U.S.) medical education, reporting that 90 percent of all physicians at the time received their training from profit-making schools, which offered few or no resources for authentic clinical training. Abraham Flexner recommended the elimination of all "diploma mills," and the tightening of education and licensing standards for North American physicians. Traditional healers, as well as black and female physicians, became easy targets for the reformed medical profession.

The Flexner Report effectively led to the closing down of schools teaching other methods of healing (herbal medicine, homeopathy, etc.), limiting the practice of medicine to those with medical science degrees. These developments awarded medical doctors the primary role in the healthcare of the population, and gave social legitimacy to *scientific medicine*—the social institution that focuses on combating disease and improving health. In the process, both the prestige and income of physicians rose dramatically; today, doctors in Canada are among the highest-paid workers in the country.

Practitioners of other approaches (such as naturopathy, midwifery, and chiropractic medicine) for a time held on to their traditional practices, but these practitioners were relegated to the fringe of the medical profession. However, chiropractic services have in the past decade gained partial coverage under some provincial healthcare systems. More recently, midwifery has also gained coverage under the provincial healthcare systems of Ontario, British Columbia, Quebec, and Manitoba (DeVries et al., 2001; Bourgeault, Benoit, & Davis-Floyd, 2004). Scientific medicine, taught in expensive, urban medical schools, also changed the social profile of doctors. As the CMA standards took hold, most physicians came from privileged backgrounds and practised in cities. Furthermore, as mentioned above, women had figured prominently in many fields of healing denigrated by the CMA. Some early medical schools did train women but, owing to the Flexner Report and declining financial resources, most of these schools soon closed. Only in recent decades have women increased their representation in the medical profession. In 1998, women accounted for 28 percent of Canada's practising physicians, up from 25 percent in 1993 (Canadian Institute for Health Information, 2000). In 2004 women made up 55 percent of all doctors in Canada (Statistics Canada, 2006).

Yet female physicians in our country tend to remain clustered in the lower-ranking medical specialties, separated by a glass ceiling from their male colleagues in top administrative and specialty posts.

HOLISTIC MEDICINE

Recently, the scientific model of medicine has been tempered by the introduction of **holistic medicine**, *an approach to healthcare that emphasizes prevention of illness and takes into account a person's entire physical and social environment.* Holistic practitioners agree on the need for drugs, surgery, artificial organs, and high technology, but they emphasize treatment of the whole person instead of symptoms, and health rather than disease. There are three foundations of holistic healthcare (Gordon, 1980; Patterson, 1998):

1. **Patients are people.** Holistic practitioners are concerned not only with symptoms but also with how people's environment and lifestyle affect health. Holistic practitioners extend the bounds of conventional

The profession of surgery has existed only for several centuries. Before that, barbers offered their services to the very sick, often cutting the skin to "bleed" a patient. Of course, this "treatment" was rarely effective, but it did produce plenty of bloody bandages, which practitioners hung out to dry. This practice identifies the origin of the red and white barber poles we see today.

Jan Sanders von Hemessen (c. 1504–1566), *The Surgeon*, oil on panel. Prado, Madrid, Spain/Giraudon/Bridgeman Art Library.

medicine, taking an active role in fighting poverty, environmental pollution, and other dangers to public health.

2. **Responsibility, not dependency.** A scientific approach to medicine puts doctors in charge of health, and patients are to follow doctors' orders. Holistic medicine tries to shift some responsibility for health from doctor to patient by emphasizing health-promoting behaviour. Holistic medicine favours an *active* approach to *health* rather than a *reactive* approach to *illness*.

3. **Personal treatment.** Scientific medicine treats patients in impersonal offices and hospitals, both disease-centred settings. Holistic practitioners favour, as much as possible, a personal and relaxed environment such as the home.

In sum, holistic health does not oppose scientific medicine but shifts the emphasis from treating disease to achieving the greatest well-being for everyone. Considering that over the last few decades many Canadian provinces have decided to certify a number of alternative and complementary health practices, there is a need for non-medical practitioners concerned with the whole patient.

PAYING FOR HEALTHCARE: A GLOBAL SURVEY

As medicine has come to rely on high technology, the costs of healthcare in high- and middle-income countries have skyrocketed. Countries throughout the world have adopted different strategies to meet these costs.

March 14, Vinales, Cuba. We have difficulty finding the hospital because there are no big signs on the modest white-washed building. Finally, we enter the large open area and encounter a friendly, efficient nurse who beckons us into an examination room. Annika has felt weak ever since we left Victoria for Havana and was not able to ride her touring bike more than a few kilometres yesterday. We explain our story in English to the Spanish-speaking doctor assigned to us; it's a challenge, but gestures and goodwill come to our aid. The hospital is spotless but crumbling. A slow leak has made a hole in the ceiling; water drops into a bucket. The X-ray machine looks as if it is hand-cranked. But, 90 minutes later, we walk out of the hospital with a firm diagnosis of pneumonia, an X-ray to take back home to our family doctor, and prescriptions for two kinds of antibiotics. To our amazement, the Cuban doctor attending our daughter declined any payment, shaking her head in seeming disbelief that we should even ask about the cost. After picking up the medicine in the local pharmacy we have spent the equivalent of $1.35! We wonder if we could have been helped so quickly and efficiently on a Saturday morning back in Canada and know that *the cost of the medicine would have been much higher back home. Why did we bother to get travellers' medical insurance?*

People's Republic of China. A poor, agrarian society in the process of industrializing, the People's Republic of China faces the immense task of providing for the health of more than 1 billion people. China has experimented with private medicine, but the government controls most healthcare.

China's "barefoot doctors," roughly comparable to paramedics or nurse practitioners in Canada, used to bring some modern methods of healthcare to peasants in rural villages, though this rural system has declined significantly in recent decades. Traditional healing arts, involving acupuncture and medicinal herbs, are still widely practised in rural and urban areas. In addition, the Chinese approach to health is based on a holistic concern for the interplay of mind and body (Sidel & Sidel, 1982b; Kaptchuk, 1985).

Russian Federation. The Russian Federation is struggling to transform a state-dominated economy into more of a market system. For this reason, healthcare in this country is in transition. Nevertheless, the idea that everyone has a right to basic healthcare remains widespread.

As in China, people in the Russian Federation do not choose a doctor but report to a local government health facility. Physicians there have much lower incomes than physicians in Canada, earning about the same salary as skilled industrial workers (Canadian doctors earn roughly five times as much as Canadian industrial workers). Also, about 70 percent of Russia's doctors are women, compared to 55 percent in Canada. Yet Russian female physicians receive comparatively low wages and have poorer working conditions than women doctors in high-income countries.

Funded by government taxes, healthcare in Russia has suffered setbacks in recent years, partly due to a falling standard of living. A rising demand for healthcare services has strained a bureaucratic system that at best provides highly standardized and impersonal care. The optimistic view is that as market reforms proceed, both living standards and the quality of health services will improve. In any case, as discussed in the Global Sociology box, what does seem certain is that inequalities in healthcare will increase (Specter, 1995; Landsberg, 1998).

Sweden. In 1891, Sweden began a compulsory, comprehensive system of government medical care. Citizens pay for this program with their taxes, which are among the highest in the world. Typically, physicians are government employees and most hospitals are government-managed. Sweden's system is called **socialized medicine,** *a medical care system in which the government owns and operates most medical facilities and employs most physicians.*

Great Britain. In 1948, Great Britain also established socialized medicine by creating a dual system of health services. All British citizens are entitled to care provided by the National Health Service, but those who can afford it can also go to doctors and hospitals that operate privately.

Japan. Physicians in Japan operate privately, but a combination of government programs and private insurance pays medical costs. As shown in Figure 14–8, the Japanese approach medical care much like the Europeans, with most medical expenses paid through the government.

The United States. With its primarily private system of medical care, the United States stands alone among industrialized societies in having no government-operated program of care for everyone. Its **direct-fee system** is *a medical care system in which patients pay directly for the services of doctors and hospitals.* Thus, whereas Europeans and Canadians look to the government to fund 70–80 percent of healthcare costs (paid for through taxation), the U.S. government pays less than half of the country's medical costs (Lohr, 1988; U.S. Census Bureau, 2001).

THE CANADIAN HEALTHCARE SYSTEM

Since 1972, Canada has had a single-payer model of healthcare that provides care to all Canadians. Like a vast insurance company, the Canadian government pays doctors and hospitals according to a set schedule of fees. Canada's "medicare" system is predominantly a publicly financed, privately delivered healthcare system. The system provides access to universal comprehensive coverage for hospital and in-patient and out-patient services that are deemed necessary by a physician. While the administration and delivery of health services is the responsibility of each individual province or territory, the system is a national one to the extent that all areas of the country are expected to adhere to national principles. The federal government sets and administers national principles, or standards, for the healthcare system under the 1984 *Canada Health Act* (the standards are universality, accessibility, portability, comprehensive coverage, and public administration). The federal government also helps to finance provincial healthcare services through monetary transfers.

For a look at the "National Dialogue" about the future of healthcare in Canada check out http://www.hc-sc.gc.ca/english/care/romanow/hcc0399.html.

When Health Fails: A Report From Russia

Night is falling in Pitkyaranta, a small town on the western edge of Russia, near the border with Finland. Andrei, a 30-year-old man with a round face and a long ponytail, weaves his way through the deepening shadows along a busy street. He has spent much of the afternoon in a bar with friends, watching music videos while drinking vodka and smoking cigarettes. Andrei is a railroad worker, but several months ago he was laid off. "Now," he explains bitterly, "I have nothing to do but drink and smoke." Andrei shrugs off a question about his health. "The only thing I care about is finding a job. I am a grown man. I don't want to be supported by my mother and father." Andrei still thinks of himself as young—yet, according to current health patterns in Russia, for a man of 30, life is half over.

After the collapse of the Soviet Union in 1991, living conditions began getting worse, year after year. One result, say doctors, is stress, especially on men who earn too little to support their families or are out of work entirely. Few people eat well anymore, and Russian men now drink and smoke as heavily as people anywhere in the world. The World Health Organization reports that alcohol abuse is Russia's number-one killer. Analysis of Russian mortality rates between 1987 and 1994 demonstrated a sharp increase, predominantly for alcohol-related deaths. This most likely reflected a combination of factors such as the reversal of the government's anti-alcohol campaign, the end of the state monopoly on alcohol imports and sales, and a reduction in the unit cost of alcohol (Ben-Shlomo, 2005).

In towns such as Pitkyaranta, the signs of poor health are everywhere: women no longer breastfeed their babies, the rate of accidents and illnesses among adults has soared, and people look old before their time. Doctors are struggling to stop the health slide, but with poorly equipped hospitals, they are simply overwhelmed. Statistically, while life expectancy has dropped several years for women, men's has plummeted and now stands at just 59 years, about where it was half a century ago. Just 150 kilometres to the west, in Finland, where economic trends are far better, the comparable figure is 74 years. In global context, life expectancy for Russian women has fallen below that in rich countries; for Russian men, life expectancy is only a little better than in some of the world's lowest-income nations.

A joke is making the rounds among young Russian men like Andrei. Their health may be failing, they say, but this cloud has a silver lining: at least they no longer have to worry about retirement.

Source: Adapted from Landsberg (1998) and Ben-Shlomo (2005).

Canada does not therefore have a system of "socialized healthcare," such as that of Sweden, where the government is the principal employer of doctors. Most Canadian physicians are instead private practitioners who work in independent or group practices and enjoy high degrees of autonomy. Private physicians are mainly paid on a fee-for-service basis and submit their service claims directly to the provincial health insurance plan for payment (Blishen, 1991; Segall & Chappell, 2000). Non-hospital dental care, many drugs, ambulance transport, private hospital beds, and other health services not covered by provincial health plans are either privately financed through employee benefit plans or paid for by individual Canadians. Total health expenditures were $97.6 billion in 2000–01, up 7.2 percent from expenditures of $91 billion in 1999–2000. This means that in 2001, $3174 was spent on the healthcare of the average person in Canada (Health Canada, 2003e)

As shown in Figure 14–8, non-insured private health costs made up 29 percent of total healthcare costs in Canada in 2004. All other G-7 countries in 2004, except for Australia (at 68 percent) and the U.S. (at 45 percent), had greater public financing on healthcare than Canada (The World Bank, 2004).

In sum, despite the many benefits of the Canadian healthcare system, there are problems that need addressing. Compared with the systems of other countries, including that of our neighbour to the south, the Canadian healthcare system makes less use of state-of-the-art technology. Some critics also point out that it responds slowly to people's needs, often requiring those facing major surgery to wait months or even a year for attention (Grant, 1984; Vayda & Deber, 1984; Rosenthal, 1991). Further, recent government cutbacks in healthcare funding have caused worry among Canadians that their much-admired healthcare system is in crisis. In fact, a recent Ipsos-Reid poll (2000) reported that most people in Canada—along with people in 16 other nations—felt that the government should spend more on healthcare.

One government-commissioned review of the healthcare system, established in 1994 and known as the "National Forum on Health," solicited opinions from the public and health providers on the way forward for coming decades. The final report, "Canada Health Action: Building on the Legacy," noted that the country is not confronting a healthcare crisis as such, yet the healthcare system is under significant stress. Though underfunding was not singled out as a main cause, the report noted the need for better strategies in spending public tax dollars on healthcare, as well as the need to focus attention on the underlying determinants of health.

A more recent 2002 report—"Building on Values: The Future of Health Care in Canada," by the Commission on the Future of Health Care in Canada headed by former premier of Saskatchewan Roy Romanow—made similar recommendations. The Commission's mandate was to review the country's healthcare system, engage Canadians in a national dialogue on its future, and make recommendations to improve the system's quality and sustainability. The report was based on comprehensive, broad-based public consultations that included 21 days of public hearings, televised in-studio policy debates with healthcare experts, 12 policy dialogues at Canadian universities, a forum on Aboriginal health, and deliberative dialogue sessions with Canadian citizens in 12 cities across Canada. In addition, more than 30 000 Canadians took part in the Commission's two consultation surveys. The results reinforce the findings of early reports on healthcare in Canada that found that Canadians wanted to keep the core principles of the medicare model that accorded with their strongly held values of universality, equal access, solidarity, and fairness. On the other hand, they also stated very strongly that the present employment of healthcare resources does not match their values of efficiency and accountability.

The proposal to create a national accountability system for Canadian healthcare was one of the recommendations to help solve such weaknesses. Some of the provinces, on

 The entire Romanow report is at this website: http://www.hc-sc.gc.ca/english/pdf/romanow/pdfs/HCC_Final_Report.pdf.

the other hand, do not agree with this recommendation because they would like more control over the healthcare in their province. This old battle between Ottawa and the provincial capitals is unlikely to be resolved in the near future and is likely to remain with us for a while yet, given that the stakes are perceived to be very high in correspondence with the large proportion of governmental budgets spent on healthcare.

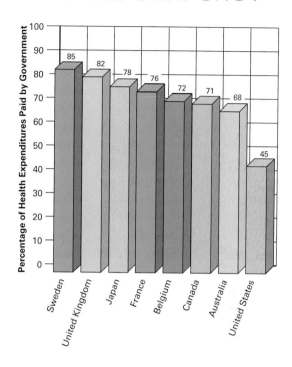

FIGURE 14-8 Extent of Socialized Medicine in Selected Countries

Sources: U.S. Census Bureau (2003) and World Bank (2004).

THE NURSING SHORTAGE

Another issue in healthcare is the shortage of nurses across Canada. In 2003, the regulated nursing work force included 241 342 registered nurses (78 percent of the total regulated nursing work force), 63 138 licensed practical nurses (20.4 percent) and 5107 registered psychiatric nurses (1.6 percent), an overall increase of 4.5 percent since 2002 (CIHI, 2004). Yet many available jobs are currently unfilled.

 The immediate cause of the shortage is that fewer people are entering the nursing profession. During the last decade, enrollments in nursing programs have dropped by one-third, even as the need for nurses (driven by the aging of the Canadian population) goes up. Why this decline? One factor is that today's young women have a wide range of job choices, and fewer are drawn to the traditionally female occupation of nursing. This fact is evident in the rising median age of working nurses, which is now 43. Another is that many of today's nurses are unhappy with their working

Throughout Canada, there is a serious shortage of nurses. One strategy for filling the need is for nursing programs to recruit more men into this profession; currently, men account for only 8 percent of nurses with R.N. degrees.

conditions, citing heavy patient loads, too much required overtime, a stressful working environment, and a lack of recognition and respect from supervisors, doctors, and hospital managers. In fact, one recent survey found that a majority of working nurses say they would not recommend the field to others, and more registered nurses are leaving the field for other jobs.

A positive sign is that the nursing shortage is bringing change to this profession. Salaries for certified nurse anesthetists are rising, although slowly. Some hospitals and doctors are also offering signing bonuses in an effort to attract new nurses. In addition, nursing programs are trying harder to recruit a more diverse population, seeking more minorities (which are currently underrepresented) and, especially, more men (who now make up only 13 percent of registered nurses) (DeFrancis, 2002a, 2002b; Dworkin, 2002; Yin, 2002; Statistics Canada, 2006).

Theoretical Analysis of Medicine

Each of the theoretical approaches in sociology helps us organize and understand facts and issues concerning human health.

STRUCTURAL-FUNCTIONAL ANALYSIS

Talcott Parsons (1951) viewed medicine as society's strategy to keep its members healthy. Parsons considered illness to be dysfunctional because it reduces people's abilities to perform their roles.

The sick role.   Society responds to illness not only by providing healthcare but also by allowing people a **sick role**, *patterns of behaviour defined as appropriate for people who are ill.* According to Parsons, the sick role releases people from everyday responsibilities. However, people cannot simply claim to be ill; they must "look the part" and, in serious cases, get the help of a medical expert. After assuming the sick role, the patient must do whatever is needed to regain good health, including cooperating with health professionals.

The physician's role.   Physicians evaluate people's claims of sickness and help restore the sick to normal routines. Because of their specialized knowledge, physicians expect patients to follow "doctor's orders" in order to complete treatment.

Critical review.   Parsons' analysis links illness and medicine to the broader organization of society. Others have extended the concept of the sick role to some non-illness situations such as pregnancy (Myers & Grasmick, 1989).

One limitation of the sick-role concept is that it applies to acute conditions (like the flu) better than to chronic illnesses (such as heart disease), which may not be reversible. In addition, a sick person's ability to assume the sick role (take time off from work to regain health) depends on the person's resources. Finally, illness is not completely dysfunctional; it can have some positive consequences. Many people who experience a serious illness consider it an opportunity to re-evaluate their lives and gain a better sense of what is truly important to them (Myers, 2000).

SYMBOLIC-INTERACTION ANALYSIS

Using the symbolic-interaction approach, society is less a grand system than a complex and changing reality. In this view, health and healthcare are socially constructed by people in everyday interaction.

Socially constructing illness.   If both health and illness are socially constructed, people in a low-income society may view malnutrition as normal. Similarly, many members of our own society give little thought to the harmful effects of a rich diet.

Our response to illness also is based on social definitions that may or may not square with medical facts. People with AIDS may be forced to deal with prejudice that has no medical basis. Students may pay no attention to symptoms of illness on the eve of a vacation but head for the infirmary

Our national view of medicine has changed during the last several decades. Television viewers in the 1970s watched doctors like Marcus Welby, M.D., confidently taking charge of situations in a fatherly—and almost godlike—manner. By the 1990s, programs like "E.R." gave a more realistic view of the limitations of medicine to address illness, as well as the violence that wracks our society.

hours before a midterm examination. In short, health is less an objective fact than a negotiated outcome.

How people define a medical situation may actually affect how they feel. Medical experts marvel at *psychosomatic* disorders (a fusion of the Greek words for "mind" and "body"), when state of mind guides physical sensations (Hamrick, Anspaugh, & Ezell, 1986). Applying sociologist W.I. Thomas's theorem (presented in Chapter 4, "Social Interaction in Everyday Life"), we can say that once health or illness is defined as real, it can become real in its consequences.

Socially constructing treatment. Also in Chapter 4 we used Erving Goffman's dramaturgical approach to explain how doctors tailor their physical surroundings (their office) and their behaviour (the "presentation of self") so that others see them as competent and in charge.

The sociologist Joan Emerson (1970) further illustrates this process of reality construction in her analysis of the gynecological examination carried out by a male doctor. The situation could be seriously misinterpreted because a man touching a woman's genitals is conventionally viewed as a sexual act and possibly an assault. To ensure that the situation is defined as impersonal and professional, medical personnel wear uniforms, and the examination room is furnished with nothing but medical equipment. The doctor's manner is designed to make the patient feel that to him, examining the genital area is no different from treating

any other part of the body. A female nurse is usually present during the examination, not only to assist the physician but also to avoid any impression that a man and woman are "alone together."

Managing situational definitions is rarely taught in medical schools. This is unfortunate, because as Emerson's analysis shows, understanding how medical personnel construct reality in the examination room is as important as mastering the medical skills needed for treatment.

Critical review. The symbolic-interaction approach reveals that what people view as healthful or harmful depends on a host of factors that are not, strictly speaking, medical. This approach also shows that in any medical procedure, both patient and medical staff engage in a subtle process of reality construction.

Critics fault the symbolic-interaction approach for implying that there are no objective standards of well-being. Certain physical conditions do indeed cause specific changes in people, regardless of how we may view those conditions. For example, people who lack sufficient nutrition and safe water suffer from their unhealthy environment, whether they define their surroundings as normal or not.

SOCIAL-CONFLICT ANALYSIS

Social-conflict analysis points out the connection between health and social inequality and, taking the lead from Karl Marx, ties medicine to the operation of capitalism.

APPLYING THEORY

HEALTH

	Structural-Functional Approach	Symbolic-Interaction Approach	Social-Conflict Approach
What is the level of analysis?	Macro-level	Micro-level	Macro-level
How does each approach relate health to society?	Illness is dysfunctional for society because it prevents people from carrying out their daily roles. The sick role releases people who are ill from responsibilities while they try to get well.	Societies define "health" and "illness" differently according to their living standards. How people define their own health affects how they actually feel (psychosomatic conditions).	Health is linked to social inequality, with rich people having more access to care than poor people. Capitalist healthcare places the drive for profits over the needs of people, treating symptoms rather than addressing poverty as a cause of illness.

Researchers have focused on three main issues: access to medical care, the effects of the profit motive, and the politics of medicine.

Access to care.   Health is important to everyone. But by requiring individuals to pay for health, capitalist societies allow the richest people to have the best health. The access problem is more serious in the U.S. than in most other high-income nations, including Canada, because the U.S. does not have a universal healthcare system to cover out-of-pocket costs for primary health and hospital care.

Yet even in our own country, as noted above, low-income people and Aboriginals are at a greater risk of mortality at birth and illness throughout their life cycle than their better-off counterparts. Conflict theorists claim that, while capitalism does provide excellent healthcare for the rich, it simply does not provide very well for the rest of the population.

The profit motive.   Some social-conflict analysts go further, arguing that the real problem is not access to healthcare but the character of capitalist medicine itself. The profit motive turns doctors, hospitals, and the pharmaceutical industry into multibillion-dollar corporations. The drive for higher profits encourages unnecessary tests and surgery and overreliance on expensive drugs rather than improving people's living conditions.

Most surgical operations performed in Canada are elective, meaning that they are intended to promote long-term health and are not prompted by a medical emergency. Of course, any medical procedure or use of drugs is risky and harms 5–10 percent of patients. Therefore, social-conflict theorists contend that surgery reflects the financial interests of surgeons and hospitals as well as the medical needs of patients (Illich, 1976; Sidel & Sidel, 1982a; Cowley, 1995; Nuland, 1999).

Finally, say conflict theorists, our society is all too tolerant of doctors having a direct financial interest in the tests and procedures they order for their patients (Pear & Eckholm, 1991). In short, healthcare should be motivated by a concern for people, not profits.

Medicine as politics.   Although science declares itself to be politically neutral, scientific medicine often takes sides on significant social issues. For example, throughout most of the twentieth century, the Canadian medical establishment mounted a strong and sustained campaign against the legalization and public funding of midwives, although the World Health Organization recommends midwives as essential healthcare providers for women. Moreover, the history of medicine shows that racial and sexual discrimination have been supported by "scientific" opinions (Leavitt, 1984). Consider the diagnosis of "hysteria," a term that has its origins in the Greek word *hyster*, meaning "uterus."

CONTROVERSY & DEBATE

The Genetic Crystal Ball: Do We Really Want to Look?

The liquid in the laboratory test tube seems ordinary enough, like a syrupy form of water. But this liquid is one of the greatest medical breakthroughs of all time; it may even hold the key to life itself. The liquid is deoxyribonucleic acid, or DNA, the spiralling molecule found in every cell of the human body that contains the blueprint for making each one of us human as well as different from every other person.

The human body is composed of some 100 trillion cells, most of which contain a nucleus of 23 pairs of chromosomes (one of each pair comes from each parent). Each chromosome is packed with DNA in segments called genes. Genes guide the production of protein, the building block of the human body.

If genetics sounds complicated (and it is), the social implications of genetic knowledge are even more complex. Scientists discovered the structure of the DNA molecule in 1952, but it wasn't until 2000 that they neared the goal of mapping the human genome. Charting our genetic landscape may lead to understanding how each bit of DNA shapes our being. But do we really want to turn the key to understand life itself? And what do we do with this knowledge once we have it?

In the Human Genome Project, many scientists see the opportunity to stop certain illnesses dead in their tracks. Research has already identified genetic abnormalities that cause some forms of cancer, sickle-cell anemia, muscular dystrophy, Huntington's disease, cystic fibrosis, and other crippling and deadly afflictions. In the future, genetic screening—a scientific "crystal ball"—could tell people their medical destiny and allow doctors to manipulate segments of DNA to prevent diseases before symptoms appear.

But many people urge caution in such research, warning that genetic information can easily be abused. At its worst, genetic mapping opens the door to Nazi-like efforts to breed a "super race." Indeed, in 1994, the People's Republic of China began to regulate marriage and childbirth with the purpose of avoiding "new births of inferior quality."

It seems inevitable that some parents will want to use genetic testing to predict the health (or even the eye colour) of their future children. What if they want to abort a fetus because it falls short of their standards? When genetic manipulations become possible, should parents be able to create "designer children"?

Then there is the issue of "genetic privacy." Should a bride-to-be be able to request a genetic evaluation of her fiancé before agreeing to marry? Should life insurance companies be able to demand genetic testing before issuing policies? Should employers be allowed to screen job applicants to weed out those whose future illnesses might drain their health-care funds? Clearly, what is scientifically possible is not always morally desirable. Society is already struggling with questions about the proper use of our expanding knowledge of human genetics. Such ethical dilemmas will only multiply as genetic research moves forward in the years to come.

Scientists are learning more and more about the genetic factors that prompt the eventual development of serious diseases. If offered the opportunity, would you want to undergo a genetic screening that would predict the future of your own health?

CONTINUE THE DEBATE . . .

1. Traditional wedding vows join couples "in sickness and in health." Do you think people have a right to know the future health prospects of their potential partner before tying the knot?

2. What do you think about the possibility of parents genetically designing their children?

3. Should private companies doing genetic research be allowed to patent their discoveries so that they alone can profit from the results, or should this valuable information be made available to all companies? Why?

Sources: Nash (1995), Thompson (1999), and Golden & Lemonick (2000).

In choosing this word to describe a wild, emotional state, the medical profession suggested that being a woman is somehow the same as being irrational.

Even today, according to conflict theory, scientific medicine explains illness in terms of bacteria and viruses, ignoring the damaging effects of poverty. In effect, scientific medicine depoliticizes health in Canada and other high-income countries by transforming social issues into simple biology.

Critical review. Social-conflict analysis provides still another view of the relationships between health, medicine, and society. According to this approach, social inequality is the reason some people have better health than others.

The most common objection to the conflict approach is that it minimizes the advances in health that can be credited to scientific medicine and higher living standards. Although there is plenty of room for improvement, health indicators for our population as a whole rose steadily over the course of the twentieth century, and they compare well with those in other high-income nations.

In sum, sociology's three major theoretical approaches explain why health and medicine are social issues. The Applying Theory table sums up what they teach us.

But advancing technology will not solve every health problem. On the contrary, as the Controversy & Debate box explains, today's advancing technology is raising new questions and concerns.

The famous French scientist Louis Pasteur (1822–1895), who spent much of his life studying how bacteria cause disease, said just before he died that health depends less on bacteria than on the social environment in which bacteria operate (Gordon, 1980:7). Explaining Pasteur's insight is sociology's contribution to human health.

LOOKING AHEAD: HEALTH IN THE TWENTY-FIRST CENTURY

In the early 1900s, deaths from infectious diseases such as diphtheria and measles were widespread. Because scientists had not yet developed penicillin and other antibiotics, even a simple infection from a minor wound was sometimes life-threatening. Today, a century later, most members of our society take good health and long life for granted. It seems reasonable to expect improvements in the health of Canadians to continue throughout the twenty-first century.

Another encouraging trend is that more people are taking responsibility for their own health (Lelonde, 1974; Segall & Chappell, 2000). Every one of us can live better and longer if we avoid tobacco, eat sensibly and in moderation, and exercise regularly.

Yet health problems will continue to plague Canadian society in the decades to come. The changing social profile of people with AIDS—which increasingly afflicts youth, the poor, Aboriginals, women, and the marginalized—reminds us that Canada has much to do to improve the health of disadvantaged members of our society. Even those among us who do not easily embrace the notion of serving as "our brother's keeper" should recognize our moral obligation to guarantee everyone the security of healthcare.

Finally, we find that health problems are far greater in low-income nations than in Canada. The good news is that life expectancy for the world as a whole has been rising—from 48 years in 1950 to 67 years today—and the biggest gains have been in low-income countries (Population Reference Bureau, 2002). But in much of Latin America, Asia, and especially Africa, hundreds of millions of adults and children lack not only medical attention but also adequate food and safe water. Improving the health of the world's poorest people is a critical challenge in the twenty-first century.

Summary

Education

1. Education is a major social institution for transmitting knowledge and skills as well as for passing on norms and values. In pre-industrial societies, education occurs informally within the family; industrial societies develop formal systems of schooling.

2. Canada was among the first countries to require mass public education, reflecting both democratic political ideals and the need for a trained industrial work force.

3. The structural-functional approach highlights the functions of schooling, including socialization, social placement, social integration, and innovation. Latent functions include child-care and building social networks.

4. Social-conflict analysis links schooling to social hierarchies involving class, race, and gender. Formal education is seen as generating conformity in order to produce obedient adult workers.

5. Most young people in Canada attend public schools largely funded through the tax system. A small proportion of young people—generally the economically advantaged—attend privately funded schools.

6. Almost half of Canadian adults over the age of 25 hold post-secondary degrees or diplomas, marking the emergence of a credential society.

7. National opinion is critical of public schools. Violence is a problem in some Canadian schools, and educational bureaucracy fosters high dropout rates and widespread student passivity.

Health and Medicine

1. Health is a social issue because well-being depends on a society's technology and distribution of resources. Culture shapes definitions of health and patterns of healthcare.

2. Low-income countries suffer from inadequate sanitation, hunger, and other problems linked to poverty. Life expectancy is about 20 years less than in Canada; in the poorest nations, half the children do not survive to adulthood.

3. Health improved dramatically in Western Europe and North America in the nineteenth century, first because of industrialization and later because of medical advances.

4. Infectious diseases were leading killers a century ago. Today, most people in Canada die in old age of chronic illnesses such as heart disease, cancer, or stroke.

5. More than three-fourths of Canadian children born today can expect to reach age 65. Women tend to live longer than men but report more lifetime illness. People of high social position enjoy better health than others.

6. Cigarette smoking is the greatest preventable cause of death in Canada.

7. The incidence of sexually transmitted infections (STIs) has risen since 1960, an exception to the general decline in infectious disease.

8. Advancing medical technology presents ethical dilemmas concerning how and when death should occur.

9. Historically a family concern, healthcare is now the responsibility of trained specialists. The model of scientific medicine underlies the Canadian medical establishment. The holistic approach seeks to give people greater responsibility for their own health.

10. Socialist societies define government healthcare as a basic right. Capitalist societies view healthcare as a commodity to be purchased, although most capitalist governments (the United States being a significant exception) help pay for healthcare through socialized medicine or national health insurance.

11. Central to the structural-functional analysis of health is the concept of the sick role, which releases sick people from routine responsibilities. The symbolic-interaction approach investigates the social construction of both health and medical treatment. Social-conflict analysis focuses on unequal access to healthcare and criticizes our medical system for its profit orientation.

KEY CONCEPTS

Education

education (p. 378) the social institution through which society provides its members with important knowledge, including basic facts, job skills, and cultural norms and values

functional illiteracy (p. 390) a lack of the reading and writing skills needed for everyday living

schooling (p. 378) formal instruction under the direction of specially trained teachers

tracking (p. 383) assigning students to different types of educational programs

Health and Medicine

direct-fee system (p. 401) a medical care system in which patients pay directly for the services of doctors and hospitals

euthanasia (p. 398) assisting in the death of a person suffering from an incurable disease; also known as *mercy killing*

health (p. 390) a state of complete physical, mental, and social well-being

holistic medicine (p. 399) an approach to healthcare that emphasizes prevention of illness and takes into account a person's entire physical and social environment

medicine (p. 391) a social institution that focuses on fighting disease and improving health

sick role (p. 404) patterns of behaviour defined as appropriate for people who are ill

social epidemiology (p. 392) the study of how health and disease are distributed throughout a society's population

socialized medicine (p. 401) a medical care system in which the government owns and operates most medical facilities and employs most physicians

CRITICAL-THINKING QUESTIONS

1. Why does industrialization lead societies to expand their system of schooling?

2. In what ways is schooling in Canada shaped by our economic system? by our cultural values? by social inequality?

3. Why is health as much a social as a biological issue?

4. Can you point to ways in which people can take responsibility for their own health? What traits of society as a whole shape patterns of health?

APPLICATIONS AND EXERCISES

1. Arrange to visit a secondary school near you. Does it have a tracking policy? If so, find out how it works. If it doesn't have one, find out why not. How much importance does a student's family background have in classroom placement?

2. Most people agree that teaching our children is a vital task. Yet most teachers earn relatively low salaries. Check the prestige ranking for teachers back in Table 8–2 on page 213. What can you find out at the library about the average salaries of teachers compared with other workers? Can you explain this pattern?

3. Arrange to speak with a midwife about her work helping women give birth. How do midwives differ in approach from obstetricians?

4. In most communities, a trip to the local courthouse is all it takes to find public records showing people's cause of death. Take a look at such records for people who lived in your community a century ago and for more recent residents. What patterns in life expectancy emerge? How do causes of death differ?

SITES TO SEE

www.pearsoned.ca/macionis

The authors and publisher of this book invite you to visit the interactive Companion Website™ that accompanies this text. Begin by clicking on the cover of your book. You will find a chapter-by-chapter study guide, practice tests, suggested weblinks, and links to other relevant material.

www.youth.society.uvic.ca/resources/wits/index.html

Read about the WITS program to reduce youth violence.

www.cmec.ca/index.en.html

Council of Ministers of Education, Canada (CMEC) is the national organization for education in Canada. It is the vehicle through which provincial ministers of education consult and act on matters of mutual interest, and the instrument through which they consult and cooperate with national education organizations and the federal government.

www.schoolnet.ca

Canada was the first country in the world to connect its public schools—including Aboriginal schools—and public libraries, through the Internet. Through the help of SchoolNet and its partners, Canadian classrooms are connected to the Internet. As of May 2000, there were nearly half a million connected computers in schools across Canada.

www.cihr-irsc.gc.ca

The Canadian Institute of Health Research (CIHR) is Canada's major federal funding agency for health research.

secure.cihi.ca/cihiweb/splash.html

The Canadian Institute for Health Information (CIHI) is an independent, national, not-for-profit organization working to improve the health of Canadians and the healthcare system by providing quality, reliable, and timely health information.

www.hc-sc.gc.ca

Health Canada is the federal department responsible for helping the people of Canada maintain and improve their health.

www.who.int/en

The World Health Organization provides health indicators for many of the world's nations and data profiling the health of the Canadian population.

www.doctorsoftheworld.org

www.imc-la.org

www.dwb.org

Here are websites for several organizations of physicians that are involved in improving health around the world. The first is operated by Doctors of the World, the second presents the International Medical Corps, and the third profiles Doctors Without Borders.

www.nedic.ca

Visit the National Eating Disorder Information Centre for information and resources on eating disorders and weight preoccupation.

 ## INVESTIGATE WITH RESEARCH NAVIGATOR™

Follow the instructions on page 33 of this text to access the features of Research Navigator™. Once at the website (**www.researchnavigator.com**), enter your login name and password. Then, to use the Content Select™ database, enter keywords such as "testing," "school violence," "euthanasia," and "AIDS," and the search engine will supply relevant and recent scholarly and popular press publications.

To reinforce your understanding of this chapter, and to identify topics for further study, visit MySocLab at **www.pearsoned.ca/mysoclab/macionis** for diagnostic tests and a multimedia ebook.

CHAPTER FIFTEEN

Population, Urbanization, and Environment

Why do many people worry about the rapid rate of global population increase?

What are the special experiences of city living?

How is the state of the natural environment a social issue?

Societies with more people and ever-larger cities challenge the natural environment as never before. To protect herself from air pollution in an industrial area of Chekka, Lebanon, this girl carries a face mask on her way to school.

Two hundred years ago, Captain Vancouver first charted the Burrard Inlet. One hundred years later, Vancouver was home to fewer than 50 000 people. Today, with a population of more than 2 million, and as the city has expanded outward, commuting for an hour to work is commonplace.

Growth like this prompted experts to coin the term "urban sprawl." Such uncontrolled growth is the result of more and more people, all of whom want bigger houses, as well as the conveniences offered by roads, schools, recreation facilities, and, of course, superstores and shopping malls. No doubt, most people in Canada see growth like this as good—the product of prosperity.

But is it that simple? This chapter examines three closely related processes: population increase, urbanization, and the state of the natural environment. As we shall see, population has soared during the past two centuries—in Canada and also around the world—and cities everywhere have grown rapidly. We shall consider how these changes have altered the shape of societies and what they mean for the future of the planet. We begin with population.

Demography: The Study of Population

When humans first began to cultivate plants some 12 000 years ago, the Earth's entire population was about 5 million, or about the population of Toronto today. Very slow growth pushed the total in 1 BCE to perhaps 300 million, or a little less than ten times the total population of Canada today (Haub, 2002a).

Around 1750, world population began to spike upward. We now add 73 million people to the planet each year, for a total of 6.5 billion in 2006.

The causes and consequences of this drama are the focus of **demography**, *the study of human population.* Demography (from Greek, meaning "description of people") is a cousin of sociology that analyzes the size and composition of a population and studies how people move from place to place. Demographers not only collect statistics but also pose important questions about the effects of population growth and suggest how it might be controlled. The following sections present basic demographic concepts.

FERTILITY

The study of human population begins with how many people are born. **Fertility** is *the incidence of childbearing in a country's population.* During her childbearing years—from the onset of menstruation (typically in the early teens) to menopause (usually in the late forties)—a woman is capable of bearing more than 20 children. But *fecundity*, or maximum possible childbearing, is sharply reduced by cultural norms, finances, and personal choice.

Demographers describe fertility using the **crude birth rate**, *the number of live births in a given year for every 1000 people in a population.* To calculate a crude birth rate, divide the number of live births in a year by the society's total population and multiply the result by 1000. In Canada in 2005, there were 339 757 live births in a population of 32 270 507, yielding a crude birth rate of 10.5 (Statistics Canada, 2006aw).

This birth rate is "crude" because it is based on the entire population—not just on women in their childbearing years. Comparing crude birth rates for various countries can be misleading, then, if one society has a larger share of women of childbearing age than another. A crude birth rate also ignores differences among various racial and ethnic categories. But this is easy to calculate and gives a good measure of a society's overall fertility. Figure 15–1 shows that, in global perspective, the crude birth rate of North Americans is low.

MORTALITY

Population size also reflects **mortality**, *the incidence of death in a country's population.* To measure mortality, demographers use a **crude death rate**, *the number of deaths in a given*

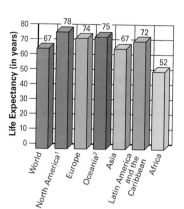

FIGURE 15–1 (a) Crude Birth Rates and Crude Death Rates, (b) Infant Mortality Rates, and (c) Life Expectancy, 2003

[1]United States and Canada.
[2]Australia, New Zealand, and South Pacific Islands.

Source: Population Reference Bureau (2004).

year for every 1000 people in a population. This time, we take the number of deaths in a year, divide by the total population, and multiply the result by 1000. In 2005, there were 236 108 deaths in the Canadian population, yielding a crude death rate of 7.3 (Statistics Canada, 2006aw). As Figure 15–1 shows, in global context, this rate is about average.

This death rate is "crude" because it is based on the entire population—it includes younger people who have a lot lower probability of dying than old people. Comparing crude death rates for various countries can be misleading, then, if one society has a larger share of old people than another country.

A third useful demographic measure is the **infant mortality rate**, *the number of deaths among infants under one year of age for each 1000 live births in a given year.* To compute infant mortality, divide the number of deaths of children under one year of age by the number of live births during the same year and multiply the result by 1000. In 2003, there were 1765 infant deaths and 335 202 live births in Canada. Dividing the first number by the second and multiplying the result by 1000 yields an infant mortality rate of 5.3 in 2003 (Statistics Canada, 2006aw, 2006ax). The second part of Figure 15–1 indicates that by world standards, North American infant mortality is low.

But remember the differences among various categories of people within a nation. For example, Aboriginals, who are twice as likely as non-Aboriginals to live below the poverty line, have an infant mortality rate almost twice as high as the national rate.

Low infant mortality greatly raises **life expectancy**, *the average life span of a country's population.* Canadian males born in 2002 can expect to live 77.2 years, and females can look forward to 82.1 years. As the third part of Figure 15–1 shows, life expectancy for North Americans is 26 years greater than that typical of low-income countries of Africa. Among high-income countries, Canada is consistently close to the top in longevity, with the United States far behind us. The life expectancy of men and women in the United States (77.2) is closer to that of Mexico (74.9) than that of Canada (79.7) (OECD, 2005).

MIGRATION

Population size is also affected by **migration**, *the movement of people into and out of a specified territory.* Movement into nations, or *immigration*, is calculated as the number of people entering a nation area for every 1000 people in the population. Movement out of a nation, or *emigration*, is

Annual Population Growth

- 3.0 percent and higher
- 2.0 to 2.9 percent
- 1.0 to 1.9 percent
- Below 1.0 percent

WINDOW ON THE WORLD

GLOBAL MAP 15–1 Population Growth in Global Perspective

The richest countries of the world—including Canada, the United States, and the nations of Europe—have growth rates below 1 percent. The nations of Latin America and Asia typically have growth rates around 1.6 percent, which double a population in 44 years. Africa has an overall growth rate of 2.4 percent, which cuts the doubling time to 29 years. In global perspective, we see that a society's standard of living is closely related to its rate of population growth: Population is rising fastest in the world regions that can least afford to support more people.

Source: Population Reference Bureau (2004); map projection from *Peters Atlas of the World* (1990).

measured as the number leaving for every 1000 people. Both types of migration usually occur at the same time, of course, and the difference between the immigration rate and the emigration rate is called the net migration rate.

All nations also experience *internal migration*—that is, movement within their borders, from one region to another. We use the terms *in-migration* and *out-migration* to describe this movement. Most internal migration con-

sists of short-distance moves. Fewer than a million Canadians moved across a provincial or territorial border between 1996 and 2001 out of the 11.7 million (one in four) Canadians who moved during this time period (Statistics Canada, 2003at).

Migration is sometimes involuntary, such as the forced transport of 10 million Africans to the Western Hemisphere as slaves during the eighteenth and nineteenth centuries.

More recently, Serb soldiers forced ethnic Albanians to flee their homes in Kosovo (Reed, 1999). Voluntary migration, on the other hand, usually results from several "push–pull" factors. Dissatisfaction with life in a poor region may "push" people to move, and the opportunity for a better life may "pull" them to the city. Glancing ahead at National Map 16–1 on page 450 we see an interesting pattern of people moving to urban areas but also to the North in Canada.

POPULATION GROWTH

Fertility, mortality, and migration all affect the size of a society's population. In general, many high-income nations (such as Canada) grow as much from immigration as natural increase—56 percent of Canada's growth between the census years 1996 and 2001 came from migration—and low-income nations (such as India) grow almost entirely from natural increase.

To calculate a population's *natural growth rate,* demographers subtract the crude death rate from the crude birth rate. The natural growth rate of the Canadian population in 2005 was 5.2 per 1000 (the crude birth rate of 10.5 minus the crude death rate of 5.3), or about 0.53 percent (*per hundred*) annual growth.

Global Map 15–1 shows that population growth in Canada and other high-income nations is well below the world average of 1.3 percent. The Earth's low-growth continents are Europe (currently posting a slight decline, expressed as −0.2 percent annual growth), North America (0.5 percent), and Oceania (1.0 percent). At the global average is Asia (1.3 percent), with Latin America (1.6 percent) slightly higher. The highest-growth region of the world is Africa (2.4 percent).

A handy rule for estimating population growth is to divide 70 by a society's population growth rate to calculate the *doubling time* in years. Thus, an annual growth rate of 2 percent (found in parts of Latin America) doubles a population in 35 years, and a 3 percent growth rate (found in some countries in Africa) drops the doubling time to just 24 years. The rapid population growth of the poorest countries is deeply troubling because these countries can barely support the populations they have now.

POPULATION COMPOSITION

Demographers also study the make-up of a society's population at a given point in time. One variable is the **sex ratio**, *the number of males for every 100 females in a nation's population.* In 2005, the sex ratio in Canada was 98, or 98 males for every 100 females. Sex ratios are usually below 100 because, on average, women outlive men. In India, however, the sex ratio is 107 because parents value sons more than daughters and may either abort a female fetus or, after birth,

give more care to a male infant, raising the odds that a female child will die.

A more complex measure is the **age–sex pyramid**, *a graphic representation of the age and sex of a population.* Figure 15–2 presents the age–sex pyramids for Canada and Yemen, a country just south of Saudi Arabia with a high birth rate (its crude birth rate is 43) and a high growth rate of 3.5 percent per year. Higher death rates as people age give these figures a rough pyramid shape. In the Canadian pyramid, the bulge corresponding to ages 40–49 reflects high birth rates during the baby boom. The contraction just below—that is, people in their thirties—reflects the subsequent baby bust when the number of births declined from a high of 479 000 in 1959 to 343 000 in 1973.

Comparison of the Canadian and Yemenite age–sex pyramids shows different demographic trends. The age–sex pyramid for Yemen, like that of other nations with high fertility, is wide at the bottom because the number of births increases every year. Yemen, in short, is a much younger population. With a larger share of females still in their childbearing years, Yemen's crude birth rate is, understand-

 To find out more about Canadian demography, go to the Statistics Canada website: **http://www.statcan.ca**.

ably, considerably higher than our own, and its annual rate of natural growth is many times higher than the Canadian rate. This illustrates what demographers call *demographic momentum*—even with a sharp reduction in the number of children per family, the large number of people in their childbearing years ensures a large number of births.

History and Theory of Population Growth

In the past, people wanted large families because human labour was the key to productivity. Moreover, until rubber condoms appeared 150 years ago, preventing pregnancy was uncertain at best. But high death rates from infectious diseases put a constant brake on population growth.

A major demographic shift, shown in Figure 15–3, began in about 1750 as the world's population turned upward, reaching the 1 billion mark by 1800. This milestone (which took all of human history to reach) was matched barely a century later in 1930, when a second billion people had been added to the planet. In other words, not only was population increasing, but the *rate* of growth was accelerating. Global population reached 3 billion by 1962 (just 32 years later) and 4 billion by 1974 (only 12 years after that). The planet passed the 5 billion mark in 1987 and the 6 billion mark late in 1999.

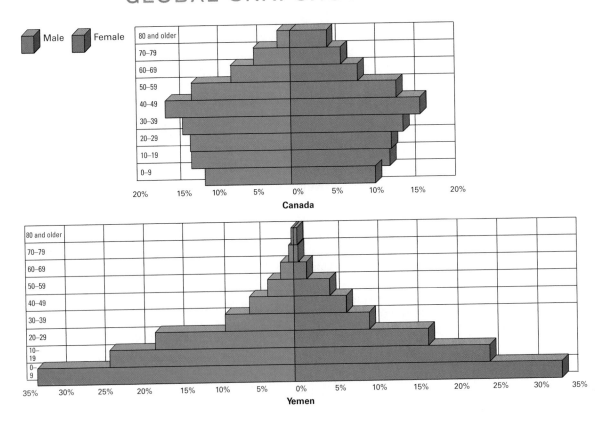

FIGURE 15–2 Age–Sex Population Pyramids for Canada and Yemen, 2005

Source: U.S. Census Bureau (2006).

In no previous century did the world's population even double. In the twentieth century, it quadrupled.

Currently, the world is gaining 75 million people each year, with 96 percent of this increase in low-income countries. The good news is that this is a substantial decrease from the late 1980s when the Earth gained almost 90 million people per year and the rate of growth has also decreased dramatically from a high of over 2 percent in the 1960s to the current rate of about 1.1 percent. Nevertheless, in large part because of demographic momentum, experts predict that the Earth's population will be 8–9 billion in 2050 (O'Neill & Balk, 2001). Given the world's troubles feeding its present population, such an increase is a matter of urgent concern.

MALTHUSIAN THEORY

The sudden population growth 250 years ago sparked the development of demography. Thomas Robert Malthus (1766–1834), an English economist and clergyman, warned that rapid population increase would lead to social chaos. Malthus (1926, orig. 1798) calculated that population would increase by what mathematicians call *geometric progression*, illustrated by the series of numbers 2, 4, 8, 16, 32, and so on. At such a rate, Malthus concluded, world population would soon soar out of control.

Food production would also increase, Malthus explained, but only in *arithmetic progression* (as in the series 2, 3, 4, 5, 6, etc.) because even with new agricultural technology, farmland is limited. Thus, Malthus presented a troubling vision of the future: people reproducing beyond what the planet could feed, leading ultimately to widespread starvation and war over what resources were left.

Malthus recognized that artificial birth control or abstaining from sex might change his prediction. But he found one morally wrong and the other quite impractical. Thus, famine and war stalked humanity in Malthus' mind, and he was justly known as "the dismal parson."

Critical review. Fortunately, Malthus' prediction was flawed. First, by 1850, the European birth rate began to drop, partly because with industrialization children were becoming an economic liability rather than an asset, and partly because people began using artificial birth control. Second, Malthus underestimated human ingenuity: modern irrigation techniques, fertilizers, and pesticides have increased farm production far more than he could have imagined.

Some criticized Malthus for ignoring the role of social inequality in world abundance and famine. For example, Karl Marx (1967, orig. 1867) objected to his view of suffering as a "law of nature" rather than the curse of capitalism. More recently, "critical demographers" claim that saying poverty is caused by a high birth rate in low-income countries amounts to blaming the victims. On the contrary, they see global inequality as the real issue (Horton, 1999; Kuumba, 1999).

Still, Malthus offers an important lesson. Habitable land, clean water, and fresh air are limited resources, and increased economic productivity has taken a heavy toll on the natural environment. In addition, medical advances have lowered death rates, pushing up world population. In principle, of course, no level of population growth can go on forever. Thus, people everywhere must become aware of the dangers of population increase.

DEMOGRAPHIC TRANSITION THEORY

A more complex analysis of population change is **demographic transition theory**, *the thesis that population patterns reflect a society's level of technological development.* Figure 15–4 shows the demographic consequences at four levels of technological development. Pre-industrial, agrarian societies (Stage 1) have high birth rates because of the economic value of children and the absence of birth control. Death rates are also high due to low living standards and limited medical technology. Outbreaks of disease neutralize births, so population rises and falls with only a modest overall increase. This was the case for thousands of years in Europe before the Industrial Revolution.

Stage 2, the onset of industrialization, brings a demographic transition as death rates fall due to greater food supplies and scientific medicine. But birth rates remain high, resulting in rapid population growth. It was during Europe's Stage 2 that Malthus formulated his ideas, which accounts for his pessimistic view of the future. The world's poorest countries today are in this high-growth stage.

In Stage 3, a mature industrial economy, the birth rate drops, curbing population growth once again. Fertility falls because most children survive to adulthood and because high living standards make raising children expensive. In

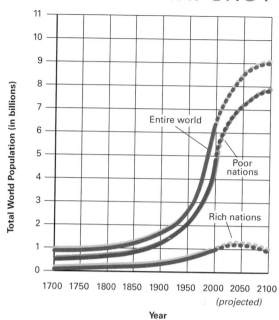

DIVERSITY SNAPSHOT

FIGURE 15-3 The Increase in World Population, 1700–2100

short, affluence transforms children from economic assets into economic liabilities. Smaller families, made possible by effective birth control, are also favoured by women working outside the home. As birth rates follow death rates downward, population growth slows further.

Stage 4 corresponds to a post-industrial economy in which the demographic transition is complete. The birth rate remains low, partly because two-income couples gradually become the norm and partly because the cost of raising children continues to increase. This trend, coupled with steady death rates, means that population grows only very slowly or even decreases. This is the case today in Japan, Europe, and Canada.

Critical review. Demographic transition theory suggests that the key to population control lies in technology. Instead of the runaway population increase feared by Malthus, this theory sees technology slowing growth and spreading material plenty.

Demographic transition theory is linked to modernization theory, one approach to global development discussed in Chapter 9 ("Global Stratification"). Modernization theorists are optimistic that poor countries will solve their population problems as they industrialize. But critics—notably dependency theorists—strongly disagree. Without a significant

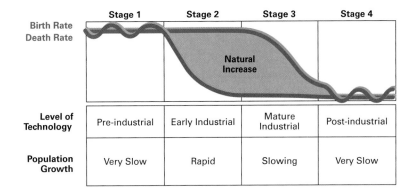

	Stage 1	Stage 2	Stage 3	Stage 4
Birth Rate Death Rate		Natural Increase		
Level of Technology	Pre-industrial	Early Industrial	Mature Industrial	Post-industrial
Population Growth	Very Slow	Rapid	Slowing	Very Slow

FIGURE 15–4 Demographic Transition Theory

redistribution of global resources, they maintain, our planet will become increasingly divided into industrialized "haves," enjoying low population growth, and non-industrialized "have-nots," struggling in vain to feed more and more people.

GLOBAL POPULATION TODAY: A BRIEF SURVEY

What can we say about population in today's world? Drawing on the discussion so far, we can identify important patterns and reach several conclusions.

 To look at the Canadian population clock go to: http://www.statcan.ca/english/edu/clock/population.htm.

The low-growth North. When the Industrial Revolution began in the Northern Hemisphere, population growth in Western Europe and North America was a high 3 percent annually. But in the centuries since, the growth rate steadily declined and in 1970 fell below 1 percent. As our post-industrial society settles into Stage 4, the Canadian birth rate is less than the replacement level of 2.1 children per woman, a point demographers call **zero population growth**, *the level of reproduction that maintains population at a steady state.* More than 60 nations, almost all of them high-income, are at or below the point of zero population growth.

Factors holding down population in these post-industrial societies include a high proportion of men and women in the labour force, rising costs of raising children, trends toward later marriage and singlehood, and widespread use of contraceptives and abortion.

In high-income nations, then, population increase is not the problem that it is in poor countries. Indeed, many governments in high-income countries are concerned about a future problem of *underpopulation,* because declining population size may be difficult to reverse and because

the swelling ranks of the elderly have fewer and fewer young people to look to for support in old age (McDonald, 2001; Kent & Mather, 2002).

The high-growth South. Population growth remains a serious threat to low-income nations of the Southern Hemisphere. No nation in the world lacks industrial technology entirely; demographic transition theory's Stage 1 applies just to remote rural areas of low-income nations. But much of Latin America, Africa, and Asia is at Stage 2, with a mix of agrarian and industrial economies. Advanced medical technology, supplied by rich societies, has sharply reduced death rates, but birth rates remain high. This is why low-income societies now account for two-thirds of the Earth's people and 96 percent of global population increase.

In low-income countries throughout the world, birth rates have fallen from an average of about six children per woman in 1950 to about four today. But fertility this high will only intensify global poverty. At a 1994 global population conference in Cairo, delegates from 180 nations agreed that a key element in controlling world population growth is to raise the status of women. The Diversity: Race, Class, & Gender box on page 422 takes a closer look.

In recent decades, the world has made significant progress in lowering fertility. Mortality also has come down. Although few people would oppose medical programs that save lives—most of them children's—lower death rates mean rising population. In fact, population growth in most low-income regions of the world results mostly from falling death rates. Around 1920, Europe and North America began taking steps to spread scientific medicine and better nutrition around the world. Since then, inoculations against infectious diseases and the use of antibiotics and insecticides have pushed down death rates with stunning effectiveness. For example, in Sri Lanka, malaria caused half of

Fertility in Canada has fallen during the past century and is now quite low. But some categories of the Canadian population have much higher fertility rates. One example is the Amish, a religious society living in rural areas of Ontario. It is common for Amish couples to have five, six, or more children. Why do you think the Amish favour large families?

all deaths in the 1930s; a decade later, use of insecticides to kill malaria-carrying mosquitoes cut the death toll from this disease in half. Although this is a great medical achievement, Sri Lanka's population began to soar. Similarly, India's infant mortality rate slid from 130 in 1975 to 64 in 2003, boosting that nation's population over the 1 billion mark so that it joined China in this exclusive club that is unlikely ever to have any more members.

In short, in much of the world, mortality is falling, especially among children. In order to limit population growth, the world—especially poor countries—must control births as successfully as it is fending off death.

Urbanization: The Growth of Cities

October 8, Hong Kong. The cable train grinds to the top of Victoria Peak, where we behold one of the world's most spectacular vistas: the city of Hong Kong at night. A million bright, colourful lights ring the harbour as ships, ferries, and traditional Chinese junks churn by. Few cities match Hong Kong for sheer energy: This small city is as economically productive as British Columbia, Alberta, and Saskatchewan combined, as productive as the entire nation of Finland. We could sit here for hours entranced by the spectacle of Hong Kong.

Throughout most of human history, the sights and sounds of great cities such as Hong Kong, New York, and Los Angeles were simply unimaginable. Our distant ancestors lived in small, nomadic groups, moving from place to

place as they depleted vegetation or hunted migratory game. The small settlements that marked the emergence of civilization in the Middle East some 12 000 years ago held only a small fraction of the Earth's people. Today, the largest three or four cities of the world hold as many people as the entire planet did back then.

Urbanization is *the concentration of humanity into cities.* Urbanization both redistributes population within a society and transforms many patterns of social life. We will trace these changes in terms of three urban revolutions: the emergence of cities beginning 10 000 years ago, the development of industrial cities after 1750, and the explosive growth of cities in poor countries today.

THE EVOLUTION OF CITIES

Cities are a relatively new development in human history. Only about 12 000 years ago did our ancestors begin founding permanent settlements, which paved the way for the *first urban revolution.*

The first cities. Hunting and gathering forced people to move all the time; however, once our ancestors discovered how to domesticate animals and cultivate crops, they were able to stay in one place. Raising their own food also created a material surplus, which freed some people from food production and allowed them to build shelters, make tools, weave cloth, and take part in religious rituals. The emergence of cities led to both specialization and higher living standards.

The first city was Jericho, which lies to the north of the Dead Sea in what is now the West Bank. Dating back 10 000 years, it was home to only 600 people. But as the centuries passed, cities grew to tens of thousands of people and

DIVERSITY: RACE, CLASS, & GENDER

Empowering Women: The Key to Controlling Population Growth

Sohad Ahmad lives with her husband in a farming village 80 kilometres south of Cairo, Egypt's capital city. Ahmad lives a poor life, like hundreds of millions of other women in the world. Yet her situation differs in an important respect: she has had only two children and will have no more.

Why do Ahmad and her husband reject the conventional wisdom that children are an economic asset? One part of the answer is that Egypt's growing population has already created such a demand for land that Ahmad's family could not afford more even if they had the children to farm it. But the main reason is that she does not want her life defined only by childbearing.

Like Ahmad, more women in Egypt are taking control of their fertility and seeking educational and economic opportunities. Indeed, this country has made great progress in reducing its annual population growth from 3.0 percent just ten years ago to 2.0 percent today.

With its focus on raising the standing of women, the 1994 Cairo conference on global population broke new ground. Past

population control programs simply tried to make birth control technology available to women, a vital effort because only half of the world's married women use effective birth control. But even with available birth control, population continues to swell in societies that define women's primary responsibility as raising children.

Dr. Nafis Sadik, an Egyptian woman who heads the United Nations' efforts at population control, sums up the new

A simple truth: Women who have more opportunity for schooling and paid work have fewer children. As more women attend school in traditional societies, the fertility rate in these countries is falling.

approach to lowering birth rates this way: *Give women more life choices, and they will have fewer children.* In other words, women with access to schooling and jobs—who can decide when and whether to marry, and who bear children as a matter of choice—will limit their own fertility. Schooling must be available to older women, too, Sadik adds, because elders exercise great influence in local communities.

Evidence from countries around the world supports the idea that controlling population and raising the social standing of women are one and the same.

WHAT DO YOU THINK?

1. Why do many analysts claim that controlling population depends on expanding women's choices?
2. What specific laws or programs can you think of that might reduce women's childbearing?
3. Is population control an issue for people in both rich and poor countries? Explain your view.

Sources: Ashford (1995), Axinn & Barber (2001), and Population Reference Bureau (2004).

became the centres of vast empires. By 3000 BCE, Egyptian cities flourished, as did cities in China by about 2000 BCE and in Central and South America by about 1500 BCE. In North America, however, only a few Native American societies formed settlements; widespread urbanization did not take place until the arrival of European settlers in the seventeenth century.

Pre-Industrial European cities. European cities date back some 5000 years to the Greeks and, later, the Romans,

both of whom formed great empires and founded cities across Europe—including Vienna, Paris, and London. With the fall of the Roman Empire, the so-called Dark Ages began as people withdrew within defensive walled settlements and warlords battled for territory. Only in the eleventh century did Europe become more peaceful; trade flourished once again, allowing cities to grow.

Medieval cities were quite different from those familiar to us today. Beneath towering cathedrals, the narrow, winding streets of London, Brussels, and Florence teemed with merchants, artisans, priests, peddlers, jugglers, nobles, and servants. Occupational groups such as bakers, carpenters, and metalworkers clustered in distinct sections or "quarters." Ethnicity also defined communities as people sought to keep out those who differed from themselves. The term "ghetto" (from the Italian word *borghetto,* meaning "outside the city walls") was first used to describe the neighbourhood into which the Jews of Venice were segregated.

Industrial European cities. As the Middle Ages came to a close, steadily increasing commerce enriched a new urban middle class called the *bourgeoisie* (French, meaning "townspeople"). With more and more money, the bourgeoisie soon rivalled the hereditary nobility.

By about 1750, the Industrial Revolution triggered a *second urban revolution,* first in Europe and then in North America. The tremendous productive power of factories caused cities to grow bigger than ever before. London, the largest European city, reached 550 000 people by 1700 and exploded to 6.5 million by 1900 (Weber, 1963, orig. 1899; Chandler & Fox, 1974).

Cities not only grew but changed shape as well. Older winding streets gave way to broad, straight boulevards to handle the increasing flow of commercial traffic. Steam and electric trolleys soon crisscrossed the expanding cities. Because land was now a commodity to be bought and sold, developers divided cities into regular-sized lots (Mumford, 1961). The centre of the city was no longer the cathedral but a bustling central business district filled with banks, retail stores, and tall office buildings.

With a new focus on business, cities became ever more crowded and impersonal. Crime rates rose. Especially at the outset, a few industrialists lived in grand style, but most men, women, and children barely survived by working in factories.

Organized efforts by workers eventually brought improvements to the workplace, better housing, and the right to vote. Public services such as water, sewer systems, and electricity further improved urban living. Today, some urbanites still live in poverty, but a rising standard of living has partly fulfilled the city's historical promise of a better life.

THE GROWTH OF NORTH AMERICAN CITIES

As noted, most of the Native Americans who inhabited North America for thousands of years before the arrival of Europeans were migratory people who formed few permanent settlements. The spread of villages and towns came after European colonization.

Colonial settlement: 1565–1800. In 1565, the Spanish built a settlement at St. Augustine, Florida, and in 1607 the English founded Jamestown, Virginia. However, the first

In the cities of the early industrial era, life was lived on the streets. This street scene in New York City almost a century ago is quite different from urban life in most cities today, where life has moved into restricted spaces, such as malls, apartment complexes, and private homes. Can you think of reasons for this change?

lasting settlement came in 1624 when the Dutch established New Amsterdam, later called New York. These settlements preceded those in Canada. For example, the first European did not reach the site that was to become Toronto until 1615.

New York, Boston (founded by the English in 1630), and Quebec City (where there was merely a trading post in 1608) started out as tiny villages in a vast wilderness. They resembled medieval towns in Europe, with narrow, winding streets that still curve through lower Manhattan, downtown Boston, and parts of Quebec City.

But economic growth soon transformed these quiet villages into thriving towns with wide streets usually laid out in a grid pattern. Montreal (founded in 1642) had grown to about 18 000 by the end of the eighteenth century, while Captain Vancouver had just explored and charted the Burrard Inlet in 1792. As the century closed, Canada was still an overwhelmingly rural society.

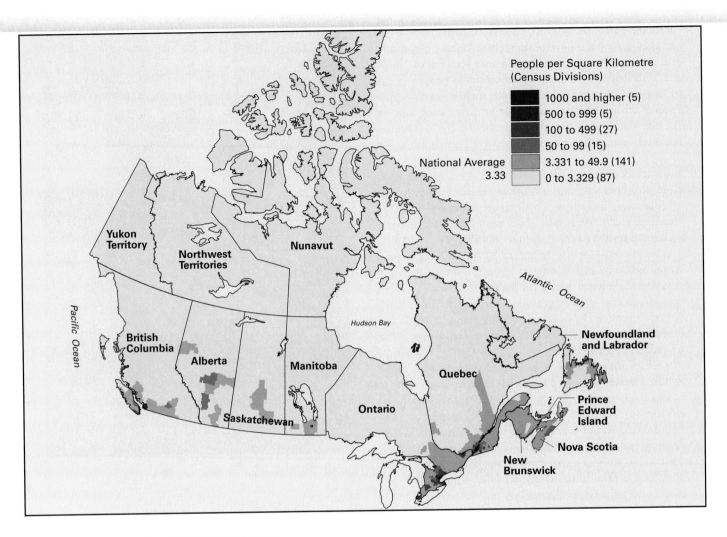

NATIONAL MAP 15-1 Population Density, Canada, 2001

The map illustrates how sparsely populated Canada is. Looking only at the population data, we see that Canada is an urban country, with most people living in urban centres. But as this map shows, from a geographical perspective these urban centres can also be thought of as exceptions. Chances are very good that you will spend all of your life living in urban areas. How will your life be different as a result of this?

Source: Statistics Canada (2003av).

Urban expansion: 1800–1860. Early in the nineteenth century, towns sprang up along the transportation routes that opened the Canadian West. First the cities along the major waterways connected to the Great Lakes emerged. By 1851, Quebec City had a population of 52 000, whereas the younger city of Montreal had already grown to 57 000.

Progress was slow away from the waterways of the Great Lakes. It was only in 1860, for example, that New Westminster (now part of the greater Vancouver area) became the first incorporated municipality west of Ontario. It was not until the completion of the Canadian Pacific Railway in 1885 that urbanization spread to the western provinces.

The metropolitan era: 1860–1950. Industrialization also gave an enormous boost to urbanization, as factories strained to produce goods. Now waves of people fled the countryside for cities in hopes of obtaining better jobs. Soon after, tens of millions of immigrants—mostly from Europe—joined the surge to the cities to form a culturally diverse urban mix.

At the time of Canadian Confederation in 1867, less than 20 percent of the population lived in urban areas. By 1951 this proportion had grown to 63 percent. Individual cities grew accordingly. By 1911 the supremacy of Montreal and Toronto (with populations of 470 000 and 377 000, respectively) was well established. The next-largest cities were Winnipeg (136 000) and Vancouver (100 000). These were still small cities compared to New York, which had already passed the 4 million mark. Such growth marked the era of the **metropolis** (from Greek words meaning "mother city"), *a large city that socially and economically dominates an urban area.* Metropolises became the economic centres of Canada.

Industrial technology further changed the physical shape of cities, pushing buildings well above the three or four storeys common up to this point. By the 1880s, steel girders and mechanical elevators raised structures more than 10 storeys high. Railroads and highways drew cities outward. By 1931, pushing upward and outward, cities were home to a majority of the Canadian population.

Urban decentralization: 1950–present. The industrial metropolis reached its peak about 1950. Since then, something of a turnaround—termed *urban decentralization*—has occurred as people have deserted downtown areas for outlying **suburbs**, *urban areas beyond the political boundaries of a city* (Balakrishnan & Jarvis, 1991). Thus the centres of the largest cities have actually experienced population decreases in the past few decades. Instead of densely packed central cities, the urban landscape has evolved into sprawling regions. Nevertheless, Canada remains a country dotted with population centres located in a vast expanse of sparsely populated land, as National Map 15–1 illustrates.

SUBURBS AND URBAN DECLINE

Imitating European nobility, some of the rich had always kept town houses in the city as well as country homes beyond the city limits. But not until after World War II did ordinary people find a suburban home within their reach. With more and more cars, new four-lane highways, affordable mortgages, and inexpensive tract homes, suburbs grew as never before. By 1981, most of the population in Canada's largest cities lived in suburbs outside the central city (McVey, Jr., & Kalbach, 1995).

Decentralization was not good news for everyone, however. Rapid suburban growth threw cities into financial chaos. Population decline meant reduced tax revenues. Further, cities that lost affluent people to the suburbs were left with the burden of providing expensive social programs to the poor who stayed behind.

Urban critic Paul Goldberger (2002) points out that the decline of central cities has led to a decline in the importance of public space. Inner-city decay has been particularly dramatic in the U.S., where deteriorating city centres have become synonymous with slum housing, crime, drugs, unemployment, poverty, and minority populations. There are similarities in Canada, Vancouver's Downtown Eastside being the most dramatic. However, marginalized populations are not as concentrated in other Canadian cities as they are in the cities of our neighbour to the south.

Canadian inner cities have fared better in large part because of early adoption of urban renewal policies. Under this program, provincial and local governments have paid for the rebuilding of many inner cities—Montreal started this as early as 1966 (Wolfe, 1992).

MEGALOPOLIS: THE REGIONAL CITY

Another result of urban decentralization is urban regions. Statistics Canada recognizes about 140 regional cities, which are called *census agglomerations* (CAs)—towns and surrounding areas where more than 10 000 people live in the urban core. The smallest CA is Labrador City, with a 2001 population of 9638 (the 1996 population was 10 460) (Statistics Canada, 2003aw). One-third of Canada's population lives in the three largest of the urban areas identified by Statistics Canada—the 27 *census metropolitan areas* (CMAs), which are cities and surrounding areas where more than 100 000 people live in the urban core. These CMAs range in size from Toronto at 4.7 million to Thunder Bay at about 122 000 (Murphy & Puderer, 2002; Statistics Canada, 2003aw).

As regional cities grow, they begin to overlap. There is now a continuous urban area from St. Catharines through Toronto to Oshawa where about 6.7 million people live. On an even larger scale, along the U.S. East Coast a 650-kilometre supercity stretches all the way from New England to Virginia. In the early 1960s, the French geographer Jean Gottmann (1961) coined the term **megalopolis** to designate *a vast urban region containing a number of cities and their surrounding suburbs.*

EDGE CITIES

Urban decentralization has also created *edge cities,* business centres some distance from the old downtowns. Edge cities—a mix of corporate office buildings, shopping malls,

Some towns in spectacular settings have grown dramatically. There are times when people living in Banff, Alberta, cannot even find a parking space.

hotels, and entertainment complexes—differ from suburbs, which contain mostly homes. The population of suburbs peaks at night, but the population of edge cities peaks during the workday.

As part of expanding urban regions, most edge cities have no clear physical boundaries, although some do have names (including Oshawa outside Toronto and Surrey outside Vancouver).

THE RURAL REBOUND

Over the course of Canadian history, the urban population of the nation has increased steadily. Immigration has played a part in this increase because most newcomers to this country settle in cities. There has also been considerable migration from rural areas to urban places, typically by people seeking greater economic opportunity.

However, in the 1990s, some areas outside of the largest cities gained population, a trend analysts have called the *rural rebound*. Most of this gain resulted from migration of people from urban areas. This trend has not affected all rural places: many small towns in rural areas are struggling simply to stay alive.

The greatest gains have come to rural communities that offer scenic and recreational attractions, such as lakes, mountains, and ski areas. People are drawn not only to the natural beauty of rural communities but also to their slower

pace: less traffic, a lower crime rate, and cleaner air. Looking ahead to National Map 16-1 on page 450, it is easy to identify some of these areas. Standing out is the whole area between Vancouver and Calgary, and also "cottage country" north of Toronto.

Urbanism as a Way of Life

Early sociologists on both sides of the Atlantic focused their attention on the rise of cities. We briefly present their accounts of urbanism as a way of life.

FERDINAND TÖNNIES: *GEMEINSCHAFT* AND *GESELLSCHAFT*

In the nineteenth century, the German sociologist Ferdinand Tönnies (1855–1937) studied how life in the new industrial metropolis differed from life in rural villages. From this contrast, he developed two concepts that have become a lasting part of sociology's terminology.

Tönnies (1963, orig. 1887) used the German word *Gemeinschaft* (meaning roughly "community") to refer to *a type of social organization in which people are closely linked by kinship and tradition.* The *Gemeinschaft* of the rural village, Tönnies explained, joins people in what amounts to a single primary group.

By and large, argued Tönnies, *Gemeinschaft* does not exist in the modern city. On the contrary, urbanization creates *Gesellschaft* (a German word, meaning roughly "association"), *a type of social organization in which people come together only on the basis of individual self-interest.* In the *Gesellschaft* way of life, individuals are motivated by their own needs rather than by a desire to help improve the well-being of everyone. By and large, city dwellers have little sense of community or common identity and look to other people mainly when they need something. Tönnies saw in urbanization the weakening of close, long-lasting social relations in favour of the brief and impersonal ties— or secondary relationships—typical of business.

EMILE DURKHEIM: MECHANICAL AND ORGANIC SOLIDARITY

The French sociologist Emile Durkheim agreed with much of Tönnies' thinking about cities. However, Durkheim countered that urbanites do not lack social bonds: they simply organize social life differently than rural people.

Durkheim described traditional, rural life as *mechanical solidarity,* social bonds based on common sentiments and shared moral values. With its emphasis on tradition, Durkheim's concept of mechanical solidarity bears a striking similarity to Tönnies' *Gemeinschaft.* Urbanization

Peasant Dance (above, c. 1565), by Pieter Breughel the Elder, conveys the essential unity of rural life forged by generations of kinship and neighbourhood. By contrast, Ernest Fiene's *Nocturne* (left) communicates the impersonality common to urban areas. Taken together, these paintings capture Tönnies' distinction between *Gemeinschaft* and *Gesellschaft*.

Pieter Breughel the Elder (c. 1525/30–1569), *Peasant Dance*, c. 1565, Kunsthistorisches Museum, Vienna/Superstock. Ernest Fiene (1894–1965), *Nocturne.* Photograph 8 Christie's Images.

erodes mechanical solidarity, Durkheim explained, but it also generates a new type of bonding, which he called *organic solidarity,* social bonds based on specialization and interdependence. This concept, which parallels Tönnies' *Gesellschaft,* reveals an important difference between the two thinkers. Both thought the growth of industrial cities weakened tradition, but Durkheim optimistically pointed to a new kind of solidarity. Where societies had been built on *sameness,* Durkheim now saw social life based on *difference.*

For Durkheim, urban society offers more individual choice, moral tolerance, and personal privacy than people find in rural villages. In sum, Durkheim thought that something is lost in the process of urbanization, but much is gained.

GEORG SIMMEL: THE BLASÉ URBANITE

The German sociologist Georg Simmel (1858–1918) offered a microanalysis of cities, studying how urban life shapes individual experience. According to Simmel, individuals see the city as a crush of people, objects, and events. To prevent being overwhelmed by all this stimulation, urbanites develop a *blasé attitude,* tuning out much of what goes on around them. Such detachment does not mean that city dwellers lack compassion for others; they simply keep their distance as a survival strategy so they can focus their

time and energy on those who really matter to them.

THE CHICAGO SCHOOL: ROBERT PARK AND LOUIS WIRTH

Sociologists in North America soon joined the study of rapidly growing cities. Robert Park (1864–1944), a leader of the first major North American sociology program at the University of Chicago, sought to add a street-level perspective by getting out and studying real cities. As he said of himself, "I suspect that I have actually covered more ground, tramping about in cities in different parts of the world, than any other living man" (1950:viii). Walking the streets, Park found the city to be an organized mosaic of distinctive ethnic communities, commercial centres, and industrial districts. Over time, he observed these "natural areas" developing and changing in relation to one another. To Park, the city was a living organism—a human kaleidoscope.

Another major figure in the Chicago School of urban sociology was Louis Wirth (1897–1952). Wirth (1938) is best known for blending the ideas of Tönnies, Durkheim, Simmel, and Park into a comprehensive theory of urban life.

Wirth began by defining the city as a setting with a large, dense, and socially diverse population. These traits result in an impersonal, superficial, and transitory way of life. Living among millions of others, urbanites come into contact with many more people than residents of rural

Trip to the Future: Census 2021 Reports That Visible Minorities Are Now a Majority in Toronto and Vancouver

According to the results of the 2001 Canadian census, 13.4 percent of Canadians—more than one in eight—belong to a visible minority group. This is an increase from 5 percent in 1981. The rapid growth of the visible minority population in Canada is expected to continue and, by 2017, it is expected that one in five Canadians will be a visible minority person, as shown in the figure below.

Why the change? By far, the most important reason is the increase in immigration and the large proportion of immigrants who are visible minorities—recall from Chapter 11 that eight of ten immigrants to Canada since 1980 arrive from Asia. Contributing factors for the increase are the younger age structure of the visible minority population—younger populations have more children—and slightly higher fertility rates.

There will be dramatic differences in the proportions of visible minorities in different parts of Canada. The greatest impact of the increase in the size and proportion of the visible minority population will be evident in Toronto and Vancouver, where visible minorities are expected to be a numerical majority by 2017—up from a little more than one-third of the population in 2001. Montreal is an interesting contrast because, with only 13 percent, it has relatively few visible minority persons.

The differences in the proportions of visible minorities in rural and urban areas are reflected in provincial differences also, with British Columbia and Ontario having the highest proportions of visible minorities. By 2017, it is expected that about one in three people in these two provinces will belong to a visible minority group.

Politicians are examining these figures closely, being mindful of the controversy resulting from former premier Jacques Parizeau's comment following the loss of the "Yes" side in the 1995 referendum that "ethnics and money" were to blame for the 1995 referendum defeat. Parti Québécois leader Bernard Landry is haunted by the comment and had to assure reporters that he did not support this interpretation when Parizeau repeated the assertion during the 2003 provincial election.

Policy makers are also mindful of these trends because the future vitality of our largest cities depends on meeting the needs and taking advantage of the contributions of their swelling visible minority populations.

WHAT DO YOU THINK?

1. Why are the minority populations of large Canadian cities increasing?
2. Why are there relatively few visible minority persons in Montreal?
3. What positive changes does a minority-majority bring to a city?
4. What challenges does a minority-majority bring to a city?

Source: Based on Bélanger & Malenfant (2005a, 2005b).

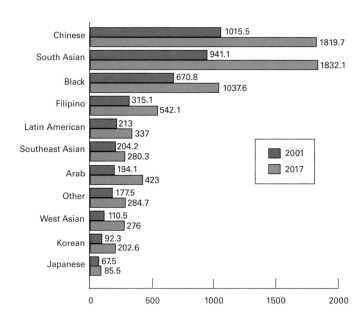

Visible Minority Population, Canada, 2001, 2017

areas. Thus, when city people notice others at all, they usually know them not in terms of *who they are* but *what they do*—as, for instance, the bus driver, the florist, or the grocery store clerk. Specialized, urban relationships sometimes are pleasant for all concerned. But we should remember that self-interest rather than friendship is the main reason for the interaction.

Finally, the impersonal nature of urban relationships, together with the great social diversity found in cities today, makes city dwellers more tolerant than rural villagers. Rural communities often jealously enforce their narrow traditions, but the heterogeneous population of a city rarely shares any single code of moral conduct (Wilson, 1985, 1995).

Critical review. In both Europe and North America, early sociologists presented a mixed view of urban living. Rapid urbanization troubled Tönnies and Wirth, who saw personal ties and traditional morality lost in the anonymous rush of the city. Durkheim and Park emphasized urbanism's positive face, pointing to more personal freedom and greater personal choice.

One problem with all of these views is that they paint urbanism in broad strokes that overlook the effects of class, race, and gender. There are many kinds of urbanites—rich and poor, black and white, Anglo and Aboriginal, women and men—all leading distinctive lives (Gans, 1968). Indeed, as the Diversity: Race, Class, & Gender box explains, the share of visible minorities in the largest Canadian cities is expected to continue growing sharply in the next decade. We see social diversity most clearly in cities, where various categories of people are large enough to form visible communities (Macionis & Parrillo, 2004).

URBAN ECOLOGY

Sociologists (especially members of the Chicago School) developed **urban ecology**, *the study of the link between the physical and social dimensions of cities.* For example, why are cities located where they are? The first cities emerged in fertile regions where the ecology favoured raising crops. Pre-industrial people, concerned with defence, built their cities on mountains (ancient Athens was perched on an outcropping of rock) or surrounded by water (Paris and Mexico City were built on islands). With the Industrial Revolution, economic considerations situated all major Canadian cities near rivers and natural harbours that facilitated trade.

Urban ecologists also study the physical design of cities. In 1925, Ernest W. Burgess, a student and colleague of Robert Park's, described land use in terms of *concentric zones*. City centres, Burgess observed, are business districts bordered by a ring of factories, followed by residential rings

with housing that becomes more expensive the farther it is from the noise and pollution of the city's centre.

Homer Hoyt (1939) refined Burgess' observations, noting that distinctive districts sometimes form *wedge-shaped sectors*. For example, one fashionable area may develop next to another, or an industrial district may extend outward from a city's centre along a train or trolley line.

Chauncy Harris and Edward Ullman (1945) added yet another insight: As cities decentralize, they lose their single-centre form in favour of a *multicentred model*. As cities grow, residential areas, industrial parks, and shopping districts typically push away from one another. Few people want to live close to industrial areas, for example, so the city becomes a mosaic of distinct districts.

Social area analysis investigates what people in particular neighbourhoods have in common. Three factors seem to explain most of the variation in neighbourhood types: family patterns, social class, and race and ethnicity (Shevky & Bell, 1955; Johnston, 1976). Families with children look for areas with large apartments or single-family homes and good schools. The rich seek high-prestige neighbourhoods, often in the central city near cultural attractions. People with a common ethnic heritage cluster in distinctive communities.

Finally, Brian Berry and Philip Rees (1969) tied together many of these insights. They explained that distinct family types tend to settle in the concentric zones described by Ernest Burgess. Specifically, households with few children tend to cluster toward the city's centre, and those with more children live farther away. Social class differences are primarily responsible for the sector-shaped districts described by Homer Hoyt; the rich occupy one "side of the tracks" and the poor the other. And racial and ethnic neighbourhoods are found at various places throughout the city, consistent with Harris and Ullman's multicentred model.

URBAN POLITICAL ECONOMY

In the late 1960s, many large North American cities were rocked by major riots. In the wake of this unrest, some analysts turned away from the ecological approach to a social-conflict understanding of city life. The *urban political economy model* applies Karl Marx's analysis of conflict in the workplace to conflict in the city (Lindstrom, 1995).

Political economists disagree with the ecological approach, which sees the city as a natural organism with particular districts and neighbourhoods developing according to an internal logic. They claim that city life is defined by people with power: corporate leaders and political officials. Capitalism, which transforms the city into real estate traded for profit and concentrates wealth in the hands of the few, is the key to understanding city life. From this point of view, for example, the development of the West Edmonton Mall and the resulting decline in downtown Edmonton can only be understood by an analysis that includes the close relationship that the developer (the Ghermezian family) had with provincial and municipal politicians.

Critical review. The fact that our largest Canadian cities appear to be in crisis, with pockets of deep poverty and high crime rates, seems to favour the political economy view over the urban ecology approach. But one criticism applies to both: they focus on Canadian cities during a limited period of history. Much of what we know about industrial cities does not apply to pre-industrial towns in our own past or the rapidly growing cities in many poor nations today. It is unlikely that any single model of city can account for the full range of urban diversity found in the world today.

URBANIZATION IN LOW-INCOME SOCIETIES

November 16, Cairo, Egypt. People call the vast Muslim cemetery in Old Cairo the "City of the Dead." In truth, it is very much alive: tens of thousands of squatters have moved into the mausoleums, making this place an eerie mix of life and death. Children run across the stone floors, clotheslines stretch between the monuments, and an occasional television antenna protrudes from a tomb roof. With Cairo gaining 1000 people a day, families live where they can.

Twice in its history, the world has experienced a revolutionary expansion of cities. The first urban revolution began about 8000 BCE with the first urban settlements and continued until permanent settlements were in place on several continents. About 1750, the second urban revolution took off; it lasted for two centuries as the Industrial Revolution spurred rapid growth of cities in Europe and North America.

A *third urban revolution* is now underway. Today, 75 percent or more of people in high-income countries are already city dwellers. But extraordinary urban growth is occurring in low-income nations. In 1950, about 25 percent of the people in low-income countries lived in cities; in 2005, the figure was close to 50 percent. In addition, in 1950, only seven cities in the world had populations over 5 million, and only two of these were in low-income countries. By 2004, 55 urban areas had passed this mark, and 38 of them were in low-income nations (Brockerhoff, 2000; *World Gazetteer*, 2004).

This third urban revolution is taking place because many low-income nations have entered the high-growth Stage 2 of demographic transition theory. Falling death rates have fuelled population increase in Latin America, Asia, and especially Africa. For urban areas, the rate of increase is *twice* as high because, in addition to the natural increase, millions of people leave the countryside each year in search of jobs, healthcare, education, and conveniences such as running water and electricity.

Cities do offer more opportunities than rural areas, but they provide no quick fix for the problems of escalating population and grinding poverty. Many cities in low-income nations—including Mexico City, Egypt's Cairo, India's Calcutta, and Manila in the Philippines—are simply unable to meet the basic needs of much of their population. All of these cities are surrounded by wretched shantytowns, settlements of makeshift homes built from discarded materials. As noted in Chapter 9 ("Global Stratification"), even city dumps are home to thousands of poor people, who pick through the waste hoping to find enough to make it through another day.

Environment and Society

The human species has prospered, rapidly increasing in population over the entire planet. An increasing share of the global population now lives in large, complex settlements that offer the promise of a better life than that found in rural villages.

But these advances have come at a high price. Never before in history have human beings placed such demands on the Earth. This disturbing development brings us to the final section of this chapter: a look at the interplay of the natural environment and society. Like demography, **ecology** is another cousin of sociology, formally defined as *the study of the interaction of living organisms and the natural environment*. Ecology rests on the research of natural scientists as well as social scientists. In this text, we focus on the aspects of ecology that involve familiar sociological concepts and issues.

The **natural environment** is *the Earth's surface and atmosphere, including living organisms, air, water, soil, and other resources necessary to sustain life*. Like every other species, humans depend on the natural environment to survive. Yet with our capacity for culture, humans stand apart from other species: we alone take deliberate action to remake the world according to our own interests and desires, for better and for worse.

Why is the environment of interest to sociologists? Environmental problems—from pollution to global warming—do not arise from the natural world operating on its own. Such problems result from the specific actions of human beings, making them social problems (Marx, 1994).

The most important insight sociology offers about our physical world is that environmental problems do not simply "happen." Rather, the state of the natural environment reflects the ways in which social life is organized—how people live and what they think is important. Moreover, the greater the technological power of a society, the greater that society's ability to threaten the natural environment.

THE GLOBAL DIMENSION

The study of the natural environment must be approached from a global perspective. Regardless of political divisions between nations, the planet is a single **ecosystem**, *a system composed of the interaction of all living organisms and their natural environment.*

The Greek meaning of *eco* is "house," reminding us that this planet is our home and that all living things and their natural environment are interrelated. A change in any part of the natural environment sends ripples through the entire global ecosystem.

Consider, from an ecological point of view, our love of eating hamburgers. People in North America (and, increasingly, around the world) have created a huge demand for beef, which has greatly expanded ranching in Brazil, Costa Rica, and other Latin American nations. To produce the lean meat sought by fast-food corporations, cattle in Latin America feed on grass, which uses a great deal of land. Latin American ranchers clear the land for grazing by destroying thousands of square miles of forests each year. These tropical forests are vital to maintaining the Earth's atmosphere. Deforestation ends up threatening everyone, including those people back in Canada enjoying their hamburgers (Myers, 1984b).

TECHNOLOGY AND THE ENVIRONMENTAL DEFICIT

Sociologists point to a simple formula: $I = PAT$, where environmental impact (I) reflects a society's population (P), its level of affluence (A), and its level of technology (T). Members of societies with simple technology—the hunters and gatherers described in Chapter 2 ("Culture")—hardly affect the environment because they are small in number, are poor, and have only simple technology. On the contrary, nature affects their lives as they follow the migration of game, watch the rhythm of the seasons, and suffer from natural catastrophes such as fires, floods, droughts, and storms.

Societies at intermediate stages of sociocultural evolution have a somewhat greater capacity to affect the environment. But the environmental impact of horticulture (small-scale farming), pastoralism (the herding of animals), and even agriculture (the use of animal-drawn plows) is limited because people still rely on muscle power for producing food and other goods.

Human control of the natural environment increased dramatically with the Industrial Revolution. Muscle power gave way to engines that burn fossil fuels—coal at first, and then oil. Such machinery affects the environment in two ways: by consuming natural resources, and by releasing pollutants into the atmosphere. Even more important, humans armed with industrial technology are able to bend nature to their will, tunnelling through mountains, damming rivers, irrigating deserts, and drilling for oil on the ocean floor. This explains why people in rich nations, who represent just 18 percent of humanity, use 80 percent of the world's energy (Miller, 1992; York, Rosa, & Deitz, 2002).

The environmental impact of industrial technology goes beyond energy consumption. Just as important is the fact that members of industrial societies produce 100 times more goods than people in agrarian societies. Higher living standards, in turn, increase the problems of solid waste

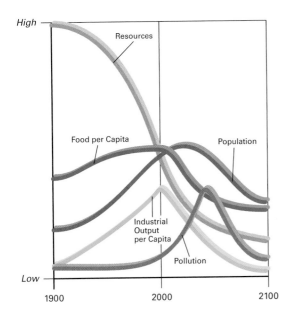

FIGURE 15-5 The Limits to Growth: Projections

Source: Based on Meadows et al. (1972).

(because people ultimately throw away most of what they produce) and pollution (industrial production generates smoke and other toxic substances).

Right from the start, people recognized the material benefits of industrial technology. But only a century later did they begin to see its long-term effects on the natural environment, which set the stage for the growth of the environmental movement. Today, we realize that the technological power to make our lives better can also put the lives of future generations at risk, and there is a national debate about how to address this issue.

Evidence is mounting that we are running up an **environmental deficit**, *profound and long-term harm to the natural environment caused by humanity's focus on short-term material affluence* (Bormann, 1990). The concept of environmental deficit is important for three reasons. First, it reminds us that the state of the environment is a social issue, reflecting choices people make about how to live. Second, it suggests that much environmental damage—to the air, land, or water—is unintended. By focusing on the short-term benefits of, say, cutting down forests, strip mining, or using throwaway packaging, we fail to see their long-term environmental effects. Third, in some respects, the environmental deficit is reversible. Inasmuch as societies have created environmental problems, societies can undo many of them.

CULTURE: GROWTH AND LIMITS

Whether we recognize environmental dangers and decide to do something about them is a cultural matter. Thus, along with technology, culture has powerful environmental consequences.

The logic of growth. One of the core values that underlie social life in Canada is *material comfort*, the belief that money and the things it buys enrich our lives. We also believe in the idea of *progress*, thinking that the future will be better than the present. In addition, we look to *science* to make our lives easier and more rewarding. In simpler terms, "having things is good," "life gets better," and "people are clever." Taken together, such cultural values form the *logic of growth*.

An optimistic view of the world, the logic of growth holds that more powerful technology has improved our lives and that new discoveries will continue to do so into the future. Throughout the history of Canada and other high-income nations, the logic of growth has been the driving force behind settling the wilderness, building towns and roads, and pursuing material affluence.

However, "progress" can lead to unexpected problems, including strain on the environment. The logic of growth responds by arguing that people (especially scientists and other technology experts) will find a way out of any problem placed in our path. If, for example, the world runs short of oil, scientists will come up with electric, solar, or nuclear engines or some as yet unknown technology to meet the world's energy needs.

Environmentalists counter that the logic of growth is flawed because it assumes that natural resources such as clean air, fresh water, and the Earth's topsoil will always be plentiful. We can and will exhaust these *finite* resources if we continue to pursue growth at any cost. Echoing Malthus, environmentalists warn that if we call on the Earth to support increasing numbers of people, we will surely destroy the environment—and ourselves—in the process.

The limits to growth. If we cannot invent our way out of the problems created by the logic of growth, perhaps we need another way of thinking about the world. Environmentalists claim that growth must have limits. Stated simply, the *limits to growth* thesis is that humanity must put in place policies to control population increase, pollution, and the use of resources in order to avoid environmental collapse.

In *The Limits to Growth,* a controversial book that had a large hand in launching the environmental movement, Donella Meadows and her colleagues (1972) used a computer model to calculate the planet's available resources, rates of population growth, amount of land available for cultivation, levels of industrial and food production, and amount of pollutants released into the atmosphere. The model reflects changes that have occurred since 1900 and projects forward to the end of the twenty-first century. The authors concede that such long-range predictions are speculative, and some critics think they are plain wrong (Simon, 1981). But right or wrong, the general conclusions of the study, shown in Figure 15–5, call for serious consideration.

According to the limits to growth thesis, we are quickly using up the Earth's finite resources. Supplies of oil, natural gas, and other energy sources are already falling sharply and will continue to drop, a little faster or more slowly depending on conservation policies in rich nations and how fast other nations industrialize. Although food production per person will continue to rise during this century, world hunger will persist because existing food supplies are distributed so unequally. By 2050, the model predicts that hunger will reach a crisis level, first stabilizing population and then sending it back downward. Sooner or later, resource depletion will cripple industrial output as well. Only then will pollution rates fall.

Limits to growth theorists are also known as neo-Malthusians because they share Malthus' pessimism about the future. They doubt that current patterns of life are sustainable for even another century. If so, we face a fundamental choice: either we make deliberate changes in how we live, or widespread calamity will force change on us.

SOLID WASTE: THE DISPOSABLE SOCIETY

Across Canada, people generate a massive amount of solid waste *each and every day*. Figure 15–6 shows the composition of a typical community's garbage.

As a rich nation containing people who value convenience, Canada has become a *disposable society*. We consume more products than virtually any other nation on Earth, many of which have throwaway packaging. For example, fast food is served in cardboard, plastic, and Styrofoam containers that we throw away within minutes. And countless other products—from toothpaste to fishhooks—are elaborately packaged to make them more attractive to the customer and to discourage tampering and theft.

Manufacturers market soft drinks, beer, and fruit juices in aluminum cans, glass bottles, and plastic containers, which not only use up finite resources but also create mountains of solid waste. Countless items are intentionally designed to be disposable: pens, razors, flashlights, batteries, and even cameras. Other goods, from light bulbs to automobiles, are designed to have a limited useful life after which they become unwanted junk. As Paul H. Connett (1991) points out, even the words we use to describe what

FIGURE 15–6 Composition of Vancouver's Trash, 2004

Source: Technology Resources Inc. (2005).

we throw away—"waste," "trash," "refuse," "garbage," "rubbish"—show how little we value what we cannot immediately use. But this was not always the case, as the Applying Sociology box explains.

Living in a rich society, the average person in North America consumes 50 times more steel, 170 times more newspaper, 250 times more gasoline, and 300 times more plastic each year than the typical person in a low-income country such as Haiti (Miller, 1992). This high level of consumption means that we in Canada not only use a disproportionate share of the planet's natural resources but also generate most of the world's refuse.

We like to say that we "throw things away." But 80 percent of our solid waste never "goes away." Rather, it ends up in landfills, which are, literally, filling up. Material in landfills also can pollute groundwater. The city of Toronto is trying to deal with this issue now. After running out of space in its own landfills, it tried to ship garbage 600 kilometres north by rail to the abandoned Adams Lake mine, close to the community of Kirkland Lake. Fierce opposition led to the garbage being shipped 400 kilometres west to Michigan instead. However, the controversy erupts again whenever an accident occurs that involves one of the hundreds of trucks that daily drive back and forth. In addition, what goes into landfills all too often stays there, sometimes for centuries. Tens of millions of tires, diapers, and other items that we bury in landfills each year do not decompose and will be an unwelcome legacy for future generations.

Environmentalists argue that we should address the problem of solid waste by doing what many of our ancestors did: turn "waste" into a resource. One way to do this is through *recycling*, reusing resources we would otherwise throw away. Recycling is an accepted practice in Japan and

Why Grandmother Had No Trash

Grandma Macionis, we always used to say, never threw away anything. She was born and raised in Lithuania—the "old country"—where life in a poor village shaped her in ways that never changed, even after she came to the United States as a young woman and settled in Philadelphia.

After opening a birthday present, she would carefully save the box, wrapping paper, and ribbon, which meant as much to her as the gift they contained. Grandma never wore new clothes, her kitchen knives were worn thin from decades of sharpening, and all of her garbage was recycled as compost for her vegetable garden.

As strange as Grandma seemed to her grandchildren, she was a product of her culture. A century ago, there was little "trash." If a pair of socks wore thin, Grandma mended them, probably more than once. When they were beyond repair, she used them as a rag for cleaning or sewed them (with other old clothing) into a quilt. For her, everything had value, if not in one way, then in another.

During the twentieth century, as women joined men working outside of the home, income went up and people spent less time at home.

Families began buying more and more "time-saving" products. Before long, few people cared about the home recycling that Grandma practised. Soon cities sent crews from block to block to pick up truckloads of discarded material. The era of "trash" had begun.

WHAT DO YOU THINK?

1. Just as Grandma Macionis was a product of her culture, so are we. What cultural values make people today demand "time-saving" products and "convenience" packaging?
2. What do you think are the prospects for expanding recycling of materials in the near future?
3. Would you support laws that limited people's trash? Why or why not?

many other nations, and it is becoming more common in Canada and the United States, where we now reuse about 30 percent of waste materials. The share is increasing as laws mandate reuse of certain materials such as glass bottles and aluminum cans. Because of our nation's market-based economy, recycling will also increase as it becomes more profitable.

WATER AND AIR

Oceans, lakes, and streams are the lifeblood of the global ecosystem. Humans depend on water for drinking, bathing, cooling, cooking, recreation, and a host of other activities.

According to what scientists call the *hydrologic cycle*, the Earth naturally recycles water and refreshes the land. The process begins as heat from the sun causes the Earth's water, 97 percent of which is in the oceans, to evaporate and form clouds. Because water evaporates at lower temperatures than most pollutants, the water vapour that rises from the seas is relatively pure, leaving various contaminants behind. Water then falls to the Earth as rain, which drains into streams and rivers and, finally, returns to the sea. Two major concerns about water, then, are supply and pollution.

Water supply.   Only about 1 percent of the Earth's water is suitable for drinking. It is not surprising, then, that for thousands of years, water rights have figured prominently in laws around the world. Today, as Global Map 15–2 shows, some regions of the world (especially the tropics) enjoy plentiful fresh water, using only a small share of the available supply. High demand, coupled with modest reserves, make water supply a matter of concern in much of North America and Asia, where people look to rivers rather than rainfall for their water. In China, deep aquifers are dropping rapidly. In the Middle East, water supply is reaching a critical level. Iran is rationing water in its capital city. In Egypt, people can consume just one-sixth as much water from the Nile River today as in 1900. Across Northern Africa and the Middle East, experts predict, as many as 1 billion people may lack the water they need for irrigation and drinking by 2025 (Postel, 1993; "China Faces Water Shortage," 2001).

Rising population and the development of more complex technology have greatly increased the world's appetite for water. The global consumption of water (now estimated at 110 billion litres per day) has doubled since 1950 and is rising steadily. As a result, even in parts of the world that receive plenty of rainfall, people are using groundwater

GLOBAL MAP 15-2 Water Consumption in Global Perspective

This map shows water consumption as a percentage of each country's renewable water resources. Nations near the equator use only a tiny share of their available resources; indeed, much of this region is covered with rainforest. Northern Africa and the Middle East are a different story, however, with dense populations drawing on very limited water resources. As a result, in countries such as Libya, Egypt, and Saudi Arabia, people (especially the poor) do not have as much water as they would like or, often, as they need.

Source: United Nations Development Programme (2000).

Water Consumption as Percentage of Natural Water Supply

- 40.0 percent or more
- 20.0 to 39.9 percent
- 10.0 to 19.9 percent
- 2.0 to 9.9 percent
- Less than 2.0 percent
- No data
- Tropical rain forest

faster than it can be replenished naturally. In the Tamil Nadu region of Southern India, for example, people are drawing so much groundwater that the local water table has fallen 30 metres over the last several decades. Mexico City—which has sprawled to some 3600 square kilometres—has pumped so much water from its underground aquifer that the city has sunk 10 metres in the past century and continues to drop about 5 centimetres per year. Closer to home,

the Colorado River often does not reach the ocean, in part because so much water is used for irrigation. While we in Canada have access to a disproportionate share of the world's fresh water, we seem to realize the importance of our resource: whenever water exports have been proposed, Canadians are up in arms in opposition.

In light of such developments, we must face the reality that water is a valuable and finite resource. Greater

Water is vital to life, and it is also in short supply. The state of Gujarat, in Western India, has experienced a decade-long drought. In the village of Natwarghad, people crowd together, lowering pots into the local well, taking what little water is left.

A special problem is *acid rain*—rain made acidic by air pollution—that destroys plant and animal life. Acid rain (or snow) begins with power plants burning fossil fuels (oil and coal) to generate electricity; this burning process releases sulfuric and nitrous oxides into the air. As the wind sweeps these gases into the atmosphere, they react with the air to form sulfuric and nitric acids, which turn atmospheric moisture acidic.

This is a clear case of one type of pollution causing another: air pollution (from smokestacks) ends up contaminating water (in lakes and streams that collect acid rain). Acid rain is truly a global phenomenon because the regions that suffer the harmful effects may be thousands of kilometres from the source of the pollution. For instance, British power plants have caused acid rain that has devastated forests and fish in Norway and Sweden, 1500 kilometres to the northeast. Similarly, U.S smokestacks have been accused of poisoning the forests in Eastern Canada.

Air pollution. Because we are surrounded by air, most people in Canada are more aware of air pollution than contaminated water. One of the unexpected consequences of industrial technology—especially the factory and the motor vehicle—has been a decline in air quality. In 1950, exhaust fumes from automobiles shrouded cities such as Vancouver, where the air is trapped between the wind from the ocean and the postcard-pretty mountains. In London, factory smokestacks, automobiles, and coal fires used to heat households all added up to what was probably the worst urban air quality of the last century. What some British jokingly called "pea soup" was, in reality, a deadly mix of pollution: during five days in 1952, an especially thick haze that hung over London killed 4000 people (Clarke, 1984a).

Air quality improved in the final decades of the last century. High-income nations passed laws that banned heavy-pollution heating, including the coal fires that choked London 50 years before. In addition, scientists devised ways to reduce the noxious output of factories and the growing numbers of automobiles and trucks. Nevertheless, even with improved technology, the impact of the internal combustion engine is significant and our reliance on private vehicles for transportation is something most of us may one day have to reconsider. National Map 15–2 shows that the vast majority of Canadians drive to work.

conservation of water by individuals (the average person consumes 45 million litres in a lifetime) is part of the answer. However, households around the world account for just 10 percent of water use. We need to curb water consumption by industry, which uses 25 percent of the global total, and farming, which consumes two-thirds of the total for irrigation.

New irrigation technology may reduce the demand for water in the future. But here again, we see how population increase, as well as economic growth, strains our ecosystem (Postel, 1993; Population Action International, 2000).

Water pollution. In large cities—from Mexico City to Cairo to Shanghai—many people have no choice but to drink contaminated water. Infectious diseases such as typhoid, cholera, and dysentery, all caused by waterborne microorganisms, spread rapidly through these populations. In addition to ensuring ample *supplies* of water, we must protect the *quality* of water.

Water quality in Canada is generally good by global standards. However, even here the problem of water pollution is growing steadily, as in the case of the raw sewage from Halifax, St. John's, and Victoria that goes straight into the ocean. Decades of heavy pollution of the Great Lakes, and of countless streams and rivers across the country, has seriously threatened plant and fish life, and for some species has resulted in extinction.

THE RAINFORESTS

Rainforests are *regions of dense forestation, most of which circle the globe close to the equator.* A glance back at

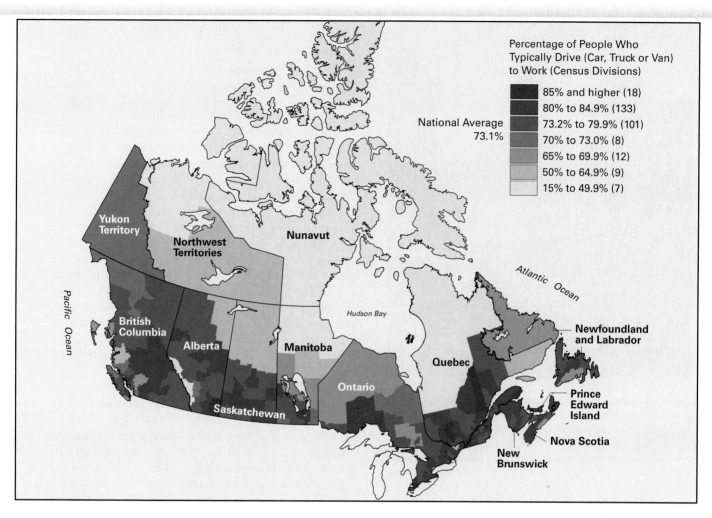

SEEING OURSELVES

NATIONAL MAP 15-2 Driving to Work, Canada, 2001

Most Canadians drive to work rather than taking public transit, riding along as a passenger, or using human-powered modes of transportation. It is not surprising that people living in the very core of the largest urban centres are less likely to drive to work. Similarly, in the North where there are few roads it is understandable that people are not likely to drive to work. But what is the explanation for the large proportion of people far away from the big cities who drive to work? Are people in small towns more or less likely to drive to work than people in the largest urban areas?

Source: Statistics Canada (2003ax).

 For more information about rainforests, visit **http://www.rainforestweb.org**.

Global Map 15–2 on page 435 shows that the largest tropical rainforests are in South America (notably Brazil), West–Central Africa, and Southeast Asia. In all, the world's rainforests cover some 7 percent of the Earth's total land surface.

Like other global resources, rainforests are falling victim to the needs and appetites of the surging world population. As noted earlier, to meet the demand for beef, ranchers in Latin America burn forested areas to increase their supply of grazing land. We are also losing rainforests to the hardwood trade. People in rich nations pay high prices for mahogany and other woods because, as environmentalist

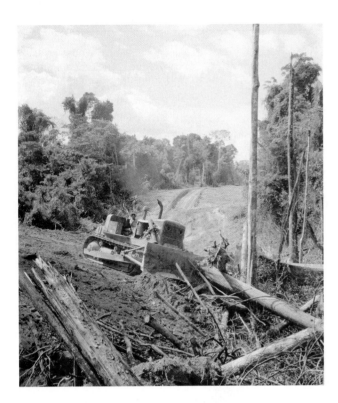

The world's rainforests continue to shrink by about 1 percent each year. The Amazon Highway, being built through the Brazilian rainforest, is to many people a welcome source of economic development. But what effect will such development have on the local environment? What difference does this make for us here in Canada?

Norman Myers (1984c:88) puts it, they have "a penchant for parquet floors, fine furniture, fancy panelling, weekend yachts, and high-grade coffins." Under such economic pressure, the world's rainforests are now just half their original size, and they continue to shrink by about 1 percent (170 000 square kilometres) annually. Unless we stop this loss, the rainforests will vanish before the end of the twenty-first century and with them, protection for the Earth's biodiversity and climate.

Global warming. Why are rainforests so important? One reason is that they cleanse the atmosphere of carbon dioxide (CO_2). Since the beginning of the Industrial Revolution, the amount of carbon dioxide produced by humans (mostly from factories and automobiles) has risen sharply. Much of this CO_2 is absorbed by the oceans. But plants take in carbon dioxide and expel oxygen. This is why the rainforests are vital to maintaining the chemical balance of the atmosphere.

 Check out this program on the Internet that estimates your eco-logical footprint based on 15 questions: **http://www.myfootprint.org**.

The problem is that production of carbon dioxide is rising while the amount of plant life on the Earth is shrinking. To make matters worse, rainforests are being destroyed mostly by burning, which releases even more carbon dioxide into the atmosphere. Experts estimate that the atmospheric concentration of carbon dioxide is now 20–30 percent higher than it was 150 years ago (Revkin, 2002).

High above the Earth, carbon dioxide acts like the glass roof of a greenhouse, letting heat from the sun pass through to the Earth while preventing much of it from radiating back away from the planet, a mechanism called the *greenhouse effect*. The result, say ecologists, is **global warming**, *a rise in the Earth's average temperature due to an increasing concentration of carbon dioxide in the atmosphere.* Over the past century, the global temperature has risen about 0.5°C (to an average of 14.5°C). Scientists warn that it could rise by 3°C to 6°C during this century, which would melt vast areas of the polar ice caps and raise the sea level to cover low-lying land around the world. Were this to happen, water would cover all of Bangladesh, for example, and much of coastal Canada. On the other hand, the Canadian Prairies, currently one of the most productive agricultural regions in the world, probably would become arid.

Not all scientists share this gloomy outlook. Some point out that global temperature changes have been taking place throughout history, apparently having little or nothing to do with rainforests. Higher concentrations of carbon dioxide in the atmosphere might speed up plant growth (because plants thrive on this gas), which would correct the imbalance and nudge the Earth's temperature downward once again. But a consensus is building that global warming is a problem that threatens the future for all of us (Begley, 1997; McDonald, 1999).

Declining biodiversity. Clearing rainforests also reduces the Earth's *biodiversity.* This is because rainforests are home to almost half of the planet's living species.

On Earth, there are as many as 30 million species of animals, plants, and microorganisms. Several dozen unique species of plants and animals cease to exist each day. But given the vast number of living species, why should we be concerned? Environmentalists give four reasons.

1. **Our planet's biodiversity provides a varied source of human food.** Using agricultural high technology, scientists can "splice" familiar crops with more exotic plant life, making food more bountiful and more resistant to insects and disease. Thus, biodiversity helps feed our planet's rapidly increasing population.

2. **Animal and plant biodiversity is a vital genetic resource.** Medical and pharmaceutical researchers rely on it to provide hundreds of new compounds each year

Members of small, simple societies—such as the Tan't Batu, who thrive in the Philippines—live in harmony with nature; such people do not have the technological means to greatly affect the natural world. Although we in complex societies like to think of ourselves as superior to such people, the truth is that there is much we can—and must—learn from them.

that cure disease and improve our lives. For example, children in Canada now have a good chance of surviving leukemia, a disease that was almost a sure killer two generations ago, because of a compound derived from a pretty tropical flower called the rosy periwinkle. The oral birth control pill, used by millions of women in this country, is another product of plant research, this one involving the Mexican forest yam.

3. **Species loss impairs the natural environment.** With the loss of any species of life—whether it is the ancient Kootenay River white sturgeon, the famed Chinese panda, the spotted owl, or even a single species of ant—the beauty and complexity of our natural environment are diminished. And there are clear warning signs: Three-fourths of the world's 9000 bird species are declining in number.

4. **Species loss is irreversible.** Unlike pollution, the extinction of any species is final—there's no bringing it back.

An important ethical question is whether people living today have the right to impoverish the world for those who will live tomorrow (Myers, 1991; Wilson, 1991; Brown et al., 1993).

ENVIRONMENTAL RACISM

Conflict theory has given birth to the concept of **environmental racism**, *the pattern by which environmental hazards are greatest for poor people, especially minorities.* Historically,

factories that spew pollution have stood near neighbourhoods housing the poor and minorities. Why? In part, the poor themselves were drawn to factories in search of work, and their low incomes often meant they could afford housing only in undesirable neighbourhoods. Sometimes the only housing that fit their budgets stood in the very shadow of the plants and mills where they worked.

Nobody wants a factory or dump nearby, of course, but powerful people are better able to present arguments leading to locating these NIMBY ("**N**ot **I**n **M**y **B**ack **Y**ard"). Accordingly, landfills are more likely to be located in areas populated by Aboriginal people, visible minorities, and rural people (Ali, 1999; Commission for Racial Justice, 1994; Bohon & Humphrey, 2000).

Looking Ahead: Toward a Sustainable Society and World

The demographic analysis presented in this chapter points to some disturbing trends. First, the Earth's population has reached record levels because birth rates remain high in poor nations and death rates have fallen just about everywhere. Reducing fertility will remain a pressing issue throughout this century. Even with some recent decline in population increase, the nightmare described by Thomas Malthus is still a real possibility.

Furthermore, population growth remains greatest in the low-income countries of the world, which lack the means to support their present populations, much less their

CONTROVERSY & DEBATE

Reclaiming the Environment: What Are You Willing to Give Up?

Surveys tell us that many people in Canada describe themselves as sympathetic to environmentalism. Yet, we are unsure that we are willing to give up very much to reclaim the ecosystem.

At the outset, the environmental movement did not ask much of us. The "first wave" of environmentalism was little more than a conservation movement that focused on protecting natural wilderness—such as the park in Banff, which was established in 1887—in the face of rapid economic development. Conservationists were responsible for pressing legislators to create scores of national parks and other protected areas where wildlife would be left undisturbed. Some Canadian conservationists became active in the U.S.-based Sierra Club and the National Audubon Society, both of which continue to monitor North American environmental issues today.

During the 1960s and early 1970s, a "second wave" of environmentalism took root, motivated predominantly by members of the upper middle class, including university and college students and people from white-collar occupations. In the 1990s, more members of the middle class, including artists and civil servants, took up the environmental cause (Hannigan, 1998). But how important is the environ-

ment to the average Canadian citizen today? As the figure shows, Canadians feel much more strongly about the environment than citizens of some other countries.

Canadian sociologist Shelley Ungar goes further and suggests that the environmental movements choose their agenda very carefully. The emphasis on recycling (rather than reducing and

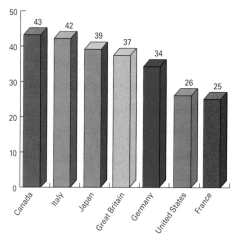

Willingness to Give Up Economic Growth for Environmental Protection, Selected Countries, 2002

Survey question: Protecting the environment should be given priority, even if it causes slower economic growth and some loss of jobs (completely agree, mostly agree, mostly disagree, completely disagree).

Source: PEW Research Center for the People and the Press (2003).

reusing), is a conscious choice taken by environmental groups. When faced with choosing between advocating car tune-up and proper tire pressure and advocating a reduction in driving, these movements choose the former because they "anticipated and actually encountered sufficient opposition from their middle-class constituency that they avoided taking challenging positions" (Ungar, 1998:269).

Perhaps our society has come to accept the idea that environmentalism is good in principle—but are we prepared to act on this idea only when other things, including jobs, are in place? Despite what people declare in response to survey questions, Canadians appear to prefer big over small when they buy vehicles and houses.

CONTINUE THE DEBATE . . .

1. Do you think that limiting economic growth is necessary to secure our environmental future? Would you be willing to accept a lower standard of living to protect the natural environment?
2. What action have you ever taken (signing a petition, participating in a demonstration, modifying your consumption patterns) to safeguard the environment?
3. Where do you think the major Canadian political parties stand on environmental issues?

Sources: Hannigan (1998); Ungar (1998).

future ones. Supporting 75 million additional people on our planet each year—72 million of whom are in low-income societies—will take a global commitment to providing not only food but also housing, schools, and

employment. The well-being of the entire world may ultimately depend on resolving the economic and social problems of these nations and bridging the widening gulf between "have" and "have-not."

Urbanization is continuing, especially in low-income countries. People have always sought out cities in the hope of finding a better life. But the sheer numbers of people who live in the emerging global supercities—including Mexico City, São Paulo (Brazil), Kinshasa (Democratic Republic of the Congo), Bombay (India), and Manila (the Philippines)—have created urban problems on a massive scale.

Throughout the world, humanity is facing a serious environmental challenge. Part of this problem is population increase, which is greatest in poor societies. But high levels of consumption, which mark rich nations such as ours, also play a role. By increasing the planet's environmental deficit, our present way of life is borrowing against the well-being of our children and their children. Globally, members of high-income societies, who currently consume so much of the Earth's resources, are mortgaging the future security of the low-income countries of the world.

 To read more about population increase, the environment, and global inequality, go to http://www.peopleandplanet.net.

The answer, in principle, is to create an **ecologically sustainable culture**, *a way of life that meets the needs of the present generation without threatening the environmental legacy of future generations.* Sustainable living depends on three strategies:

1. **Be proactive about population growth.** The current population of 6.4 billion is already straining the natural environment. Clearly, the higher world population climbs, the more difficult environmental problems will become, to the point of imposing changes in our behaviour. Even if the recent slowing of population growth continues, the world will have 8 billion people by 2050. This many people cannot consume at the current level of people in the high-income countries. Analysts are divided, with some arguing that we must hold the line at about 7 billion, and some maintaining that we must *decrease* population in the coming decades (Smail, 2004).

2. **Conserve finite resources.** This means meeting our needs with a responsible eye toward the future by using resources efficiently, seeking alternative sources of energy, and, in some cases, learning to live with less.

3. **Reduce waste.** Whenever possible, simply using less is the best way to do this. But recycling programs are also part of the answer.

In the end, making all three of these strategies work depends on a more basic change in the way we think about ourselves and our world. Our *egocentric* outlook sets our own interests as standards for how to live; a sustainable environment demands an *ecocentric* outlook that helps us see that the present is tied to the future and that everyone must work together. Most nations in the southern half of the world are economically *underdeveloped*, unable to meet the basic needs of their people. At the same time, most countries in the northern half of the world are economically *overdeveloped*, using more resources than the Earth can sustain over time. Changes needed to create a sustainable ecosystem will not come easily, but the consequences of not responding to the growing environmental deficit will certainly be more difficult to endure (Kellert & Bormann, 1991; Brown et al., 1993; Population Action International, 2000).

Finally, consider that the great dinosaurs dominated this planet for some 160 million years and then perished forever. Humanity is far younger, having existed for a mere 250 000 years. Compared to the rather dim-witted dinosaurs, our species has the gift of great intelligence. But how will we use this ability? What are the chances that humans will continue to flourish 160 million years—or even 1000 years—from now? The answer depends on the choices made by one of the 30 million species living on Earth: human beings.

Summary

Population

1. Fertility and mortality, measured as crude birth rates and crude death rates, are major factors affecting population size. In global terms, Canadian population growth is low.

2. Migration, another key demographic concept, has special importance to population increase in Canada and to the growth of cities everywhere.

3. Demographers use age–sex pyramids to graphically show the composition of a population and to project population trends. The sex ratio is a society's balance of males to females.

4. Historically, world population grew slowly because high birth rates were largely offset by high death rates. About 1750, a demographic transition began as world population rose sharply, mostly because of falling death rates.

5. Thomas Robert Malthus warned that population growth would outpace food production, resulting in social calamity. Demographic transition theory, however, contends that technological advances gradually slow population increase.

6. World population is expected to reach 8–9 billion by 2050. Such an increase will likely overwhelm many low-income societies, where most of the increase will take place.

Urbanization

1. The first urban revolution began with the appearance of cities about 8000 BCE. By the start of the common era, cities had emerged in most regions of the world except North America.

2. Pre-industrial cities have low-rise buildings, narrow, winding streets, and personal social ties.

3. A second urban revolution began in about 1750 as the Industrial Revolution propelled rapid urban growth in Europe. The physical form of cities changed as planners created wide, regular streets to facilitate trade. The focus on commerce, as well as swelling population, made urban life more anonymous.

4. Urbanism came to North America with Europeans, who settled in a string of colonial towns dotting the Atlantic coastline. By 1850, hundreds of new cities had been founded from coast to coast.

5. By 1931, a majority of the Canadian population lived in urban areas.

6. Rapid urbanization in Europe during the nineteenth century led early sociologists to contrast rural and urban life. Ferdinand Tönnies built his analysis on the concepts of *Gemeinschaft* and *Gesellschaft*, and Emile Durkheim devised parallel concepts of mechanical solidarity and organic solidarity. Georg Simmel claimed that the overstimulation of city life produced a blasé attitude in urbanites.

7. At the University of Chicago, Robert Park taught that cities permit great social freedom. Louis Wirth saw large, dense, heterogeneous populations creating an impersonal and self-interested but tolerant way of life. Other researchers have explored urban ecology and urban political economy.

8. A third urban revolution is now occurring in low-income countries, where most of the world's largest cities will soon be found.

Environment

1. A key factor affecting the natural environment is how human beings organize social life. Therefore, ecologists study how living organisms interact with their environment.

2. Societies increase the environmental deficit by focusing on short-term benefits and ignoring the long-term consequences of their way of life.

3. Our ability to alter the natural world lies in our capacity for culture. Humanity's effect on the environment has increased along with the development of complex technology.

4. The "logic of growth" thesis supports economic development, claiming that people can solve environmental problems as they arise. The opposing "limits to growth" thesis states that societies must curb development to prevent eventual environmental collapse.

5. Environmental issues include disposing of solid waste and protecting the quality of air and water. The supply of clean water is already low in some parts of the world.

6. Rainforests help remove carbon dioxide from the atmosphere and are home to a large share of this planet's living species. Under pressure from commercial interests, the world's rainforests are now half their original size and are shrinking by about 1 percent annually.

7. Environmental racism is the pattern by which the poor, especially minorities, suffer most from environmental hazards.

8. A sustainable environment does not threaten the well-being of future generations. Achieving this goal requires controlling world population, conserving finite resources, and reducing waste and pollution.

KEY CONCEPTS

Population

age–sex pyramid (p. 417) a graphic representation of the age and sex of a population

crude birth rate (p. 414) the number of live births in a given year for every 1000 people in a population

crude death rate (p. 414) the number of deaths in a given year for every 1000 people in a population

demographic transition theory (p. 419) the thesis that population patterns reflect a society's level of technological development

demography (p. 414) the study of human population

fertility (p. 414) the incidence of childbearing in a country's population

infant mortality rate (p. 415) the number of deaths among infants under one year of age for each 1000 live births in a given year

life expectancy (p. 415) the average life span of a country's population

migration (p. 415) the movement of people into and out of a specified territory

mortality (p. 414) the incidence of death in a country's population

sex ratio (p. 417) the number of males for every 100 females in a nation's population

zero population growth (p. 420) the level of reproduction that maintains population at a steady state

Urbanization

Gemeinschaft (p. 426) a type of social organization in which people are closely linked by kinship and tradition

Gesellschaft (p. 426) a type of social organization in which people come together only on the basis of individual self-interest

megalopolis (p. 425) a vast urban region containing a number of cities and their surrounding suburbs

metropolis (p. 425) a large city that socially and economically dominates an urban area

suburbs (p. 425) urban areas beyond the political boundaries of a city

urban ecology (p. 429) the study of the link between the physical and social dimensions of cities

urbanization (p. 421) the concentration of humanity into cities

Environment

ecologically sustainable culture (p. 441) a way of life that meets the needs of the present generation without threatening the environmental legacy of future generations

ecology (p. 430) the study of the interaction of living organisms and the natural environment

ecosystem (p. 431) a system composed of the interaction of all living organisms and their natural environment

environmental deficit (p. 432) profound and long-term harm to the natural environment caused by humanity's focus on short-term material affluence

environmental racism (p. 439) the pattern by which environmental hazards are greatest for poor people, especially minorities

global warming (p. 438) a rise in the Earth's average temperature due to an increasing concentration of carbon dioxide in the atmosphere

natural environment (p. 430) the Earth's surface and atmosphere, including living organisms, air, water, soil, and other resources necessary to sustain life

rainforests (p. 436) regions of dense forestation, most of which circle the globe close to the equator

CRITICAL-THINKING QUESTIONS

1. What are fertility and mortality rates? Which one has been more important in increasing global population?

2. Evaluate the environmental prediction of Thomas Robert Malthus. On balance, do you think he was more wrong or more right? Why?

3. According to demographic transition theory, how does economic development affect population patterns?

4. According to Ferdinand Tönnies, Emile Durkheim, Georg Simmel, and Louis Wirth, what characterizes urbanism as a way of life? Note several differences in the ideas of these thinkers.

APPLICATIONS AND EXERCISES

1. Here is an illustration of the problem of runaway growth (Milbrath, 1989:10): *A pond has a single water lily growing on it. The lily doubles in size each day. In 30 days, it covers the entire pond. On which day does it cover half the pond?* Discuss the implications of your answer for population increase.

2. Draw a map of a city familiar to you with as much detail of specific places, districts, roads, and transportation facilities as you can. Compare your map with a published one or, better yet, a map drawn by someone you know. Try to account for the differences.

3. Get a plastic garbage bag, and carry it around with you for one full day. Put everything you throw away in the bag. At the end of the day, weigh the bag and its contents; multiply this amount by 365 to estimate your yearly "trash factor." Multiply this amount by 33 million to estimate the annual waste of the entire Canadian population.

 SITES TO SEE

www.pearsoned.ca/macionis

The authors and publisher of this book invite you to visit the interactive Companion Website™ that accompanies this text. Begin by clicking on the cover of your book. You will find a chapter-by-chapter study guide, practice tests, suggested weblinks, and links to other relevant material.

www.eclac.org/default.asp?idioma=IN

This site, created by the Economic Commission for Latin America and the Caribbean (part of the United Nations), provides statistics on population patterns for this region of the world. Most of the site is available in both English and Spanish.

www.un.org/popin/wdtrends.htm

Want to learn more about global population trends? Read this report from the United Nations.

www.rioting.com/rioting/index.php?page=webcam

Watch big-city life from the comfort of your own home: this site uses a webcam to show the action at New York City's Fifth Avenue and Forty-Fifth Street. What can you learn from "people watching" in this way? What does this observation *not* tell you about urban life?

www.sierraclub.org

www.greenpeace.org

Here are two environmental sites, maintained by the Sierra Club and Greenpeace, respectively. Visit the sites and see how these two organizations are similar to one another and how they differ.

www.wri.org

The World Resources Institute provides information on the state of the planet's environment.

Follow the instructions on page 33 of this text to access the features of Research Navigator™. Once at the website (**www.researchnavigator.com**), enter your login name and password. Then, to use the Content Select™ database, enter keywords such as "demography," "urbanism," and "global warming," and the search engine will supply relevant and recent scholarly and popular press publications.

To reinforce your understanding of this chapter, and to identify topics for further study, visit MySocLab at **www.pearsoned.ca/mysoclab/macionis** for diagnostic tests and a multimedia ebook.

CHAPTER SIXTEEN

Social Change: Modern and Postmodern Societies

Why do societies change?

How do social movements both encourage
and resist social change?

What have important sociologists said is
good and bad about modern society?

Social change often brings together traditional and modern ways of life. These Aboriginal boys in Australia are discovering the world of the Internet.

In 1900, people lined up at the Paris Exposition to catch a glimpse of some of the world's latest inventions, including something called a "voice recorder" and the Kodak company's first small camera, the "Brownie." The same year, not far away in Germany, a physicist named Max Planck had just discovered atomic radiation, although he was not sure exactly what it was and had little idea of what people might do with it. A doctor named Sigmund Freud, published a book on the interpretation of dreams, which few people found very convincing. Farther east in Russia, a young man named Vladimir Lenin published his first newspaper article calling for a people's revolution to overthrow the government. In China, a rebellion against exploitation by foreign powers started the world thinking about the evils of colonialism. Much farther east and a year later, in Newfoundland, 1901 saw Gugliemo Marconi receiving the first wireless telegraph signal, sent across the Atlantic from Cornwall, England. The young Marconi, then only 27 years of age, had amazed leading physicists all over the world.

It is scarcely possible for people today to imagine how different life was a century ago. Most people in Canada still lived in small towns and on farms. They had no computers, televisions, or radios. Most homes did not even have electricity. There were no superhighways—only a few people had ever seen an automobile (known back then as a "horseless carriage"). Most people travelled around their communities by foot or on horseback, and a few went greater distances by railroad, in passenger cars pulled by steam-powered locomotives. Almost all women worked only in the home; none was permitted by law to vote. For both women and men, life was also much shorter: on average, people lived only about 50 years.

Learn about the lives of men and women in Newfoundland a century ago at http://www.ourroots.ca/e/toc.aspx?id=1327.

It is difficult for us to imagine how different life was a hundred years ago. Not only was life much harder back then, but it was also much shorter. Over the course of the twentieth century, much changed for the better. Yet as this chapter explains, social change is not all positive. On the contrary, change has negative consequences, too, creating unexpected new problems. Early sociologists were mixed in their assessment of *modernity*, changes brought about by the Industrial Revolution. In the same way, today's sociologists point to both good and bad aspects of *postmodernity*, the recent transformations caused by the Information Revolution and the post-industrial economy. One thing is clear: for better or worse, the rate of change has never been faster than it is now.

What Is Social Change?

In earlier chapters, we examined relatively fixed or *static* social patterns, including status and role, social stratification, and social institutions. We also looked at the *dynamic* forces that have shaped our way of life, ranging from innovations in technology to the growth of bureaucracy and the expansion of cities. All of these trends are dimensions of **social change**, *the transformation of culture and social institutions over time*. This complex process has four major characteristics:

1. **Social change happens all the time.** "Nothing is certain except death and taxes," goes the old saying. Yet our thoughts about death have changed dramatically as life expectancy in Canada has doubled since 1850 (Beaujot, 1991). Taxes, meanwhile, were unknown through most of human history, beginning only as societies grew in

size several thousand years ago. In short, virtually everything is subject to the twists and turns of change.

Still, some societies change faster than others. As Chapter 2 ("Culture") explained, hunting and gathering societies change quite slowly; members of technologically complex societies, on the other hand, can witness significant change within a single lifetime.

It is also true that in a given society, some cultural elements change faster than others. William Ogburn's theory of *cultural lag* (see Chapter 2) asserts that material culture (that is, things) usually changes faster than

 Read about how Canadian research granting agencies try to deal with ethics and research using genetic materials, at **http://www.pre.ethics.gc.ca**.

non-material culture (ideas and attitudes). For example, genetic technology that allows scientists to alter and perhaps even create life has developed more rapidly than have our ethical standards for deciding when and how to use it.

2. **Social change is sometimes intentional but often unplanned.** Industrial societies actively promote many types of change. Scientists seek more efficient forms of energy, and advertisers try to convince us that life is incomplete without this or that new gadget. Yet rarely can anyone envision all of the consequences of changes as they are set in motion.

Back in 1900, when the country still relied on horses for transportation, people looked ahead to motor vehicles that would take a single day to carry them distances that used to take weeks or months. But no one could see how much the mobility provided by automobiles would alter life in Canada, scattering family members, threatening the environment, and reshaping cities and suburbs. Nor could automotive pioneers have predicted the more than 3000 deaths that occur in car accidents each year in this country alone.

3. **Social change is controversial.** The history of the automobile shows that social change brings both good and bad consequences. Capitalists welcomed the Industrial Revolution because advancing technology increased productivity and swelled profits. However, workers feared that machines would make their skills obsolete and resisted the push toward "progress." In Canada, changing patterns of social interaction between Aboriginals, visible minorities, and other Canadians, women and men, and gays and heterosexuals give rise to both celebration and backlash as people disagree about how we ought to live.

4. **Some changes matter more than others.** Some changes (such as clothing fads) have only passing sig-

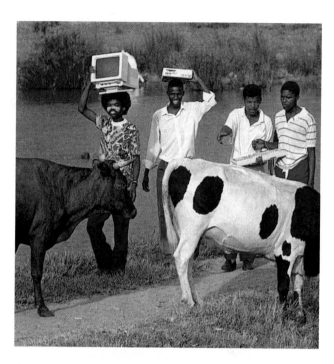

Today, most of the people with access to computers live in high-income countries such as Canada. But the number of people in low-income nations going online is on the rise. How do you think the introduction of new information technology will change more traditional societies? Are all of the changes likely to be for the good?

nificance; other changes (like computers) last a long time and may change the entire world. Will the Information Revolution turn out to be as important as the Industrial Revolution? Like the automobile and television, computers have both positive and negative effects, providing new kinds of jobs while eliminating old ones, isolating people in offices while linking people in global electronic networks, offering vast amounts of information while threatening personal privacy.

Causes of Social Change

Social change has many causes. In a world linked by sophisticated communication and transportation technology, change in one place often sets off change elsewhere.

CULTURE AND CHANGE

Chapter 2 ("Culture") identified three important sources of cultural change. First, *invention* produces new objects, ideas, and social patterns. Rocket propulsion research, which began in the 1940s, has produced sophisticated

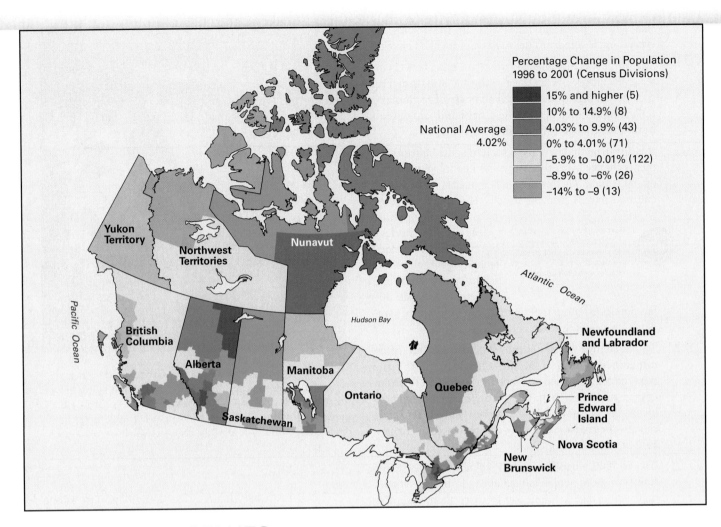

SEEING OURSELVES

NATIONAL MAP 16-1 Population Change, Canada, 1996–2001

The population of the south coast of Newfoundland declined by almost 14 percent between 1996 and 2001. This is a sparsely populated area with fewer than 20 000 people today. Nevertheless, this decline is a tremendous change for these small outports and for the individuals living there—imagine leaving home to go away to your college or university and coming home after graduation to find that every eighth house in your old neighbourhood is now empty. At the same time, York regional municipality outside Toronto grew by almost 25 percent over the same period. What kind of impact do you think rapid demographic change like this has on communities?

Source: Statistics Canada (2003ay).

spacecraft that can reach toward the stars. Today we take such technology for granted; during the present century, a significant number of people will probably experience space travel.

Second, *discovery* occurs as people take notice of existing elements of the world. For example, medical advances offer a growing understanding of the human body. Beyond

their direct effects on human health, medical discoveries have extended life expectancy, setting in motion the "greying" of Canadian society (see Chapter 3, "Socialization: From Infancy to Old Age").

Third, *diffusion* creates change as products, people, and information spread from one society to another. Ralph Linton (1937a) recognized that many familiar aspects of our culture came from other lands. For example, the cloth used to make our clothing was developed in Asia, the clocks we see all around us were invented in Europe, and the coins we carry in our pockets were devised in Turkey.

In general, material things diffuse more easily than cultural ideas. That is, new breakthroughs such as the science of cloning occur faster than our understanding of when—and even whether—they are morally desirable.

CONFLICT AND CHANGE

Tension and conflict within a society also produce change. Karl Marx saw class conflict as the engine that drives societies from one historical era to another. In industrial–capitalist societies, he maintained, the struggle between capitalists and workers pushes society toward a socialist system of production.

More than a century after Marx's death, this model has proven simplistic. Yet Marx correctly foresaw that social conflict arising from inequality (involving not just class but race and gender as well) would force changes in every society, including our own.

IDEAS AND CHANGE

Max Weber also contributed to our understanding of social change. Although Weber acknowledged that conflict could bring about change, he traced the roots of most social changes to ideas. For example, people with charisma (Martin Luther King, Jr., is one example) can carry a message that sometimes changes the world.

Weber highlighted the importance of ideas by revealing how the religious beliefs of early Protestants set the stage for the spread of industrial capitalism (see Chapter 13, "Family and Religion"). The fact that industrial capitalism developed primarily in areas of Western Europe where the Protestant work ethic was strong proved to Weber the power of ideas to bring about change (1958, orig. 1904–05).

DEMOGRAPHIC CHANGE

Population patterns can also transform a society. Profound change is taking place as our population, collectively speaking, grows older. As Chapter 3 ("Socialization: From Infancy to Old Age") explained, 12.8 percent of the Canadian population in 2003 was over age 65, more than twice the proportion in 1900. By the year 2040, seniors will account for 25 percent of the total. Medical research and healthcare services already focus extensively on the elderly, and life will change in countless additional ways as homes and household products are redesigned to meet the needs of growing ranks of older consumers.

Migration within and among societies is another demographic factor that promotes change. Between 1870

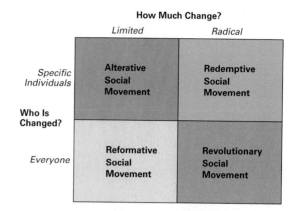

How Much Change?

FIGURE 16–1 Four Types of Social Movements

Source: Based on Aberle (1966).

and 1930, millions of immigrants entered industrial cities. Thousands more from rural areas joined the rush. As a result, farm communities declined, metropolises expanded, and Canada for the first time became a predominantly urban nation. Similar changes are taking place today as people moving from Moncton to Prince George mix with new immigrants from Latin America, Asia, and India.

Where in Canada have demographic changes been greatest? National Map 16–1 provides one answer, showing where population is growing and where it is declining.

SOCIAL MOVEMENTS AND CHANGE

A final cause of social change lies in our own efforts. People commonly band together to form a **social movement**, *an organized activity that encourages or discourages social change.* Our nation's history is the story of all kinds of social movements, from the colonial drive for independence to today's organizations supporting or opposing abortion, gay rights, and gun control.

Types of social movements. Researchers classify social movements according to the type of change they seek (Aberle, 1966; Cameron, 1966; Blumer, 1969). One variable asks, *Who is changed?* Some movements target selected people, and others try to change everyone. A second variable asks, *How much change?* Some movements attempt only superficial change; others pursue a radical transformation of society. Combining these variables results in four types of social movements, as shown in Figure 16–1.

Alterative social movements are the least threatening to the status quo because they seek limited change in only part of the population. Their aim is to help certain people *alter*

One example of a new social movement is the worldwide effort to eliminate land mines. Years after hostilities cease, these mines still remain in place and take a staggering toll in civilian lives. At a protest in Berlin, Germany, a mountain of shoes stands as a memorial to the tens of thousands who have been crippled or died as a result of stepping on buried mines.

their lives. Promise Keepers is one example of an alterative social movement; it encourages Christian men to be more spiritual and supportive of their families.

Visit the Promise Keepers website at **http://www. promisekeepers.org**. *Redemptive social movements* also target specific individuals, but they seek more radical change. Their aim is to help certain people *redeem* their lives. For example, Alcoholics Anonymous is an organization that helps people with an alcohol addiction achieve a sober life.

Reformative social movements aim for only limited change but target everyone. The environmental movement seeks to interest everyone in protecting the natural environment.

Revolutionary social movements are the most extreme of all, striving for major transformation of an entire society. Sometimes pursuing specific goals, sometimes spinning utopian dreams, these social movements—including both the left-wing Communist party (seeking government control of the economy) and right-wing militia groups (seeking the destruction of "big government")—attempt to radically change major social institutions.

Explaining social movements. Sociologists have developed several explanations of both contemporary and historical social movements (Hallgrimsdottir, in press).

Deprivation theory holds that social movements arise among people who feel deprived of something, such as income, safe working conditions, or political rights. Whether you feel deprived or not, of course, depends on your expectations. Thus, people band together in response to **relative deprivation**, *a perceived disadvantage arising from a specific comparison*. This concept helps explain why movements for change surface in both good and bad times: It is not people's absolute standing that counts but how they perceive their own situation in relation to the situations of others (Davies, 1962; Merton, 1968).

Mass-society theory, a second explanation, argues that social movements attract socially isolated people who seek a sense of identity and purpose through their membership. From this point of view, social movements have a personal as well as a political agenda (Melucci, 1989).

Resource mobilization theory, a third theoretical scheme, links the success of any social movement to available resources, including money, human labour, and the mass media. Because most social movements begin small, they must look beyond themselves to mobilize the resources required for success (Meyer & Whittier, 1994; Valocchi, 1996; Zhao, 1998).

Culture theory points out that social movements depend not only on material resources but also on cultural symbols. People must have a shared understanding of injustice in the world before they can mobilize to bring about change. In addition, specific symbols help mobilize people to act (for example, photographs of the burning World Trade Center after the September 11 attacks inspired people to support the military campaigns in Afghanistan and Iraq) (McCarthy & Zald, 1996; J. Williams, 2002).

Visit the Greenpeace website at **http://www.greenpeace.ca**. *New social movements theory* points out the distinctive character of recent social movements in post-industrial societies.

Not only are these movements typically national or international in scope, but most focus on quality-of-life issues—including the natural environment, world peace, animal rights, and gender rights—rather than the traditional concern with economic issues (Tindall, 1994; Tyyskä, 1998). This broader scope of contemporary social movements results from closer ties between governments and between ordinary people around the world, who are now linked by the mass media and new information technology (McAdam, McCarthy, & Zald, 1988; Kriesi, 1989; Pakulski, 1993; Jenkins & Wallace, 1996).

Stages in social movements. Social movements typically unfold in stages. The *emergence* of social movements occurs as people think that all is not well. Some, such as the civil rights and women's movements, are born of widespread dissatisfaction. Others emerge as a small group tries to mobilize the population, as when gay activists raised public concern about AIDS.

Coalescence takes place when a social movement defines itself and develops a strategy for attracting new members and "going public." Leaders determine policies and decide on tactics, which may include demonstrations or rallies to attract media attention.

As it gains members and resources, a social movement may undergo *bureaucratization*. As a movement becomes established, it depends less on the charisma and talents of a few leaders and more on a professional staff, which increases the chances for the movement's long-term survival.

Finally, social movements *decline* as resources dry up, the group faces overwhelming opposition, or members achieve their goals and lose interest. Some well-established organizations outlive their original causes and move on to new crusades; others lose touch with the idea of changing society and choose, instead, to become part of the "system" (Piven & Cloward, 1977; Miller, 1983; Kaufman, 2004).

Modernity

A central concept in the study of social change is **modernity**, *social patterns resulting from industrialization.* In everyday terms, modernity (its Latin root means "lately") refers to the present in relation to the past. Sociologists use this catch-all concept to describe the many social patterns set in motion by the Industrial Revolution, which began in Western Europe in the mid-eighteenth century. **Modernization**, then, is *the process of social change begun by industrialization.* The timeline inside the front cover of this book highlights important events that mark the emergence of modernity.

Peter Berger (1977) identified four major characteristics of modernization:

1. **The decline of small, traditional communities.** Modernity involves "the progressive weakening, if not destruction, of the ... relatively cohesive communities in which human beings have found solidarity and meaning throughout most of history" (Berger, 1977:72). For thousands of years, in the camps of hunters and gatherers and in the rural villages of Europe and North America, people lived in small communities where life revolved around family and neighbourhood. Such traditional worlds give each person a well-defined place that, while limiting choice, offers a strong sense of identity, belonging, and purpose.

Small, isolated communities still exist in Canada, of course, but they are home to only a tiny percentage of our nation's people. These days, their isolation is only geographic: cars, telephones, television, and computers give most rural families the pulse of the larger society and connect them to the entire world.

 Read about Canada's rural profiles at http://www.rural.gc.ca/ research/profile/index_e.phtml.

2. **The expansion of personal choice.** People in traditional, pre-industrial societies view their lives as shaped by forces—gods, spirits, or simply fate—beyond human control. As the power of tradition weakens, people come to see their lives as an unending series of options, a process Berger calls *individualization*. For instance, many people in Canada choose a particular "lifestyle" (sometimes adopting one after another), showing an openness to change. Indeed, it is a common belief that people *should* take control of their lives.

3. **Increasing social diversity.** In pre-industrial societies, strong family ties and powerful religious beliefs enforce conformity and discourage diversity and change. Modernization promotes a more rational, scientific world-view as tradition loses its hold and people gain more and more individual choice. The growth of cities, the expansion of impersonal bureaucracy, and the social mix of people from various backgrounds combine to encourage diverse beliefs and behaviour.

4. **Orientation toward the future and a growing awareness of time.** Premodern people focus on the past; people in modern societies think more about the future. Modern people are not only forward-looking but also optimistic that new inventions and discoveries will improve their lives.

Modern people organize daily routines down to the very minute. With the introduction of clocks in the late Middle Ages, Europeans began to think not in terms of sunlight and seasons but in terms of hours and minutes. Focused on personal gain, modern people demand precise measurement of time and are likely to agree that "time is money." According to Berger, one indicator of a society's degree of industrialization is the share of people wearing wristwatches.

Finally, recall that modernization touched off the development of sociology itself. As Chapter 1 ("Sociology: Perspective, Theory, and Method") explained, the discipline originated in the wake of the Industrial Revolution in Western Europe, at a point when social change was proceeding rapidly. Early European and North American sociologists

George Tooker's 1950 painting *The Subway* depicts a common problem of modern life: weakening social ties and eroding traditions create a generic humanity in which everyone is alike yet each person is an anxious stranger in the midst of others.

George Tooker, *The Subway*, 1950, egg tempera on gesso panel, 18 1/8" × 36 1/8", Whitney Museum of American Art, New York. Purchased with funds from the Juliana Force Purchase Award, 50.23. Photograph © 2000 Whitney Museum of American Art.

tried to analyze the rise of modern society and its consequences, both good and bad, for human beings.

FERDINAND TÖNNIES: THE LOSS OF COMMUNITY

The German sociologist Ferdinand Tönnies (1855–1937) produced a lasting account of modernization in his theory of *Gemeinschaft* and *Gesellschaft* (see Chapter 15, "Population, Urbanization, and Environment"). Like Peter Berger, whose work he influenced, Tönnies (1963, orig. 1887) viewed modernization as the progressive loss of *Gemeinschaft*, or human community. As Tönnies saw it, the Industrial Revolution weakened the social fabric of family and tradition by introducing a businesslike emphasis on facts, efficiency, and money. European and North American societies gradually became rootless and impersonal as people came to associate with one another mostly on the basis of self-interest, the state Tönnies termed *Gesellschaft.*

For a short biography of Ferdinand Tönnies, visit the Gallery of Sociologists at **http://www.TheSociologyPage.com.**

Early in the twentieth century, at least some parts of Canada could be described using Tönnies' concept of *Gemeinschaft.* Families that had lived for many generations in small villages and towns were bound together into a hardworking, slow-moving way of life. Telephones (invented in 1876) were rare (see the timeline inside the front cover of this book); it wasn't until 1915 that someone placed the first coast-to-coast call. Living without television (introduced in 1933 and widespread after 1950), families entertained themselves, often gathering with friends in the evening to share stories, sorrows, or songs. Without rapid transportation (Henry Ford's assembly line began in 1908, but cars became common only after World War II), for many people, the town in which they lived was their entire world.

Inevitable tensions and conflicts divided these communities of the past. But according to Tönnies, the traditional spirit of *Gemeinschaft* meant that people were "essentially united in spite of all separating factors" (1963:65, orig. 1887).

Modernity turns society inside out so that, as Tönnies put it, people are "essentially separated in spite of uniting factors" (1963:65, orig. 1887). This is the world of *Gesellschaft,* where, especially in large cities, most people live among strangers and ignore the people they pass on the street. Trust is hard to come by in a mobile and anonymous society in which, according to researchers, people tend to put their personal needs ahead of group loyalty and an increasing majority of adults believe that "you can't be too careful" in dealing with people (NORC, 2003:181). No wonder researchers conclude that even as we have become more affluent, the social health of modern societies has declined (Myers, 2000).

Critical review. Tönnies' theory of *Gemeinschaft* and *Gesellschaft* is widely used to describe modernization. The theory's strength lies in its synthesis of various dimensions of change: growing population, the rise of cities, and increasingly impersonal interaction. But modern life, though often impersonal, still has some degree of *Gemeinschaft.* Even in a world of strangers, modern friendships can be strong and lasting (Wellman, 1999). In addition, some analysts think that Tönnies favoured—perhaps even romanticized—traditional societies while overlooking bonds of family and friendship that continue to flourish in modern societies.

EMILE DURKHEIM: THE DIVISION OF LABOUR

The French sociologist Emile Durkheim shared Tönnies' interest in the important social changes that resulted from the Industrial Revolution. For Durkheim (1964a, orig. 1893), modernization was marked by an increasing **division of labour**, or *specialized economic activity*. Every member of a traditional society performs more or less the same activities; modern societies function by having people perform highly specialized roles.

Durkheim explained that pre-industrial societies are held together by *mechanical solidarity,* or shared moral sentiments (see Chapter 15). Thus, members of such societies view everyone as basically alike, doing the same work and belonging together. Durkheim's concept of mechanical solidarity is virtually the same as Tönnies' *Gemeinschaft*.

With modernization, the division of labour becomes more and more pronounced. To Durkheim, this change means less mechanical solidarity but more of another kind of tie: *organic solidarity,* or mutual dependency between people engaged in specialized work. Put simply, modern societies are held together not by likeness but by difference: All of us must depend on others to meet most of our needs. Organic solidarity corresponds to Tönnies' concept of *Gesellschaft*.

Despite obvious similarities in their thinking, Durkheim and Tönnies viewed modernity somewhat differently. To Tönnies, modern *Gesellschaft* amounted to the loss of social solidarity because people lose the "natural" and "organic" bonds of the rural village, leaving only the "artificial" and "mechanical" ties of the big city. Durkheim had a different view of modernity, even reversing Tönnies' language to bring home the point. Durkheim labelled modern society "organic," arguing that modern society is no less natural than any other, and he described traditional societies as "mechanical" because they are so regimented. Durkheim viewed modernization not so much as a loss of community as a change from community based on bonds of likeness (kinship and neighbourhood) to community based on economic interdependence (the division of labour). Durkheim's view of modernity is thus both more complex and more positive than Tönnies' view.

Critical review. Durkheim's work, which resembles that of Tönnies, is a highly influential analysis of modernity. Of the two, Durkheim was the more optimistic; still, he feared that modern societies might become so diverse that they would collapse into **anomie**, *a condition in which society provides little moral guidance to individuals.* Living with weak moral norms, modern people can become egocentric, placing their own needs above those of others and finding little purpose in life.

The suicide rate, which Durkheim considered a good index of anomie, did in fact increase in Canada over the course of the twentieth century. The vast majority of North American adults report that they see moral questions not in clear terms of right and wrong but as confusing "shades of grey," also supporting Durkheim's view (NORC, 2003:359). Yet shared norms and values seem strong enough to give most people a sense of meaning and purpose. Whatever the hazards of anomie, most people value the personal freedom modern society gives us.

MAX WEBER: RATIONALIZATION

For Max Weber, modernity meant replacing a traditional worldview with a rational way of thinking. In pre-industrial societies, tradition acts as a constant brake on social change. To traditional people, "truth" is roughly the same as "what has always been" (1978:36, orig. 1921). To modern people, by contrast, truth is the result of rational calculation. Because they value efficiency and have little reverence for the past, modern people will adopt whatever social patterns allow them to achieve their goals.

Echoing Tönnies' and Durkheim's claim that industrialization weakens tradition, Weber declared modern society to be "disenchanted." The unquestioned truths of an earlier time had been challenged by rational thinking. In short, said Weber, modern society turns away from the gods. Throughout his life, Weber studied various modern "types"—the scientist, the capitalist, the bureaucrat—all of whom share the detached worldview that he believed was coming to dominate humanity.

Critical review. Compared with Tönnies and especially Durkheim, Weber was very critical of modern society. He knew that science could produce technological and organizational wonders, yet he worried that science was carrying us away from more basic questions about the meaning and purpose of human existence. Weber feared that rationalization, especially in bureaucracies, would erode the human spirit with endless rules and regulations.

Some of Weber's critics think that the alienation Weber attributed to bureaucracy actually stemmed from social inequality. This issue leads us to the ideas of Karl Marx.

KARL MARX: CAPITALISM

For Karl Marx, modern society was synonymous with capitalism; he saw the Industrial Revolution primarily as a *capitalist revolution.* Marx traced the emergence of the bourgeoisie in medieval Europe to the expansion of commerce. The bourgeoisie gradually displaced a feudal aristocracy as the Industrial Revolution gave it control of a powerful new productive system.

Max Weber maintained that the distinctive character of modern society was its rational worldview. Virtually all of Weber's work on modernity centred on types of people he considered typical of their age: the scientist, the capitalist, and the bureaucrat. Each is rational to the core: the scientist is committed to the orderly discovery of truth, the capitalist to the orderly pursuit of profit, and the bureaucrat to orderly conformity to a system of rules.

Marx agreed that modernity weakened small communities (as described by Tönnies), increased the division of labour (as noted by Durkheim), and encouraged a rational worldview (as Weber claimed). But he saw these simply as conditions necessary for capitalism to flourish. According to Marx, capitalism draws population from farms and small towns into an ever-expanding market system centred in the cities; specialization is needed for efficient factories, and rationality is illustrated by the capitalists' endless pursuit of profit.

 For more on Durkheim, Weber, and Marx, visit the Gallery of Sociologists at **http://www.TheSociologyPage.com**.

Earlier chapters have painted Marx as a spirited critic of capitalist society, but his vision of modernity also incorporates a considerable measure of optimism. Unlike Weber, who viewed modern society as an "iron cage" of bureaucracy, Marx believed that social conflict in capitalist societies would sow the seeds of revolutionary change, leading to an egalitarian socialism. Such a society, as he saw it, would harness the wonders of industrial technology to enrich people's lives and rid the world of classes, the source of social conflict and so much suffering. Although Marx's evaluation of modern capitalist society was highly negative, he imagined a future of human freedom, creativity, and community.

Critical review. Marx's theory of modernization is a complex theory of capitalism. But he underestimated the dominance of bureaucracy in shaping modern societies. In socialist societies, in particular, the stifling effects of bureaucracy have turned out to be as bad as, or even worse than, the dehumanizing aspects of capitalism. The upheavals in Eastern Europe and the former Soviet Union in the 1990s reveal the depth of popular opposition to oppressive state bureaucracies.

Structural-Functional Analysis: The Theory of Mass Society

 June 16, Shelbourne Street at McKenzie. From the car window, we see CIBC, Shell and Petro-Canada gas stations, a Home Depot, Canadian Tire, Safeway, Boston Pizza, and Tim Hortons. This road stop happens to be in Victoria, BC, but it could be just about any city in Canada.

The rise of modernity is a complex process involving many dimensions of change, described in previous chapters and reviewed in the Summing Up table on page 458. How can we make sense of so many changes going on at once? Sociologists have two broad explanations of modern society, one guided by the structural-functional approach and the other based on social-conflict theory.

The first explanation—guided by the structural-functional approach and drawing on the ideas of Tönnies, Durkheim, and Weber—understands modernity as the emergence of *mass society* (Kornhauser, 1959; Nisbet, 1969; Berger, Berger, & Kellner, 1974; Pearson, 1993). A **mass society** is *a society in which prosperity and bureaucracy have weakened traditional social ties.* A mass society is productive; on average, people have more income than ever. At the same time, it is marked by weak kinship and impersonal neighbourhoods, so individuals often feel socially isolated. Although many people have material plenty, they are spiritually weak and often experience more uncertainty about how to live.

THE MASS SCALE OF MODERN LIFE

Mass-society theory argues, first, that the scale of modern life has greatly increased. Before the Industrial Revolution, Europe and North America formed a mosaic of countless rural villages and small towns. In these local communities, which inspired Tönnies' concept of *Gemeinschaft,* people lived out their lives surrounded by kin and guided by a shared heritage. Gossip was an informal yet highly effective means of ensuring conformity to community standards. Such small communities tolerated little social diversity— the state of mechanical solidarity described by Durkheim.

For example, before 1690, English law demanded that everyone participate regularly in the Christian ritual of Holy Communion (Laslett, 1984). Because social differences were repressed in favour of conformity to established norms, subcultures and countercultures were few, and change proceeded slowly.

Increasing population, the growth of cities, and specialized economic activity driven by the Industrial Revolution gradually altered this pattern. People came to know one another by their jobs (for example, as "the doctor" or "the bank clerk") rather than by their kinship group or hometown. People looked on most others simply as strangers. The face-to-face communication of the village was eventually replaced by the impersonal mass media: newspapers, radio, television, and, more recently, computer networks. Large organizations steadily assumed more and more responsibility for the daily needs that had once been fulfilled by family, friends, and neighbours; public education drew more and more people to schools; police, lawyers, and courts supervised a formal criminal justice system. Even charity became the work of faceless bureaucrats working for various social welfare agencies.

Geographic mobility, mass communication, and exposure to diverse ways of life all weaken traditional values. People become more tolerant of social diversity, defending individual rights and freedom of choice. Treating people differently because of their race, sex, or religion comes to be defined as backward and unjust. In the process, minorities at the margins of society gain greater power and broader participation in public life.

The mass media give rise to a national culture that washes over the traditional differences that used to set one region off from another. Mass-society theorists fear that the transformation of people of various backgrounds into a generic mass may end up dehumanizing everyone.

THE EVER-EXPANDING STATE

In the small-scale pre-industrial societies of Europe, government amounted to little more than a local noble. A royal family formally reigned over an entire nation, but in the absence of swift transportation and efficient communication, even the power of absolute monarchs fell far short of that wielded by today's political leaders.

As technological innovation allowed government to expand, the centralized state grew in size and importance. At the time of Confederation, the Canadian government was a tiny organization whose prime function was collecting and allocating taxes to different regions of the country. Since then, government has assumed responsibility for more and more areas of social life—schooling the population, regulating wages and working conditions, establishing standards for products of all sorts, administering healthcare, and offering financial assistance to the ill and the unemployed. To pay for such programs, taxes have soared: today's average Canadian worker labours more than six months a year just to pay for the broad array of services the government provides.

In a mass society, power resides in large bureaucracies, leaving people in local communities little control over their lives. For example, provincial officials mandate that local schools must meet educational standards, local products must be government-certified, and every citizen must maintain extensive tax records. While such regulations may protect people and enhance social equality, they also force us to deal increasingly with nameless officials in distant and often unresponsive bureaucracies, and they undermine the autonomy of families and local communities.

Critical review. The growing complexity of modern life may have positive aspects, but only at the cost of our losing our cultural heritage. Modern societies increase individual rights, tolerate social differences, and raise living standards. But they are prone to what Weber feared most—excessive

Traditional and Modern Societies: The Big Picture

Elements of Society	Traditional Societies	Modern Societies
Cultural Patterns		
Values	Homogeneous; sacred character; few subcultures and countercultures	Heterogeneous; secular character; many subcultures and countercultures
Norms	Great moral significance; little tolerance of diversity	Variable moral significance; high tolerance of diversity
Time orientation	Present linked to past	Present linked to future
Technology	Pre-industrial; human and animal energy	Industrial; advanced energy sources
Social Structure		
Status and role	Few statuses, most ascribed; few specialized roles	Many statuses, some ascribed and some achieved; many specialized roles
Relationships	Typically primary; little anonymity or privacy	Typically secondary; much anonymity and privacy
Communication	Face-to-face	Face-to-face communication supplemented by mass media
Social control	Informal gossip	Formal police and legal system
Social stratification	Rigid patterns of social inequality; little mobility	Fluid patterns of social inequality; high mobility
Gender patterns	Pronounced patriarchy; women's lives centred on the home	Declining patriarchy; increasing number of women in the paid labour force
Settlement patterns	Small-scale; population typically small and widely dispersed in rural villages and small towns	Large-scale; population typically large and concentrated in cities
Social Institutions		
Economy	Based on agriculture; much manufacturing in the home; little white-collar work	Based on industrial mass production; factories become centres of production; increasing white-collar work
State	Small-scale government; little state intervention in society	Large-scale government; much state intervention in society
Family	Extended family as the primary means of socialization and economic production	Nuclear family retains some socialization functions but is more a unit of consumption than of production
Religion	Religion guides worldview; little religious pluralism	Religion weakens with the rise of science; extensive religious pluralism
Education	Formal schooling limited to elites	Basic schooling becomes universal, with growing proportion receiving advanced education
Health	High birth and death rates; short life expectancy because of low standard of living and simple medical technology	Low birth and death rates; longer life expectancy because of higher standard of living and sophisticated medical technology
Social Change	Slow; change evident over many generations	Rapid; change evident within a single generation

bureaucracy—as well as to Tönnies' self-centredness and Durkheim's anomie. The size, complexity, and tolerance of diversity in modern societies all but doom traditional values and family patterns, leaving individuals isolated, powerless, and materialistic. As Chapter 12 ("Economics and Politics") noted, voter apathy is a serious and growing problem in Canada. But should we be surprised that individuals in vast, impersonal societies end up thinking that no one person can make a difference?

Many people marvelled at the industrial technology that was changing the world a century ago. But some critics pointed out that the social consequences of the Industrial Revolution were not all positive. The painting *Trabajadores* (Workers) by Mirta Cerra portrays the exhausting and mind-numbing routines of manual workers.

Mirta Cerra (1904–1986), *Trabajadores,* oil on canvas laid down on panel, 46 × 62 in. (107.3 × 157.5 cm). © Christie's Images.

Critics sometimes say that mass-society theory romanticizes the past. They remind us that many people in the small towns of our past were eager to pursue a better standard of living in cities. This approach also ignores problems of social inequality. Critics say mass-society theory attracts social and economic conservatives who defend conventional morality and are indifferent to the historical inequality of women and other minorities.

Social-Conflict Analysis: The Theory of Class Society

The second explanation of modernity derives mostly from the ideas of Karl Marx. From a social-conflict perspective, modernity takes the form of a **class society**, *a capitalist society with pronounced social stratification.* While agreeing that modern societies have expanded to a mass scale, this approach views the heart of modernization as an expanding capitalist economy, marked with inequality (Habermas, 1970; Polenberg, 1980; Blumberg, 1981; Harrington, 1984).

CAPITALISM

Class-society theory follows Marx in claiming that the increasing scale of social life in modern times has resulted from the growth and greed unleashed by capitalism. Because a capitalist economy pursues ever-greater profits, both production and consumption steadily increase.

According to Marx, capitalism rests on "naked self-interest" (Marx & Engels, 1972:337, orig. 1848). This self-centredness weakens the social ties that once united small-scale communities. Capitalism also treats people as commodities: a source of labour and a market for capitalist products.

Capitalism supports science not just as the key to greater productivity but as an ideology that justifies the status quo. Modern societies encourage people to view human well-being as a technical puzzle that can be solved by engineers and other experts rather than through the pursuit of social justice. For example, a capitalist culture seeks to improve health through advances in scientific medicine rather than by eliminating poverty, which is a core cause of poor health.

Businesses also raise the banner of scientific logic, trying to increase profits through greater efficiency. As Chapter 12 ("Economics and Politics") explained, capitalist corporations have reached enormous size and control unimaginable wealth by "going global" as multinationals. From the class-society point of view, the expanding scale of life is less a function of *Gesellschaft* than the expected and destructive consequence of capitalism.

PERSISTENT INEQUALITY

Modernity has gradually worn away some of the rigid categories that divided pre-industrial societies. But class-society theory maintains that elites persist as capitalist millionaires

SUMMING UP

Two Interpretations of Modernity

	Mass Society	Class Society
Process of modernization	Industrialization; growth of bureaucracy	Rise of capitalism
Effects of modernization	Increasing scale of life; rise of the state and other formal organizations	Expansion of the capitalist economy; persistence of social inequality

rather than nobles born to wealth and power. Canada may have no hereditary monarchy, but the richest 20 percent of families own roughly 80 percent of the country's entire wealth. The wealthiest 10 percent of families—the "very rich"—control over 50 percent of all property, but the richest 5 percent of Canadian families control more than 40 percent of the total wealth in Canada.

What of the state? Mass-society theorists argue that the state works to increase equality and fight social problems. Marx disagreed; he doubted that the state could accomplish more than minor reforms because, as he saw it, real power lies in the hands of capitalists who control the economy. Other class-society theorists add that to the extent that working people and minorities do enjoy greater political rights and a higher standard of living today, these changes came about because of political struggle, not government goodwill. They conclude that despite our pretensions of democracy, most people are still powerless in the face of wealthy elites.

Critical review. Class-society theory dismisses Durkheim's argument that people in modern societies suffer from anomie, claiming instead that most people deal with alienation and powerlessness. Not surprisingly, the class-society interpretation of modernity enjoys widespread support among liberals (and radicals) who favour greater equality and seek extensive regulation (or abolition) of the capitalist marketplace.

A basic criticism of class-society theory is that it overlooks the increasing prosperity of modern societies and the fact that discrimination based on race, ethnicity, religion, and gender is now illegal and is widely regarded as a social problem. Furthermore, a sizable number of Canadians do not want an egalitarian society; they prefer a system of unequal rewards that reflects personal differences in talent and effort.

Based on socialism's failure to generate a high overall standard of living, few observers think that a centralized economy would cure the ills of modernity. Many other problems in Canada—from unemployment, homelessness, and industrial pollution to unresponsive government—are also found in socialist nations such as the former Soviet Union.

The Summing Up table compares views of modern society offered by mass-society theory and class-society theory. Mass-society theory focuses on the increasing impersonality of social life and the growth of government; class-society theory stresses the expansion of capitalism and the persistence of inequality.

Modernity and the Individual

Both mass- and class-society theories look at the broad patterns of change since the Industrial Revolution. From these macro-level approaches, we can also draw micro-level insights into how modernity shapes individual lives.

MASS SOCIETY: PROBLEMS OF IDENTITY

Modernity liberated individuals from the small, tightly knit communities of the past. Most members of modern societies have privacy and freedom to express their individuality. However, mass-society theory suggests that extensive social diversity, isolation, and rapid social change make it difficult for many people to establish any coherent identity at all (Wheelis, 1958; Berger, Berger, & Kellner, 1974).

Chapter 3 ("Socialization: From Infancy to Old Age") explained that people's personalities are mostly a product of their social experiences. The small, homogeneous, and slowly changing societies of the past provided a firm (if narrow) foundation for building a personal identity. Even today, Hutterite communities that flourish in Canada teach young men and women "correct" ways to think and behave. Not everyone born into a Hutterite community can tolerate such rigid demands for conformity, but most members establish a well-integrated and satisfying personal identity (Curtis & Lambert, 1990).

Mass societies are quite another story. Socially diverse and rapidly changing, they offer only shifting sands on

Mass-society theory relates feelings of anxiety and lack of meaning in the modern world to rapid social change that washes away tradition. This notion of modern emptiness is captured in the photo on the left. Class-society theory, by contrast, ties such feelings to social inequality, by which some categories of people are made into second-class citizens (or not made citizens at all), an idea expressed in the photo on the right.

which to build a personal identity. Left to make many life decisions on their own, people—especially those with greater wealth—face a confusing range of options. The freedom to choose has little value without standards to guide the selection process; in a tolerant mass society, people may find little reason to choose one path over another. As a result, many people shuttle from one identity to another, changing their lifestyles, relationships, and even religions in search of an elusive "true self." Given the widespread relativism of modern societies, people without a moral compass lack the security and certainty once provided by tradition.

To David Riesman (1970, orig. 1950), modernization brings changes in **social character**, *personality patterns common to members of a particular society.* Pre-industrial societies promote what Riesman calls **tradition-directedness**, *rigid conformity to time-honoured ways of living.* Members of such societies model their lives on those of their ancestors, so that "living the good life" amounts to "doing what people have always done."

Tradition-directedness corresponds to Tönnies' *Gemeinschaft* and Durkheim's mechanical solidarity. Culturally conservative, tradition-directed people think and act alike. Unlike the conformity often found in modern societies, the uniformity of tradition-directedness is not an effort to imitate a popular celebrity or follow the latest

trend. Instead, people are alike because they all draw on the same solid cultural foundation. Hutterite women and men exemplify tradition-directedness; in the Hutterite culture, tradition ties everyone to ancestors and descendants in an unbroken chain of righteous living.

Members of diverse and rapidly changing societies define a tradition-directed personality as deviant because it seems so rigid. Modern people prize personal flexibility, the capacity to adapt, and sensitivity to others. Riesman calls this type of social character **other-directedness**, *openness to the latest trends and fashions, often expressed by imitating others.* Because their socialization occurs within societies that are continuously in flux, other-directed people develop fluid identities marked by superficiality, inconsistency, and change. They try on different "selves" almost like new clothing, seek out role models, and engage in varied performances as they move from setting to setting (Goffman, 1959). In a traditional society, such "shiftiness" marks a person as untrustworthy, but in a changing, modern society, the chameleonlike ability to fit in virtually anywhere is very useful.

In societies that value the up-to-date rather than the traditional, people anxiously look to others for approval, using members of their own generation rather than elders as role models. Peer pressure can be irresistible to people without strong standards to guide them. Our society urges people to be true to themselves, but when social surroundings

CRITICAL THINKING
Does "Modern" Mean "Progress"? Brazil's Kaiapo Community

The firelight flickers in the gathering darkness. Chief Kanhonk sits, as he has done at the end of the day for many years, ready to begin an evening of animated talk and storytelling (Simons, 2004). This is the hour when the Kaiapo, a small society in Brazil's lush Amazon region, celebrate their heritage. Because the Kaiapo are a traditional people with no written language, the elders rely on evenings by the fire to pass along their culture to their children and grandchildren. In the past, evenings like this have been filled with tales of brave Kaiapo warriors fighting off Portuguese traders in pursuit of slaves and gold.

But as the minutes pass, only a few older villagers assemble for the evening ritual. "It is the Big Ghost," one man grumbles, explaining the poor turnout. The "Big Ghost" has indeed

descended on them: its bluish glow spills from windows throughout the village. The Kaiapo children—and many adults as well—are watching sitcoms on television. Buying a television several years ago has had consequences far greater than anyone imagined. In the end, what their enemies failed to do with guns, the Kaiapo may well do to themselves with prime-time programming.

The Kaiapo are among the 230 000 native people who inhabit Brazil. They stand out because of their striking body paint and ornate ceremonial dress. During the 1980s, they became rich from gold mining and harvesting mahogany trees. Now they must decide if their new-found fortune is a blessing or a curse.

 To see pictures of Brazil's Kaiapo, go to **http://www. ddbstock.com/largeimage/ amindns.html**.

WHAT DO YOU THINK?

1. Why is social change both a winning and a losing proposition for traditional people?
2. Do the changes described here improve the lives of the Kaiapo?
3. Do traditional people have any choice about becoming more modern? Explain your view.

Source: Based on Simons (2004).

---

change so rapidly, how can people develop the self to which they should be true? This problem lies at the root of the identity crisis so widespread in industrial societies today. *Who am I?* and *What is right?* are nagging questions that many of us struggle to answer. In truth, this problem is not so much us as the inherently unstable mass society in which we live.

CLASS SOCIETY: PROBLEMS OF POWERLESSNESS

Class-society theory paints a different picture of modernity's effects on individuals. This approach maintains that persistent inequality undermines modern society's promise of individual freedom. For some, modernity serves up great privilege, but for many, everyday life means coping with

economic uncertainty and a gnawing sense of powerlessness (Newman, 1993; Ehrenreich, 2001; Myles, 2003).

For Aboriginal peoples and Canada's racial and ethnic minorities, the problem of relative disadvantage looms even larger (Leach, 2002). Similarly, although women participate more broadly in modern societies, they continue to run up against traditional barriers of sexism (Blackburn, Brooks, & Jarman, 2003). This approach rejects mass-society theory's claim that people suffer from too much freedom; according to class-society theory, our society still denies a majority of people full participation in social life.

As Chapter 9 ("Global Stratification") explained, the expanding scope of world capitalism has placed more of the Earth's population under the influence of multinational corporations. As a result, more than 75 percent of the world's income is concentrated in high-income nations, where just 18 percent of its people live. Is it any wonder, class-society theorists ask, that people in poor nations seek greater power to shape their own lives?

The problem of widespread powerlessness led Herbert Marcuse (1964) to challenge Max Weber's claim that modern society is rational. Marcuse condemned modern society as irrational for failing to meet the needs of so many people. Although modern capitalist societies produce unparalleled wealth, poverty remains the daily plight of more than 1 billion people. Marcuse added that technological advances further reduce people's control over their own lives. The advent of high technology has generally conferred a great deal of power on a core of specialists—not the majority of people—who now dominate discussion of events such as computing, energy production, and healthcare. Countering the popular view that technology *solves* the world's problems, Marcuse suggested that it is more accurate to say that science *causes* them. In sum, class-society theory asserts that people suffer because modern societies have concentrated both wealth and power in the hands of a privileged few.

Modernity and Progress

In modern societies, most people expect—and applaud—social change. We link modernity to the idea of *progress* (from Latin, meaning "moving forward"), a state of continual improvement. By contrast, we see stability as stagnation.

Given our bias in favour of change, members of our society tend to regard traditional cultures as backward. But change, particularly toward material affluence, is a mixed blessing. As the Critical Thinking box shows, social change is too complex simply to equate with progress.

Even getting rich has both advantages and disadvantages, as the case of the Kaiapo shows. Historically, among people in Canada, a rising standard of living has made lives longer and materially more comfortable. At the same time, many people wonder whether today's routines are too stressful, with families often having little time to relax or simply spend time together. Indeed, in most high-income countries, measures of happiness show a decline over the course of recent decades (Myers, 2000).

Science, too, has its pluses and minuses. As Figure 16–2 shows, people in Canada have considerable confidence—more so than those in most other societies apart from Spain, Nigeria, Russia and the U.S.—that science improves our lives. But surveys also show that many North Americans feel that science "makes our way of life change too fast" (NORC, 2003:346).

New technology has always sparked controversy. A century ago, the introduction of automobiles and telephones allowed more rapid transportation and more efficient

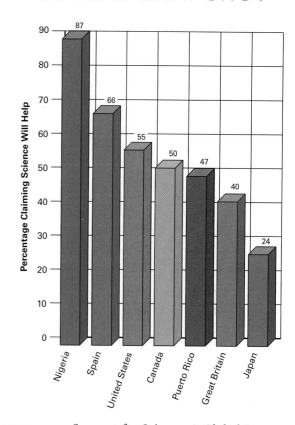

FIGURE 16-2 Support for Science: A Global Survey

Survey question: "In the long run, do you think the scientific advances we are making will help or harm humankind?"

Source: European Values Study Group and World Values Survey Association (2006).

communication. At the same time, such technology also weakened traditional attachments to hometowns and even to families. Today, people might wonder whether computer technology will do the same thing: giving us access to people around the world but shielding us from the community right outside our doors; providing more information than ever before but in the process threatening personal privacy.

In short, we all realize that social change comes faster all the time, but we may disagree about whether a particular change is good or bad for society.

Modernity: Global Variation

 October 1, Kobe, Japan. Riding the computer-controlled monorail high above the streets of Kobe or the

300-kilometre-per-hour bullet train to Tokyo, we see Japan as the society of the future, in love with high technology. Yet the Japanese remain strikingly traditional in other respects: few corporate executives and almost no politicians are women, young people still show seniors great respect, and public orderliness contrasts with the chaos of Canadian cities.

Japan is a nation at once traditional and modern. This contradiction reminds us that although it is useful to contrast traditional and modern social patterns, the old and the new often coexist in unexpected ways. In the People's Republic of China, ancient Confucian principles are mixed with contemporary socialist thinking. In Saudi Arabia and Qatar, a love of the latest modern technology is mixed with respect for the ancient principles of Islam. Likewise, in Mexico and much of Latin America, people observe centuries-old Catholic rituals even as they struggle to move ahead economically. In short, combinations of traditional and modern are far from unusual—rather, they are found throughout the world.

Postmodernity

If modernity was the product of the Industrial Revolution, is the Information Revolution creating a postmodern era? A number of scholars use the term **postmodernity** to refer to *social patterns characteristic of post-industrial societies.*

The term *postmodernism* has been used for decades in literary, philosophical, and even architectural circles. It has moved into sociology on a wave of social criticism that has been building since the spread of left-leaning politics in the 1960s. Although there are many variations of postmodern thinking, all share the following five themes (Hall & Neitz, 1993; Inglehart, 1997; Rudel & Gerson, 1999):

1. **In important respects, modernity has failed.** The promise of modernity was a life free from want. As many postmodernist critics see it, however, the twentieth century was unsuccessful in solving social problems such as poverty, evidenced by the fact that many people still lack financial security.

2. **The bright light of "progress" is fading.** Modern people look to the future expecting that their lives will improve in significant ways. Members (and even leaders) of a postmodern society have less confidence about what the future holds. The strong optimism that carried society into the modern era more than a century ago has given way to widespread pessimism: many people in Canada and the U.S., for example, believe that

life is getting worse (Angus Reid Group Inc., 1998g; NORC, 2003:208).

3. **Science no longer holds the answers.** The defining trait of the modern era was a scientific outlook and a confident belief that technology would make life better. But postmodern critics argue that science has failed to solve many old problems (such as poor health) and has even created new problems (such as pollution and resource depletion).

   Postmodernist thinkers discredit science for implying a singular truth. On the contrary, they maintain, there is no one "Truth." This means that objective reality does not exist; rather, many realities result from "social construction."

4. **Cultural debates are intensifying.** Now that more people have all the material things they really need, ideas are taking on more importance. In this sense, postmodernity is also a postmaterialist era, in which issues such as social justice, the environment, and animal rights command more and more public attention.

5. **Social institutions are changing.** Just as industrialization brought sweeping transformation to social institutions, the rise of a post-industrial society is remaking society all over again. For example, the Industrial Revolution placed *material things* at the centre of productive life; the Information Revolution emphasizes *ideas*. Similarly, the postmodern family no longer conforms to any one pattern; on the contrary, individuals are choosing between many family forms.

Critical review. Analysts who claim that Canada and other high-income countries are entering a postmodern era criticize modernity for failing to meet human needs. In defence of modernity, there have been marked increases in longevity and living standards over the past century. Even if we were to accept postmodernist views that science is bankrupt and progress is a sham, what are the alternatives?

 Check out the Atlas of Canada to find out about our quality of life at **http://atlas.nrcan.gc.ca/site/ english/maps/peopleandsociety/ QOL**.

The Applying Sociology box offers evidence suggesting life in Canada is and is not getting better.

Looking Ahead: Modernization and Our Global Future

Imagine the entire world's population reduced to a single village of 1000 people. About 180 residents of this "global

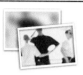

Tracking Change: Is Life in Canada Getting Better or Worse?

We began this chapter with a look at what life was like in 1900—more than a century ago. It is easy to see that in many ways, life is far better today than it was for our grandparents and great-grandparents. But especially in recent decades, the indicators are not so clear-cut. Life may be improving in some respects, but in others it is getting worse. Here is a look at some trends shaping Canada since 1970.

First, the good news: by some measures life in this region is clearly improving. Infant mortality has fallen steadily, meaning that fewer children die soon after birth. In addition, an increasing share of people are reaching old age and, after reaching age 65, are living longer than ever. More good news: the poverty rate among the elderly is well below what it was in 1970. Schooling is another area of improvement: the share of people dropping out of high school is down, while the share completing uni-versity is up, compared to a generation ago.

Now, the bad news: by some measures—several having to do with children—the quality of life in Canada has actually fallen in recent decades. The official rate of child abuse is up, as is the rate of suicide among youths, especially males, and the level of poverty among children is higher than for any other age group. Although the level of violent crime fell through most of the 1990s, it is still above the 1970 level. Economic inequality in this country has also been increasing and we have dropped to eighth place, behind the United States, on the Human Development Index list (United Nations Development Programme, 2003). For almost a decade (up to the year 2001), Canada was ranked number one among 175 countries in the United Nations' Quality of Life survey. In 2004, Canada had dropped to fourth place. According to the United Nations' Gender-Related Development Index, Canada ranks well in this category: 2nd in 2002; however, it was in first place in 1997.

Overall, then, the evidence does not support any simple ideas about "progress over time." Social change has been—and probably will continue to be—a complex process that reflects the kinds of priorities we set for this nation as well as our will to achieve them.

WHAT DO YOU THINK?

1. Some analysts claim that Canadian society contains a contradiction: Over recent decades, we see increasing economic health but declining social health. Based on the data presented here, do you agree? Why or why not?
2. Which of these trends do you find most important? Why?
3. Overall, do you think the quality of life in Canada is improving or not? Why?

village" come from high-income countries. Another 180 people are so poor that their lives are at risk.

The tragic plight of the world's poor shows that some desperately needed change has not yet occurred. Chapter 9 ("Global Stratification") presented two competing views of why 1 billion people the world over are poor. *Modernization theory* claims that in the past, the entire world was poor and technological change, especially the Industrial Revolution, enhanced human productivity and raised living standards in many nations. From this point of view, the solution to global poverty is to promote technological development around the world.

For reasons suggested earlier, however, global modernization may be difficult. Recall that David Riesman portrayed pre-industrial people as *tradition-directed* and likely to resist change. So modernization theorists urge the world's high-income nations to help low-income countries grow economically. The former can speed development by exporting technology to poor regions, welcoming students from these countries, and providing foreign aid to stimulate economic growth.

The review of modernization theory in Chapter 9 points to some success for these policies in Latin America and more dramatic results in the small Asian countries of Taiwan, South Korea, and Singapore, and what is now the Chinese special administrative region of Hong Kong. But jump-starting development in the poorest countries of the world poses greater challenges. Even where dramatic change has occurred, modernization involves a trade-off. Traditional people, such as Brazil's Kaiapo, may gain wealth through economic development, but only at the cost of losing their traditional identity and values as they are drawn into a global "McCulture" based on Western materialism,

Personal Freedom and Social Responsibility: Can We Have It Both Ways?

Shortly after midnight on a crisp March evening in 1964, Kitty Genovese drove into the parking lot of her New York apartment complex. She turned off the headlights, locked the car doors, and headed across the pavement toward the entrance to her building. Out of nowhere, a man holding a knife lunged at her, and as she shrieked in terror, he stabbed her repeatedly. Windows opened above as curious neighbours looked down to see what was going on. The attacker stopped for a moment, but when the windows closed, he went back to his deadly business. The attack continued for more than 30 minutes until Genovese lay dead in her doorway. A follow-up investigation failed to identify the assailant but did confirm a stunning fact: *dozens of neighbours had witnessed the attack on Kitty Genovese, but not one helped her or even called the police.*

Decades later, people still recall the Genovese tragedy in discussions of what we owe one another. As members of a modern, post-industrial society, we prize our individual rights and personal privacy, but we sometimes withdraw from public responsibility and turn a cold shoulder to people in need. When a cry for help is met with indifference, have we pushed our modern idea of personal freedom too far? How can "free" individuals keep a sense of human community?

These questions highlight the tension between traditional and modern social systems, which is evident in the writings of all of the sociologists discussed in this chapter. Tönnies, Durkheim, and others concluded that in some respects, traditional community and modern individualism don't go together. Society can unite its members as a moral community only by limiting their range of personal choices about how to live. In short, although we value both community and freedom, we can't have it both ways.

The sociologist Amitai Etzioni (1993, 1996, 2003) has tried to strike a middle ground. The communitarian movement rests on the simple idea that "strong rights presume strong responsibilities." Put another way, an individual's pursuit of self-interest must be balanced by a commitment to the larger community.

Etzioni claims that modern people have become too focused on individual rights. People expect the system to provide for them, but they are reluctant to support the system. Although most of us believe in the principle of trial by a jury of one's peers, fewer and fewer people today are willing to perform jury duty. Similarly, the public is quick to accept government services but increasingly reluctant to pay for these services through taxes.

Communitarians advance four proposals aimed at balancing individual rights with public responsibilities. First, our society should halt the expanding "culture of rights" by which people have placed their own interests ahead of social involvement (after all, nothing in the Canadian *Charter of Rights and Freedoms* allows us to do whatever we want to). Second, communitarians remind us, all rights involve responsibilities (we cannot simply take from society without giving something back). Third, some responsibilities, such as upholding the law or protecting the natural environment, are too important for anyone to ignore. Fourth, defending legitimate community interests may mean limiting individual rights (protecting public safety, for example, might mean subjecting workers to drug tests).

---

pop music, trendy clothes, and fast food. One Brazilian anthropologist expressed optimism about the future of the Kaiapo: "At least they quickly understood the consequences of watching television. . . . Now [they] can make a choice" (Simons, 2004:495).

Not everyone thinks that modernization is really an option. According to *dependency theory,* a second approach to global stratification presented in Chapter 9, today's poor societies struggle to modernize, even if they want to. From this point of view, the major barrier to economic development is not traditionalism but global domination by rich capitalist societies.

In effect, dependency theory asserts that high-income nations achieved their modernization at the expense of low-income countries, which provided them with valuable natural resources and human labour. Even today, the world's poorest countries remain locked in a disadvantageous economic relationship with rich nations, dependent on wealthy countries to buy their raw materials and in return provide them with whatever manufactured products they can afford. According to this view, continuing ties with rich societies will only perpetuate current patterns of global inequality.

Whichever approach one finds more convincing, we can no longer isolate the study of Canada from the rest of

The communitarian movement appeals to many people who, along with Etzioni, seek to balance personal freedom with social responsibility. But critics from both ends of the political spectrum have attacked this initiative. To those on the left, problems ranging from voter apathy to street crime cannot be solved by some vague idea of "social reintegration." Instead, we need expanded government programs to increase social equality. Specifically, these critics say, we must curb the political influence of the rich and actively fight racism and sexism.

Conservatives on the political right find fault with Etzioni's proposals for different reasons (Pearson, 1995). To them, the communitarian movement amounts to little more than a rerun of the 1960s leftist agenda. The communitarian vision of a good society favours liberal goals (such as protecting the environment) but says little about conservative goals such as allowing organized prayer in school or restoring the strength of traditional families. Conservatives ask whether a free society should permit the kind of social engineering that Etzioni advocates, such as instituting anti-prejudice programs in schools and requiring people to perform a year of national service.

Perhaps, as Etzioni himself has suggested, the fact that both the left and the right find fault with his views indicates that he has identified a moderate, sensible answer to a serious problem. But it may also be that people in a society as diverse as Canada will not easily agree about what they owe to themselves and to one another.

CONTINUE THE DEBATE . . .

1. Have you ever chosen not to come to the aid of someone in need or in danger? Why?
2. Some argue that young people today have a strong sense of "self-entitlement." Do you believe that you differ from your parents in this respect?
3. Do you agree or disagree that our society needs to balance rights with more responsibility? Explain your position.

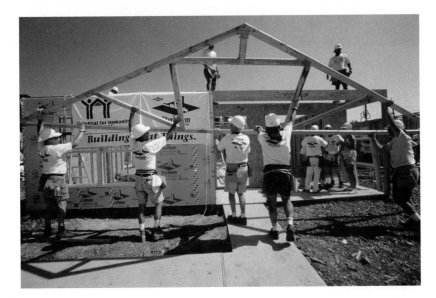

In today's world, people can find new ways to express age-old virtues such as concern for their neighbours and extending a hand to those in need. Habitat for Humanity, an organization with chapters in cities and towns across North America, is made up of people who want to help local families realize their dream of owning a home.

the world. At the beginning of the twentieth century, a majority of people in even the richest nations lived in relatively small settlements with limited awareness of the larger world. Now, with advancing communications technology, the entire world has become one human village because the lives of all people are increasingly linked.

The last century witnessed unprecedented human achievement. Yet solutions to many problems of human existence—including finding meaning in life, resolving conflicts between societies, and eliminating poverty—have eluded us. The Controversy & Debate box on pages 466–67 examines one dilemma of our post-industrial society: balancing individual freedom and personal responsibility. To the list of pressing matters new concerns have been added, such as controlling population growth and establishing a sustainable natural environment. In the future, we must be prepared to tackle such problems with imagination, compassion, and determination. Our growing understanding of human society gives us reason to look to the task with optimism.

Many people see modernity as a mix of promise and danger. The mural *Read Between the Lines* by Mexican-American artist David Botello (1975), found in East Los Angeles, contains the words, "Cuisense Amigos" ("Be careful, friends"). Looking at the mural, what is it about contemporary life in high-income countries such as Canada that Botello is worried about?

David Botello, *Read Between the Lines*, 1975, mural on Ford and Olympic Boulevards, East Los Angeles, acrylic on stucco, 10 × 20 ft.

SUMMARY

1. All societies change, some more quickly than others. Social change often generates controversy.

2. Social change is the result of invention, discovery, and cultural diffusion as well as social conflict.

3. Social movements are deliberate efforts to promote or resist change. Analysts link social movements to relative deprivation, the rootlessness of mass society, an organization's ability to obtain resources, cultural symbols that encourage change, and the operation of the capitalist economy.

4. Modernity results from the process of industrialization, which, according to Peter Berger, includes the weakening of traditional communities, expansion of personal choice, increasingly diverse beliefs, and keen awareness of the future.

5. Ferdinand Tönnies described modernization as the transition from *Gemeinschaft* to *Gesellschaft*, which signifies the progressive loss of community amid growing individualism.

6. Emile Durkheim saw modernization as a function of society's expanding division of labour. Mechanical solidarity, based on shared activities and beliefs, gradually gives way to organic solidarity, in which specialization makes people interdependent.

7. According to Max Weber, modernity replaces traditional thinking with rationality. Weber feared the dehumanizing effects of rational organization.

8. Karl Marx saw modernity as the triumph of capitalism over feudalism. Viewing capitalist societies as arenas of conflict,

Marx spoke out for revolutionary change to achieve a more egalitarian socialist society.

9. According to mass-society theory, modernity increases the scale of life, enlarging the role of government and other formal organizations in carrying out tasks previously performed by family members and neighbours. Cultural diversity and rapid social change make it difficult for people in modern societies to define what is morally good, develop stable identities, and find meaning in their lives.

10. According to class-society theory, capitalism is central to Western modernization. This approach charges that by concentrating wealth in the hands of a few, capitalism generates widespread feelings of powerlessness.

11. Social change is too complex and controversial to be equated simply with progress.

12. "Postmodernity" refers to cultural traits typical of postindustrial societies. Postmodern criticism of society centres on the failure of modernity, especially science, to fulfill its promise of prosperity and well-being.

13. In a global context, modernization theory links global poverty to the power of tradition. Some modernization theorists support policies by high-income societies to assist the economic development of economically less well-off nations.

14. Dependency theory explains global poverty as the product of the world economic system. The operation of multinational corporations ensures that poor nations will remain economically dependent on rich nations.

KEY CONCEPTS

anomie (p. 455) Durkheim's term for a condition in which society provides little moral guidance to individuals

class society (p. 459) a capitalist society with pronounced social stratification

division of labour (p. 455) specialized economic activity

mass society (p. 457) a society in which prosperity and bureaucracy have weakened traditional social ties

modernity (p. 453) social patterns resulting from industrialization

modernization (p. 453) the process of social change begun by industrialization

other-directedness (p. 461) openness to the latest trends and fashions, often expressed by imitating others

postmodernity (p. 464) social patterns characteristic of post-industrial societies

relative deprivation (p. 452) a perceived disadvantage arising from a specific comparison

social change (p. 448) the transformation of culture and social institutions over time

social character (p. 461) personality patterns common to members of a particular society

social movement (p. 451) an organized activity that encourages or discourages social change

tradition-directedness (p. 461) rigid conformity to time-honoured ways of living

CRITICAL-THINKING QUESTIONS

1. How well do you think Tönnies, Durkheim, Weber, and Marx predicted the character of modern society? How are their visions of modernity the same? How do they differ?

2. What traits lead some to call North America a "mass society"? Why do other analysts describe Canada and the United States as "class societies"?

3. What is the difference between *anomie* (a trait of mass society) and *alienation* (a characteristic of class society)? Among which categories of the Canadian population would you expect each to be more pronounced?

4. Why do some analysts believe that Canada has become a postmodern society? Do you agree? Why or why not?

APPLICATIONS AND EXERCISES

1. Most older people will be happy to tell you about the social changes they have seen in their lifetimes. Ask an elderly relative or friend to share this information with you.

2. Ask people in your class or friendship group to make five predictions about Canadian society in the year 2050, when today's 20-year-olds will be senior citizens. On what issues do you agree? disagree?

3. Has the rate of social change been increasing? Do some research about inventions over time to answer this question. For example, consider modes of travel—including walking, riding animals, riding in trains, cars, and airplanes, and flying rockets in space. Walking and riding animals characterized society for tens of thousands of years; the last four modes of transportation emerged in barely two centuries.

 SITES TO SEE

www.pearsoned.ca/macionis

The authors and publisher of this book invite you to visit the interactive Companion Website™ that accompanies this text. Begin by clicking on the cover of your book. You will find a chapter-by-chapter study guide, practice tests, suggested weblinks, and links to other relevant material.

www.utoronto.ca/utopia

Deliberate change sometimes is inspired by visions of utopia—ideal societies that exist nowhere. Read about the Society for Utopian Studies at this website.

www.canadians.org

The Council of Canadians claims to be an independent non-partisan group providing a critical and progressive voice on key national issues.

www.gwu.edu/~ccps

This website describes the goals of the Communitarian Network.

www.acdi-cida.gc.ca//index-e.htm

The Canadian International Development Agency's purpose is to support sustainable development in low-income countries in order to reduce poverty and contribute to a more equitable and prosperous world. The site offers extensive information on the agency's policies and projects.

www.habitat.ca

Habitat for Humanity Canada is a national affiliate of Habitat for Humanity, a non-profit, ecumenical Christian housing ministry dedicated to ending substandard housing and homelessness around the globe.

http://stemcells.nih.gov/index.asp

For an introduction to the recent controversy over stem cell research, check out this website.

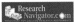
Follow the instructions on page 33 of this text to access the features of Research Navigator™. Once at the website (**www.research navigator.com**), enter your login name and password. Then, to use the Content Select™ database, enter keywords such as "social change," "modernity," and "postmodernity," and the search engine will supply relevant and recent scholarly and popular press publications.

Finally, on a personal note, we hope this book has helped you and will be a useful resource to keep for courses later on. Please visit our webpages and send an email message (**macionis@kenyon.edu; mjansson@uvic.ca; cbenoit@uvic.ca**) with your thoughts and suggestions. And, yes, we will write back!

—John J. Macionis

—S. Mikael Jansson

—Cecilia M. Benoit

www.TheSociologyPage.com
www.macionis.com
http://web.uvic.ca/~cbenoit

To reinforce your understanding of this chapter, and to identify topics for further study, visit MySocLab at **www.pearsoned.ca/mysoclab/macionis** for diagnostic tests and a multimedia ebook.

GLOSSARY

abortion (p. 162) the deliberate termination of a pregnancy

absolute poverty (p. 220) a deprivation of resources that is life-threatening

achieved status (p. 89) a social position a person takes on voluntarily that reflects personal ability and effort

age–sex pyramid (p. 418) a graphic representation of the age and sex of a population

ageism (p. 80) prejudice and discrimination against older people

agriculture (p. 46) large-scale cultivation using plows harnessed to animals or more powerful energy sources

alienation (p. 206) the experience of isolation and misery resulting from powerlessness

animism (p. 365) the belief that elements of the natural world are conscious life forms that affect humanity

anomie (p. 455) Durkheim's term for a condition in which society provides little moral guidance to individuals

anticipatory socialization (p. 72) learning that helps a person achieve a desired position

ascribed status (p. 89) a social position a person receives at birth or takes on involuntarily later in life

asexuality (p. 148) no sexual attraction to people of either sex

assimilation (p. 293) the process by which minorities gradually adopt patterns of the dominant culture

authoritarianism (p. 322) a political system that denies the people participation in government

authority (p. 320) power that people perceive as legitimate rather than coercive

beliefs (p. 43) specific statements that people hold to be true

bisexuality (p. 148) sexual attraction to people of both sexes

blue-collar occupations (p. 207) lower-prestige jobs that involve mostly manual labour

bureaucracy (p. 123) an organizational model rationally designed to perform tasks efficiently

bureaucratic inertia (p. 126) the tendency of bureaucratic organizations to perpetuate themselves

bureaucratic ritualism (p. 125) a focus on rules and regulations to the point of undermining an organization's goals

capitalism (p. 310) an economic system in which natural resources and the means of producing goods and services are privately owned

capitalists (p. 206) people who own and operate factories and other businesses in pursuit of profits

caste system (p. 199) social stratification based on ascription, or birth

cause and effect (p. 17) a relationship in which change in one variable (the independent variable) causes change in another (the dependent variable)

charisma (p. 365) extraordinary personal qualities that can infuse people with emotion and turn them into followers

church (p. 364) a type of religious organization that is well integrated into the larger society

civil religion (p. 368) a quasi-religious loyalty binding individuals in a basically secular society

class society (p. 459) a capitalist society with pronounced social stratification

class system (p. 200) social stratification based on both birth and individual achievement

cohabitation (p. 354) the sharing of a household by an unmarried couple

cohort (p. 81) a category of people with a common characteristic, usually their age

colonialism (p. 240) the process by which some nations enrich themselves through political and economic control of other nations

community-based corrections (p. 190) correctional programs operating within society at large rather than behind prison walls

concept (p. 17) a mental construct that represents some part of the world in a simplified form

concrete operational stage (p. 67) Piaget's term for the level of human development at which individuals first see causal connections in their surroundings

corporate crime (p. 178) the illegal actions of a corporation or people acting on its behalf

corporation (p. 318) an organization with a legal existence, including rights and liabilities, apart from that of its members

correlation (p. 17) a relationship in which two (or more) variables change together

counterculture (p. 52) cultural patterns that strongly oppose those widely accepted within a society

crime (p. 169) the violation of a society's formally enacted criminal law

crimes against property (property crimes) (p. 181) crimes that involve theft of goods belonging to others

crimes against the person (violent crimes) (p. 181) crimes that direct violence or the threat of violence against others

criminal justice system (p. 169) a formal response by police, courts, and prison officials to alleged violations of the law

criminal recidivism (p. 189) later offences by people previously convicted of crimes

critical sociology (p. 20) the study of society that focuses on the need for social change

crude birth rate (p. 414) the number of live births in a given year for every 1000 people in a population

crude death rate (p. 414) the number of deaths in a given year for every 1000 people in a population

cult (p. 365) a religious organization that is largely outside a society's cultural traditions

cultural integration (p. 52) the close relationships among various elements of a cultural system

cultural lag (p. 52) the fact that some cultural elements change more quickly than others, disrupting a cultural system

cultural relativism (p. 54) the practice of evaluating a culture by its own standards

cultural transmission (p. 40) the process by which one generation passes culture to the next

cultural universals (p. 56) traits that are part of every known culture

culture shock (p. 37) personal disorientation when experiencing an unfamiliar way of life

culture (p. 36) the values, beliefs, behaviour, and material objects that together form a people's way of life

Davis-Moore thesis (p. 205) the assertion that social stratification exists in every society because it has beneficial consequences for the operation of society

democracy (p. 322) a type of political system that gives power to the people as a whole

demographic transition theory (p. 419) the thesis that population patterns reflect a society's level of technological development

demography (p. 414) the study of human population

denomination (p. 364) a church, independent of the state, that recognizes religious pluralism

dependency theory (p. 244) a model of economic and social development that explains global inequality in terms of the historical exploitation of low-income nations by high-income ones

descent (p. 342) the system by which members of a society trace kinship over generations

deterrence (p. 188) the attempt to discourage criminality through the use of punishment

deviance (p. 169) the recognized violation of cultural norms

direct-fee system (p. 402) a medical care system in which patients pay directly for the services of doctors and hospitals

discrimination (p. 291) treating various categories of people unequally

division of labour (p. 455) specialized economic activity

dramaturgical analysis (p. 95) Erving Goffman's term for the study of social interaction in terms of theatrical performance

dyad (p. 117) a social group with two members

ecologically sustainable culture (p. 441) a way of life that meets the needs of the present generation without threatening the environmental legacy of future generations

ecology (p. 430) the study of the interaction of living organisms and the natural environment

economy (p. 306) the social institution that organizes a society's production, distribution, and consumption of goods and services

ecosystem (p. 431) a system composed of the interaction of all living organisms and their natural environment

education (p. 378) the social institution through which society provides its members with important knowledge, including basic facts, job skills, and cultural norms and values

ego (p. 66) Freud's term for a person's conscious efforts to balance innate pleasure-seeking drives with the demands of society

endogamy (p. 342) marriage between people of the same social category

environmental deficit (p. 432) profound and long-term harm to the natural environment caused by humanity's focus on short-term material affluence

environmental racism (p. 439) the pattern by which environmental hazards are greatest for poor people, especially minorities

ethnicity (p. 284) a shared cultural heritage

ethnocentrism (p. 53) the practice of judging another culture by the standards of one's own culture

ethnomethodology (p. 93) Harold Garfinkel's term for the study of the way people make sense of their everyday surroundings

Eurocentrism (p. 49) the dominance of European (especially English) cultural patterns

euthanasia (p. 396) assisting in the death of a person suffering from an incurable disease; also known as *mercy killing*

exogamy (p. 342) marriage between people of different social categories

experiment (p. 23) a research method for investigating cause and effect under highly controlled conditions

expressive leadership (p. 114) group leadership that focuses on the group's well-being

extended family (p. 341) a family unit that includes parents and children as well as other kin; also known as the *consanguine family*

faith (p. 360) belief based on conviction rather than scientific evidence

family unit (p. 341) a social group of two or more people, related by blood, marriage, or adoption, who usually live together

family (p. 341) a social institution that unites people in cooperative groups to oversee the bearing and raising of children

feminism (p. 274) the advocacy of social equality for women and men, in opposition to patriarchy and sexism

feminization of poverty (p. 221) the trend of women making up an increasing proportion of the poor

fertility (p. 414) the incidence of childbearing in a country's population

folkways (p. 44) norms for routine or casual interaction

formal operational stage (p. 67) Piaget's term for the level of human development at which individuals think abstractly and critically

formal organizations (p. 122) large secondary groups organized to achieve their goals efficiently

functional illiteracy (p. 389) a lack of the reading and writing skills needed for everyday living

fundamentalism (p. 370) a conservative religious doctrine that opposes intellectualism and worldly accommodation in favour of restoring traditional, otherworldly religion

Gemeinschaft (p. 426) a type of social organization in which people are closely linked by kinship and tradition

gender stratification (p. 256) the unequal distribution of wealth, power, and privilege between men and women

gender (p. 22) the personal traits and social positions that members of a society attach to being female or male

gender (p. 256) the personal traits and social positions that members of a society attach to being female or male

generalized other (p. 69) Mead's term for widespread cultural norms and values we use as a reference in evaluating ourselves

genocide (p. 294) the systematic killing of one category of people by another

gerontocracy (p. 80) a form of social organization in which the elderly have the most wealth, power, and prestige

gerontology (p. 79) the study of aging and the elderly

Gesellschaft (p. 426) a type of social organization in which people come together only on the basis of individual self-interest

global economy (p. 308) expanding economic activity that crosses national borders

global perspective (p. 8) the study of the larger world and our society's place in it

global stratification (p. 230) patterns of social inequality in the world as a whole

global warming (p. 438) a rise in the Earth's average temperature due to an increasing concentration of carbon dioxide in the atmosphere

government (p. 320) a formal organization that directs the political life of a society

groupthink (p. 116) the

tendency of group members to conform, resulting in a narrow view of some issue

hate crime (p. 179) a criminal act against a person or a person's property by an offender motivated by racial or other bias

health (p. 390) a state of complete physical, mental, and social well-being

heterosexism (p. 162) a view stigmatizing anyone who is not heterosexual as "queer"

heterosexuality (p. 148) sexual attraction to someone of the other sex

high-income countries (p. 8) the richest nations with the highest overall standards of living

high-income countries (p. 231) the richest nations with the highest overall standards of living

high culture (p. 48) cultural patterns that distinguish a society's elite

holistic medicine (p. 400) an approach to healthcare that emphasizes prevention of illness and takes into account a person's entire physical and social environment

homogamy (p. 346) marriage between people with the same social characteristics

homophobia (p. 151) the fear of close personal interaction with people thought to be gay, lesbian, or bisexual

homosexuality (p. 148) sexual attraction to someone of the same sex

horticulture (p. 45) the use of hand tools to raise crops

hunting and gathering (p. 45) the use of simple tools to hunt animals and gather vegetation for food

id (p. 66) Freud's term for the human being's basic drives

ideology (p. 204) cultural beliefs that justify particular social arrangements, including patterns of inequality

in-group (p. 117) a social group toward which a member feels respect and commitment

incest taboo (p. 143) a cultural norm that forbids sex or marriage between certain relatives

incest taboo (p. 344) a norm forbidding sexual relations or marriage between certain relatives

income (p. 201) wages or salary from work and earnings from investments

industry (p. 46) the production of goods using advanced sources of energy to drive large machinery

infant mortality rate (p. 415) the number of deaths among infants under one year of age for each 1000 live births in a given year

institutional prejudice and discrimination (p. 292) bias built into the operation of society's institutions

instrumental leadership (p. 114) group leadership that focuses on the completion of tasks

intergenerational social mobility (p. 217) upward or downward social mobility of children in relation to their parents

interpretive sociology (p. 20) the study of society that focuses on the meanings people attach to their social world

intersection theory (p. 270) the investigation of the interplay of race, class, and gender, often resulting in multiple dimensions of disadvantage

intersexed person (p. 141) a human being with some combination of female and male genitalia

intragenerational social mobility (p. 217) a change in social position occurring during a person's lifetime

kinship (p. 341) a social bond based on blood, marriage, or adoption

labelling theory (p. 173) the assertion that deviance and conformity result not so much from what people do as from how others respond to those actions

language (p. 40) a system of symbols that allows people to communicate with one another

latent functions (p. 13) the unrecognized and unintended consequences of any social pattern

liberation theology (p. 363) the combining of Christian principles with political activism, often Marxist in character

life expectancy (p. 415) the average life span of a country's population

looking-glass self (p. 69) Charles Horton Cooley's term for a self-image based on how we think others see us

low-income countries (p. 8, 231) nations with a low standard of living in which most people are poor

macro-level orientation (p. 15) a broad focus on social structures that shape society as a whole

manifest functions (p. 13) the recognized and intended consequences of any social pattern

marriage (p. 341) a legal relationship usually involving economic cooperation as well as sexual activity and childbearing—that people expect to last

Marxist political-economy model (p. 328) an analysis that explains politics in terms of the operation of a society's economic system

mass media (p. 73) the means for delivering impersonal communications to a vast audience

mass society (p. 457) a society in which prosperity and bureaucracy have weakened traditional social ties

master status (p. 89) a status that has special importance for social identity, often shaping a person's entire life

matriarchy (p. 258) a form of social organization in which females dominate males

measurement (p. 17) a procedure for determining the value of a variable in a specific case

medicalization of deviance (p. 175) the transformation of moral and legal deviance into a medical condition

medicine (p. 390) a social institution that focuses on fighting disease and improving health

megalopolis (p. 425) a vast urban region containing a number of cities and their surrounding suburbs

meritocracy (p. 201) social stratification based on personal merit

metropolis (p. 425) a large city that socially and economically dominates an urban area

micro-level orientation (p. 15) a close-up focus on social interaction in specific situations

middle-income countries (p. 8) nations with a standard of living about average for the world as a whole

middle-income countries (p. 231) nations with a standard of living about average for the world as a whole

migration (p. 415) the movement of people into and out of a specified territory

military-industrial complex (p. 332) the close association of the federal government, the military, and defence industries

minority (p. 285) any category of people distinguished by physical or cultural difference that a society sets apart and subordinates

miscegenation (p. 293) biological reproduction by partners of different racial categories

modernity (p. 453) social patterns resulting from industrialization

modernization theory (p. 242) a model of economic and social development that explains global inequality in terms of technological and cultural differences between nations

modernization (p. 453) the process of social change begun by industrialization

monarchy (p. 321) a type of political system in which a single family rules from generation to generation

monogamy (p. 342) marriage that unites two partners

monopoly (p. 318) the domination of a market by a single producer

mores (p. 44) norms that are widely observed and have great moral significance

mortality (p. 414) the incidence of death in a country's population

multiculturalism (p. 49) an educational program recognizing the cultural diversity of Canada and promoting the equality of all cultural traditions

multinational corporation (p. 241) a large business that operates in many countries

natural environment (p. 430) the Earth's surface and atmosphere, including living organisms, air, water, soil, and other resources necessary to sustain life

neocolonialism (p. 241) a new form of global power relationships that involves not direct political control but economic exploitation by multinational corporations

network (p. 119) a web of weak social ties

nonverbal communication (p. 96) communication using body movements, gestures, and facial expressions rather than speech

norms (p. 44) rules and expectations by which a society guides the behaviour of its members

nuclear family (p. 341) a family unit composed of one or two parents and their children; also known as the *conjugal family*

oligarchy (p. 126) the rule of the many by the few

oligopoly (p. 318) the domination of a market by a few producers

organizational environment (p. 124) factors outside an organization that affect its operation

organized crime (p. 178) a business supplying illegal goods or services

other-directedness (p. 461) openness to the latest trends and fashions, often expressed by imitating others

out-group (p. 117) a social group toward which a person feels a sense of competition or opposition

participant observation (p. 25) a research method in which investigators systematically observe people while joining them in their routine activities

pastoralism (p. 46) the domestication of animals

patriarchy (p. 258) a form of social organization in which males dominate females

peer group (p. 72) a social group whose members have interests, social position, and age in common

personal space (p. 97) the surrounding area over which a person makes some claim to privacy

personality (p. 64) a person's fairly consistent patterns of acting, thinking, and feeling

plea bargaining (p. 187) a legal negotiation in which a prosecutor reduces a charge in exchange for a defendant's guilty plea

pluralism (p. 292) a state in which people of all races and ethnicities are distinct but have equal social standing

pluralist model (p. 328) an analysis of politics that sees power as spread among many competing interest groups

political revolution (p. 329) the overthrow of one political system in order to establish another

politics (p. 320) the social institution that distributes power, sets a society's goals, and makes decisions

polygamy (p. 342) marriage that unites three or more people

popular culture (p. 48) cultural patterns that are widespread among a society's population

pornography (p. 152) sexually explicit material that causes sexual arousal

positivism (p. 12) a way of understanding based on science

post-industrial economy (p. 307) a productive system based on service work and high technology

postmodernity (p. 464) social patterns characteristic of post-industrial societies

power-elite model (p. 328) an analysis of politics that sees power as concentrated among the rich

power (p. 320) the ability to achieve desired ends despite resistance from others

prejudice (p. 286) a rigid and unfair generalization about an entire category of people

preoperational stage (p. 67) Piaget's term for the level of human development at which individuals first use language and other symbols

presentation of self (p. 95) Goffman's term for a person's efforts to create specific impressions in the minds of others

primary group (p. 113) a small social group whose members share personal and lasting relationships

primary sector (p. 308) the part of the economy that draws raw materials from the natural environment

primary sex characteristics (p. 141) the genitals, organs used for reproduction

profane (p. 357) an ordinary element of everyday life

profession (p. 314) a prestigious, white-collar occupation that requires extensive formal education

proletarians (p. 206) people who sell their productive labour for wages

prostitution (p. 153) the selling of sexual services

queer theory (p. 162) a growing body of research findings that challenges the heterosexual bias in North American society

race (p. 283) a socially constructed category composed of people who share biologically transmitted traits that members of a society consider important

racism (p. 289) the belief that one racial category is innately superior or inferior to another

rainforests (p. 437) regions of dense forestation, most of which circle the globe close to the equator

rationality (p. 122) a way of thinking that emphasizes deliberate, matter-of-fact calculation of the most efficient means to accomplish a particular task

rationalization of society (p. 122) Weber's term for the historical change from tradition to rationality as the dominant mode of human thought

reference group (p. 116) a social group that serves as a point of reference in making evaluations and decisions

rehabilitation (p. 188) a program for reforming the offender to prevent later offences

relative deprivation (p. 452) a perceived disadvantage arising from a specific comparison

relative poverty (p. 220) the deprivation of some people in relation to those who have more

reliability (p. 17) consistency in measurement

religion (p. 360) a social institution involving beliefs and practices based on a conception of the sacred

religiosity (p. 367) the importance of religion in a person's life

research method (p. 23) a systematic plan for doing research

resocialization (p. 81) radically changing an inmate's personality by carefully controlling the environment

retribution (p. 188) an act of moral vengeance by which society makes the offender suffer as much as the suffering caused by the crime

role conflict (p. 90) conflict among the roles corresponding to two or more statuses

role set (p. 90) a number of roles attached to a single status

role strain (p. 90) tension among the roles connected to a single status

role (p. 90) behaviour expected of someone who holds a particular status

routinization of charisma (p. 320) the transformation of charismatic authority into some combination of traditional and bureaucratic authority

sacred (p. 357) set apart as extraordinary, inspiring awe and reverence

Sapir–Whorf thesis (p. 43) the idea that people perceive the world through the cultural lens of language

scapegoat (p. 291) a person or category of people, typically with little power, whom people unfairly blame for their own troubles

schooling (p. 378) formal instruction under the direction of specially trained teachers

science (p. 16) a logical system that bases knowledge on direct, systematic observation

scientific management (p. 127) Frederick Taylor's term for the application of scientific principles to the operation of a business or other large organization

secondary group (p. 113) a large and impersonal social group whose members pursue a specific goal or activity

secondary sector (p. 308) the part of the economy that transforms raw materials into manufactured goods

secondary sex characteristics (p. 141) bodily development, apart from the genitals, that distinguishes biologically mature females and males

sect (p. 364) a type of religious organization that stands apart from the larger society

secularization (p. 368) the historical decline in the importance of the supernatural and the sacred

segregation (p. 293) the physical and social separation of categories of people

self (p. 68) George Herbert Mead's term for the part of an individual's personality composed of self-awareness and self-image

sensorimotor stage (p. 67) Piaget's term for the level of human development at which individuals experience the world only through their senses

sex ratio (p. 418) the number of males for every 100 females in a nation's population

sex (p. 141) the biological distinction between females and males

sexism (p. 260) the belief that one sex is innately superior to the other

sexual harassment (p. 271) comments, gestures, or physical contact of a sexual nature that are deliberate, repeated, and unwelcome

sexual orientation (p. 148) a person's preference in terms of sexual partners: same sex, other sex, either sex, neither sex

sick role (p. 404) patterns of behaviour defined as appropriate for people who are ill

significant others (p. 69) people—such as parents—who have special importance for socialization

social-conflict approach (p. 14) a framework for building theory that sees society as an arena of inequality that generates conflict and change

social change (p. 448) the transformation of culture and social institutions over time

social character (p. 461) personality patterns common to members of a particular society

social construction of reality (p. 92) the process by which people creatively shape reality through social interaction

social control (p. 169) attempts by society to regulate people's thoughts and behaviour

social dysfunction (p. 14) any social pattern that may disrupt the operation of society

social epidemiology (p. 392) the study of how health and disease are distributed throughout a society's population

social functions (p. 13) the consequences of any social pattern for the operation of society as a whole

social group (p. 112) two or more people who identify and interact with one another

social institution (p. 306) a major sphere of social life, or societal subsystem, organized to meet human needs

social interaction (p. 88) the process by which people act and react in relation to others

social mobility (p. 198) a change in position within the social hierarchy

social movement (p. 451) an organized activity that encourages or discourages social change

social stratification (p. 198) a system by which a society ranks categories of people in a hierarchy

social structure (p. 13) any relatively stable pattern of social behaviour

socialism (p. 310) an economic system in which natural resources and the means of producing goods and services are collectively owned

socialization (p. 64) the lifelong social experience by which individuals develop their human potential and learn culture

socialized medicine (p. 402) a medical care system in which the government owns and operates most medical facilities and employs most physicians

societal protection (p. 189) rendering an offender incapable of further offences temporarily through imprisonment or permanently by execution

society (p. 36) people who interact in a defined territory and share a culture

sociobiology (p. 56) a theoretical approach that explores ways in which human biology affects how we create culture

socioeconomic status (SES) (p. 208) a composite ranking based on various dimensions of social inequality

sociology (p. 4) the systematic study of human society

state capitalism (p. 311) an economic and political system in which companies are privately owned but cooperate closely with the government

state church (p. 364) a church formally allied with the state

status consistency (p. 201) the degree of consistency in a person's social standing across various dimensions of social inequality

status set (p. 89) all the statuses a person holds at a given time

status (p. 89) a social position that a person holds

stereotypes (p. 25) exaggerated descriptions applied to every person in some category

stereotypes (p. 287) exaggerated descriptions applied to every person in some category

stigma (p. 174) a powerfully negative label that greatly changes a person's self-concept and social identity

structural-functional approach (p. 13) a framework for building theory that sees society as a complex system whose parts work together to promote solidarity and stability

structural social mobility (p. 203) a shift in the social position of large numbers of people due more to changes in society than to individual efforts

subculture (p. 49) cultural patterns that set apart some segment of a society's population

suburbs (p. 425) urban areas beyond the political boundaries of a city

superego (p. 66) Freud's term for the cultural values and norms internalized by an individual

survey (p. 24) a research method in which subjects respond to a series of statements or questions in a questionnaire or an interview

symbolic-interaction approach (p. 15) a framework for building theory that sees society as the product of the everyday interactions of individuals

symbols (p. 40) anything that carries a particular meaning recognized by people who share a culture

technology (p. 45) knowledge that people use to make a way of life in their surroundings

terrorism (p. 330) acts of violence or the threat of such violence used as a political strategy by an individual or a group

tertiary sector (p. 308) the part of the economy that involves services rather than goods

theoretical approach (p. 13) a basic image of society that guides thinking and research

theory (p. 13) a statement of how and why specific facts are related

Thomas theorem (p. 93) W.I. Thomas's statement that situations defined as real are real in their consequences

total institution (p. 81) a setting in which people are isolated from the rest of society and manipulated by an administrative staff

totalitarianism (p. 322) a highly centralized political system that extensively regulates people's lives

totem (p. 360) an object in the natural world collectively defined as sacred

tracking (p. 383) assigning students to different types of educational programs

tradition-directedness (p. 461) rigid conformity to time-honoured ways of living

tradition (p. 122) values and beliefs passed from generation to generation

transsexuals (p. 142) people who feel they are one sex even though biologically they are the other

triad (p. 117) a social group with three members

urban ecology (p. 429) the study of the link between the physical and social dimensions of cities

urbanization (p. 421) the concentration of humanity into cities

validity (p. 17) actually measuring exactly what you intend to measure

values (p. 43) culturally defined standards that people use to assess desirability, goodness, and beauty and that serve as broad guidelines for social living

variable (p. 17) a concept whose value changes from case to case

victimless crimes (crimes without complaint) (p. 181) violations of law in which there are no obvious victims

war (p. 330) organized, armed conflict among the people of various nations, directed by their governments

wealth (p. 212) the total value of money and other assets, minus outstanding debts

welfare capitalism (p. 311) an economic and political system that combines a mostly market-based economy with extensive social welfare programs

welfare state (p. 325) a range of government agencies and programs that provide benefits to the population

white-collar crime (p. 178) crime committed by people of high social position in the course of their occupations

white-collar occupations (p. 207) higher-prestige jobs that involve mostly mental activity

zero population growth (p. 420) the level of reproduction that maintains population at a steady state

REFERENCES

ABBOTT, ANDREW. *The System of Professions: An Essay on the Division of Expert Labor.* Chicago: University of Chicago Press, 1988.

ABERLE, DAVID F. *The Peyote Religion Among the Navaho.* Chicago: Aldine, 1966.

ABRAHAMSON, PAUL R. "Postmaterialism and Environmentalism: A Comment on an Analysis and a Reappraisal." *Social Science Quarterly.* Vol. 78, No. 1 (March 1997):21–23.

ABRAHAMSON, PETER. "The Scandinavian Model of Welfare." Conference proceedings in *Comparing Social Welfare Systems in Nordic Europe and France.* Vol. 4 (1999):31–60.

ADAMS, MICHAEL. *Fire and Ice: The United States and Canada and the Myth of Converging Values.* Toronto, ON: Penguin Canada, 2003.

_____. *Sex in the Snow: Canadian Social Values at the End of the Millennium.* Toronto, ON: Penguin Canada, 1997.

ADLER, JERRY. "When Harry Called Sally..." *Newsweek.* (October 1, 1990):74.

ADORNO, T.W. et al. *The Authoritarian Personality.* New York: Harper & Brothers, 1950.

AKERS, RONALD L., MARVIN D. KROHN, LONN LANZA-KADUCE, and MARCIA RADOSEVICH. "Social Learning and Deviant Behavior." *American Sociological Review.* Vol. 44, No. 4 (August 1979):636–55.

ALAM, SULTANA. "Women and Poverty in Bangladesh." *Women's Studies International Forum.* Vol. 8, No. 4 (1985):361–71.

ALI, S. HARRIS. "The Search for a Landfill Site in the Risk Society." *Canadian Review of Sociology and Anthropology.* Vol. 36, No. 1 (February 1999):1–19.

ALLAN, EMILIE ANDERSEN, and DARRELL J. STEFFENSMEIER. "Youth, Underemployment, and Property Crime: Differential Effects of Job Availability and Job Quality on Juvenile and Young Adult Arrest Rates." *American Sociological Review.* Vol. 54, No. 1 (February 1989):107–23.

ALLEN, THOMAS B., and CHARLES O. HYMAN. *We Americans: Celebrating a Nation, Its People, and Its Past.* New York: National Geographic Society, 1999.

ALPHONSO, CAROLINE. "Girl's Death to Escape Bullying Shocks Town." *The Globe and Mail.* (November 17, 2000):A7.

ALTER, JONATHAN. "The Death Penalty on Trial." *Newsweek* (June 12, 2000):24–34.

ALVERSON, HOYT. *Mind in the Heart of Darkness.* New Haven, CT: Yale University Press, 1978.

AMATO, PAUL R. "What Children Learn From Divorce." *Population Today.* Vol. 29, No. 1 (January 2001):1, 4.

AMBERT, ANNE-MARIE. "Toward a Theory of Peer Abuse." *Sociological Studies of Children.* Vol. 7 (1995):177–205.

AMNESTY INTERNATIONAL. "The Death Penalty: List of Abolitionist and Retentionist Countries." [Online] **www.amnesty.org/ailib/intcam/dp/abrelist.htm,** April 3, 2000.

ANDERSON, ELIJAH. "The Code of the Streets." *Atlantic Monthly.* Vol. 273 (May 1994):81–94.

ANDERSON, JOHN WARD. "Early to Wed: The Child Brides of India." *Washington Post.* (May 24, 1995):A27, A30.

ANDERSON, TAMMI L., and LYNN BONDI. "Exiting the Drug-Addict Role: Variations by Race and Gender." *Symbolic Interaction.* Vol. 21, No. 2 (1998):155–74.

ANG, IEN. *Watching Dallas: Soap Opera and the Melodramatic Imagination.* London: Methuen, 1985.

ANGIER, NATALIE. "Scientists, Finding Second Idiosyncrasy in Homosexuals' Brains, Suggest Orientation is Physiological." *New York Times.* (August 1, 1992):A7.

ANGUS REID GROUP INC. *Multiculturalism and Canadians: National Attitude Survey, 1991.* Ottawa: Multiculturalism and Citizenship Canada, 1991.

_____. *The Federal Political Scene.* Public release (December 28, 1995). [Online] **www.angusreid.com/pressrel/DecFedPolScene.html**

_____. *Canadian Views on the Public Education System.* Table accompanying public release (September 7, 1996a). [Online] **www.angusreid.com/pressrel/pubedspt96.html**

_____. *Federal Political Trends and the Public Agenda.* Public release (December 9, 1996b). [Online] **www.angusreid.com/pressrel/fedpoltrendsdec96.html**

_____. *Ontarians' Belief in Miracles & Angels.* Public release (December 25, 1996c). [Online] **www.angusreid.com/pressrel/miraclesdec96.html**

_____. *Public Attitudes on Some Specific Gay Rights Issues.* Public release (June 7, 1996d). [Online] **www.angusreid.com/pressrel/ gayrights.html**

_____. *Public Support for the Federal Gun Control Legislation.* Public release (Dec-ember 23, 1996e). [Online] **www.angusreid.com/pressrel/guncontrol.html**

_____. *Canadians' Attitudes Toward Cloning.* Public release (December 16, 1997a. [Online] **www.angusreid.com/pressrel/pr161297_2.html**

_____. *Infidelity.* Public release (September 14, 1997b). [Online] **www.angusreid.com/pressrel/FIDEL1.html**

_____. *The '97 Election: Late Campaign.* Public release (May 29, 1997c). [Online] **www.angusreid.com/pressrel/97fedelect_latecampaign.htm**

_____. *Women in Politics.* Special report (May 13, 1997d). [Online] **www.angusreid.com/wip/index.htm**

_____. *Canadian Investors Suffered Losses During Stock Market Tumble.* Public release (October 5, 1998a).

_____. *Canadians' Views on Including Sexual Orientation in Human Rights Legislation.* Public release (May 10, 1998b). [Online] **www.angusreid.com/pressrel/pr100598.html**

_____. *Chrétien Continues to Ride High in Public Esteem, But Slight Majority (58%) Would Support Change in Party Leadership Before Next Election.* Tables accompanying press release (July 10, 1998c). [Online] **www.angusreid.com/pressrel/pr100798.html**

_____. *Healthcare Overtakes All Issues on Public Agenda.* Tables accompanying public release (July 11, 1998d). [Online] **www.angusreid.com/pressrel/pr110798.html**

_____. *Let's Talk About Sex, Tables.* Public release (March 3, 1998e). [Online] **www.ipsos-reid.com/media/content/pdf/pr030398tb.pdf**

_____. *The Public Agenda.* Public release (November 24, 1998f). [Online] **www.ipsos-reid.com/media/content/pdf/pr241198_1.PDF**

_____. *Six in Ten Canadians Believe That Younger Generations Will Be Worse Off Financially Than Their Own.* Public release (August 4, 1998g). [Online] **www.angusreid.com/pressrel/pr040898.html**

_____. *Canadian Teens Voice Their Opinions on Violence in Their Schools.* Public release (May 3, 1999a).

_____. *Canadians' Assessment and Views of the Educational System.* Public release (June 22, 1999b).

_____. *Liberals (47%) Still Tops in Federal Vote and Overall Performance Approval (62%).* Public release (June 17, 1999c), Table 2. [Online] **www.ipsosreid.com/media/content/pdf/pr990617_t2.pdf**

_____. "Click and Connect: New Study Shows that the Internet Has Re-Defined The Social Interactions Of Canadians, By Helping Start New Relationships." (October, 2000a).

_____. *Federal Election Poll: November 24, 2000.* Tables accompanying press release (November 24, 2000b). [Online] **www.ipsos-reid.com/media/content/pdf/mr001124_1t.pdf**

_____. *Federal Political Scene March 2000.* Public release (March 13, 2000c), Tables. [Online] **www.ipsos-reid.com/media/content/pdf/mr000313tb.pdf**

_____. *Federal Political Scene Late May 2000.* Public release (June 2, 2000d), Tables. [Online] **www.ipsosreid.com/media/content/pdf/mr0602tb.pdf**

_____. *Federal Political Scene August 2000.* Public release

(August 18, 2000e), Tables. [Online] www.ipsos-reid.com/media/content/pdf/mr000818tb_2.pdf

_____. *Federal Political Scene Late August 2000.* Public release (August 30, 2000f), Tables. [Online] www.ipsos-reid.com/media/content/pdf/mr000830_1t.pdf

_____. *Federal Political Scene Early October 2000.* Public release (October 16, 2000g), Tables. [Online] www.ipsos-reid.com/media/content/pdf/mr001016tb_2.pdf

_____. *Top Issues on the Public Agenda and Federal Voting Intentions.* Public release (February 6, 2000h), Tables. [Online] www.ipsos-reid.com/media/content/pdf/mr000206_3tb.pdf

ANNAN, KOFI. "Astonishing Facts." *New York Times.* (September 27, 1998):16.

ANNANDALE, ELLEN, and KATE HUNT, eds. *Gender Inequalities in Health.* Philadelphia, PA: Open University Press, 2000.

ANNIS, ROBERT C. "Effect of Test Language and Experimenter Race on Canadian Indian Children's Racial and Self-Identity." *Journal of Social Psychology.* Vol. 126, No. 6 (December 1986):761–73.

APA. *Violence and Youth: Psychology's Response.* Washington, DC: American Psychological Association, 1993.

APPLEBAUM, EILEEN, and ROSEMARY BATT. *The New American Workplace: Transforming Work Systems in the United States.* Ithaca, NY: ILR Press, 1994.

ARAT-KOC, SEDEF. "In the Privacy of Our Own Home: Foreign Domestic Workers as Solution to the Crisis in the Domestic Sphere in Canada." *Studies in Political Economy.* Vol. 28 (Spring 1989):33–58.

ARCHER, DANE, and ROSEMARY GARTNER. *Violence and Crime in Cross-National Perspective.* New Haven, CT: Yale University Press, 1987.

ARIÈS, PHILIPPE. *Centuries of Childhood: A Social History of Family Life.* New York: Vintage Books, 1965.

ARMSTRONG, PAT. "Caring and Women's Work." *Health and Canadian Society.* Vol. 2, No. 1 (1994):109–18.

ARMSTRONG, PAT, and HUGH ARMSTRONG. *Wasting Away: The Undermining of Canadian Health Care.* Toronto: Oxford University Press, 1996.

_____. *Wasting Away—The Undermining of Canadian Health Care.* 2nd ed. Toronto: Oxford University Press, 2003.

ARTZ, SIBYLLE. *Sex, Power, & the Violent School Girl.* Toronto: Trifolium Books, 1998.

ASANTE, MOLEFI KETE. *Afrocentricity.* Trenton, NJ: Africa World Press, 1988.

ASCH, SOLOMON. *Social Psychology.* Englewood Cliffs, NJ: Prentice Hall, 1952.

ASHFORD, LORI S. "New Perspectives on Population: Lessons From Cairo." *Population Bulletin.* Vol. 50, No. 1 (March 1995).

_____. "Young Women in Sub-Saharan Africa Face a High Risk of HIV Infection." *Population Today.* Vol. 30, No. 2 (February/March 2002):3, 6.

ASSESSMENT OF COMMON ASSUMPTIONS." *Social Science Quarterly.* Vol. 75, No. 3 (September 1994):560–79.

ASTONE, NAN MARIE, and SARA S. MCLANAHAN. "Family Structure, Parental Practices and High School Completion." *American Sociological Review.* Vol. 56, No. 3 (June 1991):309–20.

ATKINSON, MICHAEL. *Tattooed: The Sociogenesis of a Body Art.* Toronto: The University of Toronto Press, 2003.

ATTORNEY GENERAL'S COMMISSION ON PORNOGRAPHY. *Final Report.* Washington, DC: U.S. Dept. of Justice, 1986.

BACHRACH, PETER, and MORTON S. BARATZ. *Power and Poverty.* New York: Oxford University Press, 1970.

BACKMAN, CARL B., and MURRAY C. ADAMS. "Self-Perceived Physical Attractiveness, Self-Esteem, Race, and Gender." *Sociological Focus.* Vol. 24, No. 4 (October 1991):283–90.

BAGLEY, ROBIN. *Sexual Offences Against Children: Report of the Committee on Sexual Offences Against Children and Youth.* Ottawa: Canadian Government Publishing, 1984.

BAILEY, WILLIAM C. "Murder, Capital Punishment, and Television: Execution Publicity and Homicide Rates." *American Sociological Review.* Vol. 55, No. 5 (October 1990):628–33.

BAILEY, WILLIAM C., and RUTH D. PETERSON. "Murder and Capital Punishment: A Monthly Time-Series Analysis of Execution Publicity." *American Sociological Review.* Vol. 54, No. 5 (October 1989):722–43.

BAKER, MARY ANNE, CATHERINE WHITE BERHEIDE, FAY ROSS GRECKEL, LINDA CARSTARPHEN GUGIN, MARCIA J. LIPETZ, and MARCIA TEXLER SEGAL. *Women Today: A Multidisciplinary Approach to Women's Studies.* Monterey, CA: Brooks/Cole, 1980.

BAKER, MAUREEN. *Canadian Family Policies: Cross-National Comparisons.* Toronto: University of Toronto Press, 1995.

BAKER, PATRICIA S., WILLIAM C. YOELS, JEFFREY M. CLAIR, and RICHARD M. ALLMAN. "Laughter in the Triadic Geriatric Encounters: A Transcript-Based Analysis." In Rebecca J. Erikson and Beverly Cuthbertson-Johnson, eds., *Social Perspectives on Emotion.* Vol. 4. Greenwich, CT: JAI Press, 1997:179–207.

BALAKRISHNAN, T.R., and FENG HOU. *The Changing Patterns of Spatial Concentration and Residential Segregation of Ethnic Groups in Canada's Major Metropolitan Areas 1981–1991.* Discussion Paper No. 95-2. London, ON: University of Western ON, Population Studies Centre, 1995.

BALAKRISHNAN, T.R., and GEORGE K. JARVIS. "Is the Burgess Concentric Zonal Theory of Spatial Differentiation Still Applicable to Urban Canada?" *Canadian Review of Sociology and Anthropology.* Vol. 28, No. 4 (November 1991):527–40.

BALAKRISHNAN, T.R., E. LAPIERRE-ADAMCYK and K.J. KROTKI. *Family and Childbearing in Canada: A Demographic Analysis.* Toronto: University of Toronto Press, 1993.

BALDUS, BERND, and MEENAZ KASSAM. "'Making Me Truthful and Mild:' Values in Nineteenth-Century Ontario Schoolbooks." *Canadian Journal of Sociology.* Vol. 21, No. 3 (1996):327–57.

BALDUS, BERND, and VERNA TRIBE. "Children's Perceptions of Inequality." In Lorne Tepperman and James Curtis, eds., *Everyday Life: A Reader.* Toronto: McGraw-Hill Ryerson, 1992:88–97.

BALTZELL, E. DIGBY. *The Protestant Establishment: Aristocracy and Caste in America.* New York: Vintage Books, 1964.

_____, ed. *The Search for Community in Modern America.* New York: Harper & Row, 1968.

_____. "The Protestant Establishment Revisited." The American Scholar. Vol. 45, No. 4 (Autumn 1976):499–518.

_____. *Philadelphia Gentlemen: The Making of a National Upper Class.* Philadelphia: University of Pennsylvania Press, 1979a; orig. 1958.

_____. *Puritan Boston and Quaker Philadelphia.* New York: Free Press, 1979b.

BARASH, DAVID. *The Whispering Within.* New York: Penguin Books, 1981.

BARKER, EILEEN. "Who'd Be a Moonie? A Comparative Study of Those Who Join the Unification Church in Britain." In Bryan Wilson, ed., *The Social Impact of New Religious Movements.* New York: The Rose of Sharon Press, 1981:59–96.

BARON, JAMES N., BRIAN S. MITTMAN, and ANDREW E. NEWMAN. "Targets of Opportunity: Organizational and Environmental Determinants of Gender Integration Within the California Civil Service, 1979–1985." *American Journal of Sociology.* Vol. 96, No. 6 (May 1991):1362–1401.

BARON, STEPHEN. "General Strain, Street Youth, and Crime: Testing Agnew's Revised Theory," *Criminology.* 42 (2004):57–483.

BARRY, KATHLEEN. "Feminist Theory: The Meaning of Women's Liberation." In Barbara Haber, ed., *The Women's Annual 1982–1983.* Boston: G. K. Hall, 1983:35–78.

BARTLETT, DONALD L., and JAMES B. STEELE. "Corporate Welfare." *Time.* Vol. 152, No. 19 (November 9, 1998):36–54.

_____. "How the Little Guy Gets Crunched." *Time.* Vol. 155, No. 5 (February 7, 2000):38–41.

BASSUK, ELLEN J. "The Homelessness Problem." *Scientific American.* Vol. 251, No. 1 (July 1984):40–45.

BAUER, P.T. *Equality, the Third World, and Economic Delusion.* Cambridge, MA: Harvard University Press, 1981.

BAYDAR, NAZLI, and JEANNE BROOKS-GUNN. "Effect of Maternal Employment and Child-Care Arrangements on Preschoolers' Cognitive and

480 REFERENCES

Behavioral Outcomes: Evidence From Children From the National Longitudinal Survey of Youth." *Developmental Psychology*. Vol. 27 (1991):932–35.

BC MINISTRY OF EDUCATION. *Uplands Elementary* (School Performance Report). (March 2003a) [Online] **www.bced.gov.bc.ca/reports/school_perf/2002/06161044.pdf**

_____ *Blanshard Elementary* (School Performance Report). (March 2003b) [Online] **www.bced.gov.bc.ca/reports/school_perf/2002/06161059.pdf**

BEATON, ALBERT E. et al. *Mathematics Achievement in the Middle School Years: IEA's Third International Mathematics and Science Study*. Chestnut Hill, MA: Center for the Study of Testing, Evaluation, and Educational Policy, Boston College, 1996.

BEATTIE, KAREN. "Adult Correctional Services in Canada, 2003/04" *Juristat*. Vol. 25, No. 8 (December 2005):1–30.

BEAUJOT, RODERIC. "Gender Models of Family and Work." *Horizons Policy Research Initiative*. Vol. 8, No. 3 (April 2006):24–26.

_____. *Population Change in Canada: The Challenge of Policy Adaptation*. Toronto: McClelland Inc., 1991.

BECKER, HOWARD S. *Outside: Studies in the Sociology of Deviance*. New York: Free Press, 1966.

BEEGHLEY, LEONARD. *The Structure of Social Stratification in the United States*. Needham Heights, MA: Allyn & Bacon, 1989.

BEGLEY, SHARON. "Gray Matters." *Newsweek*. (March 7, 1995):48–54.

_____. "How to Beat the Heat." *Newsweek*. (December 8, 1997):34–38.

BELANGER, ALAIN, and ERIC CARON MALENFANT. "Ethnocultural Diversity in Canada: Prospects for 2017." *Canadian Social Trends*. No. 79 (Winter 2005):18–21.

_____. *Population Projections of Visible Minority Groups, Canada, Provinces and Regions, 2001–2017*. Ottawa: Statistics Canada, Catalogue No. 91-514-XIE. 2005a.

BELL, ALAN P., MARTIN S. WEINBERG, and SUE KIEFER-HAMMERSMITH. *Sexual Preference: Its Development in Men and Women*. Bloomington: Indiana University Press, 1981.

BELL, DAVID, and LORNE TEPPERMAN. *The Roots of Disunity: A Look at Canadian Political Culture*. Toronto: McClelland & Stewart, 1979.

BELLAH, ROBERT N. *The Broken Covenant*. New York: Seabury Press, 1975.

BELLAS, MARCIA L. "Comparable Worth in Academia: The Effects on Faculty Salaries of the Sex Composition and Labor-Market Conditions of Academic Disciplines." *American Sociological Review*. Vol. 59, No. 6 (December 1994):807–21.

BELTRAME, JULIAN, and BRENDA BRANSWELL. "The Enemy Within." *Maclean's*. Vol. 113, Issue 43 (October 23, 2000):36–38.

BEM, SANDRA LIPSITZ. *The Lenses of Gender: Transforming the Debate on Sexual Inequality*. New Haven, CT: Yale University Press, 1993.

BENEDICT, RUTH. "Continuities and Discontinuities in Cultural Conditioning." *Psychiatry*. Vol. 1 (May 1938):161–67.

_____. *The Chrysanthemum and the Sword: Patterns of Japanese Culture*. New York: New American Library, 1974; orig. 1946.

BENJAMIN, LOIS. *The Black Elite: Facing the Color Line in the Twilight of the Twentieth Century*. Chicago: Nelson-Hall, 1991.

BENNETT, STEPHEN EARL. "Left Behind: Exploring Declining Turnout Among Non-College Young Whites, 1964–1988." *Social Science Quarterly*. Vol. 72, No. 2 (June 1991):314–33.

BENNETT, WILLIAM J. "School Reform: What Remains to Be Done." *Wall Street Journal* (September 2, 1997):A18.

BENOIT, C., and F. SHAVER, eds. "Critical Perspectives on Sex Work in Canada." Special issue. *Canadian Review of Sociology and Anthropology*. Forthcoming (2006).

BENOIT, CECILIA. "Gender, Work and Social Rights: Canada, the United States and Sweden as Case Examples." Paper presented at the ISA 14th World Congress in Sociology, Montreal, Canada, July 28, 1998.

_____. "Rediscovering Appropriate Care: Maternity Traditions and Contemporary Issues in Canada." In David Coburn et al., eds., *Health and Canadian Society*. 3rd ed. Toronto: University of Toronto Press, 1998b.

_____. *Women, Work and Social Rights: Canada in Historical and Comparative Perspective*. Scarborough, ON: Prentice Hall Canada, 2000a.

_____. "Variation Within Post-Fordist and Liberal Welfare State Countries: Women's Work and Social Rights in Canada and the United States." In Thomas Boje and Arnlaug Leira, eds. *Gender, Welfare State and the Market: Towards a New Division of Labour*. London: Routledge, 2000b:71–88.

BENOIT, CECILIA, and ALENA HEITLINGER. "Women's Health Caring Work in Comparative Perspective: Canada, Sweden and Czechoslovakia/Czech Republic as Case Examples." *Social Science and Medicine*. Vol. 47, No. 8 (August, 1998): 1101–11.

BENOIT, CECILIA, and ALISON MILLAR. *Dispelling Myths and Understanding Realities: Working Conditions, Health Status, and Exiting Experiences of Sex Workers*. Sponsored by Prostitutes Empowerment, Education and Resource Society (PEERS). Funded by BC Health Research Foundation, Capital Health District, and BC Centre of Excellence on Women's Health, 2001.

BENOIT, CECILIA, and DENA CARROLL. "Aboriginal Midwifery in British Columbia: A Narrative Still Untold." *Western Geographic Series*. Vol. 30 (1995):221–46.

BENOIT, CECILIA, MIKAEL JANSSON, and MURRAY ANDERSON. "Understanding Health Disparities Among Female Street Youth." In Bonnie Leadbeater and Niobe Way, eds., *Urban Girls; Volume II: Building Strengths*. New York: New York University Press, forthcoming.

BENOKRAITIS, NIJOLE, and JOE FEAGIN. *Modern Sexism: Blatant, Subtle, and Overt Discrimination*. 2nd ed. Englewood Cliffs, NJ: Prentice Hall, 1995.

BEN-SHLOMO, YOAV. "Real Epidemiologists Don't Do Ecological Studies?" *International Journal of Epidemiology*. Vol. 34, No. 6 (2005):1181–1182.

BENSON, MICHAEL L., and FRANCIS T. CULLEN. *Combating Corporate Crime*. Boston: Northeastern University Press, 1998.

BERGAMO, MONICA, and GERSON CAMAROTTI. "Brazil's Landless Millions." *World Press Review*. Vol. 43, No. 7 (July 1996):46–47.

BERGER, PETER L. *Invitation to Sociology*. New York: Anchor Books, 1963.

_____. *The Sacred Canopy: Elements of a Sociological Theory of Religion*. Garden City, NY: Doubleday, 1967.

_____. *Facing Up to Modernity: Excursions in Society, Politics, and Religion*. New York: Basic Books, 1977.

_____. *The Capitalist Revolution: Fifty Propositions About Prosperity, Equality, and Liberty*. New York: Basic Books, 1986.

BERGER, PETER, BRIGITTE BERGER, and HANSFRIED KELLNER. *The Homeless Mind: Modernization and Consciousness*. New York: Vintage Books, 1974.

BERGER, PETER L., and HANSFRIED KELLNER. *Sociology Reinterpreted: An Essay on Method and Vocation*. Garden City, NY: Anchor Books, 1981.

BERGESEN, ALBERT, ed. *Crises in the World-System*. Beverly Hills, CA: Sage, 1983.

BERNARD, JESSIE. *The Future of Marriage*. New Haven, CT: Yale University Press, 1982; orig. 1973.

_____. *The Female World*. New York: Free Press, 1981.

BERNARD, LARRY CRAIG. "Multivariate Analysis of New Sex Role Formulations and Personality." *Journal of Personality and Social Psychology*. Vol. 38, No. 2 (February 1980):323–36.

BERNSTEIN, RICHARD J. *The New Constellation: The Ethical-Political Horizons of Modernity/Postmodernity*. Cambridge, MA: MIT Press, 1992.

BERNSTEIN, NINA. "On Frontier of Cyberspace, Data Is Money, and a Threat." *New York Times* (June 12, 1997):A1, B14–15.

BERRY, BRIAN L., and PHILIP H. REES. "The Factorial Ecology of Calcutta." *American Journal of Sociology*. Vol. 74, No. 5 (March 1969):445–91.

BERSCHEID, ELLEN, and ELAINE HATFIELD. *Interpersonal Attraction*. 2nd ed. Reading, MA: Addison-Wesley, 1983.

BERTRAND, JANE, MARGARET MCCAIN, J. FRASER MUSTARD, and J. DOUGLAS WILLIAMS. "A First Tier for Canadian Children: Findings From the Early Years Study in Ontario." *Atlantic Centre for Policy Research*. Fredericton, NB: University of New Brunswick. No. 6 (July 1999):1–4.

BESSERER, SANDRA, and CATHERINE TRAINOR. "Criminal Victimization in Canada, 1999." *Juristat*. Statistics Canada Catalogue No. 85-002-XIE. Vol. 20, No. 10 (November 2000):1–16.

BEST, RAPHAELA. *We've All Got Scars: What Boys and Girls Learn in Elementary School.* Bloomington, IN: Indiana University Press, 1983.

BIANCHI, SUZANNE M., and DAPHNE SPAIN. "Women, Work, and Family in America." *Population Bulletin.* Vol. 51, No. 3 (December 1996).

BIBBY, REGINALD W. *Fragmented Gods: The Poverty and Potential of Religion in Canada.* Toronto: Irwin, 1987.

———. *Unknown Gods: The Ongoing Study of Religion in Canada.* Toronto: Stoddart, 1993.

———. *Restless Gods: The Renaissance of Religion in Canada.* Toronto: Stoddart, 2002.

BIBBY, REGINALD, and MERLIN BRINKERHOFF. "Circulation of the Saints 1966–1990: New Data, New Reflections." *Journal of the Scientific Study of Religion.* Vol. 33 (1994):273–80.

BIBLARZ, TIMOTHY J., and ADRIAN E. RAFTERY. "The Effects of Family Disruption on Social Mobility." *American Sociological Review.* Vol. 58, No. 1 (February 1993):97–109.

BIERNACKI, PATRICK. *Pathways From Heroin Addiction: Recovery Without Treatment.* Philadelphia: Temple University Press, 1986.

BIGGS, LESLEY. "The Case of the Missing Midwives: A History of Midwifery in Ontario From 1795–1900." Ontario History. Vol. 75 (1983):21–35.

BILLSON, JANET MANCINI, and BETTINA J. HUBER. *Embarking Upon a Career With an Undergraduate Degree in Sociology.* 2nd ed. Washington, DC: American Sociological Association, 1993.

BLACKBURN, ROBERT, BRADLEY BROOKS, and JENNIFER JARM. "Occupational Gender Segregation in Canada, 1981–1996: Overall, Vertical and Horizontal Segregation." *Canadian Review of Sociology and Anthropology.* Vol. 40 (2003):197.

BLAU, JUDITH R., and PETER M. BLAU. "The Cost of Inequality: Metropolitan Structure and Violent Crime." *American Sociological Review.* Vol. 47, No. 1 (February 1982):114–29.

BLAU, PETER M. *Exchange and Power in Social Life.* New York: Wiley, 1964.

———. *Inequality and Heterogeneity: A Primitive Theory of Social Structure.* New York: Free Press, 1977.

BLAU, PETER M., and OTIS DUDLEY DUNCAN. *The American Occupational Structure.* New York: Wiley, 1967.

BLAU, PETER M., TERRY C. BLUM, and JOSEPH E. SCHWARTZ. "Heterogeneity and Intermarriage." *American Sociological Review.* Vol. 47, No. 1 (February 1982):45–62.

BLISHEN, BERNARD. *Doctors in Canada.* Toronto: University of Toronto Press, 1991.

BLUMBERG, PAUL. *Inequality in an Age of Decline.* New York: Oxford University Press, 1981.

BLUMER, HERBERT G. "Collective Behavior." In Alfred McClung Lee, ed., *Principles of Sociology.* 3rd ed. New York: Barnes & Noble, 1969: 65–121.

BLUMSTEIN, PHILIP, and PEPPER SCHWARTZ. *American Couples.* New York: William Morrow, 1983.

BOBO, LAWRENCE, and VINCENT L. HUTCHINGS. "Perceptions of Racial Group Competition: Extending Blumer's Theory of Group Position to a Multiracial Social Context." *American Sociological Review.* Vol. 61, No. 6 (December 1996): 951–72.

BOETHUS, MARIA-PIA. "The End of Prostitution in Sweden?" Stockholm: Swedish Institute. No. 426 (October), 1999. [Online] www.si.se/eng/esverige/cs426.html

BOFF, LEONARD, and CLODOVIS BOFF. *Salvation and Liberation: In Search of a Balance Between Faith and Politics.* Maryknoll, NY: Orbis Books, 1984.

BOGARDUS, EMORY S. "Comparing Racial Distance in Ethiopia, South Africa, and the United States." *Sociology and Social Research.* Vol. 52, No. 2 (January 1968):149–56.

BOHANNAN, CECIL. "The Economic Correlates of Homelessness in Sixty Cities." *Social Science Quarterly.* Vol. 72, No. 4 (December 1991): 817–25.

BOHLEN, CELESTINE. "Facing Oblivion, Rust-Belt Giants Top Russian List of Vexing Crises." *New York Times* (November 8, 1998):1, 6.

BOHM, ROBERT M. "American Death Penalty Opinion, 1936–1986: A Critical Examination of the Gallup Polls." In Robert M. Bohm, ed., *The Death Penalty in America: Current Research.* Cincinnati: Anderson Publishing Co., 1991: 113–45.

BOJE, THOMAS, and ARNLAUG LEIRA. *Gender, Welfare State and the Market: Towards a New Division of Labour.* London: Routledge, 2000.

BOLI, JOHN, and GEORGE M. THOMAS. "World Culture in the World Polity: A Century of International Non-Governmental Organization." *American Sociological Review.* Vol. 62, No. 2 (April 1997):171–90.

BONNER, JANE. Research presented in *The Two Brains.* Public Broadcasting System telecast, 1984.

BOOTH, ALAN, and LYNN WHITE. "Thinking About Divorce." *Journal of Marriage and the Family.* Vol. 42, No. 3 (August 1980):605–16.

BORGMANN, ALBERT. *Crossing the Postmodern Divide.* Chicago: University of Chicago Press, 1992.

BORITCH, HELEN. *Fallen Women: Female Crime and the Criminal Justice System in Canada.* Toronto: ITP Nelson, 1997.

BORMANN, F. HERBERT. "The Global Environmental Deficit." *Bioscience.* Vol. 40 (1990):74.

BORMANN, F. HERBERT, and STEPHEN R. KELLERT. "The Global Environmental Deficit." In Herbert F. Bormann and Stephen R. Kellert, eds., *Ecology, Economics, and Ethics: The Broken Circle.* New Haven, CT: Yale University Press, 1991: ix–xviii.

BOTT, ELIZABETH. *Family and Social Network.* New York: Free Press, 1971; orig. 1957.

BOUCHARD, BRIGITTE, and JOHN ZHAO. "University Education: Recent Trends in Participation." *Education Quarterly Review.* Vol. 6, No. 4 (August 2000):24–32.

BOURDIEU, PIERRE and JEAN-CLAUDE PASSERON. *Reproduction in Education, Society and Culture.* Newbury Park, CA: Sage, 1990.

BOURGEAULT, IVY, CECILIA BENOIT, and ROBBIE DAVIS-FLOYD, eds. *Reconceiving Midwifery.* Montreal-Kingston: McGill-Queen's University Press, 2004.

BOWLBY, GEOFF. "The Labour Market Review." Perspectives on Labour and Income. Statistics Canada Catalogue No. 75-001-XIE. Vol. 2, No. 1 (January 2001):5–35.

BOWLES, SAMUEL, and HERBERT GINTIS. *Schooling in Capitalist America: Educational Reform and the Contradictions of Economic Life.* New York: Basic Books, 1976.

BOYCE, WILLIAM. "Young People in Canada: Their Health and Well-Being." Ottawa: Health Canada. Canada Catalogue No. h39-498/2004e

BOYCE, WILLIAM, Doherty, MacKinnon, and Fortin (2003). "Canadian Youth, Sexual Health and HIV/AIDS Study: Factors Influencing Knowledge, Attitudes and Behaviours." Toronto: Council of Ministers of Education, Canada. [Online] http://www.cmec.ca/publications/aids/

BOYD, DAVID. (2003) "Thanks to a Tax Loophole, Corporate Crime Does Pay." *The Globe and Mail.* (March 28, 2003):A17.

BOYER, DEBRA. "Male Prostitution and Homosexual Identity." *Journal of Homosexuality.* Vol. 17, Nos. 1, 2 (1989):151–84.

BOZA, TANYA GOLASH. Proposed American Sociological Association Statement on "Race." [Online] www.unc.edu/~tatiana/, available October 24, 2002.

BRADY Campaign to Prevent Gun Violence. "Did you know?" 2003. [Online] www.bradycampaign.org/about/contact/index.asp

BRAITHWAITE, JOHN. "The Myth of Social Class and Criminality Reconsidered." *American Sociological Review.* Vol. 46, No. 1 (February 1981):36–57.

BRAND, DIONNE. No Burden to Carry: Narrative of Black Working Women in Ontario, 1920s to 1950s. Toronto: Women's Press, 1992.

BRETON, RAYMOND. *Ethnic Relations in Canada: Institutional Dynamics.* Montreal/Kingston: McGill-Queen's University Pres, 2005.

BRETON, RAYMOND, NORBERT HARTMANN, JOS LENNARDS, and PAUL B. REED. *A Fragile Social Fabric? Fairness, Trust, and Commitment in Canada.* Montreal/Kingston: McGill-Queen's University Press, 2004.

BRINTON, CRANE. *The Anatomy of Revolution.* New York: Vintage Books, 1965.

BRINTON, MARY C. "The Social-Institutional Bases of Gender Stratification:

Japan as an Illustrative Case." *American Journal of Sociology.* Vol. 94, No. 2 (September 1988):300–34.

BROCK, DEBORAH. *Making Work, Making Trouble: Prostitution as a Social Problem.* Toronto: University of Toronto Press, 1998.

BROCKERHOFF, MARTIN P. "An Urbanizing World." *Population Bulletin.* Vol. 55, No. 3 (September 2000).

BROWN, J. DAVID. "The Professional Ex-: An Alternative for Exiting the Deviant Career." In E. Rubington and M. Weinberg, eds., *Deviance: The Symbolic Interactionist Perspective.* 6th ed. Boston: Allyn and Bacon, 1996:439–56.

BROWN, LESTER R. et al., eds. *State of the World 1993: A Worldwatch Institute Report on Progress Toward a Sustainable Society.* New York: Norton, 1993.

BROWN, MARY ELLEN, ed. *Television and Women's Culture: The Politics of the Popular.* Newbury Park, CA: Sage, 1990.

BROWNING, CHRISTOPHER R., and EDWARD O. LAUMANN. "Sexual Contact Between Children and Adults: A Life Course Perspective." *American Sociological Review.* Vol. 62, No. 5 (August 1997):540–60.

BRUCKERT, C., C. PARENT, and P. ROBITAILLE. "Erotic Service/Erotic Dance Establishments: Two Types of Marginalized Labour." Ottawa: The Law Commission of Canada, 2003.

BRYM, ROBERT J., and BONNIE J. FOX. *From Culture to Power: The Sociology of English Canada.* Toronto: Oxford University Press, 1989.

BURAWAY, MICHAEL. "Review Essay: The Soviet Descent Into Capitalism." *American Journal of Sociology.* Vol. 102, No. 5 (March 1997):1430–44.

BURKE, TOM. "The Future." In Sir Edmund Hillary, ed., *Ecology 2000: The Changing Face of the Earth.* New York: Beaufort Books, 1984:227–41.

BURKETT, ELINOR. "God Created Me to Be a Slave." *New York Times Sunday Magazine* (October 12, 1997):56–60.

BURR, GRANT N., STEPHEN WONG, SARAH VANDER VEEN, and DEQIANG GU. "Three Strikes and You're Out: An Investigation of False Positive Rates Using a Canadian Sample." *Federal Probation.* Vol. 64, No. 1 (June 2000):3–6.

BURSTEIN, PAUL. "Legal Mobilization as a Social Movement Tactic: The Struggle for Equal Employment Opportunity." *American Journal of Sociology.* Vol. 96, No. 5 (March 1991):1201–25.

BUSINESS WEEK. "Online Privacy: It's Time for Rules in Wonderland." *Business Week.* March 20, 2000:82–96.

BUSSIÈRE, PATRICK, FERNADO CARTWRIGHT, and TAMARA KNIGHTON. *Measuring Up: Canadian Results of the OECD PISA Study.* Ottawa: Statistics Canada, 2004.

BUTLIN, GEORGE. "Determinants of University and Community College Leaving." *Education Quarterly Review.* Statistics Canada No. 81-003-XIE. Vol. 6, No. 4 (August 2000):8–23.

CALLAHAN, DANIEL. *Setting Limits: Medical Goals in an Aging Society.* New York: Simon & Shuster, 1987.

CAMPBELL, ANNE. *The Girls in the Gang: A Report From New York City.* Oxford: Basil Blackwell, 1984.

CAMERON, WILLIAM BRUCE. *Modern Social Movements: A Sociological Outline.* New York: Random House, 1966.

CAMPBELL, ROBERT A., and JAMES E. CURTIS. "Religious Involvement Across Societies." *Journal for the Scientific Study of Religion.* Vol. 33, No. 3 (September 1994):217–29.

CANADIAN CENTRE FOR DRUG-FREE SPORT. *Over 80 000 Young Canadians Using Anabolic Steroids.* Ottawa: News Release, 1993. [Online] **www.hc-sc.gc.ca/main/hppb/nutrition/pube/vtlk/vitlk07.htm**

CANADIAN GEOGRAPHIC. "Landfill Landscape." Vol. 111, No. 4 (May/June 1999):56–65.

CANADIAN INSTITUTE FOR HEALTH INFORMATION. *Health Care in Canada: A First Annual Report.* Ottawa: Statistics Canada, 2000.

CANADIAN INSTITUTE FOR HEALTH INFORMATION. *Nursing Workforce Getting Older: One in Three Canadian Nurses is 50 or Older.* Ottawa, 2004. [Online] **http://secure.cihi.ca/cihiweb/dispPage.jsp?cw_page=media_14dec2004_e**

CANADIAN MEDICAL ASSOCIATION JOURNAL. Editorial. "Prostitution Laws: Health Risks and Hypocrisy." *Canadian Medical Association Journal.* Vol. 171, No. 2 (2004):109–110.

CANADIAN PRESS NEWSWIRE. *Reporter Recovering From Murder Attempt Says Tougher Biker Laws Needed.* October 21, 2000.

CANADIAN SOCIOLOGY AND ANTHROPOLOGY ASSOCIATION. 1994. [Online] **www.arts.ubc.ca/csaa/eng/englcode.htm**

CANTOR, MURIAL G., and SUZANNE PINGREE. *The Soap Opera.* Beverly Hills, CA: Sage, 1983.

CAPLOW, THEODORE et al. *Middletown Families.* Minneapolis: University of Minnesota Press, 1982.

CAPLOW, THEODORE, HOWARD M. BAHR, JOHN MODELL, and BRUCE A. CHADWICK. *Recent Social Trends in the United States, 1960–1990.* Montreal: McGill-Queen's University Press, 1991.

CARLEY, KATHLEEN. "A Theory of Group Stability." *American Sociological Review.* Vol. 56, No. 3 (June 1991):331–54.

CARLSON, NORMAN A. "Corrections in the United States Today: A Balance Has Been Struck." *The American Criminal Law Review.* Vol. 13, No. 4 (Spring 1976):615–47.

CARMICHAEL, STOKELY, and CHARLES V. HAMILTON. *Black Power: The Politics of Liberation in America.* New York: Vintage Books, 1967.

CARROLL, JAMES R. "Congress Is Told of Coal-Dust Fraud UMW; Senator From Minnesota Rebukes Industry." *Louisville Courier Journal* (May 27, 1999):1A.

CASSIDY, BARBARA, ROBINA LORD, and NANCY MANDELL. "Silenced and Forgotten Women: Race, Poverty, and Disability." In Nancy Mandell, ed., *Feminist Issues: Race, Class, and Sexuality.* Scarborough, ON: Prentice Hall Allyn and Bacon Canada, 1998:26–54.

CASTELLANO, BRANT. *Aboriginal Family Trends: Extended Families, Nuclear Families, Families of the Heart.* Ottawa: The Vanier Institute of the Family.

CATALYST. "2002 Catalyst Census of Women Corporate Officers and Top Earners of Canada." 2003. [Online] **www.catalystwomen.org/press_room/factsheets/2002_cote_canada_factsheet.pdf**

CBC. "Court Approves $20 Million Hip Replacement Settlement." October 21, 2003. [Online] **www.cbc.ca/stories/2003/08/20/Consumers/hiplawsuit_030820**

CENTER FOR THE STUDY OF SPORT IN SOCIETY. *1998 Racial and Gender Report Card.* February 19, 2000. [Online] **www.sportinsociety.org**

CERNETIG, MIRO. "Ebbers' Neighbours are Forgiving, For Now: WorldCom Investors in Mississippi Pray as They Wait to See How Scandal Unfolds." *The Globe and Mail.* June 29, 2002:1.

CHAGNON, NAPOLEON A. *Y[[No mapping for (238) \'b9]]?nomamö: The Fierce People.* 4th ed. New York: Holt, Rinehart & Winston, 1992.

CHANDLER, TERTIUS, and GERALD FOX. *3000 Years of Urban History.* New York: Academic Press, 1974.

CHANGE, KWANG-CHIH. *The Archaeology of Ancient China.* New Haven, CT: Yale University Press, 1977.

CHAPKIS, WENDY. *Live Sex Acts: Women Performing Erotic Labor.* New York: Routledge, 1997.

CHAPPELL, NEENA, LYNN MacDONALD, and MICHAEL STONES. *Aging in Contemporary Canada,* 2nd ed., Toronto: Prentice Hall, 2005.

CHARLES, MARIA. "Cross-National Variation in Occupational Segregation." *American Sociological Review.* Vol. 57, No. 4 (August 1992): 483–502.

CHAUNCEY, GEORGE. *Gay New York: Gender, Urban Culture, and the Making of the Gay Male World 1890–1940.* New York: Basic Books, 1994.

CHENEY, PETER. "Is Pornography Out of Control?" *The Globe and Mail.* (December 2, 2000):F4–5.

CHESNAIS, JEAN-CLAUDE. "The Demographic Sunset of the West?" *Population Today.* Vol. 25, No. 1 (January 1997):4–5.

CHESNEY-LIND, MEDA, and JOHN M. HAGEDORN, eds. *Female Gangs in America: Essays on Girls, Gangs, and Gender.* Chicago: Lakeview Press, 1999.

CHILD AND FAMILY CANADA. How Families Are Doing in the '90s. (2003) [Online] **www.cfc-efc.ca/docs/vocfc/00001083.htm**

CHRISTIAN SCIENCE MONITOR. "Women and Power." (September 6, 1995):1, 9, 10, 11.

CHRISTIANO, KEVIN, WILLIAM H. SWATOS, JR., and PETER KIVISTO. *Sociology of Religion: Contemporary Developments*. Walnut Creek, CA: AltaMira Press, 2001.

CHRISTIE, NANCY. *Engendering the State: Family, Work, and Welfare in Canada*. Toronto: University of Toronto Press, 2000.

CHURCH, GEORGE J. "Unions Arise—With New Tricks." *Time*. Vol. 143, No. 24 (June 13, 1994):56–58.

CIMINO, RICHARD, and DON LATTIN. "Choosing My Religion." American Demographics. Vol. 21, No. 4 (April 1999):60–65.

CITIZENS' FORUM ON CANADA'S FUTURE. *Report to the People and Government of Canada*. Ottawa: Minister of Supply and Services Canada, 1991.

CLARK, MARGARET S., ed. *Prosocial Behavior*. Newbury Park, CA: Sage, 1991.

CLARK, WARREN. "Patterns of Religious Attendance." *Canadian Social Trends*. Ottawa: Statistics Canada. No. 59 (Winter 2000):23–27.

CLARKE, PAT. "So Where Are the Boys?" *Teacher*, Vol. 9, No. 4 (Jan/Feb 1977). [Online] **www.bctf.ca/ezine/archive/1997-01/support/Clarke.html**

CLARKE, ROBIN. "Atmospheric Pollution." In Sir Edmund Hillary, ed., *Ecology 2000: The Changing Face of the Earth*. New York: Beaufort Books, 1984a:130–48.

_____. "What's Happening to Our Water?" In Sir Edmund Hillary, ed., *Ecology 2000: The Changing Face of the Earth*. New York: Beaufort Books, 1984b:108–29.

CLEMENT, WALLACE. *The Canadian Corporate Elite*. Toronto: McClelland and Stewart, 1975.

CLINARD, MARSHALL, and DANIEL ABBOTT. *Crime in Developing Countries*. New York: Wiley, 1973.

CLOWARD, RICHARD A., and LLOYD E. OHLIN. *Delinquency and Opportunity: A Theory of Delinquent Gangs*. New York: Free Press, 1966.

COAKLEY, JAY J. *Sport in Society: Issues and Controversies*. 4th ed. St. Louis, MO: Mosby, 1990.

COE, MICHAEL D., and RICHARD A. DIEHL. *In the Land of the Olmec*. Austin: University of Texas Press, 1980.

COHEN, ALBERT K. *Delinquent Boys: The Culture of the Gang*. New York: Free Press, 1971; orig. 1955.

COHEN, LLOYD R. "Sexual Harassment and the Law." *Society*. Vol. 28, No. 4 (May–June 1991): 8–13.

COHEN, MARK NATHAN. *Health and the Rise of Civilization*. New Haven, CT: Yale University Press, 1989.

COLEMAN, JAMES S. "The Design of Organizations and the Right to Act." *Sociological Forum*. Vol. 8, No. 4 (December 1993):527–46.

COLEMAN, JAMES, THOMAS HOFFER, and SALLY KILGORE. *Public and Private Schools: An Analysis of Public Schools and Beyond*. Washington, DC: National Center for Education Statistics, 1981.

COLEMAN, RICHARD P., and LEE RAINWATER. *Social Standing in America*. New York: Basic Books, 1978.

COLLINS, RANDALL. "A Conflict Theory of Sexual Stratification." *Social Problems*. Vol. 19, No. 1 (Summer 1971):3–21.

_____. *The Credential Society: An Historical Sociology of Education and Stratification*. New York: Academic Press, 1979.

_____. *Sociological Insight: An Introduction to Nonobvious Sociology*. New York: Oxford University Press, 1982.

COLLOWAY, N.O., and PAULA L. DOLLEVOET. "Selected Tabular Material on Aging." In Caleb Finch and Leonard Hayflick, eds., *Handbook of the Biology of Aging*. New York: Van Nostrand-Reinhold, 1977:666–708.

COLTON, HELEN. *The Gift of Touch: How Physical Contact Improves Communication, Pleasure, and Health*. New York: Seaview/Putnam, 1983.

THE COMMISSION ON SYSTEMATIC RACISM IN THE ONTARIO CRIMINAL JUSTICE SYSTEM. *Report*. Toronto: Queen's Printer for Ontario, 1995.

COMTE, AUGUSTE. *Auguste Comte and Positivism: The Essential Writings*. Gertrud Lenzer, ed. New York: Harper Torchbooks, 1975.

CONFERENCE BOARD OF CANADA. *Performance and Potential, 2000–2001*. Ottawa: The Conference Board of Canada, 2000. [Online] **www.conferenceboard.ca/pdfs/pp_00kf.pdf**

CONNELL, ROBERT W. "Cool Guys, Swots, and Wimps: The Interplay of Masculinity and Education." *Oxford Review of Education*. Vol. 15 (1989):291–303.

CONNETT, PAUL H. "The Disposable Society." In F. Herbert Bormann and Stephen R. Kellert, eds., *Ecology, Economics, and Ethics: The Broken Circle*. New Haven, CT: Yale University Press, 1991:99–122.

COOLEY, CHARLES HORTON. *Human Nature and the Social Order*. New York: Schocken Books, 1964; orig. 1902.

CORAK, MILES. "Equality of Opportunity and Inequality Across the Generations: Challenges Ahead." *Horizons: Policy Research Initiative*. Vol. 8, No. 3 (April 2006):43–50.

CORELLI, RAE. "Winter of Discontent: Welfare Cuts and Layoffs Add to the Ranks of Canada's Homeless." *Maclean's*. Toronto ed. Vol. 109, No. 6 (February 5, 1996):46–48.

CORLEY, ROBERT N., O. LEE REED, PETER J. SHEDD, and JERE W. MOREHEAD. *The Legal and Regulatory Environment of Business*. 9th ed. New York: McGraw-Hill, 1993.

CORRELL, SHELLEY J. "Gender and the Career Choice Process: The Role of Biased Self-Assessment." *American Journal of Sociology*. Vol. 106, No. 6 (May 2001):1691–1730.

COULOMBE, S., J.F. TREMBLAY, and S. MARCHAND. *Literacy Scores, Human Capital and Growth Across 14 OECD*. Ottawa: Statistics Canada, 2004.

COUNCIL OF MINISTERS OF EDUCATION. *Canadian Youth, Sexual Health and HIV/AIDS Study*. Toronto: Council of Ministers of Education, 2003.

COUNCIL ON FAMILIES IN AMERICA. *Marriage in America: A Report to the Nation*. New York: Institute for American Values, 1995.

COUNTS, G.S. "The Social Status of Occupations: A Problem in Vocational Guidance." *School Review*. Vol. 33 (January 1925):16–27.

COURTNEY, ALICE E., and THOMAS W. WHIPPLE. *Sex Stereotyping in Advertising*. Lexington, MA: DC Heath, 1983.

COWAN, CAROLYN POPE. *When Partners Become Parents*. New York: Basic Books, 1992.

COWLEY, GEOFFREY. "The Prescription That Kills." *Newsweek* (July 17, 1995):54.

COX, HARVEY. *The Secular City*. Rev. ed. New York: Macmillan, 1971; orig. 1965.

COYOTE (CALL OFF YOUR OLD TIRED ETHICS). April 2, 2000. [Online] **www.freedomusa.org/coyotela/what_is.html**

CROCKER, DIANE, and VALERY KALEMBA. "The Incidence and Impact of Women's Experiences of Sexual Harassment in Canadian Workplaces." *The Canadian Review of Sociology and Anthropology*. Vol. 36, No. 4 (November 1999):541–558.

CROOK, STEPHAN, JAN PAKULSKI, and MALCOLM WATERS. *Postmodernity: Change in Advanced Society*. Newbury Park, CA: Sage, 1992.

CROUSE, JAMES, and DALE TRUSHEIM. *The Case Against the SAT*. Chicago: University of Chicago Press, 1988.

CROWLEY, DAVID. "Where Are We Now? Contours of the Internet in Canada." *Canadian Journal of Communication*, Vol. 27, No. 4 (2002):469–507.

CUKIER, WENDY. "Firearms Regulation: Canada in the International Context." *Chronic Diseases in Canada*. Vol. 19, No. 1 (1998):25–43.

CUMMINGS, SCOTT, and THOMAS LAMBERT. "Anti-Hispanic and Anti-Asian Sentiments Among African Americans." *Social Science Quarterly*. Vol. 78, No. 2 (June 1997):338–53.

CURRIE, ELLIOTT. *Confronting Crime: An American Challenge*. New York: Pantheon Books, 1985.

CURTIS, BRUCE. *Building the Educational State: Canada West, 1831–1871*. London, ON: Althouse Press, 1988.

CURTIS, JAMES E., EDWARD G. GRABB, and DOUGLAS BAER. "Voluntary Association Membership in Fifteen Countries: A Comparative Analysis." *American Sociological Review*. Vol. 57, No. 2 (April 1992):139–52.

CURTIS, JAMES E., EDWARD G. GRABB, and NEIL GUPPY. *Social Inequality in Canada*. Scarborough, ON: Prentice Hall, 1999.

CURTIS, JAMES E., and RONALD D. LAMBERT. "Culture." In Robert Hagedorn, ed., *Sociology*. Toronto: Holt, Rinehart and Winston of Canada, 1990:21–59.

CURTISS, SUSAN. *Genie: A Psycholinguistic Study of a Modern-Day "Wild Child."* New York: Academic Press, 1977.

DAFOE, CHRIS. "The Resurrection of Big Bear." *Globe and Mail.* (July 18, 1998): C1, C3.

DAHL, ROBERT A. *Who Governs?* New Haven, CT: Yale University Press, 1961.

_____. *Dilemmas of Pluralist Democracy: Autonomy vs. Control.* New Haven, CT: Yale University Press, 1982.

DAHRENDORF, RALF. *Class and Class Conflict in Industrial Society.* Stanford, CA: Stanford University Press, 1959.

DALY, MARTIN, and MARGO WILSON. *Homicide.* New York: Aldine, 1988.

DARROCH, JACQUELINE E., JENNIFER J. FROST, SUSHEELA SINGH, and THE STUDY TEAM. "Teenage Sexual and Reproductive Behavior in Developed Countries: Can More Progress Be Made?" New York: The Alan Guttmacher Institute (November 2001). August 14, 2002. [Online] **www.agi-usa.org/pubs/eurosynth_rpt.pdf**

DARROCH, JACQUELINE E., SUSHEELA SINGH, JENNIFER J. FROST, and THE STUDY TEAM. "Differences in Teenage Pregnancy Rates Among Five Developed Countries: The Roles of Sexual Activity and Contraceptive Use." *Family Planning Perspectives*, 2001, 33(6):244–250, 281

DARWIN, CHARLES. *On the Origin of Species by Means of Natural Selection, or the Preservation of Favoured Races in the Struggle for Life.* London: John Murray, 1859. [Online] **www.literature.org/authors/darwin-charles/the-origin-of-species/index.html**

DAVIDSON, JULIA O'CONNELL. *Prostitution, Power, and Freedom.* Ann Arbor: University of Michigan Press, 1998.

DAVIES, JAMES C. "Toward a Theory of Revolution." *American Sociological Review.* Vol. 27, No. 1 (February 1962):5–19.

DAVIES, J.B. "The Distribution of Wealth in Canada." In Edward Wolff, ed., *Research in Economic Inequality.* Greenwich, CT: JAI Press, 1993:159–80.

DAVIES, MARK, and DENISE B. KANDEL. "Parental and Peer Influences on Adolescents' Educational Plans: Some Further Evidence." *American Journal of Sociology.* Vol. 87, No. 2 (September 1981):363–87.

DAVIES, SCOTT. "In Search of Resistance and Rebellion Among High School Dropouts." *Canadian Journal of Sociology.* Vol. 19, No. 3 (Summer 1994):331–50.

DAVIES, SCOTT, and NEIL GUPPY. "Race and Canadian Education" in Vic Satzewich, ed., *Racism & Social Inequality in Canada.* Toronto: Thompson Educational Publishing, Inc., 1998:131–55.

DAVIS, DONALD M. Cited in "T.V. Is a Blonde, Blonde World." *American Demographics*, special issue: Women Change Places. Ithaca, NY: 1993.

DAVIS, KATHY. "A Dubious Equality: Men, Women and Cosmetic Surgery." *Body & Society.* Vol. 8, No. 1 (2002):49–65.

DAVIS, KINGSLEY. "Extreme Social Isolation of a Child." *American Journal of Sociology.* Vol. 45, No. 4 (January 1940):554–65.

_____. "Final Note on a Case of Extreme Isolation." *American Journal of Sociology.* Vol. 52, No. 5 (March 1947):432–37.

_____. "Sexual Behavior." In Robert K. Merton and Robert Nisbet, eds., *Contemporary Social Problems.* 3rd ed. New York: Harcourt Brace Jovanovich, 1971:313–60.

DAVIS, KINGSLEY, and WILBERT MOORE. "Some Principles of Stratification." *American Sociological Review.* Vol. 10, No. 2 (April 1945):242–49.

DAVIS, SCOTT, and NEIL GUPPY. "Fields of Study, College Selectivity, and Student Inequalities in Higher Education." *Social Forces.* Vol. 75, No. 4 (June 1977):1417–1438.

DAVIS, SHARON A., and EMIL J. HALLER. "Tracking, Ability, and SES: Further Evidence on the 'Revisionist-Meritocratic Debate.'" *American Journal of Education.* Vol. 89 (May 1981):283–304.

DAWSON, LORNE. *Comprehending Cults: The Sociology of New Religious Movements.* Toronto: University of Toronto Press, 1998.

DAWSON, LORNE L., ed. *Cults in Context: Readings in the Study of New Religious Movements.* Toronto: Canadian Scholar's Press, 1996.

DE BROUKER, PATRICE, and LAVAL LAVALLÉE. "Getting Ahead: Does Your Parents' Education Count?" *Education Quarterly Review.* Statistics Canada Catalogue No. 81-003XIE. Vol. 5, No. 1 (August 1998):22–28.

DECKARD, BARBARA SINCLAIR. *The Women's Movement: Political, Socioeconomic, and Psychological Issues.* 2nd ed. New York: Harper & Row, 1979.

DEDRICK, DENNIS K., and RICHARD E. YINGER. "MAD, SDI, and the Nuclear Arms Race." Manuscript in development. Georgetown, KY.: Georgetown College, 1990.

DELACROIX, JACQUES, and CHARLES C. RAGIN. "Structural Blockage: A Cross-national Study of Economic Dependency, State Efficacy, and Underdevelopment." *American Journal of Sociology.* Vol. 86, No. 6(May 1981):1311–47.

DELUCA, TOM. "Joe the Bookie and the Class Voting Gap." *American Demographics.* Vol. 20, No. 11 (November 1998):26–29.

DEMERATH, NJ, III. "Who Now Debates Functionalism? From System, Change, and Conflict to 'Culture, Choice, and Praxis.'" *Sociological Forum.* Vol. 11, No. 2 (June 1996):333–45.

DER SPIEGEL. "Third World Metropolises Are Becoming Monsters; Rural Poverty Drives Millions to the Slums." *World Press Review.* (October 1989).

DE TOCQUEVILLE, ALEXIS. *The Old Regime and the French Revolution.* Stuart Gilbert, trans. Garden City, NY: Anchor/Doubleday Books, 1955; orig. 1856.

DEVINE, JOEL A. "State and State Expenditure: Determinants of Social Investment and Social Consumption Spending in the Postwar United States." *American Sociological Review.* Vol. 50, No. 2 (April 1985):150–65.

DEVOR, HOLLY. *FTM: Female-to-Male Transsexuals in Society.* Bloomington, IN: Indiana University Press, 1997.

DEVRIES, R., C. BENOIT, E. VAN TEIJLINGEN, and SIRPA WREDE, eds. *Birth by Design: The Social Shaping of Maternity Care in Northern Europe and North America.* London: Routledge, 2001.

DIAMOND, JARED. "The Worst Mistake in the History of the Human Race." *Discover* (May 1987):64–66.

DICKASON, OLIVE PATRICIA. *Canada's First Nations: A History of Founding Peoples From Earliest Times.* Toronto: McClelland and Stewart Inc., 1992.

DIXON, WILLIAM J., and TERRY BOSWELL. "Dependency, Disarticulation, and Denominator Effects: Another Look at Foreign Capital Penetration." *American Journal of Sociology.* Vol. 102, No. 2 (September 1996):543–62.

DIZARD, JAN E., and HOWARD GADLIN. *The Minimal Family.* Amherst: The University of Massachusetts Press, 1990.

DOBYNS, HENRY F. "An Appraisal of Techniques With a New Hemispheric Estimate." *Current Anthropology.* Vol. 7, No. 4 (October 1966):395–446.

DOLLARD, JOHN et al. *Frustration and Aggression.* New Haven, CT: Yale University Press, 1939.

DOMHOFF, G. WILLIAM. *Who Rules America Now? A View of the '80s.* Englewood Cliffs, NJ: Prentice Hall, 1983.

DONALD, LELAND. *Aboriginal Slavery on the Northwest Coast of North America.* Berkeley: University of California Press, 1997.

DONOVAN, VIRGINIA K., and RONNIE LITTENBERG. "Psychology of Women: Feminist Therapy." In Barbara Haber, ed., *The Women's Annual 1981: The Year in Review.* Boston: G. K. Hall, 1982:211–35.

DOOB, ANTHONY N. "Transforming the Punishment Environment: Understanding Public Views of What Should Be Accomplished at Sentencing." *Canadian Journal of Criminology.* Vol. 42, No. 3 (July 2000):323–47.

DOWELL, WILLIAM. "Addressing Africa's Agony." *Time.* Vol. 155, No. 3 (January 24, 2000):36.

DOYLE, JAMES A. *The Male Experience.* Dubuque, IA: William C. Brown, 1983.

DOYLE, RICHARD F. *A Manifesto of Men's Liberation.* 2nd ed. Forest Lake, Minn.: Men's Rights Association, 1980.

DRIEDGER, LEO. *Multi-Ethnic Canada: Identities and Inequalities.* Toronto: Oxford University Press, 1996.

DROLET, MARIE. "The Persistent Gap: New Evidence of the Canadian Gender Wage Gap." Ottawa: Statistics Canada, Business and Labour Market Analysis Division. Catalogue No. 11F0019MPE, No. 157. (2001) [Online] **www.statcan.ca/english/research/11F0019MIE/ 11F0019MIE2001157.pdf**

_____. "Wives, Mothers and Wages: Does Timing Matter?" *Analytical Studies Branch Research Paper Series.* No. 186, Ottawa: Statistics Canada, 2002.

DRYBURGH, HEATHER. "Teenage Pregnancy." *Health Reports*. Statistics Canada Catalogue No. 92-003-XIE. Vol. 12, No. 1 (October 2000):9–19.

DU BOIS, W. E. B. *The Philadelphia Negro: A Social Study*. New York: Schocken Books, 1967; orig. 1899.

DUBOS, RENÉ. *Man Adapting*. New Haven, CT: Yale University Press, 1980; orig. 1965.

DUFFY, ANN. "The Feminist Challenge: Knowing and Ending the Violence." In Nancy Mandell, ed., *Feminist Issues: Race, Class, and Sexuality*. 2nd ed. Scarborough, ON: Prentice Hall Allyn and Bacon Canada, 1998:132–59.

DUHL, LEONARD J. "The Social Context of Health." In Arthur C. Hastings et al., eds., *Health for the Whole Person: The Complete Guide to Holistic Medicine*. Boulder, Colo.: Westview Press, 1980:39–48.

DUMAS, JEAN. *Report on the Demographic Situation in Canada 1993*. Statistics Canada Catalogue No. ASDF91-209E. Ottawa: Statistics Canada, Demography Division, 1994.

DUNCAN, CYNTHIA M. *Worlds Apart: Why Poverty Persists in Rural America*. New Haven, CT: Yale University Press, 1999.

DUNCAN, GREG J., W. JEAN YEUNG, JEANNE BROOKS-GUNN, and JUDITH R. SMITH. "How Much Does Childhood Poverty Affect the Life Chances of Children?" *American Sociological Review*. Vol. 63, No. 3 (June 1998):406–23.

DUNN, JOHN. "Peddling Big Brother." *Time*. Vol. 137, No. 25 (June 24, 1991):62.

DURKHEIM, EMILE. *Moral Education*. New York: Free Press, 1961; orig. 1902–3.

_____. *The Division of Labor in Society*. New York: Free Press, 1964a; orig. 1895.

_____. *The Rules of Sociological Method*. New York: Free Press, 1964b; orig. 1893.

_____. *The Elementary Forms of Religious Life*. New York: Free Press, 1965; orig. 1915.

DURKIN, KEVIN. *Television, Sex Roles and Children*. Milton Keynes: Open University Press, 1985.

DWORKIN, ANDREA. *Intercourse*. New York: Free Press, 1987.

EBAUGH, HELEN ROSE FUCHS. *Becoming an EX: The Process of Role Exit*. Chicago: University of Chicabo Press, 1988.

THE ECONOMIST. "Cockfighting: 'Til Death Us Do Part." Vol. 330, No. 7851 (February 19, 1994):30.

_____. "WorldCom's Cowboy Bites the Dust; Corporate Crime (Bernie Ebbers Learns Where the Buck Stops)." March 19, 2005:67.

EDIN, KATHRYN, and LAURA LEIN. "Work, Welfare, and Single Mothers' Economic Survival Strategies." *American Sociological Review*. Vol. 62, No. 2 (April 1996):253–66.

EDMONDSON, BRAD. "The Facts of Death." *American Demographics*. Vol. 49, No. 4 (April 1997):47–53.

EDWARDS, DAVID V. *The American Political Experience*. 3rd ed. Englewood Cliffs, NJ: Prentice Hall, 1985.

EDWARDS, RICHARD. *Contested Terrain: The Transformation of the Workplace in the Twentieth Century*. New York: Basic Books, 1979.

EHRENREICH, BARBARA. The Hearts of Men: American Dreams and the Flight From Commitment. Garden City, NY: Anchor Books, 1983.

_____. "The Real Truth About the Female Body." *Time*. Vol. 153, No. 9 (March 15, 1999):56–65.

EHRENREICH, JOHN. "Introduction." In John Ehrenreich, ed., *The Cultural Crisis of Modern Medicine*. New York: Monthly Review Press, 1978:1–35.

EICHLER, MARGRIT. *Nonsexist Research Methods: A Practical Guide*. Winchester, MA: Unwin Hyman, 1988.

_____. *Family Shifts: Families, Policies, and Gender Equality*. Toronto: Oxford University Press, 1997.

EISENBERG, DANIEL. "Rise of the Permatemp." *Time*. Vol. 154, No. 2 (July 12, 1999):48.

EISENSTEIN, ZILLAH R., ed. *Capitalist Patriarchy and the Case for Socialist Feminism*. New York: Monthly Review Press, 1979.

EKMAN, PAUL. "Biological and Cultural Contributions to Body and Facial Movements in the Expression of Emotions." In A. Rorty, ed., *Explaining Emotions*. Berkeley: University of California Press, 1980a:73–101.

_____. *Face of Man: Universal Expression in a New Guinea Village*. New York: Garland Press, 1980b.

_____. *Telling Lies: Clues to Deceit in the Marketplace, Politics, and Marriage*. New York: Norton, 1985.

ELIAS, JAMES, VERN BULLOUGH, VERONICA ELIAS, and JOYCELYN ELDERS, eds. *Prostitution: On Whores, Hustlers, and Johns*. New York: Promethus Books, 1998.

ELIAS, ROBERT. *The Politics of Victimization: Victims, Victimology and Human Rights*. New York: Oxford University Press, 1986.

ELLIOTT, DELBERT S., and SUZANNE S. AGETON. "Reconciling Race and Class Differences in Self-Reported and Official Estimates of Delinquency." *American Sociological Review*. Vol. 45, No. 1 (February 1980):95–110.

ELLISON, CHRISTOPHER G., and DARREN E. SHERKAT. "Conservative Protestantism and Support for Corporal Punishment." *American Sociological Review*. Vol. 58, No. 1 (February 1993):131–44.

ELLISON, CHRISTOPHER G., JOHN P. BARTKOWSKI, and MICHELLE L. SEGAL. "Do Conservative Protestant Parents Spank More Often? Further Evidence From the National Survey of Families and Households." *Social Science Quarterly*. Vol. 77, No. 3 (September 1996):663–73.

ELMER-DeWITT, PHILIP. "First Nation in Cyberspace." *Time*. Vol. 142, No. 24 (December 6, 1993):62–64.

_____. "Battle for the Internet." *Time*. Vol. 144, No. 4 (July 25, 1994):50–56.

EMBER, MELVIN, and CAROL R. EMBER. "The Conditions Favoring Matrilocal Versus Patrilocal Residence." *American Anthropologist*. Vol. 73, No. 3 (June 1971):571–94.

_____. *Anthropology*. 6th ed. Englewood Cliffs, NJ: Prentice Hall, 1991.

EMERSON, JOAN P. "Behavior in Private Places: Sustaining Definitions of Reality in Gynecological Examinations." In H.P. Dreitzel, ed., *Recent Sociology*. Vol. 2. New York: Collier, 1970:74–97.

ENEMARK, DANIEL. "Backstory: Tapping the World." *Christian Science Monitor*. March 22, 2006, edition. [Online] **www.csmonitor.com/ 2006/0322/p20s01-sten.html**

ENGELS, FRIEDRICH. *The Origin of the Family*. Chicago: Charles H. Kerr & Co., 1902; orig. 1884.

ENGLAND, PAULA. *Comparable Worth: Theories and Evidence*. Hawthorne, NY: Aldine, 1992.

ENSIGN, JOSEPHINE, and MICHELLE BELL. "Illness Experiences of Homeless Youth." *Qualitative Health Research*. Vol. 14, No. 9 (2004):1239–1254.

ENVIRONICS RESEARCH GROUP. "Canadians for Equal Marriage June 2006." (May 25–June 2, 2006) [Online] **http://erg.environics.net/news/ equal_marriage/**

ERIKSON, ERIK H. *Childhood and Society*. New York: Norton, 1963; orig. 1950.

ERIKSON, ROBERT S., NORMAN R. LUTTBEG, and KENT L. TEDIN. *American Public Opinion: Its Origins, Content, and Impact*. 2nd ed. New York: Wiley, 1980.

ESHLEMAN, J.R., and S.J. WILSON. *The Family*. Scarborough, ON: Prentice Hall, 1998.

ESPING-ANDERSEN, GÖSTA. *The Three Worlds of Welfare Capitalism*. Princeton: Princeton University Press, 1990.

ETZIONI, AMITAI. *A Comparative Analysis of Complex Organization: On Power, Involvement, and Their Correlates*. Rev. and enlarged ed. New York: Free Press, 1975.

_____. "How to Make Marriage Matter." *Time*. Vol. 142, No. 10 (September 6, 1993):76.

ETZIONI-HALEVY, EVA. *Bureaucracy and Democracy: A Political Dilemma*. Rev. ed. Boston: Routledge & Kegan Paul, 1985.

EUROPEAN VALUES STUDY GROUP and WORLD VALUES SURVEY ASSOCIATION. European and World Values Surveys Four-Wave Integrated Data File, 1981–2004, V.20060423, (2006). Aggregate File Producers: Análisis Sociológicos Económicos y Políticos (ASEP) and JD Systems (JDS), Madrid, Spain/Tilburg University, Tilburg, The Netherlands. Data File

Suppliers: Analisis Sociologicos Economicos y Politicos (ASEP) and JD Systems (JDS), Madrid, Spain/Tillburg University, Tillburg, The Netherlands/Zentralarchiv fur Empirische Sozialforschung (ZA), Cologne, Germany. Aggregate File Distributors: Análisis Sociológicos Económicos y Políticos (ASEP) and JD Systems (JDS), Madrid, Spain/Tillburg University, Tilburg, The Netherlands/Zentralarchiv fur Empirische Sozialforschung (ZA) Cologne, Germany.

FALK, GERHARD. Personal communication, 1987.

FALKENMARK, MALIN, and CARL WIDSTRAND. "Population and Water Resources: A Delicate Balance." *Population Bulletin.* Vol. 47, No. 3 (November 1992). Washington, DC: Population Reference Bureau.

FALLON, A.E., and P. ROZIN. "Sex Differences in Perception of Desirable Body Shape." *Journal of Abnormal Psychology.* Vol. 94, No. 1 (1985):100–105.

FARRELL, MICHAEL P., and STANLEY D. ROSENBERG. *Men at Midlife.* Boston: Auburn House, 1981.

FEATHERMAN, DAVID L., and ROBERT M. HAUSER. *Opportunity and Change.* New York: Academic Press, 1978.

FEATHERSTONE, MIKE, ed. *Global Culture: Nationalism, Globalization, and Modernity.* London: Sage, 1990.

FEDERAL, PROVINCIAL AND TERRITORIAL ADVISORY COMMITTEE ON POPULATION HEALTH. *Report on the Health of Canadians.* Ottawa: Minister of Supply and Services Canada, 1996.

_____. *Statistical Report on the Health of Canadians.* Health Canada: Ministry of Public Works and Government Services Canada, 1999. Catalogue No. H39-467/1999E.

_____. *Statistical Report on the Health of Canadians.* Revised Version (March 2000). Statistics Canada Catalogue No. 82-570-XIE. Ottawa: Minister of Public Works and Government Services Canada.

FEDERAL, PROVINCIAL/TERRITORIAL MINISTERS RESPONSIBLE FOR THE STATUS OF WOMEN. *Economic Gender Equality Indicators.* Ottawa: Status of Women, 1997.

FELLMAN, BRUCE. "Taking the Measure of Children's T.V." *Yale Alumni Magazine* (April 1995):46–51.

FENNELL, TOM, and SHENG XUE. "The Smuggler's Slaves." *Maclean's.* Vol. 111, No. 50 (December 12, 2000):14–19.

FERGUSON, R. BRIAN. *Y?nomami Warfare: A Political History.* Santa Fe, NM: School of American Research Press, 1995.

FERGUSON, TOM. "Medical Self-Care: Self Responsibility for Health." In Arthur C. Hastings et al., eds., *Health for the Whole Person: The Complete Guide to Holistic Medicine.* Boulder, Colo.: Westview Press, 1980:87–109.

FERNANDEZ, ROBERTO M., and NANCY WEINBERG. "Sifting and Sorting: Personal Contacts and Hiring in a Retail Bank." *American Sociological Review.* Vol. 62, No. 6 (December 1997):883–902.

FERREE, MYRA MARX, and ELAINE J. HALL. "Rethinking Stratification From a Feminist Perspective: Gender, Race, and Class in Mainstream Textbooks." *American Sociological Review.* Vol. 61, No. 6 (December 1996):929–50.

FETTO, JOHN. "Down for the Count." *American Demographics.* Vol. 21, No. 11 (November 1999): 46–47.

FINKELSTEIN, NEAL W., and RON HASKINS. "Kindergarten Children Prefer Same-Color Peers." *Child Development.* Vol. 54, No. 2 (April 1983):502–508.

FINN, CHESTER E., JR., and HERBERT J. WALBERG. "The World's Least Efficient Schools." *Wall Street Journal* (June 22, 1998):A22.

FINN, CHESTER E., JR., and REBECCA L. GAU. "New Ways of Education." *The Public Interest.* Vol. 130 (Winter 1998):79–92.

FIORENTINE, ROBERT. "Men, Women, and the Premed Persistence Gap: A Normative Alternatives Approach." *American Journal of Sociology.* Vol. 92, No. 5 (March 1987):1118–39.

FIORENTINE, ROBERT, and STEPHEN COLE. "Why Fewer Women Become Physicians: Explaining the Premed Persistance Gap." *Sociological Forum.* Vol. 7, No. 3 (September 1992):469–96.

FIREBAUGH, GLENN. "Does Foreign Capital Harm Poor Nations? New Estimates Based on Dixon and Boswell's Measures of Capital Penetration." *American Journal of Sociology.* Vol. 102, No. 2 (September 1996):563–75.

_____. "Empirics of World Income Inequality." *American Journal of Sociology.* Vol. 104, No. 6 (May 1999):1597–1630.

_____. "Growth Effects of Foreign and Domestic Investment." *American Journal of Sociology.* Vol. 98, No. 1 (July 1992):105–30.

_____. "The Trend in Between-Nation Income Inequality." *Annual Review of Sociology.* Vol. 26 (2000):323–39.

FIREBAUGH, GLENN, and DUMITRU SANDU. "Who Supports Marketization and Democratization in Post-Communist Romania?" *Sociological Forum.* Vol. 13, No. 3 (September 1998):521–41.

FIREBAUGH, GLENN, and FRANK D. BECK. "Does Economic Growth Benefit the Masses? Growth, Dependence, and Welfare in the Third World." *American Sociological Review.* Vol. 59, No. 5 (October 1994):631–53.

FISHER, ELIZABETH. *Woman's Creation: Sexual Evolution and the Shaping of Society.* Garden City, NY: Anchor/Doubleday, 1979.

FISKE, ALAN PAIGE. "The Cultural Relativity of Selfish Individualism: Anthropological Evidence that Humans Are Inherently Sociable." In Margaret S. Clark, ed., *Prosocial Behavior.* Newbury Park, CA: Sage, 1991:176–214.

FLAHERTY, MICHAEL G. "A Formal Approach to the Study of Amusement in Social Interaction." *Studies in Symbolic Interaction.* Vol. 5. New York: JAI Press, 1984:71–82.

_____. "Two Conceptions of the Social Situation: Some Implications of Humor." *The Sociological Quarterly.* Vol. 31, No. 1 (Spring 1990).

FORBES.COM. *The World's Richest People.* (2003) [Online] **www.forbes.com/2003/02/26/billionaireland.html**

FORD, CLELLAN S., and FRANK A. BEACH. *Patterns of Sexual Behavior.* New York: Harper & Row, 1951.

FOUCAULT, MICHEL. *The History of Sexuality: An Introduction.* Vol. 1. Robert Hurley, trans. New York: Vintage, 1990; orig. 1978.

FOX, BONNIE, ed. *Family Patterns/Gender Relations.* Toronto: Oxford University Press, 2001.

FOX, BONNIE, and MEG LUXTON. "Conceptualizing Family." In Bonnie Fox, ed., *Family Patterns/Gender Relations.* Toronto: Oxford University Press, 2001:22–33.

FRAGER, RUTH A. *Sweatshop Strife: Class, Ethnicity, and Gender in the Jewish Labour Movement in Toronto, 1900–1939.* Toronto: University of Toronto Press, 1992.

FRANK, ANDRÉ GUNDER. *On Capitalist Underdevelopment.* Bombay: Oxford University Press, 1975.

_____. *Crisis: In the World Economy.* New York: Holmes & Meier, 1980.

_____. *Reflections on the World Economic Crisis.* New York: Monthly Review Press, 1981.

FRANKLIN ASSOCIATES. *Characterization of Municipal Solid Waste in the United States, 1960–2000.* Prairie Village, Kans.: Franklin Associates, 1986.

FRAZIER, E. FRANKLIN. *Black Bourgeoisie: The Rise of a New Middle Class.* New York: Free Press, 1965.

FREDRICKSON, GEORGE M. *White Supremacy: A Comparative Study in American and South African History.* New York: Oxford University Press, 1981.

FREE, MARVIN D. "Religious Affiliation, Religiosity, and Impulsive and Intentional Deviance." *Sociological Focus.* Vol. 25, No. 1 (February 1992): 77–91.

FREEDOM HOUSE. *Freedom in the World 2001–2002.* New York: Freedom House, 2002.

FRENCH, MARILYN. *Beyond Power: On Women, Men, and Morals.* New York: Summit Books, 1985.

FRIEDMAN, MEYER, and RAY H. ROSENMAN. *Type A Behavior and Your Heart.* New York: Fawcett Crest, 1974.

FRIENDLY, MARTHA, JANE BEACH, and MICHELLE TURIANO. *Early Childhood Education and Care in Canada 2001.* Toronto: Childcare Resource and Research Unit, University of Toronto, 2005.

FRY, CRAIG. "Safer Injecting Facilities in Vancouver: Considering Issues Beyond Potential Use. *Canadian Medical Association Journal.* Vol. 169, No. 8 (October 2003):777–778.

FUCHS, VICTOR R. "Sex Differences in Economic Well-Being." *Science.* Vol. 232 (April 25, 1986): 459–64.

FULLER, REX, and RICHARD SCHOENBERGER. "The Gender Salary Gap: Do Academic Achievement, Intern Experience, and College Major Make a Difference?" *Social Science Quarterly.* Vol. 72, No. 4 (December 1991):715–26.

FURSTENBERG, FRANK F., JR., and ANDREW CHERLIN. *Divided Families: What Happens to Children When Parents Part.* Cambridge, MA: Harvard University Press, 1991.

GAGLIANI, GIORGIO. "How Many Working Classes?" *American Journal of Sociology.* Vol. 87, No. 2 (September 1981):259–85.

GAGNÉ, PATRICIA, and RICHARD TEWKSBURY. "Conformity Pressures and Gender Resistance Among Transgendered Individuals." *Social Problems.* Vol. 45, No. 1 (February 1998):81–101.

GALLUP ORGANIZATION, The. *The Gallup Poll Monthly.* December, 1993.

_____. *Special Reports: Global Study of Family Values.* Princeton, NJ: The Gallup Organization, November 7, 1997.

_____. Poll results reported in "Numbers," *Time,* Vol. 155, No. 9 (February 28, 2000):25.

GAMORAN, ADAM. "The Variable Effects of High-School Tracking." *American Sociological Review.* Vol. 57, No. 6 (December 1992):812–28.

GANNON, MARIE, and KAREN MIHOREAN. "Criminal Victimization in Canada, 2004." *Juristat.* Vol. 25, No. 7 (November 2005):1–26.

GANS, HERBERT J. *People and Plans: Essays on Urban Problems and Solutions.* New York: Basic Books, 1968.

_____. *Deciding What's News: A Study of CBS Evening News, NBC Nightly News, Newsweek and Time.* New York: Vintage Books, 1980.

_____. *The Urban Villagers: Group and Class in the Life of Italian-Americans.* New York: Free Press, 1982; orig. 1962.

GARDNER, ARTHUR. "Their Own Boss: The Self-Employed in Canada." *Canadian Social Trends.* No. 37 (Summer 1995):26–29.

GARDNER, MARILYN. "At-Home Dads Give Their New Career High Marks." *Christian Science Monitor* (May 30, 1996):1, 12.

GARFINKEL, HAROLD. "Conditions of Successful Degradation Ceremonies." *American Journal of Sociology.* Vol. 61, No. 2 (March 1956):420–24.

_____. *Studies in Ethnomethodology.* Cambridge: Polity Press, 1967.

GEE, ELLEN. "Population." In Robert Hagedorn, ed., *Sociology.* 4th ed. Toronto: Holt, Rinehart & Winston, 1990:195–226.

GEE, ELLEN, and GLORIA GUTMAN. *Overselling of Population Aging: Apocalyptic Demography, Intergenerational Challenges and Social Policy.* Toronto: Oxford University Press, 2000.

GEERTZ, CLIFFORD. "Common Sense as a Cultural System." *The Antioch Review.* Vol. 33, No. 1 (Spring 1975):5–26.

GELLES, RICHARD J., and CLAIRE PEDRICK CORNELL. *Intimate Violence in Families.* 2nd ed. Newbury Park, CA: Sage, 1990.

GELMAN, DAVID. "Who's Taking Care of Our Parents?" *Newsweek.* (May 6, 1985):61–64, 67–68.

_____. "Born or Bred?" *Newsweek.* (February 24, 1992):46–53.

GEORGE, M.V., SHIRLEY LOH, RAVI B.P. VERMA, and Y. EDWARD SHIN. *Population Projections for Canada, Provinces and Territories 2000–2026.* (2001) Statistics Canada Catalogue No. 91-520-XPB.

GERBER, THEODORE P., and MICHAEL HOUT. "More Shock than Therapy: Market Transition, Employment, and Income in Russia, 1991–1995." *American Journal of Sociology.* Vol. 104, No. 1 (July 1998):1–50.

GERLACH, MICHAEL L. *The Social Organization of Japanese Business.* Berkeley and Los Angeles: University of California Press, 1992.

GERSTEL, NAOMI. "Divorce and Stigma." *Social Problems.* Vol. 43, No. 2 (April 1987):172–86.

GESCHWENDER, JAMES A. Racial Stratification in America. Dubuque, IA: William C. Brown, 1978.

GEWERTZ, DEBORAH. "A Historical Reconsideration of Female Dominance Among the Chambri of Papua New Guinea." *American Ethnologist.* Vol. 8, No. 1 (1981):94–106.

GHOSH, RATNA. *Redefining Multicultural Education.* Toronto: Harcourt Brace Canada, 1996.

GIBBONS, DON C., and MARVIN D. KROHN. *Delinquent Behavior.* 4th ed. Englewood Cliffs, NJ: Prentice Hall, 1986.

GIBBONS, JACQUELINE. "Indo-Canadian 'Mixed' Marriage: Context and Dilemmas." *Polyphony.* Vol. 12 (1990):93–98.

GIBBS, NANCY. "When Is It Rape?" *Time.* Vol. 137, No. 22 (June 3, 1991a):48–54.

_____. "The Clamor on Campus." *Time.* Vol. 137, No. 22 (June 3, 1991b):54–55.

_____. "How Much Should We Teach Our Children About Sex?" *Time.* Vol. 141, No. 21 (May 24, 1993):60–66.

_____. "What Kids (Really) Need." *Time.* Vol. 157, No. 17 (April 30, 2001):48–49.

_____. "If You Want to Humble an Empire." *Time.* September 11, 2001. Special issue.

GIDDENS, ANTHONY. *Sociology: A Brief but Critical Introduction.* New York: Harcourt Brace Jovanovich, 1982.

_____. *The Transformation of Intimacy.* Cambridge, UK: Polity Press, 1992.

GIDDENS, ANTHONY, and JONATHAN TURNER. *Social Theory Today.* Stanford, CA: Stanford University Press, 1987.

GIELE, JANET Z. "Gender and Sex Roles." In Neil J. Smelser, ed., *Handbook of Sociology.* Newbury Park, CA: Sage, 1988:291–323.

GIGLIOTTI, RICHARD J., and HEATHER K. HUFF. "Role Related Conflicts, Strains, and Stresses of Older-Adult College Students." *Sociological Focus.* Vol. 28, No. 3 (August 1995):329–42.

GILBERT, NEIL. "Realities and Mythologies of Rape." *Society.* Vol. 29, No. 4 (May–June 1992):4–10.

GILLIGAN, CAROL. *In a Different Voice: Psychological Theory and Women's Development.* Cambridge, MA: Harvard University Press, 1982.

GILLON, RAANAN. "Euthanasia in the Netherlands—Down the Slippery Slope?" *Journal of Medical Ethics.* Vol. 25, No. 1 (February 1999):3–4.

GIMENEZ, MARTHA E. "Silence in the Classroom: Some Thoughts About Teaching in the 1980s." *Teaching Sociology.* Vol. 17, No. 2 (April 1989): 184–91.

GINSBURG, FAYE, and ANNA LOWENHAUPT TSING, eds. *Uncertain Terms: Negotiating Gender in American Culture.* Boston: Beacon Press, 1990.

GIOVANNINI, MAUREEN. "Female Anthropologist and Male Informant: Gender Conflict in a Sicilian Town." In John J. Macionis and Nijole V. Benokraitis, eds., *Seeing Ourselves: Classic, Contemporary, and Cross-Cultural Readings in Sociology.* 2nd ed. Englewood Cliffs, NJ: Prentice Hall, 1992:27–32.

GIUGNI, MARCO G. "Structure and Culture in Social Movements Theory." *Sociological Forum.* Vol. 13, No. 2 (June 1998):365–75.

GLADUE, BRIAN A., RICHARD GREEN, and RONALD E. HELLMAN. "Neuroendocrine Response to Estrogen and Sexual Orientation." Science. Vol. 225, No. 4669 (September 28, 1984):1496–99.

GLASER, NONA. Y. *Women's Paid and Unpaid Labour: The Work Transfer in Health Care and Retailing.* Philadelphia: Temple University Press, 1993.

GLEICK, ELIZABETH. "The Marker We've Been Waiting For." *Time.* Vol. 149, No. 14 (April 7, 1997):28–42.

GLENN, NORVAL D., and BETH ANN SHELTON. "Regional Differences in Divorce in the United States." *Journal of Marriage and the Family.* Vol. 47, No. 3 (August 1985):641–52.

THE GLOBE AND MAIL. "Locking Up Ebbers." Editorial. *The Globe and Mail.* July 15, 2005:A14.

GLOBEINVESTOR.COM. "Top 300 Private Companies." (2003) [Online] **www.globeinvestor.com/series/top1000/tables/private/2003/**

GLUECK, SHELDON, and ELEANOR GLUECK. *Unraveling Juvenile Delinquency.* New York: Commonwealth Fund, 1950.

GNIDA, JOHN J. "Teaching 'Nature versus Nurture': The Case of African American Athletic Success." *Teaching Sociology.* Vol. 23, No. 4 (October 1995):389–95.

GOFFMAN, ERVING. *The Presentation of Self in Everyday Life.* Garden City, NY: Anchor Books, 1959.

_____. *Asylums: Essays on the Social Situation of Mental Patients and Other Inmates.* Garden City, NY: Anchor Books, 1961.

_____. *Stigma: Notes on the Management of Spoiled Identity.* Englewood Cliffs, NJ: Prentice Hall, 1963.

_____. *Interactional Ritual: Essays on Face to Face Behavior.* Garden City, NY: Anchor Books, 1967.

_____. *Gender Advertisements.* New York: Harper & Row, 1979.

GOLDBERG, STEVEN. *The Inevitability of Patriarchy.* New York: William Morrow, 1974.

_____. Personal communication, 1987.

GOLDEN, FREDERIC, and MICHAEL D. LEMONICK. "The Race Is Over." *Time.* Vol. 156, No. 1 (July 3, 2000):18–23.

GOLDFARB, WILLIAM. "Groundwater: The Buried Life." In F. Herbert Bormann and Stephen R. Kellert, eds., *Ecology, Economics, and Ethics: The Broken Circle.* New Haven, CT: Yale University Press, 1991:123–35.

GOLDSCHEIDER, FRANCES KOBRIN, and LINDA J. WAITE. "Sex Differences in the Entry Into Marriage." *American Journal of Sociology.* Vol. 92, No. 1 (July, 1986):91–109.

GOLDSMITH, H.H. "Genetic Influences on Personality From Infancy." *Child Development.* Vol. 54, No. 2 (April 1983):331–35.

GOODE, WILLIAM J. "The Theoretical Importance of Love." *American sSociological Review.* Vol. 24, No. 1 (February 1959):38–47.

_____. "Encroachment, Charlatanism, and the Emerging Profession: Psychology, Sociology and Medicine." *American Sociological Review.* Vol. 25, No. 6 (December 1960):902–14.

GORDON, JAMES S. "The Paradigm of Holistic Medicine." In Arthur C. Hastings et al., eds., *Health for the Whole Person: The Complete Guide to Holistic Medicine.* Boulder, Colo.: Westview Press, 1980:3–27.

GORDON, SOL, and CRAIG W. SNYDER. *Personal Issues in Human Sexuality: A Guidebook for Better Sexual Health.* 2nd ed. Boston: Allyn & Bacon, 1989.

GORING, CHARLES BUCKMAN. *The English Convict: A Statistical Study.* Montclair, NJ: Patterson Smith, 1972; orig. 1913.

GOTTFREDSON, MICHAEL R., and TRAVIS HIRSCHI. "National Crime Control Policies." *Society.* Vol. 32, No. 2 (January-February 1995):30–36.

GOTTMANN, JEAN. *Megalopolis.* New York: Twentieth Century Fund, 1961.

GOUGH, KATHLEEN. "The Origin of the Family." *Journal of Marriage and the Family.* Vol. 33, No. 4 (November 1971):760–71.

GOULD, STEPHEN J. "Evolution as Fact and Theory." *Discover.* (May 1981):35–37.

GOYDER, JOHN, NEIL GUPPY, and MARY THOMPSON. "The Allocation of Male and Female Occupational Prestige in an Ontario Urban Area: A Quarter-Century Replication." *Canadian Review of Sociology and Anthropology.* Vol. 40, No. 4 (November 2003):417–439.

GRANT, KAREN R. "The Inverse Care Law in the Context of Universal Free Health Insurance in Canada: Toward Meeting Health Needs through Public Policy." *Sociological Focus.* Vol. 17, No. 2 (April 1984):137–55.

GREELEY, ANDREW M. *Religious Change in America.* Cambridge, MA: Harvard University Press, 1989.

GREEN, JOHN C. "Pat Robertson and the Latest Crusade: Resources and the 1988 Presidential Campaign." *Social Sciences Quarterly.* Vol. 74, No. 1 (March 1993):156–68.

GREENBERG, DAVID F. *The Construction of Homosexuality.* Chicago: University of Chicago Press, 1988.

GREENFIELD, LAWRENCE A. *Child Victimizers: Violent Offenders and Their Victims.* Washington, DC: U.S. Bureau of Justice Statistics, 1996.

GREENSPOON, EDWARD. "Pay-Equity Costs Too High: Chrétien." *The Globe and Mail.* (August 18, 1998):A3.

GREER, SCOTT. *Urban Renewal and American Cities.* Indianapolis, Ind.: Bobbs-Merrill, 1965.

GREGORY, PAUL R., and ROBERT C. STUART. *Comparative Economic Systems.* 2nd ed. Boston: Houghton Mifflin, 1985.

GROSS, JANE. "New Challenge of Youth: Growing Up in a Gay Home." *New York Times.* (February 11, 1991):A1, B7.

GUINDON, HUBERT. "Quebec and the Canadian Question." In James Curtis and Lorne Tepperman, eds., *Images of Canada: The Sociological Tradition.* Scarborough, ON: Prentice-Hall, Inc., 1990:30–41.

GWARTNEY-GIBBS, PATRICIA A., JEAN STOCKARD, and SUSANNE BOHMER. "Learning Courtship Agression: The Influence of Parents, Peers, and Personal Experiences." *Family Relations.* Vol. 36, No. 3 (July 1987):276–82.

GWYNNE, S. C., and JOHN F. DICKERSON. "Lost in the E-Mail." *Time.* Vol. 149, No. 15 (April 21, 1997):88–90.

GYPPY L.N., and J.L. SILTANEN. "A Comparison of the Allocation of Male and Female Occupational Prestige." *The Canadian Review of Sociology and Anthropology.* Vol. 14, No, 3 (1977):320–330.

HABERMAS, JÜRGEN. *Toward a Rational Society: Student Protest, Science, and Politics.* Jeremy J. Shapiro, trans. Boston: Beacon Press, 1970.

HABTU, ROMAN, and ANDRIJA POPOVIC. "Informal Caregivers: Balancing Work and Life Responsibilities." *Horizons.* Vol. 8 (April 2006):27–34.

HACKER, HELEN MAYER. "Women as a Minority Group." *Social Forces.* Vol. 30 (October 1951): 60–69.

_____. "Women as a Minority Group: 20 Years Later." In Florence Denmark, ed., *Who Discriminates Against Women?* Beverly Hills, CA: Sage, 1974:124–34.

HACKEY, ROBERT B. "Competing Explanations of Voter Turnout Among American Blacks." *Social Science Quarterly.* Vol. 73, No. 1 (March 1992): 71–89.

HACKLER, JIM. "Criminalizing Sex." In Jim Hackler, ed., *Canadian Criminology: Strategies and Perspectives.* Scarborough, ON: Prentice Hall Canada, 1999:254–67.

HADAWAY, C. KIRK, PENNY LONG MARLER, and MARK CHAVES. "What the Polls Don't Show: A Closer Look at U.S. Church Attendance." *American Sociological Review.* Vol. 58, No. 6 (December 1993):741–52.

HADDEN, JEFFREY K., and CHARLES E. SWAIN. *Prime-Time Preachers: The Rising Power of Televangelism.* Reading, MA: Addison-Wesley, 1981.

HAFNER, KATIE. "Making Sense of the Internet." *Newsweek.* (October 24, 1994):46–48.

HAGAN, JACQUELINE MARIA. "Social Networks, Gender, and Immigrant Incorporation: Resources and Restraints." *American Sociological Review.* Vol. 63, No. 1 (February 1998):55–67.

HAGAN, JOHN, and BILL MCCARTHY. *Mean Streets: Youth Crime and Homelessness.* New York: Cambridge University Press, 1997.

HAGAN, JOHN, and FIONA KAY. *Gender in Practice: A Study of Lawyers' Lives.* New York Oxford University Press, 1995.

HAGAN, JOHN, and PATRICIA PARKER. "White-Collar Crime and Punishment: The Class Structure and Legal Sanctioning of Securities Violations." *American Sociological Review.* Vol. 50, No. 3 (June 1985):302–16.

HAIG, ROBIN ANDREW. *The Anatomy of Humor: Biopsychosocial and Therapeutic Perspectives.* Springfield, Ill.: Charles C. Thomas, 1988.

HALBERSTAM, DAVID. *The Reckoning.* New York: Avon Books, 1986.

HALL, JOHN R., and MARY JO NEITZ. *Culture: Sociological Perspectives.* Englewood Cliffs, NJ: Prentice Hall, 1993.

HALL, STUART M. *Policing the Crisis: Mugging, the State, and Law and Order.* London: Macmillan. 1978.

HALLGRIMSDOTTIR, HELGA KRISTIN. "The Knights of Labour and the Failure of the Arbitration Platform, 1886–1887: Ideology, Hegemony, and Contextually Generated Opportunities for Frame Success." *The Sociological Quarterly,* in press.

HALLGRIMSDOTTIR, HELGA, RACHEL PHILLIPS, and CECILIA BENOIT. "Fallen Women and Rescued Girls: Social Stigma and Media Narratives of the Sex Industry in Victoria, BC, from 1980 to 2005." *Canadian Review of Sociology and Anthropology.* In press (2006).

HALLINAN, MAUREEN T., and RICHARD A. WILLIAMS. "Interracial Friendship Choices in Secondary Schools." *American Sociological Review.* Vol. 54, No. 1 (February 1989):67–78.

HAMER, DEAN, and PETER COPELAND. *The Science of Desire: The Search for the Gay Gene and the Biology of Behavior.* New York: Simon & Schuster, 1994.

HAMRICK, MICHAEL H., DAVID J. ANSPAUGH, and GENE EZELL. *Health.* Columbus, Ohio: Merrill, 1986.

HANNIGAN, JOHN. "Sociology and the Environment." In Robert J. Brym, ed., *New Society: Sociology for the 21st Century*. Toronto: Harcourt-Brace, 1998:360–82.

HANSON, R. KARL, HEATHER SCOTT, and RICHARD A. STEFFY. "A Comparison of Child Molesters and Nonsexual Criminals: Risk Predictors and Long-term Recidivism." *Journal of Research in Crime and Delinquency*. Vol. 32, No. 3 (August 1995):327–37.

HAREVEN, TAMARA K. "The Life Course and Aging in Historical Perspective." In Tamara K. Hareven and Kathleen J. Adams, eds., *Aging and Life Course Transitions: An Interdisciplinary Perspective*. New York: Guilford Press, 1982:1–26.

HARLOW, HARRY F., and MARGARET KUENNE HARLOW. "Social Deprivation in Monkeys." *Scientific American*. Vol. 207 (November 1962):137–46.

HARMAN, LESLEY D., and PETRA REMY. "When Life Gets in the Way of Life: Work/Family Struggles Among Female and Male Academics." In Swani Vethamany-Globus, Linda Paul, and Elena Hannah, eds., *Women in the Canadian Academic Tundra: The Trails, Trials, and Triumphs*. Montreal/Kingston: McGill-Queen's University Press, 2002:104–111.

HARPSTER, PAULA, and ELIZABETH MONK-TURNER. "Why Men Do Housework: A Test of Gender Production and the Relative Resources Model." *Sociological Focus*. Vol. 31, No. 1 (February 1998):45–59.

HARRIES, KEITH D. *Serious Violence: Patterns of Homicide and Assault in America*. Springfield, Ill.: Charles C. Thomas, 1990.

HARRIGAN, PATRICK J. "The Schooling of Boys and Girls in Canada." *Journal of Social History*. Vol. 23, No. 4 (Summer 1990):803–26.

HARRINGTON, MICHAEL. *The New American Poverty*. New York: Penguin Books, 1984.

HARRIS, CHAUNCEY D., and EDWARD L. ULLMAN. "The Nature of Cities." *The Annals*. Vol. 242 (November 1945):7–17.

HARRIS, JACK DASH. "Lecture on Cockfighting in the Philippines." *Semester at Sea* (October 27, 1994).

HARRIS, MARVIN. "Why Men Dominate Women." *New York Times Magazine*. (November 13, 1977):46, 115–23.

_____. *Cultural Anthropology*. 1st ed., 1983; 2nd ed. New York: Harper & Row, 1987.

HARRISON, DEBORAH, and LUCIE LALIBERTÉ. *No Life Like It: Military Wives in Canada*. Toronto: James Lorimer & Company, Publishers, 1994.

HARTLEY, THOMAS, and JOSEPHINE MAZZUCA. *Fewer Canadians Favour Legalized Abortion Under Any Circumstance*. The Gallup Poll, Vol. 61, No. 85 (December 12, 2001):1–4. [Online] **www.cric.ca/pdf/gallup/gallup_12.12.01_abortion.pdf**

HAWTHORNE, PETER. "South Africa's Makeover." *Time*. Vol. 154, No. 2 (July 12, 1999).

_____. "An Epidemic of Rapes." *Time*. Vol. 154, No. 18 (November 1, 1999):59.

HAYNEMAN, STEPHEN P., and WILLIAM A. LOXLEY. "The Effect of Primary-School Quality on Academic Achievement Across Twenty-Nine High- and Low-Income Countries." American Journal of Sociology. Vol. 88, No. 6 (May 1983):1162–94.

HEALTH CANADA. *1998–1999 Canadian Sexually Transmitted Diseases (STD) Surveillance Report*. Ottawa: Health Canada, Laboratory Centre for Disease Control. Vol. 2656 (October 2000a).

_____. *HIV and AIDS in Canada: Surveillance Report to June 30, 2000*. Ottawa: Minister of Public Works and Government Services Canada. 2000b.

_____. *Infectious Syphilis in Canada*. Epi Update (February 2002). [Online] **www.hc-sc.gc.ca/pphb-dgspsp/publicat/epiu-aepi/std-mts/infsyph_e.html**

_____. *Cancer, Lung Cancer*. Centre for Chronic Disease Prevention and Control. (2003a) [Online] **www.hc-sc.gc.ca/pphb-dgspsp/ccdpc-cpcmc/cancer/publications/lung_e.html**

_____. *STD Data Tables*. (2003b) [Online] **www.hc-sc.gc.ca/pphb-dgspsp/std-mts/stddata1201/tab2-2_e.html**

_____. *Prevalent HIV Infections in Canada: Up to One-Third May Not Be Diagnosed*. Epi Update (April 2003c). [Online] **www.hc-sc.gc.ca/pphb-dgspsp/publicat/epiu-aepi/hiv-vih/hivtest_e.html**

_____. *National HIV Prevalence and Incidence Estimates for 1999: No Evidence of a Decline in Overall Incidence*. Epi Update (April 2003d). [Online] **www.hc-sc.gc.ca/pphb-dgspsp/publicat/epiu-aepi/hiv-vih/pdf/epiact_0403_e.pdf**

_____. *Health Spending* (2003e). [Online] **www.hc-sc.gc.ca/english/care/spending.html**

HEATH, JULIA A., and W. DAVID BOURNE. "Husbands and Housework: Parity or Parody?" *Social Science Quarterly*. Vol. 76, No. 1 (March 1995):195–202.

HECKATHORN, DOUGLAS. "Respondent-Driven Sampling: A New Approach to the Study of Hidden Populations." *Social Problems*. Vol. 44, No. 2 (1997):174–99.

HEDLEY, ALAN. "Convergence in Natural, Social, and Technical Systems: A Critique." *Current Science*. Vol. 79, No. 5 (September 2000):592–601.

_____. *Running Out of Control: Dilemmas of Globalization*. Bloomfield, CN: Kumarian Press, 2002.

HELGESEN, SALLY. *The Female Advantage: Women's Ways of Leadership*. New York: Doubleday, 1990.

HELIN, DAVID W. "When Slogans Go Wrong." *American Demographics*. Vol. 14, No. 2 (February 1992):14.

HENDRICK, DIANNE, and LEE FARMER. *Adult Correctional Services in Canada, 2001/01*. (2002) *Juristat* Vol. 22, No. 10 (October). Statistics Canada Catalogue No. 85-002-XIE.

HENLEY, NANCY, MYKOL HAMILTON, and BARRIE THORNE. "Womanspeak and Manspeak: Sex Differences in Communication, Verbal and Nonverbal." In John J. Macionis and Nijole V. Benokraitis, eds., *Seeing Ourselves: Classic, Contemporary, and Cross-Cultural Readings in Sociology*. 2nd ed. Englewood Cliffs, NJ: Prentice Hall, 1992:10–15.

HENRY, FRANCES, CAROL TATOR, WINSTON MATTIS, and TIM REES. *The Colour of Democracy: Racism in Canadian Society*. Toronto: Harcourt Brace, 1995.

HENRY, WILLIAM A., III. "Gay Parents: Under Fire and On the Rise." *Time*. Vol. 142, No. 12 (September 20, 1993):66–71.

HERDT, GILBERT H. "Semen Transactions in Sambian Culture." In David N. Suggs and Andrew W. Miracle, eds., *Culture and Human Sexuality*. Pacific Grove, CA: Brooks Cole, 1993:298–327.

HEREK, GREGORY M. "Myths About Sexual Orientation: A Lawyer's Guide to Social Science Research." *Law and Sexuality*. No. 1 (1991): 133–72.

HERMAN, DIANNE. "The Rape Culture." In John J. Macionis and Nijole V. Benokraitis, eds., *Seeing Ourselves: Classic, Contemporary, and Cross-Cultural Readings in Sociology*. 5th ed. Upper Saddle River, NJ: Prentice Hall, 2001.

HERMAN, DIDI. *Rights of Passage: Struggles for Lesbian and Gay Legal Rights*. Toronto: University of Toronto Press, 1994.

HERMAN, EDWARD S. *Corporate Control, Corporate Power: A Twentieth Century Fund Study*. New York: Cambridge University Press, 1981.

HERRNSTEIN, RICHARD J., and CHARLES MURRAY. *The Bell Curve: Intelligence and Class Structure in American Life*. New York: Free Press, 1994.

HERTZ, R. *More Equal Than Others: Women and Men in Dual-Career Marriages*. Berkeley: University of California Press, 1986.

HERTZMAN, CLYDE. "The Biological Embedding of Early Experience and Its Effects on Health in Adulthood." *Annals of the New York Academy of Sciences* 896, 1999:85–95.

HESS, BETH B. "Breaking and Entering the Establishment: Committing Social Change and Confronting the Backlash." *Social Problems*. Vol. 46, No. 1 (February 1999):1–12.

HIRSCHI, TRAVIS. *Causes of Delinquency*. Berkeley: University of California Press, 1969.

HOBART, CHARLES. *Premarital Sexual Standards Among Canadian Students at the End of the Eighties*. Unpublished manuscript. Edmonton: University of Alberta, 1990.

HOBERMAN, JOHN. *Darwin's Athletes: How Sport Has Damaged Black America and Preserved the Myth of Race*. Boston: Houghton Mifflin, 1997.

_____. "Response to Three Reviews of Darwin's Athletes." *Social Science Quarterly*. Vol. 79, No. 4 (December 1998):898–903.

HOCHSCHILD, ARLIE. "Emotion Work, Feeling Rules, and Social Structure."

American Journal of Sociology. Vol. 85, No. 3 (November 1979):551–75.

_____. *The Managed Heart : Commercialization of Human Feeling.* Berkeley: University of California Press, 1983.

_____. *The Time Bind: When Work Becomes Home and Home Becomes Work.* New York: Metropolitan Books, 1997.

HOCHSCHILD, ARLIE, and ANNE MACHUNG. *The Second Shift: Working Parents and the Revolution at Home.* New York: Viking Books, 1989.

HODGE, ROBERT W., DONALD J. TREIMAN, and PETER H. ROSSI. "A Comparative Study of Occupational Prestige." In Reinhard Bendix and Seymour Martin Lipset, eds., *Class, Status, and Power: Social Stratification in Comparative Perspective.* 2nd ed. New York: Free Press, 1966:309–21.

HOLMES, STEVEN A. "For Hispanic Poor, No Silver Lining." *New York Times.* (October 13, 1996): sec. 4, p. 5.

HORTON, HAYWARD DERRICK. "Critical Demography: The Paradigm of the Future?" *Sociological Forum.* Vol. 14, No. 3 (September 1999):363–67.

HOSTETLER, JOHN A. *Amish Society.* 3rd ed. Baltimore: Johns Hopkins University Press, 1980.

HOUT, MICHAEL. "More Universalism, Less Structural Mobility: The American Occupational Structure in the 1980s." *American Journal of Sociology.* Vol. 95, No. 6 (May 1998):1358–1400.

HOYT, HOMER. *The Structure and Growth of Residential Neighborhoods in American Cities.* Washington, DC: Federal Housing Administration, 1939.

HSU, FRANCIS L. K. *The Challenge of the American Dream: The Chinese in the United States.* Belmont, CA: Wadsworth, 1971.

HUCHINGSON, JAMES E. "Science and Religion." *The Herald.* (Dade County, Florida) (December 25, 1994):1M, 6M.

HUFFMAN, MATT L., STEVEN C. VELASCO, and WILLIAM T. BIELBY. "Where Sex Composition Matters Most: Comparing the Effects of Job Versus Occupational Sex Composition of Earnings." *Sociological Focus.* Vol. 29, No. 3 (August 1996):189–207.

HULS, GLENNA. Personal communication, 1987.

HUMAN RIGHTS WATCH. "Children's Rights: Child Labor" (2001). September 25, 2002. [Online] **www.hrw.org/children/labor.htm**

HUMPHREY, CRAIG R., and FREDERICK R. BUTTEL. *Environment, Energy, and Society.* Belmont, CA: Wadsworth, 1982.

HUMPHRIES, HARRY LEROY. *The Structure and Politics of Intermediary Class Positions: An Empirical Examination of Recent Theories of Class.* Unpublished Ph.D. dissertation. Eugene: University of Oregon, 1984.

HUNTER, JAMES DAVISON. *American Evangelicalism: Conservative Religion and the Quandary of Modernity.* New Brunswick, NJ: Rutgers University Press, 1983.

_____. "Conservative Protestantism." In Philip E. Hammond, ed., *The Sacred in a Secular Age.* Berkeley: University of California Press, 1985: 50–66.

_____. *Evangelicalism: The Coming Generation.* Chicago: University of Chicago Press, 1987.

HUNTINGTON, S.P. *The Clash of Civilizations and the Future of the West.* New York: Simon & Schuster, 1996.

HYMOWITZ, CAROL. "World's Poorest Women Advance by Entrepreneurship." *Wall Street Journal* (September 9, 1995):B1.

IACOVETTA, FRANCA. "Remaking Their Lives: Immigrants, Survivors, and Refugees." In Joy Parr, ed., *A Diversity of Women: Ontario, 1945–1980.* Toronto: University of Toronto Press, 1995: 135–67.

IANNACCONE, LAURENCE R. "Why Strict Churches Are Strong." *American Journal of Sociology.* Vol. 99, No. 5 (March 1994):1180–1211.

IDE, THOMAS R., and ARTHUR J. CORDELL. "Automating Work." *Society.* Vol. 31, No. 6 (September-October 1994):65–71.

ILLICH, IVAN. *Medical Nemesis: The Expropriation of Health.* New York: Pantheon Books, 1976.

INGLEHART, RONALD. *Modernization and Postmodernization: Cultural, Economic, and Political Change in 43 Societies.* Princeton, NJ: Princeton University Press, 1997.

INGLEHART, RONALD, et al. *World Values Surveys and European Values Surveys, 1981–1984, 1990–1993, and 1995–1997.* [Computer file]

ICPSR version. Ann Arbor, MI: Interuniversity Consortium for Political and Social Research, 2000.

INSTITUTE FOR PHILOSOPHY AND PUBLIC POLICY. "The Greying of America." Vol. 8, No. 2 (Spring 1988):1–5.

INTERNATIONAL MONETARY FUND. *World Economic Outlook* (April 2000). [Online] **www.imf.org/external/pubs/ft/weo/2000/01/index.htm**

INTER-PARLIAMENTARY UNION. *Women in National Parliaments.* Geneva: 2006. [Online] **www.ipu.org/wmn-e/classif.htm**

INTER-PARLIAMENTARY UNION. *Women in Politics: 2005.* 2005. [Online] **www.ipu.org/pdf/publications/wmnmap05_en.pdf**

IPSOS-REID. "17-Country Poll on Taxes, Spending and Priorities." Media release (March 16, 2000a). [Online] **www.ipsos-reid.com/media/ dsp_displaypr_cdn.cfm?id_to_view=999**

_____. "Money is Not Enough: University Students Personify New Economics of 'The Canadian Dream.'" Press release (December 8, 2000b). [Online] **www.ipsos-reid.com/ media/dsp_displaypr_cdn.cfm?id_to_view=1129**

_____. "Marital Infidelity." Public release (March 14, 2001a). [Online] **www.ipsos-reid.com/media/dsp_displaypr_cdn.cfm?id_to_view=1186**

_____. "Health Care (36%) Increases 14 Points to Return as Most Important Issue Facing the Country According to Canadians." Public release (November 22, 2001b).

_____. "Federal Political Scene, March 2001." Tables accompanying press release March 12, 2001c. [Online] **www.ipsos_reid.com/pdf/media/ mr010312tb_5.pdf**

_____. "Federal Political Scene, Late April 2001." Tables accompanying press release April 27, 2001d. [Online] **www.ipsos_reid.com/pdf/media/ mr010427tb_8.pdf**

_____. "Federal Political Scene, July 2001." Tables accompanying press release July 9, 2001e. [Online] **www.ipsos_reid.com/pdf/media/ mr010709_3t.pdf**

_____. "Federal Liberals Lead in Every Province/ Region in the Country." Tables accompanying press release August 29, 2001f. [Online] **www.ipsos_reid.com/pdf/media/mr010829tb_3.pdf**

_____. "Two-thirds (63%) of Canadians Approve of Prime Minister's Performance." Tables accompanying press release September 28, 2001g. [Online] **www.ipsos_reid.com/pdf/media/mr010928tb.pdf**

_____. "Liberals Continue to Hold Support of Half (49%) of Decided Voters in the Country." Tables accompanying press release November 23, 2001h. [Online] **www.ipsos_reid.com/pdf/media/mr011123_1tb.pdf**

_____. "Federal Liberals (47%) at Lowest Level Since 2000 Election—But Lead Still Comfortable With What Would Be A Sweeping Majority." Tables accompanying press release, March 8, 2002a. [Online] **www.ipsos_reid.com/pdf/media/mr020308tb.pdf**

_____. "Seven in Ten (68%) Canadians Say That Prime Minister Should Step Down—Including 58% of Liberal Supporters." Tables accompanying press release May 31, 2002b. [Online] **www.ipsos-reid.com/pdf/ media/mr020531_2tb.pdf**

_____. "Despite Continued Controversies, Liberal Vote (43%) Holds Static Since May." Tables accompanying press release June 21, 2002c. [Online] **www.ipsos_reid.com/pdf/media/mr020621_1tb_2.pdf**

_____. "Despite Party In-Fighting, Support for Liberals (46%) Climbs." Tables accompanying press release July 19, 2002d. [Online] **www.ipsos_reid.com/pdf/media/mr020719_2tb.pdf**

_____. "The Green Party (4%) Shows Up on Radar Screen...Especially in British Columbia." Tables accompanying press release October 11, 2002e. [Online] **www.ipsos-reid.com/pdf/media/mr021011_1tb.pdf**

_____. "A Reader's Digest Poll: Marriage in Canada." Media release (March 24, 2003a). [Online] **www.angusreid.com/media/dsp_ displaypr_cdn.cfm?id_to_view=1777**

_____. "So, Whom Do We Trust?" Media release (January 22, 2003b). [Online] **www.ipsos-reid.com/pdf/media/mr030122-2.pdf**

_____. "Albertans Oppose Same-Sex Marriages." July 17, 2003c. [Online] **www.ipsos-reid.com/search/pdf/media/mr030717%2D1.pdf**

_____. "Slim Majority (54%) Support Same-Sex Marriages." Public release (June 13, 2003d). [Online] **www.ipsos-reid.com/search/pdf/ mediamr030613%2D1.pdf**

_____. "Same-Sex Marriage: The Debate Enjoined." Public release (August 8, 2003e). [Online] www.ipsos-reid.com/media/dsp_displaypr_cdn.cfm?id_to_view=1877

_____. "God and Other Mysteries: A Look Into the Religious and Spiritual Beliefs of Canadians." Media release (November 1, 2003f) [Online] www.ipsos-reid.com/media/dsp_displaypr_cdn.cfm?id_to_view=1957

_____. "Federal Liberals (50%) Continue to Hold Resounding Lead." Tables accompanying press release (April 27, 2003g). [Online] www.ipsos_reid.com/pdf/media/mr030427_1tb.pdf

_____. "New PC Leader MacKay Convention Fallout." Tables accompanying press release (June 6, 2003h). [Online] www.ipsos_reid.com/pdf/media/mr030606_4tb.pdf

_____. "Uniting the Right . . . ?" Tables accompanying press release (October 5, 2003i). [Online] www.ipsos_reid.com/pdf/media/mr031005_1tb.pdf

_____. "Support for New Conservative Party Drops With Official Announcement of Merger." Tables accompanying press release (October 24, 2003j). [Online] www.ipsos_reid.com/pdf/media/mr031024_3tb.pdf

_____. "Federal Politics: Bouncing Back." Vol. 19, No. 5 (September/October 2004a).

_____. "Federal Liberals Reach 40% for First Time Since May 2004." News release dated October 13, 2004b.

_____. "Federal Vote." News release dated November 2, 2004c.

_____. "Following Loss of Confidence Vote." News release dated May 14, 2005a.

_____. "The Federal Political Landscape." News release dated June 20, 2005b.

_____. "At the One Year Anniversary of the Federal Election." News release dated June 28, 2005c.

_____. "As Liberal Caucus Meets in Regina." News release dated August 22, 2005d.

_____. "Federal Poll." News release dated October 3, 2005e.

_____. "Majority of Canadians (57%) Feel Spring is Best Time to Hold Elections." News release dated November 12, 2005f.

_____. "Most Canadians (78%) Say Election Over Holidays Won't Affect Their Party Vote." News release dated November 17, 2005g.

_____. "Liberals (34% v. 30% Tories) Hold Slim Lead on Eve of Election Call as Canadians Warm to Idea of Potential Harper Minority." News release dated November 17, 2005h.

_____. "Decision Canada." News release dated November 29, 2005i.

_____. "Decision Canada." News release dated December 3, 2005j.

_____. "Grits (34%, +1 Point Have Minor Edge." News release dated December 10, 2005k.

_____. "Liberals (36%, +2 Points) Ahead of Conservatives." News release dated December 13, 2005l.

_____. "Election Prelude Ends With Tight Race." News release dated December 24, 2005m.

_____. "With Three Weeks to Election Day the Tight Race Tilts Tory." News release dated January 2, 2006a.

_____. "As Final Week of 2006 Election Begins, Tories Within Close Striking Distance of Winning Majority Government." News release dated January 17, 2006b.

_____. "Federal Landscape at One Month After Election." News release dated February 23, 2006c.

Isay, Richard A. _Being Homosexual: Gay Men and Their Development._ New York: Farrar, Straus & Giroux, 1989.

Jacobs, Jane. _The Death and Life of Great American Cities._ New York: Random House, 1961.

_____. _The Economy of Cities._ New York: Vintage Books, 1970.

Jacoby, Russell, and Naomi Glauberman, eds., _The Bell Curve Debate._ New York: Random House, 1995.

Jacquet, Constant H., and Alice M. Jones. _Yearbook of American and Canadian Churches 1991._ Nashville, Tenn.: Abingdon Press, 1991.

Jaffe, A.J. _The First Immigrants From Asia: A Population History of the North American Indians._ New York and London: Plenum Press, 1992.

Jagger, Alison. "Political Philosophies of Women's Liberation." In Laurel Richardson and Verta Taylor, eds., _Feminist Frontiers: Rethinking Sex, Gender, and Society._ Reading, MA: Addison-Wesley, 1983.

James, Carl E. "Up to No Good: Black on the Streets and Encountering Police." In Vic Satzewich, ed., _Racism & Social Inequality in Canada._ Toronto: Thompson Educational Publishing Inc. 1998:157–76.

Jamieson, Kathleen. "Sex Discrimination and the _Indian Act._" In J. Rick Ponting, ed., _Arduous Journey: Canadian Indians and Decolonialization._ Toronto: McClelland & Stewart, 1986:112–36.

Janis, Irving. _Victims of Groupthink._ Boston: Houghton Mifflin, 1972.

_____. _Crucial Decisions: Leadership in Policymaking and Crisis Management._ New York: Free Press, 1989.

Janus, Christopher G. "Slavery Abolished? Only Officially." _Christian Science Monitor._ (May 17, 1996):18.

Japanese Ministry of Health, Labour, and Welfare. Statistics and Information Department. _International Divorce Rates._ November 5, 2002. [Online] www.jinjapan.org/stat/stats/02VIT33.html

Jeffries, T. "Sechelt Women and Self-Government." In G. Creese and V. Strong-Boag, eds., _British Columbia Reconsidered: Essays on Women._ Vancouver: Press Gang Publishers, 1992:90–95.

Jencks, Christopher. "Genes and Crime." _New York Review._ (February 12, 1987):33–41.

Jenkins, J. Craig, and Michael Wallace. "The Generalized Action Potential of Protest Movements: The New Class, Social Trends, and Political Exclusion Explanations." _Sociological Forum._ Vol. 11, No. 2 (June 1996):183–207.

Jhaa, Prabhat, Rajesh Kumarb, Priya Vasaa, Neeraj Dhingraa, Deva Thiruchelvama, and Rahim Moineddina. "Low Male-to-Female Sex Ratio of Children Born in India: National Survey Of 1·1 Million Households." _The Lancet_, Volume 367, Issue 9506 (21 January 2006–27 January 2006):211–218.

Johnson, Holly. _Dangerous Domains: Violence Against Women in Canada._ Toronto: Nelson, 1996.

Johnson, Holly, and Cathy Au Coin. "Family Violence in Canada: A Statistical Profile." Ottawa: Canadian Centre for Justice Statistics. Statistics Canada, 2003. Catalogue No. 85-224-XIE. [Online] www.statcan.ca/english/freepub/85_224_XIE/85_224_XIE03000.pdf

Johnson, Paul. "The Seven Deadly Sins of Terrorism." In Benjamin Netanyahu, ed., _International Terrorism._ New Brunswick, NJ: Transaction Books, 1981:12–22.

Johnson, Roland. 1996. [Online] www.PersonalWebs.myriad.net/Roland

Johnston, R.J. "Residential Area Characteristics." In D.T. Herbert and R.J. Johnston, eds., _Social Areas in Cities. Vol. 1: Spatial Processes and Form._ New York: Wiley, 1976:193–235.

Jones, Judy. "More Miners Will Be Offered Free X-Rays; Federal Agency Wants to Monitor Black-Lung Cases." _Louisville Courier Journal._ (May 13, 1999):1A.

Josephy, Alvin M., Jr. _Now That the Buffalo's Gone: A Study of Today's American Indians._ New York: Alfred A. Knopf, 1982.

Kadushin, Charles. "Friendship Among the French Financial Elite." _American Sociological Review._ Vol. 60, No. 2 (April 1995):202–21.

Kahne, Hilda, and Janet Giele, eds. _Women's Work and Women's Lives: The Continuing Struggle Worldwide._ Bounder: Westview Press, 1992.

Kain, Edward L. "A Note on the Integration of AIDS Into the Sociology of Human Sexuality." _Teaching Sociology._ Vol. 15, No. 4 (July 1987):320–23.

_____. _The Myth of Family Decline: Understanding Families in a World of Rapid Social Change._ Lexington, MA: Lexington Books, 1990.

Kain, Edward L., and Shannon Hart. "AIDS and the Family: A Content Analysis of Media Coverage." Presented to National Council on Family Relations, Atlanta, 1987.

Kalbach, Warren E., and Wayne W. McVey. _The Demographic Basis of Canadian Society._ 2nd ed. Toronto: McGraw-Hill Ryerson, 1979.

Kaminer, Wendy. "Volunteers: Who Knows What's In It For Them." _Ms._

(December 1984): 93–94, 96, 126–28.

KAMALA, KEMPADOO, and JO DOEZEMA. *Global Sex Workers: Rights, Resistence, and Redefinition.* New York and London: Routledge, 1998.

KAMIYA, GARY. "Cablinasian Like Me." *Salon.* March 5, 2001. [Online] **www.salon.com/april97/tiger970430.html**

KANTER, ROSABETH MOSS. *Men and Women of the Corporation.* New York: Basic Books, 1977.

KANTER, ROSABETH MOSS, and BARRY A. STEIN. "The Gender Pioneers: Women in an Industrial Sales Force." In R.M. Kanter and B.A. Stein, eds., *Life in Organizations.* New York: Basic Books, 1979:134–60.

KAPLAN, DAVID E., and MICHAEL SCHAFFER. "Losing the Psywar." *U.S. News & World Report* (October 8, 2001):46.

KAPLAN, ERIC B. et al. "The Usefulness of Preoperative Laboratory Screening." *JAMA, Journal of the American Medical Association.* Vol. 253, No. 24 (June 28, 1985):3576–81.

KAPTCHUK, TED. "The Holistic Logic of Chinese Medicine." In Shepard Bliss et al., eds., *The New Holistic Health Handbook.* Lexington, MA: The Steven Greene Press/Penguin Books, 1985:41.

KARP, DAVID A., and WILLIAM C. YOELS. "The College Classroom: Some Observations on the Meaning of Student Participation." *Sociology and Social Research.* Vol. 60, No. 4 (July 1976): 421–39.

KATES, ROBERT W. "Ending Hunger: Current Status and Future Prospects." *Consequences.* Vol. 2, No. 2 (1996):3–11.

KAUFMAN, JASON. "Endogenous Explanation in the Sociology of Culture." *Annual Review of Sociology.* Vol. 30 (2004):335–357.

KAUFMAN, WALTER. *Religions in Four Dimensions: Existential, Aesthetic, Historical and Comparative.* New York: Reader's Digest Press, 1976.

KEISTER, LISA A., and STEPHANIE MOLLER. "Wealth Inequality in the United States." *Annual Review of Sociology.* Vol. 26 (2000):63–81.

KELLERT, STEPHEN R., and F. HERBERT BORMANN. "Closing the Circle: Weaving Strands Among Ecology, Economics, and Ethics." In F. Herbert Bormann and Stephen R. Kellert, eds., *Ecology, Economics, and Ethics: The Broken Circle.* New Haven, CT: Yale University Press, 1991:205–10.

KENTOR, JEFFREY. "The Long-Term Effects of Foreign Investment Dependence on Economic Growth, 1940–1990." *American Journal of Sociology.* Vol. 103, No. 4 (January 1998):1024–46.

KERCKHOFF, ALAN C., RICHARD T. CAMPBELL, and IDEE WINFIELD-LAIRD. "Social Mobility in Great Britain and the United States." *American Journal of Sociology.* Vol. 91, No. 2 (September 1985):281–308.

KERR, THOMAS, MARK TYNDALL, KATHY LI, JULIO S.G. MONTANER, and EVAN WOOD. "Safer Injection Facility Use and Syringe Sharing in Injection Drug Users." *Lancet.* Vol. 366 (2005):316–318.

KEYS, JENNIFER. "Feeling Rules that Script the Abortion Experience." Paper presented at the annual meeting of the American Sociological Association, Chicago, August 2002.

KIDD, QUENTIN, and AIE-RIE LEE. "Postmaterialist Values and the Environment: A Critique and Reappraisal." *Social Science Quarterly.* Vol. 78, No. 1 (March 1997):1–15.

KIDRON, MICHAEL, and RONALD SEGAL. *The New State of the World Atlas.* New York: Simon & Schuster, 1991.

KIELY, RAY. "Globalization, Post-Fordism and the Contemporary Context of Development." *International Sociology.* Vol. 13, No. 1 (March 1998):95–116.

KILBOURNE, BROCK K. "The Conway and Siegelman Claims Against Religious Cults: An Assessment of Their Data." *Journal for the Scientific Study of Religion.* Vol. 22, No. 4 (December 1983):380–85.

KILBOURNE, JEAN. *Slim Hopes: Advertising and the Obsession With Thinness.* Video presentation. Northampton, MA: The Media Education Foundation, 1995.

KILGORE, SALLY B. "The Organizational Context of Tracking in Schools." *American Sociological Review.* Vol. 56, No. 2 (April 1991):189–203.

KILLIAN, LEWIS M. "Organization, Rationality and Spontaneity in the Civil Rights Movement." *American Sociological Review.* Vol. 49, No. 6 (December 1984):770–83.

KING, KATHLEEN PIKER, and DENNIS E. CLAYSON. "The Differential Percep-

tions of Male and Female Deviants." *Sociological Focus.* Vol. 21, No. 2 (April 1988):153–64.

KINSEY, ALFRED et al. *Sexual Behavior in the Human Male.* Philadelphia: Saunders, 1948.

_____. *Sexual Behavior in the Human Female.* Philadelphia: Saunders, 1953.

KITZINGER, JENNY. "Media Templates: Patterns of Association and the (Re)Construction of Meaning Over Time." *Media, Culture, and Society.* 22 (2000):61–84.

KLEINER, CAROLYN. "What's So Funny?" *U.S. News & World Report.* Vol. 132, No. 9 (March 25, 2002):38–39.

KLEINFELD, JUDITH. "Student Performance: Males Versus Females." *The Public Interest.* No. 134 (Winter, 1999):3–20.

KLUCKHOHN, CLYDE. "As An Anthropologist Views It." In Albert Deuth, ed., *Sex Habits of American Men.* New York: Prentice Hall, 1948.

KOBASA, SUZANNE. "Stressful Life Events, Personality and Health: An Inquiry Into Hardiness." *Journal of Personality and Social Psychology.* Vol. 37, No. 1 (1979):1–11.

KOGAWA, JOY. *Obasan.* Markham: Penguin Books, 1981.

KOHEN, D.E., JEANNE BROOKS-GUNN, TAMA LEVENTHAL, and CLYDE HERTZMAN. "Neighborhood Income and Physical and Social Disorder in Canada: Associations with Young Children's Competencies." *Child Development.* Volume 73, Issue 6, 2002:1844–1860.

KOHLBERG, LAWRENCE. *The Psychology of Moral Development: The Nature and Validity of Moral Stages.* New York: Harper & Row, 1981.

KOHLBERG, LAWRENCE, and CAROL GILLIGAN. "The Adolescent as Philosopher: The Discovery of Self in a Postconventional World." *Daedalus.* Vol. 100 (Fall 1971):1051–86.

KOHN, MELVIN L. *Class and Conformity: A Study in Values.* 2nd ed. Homewood, IL: Dorsey Press, 1977.

KOMAROVSKY, MIRRA. *Blue Collar Marriage.* New York: Vintage Books, 1967.

_____. "Cultural Contradictions and Sex Roles: The Masculine Case." *American Journal of Sociology.* Vol. 78, No. 4 (January 1973):873–84.

KONO, CLIFFORD, DONALD PALMER, ROGER FRIEDLAND, and MATTHEW ZAFONTE. "Lost in Space: The Geography of Corporate Interlocking Directorates." *American Journal of Sociology.* Vol. 103, No. 4 (January 1998):863–911.

KORNHAUSER, WILLIAM. *The Politics of Mass Society.* New York: Free Press, 1959.

KOZOL, JONATHAN. *Rachel and Her Children: Homeless Families in America.* New York: Crown Publishers, 1988.

_____. *Savage Inequalities: Children in America's Schools.* New York: Harper Perennial, 1992.

KRAHN, HARVEY J., and GRAHAM S. LOWE. *Work, Industry, and Canadian Society.* 3rd ed. Toronto: ITP Nelson, 1998.

_____. *Work, Industry, and Canadian Society.* 4th ed. Toronto: Nelson, 2002.

KRIEGER, NANCY. "Embodiment: A Conceptual Glossary for Epidemiology." *Journal of Epidemiology and Community Health.* 59 (2005):350–357.

KRIESI, HANSPETER. "New Social Movements and the New Class in the Netherlands." *American Journal of Sociology.* Vol. 94, No. 5 (March 1989):1078–1116.

KRUEGER, INGRID. "Commitment Gives Way to Convenience." *Alberta Report/Western Report.* Vol. 24, No. 46 (October 27, 1997):45–46.

KRUKS, GABRIEL N. "Gay and Lesbian Homeless/Street Youth: Special Issues and Concerns." *Journal of Adolescent Health.* Special Issue, No. 12 (1991):515–18.

KÜBLER-ROSS, ELISABETH. *On Death and Dying.* New York: Macmillan, 1969.

KUDRLE, ROBERT T., and THEODORE R. MARMOR. "The Development of the Welfare States in North America." In Peter Flora and Arnold J. Heidenheimer, eds., *The Development of Welfare States in North America.* London: Transaction Books, 1981.

KUHN, THOMAS. *The Structure of Scientific Revolutions.* 2nd ed. Chicago: University of Chicago Press, 1970.

KUUMBA, M. BAHATI. "A Cross-Cultural Race/Class/Gender Critique of

Contemporary Population Policy: The Impact of Globalization." *Sociological Forum.* Vol. 14, No. 3 (March 1999):447–63.

KUZNETS, SIMON. "Economic Growth and Income Inequality." *The American Economic Review.* Vol. XLV, No. 1 (March 1955):1–28.

_____. *Modern Economic Growth: Rate, Structure, and Spread.* New Haven, CT: Yale University Press, 1966.

LADD, JOHN. "The Definition of Death and the Right to Die." In John Ladd, ed., *Ethical Issues Relating to Life and Death.* New York: Oxford University Press, 1979:118–45.

LAI, H. M. "Chinese." In *Harvard Encyclopedia of American Ethnic Groups.* Cambridge, MA: Harvard University Press, 1980:217–33.

LAMBERG-KARLOVSKY, C.C., and MARTHA LAMBERG-KARLOVSKY. "An Early City in Iran." In *Cities: Their Origin, Growth, and Human Impact.* San Francisco: Freeman, 1973:28–37.

LANDERS, ANN. Syndicated column. *Dallas Morning News* (July 8, 1984):4F.

LANDERS, RENE M. "Gender, Race, and the State Courts." *Radcliffe Quarterly.* Vol. 76, No. 4 (December 1990):6–9.

LANDSBERG, MITCHELL. "Health Disaster Brings Early Death in Russia." *Washington Times* (March 15, 1998):A8.

LAPPÉ, FRANCES MOORE, and JOSEPH COLLINS. *World Hunger: Twelve Myths.* New York: Grove Press/Food First Books, 1986.

LAPPÉ, FRANCES MOORE, JOSEPH COLLINS, and DAVID KINLEY. *Aid as Obstacle: Twenty Questions About Our Foreign Policy and the Hungry.* San Francisco: Institute for Food and Development Policy, 1981.

LAPRAIRIE, CAROL. " *The 'New' Justice: Some Implications for Aboriginal Communities.*" *Canadian Journal of Criminology.* Vol. 40, No. 1 (January 1998):61–79.

LARMER, BROOK. "Dead End Kids." *Newsweek.* (May 25, 1992):38–40.

LARSON, LYLE E., J. WALTER GOLTZ, and CHARLES HOBART. *Families in Canada.* Scarborough: Prentice Hall Canada Inc., 1994.

LASLETT, PETER. *The World We Have Lost: England Before the Industrial Age.* 3rd ed. New York: Charles Scribner's Sons, 1984.

LAUMANN, EDWARD O., JOHN H. GAGNON, ROBERT T. MICHAEL, and STUART MICHAELS. *The Social Organization of Sexuality: Sexual Practices in the United States.* Chicago: University of Chicago Press, 1994.

LEACH, WAYNE COLIN. "Democracy's Dilemma: Explaining Racial Inequality in Egalitarian Societies." *Sociological Forum.* Volume 17, Number 4 (2002):681–696.

LEACOCK, ELEANOR. "Women's Status in Egalitarian Societies: Implications for Social Evolution." *Current Anthropology.* Vol. 19, No. 2 (June 1978):247–75.

LEACY, F.H. *Historical Statistics of Canada.* 2nd ed., electronic ed. Statistics Canada Catalogue No. 11-516-XIE. Ottawa: Statistics Canada, 1999.

LEADBEATER, BONNIE. "Introduction: Urban Girls: Building Strengths in Contexts of Adversity and Support." In Bonnie Leadbeater and Niobe Way, eds., *Urban Girls; Volume II: Building Strengths.* New York: New York University Press, forthcoming.

LEADBEATER, BONNIE, J. ROSS, and NIOBE WAY. *Urban Girls: Resisting Sterotypes, Creating Identities.* New York: New York University Press, 1996.

LEAVITT, JUDITH WALZER. "Women and Health in America: An Overview." In Judith Walzer Leavitt, ed., *Women and Health in America.* Madison: University of Wisconsin Press, 1984:3–7.

LEERHSEN, CHARLES. "Unite and Conquer." *Newsweek.* (February 5, 1990):50–55.

LEIRA, ARNLAUG. *Welfare States and Working Mothers: The Scandinavian Experience.* New York: Cambridge University Press, 1992.

_____. "Combining Work and Family: Nordic Policy Reforms in the 1990s." In Thomas Boje and Arnlaug Leira, eds., *Gender, Welfare State and the Market: Towards a New Division of Labour.* London: Routledge, 2000:157–74.

LELAND, JOHN. "Bisexuality." *Newsweek.* (July 17, 1995):44–49.

LELONDE, MARK. *A New Perspective on the Health of Canadians: Working Paper.* Ontario: Health and Welfare Canada.

LEMERT, EDWIN M. *Social Pathology.* New York: McGraw-Hill, 1951.

_____. *Human Deviance, Social Problems, and Social Control.* 2nd ed. Englewood Cliffs, NJ: Prentice Hall, 1972.

LENGERMANN, PATRICIA MADOO, and RUTH A. WALLACE. *Gender in America: Social Control and Social Change.* Englewood Cliffs, NJ: Prentice Hall, 1985.

LENNON, MARY CLARE. "Sex Differences in Distress; The Impact of Gender and Work Roles." *Journal of Health and Social Behavior.* Vol. 28, No. 3 (1987):290–305.

LENNON, MARY CLARE, and SARAH ROSENFELD. "Relative Fairness and the Doctrine of Housework: The Importance of Options." *American Journal of Sociology.* Vol. 100, No. 2 (September 1994): 506–31.

LENSKI, GERHARD E. *Power and Privilege: A Theory of Social Stratification.* New York: McGraw-Hill, 1966.

LENSKI, GERHARD, JEAN LENSKI, and PATRICK NOLAN. *Human Societies: An Introduction to Macrosociology.* 7th ed. New York: McGraw-Hill, 1995.

LEONARD, EILEEN B. *Women, Crime, and Society: A Critique of Theoretical Criminology.* New York: Longman, 1982.

LESTER, DAVID. *The Death Penalty: Issues and Answers.* Springfield, IL: Charles C. Thomas, 1987.

LeVAY, SIMON. *The Sexual Brain.* Cambridge, MA: MIT Press, 1993.

LEVER, JANET. "Sex Differences in the Complexity of Children's Play and Games." *American Sociological Review.* Vol. 43, No. 4 (August 1978): 471–83.

LEVINE, MICHAEL. *Student Eating Disorders: Anorexia Nervosa and Bulimia.* Washington, DC: National Educational Association, 1987.

_____. "Reducing Hostility Can Prevent Heart Disease." Mount Vernon News (August 7, 1990):4A.

LEVINE, ROBERT V. "Is Love a Luxury?" *American Demographics.* Vol. 15, No. 2 (February 1993): 27–28.

LEVINSON, DANIEL J., with CHARLOTTE N. DARROW, EDWARD B. KLEIN, MARIA H. LEVINSON, and BRAXTON McKEE. *The Seasons of a Man's Life.* New York: Alfred A. Knopf, 1978.

LÉVI-STRAUSS, CLAUDE. *The Elementary Structures of Kinship.* London: Eyre and Spottiswoode, 1969.

LEWIS, FLORA. "The Roots of Revolution." *New York Times Magazine.* (November 11, 1984): 70–71, 74, 77–78, 82, 84, 86.

LEWIS, J., and E. MATICKA-TYNDALE. *Escort Services in a Border Town: Methodological Challenges Conducting Research Related to Sex Work.* Health Canada, Ottawa: Division of STD Prevention and Control, 1999.

LEWIS, OSCAR. *The Children of Sachez.* New York: Random House, 1961.

LEWIS, PIERCE, CASEY McCRACKEN, and ROGER HUNT. "Politics: Who Cares?" *American Demographics.* Vol. 16, No. 10 (October 1994):20–26.

LI, JIANG HONG, and ROGER A. WOJTKIEWICZ. "A New Look at the Effects of Family Structure on Status Attainment." *Social Science Quarterly.* Vol. 73, No. 3 (September 1992):581–95.

LIAZOS, ALEXANDER. "The Poverty of the Sociology of Deviance: Nuts, Sluts and Preverts." *Social Problems.* Vol. 20, No. 1 (Summer 1972): 103–20.

_____. *People First: An Introduction to Social Problems.* Boston: Allyn and Bacon, 1982.

LIGHT, PAUL C. "Big Government Is Bigger than You Think." *Wall Street Journal* (January 13, 1999):A22.

LIN, NAN, and WEN XIE. "Occupational Prestige in Urban China." *American Journal of Sociology.* Vol. 93, No. 4 (January 1988):793–832.

LINDEN, EUGENE. "More Power to Women, Fewer Mouths to Feed." *Time.* Vol. 144, No. 13 (September 26, 1994):64–65.

LINDSTROM, BONNIE. "Chicago's Post-Industrial Suburbs." *Sociological Focus.* Vol. 28, No. 4 (October 1995):399–412.

LINK, BRUCE, and JO PHELAN. "Social Conditions as Fundamental Causes of Disease." *Journal of Health and Social Behavior.* Extra Issue, 1995:80–94.

LINTON, RALPH. "One Hundred Percent American." *The American Mercury.* Vol. 40, No. 160 (April 1937a):427–29.

_____. *The Study of Man.* New York: D. Appleton-Century, 1937b.

LIPS, HILARY. *Sex and Gender: An Introduction.* 2nd ed. Mountain View, CA:

Mayfield Publishing Co., 1993.

LIPSET, SEYMOUR MARTIN. "Canada and the United States: The Cultural Dimension." In Charles F. Doran and John H. Sigler, eds., *Canada and the United States.* Englewood Cliffs, NJ: Prentice-Hall, 1985:109–60.

LISKA, ALLEN E. *Perspectives on Deviance.* 3rd ed. Englewood Cliffs, NJ: Prentice Hall, 1991.

LISKA, ALLEN E., and BARBARA D. WARNER. "Functions of Crime: A Paradoxical Process." *American Journal of Sociology.* Vol. 96, No. 6 (May 1991):1441–63.

LITT, JACQUELYN S., and MARY K. ZIMMERMAN. "Guest Editors' Introduction: Global Perspectives on Gender and Carework: An Introduction." *Gender & Society,* Vol. 17, No. 2 (April 2003):156–165.

LIVERNASH, ROBERT, and ERIC RODENBURG. "Population Change, Resources, and the Environment." *Population Bulletin.* Vol. 53, No. 1 (March 1998).

LOCK, MARGARET. "Cultivating the Body: Anthropology and Epistemology of Bodily Practice and Knowledge." *Annual Review of Anthropology.* Vol. 22 (1993):133–155.

LOHR, STEVE. "British Health Service Faces a Crisis in Funds and Delays." *New York Times.* (August 7, 1988):1, 12.

LOOKER, E. DIANNE, and VICTOR THIESSEN. "Images of Work: Women's Work, Men's Work, Housework." *The Canadian Journal of Sociology.* Vol. 24, No. 2 (Spring 1999):225–254.

LORD, WALTER. *A Night to Remember.* Rev. ed. New York: Holt, Rinehart & Winston, 1976.

LORENZ, KONRAD. *On Aggression.* New York: Harcourt, Brace & World, 1966.

LOWE, GRAHAM. S. *The Quality of Work: A People-Centred Agenda.* Toronto: Oxford University Press, 2000.

LOWE, GRAHAM, and HARVEY KRAHN. "Work Aspirations and Attitudes in an Era of Labour Market Restructuring: A Comparison of Two Canadian Youth Cohorts." *Work, Employment and Society.* Vol. 14, No. 1 (2000):1–22.

LOWMAN, JOHN. "Taking Young Prostitutes Seriously." *Canadian Review of Sociology and Anthropology.* Vol 24, No. 1 (1987):99–116.

_____. "Notions of Equality Before the Law: The Experience of Street Prostitutes and Their Customers." *Journal of Human Justice.* Vol. 1, No. 2 (1990):55–76.

LOWMAN, JOHN, and LAURA FRASER. *Violence Against Persons Who Prostitute: The Experience in British Columbia.* Technical Report No. TR1996-14e. Ottawa: Department of Justice Canada, 1996. [Online] **http://mypage.uniserve.ca/~lowman/violence/title.htm**

LUKER, KRISTEN. *Abortion and the Politics of Motherhood.* Berkeley: University of California Press, 1984.

LUND, DALE A. "Caregiving." *Encyclopedia of Adult Development.* Phoenix, Ariz.: Oryx Press, 1993: 57–63.

LUO, JAR-DER. "The Significance of Networks in the Initiation of Small Businesses in Taiwan." *Sociological Focus.* Vol. 12, No. 2 (June 1997): 297–317.

LUTZ, CATHERINE A. *Unnatural Emotions: Everyday Sentiments on a Micronesia Atoll and Their Challenge to Western Theory.* Chicago: University of Chicago Press, 1988.

LUTZ, CATHERINE A., and GEOFFREY M. WHITE. "The Anthropology of Emotions." *Annual Review of Anthropology.* Vol. 15 (1986):405–36.

LUXTON, MEG. *More Than a Labour of Love: Three Generations of Women in the Home.* Toronto: Women's Press, 1980.

_____. "Wives and Husbands." In Bonnie Fox, ed., *Family Patterns/Gender Relations.* Toronto: Oxford University Press, 2001:176–198.

LYND, ROBERT S., and HELEN MERRELL LYND. *Middletown in Transition.* New York: Harcourt, Brace & World, 1937.

LYNN, MARION, and MILANA TODOROFF. "Women's Work and Family Lives." In Nancy Mandell, ed., *Feminist Issues: Race, Class, and Sexuality.* 2nd ed. Scarborough, ON: Prentice Hall Allyn and Bacon Canada, 1998:208–32.

MA, LI-CHEN. Personal communication, 1987.

MABRY, MARCUS. "New Hope for Old Unions?" *Newsweek.* (February 24, 1992):39.

MABRY, MARCUS, and TOM MASLAND. "The Man After Mandela." *Newsweek.* (June 7, 1999):54–55.

MACCOBY, ELEANOR EMMONS, and CAROL NAGY JACKLIN. *The Psychology of Sex Differences.* Palo Alto, CA: Stanford University Press, 1974.

MACE, DAVID, and VERA MACE. *Marriage East and West.* Garden City, NY: Doubleday (Dolphin), 1960.

MACIONIS, JOHN J. "Intimacy: Structure and Process in Interpersonal Relationships." *Alternative Lifestyles.* Vol. 1, No. 1 (February 1978): 113–30.

_____. "A Sociological Analysis of Humor." Presentation to the Texas Junior College Teachers Association, Houston, 1987.

_____. "Making Society (and, Increasingly, the World) Visible." In Earl Babbie, ed., *The Spirit of Sociology.* Belmont, CA: Wadsworth, 1993: 221–24.

_____. *Society: The Basics.* 7th U.S. ed. Upper Saddle River, NJ: Pearson Education, 2004.

MACIONIS, JOHN J., and KEN PLUMMER. *Sociology: A Global Introduction.* New York: Prentice Hall Europe, 1997.

MACIONIS, JOHN J., and LINDA GERBER. *Sociology.* 3d Can. ed. Scarborough, ON: Prentice Hall Allyn & Bacon Canada, 2001.

MACIONIS, JOHN J., and VINCENT R. PARRILLO. *Cities and Urban Life.* 2nd ed. Upper Saddle River, NJ: Prentice Hall, 2001.

MACKAY, DONALD G. "Prescriptive Grammar and the Pronoun Problem." In Barrie Thorne, Cheris Kramarae, and Nancy Henley, eds., *Language, Gender and Society.* Rowley, MA: Newbury House, 1983:38–53.

MACKAY, JUDITH. *The Penguin Atlas of Human Sexual Behavior.* New York: Penguin Group, 2000.

MACKIE, MARLENE. *Constructing Women and Men: Gender Socialization.* Toronto: Holt, Rinehart and Winston, 1985.

MACLEAN'S. "Classes Taught by Tenured Faculty." *Maclean's.* Vol. 113, Issue 47 (November 20, 2000):78.

MADDOX, SETMA. "Organizational Culture and Leadership Style: Factors Affecting Self-Managed Work Team Performance." Paper presented at the annual meeting of the Southwest Social Science Association, Dallas, February 1994.

MADSEN, AXEL. *Private Power: Multinational Corporations for the Survival of Our Planet.* New York: William Morrow, 1980.

MAHON, RIANNE. "Rescaling Social Reproduction: Childcare in Toronto/Canada and Stockholm/Sweden." *International Journal of Urban and Regional Research.* Vol. 29, No. 2 (2005):341–357.

MALAMUTH, N.M., and F. DONNERSTEIN. *Pornography and Sexual Aggression.* Orlando, Florida: Academic Press, 1984.

MALTHUS, THOMAS ROBERT. *First Essay on Population 1798.* London: Macmillan, 1926; orig. 1798.

MANDELL, NANCY, and ANN DUFFY, eds. *Canadian Families: Diversity, Conflict, and Change.* 2nd ed. Scarborough: ITP Nelson, 2000.

_____, eds. *Canadian Families: Race, Class, Gender and Sexuality.* 3rd ed. Toronto: Harcourt, Brace & Co., 2004.

MANZA, JEFF, and CLEM BROOKS. "The Religious Factor in U.S. Presidential Elections, 1960–1992." *American Journal of Sociology.* Vol. 103, No. 1 (July 1997):38–81.

MARCUSE, HERBERT. *One-Dimensional Man.* Boston: Beacon Press, 1964.

MARE, ROBERT D. "Five Decades of Educational Assortative Mating." *American Sociological Review.* Vol. 56, No. 1 (February 1991):15–32.

MARKOFF, JOHN. "Remember Big Brother? Now He's a Company Man." *New York Times.* (March 31, 1991):7.

MARKOVSKY, BARRY, JOHN SKVORETZ, DAVID WILLER, MICHAEL J. LOVAGLIA, and JEFFREY ERGER. "The Seeds of Weak Power: An Extension of Network Exchange Theory." *American Sociological Review.* Vol. 58, No. 2 (April 1993):197–209.

MARQUAND, ROBERT. "Worship Shift: Americans Seek Feeling of 'Awe.'" *Christian Science Monitor.* (May 28, 1997):1, 8.

MARQUAND, ROBERT, and DANIEL B. WOOD. "Rise in Cults as Millennium Approaches." *Christian Science Monitor.* (March 28, 1997):1, 18.

MARSHALL, KATHERINE. "Part-time by Choice." *Perspectives on Labour and Income*. Statistics Canada Catalogue No. 75-001-XIE. Vol. 1, No. 2 (November 2000):5–12.

MARSHALL, SUSAN E. "Ladies Against Women: Mobilization Dilemmas of Antifeminist Movements." *Social Problems*. Vol. 32, No. 4 (April 1985):348–62.

MARTIN, JOHN M., and ANNE T. ROMANO. *Multinational Crime: Terrorism, Espionage, Drug and Arms Trafficking*. Newbury Park, CA: Sage, 1992.

MARTINDALE, KATHLEEN. "What Makes Lesbianism Thinkable?: Lesbianism From Adrienne Rich to Queer Theory." In Nancy Mandell, ed., *Feminist Issues: Race, Class, and Sexuality*. Scarborough, ON: Prentice Hall Allyn and Bacon Canada, 1998:55–76.

MARULLO, SAM. "The Functions and Dysfunctions of Preparations for Fighting Nuclear War." *Sociological Focus*. Vol. 20, No. 2 (April 1987): 135–53.

MARX, KARL. *Karl Marx: Selected Writings in Sociology and Social Philosophy*. T. B. Bottomore, trans. New York: McGraw-Hill, 1964; orig. 1848.

_____.*Capital*. Friedrich Engels, ed. New York: International Publishers, 1967; orig. 1867.

MARX, KARL, and FRIEDRICH ENGELS. "Manifesto of the Communist Party." In Robert C. Tucker, ed., *The Marx-Engels Reader*. New York: Norton, 1972:331–62; orig. 1848.

_____. *The Marx-Engels Reader*. 2d ed. Robert C. Tucker, ed. New York: Norton, 1978.

MARX, LEO. "The Environment and the 'Two Cultures' Divide." In James Rodger Fleming and Henry A. Gemery, eds., *Science, Technology, and the Environment: Multidisciplinary Perspectives*. Akron, OH: University of Akron Press, 1994: 3–21.

MASON, MARY ANN, and MARC GOULDEN. "Do Babies Matter (Part II)? Closing the Baby Gap." *Academe* (November–December 2004) [Online] **www.aaup.org/publications/Academe/2004/04nd/04ndmaso.htm**

MATAS, ROBERT, and CRAIG MCINNES. "Critics of Nisga'a Treaty Demand Referendum." *Globe and Mail*. (July 23, 1998):A1, A5.

MATICKA-TYNDALE, ELEANOR, NATHALIE BAJOS, KAYE WELLINGS, MARIA DANIELSSON, and JACQUELINE E. DARROCH. "Can More Progress Be Made? Teenage Sexual and Reproductive Behavior in Developed Countries." Alan Guttmacher Institute (Monday, December 10, 2001). [Online] **www.aegis.com/news/ads/2001/AD012130.html**

MATTHIESSEN, PETER. *Indian Country*. New York: Viking Press, 1984.

MAXWELL, MARY PERCIVAL, and JAMES MAXWELL. "Going Co-Ed: Elite Private Schools in Canada." *Canadian Journal of Sociology*. Vol. 20, No. 3 (Summer 1995):333–57.

MAYO, KATHERINE. *Mother India*. New York: Harcourt, Brace, 1927.

MCADAM, DOUG, JOHN D. MCCARTHY, and MAYER N. ZALD. "Social Movements." In Neil J. Smelser, ed., *Handbook of Sociology*. Newbury Park, CA: Sage, 1988:695–737.

MCBROOM, WILLIAM H., and FRED W. REED. "Recent Trends in Conservatism: Evidence of Non-Unitary Patterns." *Sociological Focus*. Vol. 23, No. 4 (October 1990):355–65.

MCCAFFREY, DAWN, and JENNIFER KEYS. "Competitive Framing Processes in the Abortion Debate: Polarization-Vilification, Frame Saving, and Frame Debunking." *Sociological Quarterly*. Vol. 41, No. 1 (Winter 2000):41–61.

MCCOLM, R. BRUCE, JAMES FINN, DOUGLAS W. PAYNE, JOSEPH E. RYAN, LEONARD R. SUSSMAN, and GEORGE ZARYCKY. *Freedom in the World: Political Rights & Civil Liberties, 1990–1991*. New York: Freedom House, 1991.

MCCORMICK, NAOMI B. *Sexual Salvation*. Westport, CT: Praeger, 1994.

MCDANIEL, SUSAN A. "Women's Changing Relations to the State and Citizenship: Caring and Intergenerational Relations in Globalizing Western Democracies." *Canadian Review of Sociology and Anthropology*. Vol. 39, No. 2 (2002):1–26.

MCDONALD, KIM A. "Debate Over How to Gauge Global Warming Heats Up Meeting of Climatologists." *Chronicle of Higher Education*. Vol. XLV, No. 22 (February 5, 1999):A17.

MCDONALD, PETER. "Low Fertility Not Politically Sustainable." *Population Today*. Vol. 29, No. 6 (August/September 2001):3, 8.

MCFARLANE, SETH, RODERIC BEAUJOT, and TONY HADDAD. "Time Constraints and Relative Resources as Determinants of the Sexual Division of Domestic Work." *The Canadian Journal of Sociology*. Vol. 25, No. 1 (Winter 2000):61–82.

MCGEARY, JOHANNA. "Nukes... They're Back." *Time*. Vol. 151, No. 20 (May 25, 1998):34–42.

MCKEE, VICTORIA. "Blue Blood and the Color of Money." *New York Times*. (June 9, 1996):49–50.

MCKENNA, BARRIE. "Milkman Becomes King of the Megadeal: Colossal Sprint Takeover Enhances the Legend of Remarkable Edmonton Native Bernard Ebbers." *The Globe and Mail*. October 6, 1999.

MCKILLOP, BARRY. *Alternative Measures in Canada—1998*. Statistics Canada Catalogue No. 85-545-XIE. Ottawa: Minister of Industry, 1999.

MCLAREN, ANGUS, and ARLENE TIGAR MCLAREN. *The Bedroom and the State: The Changing Practices and Politics of Contraception and Abortion in Canada 1880–1980*. Toronto: McClelland and Stewart, 1986.

MCLEAN, CANDIS. "Shacking Up and Breaking Down." *Alberta Report /Western Report*. Vol. 25, No. 27 (June 6, 1998):28–30.

MCLEAN, SCOTT. "Objectifying and Naturalizing Individuality: A Study of Adult Education in the Canadian Arctic." *Canadian Journal of Sociology*. Vol. 22, No.1 (Winter 1997):1–30.

MCLEOD, JANE D., and MICHAEL J. SHANAHAN. "Poverty, Parenting, and Children's Mental Health." *American Sociological Review*. Vol. 58, No. 3 (June 1993):351–66.

MCLEOD, JAY. *Ain't No Makin' It: Aspirations and Attainment in a Low-Income Neighborhood*. Boulder, CO: Westview Press, 1995.

MCVEY, JR, WAYNE W., and WARREN E. KALBACH. *Canadian Population*. Toronto: Nelson Canada, 1995.

MEAD, GEORGE HERBERT. *Mind, Self, and Society*. Charles W. Morris, ed. Chicago: University of Chicago Press, 1962; orig. 1934.

MEAD, MARGARET. *Sex and Temperament in Three Primitive Societies*. New York: William Morrow, 1963; orig. 1935.

MEADOWS, DONELLA H., DENNIS L. MEADOWS, JORGAN RANDERS, and WILLIAM W. BEHRENS, III. *The Limits to Growth: A Report on the Club of Rome's Project on the Predicament of Mankind*. New York: Universe, 1972.

MELTZER, BERNARD N. "Mead's Social Psychology." In Jerome G. Manis and Bernard N. Meltzer, eds., *Symbolic Interaction: A Reader in Social Psychology*. 3rd ed. Needham Heights, MA: Allyn & Bacon, 1978.

MELUCCI, ALBERTO. "The New Social Movements: A Theoretical Approach." *Social Science Information*. Vol. 19, No. 2 (May 1980):199–226.

_____. *Nomads of the Present: Social Movements and Individual Needs in Contemporary Society*. Philadelphia: Temple University Press, 1989.

MENCKEN, F. CARSON, and IDEE WINFIELD. "Employer Recruiting and the Gender Composition of Jobs." *Sociological Focus*. Vol. 32, No. 2 (May 1999): 210–20.

MERTON, ROBERT K. "Social Structure and Anomie." *American Sociological Review*. Vol. 3, No. 6 (October 1938):672–82.

_____. *Social Theory and Social Structure*. New York: Free Press, 1968.

MEYER, DAVIS S., and NANCY WHITTIER. "Social Movement Spillover." *Social Problems*. Vol. 41, No. 2 (May 1994):277–98.

MICHELS, ROBERT. *Political Parties*. Glencoe, IL: Free Press, 1949; orig. 1911.

MILBRATH, LESTER W. *Envisioning A Sustainable Society: Learning Our Way Out*. Albany: State University of New York Press, 1989.

MILGRAM, STANLEY. "Behavioral Study of Obedience." *Journal of Abnormal and Social Psychology*. Vol. 67, No. 4 (1963):371–78.

_____. "Some Conditions of Obedience and Disobedience to Authority." *Human Relations*. Vol. 18 (February 1965):57–76.

MILIBAND, RALPH. *The State in Capitalist Society*. London: Weidenfeld and Nicolson, 1969.

MILL, JUDY E. "HIV Risk Behaviors Become Survival Techniques for Aboriginal Women." *Western Journal of Nursing Research*. Vol. 19, No. 4 (August 1997):466–90.

MILLER, ARTHUR G. *The Obedience Experiments: A Case of Controversy in Social Science.* New York: Praeger, 1986.

MILLER, FREDERICK D. "The End of SDS and the Emergence of Weatherman: Demise Through Success." In Jo Freeman, ed., *Social Movements of the Sixties and Seventies.* New York: Longman, 1983:279–97.

MILLER, G. TYLER, JR. *Living in the Environment: An Introduction to Environmental Science.* Belmont, CA: Wadsworth, 1992.

MILLER, MICHAEL. "Lawmakers Begin to Heed Calls to Protect Privacy." *Wall Street Journal* (April 11, 1991):A16.

MILLET, KATE. *Sexual Politics.* Garden City, NY: Doubleday, 1970.

MILLS, C. WRIGHT. *The Power Elite.* New York: Oxford University Press, 1956.

_____. *The Sociological Imagination.* New York: Oxford University Press, 1959.

MINK, BARBARA. "How Modernization Affects Women." *Cornell Alumni News.* Vol. III, No. 3 (April 1989):10–11.

MINTZ, BETH, and MICHAEL SCHWARTZ. "Interlocking Directorates and Interest Group Formation." *American Sociological Review.* Vol. 46, No. 6 (December 1981):851–69.

MIROWSKY, JOHN. "The Psycho-Economics of Feeling Underpaid: Distributive Justice and the Earnings of Husbands and Wives." *American Journal of Sociology.* Vol. 92, No. 6 (May 1987):1404–34.

MIROWSKY, JOHN, and CATHERINE ROSS. "Working Wives and Mental Health." Presentation to the American Association for the Advancement of Science, New York, 1984.

MODRCIN, NANCY K. "Slim Options for Battered Men." *Peak,* Simon Fraser University's Student Newspaper, Vol. 98, No. 5 (February 9, 1998). [Online] **www.peak.sfu.ca/the-peak/98-1/issue5/battered.html**

MOFINA, RICK. "Canadians Warming to Gay Marriage: Poll." *Ottawa Citizen.* January 3, 2003. [Online] **www.canada.com/search/story.aspx?id=d26acd49-b3ac-4257-b11b-c15515a4700e**

MOLM, LINDA D. "Risk and Power Use: Constraints on the Use of Coercion in Exchange." *American Sociological Review.* Vol. 62, No. 1 (February 1997):113–33.

MONTAGU, ASHLEY. *The Nature of Human Aggression.* New York: Oxford University Press, 1976.

MOONEY, PAUL, and SHENG XUE. "*The Impossible Dream.*" *Maclean's.* Vol. 113, No. 50 (December 12, 2000):20–21.

MOORE, GWEN. "Structural Determinants of Men's and Women's Personal Networks." *American Sociological Review.* Vol. 55, No. 5 (October 1991):726–35.

_____. "Gender and Informal Networks in State Government." *Social Science Quarterly.* Vol. 73, No. 1 (March 1992):46–61.

MOORE, WILBERT E. "Modernization as Rationalization: Processes and Restraints." In Manning Nash, ed., *Essays on Economic Development and Cultural Change in Honor of Bert F. Hoselitz.* Chicago: University of Chicago Press, 1977:29–42.

_____. *World Modernization: The Limits of Convergence.* New York: Elsevier, 1979.

MORRISETTE, RENE, GRANT SCHELLENBERG, and ANICK JOHNSON. "Diverging Trends in Unionization." *Perspectives on Labour and Income.* Vol. 6, No. 4 (April 2005):5–12.

MORISSETTE, RENE, XUELIN ZHANG, and MARIE DROLET. "Wealth Inequality." *Perspectives on Labour and Income.* Vol. 3, No. 2 (February 2002a): 5–12. (2002a) Statistics Canada Catalogue No. 75-001-XIE.

_____. *The Evolution of Wealth Inequality in Canada, 1984–1999.* Analytical Studies Branch Research Paper Series No. 187. (2002b) Statistics Canada Catalogue No. 11F0019MIE2002187. [Online] **www.statcan.ca/english/research/11F0019MIE/11F0019MIE2002187.pdf**

MORRA, NORMAN, and MICHAEL D. SMITH. "Men in Feminism: Reinterpreting Masculinity and Femininity." In Nancy Mandell, ed., *Feminist Issues: Race, Class, and Sexuality.* 2nd ed. Scarborough, ON: Prentice Hall Allyn and Bacon Canada, 1998:160–78.

MORRIS, A.D., and C.M. MUELLER, eds. *Frontiers in Social Movement Theory.* New Haven, CT: Yale University Press, 1992.

MORTON, F.L. *Morgentaler v. Borowski: Abortion, the Charter, and the Courts.* Toronto: McClelland and Stewart, 1993.

MOSLEY, W. HENRY, and PETER COWLEY. "The Challenge of World Health." *Population Bulletin.* Vol. 46, No. 4 (December 1991). Washington, DC: Population Reference Bureau.

MULFORD, MATTHEW, JOHN ORBELL, CATHERINE SHATTO, and JEAN STOCKARD. "Physical Attractiveness, Opportunity, and Success in Everyday Exchange." *American Journal of Sociology.* Vol. 106, No. 6 (May 1998):1565–92.

MUMFORD, LEWIS. *The City in History: Its Origins, Its Transformations, and Its Prospects.* New York: Harcourt, Brace & World, 1961.

MURDOCK, GEORGE PETER. "Comparative Data on the Division of Labor by Sex." *Social Forces.* Vol. 15, No. 4 (May 1937):551–53.

_____. "The Common Denominator of Cultures." In Ralph Linton, ed., *The Science of Man in World Crisis.* New York: Columbia University Press, 1945:123–42.

_____. *Social Structure.* New York: Free Press, 1965; orig. 1949.

MURPHY, PETER, and HENRY PUDERER. *Census Metropolitan Areas and Census Agglomerations With Census Tracts for the 2001 Census.* Geography Working Paper Series No. 2002-1. Statistics Canada Catalogue No. 92F0138MIE, No. 2002-1 (2002). Ottawa: Statistics Canada, Geography Division. [Online] **www.statcan.ca/english/research/92F0138MIE/02001/cma2001.pdf**

MURRAY, ROBIN. "Fordism and Post-Fordism." In Stuart Hall and Martin Jacques, eds., *New Times.* London: Lawrence & Wishart, 1989:38–52.

MYERS, DAVID G. *The American Paradox: Spiritual Hunger in an Age of Plenty.* New Haven and London: Yale University Press, 2000.

MYERS, NORMAN. "Humanity's Growth." In Sir Edmund Hillary, ed., *Ecology 2000: The Changing Face of the Earth.* New York: Beaufort Books, 1984a:16–35.

_____. "The Mega-Extinction of Animals and Plants." In Sir Edmund Hillary, ed., *Ecology 2000: The Changing Face of the Earth.* New York: Beaufort Books, 1984b:82–107.

_____. "Disappearing Cultures." In Sir Edmund Hillary, ed., *Ecology 2000: The Changing Face of the Earth.* New York: Beaufort Books, 1984c:162–69.

_____. "Biological Diversity and Global Security." In F. Herbert Bormann and Stephen R. Kellert, eds., *Ecology, Economics, and Ethics: The Broken Circle.* New Haven, CT: Yale University Press, 1991:11–25.

MYERS, SHEILA, and HAROLD G. GRASMICK. "The Social Rights and Responsibilities of Pregnant Women: An Application of Parsons' Sick Role Model." Paper presented to Southwestern Sociological Association, Little Rock, Arkansas, March 1989.

MYLES, JOHN. "When Markets Fail: Social Welfare in Canada and the United States." In Gösta Esping-Andersen, ed., *Welfare States in Transition: National Adaptations in Global Economies.* London: Sage, 1996:116–40.

MYLES, JOHN. "Where Have All the Sociologists Gone? Explaining Economic Inequality. Note on the Discipline." *Canadian Journal of Sociology.* Vol. 28, No. 4 (Fall 2003):551–559.

MYLES, JOHN, and DENNIS FORCESE. "Voting and Class Politics in Canada and the United States." *Comparative Social Research.* Vol. 4 (1981):3–31.

NAGEL, JOANE. "Constructing Ethnicity: Creating and Recreating Ethnic Identity and Culture." *Social Problems.* Vol. 41, No. 1 (February 1994): 152–76.

NAJAFIZADEH, MEHRANGIZ, and LEWIS A. MENNERICK. "Sociology of Education or Sociology of Ethnocentrism: The Portrayal of Education in Introductory Sociology Textbooks." *Teaching Sociology.* Vol. 20, No. 3 (July 1992):215–21.

NANCARROW CLARKE, JUANNE, and LAUREN NANCARROW CLARKE. *Finding Strength. A Mother and Daughter's Story of Childhood Cancer.* Toronto: Oxford University Press, 1999.

NASH, J. MADELEINE. "To Know Your Own Fate." *Time.* Vol. 145, No. 14 (April 3, 1995):62.

NELSON, E.D., and B.W. ROBINSON. *Gender in Canada.* Scarborough, ON: Prentice Hall, 1999.

NEUHOUSER, KEVIN. "The Radicalization of the Brazilian Catholic Church in Comparative Perspective." *American Sociological Review.* Vol. 54, No. 2 (April 1989):233–44.

NEUMAN, W. LAURENCE. *Social Research Methods: Qualitative and Quantitative Approaches.* 3rd ed. Boston: Allyn and Bacon, 1997.

NEWMAN, KATHERINE S. *Declining Fortunes: The Withering of the American Dream.* New York: Basic Books, 1993.

NEWMAN, PETER. *The Canadian Establishment.* Vol. 1. Toronto: McClelland & Stewart, 1975.

NEWMAN, WILLIAM M. *American Pluralism: A Study of Minority Groups and Social Theory.* New York: Harper & Row, 1973.

NG, ROXANNE. "Racism, Sexism and Immigrant Women." In Sandra Burt, Lorraine Code, and Lindsay Dorney, eds., *Changing Patterns: Women in Canada.* 2nd ed. Toronto: McClelland and Stewart, 1993:279–307.

NG, ROXANNE, and TANIA DAS GUPTA. "Nation Builders? The Captive Labour Force of Non-English Speaking Immigrant Women." *Canadian Women's Studies.* Vol. 3, No. 1 (1993):83–85.

NIELSEN, FRANCOIS, and ARTHUR S. ALDERSON. "The Kuznets Curve: The Great U-Turn: Income Inequality in U.S. Counties, 1970 to 1990." *American Sociological Review.* Vol. 62, No. 1 (February 1997):12–33.

NIELSEN, JOYCE MCCARL, ed. *Feminist Research Methods: Exemplary Readings in the Social Sciences.* Boulder, Colo.: Westview, 1990.

1991 GREEN BOOK. U.S. House of Representatives. Washington, DC: U.S. Government Printing Office, 1991.

NIPPERT-ENG, CHRISTENA E. *Home and Work: Negotiating Boundaries Through Everyday Life.* Chicago: The University of Chicago Press, 1995.

NISBET, ROBERT A. *The Sociological Tradition.* New York: Basic Books, 1966.

_____. *The Quest for Community.* New York: Oxford University Press, 1969.

NOLAN, PATRICK, and GERHARD LENSKI. *Human Societies: An Introduction to Macrosociology.* 8th ed. New York: McGraw-Hill, 1999.

NORC. *General Social Surveys, 1972–1998: Cumulative Codebook.* Chicago: National Opinion Research Center, 1999.

_____. *General Social Surveys, 1972–2000: Cumulative Codebook.* Chicago: National Opinion Research Center, 2001.

NOVAK, VIVECA. "The Cost of Poor Advice." *Time.* Vol. 154, No. 1 (July 5, 1999):38.

NUNN, CLYDE Z., HARRY J. CROCKETT, JR., and J. ALLEN WILLIAMS, JR. *Tolerance for Nonconformity.* San Francisco: Jossey-Bass, 1978.

OAKES, JEANNIE. "Classroom Social Relationships: Exploring the Bowles and Gintis Hypothesis." *Sociology of Education.* Vol. 55, No. 4 (October 1982):197–212.

_____. *Keeping Track: How High Schools Structure Inequality.* New Haven, CT: Yale University Press, 1985.

O'BRIEN, DAVID J., EDWARD W. HASSINGER, and LARRY DERSHEM. "Size of Place, Residential Stability, and Personal Social Networks." *Sociological Focus.* Vol. 29, No. 1 (February 1996):61–72.

O'BRIEN, MARY. *The Politics of Reproduction.* Boston: Routledge & Kegan Paul, 1983.

O'CONNOR, RORY J. "Internet Declared Protected Speech." *Post-Star* (Glens Fall, NY). (June 27, 1997):A1–A2.

OECD. *Education at a Glance: 2000 Edition.* Paris: OECD, 2000.

_____. *Education at a Glance: 2002 Edition.* Paris: OECD, 2002.

_____. "Health Data." Accessed April 23, 2006. [Online] **http://ocde.p4.siteinternet.com/publications/doifiles/812005171G001.xls**

OFFIR, CAROLE WADE. *Human Sexuality.* New York: Harcourt Brace Jovanovich, 1982.

OGBURN, WILLIAM F. *On Culture and Social Change.* Chicago: University of Chicago Press, 1964.

OGMUNDSON, R., and J. MCLAUGHLIN. "Changes in An Intellectual Elite 1960–1990: The Royal Society Revisited." *Canadian Review of Sociology & Anthropology.* Vol. 31, No. 1 (February 1994): 1–13.

OKRENT, DANIEL. "Raising Kids Online: What Can Parents Do?" *Time.* Vol. 154, No. 18 (May 10, 1999):38–43.

OLSEN, DENIS. *The State Elite.* Toronto: McClelland and Stewart, 1980.

OLSEN, GREGG M. "Locating the Canadian Welfare State: Family Policy and Health Care in Canada, Sweden, and the United States." *Canadian Journal of Sociology.* Vol. 19, No. 1 (1994):1–20.

_____. "Re-Modeling Sweden: The Rise and Demise of the Compromise in a Global Economy." *Social Problems.* Vol. 43, No. 1 (February 1996):1–20.

OLZAK, SUSAN. "Labor Unrest, Immigration, and Ethnic Conflict in Urban America, 1880–1914." *American Journal of Sociology.* Vol. 94, No. 6 (May 1989):1303–33.

OMATSU, MARYKA. *Bittersweet Passage: Redress and the Japanese Canadian Experience.* Toronto: Between the Lines, 1992.

O'NEIL, PETER. "Use of Pepper Spray Was Reasonable, Chrétien Says." *Montreal Gazette.* (November 28, 1997):A15.

OREOPOULOS, PHILIP. "The Compelling Effects of Compulsory Schooling: Evidence From Canada." *Canadian Journal of Economics.* Vol. 39, No. 1 (2006):22–52.

ORLANSKY, MICHAEL D., and WILLIAM L. HEWARD. *Voices: Interviews With Handicapped People.* Columbus, Ohio: Merrill, 1981:85, 92, 133–34, 172.

OSGOOD, D. WAYNE, JANET K. WILSON, PATRICK M. O'MALLEY, JERALD G. BACHMAN, and LLOYD D. JOHNSTON. "Routine Activities and Individual Deviant Behavior." *American Sociological Review.* Vol. 61, No. 4 (August 1996):635–55.

OSTRANDER, SUSAN A. "Upper Class Women: The Feminine Side of Privilege." *Qualitative Sociology.* Vol. 3, No. 1 (Spring 1980):23–44.

_____. *Women of the Upper Class.* Philadelphia: Temple University Press, 1984.

OUCHI, WILLIAM. *Theory Z: How American Business Can Meet the Japanese Challenge.* Reading, MA: Addison-Wesley, 1981.

OVADIA, SETH. "Race, Class, and Gender Differences in High School Seniors' Values: Applying Intersection Theory in Empirical Analysis." *Social Science Quarterly.* Vol. 82, No. 2 (June 2001):341–56.

OWEN, DAVID. *None of the Above: Behind the Myth of Scholastic Aptitude.* Boston: Houghton Mifflin, 1985.

PACQUET, BERNARD. *Low-Income Cutoffs From 1992 to 2001 and Low Income Measures From 1991 to 2000.* (2002) Statistics Canada Catalogue No. 75F0002MIE, No. 005. [Online] **www.statcan.ca/english/research/75F0002MIE/75F0002MIE2002005.pdf**

PAKULSKI, JAN. "Mass Social Movements and Social Class." *International Sociology.* Vol. 8, No. 2 (June 1993):131–58.

PALLONE, NATHANIEL J., and JAMES J. HENNESSY. "Brain Dysfunction and Criminal Violence." *Society.* Vol. 35, No. 6 (September–October 1998):20–27.

PAMMET, JON H., and LAWRENCE LEDUC. "Explaining the Turnout Decline in Canadian Federal Elections: A New Survey of Non-Voters." Ottawa: Elections Canada. (2003). [Online] **www.elections.ca/loi/tur/tud/TurnoutDecline.pdf**

PARCEL, TOBY L., CHARLES W. MUELLER, and STEVEN CUVELIER. "Comparable Worth and Occupational Labor Market: Explanations of Occupational Earnings Differentials." Paper presented at the American Sociological Association, New York, 1986.

PARENTI, MICHAEL. *Inventing Reality: The Politics of the Mass Media.* New York: St. Martin's Press, 1986.

PARK, ALICE. "Suffer the Children." *Time.* Vol. 156, No. 2 (July 10, 2000):99.

PARK, ROBERT E. *Race and Culture.* Glencoe, IL: Free Press, 1950.

PARSONS, TALCOTT. "Age and Sex in the Social Structure of the United States." *American Sociological Review.* Vol. 7, No. 4 (August 1942):604–16.

_____. *The Social System.* New York: Free Press, 1964; orig. 1951.

_____. *Essays in Sociological Theory.* New York: Free Press, 1954.

_____. *Societies: Evolutionary and Comparative Perspectives.* Englewood Cliffs, NJ: Prentice Hall, 1966.

PARSONS, TALCOTT, and ROBERT F. BALES, eds. *Family, Socialization and Interaction Process.* New York: Free Press, 1955.

PASTOR, ROBERT. "America Observed: Why Foreign Election Observers Would Rate the United States Near the Bottom." *The American Prospect*

Online Edition. Vol. 01, No. 04. (2005) [Online] **www.prospect.org/web/page.ww?section=root&name=ViewPrint&articleId=8960**

PATEMAN, CAROLE. *The Sexual Contract.* Cambridge: Polity Press, 1988.

PAUL, ELLEN FRANKEL. "Bared Buttocks and Federal Cases." *Society.* Vol. 28, No. 4 (May–June, 1991):4–7.

PEAR, ROBERT. "Women Reduce Lag in Earnings, But Disparities With Men Remain." *New York Times.* (September 4, 1987):1, 7.

PEARSON, DAVID E. "Post-Mass Culture." *Society.* Vol. 30, No. 5 (July–August 1993):17–22.

_____. "Community and Sociology." *Society.* Vol. 32, No. 5 (July–August 1995):44–50.

PEASE, JOHN, and LEE MARTIN. "Want Ads and Jobs for the Poor: A Glaring Mismatch." *Sociological Forum.* Vol. 12, No. 4 (December 1997):545–64.

PEAT MARWICK AND PARTNERS. "Canadians' Attitudes Toward and Perceptions of Pornography and Prostitution." *Working Papers on Pornography and Prostitution #6.* Ottawa: Department of Justice, 1984.

PERSELL, CAROLINE HODGES. *Education and Inequality: A Theoretical and Empirical Synthesis.* New York: Free Press, 1977.

PESSEN, EDWARD. *Riches, Class, and Power: America Before the Civil War.* New Brunswick, NJ: Transaction, 1990.

PETERS ATLAS OF THE WORLD. New York: Harper & Row, 1990.

PETERSEN, TROND, ISHAK SAPORTA, and MARC-DAVID L. SEIDEL. "Offering a Job: Meritocracy and Social Networks." *American Journal of Sociology.* Vol. 106, No. 3 (November 2000):763–816.

PEW RESEARCH CENTER FOR THE PEOPLE AND THE PRESS. "Views of a Changing World: Summer 2002 44-Nation Survey." (2003). [Electronic Data File.]

PEW RESEARCH CENTER FOR THE PEOPLE AND THE PRESS. *Views of a Changing World, 2003.* Washington, DC: The Pew Research Center For The People & The Press, 2003.

PHILLIPS, RACHEL, and CECILIA BENOIT. "Social Determinants of Health Care Access Among Sex Industry Workers in Canada." *Sociology of Health Care.* Vol. 23 (2005):79–104.

PHIPPS, SHELLEY. "Working for Working Parents: The Evolution of Maternity and Parental Benefits in Canada." *Choices.* Vol. 12, No. 2 (2006):2–40.

PINCHOT, GIFFORD, and ELIZABETH PINCHOT. *The End of Bureaucracy and the Rise of the Intelligent Organization.* San Francisco: Berrett-Koehler, 1993.

PINES, MAYA. "The Civilization of Genie." *Psychology Today.* Vol. 15 (September 1981):28–34.

PINHEY, THOMAS K., DONALD H. RUBINSTEIN, and RICHARD S. COLFAX. "Overweight and Happiness: The Reflected Self-Appraisal Hypothesis Reconsidered." *Social Science Quarterly.* Vol. 78, No. 3 (September 1997):747–55.

PIRANDELLO, LUIGI. "The Pleasure of Honesty." In *To Clothe the Naked and Two Other Plays.* New York: Dutton, 1962:143–98.

PIVEN, FRANCES FOX, and RICHARD A. CLOWARD. *Poor People's Movements: Why They Succeed, How They Fail.* New York: Pantheon Books, 1977.

PLOMIN, ROBERT, and TERRYL T. FOCH. "A Twin Study of Objectively Assessed Personality in Childhood." *Journal of Personality and Social Psychology.* Vol. 39, No. 4 (October 1980):680–88.

PODOLNY, JOEL M., and JAMES N. BARON. "Resources and Relationships: Social Networks and Mobility in the Workplace." *American Sociological Review.* Vol. 62, No. 5 (October 1997):673–93.

POHL, RUDIGER. "The Transition From Communism to Capitalism in East Germany." *Society.* Vol. 33, No. 4 (June 1996):62–65.

POLENBERG, RICHARD. *One Nation Divisible: Class, Race, and Ethnicity in the United States since 1938.* New York: Pelican Books, 1980.

POLLACK, ANDREW. "Overseas, Smoking Is One of Life's Small Pleasures." *New York Times* (August 17, 1997):E5.

POLSBY, NELSON W. "Three Problems in the Analysis of Community Power." *American Sociological Review.* Vol. 24, No. 6 (December 1959):796–803.

PONTING, J. RICK. "Racial Conflict: Turning Up the Heat." In Dan Glenday and Ann Duffy, eds., *Canadian Society: Understanding and Surviving the 1990s.* Toronto: McClelland and Stewart, 1994:86–118.

PONTING, J. RICK, and JERILYNN KIELY. "Disempowerment: 'Justice,' Racism, and Public Opinion." In J. Rick Ponting, ed., *First Nations in Canada: Perspectives on Opportunity, Empowerment, and Self-Determination.* Whitby, ON: McGraw-Hill Ryerson, 1997.

POPENOE, DAVID. "American Family Decline, 1960–1990: A Review and Appraisal." *Journal of Marriage and the Family.* Vol. 55, No. 3 (August 1993a):527–55.

_____. "Parental Androgyny." *Society.* Vol. 30, No. 6 (September–October 1993b):5–11.

_____. "Can the Nuclear Family Be Revived?" *Society.* Vol. 36, No. 5 (July–August 1999):28–30.

POPKIN, SUSAN J. "Welfare: Views From the Bottom." *Social Problems.* Vol. 17, No. 1 (February 1990):64–79.

POPLINE. "China Faces Water Shortage." Vol. 23 (December 2001):1–4.

POPULATION ACTION INTERNATIONAL. *People in the Balance: Population and Resources at the Turn of the Millennium.* Washington, DC: PAI, 2000.

POPULATION REFERENCE BUREAU. *World Population Data Sheet 2000.* Washington, DC: The Bureau, 2002.

_____. *Women of Our World 2005; Demographic and Health Surveys.* Washington, DC: PRB, 2005. [Online] **www.prb.org/womenofourworld**

PORTER, JOHN. *The Vertical Mosaic.* Toronto: University of Toronto Press, 1965.

POSTEL, SANDRA. "Facing Water Scarcity." In Lester R. Brown et al., eds., *State of the World 1993: A Worldwatch Institute Report on Progress Toward a Sustainable Society.* New York: Norton, 1993:22–41.

POWELL, CHRIS, and GEORGE E.C. PATON, eds. *Humour in Society: Resistance and Control.* New York: St. Martin's Press, 1988.

PRENTICE, ALISON. *The School Promoters.* Toronto: McClelland and Stewart, 1977.

PRENTICE, ALISON, PAULA BOURNE, GAIL GUTHBERT BRANDT, BETH LIGHT, WENDY MITCHINSON, and NAOMI BLACK. *Canadian Women: A History.* 2nd ed. Toronto: Harcourt Brace & Company, 1996.

PRESSLEY, SUE ANNE, and NANCY ANDREWS. "For Gay Couples, the Nursery Becomes the New Frontier." *Washington Post.* (December 20, 1992):A1, A22–23.

PRIMEGGIA, SALVATORE, and JOSEPH A. VARACALLI. "Southern Italian Comedy: Old to New World." In Joseph V. Scelsa, Salvatore J. LaGumina, and Lydio Tomasi, eds., *Italian Americans in Transition.* New York: The American Italian Historical Association, 1990:241–52.

PRIVACY COMMISSIONER OF CANADA. *Privacy Legislation in Canada.* (2003) [Online] **www.privcom.gc.ca/fs-fi/fs2001-02_e.asp**

PUBLIC HEALTH AGENCY OF CANADA. 2004 Canadian Sexually Transmitted Infections Surveillance Report: Pre-Release: STI Data Tables, Table 2.1 Reported Gonorrhea Cases and Rates in Canada by Age Group and Sex, 1980–2004. (2006) [Online] **www.phac-aspc.gc.ca/std-mts/stddata_pre06_04/tab2-1_e.html**

PULLIAM, SUSAN, DEBORAH SALOMON, and CARRICK MOLLENKAMP. "Former WorldCom CEO Built an Empire on Mountain of Debt." *The Wall Street Journal.* December 31, 2002:1.

PUTERBAUGH, GEOFF, ed. *Twins and Homosexuality: A Casebook.* New York: Garland, 1990.

PUTKA, GARY. "SAT To Become A Better Gauge." *Wall Street Journal.* (November 1, 1990):B1.

QUEENAN, JOE. "The Many Paths to Riches." *Forbes.* Vol. 144, No. 9 (October 23, 1989):149.

QUINNEY, RICHARD. *Class, State and Crime: On the Theory and Practice of Criminal Justice.* New York: David McKay, 1977.

RANKIN, BRUCE, and ISIK AYTAC. "Gender Inequality in Schooling: The Case of Turkey." *Sociology of Education.* Vol. 79 (2006):25–43.

RAPHAEL, RAY. *The Men From the Boys: Rites of Passage in Male America.* Lincoln and London: University of Nebraska Press, 1988.

RECKLESS, WALTER C., and SIMON DINITZ. "Pioneering With Self-Concept as a Vulnerability Factor in Delinquency." *Journal of Criminal Law, Criminology, and Police Science.* Vol. 58, No. 4 (December 1967):515–23.

REED, HOLLY E. "Kosovo and the Demography of Forced Migration." *Population Today*. Vol. 27, No. 6 (June 1999):4.

REID, ANGUS. *Shakedown: How the New Economy is Changing Our Lives*. Toronto: Doubleday Canada, 1996.

REIMAN, JEFFREY. *The Rich Get Richer and the Poor Get Prison: Ideology, Class, and Criminal Justice*. Boston: Allyn and Bacon, 1998.

REINHARZ, SHULAMIT. *Feminist Methods in Social Research*. New York: Oxford University Press, 1992.

REISSMAN, CATERINE K. "Stigma and Everyday Resistance Practices: Childless Women in South Africa." *Gender and Society*. Vol. 14, No. 1 (2000):111–135.

REITZ, JEFFREY G. *The Survival of Ethnic Groups*. Toronto: McGraw-Hill Ryerson, 1980.

REITZ, JEFFREY, and RAYMOND BRETON. *The Illusion of Difference: Realities of Ethnicity in Canada and the United States*. Toronto: C.D. Howe Institute, 1994.

REMOFF, HEATHER TREXLER. *Sexual Choice: A Woman's Decision*. New York: Dutton/Lewis, 1984.

REMY, JACQUELINE. "Interview With Agnes Fournier de Saint-Maur, Interpol Police Lieutenant." For *L'Express*; reprinted in *World Press Review*. (November 1996):7.

RESKIN, BARBARA F., and DEBRA BRANCH MCBRIER. "Why Not Ascription? Organizations' Employment of Male and Female Managers." *American Sociological Review*. Vol. 65, No. 2 (April 2000):210–33.

RICHARDSON, C.J. "Divorce and Remarriage." In Maureen Baker, ed., *Families: Changing Trends in Canada*. 3rd ed. Toronto: McGraw-Hill Ryerson, 1996:315–49.

RICHARDSON, JAMES T. "Definitions of Cult: From Sociological–Technical to Popular Negative." Paper presented to the American Psychological Association, Boston, August, 1990.

RICHER, STEPHEN. "Sex-Role Socialization and Early Schooling." *Canadian Review of Sociology and Anthropology*. Vol. 16, No. 2 (1979):195–205.

RIDGEWAY, CECILIA L. *The Dynamics of Small Groups*. New York: St. Martin's Press, 1983.

RIESMAN, DAVID. *The Lonely Crowd: A Study of the Changing American Character*. New Haven, CT: Yale University Press, 1970; orig. 1950.

RIIS, OLE. "Religion Re-Emerging: The Role of Religion in Legitimating Integration and Power in Modern Societies." *International Sociology*. Vol. 13, No. 2 (June 1998):249–72.

RILEY, MATILDA WHITE, ANNE FONER, and JOAN WARING. "Sociology of Age." In Neil J. Smelser, ed., *Handbook of Sociology*. Newbury Park, CA: Sage, 1988:243–90.

RILEY, NANCY E. "Gender, Power, and Population Change." *Population Bulletin*. Vol. 52, No. 1 (May 1997).

RIORDAN, CORNELIUS. "Failing in School: Yes; Victims of War? No." *Sociology of Education*. Vol. 76 (2003):369–72.

RISKA, ELIANNE. "The Rise and Fall of Type A Man." *Social Science & Medicine*, Volume 51, Issue 11, 1 (2000):1665–1674.

_____. "From Type A Man to the Hardy Man: Masculinity and Health." *Sociology of Health & Illness*. 24 (3) (2002):347–358.

RISKA, ELIANNE, and KATARINA WEGAR, eds. *Gender, Work, and Medicine: Women and the Medical Division of Labour*. Newbury Park, CA: Sage, 1993.

RITZER, GEORGE. *The McDonaldization of Society: An Investigation Into the Changing Character of Contemporary Social Life*. Revised ed. Thousand Oaks, CA: Sage, 1996.

_____. *The McDonaldization Thesis: Explorations and Extensions*. Thousand Oaks, CA: Sage, 1998.

_____. "The Globalization of McDonaldization." *The Spark* (February 2000):8–9.

RITZER, GEORGE, and DAVID WALCZAK. *Working: Conflict and Change*. 4th ed. Englewood Cliffs, NJ: Prentice Hall, 1990.

ROACH, KENT. "Changing Punishment at the Turn of the Century: Restorative Justice on the Rise." *Canadian Journal of Criminology*. Vol. 42 No. 3 (July 2000):249–280.

ROBERTS, J. DEOTIS. *Roots of a Black Future: Family and Church*. Philadelphia: The Westminster Press, 1980.

ROBERTS, JULIAN V. *Disproportionate Harm: Hate Crime in Canada*. Working document prepared for Research, Statistics and Evaluation Directorate, Policy Sector, Justice Canada. Document No. WD1995-11e (1995). Ottawa: Justice Canada.

ROBERTSON, TODD. "Changing patterns of university finance." *Education Quarterly Review*. Vol. 9, No. 2. Catalogue No. 81-003-XIE (June 2003):9–17.

ROBINSON, JOYCE, and GLENNA SPITZE. "Whistle While You Work? The Effect of Household Task Performance on Women's and Men's Well-Being." *Social Science Quarterly*. Vol. 73, No. 4 (December 1992):844–61.

ROBINSON, THOMAS N., MARTA L. WILDE, LISA C. NAVRACRUZ, K. FARISH HAYDEL, and ANN VARADY. "Effects of Reducing Children's Television and Video Game Use on Aggressive Behavior." *Archives of Pediatrics and Adolescent Medicine*. Vol. 155 (January 2001):17–23.

ROBINSON, VERA M. "Humor and Health." In Paul E. McGhee and Jeffrey H. Goldstein, eds., *Handbook of Humor Research. Vol. II. Applied Studies*. New York: Springer-Verlag, 1983:109–28.

ROCHER, GUY. "The Quiet Revolution in Quebec." In James Curtis and Lorne Tepperman, eds., *Images of Canada: The Sociological Tradition*. Scarborough, ON: Prentice Hall, 1990:22–29.

ROCKETT, IAN R. H. "Population and Health: An Introduction to Epidemiology." *Population Bulletin*. Vol. 49, No. 3 (November 1994). Washington, DC: Population Reference Bureau.

ROESCH, ROBERTA. "Violent Families." *Parents*. Vol. 59, No. 9 (September 1984):74–76, 150–52.

ROHLEN, THOMAS P. *Japan's High Schools*. Berkeley: University of California Press, 1983.

RÓNA-TAS, ÁKOS. "The First Shall Be Last? Entrepreneurship and Communist Cadres in the Transition From Socialism." *American Journal of Sociology*. Vol. 100, No. 1 (July 1994):40–69.

ROOF, WADE CLARK, and WILLIAM MCKINNEY. *American Mainline Religion: Its Changing Shape and Future*. New Brunswick, NJ: Rutgers University Press, 1987.

ROSEN, JEFFREY. *The Unwanted Gaze*. New York: Random House, 2000.

ROSENDAHL, MONA. *Inside the Revolution: Everyday Life in Socialist Cuba*. Ithaca, NY: Cornell University Press, 1997.

ROSENFELD, MEGAN. "Little Boys Blue: Reexamining the Plight of Young Males." *Washington Post*. (March 26, 1998):A1, A17–A18.

ROSENTHAL, ELIZABETH. "Canada's National Health Plan Gives Care to All, With Limits." *New York Times*. (April 30, 1991):A1, A16.

ROSS, CATHERINE E., JOHN MIROWSKY, and JOAN HUBER. "Dividing Work, Sharing Work, and In-Between: Marriage Patterns and Depression." *American Sociological Review*. Vol. 48, No. 6 (December 1983):809–23.

ROSS, DAVID, KATHERINE SCOTT, and PETER SMITH. *The Canadian Fact Book on Poverty 2000*. Ottawa: Council on Social Development, 2000.

ROSS, JOHN. "To Die in the Street: Mexico City's Homeless Population Boom as Economic Crisis Shakes Social Protections." *SSSP Newsletter*. Vol. 27, No. 2 (Summer 1996):14–15.

ROSSI, ALICE S. "Gender and Parenthood." In Alice S. Rossi, ed., *Gender and the Life Course*. New York: Aldine, 1985:161–91.

ROSTOW, WALT W. *The Stages of Economic Growth: A Non-Communist Manifesto*. Cambridge: Cambridge University Press, 1960.

_____. *The World Economy: History and Prospect*. Austin: University of Texas Press, 1978.

ROTHMAN, STANLEY, and AMY E. BLACK. "Who Rules Now? American Elites in the 1990s." *Society*. Vol. 35, No. 6 (September–October 1998):17–20.

ROWE, DAVID C. "Biometrical Genetic Models of Self-Reported Delinquent Behavior: A Twin Study." *Behavior Genetics*. Vol. 13, No. 5 (1983):473–89.

ROWE, DAVID C., and D. WAYNE OSGOOD. "Heredity and Sociological Theories of Delinquency: A Reconsideration." *American Sociological Review*. Vol. 49, No. 4 (August 1984):526–40.

ROWLAND, CHRISTOPHER, ed. *The Cambridge Companion to Liberation Theology*. Cambridge, UK: Cambridge University Press, 1999.

Rozell, Mark J., Clyde Wilcox, and John C. Green. "Religious Constituencies and Support for the Christian Right in the 1990s." *Social Science Quarterly.* Vol. 79, No. 4 (December 1998):815–27.

Rubin, Lillian Breslow. *Worlds of Pain: Life in the Working-Class Family.* New York: Basic Books, 1976.

Ruck, Martin D., and Scot Wortley. "Racial and Ethnic Minority High School Students' Perceptions of School Disciplinary Practices: A Look at Some Canadian Findings." *Journal of Youth and Adolescence.* Vol. 31, No. 3 (2002):185–195.

Rudel, Thomas K., and Judith M. Gerson. "Postmodernism, Institutional Change, and Academic Workers: A Sociology of Knowledge." *Social Science Quarterly.* Vol. 80, No. 2 (June 1999):213–28.

Rudmin, Floyd W. "Cross-Cultural Psycholinguistic Field Research: Verbs of Ownership and Possession." *Journal of Cross-Cultural Psychology.* Vol. 25, No. 1 (March 1994):118–32.

Rudy, Laura. "Under the Knife: Society's Quest for Perfection." *The McGill Tribune.* Issue date: 10/22/02 (April 4, 2006) [Online] **www.mcgilltribune.com/media/storage/paper234/news/2002/10/22/Features/ Under.The.Knife.Societys.Quest.For.Perfection-303273.shtml?norewrite 200605211931&sourcedomain=www.mcgilltribune.com**

Rule, James, and Peter Brantley. "Computerized Surveillance in the Workplace: Forms and Delusions." *Sociological Forum.* Vol. 7, No. 3 (September 1992):405–23.

Rushton, Philippe, and Anthony Bogaert. "Race Differences in Sexual Behaviour: Testing an Evolutionary Hypothesis." *Journal of Research on Personality* 21 (1987):529–51.

Russell, Diana E. *The Secret Trauma: Incest in the Lives of Girls and Women.* New York: Basic Books, 1986.

Ryan, William. *Blaming the Victim.* Rev. ed. New York: Vintage Books, 1976.

Rymer, Russ. *Genie.* New York: HarperPerennial, 1994.

Sachs-Ericsson, Natalie, and James A. Ciarlo. "Gender, Social Roles, and Mental Health: An Epidemiological Perspective." *Sex Roles.* Vol. 43, Nos. 9–10 (2000):605–628.

Sacks, Valerie. "Women and AIDS: An Analysis of Media Misrepresentations." *Social Science and Medicine* 42 (1996):59–73.

Sainsbury, Diane. *Gender, Equality and Welfare States.* Cambridge, MA: Cambridge University Press, 1996.

St. Jean, Yanick, and Joe R. Feagin. *Double Burden: Black Women and Everyday Racism.* Armonk, NY: M.E. Sharpe, 1998.

Sale, Kirkpatrick. *The Conquest of Paradise: Christopher Columbus and the Columbian Legacy.* New York: Alfred A. Knopf, 1990.

Saliba, John. *Perspectives on New Religious Movements.* London: Geoffrey Chapman, 1995.

Sampson, Robert J., and John H. Laub. "Crime and Deviance Over the Life Course: The Salience of Adult Social Bonds." *American Sociological Review.* Vol. 55, No. 5 (October 1990): 609–27.

Samuel, John T. *Visible Minorities in Canada: A Projection.* Toronto: Canadian Advertising Foundation, Race Relations Advisory Council on Advertising, June 1992.

Sanders, Trevor. "Sentencing of Young Offenders in Canada, 1998/99." *Juristat.* Statistics Canada Catalogue No. 85-002-XIE. Vol. 20, No. 7 (September 2000):1–15.

Santoli, Al. "Fighting Child Prostitution." *Freedom Review.* Vol. 25, No. 5 (September–October 1994):5–8.

Sapir, Edward. "The Status of Linguistics as a Science." *Language.* Vol. 5 (1929):207–14.

_____. *Selected Writings of Edward Sapir in Language, Culture, and Personality.* David G. Mandelbaum, ed. Berkeley: University of California Press, 1949.

Satzewich, Vic. "Race, Racism and Racialization: Contested Concepts." In Vic Satzewich, ed., *Racism and Social Inequality in Canada: Concepts, Controversies & Strategies of Resistance.* Toronto: Thompson Educational Publishing, Inc., 1998:25–46.

Satzewich, Vic, ed. *Racism and Social Inequality in Canada. Concepts,*

Controversies & Strategies of Resistance. Toronto: Thomson Educational Publishing, 1998.

Saunders, Ron. *Defining Vulnerability in the Labour Market.* Research paper W 2/21. Research Network. November, 2003. Ottawa: Canadian Policy Research Network Inc. [Online] **www.cprn.org/en/ doc.cfm?doc=468**

Sauve, Julie. "Crime Statistics in Canada, 2004." *Juristat.* Vol. 25, No. 5 (July 2002):2–27.

Savoi, Josee. "Homicide in Canada, 2002." (2003) *Juristat.* Vol. 23, No. 8 (October). Statistics Canada Catalogue No. 85-002-XIE.

Scaff, Lawrence A. "Max Weber and Robert Michels." *American Journal of Sociology.* Vol. 86, No. 6 (May 1981):1269–86.

Scambler, Graham, and Annette Scambler. *Rethinking Prostitution: Purchasing in the 1990s.* London and NY: Routledge, 1997.

Scanlon, James P. "The Curious Case of Affirmative Action for Women." *Society.* Vol. 29, No. 2 (January–February 1992):36–42.

Scheff, Thomas J. *Being Mentally Ill: A Sociological Theory.* 2nd ed. New York: Aldine, 1984.

Scheper-Hughes, Nancy. "Embodied Knowledge: Thinking With the Body in Critical Medical Anthropology." In Robert Borofsky, ed., *Assessing Cultural Anthropology.* New York. McGraw-Hill, 1993:229–239.

Scherer, Ron. "Worldwide Trend: Tobacco Use Grows." *Christian Science Monitor.* (July 17, 1996):4, 8.

Schiller, Bradley. "Who Are the Working Poor?" *The Public Interest.* Vol. 155 (Spring 1994):61–71.

Schissel, Bernard. *Social Dimensions of Canadian Youth Justice.* Toronto: Oxford University Press, 1993.

Schlesinger, Arthur. "The Cult of Ethnicity: Good and Bad." *Time.* Vol. 137, No. 27 (July 8, 1991):21.

Schultz, T. Paul. "Inequality in the Distribution of Personal Income in the World: How It Is Changing and Why." *Journal of Population Economics.* Vol. 11, No. 2 (1998):307–44.

Schutt, Russell K. "Objectivity Versus Outrage." *Society.* Vol. 26, No. 4 (May/June 1989):14–16.

Schwartz, Barry. "Memory as a Cultural System: Abraham Lincoln in World War II." *American Sociological Review.* Vol. 61, No. 5 (October 1996):908–27.

Schwartz, Felice N. "Management, Women, and the New Facts of Life." *Harvard Business Review.* Vol. 89, No. 1 (January–February 1989):65–76.

Schwartz, Martin D. "Gender and Injury in Spousal Assault." *Sociological Focus.* Vol. 20, No. 1 (January 1987):61–75.

Scott, John, and Catherine Griff. *Directors of Industry: The British Corporate Network, 1904–1976.* New York: Blackwell, 1985.

Scott, Katherine. *The Progress of Canada's Children 1996.* Ottawa: Canadian Council on Social Development, 1996.

Scott, W. Richard. *Organizations: Rational, Natural, and Open Systems.* Englewood Cliffs, NJ: Prentice Hall, 1981.

Scupin, Ray. Personal communication, 2000.

Seager, Joni. *The State of Women in the World Atlas.* 2d ed. New York: Penguin, 1997.

Seale, Clive. "Health and Media: An Overview." *Sociology of Health and Illness* 25 (2003):513–531.

Segall, Alexander, and Neena Chappell. *Health and Health Care in Canada.* Toronto: Prentice Hall, 2000.

Seidman, Steven. *Queer Theory/Sociology.* Oxford, UK: Blackwell, 1996.

Sekulic, Dusko, Garth Massey, and Randy Hodson. "Who Were the Yugoslavs? Failed Sources of Common Identity in the Former Yugoslavia." *American Sociological Review.* Vol. 59, No. 1 (February 1994):83–97.

Sellin, Thorsten. *The Penalty of Death.* Beverly Hills, CA: Sage, 1980.

Sen, Amartya. "Missing Women—Revisited: Reduction in Female Mortality Has Been Counterbalanced By Sex Selective Abortions." *British Medical Journal.* (6 December 2003):1297–1298.

Sennett, Richard. *The Corrosion of Character: The Personal Consequences of Work in the New Capitalism.* New York: Norton, 1998.

SENNETT, RICHARD, and JONATHAN COBB. *The Hidden Injuries of Class.* New York: Vintage Books, 1973.

THE SENTENCING PROJECT. October 18, 2000. [Online] www.sentencingproject.org/brief/facts-pp.pdf

_____. "New Prison Population Figures Show Slowing of Growth but Uncertain Trends." August 14, 2002. [Online] www.sentencingproject.org/brief/pub1044.pdf

SHAPIRO, JOSEPH P., and JOANNIE M. SCHROF. "Honor Thy Children." *U.S. News and World Report.* Vol. 118, No. 8 (February 27, 1995):39–49.

SHAVER, FRANCES. "Prostitution: A Female Crime?" In Ellen Adelberg and Claudia Currie, eds., *In Conflict With the Law: Women and the Canadian Justice System.* Vancouver: Press Gang Publishers, 1993.

SHAWCROSS, WILLIAM. *Sideshow: Kissinger, Nixon and the Destruction of Cambodia.* New York: Pocket Books, 1979.

SHEA, RACHEL HARTIGAN. "The New Insecurity." *U.S. News & World Report.* Vol. 132, No. 9 (March 25, 2002):40.

SHEEHAN, TOM. "Senior Esteem as a Factor in Socioeconomic Complexity." *The Gerontologist.* Vol. 16, No. 5 (October 1976):433–40.

SHEEHY, GAIL. *Understanding Men's Passages: Discovering the New Map of Men's Lives.* Toronto: Random House of Canada, 1998.

SHELDON, WILLIAM H., EMIL M. HARTL, and EUGENE MCDERMOTT. *Varieties of Delinquent Youth.* New York: Harper, 1949.

SHELEY, JAMES F., JOSHUA ZHANG, CHARLES J. BRODY, and JAMES D. WRIGHT. "Gang Organization, Gang Criminal Activity, and Individual Gang Members' Criminal Behavior." *Social Science Quarterly.* Vol. 76, No. 1 (March 1995):53–68.

SHERMAN, LAWRENCE W., and DOUGLAS A. SMITH. "Crime, Punishment, and Stake in Conformity: Legal and Informal Control of Domestic Violence." *American Sociological Review.* Vol. 57, No. 5 (October 1992):680–90.

SHEVKY, ESHREF, and WENDELL BELL. *Social Area Analysis.* Stanford, CA: Stanford University Press, 1955.

SHIPLEY, JOSEPH T. *Dictionary of Word Origins.* Totowa, NJ: Roman & Allanheld, 1985.

SHIVELY, JOELLEN. "Cowboys and Indians: Perceptions of Western Films Among American Indians and Anglos." *American Sociological Review.* Vol. 57, No. 6 (December 1992):725–34.

SHKOLNIKOV, V., M. MCKEE, and D.A. LEON. "Changes in Life Expectancy in Russia in the Mid-1990s." *Lancet.* Vol. 357, No. 9260, 2001:917–21.

SHU, XIAOLING. "Education and Gender Egalitarianism: The Case of China." *Sociology of Education.* Vol. 77 (2004):311–36.

SHUPE, ANSON. *In the Name of All That's Holy: A Theory of Clergy Malfeasance.* Westport, CT: Praeger, 1995.

SHUPE, ANSON, WILLIAM A. STACEY, and LONNIE R. HAZLEWOOD. *Violent Men, Violent Couples: The Dynamics of Domestic Violence.* Lexington, MA: Lexington Books, 1987.

SIDEL, RUTH, and VICTOR W. SIDEL. *A Healthy State: An International Perspective on the Crisis in United States Medical Care.* Rev. ed. New York: Pantheon Books, 1982a.

_____. *The Health Care of China.* Boston: Beacon Press, 1982b.

SILVER, WARREN, KAREN MIHOREAN, and ANDREA TAYLOR-BUTTS. "Hate Crime in Canada." *Juristat.* Vol. 24, No. 4 (June 2004):2–18.

SILVERBERG, ROBERT. "The Greenhouse Effect: Apocalypse Now or Chicken Little?" *Omni.* (July 1991):50–54.

SIMMEL, GEORG. *The Sociology of Georg Simmel.* Kurt Wolff, ed. New York: Free Press, 1950: 118–69.

SIMON, JULIAN. *The Ultimate Resource.* Princeton, NJ: Princeton University Press, 1981.

SIMONS, CAROL. "Japan's *Kyoiku* Mamas." In John J. Macionis and Nijole V. Benokraitis, eds., *Seeing Ourselves: Classic, Contemporary, and Cross-Cultural Readings in Sociology.* Englewood Cliffs, NJ: Prentice Hall, 1989:281–86.

SIMONS, MARLISE. "The Price of Modernization: The Case of Brazil's Kaiapo Indians." In John J. Macionis and Nijole V. Benokraitis, eds., *Seeing Ourselves: Classic, Contemporary, and Cross-Cultural Readings in Sociology.* 5th ed. Upper Saddle River, NJ: Prentice Hall, 2001:496–502.

SINGER, JEROME L., and DOROTHY G. SINGER. "Psychologists Look at Television: Cognitive, Developmental, Personality, and Social Policy Implications." *American Psychologist.* Vol. 38, No. 7 (July 1983):826–34.

SIVARD, RUTH LEGER. *World Military and Social Expenditures, 1987–88.* 12th ed. Washington, DC: World Priorities, 1988.

SIZER, THEODORE R. *Horace's Compromise: The Dilemma of the American High School.* Boston: Houghton Mifflin, 1984.

SKOCPOL, THEDA. *States and Social Revolutions: A Comparative Analysis of France, Russia, and China.* Cambridge, UK: Cambridge University Press, 1979.

SKOLNICK, ARLENE. *The Intimate Environment: Exploring Marriage and the Family.* 6th ed. New York: HarperCollins, 1996.

SMAIL, J. KENNETH. "Let's Reduce Global Population!" In John J. Macionis and Nijole V. Benokraitis, eds., *Seeing Ourselves: Classic, Contemporary, and Cross-Cultural Readings in Sociology.* 6th ed. Upper Saddle River, NJ: Prentice Hall, 2004:422–26

SMITH, ADAM. *An Inquiry Into the Nature and Causes of the Wealth of Nations.* New York: The Modern Library, 1937; orig. 1776.

SMITH, ALLAN. "Seeing Things: Race, Image, and National Identity in Canadian and American Movies and Television." *Canadian Review of American Studies.* Vol. 26, No. 3 (Autumn 1996):367–91.

SMITH, DOROTHY. *The Everyday World as Problematic: A Feminist Sociology.* Toronto: University of Toronto Press, 1987.

_____. *Writing the Social: Critique, Theory and Investigations.* Toronto: University of Toronto Press, 1999.

_____ *Institutional Ethnography: A Sociology for People.* Toronto: AltaMira Press, 2005.

SMITH, DOUGLAS A. "Police Response to Interpersonal Violence: Defining the Parameters of Legal Control." *Social Forces.* Vol. 65, No. 3 (March 1987):767–82.

SMITH, DOUGLAS A., and PATRICK R. GARTIN. "Specifying Specific Deterrence: The Influence of Arrest on Future Criminal Activity." *American Sociological Review.* Vol. 54, No. 1 (February 1989):94–105.

SMITH, DOUGLAS A., and CHRISTY A. VISHER. "Street-Level Justice: Situational Determinants of Police Arrest Decisions." *Social Problems.* Vol. 29, No. 2 (December 1981):167–77.

SMITH, EARL, and WILBERT M. LEONARD, II. "Twenty-Five Years of Stacking Research in Major League Baseball: An Attempt at Explaining this Re-Occurring Phenomenon." *Sociological Focus.* Vol. 30, No. 4 (October 1997):321–31.

SMITH-LOVIN, LYNN, and CHARLES BRODY. "Interruptions in Group Discussions: The Effects of Gender and Group Composition." *American Journal of Sociology.* Vol. 54, No. 3 (June 1989): 424–35.

SMOLOWE, JILL. "When Violence Hits Home." *Time.* Vol. 144, No. 1 (July 4, 1994):18–25.

SNELL, MARILYN BERLIN. "The Purge of Nurture." *New Perspectives Quarterly.* Vol. 7, No. 1 (Winter 1990):1–2.

SNOW, DAVID A., E. BURKE ROCHFORD, JR., STEVEN K. WORDEN, and ROBERT D. BENFORD. "Frame Alignment Processes, Micromobilization, and Movement Participation." *American Sociological Review.* Vol. 51, No. 4 (August 1986):464–81.

SOMMERS, CHRISTINA HOFF. *The War Against Boys: How Misguided Feminism is Harming Our Young Men.* New York: Simon & Schuster, 2000.

SOUTH, SCOTT J., and STEVEN F. MESSNER. "Structural Determinants of Intergroup Association: Interracial Marriage and Crime." *American Journal of Sociology.* Vol. 91, No. 6 (May 1986): 1409–30.

SOWELL, THOMAS. *Race and Culture.* New York: Basic Books, 1994.

_____. "Ethnicity and IQ." In Steven Fraser, ed., *The Bell Curve Wars: Race, Intelligence and the Future of America.* New York: Basic Books, 1995:70–79.

SPATES, JAMES L. "Counterculture and Dominant Culture Values: A Cross-National Analysis of the Underground Press and Dominant Culture Magazines." *American Sociological Review.* Vol. 41, No. 5 (October 1976):868–83.

SPATES, JAMES L., and H. WESLEY PERKINS. "American and English Student

Values." *Comparative Social Research.* Vol. 5. Greenwich, CT: JAI Press, 1982:245–68.

SPECTER, MICHAEL. "Plunging Life Expectancy Puzzles Russia." *New York Times.* (August 2, 1995):A1, A2.

_____. "Deep in the Russian Soul, a Lethal Darkness." *New York Times.* (June 8, 1997): sec. 4, pp. 1, 5.

SPEER, JAMES A. "The New Christian Right and Its Parent Company: A Study in Political Contrasts." In David G. Bromley and Anson Shupe, eds., *New Christian Politics.* Macon, GA: Mercer University Press, 1984:19–40.

SPEIER, HANS. "Wit and Politics: An Essay on Laughter and Power." In Robert Jackall, ed. and trans., *American Journal of Sociology.* Vol. 103, No. 5 (March 1998):1352–1401.

SPENCER, MARTIN E. "Multiculturalism, 'Political Correctness,' and the Politics of Identity." *Sociological Forum.* Vol. 9, No. 4 (December 1994):547–67.

SPITZER, STEVEN. "Toward a Marxian Theory of Deviance." In Delos H. Kelly, ed., *Criminal Behavior: Readings in Criminology.* New York: St. Martin's Press, 1980:175–91.

SPREEN, MARIUS, and RONALD ZWAAGSTRA. "Personal Network Sampling, Outdegree Analysis and Multilevel Analysis: Introducing the Network Concept in Studies of Hidden Populations." *International Sociology.* Vol. 9 (1994): 475–91.

ST-ARNAUD, JULIE, MARIE P. BEAUDET, and PATRICIA TULLY. "Life Expectancy." *Health Reports.* Statistics Canada Catalogue No. 82-003-XIE. Vol. 17, No. 1 (Nov. 2005):43–47.

STACEY, JUDITH. *Patriarchy and Socialist Revolution in China.* Berkeley: University of California Press, 1983.

_____. *Brave New Families: Stories of Domestic Upheaval in Late Twentieth-Century America.* New York: Basic Books, 1990.

_____. "Good Riddance to 'The Family': A Response to David Popenoe." *Journal of Marriage and the Family.* Vol. 55, No. 3 (August 1993):545–47.

STAGGENBORG, SUZANNE. "Social Movement Communities and Cycles of Protest: The Emergence and Maintenance of a Local Women's Movement." *Social Problems.* Vol. 45, No. 2 (May 1998):180–204.

STANLEY, LIZ, ed. *Feminist Praxis: Research, Theory, and Epistemology in Feminist Sociology.* London: Routledge & Kegan Paul, 1990.

STARK, RODNEY. *Sociology.* Belmont, CA: Wadsworth, 1985.

STARK, RODNEY, and WILLIAM SIMS BAINBRIDGE. "Of Churches, Sects, and Cults: Preliminary Concepts for a Theory of Religious Movements." *Journal for the Scientific Study of Religion.* Vol. 18, No. 2 (June 1979):117–31.

_____. "Secularization and Cult Formation in the Jazz Age." *Journal for the Scientific Study of Religion.* Vol. 20, No. 4 (December 1981):360–73.

STATISTICS CANADA. *Religions in Canada.* Catalogue No. 93-319-XPB. Ottawa: Minister of Industry, 1993a.

_____. "The Violence Against Women Survey: Highlights." *The Daily.* Ottawa: Minister of Industry, Science and Technology, 1993b.

_____. *Report on the Demographic Situation in Canada, 1994.* Catalogue No. 91-209-XPE. (November 1994a):111–35.

_____. *Women in the Labour Force.* 1994 ed. Catalogue No. 75-50X-XPB. Ottawa: Minister of Industry, 1994b.

_____. *Women in Canada: A Statistical Report.* 3rd ed. Ottawa: Minister of Industry, 1995a.

_____. *National Population Health Survey Overview, 1994–95.* Ottawa: Minister of Industry, 1995b.

_____. *The Daily* (June 19, 1996). [Online] **www.statcan.ca/Daily/English/960619/d960619.htm**

_____. *Canada's Culture, Heritage and Identity: A Statistical Perspective.* 1997 ed. Catalogue No. 87-211-XIB. Ottawa: Minister of Industry, 1997a.

_____. *The Daily* (October 14, 1997b). [Online] **www.statcan.ca/Daily/English/971014/d971014.htm**

_____. *The Daily* (November 4, 1997c). [Online] **www.statcan.ca/Daily/English/971104/d971104.htm**

_____. *The Daily* (November 27, 1997d). [Online] **www.statcan.ca/Daily/English/971104/d971104.htm**

_____. *Education in Canada, 1996.* Catalogue No. 81-229-XIB. Ottawa: Minister of Industry, 1997e.

_____. "Homicide in Canada 1996." *Juristat.* Catalogue No. 85-002-XPE. Vol. 17, No 9 (July, 1997f):1–14.

_____. "Street Prostitution in Canada." *Juristat.* Catalogue No. 85-002-XPE. Vol. 17, No. 2 (February, 1997g):1–12.

_____. *1996 General Social Survey.* [Electronic Data File.] 1998a.

_____. *Area Profiles: 1996 Census of Population.* [Electronic Data File.] Statistics Canada Catalogue No. 95F0181XDB96001, Table prcumcsd.ivt, 1998b.

_____. *The Daily* (January 13, 1998c). [Online] **www.statcan.ca/Daily/English/980113/d980113.htm**

_____. *The Daily* (February 5, 1998d). [Online] **www.statcan.ca/Daily/English/980205/d980205.htm**

_____. *The Daily* (February 17, 1998e). [Online] **www.statcan.ca/Daily/English/980217/d980217.htm**

_____. *The Daily* (March 17, 1998f). [Online] **www.statcan.ca/Daily/English/980317/d980317.htm**

_____. *The Daily* (April 14, 1998g). [Online] **www.statcan.ca/Daily/English/980414/d980414.htm**

_____. *The Daily* (April 16, 1998h). [Online] **www.statcan.ca/Daily/English/980416/d980416.htm**

_____. *The Daily* (May 12, 1998i). [Online] **www.statcan.ca/Daily/English/980512/d980512.htm**

_____. *The Daily* (May 28, 1998j). [Online] **www.statcan.ca/Daily/English/980528/d980528.htm**

_____. *The Daily* (June 2, 1998k). [Online] **www.statcan.ca/Daily/English/980602/d980602.htm**

_____. *The Daily* (September 4, 1998l). [Online] **www.statcan.ca/Daily/English/980904/d980904.htm**

_____. *The Daily* (September 17, 1998m). [Online] **www.statcan.ca/Daily/English/980917/d980917.htm**

_____. *Earnings of Men and Women, 1996.* Catalogue No. 13-217-XPB. Ottawa: Minister of Industry, 1998n.

_____. *Income After Tax, Distributions by Size in Canada, 1996.* Catalogue No. 13-210-XPB. Ottawa: Minister of Industry, 1998o.

_____. *The Nation: 1996 Census of Canada.* [Electronic Data File.] Statistics Canada Catalogue No. 93F0027XDB96004, Table 7_T4, 1998p.

_____. *The Nation: 1996 Census of Canada.* [Electronic Data File.] Statistics Canada Catalogue No. 93F0029XDB96005, Table n05_1205, 1998q.

_____. *The Nation: 1996 Census of Canada.* [Electronic Data File.] Statistics Canada Catalogue No. 93F0027XDB96007, Table n07_T7, 1998r.

_____. *The Nation: 1996 Census of Canada.* [Electronic Data File.] Statistics Canada Catalogue No. 93F0029XDB96007, Table n07_1205, 1998s.

_____. *The Nation: 1996 Census of Canada.* [Electronic Data File.] Statistics Canada Catalogue No. 95F0182XDB-8, Table pr8cma, 1998t.

_____. "Education at a Glance." *Educational Quarterly Review.* Catalogue No. 81-003-XIB Vol. 5, No. 1 (August, 1998u):42–51.

_____. "Census Families in Private Households by Family Structure, Presence of Children and Labour Force Activity." 1999a. [Online] **www.statcan.ca/english/census96/june9/f3can.htm**

_____. *The Daily* (January 29, 1999b). [Online] **www.statcan.ca/Daily/English/990129/d990129.htm**

_____. *Low Income Persons, 1980 to 1997.* Ottawa: Minister of Industry. Catalogue No. 13-569-XIB, 1999c.

_____. *Statistical Report on the Health of Canadians.* Federal, Provincial and Territorial Committee on Population Health, 1999d.

_____. *Statistics Canada's Survey of Financial Security: Update July 1999.* Ottawa: Income Statistics Division. Catalogue No. 13F0026MIE, 1999e.

_____. "General Social Survey: Time Use." *The Daily* (Tuesday, November 9, 1999f) [Online] **www.statcan.ca/Daily/English/991109/d991109a.htm**

_____. *Low Income After Tax, 1997.* (1999g) Statistics Canada Catalogue No. 13-592-XIB.

_____. *Historical statistics of Canada.* Catalogue No. 11-516-XIE. (1999h. Orig. 1983) [Online] www.statcan.ca/english/freepub/11-516-XIE/sectiona/toc.htm

_____. *Annual Demographic Statistics, 1999.* Ottawa: Ministry of Industry. Catalogue No. 91-213-XIB, 2000a.

_____. *Average Hours per Week of Television Viewing.* November 25, 2000b. [Online] www.statcan.ca/english/Pgdb/People/Culture/arts23.htm

_____. *The Daily.* (January 20, 2000c). [Online] www.statcan.ca/Daily/English/000120/d000120.pdf

_____. *The Daily* (Thursday, March 16, 2000d). [Online] www.statcan.ca/Daily/English/000316/d000316.pdf

_____. *The Daily.* (Friday, June 16, 2000e). "Exploring Patterns of Corporate Diversification in Canada." [Online] www.statcan.ca/Daily/English/000616/d000616c.htm

_____. *The Daily* (Thursday, September 28, 2000f). [Online] www.statcan.ca/Daily/English/000928/d000928.pdf

_____. "Education at a Glance." *Education Quarterly Review.* Statistics Canada Catalogue No. 81-003-XIE. Vol. 7, No.1 (November 2000g): 56–60.

_____. *Education in Canada, 1999.* Statistics Canada Catalogue No. 81-229-XIE, May 2000h.

_____. *Education Indicators in Canada: Report of the Pan-Canadian Education Indicators Program, 1999.* Statistics Canada Catalogue No. 81-582-XIE. Ottawa: Canadian Education Statistics Council, 2000i.

_____. *Education Quarterly Review.* Vol. 7, No. 1. Catalogue No. 81-003-XIE, 2000j.

_____. "The Justice Factfinder, 1998." *Juristat.* Statistics Canada Catalogue No. 85-002-XIE. Vol. 20, No. 4 (June 2000k):1–12.

_____. *Quarterly Demographic Statistics, January–March 2000.* Ottawa: Ministry of Industry. Catalogue No. 91-002-XIB, 2000l.

_____. *Women in Canada 2000: A Gender-based Statistical Report.* Ottawa: Housing, Family and Social Statistics Division. Catalogue No.89-503-XPE. Ottawa: Ministry of Industry, 2000m.

_____. "Teenage Pregnancy." *Health Reports.* Vol. 12, No. 1 (Summer 2000):9–20. Ottawa: Health Statistics Division, 2000n.

_____. *Income in Canada 1998.* Ottawa: Ministry of Industry. Catalogue No. 75-202-XIE, 2000o.

_____. CANSIM Database Retrieval Output, Series C115100. Ottawa: Statistics Canada, 2000p.

_____. CANSIM Database Retrieval Output, Series C115103. Ottawa: Statistics Canada, 2000q.

_____. CANSIM Database Retrieval Output, Series D125599. Ottawa: Statistics Canada, 2000r.

_____. *Perspectives on Labour and Income.* Vol. 2, No. 1 (January 2001a). [Online] www.statcan.ca/english/indepth/75-001/online/00101/kl-ic_a.html

_____. *Selected Leading Causes of Death by Sex.* February 8, 2001b. [Online] www.statcan.ca/english/Pgdb/People/Health/health36.htm

_____. *Education in Canada, 2000.* Statistics Canada Catalogue No. 81-229-XIB, May 2001c.

_____. *Hate Crime in Canada: An Overview of Issues and Data Sources.* Catalogue No. 85-551-XIE. Ottawa: Statistics Canada, 2001d.

_____. "2001 Census: Marital Status, Common-law Status, Families, Dwellings and Households." *The Daily* (October 22, 2002a) [Online] www.statcan.ca/Daily/English/021022/td021022a.htm

_____. "Trends in Canadian and American Fertility." *The Daily* (July 3, 2002b). [Online] www.statcan.ca/Daily/English/020703/d020703a.htm

_____. "Divorces." *The Daily* (December 2, 2002c) [Online] www.statcan.ca/Daily/English/021202/d021202f.htm

_____. Number of Children at Home (8) and Family Structure (7) for Census Families in Private Households, for Canada, Provinces, Territories, Census Divisions and Census Subdivisions, 2001 Census—20% Sample Data. (2002d) [Electronic Data File.] Catalogue No. 95F0312XCB01006.

_____. Immigrant Status and Place of Birth of Respondent (21), Sex (3) and Age Groups (7B) for Population, for Canada, Provinces, Territories, Census Divisions and Census Subdivisions, 2001 Census—20% Sample Data (2002e). [Electronic Data File.] Catalogue No. 95F0357XCB01006.

_____. *Profile of the Canadian Population by Age and Sex: Canada Ages.* (2002f) Catalogue No. 96F0030XIE2001002.

_____. *Life Tables: Canada, Provinces and Territories, 1995–1997.* Catalogue No. 84-537-XIE. Ottawa: Minister of Industry, 2002g. [Online] www.statcan.ca/english/freepub/84-537-XIE/free.htm

_____. "Television Viewing." *The Daily* (December 2, 2002h) [Online] www.statcan.ca/Daily/English/021202/d021202a.htm

_____. "Therapeutic Abortions." *The Daily.* (January 18, 2002i) [Online] www.statcan.ca/Daily/English/020118/d020118d.htm

_____. "Perspectives on Labour and Income: Fact-sheet on Unionization." The online edition. Ottawa: Statistics Canada. Vol. 3, No. 9, September 20, 2002j, pp. 1–25. [Online] www.statcan.ca/english/indepth/75_001/online/00902/kl_ic_a.html

_____. "Survey of Self-Employed." *The Daily* (January 29, 2002k). [Online] www.statcan.ca/Daily/English/020129/d020129d.htm

_____. CANSIM Data Base Retrieval Output, Table 102-0540. Ottawa: Statistics Canada, 2003a.

_____. *Annual Demographic Statistics 2002.* Catalogue No. 91-213-XPB. Ottawa: Statistics Canada, 2003b.

_____. 2001 Census: Analysis Series. Education in Canada: Raising the Standard. Catalogue No. 96F0030XIE2001012, 2003c.

_____. *Education Quarterly Review,* Vol. 9, No. 2. Catalogue No. 81-003-XIE, June 2003d.

_____. School Attendance (4), Highest Level of Schooling (12), Age Groups (13B) and Sex (3) for Population 15 Years and Over, for Canada, Provinces, Territories, Census Divisions and Census Subdivisions, 2001 Census—20% Sample Data. (2003e) Catalogue No. 95F0418XCB01006.

_____. *The People: Student Indebtedness.* (2003f) [Online] http://142.206.72.67/02/02c/02c_007b_e.htm

_____. Overview: University Education, Experience Pay Off in Higher Earnings. (2003g) [Online] www12.statcan.ca/english/census01/Products/Analytic/companion/earn/canada.cfm#9

_____. Number and Average Employment Income (2) in Constant (2000) Dollars, Sex (3), Work Activity (3), Age Groups (7) and Historical Highest Level of Schooling (6) for Population 15 Years and Over With Employment Income, for Canada, Provinces, Territories, Census Metropolitan Areas and Census Agglomerations, 1995 and 2000—20% Sample Data. (2003h) [Electronic Data File.] Catalogue No. 97F0019XCB01002.

_____. Selected Leading Causes of Death by Sex. 2003i [Online] www.statcan.ca/english/Pgdb/health36.htm

_____. Health Indicators. Statistics Canada Catalogue No. 82-221-XIE (May 2003j). [Online] www.statcan.ca/english/freepub/82-221-XIE/00503/tables/html/2115.htm

_____. Census Families by Number of Children at Home. 2003k. [Online] www.statcan.ca/english/Pgdb/famil50a.htm

_____. Profile of Canadian Families and Households: Diversification Continues. (2003l) Ottawa: Statistics Canada. Catalogue No. 96F0030XIE2001003. [Online] www12.statcan.ca/english/census01/products/analytic/companion/fam/pdf/96F0030XIE2001003.pdf

_____. Family Violence in Canada: A Statistical Profile 2003. (2003m). Ottawa: Minister of Industry. Catalogue No. 85-224-XIE.

_____. Census Families, Number and Average Size. (2003n) [Online] www.statcan.ca/english/Pgdb/famil40b.htm

_____. Aboriginal Peoples in Canada: A Demographic Profile. (2003o) Ottawa: Minister of Industry. Catalogue No. 96F0030XIE2001007.

_____. Annual Demographic Statistics, 2002. (2003p) Ottawa: Minister of Industry. Catalogue No. 91-213-XPB.

_____. Canada e-Book. (2003q). Statistics Canada Catalogue No. (11-404-XIE). [Online] http://142.206.72.67/r000_e.htm

_____. Religion (13) and Age Groups (8) for Population, for Canada, Provinces, Territories, Census Metropolitan Areas and Census Agglomerations, 2001 Census—20% Sample Data. (2003r) [Electronic Data File.] Catalogue No. 95F0450XCB01004.

_____. Ethnic Origin (232), Sex (3) and Single and Multiple Responses (3) for Population, for Canada, Provinces, Territories, Census Metropolitan Areas and Census Agglomerations, 2001 Census—20% Sample Data (2003s) [Electronic Data File]. Catalogue No. 97F0010XCB01001.

_____. Canada's Ethnocultural Portrait: The Changing Mosaic. 2003t. Ottawa: Minister of Industry. Catalogue No. 96F0030XIE2001008.

_____. Selected Dwelling Characteristics and Household Equipment. (2003u). [Online] **www.statcan.ca/english/Pgdb/famil09c.htm**

_____. CANSIM Data Base Retrieval Output, Table 2020802. Ottawa: Statistics Canada, 2003v.

_____. Teen Pregnancy, by Outcome of Pregnancy and Age Group, Count and Rate per 1000 Women Aged 15 to 19, Canada, Provinces and Territories, 1998. (2003w). [Online] **www.statcan.ca/english/freepub/ 82-221-XIE/00503/tables/html/411.htm**

_____. "Sexual Offences in Canada." *Juristat*. Catalogue No. 85-002-XIE, Vol. 23. No. 6, 2003x.

_____. Occupation—2001 National Occupational Classification for Statistics (50), Class of Worker (6) and Sex (3) for Labour Force 15 Years and Over, for Canada, Provinces, Territories, Census Metropolitan Areas and Census Agglomerations, 2001 Census—20% Sample Data. (2003y). [Electronic Data File.] Catalogue No. 97F0012XCB01019.

_____. Various Non-official Languages Spoken (76), Age Groups (13) and Sex (3) for Population, for Canada, Provinces, Territories, Census Divisions and Census Subdivisions, 2001 Census—20% Sample Data. (2003z) [Electronic Data File.] Catalogue No. 95F0338XCB01006.

_____. Age (122) and Sex (3) for Population, for Canada, Provinces, Territories, Census Divisions and Census Subdivisions, 2001 Census—100% Data (2003aa). [Electronic Data File.] Catalogue No. 95F0300XCB01006.

_____. Detailed Language Spoken at Home (72), Frequency of Language Spoken at Home (5) and Sex (3) for Population, for Canada, Provinces, Territories, Census Divisions and Census Subdivisions, 2001 Census—20% Sample Data. (2003ab) [Electronic Data File.] Catalogue No. 95F0335XCB01006.

_____ "Family Income." *The Daily*. June 25, 2003. (2003ac) [Online] **www.statcan.ca/Daily/English/030625/d030625b.htm**

_____. *Income in Canada 2001*. (2003ad) Catalogue No. 75-202-XIE.

_____. Family Income Groups (22) in Constant (2000) Dollars, Census Family Structure (6) and Immigrant Status and Period of Immigration of Male Spouse or Partner or Lone Parent (10) for Census Families in Private Households, for Canada, Provinces and Territories, 1995 and 2000—20% Sample Data. [Electronic Data File.] (2003ae) Catalogue No. 97F0020XCB01009.

_____. Period of Construction (9), Condition of Dwelling (4) and Tenure (4) for Occupied Private Dwellings, for Canada, Provinces, Territories, Census Divisions and Census Subdivisions, 2001 Census—20% Sample Data. (2003af) [Electronic Data File.] Catalogue No. 95F0325XCB01006.

_____. Labour Force Activity (8), Highest Level of Schooling (11), Age Groups (11) and Sex (3) for Population 15 Years and Over, for Canada, Provinces, Territories and Federal Electoral Districts (1996 Representation Order), 2001 Census—20% Sample Data. (2003ag) Catalogue No. 95F0380XCB01003.

_____. Selected Income Characteristics (35), Age Groups (6), Sex (3) and Visible Minority Groups (15) for Population, for Canada, Provinces, Territories and Census Metropolitan Areas, 2001 Census—20% Sample Data. (2003ah) Catalogue No. 97F0010XCB01047.

_____. Average Earnings By Sex and Work Pattern. (2003ai) [Online] **www.statcan.ca/english/Pgdb/labor01b.htm**

_____. Number Reporting and Aggregate Amount Reported for Sources of Census Family Income (26) and Selected Income, Earnings and Family

Characteristics (155) for Census Families in Private Households With Income, for Canada, Provinces and Territories, 2000—20% Sample Data. (2003aj) Catalogue No. 97F0020XCB01074.

_____. Number and Average Wages and Salaries (2) in Constant (2000) Dollars, Sex (3), Work Activity (3), Historical Highest Level of Schooling (6), Age Groups (5) and Occupation—1991 Standard Occupational Classification (Historical) (706A) for Paid Workers 15 Years and Over With Wages and Salaries, for Canada, Provinces and Territories, 1995 and 2000—20% Sample Data. (2003ak) [Electronic Data File]. Catalogue No. 97F0019XCB01060.

_____. Income Status (4) and Census Family Structure for Census Families, Sex, Age Groups and Household Living Arrangements for Non-family Persons 15 Years and Over and Sex and Age Groups for Persons in Private Households (87), for Canada, Provinces, Census Metropolitan Areas and Census Agglomerations, 1995 and 2000—20% Sample Data. (2003al) [Electronic Data File.] Catalogue No. 97F0020XCB01006.

_____. 2001 Census: Analysis Series. Income of Canadian Families. (2003am). Statistics Canada Catalogue No. 96F0030XIE2001014. [Online] **www12.statcan.ca/english/census01/products/analytic/ companion/inc/pdf/96F0030XIE2001014.pdf**

_____. Quarterly Demographic Statistics, July– September 2002. Catalogue No. 91-002-XIB. Vol. 16, No. 3 (2003an). Ottawa: Minister of Industry.

_____. Quarterly Demographic Statistics, October–December 2002. Catalogue No. 91-002-XIB. Vol. 16, No. 4 (2003ao). Ottawa: Minister of Industry.

_____. Quarterly Demographic Statistics, January–March 2003. Catalogue No. 91-002-XIB. Vol. 17, No. 1 (2003ap). Ottawa: Minister of Industry.

_____. Quarterly Demographic Statistics, April–June 2003. Catalogue No. 91-002-XIB. Vol. 17, No. 2 (2003aq). Ottawa: Minister of Industry.

_____. CANSIM Data Base Retrieval Output, Table 510002. Ottawa: Statistics Canada, 2003ar.

_____. "Deaths." *The Daily*. (September 25, 2003as). [Online] **www.statcan.ca/Daily/English/030925/d030925c.htm**

_____. 2001 Census: Analysis Series. Profile of the Canadian Population by Mobility Status: Canada, a Nation on the Move. Catalogue No. 96F0030XIE2001006, 2003at.

_____. Population by Sex and Age Group. (2003au) [Online] **www.statcan.ca/english/Pgdb/demo10a.htm**

_____. Population and Dwelling Counts, for Census Divisions, Census Subdivisions (Municipalities) and Designated Places, 2001 and 1996 Censuses—100% Data. (2003av) [Electronic Data File.] Catalogue No. 93F0050XCB01003.

_____. Population and Dwelling Counts, for Census Metropolitan Areas and Census Agglomerations, 2001 and 1996 Censuses—100% Data. (2003aw) [Electronic Data File.] Catalogue No. 93F0050XCB01001.

_____. Mode of Transportation (9), Total Income Groups (12), Age Groups (7) and Sex (3) for Employed Labour Force 15 Years and Over Having a Usual Place of Work, for Canada, Provinces, Territories, Census Divisions and Census Subdivisions of Work, 2001 Census—20% Sample Data. (2003ax) [Electronic Data File.] Catalogue No. 97F0015XCB01041.

_____. Population and Dwelling Counts, for Census Divisions, Census Subdivisions (Municipalities) and Designated Places, 2001 and 1996 Censuses—100% Data. (2003ay) [Electronic Data File.] Catalogue No. 93F0050XCB01003.

_____. Profile of Income of Individuals, Families and Households, Social and Economic Characteristics of Individuals, Families and Households, Housing Costs, and Religion, for Canada, Provinces, Territories, Census Divisions and Census Subdivisions, 2001 Census. (2003az) [Electronic Data File.] Catalogue No. 95F0492XCB01001.

_____. Selected Demographic and Cultural Characteristics (102), Visible Minority Groups (15), Age Groups (6) and Sex (3) for Population, for Canada, Provinces, Territories and Census Metropolitan Areas, 2001

Census—20% Sample Data. (2003ba) [Electronic Data File.] Catalogue No. 97F0010XCB01044.

_____. CANSIM II Data Base Retrieval Output, Table 530002. Ottawa: Statistics Canada, 2003bb.

_____. *Education Indicators in Canada: Report of the Pan-Canadian Education Indicators Program 2003*. Ottawa: Canadian Education Statistics Council (2003bc).

_____. *Earnings of Canadians: Making a Living in the New Economy*. Catalogue No. 96F0030XIE2001013. Ottawa: Minister of Industry, 2003bd. [Online] **www12.statcan.ca/english/census01/Products/Analytic/companion/earn/pdf/96F0030XIE2001013.pdf**

_____. "University Degrees, Diplomas and Certificates Awarded." *The Daily*, 2003be. [Online] **www.statcan.ca/Daily/English/030708/d030708a.htm**

_____. Unpaid Work (20), Age Groups (7) and Sex (3) for Population 15 Years and Over, for Canada, Provinces, Territories, Census Divisions and Census Subdivisions, 2001 Census—20% Sample Data. (2003bf) [Electronic Data File.] Catalogue No. 95F0390XCB01006.

_____. Employment Income Groups (22) in Constant (2000) Dollars, Sex (3) and Aboriginal Groups (11) for Population 15 Years and Over, for Canada, Provinces and Territories, 1995 and 2000—20% Sample Data. (2003bg) [Electronic Data File]. Catalogue No. 97F0019XCB01048.

_____. Employment Income Groups (22) in Constant (2000) Dollars, Sex (3), Visible Minority Groups (14) and Immigrant Status (3) for Population 15 Years and Over, for Canada, Provinces and Territories, 1995 and 2000—20% Sample Data. (2003bh) [Electronic Data File.] Catalogue No. 97F0019XCB01047.

_____."Women in Canada: Work Chapter Updates." Ottawa: Statistics Canada, 2003bi. Catalogue No. 89F0133XIE. [Online] **www.statcan.ca/english/freepub/89F0133XIE/89F0133XIE02001.pdf**

_____. Immigrant Status and Period of Immigration (10A) and Place of Birth of Respondent (260) for Immigrants and Non-permanent Residents, for Canada, Provinces, Territories, Census Metropolitan Areas and Census Agglomerations, 2001 Census—20% Sample Data. (2003bj) [Electronic Data File.] Catalogue No. 97F0009XCB01002.

_____. Visible Minority Groups (15), Sex (3) and Age Groups (8) for Population, for Canada, Provinces, Territories, Census Divisions and Census Subdivisions, 2001 Census—20% Sample Data. (2003bk) [Electronic Data File.] Catalogue No. 95F0363XCB01006.

_____. Aboriginal Identity Population (3), Registered Indian Status (3), Age Groups (11B), Sex (3) and Area of Residence (7) for Population, for Canada, Provinces and Territories, 2001 Census—20% Sample Data. (2003bl) [Electronic Data File.] Catalogue No. 97F0011XCB01005.

_____. Employment by Industry and Sex. Ottawa: Statistics Canada. November 25, 2003bm. [Online] **www.statcan.ca/english/Pgdb/labor10b.htm**

_____. The People: Employers. Canada E-Book. Ottawa: Statistics Canada, November 19, 2003bn. [Online] **http://142.206.72.67/02/02e/02e_002_e.htm**

_____. Experienced Labour Force 15 Years and Over by Class of Worker, Provinces and Territories." Ottawa: Statistics Canada, 2003bo. [Online] **www.statcan.ca/english/Pgdb/labor43d.htm**

_____. Selected Labour Force Characteristics (50), Aboriginal Identity (8), Age Groups (5A), Sex (3) and Area of Residence (7) for Population 15 Years and Over, for Canada, Provinces and Territories, 2001 Census—20% Sample Data. (2003bp) [Electronic Data File.] Catalogue No. 97F0011XCB01044.

_____. Selected Cultural and Labour Force Characteristics (58), Age Groups (5A), Sex (3) and Visible Minority Groups (15) for Population 15 Years and Over, for Canada, Provinces, Territories and Census Metropolitan Areas, 2001 Census—20% Sample Data (2003bq) [Electronic Data File.] Catalogue No. 97F0010XCB01046.

_____. Labour Force Activity (8), Age Groups (17B), Marital Status (7B)

and Sex (3) for Population 15 Years and Over, for Canada, Provinces, Territories, Census Divisions and Census Subdivisions, 2001 Census—20% Sample Data. (2003br) [Electronic Data File.] Catalogue No. 95F0377XCB01006.

_____. Visible Minority Groups (15) and Immigrant Status and Periods of Immigration (11) for Population, for Canada, Provinces, Territories, Census Metropolitan Areas and Census Agglomerations, 2001 Census—20% Sample Data (2003bs). [Electronic Data File.] Catalogue No. 97F0010XCB01003.

_____. Selected Income Characteristics (35A), Aboriginal Identity (8), Age Groups (6), Sex (3) and Area of Residence (7) for Population, for Canada, Provinces and Territories, 2001 Census—20% Sample Data. (2003bt). [Electronic Data file.] Catalogue No. 97F0011XCB2001046.

_____. Selected Income Characteristics (35), Aboriginal Identity (8), Age Groups (6) and Sex (3) for Population, for Canada, Provinces, Territories and Census Metropolitan Areas, 2001 Census—20% Sample Data (2003bu). [Electronic Data File.] Catalogue No. 97F0011XIE2001047.

_____. Profile of Citizenship, Immigration, Birthplace, Generation Status, Ethnic Origin, Visible Minorities and Aboriginal Peoples, for Canada, Provinces, Territories, Census Divisions and Census Subdivisions, 2001 Census (2003bv). [Electronic Data File.] Catalogue No. 95F0489XCB2001001.

_____. Number and Average Economic Family Income (2) in Constant (2000) Dollars, Earning Status of Spouses or Partners (8) and Selected Demographic, Educational, Cultural, Language and Labour Force Characteristics of Couple Economic Families (282) for Couple Economic Families in Private Households, for Canada, Provinces and Territories, 1995 and 2000—20% Sample Data. (2004a). [Electronic Data file.] Catalogue No. 97F0020XCB2001070.

_____. *The Daily* (June 15, 2004a) [Online] **www.statcan.ca/Daily/English/040615/d040615.pdf**

_____. *The Daily* (Monday, September 27, 2004) [Online] **www.statcan.ca/Daily/English/040927/d040927a.htm**

_____. "Pregnancies." *The Daily* (Wednesday, October 27, 2004b). [Online] **www.statcan.ca/Daily/English/041027/d041027d.htm**

_____. *The Daily*. "Smoking: One Step Forward, One Step Back." (Wednesday, November 24, 2004). [Online] **www.statcan.ca/Daily/English/041124/d041124b.htm**

_____. Projections of the Aboriginal Populations, Canada, Provinces, and Territories: 2001 to 2017. (2005) Catalogue No. 91-547-XIE.

_____. *The Daily*. "Shelters for Abused Women: 2003/04." (Wednesday, June 15, 2005). [Online] **http://www.statcan.ca/Daily/English/050615/d050615a.htm**

_____. *Education Indicators in Canada: Report of the Pan-Canadian Education Indicators Program 2005*. Ottawa: Statistics Canada, 2005.

_____. CANSIM II: Canadian Socio-Economic Information Management System [Computer File]. Series V1. Ottawa: Statistics Canada, 2006i.

_____. CANSIM II Database Retrieval Output, Series V107. Ottawa: Statistics Canada, 2006av.

_____. CANSIM II: Canadian Socio-Economic Information Management System [Computer File]. Series V101683. Ottawa: Statistics Canada, 2006j.

_____. CANSIM II: Canadian Socio-Economic Information Management System [Computer File]. Series V101684. Ottawa: Statistics Canada, 2006k.

_____. CANSIM II: Canadian Socio-Economic Information Management System [Computer File]. Series V101686. Ottawa: Statistics Canada, 2006l.

_____. CANSIM II: Canadian Socio-Economic Information Management System [Computer File]. Series V101687. Ottawa: Statistics Canada, 2006m.

_____. CANSIM II: Canadian Socio-Economic Information Management System [Computer File]. Series V101689. Ottawa: Statistics Canada, 2006n.

_____. CANSIM II: Canadian Socio-Economic Information Management

System [Computer File]. Series V101691. Ottawa: Statistics Canada, 2006o.

_____. CANSIM II: Canadian Socio-Economic Information Management System [Computer File]. Series V101691. Ottawa: Statistics Canada, 2006p.

_____. CANSIM II: Canadian Socio-Economic Information Management System [Computer File]. Series V101692. Ottawa: Statistics Canada, 2006q.

_____. CANSIM II: Canadian Socio-Economic Information Management System [Computer File]. Series V101693. Ottawa: Statistics Canada, 2006r.

_____. CANSIM II: Canadian Socio-Economic Information Management System [Computer File]. Series V12397902. Ottawa: Statistics Canada, 2006s.

_____. CANSIM II: Canadian Socio-Economic Information Management System [Computer File]. Series V12398065. Ottawa: Statistics Canada, 2006t.

_____. CANSIM II: Canadian Socio-Economic Information Management System [Computer File]. Series V12400500. Ottawa: Statistics Canada, 2006u.

_____. CANSIM II: Canadian Socio-Economic Information Management System [Computer File]. Series V12401144. Ottawa: Statistics Canada, 2006v.

_____. CANSIM II: Canadian Socio-Economic Information Management System [Computer File]. Series V12401796. Ottawa: Statistics Canada, 2006w.

_____. CANSIM II: Canadian Socio-Economic Information Management System [Computer File]. Series V12401952. Ottawa: Statistics Canada, 2006x.

_____. CANSIM II: Canadian Socio-Economic Information Management System [Computer File]. Series V12402097. Ottawa: Statistics Canada, 2006y.

_____. CANSIM II: Canadian Socio-Economic Information Management System [Computer File]. Series V12402260. Ottawa: Statistics Canada, 2006z.

_____. CANSIM II: Canadian Socio-Economic Information Management System [Computer File]. Series V12402417. Ottawa: Statistics Canada, 2006aa.

_____. CANSIM II: Canadian Socio-Economic Information Management System [Computer File]. Series V12403508. Ottawa: Statistics Canada, 2006ab.

_____. CANSIM II: Canadian Socio-Economic Information Management System [Computer File]. Series V12404160. Ottawa: Statistics Canada, 2006ac.

_____. CANSIM II: Canadian Socio-Economic Information Management System [Computer File]. Series V12404323. Ottawa: Statistics Canada, 2006ad.

_____. CANSIM II: Canadian Socio-Economic Information Management System [Computer File]. Series V12404975. Ottawa: Statistics Canada, 2006ae.

_____. CANSIM II: Canadian Socio-Economic Information Management System [Computer File]. Series V12405790. Ottawa: Statistics Canada, 2006af.

_____. CANSIM II: Canadian Socio-Economic Information Management System [Computer File]. Series V12406589. Ottawa: Statistics Canada, 2006ag.

_____. CANSIM II: Canadian Socio-Economic Information Management System [Computer File]. Series V12407404. Ottawa: Statistics Canada, 2006ah.

_____. CANSIM II: Canadian Socio-Economic Information Management System [Computer File]. Series V1546515. Ottawa: Statistics Canada, 2006ai.

_____. CANSIM II: Canadian Socio-Economic Information Management System [Computer File]. Series V1546516. Ottawa: Statistics Canada, 2006aj.

_____. CANSIM II: Canadian Socio-Economic Information Management

System [Computer File]. Series V1546517. Ottawa: Statistics Canada, 2006ak.

_____. CANSIM II: Canadian Socio-Economic Information Management System [Computer File]. Series V1546518. Ottawa: Statistics Canada, 2006al.

_____. CANSIM II: Canadian Socio-Economic Information Management System [Computer File]. Series V1546519. Ottawa: Statistics Canada, 2006am.

_____. CANSIM II: Canadian Socio-Economic Information Management System [Computer File]. Series V1560785. Ottawa: Statistics Canada, 2006aq.

_____. CANSIM II: Canadian Socio-Economic Information Management System [Computer File]. Series V1560786. Ottawa: Statistics Canada, 2006ar.

_____. CANSIM II: Canadian Socio-Economic Information Management System [Computer File]. Series V1560774. Ottawa: Statistics Canada, 2006ao.

_____. CANSIM II: Canadian Socio-Economic Information Management System [Computer File]. Series V1560777. Ottawa: Statistics Canada, 2006as.

_____. CANSIM II: Canadian Socio-Economic Information Management System [Computer File]. Series V1560778. Ottawa: Statistics Canada, 2006at.

_____. CANSIM II: Canadian Socio-Economic Information Management System [Computer File]. Series V1560773. Ottawa: Statistics Canada, 2006ap.

_____. CANSIM II: Canadian Socio-Economic Information Management System [Computer File]. Series V21222032 Ottawa: Statistics Canada, 2006ax.

_____. Low Income Cut-Offs for 2005 and Low Income Measures for 2004. (2006an) Catalogue No. 75F0002MIE, Vol. 4. Ottawa: Statistics Canada.

_____. CANSIM II Database Retrieval Output, Series V21074181. Ottawa: Statistics Canada, 2006a.

_____. CANSIM II Database Retrieval Output, Series V21074694. Ottawa: Statistics Canada, 2006b.

_____. CANSIM II Database Retrieval Output, Series V21075207. Ottawa: Statistics Canada, 2006c.

_____. CANSIM II Database Retrieval Output, Series V14225283. Ottawa: Statistics Canada, 2006e.

_____. CANSIM II Database Retrieval Output, Series V14225285. Ottawa: Statistics Canada, 2006f.

_____. CANSIM II Database Retrieval Output, Series V14225287. Ottawa: Statistics Canada, 2006g.

_____. CANSIM II Database Retrieval Output, Series V14225289. Ottawa: Statistics Canada, 2006h.

_____. Quarterly Demographic Statistics: October–December 2005. Catalogue No. 91-002-XIE. Vol. 19, No. 4 (2006aw).Ottawa: Minister of Industry.

_____. Women in Canada: A Gender-Based Statistical Analysis. 5th ed. Ottawa: Statistics Canada. Catalogue no.89-503-XIE, 2006au.

_____. Women in Canada: A Gender-Based Statistical Report. 5th ed. Statistics Canada Catalogue No. 89-503-XPB, March 2006d.

STATISTICS CANADA and OECD. Learning a Living: First Results of the Adult Literacy and Life Skills Survey. Ottawa: Statistics Canada. Catalogue no.: 89-603-XWE. [Online] **www.statcan.ca/english/freepub/89-603-XIE/ 2005001/pdf.htm**

_____. Learning a Living: First Results of the Adult Literacy and Life Skills Survey. Catalogue no.89-603-XWE. Ottawa: Minister of Industry, Canada, and Organization for Economic Cooperation and Development (OECD), 2005.

STEBEN, MARC, and STEPHEN L. SACKS. "Genital Herpes: The Epidemiology and Control of a Common Sexually Transmitted Disease." The Canadian Journal of Human Sexuality. Vol. 6, No. 2 (1997):127–34.

STEELE, SHELBY. The Content of Our Character: A New Vision of Race in America. New York: St. Martin's Press, 1990.

STEIN, MAURICE R. *The Eclipse of Community: An Interpretation of American Studies.* Princeton, NJ: Princeton University Press, 1972.

STEPHENS, JOHN D. *The Transition From Capitalism to Socialism.* Urbana: University of Illinois Press, 1986.

STEPHENS T., C. DULBERG, and N. JOUBERT. "Mental Health of the Canadian Population: A Comprehensive Analysis." *Chronic Diseases in Canada* Vol. 20, No. 3 (1999):118–126.

STERN, LARRY. Personal communication, 1998.

STEVENSON, KATHRYN. "Family Characteristics of Problem Kids." *Canadian Social Trends.* Vol. 55 (Winter 1999):2–6.

STIER, HAYA. "Continuity and Change in Women's Occupations Following First Childbirth." *Social Science Quarterly.* Vol. 77, No. 1 (March 1996):60–75.

STODGHILL, RON, II. "Where'd You Learn That?" *Time.* Vol. 151, No. 23 (1998).

STONE, LAWRENCE. *The Family, Sex and Marriage in England 1500–1800.* New York: Harper & Row, 1977.

STONE, ROBYN, GAIL LEE CAFFERATA, and JUDITH SANGL. *Caregivers of the Frail Elderly: A National Profile.* Washington, DC: U.S. Department of Health and Human Services, 1987.

STOUFFER, SAMUEL A., et al. *The American Soldier: Adjustment During Army Life.* Princeton, NJ: Princeton University Press, 1949.

STRAUS, MURRAY A. "Physical Assaults by Wives—A Major Social Problem." In Richard Gelles and Donileen Loseke, eds., *Current Controversies on Family Violence.* Newbury Park, CA: Sage, 1993.

STRAUS, MURRAY A., and RICHARD J. GELLES."Societal Change and Change in Family Violence From 1975 to 1985 as Revealed by Two National Surveys." *Journal of Marriage and the Family.* Vol. 48, No. 4 (August 1986):465–79.

STROHSCHEIN, LISA A. "Parental Divorce and Child Mental Health Trajectories." *Journal of Marriage and Family.* Vol. 67 (2005):1286–1300.

STROSS, RANDALL E. "The McPeace Dividend." *U.S. News & World Report.* Vol. 132, No. 10 (April 1, 2002):36.

SULLIVAN, BARBARA. "McDonald's Sees India as Golden Opportunity." *Chicago Tribune,* Business section (April 5, 1995):1.

SUMNER, WILLIAM GRAHAM. *Folkways.* New York: Dover, 1959; orig. 1906.

SUNG, BETTY LEE. *Mountains of Gold: The Story of the Chinese in America.* New York: Macmillan, 1967.

SUSSMAN, DEBORAH, and LAHOUARIA YSSAAD. "The Rising Profile of Women Academics." *Perspectives on Labour and Income.* Ottawa: Statistics Canada. Catalogue No. 75-001-XIE), 2005.

SUTHERLAND, EDWIN H. "White Collar Criminality." *American Sociological Review.* Vol. 5, No. 1 (February 1940):1–12.

SUTHERLAND, EDWIN H., and DONALD R. CRESSEY. *Criminology.* 10th ed. Philadelphia: J.B. Lippincott, 1978.

SUTTON, JOHN R. "Imprisonment and Social Classification in Five Common-Law Democracies: 1955–1985." *American Journal of Sociology.* Vol. 106, No. 2 (September 2000):350–86.

SWANK, DUANE. *Global Capital, Political Institutions, and Policy Change in Developed Welfare States.* Cambridge, UK and New York, USA: Cambridge University Press, 2002.

SYNNOTT, ANTHONY. "Little Angels, Little Devils: A Sociology of Children." *Canadian Review of Sociology and Anthropology.* Vol. 20, No. 1 (February 1983):79–95.

SYZMANSKI, ALBERT. *Class Structure: A Critical Perspective.* New York: Praeger, 1983.

SZASZ, THOMAS S. *The Manufacturer of Madness: A Comparative Study of the Inquisition and the Mental Health Movement.* New York: Dell, 1961.

———. *The Myth of Mental Illness: Foundations of a Theory of Personal Conduct.* New York: Harper & Row, 1970; orig. 1961.

———. "Mental Illness Is Still a Myth." *Society.* Vol. 31, No. 4 (May–June 1994):34–39.

———. "Idleness and Lawlessness in the Therapeutic State." *Society.* Vol. 32, No. 4 (May–June 1995):30–35.

TAJFEL, HENRI. "Social Psychology of Intergroup Relations." *Annual Review of Psychology.* Palo Alto, CA: Annual Reviews, 1982:1–39.

TALLICHET, SUZANNE E. "Barriers to Women's Advancement in Underground Coal Mining." *Rural Sociology.* Vol. 65, No. 2 (June 2000): 234–52.

TANBER, GEORGE J. "Freed From Death Row." *Toledo Blade* (November 22, 1998):B1, B2.

TANNAHILL, REAY. *Sex in History.* New York: Scarborough House Publishers, 1982.

TANNEN, DEBORAH. *You Just Don't Understand: Women and Men in Conversation.* New York: William Morrow, 1990.

———. *Talking From 9 to 5: How Women's and Men's Conversational Styles Affect Who Gets Heard, Who Gets Credit, and What Gets Done at Work.* New York: William Morrow, 1994.

TANNER, JULIAN, HARVEY KRAHN, and TIMOTHY F. HARTNAGEL. *Fractured Transitions From School to Work: Revisiting the Dropout Problem.* Toronto: Oxford University Press, 1995.

TAYLOR, ALISON, and HARVEY KRAHN. "Aiming High: Educational Aspirations of Visible Minority Immigrant Youth." *Canadian Social Trends.* No. 79 (Winter 2005):8–12.

TAYLOR, FREDERICK WINSLOW. *The Principles of Scientific Management.* New York: Harper & Brothers, 1911.

TAYLOR-BUTTS, ANDREA. "Private Security and Public Policing in Canada, 2001." *Juristat.* Vol. 24, No. 7 (August 2004):1–15.

TECHNOLOGY RESOURCES INC. "Solid Waste Composition Study: Executive Summary." Vancouver: Technology Resource Inc., 2005. Accessed June 12, 2006. [Online] **www.gvrd.bc.ca/recycling-and-garbage/pdfs/2004CompositionExecSummary.pdf**

THIRUNARAYANAPURAM, DESIKAN. "Population Explosion Is Far From Over." *Popline.* Vol. 20 (January–February 1998):1, 4.

THOMAS, EVAN, JOHN BARRY, and MELINDA LIU. "Ground Zero." *Newsweek.* (May 25, 1998):28–32A.

THOMAS, JENNIFER. "Adult Correctional Services in Canada, 1998–99." *Juristat.* Statistics Canada Catalogue No. 85-002-XIE. Vol. 20, No 3 (June 2000):1–16.

THOMAS, W.I. "The Relation of Research to the Social Process." In Morris Janowitz, ed., *W.I. Thomas on Social Organization and Social Personality.* Chicago: University of Chicago Press, 1966:289–305; orig. 1931.

THOMMA, STEVEN. "Christian Coalition Demands Action From GOP." *Philadelphia Inquirer.* (September 14, 1997):A2.

THOMPSON, DICK. "Gene Maverick." *Time.* Vol. 153, No. 1 (January 11, 1999):54–55.

THOMPSON, JON, PATRICIA BAIRD, and JOCELYN DOWNIE. *Report of the Committee of Inquiry of the Case Involving Dr. Nancy Olivieri, the Hospital for Sick Children, the University of Toronto, and Apotex, Inc.* Ottawa: Canadian Association of University Teachers, 2001.

THORLINDSSON, THOROLFLEUR, and THORODDUR BJARNASON. "Modeling Durkheim on the Micro Level: A Study of Youth Suicidality." *American Sociological Review.* Vol. 63, No. 1 (February 1998):94–110.

THORNBERRY, TERRANCE, and MARGARET FARNSWORTH. "Social Correlates of Criminal Involvement: Further Evidence on the Relationship Between Social Status and Criminal Behavior." *American Sociological Review.* Vol. 47, No. 4 (August 1982):505–18.

THORNE, BARRIE. *Gender Play: Girls and Boys in School.* New Brunswick, NJ: Rutgers University Press, 1993.

THORNE, BARRIE, CHERIS KRAMARAE, and NANCY HENLEY, eds. *Language, Gender and Society.* Rowley, MA: Newbury House, 1983.

THORNTON, ARLAND. "Changing Attitudes toward Separation and Divorce: Causes and Consequences." *American Journal of Sociology.* Vol. 90, No. 4 (January 1985):856–72.

THUROW, LESTER C. "A Surge in Inequality." *Scientific American.* Vol. 256, No. 5 (May 1987):30–37.

TILLY, CHARLES. "Does Modernization Breed Revolution?" In Jack A. Goldstone, ed., *Revolutions: Theoretical, Comparative, and Historical Studies.* New York: Harcourt Brace Jovanovich, 1986:47–57.

TINDALL, DAVID. *Collective Action in the Rain Forest: Personal Networks,*

Collective Identity, and Participation in the Vancouver Island Wilderness Preservation Movement. Ph.D. thesis, Department of Sociology, University of Toronto, 1994.

TITTLE, CHARLES R., and WAYNE J. VILLEMEZ. "Social Class and Criminality." *Social Forces.* Vol. 56, No. 22 (December 1977):474–502.

TITTLE, CHARLES R., WAYNE J. VILLEMEZ, and DOUGLAS A. SMITH. "The Myth of Social Class and Criminality: An Empirical Assessment of the Empirical Evidence." *American Sociological Review.* Vol. 43, No. 5 (October 1978):643–56.

TOEWS, MIRIAM. *A Complicated Kindness.* New York: Counterpoint Press, 2005.

TOLSON, JAY. "The Trouble With Elites." *The Wilson Quarterly.* Vol. XIX, No. 1 (Winter 1995):6–8.

TOMKOWICZ, JOANNA, and TRACEY BUSHNIK. *Who Goes to Post-Secondary Education and When: Pathways Chosen by 20-Year-Olds.* Education Skills and Learning—Research Papers. Statistics Canada Catalogue No. 81-595-MIE. Ottawa: Statistics Canada. 2003 [Online] **www.statcan.ca/english/research/81-595-MIE/81-595-MIE2003006.pdf**

TÖNNIES, FERDINAND. *Community and Society (*Gemeinschaft und Gesellschaft*).* New York: Harper & Row, 1963; orig. 1887.

TORRES, LISA, and MATT L. HUFFMAN. "Social Networks and Job Search Outcomes Among Male and Female Professional, Technical, and Managerial Workers." *Sociological Focus.* Vol. 35, No. 1 (February 2002):25–42.

TRAYNOR, IAN. "Immigrants Targeted in Wake of Far-Right Win." *Guardian Weekly.* (May 10, 1998):4.

TREAS, JUDITH. "Older Americans in the 1990s and Beyond." *Population Bulletin.* Vol. 50, No. 2 (May 1995). Washington, DC: Population Reference Bureau.

TREIMAN, DONALD. *Occupational Prestige in Comparative Perspective.* New York: Academic Press, 1977.

TREMBLAY, STEPHANE, NANCY ROSS, and JEAN-MARIE BERTHELOT. "Ontario Grade 3 Student Achievement." *Canadian Social Trends.* No. 65 (Summer 2002):15–19. Statistics Canada Catalogue No. 11-008-XPE.

TREVIÑO, JAVIER, ed. *Goffman's Legacy.* Lanham: Rowman & Littlefield Publishers, Inc., 2003.

TROELTSCH, ERNST. *The Social Teaching of the Christian Churches.* New York: Macmillan, 1931.

TROIDEN, RICHARD R. *Gay and Lesbian Identity: A Sociological Analysis.* Dix Hills, NY: General Hall, 1988.

TROY, TOM. "Money Does Matter." *Toledo Blade* (October 23, 2000):A1, 5, 7.

TUMIN, MELVIN M. "Some Principles of Stratification: A Critical Analysis." *American Sociological Review.* Vol. 18, No. 4 (August 1953):387–94.

_____. *Social Stratification: The Forms and Functions of Inequality.* 2nd ed. Englewood Cliffs, NJ: Prentice Hall, 1985.

TURCOTTE, PIERRE, and ALAIN BÉLANGER. *The Dynamics of Formation and Dissolution of First Common-Law Unions in Canada.* Research report. Ottawa: Statistics Canada, 1998.

TURNER, JONATHAN. *On the Origins of Human Emotions: A Sociological Inquiry Into the Evolution of Human Emotions.* Stanford: Stanford University Press, 2000.

TYLER, S. LYMAN. *A History of Indian Policy.* Washington, DC: U.S. Department of the Interior, Bureau of Indian Affairs, 1973.

TYYSKÄ, VAPPU. "Insiders and Outsiders: Women's Movements and Organizational Effectiveness." *The Canadian Review of Sociology and Anthropology.* Vol. 35, No. 3 (August 1998):391–410.

UDRY, J. RICHARD. "Biological Limitations of Gender Construction." *American Sociological Review.* Vol. 65, No. 3 (June 2000):443–57.

UGGEN, CHRISTOPHER. "Ex-Offenders and the Conformist Alternative: A Job-Quality Model of Work and Crime." *Social Problems.* Vol. 46, No. 1 (February 1999):127–51.

UNGERLEIDER, C.S. "Media, Minorities and Misconceptions: The Portrayal of Minorities in Canadian News Media." *Canadian Ethnic Studies.* XXIII(3) (1991):158–164.

UNGAR, SHELLEY. "Recycling and the Dampening of Concern: Comparing the Roles of Large and Small Actors in Shaping the Environmental Discourse." *Canadian Review of Sociology and Anthropology.* Vol. 35, No. 2 (May 1998):253–276.

UNITED NATIONS DEVELOPMENT PROGRAMME. *Human Development Report 1990.* New York: Oxford University Press, 1990.

_____. *Human Development Report 1995.* New York: Oxford University Press, 1995.

_____. *Human Development Report 1996.* New York: Oxford University Press, 1996.

_____. *Human Development Report 1997.* New York: Oxford University Press, 1997.

_____. *Human Development Report 1998.* New York: Oxford University Press, 1998.

_____. *Human Development Report 1999.* New York: Oxford University Press, 1999.

_____. *Human Development Report 2000.* New York: Oxford University Press, 2000.

_____. *Human Development Report 2001.* New York: Oxford University Press, 2001.

_____. *Human Development Report 2002.* New York: Oxford University Press, 2002.

_____. *Human Development Report 2003.* New York: Oxford University Press, 2003.

_____. *Human Development Report 2005.* New York: United Nations Development Program, 2005.

UNRUH, JOHN D., JR. *The Plains Across.* Urbana, IL: University of Illinois Press, 1979.

U.S. BUREAU OF THE CENSUS. International Database. May 12, 2001a. [Online] **www.census.gov/cgi-bin/ipc/idbsum?cty=MX**

_____. *Statistical Abstract of the United States: 2001.* Washington, DC: U.S. Government Printing Office, 2001b.

U.S. CENSUS BUREAU. International Database. Summary Demographic Data—Yemen and Canada. Accessed May 4, 2006. [Online]

U.S. CENTERS FOR DISEASE CONTROL AND PREVENTION. *Morbidity and Mortality Weekly Report.* Vol. 49, No. 43 (November 3, 2000):978–92.

U.S. DEPARTMENT OF LABOR. BUREAU OF LABOR STATISTICS. *Employment and Earnings.* Vol. 47, No. 1 (January 2000).

U.S. FEDERAL BUREAU OF INVESTIGATION. *Crime Trends: 2001 Preliminary Figures.* August 15, 2002. [Online] **www.fbi.gov/ucr/01prelim.pdf** and **www.fbi.gov/pressrel/pressrel02/01bprelimcius.htm**

U.S. HOUSE OF REPRESENTATIVES. "Street Children: A Global Disgrace." Hearing on November 7, 1991. Washington, DC: U.S. Government Printing Office, 1992.

VALLAS, STEPHEN P., and JOHN P. BECK. "The Transformation of Work Revisited: The Limits of Flexibility in American Manufacturing." *Social Problems.* Vol. 43, No. 3 (August 1996):339–61.

VALOCCHI, STEVE. "The Emergence of the Integrationist Ideology in the Civil Rights Movement." *Social Problems.* Vol. 43, No. 1 (February 1996): 116–30.

VAN BIEMA, DAVID. "Parents Who Kill." *Time.* Vol. 144, No. 20 (November 14, 1994):50–51.

_____. "Strangers in a Land of Strange Mountains." *Time.* Vol. 156, No. 11 (September 11, 2000):7.

VAN DEN HAAG, ERNEST, and JOHN P. CONRAD. *The Death Penalty: A Debate.* New York: Plenum Press, 1983.

VAUGHAN, MARY KAY. "Multinational Corporations: The World as a Company Town." In Ahamed Idris-Soven et al., eds., *The World as a Company Town: Multinational Corporations and Social Change.* The Hague: Mouton Publishers, 1978:15–35.

VAYDA, EUGENE, and RAISA B. DEBER. "The Canadian Health Care System: An Overview." *Social Science and Medicine.* Vol. 18, No. 3 (1984):191–97.

VEENHOF, B., P. NEOGI, and B. VAN TOL. 2003. *High Speed on the Information Highway: Broadband in Canada.* Ottawa: Statistics Canada Catalogue No. 56F0004MIE, No. 10.

VOGEL, EZRA F. *The Four Little Dragons: The Spread of Industrialization in East Asia.* Cambridge, MA: Harvard University Press, 1991.

VOGEL, LISE. *Marxism and the Oppression of Women: Toward a Unitary Theory.* New Brunswick, NJ: Rutgers University Press, 1983.

VOLD, GEORGE B., and THOMAS J. BERNARD. *Theoretical Criminology.* 3rd ed. New York: Oxford University Press, 1986.

VON HIRSH, ANDREW. *Past or Future Crimes: Deservedness and Dangerousness in the Sentencing of Criminals.* New Brunswick, NJ: Rutgers University Press, 1986.

VOSS, JACQUELINE, and LORI KOGAN. Research reported in Keith Mulvihill, "Sex Education Does Not Up Sexual Activity: Study." May 1, 2001. [Online] http://dailynews.yahoo.com

VOYDANOFF, PATRICIA, and BRENDA W. DONNELLY. Adolescent Sexuality and Pregnancy. Newbury Park, CA: Sage, 1990.

WADHERA, SURINDER, and WAYNE J. MILLAR. "Teenage Pregnancies, 1974 to 1994." *Health Reports.* Vol. 8, No. 3 (Winter 1996):9–17.

WAITE, LINDA J., GUS W. HAGGSTROM, and DAVID I. KANOUSE. "The Consequences of Parenthood for the Marital Stability of Young Adults." *American Sociological Review.* Vol. 50, No. 6 (December 1985):850–57.

WALBY, KEVIN. "Open-Street Camera Surveillance and Governance in Canada." *Canadian Journal of Criminology and Criminal Justice.* Vol. 47, No. 4 (October 2005):655–683.

WALDFOGEL, JANE. "The Effect of Children on Women's Wages." *American Sociological Review.* Vol. 62, No. 2 (April 1997):209–17.

WALDRAM, JAMES B. "Native Employment and Hydroelectric Development in Northern Manitoba." In Graham S. Lowe and Harvy J. Krahn, eds., *Work in Canada: Readings in the Sociology of Work and Industry.* Scarborough, ON: Nelson Canada, 1993:172–80.

WALKER, KAREN. "'Always There For Me': Friendship Patterns and Expectations Among Middle- and Working-Class Men and Women." *Sociological Forum.* Vol. 10, No. 2 (June 1995):273–96.

WALL, THOMAS F. *Medical Ethics: Basic Moral Issues.* Washington, DC: University Press of America, 1980.

WALLACE, MARNICE. "Crime Statistics in Canada, 2002." (2003) *Juristat.* Vol. 23, No. 5 (July). Statistics Canada Catalogue No. 85-002-XIE.

WALLER, DOUGLAS. "Onward Cyber Soldiers." *Time.* Vol. 146, No. 8 (August 21, 1995):38–44.

WALLERSTEIN, IMMANUEL. *The Modern World-System: Capitalist Agriculture and the Origins of the European World-Economy in the Sixteenth Century.* New York: Academic Press, 1974.

_____. *The Capitalist World-Economy.* New York: Cambridge University Press, 1979.

_____. "Crises: The World Economy, the Movements, and the Ideologies." In Albert Bergesen, ed., *Crises in the World-System.* Beverly Hills, CA: Sage, 1983:21–36.

_____. *The Politics of the World Economy: The States, the Movements, and the Civilizations.* Cambridge, UK: Cambridge University Press, 1984.

WALLERSTEIN, JUDITH S., and SANDRA BLAKESLEE. *Second Chances: Men, Women, and Children a Decade After Divorce.* New York: Ticknor & Fields, 1989.

WALTON, JOHN, and CHARLES RAGIN. "Global and National Sources of Political Protest: Third World Responses to the Debt Crisis." *American Sociological Review.* Vol. 55, No. 6 (December 1990):876–90.

WARD, MARGARET. *The Family Dynamic: A Canadian Perspective.* 3rd ed. Toronto: ITP Nelson, 2002.

WARNER, MICHAEL. "Fear of a Queer Planet." *Social Text.* Vol. 29 (1991):3–17.

WARNER, R. STEPHEN. "Work in Progress toward a New Paradigm for the Sociological Study of Religion in the United States." *American Journal of Sociology.* Vol. 98, No. 5 (March 1993): 1044–93.

WARNER, W. LLOYD, and PAUL S. LUNT. *The Social Life of a Modern Community.* New Haven, CT: Yale University Press, 1941.

WARR, MARK, and CHRISTOPHER G. ELLISON. "Rethinking Social Reactions to Crime: Personal and Altruistic Fear in Family Households." *American Journal of Sociology.* Vol. 106, No. 3 (November 2000):551–78.

WATKINS, S. CRAIG, and RANA EMERSON. "Feminist Media Practices and Feminist Media Criticism." *Annals of the American Academy of Political and Social Science.* 571 (2000):151–166.

WATTENBERG, BEN J. "The Population Explosion Is Over." *New York Times Magazine* (November 23, 1997):60–63.

WEB MARKETING ASSOCIATES. *Marathon Records.* (2002) [Online] www.marathonguide.com

WEBER, ADNA FERRIN. *The Growth of Cities.* New York: Columbia University Press, 1963; orig. 1899.

WEBER, MAX. *The Protestant Ethic and the Spirit of Capitalism.* New York: Charles Scribner's Sons, 1958; orig. 1904–5.

_____. *Economy and Society.* G. Roth, and C. Wittich, eds. Berkeley: University of California Press, 1978; orig. 1921.

WEBSTER, PAMELA S., TERRI ORBUCH, and JAMES S. HOUSE. "Effects of Childhood Family Background on Adult Marital Quality and Perceived Stability." *American Journal of Sociology.* Vol. 101, No. 2 (September 1995):404–32.

WEEKS, JEFFREY. *Sexuality and Its Discontent.* New York: Routledge, 1985.

WEIDENBAUM, MURRAY. "The Evolving Corporate Board." *Society.* Vol. 32, No. 3 (March–April 1995):9–20.

WEINBERG, GEORGE. *Society and the Healthy Homosexual.* Garden City, NY: Anchor Books, 1973.

WEINBERG, MARTIN, FRANCES SHAVER, and COLIN WILLIAMS. "Gendered Sex Work in the San Francisco Tenderloin." *Archives of Sexual Behaviour,* 2000.

WEINER, TIM. "Head of C.I.A. Plans Center to Protect U.S. Cyberspace." *New York Times.* (June 26, 1996):B7.

WEINRICH, JAMES D. *Sexual Landscapes: Why We Are What We Are, Why We Love Whom We Love.* New York: Charles Scribner's Sons, 1987.

WEISBERG, D. KELLY. *Children of the Night: A Study of Adolescent Prostitution.* Lexington, MA: DC Heath, 1985.

WEISBURD, DAVID, STANTON WHEELER, ELIN WARING, and NANCY BODE. *Crimes of the Middle Class: White Collar Defenders in the Courts.* New Haven, CT: Yale University Press, 1991.

WEISNER, THOMAS S., and BERNICE T. EIDUSON. "The Children of the '60s as Parents." *Psychology Today.* (January 1986):60–66.

WEISS, M.G., and J. RAMAKRISHNA. "Stigma Interventions and Research for International Health." Stigma and Global Health: Developing a Research Agenda: An International Conference. September 2001.

WEITZMAN, LENORE J. *The Divorce Revolution: The Unexpected Social and Economic Consequences for Women and Children in America.* New York: Free Press, 1985.

_____. "The Economic Consequences of Divorce Are Still Unequal: Comment on Peterson." *American Sociological Review.* Vol. 61, No. 3 (June 1996):537–38.

WELLFORD, CHARLES. "Labeling Theory and Criminology: An Assessment." In Delos H. Kelly, ed., *Criminal Behavior: Readings in Criminology.* New York: St. Martin's Press, 1980:234–47.

WELLMAN, BARRY, ed. *Networks in the Global Village.* Boulder, CO: Westview Press, 1999.

WELLMAN, BARRY, and KEITH HAMPTON. "Living Networked On and Offline." *Contemporary Sociology.* Vol. 28, No. 6 (November 1999): 648–54.

WESTERN, BRUCE. "Postwar Unionization in Eighteen Advanced Capitalist Countries." *American Sociological Review.* Vol. 58, No. 2 (April 1993): 266–82.

_____. "A Comparative Study of Working-Class Disorganization: Union Decline in Eighteen Advanced Capitalist Countries." *American Sociological Review.* Vol. 60, No. 2 (April 1995): 179–201.

WHEELIS, ALLEN. *The Quest for Identity.* New York: Norton, 1958.

WHITE, RALPH, and RONALD LIPPITT. "Leader Behavior and Member Reaction in Three 'Social Climates.'" In Dorwin Cartwright and Alvin Zander, eds., *Group Dynamics.* Evanston, IL: Row, Peterson, 1953:586–611.

WHITMAN, DAVID. "Shattering Myths About the Homeless." *U.S. News & World Report* (March 20, 1989):26, 28.

WHO (WORLD HEALTH ORGANIZATION). *Constitution of the World Health Organization.* New York: World Health Organization Interim Commission, 1946.

_____. *Suicide Rates.* July 6, 2003. [Online] **www.who.int/mental_health/ prevention/suicide/suiciderates/en/**

WHORF, BENJAMIN LEE. "The Relation of Habitual Thought and Behavior to Language." In *Language, Thought, and Reality.* Cambridge, MA: The Technology Press of MIT/New York: Wiley, 1956:134–59; orig. 1941.

WHYTE, WILLIAM FOOTE. *Street Corner Society: The Social Structure of an Italian Slum.* 4th ed. Chicago: University of Chicago Press, 1993.

WIARDA, HOWARD J. "Ethnocentrism and Third World Development." *Society.* Vol. 24, No. 6 (September–October 1987):55–64.

WIATROWSKI, MICHAEL A., DAVID B. GRISWOLD, and MARY K. ROBERTS. "Social Control Theory and Delinquency." *American Sociological Review.* Vol. 46, No. 5 (October 1981):525–41.

WIDOM, CATHY SPATZ. "Childhood Sexual Abuse and its Criminal Consequences." *Society.* Vol. 33, No. 4 (May–June 1996):47–53.

WILES, P.J.D. *Economic Institutions Compared.* New York: Halsted Press, 1977.

WILKINS, RUSSELL, JEAN-MARIE BERTHELOT, and EDWARD NG. *Trends in Mortality by Neighbourhood Income in Urban Canada From 1971 to 1996.* Supplements to Health Reports, Vol. 13. Statistics Canada Catalogue No. 82-003-SIE, 2002.

WILLIAMS, CARA. "Family Disruptions and Childhood Happiness." *Canadian Social Trends.* No. 62 (Autumn 2002):2–4. Statistics Canada Catalogue No. 11-008-XPE.

WILLIAMS, RHYS H., and N.J. DEMERATH, III. "Religion and Political Process in an American City." *American Sociological Review.* Vol. 56, No. 4 (August 1991):417–31.

WILLIAMS, ROBIN M., JR. *American Society: A Sociological Interpretation.* 3rd ed. New York: Alfred A. Knopf, 1970.

WILLIAMSON, JEFFREY G., and PETER H. LINDERT. *American Inequality: A Macroeconomic History.* New York: Academic Press, 1980.

WILLIS, ANDREW, and GAYLE MACDONALD. "The Gap Between the Rich and the Poor." *The Globe and Mail* (July 5, 2003):F4.

WILSON, BARBARA. "National Television Violence Study." Reported by Julia Duin, "Study Finds Cartoon Heroes Initiate Too Much Violence." *Washington Times.* (April 17, 1998):A4.

WILSON, CLINT C., II, and FELIX GUTIERREZ. *Minorities and Media: Diversity and the End of Mass Communication.* Beverly Hills, CA: Sage, 1985.

WILSON, JAMES Q. *Bureaucracy: What Government Agencies Do and Why They Do It.* New York: Basic Books, 1991.

WILSON, JAMES Q., and RICHARD J. HERRNSTEIN. *Crime and Human Nature.* New York: Simon & Schuster, 1985.

WILSON, S. J. *Women, Families and Work.* 4th ed. Toronto: McGraw-Hill Ryerson, 1996.

WILSON, THOMAS C. "Urbanism and Tolerance: A Test of Some Hypotheses Drawn From Wirth and Stouffer." *American Sociological Review.* Vol. 50, No. 1 (February 1985):117–23.

_____. "Urbanism and Unconventionality: The Case of Sexual Behavior." *Social Science Quarterly.* Vol. 76, No. 2 (June 1995):346–63.

WILSON, WILLIAM JULIUS. *When Work Disappears: The World of the New Urban Poor.* New York: Alfred A. Knopf, 1996a.

_____. "Work." *New York Times Magazine.* (August 18, 1996b):26–31, 40, 48, 52, 54.

WIRTH, LOUIS. "Urbanism as a Way of Life." *American Journal of Sociology.* Vol. 44, No. 1 (July 1938):1–24.

WITKIN-LANOIL, GEORGIA. *The Female Stress Syndrome: How to Recognize and Live With It.* New York: Newmarket Press, 1984.

WOLF, DIANE L., ed. *Feminist Dilemma of Fieldwork.* Boulder, CO: Westview Press, 1996.

WOLF, NAOMI. *The Beauty Myth: How Images of Beauty are Used against Women.* New York: William Morrow, 1990.

WOLFE, JEANNE M. "Canada's Liveable Cities." *Social Policy.* Vol. 23, No. 1 (Summer 1992): 56–65.

WOLFGANG, MARVIN E., ROBERT M. FIGLIO, and THORSTEN SELLIN. *Delinquency in a Birth Cohort.* Chicago: University of Chicago Press, 1972.

WOLFGANG, MARVIN E., TERRENCE P. THORNBERRY, and ROBERT M. FIGLIO. *From Boy to Man, From Delinquency to Crime.* Chicago: University of Chicago Press, 1987.

WOMEN'S INTERNATIONAL NETWORK NEWS. "USA: Utah Polygamist is Sentenced for Child Rape." Vol. 28, No. 4 (Autumn 2002):90.

WONDERS, NANCY A., and RAYMOND MICHALOWSKI. "Bodies, Borders, and Sex Tourism in a Globalized World: A Tale of Two Cities—Amsterdam and Havana." *Social Problems.* Vol. 48, No. 4 (November 2001):545–71.

WOOD, EVAN, THOMAS KERR, WILL SMALL, KATHY LI, DAVID C. MARSH, JULIO S.G. MONTANER, and MARK W. TYNDALL. "Changes in Public Order After the Opening of a Medically Supervised Safer Injecting Facility for Illicit Injection Drug Users." *Canadian Medical Association Journal.* Vol. 170, No. 10 (May 2004):1551–1556.

_____. "Changes in Public Order After the Opening of a Medically Supervised Safer Injecting Facility for Illicit Injection Drug Users." *Canadian Medical Association Journal.* Vol. 171 (2004):7.

WOODS, DANIEL. "Bountiful, BC: It's a Remote Town in an Idyllic Valley Where Polygamy is the Norm and the Neighbours Don't Seem to Mind." *Saturday Night.* Vol. 116, No. 28 (August 4, 2001):24–31.

WOODWARD, KENNETH L. "Feminism and the Churches." *Newsweek.* Vol. 13, No. 7 (February 13, 1989):58–61.

_____. "Talking to God." *Newsweek.* Vol. 119, No. 1 (January 6, 1992):38–44.

WORKPLACE DIVERSITY UPDATE. "Ernst & Young: Recognized Diversity Pioneer." Vol. 12, No. 4 (April 2004):1–2.

WORLD ALMANAC, THE. *The World Almanac and Book of Facts 1999.* Mahwah, NJ: World Almanac Books, 1999.

_____. *The World Almanac and Book of Facts 2001.* Mahwah, NJ: World Almanac Books, 2000.

WORLD BANK, THE. *World Development Report 1993.* New York: Oxford University Press, 1993.

_____. *World Development Report 2000/2001.* New York: Oxford University Press, 2000.

_____. *World Development Indicators 2001.* Washington, DC: The World Bank, 2001.

_____. *World Development Indicators 2002.* Washington, DC: The World Bank, 2002.

_____. *World Development Indicators 2003.* Washington, DC: The World Bank, 2003.

_____. *World Development Indicators 2005.* Washington, DC: The World Bank, 2005.

WORLD RESOURCES INSTITUTE. *World Resources 2000/2001.* Washington, DC: World Resources Institute, 2000.

WORLD VALUES SURVEY, *1990–1993.* Ann Arbor, MI: Inter-university Consortium for Political and Social Research, 1994.

_____. 2000, Canada, Question D056. [Electronic File] **www.worldvaluessurvey.org**

WORSLEY, PETER. "Models of the World System." In Mike Featherstone, ed., *Global Culture: Nationalism, Globalization, and Modernity.* Newbury Park, CA: Sage, 1990:83–95.

WREN, CHRISTOPHER S. "In Soweto-by-the-Sea, Misery Lives on as Apartheid Fades." *New York Times.* (June 9, 1991):1, 7.

WRIGHT, ERIK OLIN, and BILL MARTIN. "The Transformation of the American Class Structure, 1960–1980." *American Journal of Sociology.* Vol. 93, No. 1 (July 1987):1–29.

WRIGHT, ERIC R. "Personal Networks and Anomie: Exploring the Sources and Significance of Gender Composition." *Sociological Focus.* Vol. 28, No. 3 (August 1995):261–82.

WRIGHT, JAMES D. "Ten Essential Observations On Guns in America." *Society.* Vol. 32, No. 3 (March–April 1995):63–68.

WRIGHT, QUINCY. "Causes of War in the Atomic Age." In William M. Evan and Stephen Hilgartner, eds., *The Arms Race and Nuclear War.* Englewood Cliffs, NJ: Prentice Hall, 1987:7–10.

WRIGHT, RICHARD A. *In Defense of Prisons*. Westport, CT: Greenwood Press, 1994.

WRIGHT, ROBERT. "Sin in the Global Village." *Time*. Vol. 152, No. 16 (October 19, 1998):130.

WU, LAWRENCE L. "Effects of Family Instability, Income, and Income Instability on the Risk of a Premarital Birth." *American Sociological Review*. Vol. 61, No. 3 (June 1996):386–406.

WU, ZHENG. "Premarital Cohabitation and the Timing of First Marriage." *Canadian Review of Sociology and Anthropology*. Vol. 36, No. 1 (February 1999):109–127.

_____. *Cohabitation: An Alternative Form of Living*. Don Mills, ON: Oxford University Press, 2000.

YAMAGATA, HISASHI, KUANG S. YEH, SHELBY STEWMAN, and HIROKO DODGE. "Sex Segregation and Glass Ceilings: A Comparative Static Model of Women's Career Opportunities in the Federal Government of a Quarter Century." *American Journal of Sociology*. Vol. 103, No. 3 (November 1997):566–632.

YANG, FENGGANG, and HELEN ROSE EBAUGH. "Transformations in New Immigrant Religions and Their Global Implications." *American Sociological Review*. Vol. 66, No. 2 (April 2001): 269–88.

YANKELOVICH, DANIEL. "How Changes in the Economy are Reshaping American Values." In Henry J. Aaron, Thomas E. Mann, and Timothy Taylor, eds., *Values and Public Policy*. Washington, DC: The Brookings Institution, 1994:20.

YEATTS, DALE E. "Self-Managed Work Teams: Innovation in Progress." *Business and Economic Quarterly*. (Fall-Winter 1991):2–6.

YEE, M. "Chinese Canadian Women: Our Common Struggle." In G. Creese and V. Strong-Boag, eds., *British Columbia Reconsidered: Essays on Women*. Vancouver: Press Gang Publishers, 1992.

YODER, JAN D., and ROBERT C. NICHOLS. "A Life Perspective: Comparison of Married and Divorced Persons." *Journal of Marriage and the Family*. Vol. 42, No. 2 (May 1980):413–19.

YOELS, WILLIAM C., and JEFFREY MICHAEL CLAIR. "Laughter in the Clinic: Humor in Social Organization." Symbolic Interaction. Vol. 18, No. 1 (1995):39–58.

YUNKER, JAMES A. "A New Statistical Analysis of Capital Punishment Incorporating U.S. Postmoratorium Data." *Social Science Quarterly*. Vol. 82, No. 2 (June 2001):297–311.

ZHAO, DINGXIN. "Ecologies of Social Movements: Student Mobilization During the 1989 Prodemocracy Movement in Beijing." *American Journal of Sociology*. Vol. 103, No. 6 (May 1998):1493–1529.

ZIMMERMAN, MARY K., JACQUELINE LITT, and CHRIS BOSE, eds. *Global Dimensions of Gender and Carework*. Palo Alto, CA: Stanford University Press, 2006.

ZIPP, JOHN F. "The Impact of Social Structure on Mate Selection: An Empirical Evaluation of an Active-Learning Exercise." *Teaching Sociology*. Vol. 30, No. 2 (April 2002):174–84.

ZUBOFF, SHOSHANA. "New Worlds of Computer-Mediated Work." *Harvard Business Review*. Vol. 60, No. 5 (September–October 1982):142–52.

CREDITS

Photo Credits

CHAPTER 1 Reproduced with the permissions of Statistics Canada, 2 (top); Archives of Ontario/F2130, 2 (left); Helen C. Abell Collection, Archival & Special Collections, University of Guelph Library, 2 (middle); Courtesy of Dorothy Smith, 2 (right); Reuters/Corbis/Bettmann, 3; EyeWire Collection/Getty Images– Photodisc, 4; Caroline Penn/Corbis/Bettmann, 6 (top left); Minh-Thu Pham, 6 (top middle); Graham, Neal/Omni-Photo Communications, Inc., 6 (top right); Paul W. Liebhardt, 6 (bottom left); Alan Evrard/Robert Harding World Imagery, 6 (bottom middle); Paul W. Liebhardt, 6 (bottom right); Lineair/Peter Arnold, Inc., 8; North Wind Picture Archives, 11; Archives of Ontario/F2130, 12 (left); Helen C. Abell Collection, Archival & Special Collections, University of Guelph Library, 12 (right); Paul Marcus/Studio SPM, Inc., 14; Lisa Harris Gallery, 15; Museum of New Mexico, 20; New York Times Pictures, 23; Courtesy of Dorothy Smith, 27; Reproduced with the permissions of Statistics Canada, 29

CHAPTER 2 The Coca-Cola Company. Coca-Cola is a trademark of The Coca-Cola Company and used with its express permission, 34 (top); Anthony Bannister/Gallo Images/Corbis/Bettmann, 34 (left); Darren Staples/Reuters/Corbis/Bettmann, 34 (middle); Margaret Courtney-Clarke/Corbis/Bettmann, 34 (right); Michael Busselle/Corbis/Bettmann, 35; Paul W. Liebhardt, 37 (top left); Carlos Humberto/TDC/Contact/Corbis/Stock Market, 37 (top middle); © Doranne Jacobson/International Images, 37 (top right); Paul W. Liebhardt, 37 (center left); David Austen/Stock Boston, 37 (center middle); Hubertus Kanus/Photo Researchers, Inc., (37 center right); © Doranne Jacobson/International Images, 37 (bottom left); Art Wolfe/Getty Images Inc. – Stone Allstock, 37 (bottom right); Dimitri Lovetsky/AP Wide World Photos, 38; Herve Collart Odinetz/Corbis/Sygma, 39; Pearson Education/PH College, 40; Penguin Books USA, Inc., 43; SuperStock, Inc., 47; Shehzad Nooran/Still Pictures/Peter Arnold, Inc., 53; Paul Soloman/Woodfin Camp & Associates, 56; Ruth Orkin/Estate of Ruth Orkin Photo Archive, 57.

CHAPTER 3 Anthony Redpath/Corbis/Bettmann, 62 (top); Pete Saloutos/Corbis/Bettmann, 62 (left); Corbis Royalty Free, 62 (middle); Corbis Royalty Free, 62 (right); Paul Chesley/Getty Images Inc.—Stone Allstock, 63; Jose Luis Pelaez/Corbis Bettmann, 64; Isaacs Gallery Toronto, 65; Gareth Brown/Corbis/ Bettmann, 67; Rimma Gerlovina and Valeriy Gerlovin, 69; Copyright© Big Soul Productions, 74; 20th Century Fox/The Kobal Collection/Brandy Eve Allen, 75; Michael Newman/PhotoEdit, 81 (left); © John Garrett/Corbis, 81 (right); Eastcott/Momatiuk/The Image Works, 82.

CHAPTER 4 © Dorling Kindersley, 86 (top); © Royalty-Free/Corbis, 86 (left); Corbis Royalty Free, 86 (middle and right);Wolfgang Kaehler/Corbis/Bettmann, 87; © www. franksiteman.com, 88; Department of Defense "Canadian Forces Photo", 89; Ron Chapple/Getty Images, Inc. – Taxi, 92; Staton R. Winter/New York Times Pictures, 94; American Sociological Association, 96; Paul Ekman, Ph.D., 98; Paul W. Liebhardt, 99; Barbara Penoya/Getty Images, Inc.- Photodisc., 100 (top left); Alan S. Weiner, 100 (top middle); Andy Crawford/© Dorling Kindersley, 100 (top right); © Guido Alberto Rossi/TIPS Images, 100 (bottom left); Chris Carroll/Corbis/Bettmann, 100 (bottom middle); Costa Manos/Magnum Photos, Inc., 100 (bottom right); Najlah Feanny/Stock Boston, 101;

CP/Andrew Vaughan, 103; Martin, Inc., Butch/Getty Images Inc.—Image Bank, 104

CHAPTER 5 Courtesy of Amnesty International Canada, 110 (top); Annie Griffiths Belt/Corbis/Bettmann, 110 (left); Richard Cummins/Corbis/Bettmann, 110 (middle); David Joel/Getty Images, Inc., 110 (right); Jerry Lampen/Reuters/Corbis/Bettmann, 111; Robert Landau/Corbis/Bettmann, 112; Aaron J.H. Walker/Getty Images, Inc., 113; Spencer Grant/PhotoEdit, 116; Cecilia Benoit, 118 (top); Jonathan Green Studios, Inc., 118 (bottom); Cliché Bibliothèque nationale de France, Paris. From The Horizon History of China by the editors of Horizon Magazine, The Horizon Publishing Co., Inc., 551 5th Avenue, New York, NY 10017. (C)1969. Bibliothèque nationale de France., 123; The Metropolitan Museum of Art, 125; Paul W.Liebhardt, 126; Courtesy: Google, 131 (left); Michael Newman/PhotoEdit, 131 (right).

CHAPTER 6 Davies & Starr/Getty Images Inc.—Stone Allstock, 138 (top); Patrik Giardino/Corbis/Bettmann, 138 (left); © Judith Miller/Dorling Kindersley/VinMagCo, 138 (middle); Maggie Hallahan/Corbis/Bettmann, 138 (right); Tony West/PICIMPACT/Corbis/Bettmann, 139; Paul Solomon/ Woodfin Camp & Associates, 140; Andre Gallant/Getty Images Inc.—Image Bank, 142 (top left); Pete Turner, 142 (top middle); Brun/Photo Researchers, Inc., 142 (top right); Bruno Hadjih/Getty Images, Inc – Liaison, 142 (bottom left); Elliot Erwitt/Magnum Photos, Inc., 142 (bottom middle); George Holton/Photo Researchers, Inc., 142 (bottom right); Dominic Harcourt-Webster/Robert Harding World Imagery, 143; Corbis/Bettmann, 144; CP/Kevin Frayer. 150; Bill Aron/PhotoEdit, 156; AKG London Ltd, 159.

CHAPTER 7 C Squared Studios/Getty Images, Inc.- Photodisc, 166 (top); Tom and Dee Ann McCarthy/Corbis/Bettmann, 166 (left); Bill Varie/Corbis/Bettmann, 166 (middle); Jack Star/Getty Images, Inc.- PhotoDisc, 166 (right); Getty Images/PNC, 168; Tony Freeman/PhotoEdit, 168; Melissa Moore/The Image Works, 169; Robert Yager/Getty Images Inc.—Stone Allstock, 173; SW Production/Index Stock Imagery, Inc., 174; Andrew Lichtenstein/The Image Works, 176; CP Photo/Jonathan Hayward, 178; CP Photo/str/Phil Snell, 181 (left); CP Photo/Frank Gunn, 181 (right); The Cartoon Bank, 183; A. Ramey/Woodfin Camp & Associates, 188; U.S. Information Agency, 189.

CHAPTER 8 Tim Graham/Corbis/Sygma, 196 (top); Kevin Fleming/Corbis/Bettmann, 196 (left); Cydney Conger/Corbis/Bettmann, 196 (middle); Ralf-Finn Hestoft/Corbis/Bettmann, 196 (right); Antoine Serra/In Visu/Corbis/Bettmann, 197; Illustration by Ken Marschall (C)1992 from Titanic: An Illustrated History, a Viking Studio/Madison Press Book, 198; Sebastiao Salgado/Contact Press Images Inc., 199; Abbas/Magnum Photos, Inc., 200; AP Wide World Photos. 202; Julia Calfee/Polaris Images, 204; © Doranne Jacobson/International Images, 208; Ed Bock/Corbis/Stock Market, 215; Russell Lee/Corbis/Bettmann, 216; The Cartoon Bank, 217; Richard Pasley/Stock Boston, 220; CP/Ryan Remiorz, 221.

CHAPTER 9 Jeremy Horner/Corbis/Bettmann, 228 (left); Daniel Laine/Corbis/Bettmann, 228 (middle); James Sparshatt/Corbis/Bettmann, 228 (right); Les Stone/Corbis/Bettmann, 229; Getty Images, Inc.—Agence France Presse, 230; Martin Benjamin/The Image Works, 232 (top left); Peter Turnley/Corbis/Bettmann, 232 (top right); Pablo Bartholomew/Getty Images, Inc – Liaison, 232 (bottom); Reuters NewMedia Inc./Corbis/Bettmann, 233 (left); Chip Hires/Gamma Press

USA, Inc., 233 (right); David Butow/Redux Pictures, 235; Yuri Cortez/Agence France Presse/Getty Images, 238; Malcolm Linton/Getty Images, Inc – Liaison, 240; Steve Maines/Stock Boston, 241; Joe McDonald/Corbis/Bettmann, 243 (left); Robert van der Hilst/Corbis/Bettmann, 243 (middle); Wolfgang Kaehler/Corbis/Bettmann, 243 (right); Mark Edwards/Still Pictures/Peter Arnold, Inc., 244.

CHAPTER 10 © Judith Miller/Dorling Kindersley/The Doll Express, 254 (top); Javier Pierini/Corbis/Bettmann, 254 (left); Jim Zuckerman/Corbis/Bettmann, 254 (middle); Digital Vision/Getty Images, Inc–Liaison, 254 (right); Gideon Mendel/Corbis/Bettmann, 255; British Columbia Archives, 256; Andy Cox/Getty Images Inc.—Stone Allstock, 258; Angela Fisher/Carol Beckwith/Robert Estall Photo Agency, 260; Tony Freeman/PhotoEdit, 263; Sonda Dawes/The Image Works, 271; Getty Images Inc.—Hulton Archive Photos, 273; Carol Beckwith/Angela Fisher/Robert Estall Photo Agency, 276; Richard B. Levine/Frances M. Roberts, 277.

CHAPTER 11 Vancouver Public Library, 280 (top); Kevin Fleming/Corbis/Bettmann, 280, (left); P. Koch/Robert Harding, 280 (middle); Sandy Huffacker/Zuma/Corbis/Bettmann, 280 (right); Gideon Mendel/Corbis/Bettmann, 281; Myrleen Ferguson Cate/PhotoEdit, 282; Joel Gordon/Joel Gordon Photography, 283 (top left); Leong Ka Tai, 283 (top middle); Owen Franken/Corbis/Bettmann, 283 (top right); Charles O'Rear/Corbis/Bettmann, 283 (bottom left); Paul W. Liebhardt, 283 (bottom middle); Lisi Dennis/Lisl Dennis, 283 (bottom right); Joel Gordon Photography, 284; Sean Sprague/Stock Boston, 287; Bob Daemmrich Photography, Inc., 288; The Slide Farm/Al Harvey, 293; CP Photo/David Rossiter, 295; PonoPress International/Luc Vidal, 298; Library and Archives Canada/C-024452, 299; A. Ramey/Woodfin Camp & Associates, 300

CHAPTER 12 CP Photo/Larry MacDougal, 304 (top); Steve Kaufman/Corbis/Bettmann, 304 (left); CP Photo/Ryan Remiorz, 304 (middle); Bernd Obermann/Corbis/Bettmann, 304 (right); Serra Antoine/Corbis/Bettmann, 305; AP Wide World Photos, 306; Catherine Karnow/Woodfin Camp & Associates, 307; Bellavia/REA/Corbis/SABA Press Photos, Inc., 311 (left); John Bryson/Corbis/Sygma, 311 (right); Gamma Press USA, Inc., 312; FSA/National Archives/Franklin D. Roosevelt Library, 315; Bob Daemmerich Photography, Inc., 317; Matthew Borkoski/Index Stock Imagery, Inc., 319; AP Wide World Photos, 321; Durand/SIPA Press, 322; Timothy Fadek/Gamma Press USA, Inc., 324 (left); Joel Gordon Photography, 324 (right); CP Photo/Ryan Remiorz, 326; David Hoffman, Photo Library, 331.

CHAPTER 13 Getty Images – Photodisc, 338 (top); Tom & Dee Ann McCarthy/Corbis/Bettmann, 338 (left); Reuters/Bazuki Muhammad/Corbis/ Bettmann, 338 (middle); Corbis Royalty Free, 338 (right); Owen Franken/Corbis/Bettmann, 339; Beth Balbierz/The Record, 340; David Botello, 341; Christian Pierre, B. 1962, I Do, American Private Collection, SuperStock, Inc., 345; AP Wide World Photos, 347; Mark J. Barrett/Creative Eye/MIRA.com, 353; Bill Bachmann/The Image Works, 354; Anglican Church of Canada, The Diocese of the Arctic, 361; David G. Wells/Corbis Digital Stock, 362; © Doranne Jacobson/International Images, 364; Philip North-Coombes/Getty Images Inc.—Stone Allstock, 369; Anna Belle Lee Washington/SuperStock, Inc., 372.

CHAPTER 14 Getty Images, Inc.- Photodisc, 376 (top); Louise Gubb/Corbis/SABA Press Photos, Inc., 376 (left); Richard T. Nowitz/Corbis/Bettmann, 376 (middle); Lynsey Addario/Corbis/Bettmann, 376 (right); Gideon Mendel/Corbis/Bettmann, 378; Getty Images, Inc., 382; Mary Kate Denny/PhotoEdit, 383 (left); Getty Images, Inc., 383 (right); British Columbia Archives, 387; Will & Deni McIntyre/Corbis/Bettmann, 389; Lawrence Migdale/Lawrence Migdale/Pix, 390; Mugshots/Corbis/Stock Market, 391; The Bridgeman Art Library International Ltd., 400; Billy E. Barnes/PhotoEdit, 404; ABC Television/Globe Photos, Inc., 405 (left); Globe

Photos, Inc., 405 (right); Steve Murez/Black Star, 407.

CHAPTER 15 Jonathan Nourok/PhotoEdit, 412 (top); Gustavo Gilabert/Corbis/SABA Press Photos, Inc., 412 (left); Sheldon Collins/Corbis/Bettmann, 412 (middle); Robert Landau/Corbis/Bettmann, 412 (right); MUNIR NASA/UNEP/Peter Arnold, Inc., 413; David Butow/Corbis/Bettmann, 414; David and Peter Turnley/Corbis/Bettmann, 421; Lauren Goodsmith/The Image Works, 422; © Bettmann/Corbis, 423; © Bettmann/Corbis, 426; SuperStock, Inc., 427 (left); Christie's Images Inc., 427 (right); James King-Holmes/Science Photo Library/Photo Researchers, Inc., 431; Dave Amit/Reuters/Landov LLC, 436; SuperStock, Inc., 438; Eric Pasquier/Corbis/Sygma, 439.

CHAPTER 16 Ryan McVay/Getty Images – Photodisc, 446 (top); Reuters/Corbis/Bettmann, 446 (left); Kevin Fleming/Corbis/Bettmann, 446 (middle); Corbis Royalty Free, 446 (right); Robert Essel NYC/Corbis/Bettmann, 447; Culver Pictures, Inc., 448; Mark Peters, 449; Hans Edinger/AP/Wide World Photos, 452; Whitney Museum of American Art, 454; Pearson Education/PH College, 456; Christie's Images Inc., 459; Ed Pritchard/Getty Images Inc.—Stone Allstock, 461 (left); Mark Richards/PhotoEdit, 461 (right); Mauri Rautkari/WWF UK (World Wide Fund For Nature), 462; Paul Howell/Getty Images, Inc – Liaison, 467; David Botello, 468.

Table and Figure Credits

CHAPTER 1 Figure 1.1, adapted from Statistics Canada publication *Annual Demographics Statistics 2002* Catalogue 91-213 and adapted from CANSIM website http:// cansim2.statcan.ca Series V21074181, V21074694 and V21075207; Map 1-2, the World Bank, *World Development Indicators 2005.* Used with permission of the International Bank for Reconstruction and Development/The World Bank; Figure 1.2, World Health Organization. Suicide Rates [Online].. Accessed July 6, 2003. Reprinted with the permission of the World Health Organization; Table, data taken from Mikael Jansson and Cecilia Benoit, "Respect or Protect? Ethical Challenges in Conducting Community-Academic Research with Street-Involved Youth," in Bonnie Leadbeater et al., eds., *Ethical Issues in Community-Based Research with Children and Youth.* Copyright © 2006 University of Toronto Press. Reprinted with the permission of the publisher.

CHAPTER 2 Global Map 2-1, map from: *Peters Atlas of the World.* New York: Harper & Row Publishers, 1990 – updated by the author; Figure 2.3, adapted from the Statistics Canada publications Catalogue 11-516, Released July 29, 1999; and Catalogue 95F0357XCB2001006, Released April 23, 2003, and Catalogue 97F0009XCB2001002, Released January 21, 2003; National Map 2-1, adapted from Statistics Canada publication *Various Non-official Languages Spoken (76), Age Groups (13) and Sex (3) for Population, for Canada, Provinces, Territories, Census Divisions and Census Subdivisions, 2001 Census – 20% Sample Data,* Catalogue 95F0338XCB2001006, Released March 13, 2003; Figure 2.4, Ipsos-Reid Press Release, "Money Is Not Enough: University Students Personify New Economics of 'The Canadian Dream,'" December 8, 2000. Used with the permission of Ipsos-Reid, Toronto, www.ipsos-reid.com.

CHAPTER 3 Figure 3.2, Ipsos-Reid Media Release, "So, Whom Do We Trust?" January 22, 2003. Used with the permission of Ipsos-Reid, Toronto,; Figure 3.3, adapted from Statistics Canada *Perspectives on Labour and Income,* Catalogue 75-001, pages 5-12, Released April 22, 2005; Figure 3.4, adapted from the Statistics Canada publication *Population Projections for Canada, Provinces and Territories 2000 to 2026,* Catalogue 91-520, Released March 13, 2001; National Map 3-1, adapted from Statistics Canada, *Age (122) and Sex (3) for Population, for Canada, Provinces, Territories, Census Divisions and Census Subdivisions, 2001 Census — 100% Data,* Catalogue 95F0300XCB2001006, Released July 16, 2002.

CHAPTER 4 Naional Map 4-1, "Do you use alternative medicine?" *Saturday Night* (December 9, 2000).

CHAPTER 5 National Map 5-1, adapted from Statistics Canada publication *Detailed Language Spoken at Home (72), Frequency of Language Spoken at Home (5) and Sex (3) for Population, for Canada, Province, Territories, Census Divisions and Census Subdivisions, 2001 Census — 20% Sample Data*, Catalogue 95F0335XCB2001006, Released March 13, 2003; Figure 5.3, adapted from Statistics Canada publication *Perspectives on Labour and Income*, Catalogue 75-001, pages 5-12, Released April 22, 2005; Figure 5.4, Adapted from Statistics Canada publication *Women in Canada: A Gender-Based Statistical Report*, 5th ed., Catalogue 89-503, page 128, Released March 13, 2006.

CHAPTER 6 Figure 6.1, Darroch J.E. et al, "Differences in Teenage Pregnancy Rates among Five Developed Countries: The Roles of Sexual Activity and Contraceptive Use," *Family Planning Perspectives* 2001 33(6): 244-250 & 281; Figure 6.2, adapted from Charles Hobart, "Premarital Sexual Standards among Canadian Students at the End of the Eighties," unpublished manuscript. Edmonton: University of Alberta, 1990. Used with the kind permission of the author; Figure 6.4, adapted from Statistics Canada publication *The Daily*, Catalogue 11-001, Released June 15, 2004 and adapted from www. statcan.ca/Daily/ English/ 040615/d040615.htm; Table 6.1, Ipsos-Reid Press Release, "Marital Infidelity," March 14, 2001. Used with the permission of Ipsos-Reid, Toronto.; Figure 6.5, PEW Global Attitudes Project, *Views of a Changing World* (2003), Washington, DC: The Pew Research Center. [Online]. Reproduced with permission. The Center bears no responsibility for the interpretation presented or conclusions reached based on analysis of the data; Figure 6.6, adapted from Statistics Canada CANSIM database, Table 106-9002, Series V14225283, V14225285, V14225287, and V14225289; Figure 6.7, "Fewer Canadians Favour Legalized Abortion under Any Circumstances," *The Gallup Poll* vol. 61, no. 85 (December 12, 2001), p. 3. [Online]. http://www.cric.ca/pdf/gallup/ gallup_12.12.01_abortion.pdf. Reprinted with permission of The Gallup Organization.

CHAPTER 7 Figure 7.2, adapted from Statistics Canada CANSIM II, Series (2006b-z); Figure 7.3, Adapted from Statistics Canada publication *Juristat*, Catalogue 85-002, Volume 23, Number 8, page 3, Released October 1, 2003; Figure 7.4, Brady Campaign to Prevent Gun Violence. "Did you know?" 2003. [Online] www. bradycampaign.org/about/contact/index.asp; Figure 7.5, The Sentencing Project (2002).

CHAPTER 8 Figure 8.1, adapted from United Nations Development Program, *Human Development Report 2005: International Cooperation at a Crossroads* (New York: Oxford University Press, 2005), Table 15; Table 8.1, adapted from Statistics Canada publication *Family Income Groups (22) in Constant (2000) Dollars, Census Family Structure (6) and Immigrant Status and Period of Immigration of Male Spouse or Partner or Lone Parent (10) for Census Families in Private Households, for Canada, Provinces and Territories, 1995 and 2000 - 20% Sample Data, 2001 Census*, Catalogue 97F0020XCB201009, Released May 13, 2003; Table 8.2, Data from John Goyder, Neil Guppy and Mary Thompson, "The Allocation of Male and Female Occupational Prestige in and Ontario Urban Area: A Quarter Century Replication," *Canadian Review of Sociology and Anthropology* 40, no. 4 (November 2003): 417-439. Reprinted with permission of the Canadian Sociology and Anthropology Association; Table 8.3, adapted from the Statistics Canada publication *Labour Force Activity (8), Highest Level of Schooling (11), Age Groups (11) and Sex (3) for Population 15 Years and Over, for Canada, Provinces, Territories and Federal Electoral Districts (1996 Representation Order), 2001 Census - 20% Sample Data*, Catalogue 95F0380XCB2001003, Released May 13, 2003; Figure 8.3, adapted from Statistics Canada publication *Income in Canada*, Catalogue 75-202, Table 7.2, pages 79, 81, Released June 25, 2003; Figure 8.4, adapted from Statistics Canada CANSIM database, Table 202-0701, Series V1546515, V1546516,

V1546517, V1546518, V1546519; National Map 8-1, adapted from Statistics Canada publication *Profile of Income of Individuals, Families and Households, Social and Economic Characteristics of Individuals, Families and Households, Housing Costs, and Religion, for Canada, Provinces, Territories, Census Divisions and Census Subdivisions, 2001 Census*, Catalogue 95F0492XCB2001001, May 13, 2003; National Map 8-2, adapted from the Statistics Canada publication *Income in Canada*, Catalogue No. 75-202, Released June 25, 2003; Figure 8.5, PEW Global Attitudes Project, *Views of a Changing World* (2003), Washington, DC: The Pew Research Center. [Online]. Reproduced with permission. The Center bears no responsibility for the interpretation presented or conclusions reached based on analysis of the data.

CHAPTER 9 Figure 9.1, The World Bank, *World Development Indicators 2005*. Used with permission of the International Bank for Reconstruction and Development/The World Bank; Figure 9.2, The World Bank, *World Development Indicators 2005*. Used with permission of the International Bank for Reconstruction and Development/The World Bank; Table 9.1, The World Bank, *World Development Indicators 2005*. Used with permission of the International Bank for Reconstruction and Development/The World Bank; Global Map 9-1, Data from the U.S. Census Bureau, International Data Base. [Online]. Retrieved July 5, 2006; Figure 9.3, adapted from United Nations Development Program, *Human Development Report 2005: International Cooperation at a Crossroads* (New York: Oxford University Press, 2005), Table 15.

CHAPTER 10 Figure 10.2, adapted from Statistics Canada publication *Women in Canada: A Gender-Based Statistical Report*, 5th ed., Catalogue 89-503, page 119, Released March 13, 2006; Figure 10.3, adapted from the Statistics Canada publication *Women in Canada 2000: A Gender-based Statistical Report*, Catalogue 89-503, 2003; National Map 10-1, adapted from Statistics Canada publication *Unpaid Work (20), Age Groups (7) and Sex (3) for Population 15 Years and Over, for Canada, Provinces, Territories, Census Divisions and Census Subdivisions, 2001 Census - 20% Sample Data*, Catalogue 95F0390XCB2001006, May 14, 2003; Natinoal Map 10-2, adapted from Statistics Canada publication *Unpaid Work (20), Age Groups (7) and Sex (3) for Population 15 Years and Over, for Canada, Provinces, Territories, Census Divisions and Census Subdivisions, 2001 Census - 20% Sample Data*, Catalogue 95F0390XCB2001006, May 14, 2003; Table 10.3, extract from the Inter-Parliamentary Union, *Women in National Parliaments, 2003* (Geneva: IPU, 2003). [Online]. http://www. ipu.org/vmn-a/class.htm; and.*Women in National Parliaments, 2006* (Geneva: IPU, 2006). [Online]. www. ipu.org.wmn-e/classif.htm. Used with permission of the IPU.

CHAPTER 11 Table 11.1, adapted from Statistics Canada publication *Ethnic Origin (232), Sex (3) and Single and Multiple Responses (3) for Population, for Canada, Provinces, Territories, Census Metropolitan Areas and Census Agglomerations, 2001 Census - 20% Sample Data*, Catalogue 97F0010XCB2001001, January 21, 2003; National Map 11-1, adapted from Statistics Canada publication *Visible Minority Groups (15), Sex (3) and Age Groups (8) for Population, for Canada, Provinces, Territories, Census Divisions and Census Subdivisions, 2001 Census - 20% Sample Data*, Catalogue 95F0363XCB2001006, Released April 23, 2003; Table 11.2, adapted from Statistics Canada publication *Aboriginal Identity Population (3), Registered Indian Status (3), Age Groups (11B), Sex (3) and Area of Residence (7) for Population, for Canada, Provinces and Territories, 2001 Census - 20% Sample Data*, Catalogue 97F0011XCB2001005, Released January 21, 2003; Table 11.3, adapted from Statistics Canada publication *Visible Minority Groups (15) and Immigrant Status and Period of Immigration (11) for Population, for Canada, Provinces, Territories, Census Metropolitan Areas and Census Agglomerations, 2001 Census - 20% Sample Data*, Catalogue 97F0010XCB2001003, 2003; Table 11.4, adapted from Statistics Canada publication *Employment Income Groups (22) in Constant (2000) Dollars, Sex (3), Visible Minority Groups (14) and Immigrant Status (3) for Population*

15 Years and Over, for Canada, Provinces and Territories, 1995 and 2000 - 20% Sample Data, Catalogue 97F0019XCB2001047, 2003; Figure 11.3, European Values Study Group and World Values Survey Association (2006).

CHAPTER 12 Figure 12.4, adapted from the Statistics Canada publication *Selected Labour Force Characteristics (50), Aboriginal Identity (8), Age Groups (5A), Sex (3) and Area of Residence (7) for Population 15 Years and Over, for Canada, Provinces and Territories, 2001 Census - 20% Sample Data*," Catalogue 97F0011XCB01044 and "*Selected Cultural and Labour Force Characteristics (58), Age Groups (5A), Sex (3) and Visible Minority Groups (15) for Population 15 Years and Over, for Canada, Provinces, Territories and Census Metropolitan Areas, 2001 Census - 20% Sample Data*, Catalogue 97F0010XCB2001046, 2003; National Map 12-1, adapted from Statistics Canada publication *Labour Force Activity (8), Age Groups (17B), Marital Status (7B) and Sex (3) for Population 15 Years and Over, for Canada, Provinces, Territories, Census Divisions and Census Subdivisions, 2001 Census - 20% Sample Data*, Catalogue 95F0377XCB2001006, 2003.

CHAPTER 13 Figure 13.2, the Gallup Organization, *Special Reports: Global Study of Family Values* (1997). Reprinted with the permission of The Gallup Organization; Table 13.1, Roman Habtu and Andrija Popovic, "Informal Caregivers: Balancing Work and Life Responsibilities," in Human Resources and Social Development Canada, *Horizons* (April 2006). Reproduced with the permission of Her Majesty the Queen in Right of Canada 2006; Figure 13.3, adapted from Statistics Canada publication *Women in Canada 2000: A Gender-Based Statistical Report*, Catalogue 89-503, 2000; Figure 13.4, adapted from Statistics Canada CANSIM database, Table 053-0002, Series V107; National Map 13-1, adapted from Statistics Canada publication *Number of Children at Home (8) and Family Structure (7) for Census Families in Private Households, for Canada, Provinces, Territories, Census Divisions and Census Subdivisions, 2001 Census - 20% Sample Data*, Catalogue 95F0312XCB2001006, 2002; Figure 13.5, World Value Survey 2000, Canada, Question, D056 [online].; Figure 13.6, adapted from the Statistics Canada publication *Religion (13) and Age Groups (8) for Population, for Canada, Provinces, Territories, Census Metropolitan Areas and Census Agglomerations, 2001 Census - 20% Sample Data*, Catalogue 95F0450XCB2001004, 2003; Figure 13.8, Warren Clark, "Patterns of Religious Attendance," from Statistics Canada publication *Canadian Social Trends* (Winter 2000), pp. 23-27.

CHAPTER 14 Table 14.1, adapted from the Statistics Canada website www.statcan.ca/bsolc/ english/bsolc?catno=96F0030X2001012; National Map 14-1, adapted from Statistics Canada publication *School Attendance (4), Highest Level of Schooling (12), Age Groups (13B) and Sex (3) for Population 15 Years and Over, for Canada, Provinces, Territories, Census Divisions and Census Subdivisions, 2001 Census – 20% Sample Data (Education in Canada: School Attendance and Levels of Schooling, 2001 Census)*, Catalogue 95F0418XCB2001006, 2003; Figure 14.2, adapted from Statistics Canada website; Table 14.2, adapted from Statistics Canada publication *Number and Average Employment Income (2) in Constant (2000) Dollars, Sex (3), Work Activity (3), Age Groups (7) and Historical Highest Level of Schooling (6) for Population 15 Years and Over with Employment Income, for Canada, Provinces, Territories, Census Metropolitan Areas and Census Agglomerations, 1995 and 2000 – 20% Sample Data*, Catalogue 97F0019XCB2001002, 2003; Figure 14.3, Adapted from Statistics Canada *Learning a Living: First Results of the Adult Literacy and Life Skills Survey*, Catalogue 89-603, page 49, Released May 11, 2005; Table 14.3, adapted from Statistics Canada publication *Women in Canada: A Gender-Based Statistical Report, 2005*, 5th ed. Catalogue 89-503, page 57, Released March 13, 2006; Figure 14.4, adapted from Statistics Canada publication *Women in Canada: A Gender-Based Statistical Report*, 5th ed., Catalogue 89-503, page 191, Released March 13, 2006; Figure 14.5, *Tuberculosis in Canada, 2001*, Public Health Agency of Canada (2001). Adapted and reproduced with the permission of the Minister of Public Works and Government Services Canada, 2006; Figure 14.6, The World Bank, *World Development Indicators 2005*. Used with permission of the International Bank for Reconstruction and Development/The World Bank; Figure 14.7, *Canada Communicable Diseases Report*, vol. 32, no. 15 (August 2006), Public Health Agency of Canada. Adapted and reproduced with the permission of the Minister of Public Works and Government Services Canada, 2006.

CHAPTER 15 Figure 15.2, Data from the U.S. Census Bureau, International Data Base. Summary Demographic Data. Yemen and Canada. [Online]. Retrieved May 4, 2006; National Map 15-1, adapted from Statistics Canada publication *Population and Dwelling Counts, for Census Divisions, Census Subdivisions (Municipalities) and Designated Places, 2001 and 1996 Censuses – 100% Data*, Catalogue 93F0050XCB2001003, 2003; National Map 15-2, adapted from Statistics Canada publication *Mode of Transportation (9), Total Income Groups (12), Age Groups (7) and Sex (3) for Employed Labour Force 15 Years and Over Having a Usual Place of Work, for Canada, Provinces, Territories, Census Divisions and Census Subdivisions of Work, 2001 Census - 20% Sample Data*, Catalogue 97F0015XCB2001041, 2003; Figure 15.6, Technology Resource Inc., *Solid Waste Composition Study for Greater Vancouver Regional District: Executive Summary*, 14 January 2005. Reprinted with permission of Greater Vancouver Regional District and Technology Resource Inc.

CHAPTER 16 Figure 16.2, European Values Study Group and World Values Survey Association (2004); National Map 6-1, adapted from Statistics Canada publication *Population and Dwelling Counts, for Census Divisions, Census Subdivisions (Municipalities) and Designated Places, 2001 and 1996 Censuses – 100% Data*, Catalogue 93F0050XCB2001003, 2003.

NAME INDEX

SUBJECT INDEX

Canadian Alliance Party (prev. Reform Party), 326
Canadian Association of Broadcasters, 74
Canadian Association of Chiefs of Police, 181, 326
Canadian Association of Independent Schools (CAIS), 384
Canadian Association of University Teachers, 8
Canadian Centre for Justice Statistics, 156, 181
Canadian Human Rights Tribunal, 267
Canadian Institute for Health Research, 396
Canadian Intellectual Property Office, 52
Canadian International Development Agency (CIDA), 122
Canadian Medical Association (CMA), 399
Canadian Pacific Railways, 424
Canadian Security Intelligence Service (CSIS), 126
Canadian Sociology and Anthropology Association (CSAA), 21
CAP. *See* Canada Assistance Plan (CAP)
capitalism, 459
   advantages of, 312
   as economic system, 310
   Protestantism and, 363
   state, 311
   welfare, 311
capitalists, 206
Capone, Al, 172
Cardinal, Lorne, 74
Carnegie, Andrew, 206
Carp, Diane, 340
CAs. *See* census agglomerations (CAs)
caste system, 199, 200, 201
Catholics, 6, 242
cause and effect, 17
census agglomerations (CAs), 425
census metropolitan areas (CMAs), 425
Chad,
   as low-income country, 233
   population of, 239
Chagnon, André, 328
Chagnon, Napoleon, 39
charisma, 365
Charter of Rights and Freedoms, 11, 152, 160, 181, 275, 297, 325, 342, 466
Charter of the French Language (Bill 101, Quebec), 50
Chicago School of urban sociology, 427–429
child abuse, 353
Child Care Act, 359
child labour, 75, 76
childbearing, 5
childhood, 75
Chile,
   as middle-income country, 233
Chowdhury, Tanveer, 230
Christianity, 46
Chukche Eskimo peoples, 148
Church of Jesus Christ of Latter-day Saints, 342, 370
church, 364
   sects and, 365
   state, 364
CIDA. *See* Canadian International Development Agency (CIDA)
cigarette smoking, 393–394, 395*f*
cities, 421, 430, 457
   concentric zones, 429

critical review of, 430
   edge, 425–426
   first, 421–422
   ghetto, 422
   Industrial European, 423
   megalopolis, 425
   metropolis, 425
   multicentred model, 429
   North American, 423, 424, 425
   Pre-Industrial European, 422–423
   social area analysis, 429
   urban political economy model, 429–430
   water pollution in, 436
   wedge-shaped sectors, 429
Citizens' Forum on Canada's Future, 43
civil law, 178
class conflict, 206
class society, 459
class system, 200–201
   average-middle class, 215
   lower class, 216
   lower-upper class, 215
   middle class, 215
   United Kingdom's, 201, 202
   upper class, 214
   upper-middle class, 215
   upper-upper class, 214–215
   working class, 215
classless societies, 202, 203, 204
closed social system, 199
Cloward, Richard, 172, 173
CMA. *See* Canadian Medical Association (CMA)
CMAs. *See* census metropolitan areas (CMAs)
Co-operative Commonwealth Federation, 7
coercive organizations, 122
Coffin, Paul, 178
cognition, 67
cognitive development. *See* human (cognitive) development
cohabitation, 354–355
Cohen, Albert, 172, 173
cohort, 81
Cold War, 120, 126, 333
Collins, Joseph, 246
colonialism, 240, 245
Columbia, 185
   immigrant workers from, 288
Columbus, Christopher, 50, 240, 295
Commission on the Future of Health Care in Canada (2002), 403
Communist Party (China), 203
Communist Party (USSR), 202
communitarian movement, 466–467
community policing, 192
community-based corrections, 190
   critical review of, 190–191
comparable worth policy, 267
Complicated Kindness, A, 56
computers in workplace, 317–318
Comte, Auguste, 11–13
concept, 17
Confederation, 49, 290, 325, 399, 425, 457
conflict subcultures, 172
conflict theory of prejudice, 290
Confucius (K'ung Fu-tzu), 11, 53, 378
conglomerates, 318
Conservative Party (prev. Progressive Conservative Party) of Canada, 325, 326, 356, 359
containment theory (of deviance), 170
conventional reality, 103
Cooley, Charles Horton, 113

Copernicus, Nicolaus, 12
Corneville, Boston, 25–27
corporate welfare, 321
corporations, 318
   competitive, 318
   global economy and, 319
   monopoly, 318
   multinational, 241, 246, 309, 319, 324, 462
   oligopoly, 318
correlation, 17
Costa Rica,
   immigrant workers from, 288
counterculture, 52
Cox, Harvey, 368
Cran, Ryan, 180
credential society, 387
Cree peoples, 22, 41
crime, 168, 181
   against property, 181
   against the person, 181
   biological theories for, 170
   corporate, 178
   global focus, 184, 185
   hate, 179–180
   organized, 179
   reduction in violent, 192
   statistics, 183
   types of, 182–183
   victimless, 182
   white-collar, 178, 184
Criminal Code of Canada, 8, 144, 152, 160, 179, 182, 183, 189, 398
criminal intent, 181
criminal justice system, 169
criminal law, 178
criminal profile, 183, 184
criminal subcultures, 172
criminal(s),
   age of, 183
   gender of, 183
   race and ethnicity of, 184
   recidivism, 189
   social class of, 183–184
CSAA. *See* Canadian Sociology and Anthropology Association
CSIS. *See* Canadian Security Intelligence Service (CSIS)
Cuba,
   deviance in, 170
   healthcare in, 400–401
   Marxist revolution in, 209
cult, 365
cultural change, 52, 53, 449–451
cultural diversity, 36, 47–48
cultural integration, 52
cultural lag, 52, 449
cultural patterns, 291
cultural relativism, 54, 55
cultural universals, 56
culture shock, 37–38, 40
culture theory of prejudice, 290
culture theory of social movements, 452
culture, 36
   components of, 40, 41
   freedom and, 58
   gender and, 258
   global, 55
   high, 48
   ideal and real, 44
   intelligence and, 38
   popular, 48, 49
   reality construction and, 94
   see also counterculture; multiculturalism; subculture
   sexuality and, 143

technology and, 45
   theoretical analysis of, 55–56
   virtual, 47
Cupid, 4
Curie, Marie, 53
Czech Republic, 126
   market reforms in, 313

Daly, Mary, 362
Dark Ages, 422
Darwin, Charles, 57, 65, 205, 371
date rape, 156–157
Davis, Kingsley, 64, 66, 158, 205
Davis-Moore thesis (on social stratification), 205–206
de Pizan, Christine, 11
de Tocqueville, Alexis, 11
death and dying, 80–81
   definition of, 398
   ethical dimensions to, 398
   median age, 236, 237
death rate, 414–415
   crude, 414–415
debt bondage, 239
deception, 98
demeanour, 97
democracy, 322
   gap, 334
democratic leadership, 114, 124
Democratic Republic of the Congo, 233
demographic change, 451
demographic momentum, 417, 439
demographic transition theory, 419, 420*f*
   critical review of, 419–420
demography, 414
Deng Xiaoping, 204
denomination, 364
deoxyribonucleic acid (DNA), 407
dependency theory of global stratification, 241, 244, 247, 466
   critical review of, 246–247
   history of, 245
   multinational corporations and, 319
deprivation theory of social movements, 452
Dershowitz, Alan, 180
descent, 342
deterrence, 188, 189–191, 333
deviance, 154
   biological context of, 169
   capitalism and, 177
   critical review of biological context of, 170
   critical review of personality factors for, 170
   definition of, 168–169
   gender and, 180–181
   labelling difference, 175
   labelling of, 173, 175
   medicalization of, 175
   personality factors for, 170
   power and, 177
   primary, 174
   race and, 179, 180
   secondary, 174
   social foundations of, 170
   subcultures, 172, 174
Dewey, John, 382
diffusion, 53, 450
Dinitz, Simon, 170
Dion, Céline, 48, 206
diplomacy, 333
disarmament, 333
discovery, 53, 450
discrimination, 290

child, 239
  in Mauritania, 239, 240
Slovakia,
  market reforms in, 313
Smith, Adam, 11, 310
Smith, Allan, 74
Smith, Goldwin, 256
Smoke Signals, 74
social behaviourism. *See* Mead's theory
  of social behaviourism
social change, 448
  causes of, 449–451
  characteristics of, 448–449
  conflict and, 451
  ideas and, 451
social character, 461
social class, 4
  accent as indicator of, 202
  criminals and, 183–184
  family and, 349
  groups and, 118
  health and, 393
  religion and, 367
  social stratification and, 225
social cohesion, 361
social construction of reality, 92, 93
social control, 169
  education as, 383
  religion and, 361
Social Credit party, 7
social distance scale, 287, 289, 289*f*
social diversity, 118, 453
  in workplace, 315, 317
social dysfunction, 14
social epidemiology, 392
social functions, 13
social groups, 112
  dynamics, 118
  in-group, 117
  out-group, 117
  size of, 117, 117*f*, 118
social inequality, 161–162, 202, 205,
  240, 459–460
  deviance and, 177
  health and, 391
  intelligence and, 291
  Kuznet's curve and, 209, 210
social institution, 306
  economy as, 306
  medicine as, 398
social integration, 6, 13, 382
social interaction, 88, 89, 90, 92
social isolation, 6, 65, 66
social marginality, 7
social mobility, 198–199, 214, 217
  downward, 217
  gender and, 218
  horizontal, 217
  income and, 218
  intergenerational, 217
  intragenerational, 217
  upward, 217
social movements, 451
  alterative, 452
  explaining, 452
  redemptive, 452
  reformative, 452
  relative deprivation, 452
  revolutionary, 452
  stages in, 453
  types of, 451, 451*f*, 452
social networks, 119–121
  Internet, 120
social patterns, 13
social placement, 382
social stratification, 16, 134, 240
  caste system, 199, 200

class system, 200–201, 212
classless societies, 202, 203, 204
conflict and, 206, 207
definition of, 198–199
economic inequality and, 208–209
education and, 212
family and, 216–217
functions of, 206
gender and, 214, 217
health and, 216
ideology of, 204
meritocracy, 201
occupational prestige and, 212, 213
politics and, 216, 224–225
race and ethnicity in, 213–214
social class and, 224–225
status consistency, 201
technology and, 209, 210
values and, 216, 224–225
wealth and, 212
welfare and, 224–225
social structure, 13
social-conflict theoretical approach,
  14–15, 21
  critical review of deviance, 179
  critical review of education, 387
  critical review of gender, 274
  critical review of medicine, 408
  critical review of modernity, 460
  critical review of religion, 362
  critical review of sexuality, 162
  critical review of social stratification,
    206–207
  deviance, 177, 178–179
  education, 383, 386–388
  family, 344, 346
  gender, 272, 273, 274
  medicine, 406, 408
  modernity, 459–460
  religion, 361–362, 363
  review of, 15
  sexuality, 158, 161, 162
  social stratification, 206, 207
  to culture, 56
  to politics, 328
  to sports, 18
social-exchange analysis, 15
  critical review of family, 345
  family and, 345
socialism,
  advantages of, 312
  as economic system, 310–311
  changes in countries, 313
socialization, 64, 66
  agents of, 70, 71, 72, 73, 75
  anticipatory, 72, 116
  education and, 382
  family, 344
  gender and, 261
  life course of, 75, 78
societal protection, 189, 191
society, 36
  categories of, 4
  environment and, 430
  health and, 391
  McDonaldization of, 131, 132
  power of, 4
  rationalization of, 122
  rules, 4
  sexual orientation and, 148–149
sociobiology, 56–57
  critical review of, 57–58
sociocultural evolution, 45
socioeconomic status (SES), 208
sociological perspective, 4, 7
  benefits of, 7
sociologists, 4

sociology, 4
  as term, 11
  Comte's stages of, 11–12
  critical, 20
  definition of, 4
  interpretive, 20
  science and, 11–12
  scientific, 16–17, 20
  sports and, 18
  stereotypes and, 30
Socrates, 378
Solar Temple cult, 365
Solis, Oscar, 235
Somalia,
  as low-income country, 242
South Africa, 285
  as middle-income country, 233
  caste system in, 200, 204
  childbearing in, 5
South Korea,
  as high-income country, 232
  GDP in, 312
  industrialization in, 242–243
  state capitalism in, 311, 333
Sowell, Thomas, 291
special interest groups, 326
Spencer, Herbert, 13, 204, 205
spirituality, 369
Spitzer, Steven, 177
Sri Lanka,
  arranged marriage in, 346
Stalin, Josef, 294
Stanford County Prison experiment,
  23, 24
Stanford University, California, 23
Stark, Rodney, 365
status consistency, 201
Status of Women Canada, 122
status, 89
  achieved, 89
  ascribed, 89
  master, 89–90
  set, 89
STDs *See* sexually transmitted diseases
  (STDs)
Steele, Shelby, 290
stereotypes, 30, 287
Stewart, Martha, 173
stigma, 174–175
Stone Age, 38
Stouffer's research (into reference
  groups), 116–117
Stouffer, Samuel A., 116
strain theory (of deviance), 171–172,
  173, 180
strategic defence initiative (SDI), 333
Street Corner Society (1943), 25
structural social mobility, 203
structural-functional theoretical
  approach, 13, 14, 15, 21
  critical review of deviance, 173
  critical review of education, 383
  critical review of family, 344
  critical review of gender, 273
  critical review of medicine, 404
  critical review of modernity,
    457–459
  critical review of religion, 361
  critical review of sexuality, 159
  critical review of social stratification,
    205–206
  culture, 55–56
  deviance, 171, 172–173, 179
  education, 382, 388
  family, 343–344, 346
  gender, 272, 273
  medicine, 404, 406

modernity, 457
politics, 328
religion, 360–361, 363
review of, 14
sexuality, 158–159
social stratification, 205, 207
sports, 18
subculture, 49
sublimation, 67
subordination, 285
suburbs, 425–426
Sudan,
  as low-income country, 231
suicide, 6, 13, 28
superego, 66, 70
Supreme Court of Canada, 50, 152,
  356, 398
surveys, 24
Sutherland's differential association
  theory, 176, 177
Sutherland, Edwin, 176, 178
Sutton, Willy, 104
Sweden, 90
  child support in, 352
  childcare in, 77, 359
  healthcare costs in, 401
  prostitution in, 154
  teenage pregnancy rates in, 140, 151,
    153
  union affiliation in, 313
  welfare capitalism in, 311
  welfare state in, 333, 354
  women in politics in, 270
symbolic institutions, 340
symbolic-interaction theoretical
  approach, 13, 15, 21
  critical review of deviance, 176–177
  critical review of family, 345
  critical review of medicine, 405
  critical review of religion, 361
  critical review of sexuality, 160
  deviance, 173, 174–175, 176, 179
  family, 344, 346
  medicine, 404, 405, 406
  religion, 361, 363
  review of, 15
  sexuality, 158, 159
symbols, 40
Szasz, Thomas, 175

table reading, 26
tact, 99
Taiwan, 75
Tannen, Deborah, 104, 129
Taylor, Frederick Winslow, 127, 130
technology,
  culture and, 45
  electronic, 10
  industrial, 10
  information, 317–318
teen pregnancy, 151
terminology, 231
terrorism, 330
  state, 330
  war and, 331–332
tertiary sector of economy, 308
test-tube babies, 356
Thailand,
  take-off stage of modernization in,
    242
thanatos, 66
theological stage of development, 11
theory of sociology, 13
third estate (England), 201
Third World, 231
This Hour Has 22 Minutes, 73
Thomas Theorem, 93, 174, 405